PH...

ST...

London

Contents

II Key to map pages

IV Administrative and Postcode boundaries

VI Key to map symbols

1 Street maps

77 Central London

77 Key to map pages and key to symbols

78 Large-scale street maps

174 Index

292 List of numbered locations

312 London Underground map

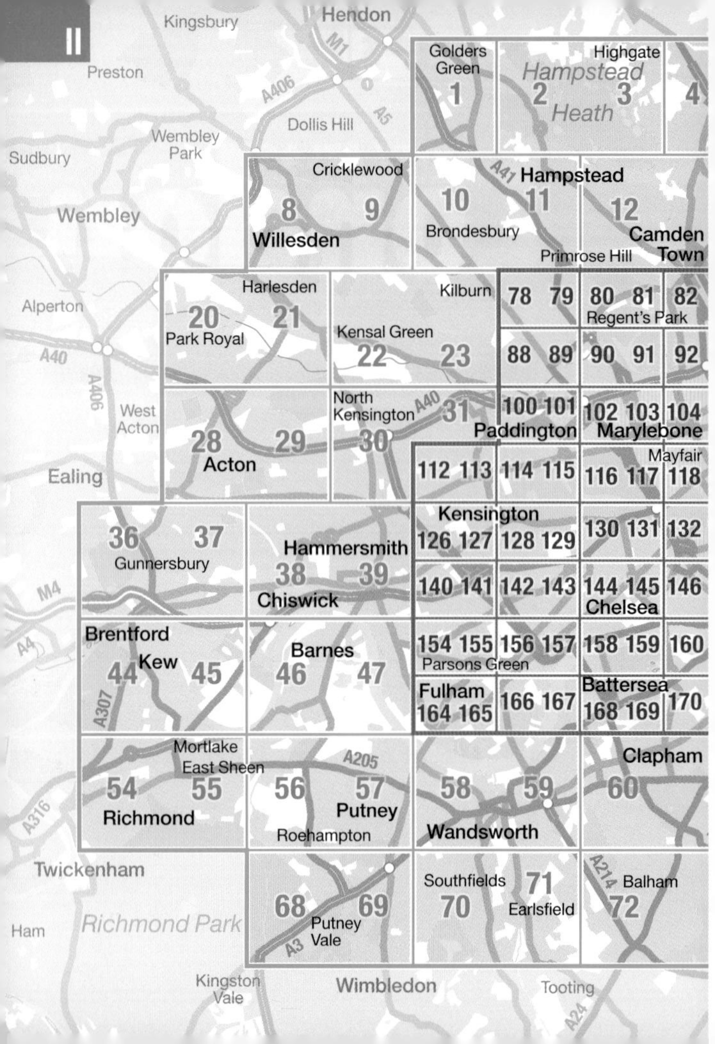

Hendon
Kingsbury
Preston
M1
A406
A5
Dollis Hill
Wembley Park
Sudbury
Wembley
Golders Green
1
Highgate
Hampstead Heath
2
3
4
Cricklewood
8
9
Willesden
A41
Hampstead
10
11
12
Brondesbury
Camden Town
Primrose Hill
Alperton
A40
A406
Harlesden
20
21
Park Royal
Kilburn
Kensal Green
22
23
78
79
80
81
82
Regent's Park
88
89
90
91
92
West Acton
North Kensington
A40
31
100
101
102
103
104
Paddington
Marylebone
28
29
30
Acton
Ealing
Mayfair
112
113
114
115
116
117
118
36
37
Gunnersbury
Kensington
126
127
128
129
130
131
132
Hammersmith
38
39
Chiswick
M4
140
141
142
143
144
145
146
Chelsea
A4
Brentford
Kew
44
45
A307
Barnes
46
47
154
155
156
157
158
159
160
Parsons Green
Fulham
164
165
166
167
Battersea
168
169
170
Mortlake
East Sheen
A205
54
55
56
57
Putney
A316
Richmond
Roehampton
58
59
Wandsworth
Clapham
60
Twickenham
Richmond Park
Ham
68
69
Putney Vale
A3
Southfields
70
71
Earlsfield
A214
Balham
72
Kingston Vale
Wimbledon
Tooting
A24

Key to map pages

Atlas pages at 3½ inches to 1 mile are shown in blue

Central London atlas pages at 7 inches to 1 mile are shown in red (See page 77)

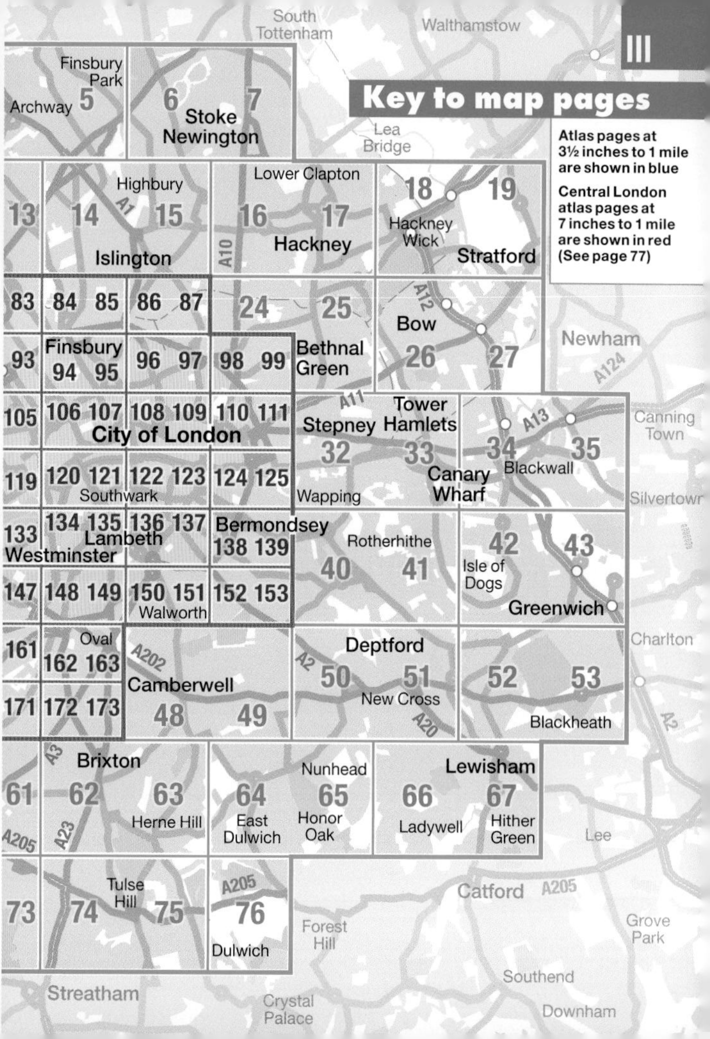

South Tottenham

Walthamstow

Finsbury Park

Archway **5**

6 Stoke Newington **7**

Lea Bridge

Highbury

13 **14** A1 **15**

Islington

Lower Clapton

16 A10 **17**

Hackney

Hackney Wick

18 **19**

Stratford

Newham A124

83 **84** **85** **86** **87**

93 Finsbury **94** **95** **96** **97** **98** **99**

24 **25**

Bethnal Green

26 A12 Bow **27**

Canning Town

Silvertown

105 **106** **107** **108** **109** **110** **111**

City of London

119 **120** **121** **122** **123** **124** **125**

Southwark

133 **134** **135** **136** **137**

Westminster Lambeth

147 **148** **149** **150** **151** **152** **153**

Walworth

Tower Hamlets

Stepney

32 **33**

Wapping

A11

34 A13 **35**

Canary Wharf Blackwall

Bermondsey **138** **139**

40 Rotherhithe **41**

42 Isle of Dogs **43**

Greenwich

Charlton

161 Oval **162** **163** A202

171 **172** **173**

Camberwell

48 **49**

Deptford

50 **51**

New Cross A20

A2

52 **53**

Blackheath

A2

61 A3 **62** **63**

Brixton

A205 A23 Herne Hill

Nunhead

64 **65**

East Dulwich Honor Oak

Lewisham

66 **67**

Ladywell Hither Green

Lee

73 **74** Tulse Hill **75** A205 **76**

Dulwich

Catford A205

Grove Park

Streatham

Forest Hill

Crystal Palace

Southend

Downham

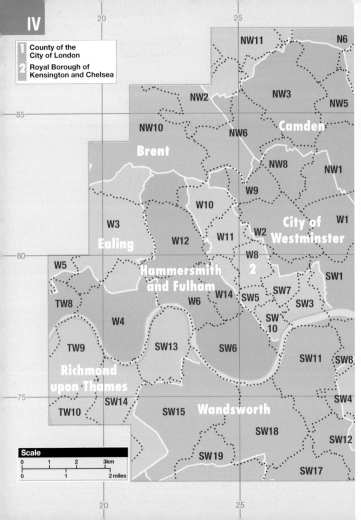

IV

1 County of the City of London
2 Royal Borough of Kensington and Chelsea

NW11
N6
NW2
NW3
NW5
NW10
Camden
Brent
NW6
NW8
NW1
W9
W10
W3
W11
W1
W12
W2
City of Westminster
Ealing
W8
W5
Hammersmith and Fulham
SW1
TW8
W14
SW5
SW7
W6
SW3
W4
SW10
SW13
SW6
SW11
SW8
TW9
Richmond upon Thames
SW4
SW14
Wandsworth
TW10
SW15
SW12
SW18
SW19
SW17

Scale
0   1   2   3km
0   1   2 miles

Administrative and Postcode boundaries

Key to map symbols

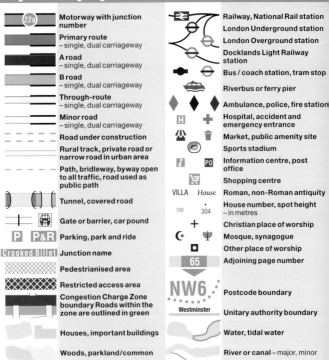

	Motorway with junction number
	Primary route – single, dual carriageway
	A road – single, dual carriageway
	B road – single, dual carriageway
	Through-route – single, dual carriageway
	Minor road – single, dual carriageway
	Road under construction
	Rural track, private road or narrow road in urban area
	Path, bridleway, byway open to all traffic, road used as public path
	Tunnel, covered road
	Gate or barrier, car pound
P **P&R**	Parking, park and ride
Crooked Billet	Junction name
	Pedestrianised area
	Restricted access area
	Congestion Charge Zone boundary Roads within the zone are outlined in green
	Houses, important buildings
	Woods, parkland/common

	Railway, National Rail station
	London Underground station
	London Overground station
	Docklands Light Railway station
	Bus / coach station, tram stop
	Riverbus or ferry pier
	Ambulance, police, fire station
H +	Hospital, accident and emergency entrance
	Market, public amenity site
	Sports stadium
i **PO**	Information centre, post office
	Shopping centre
VILLA *House*	Roman, non-Roman antiquity
100 · 304	House number, spot height – in metres
+	Christian place of worship
☪★ ♔	Mosque, synagogue
◻	Other place of worship
65	Adjoining page number
NW6	Postcode boundary
Westminster	Unitary authority boundary
	Water, tidal water
	River or canal – major, minor

The map scale on the pages numbered in blue is 3½ inches to 1 mile
5.52 cm to 1 km • 1:18 103

0	¼ mile	½ mile

0	250m	500m	750m	1km

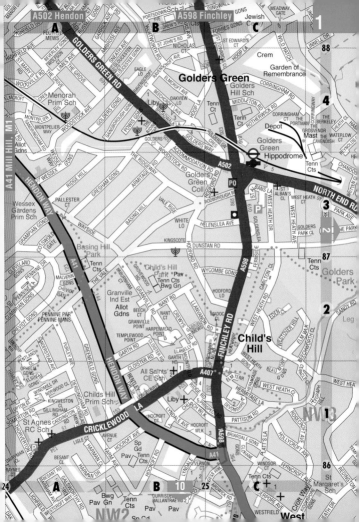

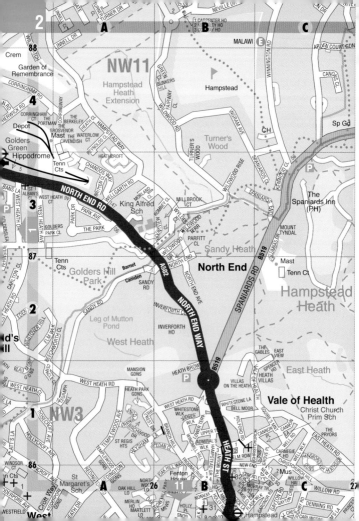

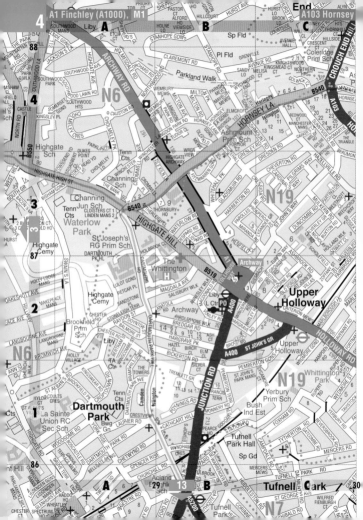

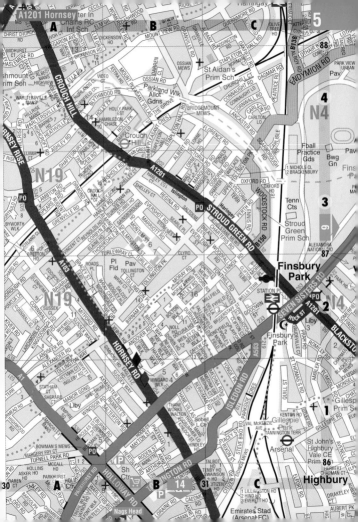

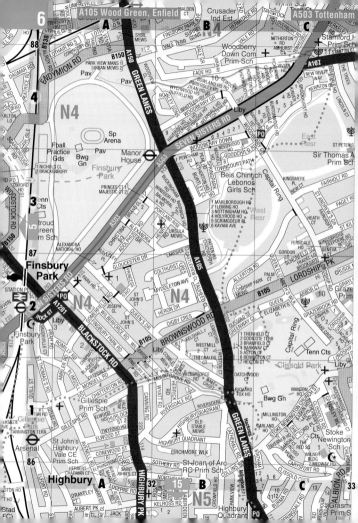

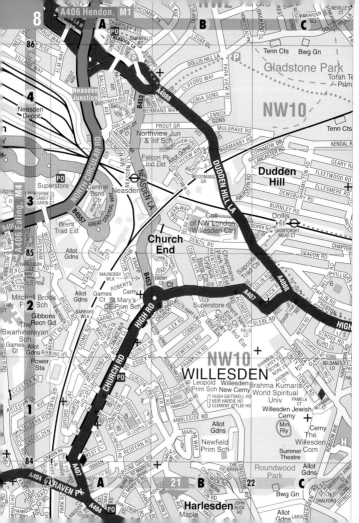

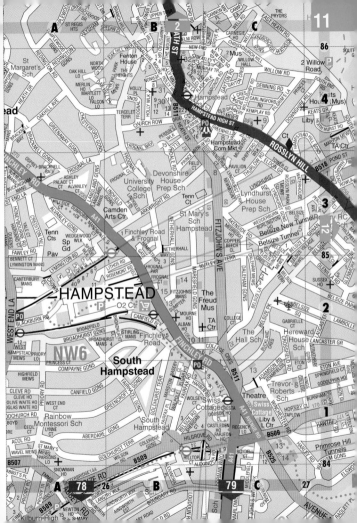

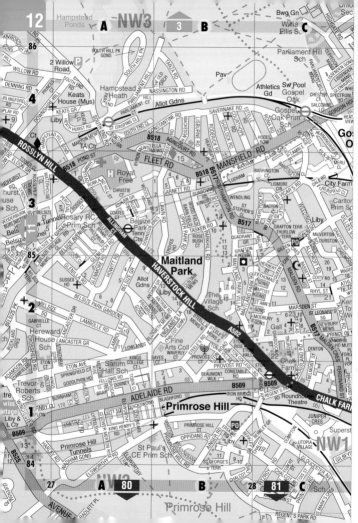

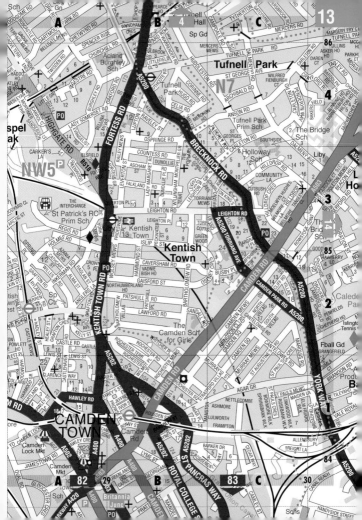

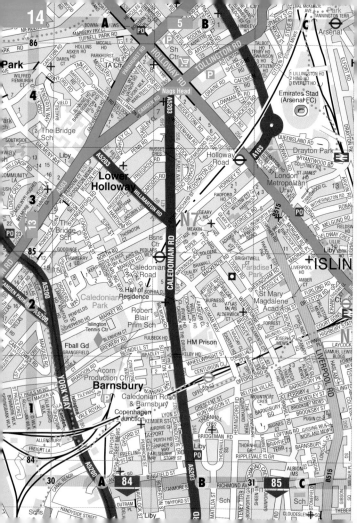

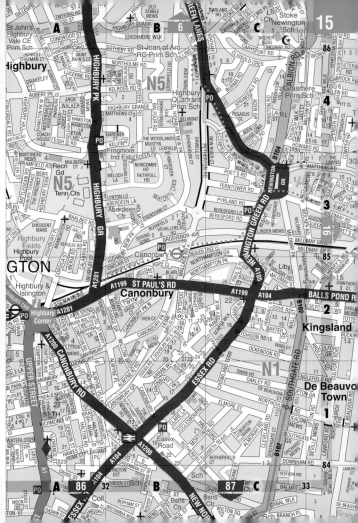

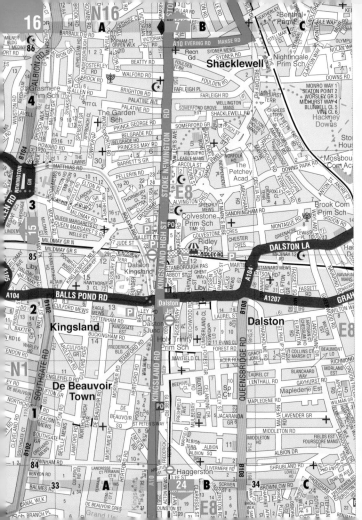

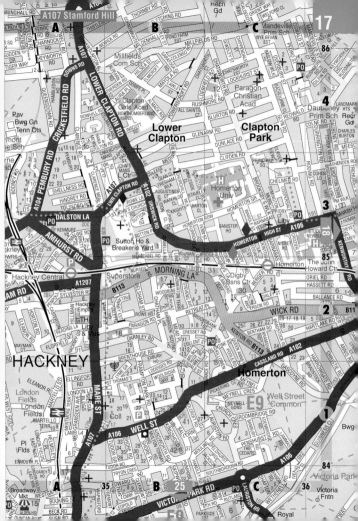

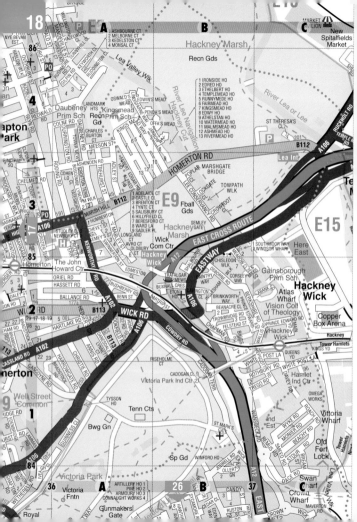

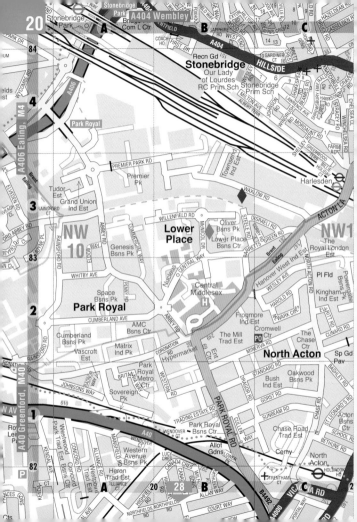

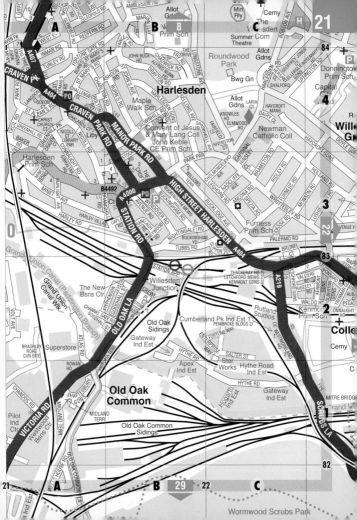

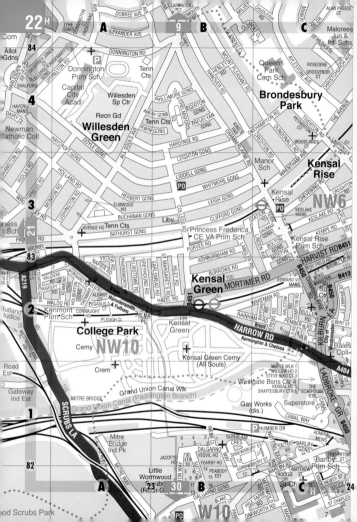

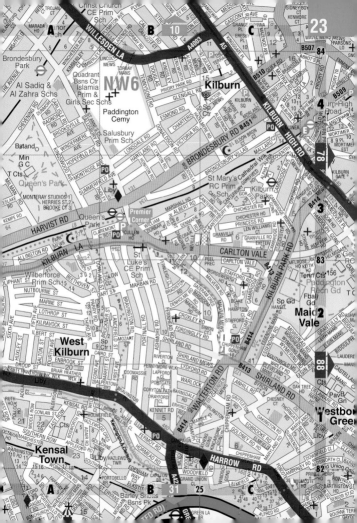

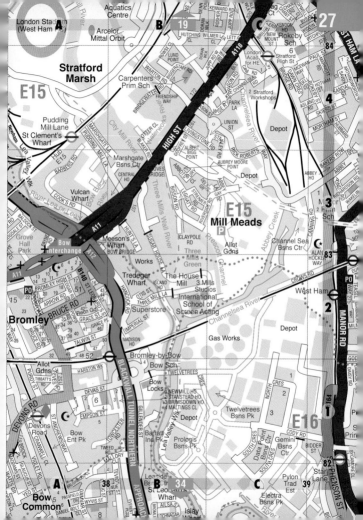

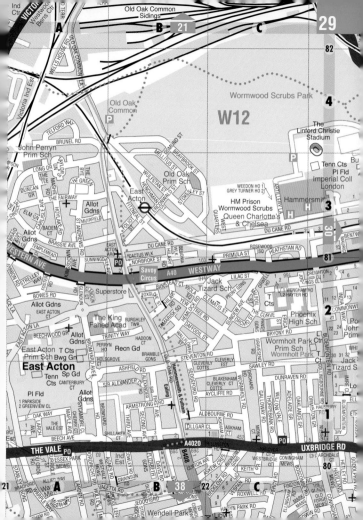

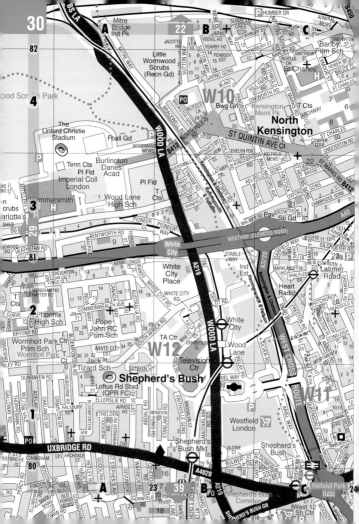

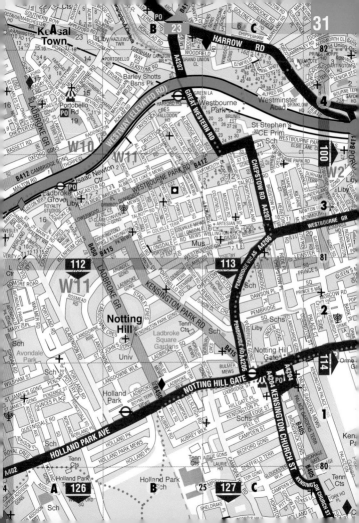

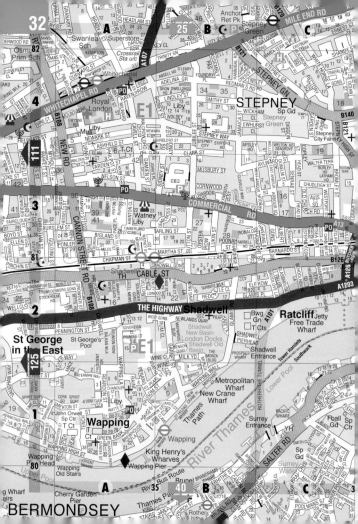

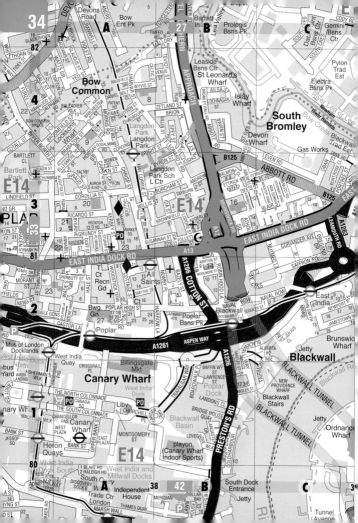

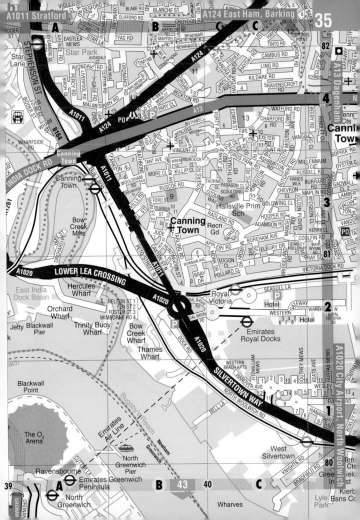

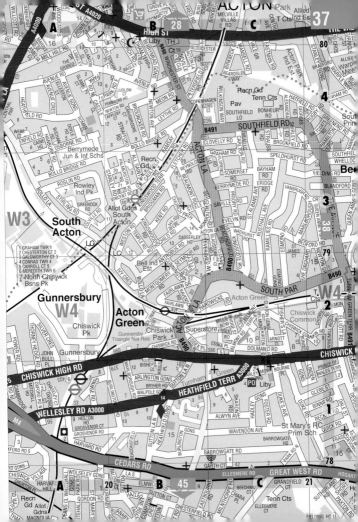

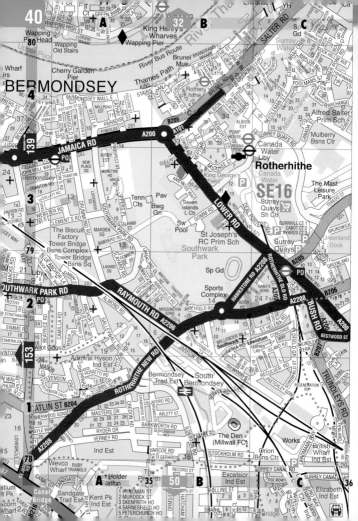

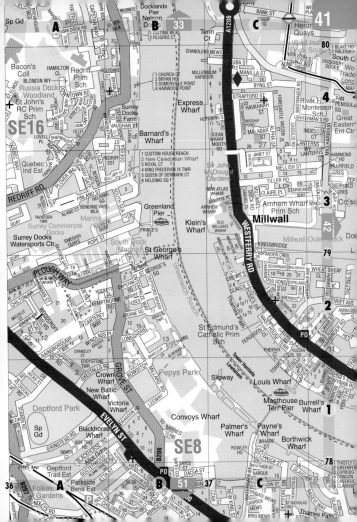

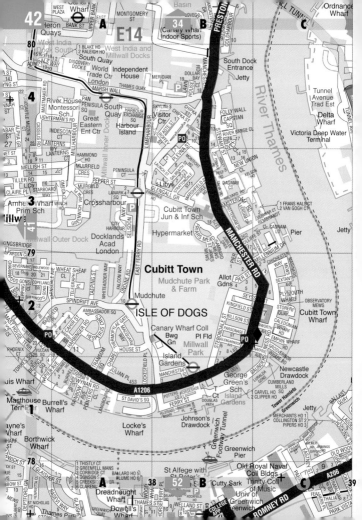

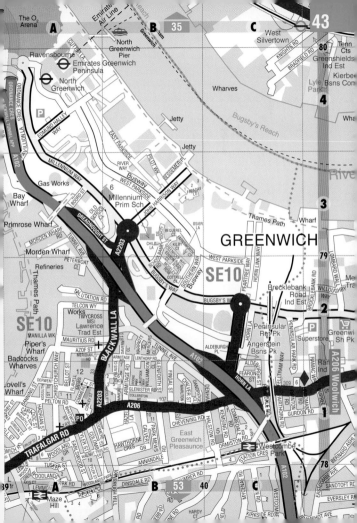

GROSVENOR CT
GROSVENOR RD
HARVARD RD
CEDARS RD
A4
GREAT WEST RD
HOGARTH
37
WAVENDON AVE
St Mary's R
Prim Sch
BARROWGATE HO
BARROWGATE RD
GARTH CT
ELLESMERE RD
PARK RD N
78
SUTTON LA N
BEACONSFIELD CL
CHISWICK VILLAGE
HARVARD HILL
CHURTON PL
WOLSELEY GDNS
BURNABY GDNS
WHITEHALL GDNS
WHITEHALL PARK RD
DEANS CL
GORDON RD
ST MARY'S GR
Recn Gd
Allot Gdns
MAGNOLIA WHARF
MAGNOLIA RD
THAMES RD
HERBERT GDNS
ERNEST GDNS
LORAINE RD
BAILEY MEWS
LC
RIVERVIEW GR
RIVERVIEW RD
GROVE PARK TERR
RANELAGH GDNS
NIGHTINGALE CL
ST THOMAS' RD
FLORENCE GDNS
FALCONBERG RD
BURNABY CRES
HAZLEDENE RD
COMPTON CRES
SUTTON CT
SUTTON COURT RD
ELMWOOD RD
LA S
FALCON CL
SUTTON CL
CHESTERFIELD RD
CHATSWORTH RD
EASTBOURNE RD
MILNTHORPE RD
CHARA PL
BEECHWOOD CT
GRANDFIELD CT
ELLESMERE CT
Tenn Cts
PARK RD
SUTHERLAND RD
SHORT RD
PAXTON RD
FIELDING HO 1
GARRICK HO 2
HAMILTON HO 3
CHISWICK SQ 4
PAGE'S YD 5
4
1 MONTGOMERY CT
2 FAUCONBERG CT
3 EGERTON HO
4 BOURNE CT
5 CHISWICK PLAZA
6 SUTTON COURT MANS
7 Grove Park Prim Sch
Chiswick House
STAVELEY RD
LAWFORD RD
GROVE PARK MEWS
CROFTON AVE
FITZROY CRES
Pav
PO
GRANTH
WHITTINGHAM CT
EDENSOR
ISIS CT
REDCLIFFE GDNS
GROVE PARK GDNS
GROVE PARK BRIDGE
GROVE PARK RD
LAKE TERR
STONE
OLANDS CT
Queen's Prim Sch
The National Archives
DORCHESTER HO
CHARLWOOD HO
BIRCHGROVE HO
STRAND DR
HARTINGTON CT
KINNAIRD AVE
STATION APP RD
BURLINGTON LA
Chiswick Sch
WAR MEMORIAL HOMES
Tenn Cts
3
ALEXANDRA GDNS
PROMENADE
Chiswick
RUSSELL KERR CL
WILMINGTON AVE
STAVELEY RD
Allot Gdns
Pav
Tenn Cts
46
DEVONSHIRE GDNS
SPENCER RD
STATION GDNS
BOLTON RD
CONISTON CL
MARAIS
KELVIN CT
1 HUNTINGDON GDNS
2 BURLINGTON CT
3 QUINTIN CT
4 WINDRUSH CL
5 THE LINDENS
Cemy
Cavendish Prim Sch
77
RIVERSIDE DR
ACQUA HO
BESSANT DR
Grove Park
CHISWICK STAITHE
ST ANDREWS CT
CAVENDISH RD
Tenn Cts
W4
The Quintin Hogg Meml Gd
CHERTSEY RD
Sp Gd
STAVELEY GDNS
Tenn Cts
Civil S Sp
Kew Ret Pk
WOODMAN MEWS
KELSALL MEWS
GREEN LINK WLK
WHITCOME MEWS
MELLISS AVE
THAMES VILLAGE
Pav
HARTINGTON RD
Tenn Cts
Stadium
GREAT
Allot Gdns
2
The Riverside Health & Racquet Club Chiswick
Marlborough Trad Est
MAGNOLIA CT
PARK AVE
BESSANT DR
ERICK FARM CL
WEST HALL RD
HAWTHORN CT
COURTLANDS AVE
CHISWICK QUAY
IBIS LA
Yacht Basin
Sp Gd
Riverside Lands School Pl Flds
221
TOWNMEAD RD
BARKER CL
Allot Gdns
CHISWICK BRIDGE
Duke's Meadows
Pav
Allot Gdns
Tenn Cts
Sp Gd
Drv Rng
TAYLOR AVE
TW9
Kew Riverside Prim Sch
Crem
CLIFFORD AVE
Pav
Tenn Cts
P
Allot Gdns
1
TIDEWAY YD 1
TIDEWAY WHARF 2
THE BROADWAY 3
RIVER HO 4
ELM BANK MANS 5
MALTINGS CL 6
MALTHOUSE PAS 7
North Sheen Cemy (Fulham)
Hammersmith New Cemy
WADHAM MEWS
THAMES BANK
VARSITY ROW
1 WATNEY COTTS
2 LANGDON PL
3 ROSEMARY LA
4 WALDECK TERR
5 ROSEMARY GDNS
6 HUNTINGDON CT
7 ST LEONARDS CT
8 MODEL COTTS
Hounslow
Richmond upon Thames
BULLS ALLEY
DUKES CT
ASHLEIGH HO 1
RIPLEY HO 2
Bwg Gn
REID CT
PARLIAMENT MEWS
COMBE HO
WILLIAMS LA
SHIP LA
A316
ERICK RD
Chalkers Cnr
ELSINORE WAY
POPHAM GDNS
LOWER RICHMOND RD
A3003
CHERTSEY CT
20
WATNEY RD
Sp Gd
Mortlake
LADY ELIZABETH
55
WALDECK RD
Mortlake
B351
VINEYARD PATH
ALDER RD
WRIGHTS WLK
MULLINS PATH
FITZGERALD RD
WORPLE ST
RIPLEY GDNS
AVONDALE RD
ASHLEIGH RD
COWLEY RD
SECOND AVE
MORTLAKE HIGH
76
PO
21
14
THE RETREAT
BUXTON RD
BROOK CT
NORTH WORPLE WAY
SHALSTONE RD
RUTLAND CL
A
B
C

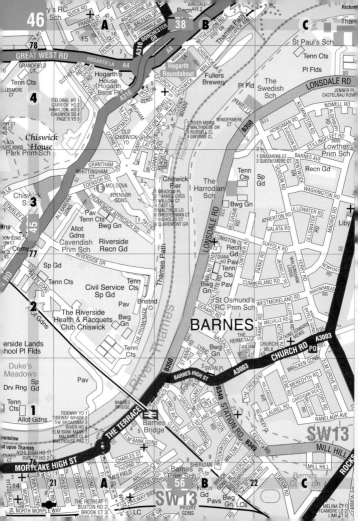

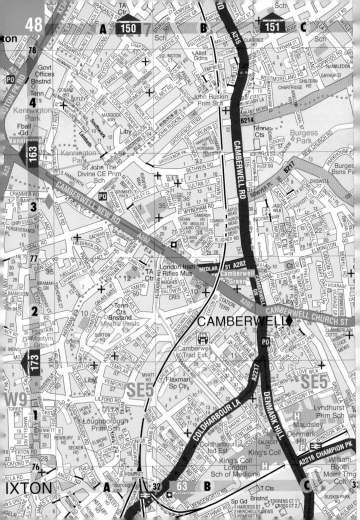

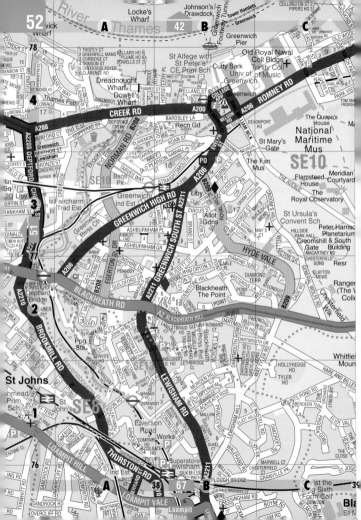

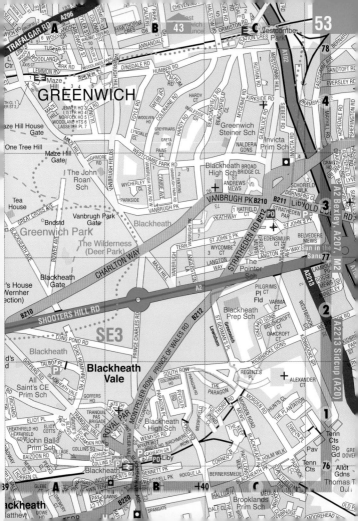

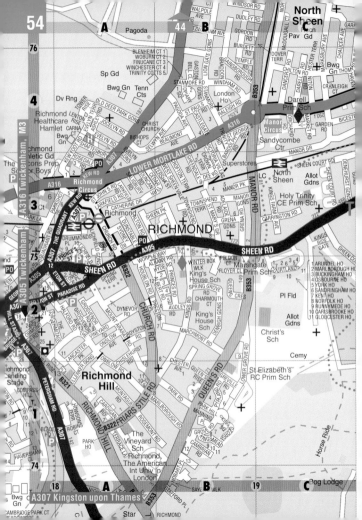

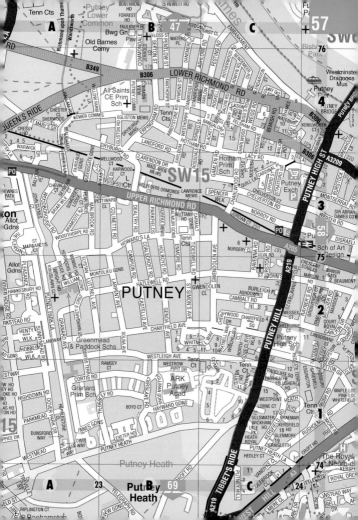

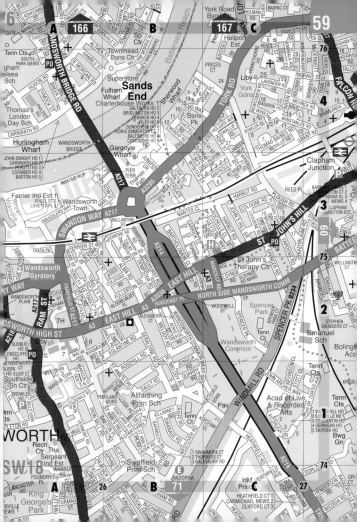

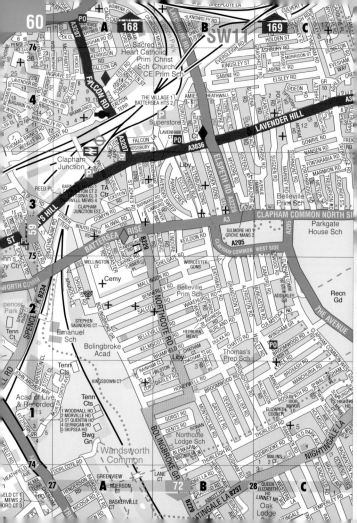

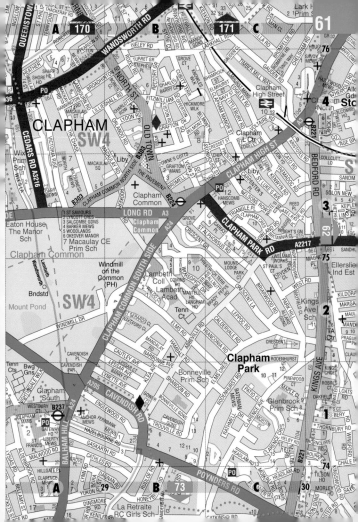

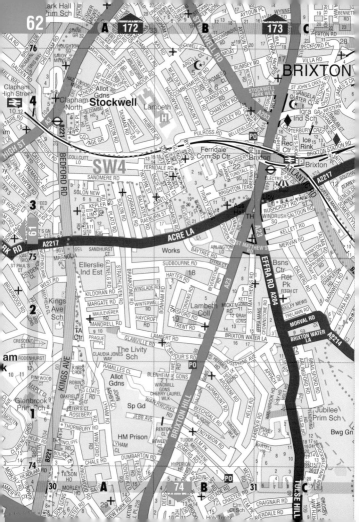

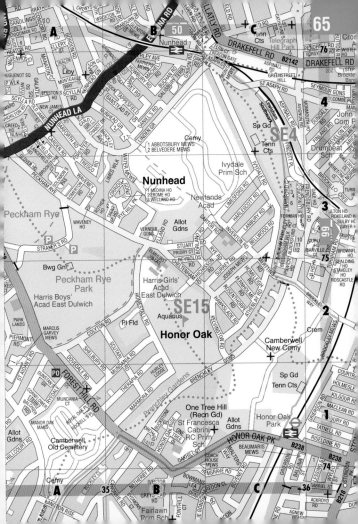

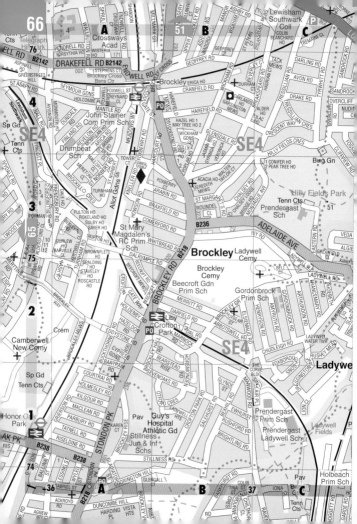

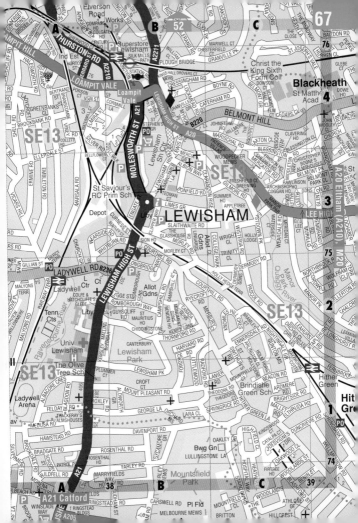

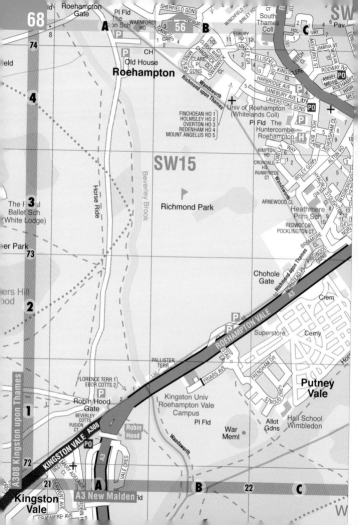

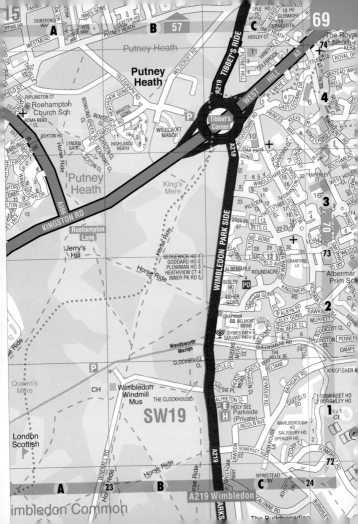

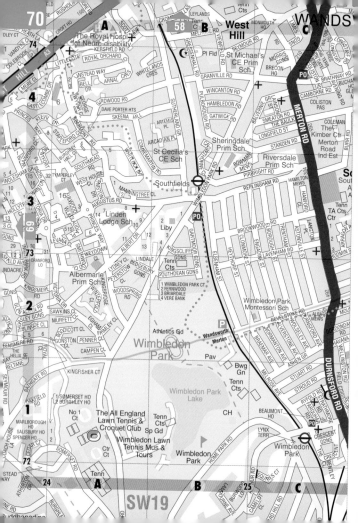

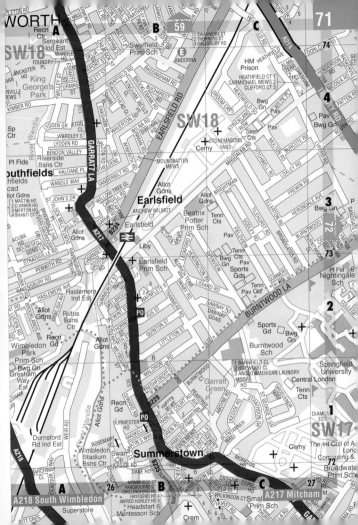

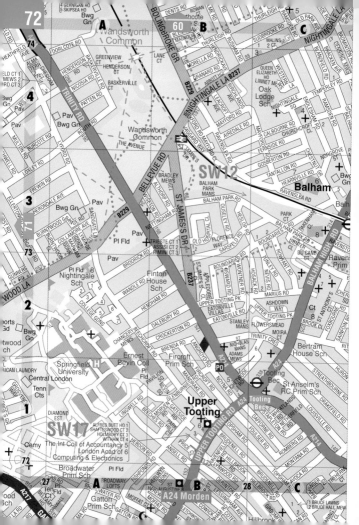

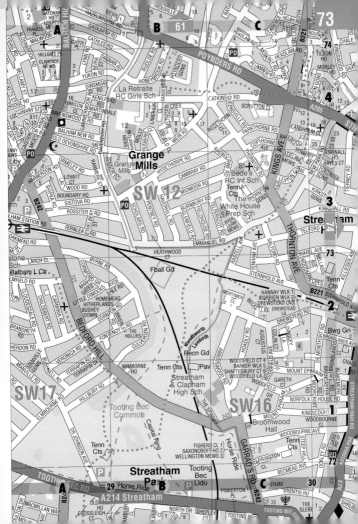

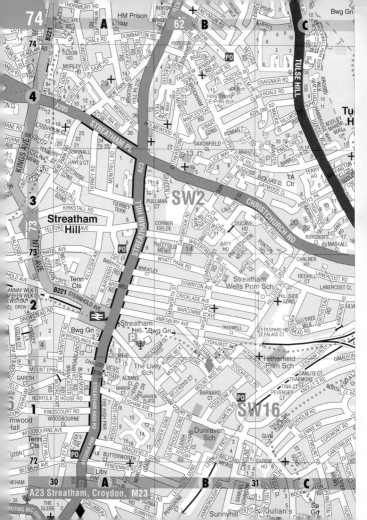

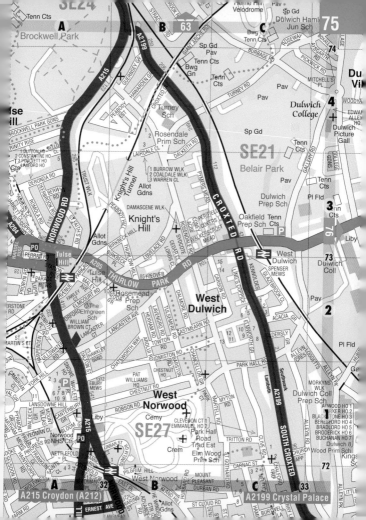

Key to central London map pages

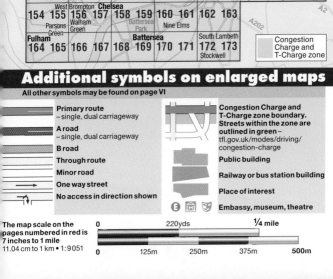

78 79 St John's Wood	Primrose Hill 80 81 Regent's	82 83 Somers	Islington 84 85 King's Cross	86 87	
Maida Vale 88 89 Westbourne Green	90 91 Lisson Grove	92 93 St Pancras Bloomsbury	Finsbury 94 95	Shoreditch 96 97	Bethnal 98 99 Green
Paddington 100 101	Marylebone 102 103	Fitzrovia 104 105	Holborn 106 107 St Giles Strand	108 109 City	Spitalfields 110 111 Whitechapel
Notting Hill 112 113	Bayswater 114 115 Kensington Gardens	Mayfair 116 117 Hyde Park	118 119 St James	120 121 South Bank	124 125 St George in the East
Kensington Holland Pk 126 127	Knightsbridge 128 129 Brompton	Green Park 130 131	Waterloo 132 133	122 123 Southwark	
West Kensington 140 141 Earl's Ct	South Kensington 142 143	Victoria 144 145 Belgravia Pimlico	Lambeth 148 149 Vauxhall Kennington	The Borough 136 137	138 139 Bermondsey
West Brompton Chelsea 154 155 Parsons Green	Walham 156 157 Green	Battersea 158 159 Park	160 161 Nine Elms	146 147	Newington 150 151 152 153 Walworth
Fulham 164 165	Battersea 166 167	168 169	170 171	South Lambeth 162 163 172 173 Stockwell	

Westminster

Congestion Charge and T-Charge zone

Additional symbols on enlarged maps

All other symbols may be found on page VI

Primary route – single, dual carriageway

A road – single, dual carriageway

B road

Through route

Minor road

One way street

No access in direction shown

Congestion Charge and T-Charge zone boundary. Streets within the zone are outlined in green – tfl.gov.uk/modes/driving/congestion-charge

Public building

Railway or bus station building

Place of interest

Ⓔ 🏛 ♟ **Embassy, museum, theatre**

The map scale on the pages numbered in red is 7 inches to 1 mile
11.04 cm to 1 km • 1:9051

0	220yds	¼ mile
0	125m	250m	375m	500m

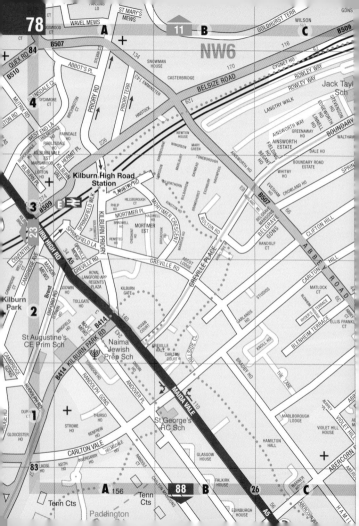

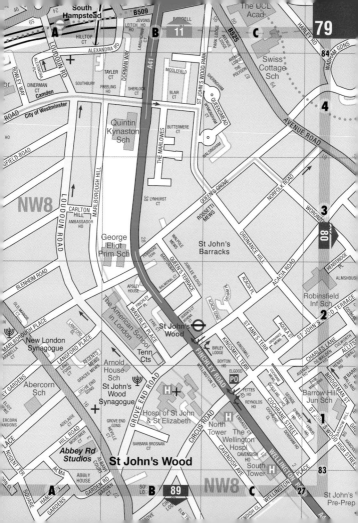

South Hampstead

B509

The UCL Acad

HARLEY GDNS

84 WADHAM GDNS

HILLTOP CT

JEVONS HO
LEITCH HO

BRIDGELL

PARK LODGE

B525

Swiss Cottage Sch

ALEXANDRA RD

LANGHORNE

MIDDLEFIELD

SHERINGHAM

THE POLYGON

4

DORMAN WAY

ROWLEY WAY

TAYLER CT

FREELING HO

SOUTHBURY

SHERLOCK CT

BLAIR CT

ST JOHN'S WOOD PARK

QUEENSMEAD

WYNDHAM CT

AVENUE ROAD

ALEXANDRA

DINERMAN CT

Camden

City of Westminster

Quintin Kynaston Sch

THE MARLOWES

BUTTERMERE CT

WALSINGHAM

GFIELD ROAD

NW8

LOUDOUN ROAD

MARLBOROUGH HILL

CARLTON HILL

AMBASSADOR HO

LYNHURST CT

QUEEN'S GROVE

ROSSETTI MEWS

NORFOLK ROAD

WORONZO

3

George Eliot Prim Sch

WALPOLE MEWS

QUEEN'S TERRACE

St John's Barracks

ORDNANCE HILL

ACACIA RD

80

HENSTRIDGE

ALMSHOU

BLENHEIM ROAD

APSLEY HOUSE

FINCHLEY PL

QUEENSWAY

BALMORAL CT

JUBILEE BLDGS

ACACIA GDNS

Robinsfield Inf Sch

The American School in London

WAVERLEY PLACE

ST JOHN'S TERRACE

2

OLD MANOR Y

MARLBOROUGH PLACE

LANGFORD PLACE

RECENTS MEWS

GRASSE MEWS

St John's Wood

ST ANN'S TERR

KINGSMILL

ORDNANCE MEWS

CHARLES LANE

AVENUE

New London Synagogue

ARIMBELA

Tenn Cts

Arnold House Sch

LANGFORD PLACE

GROVE END GDNS

BIRLEY LODGE

BOYTON

KINGSMILL TERR

FETTES HO

COCHRANE STREET

Barrow Hill Jun Sch

ALLITS

ABERCORN Sch

St John's Wood Synagogue

FINCHLEY ROAD

WELLINGTON CT

ELGOOD

PO

REYNOLDS HO

COCHRANE HO

1

ELIOT

ERCORN ANSIONS

HILL ROAD

ADELAIDE RD

Hosp of St John & St Elizabeth

CIRCUS ROAD

North Tower

H

The Wellington Hospl

DRISKMAN RD

ST JOHN'S WOOD HIGH STREET

LACE

GROVE END ROAD

MORTIMER CT

GROVE END GDNS

NEVILLE CT

BARBARA BROSNAN CT

CAVENDISH

H

South Tower

H

83

Abbey Rd Studios

St John's Wood

ALMA

ABBEY HOUSE

GARDEN RD

CAVENDISH AVE

WELLINGTON ROAD

WELLINGTON PLACE

St John's Pre-Prep

NUGENT TER

SQUARE

HALL

GARDENS

B

89

NW8

C

27

ABBEY RD

ALBANY COURT

ELM T

MDISH CL

GROVE

A4

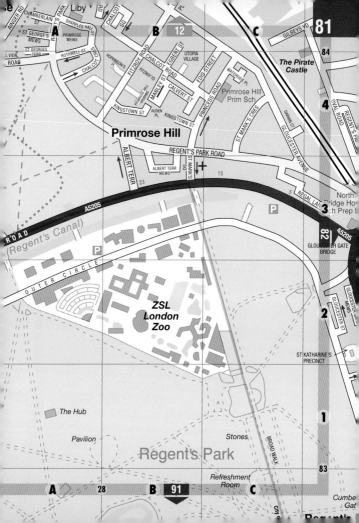

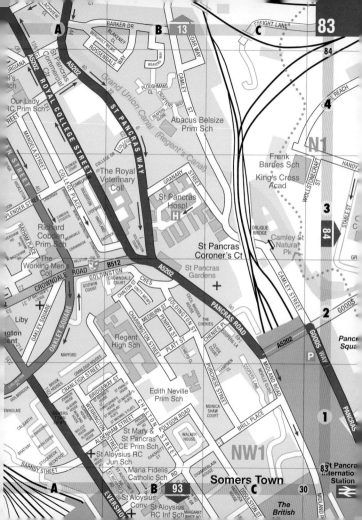

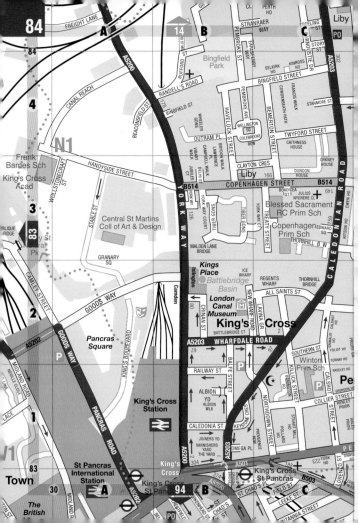

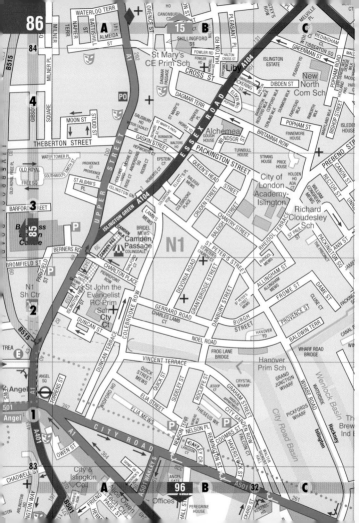

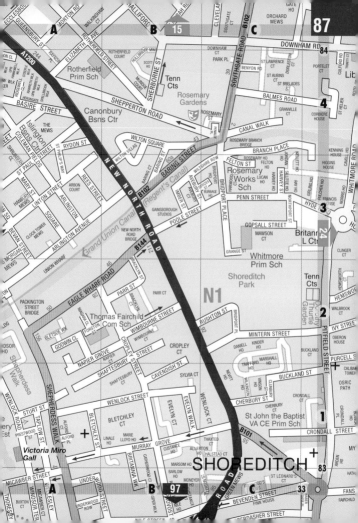

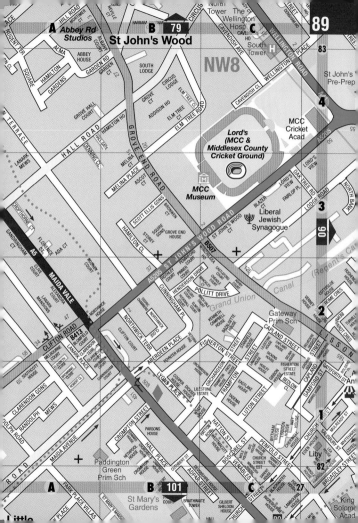

Abbey Rd Studios

St John's Wood

NW8

St John's Pre-Prep

Lord's (MCC & Middlesex County Cricket Ground)

MCC Cricket Acad

MCC Museum

Liberal Jewish Synagogue

LORD'S VIEW

NORTH BANK

ST JOHN'S WOOD ROAD

Grand Union

MAIDA VALE

(Regent's Canal)

Canal

Gateway Prim Sch

CUNNINGHAM PL

CLIFTON ROAD

POLLITT DRIVE

Capland Street

CAPLAND STREET

HENDERSON DRIVE

NORTHWICK TERR

ABERDEEN PLACE

FISHERTON STREET

FISHERTON STREET ESTATE

LISSON

LYONS PLACE

CROMPTON STREET

FRAMPTON STREET

ORCHARDSON STREET

LUTON STREET

PENFOLD STREET

CHURCH STREET

PARSONS HOUSE

HALL PLACE

Clarendon Mews

Randolph Mews

MAIDA AVENUE

Paddington Green Prim Sch

HATTON STREET

BOSCOBEL ST

VENABLES ST

BROADLEY STREET

Liby

St Mary's Gardens

King Solomon Acad

Little

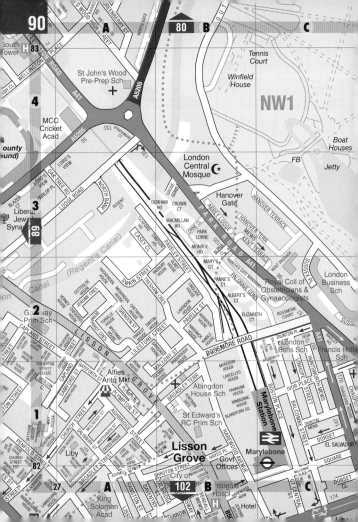

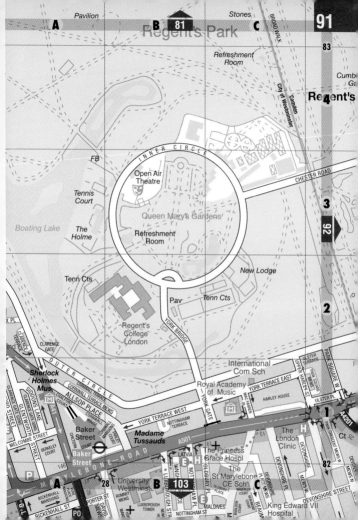

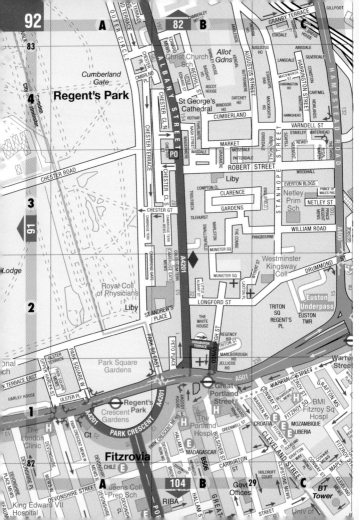

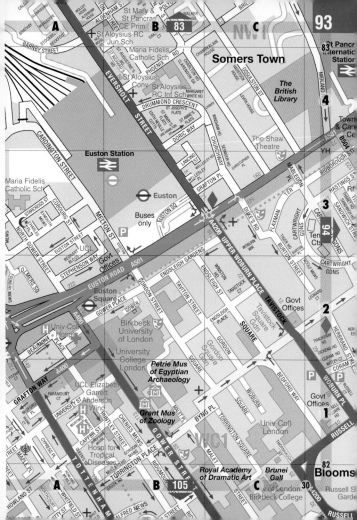

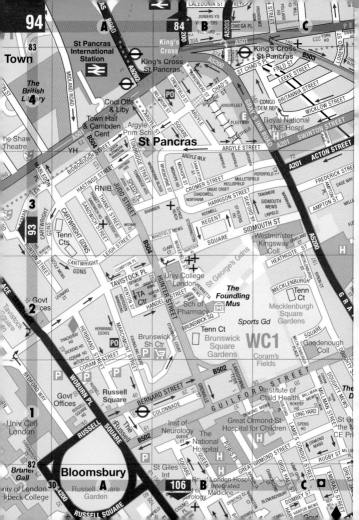

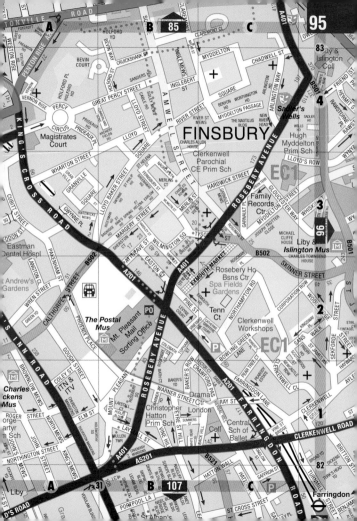

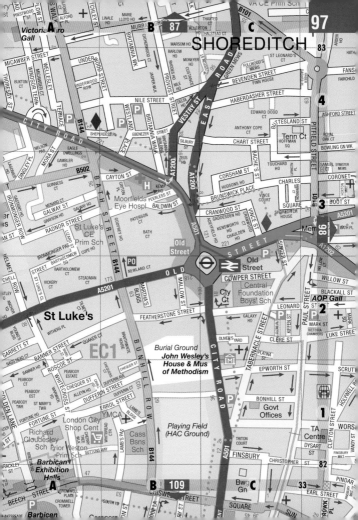

Victoria Miro
Gall

SHOREDITCH

CITY ROAD

B144

SHEPHERDESS PL

NILE STREET

VESTRY ST

EAST ROAD

B101

VA CE Prim Sch

ALLERTON   THAXTED

MARSOM HO

BARLOW HO
MONEYER
COSTARD HO

MILE
END

GREEN MEWS

FULLWOOD'S
MEWS

ST LEONARD'S

BEVENDEN STREET
FINN HOUSE

HABERDASHER STREET

EDWARD DODD
CT

ANTHONY COPE
CT

BATTLESLAND ST

Tenn Ct
HOFFMAN
SQ

ASHFORD STREET

ROYAL
OAK CT

PITFIELD STREET

BOWLING GN WK

SAMUEL SYMSTER
STREET

CORONET

BOOT ST

A5201

BATH ST

CAYTON ST

B502

GUINNESS
CT

GALWAY ST   GALWAY HO

RADNOR STREET   GRAYSON HO

BATH STREET

IRONMONGER PAS

BARTHOLOMEW
ST   COPE HO

St Luke's CE
Prim Sch

PATERSON
CT

GODFREY HO

BATH
CT

Moorfields
Eye Hospi

KEMP
CT   CAYTON
ST

PEERLESS ST

PEERLESS ST

BALDWIN ST

CRANWOOD ST

KENSWORTH HO
GADDESDEN HO
CHADULDEN
221

CORSHAM ST

HUDSONS HO

BRUNSWICK PLACE

CHARLES
SQUARE

VINCE
COURT

SHOREDITCH
HOUSE

A1202

OLD   STREET

Old
Street

Old
Street

St Luke's

PO

HELMET
ROW   St LUKE'S SQ

VICKERY
CT

STEDMAN
CT

173

B144

NEWLAND CT

MARTHA'S
BLDGS

A5201

MALLOW ST

COWPER STREET

Cty
Ct

Central
Foundation
Boys' Sch

SINGER STREET

WILLOW ST

BLACKALL ST

AOP Gall

PAUL STREET

LEONARD
ST   GALAXY
HO

MARK ST

VICTORIA
CHAMBERS

LUKE STREET

FEATHERSTONE STREET

CLERE ST

PLATINA
ST

SCRUT

GARRETT ST

BANNER STREET

ROSCOE ST

PEABODY
ESTATE

BUNHILL ROW

QUAKER CT

BRIGHTWATER
CT

DUFFERIN
AVE

OLIVER'S YARD

TABERNACLE STREET

EPWORTH ST

EC1

Burial Ground
John Wesley's
House & Mus
of Methodism

CITY ROAD

EPWORTH ST

BONHILL ST

HOLWELL RO

Govt
Offices

GOLDEN LANE

PEABODY
TWR   ST MARY'S
TWR

FORTUNE HO

FORTUNE ST

WHITECROSS STREET

CHEQUER ST

ALLEYN HO

DUFFERIN ST

DUFFERIN CT

London City
Shop Cent

YMCA

LAMB'S BLDGS

Cass
Bsns
Sch

B144

Playing Field
(HAC GROUND)

CLIFTON STREET

TA
Centre   FINSBURY
MKT

WORS

DYSART
ST

Richard
Cloudesley
Sch   Prior Weston
Prim Sch

SUTTONS WAY

TRITON
COURT

A501   FINSBURY

CHRISTOPHER   ST

PINDAR

Barbican
Exhibition
Halls

A   B   109   C

CROMWELL
PLACE

CROMWELL RD

CROMWELL
TOWER

BEECH ST   P   Barbican

SQUARE   Bwg
Gn

EARL STREET

CROWN
PL

SUN

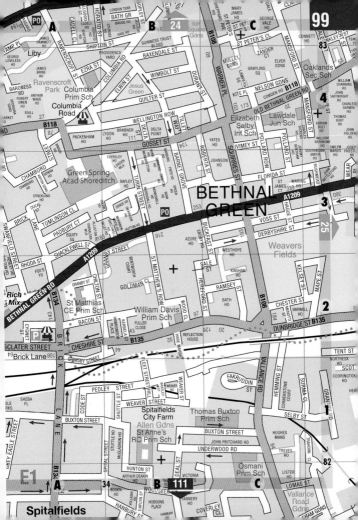

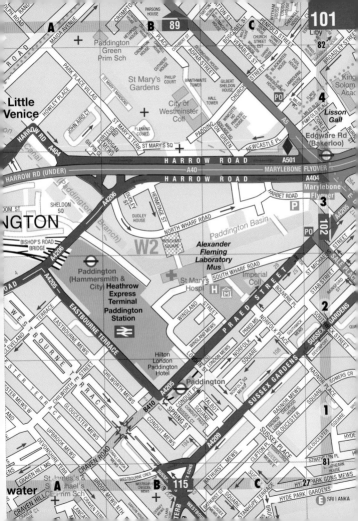

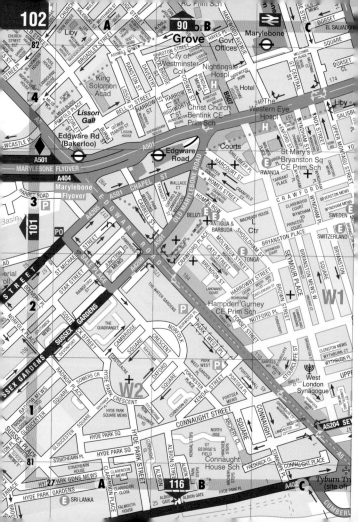

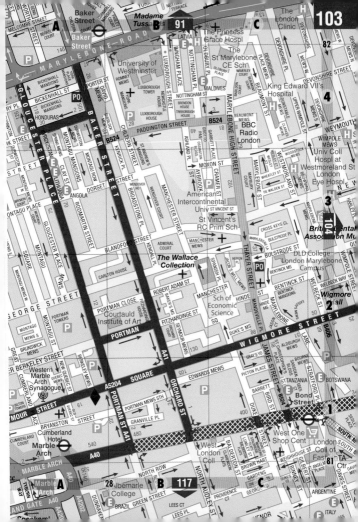

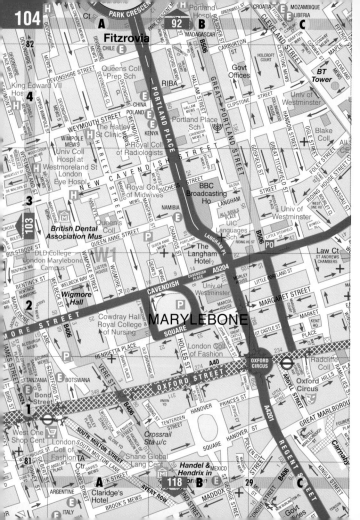

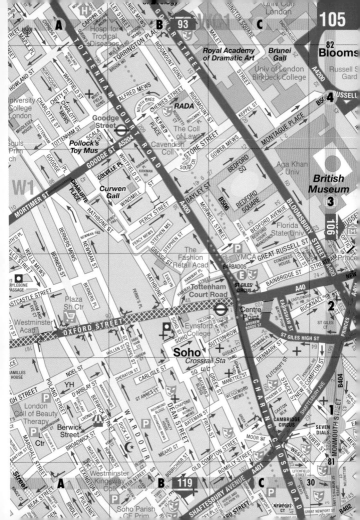

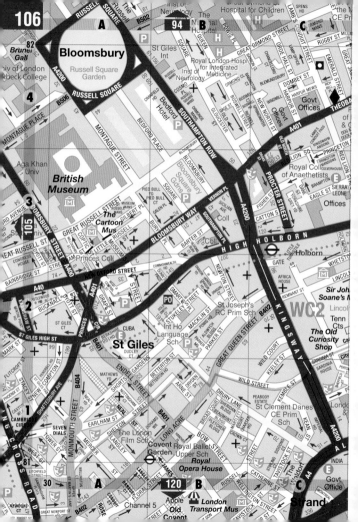

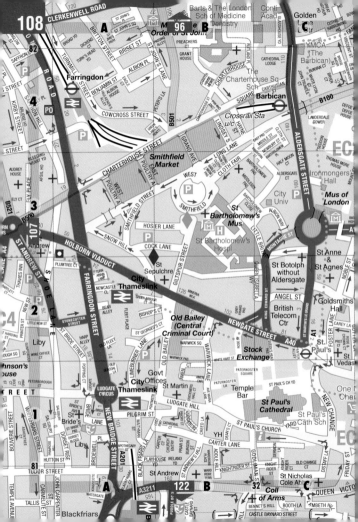

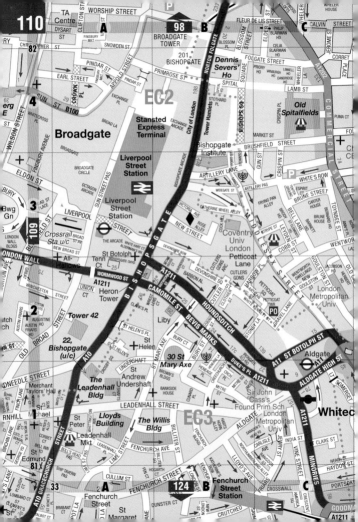

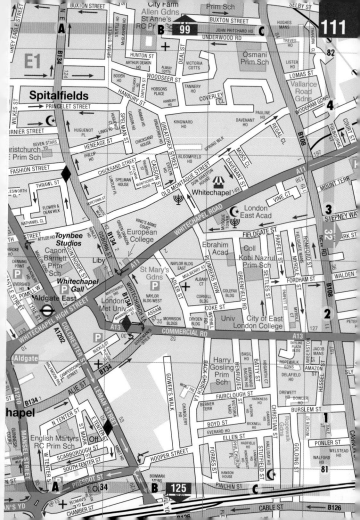

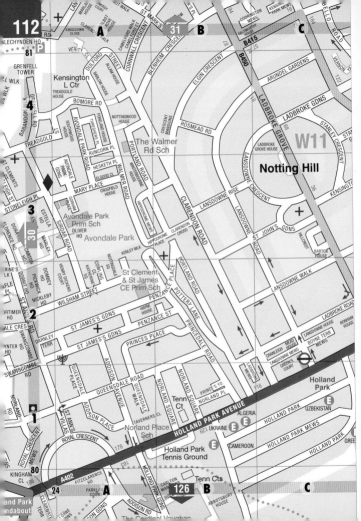

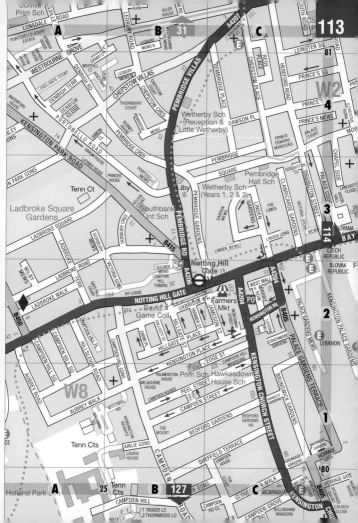

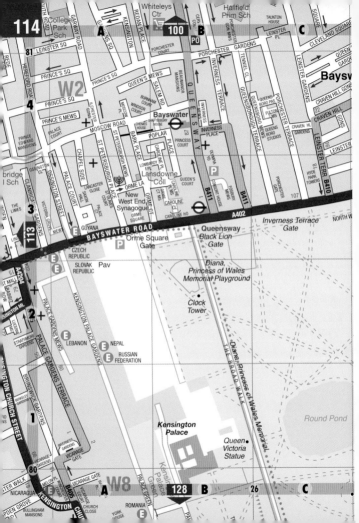

College Park Sch
Whiteleys Ctr
Hallfield Prim Sch
TAUNTON HOUSE
LEINSTER SQUARE

A
B
C

100

PO

GARWAY ROAD
REDAN PLACE
KENSINGTON
PRINCE'S SQ
QUEEN'S SQ
HEREFORD ROAD
REDE
81
LEINSTER SQ
PORCHESTER COURT
PORCHESTER GARDENS
CLEVELAND SQUARE
LEINSTER PL
QUEENS GARDENS

W2
4
PRINCE'S MEWS
PRINCE'S SQ
BEAUMANOR MANSIONS
INVERNESS TERRACE
LEINSTER GARDENS
Baysw
QUEEN'S MEWS
SALEM RD
PORCHESTER TERRACE
CRAVEN HILL
CRAVEN HILL GDNS
22

PRINCE'S MEWS
ILCHESTER GDNS
BURNHAM COURT
MOSCOW ROAD
WINDSOR COURT
Bayswater
QUEENSWAY
QUEEN'S BORO PASS
QUEENS BORO MAS
FULTON MS
CRAVEN HILL
CRAVEN HILL STUDIOS
QUEENS BORO STUDIOS
LEINSTER TERRACE
LEINSTER

PRINCE EDWARD MANSIONS
PALACE COURT
MOSCOW ROAD
CHENIES HOUSE
SHAFTESBURY
POPLAR PLACE
BARK PLACE
PRINCESS CT
INVERNESS MEWS
INVERNESS PLACE
QUEENSBOROUGH TERRACE
HYDE PARK TOWERS
B410

bridge I Sch
OSSINGTON CL
CHAPEL SIDE
ST PETERSBURGH MEWS
ST PETERSBURGH PLACE
CAROLINE PL
LOMBARD LPK
CAROLINE PL MS
OLYMPIA YD
QUEEN'S COURT
PORCHESTER GATE
107

THE LIMES
CLANRICARDE GARDENS
PALACE COURT
VICTORIA GROVE
LANCASTER CLOSE
SAXON HALL
ORME LA
New West End Synagogue
Lansdowne Coll
ORME LA
ST STOKES
CAROLINE
CAROLINE HO
FOSSBURY MEWS
B411
B411
PEMBRIDGE GATE

3
113
GUYANA
ORME SQUARE
BAYSWATER ROAD
A402
Inverness Terrace Gate
NORTH W

E
Orme Square Gate
P
Queensway Black Lion Gate
Inverness Terrace Gate

CZECH REPUBLIC
SLOVAK REPUBLIC
Pav
Diana, Princess of Wales Memorial Playground

2
SINGTON ML
STRATHMORE GARDENS
PALACE GARDENS MEWS
KENSINGTON PALACE GARDENS
Clock Tower

AM204
E LEBANON
E NEPAL
E RUSSIAN FEDERATION

1
INVERNESS GARDENS
Kensington Palace
Queen Victoria Statue
Round Pond

ON CHURCH STREET
BRUNSWICK GARDENS
PALACE GARDENS TERRACE
BERKELEY GDNS

80
VICARAGE GDNS
VICARAGE GATE
INVERNESS
NICARAGUA
VICARAGE COURT
CHURCH CLOSE
YORK HOUSE
E ROMANIA
W8
A
128
B
26
C
KENSINGTON
KENSINGTON PALACE GREEN
TER WALK
PINE GROVE
BILLINGHAM MANSIONS
COURT

THE BROAD WALK
Diana, Princess of Wales Memorial

A MEWS

URBA

DEVONSHIRE TERR

CRAVEN HILL MS

CRAVEN HILL

CRAVEN ROAD

B 101

CONDUIT MS

ING ST

A209

A4209

SUSSEX GDNS

C

SUSSEY PLACE

GLOUCESTER SQUARE

GLOUCESTER

STRATH

8¹ PL

HYD

STRATHEARN GDNS

HYDE PARK GDNS MEWS

E SRI LANKA

4

vater

St James & St Michael's CE Prim Sch

CRAVEN HILL LODGE

CRAVEN EL

LANCASTER MEWS

LANCASTER GATE

LANCASTER COURT

WESTBOURNE CRES

BROOK MEWS NTH

GLOUCESTER TERR

WESTBOURNE CRESCENT MEWS

GARDEN RD

CARROLLS HOUSE

ELMS MEWS

GILBERT RD

LANCASTER TERR

BATHURST MEWS

SUSSEX SQUARE

CLIFTON PL

SUSSEX SQUARE

STANHOPE TERRACE

HYDE PARK GDNS

BROOK ST

HYDE PARK GARDENS MEWS

A4209

Royal Lancaster Hotel

A402

Victoria Gate

E COSTA RICA

LANCASTER GATE

LANCASTER GATE

BARRIE HOUSE

SPIRE HOUSE

Lancaster Gate

Westbourne Gate

B A Y S W A T E R   R O A D

NORTH FLOWER WALK

Marlborough Gate

Lancaster Gate

St Agnes' Well

The Fountains

3

WEST CARRIAGE DRIVE

BIRTH RIDE

116

Bayswater Road Mkt

Lancaster Gate

ALK

Bayard's Watering Place (site of)

BUCK HILL WALK

BUDGES WALK

Speke's Monument

LANCASTER WALK

W2

Peter Pan Statue

The Long Water

2

Serpentine Sackler Gallery

P

Diana, Princess of Wales Memorial Walk

Physical Energy Statue

Temple Lodge

Serpentine Bridge

1

Kensington Gardens

P

LANCASTER WALK

A

Bandstand

B 129

ntine Gallery

Diana, Princess of Wales Memorial

C

80

Diana, Princ

27

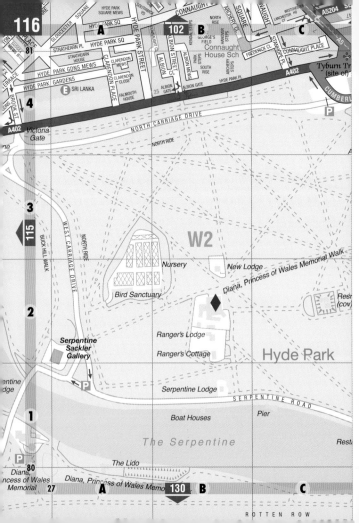

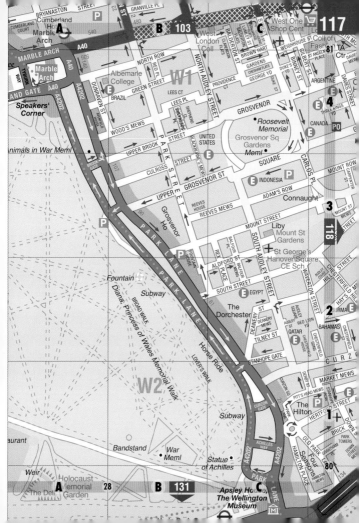

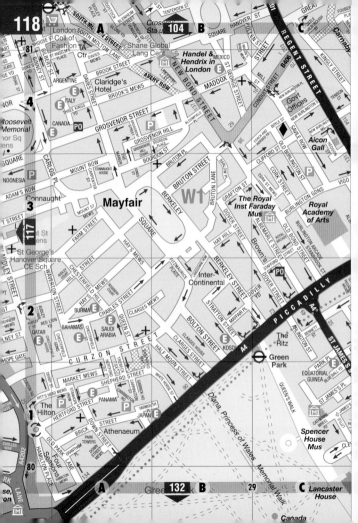

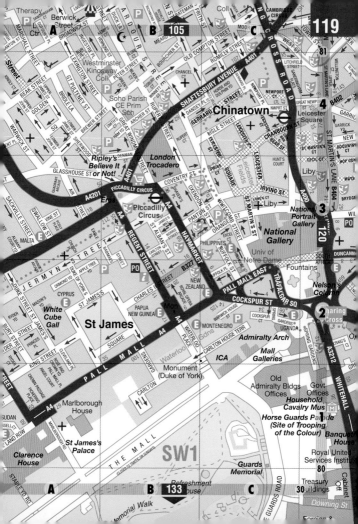

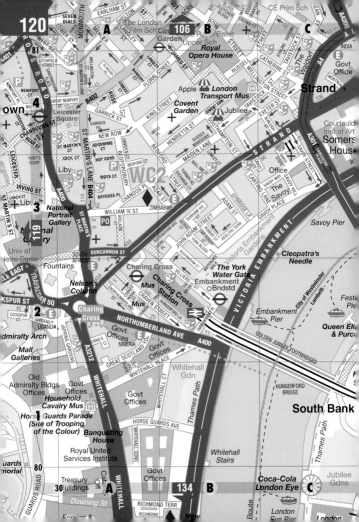

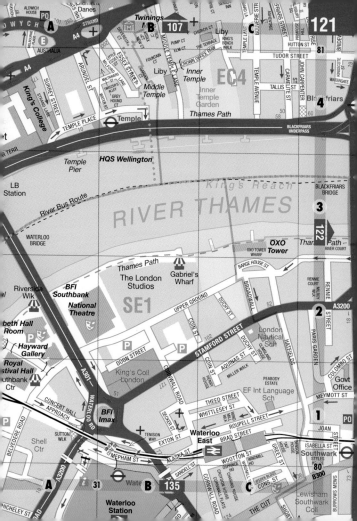

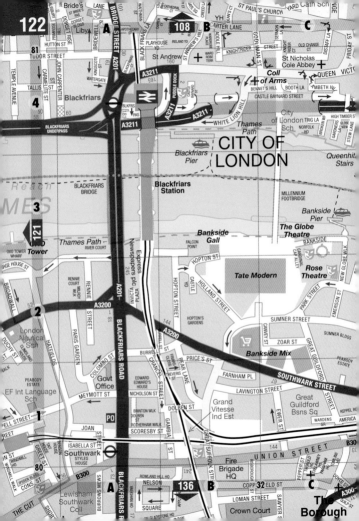

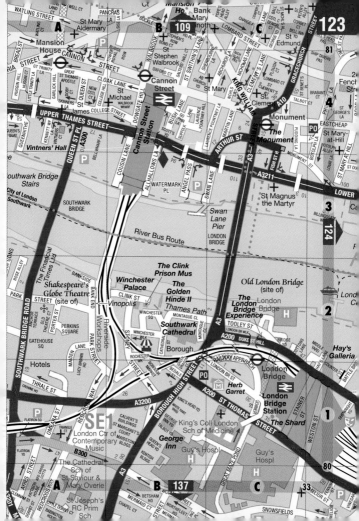

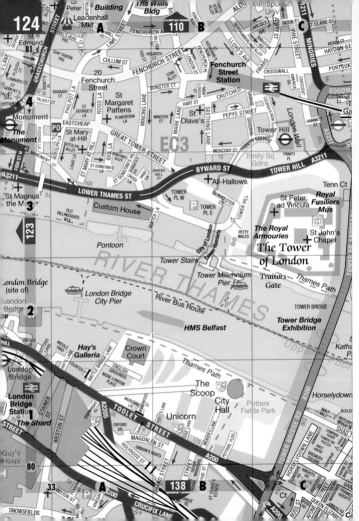

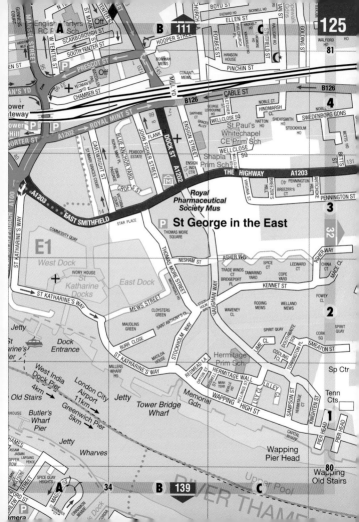

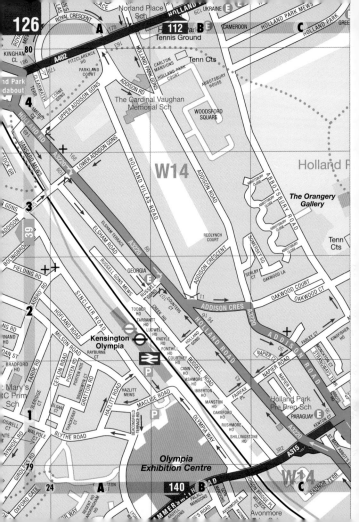

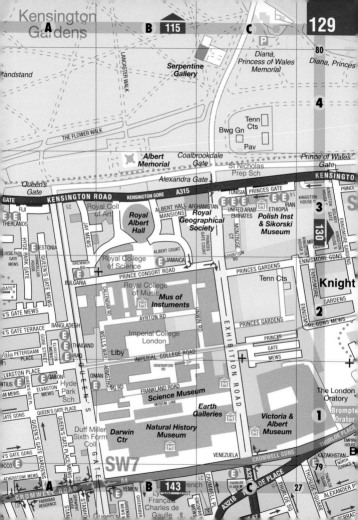

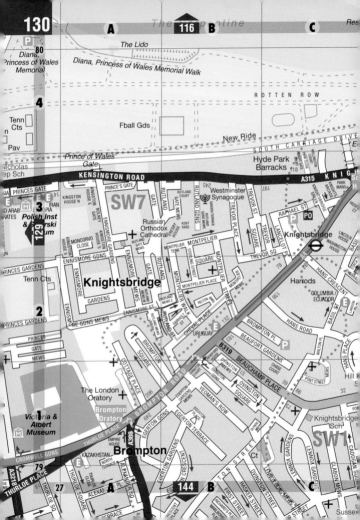

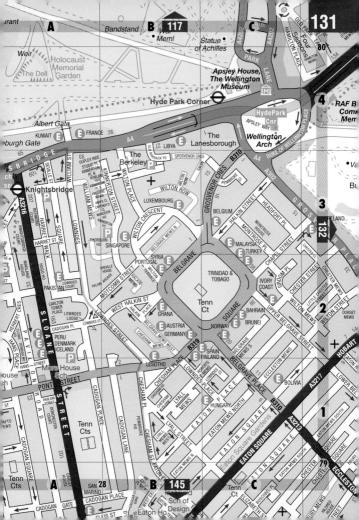

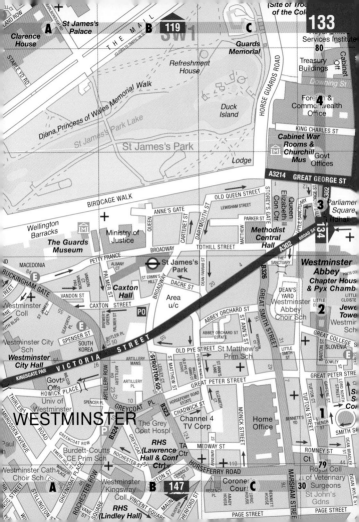

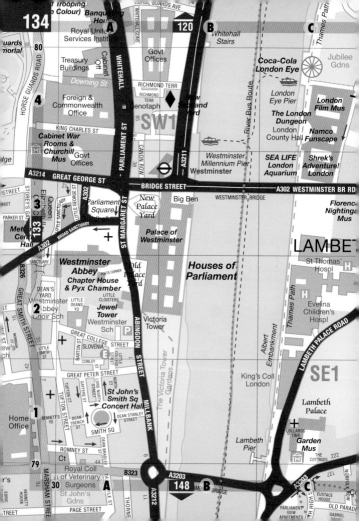

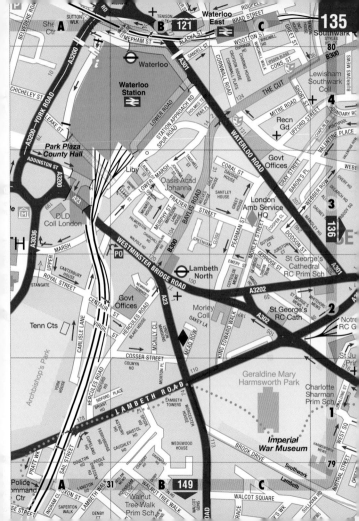

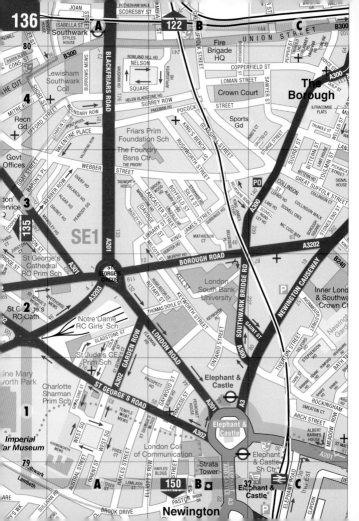

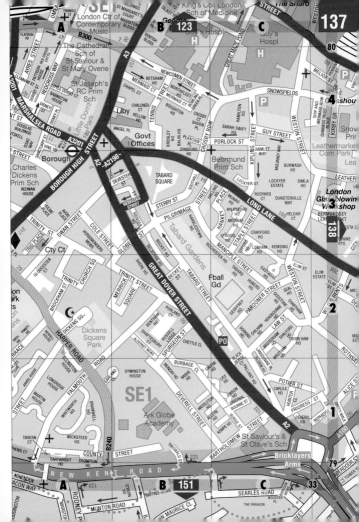

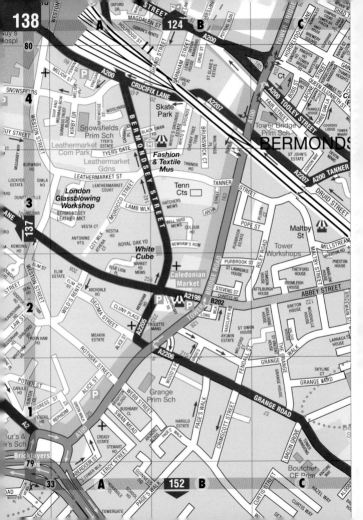

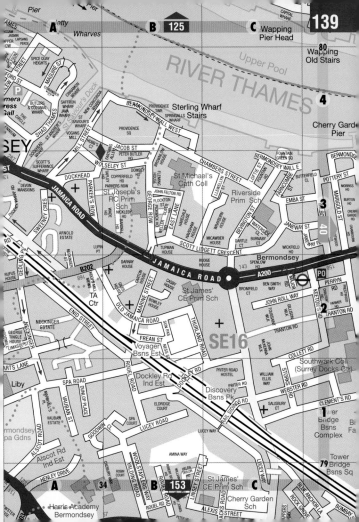

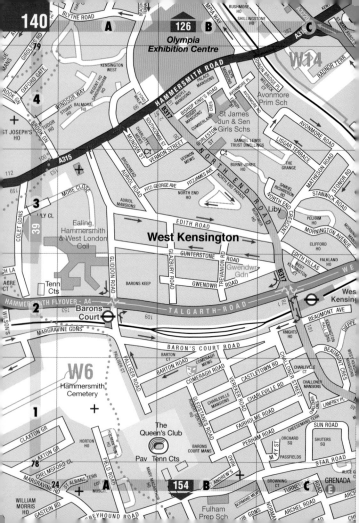

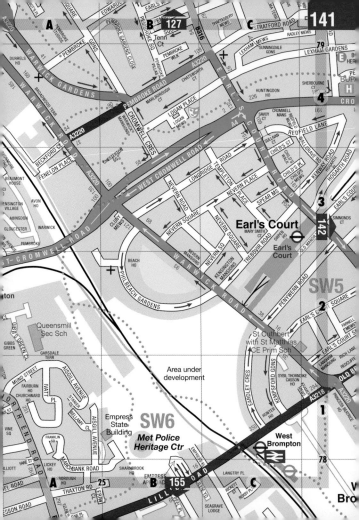

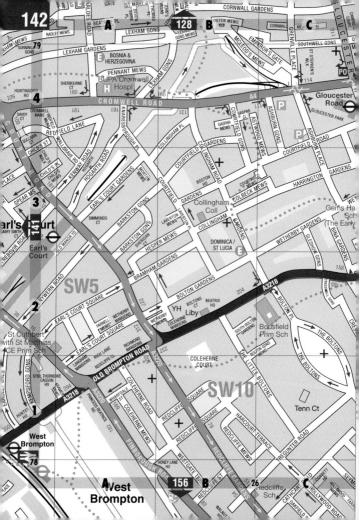

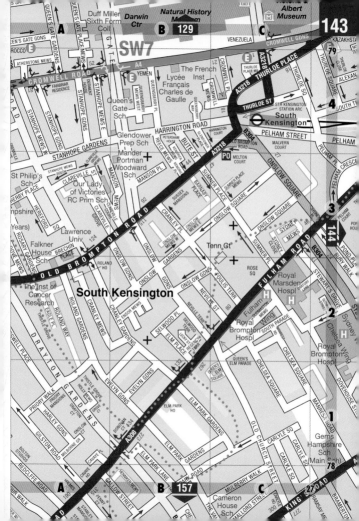

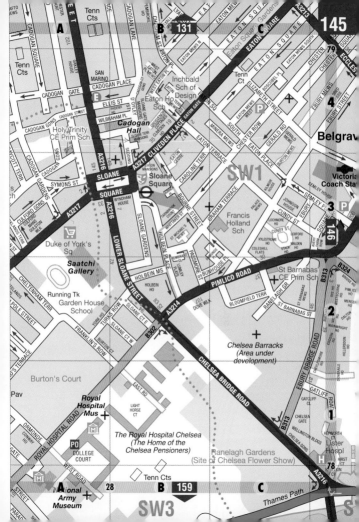

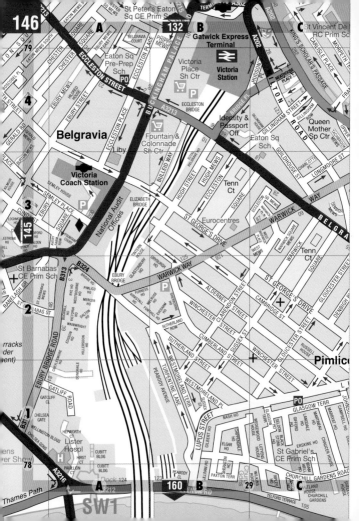

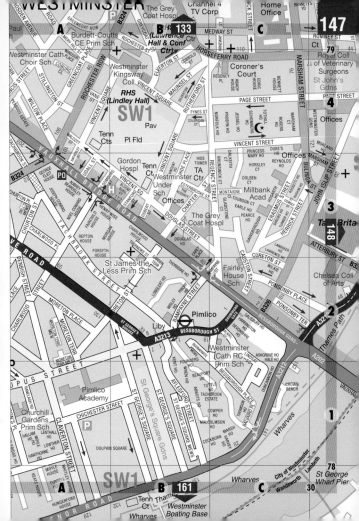

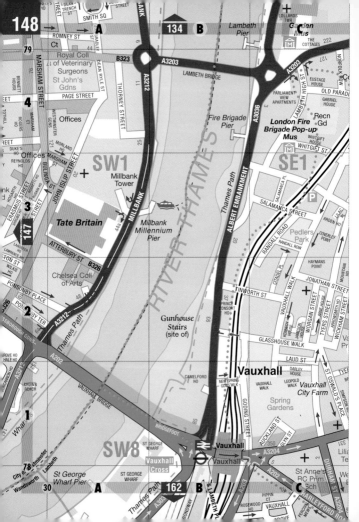

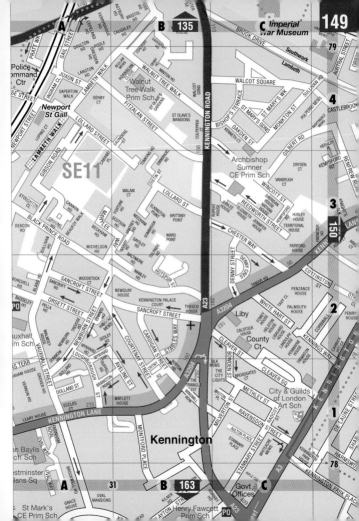

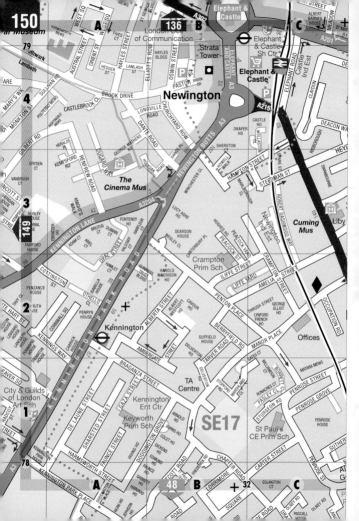

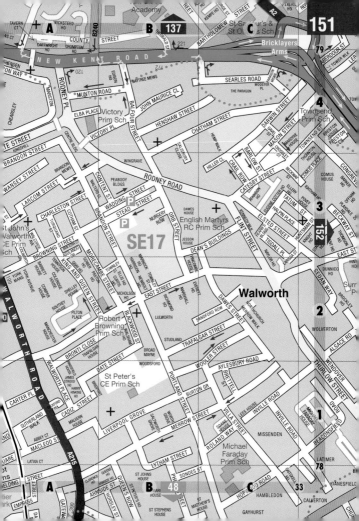

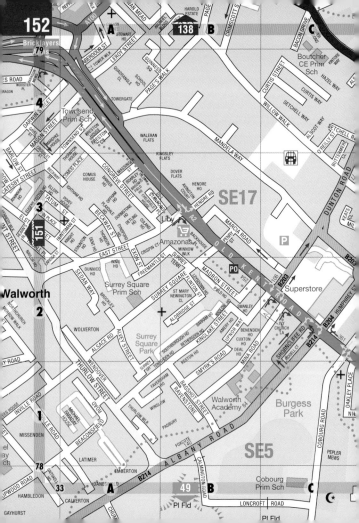

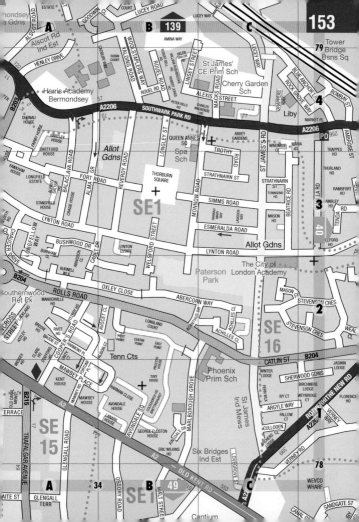

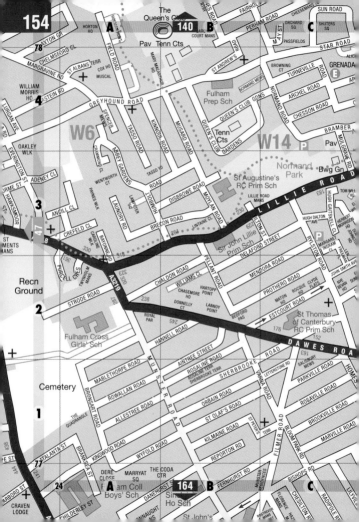

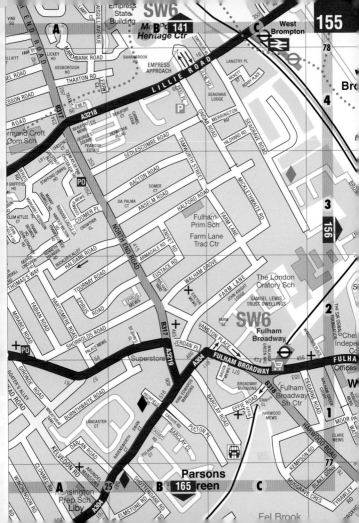

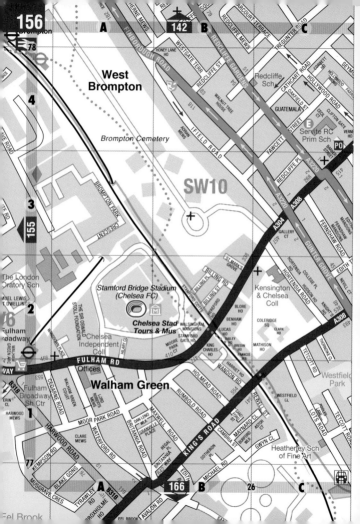

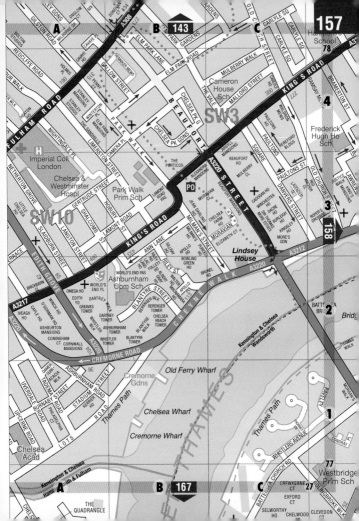

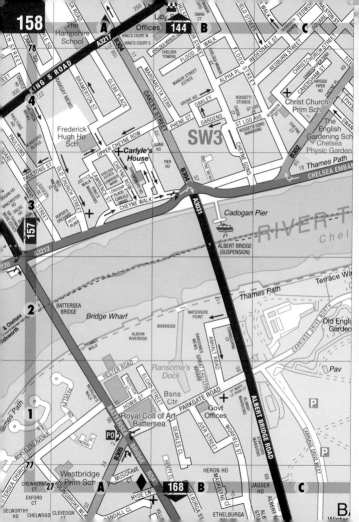

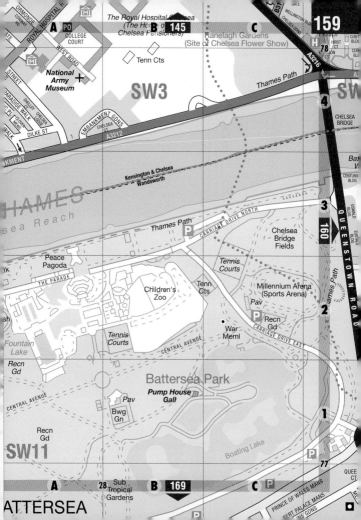

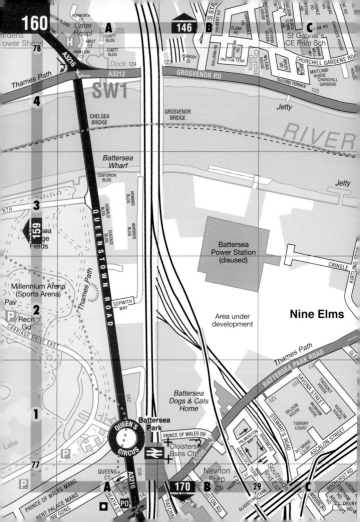

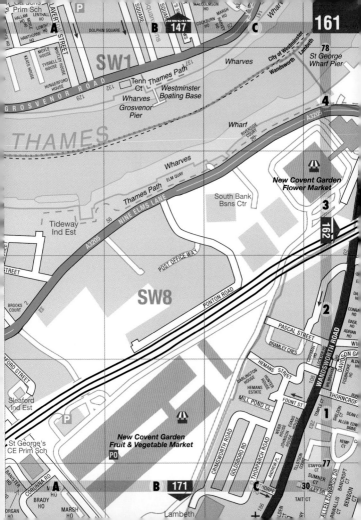

A **B** **147** **C**

SQUARE

MacCOLSON
COCKBURN HO MARSH HO
Wharf
DOLPHIN SQUARE

City of Westminster
Wandsworth Lambeth

78
St George
Wharf Pier

Wharves

SW1

Tenn Thames Path
Ct
Wharves
Westminster
Boating Base
*Grosvenor
Pier*

4

HALLAM
HAWTHORNE HO
LENTHALL
WHITLEY HO
MOYLE HOUSE
TYRRELEY HOUSE
KEATS HOUSE
HUNGERFORD HOUSE

GROSVENOR ROAD 129 132 137

Wharves
Wharf
RIVERSIDE
COURT

THAMES

A3205

Wharves

New Covent Garden
Flower Market

ELM QUAY

Thames Path

3

NINE ELMS LANE

162

56

Tideway
Ind Est

South Bank
Bsns Ctr

A3205

POST OFFICE WAY

SW8

PONTON ROAD

2

BROOKS
COURT

PASCAL STREET

BRAMLEY CRES

HEMANS STREET

BARLINGTON
HOUSE
PAINTERS
HOUSE
HEMANS
ESTATE

MILL POND CL

FOUNT ST

WANDSWORTH ROAD

CONRAD
HO
BASIL
HO
ADRIAN
HO
WI
LOCKYER ST
FOXBOURNE

1

Sleaford
Ind Est

ST FORD STREET

P

St George's
CE Prim Sch

New Covent Garden
Fruit & Vegetable Market

PO

CRIMSWORTH ROAD

GOLDSBORO RD

THORPARCH ROAD

ANDREW PL

WEBB
HOUSE
EVANS
HOUSE
JOHNSON
HOUSE

ELLINGTON
PL

STAFFORD
CT
SUMNER
CT

BANCROFT
CT

BENSON
CT

THORNCROFT ST
DEAN CL
ALLEN EDW
DRIVE
KEMP CT
SHELDON
CT

THORNCROFT
DAVIDSON GA

TEMPLE CT

SHELDON

DEAN

HOLBROUGH

77

CORUNNA RD
A
B **171** **C**

BRADY
HO
MARSH
HO
ORGAN HO

TAIT CT
ALLEN EDWARDS DRIVE
THORPE
TURNWALLIS CT
CRIMWALLIS

30
LEY DR

Lambeth

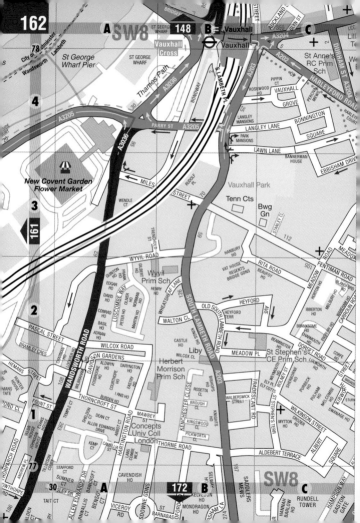

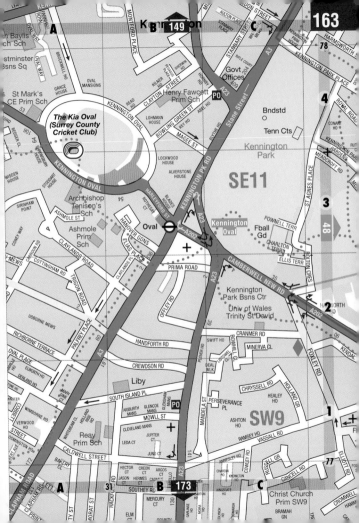

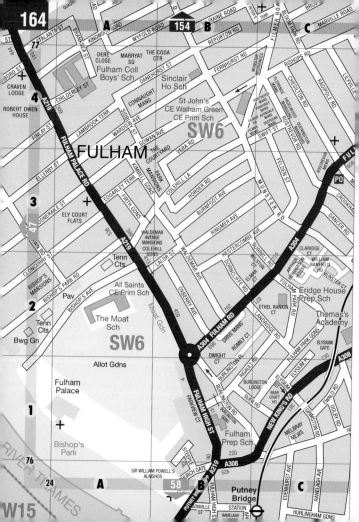

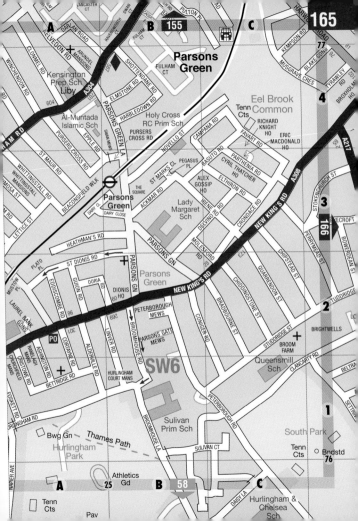

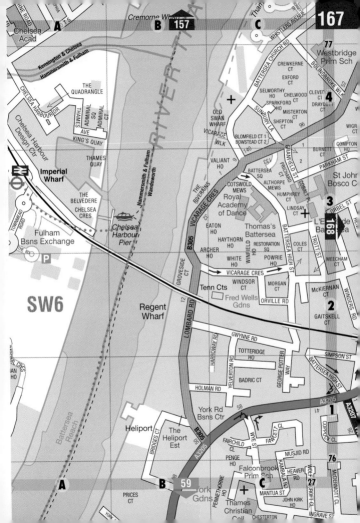

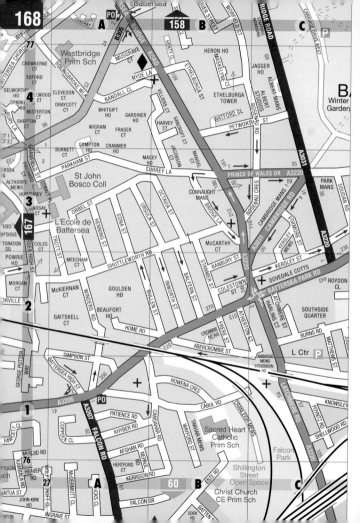

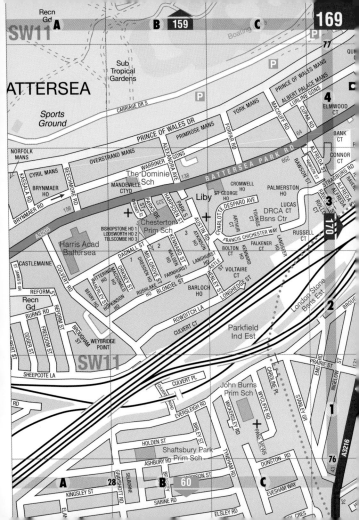

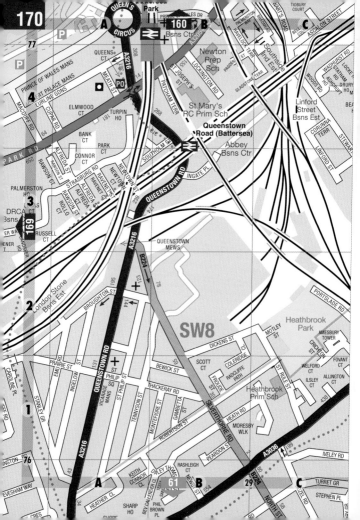

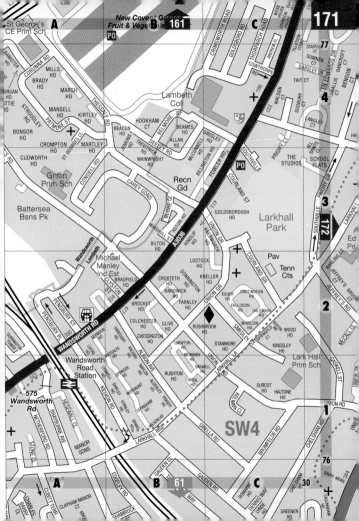

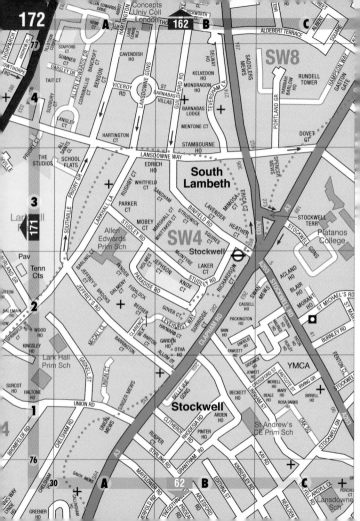

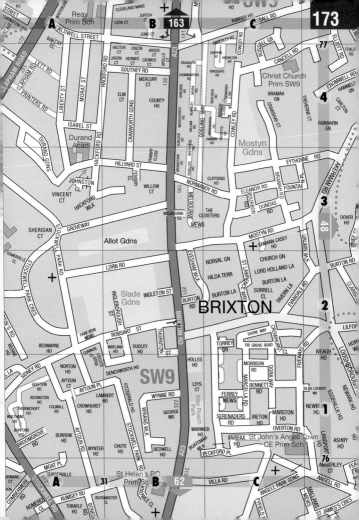

Church Rd 6 Beckenham BR2..........**53** C6 **228** C6

Place name	Location number	Locality, town or village	Postcode district	Standard scale reference	Enlarged scale reference
May be abbreviated on the map	Present when a number indicates the place's position in a crowded area of mapping	Shown when more than one place (outside London postal districts) has the same name	District for the indexed place	Page number and grid reference for the standard mapping	Page number and grid reference for the central London enlarged mapping, underlined in red

Public and commercial buildings are highlighted in magenta.
Places of interest are highlighted in blue
Cities, towns and villages are listed in CAPITAL LETTERS

Abbreviations used in the index

Acad	Academy	Ct	Court	Int	International	Prom	Promenade
App	Approach	Ctr	Centre	Intc	Interchange	RC	Roman Catholic
Arc	Arcade	Crkt	Cricket	Jun	Junior	Rd	Road
Art Gall	Art Gallery	Ctry Pk	Country Park	Junc	Junction	Rdbt	Roundabout
Ave	Avenue	Cty	County	La	Lane	Ret Pk	Retail Park
Bglws	Bungalows	Ctyd	Courtyard	L Ctr	Leisure Centre	Sch	School
Bldgs	Buildings	Dr	Drive	Liby	Library	Sec	Secondary
Bsns Ctr	Business Centre	Ent Ctr	Enterprise Centre	Mans	Mansions	Sh Ctr	Shopping Centre
Bsns Pk	Business Park	Ent Pk	Enterprise Park	Mdw/s	Meadow/s	Sp	Sports
Bvd	Boulevard	Est	Estate	Meml	Memorial	Specl	Special
Cath	Cathedral, Catholic	Ex Ctr	Exhibition Centre	Mid	Middle	Sports Ctr	Sports Centre
CE	Church of England	Ex Hall	Exhibition Hall	Mix	Mixed	Sq	Square
Cemy	Cemetery	Fst	First	Mkt	Market	St	Street, Saint
Cir	Circus	Gdn	Garden	Mon	Monument	Sta	Station
Circ	Circle	Gdns	Gardens	Mus	Museum	Stad	Stadium
Cl	Close	Gn	Green	Obsy	Observatory	Tech	Technical Technology
Cnr	Corner	Gr	Grove	Orch	Orchard		
Coll	College	Gram	Grammar	Par	Parade	Terr	Terrace
Com	Community	Her Ctr	Heritage Centre	Pas	Passage	Trad Est	Trading Estate
Comm	Common	Ho	House	Pav	Pavilion	Twr/s	Tower/s
Comp	Comprehensive	Hospl	Hospital	Pk	Park	Univ	University
Con Ctr	Conference Centre	Hts	Heights	Pl	Place	Wlk	Walk
Cotts	Cottages	Ind Est	Industrial Estate	Prec	Precinct	Yd	Yard
Cres	Crescent	Inf	Infant	Prep	Preparatory		
Cswy	Causeway	Inst	Institute	Prim	Primary		

2 Willow Rd NW3 . . . .12 A4
3 Mills Studios
E16 . . . . .27 B2
22, Bishopgate
EC2 . . . . 110 A1
30 St Mary Axe (The
Gherkin) EC2 . . . . 110 B2
176 Gall NW5 . . . . . .12 C2
201 Bishopgate
EC2 . . . . 110 A1
575 Wandsworth Rd
SW8 . . . . 171 A1

A

Abacus Belsize Prim
Sch NW1 . . . . .83 B4
Abadey Ho SW4 . . . .147 C4
Abady Mews 9
SW8 . . . . .61 A4
Abbess Cl SW2 . . . . .75 A3
Abbeville Mews 3
SW4 . . . . .61 C3
Abbeville Rd SW4 . . .61 B2
Abbey Bsns Ctr
SW8 . . . . 170 B4
Abbey Ct
6 Bedford Pk
W12 . . . . .38 A3
Camberwell SE17 . . .151 A1
St John's Wood
NW8 . . . . .78 C2
Abbeyfield Rd
SE16 . . . . .40 B2
Abbey Gdns
10 Bermondsey
SE16 . . . . 153 C4
St John's Wood
NW8 . . . . .79 A1
West Kensington
W6 . . . . 154 A3
Abbey Ho NW8 . . . . .89 A4
Abbey La E15 . . . . . .27 C3
Abbey Lo NW8 . . . . . .90 B3
Abbey Orchard St
SW1 . . . . 133 C2
Abbey Orchard Street
Est SW1 . . . . 133 C2
Abbey Rd
St John's Wood
NW8 . . . . .78 C2
Wembley NW10 . . . . .20 A3
Abbey Rd Studios
NW8 . . . . .79 A1
Abbot Cl SW8 . . . . . 138 C2
Abbot Cl SW8 . . . . . 162 A1
Abbot Ho 10 E14 . . . .34 A2
Abbotsbury Cl
Kensington W14 . . . .126 C3
Mill Meads E15 . . . . .27 B3
Abbotsbury Ho
W14 . . . . 126 B4
Abbotsbury Mews
SE15 . . . . .65 B4
Abbotsbury Rd
W14 . . . . 126 C3
Abbotshade Rd 13
SE16 . . . . .32 C1
Abbots Ho
Kensington W14 . . . .126 C1
Pimlico SW1 . . . . . . 147 B1
Abbots La SE1 . . . . . 124 B1
Abbots Pk SW2 . . . . .74 C3
Abbot's PI NW6 . . . . .78 A4
Abbot St E8 . . . . .16 B2

Abbotstone Ho 4
E5 . . . . .7 C2
Abbotstone Rd
SW15 . . . . .57 B4
Abbotswell Rd
SE4 . . . . .66 B2
Abbotswood Rd
London SE22 . . . . . . .64 A3
Streatham SW16 . . . .73 C1
Abbott Ho SW12 . . . .72 B4
Abbott Rd E14 . . . . . .34 C3
Abbotts Cl N1 . . . . . .15 B2
Abbotts Wharf 4
E14 . . . . .33 C3
Abchurch La EC2,
EC4 . . . . 123 C4
Abchurch Yd EC4 . . 123 B4
Abdale Rd W12 . . . . .30 A1
Abel Ho 11 SE11 . . . 163 B4
Aberavon Rd E3 . . . .26 A2
Abercorn Cl NW8 . . . .88 C4
Abercorn Mans
NW8 . . . . .79 A1
Abercorn Mews 10
TW10 . . . . .54 B3
Abercorn PI NW8 . . . .78 C1
Abercorn Sch
NW8 . . . . .79 A1
Abercorn Way
SE1 . . . . 153 B2
Abercorn Wlk
NW8 . . . . .88 C4
Abercrombie Ho 1
W12 . . . . .30 A2
Abercrombie Rd
E15 . . . . .19 C3
Abercrombie St
SW11 . . . . 168 B2
Aberdale Ct 22
SE16 . . . . .40 C4
Aberdare Gdns
NW6 . . . . .11 A1
Aberdeen Ct
Canonbury N5 . . . . . .15 B3
Paddington W2 . . . . .89 B1
Aberdeen Ctr N5 . . . .15 B3
Aberdeen La N5 . . . . .15 B3
Aberdeen Mans
WC1 . . . . .94 A2
Aberdeen PI N5 . . . . .15 B3
Aberdeen PI NW8 . . . .89 B2
Aberdeen Rd
Canonbury N5 . . . . . .15 B4
Dudden Hill NW10 . . . .8 B3
Aberdeen Terr
SE3 . . . . .52 C1
Aberdour St SE1 . . . 152 A4
Aberfeldy Ho SE5 . . .48 A3
Aberfeldy St E14 . . . .34 B3
Abersham Rd E8 . . . .16 B3
Ability Plaza 3 E8 . . .16 B1
Ability Twrs EC1 . . . . .96 C4
Abingdon W14 . . . . . 141 A3
Abingdon Cl
Fulham SE1 . . . . 153 A2
Kentish Town NW1 . . .13 C2
Abingdon Ct W8 . . . 127 C1
Abingdon Gdns
W8 . . . . 127 C1
Abingdon Ho
E2 . . . . .24 B1 98 C2
Abingdon House Sch
NW1 . . . . .90 B1
Abingdon Mans
W8 . . . . 127 B2
Abingdon Rd W8 . . . 127 C1

Abingdon St SW1 . . 134 A2
Abingdon Villas
W8 . . . . 127 C1
Abinger Gr SE8 . . . . .51 B4
Abinger Ho SE1 . . . . .7 B2
Abinger Mews W9 . . .23 C1
Abinger Rd W4 . . . . .38 A3
Ablett St SE16 . . . . . .40 B1
Abney Gdns 5 N16 . .7 B2
Abney Park Cemetery
N16 . . . . .7 A2
Abney Park Ct N16 . .7 B2
Aboyne Rd SW17 . . .71 C1
Abyssinia Cl SW11 . .60 A3
Abyssinia Rd
SW11 . . . . .60 A3
Acacia Cl SE8 . . . . . .41 A2
Acacia Gdns NW8 . . .79 C2
Acacia Gr SE21 . . . . .75 C2
Acacia Ho
Brockley SE4 . . . . . . .66 B3
Stoke Newington
N16 . . . . .6 C2
Acacia PI NW8 . . . . . .79 C2
Acacia Rd
Acton W3 . . . . .28 B2
St John's Wood
NW8 . . . . .79 C2
Acacia Wlk SW10 . . 157 A1
Academy Ct 13 E2 . .25 B2
Academy Gdns
W8 . . . . 127 B4
Academy Sch The 3
NW3 . . . . .11 C4
Academy The 2
N19 . . . . .4 B3
Acad of Live &
Recorded Arts
SW18 . . . . .59 C1
Acanthus Dr SE1 . . . 153 B2
Acanthus Rd
SW11 . . . . .60 C4
Accommodation Rd
NW11 . . . . .1 B3
Acer Ct 11 NW2 . . . . .9 C4
Acer Rd E8 . . . . .16 C1
Acfold Rd SW6 . . . . 166 A3
Achilles Cl SE1 . . . . 153 C2
Achilles Ho 12 E2 . . .25 A3
Achilles Rd NW6 . . . .10 C3
Achilles St SE14 . . . .51 A3
Achilles Way 1 . . . . 117 C1
Acklam Rd W10 . . . . .31 B4
Ackmar Rd SW6 . . . 165 B3
Ackroyd Dr E3 . . . . . .33 C4
Acland Burghley Sch
NW5 . . . . .13 A4
Acland Cres SE5 . . . .63 C4
Acland Ho SW9 . . . . 172 C2
Acland Rd NW2 . . . . . .9 A2
Acol Ct 3 NW6 . . . . .10 C1
Acol Rd NW6 . . . . . . .11 A1
Acorn Ct 5 E3 . . . . . .26 C3
Acorn Gdns W3 . . . . .28 C4
Acorn Par 7 SE15 . . .50 A3
Acorn Production Ctr
N7 . . . . .14 A1
Acorns The 21
SW19 . . . . .69 C3
Acorn Wharf SE15 . . .49 C4
Acorn Wlk SE16 . . . . .33 A1
Acqua Ho TW9 . . . . . .45 A3
Acre Dr SE22 . . . . . . .64 C3
Acre La SW2 . . . . . . .62 B3
Acris St SW18 . . . . . .59 B2

ACTON 28 C1
Acton Bsns Ctr 28 C1
Acton Central Ind Est
4 W3 . . . . .28 B2
Acton Central Sta
W3 . . . . .28 C2
Acton High Sch
W3 . . . . .36 C4
Acton Hill Mews
W3 . . . . .28 A1
Acton Ho
8 Acton W3 . . . . . . .28 B3
11 Haggerston E8 . . .24 B4
Acton La
Acton Green W4 . . . .37 B3
Harlesden NW10 . . . .20 C3
Acton Main Line Sta
W3 . . . . .28 B3
Acton Mews E8 . . . . .24 B4
Acton Park Ind Est
W3 . . . . .37 C4
Acton St WC1 . . . . . .94 C3
Acton Town Sta
W3 . . . . .36 C4
Acton Vale Ind Pk
W3 . . . . .29 B1
Acuba Ho SW18 . . . .71 A3
Acuba Rd SW18 . . . . .71 A2
Ada Ct
Islington N1 . . . . .86 C3
St John's Wood W9 . .89 A3
Ada Ho 29 E2 . . . . . .24 C4
Adair Ho SW3 . . . . . 158 B4
Adair Rd W10 . . . . . . .23 A1
Adair Twr 7 W10 . . . .23 A1
Ada Kennedy Ct 6
SE10 . . . . .52 B3
Adam & Eve Ct
W1 . . . . 105 A2
Adam & Eve Mews
W8 . . . . 127 C2
Adamfields 3 . . . . . .11 C2
Adams Gardens Est 5
SE16 . . . . .40 B4
Adams Ho 3 E14 . . . .34 C3
Adams Mews
SW17 . . . . .72 B2
Adamson Rd
Hampstead NW3 . . . .11 C1
Newham E16 . . . . . . .35 C3
Adams' Row W1 . . . 117 C3
Adam St WC2 . . . . . 120 B3
Adam Wlk SW6 . . . . .47 B3
Ada PI E2 . . . . .24 C4
Ada Rd SE5 . . . . .49 A3
Adare Wlk SW16 . . . .74 B1
Ada St E8 . . . . .25 A4
Adderley Gr SW11 . . .60 C2
Adderley St E14 . . . . .34 B3
Addey Ho SE8 . . . . . .51 B3
Addey & Stanhope
Sch 11 SE14 . . . . . .51 C2
Addington Ct 7
SW14 . . . . .55 C4
Addington Ho 13
SW9 . . . . 173 A1
Addington Rd E3 . . . .26 C2
Addington Sq SE5 . . .48 C3
Addington St SE1 . . 135 A3

Addis Ho 13 E1 . . . . .32 B4
Addison Ave
W11 . . . . . . .31 A1 112 A1
Addison Bridge PI
W14 . . . . 140 C4
Addison Cres
W14 . . . . 126 B2
Addison Gdns
W14 . . . . .39 C3
Addison Gr W4 . . . . .38 A3
Addison Ho NW8 . . . .89 B4
Addison Park Mans 1
W14 . . . . .39 C3
Addison PI
W11 . . . . . . .31 A1 112 A1
Addison Prim Sch
W14 . . . . .39 C3
Addison Rd W14 . . . 126 C2
Addle Hill EC4 . . . . . 108 B1
Addlestone Ho 6
W10 . . . . .30 B2
Adela Ho 9 W6 . . . . .39 B1
Adelaide Ave SE4 . . .66 C3
Adelaide Ct SW9 . . .62 C3
Adelaide Ct
Hackney E5 . . . . .18 A3
St John's Wood
NW8 . . . . .79 A1
Adelaide Gr W12 . . . .29 C1
Adelaide Rd
Primrose Hill
NW3 . . . . .12 A1
Richmond TW9 . . . . . .54 B3
2 Wandsworth
SW18 . . . . .58 C2
Adelaide St WC2 . . . 120 A3
Adela St W10 . . . . . . .23 A1
Adelina Gr E1 . . . . . .32 B4
Adelina Mews
SW12 . . . . .73 C3
Adeline PI WC1 . . . . 105 C3
Adelphi Ct 20
SE16 . . . . .40 C4
Adelphi Terr WC2 . . 120 B3
Adeney Cl W6 . . . . . .47 C4
Aden Gr N16 . . . . . . .15 C4
Aden Ho 15 E1 . . . . .32 C4
Aden Lo N16 . . . . . . .15 C4
Adeyfield Ho EC1 . . . .97 C3
Adie Rd W6 . . . . .39 B3
Adisham Ho 4 E5 . . .17 A3
Adler St E1 . . . . 111 B2
Adley St E5 . . . . .18 A3
Admiral Ct
Chelsea SW10 . . . . . 167 A4
Marylebone W1 . . . . 103 B3
Admiral Hyson Ind Est
SE16 . . . . .40 A1
Admiral Mews
W10 . . . . .22 C1
Admiral PI SE16 . . . . .33 A1
Admirals Ct
Bermondsey SE1 . . . 124 C1
32 Putney SW19 . . . .69 C3
Admirals Gate
SE10 . . . . .52 A2
Admiral Sq SW10 . . 167 A4
Admiral St SE8 . . . . .51 C2
Admirals Way E14 . . .41 C4
Admiral's Wlk NW3 . .2 B1
Admiralty Arch
SW1 . . . . 119 C2

Admiralty Cl [1]
SE8 . . . .**51** C2
Admiral Wlk W9 . . . . . .**31** C4
Adolphus Rd N4 . . . . . .**6** A3
Adolphus St SE8 . . . . . .**51** B3
Adpar St W2 . . . .**101** B4
Adrian Bolt Ho [7]
E2 . . . .**25** A2
Adrian Ho
Islington N1 . . . .**85** A3
South Lambeth
SW8 . . . .**162** A2
Stratford E15 . . . .**19** C1
Adrian Mews
SW10 . . . .**156** B4
Adriatic Bldg [18]
E14 . . . .**33** A2
Adriatic Ho [18] EL **25** C1
Adron Ho [13] SE16 . . . .**40** B2
Adstock Ho [5] N1 . . . . .**15** A1
Adventurers Ct [17]
E14 . . . .**34** C2
Adys Lawn NW2 . . . . . .**9** A2
Adys Rd SE15 . . . .**64** B4
Aegean Apts [7]
E16 . . . .**35** C2
Aegon Ho [8] E14 . . . . .**42** A3
Affleck St N1 . . . .**85** A1
Afghan Rd SW11 . . . . .**168** A1
Africa Ho WC2 . . . . . .**106** C2
Afsil Ho S1 . . . .**107** C3
Aga Khan Univ
WC1 . . . .**105** C3
Agamemnon Rd
NW6 . . . .**10** B3
Agar Gr NW1 . . . .**13** C1
Agar PI NW1 . . . .**13** B1
Agar St WC2 . . . .**120** B3
Agate Rd W6 . . . .**39** B3
Agatha Cl E1 . . . .**32** B1
Agave Rd NW2 . . . .**9** B4
Agdon St EC1 . . . .**96** A2
Agincourt Rd NW3 . . . .**12** B4
Agnes Ct [11] SW18 . . . .**59** C3
Agnes Ho [11] W11 . . . . .**30** C2
Agnes Rd W3 . . . .**38** B4
Agnes St E14 . . . .**33** B3
Aicon Gall SW1 . . . . . .**118** C4
Aigburth Mans [5]
SW9 . . . .**163** B1
Ailsa St E14 . . . .**34** B4
Ainger Rd NW3 . . . . . .**12** B1
Ainsdale NW1 . . . .**92** C4
Ainsdale Dr SE1 . . . . .**153** B1
Ainsley St E2 . . . .**25** A2
Ainslie Wlk [8]
SW12 . . . .**73** A4
Ainsty St [20] SE16 . . . .**40** B4
Ainsworth Cl SE5 . . . . .**49** A1
Ainsworth Est
NW8 . . . .**78** C4
Ainsworth Ho NW8 . . . .**78** B3
Ainsworth Rd E9 . . . . .**17** B1
Ainsworth Way
NW8 . . . .**78** C4
Aintree St SW6 . . . . . .**154** B2
Aird Ho SE1 . . . .**136** C1
Airdrie Cl N1 . . . .**14** B1
Airedale Ave W4 . . . . . .**38** B1
Airedale Ave S W4 . . . . .**38** B1
Airedale Rd SW12 . . . . .**72** B4
Airlie Gdns
W8 . . . .**31** C1 **113** B1
Air St W1 . . . .**119** A3

Aisgill Ave SW5 . . . . .**141** A1
Aiten PI W6 . . . .**38** C2
Aithan Ho [18] E14 . . . . .**33** B3
Aitken Cl E8 . . . .**24** C4
Ajax Ho [16] E2 . . . .**25** A3
Ajax Rd NW6 . . . .**10** C3
Akbar Ho [7] E14 . . . . . .**42** A2
Akehurst St SW15 . . . . .**68** C4
Akenside Ct [3]
NW3 . . . .**11** C3
Akenside Rd NW3 . . . . .**11** C3
Akerman Rd SW9 . . . . .**48** A2
Akintaro Ho [7]
SE8 . . . .**51** B4
Alamaro Lo [5]
SE10 . . . .**43** B3
Aland Ct SE16 . . . .**41** A3
Alan Preece Ct
NW6 . . . .**9** C1
Alaska Bldg [12]
SE13 . . . .**52** A2
Alaska St SE1 . . . .**121** B1
Alastor Ho [10] E14 . . . .**42** B3
Albacore Cres
SE13 . . . .**67** A1
Alba Mews SW18,
SW19 . . . .**70** C2
Alban Ho
Hampstead NW3 . . . . . .**11** B2
New Cross SE14 . . . . . .**51** B2
Albans Cl SW16 . . . . . .**74** A1
Albany W1 . . . .**118** C3
Albany Cl SW14 . . . . . .**55** A3
Albany Ct
College Pk NW10 . . . . . .**22** A2
NW8 . . . .**79** B1
Westminster SW1 . . . .**133** B2
[8] Whitechapel E1 . . .**111** B2
Albany Ho [8] TW8 . . . . .**44** A4
Albany Mans
SW11 . . . .**158** B1
Albany Par [4]
TW8 . . . .**44** A4
Albany Pas [12]
TW10 . . . .**54** A2
Albany Rd
Camberwell SE5 . . . . . .**49** A4
Richmond TW10 . . . . . .**54** A2
Albany St NW1 . . . .**92** B4
Albany Terr [6]
TW10 . . . .**54** A2
Alba PI W11 . . . .**31** B3
Albemarle SW19 . . . . . .**69** C2
Albemarle Coll
W1 . . . .**117** A4
Albemarle Ho
[6] Brixton SW9 . . . . . .**62** C4
Rotherhithe SE8 . . . . . .**41** B2
Albemarle Mans
NW3 . . . .**11** A4
Albemarle Prim Sch
SW19 . . . .**70** A2
Albemarle St W1 . . . . .**118** C3
Albemarle Way
EC1 . . . .**96** A1
Alberta Ct [1]
TW10 . . . .**54** B2
Alberta Ho E14 . . . .**34** B1
Alberta St SE17 . . . . . .**150** B2
Albert Ave SW8 . . . . . .**162** C1
Albert Barnes Ho
SE1 . . . .**136** C1

Albert Bigg Point
E15 . . . .**27** B4
Albert Bridge Rd
SW11 . . . .**158** C1
Albert Cl [1] E9 . . . .**25** A4
Albert Cotts [2]
E1 . . . .**111** B4
Albert Ct
Knightsbridge
SW7 . . . .**129** B3
[8] Putney SW19 . . . . . .**70** A3
Albert Dr SW19 . . . .**70** A3
Albert Emb SE1 . . . . . .**148** B3
Albert Gate Ct
SW1 . . . .**130** C3
Albert Gdns E1 . . . .**32** C3
Albert Gray Ho
SW7 . . . .**129** B3
Albert Hall Mans
SW7 . . . .**129** B3
Albert Mans
Battersea SW11 . . . . . .**168** C4
Hornsey N8 . . . .**5** A4
Albert Meml SW7 . . . .**129** B3
Albert Palace Mans
SW11 . . . .**169** C4
Albert PI W8 . . . .**128** B3
Albert Rd
Finsbury Pk N4 . . . .**5** B4
[7] Kilburn NW6 . . . . . .**23** B3
Richmond TW10 . . . . . .**54** B2
Albert's Ct NW1 . . . . . .**90** B2
Albert Sq SW8 . . . .**162** C1
Albert St NW1 . . . .**82** B3
Albert Starr Ho [7]
SE8 . . . .**40** C2
Albert Studios
SW11 . . . .**168** C4
Albert Terr
Camden Town
NW1 . . . .**81** B3
Stonebridge NW10 . . . . .**20** B4
Albert Terr Mews
NW1 . . . .**81** B3
Albert Way SE15 . . . . . .**50** A3
Albert Westcott Ho
SE17 . . . .**150** B2
Albion Ave SW8 . . . . . .**171** B1
Albion Cl W2 . . . .**116** B4
Albion Dr E8 . . . .**16** C1
Albion Est SE16 . . . .**40** B4
Albion Gate W2 . . . . . .**116** B4
Albion Gdns [1]
W6 . . . .**39** A2
Albion Gr N16 . . . .**7** A1
Albion Ho
[1] Deptford SE8 . . . . . .**51** C3
E16 . . . .**35** C1
Albion Mews
Bayswater W2 . . . .**116** B4
[6] Hammersmith
W6 . . . .**39** A2
Islington N1 . . . .**85** B4
Albion PI
Broadgate EC2 . . . .**109** C3
Hammersmith EC1 . . . .**108** A4
Hammersmith W6 . . . . .**39** A2
Albion Prim Sch [34]
SE16 . . . .**40** B4
Albion Rd N16 . . . .**15** C4
Albion Riverside
SW11 . . . .**158** A2
Albion Sq E8 . . . .**16** B1

Albion St
Bayswater W2 . . . .**116** B4
Rotherhithe SE16 . . . . . .**40** B4
Albion Terr E8 . . . .**16** B1
Albion Way
Barbican EC2 . . . .**108** C3
Lewisham SE13 . . . .**67** B3
Albion Wlk N1 . . . .**84** B1
Albion Works Studios
E8 . . . .**16** C3
Albion Yd N1 . . . .**84** B1
Albon Ho SW18 . . . .**59** A1
Albrighton Rd SE5,
SE22 . . . .**64** A4
Albury Bldgs SE1 . . . .**136** B3
Albury Ct SE8 . . . .**51** C4
Albury St SE8 . . . .**51** C4
Albyn Rd SE8 . . . .**51** C2
Alchemea Coll of
Audio Engineering
N1 . . . .**86** B4
Alconbury Rd E5 . . . .**7** C2
Aldbourne Rd
W12 . . . .**29** C1
Aldbridge St SE17 . . . .**152** B2
Aldburgh Mews
W1 . . . .**103** C2
Aldebert Terr
SW8 . . . .**162** C1
Aldeburgh PI SE10 . . . . .**43** C2
Aldeburgh St SE10 . . . . .**43** C1
Aldenham Ho NW1 . . . . .**83** A1
Aldenham St NW1 . . . . .**83** B1
Alden Ho E8 . . . .**25** A4
Aldensley Rd W6 . . . . . .**39** A3
Alderbrook Prim Sch
[5] SW12 . . . .**73** A4
Alderbrook Rd
SW12 . . . .**61** A1
Alderbury Rd
SW13 . . . .**46** C4
Aldergrove Ho [3]
E5 . . . .**7** C2
Alder Ho
Camberwell SE15 . . . . . .**49** B4
[1] Maitland Pk
NW3 . . . .**12** B2
SE4 . . . .**66** C4
Alderley Ho [36]
SW8 . . . .**171** B1
Alder Lo SW6 . . . .**47** C2
Aldermanbury
EC2 . . . .**109** A2
Aldermanbury Sq
EC2 . . . .**109** A3
Alderman's Wlk
EC2 . . . .**110** A3
Alder Mews [13] N19 . . . .**4** B2
Alderney Ho [20]
N1 . . . .**15** B2
Alderney Mews
SE1 . . . .**137** B2
Alderney Rd EL **25** C1
Alderney St SW1 . . . . .**146** B2
Alder Rd SW14 . . . .**55** C4
Aldersford Cl SE4 . . . . .**65** C3
Aldersgate Ct
EC1 . . . .**108** C3
Aldersgate St EC1 . . . .**108** C3
Aldershot Rd NW6 . . . . .**23** B4
Alderson St W10 . . . . . .**23** A1
Alderton Rd SE24 . . . . .**63** B4
Alderville Rd
SW6 . . . .**165** A2

Alderwick Ct N7 . . . . . .**14** B2
Alford St W1 . . . .**117** C2
Aldgate EC3 . . . .**110** B1
Aldgate East Sta
E1 . . . .**111** A2
Aldgate High St
EC3 . . . .**110** C1
Aldgate Sta EC3 . . . . . .**110** C1
Aldham Ho SE4 . . . .**51** B2
Aldine Ct W12 . . . .**30** B1
Aldine St W12 . . . .**39** B4
Aldington Ct [1]
E8 . . . .**16** C1
Aldred Rd NW6 . . . .**10** C3
Aldren Rd SW17 . . . . . .**71** B1
Aldrich Terr SW18 . . . . .**71** B2
Aldrick Ho N1 . . . .**85** A2
Aldridge Ct W11 . . . .**31** B4
Aldridge Rd Villas
W11 . . . .**31** B4
Aldsworth Cl W9 . . . . . .**88** A1
Aldwich Ho WC2 . . . . .**107** A1
Aldworth Gr SE13 . . . . .**67** B1
Aldwych WC2 . . . .**107** A1
Aldwych Bldgs
WC2 . . . .**106** B2
Aldwyn Ho SW8 . . . . . .**162** A1
Alexander Ave
NW10 . . . .**9** A1
Alexander Ct
SW18 . . . .**59** B2
Alexander Fleming
Laboratory Mus
W2 . . . .**101** C2
Alexander Ho [15]
E14 . . . .**41** C3
Alexander Mews [2]
W2 . . . .**100** A2
Alexander PI SW7 . . . .**144** A4
Alexander Rd N19 . . . . . .**5** A2
Alexander Sq
SW3 . . . .**144** A4
Alexander St W2 . . . . . .**31** C3
Alexandra Ave
SW11 . . . .**169** B3
Alexandra Cl SE8 . . . . . .**51** B4
Alexandra Cotts
SE14 . . . .**51** B2
Alexandra Ct
Paddington W9 . . . .**89** A2
[4] Shacklewell N16 . . . .**16** B4
[5] Shepherd's Bush
W12 . . . .**38** C4
Alexandra Gdns
W4 . . . .**46** A3
Alexandra Gr N4 . . . .**6** A3
Alexandra Mans
Chelsea SW3 . . . .**157** B3
Cricklewood NW2 . . . . . .**9** C3
[6] Hampstead
NW6 . . . .**11** B2
[9] Shepherd's Bush
W12 . . . .**30** B1
Alexandra National
Ho N4 . . . .**6** A2
Alexandra Rd
Acton W4 . . . .**37** C4
Hampstead NW8 . . . . . .**11** C1
Mortlake SW14 . . . .**55** C4
Richmond TW9 . . . .**44** B1
Alexandra St
[5] Deptford SE14 . . . . .**51** A3
Newham E16 . . . .**35** C4

Alex Gossip Ho
SW6 . . . . **165** B3
Alexis St SE16 . . . . **153** C4
Alfearn Rd E5 . . . . **17** B4
Alfies Antique Mkt
NW8 . . . . **90** A1
Alford Ct N1 . . . . . . **87** A1
Alford Pl N1 . . . . . . **87** A1
Alfreda Ct SW11 . . **170** A3
Alfreda St SW11 . . **170** A3
Alfred Butt Ho
SW17 . . . . **72** B1
Alfred Cl W4 . . . . . . **37** C2
Alfred Ho E9 . . . . . . **18** A3
Alfred Mews W1,
WC1 . . . . **105** B4
Alfred Nunn Ho
NW10 . . . . **21** B4
Alfred Pl WC1 . . . . **105** B4
Alfred Rd
Acton W3 . . . . **28** B1
Paddington W2 . . . . **31** C4
Alfred Salter Ho
SE1 . . . . **153** A3
Alfred Salter Prim
Sch SE16 . . . . **40** C4
Alfred St E3 . . . . . . **26** B2
Alfreton Cl SW19 . . **69** C1
Alfriston Rd SW11 . **60** B2
Algar Ho SE1 . . . . **136** A3
Algarve Rd SW18 . . **71** A3
Algernon Rd
Kilburn NW6 . . . . . . **23** C4
Lewisham SE13 . . . . **67** A2
Algiers Rd SE13 . . . **66** C3
Alice Gilliott Ct
W14 . . . . **155** A4
Alice La E3 . . . . **26** B4
Alice Owen Tech Cty
EC1 . . . . **96** A4
Alice Shepherd Ho [2]
E14 . . . . **42** B4
Alice St SE1 . . . . . **138** A1
Alice Walker Cl [8]
SE24 . . . . **63** A3
Alie St E1 . . . . **111** A1
Aliwal Rd SW11 . . . . **60** A3
Alkerden Rd W4 . . . **38** A1
Alkham Rd N16 . . . . . **7** B2
Allam Ho
W11 . . . . . . **31** A2 **112** A4
Allanbridge N16 . . . . **7** A4
Allan Ho SW8 . . . . **171** B4
Allan Way W3 . . . . . **28** B4
Allard Gdns SW4 . . . **61** C2
Allardyce St SW4,
SW9 . . . . **62** B3
Allbrook Ho [3]
SW15 . . . . **68** C4
Allcroft Rd NW5 . . . . **12** C2
Allendale Cl SE5 . . . **48** C1
Allen Edwards Dr
SW8 . . . . **172** A4
Allen Edwards Prim
Sch SW4 . . . . **172** A3
Allenford Ho
SW15 . . . . **56** B1
**All England Lawn
Tennis & Croquet
Club The** SW19 . . . **70** A1
Allen Ho W8 . . . . . **127** C2
Allen Mans W8 . . . **127** C2
Allen Rd
Old Ford E3 . . . . **26** B3
Stoke Newington
N16 . . . . **16** A4

Allensbury Pl
[7] Camden Town
NW1 . . . . **13** C1
Camden Town NW1 . . **14** A1
Allen St W8 . . . . . **127** C1
Allenswood [12]
SW19 . . . . **70** A3
Allerdale Ho [7] N4 . . **6** C4
Allerford Rd SE6 . . . **87** C1
Allerton Ho N1 . . . . **87** C1
Allerton Rd N16 . . . . . **6** C2
Allerton St N1 . . . . . **97** C4
Allerton Wlk [11] N7 . . **5** B2
Allestree Rd SW6 . . **154** A1
Alleyn Cres SE21 . . . **75** C2
Alleyn Ho
Bermondsey SE1 . . . **137** B1
St Luke's EC1 . . . . . . **97** A1
Alleyn Pk SE21 . . . . **76** A1
Alleyn Rd SE21 . . . . **76** A1
Alleyn's Sch SE22 . . . **64** A2
Allfarthing La
SW18 . . . . **59** B1
Allfarthing Prim Sch
SW18 . . . . **59** B1
Allgood St [16] E2 . . **24** B3
Allhallows Rd EC4 . **123** B3
Alliance Ct W3 . . . . **28** A4
Alliance Rd W3 . . . . **28** A4
Allied Ind Est W3 . . **29** A1
Allied Way W3 . . . . . **38** A4
Allingham Mews
N1 . . . . **86** C2
Allingham St
N1 . . . . **86** C2
Allington Ct [8]
SW8 . . . . **170** C1
Allington Rd W10 . . . **23** A3
Allington St SW1 . . **132** B1
Allison Cl SE10 . . . . **52** B2
Allison Gr SE21 . . . . **76** A3
Allison Rd W3 . . . . . **28** B2
Allison Ho [27]
E2 . . . . **24** B2 **99** A3
Allitsen Rd NW8 . . . . **80** A2
All Nations Ho [8]
E8 . . . . **17** A1
Allnutt Way SW4 . . . **61** C2
Alloa Rd SE8 . . . . . **40** C1
Allom Ct [8] SW4 . . **172** B1
Allonby Ho E14 . . . . . **33** A4
Alloway Rd E3 . . . . . **26** A2
Allport Ho SE5 . . . . . **63** C4
Allport Mews [5]
E1 . . . . **25** B1
**All Saints CE Prim
Sch**
[8] Fulham SW6 . . . **164** A4
Putney SW15 . . . . . . **57** B4
**All Saints' CE Prim
Sch** SE3 . . . . **53** A1
All Saints' CE Sch
NW2 . . . . **9** C2
All Saints Church [9]
N19 . . . . **4** C1
All Saints Ct
Lower Clapton E5 . . . **17** B4
[10] Shadwell E1 . . . . **32** B2
All Saints Dr SE3 . . . **53** B1
All Saints Ho [2]
W11 . . . . **31** B4
All Saints Pas
SW18 . . . . **58** C2
All Saints Rd W11 . . . **31** B3
All Saints' Rd W3 . . . **37** B3
All Saints St N1 . . . . **84** C2
All Saints Sta E14 . . . **34** A2
Allsop Pl NW1 . . . . . **91** A1

All Souls Ave
NW10 . . . . **22** A4
All Souls CE Prim Sch
W1 . . . . **104** C4
All Souls Pl W1 . . . **104** B3
Alma [8]
Camden Town
NW5 . . . . **13** A4
Stratford New Town
E15 . . . . **19** C2
Alma Birk Ho [1]
NW6 . . . . **10** B1
Almack Rd E5 . . . . . **17** B4
Alma Gr SE1 . . . . . **153** A3
Alma Ho [3] TW8 . . . **44** A4
Alma Pl NW10 . . . . . **22** A2
Alma Rd SW18 . . . . . **59** B2
Alma Sq NW8 . . . . . **89** A4
Alma St
Camden Town
NW5 . . . . **13** A3
Alma Terr
Earl's Ct W8 . . . . . . **127** C1
Wandsworth SW18 . . **71** C4
Almeida St [10] N1 . . **15** A1
Almeric Rd SW11 . . . **60** B3
Almington St N4 . . . . **5** B3
Almond Ave W5 . . . . **36** A3
Almond Cl SE15 . . . . **49** C1
Almond Rd SE16 . . . **40** A2
Almorah Rd N1 . . . . **15** C1
Al-Muntada Islamic
. . . . **165** A4
Alperton St W10 . . . . **23** B1
Alphabet Sq E3 . . . . . **33** C4
Alpha Cl NW8 . . . . . **90** B3
Alpha Ct [8] NW5 . . . **13** A2
Alpha Gr E14 . . . . . . **41** C4
Alpha Ho
[4] Brixton SW4 . . . . **62** B3
Kilburn NW6 . . . . . . **23** C3
Lisson Gr NW8 . . . . . **90** B1
Alpha Pl
Chelsea SW3 . . . . . **158** B4
Kilburn NW6 . . . . . . **23** C3
Alpha Rd SE14 . . . . . **51** B2
Alpha St SE15 . . . . . **49** C1
Alpine Gr [27] E9 . . . **17** B1
Alpine Rd SE16 . . . . . **40** C1
Alroy Rd N4 . . . . **5** C4
Alsace Rd SE17 . . . . **152** A2
Al Sadiq & Al Zahra
Schs **23** A4
Alscot Rd SE1 . . . . **139** A1
Alscot Way SE1 . . . **152** C4
Altair Ct N1 . . . . **15** C2
Altenburg Gdns
SW11 . . . . **60** B3
Althea St SW6 . . . . . **59** A4
Althorpe Mews
SW11 . . . . **167** C3
Althorp Rd SW17 . . . **72** B3
Altima Ct SE22 . . . . **64** C3
Alton Ho [3] E3 . . . . . **27** A2
Alton Rd
Richmond TW10,
TW9 . . . . **54** A3
Roehampton SW15 . . **68** C3
Alton Sch The
SW15 . . . . **56** A1
Alton St E14 . . . . **34** A4
Alumni Ct SE1 . . . . **139** A4
Alvanley Ct NW3 . . . . **11** A3
Alvanley Gdns
NW6 . . . . **11** A3

Alvanley Ho [14]
SW9 . . . . **173** B4
Alverstone Ave
SW19 . . . . **70** C2
Alverstone Ho [11]
SE11 . . . . **163** B3
Alverstone Rd NW2 . . **9** B1
Alverton St SE8 . . . . **51** B4
Alvey St SE17 . . . . . **152** A2
Alvington Cres E8 . . . **16** B3
Alwyn Ave W4 . . . . . **37** C1
Alwyne La N1 . . . . . . **15** A1
Alwyne Pl N1 . . . . . . **15** B2
Alwyne Rd N1 . . . . . . **15** B1
Alwyne Sq N1 . . . . . . **15** B2
Alwyne Villas N1 . . . **15** A1
Alwyn Gdns W3 . . . . **28** A3
Alzette Ho [11] E2 . . . **25** C3
Aman Dalvi Ho [2]
SW9 . . . . **63** A4
Amazonas SE1 . . . . **152** B3
Amazon St E1 . . . . . **32** A3
Ambassador Ct [5]
NW6 . . . . **10** C3
Ambassador Ho
NW8 . . . . **79** A4
Ambassador Sq
E14 . . . . **42** A2
Amber Ct N7 . . . . . **14** C2
Ambergate St
SE17 . . . . **150** B2
Amberley Ct [8]
SW9 . . . . **63** A4
Amberley Rd W9 . . . . **31** C4
Amber Wharf [29]
E2 . . . . **24** B4
Amblecote [18]
SE12 . . . . **87** A4
Amblecote Cl SE12 . . **87** A4
Amblecote Rd
SE12 . . . . **87** A4
Ambleside [6]
Regent's Pk NW1 . . . **82** B1
Putney SW19 . . . . . . **70** A3
Ambleside Cl [5] E9 . . **17** B3
Ambleside Point [3]
SE15 . . . . **50** B3
Ambleside Rd
NW10 . . . . **8** B1
Ambrose Ho [3]
E14 . . . . **33** C4
Ambrose Mews [2]
SW11 . . . . **168** C2
Ambrose St SE16 . . . **40** A2
Ambrose Wlk E3 . . . . **26** C3
AMC Bsns Ctr
. . . . **79** A4
Amelia Cl W3 . . . . . . **37** A4
Amelia Ho [5] W6 . . . **39** B1
Amelia St SE17 . . . **150** C2
Amen Cnr EC4 . . . . **108** B1
Amen Ct EC4 . . . . . **108** B1
**American
Intercontinental
Univ** W1 . . . . **103** C3
**American Sch in
London The** NW8 . . **79** B2
America Sq EC3 . . . **124** C4
America St SE1 . . . **122** C1
Amerland Rd
SW18 . . . . **58** B1
Amersham Gr
SE14 . . . . **51** B3
Amersham Rd
SE14 . . . . **51** B2

Amersham Vale SE14,
SE8 . . . . **51** B3
Amery Gdns NW10 . . **22** A4
Amery Ho SE17 . . . **152** B2
Amesbury Ave
SW2 . . . . **74** B2
Amesbury Twr [8]
SW8 . . . . **170** C2
Ames Cotts [12] E3 . . **33** A4
Ame Ho E2 . . . . . . **25** C3
Amethyst Rd E15 . . . **19** C4
Amhurst Ct N4 . . . . . . **6** C4
Amhurst Par N16 . . . . **7** B4
Amhurst Pk N4, N16 . . **7** A4
Amhurst Rd E8,
N16 . . . . **16** C4
Amhurst Terr E8 . . . . **16** C4
Amias Ho EC1 . . . . . **96** C2
Amiel St [11] E1 . . . . **25** B1
Amies St SW11 . . . . . **60** B4
Amigo Ho SE1 . . . . **135** C2
Amina Way SE16 . . . **139** B1
Amner Rd SW11 . . . . **60** C1
Amory Ho N1 . . . . . . **85** A2
Amott Rd SE15 . . . . . **64** C4
Amoy Pl E14 . . . . . . **33** C2
Ampton Pl WC1 . . . . **94** C3
Ampton St WC1 . . . . **94** C3
Amstel Ct [17] SE15 . . **49** B3
Amsterdam Rd
E14 . . . . **42** B3
Amundsen Ct [7]
E14 . . . . **41** C1
Amwell St EC1 . . . . . **95** B4
Amyruth Rd SE4 . . . . **66** C2
Anatola Rd N19 . . . . . **4** B2
Anchorage Point [1]
E14 . . . . **41** C4
Anchor Ho [1]
SW12 . . . . **61** A1
Anchor Ret Pk E1 . . . **25** B1
Anchor St SE16 . . . . **40** A2
Anchor Terr SE1 . . . **123** A2
Anchor Yd EC1 . . . . . **97** A2
Ancill Cl W6 . . . . . . **154** A3
Ancona Rd NW10 . . . **21** C3
Andalus Rd SW9 . . . . **62** A4
Andaman Ho [3]
E1 . . . . **33** A4
Andersens Wharf [9]
E14 . . . . **33** A3
Anderson Cl W3 . . . . **28** C3
Anderson Ho [10]
E14 . . . . **34** B2
Anderson Rd E9 . . . . **17** C2
Andersons Sq N1 . . . **86** A3
Anderson St SW3 . . **144** C2
Anderton Cl SE5 . . . . **63** C4
Andover Ho [5] N7 . . . . **5** B2
Andover Pl NW6 . . . . **78** A1
Andover Rd N7 . . . . . . **5** B2
Andoversford Ct [7]
SE15 . . . . **49** A4
Andre St E8 . . . . **16** C3
Andrew Borde St
WC2 . . . . **105** C2
Andrewes Ho EC2 . . **109** A3
Andrew Ho
New Cross SE4 . . . . . **51** B1
Putney SW15 . . . . . . **57** C2
Andrew Marvell Ho [12]
N16 . . . . **16** A4

Andrew Pl SW8... **171** C4
Andrew Reed Ho **3**
SW18 ....70 A4
Andrews Crosse
WC2 ....**107** B1
Andrew's Rd E8 ..25 A4
Andrew St E14 ...34 B3
Andrews Wharf **4**
E8 ....25 A4
Andrews Wlk SE17 ..48 A4
Andrew Wilmot Ct
SW18 ....71 B3
Anerley St SW11 .**169** A2
Anfield Cl SW12 ..73 B4
Angel EC1 ....86 B1
Angela Carter Cl
SW9 ....62 C4
Angela Davis Ind Est
20 SW9 ....63 A3
Angel Ct
Broadgate EC2 ....**109** C2
St James SW1 ....**119** A1
5 Willesden NW2 ...8 C2
Angel Gate EC1 ...96 B4
Angel Ho N1 ....85 C1
Angelina Ho **2**
SE15 ....49 C2
Angelis Appartments
N1 ....86 B1
Angel La E15 ......19 C2
Angel Park Gdns **4**
SW9 ....62 C4
Angel Rd SW9 ....63 A4
Angel Mews
Finsbury N1 ....85 C1
Putney SW15 .....68 C4
Stepney E1 ....32 A2
Angel Oak Acad
SE15 ....49 A3
Angel Pas EC4 ...**123** B3
Angel Pl SE1 ......**137** B4
Angel Sq N1 ....85 C1
Angel St EC1 ......**108** C2
Angel Sta EC1 ....85 C1
Angel Wlk W6 ....39 B2
Angerstein Bsns Pk
SE10 ....43 C2
Angerstein La SE3 .53 B2
Anglebury **5** W2 ..31 C3
Anglers La NW5 ..13 A2
Anglesey Ho **13**
E14 ....33 C3
Anglia Ho **15** E14 .33 A3
Anglo American
Laundry SW17 ...71 B1
Anglo Rd **10** E3 ..26 B3
Angrave Ct **8** E8 .24 B4
Angrave Pas **3** E8 .24 B4
Angus Ho **3**
SW12 ....73 C4
Angus St SE14 ...51 A3
Anhalt Rd SW11 .**158** B2
Animals in War Meml
W1 ....**117** A4
Anley Rd W14 ....39 C4
Annabel Cl E14 ..34 A3
Anna Cl E8 ....24 B4
Annandale Rd
Chiswick W4 ......38 A1
Greenwich SE10 ..43 B1
Anne Goodman Ho **3**
E1 ....32 B3
Anne Kerr Ct **18**
SW15 ....57 C1

Anne's Ct NW8 .....90 B2
Annesley Ho **1**
SW9 ....**173** B4
Annesley Wlk N19 ...4 B2
Annette Cres **10**
N1 ....15 B1
Annette Ct N7 ......5 B1
Annette Rd N7 .....14 B4
Annie Besant Cl
E3 ....26 B4
Anning St
EC2 ....24 A1 98 B2
Annis Rd E9 ....18 A2
Ann La SW10 .....**157** B3
Ann Moss Way
SE16 ....40 B3
Ann's Cl SW1 ....**131** B3
Ann's Pl E1 ....**110** C3
Ann St N1 ....86 C2
Ansdell Rd SE15 ..50 B1
Ansdell St W8 ....**128** B2
Ansdell Terr W8 ..**128** B2
Ansell Ho E1 ......32 B4
Ansell Rd SW17 ..72 B1
Anselm Rd SW6 .**155** B3
Ansleigh Pl W11 ...30 C2
Anson Ho
Pimlico SW1 ......**160** C4
7 Tower Hamlets
E1 ....26 A1
Anson Prim Sch
N7 ....9 C3
Anson Rd
Cricklewood NW2 .9 B3
Tufnell Pk N7 .....13 C4
Anstey Ct **3** W3 ...37 A4
Anstey Ho **7** E9 ..25 B4
Anstice Cl W4 .....46 A3
Antenor Ho **11** E2 .25 A3
Anthems Way E15 .19 A2
Anthony Cope Ct
N1 ....97 C4
Anthony Ho NW8 .90 A1
Anthony St E1 ....32 A3
Antilles Bay **19**
E14 ....42 B4
Antill Ho **3** SW11 ..28 C3
Antill Rd E3 ....26 A2
Antill Terr **8** E1 ..32 C3
Antoine Hts **13** ...**138** A3
Anton St E8 ....16 C3
Antony Ho
4 Deptford SE14 ..50 C3
3 Rotherhithe
SE16 ....40 B2
Antrim Gr NW3 ...12 B2
Antrim Ho SW11 ..60 C4
Antrim Mans NW3 .12 B2
Antrim Rd NW3 ...12 B2
Antrobus Rd W4 .37 B3
AOP Gall SE14 ....98 A2
Apex Ind Est
NW10 ....21 B1
Aphrodite Ct **11**
E14 ....41 C2
Apollo Bldg **2**
E14 ....41 C2
Apollo Ho
Chelsea SW10 ...**157** B3
32 Hackney E2 ...25 A3
Highgate N6 ....3 B4
AOP Ind Bsns Ctr **32**
SE8 ....50 C4
Apollo Pl SW10 ..**157** B2

Apollo Studios **18**
NW5 ....13 C3
Apothecary St
EC4 ....**108** A1
Appach Rd SW12 .62 C1
Appleby Ct W3 ....37 B4
Appleby Rd
Hackney E8 ....16 C1
Newham E16 .....35 C3
Appleby St E2 ....24 B3
Appledore Cl SW12,
SW17 ....72 B2
Appleford Ho **5**
W10 ....23 A1
Appleford Rd W10 .23 A1
Applegarth Ho
Borough The SE1 ..**136** B4
6 Camberwell
SE5 ....48 B3
Applegarth Rd
W14 ....39 C3
Apple Mkt WC2 ..**120** B4
Appleshaw Ho **5**
SE5 ....64 A4
Appleton Ct **30** E8 .17 A3
Appletree Ct SE13 .67 C3
Apple Tree Yd
SW1 ....**119** A2
Appold St EC2 ....**110** A4
Appold Ct **7**
SW9 ....**173** B4
Approach Cl N16 ..16 A4
Approach Rd E2 ..25 B3
Approach The W3 .28 C3
April Ct **10** E2 ....24 C3
April St E8 ....16 B4
Apsley Ho
Stepney E1 ....32 B4
8 St John's Wood
NW8 ....**79** B2
Apsley Ho, The
Wellington Mus
SW1 ....**131** C4
Apsley Way W1 ..**131** C4
Aquila St NW8 ....**79** C2
Aquinas St SE1 ..**121** C1
Arabella Ct NW8 .**79** A2
Arabella Dr SW15 .56 A3
Arabian Ho **3** E1 .26 A1
Arabin Rd SE4 ....66 B3
Aragon Twr SE8 ..41 B2
Arakan Ho **4** N16 .15 C4
Aral Ho **4** E1 .....25 C1
Arapiles Ho **8**
E14 ....34 C3
Arbery Rd E3 ......26 A3
Arbon Ct N1 ....87 A3
Arbor Ct N16 ......6 C2
Arborfield Cl SW2 .74 B3
Arborfield Ho **7**
E14 ....33 C2
Arbour Ho **3** E1 .32 C3
Arbour Sq E1 .....32 C3
Arbuthnot Rd
SE14 ....50 C1
Arbutus St E8 ....24 B4
Arcade The
Broadgate EC2 ....**110** A3
1 Tufnell Pk N7 ..14 A4
Arcadian Ho SW6 **167** A1
Arcadian Pl SW18 .70 B4
Arcadia St E14 ...33 C3

Arcelor Mittal Orbit
E15 ....19 A1
Archangel St SE16 .40 C4
Archbishop Coggan
Ho SE13 ....67 C3
Archbishop's Pl **1**
SW2 ....74 B4
Archbishop Sumner
CE Prim Sch
SE11 ....**149** C3
Archbishop Tenison's
Sch SE11 ....163 A3
Archdale Ct W12 ..30 A1
Archdale Ho SE1 .**138** A2
Archdale Rd SE22 .64 B3
Archel Rd W14 ...**154** C4
Archer Ho
1 Battersea
SW11 ....**169** C2
5 Hoxton N1 ....24 A4
1 New Cross SE14 .51 A2
Notting Hill
W11 ....31 B2 **113** A4
Archers Lo **3**
SE16 ....**153** C1
Archer Sq SE14 ..51 A4
Archer St W1 .....**119** B4
Archery Cl W2 ....**102** B1
Archery Fields Ho
WC1 ....95 B4
Archery Stps **2** SW1 .**116** B3
Arches The WC2 ..**120** B2
Archibald Mews
W1 ....**118** A3
Archibald Rd N7 ..13 C4
Archibald St E3 ..26 C2
Archie St SE1 ....**138** B3
Arch St SE1 ......**136** C1
Archway N19 ......4 C1
Archway Bsns Ctr **5**
N19 ....4 C1
Archway Cl
North Kensington
W10 ....30 C4
2 Upper Holloway
N19 ....4 B2
Archway Hts **5** N19 .4 B3
Archway L Ctr N19 .4 B2
Archway Mews
SW15 ....58 A3
Archway Rd N6 ...4 A4
Archway St SW13, ..
SW14 ....56 A4
Archway Sta N19 ..4 B2
Arcola St E8 ....16 B3
Arctic St NW5 ....13 A3
Ardbeg Rd SE24 .63 C2
Arden **17** SW19 ..69 C3
Arden Cres E14 ..41 C2
Arden Ho
21 Hoxton N1 ....24 A3
55 Stockwell SW9 .**172** B1
Vauxhall SE11 ...**148** C3
Ardent Ho **20** E3 ..26 A3
Ardilaun Rd N5 ...15 B4
Ardleigh Rd N1 ..16 A2
Ardlui Rd SE27 ...75 B2
Ardmere Rd SE13 .67 C1
Ardshiel Cl **6**
SW15 ....57 C4
Ardwell Rd SW2 ..74 A2
Ardwick Rd NW2 .10 C4
Ares Ct **18** E14 ...41 C2
Arethusa Ho **8**
E14 ....42 A2

Argo Bsns Ctr **4**
NW6 ....23 C2
Argon Mews SW6 **155** C1
Argos Ct **2** SW9 .**173** B4
Argos Ho **8** E2 ....25 A3
Argosy Ho
Fitzrovia W1 ......92 B1
Rotherhithe SE8 ..41 A2
Argyle Mans **4**
NW2 ....9 C4
Argyle Ho **16** 39 A2
Argyle Prim Sch
WC1 ....94 C4
Argyle Rd E1 .....25 C1
Argyle Sq WC1 ...94 B4
Argyle St WC1 ...94 B4
Argyle Way SE16 .**153** C1
Argyle Wlk WC1 ..94 B3
Argyll Cl SW9 ....62 B4
Argyll Ct **15** SW2 ..74 A4
Argyll Mans
Chelsea SW3 .....**157** F4
West Kensington
W14 ....**140** B4
Argyll Rd W8 .....**127** C3
Argyll St W1 ......**104** C1
Arica Ho SE16 ....40 A3
Arica Rd SE4 .....66 A4
Ariel Ct
5 Hammersmith
W12 ....38 C3
Newington SE11 ..**150** A3
Ariel Rd NW6 .....10 C2
Ariel Way W11, ...
W12 ....30 C1
Aristotle Rd SW4 .61 C4
Arizona Bldg **10**
SE13 ....52 A2
Ark All Saints Acad
SE5 ....48 B3
Arkansas Ho **21**
N19 ....4 C4
Ark Atwood Primary
Acad W9 ....100 A4
Ark Brunel Prim Acad
21 W10 ....23 B2
Ark Ct N10 ....7 B2
Ark Globe Acad
SE1 ....137 C1
Arklow Ho SE17 ..48 C4
Arklow Rd SE14 ..51 B4
Arklow Road Trad Est
SE14 ....51 B4
Ark Priory Prim Acad
12 W3 ....37 B4
ARK Putney Acad
SW15 ....57 C2
Arkwright Ho **23**
SW2 ....74 A4
Arkwright Mans **1**
NW3 ....11 B3
Arkwright Rd NW3 .11 B3
Arlesey Cl SW15 .58 A2
Arlesford Rd SW9 .62 A4
Arlidge Ho EC1 ..107 C4
Arlingford Rd
SW2 ....62 C1
Arlington Ave N1 .87 A3
Arlington Cl SE13 .67 C2
Arlington Ct **3**
W3 ....28 A1
Arlington Gdns
W4 ....37 B1
Arlington Ho
3 Deptford SE8 ..51 C4

Arlington Ho *continued*
Finsbury EC1 . . . . . . **95** C4
1 Shepherd's Bush
  W12 . . . . .30 A1
Arlington Lo SW2 . . .62 B3
Arlington Park Mans
1 W4. . . . . .37 B1
Arlington Pl
10 Greenwich
  SE10 . . . . .52 B3
7 SE10 . . . . .52 B3
Arlington Rd NW1. . .82 B3
Arlington Sq N1 . . . .87 A3
Arlington St SW1 . . 118 C2
Arlington Way EC1 . .95 C4
Armada Ct **11** SE8 . .51 C4
Armadale Rd
  SW6 . . . . 155 B3
Armada St **10** SE8 . .51 C4
Armagh Rd E3. . . . . .26 B4
Arminger Rd W12 . . .30 A1
Armitage Ho
  NW1 . . . . 102 B4
Armitage Rd
  Golders Green
  NW11 . . . . .1 B3
  Greenwich SE10 . . .43 B1
Armour Cl N7 . . . . . .14 B2
Armoury Ho E3 . . . . .26 A4
Armoury Rd SE8 . . . .52 A1
Armoury Way
  SW18 . . . . .58 C2
Armsby Ho **17** E1. . .32 B4
Armstrong Ho **8**
  SW15 . . . . .57 C1
Armstrong Rd
  East Acton W3 . . . .29 B1
  Knightsbridge
  SW7 . . . . 129 B1
  9 Willesden NW10 . .9 A1
Arnal Cres SW18 . . .70 A4
Arncliffe NW6 . . . . . .78 B3
Arndale Wlk **6**
  SW18 . . . . .59 A2
Arne Ho SE11 . . . . . 148 C2
Arne St WC2 . . . . . . 106 B1
Arneway St SW1 . . . 133 C1
Arnewood Cl
  SW15 . . . . .68 C3
Arnhem Pl E14 . . . . .41 C3
Arnhem Way **3**
  SE22. . . . . .64 A2
Arnhem Wharf
  E14 . . . . .41 C3
Arnhem Wharf Prim
  Sch E14 . . . . .41 C3
Arnold Cir
  E2 . . . . .24 B2 98 C3
Arnold Est SE1 . . . . 139 A3
Arnold Ho
  Newington SE17. . . 150 B1
  5 Stoke Newington
  N16. . . . . .7 A1
Arnold House Sch
  NW8 . . . . .79 B1
Arnold Rd E3 . . . . . .26 C2
Arnot Ho **22** SE5. . . .48 B3
Arnott Cl W4 . . . . . .37 C2
Arnould Ave SE5 . . .63 C3
Arnside Ho **2**
  SE17. . . . . .48 C4
Arnside St SE17 . . . .48 C4
Arodene Rd SW2 . . .62 B1
Arragon Rd SW18 . . .70 C3

Arran Ho
1 Canary Wharf
  E14. . . . . .34 B1
  Stoke Newington
  N16. . . . . .7 B3
Arran Wlk N1 . . . . . .15 B1
Arrol Ho SE1 . . . . . . 137 A1
Arrowe Ct **8** E5. . . .17 A4
Arrow Ho **24** N1 . . .24 A4
Arrow Rd E3 . . . . . . .27 A2
Arrowsmith Ho
  SE11 . . . . 148 C2
Arsenal Sta N5 . . . . .5 C1
Arta Ho **28** E1 . . . . .32 B3
Artemis Ct **14** E14 . .41 C2
Artemis Pl SW18 . . .70 B4
Artesian Rd W2 . . . .31 C3
Arthur Ct
  Battersea SW11 . . . 169 C3
  10 North Kensington
  W10 . . . . .30 C3
  Paddington W2. . . . 100 A2
Arthur Deakin Ho **1**
  E1 . . . . 111 B4
Arthurdon Rd SE4 . .66 C2
Arthur Henderson Ho
  1 Crouch End N19 . . .4 C4
  2 Fulham SW6 . . . 164 C2
Arthur Newton Ho **1**
  SW11 . . . . .59 C4
Arthur Rd N7. . . . . . .14 B4
Arthur St EC4 . . . . . 123 C4
Arthur Wade Rd **7**
  E2 . . . . .24 B2 99 A4
Artichoke Hill **1**
  E1 . . . . .32 A2
Artichoke Mews **5**
  SE5 . . . . .48 C2
Artichoke Pl SE5 . . .48 C2
Artillery Ho
  Bow E3 . . . . .26 A4
  Westminster SW1 . . 133 B1
Artillery La
  Broadgate E1 . . . . 110 B3
  North Kensington
  W12 . . . . .29 C3
Artillery Pas E1 . . . 110 B3
Artillery Pl SW1 . . . 133 B1
Artillery Row
  SW1 . . . . 133 B1
Artisan Ct E8 . . . . . .16 C2
Artisan Mews **9**
  NW10 . . . . .22 C2
Artisan Quarter **10**
  NW10 . . . . .22 C2
Artizan St E1 . . . . . . 110 B2
Arton Wilson Ho **10**
  SW15 . . . . .56 C2
Arts Educational
  Schools London **14**
  W4. . . . . .38 A2
Arts La SE16. . . . . . . 139 A1
Arundel Bldgs
  SE1 . . . . 138 B1
Arundel Cl SW11 . . .60 A2
Arundel Ct
  Barnes SW13 . . . . .47 A4
  Chelsea SW3 . . . . . 144 B2
  Putney SW15 . . . . .57 C2
Arundel Gdns
  W11 . . . . . .31 B2 112 C4
Arundel Gr N16. . . . .16 A3
Arundel Ho
  Islington N1 . . . . . .86 B4
  3 South Acton W3 . . .37 A4

Arundel Lo **3** N19 . . .5 A2
Arundel Mans
  Barnes SW13 . . . . .47 A4
  Fulham SW6 . . . . . 165 A4
Arundel Pl N1, N7 . . .14 C2
Arundel Sq N7 . . . . .14 C2
Arundel St WC2 . . . 121 A4
Arundel Terr
  SW13 . . . . .47 A4
Arungford Mews **12**
  SW2 . . . . .62 C2
Arvon Rd N5 . . . . . . .14 C3
Asaph Ho SE14 . . . . .51 B2
Ascalon Ct **16** SW2 .74 B4
Ascalon Ho SW8. . . 160 C1
Ascalon St SW8 . . . 160 C1
Ascham St NW5 . . . .13 B3
Ascot Ct
  Brixton SW4 . . . . . .62 A3
  St John's Wood
  NW8 . . . . .89 B3
Ascot Ho
  6 Acton Green
  W4 . . . . .37 B1
  1 Paddington W9 . .31 C4
  Regent's Pk NW1 . . .92 B4
Ascot Lo NW6 . . . . . .78 B2
Ascot Par **3** SW4 . .62 A3
Ascott Ave W5. . . . . .36 A4
Ashbourne Ct E5 . . .18 A4
Ashbourne Gr
  Chiswick W4 . . . . . .38 A1
  East Dulwich SE22 . .64 B3
Ashbourne
  Independent Sixth
  Form Coll W8 . . . . 128 A3
Ashbridge Ct **4**
  W6 . . . . .39 A3
Ashbridge St NW8. . .90 A1
Ashbrook Rd N19. . . .4 C3
Ashburn Gdns
  SW7 . . . . 142 C4
Ashburnham Com Sch
  SW10 . . . . 157 B2
Ashburnham Gr
  SE10 . . . . .52 A3
Ashburnham Pl
  SE10 . . . . .52 A3
Ashburnham Rd
  Chelsea SW10 . . . . 157 A1
  Kensal Rise NW10 . .22 B2
Ashburnham Retreat
  4 SE10 . . . . .52 A3
Ashburnham Twr
  SW10 . . . . 157 B2
Ashburn Mews
  SW7 . . . . 142 C3
Ashburn Pl SW7 . . . 142 C3
Ashburton Mans
  SW10 . . . . 157 A2
Ashburton Rd E16 . .35 C3
Ashbury Rd SW11 . .60 C4
Ashby Ct NW8 . . . . . .89 C2
Ashby Gr N1 . . . . . . .15 B1
Ashby Ho
  1 Brixton SW9 . . . .48 A1
  10 Islington N1 . . .15 B1
Ashby Mews
  4 Clapham Pk
  SW2 . . . . .62 A2
  New Cross SE4. . . . .51 B1
Ashby Rd SE4 . . . . . .51 B1
Ashby St EC1. . . . . . .96 B3
Ashchurch Ct **2**
  W12 . . . . .38 C3
Ashchurch Gr
  W12 . . . . .38 C3

Ashchurch Park Villas
  W12 . . . . .38 C3
Ashchurch Terr
  W12 . . . . .38 C3
Ashcombe Ct **4**
  SW15 . . . . .58 A2
Ashcombe Ho **39**
  E3 . . . . .27 A2
Ashcombe St
  SW6 . . . . 166 A1
Ashcroft Ho SW8 . . 170 C4
Ashcroft Rd E3 . . . . .26 A2
Ashcroft Sq **3** W6. .39 B2
Ashcroft Tech Acad
  SW15 . . . . .58 B2
Ash Ct
  Clapham SW11 . . . .60 C2
  Marylebone W1 . . . 102 C2
  6 Rotherhithe
  SE16 . . . . .33 A1
  Upper Holloway N19 . .4 B2
Ashdale Ho N4 . . . . . .6 C4
Ashdene **6** SE15 . . .50 A3
Ashdon Rd NW10 . . .21 B4
Ashdown N19 . . . . . . .5 A2
Ashdown Cres
  NW5 . . . . .12 C3
Ashdown Ct SE22 . . .76 C3
Ashdown Ho **7**
  SW1 . . . . .72 C4
Ashdown Wlk **20**
  E14 . . . . .41 C2
Ashenden SE17 . . . . 151 A4
Ashenden Rd E5 . . . .18 A3
Ashen Gr SW19 . . . . .70 C2
Ashentree Ct EC4 . . 107 C1
Asher Way E1 . . . . . 125 C3
Ashfield Ho **5** N5 . .15 B3
Ashfield Rd W3 . . . . .29 B1
Ashfield St
  E1 . . . . .32 B4
  4 Whitechapel E1. .32 A4
Ashfield Yd **21** E1. .32 A4
Ashford Ct NW2 . . . . .9 C4
Ashford Ho
  8 Brixton SW9 . . . .63 A3
  1 Deptford SE8. . . .51 B4
Ashford Rd NW2 . . . .9 C4
Ashford St
  N1 . . . . .24 A2 98 A4
Ash Gr
  Cricklewood NW2 . .10 A4
  Ealing W5 . . . . .36 A3
  Hackney E8. . . . . . .25 A4
Ashgrove Ct **2**
  W9 . . . . .31 C4
Ashgrove Ho SW1 . . 147 C2
Ash Ho
  5 Canary Wharf
  E14. . . . . .42 B4
  Fulham SE1 . . . . . . 153 A3
Ashington Rd
  SW6 . . . . 165 A1
Ashland Pl W1 . . . . . 103 B4
Ashleigh Ho SW14 . .56 A4
Ashleigh Rd SW14 . .56 A4
Ashley Cres SW11 . .60 C4
Ashley Ct
  Hampstead NW3 . . .11 A3
  16 Kingsland N16. .16 A4
Ashley Pl SW1 . . . . . 132 C1

Ashley Rd
  Hornsey N19. . . . . . .5 A4
  Richmond TW9 . . . . .54 A4
Ashlin Rd E15 . . . . . .19 C4
Ash Lo SW6 . . . . .47 C2
Ashlone Rd SW15. . .57 C4
Ashmead Bsns Ctr **7**
  E16 . . . . .27 C1
Ashmead Ho **9** E9 . .18 A3
Ashmead Mews **1**
  SE8 . . . . .51 C1
Ashmead Prim Sch
  SE8 . . . . .51 C1
Ashmead Rd SE8 . . .51 C1
Ashmere Gr **11** SW2,
  SW4 . . . . .62 A3
Ashmere Ho **10**
  E3 . . . . .62 A3
Ashmill St NW8. . . . 102 A4
Ashmole Prim Sch
  SW8 . . . . 163 A3
Ashmole St SW8. . . 163 A3
Ashmore NW1 . . . . . .13 C1
Ashmore Cl SE15 . . .49 B3
Ashmore Ho W14 . . 126 B1
Ashmore Rd W9 . . . .23 B2
Ashmount Prim Sch
  London N19 . . . . . . .4 B4
  Upper Holloway N19 . .5 A4
Ashmount Rd N19 . . .4 C4
Ashness Rd SW11 . .60 B2
Ashpark Ho **4**
  E14 . . . . .33 A3
Ashtead Ct **15**
  SW19 . . . . .69 C3
Ashtead Rd E5 . . . . . .7 C4
Ashton Ho
  16 Kennington
  SW9 . . . . 163 C1
  Roehampton SW15. .69 A4
Ashton Rd E15 . . . . .19 C3
Ashton St E14 . . . . . .34 B2
Ashurst Lo **4** N5 . . .15 A3
Ashwin St E8. . . . . . .16 B2
Ashworth Cl SE5 . . .48 C1
Ashworth Mans
  W9 . . . . .88 B4
Ashworth Rd W9 . . . .88 B4
Aske Ho **2**
  N1 . . . . .24 A2 98 A4
Asker Ho N7 . . . . . . .14 A4
Aske St N1 . . . .24 A2 98 A4
Askew Cres W12. . . .38 C4
Askew Mans **14**
  W12 . . . . .38 C4
Askew Rd W12 . . . . .29 C1
Askham Ct W12 . . . .29 C1
Askham Rd W12 . . . .29 C1
Askill Dr SW15 . . . . .58 A2
Asland Rd E15 . . . . .27 C4
Aslett St SW18 . . . . .71 B4
Asmara Rd NW2 . . . .10 A3
Asolando Dr SE17 . . 151 A3
Aspect Ho **7** E14. . .42 B4
Aspen Cl
  Ealing W5 . . . . .36 B4
  15 Upper Holloway
  N19 . . . . .4 B2
Aspen Ct
  10 Acton W3 . . . . .28 B3
  12 Hackney E8. . . .16 C3
  Richmond TW9 . . . .44 C3
Aspen Gdns **3**
  W6 . . . . .39 A1

Aspen Ho
8 Deptford SE15 . . . . 50 B4
4 Maitland Pk
NW3 . . . . 12 B2
Richmond TW9 . . . . . . 44 C4
Aspenlea Rd W6 . . . . 47 C4
Aspen Way E14 . . . . 34 B2
Aspern Gr NW3 . . . . 12 A3
Aspinall Ho SW12 . . . 74 A3
Aspinall Rd SE4 . . . . 65 C4
Aspinden Rd SE16 . . 40 A2
Aspire Bldg **10**
SW15 . . . . 58 A2
Aspley Rd SW18 . . . . 59 A2
Assam SE1 . . . . 125 A1
Assam St E1 . . . . . . 111 B2
Assata Mews N1 . . . 15 A2
Assembly Pas E1 . . . 32 B4
Assisi Ct SW12 . . . . 72 B3
Astbury Bsns Pk **5**
SE15 . . . . 50 B2
Astbury Ho SE11 . . 135 B1
Astbury Rd SE15 . . . 50 B2
Astell St SW3 . . . . . 144 B2
Aster Ho **3** SE13 . . 52 B1
Aste St E14 . . . . 42 B4
Astey's Row **1** N1 . 15 B1
Aston Ct SW11 . . . . 169 C2
Astley Ave NW2 . . . . 9 B3
Astley Ho
Fulham SE1 . . . . . . 153 A2
30 Paddington W2 . . 31 C4
Aston Ct N4 . . . . 6 B2
Aston Ho
Notting Hill
W11 . . . 31 B2 113 A4
South Lambeth
SW8 . . . . 171 B3
Aston St E14 . . . . . . 33 A4
Astonville St
SW18 . . . . 70 C3
Astor Ct SW6 . . . . . 156 C1
Astoria Mans **18**
SW16 . . . . 74 A1
Astoria Par SW16 . . 74 A1
Astoria Wlk SW9 . . . 62 C4
Astra Ho
3 Bow E3 . . . . 26 B2
Hornsey N4 . . . . 5 B4
Astrop Mews W6 . . . 39 B3
Astrop Terr W6 . . . . 39 B4
Astwood Mews
SW7 . . . . 142 C4
Asylum Rd SE15 . . . 50 A3
Atalanta St
SW6 . . . . . 47 C3 154 A1
Atheldene Rd
SW18 . . . . 71 B3
Athelstane Gr E3 . . . 26 B3
Athelstane Mews
N4 . . . . 5 C3
Athelstan Gdns **8**
NW6 . . . . 10 A1
Athelstan Ho
Hackney Wick E9 . . . 18 B3
Stoke Newington
N16 . . . . 16 A4
Athena Ct
Bermondsey SE1 . . 138 A3
St John's Wood
NW8 . . . . 79 B2
Athenia Ho **7** E14 . 34 C3
Athenlay Rd SE15 . . 65 C3
Athenoeum Ct N5 . . 15 B4

Athens Gdns W9 . . . 23 C1
Atherden Rd E5 . . . . 17 B4
Atherfield Ct
SW18 . . . . 59 A1
Atherfold Rd SW9 . . 62 A4
Atherstone Ct W2 . 100 B4
Atherstone Mews
SW7 . . . . 143 A4
Atherton Rd SW13 . . 46 C3
Atherton St SW11 . 168 C2
Athlone Cl **24** E5 . . 17 A3
Athlone Gate **10**
W10 . . . . 31 A4
Athlone Ho
16 Camden Town
NW5 . . . . 12 C2
9 Stepney E1 . . . . 32 B3
Athlone Rd SW2 . . . 74 C4
Athlone St NW5 . . . . 12 C2
Atholl Ho W9 . . . . . . 88 C3
Athol Sq E14 . . . . . . 34 B3
Atkins Ct E3 . . . . . . 26 B4
Atkins Lo W8 . . . . . 127 B4
Atkinson Ho
Battersea SW11 . . . 169 B3
15 Hackney E2 . . . 24 C3
Walworth SE17 . . . 151 C3
Atkins Rd SW4,
SW12 . . . . 73 C4
Atlanta Bldg **3**
SE13 . . . . 52 A2
Atlantic Ct **16** E14 . 34 C2
Atlantic Ho
1 Putney SW15 . . . 58 B2
2 Tower Hamlets
E1 . . . . 33 A4
Atlas Mews
Dalston E8 . . . . 16 B2
Islington N7 . . . . 14 B2
Atlas Rd NW10 . . . . 21 A2
Atney Rd SW15 . . . . 58 A3
Atterbury St SW1 . 148 A3
Attilburgh Ho SE1 138 C2
Attlee Ho E1 . . . . . 111 A3
Attneave St WC1 . . . 95 B3
Atwater Cl SW2 . . . 74 C3
Atwell Rd **6** SE15 . . 49 C1
Atwood Ave TW9 . . . 44 C1
Atwood Ho SE21 . . . 76 A1
Atwood Rd W6 . . . . 39 A2
Aubert Ct N5 . . . . . . 15 A4
Aubert Pk N5 . . . . . 15 A4
Aubert Rd N5 . . . . . 15 A4
Aubrey Beardsley Ho
SW1 . . . . 147 A3
Aubrey Mans
NW1 . . . . 102 A4
Aubrey Moore Point
E15 . . . . 27 B3
Aubrey Pl NW8 . . . . 78 C1
Aubrey Rd
W14 . . . . 31 B1 113 A1
Aubrey Wlk
W14 . . . . 31 B1 113 A1
Auburn Cl SE14 . . . . 51 A3
Aubyn Sq SW15 . . . 56 C2
Auckland Ho **11**
W12 . . . . 30 A2
Auckland Rd
SW11 . . . . 60 A3
Auckland St SE11 148 C1
Auden Pl NW1 . . . . . 81 B4

Audley Cl **9** SW11 . . 60 C4
Audley Ct W1 . . . . . 118 A2
Audley Rd TW10 . . . 54 B2
Audley Sq W1 . . . . . 117 C2
Audley St W1 . . . . . 117 C2
Audrey Ho EC1 . . . . 107 C3
Audrey St E2 . . . . . . 24 C3
Augusta St E14 . . . . 34 A3
Augustine Ho
Broadgate EC2 . . . 109 C2
New Cross SE4 . . . . 51 B2
Augustine Rd W14 . . 39 C3
Augustines Ct E9 . . 17 B3
Augustus Cl W12 . . 39 A3
Augustus Ct
8 Putney SW19 . . . 70 A3
Streatham SW16 . . . 74 A2
Augustus Ho NW1 . . 92 C4
Augustus Rd
52 Putney SW19 . . 69 C3
Putney SW19 . . . . . 70 A3
Augustus St NW1 . . 92 B4
Aulton Pl SE11 . . . . 149 C1
Aura Ho **3** TW9 . . . 45 A2
Auriga Mews N1 . . . 15 C3
Auriol Mans W14 . . 140 A3
Auriol Rd W14 . . . . 140 A3
Aurora Bldg **4**
E14 . . . . 34 B1
Aurora Ho E14 . . . . 34 A3
Austen Ho **5** NW6 . 23 C2
Austin Friars EC2 . . 109 C2
Austin Friars Ho
EC2 . . . . 109 C2
Austin Friars Sq
EC2 . . . . 109 C2
Austin Ho
8 Brixton SW2 . . . 62 B2
1 New Cross SE14 . 51 B3
Austin Rd SW11 . . . 169 B3
Austin St E2 . . . . . . 98 C3
Australia Rd W12 . . 30 A2
Austral St SE11 . . . 150 A4
Autumn Rise **9**
W4 . . . . 37 C1
Autumn St E3 . . . . . 26 C4
Avalon Rd SW6 . . . . 166 A4
Avebury Ct N1 . . . . . 87 C3
Avebury St N1 . . . . . 87 C3
Aveline St SE11 . . . 149 B1
Aveling Ho **12** N19 . 4 B1
Ave Maria La EC4 . . 108 B1
Avenell Mans N5 . . . 15 A4
Avenell Rd N5 . . . . . 6 A1
Avenfield Ho W1 . . . 117 A4
Avening Rd SW18 . . 70 C4
Avening Terr
SW18 . . . . 70 C4
Avenue Cl NW8 . . . . 80 B3
Avenue Cres W3 . . . 37 A4
Avenue Ct
Chelsea SW3 . . . . . 144 C3
Cricklewood NW2 . . . 1 A1
Avenue Gdns
Mortlake SW14 . . . . 56 A4
South Acton W3 . . . . 37 A4
Avenue Lo **12**
NW8 . . . . 11 C1

Avenue Mans
Clapham SW11 . . . . 60 C3
Hampstead NW3 . . . 11 A3
Willesden NW2 . . . . . 9 C2
Avenue Park Rd SE21,
SE27 . . . . 75 A2
Avenue Rd
Crouch End N6 . . . . . 4 C4
Harlesden NW10 . . . 21 B3
Primrose Hill NW8 . . 80 A4
South Acton W3 . . . . 37 A4
Avenue The
Bedford Pk W4 . . . . 38 A3
Brondesbury Pk
NW6 . . . . 23 A4
Clapham SW4 . . . . . 60 C2
Greenwich SE10 . . . 52 C3
Richmond TW9 . . . . 44 B1
Wandsworth SW18,
SW12 . . . . 72 A4
Averill St W6 . . . . . . 47 C4
Avery Farm Row
SW1 . . . . 146 A3
Avery Row **1** W1 . 118 B4
Aviary Cl E16 . . . . . 35 B4
Avignon Rd SE4 . . . 65 C4
Avingdor Ct **10**
W3 . . . . 28 B1
Avington Ct SE1 . . . 152 B3
Avis Sq E1 . . . . 32 C3
Avocet Cl SE1 . . . . 153 C2
Avon Ct
1 Acton W3 . . . . . 28 B3
10 Putney SW15 . . 58 A2
Avondale Ct E16 . . . 35 A4
Avondale Ho
11 Bermondsey
SE1 . . . . 153 B1
6 Mortlake SW14 . 55 C4
Avondale Mans
SW6 . . . . 164 C4
Avondale Park Gdns
W11 . . . . 31 A2 112 A3
Avondale Park Prim
Sch W11 . . 31 A2 112 A3
Avondale Park Rd
W11 . . . . 31 A2 112 A3
Avondale Rise
SE15 . . . . 64 B4
Avondale Sq SE1 . . 153 B1
Avon Ho
2 Islington N1 . . . 14 C1
14 Stoke Newington
N16 . . . . 15 C4
West Kensington
W14 . . . . 141 A3
Avonhurst Ho
NW6 . . . . 10 A1
Avonley Rd SE14 . . . 50 B3
Avonmore Gdns
W14 . . . . 141 A3
Avonmore Pl
W14 . . . . 140 B4
Avonmore Prim Sch
W14 . . . . 140 B4
Avonmore Rd
W14 . . . . 140 C4
Avonmouth St
SE1 . . . . 136 C2
Avon Pl SE1 . . . . . . 137 A3
Avon Rd SE4 . . . . . . 66 C4
Avriol Ho W12 . . . . . 30 A1
Avro Ct E9 . . . . 18 A3

Axford Ho SW2 . . . . 75 A3
Axis St SE10 . . . . . . 53 A4
Axminster Rd N7 . . . . 5 B1
Aybrook St W1 . . . 103 B3
Aycliffe Rd W12 . . . 29 C1
Aylesbury Ho **13**
SE15 . . . . 49 C4
Aylesbury Rd
SE17 . . . . 151 C1
Aylesbury St EC1 . . 96 A1
Aylesford Ho SE1 . 137 C3
Aylesford St SW1 . 147 B1
Aylesham Sh Ctr
SE15 . . . . 49 C2
Aylestone Ave
NW6 . . . . 22 C4
Aylmer Ho SE10 . . . 42 C1
Aylmer Rd W12 . . . . 38 B4
Aylton Est **3** SE16 . 40 B4
Aylward St E1 . . . . . 32 C3
Aylwin Est SE1 . . . 138 B2
Aynhoe Mans W14 . 39 C2
Aynhoe Rd W14 . . . 39 C3
Ayres St SE1 . . . . . 137 A4
Ayrsome Rd N16 . . . . 7 A1
Ayrton Gould Ho **9**
E2 . . . . 25 C2
Ayrton Rd SW7 . . . 129 B2
Aysgarth Rd SE21 . . 76 A4
Ayshford Ho E1 . . . 25 A2
Ayston Ho **10** SE8 . 40 C2
Aytoun Ct **17** SW9 173 A1
Aytoun Pl SW9 . . . 173 A1
Aytoun Rd SW9 . . . 173 A1
Azalea Ho SE14 . . . 51 B3
Azania Mews NW5 . 13 A2
Azenby Rd SE15 . . . 49 B1
Azof St SE10 . . . . . . 43 A2
Azov Ho **10** E1 . . . . 26 A1
Aztec Ct **8** N16 . . . 16 A2
Azure Ho **28**
E2 . . . . 24 C2 99 B3

B

Baalbec Rd N5 . . . . 15 A3
Babington Ct
WC1 . . . . 106 B4
Babington Ho
SE1 . . . . 137 A4
Babmaes St SW1 . . 119 B3
Bacchus Wlk **12**
N1 . . . . 24 A3
Bache's St N1 . . . . . 97 C3
Back Church La
E1 . . . . 111 B1
Back Hill EC1 . . . . . 95 C1
Backhouse Pl SE1 . 152 B3
Back La NW3 . . . . . . 11 B4
Bacon Gr SE1 . . . . 138 C1
Bacon's Coll SE16 . . 41 A4
Bacon St E2 . . . 24 B1 99 A2
Bacon's La N6 . . . . . . 3 C3
Bacton NW5 . . . . . . 12 C3
Bacton St E2 . . . . . . 25 B2
Baddeley Ho
SE11 . . . . 149 A2
Baddow Wlk N1 . . . . 86 C4
Baden Cl SW3 . . . . 144 B2
Baden Pl SE1 . . . . . 137 B4
Bader Wy **2**
SW15 . . . . 56 C1
Badminton Ct **9**
N4 . . . . 6 B4

Badminton Ho
SE22 . . . . 64 A3
Badminton Mews 9
E16 . . . . 35 C1
Badminton Rd
SW12 . . . . .60 C1
Badric Ct SW11 . . . 167 C1
Badsworth Rd 8
SE5 . . . . 48 B2
Baffin Wy E14 . . . . . . 34 B2
Bagley's La SW6 . . 166 B3
Bagnigge Ho WC1 . . 95 B3
Bagshot Ho NW1 . . . 92 B4
Bagshot St SE17 . . 152 B1
Baildon 27 E2 . . . . . . 25 B3
Baildon St SE8 . . . . . 51 B3
Bailey Cl E17 . . . . 38 C4
Bailey Ho SW10 . . 156 B2
Bailey Mews
Brixton SW2 . . . . 62 C2
Chiswick W4 . . . . 45 B4
Bainbridge St
WC1 . . . . 105 C2
Bain Ho 22 SW9 . . 172 B2
Baird Ho 22 W12 . . . 30 A2
Baird St EC1 . . . . 97 A2
Baizdon Rd SE3 . . . . 53 A1
Baker Ho 22 E3 . . . . . 27 A2
Baker Rd NW10 . . . . 21 A4
Bakers Field N7 . . . . 14 A4
Bakers Hall Ct
EC3 . . . . 124 B3
Baker's Mews 11 103 B2
Bakers Pas 27
NW3 . . . . 11 B4
Bakers Rents 18
E2 . . . . 24 B2 98 B3
Baker's Row EC1 . . . 95 B1
Baker St W1 . . . . . . 103 A4
Baker Street W1 . . 103 A4
Baker Street Sta
NW1 . . . . 91 A1
Baker's Yd EC1 . . . . . 95 B1
Bakery Gr SW9 . . . 163 A1
Balaclava Rd SE1 . 153 A3
Balchier Rd SE22 . . 65 A1
Balcombe Ho
Lisson Gr NW1 . . . . . . 90 C2
1 Streatham SW2 . . 74 B3
Balcombe St NW1 . . 90 C1
Balcorne St 17 E9 . . 17 B1
Balderton Flats
W1 . . . . 103 C1
Balderton St W1 . . 103 C1
Baldock Ho 81
SE5 . . . . 48 B1
Baldock St E3 . . . . . . 27 A3
Baldrey Ho 11
SE10 . . . . 43 B1
Baldwin Cres SE5 . . 48 B2
Baldwin Ho 18
SW2 . . . . 74 C3
Baldwin Rd SW11 . . 60 C1
Baldwin's Gdns
EC1 . . . . 107 B4
Baldwin St EC1 . . . . . 97 B3
Baldwin Terr N1 . . . . 86 C2
Baldwyn Gdns W3 . . 28 C2
Balearic Apts 8
E16 . . . . 35 C2
Bale Rd E1 . . . . 33 A4
Bales Coll W10 . . . . . 22 C2
Balfern Gr W4 . . . . . 38 A1
Balfern St SW11 . . 168 B2
Balfe St N1 . . . . 84 B1

Balfour Ho 4
W10 . . . . 30 C4
Balfour Mews W1 117 C2
Balfour Pl
Mayfair W1 . . . . 117 C3
Putney SW15 . . . . . . 57 A3
Balfour Rd
Highbury N5 . . . . 15 B4
North Acton W3 . . . . 28 B4
Balfour St SE17 . . . 151 B4
Balfron Twr 4
E14 . . . . 34 B3
BALHAM 72 C3
Balham Gr SW12 . . . 72 C4
Balham High Rd SW12,
SW17 . . . . 72 C3
Balham Hill SW12 . . 61 A1
Balham L Ctr
SW12 . . . . 73 A2
Balham New Rd
SW12 . . . . 73 A4
Balham Park Mans
SW12 . . . . 72 B3
Balham Park Rd SW12,
SW17 . . . . 72 C3
Balham Station Rd
SW12 . . . . 73 A3
Balin Ho SE1 . . . . . 137 B4
Balkan Wlk E1 . . . . . 32 A2
Balladier Wlk E14 . . 34 A4
Ballance Rd E9 . . . . . 18 A2
Ballantine St
SW18 . . . . 59 B3
Ballantrae Ho
NW2 . . . . 10 B4
Ballard Ho SE10 . . . 52 A4
Ballast Quay SE10 . 42 C1
Ballater Rd SW2,
SW4 . . . . 62 A3
Ball Ct EC3 . . . . 109 C1
Ballin Ct 14 E14 . . . 42 B4
Ballingdon Rd
SW11 . . . . 60 C1
Ballinger Point 18
E3 . . . . 27 A2
Balliol Ho 4
SW15 . . . . 57 C1
Balliol Rd W10 . . . . . 30 C3
Ballogie Ave NW10 . 8 A4
Ballow Cl 15 SE5 . . 49 A3
Ball's Pond Pl 3
N1 . . . . 15 C2
Ball's Pond Rd N1 . . 16 A2
Balman Ho 3
SE16 . . . . 40 C2
Balmer Rd E3 . . . . . . 26 B3
Balmes Rd N1 . . . . . . 87 C4
Balmoral Cl 1
SW15 . . . . 57 C1
Balmoral Ct
11 Rotherhithe
SE16 . . . . 32 C1
St John's Wood
NW8 . . . . 79 B2
Balmoral Gr N7 . . . . 14 B2
Balmoral Ho
2 Isle Of Dogs
E14 . . . . 42 A3
Stoke Newington N4 . 6 B3
West Kensington
W14 . . . . 140 A4
Balmoral Mews
W12 . . . . 38 B3
Balmoral Rd NW2 . . 9 A2
Balmore Cl E14 . . . . 34 B3

Balmore St N19 . . . . 4 A2
Balmuir Gdns
SW15 . . . . 57 B3
Balnacraig Ave
NW10 . . . . 8 A4
Balsam Ho 9 E14 . . 34 A2
Baltic Apts 8 E16 . . 35 C2
Baltic Ho 7 SE5 . . . 48 B1
Baltic St E EC1 . . . . . 96 C1
Baltic St W EC1 . . . . 96 C1
Baltimore Ho
Clapham SW18 . . . . . 59 B3
Kennington SE11 . . 149 B2
Balvaird Pl SW1 . . 147 C1
Balvernie Gr SW18 . 70 C4
Bamber Rd 5
SE15 . . . . 49 B2
Bamborough Gdns 11
W12 . . . . 39 B4
Banbury Ct WC2 . . 120 A4
Banbury Ho 8 E9 . . 17 C1
Banbury Rd E9 . . . . . 17 C1
Banbury St 3
SW11 . . . . 168 B2
Bancroft Ct SW8 . . 172 A4
Bancroft Ho 4
E1 . . . . 25 C1
Bancroft Rd E1 . . . . . 25 C1
Banfi Ho 4 NW3 . . . 12 A2
Banfield Rd SE15 . . 65 A4
Bangabandhu Prim
Sch 22 E2 . . . . 25 B2
Bangalore St
SW15 . . . . 57 C4
Banim St W6 . . . . . . 39 A2
Banister Ho
Hackney E9 . . . . 17 C3
Nine Elms SW8 . . . 171 A4
9 West Kilburn
W10 . . . . 23 A2
Banister Rd W10 . . . 22 C2
Bank Ct SW11 . . . . 170 A4
Bank End SE1 . . . . . 123 A2
Bank La SW15 . . . . . 56 A2
Bankes Ct SE1 . . . . 135 C3
Banks Ho SE1 . . . . . 136 C1
Bankside
Borough The SE1 . . 122 C3
Borough The SE1 . . 123 A2
Bankside Ave 1
SE13 . . . . 67 B4
Bankside Gall
SE1 . . . . 122 B3
Bankside Ho EC3 . . 110 B1
Bankside Mix SE1 . 122 C2
Bankside Pier
SE1 . . . . 122 C3
Bank Sta EC3 . . . . . 109 C1
Bank The N6 . . . . 4 A3
Bankton Rd SW2 . . . 62 C3
Banner Ho 11 SE16 . 40 B2
Banner Rd EC1 . . . . . 97 A1
Bannerman Ho
SW8 . . . . 162 C3
Banner St EC1 . . . . . . 97 A2
Banning Ho 4
SW19 . . . . 69 C3
Banning St SE10 . . . 43 A1
Bannister Cl SW2 . . 74 C3
Bannister Ho 20
SE14 . . . . 50 C4

Banqueting Ho
SW1 . . . . 120 A1
Banstead Ct
East Acton W12 . . . . 29 B2
Stoke Newington N4 . 6 B3
Banstead St SE15 . . 65 B4
Bantock Ho 9
W10 . . . . 23 A2
Bantry Ho 18 E1 . . . . 25 C1
Bantry St SE5 . . . . . . 48 C3
Banville Ho SW8 . . 163 A1
Banyan Ho 4
NW3 . . . . 11 A2
Banyard Rd SE16 . . 40 A3
Baptist Gdns NW5 . 12 C2
Barandon Wlk 6
W11 . . . . 30 C2
Barbanel Ho 21 E1 . 25 B1
Barbara Brosnan Ct
NW8 . . . . 79 B1
Barbara Castle Cl
SW6 . . . . 155 A3
Barbara Rudolph Ct
5 N19 . . . . 5 A4
Barbauld Rd N16 . . . 7 A1
Barber Beaumont Ho
2 E1 . . . . 25 C2
Barbers Rd E15 . . . . 27 A3
BARBICAN 109 A3
Barbican Ctr EC2 . . 109 A4
Barb Mews W6 . . . . 39 B3
Barbon Alley EC3 . . 110 B2
Barbon Cl WC1 . . . 106 C4
Barbrook Ho E9 . . . . 17 B2
Barchard St SW18 . . 59 A2
Barchester St E14 . . 34 A4
Barclay Cl SW6 . . . 155 B1
Barclay Ho 22 E9 . . 17 B1
Barclay Rd SW6 . . . 155 C1
Barcombe Ave
SW2 . . . . 74 B2
Bardell Ho 17 SE1 . 139 B3
Bardolph Rd
Richmond TW9 . . . . . 54 B4
Tufnell Pk N7 . . . . . . 14 A4
Bard Rd W10 . . . . . . 30 C2
Bardsey Pl 4 E1 . . . 25 B1
Bardsey Wlk 8
N1 . . . . 15 B2
Bardsley Ho 6
SE10 . . . . 52 B4
Bardsley La SE10 . . 52 B4
Barents Ho 11 E1 . . 25 C1
Barfett St W10 . . . . . 23 B1
Barfleur La SE8 . . . . 41 B2
Barford Ho 22 E3 . . 26 B3
Barford St N1 . . . . . . 85 C3
Barforth Rd SE15 . . 65 B4
Barge House St
SE1 . . . . 121 C2
Barge La 10 E3 . . . . 26 B4
Baring Ho 15 E14 . . 33 C3
Baring St N1 . . . . 87 B3
Barker Cl TW9 . . . . . 45 A1
Barker Dr NW1 . . . . 13 C1
Barker Ho
Dulwich SE21 . . . . . . 76 A1
Walworth SE17 . . . 152 A3
Barker Mews SW4 . 61 A3
Barker St SW10 . . . 156 C4
Barker Wlk SW16 . . 73 C1
Bark Pl W2 . . . . 114 A4
Barkston Gdns
SW5 . . . . 142 A3

Barkway Ct N4 . . . . . . 6 B2
Barkwith Ho 27
SE14 . . . . 50 C4
Barkworth Rd
SE16 . . . . 40 B1
Barlborough St
SE14 . . . . 50 C3
Barlby Gdns W10 . . 22 C1
Barlby Prim Sch
W10 . . . . 22 C1
Barlby Rd W10 . . . . . 30 C4
Barleycorn Way
E14 . . . . 33 B2
Barley Mow Pas
Chiswick W4 . . . . 37 C1
Clerkenwell EC1 . . . 108 B3
Barley Shotts Bsns Pk
W10 . . . . 31 B4
Barling 6 NW1 . . . . . 13 A1
Barling Ct 1
SW9 . . . . 172 A2
Barlings Ho 2
SE4 . . . . 65 C3
Barloch Ho 14
SW11 . . . . 169 B2
Barlow Ho
14 Bermondsey
SE16 . . . . 40 A2
Notting Hill
W11 . . . . 31 A2 112 A4
Shoreditch N1 . . . . . . 97 B4
Barlow Pl W1 . . . . . 118 B3
Barlow Rd
Acton W3 . . . . 28 A1
Brondesbury NW6 . . 10 B2
5 Hammersmith
W6 . . . . 39 A2
Barlow St SE17 . . . 151 C3
Barmouth Ho 6 N7 . 5 B2
Barmouth Rd
SW18 . . . . 59 B1
Barnabas Ho EC1 . . 96 C3
Barnabas Lo SW8 . 172 B4
Barnabas Rd E9 . . . 17 C3
Barnaby Pl SW7 . . 143 B3
Barnado Gardens
E1 . . . . 32 C2
Barnard Ct SW16 . . 74 B1
Barnard Ho 16 E2 . . 25 A2
Barnard Lo 10 W9 . 31 C4
Barnard Mews
SW11 . . . . 60 A3
Barnardo Gdns 1
E1 . . . . 32 C2
Barnardo St E1 . . . . 32 C3
Barnard Rd SW11 . . 60 A3
Barnard's Inn EC1 107 C2
Barnbrough NW1 . . 82 C3
Barnby St NW1 . . . . 93 A4
Barn Cl 19 NW5 . . . 13 C3
Barn Elms Sp Ctr
SW15 . . . . 47 B2
Barnersbury Ho
N7 . . . . 14 A4
BARNES 46 B2
Barnes Ave SW13 . . 46 C3
Barnes Bridge Sta
SW13 . . . . 46 A1
Barnes Common
SW13 . . . . 56 C4
Barnes Ct N1 . . . . . . 14 C1
Barnes High St
SW13 . . . . 46 B1
Barnes Ho
14 Bethnal Green
E2 . . . . 25 B3

Barnes Ho continued
Camden Town NW1 .. **82** B4
26 Deptford SE14 .... **50** C4
Hornsey N19............ **5** A4

Barnes Hospl
SW14 .... **56** A4

Barnes Prim Sch
SW13 .... **56** B4

Barnes St E14 .... **33** A3
Barnes Sta SW13 ... **56** C4
Barnes Terr SE8 ..... **41** B1

Barnet Gr
E2 .... **24** C2 **99** B3

Barnet Ho **33** SE5... **48** B1
Barnett St E1 .... **32** A3
Barn Field NW3 ..... **12** B3

Barnfield Cl
London N4 .... **5** A4
Wandsworth SW17 ... **71** B1

Barnfield Pl E14 .... **41** C2
Barnham St SE1 ... **138** B4
BARNSBURY **14** A1
Barnsbury Gr N7 ..... **14** B1
Barnsbury Ho **12**
SW4 .... **61** C1
Barnsbury Pk N1 ... **14** C1
Barnsbury Rd N1 ... **85** B3
Barnsbury Sq N1 ... **14** C1
Barnsbury St N1 ... **14** C1
Barnsbury Terr N1 .. **14** B1
Barnsdale Ave
E14 .... **41** C2
Barnsdale Rd W9 ... **23** B1
Barnsley St E1 ..... **25** A1
Barn St N16 .... **7** A2
Barnstaple La
SE13 .... **67** B3
Barnston Wlk N1 ... **86** C4
Barnwell Ho **1**
SE5 .... **49** A2
Barnwell Rd SW2 ... **62** C2
Barnwood Cl W9 .... **88** B1
Baron Cl N1 .... **85** B2
Baroness Rd **8**
E2 .... **24** B2 **99** A4
Barons Court Mans
W14 .... **140** B1
Baron's Court Rd
W14 .... **140** B2
Barons Court Sta
W14 .... **140** A2
Barons Gate **13**
W4 .... **37** B3
Barons Keep W14 . **140** B2
Barons Lo **9** E14 ... **42** B2
Baronsmead Rd
SW13 .... **46** C2
Baronsmede W5 .... **36** A4
Baron's Pl SE1 ... **135** C3
Baron St N1 .... **85** B2
Baron Wlk E16 ...... **35** B4
Barque Mews SE8 .. **51** C4
Barradell Ho **13**
W14 .... **39** C3
Barratt Ho **1** N1 ... **15** A1
Barratt Ind Pk E3 .. **27** B4
Barret Ho NW6 ...... **23** C4
Barrett Ct **2**
NW10 .... **21** A3
Barrett's Gr N16.... **16** A3
Barretts Green Rd
NW10 .... **20** C3
Barrett St W1 ..... **103** C1

Barrhill Rd SW2 .... **74** A2
Barriedale SE14 .... **51** A1

Barrie Ho
Acton W3 .... **37** B4
Bayswater W2 ...... **115** A3
Primrose Hill NW8 .. **80** B3
8 Stoke Newington
N16.................. **7** A1

Barrington Cl
NW5.................. **12** C3

Barrington Ct
Acton W3 .... **37** A4
Kentish Town NW5.. **12** C3
51 South Lambeth
SW9 .... **172** B1

Barrington Rd
SW9 .... **63** A4

Barrowgate Ho
W4 .... **37** C1

Barrowgate Rd
W4 .... **37** C1

Barrow Hill Est
NW8 .... **80** A1

Barrow Hill Jun Sch
NW8 .... **80** A1

Barrow Hill Rd
NW8 .... **80** A1

Barry Ct SW4........ **61** B1
Barry Ho **3** SE16 ... **40** A1
Barry Lo N4 .... **5** B4
Barry Par SE22 ...... **64** C3
Barry Rd SE22 ...... **64** C2
Barset Rd SE15 ..... **65** B4
Barston Rd SE27 ... **75** B1
Barstow Cres SW2 . **74** B3
Bartell Ho SW2 ..... **62** C1
Barter St WC1 .... **106** B3
Bartholomew Cl
18 Blackwall E14 .... **34** C2
St Luke's EC1 .... **97** A2

Bartholomew Ct
EC1 .... **108** C3

Bartholomew Ho **22**
SE5 .... **48** B1

Bartholomew La
EC2 .... **109** C1

Bartholomew Pas
EC1 .... **108** B3

Bartholomew Pl
EC1 .... **108** C3

Bartholomew Rd
NW5 .... **13** B2

Bartholomew Sq
18 Bethnal Green
E1 .... **25** A1
St Luke's EC1 .... **97** A2

Bartholomew St
SE1 .... **137** C1

Bartholomew Villas
NW5 .... **13** B2
Bartle Rd W11 ...... **31** A3
Bartlett Cl E14 .... **33** C3
Bartlett Ct EC4 ... **107** C2
Bartok Ho
W11................. **31** B2 **112** C3

Barton Cl
Hackney E9 .... **17** B3
Peckham SE15 .... **65** A4

Barton Ct
3 South Lambeth
SW4 .... **172** A2
West Kensington
W14 .... **140** B2

Barton Ho
8 Bromley E3 ...... **27** A2

Barton Ho continued
Islington N1.......... **15** A1
Sands End SW6 ..... **59** A4
Barton Rd W14 .... **140** B1
Barton St SW1 .... **134** A2
Bartonway NW8 .... **79** B2
Bartram Rd SE4 .... **66** A1
Bartrip St E9 .... **18** B2
**Bars & The London
Sch of Medicine &
Dentistry** EC1 ..... **96** B1
Barville Cl SE4 ..... **66** A3
Barwell Ho **7**
E2 .... **24** C1 **99** C2
Barwick Ho **7** W3 . **37** B4
Bascome St **13**
SW2 .... **62** C1
Base Apartments **11**
N1 .... **15** B1
**Baseline Business
Studios** **4** W11 ... **30** C1
Basevi Way SE8 ..... **52** A4
Bashley Rd NW10... **20** C1
Basildon Ct W1 ... **103** C4
Basil Ho
South Lambeth
SW8 .... **162** A2
47 Whitechapel E1 . **111** C2
Basil Mans SW1 .. **130** C3
Basil St
Knightsbridge
SW1 .... **130** C2
Knightsbridge SW1,
SW3 .... **130** C2
Basin App **20** E14... **33** A3
Basing Ct **5** SE15 . **49** B2
Basingdon Way
SE5 .... **63** C3
Basinghall Ave
EC2 .... **109** B2
Basinghall St EC2 **109** B2
Basing Hill NW11 ... **1** B3
Basing House Yd **22**
E2 .... **24** B2 **98** B4
Basing Pl E2 ..... **24** B2 **98** B4
Basing St W11 ...... **31** B3
Basire St N1 .... **87** A4
Baskerville Ct
SW18 .... **72** A4
Baskerville Gdns
NW10 .... **8** A4
Baskerville Rd
SW18 .... **72** A4
Baslow Wlk E5 .... **17** C4
Basnett Rd **9**
SW11 .... **60** C4
Basque Ct **21** SE16.. **40** C4
Bassano St SE22 .... **64** B2
Bassein Park Rd
W12 .... **38** B4
Bassett House Sch **22**
W10 .... **30** C3
Bassett Rd W10 .... **30** C3
Bassett St NW5 ..... **12** C2
Bassingbourn Ho **3**
N1 .... **15** A1
Bassingham Rd
SW18 .... **71** B4
Bassishaw Highwalk
EC2 .... **109** B3
Basswood Cl **5**
SE15 .... **65** A4
Basterfield Ho EC1 . **96** C1
Bastion Highwalk
EC2 .... **108** C3
Bastwick St EC1 .... **96** C2

Basuto Rd SW6.... **165** C3
Batavia Ho **1**
SE14 .... **51** A3
Batavia Mews **3**
SE14 .... **51** A3
Batavia Rd SE14.... **51** A3
Batchelor St N1 .... **85** C3
Bateman Ho **6**
SE17 .... **48** A4
Bateman Mews
SW4 .... **61** C1
Bateman's Bldgs
W1 .... **105** B1
Bateman's Row
EC2 .... **24** A1 **98** B2
Bateman St W1 ... **105** B1
Bate St **10** E14 ..... **33** B2
Bath Cl SE15 ...... **50** B3
Bath Ct
Finsbury EC1 .... **97** B3
3 Forest Hill SE26 . **76** C1
Holborn EC1 .... **95** B1
Bathgate Ho **8**
SW9 .... **48** A2
Bathgate Rd SW19 **69** C1
Bath Gr E2 .... **24** C3
Bath Ho
Bethnal Green
E2 .... **24** C1 **99** C2
Borough The SE1 .. **137** A2
Bath Pl
14 Hammersmith
W6 .... **39** B1
8 Shoreditch
EC2 .... **24** A2 **98** A3
Bath Rd W4 .... **38** A2
Bath St EC1 .... **97** B3
Bath Terr SE1 .... **137** A2
Bathurst Gdns
NW10 .... **22** A3
Bathurst Ho **2**
W12 .... **30** A2
Bathurst Mews
W2 .... **115** C4
Bathurst St W2 ... **115** C4
Batley Pl **3** N16.... **7** B1
Batley Rd N16 ...... **7** B1
Batman Cl W12..... **30** A1
Batoum Gdns W6... **39** B3
Batson Ho **29** E1 .. **111** C1
Batson St W12 ..... **38** C4
Batten Ho
7 London SW4 .... **61** B2
8 West Kilburn
W10 .... **23** A2
Batten St SW11 .... **60** A4
BATTERSEA **169** A4
Battersea Bridge Rd
SW11 .... **158** A1
Battersea Bsns Ctr
SW11 .... **60** C4
Battersea Bsns Pk
SW8 .... **171** A3
Battersea Church Rd
SW11 .... **167** C4
**Battersea Dogs & Cats
Home** SW8........ **160** B1
Battersea High St
SW11 .... **167** B1
Battersea Hts
SW11 .... **60** B4
Battersea Park ... **159** B1
Battersea Park Rd
SW11, SW8 .... **169** A3

Battersea Park Sta
SW8 .... **160** A1
**Battersea Power
Station(dis)**
SW8 .... **160** B4
Battersea Rise
SW11 .... **60** A3
Battersea Sq
SW11 .... **167** C3
Battishill St N1 .... **15** A1
Battlebridge Ct
NW1 .... **84** B2
Battle Bridge La
SE1 .... **124** A1
Battledean Rd N5 .. **15** A3
Battle Ho **8** SE15 . **49** C4
Batty St E1 .... **111** C2
Batty Ho SW2 ...... **74** B3
Baulk The SW18 .... **70** C4
Bavaria Rd N19..... **5** A2
Bavent Rd SE5 ..... **48** B1
Bawdale Rd SE22... **64** B2
Bawtree Rd SE14 ... **51** A3
Baxendale St
E2 .... **24** C2 **99** B4
Baxter Ho **11** E3 ... **27** A2
Baxter Rd N1 .... **15** C2
Baycliffe Ho **8** E9 . **17** C2
Bay Ct
7 Ealing W5 .... **36** A3
7 Stepney E1 ...... **25** C1
Bayer Ho EC1 ...... **96** C1
Bayes Ct NW3 ...... **12** B1
Bayfield Ho **8**
SE4 .... **65** C3
Bayford Ho NW10... **22** C2
Bayford St Ind Ctr **3**
E8 .... **17** A1
Bayford St **4** E8 ... **17** A1
Bayham Pl NW1 .... **83** A3
Bayham Rd W4 ..... **37** C3
Bayham St NW1 .... **82** C3
Bayhurst Ho N4 ..... **6** B4
Bayley St WC1 .... **105** B3
Baylis Rd SE1 ..... **135** B3
Baynes Mews **2**
NW3 .... **11** C2
Baynes St NW1 .... **13** B1
Bayon Ho **27** N19... **4** C4
Bayonne Rd W6 ... **154** A3
Bayston Rd N16 .... **7** B1
BAYSWATER **114** C4
Bayswater Rd W2 **115** B3
Bayswater Sta
W2 .... **114** B3
Bayton Ct **2** E8 .... **16** C1
Baytree Mews
SE17 .... **151** B4
Baytree Rd SW2 .... **62** B3
Bazalgette Ho
NW8 .... **89** C2
Bazely Ho SE1... **136** A2
Bazely St E14 ...... **34** B2
Beach Ho SW5 .... **141** B2
Beachy Rd E3 ...... **18** C4
**Beaconfield Terrace
Rd** W14 .... **126** A3
Beacon Gate SE14 . **65** C4
Beacon Hill N7 ..... **14** A3
Beacon Ho
11 Camberwell
SE5 .... **49** A3
7 Isle Of Dogs
E14 .... **42** A1

Beacon Ho continued
South Lambeth
  SW8 . . . . **171** B4
Beacon Rd SE13 . . . .**67** C1
Beaconsfield Cl
  Acton Green W4 . . . . .37 B1
  Greenwich SE3 . . . . .53 C4
Beaconsfield Rd
  Acton W4 . . . . .37 C3
  Greenwich SE3 . . . . .53 C3
  Walworth SE17 . . . . **152** A1
  Willesden NW10 . . . . .8 B2
Beaconsfield St
  N1 . . . . **84** A4
Beaconsfield Wlk 28
  SW6 . . . . **165** A3
Beadon Rd W6 . . . . .**39** B2
Beak St W1 . . . . . . **119** A4
Beale PI E3 . . . . . . **172** C1
Beale Rd E3 . . . . . . .26 B4
Beames Ho 3 SW8. .**171** B4
Beames Rd NW10. . .20 C4
Beaminster Ho
  SW8 . . . . **162** C2
Beamish Ho 7
  SE16 . . . . .40 B2
Bear Alley EC4 . . . . **108** A2
Bear Croft Ho 6
  SW6 . . . . **164** C1
Beardsley Way
  W3 . . . . .37 C4
Bear Gdns SE1 . . . . **122** C2
Bear La SE1 . . . . . . **122** B1
Bear St WC2 . . . . . . **119** C4
Bearstead Rise
  SE4 . . . . .66 B2
Beaton Cl SE15 . . . .49 B2
Beatrice Ho
  1 Brixton SW2 . . . .62 B2
  4 Hammersmith
    W6 . . . . .39 B1
  8 Stepney E1 . . . . .32 C4
Beatrice PI W8 . . . . **128** A1
Beatrice Rd
  Bermondsey SE1 . . . **153** C3
  Finsbury Pk N4 . . . . .5 C4
  8 Richmond
    TW9 . . . . .54 B3
  5 Peckham SE15 . . .49 C1
Beatrice Tate Sch
  E2 . . . . .25 A2
Beatrice Webb Ho 4
  E3 . . . . .26 A3
Beatrix Potter Prim
  Sch SW18 . . . . . . .71 B3
Beatson Wlk 25
  SE16 . . . . .32 C1
Beattie Ho SW8 . .**171** A4
Beatty Ho 16 E14 . .41 C4
Beatty Rd N16 . . . . .16 A4
Beatty St NW1 . . . .**82** C2
Beauchamp Cl 7
  W4 . . . . .37 B3
Beauchamp Pl
  SW3 . . . . **130** B1
Beauchamp Rd
  SW11 . . . . .60 B3
Beauchamp St
  EC1 . . . . **107** B3
Beauchamp Terr
  SW15 . . . . .57 A4
Beauclerc Rd W6 . .39 A3
Beauclerk Ho 10
  . . . . .74 A1

Beaufort Cl SW19. . .69 A4
Beaufort Ct SW6 . .**155** B4
Beaufort Gdns
  SW3 . . . . **130** B2
Beaufort Ho
  Battersea SW11 . . .**168** A2
  Chelsea SW3 . . . .**157** C3
  20 Millwall E14 . .41 C4
  Pimlico SW1 . . . .**147** A1
Beaufort Mans
  SW3 . . . . **157** C3
Beaufort Mews
  SW6 . . . . **155** A4
Beaufort St SW3 . .**157** B3
Beaufoy Ho
  South Lambeth
  SW8 . . . . **162** C2
  3 West Norwood
  SE27 . . . . .75 A1
Beaufoy Rd 11
  SW8 . . . . .61 A4
Beaufoy Wlk
  SE11 . . . . **149** A3
Beaulieu Cl SE5 . . .63 C4
Beaumanor Mans
  W2 . . . . **114** B4
Beaumaris Mews
  SE23 . . . . .65 C1
Beaumaris Twr 2
  W3 . . . . .37 A4
Beaumont SW15. . .58 A2
Beaumont Ave
  Richmond TW9 . . . .54 B4
  West Kensington
  W14 . . . . **140** C2
Beaumont Bldgs
  WC2 . . . . **106** B1
Beaumont Cres
  W14 . . . . **140** C1
Beaumont Ct
  20 Acton Green
    W4 . . . . .37 B1
  Marylebone W1 . . .**103** C4
  1 Mile End E1 . . . .26 A2
Beaumont Gdns
  NW3 . . . . .1 C1
Beaumont Gr E1 . . .25 C1
Beaumont Ho
  2 Streatham
    SW2 . . . . .74 A3
  West Kensington
  W14 . . . . **141** A3
  Wimbledon SW19 . .70 C1
Beaumont Lo 6 . . .16 C2
Beaumont Pl NW1,
  WC1, W1 . . . .**93** A2
Beaumont Rd
  2 Acton W4 . . . . . .38 A2
  7 Stockwell SW4 . .62 A3
Beaumont Rise N19 . .4 C3
Beaumont Sq E1 . . .32 C4
Beaumont St W1 . .**103** C4
Beaumont Wlk
  NW3 . . . . .12 B1
Beauval Rd SE22 . .64 B1
Beavis Ho N16 . . . . . .7 A1
Beavor La W6 . . . . .38 C1
Beccles St E14 . . . . .33 B2
Beck Cl SE13 . . . . . .52 A2
Beckers The N16 . . .16 C4
Becket Ho SE1 . . . .**137** B3
Becket St SE1 . . . .**137** B2

Beckett Cl
  Streatham SW16 . . .73 C2
  Willesden NW10 . . . .8 A2
Beckett Ho
  16 London SW9 . .**172** B1
  15 Stepney E1 . . . .32 B4
Beckfoot NW1. . . . .**83** A1
Beckford Cl W14 . .**141** A3
Beckford Ho 18
  N16 . . . . .16 A3
Beckford Pl SE17 . **151** A1
Beckford Prim Sch
  NW6 . . . . 10 B2
Beckham Ho
  SE11 . . . . **149** A3
Beck Ho N16 . . . . . .7 A1
Beckington 18
  NW5 . . . . .12 C2
Beckley Ho E3. . . . .26 B1
Becklow Gdns
  Chiswick W12. . . . .38 B4
  12 Shepherd's Bush
    W12 . . . . .38 C4
Becklow Mews 7
  W12 . . . . .38 C4
Becklow Rd W12 . . .38 C4
Beck Rd E8 . . . . . . .25 A4
Beckton Rd E16 . . . .35 B4
Beckway St SE17 . .**152** A3
Beckwith Ho 27
  E2 . . . . .25 A3
Beckwith Rd SE24 .63 C2
Bective PI SW15 . . .58 B3
Bective Rd SW15 . . .58 B3
Bedale St SE1 . . . . **123** B1
Bedefield WC1 . . . . .**94** B3
Bede Ho
  London SE14. . . . . .51 B2
  5 Putney SW15 . . . .57 C1
Bedford Ave WC1 . .**105** C3
Bedfordbury WC2 . .**120** A3
Bedford Cnr 5
  W4 . . . . .38 A2
Bedford Court Mans
  WC1 . . . . **105** C3
Bedford Ct
  6 Richmond
    TW9 . . . . .54 B3
  St James WC2 . . . .**120** A3
Bedford Gdns
  W8 . . . . . . .31 C1 **113** C1
Bedford Hill SW12 .73 A2
Bedford Ho
  2 Acton W4 . . . . . .38 A2
  4 Stockwell SW4 . .62 A3
BEDFORD PARK . .38 A3
Bedford Park Mans 5
  W4 . . . . .38 A2
Bedford Pas SW6. .**154** B2
Bedford PI WC1 . . .**106** A4
Bedford Rd
  Acton W4 . . . . .38 A2
  Stockwell SW2,
    SW4 . . . . .62 A3
Bedford Row
  WC1 . . . . **107** A3
Bedford Sq WC1 . .**105** C3
Bedford St WC2 . . .**120** B3
Bedford Way WC1 . .93 C1
Bedgebury Gdns
  SW19 . . . . .70 A2

Bedlam Mews
  SE11 . . . . **149** B4
Bedlow Cl NW8. . . .**89** C1
Bedser Cl SE11 . . .**163** A4
Bedser Ct 7 SW4 .**172** A2
Bedwell Ho
  SW9 . . . . **173** B1
Beech Ave W3. . . . .29 A1
Beech Cl
  Deptford SE8 . . . . .51 B4
  Putney SW15 . . . . .68 C4
Beechcroft Ave
  NW11 . . . . .1 B4
Beech Ct
  5 Golders Green
    NW11 . . . . .1 B4
  Greenwich SE3 . . . .53 C2
Beech Croft Ct N5 .15 B4
Beechcroft Rd
  Mortlake SW14 . . . .55 B4
  Upper Tooting
    SW17 . . . . .72 A2
Beechcroft Way
  N19 . . . . .4 C3
Beechdale 2 . . . . . .62 B1
Beechdene 4
  SE15 . . . . .50 A2
Beeches The 1
  N19 . . . . .5 A3
Beeches Rd SW17 .72 B1
Beechey Ho 30 E1 .32 A1
Beech Gdns 5 W5 .36 A3
Beech Ho
  5 Maitland Pk
    NW3 . . . . .12 B2
  22 Rotherhithe
    SE16 . . . . .40 B4
  5 Stoke Newington
    N16 . . . . .6 C2
Beechmore Rd
  SW11 . . . . **169** A3
Beech St EC2. . . . .**109** A4
Beech Tree Cl 1
  N1 . . . . .14 C1
Beechwood Ave
  TW9 . . . . .44 C2
Beechwood Ct
  Chiswick W4. . . . . .45 C4
  Stamford Hill N16. . . .7 A4
Beechwood Gr
  W3 . . . . .29 A2
Beechwood Ho 23
  E2 . . . . .24 C3
Beechwood Rd E8. .16 B2
Beechworth Cl
  NW3 . . . . .1 C2
Beecroft Garden Prim
  Sch SE4 . . . . .66 A2
Beecroft La SE4. . .66 A2
Beecroft Mews
  SE4 . . . . .66 A2
Beecroft Rd SE4. . .66 A2
Beehive Cl E8 . . . . .16 B1
Beehive Pl SW9 . . .62 C4
Beeston Cl 8 E8 . . .16 C3
Beeston PI SW1 . .**132** B2
Beeston's Ho SE15 .65 A4
Beethoven St W10. .23 A2
Begbie Ho SW9. . .**173** A2
Begonia Wlk W12 . .29 B3

Beira St SW12. . . . .73 A4
Beis Chinuch Lebonos
  Girls Sch N4 . . . . . .6 B4
Beis Malka Girls Sch
  N16 . . . . .7 B4
Beis Rochel d'Satmar
  Girls Sch 1 N16. . . .7 A4
Beis Yaakov Girls Sch
  10 N16 . . . . .6 C2
Bekesbourne St 17
  E14 . . . . .33 A3
Beldanes Lo NW10 . .8 C1
Belenoid Ct SW16 . .74 B1
Belfast Rd N16 . . . . .7 B2
Belfont Wlk N7. . . . .14 A4
Belford Ho 7 E8. . . .24 B4
Belfort Rd SE15 . . . .50 B1
Belfry Cl 33 SE16 . . .40 A1
Belgrade Ho N16 . . .16 A4
Belgrade Rd N16 . . .16 A4
Belgrave Cl 1 W3 . .37 A4
Belgrave Ct
  Acton Green
    W4 . . . . .37 B1
  2 Limehouse E14 . .33 B2
  Nine Elms SW8. . . .**160** C1
Belgrave Gdns
  Kilburn NW8. . . . . . **78** C3
  St John's Wood
    NW8 . . . . **78** C3
Belgrave Mews N
  SW1 . . . . **131** B3
Belgrave Mews S
  SW1 . . . . **131** B2
Belgrave Mews W
  SW1 . . . . **131** B2
Belgrave PI SW1 . . **131** C1
Belgrave Rd
  Barnes SW13 . . . . .46 B3
  Westminster SW1. .**146** C3
Belgrave Sq SW1. .**131** C2
Belgrave St E1. . . . .32 C3
Belgrave Yd SW1 . .**132** A1
BELGRAVIA **146** A4
Belgravia Ct SW1. .**132** A1
Belgravia Ho 11
  SW4 . . . . .61 C1
Belgrove St WC1 . . .**94** B4
Belham Wlk 13
  SE5 . . . . .48 C2
Belinda Rd 8
  SW9 . . . . .63 A4
Belitha Villas N1. . .14 C1
Bellamy Cl
  10 Millwall E14 . . . .41 C4
  West Kensington
    SW5 . . . . **141** A1
Bellamy's Ct 10
  SE16 . . . . .32 C1
Bellamy St SW12. . .73 A4
Bellasis Ave SW2. . .74 A2
Bell Ct SE13 . . . . . .52 C2
Bell Dr SW18 . . . . . .70 A4
Bellefields Rd
  SW9 . . . . .62 B4
Bellenden Prim Sch
  SE15 . . . . .64 C4
Bellenden Rd
  SE15 . . . . .49 B1
Bellenden Rd Ret Pk
  SE15 . . . . .49 C2

Bellendon Road Bsns
Ctr SE15 . . . . 49 B1
Bellerbys Coll SE8 . . 51 C4
Belleville Primary Sch
SW11 . . . . 60 C3
Belleville Prim Sch
SW11 . . . . 60 B2
Belleville Rd SW11 . 60 B2
Belle Vue Gdns
SW9 . . . . 172 B1
Bellevue PI E1 . . . . . 25 B1
Bellevue Rd
Barnes SW13 . . . . 46 C1
Upper Tooting
SW17 . . . . 72 B3
Bellew St SW17 . . . . 71 B1
Bell Flats 4 NW2 . . . 8 C2
Bellflower Ct SE13 . 67 A3
Bellgate Mews
NW5 . . . . 4 A1
Bellgrave Lo 9
W4 . . . . 37 A1
Bell Ho
Greenwich SE10 . . . . 52 B4
15 Streatham SW2 . 74 C4
Bellina Mews NW5 . 13 B4
Bell Ind Est 2 W4 . . 37 B2
Bell Inn Yd EC3 . . . 109 C1
Bell La
Newham E16 . . . . 35 C1
Spitalfields E1 . . . . 111 A3
Bellmaker Ct 1
E3 . . . . 33 C4
Bell Moor NW3 . . . . . 2 C1
Bello Cl SE24, SW2 . 75 A3
Bellot Gdns 1
SE10 . . . . 43 A1
Bellot St SE10 . . . . . 43 A1
Bell St NW1 . . . . . . 102 A4
Bell Wharf La
EC4 . . . . 123 A4
Bellwood Rd SE15 . 65 C3
Bell Yard Mews
SE1 . . . . 138 B3
Bell Yd WC2 . . . . . . 107 B1
Belmont Cl SW4 . . . . 61 B4
Belmont Ct
Highbury N5 . . . . 15 B4
5 Stamford Hill N16 . 7 A3
Belmont Gr
Chiswick W4 . . . . 37 C2
Lewisham SE13 . . . . 67 C4
Belmont Hall Ct
SE13 . . . . 67 C4
Belmont Hill SE13 . 67 C4
Belmont Mews
SW19 . . . . 69 C2
Belmont Prim Sch 10
W4 . . . . 37 C2
Belmont Rd
Clapham SW4 . . . . . . 61 B4
London W4 . . . . 37 C2
Belmont St NW1 . . . 12 C1
Belmont Terr W4 . . . 37 C2
Belmore Ho N7 . . . . 13 C3
Belmore La N7 . . . . . 13 C3
Belmore St SW8 . . 171 B4
Beloe Cl SW15 . . . . . 56 C3
Belper Ct 1 E5 . . . . . 17 C4
Belsham St E9 . . . . . 17 B2
Belsize Ave NW3 . . 12 A3
Belsize Court Garages
1 NW3 . . . . 11 C3
Belsize Cres NW3 . . 11 C3

Belsize Ct NW3 . . . . 11 C3
Belsize Gr NW3 . . . 12 A2
Belsize La NW3 . . . . 11 C3
Belsize Mews
NW3 . . . . 11 C2
Belsize Park Gdns
NW3 . . . . 12 A3
Belsize Park Mews 1
NW3 . . . . 11 C2
Belsize Park Sta
NW3 . . . . 12 A3
Belsize Pk NW3 . . . . 11 C2
Belsize Pl NW3 . . . . 11 C3
Belsize Rd NW6 . . . 78 B4
Belsize Sq NW3 . . . . 11 C2
Belsize Terr NW3 . . 11 C2
Beltane Dr SW19 . . . 69 C1
Belthorn Cres
SW12 . . . . 73 B4
Belton Rd NW2 . . . . . 8 C2
Belton Way E3 . . . . . 33 C4
Beltran Rd SW6 . . . 166 A1
Belvedere Bldgs
SE1 . . . . 136 B3
Belvedere Ct
Brondesbury NW2 . . . 9 C2
7 Clapham Pk
SW4 . . . . 61 C1
Putney SW15 . . . . . . 57 B3
13 Shoreditch N1 . . . 24 A4
Belvedere Htss
NW8 . . . . 90 A2
Belvedere Mews
SE15 . . . . 65 B4
Belvedere Pl
Brixton SW2 . . . . 62 B3
Lambeth SE1 . . . . . . 136 B3
Belvedere Rd SE1 . 121 A1
Belvedere The
SW10 . . . . 167 A3
Belvoir Lo SE22 . . . . 76 C4
Belvoir Rd SE22 . . . . 76 C4
Bembridge Cl
NW6 . . . . 10 A1
Bembridge Ho
9 Deptford SE8 . . . . 41 B2
Wandsworth SW18 . 59 A1
Bemerton St N1 . . . . 84 C4
Bemish Rd SW15 . . 57 C4
Benabo Ct 6 E8 . . . 16 C3
Benbow Ct W6 . . . . . 39 A3
Benbow Ho 12
SE8 . . . . 51 C4
Benbow Rd W6 . . . . 39 A3
Benbow St SE8 . . . . 51 C4
Bence Ho 13 SE8 . . 41 A2
Bendall Mews
NW1 . . . . 102 B4
Bendemeer Rd
SW15 . . . . 57 C4
Bendon Valley
SW18 . . . . 71 A4
Benedict Rd SW9 . . 62 B4
Benenden Ho
SE17 . . . . 152 B2
Ben Ezra Ct SE17 . 151 A3
Benfleet Ct 6 E8 . . 24 B4
Bengal Ct EC3 . . . . 109 C1
Bengal Ho E1 . . . . . 32 C4
Bengeworth Rd
SE5 . . . . 63 B4
Benham Cl 2
SW11 . . . . 59 C4
Benham Ho SW10 . 156 B2

Benham's Pl 11
NW3 . . . . 11 B4
Benhill Rd SE5 . . . . 48 C2
Benington Ct N4 . . . . 6 B2
Benjamin Cl E8 . . . . 24 C4
Benjamin Franklin
House SW1 . . . . 120 A2
Benjamin Ho 12
W3 . . . . 28 A1
Benjamin Mews
SW12 . . . . 73 B4
Benjamin St EC1 . . 108 A4
Ben Jonson Ct 10
N1 . . . . 24 A3
Ben Jonson Prim Sch
E1 . . . . 26 A1
Ben Jonson Rd E1 . 33 A4
Benkart Mews 6
SW15 . . . . 56 C1
Benledi Rd E14 . . . . 34 C3
Bennelong Cl 4
SW11 . . . . 60 A4
Bennet's Hill EC4 . 122 B4
Bennett Ct
Hampstead NW6 . . . 11 A2
Lower Holloway N7 . . 5 B1
7 South Acton W3 . . 37 A4
Bennett Gr SE13 . . . 52 A2
Bennett Ho
1 Streatham
SW4 . . . . 73 C4
Westminster SW1 . 147 C4
Bennett St
Chiswick W4 . . . . 38 A1
St James SW1 . . . . 118 C2
Bennett's Yd SW1 . 133 C1
Benn Ho E2 . . . . . . 24 C2 99 B3
Benns Wlk 5 TW9 . 54 A3
Bensbury Cl SW15 . 69 B4
Ben Smith Way 4
SE16 . . . . 139 C2
Benson Ct
South Lambeth
SW8 . . . . 172 A4
1 Tufnell Pk N19 . . . 13 B4
Benson Ho
Lambeth SE1 . . . . . . 121 C1
Shoreditch
E2 . . . . 24 B1 98 C2
Benson Quay E1 . . . 32 B2
Benthal Ct N16 . . . . . 7 C1
Benthal Prim Sch
N16 . . . . 7 C1
Benthal Rd N16 . . . . 7 C1
Bentham Ct 11 N1 . . 15 B1
Bentham Ho SE1 . . 137 B2
Bentham Rd E9 . . . . 17 C2
Bentinck Cl NW8 . . 80 B1
Bentinck Ho 8
W12 . . . . 30 A2
Bentinck Mans
W1 . . . . 103 C2
Bentinck Mews
W1 . . . . 103 C2
Bentinck St W1 . . . 103 C2
Bentley Cl SW19 . . . 70 C1
Bentley Ct SE13 . . . 67 B3
Bentley Dr NW2 . . . 10 B1
Bentley Ho
6 Bow E3 . . . . 26 C1
4 Camberwell SE5 . 49 A2
Bentley Rd N1 . . . . . 16 A2
Bentworth Ct 5
E2 . . . . 24 C1 99 B3

Bentworth Prim Sch
W12 . . . . 30 A3
Bentworth Rd
W12 . . . . 30 A3
Benwell Rd N7 . . . . 14 C3
Benwick Cl SE16 . . . 40 A2
Benworth St E3 . . . . 26 B2
Benyon Ho EC1 . . . . 95 C4
Benyon Rd N1 . . . . . 87 C4
Benyon Wharf 87
E8 . . . . 24 A4
Beormund Prim Sch
SE1 . . . . 137 C3
Bequerel Ct SE10 . . 43 B3
Berberis Ho 17 E3 . 33 C4
Berber Pl 2 E14 . . . 33 C2
Berber Rd SW11 . . . 60 B2
Berebinder Ho 21
E3 . . . . 26 B3
Berenger Twr
SW10 . . . . 157 B2
Berenger Wlk
SW10 . . . . 157 B2
Berens Rd NW10 . . . 22 C2
Beresford Ct E9 . . . . 18 A3
Beresford Ho
Dulwich SE21 . . . . . . 76 A1
15 Stockwell SW4 . . 62 A3
Beresford Lo N4 . . . 15 C3
Beresford Rd N5 . . . 15 C3
Beresford Terr 3
N5 . . . . 15 B3
Bere St E1 . . . . 32 C2
Berestede Rd 4
W6 . . . . 38 B1
Bergen Ho 1 SE5 . . 48 B1
Bergen Sq SE16 . . . 41 A3
Berger Prim Sch 82
E9 . . . . 17 C2
Berger Rd E9 . . . . . . 17 C2
Berghem Mews
W14 . . . . 39 C3
Bergholt Cres N16 . . 7 A4
Bergholt Mews 4
NW1 . . . . 13 B1
Berglen Ct E14 . . . . 33 A2
Bering Sq E14 . . . . . 41 C1
Berisford Mews
SW18 . . . . 59 B1
Berkeley Ct
1 Golders Green
NW11 . . . . 1 B4
Marylebone NW1 . . . 91 A1
Willesden NW10 . . . . 8 A4
Berkeley Gdns
W8 . . . . 31 C1 113 C1
Berkeley Ho
17 Bow E3 . . . . 26 C2
Deptford SE8 . . . . . . 41 B1
Berkeley Mews
W1 . . . . 103 A1
Berkeley Rd SW13 . 46 C2
Berkeley Sq W1 . . . 118 B3
Berkeley St W1 . . . 118 B2
Berkeley The NW11 . 2 A4
Berkeley Wlk 1 N7 . 5 B2
Berkley Gr NW1 . . . 12 C1
Berkley Rd NW1 . . . 12 B1
Berkshire Ho
WC2 . . . . 106 A2
Berkshire Rd E9 . . . 18 B2
Bermans Way
NW10 . . . . 8 B4
BERMONDSEY 40 A4
Bermondsey Leather
Mkt SE1 . . . . 138 A3

Bermondsey Sq
SE1 . . . . 138 B?
Bermondsey St
SE1 . . . . 138 A?
Bermondsey Sta
SE16 . . . . 40 A4
Bermondsey Trad Est
SE16 . . . . 40 B2
Bermondsey Wall E
SE16 . . . . 139 C4
Bermondsey Wall W
SE1, SE16 . . . . 139 B
Bernard Angell Ho 6
SE10 . . . . 52 C
Bernard Cassidy St 2
E16 . . . . 35 B
Bernard Ho E1 . . . . 110 C
Bernard Shaw Ct 5
NW1 . . . . 13 B
Bernard Shaw Ho 2
NW10 . . . . 20 C
Bernard St WC1 . . . . 94 B
Bernay's Gr SW9 . . 62 B
Berners Ho N1 . . . . . 85 B
Berners Mews
W1 . . . . 105 A
Berners Pl W1 . . . . 105 A
Berners Rd N1 . . . . . 86 A
Berners St W1 . . . . 105 A
Berner Terr 7 E1 . . 111 C
Bernhard Baron Ho 23
E1 . . . . 111 C
Bernhardt Cres
NW8 . . . . 90 A
Bernie Grant Ho 40
E9 . . . . 17 B
Bernwood Ho 6
N4 . . . . 6 C
Berridge Mews
NW6 . . . . 10 C
Berriman Rd N7 . . . . 5 B
Berry Cotts 2 E14 . 33 A
Berryfield Rd
SE17 . . . . 150 B
Berry Ho
10 Battersea
SW11 . . . . 169 A
5 Bethnal Green
E1 . . . . 25 A
Berrymead Gdns
W3 . . . . 37 B
Berrymede Inf Sch
W3 . . . . 37 A
Berrymede Jun Sch
W3 . . . . 37 A
Berrymede Rd W4 . 37 C
Berry Pl EC1 . . . . . . 96 B
Berry St EC1 . . . . . . 96 B
Berry Way W5 . . . . . 36 A
Bertha Neubergh Ho
1 SE5 . . . . 48 B
Berthon St SE8 . . . . 51 C
Bertie Rd NW10 . . . 8 C
Bertram St N19 . . . . 4 A
Bertrand Ho 11
SW16 . . . . 74 A
Bertrand St SE13 . . 67 A
Bertrum House Sch
SW17 . . . . 72 B
Berwick St W1 . . . . 105 A
Berwick Street Mkt
W1 . . . . 105 A
Berwyn Ho 3 N16 . 7 B
Berwyn Rd
Mortlake SW14,
TW10 . . . . 55 A

erwyn Rd continued
Streatham SE24 . . . .75 A3
eryl Rd W6 . . . . .39 C1
esant Cl NW2 . . . . . . .1 A1
esant Ho NW8 . . . .78 C3
esant Pl SE22 . . . . . .64 B3
esant Rd NW2 . . . . . .10 A4
esant Wlk N7 . . . . . . .5 B2
essborough Gdns
SW1 . . . . .147 C2
essborough Pl
SW1 . . . . .147 C2
essborough Rd
SW1 . . . . .68 C3
essborough St
SW1 . . . . .147 B2
essemer Ct [7]
NW1 . . . . .13 B1
essemer Grange
Prim Sch SE5 . . . .64 A3
essemer Park Ind
Est [8] SE24 . . . . . . .63 A3
essemer Pl SE10 . . .43 B3
essemer Rd SE5 . . . .48 B1
essingham Wlk
SE4 . . . . .65 C2
esson St SE14 . . . . . .50 C2
estwood St SE8 . . . .40 C2
eswick Mews [1]
NW6 . . . . .11 A1
eta Pl [20] SW4 . . . . .62 B3
etchworth Ho [1]
N7 . . . . .13 C3
ethersden Ho
SE17 . . . . .152 B2
ethlehem Ho [13]
E14 . . . . .33 B2
ETHNAL GREEN . .25 A2
ethnal Green Rd
Bethnal Green
E2 . . . . .24 C2 99 B3
Shoreditch E1,
E2 . . . . .24 B1 99 A2
ethnal Green Sta
Bethnal Green E2 . . .25 A1
Bethnal Green E2 . . .25 B2
ethune Rd
North Acton
W10 . . . . .20 C1
Stamford Hill N16 . . . .7 A4
ethwin Rd SE5 . . . . .48 B3
etsham Ho SE1 . . . .137 B4
etterton St
WC2 . . . . .106 B1
etterton St WC2 . .106 B1
ettridge Rd SW6 165 A1
etts Ho E1 . . . . .32 A2
etts St E1 . . . . .32 A2
etty Layward Prim
Sch N16 . . . . .7 A1
etty May Gray Ho [2]
E14 . . . . .42 B2
evan St N1 . . . . .87 A3
ev Callender Cl [5]
SW8 . . . . .61 A4
evenden St N1 . . . .97 C4
everidge Rd [1]
NW10 . . . . .8 A1
everley Cl
Barnes SW13 . . . . . .46 C1
[6] Wandsworth
SW11 . . . . .59 C3

Beverley Cotts
SW15 . . . . .68 A1
Beverley Ct
[9] Acton Green
W4 . . . . .37 B1
[5] Acton W12 . . . . . .38 A4
Brockley SE4 . . . . . . .66 A3
Islington N5 . . . . .15 A2
Beverley Gdns
Barnes SW13 . . . . . .56 B4
Hendon NW11 . . . . . . .1 A4
Beverley Lo [6]
SW13 . . . . .54 A2
Beverley Path [9]
SW13 . . . . .46 B1
Beverley Rd
Barnes SW13 . . . . . .56 B4
Chiswick W4 . . . . . . .38 B1
Beversbrook Rd
N19 . . . . .4 C1
Beverstone Rd
SW2 . . . . .62 B2
Beverston Mews
NW1 . . . . .102 C3
Bevin Cl SE16 . . . . . .33 A1
Bevin Ct WC1 . . . . . .95 A4
Bevington Prim Sch
[2] W10 . . . . .31 A4
Bevington Rd W10 . .31 A4
Bevington St
SE16 . . . . .139 C3
Bevin Ho
[3B] Bethnal Green
E2 . . . . .25 B2
[3] Bow E3 . . . . .26 C2
Bevin Sq SW17 . . . . .72 B1
Bevin Way WC1 . . . . .95 B4
Bevis Marks EC3 . .110 B2
Bew Ct SE21 . . . . . . .76 C4
Bewdley Ho N4 . . . . . .6 B4
Bewdley St N1 . . . . . .14 C1
Bewick Mews
SE15 . . . . .50 A3
Bewick St SW8 . . . .170 B1
Bewley Ct SW2 . . . . .62 B1
Bewley Ho [7] E1 . . . .32 A2
Bewley St [7] E1 . . . .32 A2
Bexhill Rd
Catford SE4 . . . . .66 B1
Mortlake SW14 . . . . . .55 B4
Bexley Ho SE4 . . . . .66 A3
BFI Imax (Cinema)
SE1 . . . . .121 B1
BFI Southbank
SE1 . . . . .121 A2
Bianca Rd SE1,
SE15 . . . . .49 C4
Bibury Cl SE15 . . . . .49 A4
Bicester Rd TW9 . . . .55 A4
Bickenhall Mans
W1 . . . . .103 A4
Bickenhall St W1 . .103 A4
Bickerton Rd N19 . . . .4 B2
Bicknell Ho [34] E1 . 111 C1
Bicknell Rd SE5 . . . . .63 B4
Bicknor Ho [2] E5 . . .17 A3
Bicycle Mews [1]
SW4 . . . . .61 C4
Bidborough St N1,
WC1 . . . . .94 A3
Biddenham Ho [8]
SE16 . . . . .40 C2
Bidder St E16 . . . . . .35 A4
Biddesden Ho
SW3 . . . . .144 C3
Biddestone Rd N7 . .14 B4

Biddulph Mans
W9 . . . . .88 B3
Biddulph Rd W9 . . . .88 B3
Bidwell St SE15 . . . . .50 A2
Big Ben SW1 . . . . . .134 B3
Biggerstaff Rd
E15 . . . . .27 B4
Biggerstaff St N4 . . . .5 C2
Bigg's Row SW15 . . .57 C4
Biggs Sq [9] 18 C2
Bigland Green Prim
Sch [43] E1 . . . . . . .32 A3
Bigland St E1 . . . . . . .32 A3
Bilberry Ho [18] E3 . .33 C4
Billie Holiday Ct
NW10 . . . . .20 C3
Billingford Cl SE4 . . .65 C3
Billing Ho [9] E1 . . . .32 C3
Billingley [1]
NW1 . . . . .82 C3
Billing Pl SW10 . . . .156 B2
Billing Rd SW10 . . . .156 B2
Billingsgate Mkt
E14 . . . . .34 A1
Billington Ho SW8 . .171 C3
Billington Rd SE14 . . .50 C3
Billiter Sq EC3 . . . . .110 B1
Billiter St EC3 . . . . .110 B1
Billson St E14 . . . . . .42 B2
Bilton Ho SW8 . . . . .171 B3
Bilton Twrs W1 . . . .103 A1
Bina Gdns SW5 . . . .142 C3
Binbrook Ho [13]
W10 . . . . .30 B4
Binden Rd W12 . . . . .38 B3
Binfield Ct SE5 . . . . .48 B1
Binfield Rd SW4 . . . .172 B3
Bingfield St N1 . . . . .84 C4
Bingham Pl W1 . . . .103 B4
Bingham St N1 . . . . .15 C2
Binley Ho SW15 . . . . .56 B1
Binney St W1 . . . . . .103 C1
Binnie Ct SE10 . . . . .52 A3
Binnie Ho SE1 . . . . .136 C1
Binns Rd W4 . . . . . . .38 A1
Binns Terr [3] W4 . . .38 A1
Binstead Ho SW18 . .59 A1
Binyon Ho [8] N16 . . .16 A4
Birbeck Ho [4] N19 . .4 C2
Bircham Path SE4 . . .65 C3
Birch Cl
Newham E16 . . . . . . .35 A4
Peckham SE15 . . . . .49 C1
Upper Holloway N19 . .4 B2
Birchdown Ho [2]
E3 . . . . .27 A2
Birches The SE5 . . . .49 A1
Birchfield Ho [3]
E14 . . . . .33 C2
Birchfield St E14 . . . .33 C2
Birchgrove Ho
TW9 . . . . .45 A3
Birch Ho
New Cross Gate
SE14 . . . . .51 B2
[4] Tulse Hill SW2 . . .62 C1
Birchington Ct [2]
NW6 . . . . .78 A4
Birchington Ho [1]
E5 . . . . .17 A3
Birchington Rd
NW6 . . . . .23 C4
Birchin La EC3 . . . . .109 C1
Birchlands Ave
SW12 . . . . .72 B4

Birchmere Lo [18]
SE16 . . . . .40 C2
Birchmere Row
SE3 . . . . .53 B1
Birchmore Wlk N5 . . .6 B1
Birch Vale Ct NW8 . .89 C2
Birchwood Dr NW3 . .2 A1
Birch Yd [18] SW11 . .46 B1
Birdcage Wlk
SW1 . . . . .133 B3
Birdhurst Rd
SW18 . . . . .59 B2
Bird In Bush Rd
SE15 . . . . .49 C3
Bird In Hand Yd [24]
NW3 . . . . .11 B4
Birdsall Ho [5] SE5 . .64 A4
Birdsfield La [12]
E3 . . . . .26 B4
Bird St W1 . . . . .103 C1
Birdwood Ave [4]
SE13 . . . . .67 C1
Birkbeck Ave W3 . . . .28 B2
Birkbeck Cl W3 . . . . .28 B2
Birkbeck Ct W3 . . . . .28 C1
Birkbeck Gr W3 . . . . .37 B4
Birkbeck Hill SE21 . .75 A3
Birkbeck Mews [5]
E8 . . . . .16 B3
Birkbeck Pl SE21 . . . .75 B2
Birkbeck Rd
Acton W3 . . . . .28 C1
Dalston E8 . . . . .16 B3
Birkbeck St E2 . . . . . .25 A2
Birkbeck Univ of
London WC1 . . . . .93 B2
Birkdale Cl [30]
SE16 . . . . .40 A1
Birkenhead Ho
N7 . . . . .14 C3
Birkenhead St
WC1 . . . . .94 B4
Birkwood Cl SW12 . .73 C4
Birley Lo NW8 . . . . . .79 C2
Birley St SW11 . . . .169 B1
Birnam Rd N4 . . . . . . .5 B2
Birrell Ho [9] SW9 . .172 C1
Birse Cres NW10 . . . . .8 A4
Birtwistle Ho [7]
E3 . . . . .26 B4
Biscay Ho [11] E1 . . .25 C1
Biscay Rd W6 . . . . . .39 C1
Biscoe Way [3] SE13 .67 C4
Biscott Ho [3] E3 . . . .27 A1
Biscuit Factory The
SE16 . . . . .40 A3
Bisham Gdns N6 . . . .3 C3
Bishop Challoner
Catholic Federation
of Schools [1] . . .32 B3
Bishop Ct [20] SW2 . .62 C1
Bishop Duppa's
Almshouses [7]
TW10 . . . . .54 A2
Bishop King's Rd
W14 . . . . .140 B4
Bishop's Ave SW6 . .164 A3
Bishop's Bridge Rd
W2 . . . . .100 B2
Bishops Cl W4 . . . . . .37 B1
Bishop's Ct EC4 N19 . .5 B2
Bishops Ct
[13] Bayswater
W2 . . . . .100 B2
Richmond TW9 . . . . .54 A4
Bishop's Ct
Holborn EC4 . . . . .108 A2

Bishop's Ct continued
Holborn WC2 . . . . .107 A2
Bishopsdale Ho [8]
NW6 . . . . .23 C4
Bishopsgate EC2 . .110 A2
Bishopsgate Arc
E1 . . . . .110 B3
Bishopsgate
Churchyard EC2 . 110 A2
Bishopsgate Inst
EC2 . . . . .110 B3
Bishops Ho SW8 . . .162 B1
Bishop's Mans
SW6 . . . . .47 C1
Bishops Mead SE5 . .48 B3
Bishop's Park Rd
SW6 . . . . .47 C1
Bishops Rd SW6 . .164 C4
Bishops Sq E1 . . . . .110 B4
Bishop St N1 . . . . . . .86 C4
Bishop's Terr
SE11 . . . . .149 C4
Bishopstone Ho [4]
SW11 . . . . .169 B2
Bishop's Way E2 . . . .25 B3
Bishopswood Rd
N6 . . . . .3 B4
Bishop Wilfred Wood
Cl SE15 . . . . .49 C1
Bisley Ho SW19 . . . .69 C2
Bissextile Ho SE13 . .52 A1
Bisson Rd E15 . . . . . .27 B3
Bittern Ct [7] SE8 . . .51 C4
Bittern Ho SE1 . . . .136 C3
Bittern St SE1 . . . . .136 C3
Blackall St
EC2 . . . . . . .24 A1 98 A2
Blackburn Ct [4]
SW2 . . . . .62 C1
Blackburne's Mews
W1 . . . . .117 B3
Blackburn Rd
NW6 . . . . .11 A2
Blackdown Ho [8]
E8 . . . . .16 C4
Blackett St SW15 . . . .57 C4
Blackfriars Bridge
EC4 . . . . .122 A3
Blackfriars Ct
EC4 . . . . .122 A4
Black Friars La
EC4 . . . . .108 A1
Blackfriars Pas
EC4 . . . . .122 A4
Blackfriars Pier
EC4 . . . . .122 A4
Blackfriars Rd
SE1 . . . . .122 A3
Blackfriars Underpass
EC4 . . . . .121 C2
Blackheath Ave
SE3 . . . . .53 A2
Blackheath Bsns Est
SE10 . . . . .52 B2
Blackheath Gr SE3 . .53 B1
Blackheath High Sch
Blackheath SE3 . . . . .53 B1
Greenwich SE3 . . . . .53 C3
Blackheath Hill
SE10 . . . . .52 B2
Blackheath Prep Sch
SE3 . . . . .53 C2
Blackheath Rd
SE10 . . . . .52 A2

Blackheath Rise
SE13 ....52 B1
BLACKHEATH
VALE 53 B1
Blackheath Vale
SE3 ....53 A1
Blackheath Village
SE3 ....53 B1
Black Horse Ct
SE1 ....137 C2
Blackhorse Rd
SE8 ....51 A4
Blacklands Terr
SW3 ....146 C2
Black Lion La W6....38 C2
Black Lion Mews
W6 ....38 C2
Blackmore Ho
Islington N1 ....85 A3
Wandsworth
SW18 ....59 A2
Blackmore Twr **1**
W3 ....37 B3
Blackpool Rd
SE15 ....49 C1
Black Prince Rd SE1,
SE11 ....149 A3
Black Roof Ho **9**
SE5 ....48 A2
Black's Rd W6.........39 B2
Blackstock Ho **2**
N5 ....6 A1
Blackstock Mews
N4 ....6 A1
Blackstock Rd N4,
N5 ....6 A1
Blackstone Ho
Dulwich SE21........76 A1
Pimlico SW1 ....146 C1
Blackstone Rd NW2 .9 B4
Black Swan Yd
SE1 ....138 A4
Blackthorn Ct
20 Camberwell
SE15 ....49 B3
4 Leyton E15 ....19 C4
Blackthorn St E3 ...26 C1
Blacktree Mews **1**
SW9 ....62 C4
BLACKWALL 34 C2
Blackwall Sta E14 ..34 B2
Blackwall Trad Est
E14 ....34 C4
Blackwall Tunnel
SE10 ....34 C1
Blackwall Tunnel App
SE10 ....43 A4
Blackwall Tunnel
Northern Approach
E14, E3 ....27 B1
Blackwall Way
E14 ....34 B2
Blackwater Ho
NW8 ....101 C4
Blackwater St
SE22 ....64 B2
Blackwell Cl **1** E5 ..17 C4
Blackwell Ho **3**
SW4 ....61 C1
Blackwood Ho **11**
E1 ....25 A1
Blackwood St
SE17 ....151 B2
Blade Mews SW15 ..58 B3

Bladen Ho **4** E1 .....32 C3
Blades Ct
4 Hammersmith
W6 ....39 A1
Putney SW15 ....58 B3
Blades Ho **3**
SE11 ....163 B3
Blades Lo **5** SW2 ..62 C1
Blagdon Rd SE13 ....67 A1
Blagrove Rd **1**
W10 ....31 B4
Blair Cl N1 ....15 B2
Blair Ct NW8 ....79 B4
Blairderry Rd SW2 ..74 A2
Blairgowrie Ct **13**
E14 ....34 C3
Blair Ho SW9 ....172 C2
Blair St E14 ....34 C3
Blake Coll **1** SE11 104 C4
Blake Ct
5 Bermondsey
SE16 ....40 A1
Kilburn NW6 ....23 C2
Blake Gdns SW6 ...166 A4
Blake Ho
2 Deptford SE8 ....51 C4
Isle of Dogs E14 .....42 A4
1 Kentish Town
N19 ....13 C3
Lambeth SE1 ....135 B2
8 Stoke Newington
N16 ....16 A4
Blake Mews **13**
TW9 ....44 C2
Blakemore Rd
SW16 ....74 A1
Blakeney Cl
5 Camden Town
NW1 ....13 C1
2 Dalston E8........16 C3
Blakenham Ct
W12 ....29 C1
Blaker Rd E15 ....27 B4
Blakes Cl W10 ....30 B4
Blake's Rd SE15 ....49 A3
Blanca Ho **10** N1 ...24 A3
Blanchard Way E8 ..16 C2
Blanch Cl SE15 ......50 B3
Blanchedowne
SE5 ....63 C3
Blandfield Rd
SW12 ....72 C4
Blandford Ct
Brondesbury Pk
NW6 ....10 A1
6 De Beauvoir Town
N1 ....16 A1
Blandford Ho
SW8 ....162 C2
Blandford Rd W4 ....38 A3
Blandford Sq NW1 ..90 B1
Blandford St W1 ...103 B3
Bland Ho SE11 .....149 A2
Blantyre St SW10 .157 B2
Blantyre Twr
SW10 ....157 B2
Blantyre Wlk
SW10 ....157 B2
Blashford NW3 ......12 B1
Blasker Wlk **8**
E14 ....42 A1
Blaxland Ho **12**
W12 ....30 A2
Blazer Ct **5** NW8 ..89 C3
Blechynden Ho **17**
W10 ....30 C3

Blechynden St
W10 ....30 C2
Bleeding Heart Yd
EC1 ....107 C3
Blemundsbury
WC1 ....106 C4
Blendworth Point **4**
SW15 ....69 A3
Blenheim **32** SE16 ..32 C1
Blenheim Cres
Notting Hill W11 ....31 A3
Notting Hill
W11 ...31 A2 112 B4
Blenheim Ct
Barnsbury N7 ....14 A2
Richmond TW9 ....54 B4
7 Rotherhithe
SE16 ....32 C1
Upper Holloway N19 ..5 A2
Blenheim Gdns
Clapham Pk SW2 ....62 B1
Dollis Hill NW2 ......9 B3
Richmond Gr SE15 ..49 C1
Blenheim Pas
NW8 ....78 C2
Blenheim Rd
Acton W4 ....38 A3
St John's Wood
NW8 ....79 A2
Blenheim St W1 ....104 A1
Blenheim Terr
NW8 ....78 C2
Blenkarne Rd
SW11 ....60 C1
Blessed Sacrament
RC Prim Sch N1 .....84 C3
Blessington Cl
SE13 ....67 C4
Blessington Rd
SE13 ....67 C3
Bletchley Ct N1 ......87 A1
Bletchley St N1 ......87 A1
Bletsoe Wlk N1 ......87 A2
Blick Ho **1** SE16 ...40 B3
Blincoe Cl SW19 ....69 C2
Bliss Cres SE13 .....52 A1
Blissett St SE10 ....52 B2
Bliss Mews **14**
W10 ....23 A2
Blisworth Ho **12**
E2 ....24 C4
Blithfield St **1** W8 128 A1
Bloemfontein Ave
W12 ....30 A1
Bloemfontein Rd
W12 ....30 A2
Blomfield Ct
Battersea SW11 ...167 C4
Paddington W9 ....89 A2
Blomfield Ho **4**
E14 ....34 A2
Blomfield Mans **3**
W12 ....30 B1
Blomfield Rd W9 ..100 C4
Blomfield St EC2 ..109 C3
Blomfield Villas
W9 ....100 C4
Blondel St SW11 ...169 B2
Blondin St E3 ....26 C3
Blondin Wy SE16 ...41 A4
Bloomberg Space
EC1 ....109 C4
Bloomburg St
SW1 ....147 A3
Bloomfield Ho **19**
E1 ....111 B3

Bloomfield PI W1...118 B4
Bloomfield Terr
SW1 ....145 C2
Bloom Gr SE27 .....75 A1
Bloom Park Rd
SW6 ....154 C1
BLOOMSBURY ...106 A4
Bloomsbury Ct
WC1 ....106 B3
Bloomsbury Ho **10**
SW4 ....61 C1
Bloomsbury
International
Language Sch
WC1 ....106 B3
Bloomsbury Pl
London SW18 ....59 B2
St Giles WC1.........106 B3
Bloomsbury Sq
WC1 ....106 B3
Bloomsbury St
WC1 ....105 C3
Bloomsbury Way
WC1 ....106 B3
Blore Cl SW8 ....171 B3
Blore Ct W1 ....119 B4
Blore Ho SW10 ....156 B2
Blossom Cl W5 ......36 A4
Blossom Pl
E1 ....24 A1 98 B1
Blossom St
E1 ....24 A1 98 B1
Blount St E14 ....33 A3
Blucher Rd SE5......48 B3
Blue Anchor Alley **1**
TW9 ....54 A3
Blue Anchor La
SE16 ....40 A2
Blue Anchor Yd
E1 ....125 B4
Blue Ball Yd SW1 .118 C1
Bluebell Cl **9** E9 ...25 B4
Blue Gate Fields Jun
& Inf Schs E1 ....32 B2
Bluegate Mews
E1 ....32 A2
Blue Lion Pl SE1 ..138 A2
Blueprint Apartments
15 SW12 ....73 A4
Blundell Cl E8 ....16 C4
Blundell St N7 ....14 A2
Blurton Rd E5 ....17 C4
Blyth Cl **4** E14 .....42 C2
Blythe Ho **8**
SE11 ....163 C4
Blythe Mews **2**
W14 ....39 C1
Blythendale Ho **34**
E2 ....24 C3
Blythe Rd W14 .....126 A1
Blythe St E2 ....25 A2
Blyth's Wharf E14 ..33 A2
Blythwood Rd N4 ...5 A4
BMI Fitzroy Square
Hospl **41** 92 C1
Bnois Jerusalem Girls
Sch **21** N16 ....6 C4
Boades Mews **3**
NW3 ....11 C4
Boadicea St N1......84 C4
Boardwalk Pl E14 ..34 B1
Boarley Ho SE17...152 A3
Boathouse Ctr The
W10 ....22 C1
Boathouse Wlk **24**
SE15 ....49 B3

Boat Lifter Way **19**
SE16 ....41 A2
Bob Anker Cl **4**
E13 ....61 B1
Bob Marley Way **10**
SE24 ....62 C3
Bocking St E8........25 A4
Boddicott Cl SW19 .70 A4
Boddington Gdns
W3 ....36 C4
Boddington Ho **2**
SE14 ....50 B2
Bodeney Ho **10**
SE5 ....49 A2
Boden Ho **4** E1 ...111 B3
Bodington Ct **2**
W12 ....39 C4
Bodley Manor Way
SW2 ....74 C4
Bodmin St SW18 ...70 C3
Bodney Rd E5, E8 ..17 A3
Bogart Ct **3** E14 ...33 C2
Bohemia Pl **1** E8 ...17 A2
Bohn Rd E1 ....33 A4
Boileau Rd SW13 ..47 A3
Boilerhouse SE1 ...124 C1
Boisseau Ho **31** E1 .32 B4
Bolden St SE8 ....52 A1
Boldero Pl NW8 ......90 A1
Boleyn Rd N16 ......16 A3
Bolina Rd SE16 .....40 B1
Bolingbroke Acad
SW11 ....60 A1
Bolingbroke Gr
SW11 ....60 B1
Bolingbroke Rd
W14 ....39 C3
Bolingbroke Wlk
SW11 ....168 A4
Bollo Bridge Rd
W3 ....37 B4
Bollo Ct **2** W3 .....37 B3
Bollo La W3............37 A4
Bolney Gate SW7 .130 A3
Bolney St SW8 .....162 C1
Bolsover St W1......92 B1
Bolt Ct EC4 ....107 C1
Bolton Cres SE5 ....48 A3
Bolton Ct SW11 ...169 C2
Bolton Gdns
Kensal Rise
NW10 ....22 C2
South Kensington
SW5 ....142 B2
Bolton Gdns Mews
SW10 ....142 C2
Bolton Ho **3** SE10 ..43 A3
Bolton Pl SW5 ......142 C2
Bolton Rd
Chiswick W4 ....45 B3
Harlesden NW10 ....21 A4
Kilburn NW8 ....78 B3
Bolton Cts SW5 ....142 B2
Bolton St W1 ....118 B2
Boltons The
SW10 ....143 A2
Bolton Studios
SW10 ....143 A1
Bolton Wlk N7 ....5 B2
Bombay Ct **8**
SE16 ....40 B4
Bombay St SE16 ....40 A2
Bomore Rd
W11 ....31 A2 112 A4
Bonar Rd SE15 .....49 C3
Bonchurch Rd
W10 ....31 A4

Bond Ct EC4...... **109** B1
Bond Ho 4 NW6..... 23 B1
Bonding Yard Wlk
 SE16...............41 A3
Bond St W4.........37 C2
Bond Street Sta
 W1............... **103** C1
Bondway SW8.... **162** B4
Bonfield Rd SE13....67 B3
Bonham Ho
 W11..........31 B1 **112** C2
Bonham Rd SW2.....62 B2
Bonheur Rd W4.....37 C4
Bonhill St EC2...... **97** C1
Bonington Ho N1.... **84** C1
Bonita Mews SE15...65 C4
Bonner Ho 3
 SW15...............56 C2
Bonner Prim Sch 20
 E2.................25 B2
Bonner Rd E2.......25 B3
Bonner St E2.......25 B3
Bonneville Gdns
 SW4...............61 B1
Bonneville Prim Sch
 SW4...............61 B1
Bonnington Sq
 SW8.............. **162** C4
Bonny St NW1.......13 B1
Bonsor Ho SW8.... **171** A4
Bonsor St SE5.......49 A3
Bonthron Ho 3
 SW15...............47 B1
Booker Cl 11 E3....33 B4
Boord St SE10.......43 A3
Boothby Rd N19.....4 C2
Booth Cl 8 E9.....25 A4
Booth Ho 2 SW2...74 C4
Booth La EC4..... **122** C4
Booth's Pl W1.... **105** A3
Boot St N1.....24 A2 **98** A3
Bordon Wlk 5
 SW15...............68 C4
Boreas Wlk N1...... **86** B1
Boreham Ave E16....35 C3
Boreman Ho 11
 SE10...............52 B4
Borland Rd SE15....65 B3
Borneo St SW15.....57 C4
Borough High St
 SE1.............. **123** B2
Borough Mkt SE1. **123** B1
Borough Rd SE1.. **136** B2
Borough Sq SE1... **136** C3
Borough Sta SE1.. **137** A3
BOROUGH THE .. **136** C4
Borrett Cl SE17... **150** C1
Borrodaile Rd
 SW18...............59 A1
Borrowdale NW1... **92** C3
Borthwick St SE8....41 C1
Boscastle Rd NW5....4 A1
Boscobel Ho 6
 E8.................17 A2
Boscobel Pl SW1. **145** C4
Boscobel St NW8... **89** C1
Boscombe Cl E5.....18 A3
Boscombe Rd
 W12...............38 C4
Boss Ho SE1...... **138** C4
Boss St SE1...... **138** C4
Boston Gdns W4....46 A4
Boscobel Ho 6
 21 Camberwell
 Earl's Ct SW5.... **142** B3

Boston Ho continued
 Lisson Gr NW1..... **90** C2
Boston Pl NW1..... **90** C1
Bosun Cl 22 E14...41 C4
Boswell Ct
 Bloomsbury WC1 .. **106** B4
 9 Hammersmith
 W6.................39 C3
Boswell Ho WC1.. **106** B4
Boswell St WC1.. **106** B4
Bosworth Ho 4
 W10...............23 A1
Bosworth Rd W10..23 A1
Bothwell Cl E16...35 C4
Bothwell St 4 W6..47 C4
Botolph Alley EC3 **124** A4
Botolph La EC3... **124** A4
Bott's Mews W2....31 C3
Boughton Ho SE1 **137** B4
Boulcott St E1.....32 C3
Boulevard The
 Chelsea SW6..... **167** A3
 4 Upper Tooting
 SW17...............72 C2
Boulogne Ho SE1 **138** C2
Boulter Ho 4
 SE14...............50 B2
Boundaries Mans 3
 SW12..............72 C3
Boundaries Rd
 SW12..............72 C3
Boundary Ho
 Balham SW12......73 A3
 11 Camberwell SE5..48 B3
 18 Notting Hill
 W11...............30 C1
Boundary La SE17..48 B4
Boundary Pas
 E2............24 B1 **98** C2
Boundary Rd NW8..79 A4
Boundary Road Est
 NW8...............78 C3
Boundary Row
 SE1.............. **136** A4
Boundary St
 E2............24 B1 **98** C2
Bourbon St SW9 **173** C3
Bourchier St W1.. **119** B4
Bourdon Pl W1... **118** B3
Bourdon St W1... **118** B3
Bourke Cl
 London SW4.......62 A1
 Willesden NW10.... 8 A2
Bourlet Cl W1.... **104** C3
Bourne Ct W4.....45 B4
Bourne Ho 5 SW4..61 B3
Bourne Mews W1. **103** C1
Bournemouth Cl
 SE15...............49 C1
Bournemouth Rd
 SE15...............49 C1
Bourne Pl W4......37 C1
Bourne St SW1... **145** B3
Bourne Terr W2.. **100** B4
Bousfield Prim Sch
 SW10............. **142** C2
Bousfield Rd SE14.50 C1
Boutcher CE Prim Sch
 SE1.............. **152** C4
Boutflower Rd
 SW11...............60 A3
Bouverie Mews
 N16...............7 A2
Bouverie Pl W2.. **101** C2
Bouverie Rd N16....7 A2

Bouverie St EC4... **107** C1
Bovingdon Cl 4
 N19................4 B2
Bovingdon Rd
 SW6............. **166** B3
BOW.................26 B3
Bowater Cl SW2...62 A1
Bowater Ho EC1.... 97 A1
Bow Brook The 20
 E2.................25 C3
Bow Church Sta
 E3.................26 C2
Bow Common La
 E3.................26 B1
Bowden Ho 20 E3...27 A2
Bowden St SE11... **149** C1
Bowditch SE8......41 B1
Bowen Ct 2 N5...15 A4
Bowen Dr SE21.....76 A1
Bowen St E14.....34 A3
Bower Ave SE3.....53 A3
Bowerdean St
 SW6............. **166** A2
Bower Ho SE14....50 C2
Bowerman Ave
 SE14...............51 A4
Bowerman Ct 11
 N19................4 C2
Bower St E1........32 C3
Bowes-Lyon Hall 11
 E16...............35 C1
Bowes Rd W3.....29 A2
Bowfell Rd W6.....47 B4
Bowhill Cl SW9... **163** C2
Bow Ho 11 E3.....26 C2
Bowie Cl SW4.....73 C4
Bow La EC2, EC4 **109** A1
Bowland Ho N4.....6 B4
Bowland Rd SW4...61 C3
Bowland Yd SW1. **131** A3
Bowl Ct EC2...24 A1 **98** B1
Bowles Rd 1 SE1..49 C4
Bowley Ho 6
 SE16.............. **139** B2
Bowling Green Cl
 SW19...............69 A4
Bowling Green Ho
 SW10............. **157** B2
Bowling Green La
 EC1............... **95** C2
Bowling Green Pl
 SE1.............. **137** B4
Bowling Green St
 SE11............. **163** B4
Bowling Green Wlk
 N1...........24 A2 **98** A4
Bowman Ave E16..35 B2
Bowman Mews
 St George in East
 E1............... **125** B4
 Wandsworth SW18.70 B3
Bowman's Mews
 N7.................5 A1
Bowman's Pl N7....5 A1
Bowmore Wlk
 NW1...............13 C1
Bowness Cl 5 E8..16 B2
Bowness Ho SE15..50 B3
Bowood Rd SW11..60 C2
Bow Rd E3........26 C2
Bow Road Sta E3..26 C2
Bowry Ho 4 E14...33 B4
Bow Sch
 19 E3.............26 C2

Bow Sch continued
 Mill Meads E16.....27 B1
Bowsprit Point 1
 E14...............41 C3
Bow St WC2...... **106** B1
Bowstead Ct
 SW11.............. **167** C3
Bow Triangle Bsns Ctr
 17 E3..............26 C1
Bowyer Ho
 27 Shoreditch N1....24 A4
 Wandsworth SW18..59 A1
Bowyer Pl SE5.....48 B3
Bowyer St 15 SE5..48 B3
Boxall Rd SE21.....64 A1
Boxley Ho 8 E5.....17 A3
Boxmoor Ho
 18 Hackney E2.....24 C4
 9 Shepherd's Bush
 W11...............30 C1
Box Tree Ho SE8...41 A1
Boxworth Gr N1.... **85** A4
Boyce Ho 6 W10...23 B2
Boyd Ct SW15.....57 B1
Boydell Ct NW8....11 C1
Boyd St E1....... **111** C1
Boyfield St SE1... **136** B3
Boyle St W1...... **118** C4
Boyne Ct NW10....8 C1
Boyne Rd SE13.....67 C4
Boyne Terr Mews
 W11..........31 B1 **112** C2
Boyson Rd 10
 SE17...............48 C4
Boyton Cl SE25.....25 C1
Boyton Ho
 Kennington SE11 .. **149** B1
 St John's Wood
 NW8............... **79** C2
Brabant Ct EC3.... **124** A4
Brabazon St E14....34 A4
Brabner Ho 3
 E2............24 C2 **99** B3
Brabourn Gr SE15..50 B1
Bracer Ho 11 N1...24 A3
Bracewell Rd W10..30 B4
Bracey Mews 14 N4..5 A2
Bracey St N4......5 A2
Bracken Ave
 SW12...............72 C4
Brackenbury N4....5 B3
Brackenbury Gdns
 W6.................39 A3
Brackenbury Prim Sch
 4 W6..............39 A2
Brackenbury Rd
 W6.................39 A3
Bracken Gdns
 SW13..............46 C1
Bracken Ho 15 E3..33 C4
Brackley Ave SE15..65 B4
Brackley Ct NW8... **89** C2
Brackley Rd W4....38 A1
Brackley St EC1... **109** A4
Brackley Terr 6
 W4.................38 A1
Bracklyn Ct N1.... **87** B2
Bracklyn St N1.... **87** B2
Bracknell Gate
 NW3...............11 A3
Bracknell Gdns
 NW3...............11 A3
Bracknell Way
 NW3...............11 A4
Bradbeer Ho 24
 E2.................25 B2

Bradbourne St
 SW6............. **165** C3
Bradbury Ct 2
 SE3................53 C3
Bradbury Ho E1... **111** A2
Bradbury St 28
 N16...............16 A3
Bradby Ho NW8.... **78** B1
Braddon Rd SW14..55 C4
Braddyll St SE10...43 A1
Bradenham 11
 SE17...............48 C4
Bradenham Cl
 SE17...............48 C4
Braden St W9...... **88** A1
Bradfield Ct 14
 NW1...............13 A1
Bradfield Ho 15
 SW8.............. **171** B2
Bradford Ho 4
 W14...............39 C3
Bradford Rd W3....38 A4
Bradgate Rd SE6...67 A1
Brading Rd SW2...74 B4
Brading Terr W12..38 C3
Bradiston Rd W9...23 B2
Bradley Cl N7......14 B2
Bradley Ho
 Bermondsey SE16 ..40 A2
 11 Bromley E3.....27 A2
Bradley Mews
 SW12...............72 B3
Bradley's Cl N1... **85** C2
Bradlord Rd SE21..76 A1
Bradmead SE6.... **160** C1
Bradmore Park Rd
 W6.................39 A2
Brad St SE1....... **121** C1
Bradstock Ho E9..18 A1
Bradstock Rd E9...17 C2
Bradwell Ho 8
 NW6...............78 A3
Bradwell St 2 E1..25 C2
Brady Ho
 London SW4.......61 C2
 South Lambeth
 SW8.............. **171** A4
Brady St E1.......25 A1
Braefoot Ct SW15..57 C2
Braemar SW15.....57 C1
Braemar Ave SW18,
 SW19...............70 C2
Braemar Ho W9... **88** C3
Braemar Mans
 W8................ **128** A1
Braes St N1.......15 A1
Braganza St SE17. **150** A1
Braham Ho SE11.. **149** A1
Brahma Kumaris
 World Spiritual Univ
 NW10...............8 C1
Braid Ave W3......29 A3
Braid Ho SE10.....52 B2
Braidwood St SE1 **124** A1
Brailsford Rd SW2..62 C1
Braintree Ho 6
 E1.................25 B1
Braintree St E2....25 B2
Braithwaite Ho
 EC1............... **97** B2
Braithwaite Twr
 W2................ **101** B4
Bramah Gn SW9.. **173** C4
Bramah Rd SW9.. **173** C3

Bramall Ct N7 . . . . . .14 B2
Bramber WC1 . . . . . .94 A3
Bramber Ct TW8 . . . .36 A2
Bramber Rd W14 . .154 C4
Brambledown **8**
N4 . . . . .5 A4
Bramble Gdns
W12 . . . . .29 B2
Bramble Ho **16** E3 . .33 C4
Brambling Ct **22**
SE8 . . . . .51 B4
Bramcote Gr SE16 . .40 B1
Bramcote Rd
SW15 . . . . .57 A3
Bramerton St
SW3 . . . . .158 A4
Bramfield Ct N4 . . . .6 B2
Bramfield Rd
SW11 . . . . .60 B2
Bramford Rd
SW18 . . . . .59 B3
Bramham Gdns
SW5 . . . . .142 B3
Bramham Ho SE22 . .64 A3
Bramlands Cl
SW11 . . . . .60 A4
Bramley Cres
SW8 . . . . .161 C2
Bramley Ct SE13 . . .67 C2
Bramley Ho
10 North Kensington
W10 . . . . .30 C3
Roehampton SW15 . .56 B1
Bramley Rd W10 . . . .30 C3
Brampton WC1 . . .106 C3
Bramshaw Rd E9 . . .17 C2
Bramshill Gdns
NW5 . . . . .4 A1
Bramshill Rd
NW10 . . . . .21 B3
Bramshurst NW8 . . .78 B3
Bramston Rd
Harlesden NW10 . . .21 C3
Wandsworth SW17 . .71 B1
Bramwell Ho
Borough The SE1 . .137 A1
Chelsea SW1 . . . .160 C4
Bramwell Mews
N1 . . . . .85 A4
Brancaster Ho
22 Globe Town
E1 . . . . .25 C2
Islington N1 . . . . . . .15 A3
Brancaster Rd
SW16 . . . . .74 A1
Branch Hill NW3 . . . .2 B1
Branch Pl N1 . . . . . .87 C4
Branch Rd E14 . . . . .33 A2
Branch St SE15 . . . .49 A3
Brand Cl N4 . . . . .6 A3
Branden Lo **18** W4 . .37 B1
Brandlehow Prim Sch
SW15 . . . . .58 B3
Brandlehow Rd
SW15 . . . . .58 B3
Brandon Mews
Barbican EC2 . . . .109 B4
Walworth SE17 . . .151 A3
Brandon Rd N7 . . . .14 A1
Brandon St SE17 . .151 A3
Brandrams Wharf
SE16 . . . . .40 B4

Brandreth Rd
SW17 . . . . .73 A2
Brand St SE10 . . . . .52 B3
Brangton Rd
SE11 . . . . .149 A1
Brangwyn Ct W14 . .126 A1
Branksea St SW6 . .154 A1
Branksome Ho
SW8 . . . . .162 C2
Branksome Rd
SW2 . . . . .62 A2
Bransby Ct **4** N16 . .16 A4
Branscombe NW1 . .83 A3
Branscombe St
SE13 . . . . .67 A4
Bransdale Cl NW6 . .23 C4
Branston Ct **9**
TW9 . . . . .44 B2
Branston Rd TW9 . .44 B2
Branston Ho N7 . . . .14 C3
Brantwood Ho **7**
SE5 . . . . .48 B3
Brantwood Rd
SE24 . . . . .63 B2
Brasenose Dr
SW13 . . . . .47 B4
Brashley Road Cvn
Site NW10 . . . . . . .21 A2
Brassey Ho **1** E14 . .42 A2
Brassey Rd NW6 . . .10 B2
Brassey Sq SW11 . . .60 C4
Brassie Ave W3 . . . .29 A3
Brass Talley Alley **31**
SE16 . . . . .40 C4
Brathay NW1 . . . . .83 A1
Brathway Rd
SW18 . . . . .70 C4
Bratley St **1**
E1 . . . . .24 C1 99 B1
Bravington Pl W9 . .23 B1
Bravington Rd W9 . .23 B2
Brawne Ho **12**
SE17 . . . . .48 A4
Braxfield Rd SE4 . . .66 B3
Bray NW3 . . . . .12 A1
Brayard's Rd SE15 . .50 A1
Braybrook St W12 . .29 B3
Brayburne Ave
SW4 . . . . .171 A1
Bray Cres SE16 . . . .40 C4
Braydon Rd N16 . . . .7 C3
Bray Dr E16 . . . . . . .35 B2
Brayfield Terr N1 . . .14 C1
Brayford Sq **12** E1 . .32 B3
Bray Pl SW3 . . . . .144 C3
Bread St EC2 EC4 . .109 A1
Breakspeare SE21 . .76 B1
Breakspears Mews
SE4 . . . . .51 C1
Breakspears Rd
SE4 . . . . .66 C4
Breakwell Ct **16**
W10 . . . . .23 A1
Breamore Cl
SW15 . . . . .68 C3
Breamore Rd
SE15 . . . . .49 C3
Bream's Bldgs
EC4 . . . . .107 B2
Bream St E3 . . . . . . .18 C1
Breasley Cl SW15 . . .57 A3
Brechin Pl SW7 . . .143 A3
Brecknock Prim Sch
10 N7 . . . . .14 A2
Brecknock Rd N19 . .13 C3

Brecon Ho
Stamford Hill N16 . . . .7 B3
Wandsworth SW18 . .70 C4
Brecon Mews **23**
N7 . . . . .13 C3
Brecon Rd W6 . . . .154 B3
Bredel Ho **1** E14 . . . .33 C4
Bredgar SE13 . . . . . .67 A2
Bredgar Rd N19 . . . . .4 B2
Bredinghurst SE22 . .76 C4
Bredinghurst Ho **10**
SW15 . . . .
Bredinghurst Sch
SE15 . . . .
Bredon Ho SW10 . .156 B2
Breer St SW6 . . . . . .59 A4
Breezer's Ct **2**
E1 . . . . .125 C3
Breezer's Hill E1 . .125 C3
Brehon Ho NW1 . . . .82 C3
Bremans Row **1**
SW18 . . . .
Bremner Rd SW7 .129 A2
Brenchley Gdns SE15,
SE22, SE23 . . . . . . .65 C1
Brenda Rd SW17 . . .72 B2
Brendon Ave NW10 . .8 A4
Brendon Ho **1** W1 .103 B4
Brendon St W1 . . .102 B2
Brenley Ho SE1 . . .137 B4
Brenley Ct **14**
SE5 . . . .
N19 . . . .
Brent Ct **5** W4 . . . .38 A3
Brentford Fountain L
Ctr W4 . . . . .36 C1
Brent Ho **19** E9 . . . .17 B2
Brenthouse Rd E9 . .17 B2
Brenthurst Rd
NW10 . . . . .8 B2
Brentwick Gdns
TW8 . . . . .36 A2
Brereton Ho **4**
SW2 . . . . .74 C4
Bressenden Pl
SW1 . . . . .132 C2
Breton Ho
Bermondsey SE1 . .138 C2
St Luke's EC2 . . . . .97 A1
Brett Cl N16 . . . . .7 A2
Brett Cres NW10 . . .20 C4
Brettell St SE17 . . .151 C1
Brett Ho **2** SW15 . . .69 C4
Brett House Ct **2**
SW15 . . . . .69 C4
Brettinghurst **3**
SE1 . . . . .153 B1
Bretton Ho N19 . . . . .5 A3
Brett Pas **28** E8 . . . .17 A3
Brett Rd E8 . . . . . . .17 A3
Brewers Bldgs EC1 .96 A4
Brewers Ct W2 . . .100 C2
Brewer's Gn SW1 . .133 B2
Brewers Hall Gdns
EC2 . . . . .109 A3
Brewer St W1 . . . .119 A4
Brewery Ind Est The
N1 . . . . .87 A1
Brewery Rd N7 . . . .14 A2
Brewery Sq
Bermondsey SE1 . .124 C1
Clerkenwell EC1 . . .96 B2

Brewhouse La
Putney SW15 . . . . . .58 A4
Wapping E1 . . . . . . .32 A1
Brewhouse Wlk
SE16 . . . . .33 A1
Brewhouse Yd EC1 .96 A2
Brewster Gdns
W10 . . . . .30 B4
Brewster Ho
Bermondsey SE1 . .153 A4
Poplar E14 . . . . . . .33 B2
Briant Ho SE1 . . . .135 A1
Briant St SE14 . . . . .50 C3
Briar Ct
7 Bow E3 . . . . .26 C3
9 Dalston E8 . . . . . .16 B1
Briardale SW19 . . . .70 B3
Briardale Gdns
NW3 . . . . .1 C1
Briardale Ho **12**
N16 . . . . .7 A3
Briar Rd NW2 . . . . . .9 B4
Briar Wlk
Putney SW15 . . . . . .57 A3
West Kilburn W10 . .23 A1
Briarwood Rd
SW4 . . . . .61 C2
Briary Cl NW3 . . . . .12 A1
Briary Ct **15** E16 . . .35 B3
Brickbarn Cl
SW10 . . . . .157 A2
Brick Ct EC4 . . . . .107 B1
Brick Farm Cl
TW9 . . . . .45 A2
Brickfield Rd
SW4 . . . . .61 C1
Brick La
Shoreditch
E2 . . . . .24 B2 99 A3
Spitalfields
E1 . . . . .24 B2 99 A3
Brick Lane Mkt E2 . .99 A2
Bricklayers Arms
SE1 . . . . .137 C1
Brick St W1 . . . . . .118 A1
Brickworth Ho **2**
SW9 . . . . .173 C4
Bridale Cl SE15 . . . . .49 B4
Bride Ct EC4 . . . . .108 A1
Bride La EC4 . . . . .108 A1
Bridel Mews N1 . . . .86 A3
Bridewain St SE1 . .138 C2
Bridewell Pl
Holborn EC4 . . . . .108 A1
20 Wapping E1 . . . . .32 A1
Bridford Mews
W1 . . . . .104 B4
Bridge Acad The
31 Bethnal Green
E2 . . . . .24 B4
Bridge App NW3 . . .12 C1
Bridge Ave W6 . . . .39 B1
Bridge Avenue Mans
1 W6 . . . . .39 B1
Bridge Ct **13** W10 . .30 C3
Bridge Field Ho **7**
W2 . . . . .100 A2
Bridgefoot SE1 . . .148 B1
Bridge Gdns
1 Brockley SE4 . . . .66 B3

Bridge Ho continued
1 Camden Town
NW1 . . . . .12 C1
Homerton E9 . . . . . .17 C3
Bridge House Quay
E14 . . . . .34 B1
Bridge La SW11 . . .168 B3
Bridgeland Rd
E16 . . . . .35 C2
Bridgeman Ho **19**
E9 . . . . .17 B1
Bridgeman Rd N1 . .14 B1
Bridgeman St
NW8 . . . . .80 A1
Bridge Meadows
SE14 . . . . .50 C4
Bridgemount Mews
N19 . . . . .5 A4
Bridgend Rd SW18 . .59 B3
Bridgen Ho **9** E1 . . .32 A3
Bridge Pk **7**
SW18 . . . . .58 C2
Bridge Pl SW1 . . . .146 B4
Bridgeport Pl **4**
E1 . . . . .125 C2
Bridge Rd
Stratford Marsh
E15 . . . . .27 C4
Willesden NW10 . . . .8 A2
Bridge Sch The
N7 . . . . .14 A3
Bridges Ct SW11 . .167 B1
Bridges Ho **15** SE5 . .48 C3
Bridge St
Chiswick W4 . . . . . .37 C2
Westminster SW1 . .134 B3
Bridge Terr E15 . . . .19 C1
Bridgeview **2** W6 . .39 B1
Bridgewater Rd
E15 . . . . .27 B4
Bridgewater Sq
EC2 . . . . .108 C4
Bridgewater St
EC2 . . . . .108 C4
Bridgeway St NW1 . .83 A1
Bridge Wharf **11**
E2 . . . . .25 C3
Bridge Yd SE1 . . . .123 C2
Bridgford St SW17,
SW18 . . . . .71 B1
Bridgman Rd W4 . . .37 B3
Bridgnorth Ho **10**
SE15 . . . . .49 C4
Bridgwater Ho
W2 . . . . .100 C2
Bridle La W1 . . . . .119 A4
Bridlington Ho
SW18 . . . .
Bridport SE17 . . . .151 A1
Bridport Ho N1 . . . .87 C3
Bridport Pl N1 . . . . .87 C3
Bridstow Pl W2 . . . .31 C3
Brief St SE5 . . . . . . .48 A2
Brierfield NW1 . . . . .82 C3
Brierley Rd
Leyton E11 . . . . . . .19 C4
Upper Tooting
SW12 . . . . .73 B2
Brierly Gdns E2 . . . .25 B3
Brigade St SE3 . . . . .53 B1
Briggeford Cl **5** E5 . .7 C2
Briggs Ho **20**
E2 . . . . .24 B2 99 A4
Brightlingsea PI **5**
E14 . . . . .33 B2

Brightman Rd SW18 ....71 C3
Brighton Bldgs SE1 ....138 A1
Brighton Ct SW15 ..58 B1
Brighton Gr SE14 ....51 A2
Brighton Ho **7** SE5 ....48 C2
Brighton Rd N16 ..16 A4
Brighton Terr SW9 ....62 B3
Brightside Rd SE13 ....67 C1
Bright St E14 ......34 A4
Brightwell Ct N7 ...14 B3
Brightwells SW6 ....166 A2
Brig Mews SE8 .....51 C4
Brigstock Ho SE5 ...48 B1
Brill Pl NW1 ......83 C1
Brimsdown Ho E3 ..27 B1
Brindisie Green SE13 ....67 C1
Brindley Ho
37 Notting Hill W2 ....31 C4
2 Streatham SW12 ....74 A4
Brindley La SE14 ...51 B2
Brine Ho **11** E3 .....26 B3
Brinklow Ho W2 ..100 A3
Brinkworth Way E9 ....18 B2
Brinsley Ho **7** E1 ..32 B3
Brinsley St **13** E1 ...32 A3
Brinton Wlk SE1 ...122 A1
Brion Pl E14 ......34 B4
Brisbane Ho **3** W12 ....30 A2
Brisbane St SE5 ...48 C3
Briset St EC1 .....96 A1
Briset Way N7 .....5 B2
Bristol Gdns
Putney SW15 ......69 B4
Westbourne Green W9 ....88 B1
Bristol Ho SE11 ...135 B1
Bristol Mews W9 ...88 B1
Bristowe Cl **2** SW2 ....62 C1
Britannia Bsns Ctr **5** NW6 ....9 C4
Britannia Building N1 ....97 B4
Britannia Cl SW4 ..61 C3
Britannia Gate **11** E16 ....35 C1
Britannia Junc NW1 ....82 B4
Britannia L Ctr N1 ..24 A4
Britannia Rd
23 Millwall E14 ....41 C2
Walham Green SW6 ....156 A1
Britannia Row N1 ..86 C4
Britannia St WC1 ..94 C4
Britannia Way NW10 ....20 A1
Britannia Wlk N1 ..97 B4
British Coll of Osteopathy NW3 ...11 B2
British Dental Association Mus W1 ....104 A3
British Gr W4 ......38 B1

British Grove Pas **2** W4 ....38 B1
British Grove S **3** W4 ....38 B1
British Library The WC1 ....93 C4
British Mus WC1 ..106 A3
British Optical Association Mus SW1 ....120 A2
British St E3 ......26 B2
British Wharf Ind Est SE14 ....50 C4
Britley Ho **8** E14 ...33 B3
Brittage Rd **8** NW10 ....8 A1
Brittany Ho SW15 ...57 B3
Brittany Point SE11 ....149 B3
Britten Cl NW11 ....2 A3
Britten Ho SW3 ...144 B2
Britten St SW3 ...144 A2
Britton St EC1 ....96 A1
BRIXTON SW9 .....62 C4
Brixton Hill Ct **5** SW2 ....62 B2
Brixton Hill Pl SW2 ....74 A4
Brixton Mkt SW9 ..62 C3
Brixton Rd SW9 ..173 B2
Brixton Rec Ctr SW9 ....62 C4
Brixton Sta SW9 ...62 C3
Brixton Station Rd SW9 ....62 C4
Brixton Water La SW2 ....62 B2
Broadbent Cl N6 ...4 A3
Broadbent St W1 ..118 A4
Broadbridge Cl SE3 ....53 C3
Broad Common Est N16 ....7 C3
Broad Ct WC2 ....106 B1
Broadfield NW6 ...11 A2
Broadfield La NW1 ..14 A1
Broadfields Way NW10 ....8 B3
Bradford Ho **12** E1 ...26 A1
BROADGATE EC2 ..110 A4
Broadgate Ct EC2 ..110 A4
Broadgate Circ EC2 ....110 A3
Broadgates Ct SE11 ....149 C1
Broadgates Rd SW18 ....71 C3
Broadgate Twr The EC2 ....98 B1
Broadhinton Rd SW4 ....61 B4
Broadhurst Cl
Hampstead NW6 ...11 B2
11 Richmond TW10 ..54 B2
Broadhurst Gdns NW6 ....11 A1
Broadhurst Mans NW6 ....11 A1
Broad La EC2 ....110 A4
Broadlands N6 .....3 C4
Broadlands Ave SW16 ....74 A2

Broadlands Cl
Highgate N6 ....3 C4
Streatham SW16 ...74 A2
Broadlands Ct TW9 ....44 C3
Broadlands Lo N6 ...3 B4
Broadlands Mans **2** SW16 ....74 A2
Broadley St NW8 ..102 A4
Broad Terr NW1 ....9 B2
Broadmayne SE17 .151 B2
Broadmead W14 ..140 A3
Broadoak Ct **8** SW9 ....62 C4
Broadoak Ho **11** NW6 ....78 B3
Broad Passage **3** W3 ....29 B1
Broad St Ann EC12 ....110 A2
Broad Sanctuary SW1 ....134 A3
Broadstone Ho SW8 ....162 C1
Broadstone Pl W1 .103 B3
Broad Street Pl EC2 ....109 C3
Broadwalk Ho SW7 ....128 C3
Broadwalk La NW11 ....1 B4
Broadwall SE1 ....121 C2
Broadway
Stratford E15 .....19 C1
Westminster SW1 .133 B2
Broadway Arc **3** W6 ....39 B2
Broadway Ho **2** E8 ...25 A4
Broadway Mans SW6 ....155 C1
Broadway Market E8 ....25 A4
Broadway Market Mews **21** E8 ....24 C4
Broadway Mews **5** N16 ....7 B4
Broadway Mkt E8 ...25 A4
Broadway Ret Pk NW2 ....9 C4
Broadway Sh Ctr **6** W6 ....39 B2
Broadway The
Barnes SW13 .....46 A1
South Acton W3 ...36 C4
Broadway Wlk **2** E14 ....41 C3
Brodwick St W1 ..105 A1
Broad Wlk
Mayfair W1 ....117 B2
Regent's Pk NW1 ..81 C1
Richmond TW9 ....44 B3
Broad Wlk The W8 ....114 B1
Broadwood Terr W14 ....141 A4
Brocas Cl NW3 ....12 A1
Brockbridge Ho SW15 ....56 B1
Brocket Ho **18** SW8 ....171 B2
Brockham Dr SW2 .74 B4
Brockham Ho
Camden Town NW1 ....83 A3

Brockham Ho continued
11 Streatham SW2 ..74 B4
Brockham St SE1 ..137 A2
Brockhurst Ho N4 ...6 C4
Brockill Cres SE4 ..66 A3
Brocklebank Rd SE7 ....43 C2
Brocklebank Road Ind Est SE7 ....43 C2
Brocklehurst St SE14 ....50 C3
BROCKLEY SE4 ...66 B3
Brockley Cross SE4 ....66 B4
Brockley Cross Bsns Ctr SE4 ....66 A4
Brockley Gdns SE4 ....51 B1
Brockley Gr SE4 ...66 B2
Brockley Hall Rd SE4 ....66 A2
Brockley Ho SE17 .152 A2
Brockley Mews SE4 ....66 A2
Brockley Prim Sch SE4 ....66 B2
Brockley Rd SE4 ...66 B2
Brockley Sta SE4 ..66 A4
Brockley Way SE4 ..66 A3
Brockmer Ho **5** E1 ..32 A2
Brock Pl E3 ....27 A1
Brock St SE15 .....65 B4
Brockweir **2** E2 ...25 B3
Brockwell Ct **2** SW2 ....62 C2
Brockwell Ho SE11 ....163 A4
Brockwell Lido SE24 ....63 A1
Brockwell Park SE24 ....63 A1
Brockwell Park Gdns SE24 ....75 A4
Brockwell Park Row SW2 ....62 C1
Broderick Ho SE21 ....76 A1
Brodia Rd N16 .....7 A1
Brodick Ho **12** E3 ...26 B3
Brodie Ho SE1 ...153 A2
Brodie St SE1 ....153 A2
Brodlove La E1 ....32 C2
Brodrick Rd SW17 .72 A2
Brody Ho E1 .....110 C3
Broken Wharf EC4 ....122 C4
Brokesley St E3 ...26 B2
Broke Wlk
Hackney E8 ....24 B4
8 Hackney E8 ...24 C4
Bromar Rd SE5 ...64 A4
Bromehead St **8** E1 ..32 B3
Bromell's Rd SW4 ..61 B3
Bromfelde Rd SW4 ....171 C1
Bromfield Ct **20** SE16 ....139 C2
Bromfield St N1 ...85 C2
Bromleigh Ho SE1 ....138 C2
BROMLEY E3 .....27 A2
Bromley-by-Bow Sta E3 ....98 A4
Bromley Hall Rd E14 ....34 B4

Bromley High St E3 ....27 A2
Bromley Lo **2** W3 ..28 B3
Bromley Pl W1 ...104 C4
Bromley St E1 .....32 C3
BROMPTON SW1 .130 A1
Brompton Arc SW1 ....131 A3
Brompton Oratory SW3 ....130 A1
Brompton Park Cres SW6 ....156 A3
Brompton Pl SW3 .130 B2
Brompton Rd SW3 ....130 A1
Brompton Sq SW3 ....130 A1
Bromstone Ho **19** SW9 ....173 B3
Bromwich Ave N6 ...3 C2
Bromwich Ho **3** TW10 ....54 A1
Bromyard Ave W3 .29 A2
Bromyard Ho
Acton W3 ....29 A1
3 Peckham SE15 ..50 A3
Bron Ct NW6 .....23 C4
BRONDESBURY NW2 ....10 A2
Brondesbury College for Boys **2** NW6 ....10 B2
Brondesbury Ct NW2 ....9 C2
Brondesbury Mews **11** NW6 ....10 C1
BRONDESBURY PARK NW2 ....22 C4
Brondesbury Park Sta NW6 ....23 A4
Brondesbury Pk NW6 ....10 A1
Brondesbury Rd NW6 ....23 C3
Brondesbury Sta NW6 ....10 B1
Brondesbury Villas NW6 ....23 C3
Bronsart Rd SW6 ..154 A1
Bronte Ct **8** W14 ...39 C3
Bronte Ho
Kilburn NW6 .....23 C2
6 Stoke Newington N16 ....16 A4
Bronti Cl SE17 ...151 A2
Bronwen Ct NW8 ...89 B3
Bronze St SE8 .....51 C3
Brookbank Rd SE13 ....67 A4
Brook Cl SW17 ....72 C2
Brook Com Prim Sch E8 ....16 C3
Brook Ct SW14 ....56 A4
Brookdale Rd SE6 ..67 A1
Brook Dr SE11 ...150 A4
Brooke Ho **4** SE14 ...51 A2
Brooke Rd E5,N16 ...7 C1
Brookes Ct EC1 ...107 B4
Brooke's Mkt EC1 .107 C4
Brooke St EC1 ....107 B3
Brookfield
Dartmouth Pk N6 ...3 C1
1 Finsbury Pk N4 ...5 C2

Brookfield Ho 28
E2 . . . . 25 A3
Brookfield Pk NW5 . . 4 A3
Brookfield Prim Sch
N19 . . . . 4 A2
Brookfield Rd
Acton W4 . . . . 37 C4
Homerton E9 . . . . . . 18 A2
Brookgate N16 . . . . . . 6 C2
Brook Gate W1 . . . 117 A3
Brook Gdns SW13 . . 56 A4
Brook Gn W6 . . . . . . 39 C2
BROOK GREEN 39 C2
Brook Green Flats 19
W14 . . . . 39 C2
Brook Ho
3 Clapham Pk
SW4 . . . . 61 B2
Ealing W3 . . . . 36 C4
4 Hammersmith
W6 . . . . 39 B2
Marylebone WC1 . . . 105 B4
Brook Hos NW1 . . . 83 A1
Brooklands Ave
SW18 . . . . 71 A2
Brooklands Court
Apartments 3
NW6 . . . . 10 B1
Brooklands Ct 2
NW6 . . . . 10 B1
Brooklyn Ct W12 . . 30 B1
Brookmarsh Ind Est
SE10 . . . . 52 A3
Brook Mews N 3
W2 . . . . 115 A4
Brookmill Rd SE8 . . 51 C2
Brooksbank Ho 7
E9 . . . . 17 B2
Brooksbank St 3
E9 . . . . 17 B2
Brooksby Ho 2
N1 . . . . 14 C1
Brooksby Mews
N1 . . . . 14 C1
Brooksby St N1 . . . 14 C1
Brooksby's Wlk E9 17 C3
Brooks Ct
3 London SW4 . . . 172 A2
Nine Elms SW8 . . . 161 A2
Brooks Ho 6 SW2 . 74 C3
Brookside Rd N19 . . 4 B2
Brooks La W4 . . . . . 44 C4
Brook's Mews W1 118 A4
Brooks Rd W4 . . . . 36 C1
Brook St
Bayswater W2 . . . 115 C4
Mayfair W1 . . . . . . 118 A4
Brookstone Ct
SE15 . . . . 65 A3
Brooksville Ave
NW6 . . . . 23 A4
Brookville Rd
SW6 . . . . 154 C1
Brookwood Ave
SW13 . . . . 46 B1
Brookwood Ho
SE1 . . . . 136 B3
Brookwood Rd
SW18 . . . . 70 C3
Broome Ct 3
TW9 . . . . 44 C2
Broome Ho 7 E5 . . 17 A3
Broome Way SE5 . . 48 C3
Broom Farm SW6 165 C2

Broomfield 7
NW1 . . . . 12 C1
Broomfield Ho
SE17 . . . . 152 A3
Broomfield House Sch
TW9 . . . . 44 B2
Broomfield Rd
TW9 . . . . 44 B2
Broomfield St E14 . 34 A4
Broomgrove Rd
SW9 . . . . 173 A1
Broomhill Rd
SW18 . . . . 58 C2
Broomhouse La
SW6 . . . . 58 C2
Broomhouse Rd
SW6 . . . . 165 B2
Broomsleigh St
NW6 . . . . 10 B3
Broomwood Hall
(Lower Sch) 42
SW12 . . . . 60 C1
Broomwood Hall Sch
(Lower Sch)
SW16 . . . . 73 C1
Broomwood Hall Sch
(Upper Sch) 45
SW12 . . . . 72 C4
Broomwood Rd
SW11 . . . . 60 C2
Brougham Rd 2
Acton W3 . . . . 28 B3
Hackney E8 . . . . 24 C4
Brougham St
SW11 . . . . 169 A2
Brough Cl SW8 . . . 162 B1
Broughton Dr 19
SW9 . . . . 63 A3
Broughton Rd
SW6 . . . . 166 B2
Broughton Road App
2 SW6 . . . . 166 A2
Broughton St
SW8 . . . . 170 A2
Brouncker Rd W3 . 37 B4
Browne Ho 13 SE8 . 51 C3
Brownfield St E14 . 34 B3
Brownflete Ho
SE4 . . . . 66 A3
Brown Hart Gdns
W1 . . . . 117 C4
Browning Cl W9 . . 89 A1
Browning Ho
1 London SE14 . . . . 51 A2
7 Shepherd's Bush
W12 . . . . 30 B3
16 Stoke Newington
N16 . . . . 16 A4
Browning Mews
W1 . . . . 103 C3
Browning St SE17 151 A3
Brownlow Ho 16
SE16 . . . . 139 B3
Brownlow Mews
WC1 . . . . 95 A1
Brownlow Rd
Hackney E8 . . . . 24 C4
Willesden NW10 . . . . 8 A1
Brownlow St WC1 107 A3
Brown's Bldgs
EC3 . . . . 110 B1
Brown St W1 . . . . . 102 C2
Brownswood Rd N4 . 6 B2
Broxash Rd SW11 . . 60 C1

Broxbourne Ho 1
E3 . . . . 27 A1
Broxholme Ho
SW6 . . . . 166 A4
Broxholm Rd SE27,
SW16 . . . . 74 C1
Broxwood Way
NW8 . . . . 80 B3
Bruce Cl W10 . . . . . 30 C4
Bruce Glasier Ho 12
N19 . . . . 4 C4
Bruce Ho
4 Clapham Pk
SW4 . . . . 61 C1
3 North Kensington
W10 . . . . 30 C4
Putney SW15 . . . . . . 57 A2
Bruce Rd E3 . . . . . . 27 A2
Bruckner St W10 . . 23 B2
Bruges Pl 14 NW1 . 13 B1
Brune Ho E1 . . . . . 110 C3
Brunei Gall The
WC1 . . . . 105 C4
Brunel Ct
3 Barnes SW13 . . . 46 B1
College Park NW1 . . 21 C3
Brunel Est W2 . . . . 31 C4
Brunel Ho
Chelsea SW10 . . . . 157 C2
4 Gospel Oak
NW5 . . . . 4 A1
Millwall E14 . . . . . . 42 A1
New Cross SE8 . . . . 51 B3
23 Streatham SW2 . 74 A4
Brunel Mews
NW10 . . . . 22 C2
Brunel Mus SE16 . . 40 B4
Brunel Rd
Acton W3 . . . . 29 A4
Wapping SE16 . . . . . 32 B1
Brunel St E16 . . . . 35 B3
Brune St E1 . . . . . . 110 C3
Brunlees Ho SE1 . . 137 A1
Bruno Ct 8 E8 . . . . 16 C2
Brunswick Ct
Bermondsey SE1 . . 138 B4
Finsbury EC1 . . . . . . 96 A3
Westminster SW1 . 147 C3
Brunswick Gdns
W8 . . . . 31 C1 113 C1
Brunswick Ho
4 Haggerston E2 . . 24 B3
Lisson Gr NW1 . . . . 90 C2
Brunswick Mews
W1 . . . . 103 A2
Brunswick Park Prim
Sch 22 SE5 . . . . 48 C3
Brunswick Pk SE5 . 49 A2
Brunswick Pl N1 . . 97 C3
Brunswick Quay
SE16 . . . . 40 C3
Brunswick Rd E14 . 34 B3
Brunswick Sh Ctr
WC1 . . . . 94 B2
Brunswick Sq WC1 94 B2
Brunswick Villas 2
SE5 . . . . 49 A2
Brunton Pl E14 . . . . 33 A3
Brushfield St E1 . . 110 C4
Brussels Rd SW11 . 59 C3
Bruton La W1 . . . . 118 B3
Bruton Pl W1 . . . . . 118 B3
Bruton St W1 . . . . 118 B3
Brutus Ct SE11 . . . 150 A3
Bryan Ave NW10 . . 9 A1
Bryan Ct W1 . . . . . 102 C2

Bryan Ho SE16 . . . . 41 B4
Bryan Rd SE16 . . . . 41 B4
Bryanston Ct W1 . 102 C2
Bryanston Ho 12
SE15 . . . . 49 B2
Bryanston Mans
W1 . . . . 102 C4
Bryanston Mews E
W1 . . . . 102 C3
Bryanston Mews W
W1 . . . . 102 C3
Bryanston Pl W1 . . 102 C3
Bryanston Sq W1 . 102 C2
Bryanston St W1 . . 103 A1
Bryant Ct
Acton W3 . . . . 28 C1
Haggerston E2 . . . . . 24 B3
Bryantwood Rd N5,
N7 . . . . 5 C2
Bryce Ho 22 SE14 . 50 C4
Brydale Ho 2
SE16 . . . . 40 C2
Brydges Pl WC2 . . 120 A3
Brydges Rd E15 . . . 19 C3
Bryden Cl SE26 . . . 76 A4
Bryer Ct EC2 . . . . . 108 C4
Bryett Rd N7 . . . . . . 5 A1
Bryher Ho W4 . . . . 37 B1
Brymay Cl E3 . . . . . 26 C3
Brymon Ct W1 . . . 103 A3
Brynmaer Ho
SW11 . . . . 169 A3
Brynmaer Rd
SW11 . . . . 169 A3
Bryony Rd W12 . . . 29 C2
BT Twr W1 . . . . 104 C4
Buccleuch Ho E5 . . 7 C4
Buchanan Ct 16
SE16 . . . . 40 C2
Buchanan Gdns
NW10 . . . . 22 A3
Buchanan Ho
Dulwich SE21 . . . . . 76 A1
Wandsworth SW18 . 70 C4
Buchan Ho W3 . . . . 37 A4
Buchan Rd SE15 . . 65 B4
Bucharest Rd
SW18 . . . . 71 B4
Buckfast St E2 . . . . 25 A2
Buck Hill Wlk W2 115 C3
Buckhold Rd
SW18 . . . . 58 C1
Buckhurst Ho 13
N7 . . . . 13 C3
Buckhurst St E1 . . . 25 A1
Buckingham Gate
SW1 . . . . 133 A2
Buckingham Ho
Finsbury Pk N4 . . . . . 6 B3
Richmond TW10 . . . 54 C2
Buckingham Mans
NW6 . . . . 11 A3
Buckingham Mews
Harlesden NW10 . . . 21 B3
7 Kingsland N1 . . . . 16 A2
Westminster SW1 . 132 C2
Buckingham Pal
SW1 . . . . 132 C2
Buckingham Palace
Rd SW1 . . . . 146 B4
Buckingham Pl
SW1 . . . . 132 C2

Buckingham Rd
Harlesden NW10 . . . 21 B3
Kingsland N1 . . . . . . 16 A2
Buckingham St
WC2 . . . . 120 B3
Buckingham Yd
NW10 . . . . 21 B3
Buckland Cres
NW3 . . . . 11 C2
Buckland Ho 3
N1 . . . . 14 A3
Buckland St N1 . . . 87 C1
Buckland Wlk 2
W3 . . . . 37 B4
Buckler's Alley
SW6 . . . . 155 A2
Bucklersbury EC2,
EC4 . . . . 109 B1
Buckle St
16 Whitechapel
E1 . . . . 111 B2
Whitechapel E1 . . . 111 A2
Buckley Ct 5
NW6 . . . . 10 B1
Buckley Rd NW6 . . 10 B1
Buckmaster Cl 1
SW9 . . . . 62 C4
Buckmaster Ho 2
N7 . . . . 14 B4
Buckmaster Rd
SW11 . . . . 60 A3
Bucknall St WC1 . . 106 A2
Bucknell Cl SW2 . . 62 B3
Buckner Rd SW2 . . 62 B3
Buckridge Bldg
EC1 . . . . 107 B4
Buckshead Ho 19
W2 . . . . 31 C4
Buck St NW1 . . . . . 13 A1
Buckstone Cl SE23 . 65 B1
Buckters Rents
SE16 . . . . 33 A1
Buckthorne Rd
SE4 . . . . 66 A2
Budge Row EC4 . . 109 B1
Budge's Wlk W2 . . 115 A2
Budleigh Ho 11
SE15 . . . . 49 C3
Buer Rd SW6 . . . . . 164 B1
Bugsby's Way
SE10 . . . . 43 B2
Buick Ho 4 E3 . . . . 26 C1
Building Crafts Coll
The E15 . . . . 27 C4
Bulbarrow NW8 . . . 78 B3
Bulinga St SW1 . . . 147 C3
Bullace Row SE5 . . 48 C2
Bullards Pl 5 E2 . . 25 C2
Bulleid Way SW1 . 146 B3
Bullen Ho 13 E1 . . 25 A1
Bullen St SW11 . . . 168 B2
Buller Cl SE15 . . . . 49 C3
Buller Rd NW10 . . . 22 C2
Bullfinch Ct 4
SE21 . . . . 75 C2
Bull Inn Ct WC2 . . 120 B3
Bullivant St 9
E14 . . . . 34 B2
Bulls Alley W4 . . . . 46 A3
Bull's Gdns SW3 . . 144 B4
Bulls Head Pas
EC3 . . . . 110 A1
Bull Yd SE15 . . . . . 49 C2

Bulmer Mews
W11 . . . . .31 C1 113 B2
Bulow Ct 3 SW6. 166 B2
Bulstrode Pl W1. . . 103 C3
Bulstrode St W1. . . 103 C2
Bulwer St W12. . . .30 B1
Bunbury Ho SE15. . .49 C3
Bunhill Row 97 B1
Bunhouse Pl
Chelsea SW11. . . 145 C2
SW1. . . 145 C2
Bunkers Hill NW11. .2 B4
Bunning Ho N7. . . .14 A4
Bunning Way N7. . .14 B1
Bunsen Ho 2 E3. . .26 A3
Bunsen St 3 E3. . .26 A3
Bunyan Ct EC2. . . 108 C4
Buonaparte Mews
SW1. . . 147 B2
Burbage Cl SE1. . . 137 B1
Burbage Ho
5 Deptford SE14. . . 50 C4
Shoreditch N1. . . 87 C3
Burbage Rd SE21,
SE24. . . 76 A4
Burcham St E14. . .34 B3
Burchell Ho SE11. . 149 A2
Burchell SE15. . . 50 A2
Burcher Gale Gr 7
SE15. . . 49 B3
Burcote Rd SW18. .71 C4
Burden Ho SW8 . 162 A1
Burdenshott Ave
TW10. . . 55 A3
Burder Cl N1. . . 16 A2
Burder Rd N1. . . 16 A2
Burdett Coutts &
Townshend CE Prim
Sch SW1. . . 133 B1
Burdett Mews 4
W2. . . 100 A2
Burdett Rd
Richmond TW9. . .54 B4
Tower Hamlets E3. .33 B4
Burdon Cl 3 E8. . .16 C2
Burford Ct SE8. . . 51 C4
Burford Ho
1 Brentford
TW8. . . 36 A1
11 South Lambeth
SW9. . . 173 A1
Burford Rd
Brentford TW8. . .36 A1
5 Stratford Marsh
E15. . . 27 C4
Burford Wlk SW6. 156 B1
Burgate Ct 9
SW9. . . 62 C4
Burgess Ho 3 SE5 . .48 C3
Burgess Ho 3 SE5 .48 B3
Burgess Park Mans
NW6. . . 10 C4
Burgess St 3 E14 . 33 C4
Burge St SE1. . . 137 C1
Burghley Hall Cl
SW19. . . 70 A4
Burghley Ho SW19. .70 A1
Burghley Rd NW5. .13 A4
Burghley Twr 3 W3. .29 B2
Burgh St N1. . . 86 B2

Burgon St EC4. . . . 108 B1
Burgos Gr SE10. . . .52 A2
Burgoyne Rd SW9 .62 B4
Burhan Uddin Ho
E1. . . . . .24 B1 98 C1
Buriton Ho 9
SW15. . . . . .69 A3
Burke Cl SW15. . . .56 A3
Burke Ho 1 SW11. .59 C3
Burke St E16. . . . . .35 B4
Burland Rd SW11. .60 B2
Burleigh Coll Ho . . 39 B2
Burleigh Ho
Chelsea SW3 . 157 C3
1 North Kensington
W10. . . . . .30 C4
Burleigh Pl SW15. .57 C2
Burleigh St WC2. . 120 C4
Burley Ho E1. . . . . .32 C3
Burlington Arc
W1. . . . . . 118 C3
Burlington Ave
TW9. . . . . .44 C2
Burlington Cl W9. . .23 C1
Burlington Ct
Chiswick W4. . . . .45 B3
Highgate N6. . . . . .3 C3
Burlington Danes
Acad W12. . . . . .30 A3
Burlington Gdns
Acton Green W4. . .37 B1
Acton W3. . . . . .28 B1
4 Fulham SW6 . 164 B1
Marylebone W1 . 118 C3
Burlington Ho
NW3. . . . . .11 B4
Burlington La W4. . .45 C3
Burlington Lodge
SW6. . . . . . 164 B1
Burlington Mews
Acton W3. . . . . .28 B1
2 Putney SW15. .58 B2
Burlington Pl
SW6. . . . . . 164 B1
Burlington Rd
Acton Green W4. . .37 B1
Fulham SW6. . . . . . 164 B1
Burma Rd N16. . . . . .15 C4
Burmarsh NW5. . . .12 C2
Burmester Ho
SW17. . . . . .71 B1
Burmester Rd
SW17. . . . . .71 B1
Burnaby Cres W4. .45 B4
Burnaby Ct 31
SE16. . . . . . 139 C3
Burnaby Gdns W4. .45 A4
Burnaby St SW10 . 157 A1
Burnand Ho 8
W14. . . . . .39 C3
Burnbury Rd SW12 .73 B3
Burne Jones Ho
W14. . . . . . 140 B3
Burnell Ho 18
SW9. . . . . .74 C3
Burnell Wlk SE1. . 153 A2
Burness Cl N7. . . .14 B2
Burne St NW1. . . 102 A4
Burnett Cl E9. . . . . .17 B3
Burnett Ct SW11. . 168 A3
Burnett Ho 6
SE13. . . . . .52 B1
Burney St SE10. . . .52 B3
Burnfoot Ave
SW6. . . . . . 164 B3
Burnham 4 NW3. . . .12 A1

Burnham Cl SE1. . 153 A3
Burnham Ct W2. . . 114 B4
Burnham Est 8
E2. . . . . .25 B2
Burnham St E2. . . .25 B2
Burnhill Cl 12
SE15. . . . . .50 A3
Burnhill Ho EC1. . . 96 C3
Burnley Rd
London SW9. . . 172 C2
Willesden NW10. . . .8 C3
Burnsall St SW3 . 144 B2
Burns Ho
10 Bethnal Green
E2. . . . . .25 B2
2 Islington N7. . . 14 C3
Kennington SE17. . 150 B1
6 Stoke Newington
N16. . . . . .16 A4
Burn's Ho NW10. . .21 A4
Burnside Cl SE16. . .32 C1
Burns Rd SW11. . . 168 C2
Burn's Rd NW10. . .21 B4
Burnthwaite Rd
SW6. . . . . . 155 A1
Burntwood Cl
SW18. . . . . .72 A3
Burntwood Ct
SW17. . . . . .71 B1
Burntwood Grange
Rd SW18. . . . . .72 A3
Burntwood La
SW17. . . . . .71 C1
Burntwood Sch
SW17. . . . . .71 C1
Buross St E1. . . . . .32 A3
Burrage Ct 17
SE16. . . . . .40 C2
Burrard Ho 11 E2. .25 B3
Burrard Rd NW6. . .10 C4
Burr Cl E1. . . . . . 125 B2
Burrell St SE1. . . 122 A2
Burrell's Wharf Sq
E14. . . . . .42 A1
Burrhill Ct SE16. . .40 C3
Burrow Ho 19
SW9. . . . . . 173 A1
Burrow Rd SE22. . .64 A3
Burrows Mews
SE1. . . . . . 136 A4
Burrows Rd NW10 .22 B2
Burrow Wlk SE21. .75 B4
Burr Rd SW18. . . . . .71 A3
Bursar St SE1. . . 124 A1
Burslem St E1. . . 111 C1
Burstock Rd SW15.58 A3
Burston Rd SW15. .57 C2
Burtley Cl N4. . . . . .6 B3
Burton Bank N1. . . .15 C1
Burton Ct SW3 . 145 A2
Burton Gr SE17. . . 151 B1
Burton Ho
7 Brixton SW9. . .62 B3
8 Bermondsey
SE16. . . . . .40 A4
Burton Lo 6
SW15. . . . . .58 B2
Burton Mews
SW1. . . . . . 145 C3
Burton Pl WC1. . . 93 C3
Burton Rd
7 Brixton SW9. . .62 C2
Brixton SW9. . .48 A1
Brondesbury NW6.10 B1
Burtons Ct E15. . .19 C1
Burton St WC1. . . 93 C2

Burtonwood Ho N4. .6 C4
Burtt Ho 9
N1. . . . . .24 A2 98 A4
Burwash Ho SE1. . 137 C3
Burwell Cl 27 E1. . .32 A3
Burwell Wlk 3
E3. . . . . .26 C1
Burwood Ho 11
SW9. . . . . .63 A3
Burwood Pl W2 . 102 C2
Bury Cl SE16. . . . . .32 C1
Bury Ct EC3. . . 110 B2
Buryfield Ct 23
SE8. . . . . .40 C2
Bury Pl WC1. . . 106 B3
Bury St
St James SW1 . 119 A2
Whitechapel EC3. . 110 B2
Bury Wlk SW3 . 144 A2
Busbridge Ho 24
E14. . . . . .33 C4
Busby Mews 5
NW1. . . . . .13 C2
Busby Pl NW5. . . .13 C2
Bushbaby Cl SE1 . 138 A1
Bushberry Rd E9. . .18 A2
Bush Cotts 12
SW18. . . . . .58 C2
Bush Ct 7 W12. . . .39 C4
Bushell Cl SW2. . . .74 B2
Bushell St 18 E1 . 125 C2
Bushey Down
SW12. . . . . .73 A2
Bushey Hall SE5. . .48 B2
Bushey Hill Rd
SE5. . . . . .49 B2
Bushfield Ho N5. . .15 B3
Bush Ind Est
London NW10. . .20 C1
Upper Holloway N19 . 4 C1
Bush La EC4. . . . 123 B4
Bushnell Rd SW17. .73 A1
Bush Rd
Bermondsey SE8 . . .40 C2
Hackney E8. . . . . .25 A4
1 Richmond TW9. . .44 C4
Bushwood Dr SE1 . 153 A3
Bushwood Rd
TW9. . . . . .44 C4
Business Design Ctr
N1. . . . . . 85 C3
Buspace Studios 3
W10. . . . . .23 A1
Butcher Row E1. . .32 C3
Butchers Rd E16. . .35 C3
Bute Gdns W6. . . . . .39 C2
Bute House Prep Sch
W6. . . . . .39 C2
Bute St SW7. . . 143 B4
Bute Wlk 14 N1. . . .15 C2
Butfield Ho 6 E9. . .17 B2
Butler Ho
32 Bethnal Green
E2. . . . . .25 B2
5 Brixton SW9. . .48 A2
10 Poplar E14. . . . . .33 B3
Butler Pl SW1 . 133 B2
Butler Rd NW10. . .8 B1
Butlers & Colonial
Wharf SE1 . 139 A4
Butler St 32 E2. . . .25 B2
Butler's Wharf W
SE1. . . . . . 124 C1
Butley Ct 8 E3. . . .26 A3
Butterfield Cl
SE16. . . . . .40 A4

Butterfly Wlk 2
SE5. . . . . .48 C2
Buttermere NW1. . . 92 B4
Buttermere Cl
Bermondsey SE1 . 152 C3
Leyton E11. . . . . .19 C4
Buttermere Ct
NW8. . . . . . 79 B4
Buttermere Dr
SW15. . . . . .58 A2
Buttermere Ho 3
E3. . . . . .26 B2
Buttermere Wlk 7
E8. . . . . .16 B2
Butterwick W6. . . . . .39 B2
Butterworth Ct
SW16. . . . . .74 A1
Buttesland St N1 . 97 C4
Buxhall Cres E9. . .18 B2
Buxted Rd
Camberwell SE22. .64 A3
Dalston E8. . . . . .16 B1
Buxton Ct N1. . . 97 A4
Buxton Gdns W3. . .28 A2
Buxton Ho 3
SW11. . . . . .59 C3
Buxton Mews
SW4. . . . . . 171 C2
Buxton Rd
Mortlake SW14. . . .56 A4
Upper Holloway N19 . 4 C3
Willesden NW2. . . . . .9 A2
Buxton St E1. . .24 B1 99 A1
Byam Ct SW6. . . 166 C1
Byards Ct SE16. . . .40 C3
Byas Ho 3 E3. . . . . .26 B2
Byefield Cl SE16. . .41 A4
Byelands Cl 12
SE16. . . . . .32 C1
Bye The W3. . . . . .28 A4
Byeway The SW14. .55 B4
Byfeld Gdns SW13.46 C2
Bygrove Prim Sch
E14. . . . . .34 A3
Bygrove St E14. . . . . .34 A3
Byng Pl WC1. . . 93 B1
Byng St E14. . . . . .41 C4
Byrne Ho 11 SW2. .62 B2
Byrne Rd SW12. . . .73 A2
Byron Cl E8. . . . . .24 C4
Byron Ct
Chelsea SW3 . 144 B3
Dulwich SE21. . . . . .76 C3
3 Hampstead
NW6. . . . . .11 B1
Paddington W9. . . . . .23 C1
St Pancras WC1. . . 94 C2
Byron Mews
Hampstead NW3 . 12 A4
2 Maida Vale W9. . .23 C1
Byron St E14. . . . . .34 B3
Bythorn St SW9. . . .62 B3
Byward St EC3. . . 124 B3
Bywater Pl SE16. . .33 A1
Bywater St SW3 . 144 C2
Bywell Pl W1. . . 104 C3
Byworth Wlk N19. . .5 A3

C

Cabanel Pl SE11 . . . **149** A3
Cabbell St NW1 . . . . **102** A3
Cabinet Off SW1 . . . **134** A4
Cabinet War Rooms &
Churchill Mus
SW1 . . . . **133** C4
Cable Ho WC1 . . . . . . **95** B4
Cable Pl SE10 . . . . . . **52** B2
Cable St E1 . . . . **32** A2
Cabot Ct SE16 . . . . . . **40** C3
Cabot Sq E14 . . . . . . **33** C1
Cabul Rd SW11 . . . . **168** B1
Cactus Cl SE5 . . . . . . **49** A1
Cactus Wlk SW12 . . . **29** B3
Cadbury Way 11
SE16 . . . . **153** B4
Caddington Rd
NW2 . . . . **1** A1
Cadell Cl E2 . . . . **24** B3
Cadell Ho 12 E2 . . . . **24** B3
Cade Rd SE10 . . . . . . **52** C2
Cader Rd SW18 . . . . . **59** B1
Cadet Dr SE1 . . . . . . **153** A2
Cade Tyler Ho 10
SE10 . . . . **52** B2
Cadiz St SE17 . . . . . **151** A1
Cadman Cl SW9 . . . . . **48** A3
Cadmore Ho 8
N1 . . . . **15** A1
Cadmus Cl 9
SW4 . . . . **61** C4
Cadmus Ct 6
SW9 . . . . **173** B4
Cadnam Point 15
SW15 . . . . **69** A3
Cadogan Cl E9 . . . . . . **18** B1
Cadogan Ct SW3 . . . **144** C3
Cadogan Ct Gdns
SW1 . . . . **145** B4
Cadogan Gate
SW1 . . . . **145** A4
Cadogan Gdns
SW3 . . . . **145** A3
Cadogan Hall
SW1 . . . . **145** B4
Cadogan Ho SW3 . . . **157** C3
Cadogan La SW1 . . . **131** B1
Cadogan Pier
SW3 . . . . **158** B3
Cadogan Pl SW1 . . . **131** A1
Cadogan Sq SW1 . . . **131** A1
Cadogan St SW3 . . . **144** C3
Cadogan Terr E9 . . . . **18** B1
Caernarvon Ho
W2 . . . . **100** C2
Caesar Ct 8 E2 . . . . . **25** C3
Cahill St EC1 . . . . **97** A1
Cahir St E14 . . . . **42** A2
Caine Ho W3 . . . . **37** A4
Caird St W10 . . . . . . **23** B2
Cairns Ho 3 N7 . . . . . **14** B4
Cairns Rd SW11 . . . . . **60** A2
Caister Ho N7 . . . . . . **14** B2
Caistor Ho 10
SW12 . . . . **73** A4
Caistor Mews
SW12 . . . . **73** A4
Caistor Rd SW12 . . . **73** A4

Caithness Ho N1 . . . . **84** C4
Caithness Rd W14 . . . **39** C3
Calabria Rd N5 . . . . . **15** A3
Calais Gate SE5 . . . . . **48** A2
Calais St SE5 . . . . **48** A2
Calbourne Rd
SW12 . . . . **72** C4
Calcraft Ho 10 E2 . . . **25** B3
Caldecot Ct SE5 . . . . **48** B1
Caldecot Rd SE5 . . . . **48** B1
Calder Ct SE16 . . . . . **33** B1
Calderon Ho NW8 . . . **80** A2
Calderon Pl
W10 . . . . **30** B4
Caldervale Rd
SW4 . . . . **61** C2
Caldew St SE5 . . . . . . **48** C3
Caldwell St SW9 . . . **163** A1
Caldy Wlk 15 N1 . . . . **15** B2
Caleb St SE1 . . . . . . **137** A4
Caledonia Ho 1
E14 . . . . **33** A3
Caledonian Market
SE1 . . . . **138** B2
Caledonian Rd
Islington N1 . . . . **84** C3
Lower Holloway N7 . . **14** B2
Caledonian Road &
Barnsbury Sta
N1 . . . . **14** B1
Caledonian Road Sta
N7 . . . . **14** B2
Caledonia Sq 6
NW1 . . . . **13** C2
Caledonia Wharf Rd
E14 . . . . **43** A2
Caledonia St N1 . . . . **84** B1
Cale St SW3 . . . . . . **144** A2
Caletock Way
SE10 . . . . **43** B1
Calgarth NW1 . . . . . . **83** A1
Calgary Ct 12 SE16 . . **40** B4
Caliban Twr 8 N1 . . . **24** A3
Calico Ho 4 SW11 . . . **59** B4
Calico Row 5
SW11 . . . . **59** B4
Calidore Cl SW2 . . . . **62** B1
California Bldg 2
SE13 . . . . **52** A2
Callaby Terr 11
N1 . . . . **15** C2
Callahan Cotts 8
E1 . . . . **32** B4
Callcott Ct NW6 . . . . **10** B1
Callcott Rd NW6 . . . . **10** B1
Callcott St
W8 . . . . **31** C1 **113** B2
Callendar Rd
SW7 . . . . **129** B2
Callingham Cl 13
E14 . . . . **33** B4
Callingham Ho 4
SW4 . . . . **62** A4
Callow St SW3 . . . . **157** B4
Calmington Rd
SE5 . . . . **49** A4
Calshot Ho N1 . . . . . **84** C2
Calshot St N1 . . . . . . **84** C1
Calstock Ho SE11 . . **149** C2
Calthorpe St WC1 . . . **95** A2
Calton Ave SE21 . . . . **64** A1
Calver 13 NW5 . . . . . **13** A4
Calverley Gr N19 . . . . **4** C3
Calvert Ave
E2 . . . . **24** B2 **98** C3

Calvert Ct
1 London N19 . . . . . . **4** B3
5 Richmond TW9 . . . **54** B3
Calverton SE5 . . . . . . **49** A4
Calvert Ho 9 W12 . . . **30** A2
Calvert Rd SE10 . . . . **43** B1
Calvert's Bldgs
SE1 . . . . **123** B1
Calvert St NW1 . . . . **81** B4
Calvin St E1 . . . **24** B1 **98** C1
Calypso Cres 6
SE15 . . . . **49** B3
Calypso Way SE16 . . **41** B2
Camaby St W1 . . . .
Camaret Ct
W11 . . . . **31** A3
Cambalt Ho 3
SW15 . . . . **57** C2
Cambalt Rd SW15 . . . **57** C2
Cambay Ho 4
E1 . . . . **26** A1
Camber Ho 7
SE15 . . . . **50** B4
Camberley Ho
NW1 . . . . **82** B1
CAMBERWELL **48** B2
Camberwell Bsns Ctr
SE5 . . . . **48** C3
Camberwell Church St
SE5 . . . . **48** C2
Camberwell Coll of
Arts
11 Camberwell
SE5 . . . . **49** A2
22 Camberwell
SE15 . . . . **49** B3
Camberwell Glebe
SE5 . . . . **49** A2
Camberwell Gn
SE5 . . . . **48** C2
Camberwell Green
SE5 . . . . **48** B2
Camberwell New Rd
SW9 . . . . **48** A3
Camberwell Rd
SE5 . . . . **48** B3
Camberwell Station
Rd SE5 . . . . **48** B2
Camberwell Trad Est
SE5 . . . . **48** B2
Camborne Rd
SW18 . . . . **70** C4
Cambourne Mews 6
W11 . . . . **31** A3
Cambray Rd SW12 . . **73** B3
Cambria Ho 14
E14 . . . . **33** A3
Cambria Lo 8
SW15 . . . . **58** B2
Cambria Rd SE5 . . . . **63** B4
Cambria St SW6 . . . **156** B1
Cambridge Ave
NW6 . . . . **23** C3
Cambridge Cir
WC2 . . . . **105** C1
Cambridge Cotts
TW9 . . . . **44** C4
Cambridge Cres 20
E2 . . . . **25** A3

Cambridge Ct continued
2 Kilburn NW6 . . . . **23** C3
Marylebone W2 . . . **102** A3
Stamford Hill N16 . . . **7** A4
Cambridge Gate
NW1 . . . . **92** A2
Cambridge Gate
Mews NW1 . . . . **92** B2
Cambridge Gdns
Kilburn NW6 . . . . . . **23** C3
North Kensington
W10 . . . . **31** A3
Cambridge Gr W6 . . . **39** A2
Cambridge Heath Rd
E1, E2 . . . . **25** A2
Cambridge Heath Sta
E2 . . . . **25** A3
Cambridge Ho
SW6 . . . . **58** A4
Cambridge Mans
SW11 . . . . **168** C3
Cambridge Pas 2
E9 . . . . **17** B1
Cambridge Pl W8 . . **128** B3
Cambridge Rd
Barnes SW13 . . . . . . **46** B1
Battersea SW11 . . . **168** C3
Kilburn NW6 . . . . . . **23** C2
Kilburn NW6 . . . . . . **23** C3
Richmond TW9 . . . . **44** C3
Cambridge Rd N
W4 . . . . **37** A1
Cambridge Rd S 3
W4 . . . . **37** A1
Cambridge Sch 15
W6 . . . . **39** A2
Cambridge Sq
W2 . . . . **102** A2
Cambridge St
SW1 . . . . **146** C2
Cambridge Terr
NW1 . . . . **92** A3
Cambridge Terr Mews
NW1 . . . . **92** B3
Cambus Rd E16 . . . . **35** C4
Cam Ct 2 SE15 . . . . . **49** B4
Camden Arts Ctr
NW2 . . . . **11** B3
Camden Gdns
NW1 . . . . **13** A1
Camden High St
NW1 . . . . **82** C3
Camden Ho 6
SE8 . . . . **41** B1
Camdenhurst St
E14 . . . . **33** A3
Camden Lock Mkt
NW1 . . . . **13** B1
Camden Lock Pl
NW1 . . . . **13** B1
Camden Mews
NW1 . . . . **13** C2
Camden Mkt NW1 . . . **82** B4
Camden Park Rd
NW1 . . . . **13** C2
Camden Pas N1 . . . . **86** A3
Camden Rd NW1 . . . . **82** C4
Camden Road Sta
NW1 . . . . **13** B1
Camden Row SE3 . . . **53** A1
Camden Sch for Girls
The NW5 . . . . **13** B2
Camden Sq NW1 . . . . **13** C2
Camden St NW1 . . . . **83** A3
Camden Studios
NW1 . . . . **83** A3

Camden Terr 17
NW1 . . . . **13** C2
CAMDEN TOWN **13** A1
Camden Town Sta
NW1 . . . . **82** B4
Camden Wlk N1 . . . . **86** A3
Cameford Ct 20
SW12 . . . . **74** A4
Camelford Ho 1
NW1 . . . . **83** A3
Camelford Ct 15
W11 . . . . **31** A3
Camelford Ho
SE11 . . . . **148** B1
Camelford Wlk 18
W11 . . . . **31** A3
Camellia Ho SE8 . . . . **51** B3
Camellia St SW8 . . . **162** A1
Camelot Ho 2
NW1 . . . . **13** C2
Camelot Prim Sch
SE15 . . . . **50** A4
Camera Pl SW10 . . . **157** B4
Camera Press Gall
SE1 . . . . **138** C3
Cameret Ct 6
W11 . . . . **39** C4
Cameron Ct 3
SW19 . . . . **70** A3
Cameron Ho
Camberwell SE5 . . . . **48** B3
St John's Wood
NW8 . . . . **80** A2
Cameron House Sch
SW10 . . . . **157** C4
Cameron Pl SW16 . . . **74** C2
Camerton Cl 8 E8 . . . **16** B2
Camilla Rd SE16 . . . . **40** A2
Camlet St
E2 . . . . **24** B1 **98** C2
Camley St Natural Pk
NW1 . . . . **83** C3
Camley St NW1 . . . . . **83** C2
Camomile St EC3 . . . **110** B2
Campaign Ct W9 . . . . **23** B1
Campana Rd SW6 . . **165** C4
Campbell Ct
Dulwich SE21 . . . . . . **76** C3
South Kensington
SW7 . . . . **128** C1
Campbell Gordon Way
NW2 . . . . **9** A4
Campbell Ho
Paddington W2 . . . . . **89** B1
Pimlico SW1 . . . . . . **146** C1
30 Shepherd's Bush
W12 . . . . **30** A2
Campbell Rd 3 E3 . . . **26** C2
Campbell Wlk N1 . . . **84** B4
Campdale Rd N7 . . . . . **4** C1
Campden Gr W8 . . . **127** C4
Campden Hill W8 . . **127** B4
Campden Hill Ct
W8 . . . . **127** C4
Campden Hill Gate
W8 . . . . **127** B4
Campden Hill Gdns
W8 . . . . **31** C1 **113** B2
Campden Hill Mans
W8 . . . . **31** C1
Campden Hill Pl
W11 . . . . **31** B1 **113** A2
Campden Hill Rd
W8 . . . . **127** B4
Campden Hill Sq
W14 . . . . **31** B1 **113** A2

Campden Ho 4
NW6 . . . . 11 C1
Campden Hos
W8 . . . . 31 C1 113 B1
Campden House Cl
W8 . . . . 127 C4
Campden St
W8 . . . . 31 C1 113 B1
Campen Cl SW19 . . 70 A2
Camperdown St
E1 . . . . 111 A1
Campion Ho 15
N16 . . . . 16 A3
Campion Rd SW15 . 57 B2
Camplin Rd SE14 . . 50 C3
Campshill Pl SE13 . 67 B2
Campshill Rd SE13 . 67 B2
Campton Hill Twrs
W8 . . . . 31 C1 113 B2
Cam Rd E15 . . . . . 27 C4
Camsey Ho 3
SW2 . . . . 62 B2
Canada Cres W3 . . 20 B1
Canada Est 8
SE16 . . . . 40 B4
Canada Gdns SE13 . 67 B2
Canada Memorial
SW1 . . . . 132 C4
Canada Rd W3 . . . 28 B4
Canada Sq E14 . . . 34 A1
Canada St SE16 . . . 40 C4
Canada Water Sta
SE16 . . . . 40 C3
Canada Way W12 . . 30 A2
Canal App SE8 . . . 51 A4
Canal Bldg N1 . . . . 86 C2
Canal Bridge SE15 . 49 C4
Canal Byd 1 NW1 . . 13 C2
Canal Cl
Mile End E1 . . . . 26 A1
North Kensington
W10 . . . . 22 C1
Canal Gr SE15 . . . 50 A4
Canal Head Public Sq
1 SE15 . . . . 49 C2
Canal Path 2 E2 . . 24 B4
Canal Reach N1 . . . 84 C4
Canalside Studios 20
N1 . . . . 24 A4
Canal St SE5 . . . . . 48 C4
Canal Way W10 . . . 22 C1
Canal Wlk N1 . . . . 87 C4
CANARY WHARF . . 34 A1
Canary Wharf E14 . 34 A1
Canary Wharf Coll
E14 . . . . 42 B2
Canary Wharf Pier
E14 . . . . 34 A1
Canary Wharf Sta
E14 . . . . 34 A1
Canary Wharf Sta
(DLR) E14 . . . . . . 33 C1
Canbury Mews
SE26 . . . . 76 C1
Cancell Rd SW9 . . 173 C4
Candahar Rd
SW11 . . . . 168 A1
Candida Ct 9
NW1 . . . . 13 A1
Candishe Ho SE1 . 138 C4
Candle Gr SE15 . . . 65 A4
Candle Ho 6
SW11 . . . . 59 C4
Candle St E1 . . . . . 33 A4
Candover St W1 . . 104 C3
Candy St E3 . . . . . 26 B4

Canfield Gdns
NW6 . . . . 11 A1
Canfield Pl NW6 . . 11 B2
Canford Rd SW11 . . 60 C2
Canham Rd W3 . . . 38 A4
Cann Ho W14 . . . . 126 B1
Canning Cross
SE5 . . . . 49 A1
Canning Ho 23
W12 . . . . 30 A2
Canning Pas W8 . . 128 C2
Canning Pl W8 . . . 128 C2
Canning Pl Mews
W8 . . . . 128 C2
Canning Rd N5 . . . 6 A1
Cannington 14
NW5 . . . . 12 C2
CANNING TOWN . . 35 B3
Canning Town
E16 . . . . 35 A3
Canning Town Sta
E16 . . . . 35 A3
Cannock Ho N4 . . . 6 C4
Cannon Dr 14 E14 . . 33 C2
Cannon Hill NW6 . . 10 C3
Cannon Ho SE11 . 149 A3
Cannon La NW3 . . . 2 C1
Cannon Pl NW3 . . . 2 C1
Cannon St EC4 . . . 123 A4
Cannon Street Rd
E1 . . . . 32 A3
Cannon Street Sta
EC4 . . . . 123 B4
Cannon Wharf Bsns
Ctr 27 SE8 . . . . . . 41 A2
Canon Barnett Prim
Sch E1 . . . . 111 A2
Canon Beck Rd
SE16 . . . . 40 B4
CANONBURY 15 B3
Canonbury Bsns Ctr
N1 . . . . 87 A4
Canonbury Cres
N1 . . . . 15 B1
Canonbury Ct 21
N1 . . . . 15 A1
Canonbury Gr N1 . . 15 B1
Canonbury Hts 6
N1 . . . . 15 C2
Canonbury La N1 . . 15 B1
Canonbury Pk N
N1 . . . . 15 B2
Canonbury Pl N1 . . 15 A2
Canonbury Prim Sch
4 N1 . . . . 15 B2
Canonbury Rd N1 . . 15 A1
Canonbury Sq N1 . . 15 A1
Canonbury St N1 . . 15 B1
Canonbury Sta N1,
N5 . . . . 15 B3
Canonbury Villas
N1 . . . . 15 A1
Canonbury Yd E 28
N1 . . . . 15 B2
Canon Murnane Rd
SE1 . . . . 138 C1
Canon Row SW1 . 134 A3
Canons Cl N2 . . . . 2 C4
Canon St N1 . . . . . 86 C3
Canrobert St E2 . . . 25 A2
Cantelowes Rd
NW1 . . . . 13 C2
Canterbury SE13 . . 67 B2

Canterbury Cl 16
SE5 . . . . 48 B1
Canterbury Cres
SW9 . . . . 62 C4
Canterbury Ct
Acton W3 . . . . . 29 A1
Kilburn NW6 . . . . 23 C3
Canterbury Gr SE27,
SW16 . . . . 74 C1
Canterbury Ho
6 Bromley E3 . . . 27 A2
Lambeth SE1 . . . 135 A2
Canterbury Ind Pk 16
SE5 . . . . 48 B4
Canterbury Mans
NW6 . . . . 11 A2
Canterbury Pl
SE17 . . . . 150 B3
Canterbury Rd
NW6 . . . . 23 C3
Canterbury Terr
NW6 . . . . 23 C3
Cantium Ret Pk
SE1 . . . . 49 C4
Canton St E14 . . . . 33 C3
Cantrell Rd E3 . . . . 26 C1
Canute Ct SW16 . . 74 C1
Canute Gdns SE16 . 40 C2
Canvey St SE1 . . . 122 C2
Cape Henry Ct 11
E14 . . . . 34 C2
Capel Ho 17 E9 . . . 17 B1
Capel Lo
6 Richmond
TW9 . . . . 44 B2
12 Streatham SW2 . 74 B4
Capener's Cl SW1 131 B3
Capern Rd SW18 . . 71 B3
Capital City Acad
NW10 . . . . 22 A4
Capital East Apts 8
E16 . . . . 35 C2
Capital Interchange
Way TW8 . . . . . . 36 C1
Capital Sh Ctrs
SW1 . . . . 133 B3
Capital Wharf 14
E1 . . . . 125 C1
Capland Ho NW8 . . 89 C2
Capland St NW8 . . 89 C2
Caple Ho SW10 . . 157 A2
Caple Rd NW10 . . . 21 B3
Capper St WC1 . . . 93 A1
Capstan Ho 6 E14 . 42 B2
Capstan Rd SE8 . . . 41 B2
Capstan Sq E14 . . . 42 B4
Capstan Way SE16 . 33 A1
Capulet Mews 1
E16 . . . . 35 C1
Caradoc Cl W2 . . . 31 C3
Caradoc St SE10 . . 43 A1
Cara Ho 10 N1 . . . . 14 C1
Caranday Villas 5
W11 . . . . 30 C1
Caravel Cl E14 . . . . 41 C3
Caravel Mews 14
SE8 . . . . 51 C4
Caraway Hts E14 . . 34 B2
Carbery Ave W3 . . 36 B4
Carbis Rd E14 . . . . 33 B3
Carbroke Ho 9
E9 . . . . 25 B4
Carburton St W1 . . 92 B1
Cardale St 11 E14 . 42 B3
Carden Rd SE15 . . . 65 A4
Cardiff Ho 9 SE15 . 49 C4

Cardigan Rd
Barnes SW13 . . . . 46 C1
Bow E3 . . . . 26 B3
Richmond TW10 . . 54 A1
Cardigan St SE11 . 149 B2
Cardigan Wlk 4
N1 . . . . 15 B1
Cardinal Bourne St
SE1 . . . . 137 C1
Cardinal Cap Alley
SE1 . . . . 122 C3
Cardinal Hinsley Cl
NW10 . . . . 21 C3
Cardinal Pl SW15 . 57 C3
Cardinal Pole RC Sch
51 Hackney E9 . . . 17 C2
London E9 . . . . . 18 A3
Cardinals Way N19 . . 4 C3
Cardinal Vaughan
Meml Sch The
W14 . . . . 126 A4
Cardinal Wlk
SW1 . . . . 132 C1
Cardine Mews
SE15 . . . . 50 A3
Cardington St
NW1 . . . . 93 A3
Cardozo Rd N7 . . . 14 A3
Cardross St W6 . . . 39 A3
Cardwell Rd 3
N7 . . . . 14 A4
Career Ct 11 SE16 . 40 C4
Carew Cl N7 . . . . . 5 B2
Carew Ct 15 SE14 . 50 C4
Carew Ho SW16 . . 74 C1
Carew St SE5 . . . . 48 B1
Carey Ct 20 SE5 . . 48 B3
Carey Gdns SW8 . 171 B3
Carey La EC2 . . . . 108 C2
Carey Pl SW1 . . . 147 B3
Carey St WC2 . . . 107 A1
Carfax Pl SW4 . . . 61 C3
Carfree Cl 5 N1 . . . 14 C1
Cargill Rd SW18 . . 71 B3
Carinthia Ct 9
SE8 . . . . 41 A2
Carisbrooke Ct
Acton W3 . . . . . 37 B4
1 Streatham
SW16 . . . . 74 B1
Carisbrooke Gdns
SE15 . . . . 49 B3
Carisbrooke Ho
TW10 . . . . 54 C2
Carker's La
Crouch End N19 . . 4 C4
Gospel Oak NW5 . 13 A3
Carleton Gdns
N19 . . . . 13 B3
Carleton Rd N7 . . . 13 C3
Carlile Cl E3 . . . . . 26 B3
Carlile Ho SE1 . . . 137 C1
Carlingford Rd
NW3 . . . . 11 C4
Carlisle Ave
Acton W3 . . . . . 29 A3
Whitechapel EC3 . 110 C1
Carlisle Ho 6
NW5 . . . . 4 B1
Carlisle La SE1 . . . 135 A2
Carlisle Mews
NW8 . . . . 89 C1
Carlisle Pl SW1 . . 132 C1
Carlisle Rd
Finsbury Pk N4 . . . 5 C4
Kilburn NW6 . . . . 23 A4
Carlisle St W1 . . . 105 B1
Carlisle Wlk 6 E8 . . 16 B2

Carlos Pl W1 . . . . 118 A3
Carlow St NW1 . . . 82 C2
Carlson Ct SW15 . . 58 B3
Carlton Cl
NW3 . . . . 1 C2
Carlton Ct
Brixton SW9 . . . . 48 A2
Kilburn NW6 . . . . 78 B2
9 Willesden NW2 . . 9 B2
Carlton Dr SW15 . . 58 A2
Carlton Gdns
SW1 . . . . 119 B1
Carlton Gr SE15 . . 50 A2
Carlton Hill NW8 . . 78 C2
Carlton Ho
6 Kilburn NW6 . . . 23 B3
Kilburn NW6 . . . . 78 B2
Marylebone W1 . . 103 A2
Carlton House Terr
SW1 . . . . 119 C2
Carlton Lo N4 . . . . 5 C4
Carlton Mans
Brixton SW9 . . . . 62 C3
Cricklewood NW2 . . 9 C3
Kensington W14 . 126 B4
Maida Vale W9 . . . 88 B4
5 South Hampstead
NW6 . . . . 10 C1
Stamford Hill N16 . . 7 B3
Carlton Prim Sch
NW5 . . . . 12 C3
Carlton Rd
Acton W4 . . . . . 37 C4
Finsbury Pk N4 . . . 5 C4
Mortlake SW13 . . 55 B3
Carlton Sq E1 . . . . 25 C1
Carlton St SW1 . . 119 B3
Carltons The 5
SW15 . . . . 58 A2
Carlton Tower Pl
SW1 . . . . 131 A2
Carlton Vale NW6 . 23 C3
Carlton Vale Inf Sch
NW6 . . . . 23 B2
Carlyle Ho
6 Camberwell
SE5 . . . . 48 B3
Chelsea SW3 . . . 157 C3
12 Stoke Newington
N16 . . . . 7 A1
Carlyle Mans
SW3 . . . . 158 A3
Carlyle Mews 24
E1 . . . . 25 C1
Carlyle Pl SW15 . . 57 C3
Carlyle Rd
10 Camberwell
SE28 . . . . 20 C4
Mortlake SW13 . . 46 B1
Carlyle's Ho SW3 . 158 A3
Carlyle Sq SW3 . . 143 C1
Carmalt Gdns
SW15 . . . . 57 B3
Carmarthen Ho 9
SW15 . . . . 69 B4
Carmarthen Pl
SE1 . . . . 138 A4
Carmel Ct W8 . . . 128 A4
Carmelite St EC4 . 121 C4
Carmel Lo SW6 . . 155 B4
Carmen St E14 . . . 34 A3
Carmichael Cl 8
SW11 . . . . 59 C4
Carmichael Ct 3
SW13 . . . . 46 B1
Carmichael Ho 5
E14 . . . . 34 B2

Carmichael Mews
SW18 ....**71** C4
Carminia Rd SW17 .**73** A2
Carnaby St W1 .....**104** C1
Carnac St SE21,
SE27 ....**75** C1
Carna Ct TW9 ....**54** A4
Carnegie Ho NW3 ...**2** C1
Carnegie PI SW19 ..**69** C1
Carnegie St N1.......**85** A3
Carnicot Ho 9
SE15......................**50** A2
Carnoustie Dr N1...**14** B1
Carnwath Ho SW6..**59** A4
Carnwath Rd SW6...**59** A4
Caroline Cl
Bayswater W2 .....**114** B3
Streatham SW16 ...**74** B1
Caroline Gdns
E2 ....**24** A2 **98** B4
Caroline Ho
Bayswater W2 .....**114** B3
20 Hammersmith
W6........................**39** B1
Caroline Martyn Ho 8
N19 ....**4** C4
Caroline PI
Bayswater W2 .....**114** B3
Clapham SW11 ....**169** C1
Caroline PI Mews
W2 ....**114** B3
Caroline St E1........**32** C3
Caroline Terr
SW1 ....**145** B3
Caroline Wlk W6 ..**154** A3
Carol St NW1 ....**82** C4
Caronia Ct 4
SE16......................**41** A2
Carpenter Ho
1 Tower Hamlets
E14........................**33** C4
5 Tufnell Pk N19 ...**13** C4
Carpenters Ct
NW1 ....**82** C4
Carpenter's PI
SW4......................**61** C3
Carpenters Prim Sch
E15 ....**27** B4
Carpenter St W1 .**118** A3
Carradale Ho 2
E14........................**34** B3
Carrara Cl SW9 ....**63** B3
Carrara Wharf
SW6......................**58** A4
Carriage Dr E
SW11 ....**159** C2
Carriage Drive E
SW11 ....**159** C2
Carriage Drive N SW11,
SW8 ....**159** C3
Carriage Dr N
Battersea SW8,
SW11 ....**158** C2
Battersea SW8,
SW11 ....**159** C3
Carriage Dr S
SW11 ....**169** B4
Carriage Dr W
SW11 ....**158** C1
Carrick Ho
Islington N7 ....**14** B2
Kennington SE11 .**150** A2
Carrick Mews SE8 ..**51** C4

Carrington Ct
SW11 ....**60** A3
Carrington Ho
W1 ....**118** A1
Carrington Lo 3
TW10 ....**54** A2
Carrington Rd
TW10 ....**54** C3
Carrington St W1 .**118** A1
Carrol Ct NW5 ......**13** A4
Carroll Ct
Acton W3 ....**37** A3
4 Shacklewell E5 ...**7** C2
Carroll Ho W2 .....**115** B4
Carron Cl E14 ....**34** A3
Carroun Rd SW8 ..**162** C2
Carr St 8 E14 ....**33** A3
Carslake Rd SW15 ..**57** B1
Carson Rd
Dulwich SE21 ....**75** C2
Newham E16 ....**35** C4
Carter Ct EC4 ......**108** B1
Carteret Ho 8
W12 ....**30** A2
Carteret St SW1 ..**133** B3
Carteret Way SE8...**41** A2
Carter Ho
11 London SW2.....**62** C2
Spitalfields E1 .....**110** C3
Carter La EC4 ......**108** B1
Carteret St E1 .....**151** A1
Carters Cl 10 NW5..**13** C2
Carter St SE17 ....**150** C1
Carter Yd SW18 ....**58** C2
Carthew Rd W6 .....**39** A3
Carthew Villas W6 .**39** A3
Carthusian St EC1 **108** C4
Carter Circ E14 .....**34** B1
Carting La WC2 ...**120** B3
Carton Ho
4 Bermondsey
SE16....................**139** B2
5 Shepherd's Bush
W11 ....**30** C2
Cartoon Mus The
WC1 ....**106** A3
Cartwright Gdns
WC1 ....**94** A3
Cartwright Ho
SE1 ....**137** A1
Cartwright St E1 .**125** A3
Cartwright Way
SW13 ....**47** A3
Carvel Ho E14 ....**42** B1
Carver Cl 19 W4 ...**37** B3
Carver Rd SE24 .....**63** B1
Carville Cres TW8 .**36** A2
Caryl Ho 9 SW9 ....**69** C3
Carysfort Rd N16 ..**15** C4
Casby Ho 32 SE16 .**139** B2
Casdar Rd SE14 .....**50** C3
Casey Cl NW8 ....**90** B3
Casino Ave SE24....**63** C2
Caspian Ho 10 E1 ..**32** C4
Caspian St SE5 ......**48** C3
Cassandra Ct 7
NW2 ....**9** B2
Cass Bsns Sch EC1 **97** B1
Cassell Ho 8
SW9 ....**172** B2
Casserley Ho W4 ...**37** C3
Cass Ho 2 E9 ....**17** C2
Cassidy Rd SW6 ..**155** B1
Cassilis Rd E14 .....**41** C4
Cassinghurst SE24..**63** C2

Cassland Rd E9......**17** C2
Casson Ho 11 E1 ..**111** B4
Casson St E1 ....**111** B3
Castalia Sq 6 E14 ..**42** B4
Castellain Mans
W9 ....**88** A2
Castellain Rd W9 ..**88** A2
Castell Ho 11 SE8..**51** C3
Castello Ave SW15 .**57** A2
Castelnau SW13 .....**47** A3
Castelnau Gdns
SW13 ....**47** A4
Castelnau Mans
SW13 ....**47** A4
Castelnau Row
SW13 ....**47** A4
Casterbridge
Kilburn NW6 ....**78** B4
3 Notting Hill W11 .**31** C3
Casterton St E8 ....**17** A2
Castleacre W2......**102** A1
Castle Baynard St
EC4 ....**122** C4
Castlebrook Cl
SE11 ....**150** A4
Castle Cl
12 Acton W3 ....**37** B3
Homerton E9 ....**18** A3
South Acton W3 .....**37** A4
Wimbledon SW19 ..**69** C1
Castlecombe Dr
SW19 ....**69** C4
Castleden Ho
NW6........................**11** C1
Castleford Ct NW8 .**89** C2
Castle Ho
Newington SE1.....**150** C4
South Lambeth
SW8 ....**162** B2
Castle Ind Est
SE17 ....**150** C4
Castle La SW1 .....**132** C2
Castlemaine 8
SW11 ....**169** A2
Castlemaine St 1
E1..........................**32** A4
Castle Mead SE5 ...**48** B3
Castle Mews NW1 .**13** A2
Castle PI
6 Acton W4 ....**38** A2
Camden Town NW1 ..**13** A2
Castle Rd NW1 ......**13** A2
Castlereagh St
W1 ....**102** C2
Castleton Ho 3
E14........................**42** B2
Castletown Rd
W14 ....**140** B1
Castleview N4 ....**6** B2
Castle Way SW19 ..**69** C1
Castlewood Ho
WC1 ....**105** C2
Castle Yd
Highgate N6 ....**3** C4
Lambeth SE1 ....**122** B2
Castor La E14 ....**34** A2
Catalpa Ct SE13 ....**67** C1
Caterham Rd SE13 .**67** C4
Catesby Ho 23 E9 ..**17** B1
Catesby St SE17 ..**151** C3

Cathay Ho SE16 ....**40** A4
Cathay St 5 SE16 .**40** A4
Cathcart Hill N19...**4** B1
Cathcart Rd
SW10 ....**156** C4
Cathcart St NW5 ...**13** A2
Cathedral Ct EC4 .**108** B1
Cathedral Lo EC1 .**108** C4
Cathedral Sch of St
Saviour & St Mary
Overie The SE1 ...**137** A4
Cathedral St SE1 .**123** B2
Cathedral Wlk
SW1 ....**132** C2
Catherall Rd N5,
N16........................**6** B1
Catherine Baird Ct 12
SW12 ....**73** A4
3 Notting Hill W11 .**31** A3
Catherine Dr TW9 .**54** A4
Catherine Gr SE10 .**52** A2
Catherine Griffiths Ct
EC1........................**95** C2
Catherine Ho 18
N1..........................**24** A4
Catherine PI SW1 .**132** C2
Catherine St WC2 .**120** C4
Catherine Wheel Alley
E1 ....**110** B3
Catherine Wheel Yd
SW1 ....**118** C1
Catherwood Ct N1 .**87** B1
Cathles Rd SW12 ...**61** A1
Cathnor Rd W12 ...**39** A4
Catlin St SE16 ....**40** A1
Catman Ho N4 ....**5** B3
Cato Rd SW4..........**61** C3
Cator St
Camberwell SE15.....**49** B4
Camberwell SE15....**49** B4
Cato St W1 ....**102** B2
Catton St WC1 .....**106** C3
Caughley Ho
SE11 ....**135** B1
Caulfield Ct 18
NW1 ....**13** B1
Caulfield Rd
Gunnersbury W3 ...**37** B3
London SE15.........**50** A1
Causeway The
SW18 ....**59** A2
Causton Cotts 3
E14........................**33** A3
Causton Ho SE5 ....**48** B3
Causton Rd N6 ....**4** A4
Cautley Ave SW4 ..**61** B2
Cavalry Gdns
SW15 ....**58** B2
Cavaye Ho SW10 ..**157** A4
Cavaye PI SW10 ...**143** A1
Cavell Ct 3 N19 .....**4** B2
Cavell Ho 8 N1 .....**24** A4
Cavell St E1 ....**32** A4
Cavendish Ave
NW8........................**79** C1
Cavendish Cl
Brondesbury NW6 ..**10** B2
3 Putney SW15 .....**58** A2
St John's Wood
NW8........................**89** C4
Cavendish Coll
WC1 ....**105** B4
Cavendish Ct EC2 .**110** B2
Cavendish Gdns
SW4......................**61** B1

Cavendish Ho
South Lambeth
SW8 ....**172** A4
St John's Wood
NW8........................**79** C1
Cavendish Mans
2 Clapham Pk
SW12 ....**61** B3
Hackney E5............**17** B3
Holborn EC1 ....**95** B1
5 West Hampstead
NW6......................**10** C3
Cavendish Mews N
W1 ....**104** B4
Cavendish Mews S
W1 ....**104** B3
Cavendish Par
SW12 ....**61** A1
Cavendish PI
Balham SW4..........**61** A1
Brondesbury NW2 ..**9** C2
Marylebone W1 ...**104** B2
Cavendish Prim Sch
W4 ....**46** A3
Cavendish Rd
Brondesbury NW6 ..**10** B1
Chiswick W4 ....**45** B2
Clapham Pk SW12 ..**61** B1
Cavendish Sch 14
SE16......................**40** B2
Cavendish Sch The
NW1 ....**82** B4
Cavendish Sq W1 .**104** B2
Cavendish St N1 ....**87** B1
Cavendish Terr 11
E3..........................**26** B2
Cavendish The
NW11 ....**2** C4
Caversham Ho 7
SE15......................**49** C4
Caversham Rd
NW5......................**13** B2
Caversham St
SW3 ....**158** C4
Caverswall St W12 .**30** B3
Cavour Ho SE17 ...**150** B2
Caxton Gr E3 ....**26** C2
Caxton Hall Rd W1 **133** B2
Caxton Rd W12 .....**39** C4
Caxton St E16 ......**35** B3
Caxton St SW1 ....**133** B2
Caxton Wlk WC2 ..**105** C1
Cayford Ho 1
NW3........................**12** B3
Cayley Prim Sch 22
E14........................**33** A3
Cayton PI EC1 ....**97** B3
Cayton St EC1 ....**97** B3
Cazenove Mans 1
N16 ....**7** C2
Cazenove Rd N16...**7** C2
Cecil Ct
Chelsea SW10 .....**156** C4
South Hampstead
NW6......................**11** A1
St James WC2 .....**120** A3
Cecil Gr NW8 ....**80** B3
Cecilia Rd E8 ....**16** C3
Cecil Mans 2
SW17......................**72** C2
Cecil Rd
Acton W3 ....**28** B4
Harlesden NW10 ...**21** A3
Cecil Rhodes Ho
NW1........................**83** B2

Cedar Cl
Old Ford E3 . . . . . . 26 B4
West Norwood
SE21 . . . . 75 B2
Cedar Ct
Islington N1 . . . . . . 15 B1
Marylebone W1 . . 102 B2
Mortlake SW14 . . . 55 B3
Wimbledon SW19 . 69 C1
Cedar Gr W5 . . . . 36 A3
Cedar Ho
5 Cubitt Town
E14 . . . . 42 B4
Kensington W8 . . 128 A2
New Cross Gate
SE14 . . . . 50 C2
5 Richmond TW9 . 45 A2
10 Rotherhithe
SE16 . . . . 40 C4
Cedar Lo
Brondesbury NW2 . 10 B2
Fulham SW6 . . . . 47 C2
Cedarne Rd SW6 . 156 A1
Cedar Rd NW2 . . . 9 B4
Cedars Cl SE13 . . 67 C4
Cedars SW15 . . . . 56 C1
Cedars Ho 21 SW2 . 62 B3
Cedars Mews SW4 . 61 A3
Cedars The E9 . . . 17 C1
Cedar Terr TW9 . . 54 A3
Cedar Way NW1 . . 83 B4
Cedra Ct N16 . . . . 7 C3
Cedric Chambers
NW8 . . . . 89 B2
Celandine Cl E3,
E14 . . . . 33 C4
Celandine Dr E8 . . 16 B1
Celbridge Mews
W2 . . . . 100 B2
Celebration Ave
E15 . . . . 19 B2
Celestial Gdns
SE13 . . . . 67 C3
Celia Blairman Ho
E1 . . . . 110 C4
Celia Ct 7 TW9 . . 44 B2
Celia Ho 10 N1 . . . 24 A3
Celia Rd N19 . . . . 13 B4
Celtic St E14 . . . . 34 A4
Cenacle Cl NW3 . . 1 C1
Cenotaph Cl 1 . . . 134 A4
Centaur Ct 3
TW8 . . . . 36 A1
Central St SE1 . . 135 A2
Central Ave SW11 159 A1
Central Bsns Ctr
NW10 . . . . 8 A3
Central Foundation
Boys' Sch EC2 . . 97 C2
Central Foundation
Upper Girls Sch The
2 E3 . . . . 26 B2
1 E3 . . . . 27 B3
Central Middlesex
Hospl W10 . . . . 20 B2
Central Par W3 . . . 37 A4
Central St Martins
Coll EC1 . . . . . . 95 C1
Central St Martins
College of Art &
Design N1 . . . . 84 A3
Central Sch of Ballet
EC1 . . . . 95 C1

Central Sch of Speech
& Drama NW3 . . 11 C1
Central St EC1 . . . 96 C3
Central Way NW10 . 20 B2
Centre Acad 2
SW11 . . . . 59 C3
Centre Ave W3 . . . 28 C1
Centre Bldg SE17 151 A4
Centre Hts 5
NW3 . . . . 11 C1
Centre Point 3
SE1 . . . . 153 B2
Centre Point Ho
WC2 . . . . 105 C2
Centre St E2 . . . . 25 A3
Centurion Bldg
SW8 . . . . 160 A3
Centurion Cl N7 . . 14 B1
Centurion La E3 . . 26 B3
Century Bldg SE13 . 52 A1
Century Mews 8
N5 . . . . 6 A1
Cephas Ave 6 E1 . . 25 B1
Cephas Ho 9 E1 . . 25 B1
Cephas St E1 . . . . 25 B1
Cerise Rd SE15 . . . 49 C2
Cerney Mews W2 . 115 B4
Cervantes Ct 12
W2 . . . . 100 B1
Cester St E2 . . . . 24 C4
Ceylon Rd
6 Hammersmith
W14 . . . . 39 C3
Kensington W14 . 126 A1
Chabot Dr SE15 . . 65 A4
Chadacre Ho 10
SW9 . . . . 63 A3
Chadbourn St E14 . 34 A4
Chadston Ho 11
N1 . . . . 15 A1
Chadswell Ho 5
Chadwell St EC1 . . 95 C4
Chadwick Cl SW15 . 68 B4
Chadwick Rd
Harlesden NW10 . 21 B4
Peckham SE15 . . . 49 B1
Chadwick St SW1 . 133 B1
Chadworth Ho
Finsbury EC1 . . . 96 C3
Finsbury Pk N4 . . . 6 B3
Chagford Ho
33 Bromley E3 . . 27 A2
Marylebone NW1 . 90 C1
Chagford St NW1 . 91 A1
Chalbury Ho 3
SW9 . . . . 62 B3
Chalbury Wlk N1 . 85 B2
Chalcot Cres NW1 . 81 A4
Chalcot Gdns NW3 . 12 B2
Chalcot Mews
SW16 . . . . 74 A1
Chalcot Rd NW1 . . 81 B4
Chalcot Sq NW1 . . 12 C1
Chaldon Rd SW6 . 154 B2
Chale Rd SW2 . . . 62 A1
Chalfont Ct NW1 . . 91 A1
Chalfont Ho 2
SE15 . . . . 49 C3
Chalford 7 NW3 . . 11 B2
Chalford Ct 13
SW15 . . . . 57 C1
Chalkers Cnr TW9 . 55 A4
Chalk Farm Sta
NW3 . . . . 12 C1
Chalk Hill Rd W6 . 39 C2

Chalkwell Ho 10
E1 . . . . 32 C3
Challenge Cl
NW10 . . . . 21 A4
Challenger Ho 7
E14 . . . . 33 A2
Challice Way 3 SW2 74 B3
Challoner Cres
W14 . . . . 140 C1
Challoner Mans
W14 . . . . 140 C1
Challoner St W14 140 C1
Chalmers Ho 15
SW11 . . . . 59 B4
Chalmer's Wlk 14
SE17 . . . . 48 A4
Chalner Ho SW2 . . 74 C3
Chaloner Ct SE1 . 137 B4
Chalsey Lodge
SE4 . . . . 66 B3
Chalsey Rd SE4 . . 66 B3
Chalton St NW1 . . 83 B1
Chamberlain Cotts
SE5 . . . . 48 C2
Chamberlain Ho 6
E1 . . . . 32 B2
Chamberlain St 7
NW1 . . . . 12 B1
Chamberlayne Mans
8 NW10 . . . . 22 C2
Chamberlayne Rd
NW10 . . . . 22 B4
Chambers La NW10 . 9 B1
Chambers Rd N7 . . 14 A4
Chambers St
SE16 . . . . 139 C3
Chamber St E1 . . 125 A4
Chambon Pl 7
W6 . . . . 38 C2
Chambord Ho 24
E2 . . . . . . 24 B2 99 A3
Chambord St E2 . 24 B2 99 A3
Champion Gr SE5 . 63 C4
Champion Hill SE5 63 C4
Champion Pk SE5 . 48 C4
Champlain Ho 20
W12 . . . . 30 A2
Chancel Ct W1 . . 119 B4
Chancellor Gr
SE21 . . . . 75 B1
Chancellor Ho
South Kensington
SW7 . . . . 129 A2
20 Wapping E1 . . 32 A1
Chancellor Pas
E14 . . . . 33 C1
Chancellors' Rd
W6 . . . . 39 B1
Chancellors St W6 . 39 B1
Chancellors Wharf 21
 . . . . 39 B1
Chancel St SE1 . . 122 A1
Chancery Bldgs 14
E1 . . . . 32 B2
Chancery Ho
WC2 . . . . 107 B3
Chancery La EC4 . 107 B2
Chancery Lane Sta
WC1 . . . . 107 B3
Chancery Mews
SW17 . . . . 72 A2
Chance St
E2 . . . . . . 24 B1 98 C2

Chandler Ave E16 . 35 C4
Chandlers Mews
E14 . . . . 41 C4
Chandler St E1 . . . 32 A1
Chandlers Way 11
SE24 . . . . 75 A4
Chandler Way
SE15 . . . . 49 B3
Chandlery Ho 23
E1 . . . . 111 B1
Chandos Pl WC2 . 120 A3
Chandos Rd
Cricklewood NW2 . 9 C3
Old Oak Comm
NW10 . . . . 21 A1
Stratford New Town
E15 . . . . 19 C3
Chandos St W1 . . 104 B3
Chandos Way NW11 2 A3
Change Alley EC3 109 C1
Channel Gate Rd
NW10 . . . . 21 A2
Channel Ho E14 . . 33 A4
Channel Sea Bsns Ctr
E15 . . . . 27 C3
Channelsea Rd
E15 . . . . 27 C4
Channing Jun Sch
N6 . . . . 3 C3
Chantrey Rd SW9 . 62 B4
Chantry Cl W9 . . . 23 B1
Chantry Cres NW10 8 B2
Chantry Sq W8 . . 128 A1
Chantry St N1 . . . 86 B3
Chant Rd E15 . . . 19 C1
Chant Sq E15 . . . . 19 C1
Chapel Cl NW10 . . 8 B2
Chapel Ct SE1 . . 137 B4
Chapel House St
E14 . . . . 42 A2
Chapel Mkt N1 . . 85 C2
Chapel Pl
Islington N1 . . . . 85 C2
Marylebone W1 . 104 A1
3 Shoreditch
EC2 . . . . 24 A2 98 A3
Chapel Side W2 . . 114 A3
Chapel St
Paddington NW1 . 102 A3
Westminster SW1 . 131 C3
Chapleton Ho
SW2 . . . . 62 C2
Chaplin Cl SE1 . . 136 A4
Chaplin Ho 6
SW9 . . . . 62 C3
Chaplin Rd NW2 . . 8 C2
Chaplow Cl SW6 . 166 C1
Chapman Ho
26 Stepney E1 . . 32 A3
West Norwood
SE27 . . . . 75 A1
Chapman Rd E9 . . 18 B2
Chapmans Park Ind
Est NW10 . . . . . . 8 B2
Chapman Sq
SW19 . . . . 69 C2
Chapman St E1 . . 32 A2
Chappell Ho SW1 . 147 B3
Chapter III 10 SW4 73 B3
Chapter House & Pyx
Chamber SW1 . . 134 A2
Chapter Rd
Kennington SE17 . 150 B1
Willesden NW2 . . . 8 C3

Chapter St SW1 . . 147 B3
Chara Pl W4 . . . . 45 C4
Charcot Ho SW15 . 56 B1
Charcroft Ct 11
W14 . . . . 39 C4
Chard Ho 7 N7 . . . 5 B2
Chardin Ho 30
SW9 . . . . 173 C4
Chardin Rd 6 W4 . 38 A2
Chardmore Rd N16 . 7 C3
Charecroft Way
W12 . . . . 39 C4
Charfield Ct W9 . . 88 B1
Charford Rd E16 . . 35 C4
Chargrove Cl
SE16 . . . . 40 C4
Charing Cross
SW1 . . . . 120 A2
Charing Cross Hospl
W6 . . . . 39 C1
Charing Cross Rd
WC2 . . . . 105 C2
Charing Cross Sta
SW1 . . . . 120 B2
Chariot Cl 3 E3 . . 26 C4
Charlbert Ct NW8 . 80 A2
Charlbert St NW8 . 80 A2
Charles Allen Ho
EC1 . . . . 95 C4
Charles Auffray Ho 30
E1 . . . . 32 B4
Charles Barry Cl
SW4 . . . . 61 B4
Charles Burton Ct
E5 . . . . 18 A4
Charles Coveney Rd
SE15 . . . . 49 B2
Charles Darwin Ho 8
E2 . . . . 25 A2
Charles Dickens Ho 1
E2 . . . . 25 A2
Charles Dickens Mus
The WC1 . . . . . . 95 A1
Charles Dickens Prim
Sch SE1 . . . . . . 136 C3
Charles Edward
Brooke Sch 11
SW9 . . . . 48 A2
Charles Flemwell
Mews 7 E16 . . . 35 C1
Charles Haller St 2
SW2 . . . . 74 C4
Charles Harrod Ct
SW13 . . . . 47 B4
Charles Hobson Ho 8
NW10 . . . . 21 B3
Charles Hocking Ho
3 W3 . . . . 37 B4
Charles II Pl SW3 . 144 C1
Charles II St SW1 . 119 B2
Charles La NW8 . . 80 A2
Charles Lamb Ct
N1 . . . . 86 B2
Charles Mackenzie Ho
7 SE16 . . . . 153 C4
Charles Rowan Ho
WC1 . . . . 95 B3
Charles Sq N1 . . . 97 C3
Charles St
Barnes SW13 . . . 46 A1
Mayfair W1 . . . . 118 A2

Charles St continued
8 Upper Holloway
N19 . . . . 5 A3
Charleston St
SE17 . . . . 151 A3
Charles Townsend Ho
EC1 . . . . 96 A2
Charles Utton Ct
E8 . . . . 16 C4
Charlesworth Ho 6
E14 . . . . 33 C3
Charleville Ct
SW5 . . . . 140 C1
Charleville Mans
W14 . . . . 140 B1
Charleville Rd
W14 . . . . 140 C1
Charlotte Ct 16
W6 . . . . 38 C2
Charlotte Despard
Ave SW11 . . . . . 169 C3
Charlotte Ho 12
W6 . . . . 39 B1
Charlotte Mews
Marylebone W1 . . 105 A4
North Kensington
W10 . . . . 30 C3
West Kensington
W14 . . . . 140 A4
Charlotte Pl
Marylebone W1 . . 105 A3
Westminster SW1 . 146 C3
Charlotte Rd
Barnes SW13 . . . . . 46 B2
Shoreditch
EC2 . . . . . . 24 A1 98 A2
Charlotte Row
SW4 . . . . 61 B4
Charlotte Sharman
Prim Sch SE11 . 136 A1
Charlotte Sq 6
TW10 . . . . 54 B1
Charlotte St W1 . 105 A4
Charlotte Terr N1 . 85 A3
Charlton Ct
25 Hackney E2 . . . 24 B4
2 Kentish Town
N7 . . . . 13 C3
Charlton Ho
5 Brentford
TW8 . . . . 44 A4
Somers Town NW1 . 93 B4
Charlton King's Rd
NW5 . . . . 13 C3
Charlton Pl N1 . . . 86 A2
Charlton Rd NW10 . 21 A4
Charlton Terr
SE11 . . . . 163 C3
Charlton Way SE10,
SE3 . . . . 53 A2
Charlwood Ho
Richmond TW9 . . . . 45 A3
1 Streatham SW2 . 74 B3
Westminster SW1 . 147 B3
Charlwood Pl
SW1 . . . . 147 A3
Charlwood Rd
SW15 . . . . 57 C4
Charlwood St
SW1 . . . . 147 A2
Charlwood Terr 5
SW15 . . . . 57 C3
Charman Ho
18 London SW2 . . . 62 C1

Charman Ho continued
South Lambeth
SW8 . . . . 162 A2
Charmian Ho 19
N1 . . . . 24 A3
Charmouth Ct
TW10 . . . . 54 B2
Charmouth Ho
SW8 . . . . 162 C2
Charnock Ho 22
W12 . . . . 30 A2
Charnwood Gdns
E14 . . . . 41 C2
Charrington Ho 45
E1 . . . . 25 B1
Charrington St
NW1 . . . . 83 B2
Charter Bldgs 14
SE10 . . . . 52 A2
Charter Ct
Finsbury Pk N4 . . . . 5 C3
Marylebone W1 . . 102 B3
Charter Ho WC2 . . 106 B1
Charterhouse Bldgs
EC1 . . . . 96 C1
Charterhouse Mews
EC1 . . . . 108 B4
Charterhouse Rd
E8 . . . . 16 C3
Charterhouse Sq
EC1 . . . . 108 B4
Charterhouse Square
Sch The EC1 . . . 108 B4
Charterhouse St
EC1 . . . . 108 A3
Charterhouse Works
SW18 . . . . 59 B3
Charteris Rd
Finsbury Pk N4 . . . . 5 C3
Kilburn NW6 . . . . . 23 B4
Charteris Sp Ctr
NW6 . . . . 23 C4
Charter Sch The
SE24 . . . . 63 C2
Chartes Ho SE1 . . 138 B2
Chartfield Ave
SW15 . . . . 57 B2
Chartfield Sq
SW15 . . . . 57 C2
Chartham Ct 12
SW9 . . . . 62 C4
Chartham Gr SE27 . 75 A1
Chartham Ho SE1 137 C2
Chart House The 5
E14 . . . . 42 A1
Chartridge SE17 . . 48 C4
Chart St N1 . . . . . . 97 C4
Chartwell 3
SW19 . . . . 69 C3
Chase Ct SW3 . . . 130 C1
Chase Ctr The
NW10 . . . . 20 C2
Chaseley St E14 . . . 33 A3
Chasemore Ho
SW6 . . . . 154 B2
Chase Rd NW10 . . . 20 C1
Chase Road Trad Est
NW10 . . . . 20 C1
Chase The SW4 . . . 61 A4
Chater Ho 6 E2 . . . 25 C2
Chatfield Rd SW11 . 59 B4
Chatham Ct SW11 160 B2
Chatham Ho 7
SE5 . . . . 49 A1
Chatham Pl E9 . . . 17 B2

Chatham Rd SW11 . 60 B2
Chatham St SE17 . 151 C4
Chatsworth Ct
Brondesbury NW2 . . . 9 C2
Clapton Pk E5 . . . . 17 C4
Earl's Ct W8 . . . . . 141 B4
Chatsworth Est E5 . 17 C4
Chatsworth Gdns
W3 . . . . 28 A1
Chatsworth Lo 1
W4 . . . . 37 C1
Chatsworth Rd
Brondesbury NW2 . . . 9 C2
Chiswick W4 . . . . . 45 B4
Clapton Pk E5 . . . . 17 C4
Chatsworth Way
SE27 . . . . 75 B1
Chattenden Ho 9
N4 . . . . 6 C4
Chatterton Ct TW9 . 44 B1
Chatterton Rd N4 . . 6 A1
Chatto Rd SW11 . . . 60 B2
Chaucer Ave TW9 . . 44 C1
Chaucer Ct 17 . . . .
Chaucer Dr SE1 . . 153 A3
Chaucer Ho SW1 . 146 C1
Chaucer Rd
Acton W3 . . . . 28 B1
Herne Hill SE24 . . . 63 A2
Chauldon Ho EC1 . . 97 C3
Cheadle Ct NW8 . . . 89 C2
Cheadle Ho 11
E14 . . . . 33 B3
Cheam St 6 SE15 . . 65 A4
Cheapside EC2 . . . 109 A1
Chearsley SE17 . . . 151 A4
Cheddington Ho 7
E2 . . . . 24 C4
Chedworth Cl E16 . . 35 B3
Chedworth Ho 2
E5 . . . . 7 C2
Cheering La E15 . . . 19 C1
Cheesemans Terr
W14 . . . . 140 C1
Chelmer Rd E9 . . . . 17 C3
Chelmsford Cl W6 . . 47 C4
Chelmsford Ho 5
N7 . . . . 14 B4
Chelmsford Sq
NW10 . . . . 22 B4
CHELSEA 144 C1
Chelsea Acad
SW10 . . . . 157 A1
Chelsea Barracks
SW1 . . . . 145 C1
Chelsea Bridge
SW1 . . . . 160 A4
Chelsea Bridge Rd
SW1 . . . . 145 C1
Chelsea Cl SW10 . . 157 A3
Chelsea Cloisters
SW3 . . . . 144 B3
Chelsea Coll of Arts
SW1 . . . . 148 A2
Chelsea Cres
Brondesbury NW2 . . 10 B2
Chelsea SW10 . . . 167 A3
Chelsea Ct SW3 . . 159 B4
Chelsea Emb
SW3 . . . . 158 C3
Chelsea Farm Ho
SW10 . . . . 157 C3
Chelsea Gate
SW1 . . . . 145 C1

Chelsea Gdns
SW1 . . . . 145 C1
Chelsea Harbour
Design Ctr
SW10 . . . . 167 A4
Chelsea Harbour Dr
SW10 . . . . 167 A4
Chelsea Harbour Pier
SW10 . . . . 167 B4
Chelsea Ind Coll
SW6 . . . . 156 A1
Chelsea Lo SW1 . . 159 A4
Chelsea Manor Ct
SW3 . . . . 158 B4
Chelsea Manor Gdns
SW3 . . . . 144 B1
Chelsea Manor St
SW3 . . . . 144 B1
Chelsea Manor
Studios SW3 . . . 144 B1
Chelsea Park Gdns
SW3 . . . . 157 B4
Chelsea Physic Gdn
SW1 . . . . 158 C3
Chelsea Reach Twr
SW10 . . . . 157 B2
Chelsea Sp Ctr
SW3 . . . . 144 B1
Chelsea Sq SW3 . . 143 C1
Chelsea Stud Tours &
Mus SW3 . . . . . . 158 B3
Chelsea Twrs
SW3 . . . . 158 B3
Chelsea &
Westminster Hospl
SW10 . . . . 157 A3
Chelsfield Ho
SE17 . . . . 152 A3
Chelsfield Point 3
E9 . . . . 17 C1
Chelsham Ho 1
SW4 . . . . 61 C4
Chelsham Rd SW4 . 61 C4
Cheltenham Pl
10 Acton W3 . . . . 28 B1
Acton W3 . . . . 37 B4
1 South Acton W3 . 37 A4
Cheltenham Rd
SE15 . . . . 65 B2
Cheltenham Terr
SW3 . . . . 145 A2
Chelverton Ct
SW15 . . . . 57 C3
Chelverton Rd
SW15 . . . . 57 C3
Chelwood NW5 . . . 12 C3
Chelwood Ct
SW11 . . . . 167 C4
Chelwood Gdns
TW9 . . . . 44 C1
Chelwood Ho W2 . 101 C1
Chenies Ho W2 . . . 114 A4
Chenies Mews
WC1 . . . . 93 B1
Chenies Pl NW1 . . . 83 C2
Chenies St WC1 . . 105 B4
Chenies The NW1 . . 83 C2
Cheniston Gdns
W8 . . . . 128 A2
Chepstow Cl
SW15 . . . . 58 A2
Chepstow Cres
W11 . . . . . . 31 C2 113 B4
Chepstow Ct
W11 . . . . . . 31 C2 113 B4

Chepstow Pl
W2 . . . . . . 31 C2 113 C4
Chepstow Rd W2 . . 31 C3
Chepstow Villas
W11 . . . . . . 31 C2 113 B4
Chequers Ct EC1 . . 97 B1
Chequers Ho NW8 . 90 A2
Chequer St EC1 . . . 97 A1
Cherbury Ct N1 . . . 87 C1
Cherbury St N1 . . . 87 C1
Cheriton Ho E5 . . . 17 A3
Cheriton Sq SW17 . 72 C2
Cherry Ct 7 W3 . . . 28 C1
Cherry Ct
Acton W3 . . . . 29 A1
5 Rotherhithe
SE16 . . . . 33 A1
Cherry Garden Ho 6
SE16 . . . . 40 A4
Cherry Garden Sch 5
SE16 . . . . 153 C3
Cherry Garden St
SE16 . . . . 40 A4
Cherry Laurel Wlk
SW2 . . . . 62 B1
Cherry Tree Cl 1
E9 . . . . 25 B4
Cherry Tree Ct
1 Camden Town
NW1 . . . . 13 B1
5 Peckham SE15 . . 50 A2
Cherry Tree Dr
SW16 . . . . 74 A1
Cherrytree Ho 8
W10 . . . . 22 C2
Cherry Tree Ho
SE14 . . . . 51 B1
Cherry Trees Sch The
3 E3 . . . . 26 C2
Cherry Tree Terr
SE1 . . . . 138 B4
Cherry Tree Wlk
EC1 . . . . 97 A1
Cherrywood Cl E3 . 26 A2
Cherrywood Dr
SW15 . . . . 57 C2
Chertsey Ct SW14 . 55 A4
Chertsey Ho 1
E2 . . . . 24 B2 98 C3
Cherwell Ho NW8 . . 89 C1
Cherwell Mews
SW11 . . . . 60 A4
Cheryls Cl SW6 . . . 166 B4
Chesham Cl SW1 . . 131 B1
Chesham Ct SW18 . 71 C4
Chesham Flats
W1 . . . . 117 C4
Chesham Ho SW1 . 131 B1
Chesham Mews
SW1 . . . . 131 B2
Chesham Pl SW1 . . 131 B1
Chesham St SW1 . . 131 B1
Cheshire St
E2 . . . . 24 B1 99 A2
Chesholm Rd N16 . . 7 A1
Cheshunt Ho 3
NW6 . . . . 78 A3
Chesil Ct
11 Bethnal Green
E2 . . . . 25 B3
Chelsea SW3 . . . . 158 B4
Chesilton Rd SW6 164 C4
Chesney Ct W9 . . . 23 C1
Chesney Ho SE13 . . 67 C3
Chesney St SW11 . 169 B3

Chessington Ho 19 .... 171 B2
Chesson Rd W14 ...... 155 A4
Chessum Ho E8 .... 16 C2
Chester Ave TW10 ..... 54 B1
Chester Cl
  Barnes SW13 .... 57 A4
  Knightsbridge
  SW1 .... 132 A3
  4 Richmond TW10 ... 54 B1
Chester Close N
  NW1 .... 92 B4
Chester Close S
  NW1 .... 92 B3
Chester Cres E8 ...... 16 B3
Chester Ct
  Bermondsey SE8 .... 40 C1
  4 Camberwell SE5 .. 48 C3
  Gospel Oak NW5 .... 12 C4
  Regent's Pk NW1 ... 92 B3
Chesterfield Ct
  SE13 .... 67 B4
Chesterfield Gdns
  Greenwich SE10 .... 52 C3
  Mayfair W1 .... 118 A2
Chesterfield Gr
  SE22 .... 64 B2
Chesterfield Hill
  W1 .... 118 A2
Chesterfield Ho
  Highgate N6 .... 3 C3
  Mayfair W1 .... 117 C2
Chesterfield Rd
  W4 .... 45 B4
Chesterfield St
  W1 .... 118 A2
Chesterfield Way
  SE15 .... 50 B3
Chesterford Gdns
  NW3 .... 11 A4
Chester Gate NW1 ... 92 B3
Chester Ho
  Dartmouth Pk N19 ... 4 A2
  1 Deptford SE8 .... 51 B4
Chesterman Ct
  W4 .... 46 A3
Chester Mews
  SW1 .... 132 A2
Chester Pl NW1 ..... 92 A4
Chester Rd
  Dartmouth Pk N19 ... 4 A2
  Regent's Pk NW1 ... 92 A3
Chester Row SW1 ... 145 C4
Chester Sq SW1 .... 146 A4
Chester Sq Mews
  SW1 .... 132 A1
Chester St
  Bethnal Green
  E2 .... 24 C1 99 C2
  Westminster SW1 .. 131 C2
Chester Terr NW1 ... 92 A4
Chesterton Cl
  SW18 .... 58 C2
Chesterton Ct 3 ... 37 A3
Chesterton Ho
  5 Battersea
  SW11 .... 59 C4
  3 Kensal Town
  W10 .... 31 A4
Chesterton Prim Sch
  SW11 .... 169 B3
Chesterton Rd
  W10 .... 31 A4
Chesterton Sq
  W8 .... 141 B3
Chester Way SE11 .. 149 C3

Chestnut Alley
  SW6 .... 155 A3
Chestnut Ave 11
  SW14 .... 55 C4
Chestnut Cl
  New Cross Gate
  SE14 .... 51 B2
  1 Stoke Newington
  N16 .... 6 C2
Chestnut Ct SW6 ... 155 A4
Chestnut Ct 2 SW12 .. 72 C3
Chestnut Grove Sch
  6 SW12 .... 72 C3
Chestnut Ho
  1 Acton W4 .... 38 A2
  Brockley SE4 ...... 66 B4
  7 Maitland Pk
  NW3 .... 12 B2
  West Norwood
  SE27 .... 75 B1
Chestnut Mews
  SW14 .... 55 B3
Chestnut Rd SE21,
  SE27 .... 75 B1
Chestnuts The 1
  N5 .... 15 A4
Chettle Cl SE1 ..... 137 B2
Chetwode Ho NW8 .. 90 A2
Chetwode Rd
  SW17 .... 72 B1
Chetwynd Rd NW5 ... 4 A1
Cheval Ct SW15 .... 57 A3
Cheval Pl SW7 ..... 130 B2
Cheval St E14 ...... 41 C3
Chevening Rd
  Cubitt Town SE10 .. 43 B1
  Kilburn NW6 .... 23 A4
Cheverell Ho 28
  E2 .... 24 C3
Cheverton Rd N19 ... 4 C3
Chevet St E9 .... 18 A3
Chevington NW2 .... 10 B2
Cheviot Ct 12 SE14 .. 50 B3
Cheviot Gate NW2 ... 1 A2
Cheviot Gdns NW2 ... 1 A2
Cheviot Ho N16 .... 7 B3
Chevron Cl E16 .... 35 C3
Cheylesmore Ho
  SW1 .... 146 A2
Cheyne Ct SW3 .... 158 C4
Cheyne Gdns
  SW3 .... 158 B3
Cheyne Mews
  SW3 .... 158 B3
Cheyne Pl SW3 .... 158 C4
Cheyne Row SW3 .. 158 B3
Cheyne Wlk
  SW10 .... 157 B2
Cheyney Ho 2 E9 .. 17 C2
Chichele Mans
  NW2 .... 9 C3
Chichele Rd NW2 ... 9 C3
Chicheley St SE1 .. 135 A4
Chichester Ct 2
  NW1 .... 13 B1
Chichester Ho
  Kilburn NW6 .... 23 C3
Chichester Rd
  Bayswater W2 ..... 100 B4
  Kilburn NW6 .... 23 C3
Chichester Rents
  WC2 .... 107 B2
Chichester St
  SW1 .... 147 A1
Chichester Way
  E14 .... 42 C2

Chicksand Ho 14
  E1 .... 111 B4
Chicksand St E1 ... 111 A3
Chicksand Street
  E1 .... 111 B3
Chiddingstone
  SE13 .... 67 B2
Chiddingstone St
  SW6 .... 165 C2
Chigwell Ct 13 E9 .. 18 A2
Chigwell Hill E1 .... 32 A2
Chiham Ho 8
  SE15 .... 50 B4
Chilcombe Ho 8
  SW15 .... 68 C3
Chilcot Cl 13 E14 .. 34 A3
Childebert Rd
  SW17 .... 73 A2
Childeric Prim Sch
  SE14 .... 51 A3
Childeric Rd SE14 .. 51 A3
Childerley St
  SW6 .... 164 A4
Childers St SE8 .... 51 B4
Child La SE10 ..... 43 B3
Childrens House
  Upper Sch 18 N1 .. 16 A2
CHILD'S HILL 1 C2
  Child's Hill Prim Sch
Child's Mews
  SW5 .... 141 C3
Child's Pl SW5 .... 141 C3
Child's St SW5 .... 141 C3
Child's Wlk SW5 ... 141 C3
Chilham Ct SW9 .... 62 C4
Chilham Ho SE1 ... 137 C2
Chillington Dr
  SW11 .... 59 C3
Chillingworth
  N7 .... 14 C3
Chiltern Ct
  13 Deptford SE14 .. 50 B3
  Marylebone NW1 .. 91 A1
Chiltern Ho
  Camberwell SE17 .. 48 C4
  4 Kensal Town
  W10 .... 31 A4
  5 Stamford Hill N16 .. 7 B3
Chiltern Rd E3 ..... 26 C1
Chiltern St W1 .... 103 B4
Chilton Gr SE8 .... 41 A2
Chiltonian Mews
  SE13 .... 67 C2
Chilton St
  E2 .... 24 B1 99 A2
Chilver St SE10 .... 43 B1
Chilworth Ct 8
  SW19 .... 69 C3
Chilworth Mews
  W2 .... 101 B1
Chilworth St W2 ... 101 A1
Chimney Ct 2 E1 ... 32 A1
China Ct 1 E1 .... 32 A1
China Hall Mews 5
  SE16 .... 40 B3
China Mews 17
  SW2 .... 74 B4
Chindit Ho 11 N16 .. 7 B3
Ching Ct WC2 ..... 106 A1
Chinnocks Wharf
  E14 .... 33 A2
Chipka St E14 ..... 42 B4
Chipley St SE14 ... 51 A4

Chippendale Ho
  SW1 .... 146 B1
Chippenham Gdns
  NW6 .... 23 C2
Chippenham Mews
  W9 .... 23 C1
Chippenham Rd
  W9 .... 23 C1
Chipstead Ho 4
  SW2 .... 74 A3
Chipstead St SW6 . 165 C2
Chirk Ct SE4 ...... 51 B1
Chisenhale Prim Sch
  38 E3 .... 26 A3
Chisenhale Rd E3 .. 26 A3
Chisholm Ct 1
  W4 .... 38 C1
Chisholm Rd 3
  TW10 .... 54 B1
Chisledon Wlk E9 .. 18 B2
Chislehurst Rd
  TW10 .... 54 A2
Chislet 6 NW5 .... 12 C2
Chiswell St
  Barbican EC1 ..... 109 B4
  Camberwell SE5 ... 48 C3
CHISWICK 38 B1
Chiswick & Bedford
  Park Prep Sch 13
  W4 .... 37 C2
Chiswick Common Rd
  W4 .... 38 A2
Chiswick Green
  Studios 1 W4 ..... 37 B2
Chiswick High Rd
  W4 .... 38 A2
Chiswick High Road
  (North Circular Rd)
  Chiswick W4 ...... 36 C1
  Chiswick Ho W4 ... 45 C4
Chiswick La W4 .... 38 B1
Chiswick La S W4 .. 46 B4
Chiswick Mall W4 .. 46 B4
Chiswick Park Sta
  W4 .... 37 A2
Chiswick Pier W4 .. 46 B3
Chiswick Quay W4 .. 45 B2
Chiswick Rd W4 .... 37 B2
Chiswick Rdbt W4 .. 36 C1
Chiswick Sch W4 ... 45 A4
Chiswick Sta W4 ... 45 A3
Chiswick Staithe
  W4 .... 45 B2
Chiswick Terr 6
  W4 .... 37 B2
Chiswick Village
  W4 .... 45 A4
Chiswick Wharf
  W4 .... 46 B4
Chitty St W1 ...... 105 A4
Chivalry Rd SW11 .. 60 A2
Chiveston 2
  SW19 .... 69 C3
Chobham Acad
  E15 .... 19 B3
Chobham Gdns
  SW19 .... 69 C2
Chobham Rd E15 .. 19 C3
Cholmeley Cres N6 .. 4 A4
Cholmeley Lo N6 ... 4 A3
Cholmeley Pk N6 ... 4 A4

Cholmley Gdns
  NW6 .... 10 C3
Cholmondeley Ave
  NW10 .... 21 C3
Chopin's Ct 1 E1 .. 32 A1
Chopwell Cl E15 ... 19 C1
Choumert Gr SE15 . 49 C1
Choumert Mews
  SE15 .... 49 C1
Choumert Rd SE15 . 49 B1
Choumert Sq 4
  SE15 .... 49 C1
Chow Sq 2 E8 .... 16 B3
Chrisp Ho SE10 .... 53 A4
Chrisp St E14 ..... 34 A3
Chris Pullen Wy 6
  N7 .... 14 A2
Christ Church
  Tump 54 A4
Christchurch Ave
  NW6 .... 10 A1
Christ Church
  Bentinck CE Prim
  Sch NW1 .... 102 B3
Christ Church CE
  Prim Sch
  Battersea SW11 ... 60 A4
  Brondesbury NW6 .. 10 B1
  Cubitt Town SE10 .. 43 A1
  12 Greenwich SE10 .. 43 A1
Christchurch CE Sch
  E1 .... 111 A3
Christ Church Ct
  1 Brondesbury Pk
  NW6 .... 10 A1
  Harlesden NW10 .. 53 A4
Christchurch Hill
  NW3 .... 11 C4
Christchurch Ho 2
  SW2 .... 74 A3
Christchurch Pas
  NW3 .... 2 B1
Christ Church Prim
  Sch
  Camberwell
  SW9 .... 173 C4
  Hampstead NW3 ... 2 C1
  SW3 .... 158 C4
Christchurch Rd
  Mortlake SW14 .... 55 B2
  Streatham SW2 .... 74 C3
Christ Church Sch
  NW1 .... 92 B3
Christchurch Sq 2
  E9 .... 25 B4
Christchurch St
  SW3 .... 158 C4
Christ Church
  Streatham CE Prim
  Sch 18 SW2 ...... 74 B3
Christchurch Terr
  SW3 .... 158 C4
Christchurch Way
  SE10 .... 43 A1
Christian Ct SE16 .. 33 B1
Christian St E1 .... 111 C1
Christie Ct
  Maitland Pk NW3 .. 12 A3
  2 Upper Holloway
  N19 .... 5 A2
Christie Ho 2
  SE10 .... 43 B1
Christie Rd E9 ..... 18 A2
Christina Sq N4 .... 6 A3

Christina St
EC2 . . . . .24 A1 **98** A2

Christopher Boone's Almshouses
SE13 . . . . .67 C3

Christopher Cl
SE16 . . . . .40 C4

Christopher France Ho 1 . . . . .26 A2

Christopher Hatton Prim Sch EC1 . . . . **95** B1

Christopher Lo 2
N6 . . . . .4 C4

Christopher Pl
NW1 . . . . **93** C3

Christopher St EC2 **97** C1

Christ's Sch TW10 . .54 C2

Christ the King RC Prim Sch 7 N4 . . . . .5 B2

Christ the King Sixth Form Coll SE13 . . .67 C4

Chryssell Rd SW9 . .163 C1

Chubworthy St 5 SE14 . . . . .51 A4

Chudleigh Rd
Hampstead NW6 . . . . . .9 C1
London SE4 . . . . .66 C2

Chudleigh St E1 . . . .32 C3

Chumleigh Gdns
SE5 . . . . .49 A4

Chumleigh St SE5 . . .49 A4

Church App SE21 . . .75 C1

Church Ave
Camden Town
NW1 . . . . .13 A2
Mortlake SW14 . . . . . .55 C4
Stockwell SW8 . . . . **128** A4

Church Cres E9 . . . .17 C1

Churchcroft Cl
SW12 . . . . .72 C4

Church Ct
Holborn EC4 . . . . . . **107** C1
Rotherhithe SE16 . . . .41 B4

Churchdale Ct 1
W4 . . . . .37 A1

CHURCH END NW10 . .8 B3

Church Entry EC4 . **108** B1

Church Estate Almshouses 4
TW9 . . . . .54 B3

Churchfield Ho
W2 . . . . **89** B1

Churchfield Mans 5
SW6 . . . . **165** A1

Churchfield Rd
W3 . . . . .28 B1

Churchfields SE10 . .52 B4

Church Garth 4
N19 . . . . .4 C2

Church Gate SW6 . . .58 A4

Church Gn 4
SW9 . . . . **173** C2

Church Gr SE13 . . . .67 A2

Church Ho EC1 . . . . **96** B2

Churchill Ct
Finsbury Pk N4 . . . . . . .5 C4
Peckham SE5 . . . . . . .49 C1
Willesden NW2 . . . . . . .9 A3

Churchill Gardens Prim Sch SW1 . . **147** A1

Churchill Gdns
SW1 . . . . **160** C4

Churchill Gdns Rd
SW1 . . . . **160** C4

Churchill Pl E14 . . . .34 A1

Churchill Rd
Gospel Oak NW5 . . . . .13 A4
Willesden NW2 . . . . . . .9 A2

Churchill Wlk E9 . . . .17 B3

Church Mead SE5 . . .48 B3

Churchmead Rd
NW10 . . . . .8 C2

Church Path W4 . . . .37 B3

Church Pl SW1 . . . **119** A3

Church Rd
Acton W3 . . . . .37 B4
Barnes SW13 . . . . . . .46 C2
24 Canonbury N1 . . . . .15 B2
Richmond TW10,
TW9 . . . . .54 A2
Willesden NW10 . . . . . .8 A1

Church Row NW3 . . .11 B4

Church St
Chiswick W4 . . . . .46 B4
Lisson Gr NW8 . . . . **90** A1

Church Street Est
NW8 . . . . **89** C1

Church Studios 1
NW1 . . . . .13 C2

Churchward Ho
Camberwell SE17 . . . .48 A4
West Kensington
SW5 . . . . **141** A1

Churchway NW1 . . . **93** C4

Churchyard Wlk
Barnes SW13 . . . . . . .46 C2
Canonbury N16 . . . . . .15 C4
Child's Hill NW2 . . . . . .1 B1
Dartmouth Pk N6 . . . . .3 C1

Churchyard Row
SE11 . . . . **150** B4

Churnfield 2 N4 . . . . .5 C2

Churston Cl 2
SW2 . . . . .74 C3

Churston Mans
WC1 . . . . **95** A1

Churton Pl
Brentford W4 . . . . .45 A4
Pimlico SW1 . . . . . . **147** A3

Churton St SW1 . . . **147** A3

Chute Ho W SW9 . . **173** B1

Chuter Ede Ho
SW6 . . . . **155** A3

Cicada Rd SW18 . . . .59 B2

Cicely Ho NW8 . . . . **79** C1

Cicely Rd SE15 . . . . .49 C2

Cinema Mus The 8
SE11 . . . . **150** A3

Cinnabar Wharf Central 11 E1 . . **125** C2

Cinnabar Wharf East 7 E1 . . . . **125** C2

Cinnabar Wharf West 17 E1 . . . . **125** C2

Cinnamon Cl 8
SE15 . . . . .49 A3

Cinnamon Row 3
SW11 . . . . .59 B4

Cinnamon St E1 . . . . .32 A1

Cinnamon Wharf
SE1 . . . . **139** A4

Circle Ho 14 E14 . . . .34 C3

Circle The SE1 . . . . **139** A4

Circus Lo NW8 . . . . **89** B4

Circus Mews W1 . . **102** C4

Circus Pl EC2 . . . . . **109** C3

Circus Rd NW8 . . . . **79** B1

Circus St SE10 . . . . .52 B3

Cirencester St
W2 . . . . **100** A4

Cissbury Ho 6
SE26 . . . . .76 C1

Citadel Pl SE11 . . . **148** C2

Citizen Ho N7 . . . . . .14 C4

Citizen Rd N7 . . . . . .14 C4

Citron Terr 4
SE15 . . . . .65 A4

Citrus Ho 4 SE8 . . . .41 B1

City Academy, Hackney The 2
E9 . . . . .17 B3

City Bsns Coll EC1 . . **96** B3

City Bsns Ctr 6 SE16 .40 B4

City Central Est
EC1 . . . . **97** A3

City Coll of London The WC1 . . . . . **107** A3

City Forum EC1 . . . **96** C4

City Garden Row
N1 . . . . **86** B1

City Gate E1 . . . . . .25 B1

City Harbour E14 . . .42 A3

City Heights Acad 22
SE22 . . . . .74 C3

City & Islington Coll
E1 . . . . .25 C1

City & Islington Coll (Ctr for Applied Sciences) EC1 . . . **96** A4

City & Islington Coll (Ctr for Bsns, Arts & Technology) 8
N7 . . . . .14 A4

City & Islington Coll (Ctr for Health, Social & Child Care) 7
N7 . . . . .14 B4

City & Islington Coll (Ctr for Lifelong Learning) 3 N4 . . . .6 A2

City Law Sch The
EC1 . . . . **107** A3

City Lights The 5
SE11 . . . . **149** C1

CITY OF LONDON 8 . . . . . . .122 B4

City of London Acad- Islington N1 . . . . . .86 C4

City of London Acad The SE1 . . . . . **153** C2

City of London Information Ctr 7
EC4 . . . . **108** B1

City of London Sch
EC4 . . . . **122** C4

City of London Sch for Girls EC2 . . . **109** A4

City of Westminster Coll W2 . . . . . **101** A4

City of Westminster Coll, Cosway Street 1 NW1 . . . . **102** B4

City of Westminster Coll, Maida Vale Ctr 1 W9 . . . . **88** C3

City of Westminster Coll, Queens Park Ctr 10 W9 . . . . .23 C2

City Rd EC1 . . . . . . **97** A4

City Thameslink Sta
EC4 . . . . **108** A1

City, University of London **96** A3

City Wlk SE1 . . . . . **138** A3

Clabon Mews
SW1 . . . . **130** C1

Clack St SE16 . . . . . .40 B4

Claire Ct NW2 . . . . . .10 A2

Claire Pl E14 . . . . . .41 C3

Clancarty Rd SW6 . **165** C1

Clandon Cl W3 . . . . .37 A4

Clandon St SE8 . . . . .51 C1

Clanfield Ho 9
SW15 . . . . .68 C3

Clanricarde Gdns
W2 . . . . . . .31 C2 **113** C3

CLAPHAM 61 A4

Clapham Common 61 A4

Clapham Common North Side SW4 . . . .61 B3

Clapham Common South Side SW4 . . . .61 B2

Clapham Common Sta
SW4 . . . . .61 B3

Clapham Common West Side
SW11, SW4, SW12 . . . . .60 C2

Clapham Computer & Secretarial Coll 2
SW11 . . . . .60 B2

Clapham Court Terr 2
SW4 . . . . .62 A2

Clapham Cres
SW4 . . . . .61 C3

Clapham Ct 3
SW4 . . . . .62 A2

Clapham High St
SW4 . . . . .61 C3

Clapham High Street Sta SW4 . . . . .61 C4

Clapham Junction Est
SW11 . . . . .60 A3

Clapham Junction Sta
SW11 . . . . .60 A4

Clapham L Ctr
SW4 . . . . .61 C3

Clapham Manor Ct 1
SW4 . . . . .61 B4

Clapham Manor Prim Sch 3 SW4 . . . .61 B4

Clapham Manor St
SW4 . . . . .61 B4

Clapham Mans
SW4 . . . . .61 A1

Clapham North Bsns Ctr 8 SW4 . . . .61 C4

Clapham North Sta
SW4 . . . . .62 A4

CLAPHAM PARK 61 C2

Clapham Park Rd
SW4 . . . . .61 C3

Clapham Park Terr 4
SW2 . . . . .62 A2

Clapham Rd
Brixton SW9 . . . . . . **173** A4
SW9 . . . . **163** A2

Clapham South Sta
SW4 . . . . .61 A2

Clapton Comm E5 . . . .7 C4

Clapton Girls' Acad
E5 . . . . .17 B4

CLAPTON PARK 17 C4

Clapton Pas E5 . . . . .17 B3

Clapton Sq E5 . . . . . .17 B3

Clapton Terr E5 . . . . . .7 C3

Clapton Way E5 . . . . .16 C4

Clara Grant Ho 10
E14 . . . . .41 C3

Clara Grant Prim Sch The 18 E3 . . . . . . .26 C1

Clare Ct WC1 . . . . . . **94** B3

Claredale Ho 1
E2 . . . . .25 A3

Claredale St E2 . . . . .24 C3

Clare Gdns W11 . . . .31 A3

Clare Ho
Bermondsey SE1 . . . **153** A2
6 Old Ford E3 . . . . . .26 B4

Clare La N1 . . . . .15 B1

Clare Lawn Ave
SW14 . . . . .55 C2

Clare Mews SW6 . . . .64 A1

Clare Mkt WC2 . . . **107** A1

Claremont 1
SW15 . . . . .58 A2

Claremont Cl
Finsbury N1 . . . . **85** C1
4 Streatham SW2 . .74 B3

Claremont Ct 1
W9 . . . . .23 B3

Claremont Gr W4 . . . .46 A3

Claremont Rd
Highgate N6 . . . . .4 B4
West Kilburn W9 . . . . .23 B3

Claremont Sq N1 . . . **85** B1

Claremont St SE10 . . .52 A4

Clarence Ave SW4 . . .61 C1

Clarence Cres
SW4 . . . . .61 C1

Clarence Ct 10
W6 . . . . .39 A2

Clarence Gate
NW1 . . . . **91** A2

Clarence Gate Gdns
NW1 . . . . **91** A1

Clarence Gdns
NW1 . . . . **92** B3

Clarence Ho SE17 . . .48 B4

Clarence Ho NW1 . . **119** A1

Clarence La SW15 . . .56 B1

Clarence Mews
Balham SW12 . . . . . . .73 A4
Hackney E5 . . . . .17 A3
1 Rotherhithe
SE16 . . . . .32 C1

Clarence Pl 22 E5 . . .17 A3

Clarence Rd
Brentford W4 . . . . .36 C1
Brondesbury NW6 . . . .10 B1
Greenwich SE8 . . . . . .52 A4
Lower Clapton E5 . . . .17 A4
Richmond TW9 . . . . . .44 C2

Clarence St 5
TW9 . . . . .54 A3

Clarence Terr
NW1 . . . . **91** A2

Clarence Way
NW1 . . . . .13 A1

Clarence Wlk 9
SW4 . . . . **172** A2

Clarendon Cl
Bayswater W2 . . . . . **116** A4
30 Hackney E9 . . . . .17 B1

Clarendon Cross
W11 . . . . .31 A2 **112** B3

Clarendon Ct
Paddington W9 . . . . . **89** A2
1 Richmond TW9 . . . .44 C2
Willesden NW2 . . . . . . .9 B1

Clarendon Dr SW15	57 B3
Clarendon Flats W1	**103** C1
Clarendon Gdns W9	89 A1
Clarendon Gr NW1	93 B4
Clarendon Ho NW1	83 A1
Clarendon Mews W2	116 A4
Clarendon Pl W2	116 A4
Clarendon Rd W11	31 A2 112 B3
Clarendon Rise SE13	67 B3
Clarendon St SW1	**146** B2
Clarendon Terr W9	89 A2
Clarendon Wlk 11 W11	31 A3
Clare Ho E3	26 B4
Clare La N1	15 B1
Clare Lawrence Ct 4 SW11	59 C4
Clare Mkt WC2	**107** A1
Clare Rd	
New Cross Gate SE14	51 B2
Willesden NW10	8 C1
Clare St E2	25 A3
Clareville Ct 7 SW7	143 A3
Clareville Gr SW7	143 A3
Clareville Grove Mews SW7	143 A3
Clareville St SW7	143 A3
Clarewood Ct W1	102 C3
Clarewood Wlk SW9	62 C3
Clarges Ho W1	118 B2
Clarges Mews W1	118 A2
Clarges St W1	118 B2
Clariat Ct W3	36 C4
Claribel Rd SW9	48 A1
Claridge Ct SW6	164 C3
Clarissa Ho 7 E14	34 A3
Clarissa St E8	24 B4
Clarke Ho 2 SW4	61 B4
Clarke Path N16	7 C3
Clarkes Mews W1	103 C4
Clark Ho SW10	156 C2
Clarkson Rd E16	35 B3
Clarkson Row NW1	82 C1
Clarkson St E2	25 A2
Clark's Pl EC2	110 A1
Clark St E1	32 B4
Classic Mans 13 E9	17 B1
Classinghall Ho 14 SW15	69 C3
Claude Rd SE15	50 A1
Claude St E14	41 C2
Claudia Jones Way SW2	62 A1
Claudia Ho N19	70 A3
Clavell St 8 SE10	52 B4
Claverdale Rd SW2	74 C4
Clavering Ave SW13	47 A4
Clavering Ho SE13	67 C3
Clavering Pl 6 SW12	60 C1
Claverton St SW1	147 A1
Clave St E1	32 B1

Claxton Gr W6	39 C1 140 A1
Claybank Gr SE13	67 A4
Claybrook Rd W6	47 C4
Claydon SE17	150 C4
Clayhall Ct 20 E3	26 B3
Claylands Pl SW8	163 B2
Claylands Rd SW8	163 A3
Claypole Rd E15	27 B3
Clayponds Ave TW8	36 A2
Clayponds Hospl W5	36 A2
Clayponds La TW8	36 A1
Clays Ct N16	7 B3
Clay St W1	103 A3
Clayton Cres N1	84 C3
Clayton Ho 2 E9	17 B1
Clayton Mews SE10	52 C2
Clayton Rd SE15	49 C2
Clayton St SE11	163 B4
Clearbrook Way 13 E1	32 B3
Clear Water Ho 9 TW10	54 A2
Clearwater Terr 4 W11	39 C4
Clearwell Dr W9	88 B1
Cleaver Ho 6 NW3	12 B1
Cleaver Sq SE11	149 C1
Cleaver St SE11	149 C2
Cleeve Ho 15 E2	24 A2 98 B3
Cleeve Way SW15	68 B4
Cleeve Workshops 14 E2	24 A2 98 B3
Clegg St 19 E1	32 A1
Cleland Ho 19 E2	25 B3
Clematis St W12	29 C2
Clem Atlee Par SW6	155 A3
Clem Attlee Ct SW6	155 A3
Clemence St E14	33 B4
Clement Attlee Ho NW10	8 B4
Clement Ave SW4	61 C3
Clement Cl	
Acton W4	37 C2
Hampstead NW6	9 B1
Clement Danes Ho 6 W12	30 A3
Clement Ho	
16 Deptford SE8	41 A2
17 North Kensington W10	30 B4
Clements Ave 1 E16	35 C2
Clements Inn WC2	107 A1
Clements Inn Pas WC2	107 A1
Clement's La EC2, EC4	123 C4
Clement's Rd SE16	40 A3
Clemson Ho 9 E8	24 B4
Clennam St SE1	137 A4
Clenston Mews W1	102 C2
Clent Ho 5 N16	7 B3
Cleopatra's Needle WC2	**120** C3

Clephane Rd 13 N1	15 B2
Clephane Rd N N1	15 C2
Clephane Rd S N1	15 C2
Clere Pl EC2	97 C2
Clere St EC2	97 C2
CLERKENWELL	96 A1
Clerkenwell Cl EC1	95 C1
Clerkenwell Gn EC1	96 A1
Clerkenwell Parochial CE Prim Sch SW1	95 B3
Clerkenwell Rd EC1	96 A1
Clerkenwell Workshops EC1	95 C2
Clermont Rd E9	25 B4
Clevedon Cl N16	7 B1
Clevedon Mans NW5	12 C4
Clevedon Mans	
Battersea SW11	168 A4
Dulwich SE21	75 C1
Cleve Ho NW6	11 A1
Cleveland Ave W4	38 B2
Cleveland Ct W1	93 A1
Cleveland Gdns	
Barnes SW13	46 B1
Paddington W2	100 C1
Cleveland Gr 32 E1	25 B1
Cleveland Mans	
3 Brixton SW9	163 B1
4 Shoreditch NW6	10 B1
Paddington W9	23 C1
Cleveland Mews W1	104 C4
Cleveland Pl SW1	119 A2
Cleveland Rd	
Barnes SW13	46 B1
Islington N1	15 C1
14 South Acton W4	37 B3
Cleveland Row SW1	119 A1
Cleveland Sq W2	100 C1
Cleveland St W1	92 C1
Cleveland Terr W2	101 A1
Cleveland Way 1 E1	25 B1
Clevendon Cl N16	7 B1
Cleverly Cotts W12	29 B1
Cleverly Est W12	29 C2
Cley Ho SE4	65 C3
Clichy Ho 22 E1	32 B4
Clifden Mews E5	17 C3
Clifden Rd E5	17 C3
Cliff Ct 14 NW1	13 C2
Cliffe Ho 4 SE10	43 B1
Clifford Ave	
Mortlake SW14	45 B1
Mortlake SW14, TW9	55 A4
Clifford Ct	
Bayswater W2	100 A3
Wandsworth SW18	71 C4
Willesden NW10	8 A4
Clifford Dr SW9	63 A3
Clifford Gdns NW10	22 B3
Clifford Haigh Ho SW6	47 C3
Clifford Ho W14	**140** C3

Clifford's Inn Pas EC4	**107** B1
Clifford St W1	118 C3
Clifford Way NW10	8 B4
Clifford Rd N1	16 A2
Cliff Rd NW1	13 C2
Cliff Road Studios 13 NW1	13 C2
Cliffsend Ho 25 SW9	173 C3
Cliff Terr SE8	51 C1
Cliffview Rd SE13	66 C4
Cliff Villas NW1	13 C2
Cliff Wlk E16	35 B4
Clifton Ave W12	29 B1
Clifton Cres SE15	50 A3
Clifton Ct	
Finsbury Pk N4	5 C2
Paddington NW8	89 B2
Peckham SE15	50 A3
Putney SW15	57 C2
Clifton Gate SW10	**156** C4
Clifton Gdns	
Chiswick W4	37 C2
Paddington W9	88 C1
Clifton Gr E8	16 C2
Clifton Hill NW8	78 C3
Clifton Ho E2	24 B1 98 C2
Clifton Mans 4 SW9	62 C3
Clifton Pl	
Paddington W2	101 C1
Rotherhithe SE16	40 B4
Clifton Rd	
Harlesden NW10	21 C3
Newham E16	35 A4
Paddington W9	89 A2
Clifton Rise SE14	51 A3
Clifton St EC2	24 A1 98 A1
Clifton Terr N4	5 C2
Clifton Villas W9	100 C4
Clifton Way SE15	50 B3
Climsland Ho SE1	121 C2
Clinch Ct 11 E16	35 C4
Clinger Ct N1	24 A4
Clink Prison Mus The SE1	123 B2
Clink St SE1	**123** B2
Clinton Rd E3	26 A2
Clipper Appts 12 SE10	52 C1
Clipper Cl 3 SE16	40 C4
Clipper Ho E14	42 B1
Clipper Way SE13	67 B3
Clipstone Ho 10 SW15	56 C2
Clipstone Mews W1	104 C4
Clipstone St W1	104 C4
Clissold Cres N16	15 C4
Clissold Ct N4	6 B2
Clissold Ho 5 N16	6 C3
Clissold Rd N16	6 C1
Clitheroe Rd SW9	172 B1
Clive Ct W9	89 A2
Cliveden Ho SW1	145 B4
Cliveden Pl SW1	145 B4
Clive Ho	
8 Clapham SW8	**171** B2
Greenwich SE10	52 B4
Clive Rd SE21, SE27	75 C1

Cloak La EC4	**123** B4
Clochar Ct NW10	21 B4
Clock Ho N16	7 B4
Clockhouse Cl SW19	69 B2
Clockhouse Pl SW15	58 A1
Clockhouse The EC2	**109** A2
Clockmakers Mus	
EC2	**109** A2
Clock Tower Mews N7	87 A3
Clock Tower Pl 1 N7	14 A2
Clock View Cres 2 N7	14 A2
Cloister Rd	
Acton W3	28 B4
Child's Hill NW2	1 B2
Cloisters Ct N6	4 C4
Cloisters The 1 SW9	173 C3
Clonbrock Rd N16	16 A4
Cloncurry St SW6	47 C1
Clone Ct 4 W12	38 A3
Clonmel Rd SW6	165 A4
Clonmore St SW18	70 B3
Clorane Gdns NW3	1 C1
Close The	
Lewisham SE3	52 C1
Mortlake TW9	55 A4
Cloth Ct EC1	108 B3
Cloth Fair EC1	108 B3
Clothier St E1	110 B2
Cloth St EC1	108 C4
Cloudesdale Rd SW17	73 A2
Cloudesley Mans N1	85 C3
Cloudesley Pl N1	85 C3
Cloudesley Rd N1	85 C3
Cloudesley Sq N1	85 C3
Cloudesley St N1	85 C3
Clove Cres E14	34 C2
Clovelly Ct NW2	9 B3
Clovelly Ho W2	100 C2
Clovelly Rd W4	37 C4
Clovelly Way E1	32 B3
Clover Mews SW3	**159** A4
Clowes Ho 3 SW4	62 A3
Cloysters Gn E1	125 B2
Club Row E2	24 B1 98 C2
Clunbury St N1	87 C1
Clunie Ho SW1	131 A2
Cluny Mews SW5	141 B3
Cluny Pl SE1	138 A2
Cluse Ct N1	86 C2
Clutton St E14	34 A4
Clyde Ct NW1	83 C2
Clyde Flats SW6	154 C2
Clydesdale Gdns TW10	55 A3
Clydesdale Ho 4 W11	31 B3
Clydesdale Rd W11	31 B3
Clyde St SE8	51 B4
Clynes Ho 3 E2	25 C2
Clyro Ct N4	5 B3
Clyston St SW8	**171** A2

Coach & Horses Yd
W1 . . . . .118 C4
Coach House La
Highbury N5 . . . . .15 A4
Wimbledon SW19 . . . .69 C1
Coach House Mews
SE23 . . . . .65 C1
Coach House Yd 5
NW3 . . . . .11 C4
Coachmaker Mews 4
W9 . . . . .62 A4
Coalbrook Mans 3
SW12 . . . . .73 A3
Coaldale Wlk SE21 . .75 B4
Coalecroft Rd
SW15 . . . . .57 B2
Coalport Ho SE11 . .149 B4
Coatbridge Ho 8
N1 . . . . .14 B1
Coates Ave SW18 . .60 A1
Coates Ct NW3 . . . .12 A3
Coate St E2 . . . . . . .24 C3
Coates Wlk TW8 . . . .36 A1
Cobalt Pl SW11 . . . .167 C3
Cobbett St SW8 . . . .163 A1
Cobble La N1 . . . . . .15 A1
Cobble Mews N4,
N5 . . . . .6 B1
Cobbold Ct SW1 . . .147 B4
Cobbold Ind Est
NW10 . . . . .8 B2
Cobbold Rd
Bedford Pk W12 . . . .38 B4
Willesden NW10 . . . . .8 B2
Cobb's Hall 1
SW6 . . . . .47 C4
Cobb St E1 . . . . . . .110 C3
Cobden Bldgs
WC1 . . . . .94 C4
Cobden Ho
11 Bethnal Green
E2 . . . . .24 C2
Regent's Pk NW1 . . . .82 C2
Cobham Cl SW11 . . .60 A1
Cobham Mews 3
NW1 . . . . .13 C1
Coborn Mews 9
E3 . . . . .26 B2
Coborn Rd E3 . . . . . .26 B2
Coborn St E3 . . . . . .26 B2
Cobourg Prim Sch
SE5 . . . . .49 B4
Cobourg Rd SE5 . . . .49 B4
Cobourg St NW1 . . . .93 A3
Coburg Cl SW1 . . . .147 A4
Coburg Cres SW2 . . .74 C3
Coburg Dwellings 11
E1 . . . . .32 B2
Coca-Cola London
Eye SE1 . . . . .134 C4
Cochrane Cl NW8 . . .79 C1
Cochrane Ho 15
E14 . . . . .41 C4
Cochrane Mews
NW8 . . . . .79 C1
Cochrane St NW8 . . .79 C1
Coci Ho W14 . . . . . .141 A3
Cockburn Ho
SW1 . . . . .147 C1
Cock Hill E1 . . . . . . .110 B3
Cock La EC1 . . . . . . .108 B3
Cockpit Yd WC1 . . . .107 A4

Cockspur Ct SW1 . .119 C2
Cockspur St SW1 . .119 C2
Coda Ctr The
SW6 . . . . .164 B4
Codicote Ho 22
SE8 . . . . .40 C2
Codicote Terr N4 . . . .6 B2
Codling Cl 12 E1 . . .125 C2
Codrington Ct 8
SE16 . . . . .33 A1
Codrington Ho 7
E1 . . . . .25 A1
Codrington Mews
W11 . . . . .31 A3
Cody Rd E16 . . . . . . .27 C1
Coffey St SE8 . . . . . .51 C3
Cohen Lo E5 . . . . . . .18 A3
Coin St SE1 . . . . . . .121 B2
Coity Rd NW5 . . . . . .12 C2
Cokers La SE21 . . . .75 C3
Coke St E1 . . . . .111 B2
Colas Mews 7
NW6 . . . . .23 C4
Colbeck Mews
SW5 . . . . .142 B3
Colberg Pl N16 . . . . . .7 B4
Colbert 1 SE5 . . . . .49 B2
Colborne Ho 8
E14 . . . . .33 C2
Colchester Ho 7
SW8 . . . . .171 B2
Colchester St E1 . . .111 A2
Coldbath Sq EC1 . . . .95 B2
Coldbath St SE13 . . .52 A1
Cold Blow La SE14 . .50 C4
Coldharbour E14 . . . .34 B1
Coldharbour Ind Est
SE5 . . . . .48 B1
Coldharbour La
SW9 . . . . .63 A4
Coldharbour Pl
SE5 . . . . .48 C1
Coldstream Gdns
SW18 . . . . .58 B1
Colebeck Mews
N1 . . . . .15 A2
Colebert Ave E1 . . . .25 B1
Colebert Ho 21 E1 . .25 B1
Colebrook Ct
SW19 . . . . .69 C4
Colebrook Ct
SW3 . . . . .144 B3
Colebrooke Pl N1 . . .86 B3
Colebrooke Row
Islington N1 . . . . .86 A4
Islington N1 . . . . .86 A2
Colebrook Ho 8
E14 . . . . .34 A3
Coleby Path 4
SE5 . . . . .48 C3
Colechurch Ho 9
SE1 . . . . .153 B1
Colefax Bldg 12
E1 . . . . .111 C2
Coleford Rd SW18 . .59 B2
Colegrave Prim Sch
E15 . . . . .19 C3
Colegrave Rd E15 . . .19 C3
Colegrove Rd
SE15 . . . . .49 B4
Coleherne Ct
SW10 . . . . .142 B1
Coleherne Mans
SW5 . . . . .142 B2

Coleherne Mews
SW10 . . . . .142 A1
Coleherne Rd
SW10 . . . . .142 A1
Colehill Gdns
SW6 . . . . .164 A3
Colehill La SW6 . . .164 B3
Cole Ho SE1 . . . . . .135 C3
Coleman Ct SW18 . .70 C4
Coleman Fields
N1 . . . . .87 A4
Coleman Mans N19 . .5 A4
Coleman Rd SE5 . . .49 A3
Coleman St EC2 . . . .109 B2
Coleman Street Bldgs
EC2 . . . . .109 B2
Colenso Rd E5 . . . . .17 B4
Coleraine Rd SE3 . . .53 B4
Coleridge Cl SW8 . .170 B1
Coleridge Ct W14 . . .39 C3
Coleridge Gdns
NW6 . . . . .11 B1
Coleridge Ho
Pimlico SW1 . . . . . . .147 A1
Walworth SE17 . . . . .151 A2
Coleridge Prim Sch
N8 . . . . .4 C4
Coleridge Rd N4,
N7 . . . . .5 C2
Coleridge Sq
SW10 . . . . .156 C2
Coles Ct SW11 . . . .167 C3
Coleshill Flats
SW1 . . . . .145 C3
Cole St SE1 . . . . . . .137 A3
Colestown St 4
SW11 . . . . .168 B2
Colet Gdns W14 . . . .39 C2
Colet Ho SE17 . . . . .150 B1
Colette Ct 5 SE16 . .40 C4
Coley St WC1 . . . . . .95 A1
Colfe & Hatchcliffe's
Glebe SE13 . . . . .67 A2
Colgate Ho SE13 . . . .52 A1
Colin Blanchard Ho
SE4 . . . . .51 C1
Colin Ct SW16 . . . . . .73 C2
Coinette Rd SW15 . .57 B3
Colin Rd NW10 . . . . . .8 C2
Colinsdale N1 . . . . . .86 A3
Colin Winter Ho 44
E1 . . . . .25 B1
Coliston Pas SW18 . .70 C4
Coliston Rd SW18 . . .70 C4
Collamore Ave
SW18 . . . . .72 A3
Collard Pl NW1 . . . . .13 A1
College App SE10 . . .52 B4
College Cl E5 . . . . . .17 B3
College Cres NW3 . .11 C2
College Cross N1 . . .14 C1
College Ct
Chelsea SW3 . . . . . . .145 A1
7 Hammersmith
W6 . . . . .39 B1
Hampstead NW3 . . . .12 A2
College Francais
Bilingue de Londres
SW5 . . . . .142 A2
College Gdns
Dulwich SE21 . . . . . . .76 A3
Upper Tooting
SW17 . . . . .72 A2
College Gr NW1 . . . .83 B4

College Green Ct
SW9 . . . . .63 A4
College Hill EC4 . . . .123 A4
College La NW5 . . . .13 A4
College Mews 3
SW18 . . . . .59 A2
COLLEGE PARK 22 A2
College Park Cl
SE13 . . . . .67 C3
College Park Sch 20
W2 . . . . .100 C2
College Pl
Camden Town
NW1 . . . . .83 A3
Chelsea SW10 . . . . .156 C2
College Rd
Dulwich SE19,
SE21 . . . . .76 A2
Kensal Green
NW10 . . . . .22 B3
College St EC4 . . . . .123 A4
College Terr E3 . . . . .26 B2
Collent Ho 9 E9 . . . .17 B2
Collent St E9 . . . . . . .17 B2
Collerston Ho
SE10 . . . . .43 B1
Collette Ho N16 . . . . .7 B3
Collett Ho SE13 . . . .67 A4
Collett Rd SE16 . . . .139 C2
Colley Ho 8 N7 . . . . .13 C3
Collier St N1 . . . . . . .84 C1
Collingbourne Rd 9
W12 . . . . .30 A1
Collingham Coll
SW5 . . . . .142 B3
Collingham Gdns
SW5 . . . . .142 B3
Collingham Pl
SW5 . . . . .142 B4
Collingham Rd
SW5 . . . . .142 B4
Collington St 7
SE10 . . . . .42 C1
Collingwood Ho
27 Bethnal Green
E1 . . . . .25 A1
Marylebone W1 . . . .104 C4
Collingwood St 1
E1 . . . . .25 A1
Collins Ct E8 . . . . . . .16 C2
Collins Ho
3 Cubitt Town
SE10 . . . . .43 B1
4 Poplar E14 . . . . . . .34 B2
Collinson Ct SE1 . . .136 C3
Collinson Ho 14
SE15 . . . . .49 C3
Collinson St SE1 . . .136 C3
Collinson Wlk
SE1 . . . . .136 C3
Collins Rd N5, N16 . .15 B4
Collins Sq SE3 . . . . . .53 B1
Collins St SE3 . . . . . .53 A1
Collins Yd N1 . . . . . . .86 A3
Collison Pl N16 . . . . . .7 A3
Coll of Arms EC4 . . .122 C4
Coll of Law The
(Bloomsbury)
EC1 . . . . .105 B4
Coll of Law The
(Moorgate) EC1 . . . . .97 B1
Coll of NW London
NW6 . . . . .23 C4
Coll of NW London
(Willesden Centre)
NW10 . . . . .9 A2
Coll of Optometrists
The SW1 . . . . .120 C2

Coll Sharp Ct 6
E2 . . . . .24 B2 98 C3
Coll's Rd SE15 . . . . . .50 B2
Collyer Pl SE15 . . . . .49 C2
Colmans Wharf 5
E14 . . . . .34 A4
Colmar Ct 3 E1 . . . . .25 C1
Colmore Mews
SE15 . . . . .50 A2
Colnbrook St SE1 . .136 A2
Colne Ho NW8 . . . . . .89 C1
Colne Rd E5 . . . . .18 A4
Cologne Rd SW11 . . .59 C3
Colombo St SE1 . . . .122 A1
Colomb St SE10 . . . .43 A1
Colonades The 4
SE5 . . . . .48 C2
Colonial Dr W4 . . . .37 B2
Colonnade WC1 . . . . .94 B1
Colonnade Ho SE3 . .53 B1
Colonnades The 8
W2 . . . . .17 A2
Colonnade The 12
SE8 . . . . .41 B2
Colorado Bldg 9
SE13 . . . . .52 A2
Colosseum Terr
NW1 . . . . .92 B2
Colour Ho SE1 . . . . .138 C3
Colstead Ho 22 E1 . .32 A3
Colston Rd SW14 . . .55 B3
Colthurst Cres N4 . . . .6 B2
Coltman Ho SE10 . . .52 B4
Coltman St E14 . . . . .33 A4
Columba Ho SE14 . . .51 B2
Columbas Dr NW3 . . .2 C3
Columbia Ho 3
E3 . . . . .26 C2
Columbia Point 7
SE16 . . . . .40 B3
Columbia Prim Sch 50
E2 . . . . .24 B2 99 A4
Columbia Rd
9 Hackney E2 . . . . . .24 C3
Shoreditch
E2 . . . . .24 B2 98 C4
Columbia Road
Flower Mkt
E2 . . . . .24 B2 99 A4
Colverson Ho 14
E1 . . . . .32 B4
Colvestone Cres
E8 . . . . .16 B3
Colvestone Prim Sch
E8 . . . . .16 B3
Colville Gdns W11 . .31 B3
Colville Ho
13 Bethnal Green
E2 . . . . .25 B3
Notting Hill W11 . . . . .31 B3
Colville Mews
W11 . . . . .31 B3
Colville Pl W1 . . . . .105 A3
Colville Prim Sch 5
W11 . . . . .31 B3
Colville Rd
Notting Hill W11 . . . . .31 B3
Notting Hill W11 . . . . .31 B3
South Acton W3 . . . . .37 A3
Colville Sq W11 . . . .31 B3
Colville Terr W11 . . .31 B3
Colwall Ho 18
SW9 . . . . .173 A1
Colwell Rd SE22 . . . .64 B2
Colwick Cl N6 . . . . . . .4 C4
Colwith Rd W6 . . . . . .47 B4
Colworth Gr SE17 . .151 A3

Colwyn Ho SE1...... **135** B1
Colyton Rd SE22....**65** A2
Combe Ave SE3 ....53 B3
Combedale Rd
SE10 ....43 C1
Combe Ho
Mortlake SW14 ....45 B1
20 Paddington W2 ..31 C4
Combemartin Rd
SW18 ....70 A3
Combe Mews
SE3 ....53 B3
Comber Gr SE5.....48 B3
Comber Grove Prim
Sch 48 B3
Comber Ho SE5 ....48 B3
Combermere Rd
SW9 ....62 B4
Combe Tho NW1 ...92 B3
Com Coll Hackney
The 11 E8.......25 A4
Comeragh Mews
W14 ....140 B1
Comeragh Rd
W14 ....140 B1
Comerford Rd SE4..66 B3
Comet PI SE8 ......51 C3
Comet St SE8 ......51 C3
Comfort St
SE15 ....49 A4
Comins Ho SE1 ....61 B2
Commercial Rd
Stepney E1........32 B3
Whitechapel E1 ...111 C2
Commercial St
E1 ....110 C4
Commercial Way
Peckham SE15 .....49 C3
Wembley NW10 ....20 A3
Commerell PI
SE10 ....43 B1
Commerell St
SE10 ....43 B1
Commodity Quay
E1 ....125 A3
Commodore Ct
SE8 ....51 C2
Commodore Ho 7
E14 ....34 B2
Commodore St E1..26 A1
Commondale
SW15 ....57 B4
Common Rd SW13..56 C4
Common View
SW15 ....57 B4
Commonwealth Ave
12 W12...........30 A2
Commonwealth Ho
WC1 ....106 B2
Community La N7..13 C3
Community Rd
E15 ....19 C3
Comodore Ho
SW18 ....59 B3
Compania Bldg 12
E1 ....32 C2
Compass Ct SE1..124 C1
Compass Ho
Bayswater W2 ....100 A1
London SE8 ....52 A1
Compass Point 10
E14 ....33 C2
Compass Sch 12
SE16 ....40 A3
Compayne Gdns
NW6 ....11 A1

Compton Ave
Islington N1........15 A2
London N6 ....3 A4
Compton CI
Camberwell SE15...49 B3
Regent's Pk NW1...92 B3
Compton Cres W4...45 B4
Compton Ho
SW11 ....168 A4
Compton Pas EC1...96 B2
Compton PI WC1 ...94 A2
Compton Rd
Islington N1........15 A2
Kensal Green
NW10 ....22 C2
Compton St EC1....96 B2
Compton Terr N1...15 A2
Comus Ho SE17 ...152 A3
Comus PI SE17 ....152 A3
Comyn Rd SW11....60 A3
Comyns CI E16.....35 B4
Conant Ho SE11 ...48 A4
Conant Mews 1
E1 ....125 B4
Concanon Rd SW2,
SW4 ....62 B3
Concepts Univ Coll
London SW8 ....162 A1
Concert Hall App
SE1 ....121 C1
Concord Bsns Ctr
W3 ....28 A4
Concorde Way
SE16 ....40 C2
Concordia Wharf 10
E14 ....34 B1
Condell Rd SW8 ..171 A3
Conder St E14.....33 A3
Condray PI SW11 .158 A1
Conduit Ct WC2 ..120 A4
Conduit Ho SE10 ..52 C2
Conduit Mews
W2 ....101 B1
Conduit Pas W2 ..101 B1
Conduit PI W2 ....101 B1
Conduit St W1 ....118 C4
Conewood St N5 ...15 A4
Coney Acre SE21...75 B3
Coney Way SW8 ..163 A3
Congers Ho SE8 ...51 C3
Congress Ho WC1.105 C2
Congreve Ho 10
N16.............16 A3
Congreve St SE17 152 A3
Conifer Ct 23
SW19 ....69 C3
Conifer Gdns
SW16 ....74 B1
Conifer Ho SE4....66 B3
Coniger Rd SW6 ..165 B2
Coningham Ct
SW10 ....157 A2
Coningham Mews
W12 ....29 C1
Coningham Rd
W12 ....39 A4
Coningsby Rd N4...6 A4
Conington Rd
SE13 ....52 B1
Conisbrough NW1..82 C3
Coniston NW1 ....92 C4
Coniston CI
Barnes SW13......46 B3
Chiswick W4.......45 B3

Coniston Ct
Marylebone W2 ...102 B1
6 Rotherhithe
SE16 ....40 C4
Conistone Way N7..14 A1
Coniston Ho
10 Bow E3 ....26 B2
12 Camberwell SE5..48 B3
Coniston Wlk E9 ..17 B3
Conlan St W10 ....23 A1
Conley Rd NW10...8 A2
Conley St SE10 ....43 A1
Connaught Ave
SW14 ....55 B3
Connaught CI W2..102 B1
Connaught Ho
College Pk NW10...22 A2
Mayfair W1.......118 A3
Connaught House Sch
W2 ....102 B1
Connaught La N4...5 C4
Connaught Mans
Battersea SW11 ...168 B3
3 Brixton SW9.....62 C3
15 Canonbury N16..15 C4
Fulham SW6......164 A4
Connaught Rd
Finsbury Pk N4 ....5 C4
Harlesden NW10...21 A3
5 Richmond TW10..54 B2
Connaught Sq
W2 ....102 C1
Connaught St W2 .102 B1
Connaught Works
E3 ....26 A4
Connell Ct 6
SE14 ....50 C4
Connor Ct SW11 ..170 A3
Connor St E9.......25 C4
Conrad Ho
6 Limehouse
SE16 ....33 A2
South Lambeth
SW8 ....162 A2
5 Stoke Newington
N16.............16 A3
Conrad Twr W3 ...37 A3
Consort Ho W2 ...114 B3
Consort Lo NW8 ...80 C3
Consort Rd SE15...50 A1
Cons St SE1 ......135 C4
Constable Ct 11
SE16 ....40 A1
Constable Ho
Millwall E14 ......41 C4
Primrose Hill NW3 ..12 B1
Constable Wlk
SE21 ....76 A1
Constant Ho 20
E14 ....34 A2
Constantine Ho
SW2 ....75 A3
Constantine Rd
NW3 ....12 A4
Constitution Hill
Hill 132 B4
Consul Ho 5 E3 ...26 C1
Content St SE17 ..151 B3
Convent Gdns
W11 ....31 B3
Convent of Jesus &
Mary Language Coll
NW10 ....21 B4

Convent of Jesus &
Mary RC Inf Sch 3
NW2 ....9 B2
Conway Gr W3 ....28 C4
Conway Ho
Chelsea SW3 .....145 A1
3 Millwall E14 ....42 A2
8 Streatham SW2 .74 A3
Conway Mews W1..92 C1
Conway St E1......32 C1
Conway St W1 .....92 C1
Conybeare NW3 ...12 A1
Conyer St E3 ......26 A3
Cookham Cres
SE16 ....40 C4
Cookham Ho
E2 ....24 B1 98 C2
Cook's Rd
Camberwell SE17..48 A4
Stratford Marsh
E15 ....27 A3
Coomassie Rd W9 .23 B1
Coombe Ho N7 ....13 C3
Coombe Rd W4 ....38 A1
Coombs St N1 .....86 B1
Coomer Mews
SW6 ....155 A3
Coomer PI SW6 ..155 A3
Cooperage The
SE1 ....124 C1
Cooper CI SE1 ...135 C3
Cooper Ho NW8 ...89 B1
Cooper Rd NW10...8 C3
Coopersale Rd E9 .17 C3
Coopers CI E1 .....25 B1
Coopers Ct
8 Acton W3 ....28 B1
3 Tower Hamlets E3..26 B2
Coopers La NW1 ...83 C1
Cooper's Lo SE1 ..138 C4
Cooper's Rd SE1 ..153 A2
Cooper's Row
EC3 ....124 C4
Coopers Yd N1 ....15 A1
Cope Ho EC1 ......97 A3
Copeland Dr E14 ..41 C2
Copeland Ho
SE11 ....135 A1
Copeland Ind Pk 7
SE15 ....49 C1
Copeland Rd SE15..50 A1
Copenhagen Gdns
W4 ....37 C4
Copenhagen Ho
N1 ....85 B3
Copenhagen PI
E14 ....33 B3
Copenhagen Prim Sch
N1 ....84 C3
Copenhagen St
N1 ....84 C3
Cope PI W8 ....127 B1
Cope St SE16 .....40 C2
Copford Wlk N1 ...86 C4
Copleston Rd
SE15 ....64 B4
Copley CI 15 SE17..48 A4
Copley St E1 ......32 C4
Coppedhall 2
SE21 ....75 C2
Copperas St SE8 ..52 A4
Copperbeech CI
NW3 ....11 C3
Copper Box Arena
E15 ....18 C2

Copperfield Ho 12
SE1 ....139 B3
Copperfield Rd E3..33 A4
Copperfields Ct
W3 ....36 C4
Copperfield St
SE1 ....136 C4
Copper Mews 13
W4 ....37 B3
Copper Row SE1 ..124 C1
Copperwood PI 17
SE10 ....52 B2
Coppice Dr SW15..57 A1
Coppin Ho SW2 ...75 A3
Coppock CI SW11 168 A1
Copse Ct SW15 ...58 A2
Copthall Ave EC2 .109 C2
Copthall Bldgs
EC2 ....109 C2
Copthall Ct EC2 ..109 C2
Copthorne Ave
SW12 ....73 C4
Coptic St WC1 ....106 A3
Corбет Ct SE15 ....33 C4
Coral Apts 6 E16..35 C2
Coral Ho 6 E1 ....26 A1
Coral Row
SW11 ....59 B4
Coral St SE1 .....135 C3
Coram Ho
Bloomsbury WC1 ..94 A2
4 Chiswick W4 ....38 A1
Coram Mans WC1 .94 C1
Coram St WC1 ....94 A2
Corben Ms SW8 ..171 A2
Corbet Ct EC3 ....109 C1
Corbet Ho N1 .....85 B3
Corbet PI E1 .....110 C4
Corbett Ho SW10 156 C4
Corbett's La SE16..40 B2
Corbetts Pas 8
SE16 ....40 B2
Corbidge Ct SE8 ..52 A4
Corbridge Cres E2..25 A3
Corbyn St N4, N19..5 A3
Corby Rd NW10 ...20 C3
Corby Way E3 .....26 C1
Cordelia CI SE24 ..63 A3
Cordelia Ho 26 N1..24 A3
Cordelia St E14 ...34 A3
Cording St E14 ....34 A4
Cordwainers Ct 19
E9 ....17 B1
Corelli Rd SE3 .....53 E1
Corfe Ho SW8 ....162 C2
Corfe Lodge 15
SE21 ....75 C2
Corfe Twr 6 W3 ...37 B4
Corfield St E2 .....25 A2
Coriander Ave E14 .34 C3
Coriander Ct SE1 139 A4
Corinne Rd N19 ...13 B4
Cork Sq E1 ....32 A1
Cork St Mews W1 118 C3
Cork St W1 ....118 C3
Corlett St NW1 ...102 A4
Cormont Rd SE5 ..48 A2
Cormorant
36 Deptford SE8 ...51 B4
13 Dulwich SE21 ..75 C2

Cornbury Ho **5**
SE8 . . . . .51 B4
Cornelia St N7 . . . .14 B2
Cornell Bldg **3**
E1 . . . . .111 B2
Corner Fielde
SW2 . . . . .74 B3
Corner House St
WC2 . . . . .120 A2
Cornerstone Ct **15**
E1 . . . . .24 C1 99 C1
Cornerways SW15 . .56 C3
Corney Rd W4 . . . . .46 A4
Corney Reach Way
W4 . . . . .46 A3
Cornflower Terr
SE22 . . . . .65 A1
Cornford Gr SW12 . .73 A2
Cornhill EC3 . . . . . .109 C1
Cornick Ho **7**
SE16 . . . . .40 A3
Cornish Ho
Brentford TW8 . . . . . .36 B1
7 Camberwell
SE17 . . . . .48 A4
Cornmill La SE13 . . .67 B4
Cornmow Dr NW10 . .8 C3
Cornwall Ave E2 . . .25 B2
Cornwall Cres
W11 . . . . .31 A3
Cornwall Flats
SE1 . . . . .135 C4
Cornwall Gdns
Kensington SW7 . . .128 B1
Willesden NW10 . . . . .9 A2
Cornwall Gdns Wlk
SW7 . . . . .128 B1
Cornwall Gr W4 . . . .38 A1
Cornwall Ho
Marylebone NW1 . . .91 A1
3 Putney SW15 . . .69 B4
Cornwallis Ct
SW8 . . . . .172 A4
Cornwallis Ho **2**
W12 . . . . .30 A2
Cornwallis Rd N19 . .5 A2
Cornwallis Sq
3 Finsbury Pk
N4 . . . . .5 C2
London N19 . . . . .5 A2
Cornwall Mans
Chelsea SW10 . . . .157 A2
Marylebone NW1 . . .91 A1
Cornwall Mews S
SW7 . . . . .128 C1
Cornwall Mews W
SW7 . . . . .128 B1
Cornwall Rd
Finsbury Pk N4 . . . . .5 C4
Lambeth SE1 . . . . . .135 C4
Cornwall Sq SE11 . .150 A2
Cornwall St **4** E1 . . .32 A2
Cornwall Terr
NW1 . . . . .91 A1
Cornwall Terrace
Mews NW1 . . . . . . .91 A1
Cornwood Dr E1 . . .32 B3
Coronation Ave **1**
N16 . . . . .16 B4
Coronation Ct **19**
W10 . . . . .30 A4
Coronet St
N1 . . . . .24 A2 98 A3

Corporation Row
EC1 . . . . .95 C2
Corporation St N7 . .14 A3
Corpus Christi RC
Prim Sch **13** SW2 . .62 B2
Corrance Rd SW2,
SW4 . . . . .62 A3
Corringham Ct
NW11 . . . . .1 C4
Corringham Ho **11**
E1 . . . . .32 C3
Corringham Rd
NW11 . . . . .1 C4
Corringway NW11 . . .2 A4
Corry Dr SW9 . . . . .63 A3
Corry Ho **2** E14 . . .34 A2
Corsham St N1 . . . .97 C3
Corsica St N5 . . . . .15 A2
Corsley Way E3 . . . .18 B2
Cortayne Rd SW6 . .165 A2
Cortis Rd SW15 . . . .57 A1
Cortis Terr SW15 . . .57 A1
Corunna Rd SW8 . .171 A4
Corunna Terr
SW8 . . . . .170 C4
Corvette Sq **5**
SE10 . . . . .52 C4
Coryton Path **9** W9 .23 B1
Cosbycote Ave
SE24 . . . . .63 B2
Cosgrove Ho **11**
E2 . . . . .24 C4
Cosmo Pl WC1 . . . .106 B4
Cosmur Cl W12 . . . .38 B3
Cossall Wlk SE15 . . .50 A2
Cossar Mews **10**
SW2 . . . . .62 C2
Cosser St SE1 . . . .135 B2
Costa St SE15 . . . . .49 C1
Coston Wlk **4**
SE4 . . . . .65 C3
Cosway Mans
NW1 . . . . .102 B4
Cosway St NW1 . . .102 B4
Cotall St E14 . . . . . .33 C4
Cotes Ho NW8 . . . . .90 A1
Cotham St SE17 . . .151 A3
Cotherstone Rd
SW2 . . . . .74 B3
Cotleigh Rd NW6 . . .10 C1
Cotman Cl SW15 . . .57 C2
Cotman Ho NW8 . . .80 A2
Cotrill Gdns E8 . . . .17 A2
Cotswold Ct EC1 . . .96 C2
Cotswold Gate NW2 . .1 A3
Cotswold Ho N16 . . .7 B3
Cotswold Mews
SW11 . . . . .167 C3
Cottage Gr SE5 . . . .48 C3
Cottage Grn SW9 . .62 A4
Cottage Pl SW3 . . .130 A1
Cottage Rd N7 . . . . .14 B3
Cottage St E14 . . . .34 A2
Cottages The SE1 . .134 C1
Cottage Wlk **2** N16 .7 B1
Cottenham Ho **3**
N19 . . . . .5 A2
Cottesbrook St **3**
SE14 . . . . .51 A3
Cottesloe Ho NW8 . .90 A2
Cottesloe Mews
SE1 . . . . .135 C2
Cottesmore Ct
W8 . . . . .128 B2
Cottesmore Gdns
W8 . . . . .128 B2

Cottingham Rd
SW8 . . . . .163 A2
Cottington St
SE11 . . . . .150 A2
Cotton Ave W3 . . . .28 C3
Cotton Ho
Bedford Pk W12 . . . .38 B4
3 Streatham
SW2 . . . . .74 B4
Cotton Row SW11 . .59 C4
Cotton's Gdns
E2 . . . . .98 B4
Cottons La SE1 . . . .123 C2
Cotton St E14 . . . . .34 B2
Cottrell Ct SE10 . . . .43 B2
Couchman Ho **8**
SW4 . . . . .61 B1
Coulgate St SE4 . . . .66 A4
Coulsdon Ho **9**
SW2 . . . . .74 A3
Coulson St SW3 . . .144 C2
Coulter Rd W6 . . . . .39 A3
Coulthurst Ho **10**
SE8 . . . . .51 B4
Coults Cres NW5 . . .3 C1
Councillor St SE5 . . .48 B3
Counter Ct SE1 . . . .123 B1
Counter St SE1 . . . .124 A1
Countess Rd NW5 . .13 B3
Countisbury Ho
SE26 . . . . .76 C1
County Gr SE5 . . . . .48 B2
County Ho
2 Herne Hill
SE24 . . . . .63 A3
3 South Lambeth
SW9 . . . . .173 B4
County St SE1 . . . . .137 A1
Courier Ho **17**
SW2 . . . . .74 C4
Courland Gr SW8 . .171 C3
Courland St SW8 . . .171 C3
Courtauld Ho **12**
E2 . . . . .24 C3
Courtauld Institute of
Art W1 . . . . .103 B2
Courtauld Inst of Art
WC2 . . . . .120 C4
Courtauld Rd N19 . . .5 A3
Courtenay Ave N6 . . .3 A4
Courtenay Sq
SE11 . . . . .149 B1
Courtenay St
SE11 . . . . .149 B2
Courtfield Gdns
SW5 . . . . .142 B3
Courtfield Ho EC1 . .107 B4
Courtfield Mews
SW7 . . . . .142 B3
Courtfield Rd
SW7 . . . . .142 C3
Courthill Rd SE13 . . .67 B3
Courthope Ho
5 Rotherhithe
SE16 . . . . .40 B3
South Lambeth
SW8 . . . . .162 A1
Courthope Rd
NW3 . . . . .12 B4
Court La SE21 . . . . .76 B4
Courtlands TW10 . . .54 C2
Courtlands Ave
SE12 . . . . .67 C1
Court Lane Gdns
SE21 . . . . .76 A4
Court Mans **8** SW6 .38 C2

Courtmead Cl
SE24 . . . . .63 B1
Courtnell St W2 . . . .31 C3
Courtney Ct N7 . . . .14 C3
Courtney Ho W14 . .126 B2
Courtney Rd N7 . . . .14 C3
Courtrai Rd SE23 . . .66 A1
Court Royal SW15 . .58 A2
Court St **3** E1 . . . . .32 A4
Courtville Ho **12**
W10 . . . . .23 A2
Court Way W3 . . . . .28 B4
Courtyard The
Fulham SW6 . . . . . .164 A3
Islington N1 . . . . .14 B1
13 Wandsworth
SW18 . . . . .59 C3
Cousin La EC4 . . . .123 B3
Couzens Ho **3** E3 . .33 B4
Coval Gdns SW14 . .55 A3
Coval La SW14 . . . . .55 A3
Coval Pas SW14 . . . .55 B3
Coval Rd SW14 . . . .55 B3
Covell Ct **16** SE8 . . .51 C3
Covent Garden Sta
WC2 . . . . .106 B1
Coventry Cl NW6 . . .23 C4
Coventry Rd E1, ...25 A1
Coventry St W1 . . . .119 B3
Coventry Univ London
EC2 . . . . .110 B3
Coverdale Rd
Brondesbury
NW2 . . . . .10 A2
Hammersmith W12 . .39 A4
Hampstead NW6 . . . .9 C1
Coverham Ho **5**
SE4 . . . . .65 C3
Coverley Cl E1 . . . . .111 C4
Coverley Point
SE11 . . . . .148 C3
Cowcross St EC1 . . .108 A4
Cowdenbeath Path
N1 . . . . .84 C4
Cowdray Hall Royal
Coll of Nursing
W1 . . . . .104 A2
Cowdray Ho **2**
SE22 . . . . .64 A4
Cowdry Rd E9 . . . . .18 B2
Cowley Rd
Brixton SW9 . . . . . .173 C4
East Acton W3 . . . . .29 B1
Mortlake SW14 . . . . .56 A4
Cowley St SW1 . . . .134 A1
Cowling Cl
W11 . . . . . .31 A1 112 A2
Cowper Ho
Pimlico SW1 . . . . . .147 C1
Walworth SE17 . . . .151 A2
Cowper Rd
Acton W3 . . . . .28 C1
Stoke Newington
N16 . . . . .7 A1
Cowper's Ct EC3 . . .109 C1
Cowper St EC1, EC2 .97 C2
Cowper Terr W10 . . .30 C4
Cowthorpe Rd
SW8 . . . . .171 C4
Cox Ho W6 . . . . . . .154 A4
Coxson Way SE1 . . .138 C3
Coysh Ct **8** SW15 . .58 A2
Crabtree Ct E3 . . . . .26 A3
Crabtree Hall SW6 . .47 B3
Crabtree La SW6 . . .47 C3

Craddock St NW5 . .12 C2
Cragie Ho SE1 . . . .153 A3
Craigleith SW15 . . . .57 C1
Craignair Rd SW2 . .74 C4
Craig's Ct SW1 . . . .120 A2
Craik Ct NW6 . . . . .23 B3
Crail Row SE17 . . . .151 C3
Cramer St W1 . . . . .103 C3
Crammond Cl W6 . .154 A3
Crampton Prim Sch
SE17 . . . . .150 B2
Crampton St SE17 . .150 C2
Cranbourn Alley
WC2 . . . . .119 C4
Cranbourne Ct
SW11 . . . . .158 B2
Cranbourne Rd
E15 . . . . .19 B4
Cranbourn Ho **6**
SE16 . . . . .40 A4
Cranbourn Pas **5**
SE16 . . . . .40 A4
Cranbourn St
WC2 . . . . .119 C4
Cranbrook NW1 . . . .83 A3
Cranbrook Ho **5**
E5 . . . . .17 A3
Cranbrook Rd
Chiswick W4 . . . . . . .38 A1
St Johns SE8 . . . . . .51 C2
Cranbrook St E2 . . . .25 C3
Cranbury Rd SW6 . .166 B1
Crandale Ho **8**
E5 . . . . .17 A3
Crandley Ct SE8 . . . .41 A2
Crane Ave W3 . . . . .28 B2
Crane Ct
2 Acton W12 . . . . .38 A4
Holborn EC4 . . . . . .107 C1
Crane Gr N7 . . . . . .14 C2
Crane Ho
2 Bow E3 . . . . . . .26 A3
10 Peckham SE15 . .49 B2
Crane Mead SE16 . . .40 C2
Crane St
Greenwich SE10 . . . .42 C1
2 Peckham SE15 . .49 B2
Cranfield Ct **1**
SW1 . . . . .75 B1
Cranfield Ct NW1 . .102 B3
Cranfield Ho WC1 . .106 B3
Cranfield Rd SE4 . . .66 B4
Cranford Cotts **8**
E1 . . . . .32 C2
Cranford Lo SW19 . .69 C2
Cranford St E1 . . . . .32 C2
Cranhurst Rd NW2 . .9 B3
Cranleigh
W11 . . . . . . .31 B1 112 C2
Cranleigh
Richmond TW9 . . . . .54 C4
4 Stamford Hill N16 .7 A3
Cranleigh Hos
NW1 . . . . .83 A1
Cranleigh Mews
SW11 . . . . .168 C1
Cranleigh St NW1 . . .83 A1
Cranley Gdns
SW7 . . . . .143 B2
Cranley Mews
SW7 . . . . .143 A2
Cranley Pl SW7 . . . .143 B3
Cranmer Ct SW3 . . .144 B3
Cranmer Ho
SW11 . . . . .168 A4
Cranmer Rd SW9 . .163 C2

Cranswick Rd
SE16 . . . . 40 A1
Cranwell Cl E3 . . . . . 27 A1
Cranwich Rd N16 . . . 7 A4
Cranwood Ct EC1 . . . 97 C3
Cranwood St EC1 . . . 97 C3
Cranworth Gdns
SW9 . . . . 173 B4
Cranworth Ho 6
N7 . . . . 14 B4
Craster Rd SW2 . . . . 74 B4
Craston Ho 2 SE5 . . 49 A1
Craven Cl N16 . . . . . 7 C4
Craven Cottage
(Fulham FC)
SW6 . . . . 47 C2
Craven Hill W2 . . . . 115 A4
Craven Hill Gdns
W2 . . . . 114 C4
Craven Hill Mews
W2 . . . . 115 A4
Craven Ho 2
SW14 . . . . 55 C4
Craven Lo
Bayswater W2 . . . . 115 A4
Fulham SW6 . . . . . . 47 C2
Craven Mews 5
SW11 . . . . 60 C4
Craven Park Mews
NW10 . . . . 21 A4
Craven Park Rd
NW10 . . . . 21 A4
Craven Pas SW1C 2 . 120 A2
Craven Pk NW10 . . . 21 A4
Craven Pl
Paddington W2 . . . . 101 A1
Stonebridge NW10 . . 20 C4
Craven St WC2 . . . . 120 A2
Craven Terr W2 . . . . 115 A4
Craven Wlk E5, N16 . 7 C4
Crawford Bldgs
NW1 . . . . 102 B3
Crawford Mews
W1 . . . . 102 C3
Crawford Pas EC1 . . 95 C1
Crawford Pl W1 . . . . 102 B3
Crawford Place
Dwellings W1 . . . . . 102 B3
Crawford Point 4
E16 . . . . 35 B3
Crawford Prim Sch
11 Camberwell
SE5 . . . . 48 B2
London SE5 . . . . 48 B2
Crawford Rd SE5 . . . 48 B2
Crawford St W1 . . . . 102 C3
Crawshay Ct SW9 . . 173 C4
Crawshay Ho 3
SE22 . . . . 64 A4
Crawthew Gr SE22 . . 64 B3
Crayford Ho
Bermondsey SE1 . . . 137 C3
5 Lower Holloway
N7 . . . . 14 A4
Crayford Rd N7 . . . . 14 A4
Crayle Ho EC1 . . . . . 96 B2
Crealock St SW18 . . . 59 A1
Creasy Est SE1 . . . . 138 A1
Crebor St SE22 . . . . 64 C1
Credenhill Ho 2
SE15 . . . . 50 A3
Crediton Hill NW6 . . . 11 A3
Crediton Rd
Brondesbury Pk
NW10 . . . . 22 C4

Crediton Rd continued
Newham E16 . . . . . . 35 C3
Credon Rd SE16 . . . . 40 A1
Creechurch La
EC3 . . . . 110 B1
Creechurch Pl
EC3 . . . . 110 B1
Creed Ct 5 E1 . . . . . 26 A2
Creed Ho SE15 . . . . 65 A4
Creed La EC4 . . . . . 108 B1
Creek Ho W14 . . . . . 126 B2
Creek Rd SE10,
SE8 . . . . 52 A4
Creek Road Ind Est
SE8 . . . . 52 A4
Creekside SE8 . . . . . 52 A3
Creekside Foyer
SE8 . . . . 52 A4
Crefeld Cl W6 . . . . . 154 A3
Creighton Cl W12 . . . 30 A2
Creighton Rd NW6 . . 22 C3
Cremer Bsns Ctr 8
E2 . . . . 24 B2 112 B4
Cremer Ho 9 SE8 . . 51 C3
Cremer St E2 . . . . . 24 B3
Cremorne Rd
SW10 . . . . 157 B2
Creon Ct 3 SW9 . . . 173 B4
Crescent EC3 . . . . . 124 C4
Crescent Arc 1
SE10 . . . . 52 B4
Crescent Court Bsns
Ctr 1 E16 . . . . 27 C1
Crescent Ct SW4 . . . 61 C2
Crescent Gdns
SW19 . . . . 70 C1
Crescent Gr SW4 . . . 61 B3
Crescent Ho SE13 . . 52 A1
Crescent La SW4 . . . 61 C3
Crescent Mans
Islington N5 . . . . . . 15 A3
Notting Hill
W11 . . . . 31 A2 112 B4
Crescent Pl SW3 . . . 144 B4
Crescent Row EC1 . . 96 C1
Crescent St N1 . . . . 14 B1
Crescent Stables
SW15 . . . . 58 A2
Crescent The
Acton W3 . . . . 29 A3
Barnes SW13 . . . . . 46 C1
Wimbledon SW19 . . . 70 C1
Crescent Way SE4 . . 66 C4
Crescent Wood Rd
SE21, SE26 . . . . 76 C1
Cresford Rd SW6 . . . 166 A3
Cressage Ho 9
TW8 . . . . 44 A4
Cressall Ho 2
E14 . . . . 41 C3
Cresset Ho 8 E9 . . . 17 B2
Cresset Rd E9 . . . . . 17 B2
Cresset St SW4 . . . . 61 C4
Cressfield Cl NW5 . . 12 C3
Cressida Rd N19 . . . 4 C3
Cressingham Rd
SE13 . . . . 67 B4
Cressington Cl 4
N16 . . . . 16 A3
Cresswell Gdns
SW5 . . . . 142 C2
Cresswell Pl
SW10 . . . . 143 A2
Cressy Ct
Hammersmith W6 . . . 39 A3
36 Stepney E1 . . . . . 32 B4

Cressy Ct continued
6 Stepney E1 . . . . . 32 B4
Cressy Hos 3 E1 . . . 32 B4
Cressy Hos 7 E1 . . . 32 B4
Cressy Pl E1 . . . . . . 32 B4
Cressy Rd NW3 . . . . 12 B4
Cresta Ho
2 Bow E3 . . . . 26 C1
Hampstead NW6 . . . . 11 C1
Crestfield St N1,
WC1 . . . . 94 B4
Crestview NW5 . . . . . 4 A1
Crestway SW15 . . . . 57 A1
Creswick Ct W3 . . . . 28 A2
Creswick Rd W3 . . . . 28 A2
Creswick Wlk 7
E3 . . . . 26 C2
Crewdson Rd
SW9 . . . . 163 B1
Crewe Pl NW10 . . . . 21 B2
Crewkerne Ct
SW11 . . . . 167 C4
Crews St E14 . . . . . 41 C2
Crewys Rd
Child's Hill NW2 . . . . 1 B2
London SE15 . . . . . . 50 A1
Crichton St SW8 . . . 170 C2
Cricketers Mews 4
SW4 . . . . 59 A2
Cricketfield Rd E5 . . 17 A4
Cricklade Ave
SW2 . . . . 74 B2
CRICKLEWOOD 9 B4
Cricklewood
Broadway NW2 . . . . 9 C4
Cricklewood La
NW2 . . . . 1 B1
Cricklewood Sta
NW2 . . . . 9 C4
Crieff Rd SW18 . . . . 59 B1
Criffel Ave SW2 . . . . 73 C3
Crimscott St SE1 . . . 138 B1
Crimsworth Rd
SW8 . . . . 161 C1
Crinan St N1 . . . . . . 84 B2
Cringle St SW8 . . . . 160 C2
Cripplegate St
EC1 . . . . 109 A4
Crispe Ho N1 . . . . . 85 A3
Crispian Cl NW10 . . . 8 A4
Crispin Ct SE17 . . . . 152 A3
Crispin Pl E1 . . . . . . 110 C4
Crispin St E1 . . . . . . 110 C3
Crisp Rd W6 . . . . . . 39 B1
Cristowe Rd SW6 . . . 165 A1
Criterion Mews
N19 . . . . 4 C2
Crockerton Rd
SW17 . . . . 72 B2
Croft Cl SE13 . . . . . 67 B1
Croftdown Rd NW5 . . 4 A1
Crofters Ct 9 SE8 . . 41 A2
Crofters Way NW1 . . 83 B4
Croft Ho
Putney SW15 . . . . . . 58 A1
7 West Kilburn
W10 . . . . 23 A2
Crofton Ave W4 . . . . 45 C3
Crofton Gate Way
SE4 . . . . 66 A2
Crofton Park Rd
SE4 . . . . 66 B1
Crofton Park Sta
SE4 . . . . 66 A2
Crofton Rd SE5 . . . . 49 A1

Crofton Terr
Homerton E5 . . . . . . 18 A3
Richmond TW9 . . . . . 54 B3
Crofts Ho 21 E2 . . . 24 C3
Crofts St E1 . . . . . . 125 B3
Croft St SE8 . . . . . . 41 A2
Croft The NW10 . . . . 21 B3
Crogsland Rd
NW1 . . . . 12 C1
Cromartie Rd N19 . . 4 C4
Cromarty Ho 8
E1 . . . . 33 A4
Crombie Mews 3
SW11 . . . . 168 B2
Cromdale Ct N16 . . . 7 B4
Cromer Ct
Streatham SW16 . . . 74 A1
Wandsworth SW18 . . 58 B1
Crome Ho N8 . . . . . 8 A2
Cromer St WC1 . . . . 94 B3
Cromer Terr E8 . . . . 16 C3
Cromer Villas Rd
SW18 . . . . 58 B1
Cromford Path 1
E5 . . . . 17 C4
Cromford Rd
SW18 . . . . 58 C2
Crompton Ct SW3 . . 144 A4
Crompton Ho
Borough The SE1 . . . 137 A1
Paddington W2 . . . . 89 B1
South Lambeth
SW8 . . . . 171 A3
Crompton St W2 . . . 89 B1
Cromwell Ave
Hammersmith W6 . . . 39 A2
Highgate N6 . . . . . . 4 A3
Cromwell Cl
Acton W3 3 . . . . . . 28 B1
2 Gunnersbury
W4 . . . . 37 A1
Cromwell Cres
SW5 . . . . 141 B4
Cromwell Ctr
NW10 . . . . 20 C2
Cromwell Gdns
SW7 . . . . 129 C1
Cromwell Gr W6 . . . 39 B3
Cromwell Ho
Battersea SW11 . . . 169 C3
Putney SW15 . . . . . 56 C3
Cromwell Hospl
(BUPA) SW5 . . . . . 142 A4
Cromwell Lo 46
E1 . . . . 25 B1
Cromwell Mans
SW5 . . . . 141 C4
Cromwell Mews
SW7 . . . . 143 C4
Cromwell Pl
5 Acton W3 . . . . . . 28 B1
Barbican EC1 . . . . . 109 A4
Highgate N6 . . . . . . 4 A3
Mortlake SW14 . . . . 55 B4
South Kensington
SW7 . . . . 143 C4
Cromwell Rd
Brixton SW9 . . . . . . 48 A2
South Kensington
SW7 . . . . 143 A4
Cromwell Twr
EC2 . . . . 109 A4
Crondace Rd
SW6 . . . . 165 C3
Crondall Ct 7 N1 . . . 24 A3
Crondall Ho SW15 . . 68 C3

Crondall Pl 15 N1 . . 24 A3
Crondall St N1 . . . . . 24 A3
Crone Ct 5 NW6 . . . 23 B3
Cronin St SE15 . . . . 49 B3
Crooked Billet Yd 8
E2 . . . . 24 A2 98 B4
Crooke Rd SE8 . . . . 41 A1
Crookham Rd
SW6 . . . . 164 C3
Croom's Hill SE10 . . 52 C3
Croom's Hill Gr
SE10 . . . . 52 B3
Cropley Ct N1 . . . . . 87 B2
Cropley St N1 . . . . . 87 B2
Cropthorne Ct W9 . . 89 A3
Crosby Ct SE1 . . . . 137 B4
Crosby Ho 18 E14 . . 42 B3
Crosby Row SE1 . . . 137 B4
Crosby Sq EC3 . . . . 110 A2
Crosby Wlk
3 Dalston E8 . . . . . 16 B2
Streatham SE24 . . . . 74 C4
Crosfield Ct 3
W10 . . . . 30 C3
Crosfield Ho
W11 . . . . 31 A2 112 A3
Crosland Pl 5
SW11 . . . . 60 C4
Crossbow Ho 15
N1 . . . . 24 A4
Cross Cl SE15 . . . . . 50 A1
Cross Ct SE5 . . . . . 63 C4
Crossfield Rd
NW3 . . . . 11 C2
Crossfield St SE8 . . . 51 C3
Crossford St SW9 . . 172 C1
Crossharbour Sta
E14 . . . . 42 A3
Cross Keys Cl W1 . . 103 C3
Cross La EC3 . . . . . 124 A3
Crossleigh Ct 3
SE14 . . . . 51 B3
Crosslet St SE17 . . . 151 C4
Crosslet Vale SE10 . 52 A2
Crossley St N7 . . . . 14 C2
Crossman Hos 15
SW12 . . . . 74 A4
Crossmount Ho 5
SE5 . . . . 48 B3
Crossrail Pl E14 . . . 34 A1
Cross St SE5 . . . . . 49 A1
Cross St
Islington N1 . . . . . . 86 B4
Mortlake SW13 . . . . 56 A4
Crossthwaite Ave SE5,
SE24 . . . . 63 C3
Crosstrees Ho 7
E14 . . . . 41 C3
Crosswall EC3 . . . . . 124 C4
Crossway E8, N16 . . 16 A3
Crossway Ct SE4 . . . 51 A1
Crossways Acad
SE4 . . . . 51 A1
Croston St E8 . . . . . 24 C4
Crouch End Hill N8 . . 4 C4
Crouch Hill N4, N8,
N19 . . . . 5 A4
Crouch Hill Sta N4 . . 5 B4
Crouchmans Cl SE21,
SE26 . . . . 76 C1
Crowder St E1 . . . . . 32 A2
Crowfield Ho N5 . . . 15 B4
Crowfoot Cl E9 . . . . 18 B3

Crowhurst Cl
SW9 . . . . **173** C2
Crowhurst Ho 21
SW9 . . . . **173** A1
Crowland Ho NW8 . **78** C3
Crowland Terr N1 . **15** C1
Crowline Wlk 1
N1 . . . . **15** B2
Crown Cl
Bow E3 . . . . **26** C4
Hampstead NW6 . . **11** A2
Crown Close Bsns Ctr
E3 . . . . **26** C4
Crown Ct
City of London
EC4 . . . . **109** A1
4 Putney SW15 . . **57** C3
St Giles WC2 . . . . **106** B1
St John's Wood
NW8 . . . . **90** B3
Crowndale Ct NW1 **83** B2
Crowndale Rd
NW1 . . . . **83** A2
Crowne Ho SE1 . . **123** A1
Crownfield Rd
E15 . . . . **19** C4
Crowngate Ho 33
E3 . . . . **26** B3
Crownhill Rd
NW10 . . . . **21** B4
Crownleigh 1
SW2 . . . . **62** C2
Crown Lo SW3 . . . **144** B3
Crown Mews 2
E1 . . . . **32** C4
Crown Office Row
EC4 . . . . **121** B4
Crown Pas SW1 . . **119** A1
Crown Pl
Broadgate EC2 . . **110** A4
Kentish Town NW5 . **13** A2
Crown Reach
SW1 . . . . **147** C1
Crown St
Acton W3 . . . . **28** A1
Camberwell SE5 . . **48** B3
Crownstone Ct 1
SW2 . . . . **62** C2
Crownstone Rd
SW2 . . . . **62** C2
Crown Terr TW9 . . **54** B3
Crows Rd E3, E15 . **27** C2
Crowther Ave
TW8 . . . . **36** A2
Crowther Cl SW6 **155** A3
Crowthorne Cl
SW18 . . . . **70** B3
Crowthorne Rd
W10 . . . . **30** C3
Croxley Rd W9 . . . **23** B2
Croxted Cl SE21 . . **75** B4
Croxted Rd SE21,
SE24 . . . . **75** C2
Croxteth Ho 11
SW8 . . . . **171** B2
Croydon Ho SE1 . **135** C4
Crozier Ho SW8 . **162** C1
Crozier Terr E9 . . . **17** C3
Crucifix La SE1 . . **138** A4
Cruden Ho
6 Bow E3 . . . . . . **26** B3
11 Camberwell
SE17 . . . . **48** A4
Cruden St N1 . . . . **86** B3

Cruickshank St
WC1 . . . . **95** B4
Cruikshank Ho 2
NW8 . . . . **80** B2
Crusader Ho EC1 . . **96** A1
Crusoe Mews N16 . . **6** C2
Crutched Friars
EC3 . . . . **124** B4
Crystal Palace Rd
SE22 . . . . **64** C2
Crystal Wharf N1 . **86** B1
Cuba St E14 . . . . . **41** C4
Cubitt Bldg SW1 . **146** A1
Cubitt Ho 4 SW4 . **61** B1
Cubitt St WC1 . . . . **95** A3
Cubitt Terr SW4 . . **61** B4
CUBITT TOWN . . . **42** B2
Cubitt Town Jun & Inf
Sch E14 . . . . **42** B3
Cuddington SE17 . **151** A4
Cudworth Ho
SW8 . . . . **171** A3
Cudworth St E1 . . **25** A1
Cuffley Ho 8 W10 . **30** B4
Cuff Point 12
E2 . . . . . . **24** B2 **98** C4
Culand Ho SE17 . . **152** A3
Culford Gdns
SW3 . . . . **145** A3
Culford Gr N1 . . . . **16** A2
Culford Mans
SW3 . . . . **145** A3
Culford Mews N1 . **16** A2
Culford Rd
Kingsland N1 . . . . **16** A2
Shoreditch N1 . . . . **24** A4
Culham Ho
2 Paddington
W2 . . . . **31** C4
9 Shoreditch
E2 . . . . . . **24** B2 **98** C3
Cullen Ho W9 . . . . **23** B3
Cullen Way NW10 . **20** B1
Culling Rd SE16 . . **40** B3
Cullingworth Rd
NW10 . . . . **9** A3
Culloden Cl 21
SE16 . . . . **153** C1
Culloden Prim Sch 10
E14 . . . . **34** B3
Cullum St EC3 . . . **124** A4
Culmore Rd SE15 . **50** B3
Culmstock Rd
SW11 . . . . **60** C2
Culpepper Ct
SE11 . . . . **149** B4
Culross Bldgs
NW1 . . . . **84** A2
Culross St W1 . . . **117** B3
Culver Ct SW18 . . . **59** A1
Culverden Rd
SW12 . . . . **73** B2
Culverhouse WC1 . **106** C3
Culverhouse Gdns
SW16 . . . . **74** B1
Culvert Ct SW11 . . **169** B2
Culvert Pl SW11 . . **169** B2
Culvert Rd SW11 . . **169** A2
Culworth Ho NW8 . **80** A1
Culworth St NW8 . . **80** A1
Culzean Cl 11
SE27 . . . . **75** A1
Cumber Ho SW18 . . **70** C3
Cumberland Ave
NW10 . . . . **20** A2

Cumberland Bsns Pk
NW10 . . . . **20** A2
Cumberland Cl E8 . **16** B2
Cumberland Cres
W14 . . . . **140** B4
Cumberland Ct
2 Paddington
W2 . . . . **103** A1
4 Willesden
NW10 . . . . **8** C1
Cumberland Gate
W1 . . . . **117** A4
Cumberland Gdns
WC1 . . . . **95** B4
Cumberland Ho
Paddington W9 . . . **88** C1
3 Putney SW15 . . **69** B4
Cumberland Mans
Marylebone W1 . . **102** C2
4 West Hampstead
NW6 . . . . **10** C3
Cumberland Mkt
NW1 . . . . **92** B4
Cumberland Mills Sq
E14 . . . . **42** C1
Cumberland Park Ind
Est NW10 . . . . . . **21** C2
Cumberland Pk
W3 . . . . **28** B2
Cumberland Pl
NW1 . . . . **92** A4
Cumberland Rd
Acton W3 . . . . **28** B2
Barnes SW13 . . . . **46** C2
Richmond TW9 . . . **44** C3
Cumberland St
SW1 . . . . **146** B2
Cumberland Terr
NW1 . . . . **82** A1
Cumberland Terrace
Mews NW1 . . . . . . **82** A1
Cumberland Villas
W3 . . . . **28** B2
Cumberland Wharf 7
SE16 . . . . **40** B4
Cumbrian Gdns
NW2 . . . . **1** A2
Cuming Mus SE17 **150** C3
Cumming St N1 . . . **85** A1
Cumnor Cl 22
SW9 . . . . **173** A2
Cunard Pl EC3 . . . **110** B1
Cunard Rd NW10 . . **20** C2
Cunard Wlk 3
SE16 . . . . **41** A2
Cundy St SW1 . . . **145** C3
Cunningham Ct
W2 . . . . **89** B1
Cunningham Ho 5
SE5 . . . . **48** C3
Cunningham Pl
NW8 . . . . **89** B2
Cunnington St W4 . **37** B2
Cupar Rd SW11 . . **169** C4
Cureton St SW1 . . **147** C3
Curlew Ho
Brockley SE4 . . . . **66** A3
7 Peckham SE15 . **49** B2
Curlew St SE1 . . . **139** A4
Curness St SE13 . . **67** B3
Curran Ho SW3 . . **144** A3
Curricle St W3 . . . **29** A1
Currie Ho 13
SW12 . . . . **73** C4
Cursitor St EC4 . . **107** B2
Curtain Pl
EC2 . . . . . . **24** A1 **98** B2
Curtain Rd
EC2 . . . . . . **24** A1 **98** B2

Curtis Dr W3 . . . . . **28** C3
Curtis Ho SE17 . . . **151** B2
Curtis St SE1 . . . . **152** C4
Curtis Way SE1 . . . **152** C4
Curve Bldg The
SE4 . . . . **66** B2
Curve The W12 . . . **29** C2
Curwen Gall W11 . **105** B3
Curwen Rd W12 . . . **38** C4
Curzon Cres NW10 . . **8** A1
Curzon Gate W1 . . **117** C1
Curzon Sq
City of London
W1 . . . . **117** C1
Curzon St W1 . . . . **118** A2
Custance Ho 1
N1 . . . . **87** B1
Custance St N1 . . . **97** B4
Custom House
EC3 . . . . **124** A3
Custom House Reach
SE16 . . . . **41** B3
Cutbush Ho N7 . . . **13** C3
Cutcombe Rd SE5 . **48** B1
Cuthbert Harrowing
Ho EC1 . . . . **96** C1
Cuthbert Ho W2 . . **101** B4
Cuthbert St W2 . . . **89** B1
Cuthill Wlk 3 SE5 . **48** C2
Cutler Ho SW11 . . **167** C2
Cutlers Gdns EC2 . **110** B2
Cutlers Gdns Arc
EC2 . . . . **110** B2
Cutlers Sq E14 . . . **41** C2
Cutler St EC2 . . . . **110** B2
Cutter La SE10 . . . **43** A4
Cut The SE1 . . . . . **135** C4
Cutty Sark SE10 . . **52** B4
Cutty Sark Ho 9
E14 . . . . **42** A2
Cutty Sark Sta
SE10 . . . . **52** B4
Cuxton Ho SE17 . . **152** B2
Cyclops Mews 12
E14 . . . . **41** C2
Cygnet Ho NW8 . . . **78** C4
Cygnet House N 8
E14 . . . . **34** A3
Cygnet House S 9
E14 . . . . **34** A3
Cygnet St
E1 . . . . **24** B1 **99** A2
Cygnus Bsns Ctr
NW10 . . . . **8** B2
Cynthia St N1 . . . . **85** A1
Cyntra Pl 8 E8 . . . . **17** A1
Cypress Cl 7 E5 . . . . **7** C2
Cypress Ct 3 E11 . . **19** C4
Cypress Gdns SE4 . **66** A2
Cypress Ho SE14 . . **50** C2
Cypress Pl W1 . . . . **93** A1
Cyprus Pl 22 E2 . . . **25** B3
Cyprus St E2 . . . . . **25** B3
Cyrena Rd SE22 . . . **64** B2
Cyril Jackson Prim
Sch (North Bldg) 23
E14 . . . . **33** B2
Cyril Jackson Prim
Sch (South Bldg) 24
E14 . . . . **33** B2
Cyril Mans SW11 . **169** A3
Cyril Thatcher Ho
SW6 . . . . **165** C3
Cyrus Ho EC1 . . . . **96** B2
Cyrus St EC1 . . . . . **96** B2
Czar St SE8 . . . . . . **51** C4

D

Dabb's La EC1 . . . . **95** C1
Dabin Cres SE10 . . **52** B2
Dacca St SE8 . . . . . **51** B4
Dace Rd E3 . . . . . . **26** C4
Dacre Ho SW3 . . . **157** C3
Dacre St SW1 . . . . **133** B2
Daffodil St W12 . . . **29** B2
Dafforne Rd SW17 . **72** C1
Dagmar Ct E14 . . . **42** B3
Dagmar Gdns
NW10 . . . . **22** C3
Dagmar Pas N1 . . . **86** B4
Dagmar Rd
Camberwell SE5 . . **49** A2
Finsbury Pk N4 . . . . **5** C4
Dagmar Terr N1 . . . **86** B4
Dagnall St SW11 . **169** B3
Dagnan Rd SW12 . . **73** B4
Dagobert Ho 27
E1 . . . . **32** B4
Daimler Ho 8 E3 . . **26** C1
Dainton Ho 22 W2 . **31** C4
Daintry Way E9 . . . **18** B2
Dairy Ho N16 . . . . . **21** C4
Dairyman Cl NW2 . . **1** A1
Daisy Dormer Ct 2
SW9 . . . . **62** B3
Daisy La SW6 . . . . . **58** C4
Dakin Pl 8 E1 . . . . **33** A4
Dakota bldg 6
SE13 . . . . **52** A2
Dalberg Rd SW2 . . **62** C2
Dalbury Ho 3
SW9 . . . . **62** B3
Dalby Rd SW18 . . . **59** B3
Dalby St NW5 . . . . **13** A2
Dalebury Rd SW17 . **72** B2
Dale Croft N4 . . . . . **6** B1
Daleham Gdns
NW3 . . . . **11** C2
Daleham Mews
NW3 . . . . **11** C2
Dale Ho
London SE4 . . . . . **66** A3
St John's Wood
NW8 . . . . **78** C4
Dalemain Ho 8
SW8 . . . . **171** C2
Dalemain Mews 12
E16 . . . . **35** C1
Dale Rd
Camberwell SE17 . **48** A4
Gospel Oak NW5 . . **12** C3
Dale Row W11 . . . . **31** A3
Dale St W4 . . . . **38** A1
Daley Ho 6 W12 . . . **30** A3
Daley St E9 . . . . . . **17** C2
Daley Thompson Way 1
SW8 . . . . **61** A4
Dalgarno Gdns
W10 . . . . **30** B4
Dalgarno Way
W10 . . . . **22** B1
Dalgleish St 1
E14 . . . . **33** A3
Daling Way E3 . . . . **26** A3
Dalkeith Ct SW1 . . **147** C3
Dalkeith Ho 6
SW9 . . . . **48** A2
Dalkeith Rd SE21 . . **75** B4
Dalling Rd W6 . . . . **39** A2

Dallington Sch
  EC1...................96 B2
Dallington St EC1....96 B2
Dalmeny Ave N7...13 C4
Dalmeny Avenue Est
  N7........................13 C4
Dalmeny Ct 4
  SW4...................172 A2
Dalmeny Rd N7....13 C4
Dalmeyer Rd NW10...8 B2
Dalmore Rd SE21...75 B2
Dalrymple Rd SE4..66 A3
DALSTON...............16 C2
Dalston Jct E8........16 B2
Dalston Junction Sta
  E8........................16 A2
Dalston Kingsland Sta
  E8........................16 B3
Dalston La E8..........16 C3
Dalton Ho
  7 Balham SW12...73 A4
  2 Bow E3..............26 A3
  19 Deptford SE14...50 C4
Dalton St SE27........75 A1
Dalwood St SE5......49 A2
Dalyell Rd SW9.......62 B4
Damascene Wlk
  SE21...................75 B3
Damer Ho 9
  TW10..................54 B1
Damer Terr SW10..157 A1
Dame St N1.............86 C2
Damien Ct 12 E1....32 A3
Damien St E1..........32 A3
Damory Ho 1
  SE16...................40 B2
Dan Bryant Ho 5
  SW12..................73 B4
Danbury St N1.........86 B2
Danby Ho
  22 Hackney E9......17 B1
  3 West Kilburn
  W10....................23 B2
Danby St SE15........64 B4
Dancer Rd
  Fulham SW6........164 C3
  Richmond TW9.....54 C4
Dandridge Cl SE10..43 B1
Dandridge Ho E1..110 C4
Daneburg 18 W10...30 B4
Danebury Ave
  SW15..................56 B1
Danecroft Rd
  SE24...................63 C2
Dane Ho 13 SE5....48 B1
Danehurst St
  SW6...................164 A4
Danemere St
  SW15..................57 B4
Dane Pl E3..............26 B3
Danes Cl NW8........80 C3
Danesdale Rd E9....18 A2
Danesfield SE5.......49 A4
Danes Ho 10 W10..30 B4
Dan St NW1............13 C1
Danette Gdns SE5...48 C1
Daneville Rd SE5....48 C2
Daniel Bolt Cl E14..34 A4
Daniel Ct W3..........29 A2
Daniel Gdns SE15...49 B3
Daniell Ho N1..........87 C2
Daniel's Rd SE15....65 B4
Dan Leno Wlk
  SW6...................156 A1
Dante Pl 1 W1.....119 B4
Dante Pl SE11......150 B3
Dante Rd SE11.....150 A4

Danube Ct 13
  SE15...................49 B3
Danube St SW3....144 B2
Danvers Ho 54 E1..111 C1
Danvers St SW3...157 C3
Da Palma Ho
  SW8...................155 B3
Daplyn St 6 E1....111 B4
D'arblay St W1....105 A1
Darcy Ho E8............25 A4
Darell Prim Sch
  TW9....................54 C4
Darell Rd TW9.........54 C4
Daren Ct 1 N7.........5 A1
Daren Ho NW8......101 C4
Darenth Rd N16.......7 B3
Darfield NW1............82 C3
Darfield Rd SE4......66 B2
Darfield Way W10...30 A4
Darfur St 2 SW15...57 C4
Darien Ho
  16 London SW11...59 C4
  1 Stepney E1........32 C4
Darien Rd SW11.....59 C4
Daring Ho 27 E3.....26 A3
Darlan Rd SW6.....155 A1
Darley Ho SE11....148 C1
Darley Rd SW11......60 B1
Darling Rd SE4.......66 C4
Darling Row 4 E1...25 A1
Darlington Ho
  SW8...................161 C1
Darnall Ho 7
  SE10...................52 B2
Darnay Ho 7
  SE10...................139 B2
Darnell Ho 8
  SE10...................52 B3
Darnley Ho 17 E14..33 A3
Darnley Rd E9........17 B2
Darnley Terr 2
  W11....................30 C1
Darrell Rd SE22.....64 C2
Darren Cl N4.............5 A4
Darsley Dr 7 SW8..172 A4
Dartford Ho SE1....153 A4
Dartford St SE17....48 B4
Dartington NW1....83 A3
Dartington Ho
  Baywater W2......100 A4
  7 London SW8....171 C2
Dartle Ct 2 SE16..139 C3
Dartmoor Wlk 9
  E14......................41 C2
Dartmouth Cl W11...31 C3
Dartmouth Ct
  SE10...................52 B2
Dartmouth Gr
  SE10...................52 B2
Dartmouth Hill
  SE10...................52 B2
Dartmouth Ho
  Dartmouth Pk N19...4 A2
  Lewisham SE10....52 B1
DARTMOUTH
  PARK...................4 A1
Dartmouth Park Ave
  NW5......................4 A1
Dartmouth Park Hill
  NW5......................4 A4
Dartmouth Park Rd
  NW5......................4 A1
Dartmouth Pl W4....46 A4
Dartmouth Rd NW2...9 C2
Dartmouth Row
  SE10...................52 B3

Dartmouth St
  SW1...................133 C3
Dartmouth Terr
  SE10...................52 C2
Darton St 1 W10....23 A1
Dartrey Twr
  SW10..................157 B2
Dartrey Wlk
  SW10..................157 A2
Dart St W10............23 B2
Darville Rd N16........7 B1
Darwen Pl 2 E2.....25 A4
Darwin Ct NW1.......81 C4
Darwin Ho 8 SW1..129 B1
Darwin Ho 8
  SE13...................151 C4
Darwin St SE17....151 C4
Daryngton Ho
  SW8...................162 A1
Dashwood Ho
  SE21...................76 B1
Data Point Bsns Ctr
  E16....................27 C1
Datchelor Pl 14
  SE5......................48 C2
Datchett Ho 40
  E2.............24 B2 98 C3
Datchwood Ct 4
  N4.........................6 B1
Datchworth Ho 8
  N1........................15 A1
Date St SE17..........151 B1
Daubeney Prim Sch
  E5.........................18 A4
Daubeney Rd E5.....18 A4
Daubeney Twr 2
  SE8.......................41 B1
Dault Rd SW18.......59 B1
Dauney Ho 11 SE1..136 A3
Davenant Ho 20
  E1........................111 C4
Davenant Rd N19...4 C2
Davenant St E1....111 C3
Davenport Ho
  SE11...................135 B1
Davenport Mews 2
  W12....................30 A1
Davenport Rd SE6..67 B1
Daventry St NW1..102 A4
Dave Porter Hts
  SW19....................70 A4
Daventry St NW1..102 A4
Davern Cl SE10......43 B2
Davey Cl N7............14 B2
Davey Rd E9............18 C1
Davey's Ct WC2....120 A4
Davey St SE15........49 B4
David Devine Ho 7
  E8........................16 C3
David Game Coll
  N16....................113 C2
Davidge Ho SE1....135 C3
Davidge St SE1......136 B3
David Hewitt Ho 3
  E3........................34 A4
David Ho
  8 Putney SW15...56 C2
  South Lambeth
  SW8...................162 A2
David Mews
  14 Greenwich
  SE10...................52 B3
  W1.....................103 A4

Davidson Gdns
  SW8...................162 A2
Davidson Ho 7
  N19......................13 B4
David St E15...........19 C3
Davies Mews W1..118 A4
Davies St W1.........118 A4
Davina Ho
  Brondesbury NW2...10 B2
  14 Hackney E5......17 A3
Da Vinci Ct 12
  SE16.....................40 A1
Davis Ho 8 W12....30 A2
Davis Rd W3...........38 A4
Davisville Rd W12...39 C4
Dawes Ho 22 SE17..151 B3
Dawes Rd SW6.....154 C2
Dawes St SE17....151 C2
Dawlish Ave SW18..71 A2
Dawlish Rd NW2......9 C2
Dawnay Gdns
  SW18.....................71 C2
Dawnay Rd SW17,
  SW18.....................71 C2
Dawn Cres E15.......27 C4
Dawson Ho
  22 Bethnal Green
  E2........................25 B2
  7 Camberwell SE5...49 A2
Dawson Pl
  W2...........31 C2 113 C4
Dawson Rd NW2......9 B4
Dawson St E2..........24 B3
Day Ho 2 SE5.........48 B3
Daynor Ho 4
  NW6......................23 C4
Daysbrook Rd
  SW2......................74 B3
Dayton Gr SE15......50 B2
Deacon Ho SE11...149 A3
Deacon Mews N1...15 C1
Deacon Rd NW2......8 C2
Deacon Way SE17 151 A4
Deal Ho
  Deptford SE15.......50 C4
  Walworth SE17....152 B2
Deal Porters Way
  SE16.....................40 C3
Deal St E1.............111 B4
Dealtry Rd SW15...57 B3
Deal Wlk 5 SW9..163 C1
Dean Bradley St
  SW1...................134 A1
Dean Cl
  Hackney E9..........17 B3
  Rotherhithe SE16...32 C1
Deancross St E1....32 B3
Dean Ct
  Acton W3..............28 C3
  South Lambeth
  SW8...................162 A1
Deanery Mews
  W1.....................117 C2
Deanery St W1.....117 C2
Dean Farrar St
  SW1...................133 C2
Deanhill Ct 2
  SW14....................55 A3
Deanhill Rd SW14..55 A3
Dean Ho
  London N4..............6 B4
  New Cross SE14....51 B3
  Stamford Hill N16...7 B3
  18 Stepney E1.......32 B3

Dean Rd NW2...........9 B2
Dean Ryle St SW1 148 A4
Dean's Bldgs
  SE17...................151 C3
Deans Cl W4...........45 A4
Dean's Ct EC4......108 B1
Dean's Gateway 7
  SE10.....................51 C2
Deanshanger Ho 2
  SE8.......................51 B4
Dean's Mews W1..104 B2
Dean St W1...........105 B1
Dean Stanley St
  SW1...................134 A1
Dean's Yd SW1....133 C2
Dean Trench St
  SW1...................134 A1
Dearmer Ho 6
  SW2......................74 C4
Deason St E15........27 B4
Deauville Ct
  14 London SW4...61 B1
  2 Rotherhithe
  SE16.....................40 C4
Deauville Mans 7
  SW4......................61 B1
De Barowe Mews
  1 Highbury N5.......15 A4
  1 London N5.........15 A3
Debdale Ho 20 E2..24 C4
De Beauvoir Cres
  N1........................24 A4
De Beauvoir Pl 5
  N1........................15 C1
De Beauvoir Prim Sch
  15 N1....................16 A2
De Beauvoir Rd
  N1........................16 A1
De Beauvoir Sq
  N1........................16 A1
DE BEAUVOIR
  TOWN..................16 A1
Debenham Ct E8....24 C4
Debnams Rd SE16...40 B2
Decima St SE1.....138 A2
Deck Cl SE16..........32 C1
De Coubertin St
  E15......................19 B2
De Crespigny Pk
  SE5.......................48 C1
Deeley Rd SW8....171 B4
Deepdale N4.............6 A1
Deepdene Gdns
  SW2......................74 B4
Deepdene Ho N16...6 C3
Deepdene Lo 5
  SW2......................74 B4
Deepdene Mans
  SW6...................164 C3
Deepdene Rd SE5,
  SE24.....................63 C3
Deerbrook Rd SE24,
  SW2......................75 A3
Dee Rd TW9.............54 B3
Deerdale Rd SE24...63 B3
Deerhurst Ho 6
  SE15.....................49 C4
Deerhurst Rd NW2...9 C2
Deer Lo SW6...........58 A4
Deeside Rd SW17...71 C1
Dee St E14...............34 B3
Defoe Ave TW9.......44 C3

Defoe Ho
Barbican EC2 .....**108** C4
5 Stoke Newington
N16 .....**7** A2
Defoe Pl EC2 .....**108** C4
Defoe Rd
Rotherhithe SE16 .....**41** B4
Stoke Newington
N16 .....**7** A2
De Gama Pl 3
E14 .....**41** C1
Dekker Ho SE5 .....**48** C3
Dekker Rd SE21 .....**64** A1
Delafield Ho 2
E1 .....**111** A2
Delaford Rd SE16 .....**40** A1
Delaford St SW6 .....**154** B3
Delamere Ho 4 SW6 .....**4** A4
Delamere Rd W5 .....**36** A4
Delamere St W2 .....**100** C3
Delamere Terr
W2 .....**100** B4
Delancey Pas NW1 .....**82** B3
Delancey St NW1 .....**82** B3
Delancey Studios
NW1 .....**82** B3
Delany Ho SE10 .....**52** B4
Delarch Ho SE1 .....**136** A1
De Laune St SE17 .....**150** A1
Delaware Rd W9 .....**88** A2
Delawyk Cres
SE24 .....**63** C1
Delft Way 2 SE22 .....**64** A2
Delhi St N1 .....**84** B3
Delia St SW18 .....**71** A4
Delius Gr E15 .....**27** B3
Dellafield N4 .....**5** C2
Dell Cl E15 .....**27** C4
Dellow Ho 6 E1 .....**32** A2
Dellow St E1 .....**32** A2
Dell's Mews SW1 .....**147** A3
Deloraine Ho SE8 .....**51** C2
Deloraine St SE8 .....**51** C2
Delorme St W6 .....**47** C4
Delta Bldg 7 E14 .....**34** B3
Delta Ho N1 .....**97** B4
Delta Pk SW18 .....**59** A3
Delta Point 5
E2 .....**24** C2 **99** B4
Delta St 4
E2 .....**24** C2 **99** B4
Delverton Ho
SE17 .....**150** B2
Delverton Rd
SE17 .....**150** B1
Delvino Rd SW6 .....**165** C3
De Montfort Ct 1
SW16 .....**74** A1
De Montfort Rd
SW16 .....**74** A2
De Morgan Rd
SW6 .....**59** A4
Dempster Rd
SW18 .....**59** B2
Denbigh Cl
W11 .....**31** B2 **113** A4
Denbigh Gdns
TW10 .....**54** B2
Denbigh Ho
Knightsbridge
SW1 .....**131** A2
7 Notting Hill **31** B3
Notting Hill
W11 .....**31** B2 **113** A4

Denbigh Mews
SW1 .....**146** C3
Denbigh Pl SW1 .....**146** C2
Denbigh Rd
W11 .....**31** B2 **113** A4
Denbigh Terr
W11 .....**31** B2 **113** A4
Denbury Ho 45 E3 .....**27** A2
Denby Ct SE11 .....**149** A4
Dence Ho
E2 .....**24** C2 **99** B3
Denchworth Ho 14
SW9 .....**173** B1
Dene Cl SE4 .....**66** A3
Denehurst Gdns
Acton W3 .....**28** A1
Richmond TW10 .....**54** C3
Dene Mans 1
NW6 .....**10** C2
Denesmead SE24 .....**63** B2
Denewood Rd N6 .....**3** B4
Dengie Wlk N1 .....**86** C4
Denham Ho 22
W12 .....**30** A2
Denham St SE10 .....**43** C1
Denholme Rd W9 .....**23** B2
Denland Ho SW8 .....**163** A1
Denman Ho N16 .....**7** A2
Denman Rd SE15 .....**49** B1
Denman St W1 .....**119** B3
Denmark Gr N1 .....**85** B2
Denmark Hill SE5 .....**48** C1
Denmark Hill Sta
SE5 .....**48** B1
Denmark Mans 14
SE5 .....**48** B1
Denmark Pl
24 Bow E3 .....**26** C2
2 Bromley E3 .....**26** C2
Soho WC2 .....**105** C2
Denmark Rd
Camberwell SE5 .....**48** B1
Kilburn NW6 .....**23** B3
Denmark St WC2 .....**105** C2
Denmead Ho
SW15 .....**56** B1
Denne Terr E8 .....**24** B4
Dennett's Gr SE14 .....**50** C1
Dennett's Rd SE14 .....**50** B2
Denning Cl NW8 .....**89** A3
Denning Mews
SW12 .....**60** C1
Denning Point 11
E1 .....**111** A2
Denning Rd NW3 .....**11** C4
Dennington Park
Mansions 12
NW6 .....**10** C3
Dennington Park Rd
NW6 .....**10** C2
Dennis Ct SE10 .....**52** B2
Dennis Ho 4 E3 .....**26** B3
Dennison Point
E15 .....**76** B1
Dennis Severs' House
E1 .....**110** C4
Dennis Way SW4 .....**61** C4
Denny Cres SE11 .....**149** C2
Denny St SE11 .....**149** C2
Densham Ho NW8 .....**79** C1
Denstone Ho 5
SE15 .....**49** C4
Den The (Millwall FC)
SE16 .....**40** B2
Dent Ho SE17 .....**152** A3
Denton NW1 .....**12** C2

Denton Ho N1 .....**15** A1
Denton St SW18 .....**59** A1
Denton St SW18 .....**60** B1
Denver Rd N16 .....**7** A4
Denyer Ho 1
NW5 .....**13** A4
Denyer St SW3 .....**144** B4
Denys Bldg EC1 .....**107** B4
Denzil Rd NW10 .....**8** B3
Deodar Rd SW15 .....**58** A3
Depot App NW2 .....**9** C4
Depot Rd W12 .....**30** B2
Depot St SE5 .....**48** C4
DEPTFORD **50** C3
Deptford Bridge
SE8 .....**51** C2
Deptford Bridge Sta
SE8 .....**51** C2
Deptford Broadway
SE8, SE14 .....**51** C2
Deptford Church St
SE8 .....**51** C3
Deptford Ferry Rd 24
E14 .....**41** C2
Deptford Gn SE8 .....**51** C4
Deptford Green Sch
SE14 .....**51** B3
Deptford Green Sch
(Annex) 4 SE14 .....**51** A3
Deptford High St
SE8 .....**51** C3
Deptford Park Prim
Sch 2 SE16 .....**41** A4
Deptford Sta SE8 .....**51** C3
Deptford Trad Est
SE8 .....**51** A4
Deptford Wharf
SE8 .....**41** B2
De Quincey Mews 3
E16 .....**35** C1
Derby Ct 5 E5 .....**18** A4
Derby Gate SW1 .....**134** A4
Derby Ho SE11 .....**149** B4
Derby Rd
Mortlake SW14 .....**55** A3
South Hackney E9 .....**25** C4
Derbyshire St
E2 .....**24** C2 **99** C3
Derby St W1 .....**117** C1
Dereham Ho 4
SE4 .....**65** C3
Dereham Pl
EC2 .....**24** A1 **98** B2
Derek Walcott Cl
SE24 .....**63** A2
Dericote St E8 .....**25** A4
Dering St W1 .....**104** B1
Dermody Gdns
SE13 .....**67** C2
Dermody Rd SE13 .....**67** C2
Deronda Rd SE24,
SW2 .....**75** A3
Derrick Ho 13
SW2 .....**74** C3
Derrycombe Ho 18
W2 .....**31** C4
Derry St W8 .....**128** A3
Dersingham Rd
NW2 .....**1** A1
Derwent NW1 .....**92** C3
Derwent Ct
3 Hammersmith
W6 .....**38** C2
5 Rotherhithe
SE16 .....**40** C4

Derwent Gr SE22 .....**64** B3
Derwent Ho
South Kensington
SW7 .....**143** A4
Tower Hamlets E3 .....**26** B1
Derwent St SE10 .....**43** A1
Derwentwater Mans
2 W3 .....**28** B1
Derwentwater Prim
Sch W3 .....**28** B1
Derwentwater Rd
W3 .....**28** B1
Desborough Cl
W2 .....**100** B4
Desborough Ho
W14 .....**155** A4
Desenfans Rd
SE21 .....**64** A1
Design Mus W8 .....**127** B2
Desmond St SE14 .....**51** A4
Despard Ho SW2 .....**74** C2
Despard Rd N19 .....**4** B3
Dethick Ct E3 .....**26** A4
Detling Ho SE17 .....**152** A3
Devas St E3 .....**27** A1
Deventer Cres 3
SE22 .....**64** A2
De Vere Cotts W8 .....**128** C2
De Vere Gdns W8 .....**128** C3
Deverell St SE1 .....**137** B1
Devereux Mews
W8 .....**128** C2
Devereux Ct WC2 .....**107** B1
Devereux Ho 7
SW15 .....**56** C2
Devereux La SW13 .....**47** A3
Devereux Rd
SW11 .....**60** B1
Devitt Ho 5 E14 .....**34** A2
Devizes St N1 .....**87** C3
Devonhurst Pl 4
W4 .....**37** C1
Devonia Rd N1 .....**86** B2
Devon Mans SE1 .....**138** B4
Devonport W2 .....**102** A2
Devonport Ho
Greenwich SE10 .....**52** B4
23 Paddington W2 .....**31** C4
Devonport Rd
W12 .....**39** A4
Devonport St E1 .....**32** B3
Devonshire Cl
W1 .....**104** A4
Devonshire Dr
SE10 .....**52** A2
Devonshire Gdns
W4 .....**45** B3
Devonshire Gr
SE15 .....**50** A4
Devonshire Hall 6
E9 .....**17** B2
Devonshire Ho
Brondesbury NW6 .....**10** B2
Newington SE1 .....**136** C2
Paddington W2 .....**101** C4
3 Putney SW15 .....**69** B4
Westminster SW1 .....**147** C2
Devonshire House
Prep Sch NW3 .....**11** B3
Devonshire Mews 2
W4 .....**38** A1

Devonshire Mews N
W1 .....**104** A4
Devonshire Mews S
W1 .....**104** A4
Devonshire Mews W
W1 .....**103** C4
Devonshire Pl
Child's Hill NW2 .....**1** C1
Kensington W8 .....**128** A1
Marylebone W1 .....**103** C4
Devonshire Place
Mews W1 .....**103** C4
Devonshire Rd
W4 .....**38** A1
Devonshire Row
EC2 .....**110** B3
Devonshire Row
Mews W1 .....**92** B1
Devonshire Sq
EC2 .....**110** B2
Devonshire St
Chiswick W4 .....**38** A1
Marylebone W1 .....**104** A4
Devonshire Terr
W2 .....**101** A1
Devons Rd E3 .....**27** A1
Devons Road Sta
E3 .....**27** B1
Devon St SE15 .....**50** A4
De Walden Ho
NW8 .....**80** A2
De Walden St W1 .....**103** C3
Dewar St SE15 .....**64** C4
Dewberry St E14 .....**34** B4
Dewey Rd N1 .....**85** B2
Dewhurst Rd W14 .....**39** C3
Dewsbury Ct 4
W4 .....**37** B2
Dewsbury Rd NW10 .....**8** C3
Dewsbury Terr
NW1 .....**82** B4
D'eynsford Rd SE5 .....**48** C2
Dhonau Ho SE16 .....**153** A4
Diadem Ct W1 .....**105** B2
Dial Wlk The W8 .....**128** B4
Diamond Est
SW17 .....**72** A1
Diamond Ho 22
E3 .....**26** A3
Diamond St SE15 .....**49** A3
Diamond Terr
SE10 .....**52** B2
Diana Cl 27 SE8 .....**51** B4
Diana Ho
Barnes SW13 .....**46** B2
1 Brixton SW2 .....**62** B2
Diana, Princess of
Wales Meml
Fountain W2 .....**129** C4
Diana, Princess of
Wales Meml Wlk
W2 .....**114** C1
Dibden Ho 8 SE5 .....**49** A3
Dibden St N1 .....**86** C4
Dibdin Ho W9 .....**78** A1
Dibdin Row SE1 .....**135** C2
Dicey Ave NW2 .....**9** B4
Dickens Ct EC1 .....**96** A1
Dickens Ho
Bloomsbury WC1 .....**94** A2
Kennington SE17 .....**150** B1
Kilburn NW6 .....**23** C2
Paddington NW8 .....**89** C2
Dickenson Rd N8 .....**5** A4
Dickens Sq SE1 .....**137** A2
Dickens St SW8 .....**170** B2

Dickinson Ho 18
E2 . . . . .24 C2 99 B3
Dicksee Ho NW8 . . .89 B1
Dick Shepherd Ct 17
SW2 . . . . .62 C1
Dickson Ho 4 E1 . .32 A3
Didbin Ho N7 . . . . . .5 B2
Dieppe Cl W14 . . .140 C2
Digby Bsns Ctr E9 .17 C2
Digby Cres N4 . . . . . .6 B2
Digby Mans W6 . . . .39 B1
Digby Rd E9 . . . . . . .17 C2
Digby St E2 . . . . .25 B2
Diggon St E1 . . . . . .32 C4
Dighton Ct SE17 . . .48 B4
Dighton Rd SW18 . .59 B3
Dignum St N1 . . . . .85 B2
Digswell St N7 . . . . .14 C2
Dilke St SW3 . . . . .159 A4
Dilston Gr SE16 . . . .40 B2
Dilton Gdns SW15 .69 A3
Dimes PI 8 W6 . . . .39 A2
Dimson Cres E3 . . .26 C2
Dinerman Ct NW8 . .79 A4
Dingle Gdns E14 . . .33 C2
Dingley La SW16 . . .73 C2
Dingley PI EC1 . . . .97 A3
Dingley Rd EC1 . . . .96 C3
Dingwall Rd SW18 .71 B4
Dinmont Ho 20 E2 . .24 C3
Dinmont St 1 E2 . . .25 A3
Dinnington Ho 16 E2 25 A1
Dinnington Ho 17
E1 . . . . .25 A1
Dinsdale Rd SE3 . . .53 B4
Dinsmore Rd
SW12 . . . . .73 A4
Dinton Ho NW8 . . . .90 A2
Dinwiddy Ho N1 . . . .84 C1
Dionis Ho SW6 . . . .165 B2
Disbrowe Rd W6 . .154 B3
Discovery Bsns Pk 13
SE16 . . . . .139 C1
Discovery Dock E
E14 . . . . .42 A4
Discovery Ho 1
E14 . . . . .34 B2
Disney PI SE1 . . . .137 A4
Disney St SE1 . . . .137 A4
Disraeli Cl 1 W4 . . .37 C2
Disraeli Gdns
SW15 . . . . .58 B3
Disraeli Rd
Acton NW10 . . . . . .20 C3
Putney SW15 . . . . .58 A3
Diss St E2 . . . .24 B2 98 C4
Distaff La EC4 . . . .122 C4
Distillery La W6 . . . .39 B1
Distillery Rd W6 . . .39 B1
Distillery Wlk 3
TW8 . . . . .44 A4
Distin St SE11 . . . .149 B3
Ditchburn St E14 . .34 B2
Ditton Ho 10 E5 . . . .17 A3
Divis Way SW15 . . .57 A1
Dixon Clark Ct N1 . .15 A2
Dixon Ho 20 NW10 .30 C3
Dixon Rd SE14 . . . .51 A2
Dixon's Alley 6
SE16 . . . . .40 A4
Dixon Way 5 NW10 .8 A1
DLD College London
Marylebone Campus
W1 . . . . .103 C2
DLD College London
SE1 . . . . .135 A3

Dobree Ave NW10 . . .9 A1
Dobson Cl NW6 . . . .11 C1
Dobson Ho 18
SE14 . . . . .50 C4
Doby Ct EC4 . . . . .123 A4
Dockers Tanner Rd 20
E14 . . . . .41 C2
Dockhead SE1 . . . .139 A3
Dockhead Wharf
SE1 . . . . .139 A4
Dock Hill Ave
SE16 . . . . .40 C4
Docklands Acad
London SE14 . . . . .42 A3
Docklands Ct 20
E14 . . . . .33 B3
Docklands Visitor Ctr
E14 . . . . .42 B4
Dockley Rd SE16 . .139 B1
Dockley Road Ind Est
SE16 . . . . .139 B1
Dock Offices 17
SE16 . . . . .40 B3
Dock Rd E16 . . . . . .35 B2
Dock St E1 . . . . . . .125 B4
Doctor Spurstowe
Almshouses 9
E8 . . . . .17 A2
Docura Ho N7 . . . . . .5 B2
Docwras Bldgs N1 .16 A2
Dodbrooke Rd
SE27 . . . . .75 A1
Dodd Ho 18 SE16 . .40 A2
Doddington Gr
SE17 . . . . .150 B1
Doddington PI 4
SE17 . . . . .48 A4
Dodson St SE1 . . . .135 C3
Dod St E14 . . . . .33 C3
Dog & Duck Yd
WC1 . . . . .106 A4
Dog Kennel Hill
SE22 . . . . .64 A4
Dog Kennel Hill Sch
SE22 . . . . .64 A4
Dog La NW10 . . . . . . .8 A4
Dolben Ct SW1 . . . .147 C3
Dolben St SE1 . . . .122 B1
Dolby Rd SW6 . . . .164 C1
Doleman Ho 18
SE10 . . . . .52 A2
Dolland Ho SE11 . .149 A1
Dolland St SE11 . . .149 A1
Dollar Bay E14 . . . .42 B4
DOLLIS HILL 9 A4
Dollis Hill Sta NW2 .8 C3
Dolman Rd W4 . . . .37 C2
Dolman St SW4 . . . .62 B3
Dolphin Cl 2
SE16 . . . . .40 C4
Dolphin Ct N7 . . . . .13 C4
Dolphin La E14 . . . .34 A2
Dolphin Sq SW1 . .147 A1
Dolphin Twr 2
SE8 . . . . .51 B4
Dombey Ho
8 Bermondsey
SE1 . . . . .139 B3
4 Shepherd's Bush
W11 . . . . .30 C1
Dombey St WC1 . . .106 C4
Domelton Ho
SW18 . . . . .59 A1
Domett Cl SE5 . . . . .63 C3
Domfe PI E5 . . . . . . .17 B4
Domingo St EC1 . . . .96 C1

Dominie Sch The
SW11 . . . . .169 B3
Dominion Dr 35
SE16 . . . . .40 C4
Dominion St EC2 . .109 C4
Donaghue Cotts 10
E14 . . . . .33 A4
Donaldson Rd
NW6 . . . . .23 B4
Donegal Ho 2 E1 . .25 B1
Donegal St N1 . . . . .85 A1
Doneraile Ho
SW1 . . . . .146 A1
Doneraile St SW6 . 47 C2
Dongola Rd E1 . . . . .33 A4
Don Gratton Ho 22
E1 . . . . .111 B3
Donkey Alley SE22 .64 C1
Donkin Ho 16
SE16 . . . . .40 A2
Donne Ct SE24 . . . . .63 B1
Donne Ho
16 Canonbury
N16 . . . . .15 C4
14 Deptford SE14 . .50 C4
10 Poplar E14 . . . . .33 C3
Donnelly Ct SW6 . .154 B2
Donne PI SW3 . . . .144 B4
Donnington Ct
1 Camden Town
NW1 . . . . .13 A1
11 Willesden NW10 . .9 A1
Donnington Ho 8
SW8 . . . . .171 B2
Donnington Prim Sch
NW10 . . . . .22 A4
Donnington Rd
NW10 . . . . .22 A4
Donovan Ct SE1 . . .143 B1
Donovan Ho 4 E1 . .32 B2
Don Phelan Cl
SE5 . . . . .48 C2
Doon St SE1 . . . . . .121 B2
Doradus Ct 20
SW19 . . . . .69 C3
Dora Ho
3 Shepherd's Bush
W11 . . . . .30 C2
1 Tower Hamlets
E14 . . . . .33 B3
Dorando Cl W12 . . .30 A2
Doran Wlk
Stratford E15 . . . . . .19 B1
Stratford Marsh
E15 . . . . .27 B4
Dora St E14 . . . . . . .33 B3
Dorcas Ct 9
SW11 . . . . .59 C4
Dorchester Ct
1 De Beauvoir Town
N1 . . . . .16 A1
Herne Hill SE24 . . .63 B2
Knightsbridge
SW1 . . . . .131 A1
3 Streatham
SW16 . . . . .74 A2
Dorchester Dr
SE24 . . . . .63 B2
Dorchester Gr W4 . .38 B1
Dorchester Ho
TW9 . . . . .45 A3
Dordrecht Rd W3 . .29 A1
Doria Rd SW6 . . . . .165 A2
Doric Ho 2 E2 . . . . .25 C3
Doric Way NW1 . . . .93 B4

Doris Emmerton Ct
SW18 . . . . .59 B3
Dorking Cl SE8 . . . . .51 B4
Dorking Ho SE1 . . .137 C2
Dorland Ct SW15 . .58 B1
Dorlcote Rd SW18 . .72 A4
Dorleston Ct N1 . . . .87 C4
Dorman Way NW8 . .79 B4
Dormay St SW18 . . .59 A2
Dormstone Ho
SE17 . . . . .152 A3
Dornberg Cl SE3 . . .53 C3
Dorncliffe Rd
SW6 . . . . .164 B2
Dorney NW3 . . . . . . .12 A1
Dorney Ct SW6 . . . . .58 A4
Dornfell St NW6 . . .10 C3
Dornoch Ho 3 E3 . .26 B3
Dornton Rd SW12,
SW17 . . . . .72 B3
Dorothy Charrington
Ho 1 SE22 . . . . .64 C2
Dorothy Rd SW11 . .60 B4
Dorrell PI 8 SW9 . .62 C4
Dorrien Wlk SW16 . .73 C2
Dorrington Point 20
E3 . . . . .27 A2
Dorrington St
EC1 . . . . .107 B4
Dorrit Ho 2 W11 . . .30 C1
Dorrit St SE1 . . . . .137 A4
Dorset Bldgs EC4 .108 A1
Dorset Cl NW1 . . . .102 C4
Dorset Ct 3 N1 . . . .16 A1
Dorset Mans 2
W6 . . . . .47 C4
Dorset Mews
SW1 . . . . .132 A2
Dorset PI E15 . . . . .19 C2
Dorset Rd SW8 . . . .162 C2
Dorset Rise EC4 . . .108 A1
Dorset Sq NW1 . . . .90 C1
Dorset St W1 . . . . .103 A3
Dorton Cl 6 SE15 . .49 A3
Dorville Cres W6 . . .39 A3
Doughty Ct 11 E1 . .32 A1
Doughty Mews
WC1 . . . . .94 C1
Doughty St WC1 . . . .94 C1
Douglas Bldgs
SE1 . . . . .137 A4
Douglas Ct 5
NW6 . . . . .10 C1
Douglas Gracey Ho 1
SW18 . . . . .70 A4
Douglas Ho
Putney SW15 . . . . . .56 C1
Westminster SW1 . .147 B3
Douglas Johnstone
Ho SW6 . . . . .154 C3
Douglas Mews
NW2 . . . . .1 A1
Douglas Path 12 E14 .42 B2
Douglas Rd
Islington N1 . . . . . .15 B1
Kilburn NW6 . . . . . .23 B4
5 Newham E16 . . . .35 C4
Douglas Rd N N1 . .15 B2
Douglas Rd S N1 . .15 B2
Douglas St SW1 . . .147 B3
Douglas Waite Ho
NW6 . . . . .11 A1
Douglas Way SE8 . .51 B3
Doulton Ho 4
SE11 . . . . .149 A4
Doulton Mews 4
NW6 . . . . .11 A2

Dounesforth Gdns
SW18 . . . . .71 A3
Douro PI W8 . . . . . .128 B2
Douro St E3 . . . . . . .26 C3
Douthwaite Sq 11
E1 . . . . .125 C2
Dovecote Gdns 8
SW14 . . . . .55 C4
Dove Ct EC2 . . . . . .109 B1
Dovedale Cotts 8
SW11 . . . . .168 C2
Dovedale Ho N16 . . .6 A4
Dovedale Rd SE22 .65 A1
Dovehouse St
SW3 . . . . .144 A1
Dove Mews SW7 . .143 A2
Dovercourt Rd
SE22 . . . . .64 B1
Dover Ct
Clerkenwell EC1 . . .96 A2
17 Greenwich SE10 .52 A2
Dove Rd N1 . . . . . . .15 C2
Doverfield Rd
SW2 . . . . .74 A4
Dover Flats SE1 . . .152 B3
Dover Ho
Brixton SE5 . . . . . . .48 A2
11 Deptford SE15 . .50 B4
Dover House Rd
SW15 . . . . .57 A2
Dover Mans 18
SW9 . . . . .62 C4
Dover Park Dr
SW15 . . . . .57 A1
Dover St W1 . . . . . .118 C2
Dover Terr TW9 . . . .44 C1
Dover Yd W1 . . . . . .118 C2
Doves Yd N1 . . . . . .85 B3
Dovet Ct SW8 . . . .172 C4
Doveton Ho 7 E1 . . .25 B1
Doveton St 6 E1 . . .25 B1
Dove Wlk SW1 . . . .145 C2
Dovey Lo 4 N1 . . . .14 C1
Dowdeny Cl 12
NW5 . . . . .13 B3
Dowdeswell Cl
SW15 . . . . .56 A3
Dowding Ho N6 . . . . .3 C4
Dowell Ho SE21 . . . .76 B1
Dowells St SE10 . . .52 A4
Dowes Ho 3
SW16 . . . . .74 A1
Dowgate Hill EC4 . .123 B4
Dowland St W10 . . .23 A2
Dowlas St SE5 . . . . .49 A3
Dowlen Ct 2 E14 . . .41 C4
Dowler Ho 2 E1 . . .111 C1
Downbarton Ho 11
SW9 . . . . .173 B4
Downbury Mews 18
SW18 . . . . .58 C2
Downend Ct 1
SE15 . . . . .49 A4
Downer's Cotts
SW4 . . . . .61 B3
Downey Ho 6 E1 . . .25 C1
Downfield Cl W9 . . .88 A1
Downham Ct 1
N1 . . . . .15 C1
Downham Rd N1 . . .15 C1
Downing Ho
2 North Kensington
W10 . . . . .30 C3

Downing Ho continued
🔢 Putney SW15......56 C2
Downing St SW1 134 A4
Down Pl W6...........39 A1
Down St Mews
W1................118 A1
Down St E16 18 .....17 A3
Downsell Prim Sch
E15.................19 C4
Downsell Rd E15 ..19 C4
Downshire Hill
NW3...............11 C4
Downside 2
SW15..............58 A2
Downside Cres
NW3................12 A3
Downs La 2 E5.....17 A4
Downs Park Rd E5,
E8................16 C4
Downs Rd E5, N16 .16 C4
Down St W1...........1 A4
Downton Ave SW2..74 B2
Downtown Rd
SE16...............41 A4
Dowrey St N1.......85 B4
Dowson CI SE5.....63 C3
Dowson Ct SE13....67 C4
Dowson Ho 8 E1 ..32 C3
Doyce St SE1.......136 C4
Doyle Gdns NW10 ..22 A4
Doyle Ho 4 W3.....37 A4
D'Oyley St SW1... 145 B4
Doynton St N19 .....4 A2
Draco St SE17......48 B4
Dragon Ct 9
SW9.............61 C1
Dragon Ct W2... 106 B2
Dragonfly Pl 1
SE4................66 A3
Dragon Rd SE15...49 A4
Dragon Yd WC1...106 B2
Dragoon Rd SE8...41 B1
Dragor Rd NW10 ..20 C1
Drake Croft N16....6 C2
Drake Ct 6 W12...39 A4
Drakefell Rd SE4,
SE14...............65 C4
Drakefield Rd
SW17.............72 C1
Drake Ho
2 Limehouse
E14................33 A2
21 Stepney E1.....32 B4
Drakeley Ct N5....15 A4
Drake Rd SE4......66 C4
Drakes Ctyd NW6...10 B1
Drake St WC1.....106 C3
Drama Ctr London
EC1................95 C1
Draper Ho SE1...150 B4
Draper Pl N1.......86 B4
Drapers Almshouses 5
E3................26 C2
Drapers Gdns
EC2...............109 C2
Drapers Rd E15 ...19 C4
Drappers Way 8
SE16.............153 C4
Draycott Ave
SW3..............144 B3
Draycott Cl SE5...48 C3
Draycott Ct SW11 168 A4
Draycott Ho SW3 144 C3

Draycott Pl SW3.. 144 C3
Draycott Terr
SW3..............145 A3
Drayford Cl W9....23 B1
Dray Gdns SW2....62 B2
Draymans Ct 4
SW9..............62 B4
Draymans Mews
SE15..............49 B1
Drayson Mews
W8................127 C3
Drayton Ct SW10 143 A1
Drayton Gdns
SW10.............143 A1
Drayton Ho 11
SE5................48 C3
Drayton Park Mews 2
N5................15 C3
Drayton Park Prim
Sch 13 N5.......14 C3
Drayton Park Sta
N5................14 C3
Drayton Pk N5, N7 .14 C4
Drayton Rd NW10 ..21 B4
DRCA Business Ctr
SW11.............169 C3
Dreadnought St
SE10..............43 A3
Dresden Cl NW6...11 A2
Dresden Ho
6 Clapham
SW11.............169 B2
Lambeth SE11.....149 A4
Dresden Rd N19....4 C3
Dressington Ave
SE4................66 C1
Drewett Ho 5 E1.111 C1
Drever Ho 10 SW16 .74 A1
Drewstead La
SW16..............73 C2
Drewstead Rd
SW16..............73 C2
Driffield Rd E3 ....26 A3
Driftway Ho 16 E3 .26 B3
Drinkwater Ho 11
SE5................48 C3
Drive Mans 1
SW6..............164 B2
Drive The
Acton W3..........28 B3
Harlesden NW10 ..21 B4
Hendon NW11 ......1 A4
Islington N7........14 B2
Dr Johnson Ave
SW17..............73 A1
Dr Johnson's House
EC4...............107 C1
Droitwich Cl SE26 .76 C1
Dromore Rd SW15 .58 A1
Dron Ho E1.........32 B4
Droop St W10......23 A1
Drovers Ct SE13 ...67 B4
Drovers Pl SE15 ...50 A3
Drovers Way N7 ...14 A2
Druce Rd SE21.....64 A1
Druid St SE1......138 C3
Drumbeat Sch
SE4................66 B4
Drummer Lo N7.....5 B1
Drummond Cres
NW1..............93 B4
Drummond Gate
SW1..............147 C2
Drummond Ho 13

Drummond Rd
SE16..............40 A3
Drummonds Pl
TW9................54 A3
Drummond St
NW1..............92 C2
Drury Ct 7 SW15...56 C1
Drury Ho SW8....170 C4
Drury La WC2....106 B1
Dryad St SW15...57 C4
Dryburgh Ho SW1 146 B2
Dryburgh Mans
SW15..............57 B4
Dryburgh Rd
SW15..............57 B4
Dryden Bldg 10
E1................111 B2
Dryden Ct SW1...61 C2
Dryden Ct SE11...149 C3
Dryden Ho
6 Camberwell
SE5................49 A2
16 Stoke Newington
N16.................7 A1
Dryden St WC2...106 B1
Dryfield Wlk 1
SE8................51 C4
Drysdale Flats 3
E8................16 B3
Drysdale Ho 10
E2................24 A2 98 B4
Drysdale Pl
N1................24 A2 98 B4
Drysdale St
N1................24 A2 98 B4
Dublin Ave 8....24 C4
Ducal St 8
E2................24 B2 99 A3
Ducane Ct 6 W12 .30 B3
Du Cane Ct SW12..72 C3
Du Cane Rd W12 ..29 C3
Ducavel Ho SW2...74 B3
Duchess Mews
W1................104 B3
Duchess of Bedford
Ho W8............127 B3
Duchess of Bedford's
Wlk W8...........127 B3
Duchess St W1...104 B3
Duchy St SE1.....121 C2
Ducie Ho 2 SW15..57 B2
Ducie St SW4......62 B3
Duckett St E1......33 A4
Duck La W1......105 B1
Du Cros Rd W3....29 A1
DUDDEN HILL La
NW10...............8 C3
Dudley Ct
Marylebone W1...102 C1
St Giles WC2.....106 A2
Dudley Ho
13 Brixton SW9... 173 B2
Paddington W2.. 101 B3
Dudley Mews 4
SW2................62 C1
Dudley Rd
Kilburn NW6......23 B3
Richmond TW9.....44 B1
Dudley St W2... 101 B3
Dudmaston Mews
SW3..............143 C2
Duffell Ho SE11...149 A1
Dufferin Ave EC1...97 B1
Dufferin Ct EC1...97 B1
Dufferin St EC1...97 A1

Duffield Ho N4......6 B4
Duff Miller Sixth Form
Coll SW7........129 A1
Duff St E14.........34 A3
Dufour's Pl W1...105 A1
Dugard Way SE11 150 A3
Dugdale Ho 10
SE1................53 A1
Duke Humphrey Rd
SE3................53 A1
Duke of Wellington Pl
SW1, W1.........131 C4
Duke of York's
SW3..............145 A3
Duke of York St
SW1..............119 A2
Duke Rd W4.......37 C1
Duke St Hill SE1..123 C2
Duke St St James's
SW1..............119 A2
Duke's Ave W4....37 C1
Dukes Ct
Dulwich SE22.....76 C3
East Dulwich SE22 .65 A2
Lewisham SE13 ...52 B1
Mortlake SW14 ....45 C1
Dukes Gate 4 W4..37 B2
Dukes Head Ho ...6 A3
Duke's Mead SW1 147 C4
Duke Shore Wharf
E14................33 B2
Dukes La W8.....128 A4
Duke's Mews W1 103 C2
Duke's Pl EC3....110 B1
Dukes Point N6....4 A3
Duke's Rd WC1...93 C3
Duke Street Mans
W1................103 C1
Duke's Yd W1....117 C4
Dulas St N4.........5 B3
Dulford St W11....31 A2 112 A4
Dulka Rd SW11....60 B2
Dulverton NW1....83 A3
Dulverton Mans
WC1................95 A1
Dulwich SE21......76 A1
Dulwich Coll SE21 .76 A2
Dulwich Coll Prep Sch
SE21..............76 A1
Dulwich Com Hospl
SE22..............64 A3
Dulwich Comm
SE21..............63 C1
Dulwich Hamlet Jun
Sch SE21.........63 C1
Dulwich Lawn Cl
SE22..............64 B2
Dulwich L Ctr
SE22..............64 C3
Dulwich Mead
SE24..............63 B1
Dulwich Mews
1 East Dulwich
SE22..............64 B3
SE22..............64 B3
Dulwich Oaks The
SE21..............76 B1
Dulwich Picture Gall
SE21..............76 A1
Dulwich Prep Sch
SE21..............75 C3
Dulwich Rd SE24..63 A1
DULWICH
VILLAGE..........76 A4

Dulwich Village
SE21..............64 A1
Dulwich Village CE Inf
Sch
Dulwich SE21.....64 A1
Dulwich SE21.....64 A1
Dulwich Wood Prim
Sch SE21.........76 B1
Dumain Ct SE11.. 150 A3
Du Maurier Ho 2
NW3................12 B3
Dumbarton Ct 18
SW2................74 A4
Dumbarton Rd
SW2................62 A1
Dumont Rd N16....7 A1
Dumphreys Ho 5
SW4................73 C4
Dumpton Pl NW1 ..12 C1
Dunbar St SE27...75 B1
Dunbar Wharf 20
E14................33 B2
Dunboyne Rd NW3 .12 B3
Dunbridge Ho
SW15..............56 B1
Dunbridge St
Bethnal Green
E2................24 C1 99 C2
Bethnal Green E2 ..25 A1
Duncan Ct 3 E14..34 B4
Duncan Gr W3 .....29 A3
Duncan Ho 3
NW3................12 B1
Duncannon Ho
SW1..............147 C1
Duncannon St
WC2..............120 A3
Duncan Rd
Hackney E8........25 A4
Richmond TW9....54 A3
Duncan St N1.......86 A2
Duncan Terr N1 ....86 A2
Dunch St E1........32 A3
Duncombe Ho 7
SW19..............69 C3
Duncombe Prim Sch
N19.................5 A3
8 Upper Holloway
N19.................5 A3
Duncrievie Rd N19 .4 C3
Dundalk Ho 2 E1.32 B3
Dundalk Rd SE4...66 A4
Dundas Ho 12 E2..25 B3
Dundas Rd
Brixton SW9.....173 C3
London SE15.....50 B1
Dundee Ct 38 E1...32 A1
Dundee Ho W9....88 C4
Dundee St E1.......32 A1
Dundee Wharf
E14................33 B2
Dundonald Rd
NW10.............22 C4
Dundry Ho 8
SE26..............76 C1
Dunelm Gr
Brixton SE27.....75 B1
West Norwood
SE27..............75 B1
Dunelm St E1.....32 C3
Dunford Rd N7....14 B4
Dungarvan Ave
SW15..............56 C3

Dungeness Ho
SW18 . . . . 59 B3
Dunhill Point 12
SW15 . . . . 69 A3
Dunkeld Ho 13
E14 . . . . 34 C3
Dunlace Rd E5 . . . . . . 17 C4
Dunlin Ct 11 SE21 . . 75 C2
Dunlin Ho 15 SE16 . . 40 C2
Dunloe Ct 7 E2 . . . . 24 B3
Dunloe St E2 . . . . . . 24 B3
Dunlop Pl SE16 . . . . 139 A1
Dunmore Point 18
E2 . . . . 98 C3
Dunmore Rd NW6 . . 23 A4
Dunmow Ho SE11 . . 149 B2
Dunmow Rd E15 . . . 19 C4
Dunmow Wlk N1 . . . 86 C4
Dunnage Cres
SE16 . . . . 41 A2
Dunne Mews 11
NW5 . . . . 13 B3
Dunnet Ho 27 E3 . . . 26 B3
Dunnico Ho SE17 . . 152 A2
Dunnock Ct 11
SE21 . . . . 75 C2
Dunn's Pas WC1 . . . 106 B2
Dunn St E8 . . . . 16 B3
Dunollie Pl NW5 . . . 13 B3
Dunollie Rd NW5 . . . 13 B3
Dunoon Ho N1 . . . . 84 C3
Dunraven Ho 12
TW9 . . . . 44 B2
Dunraven Rd W12 . . 29 C1
Dunraven Sch
SW16 . . . . 74 B1
Dunraven St W1 . . . 117 A4
Dunrobin Ct N3 . . . . 11 A3
Dunsany Rd W14 . . . 39 C3
Dunsfold Ho 4
SW2 . . . . 74 B4
Dunsford Way
SW15 . . . . 57 A1
Dunsmure Rd N16 . . 7 A3
Dunstable Ct 3
SE3 . . . . 53 C3
Dunstable Mews
W1 . . . . 103 C4
Dunstable Rd TW10,
TW9 . . . . 54 A3
Dunstall Ho 9
SE15 . . . . 49 C2
Dunstan Ho SE4 . . . 51 B1
Dunstan Hos 5
E1 . . . . 32 B4
Dunstan Rd NW11 . . 1 C3
Dunstan's Gr SE22 . . 65 A1
Dunstan's Rd SE22 . . 64 C1
Dunster Ct EC3 . . . . 124 B4
Dunster Gdns
NW6 . . . . 10 B1
Dunsterville Way
SE1 . . . . 137 C3
Dunston Rd
Clapham SW11 . . . . 169 C1
Hackney E8 . . . . 24 B4
Dunston St E8 . . . . . 24 B4
Dunton Ho 14
SW16 . . . . 74 A1
Dunton Rd SE1 . . . . 152 C3
Duntshill Rd SW18 . 71 A3
Dunworth Mews
W11 . . . . 31 B3
Duplex Ride SW1 . . 131 A3
Durand Acad
SW9 . . . . 173 A3

Durand Gdns
SW9 . . . . 173 A3
Durant St
E2 . . . . 24 C2 99 B4
Durban Ho 28
W12 . . . . 30 A2
Durdans Ho 8
NW1 . . . . 13 B1
Durfey Pl SE5 . . . . . 48 C3
Durford Cres
SW15 . . . . 69 A3
Durham Ct
Brockley SE4 . . . . . . 66 C4
4 Kilburn NW6 . . . . 23 C3
Durham Ho
7 Dartmouth Pk
N6 . . . . 4 B4
10 Kilburn NW6 . . . 90 B3
Durham House St
WC2 . . . . 120 B3
Durham Pl SW3 . . . 144 C1
Durham Rd N4, N7 . . 5 B2
Durham Row E1 . . . 33 A4
Durham St SE11 . . . 162 C4
Durham Terr W2 . . . 100 A2
Durley Rd N16 . . . . . 7 A4
Durlock Ho 8
SW9 . . . . 173 B4
Durnford Ho 5
SE10 . . . . 52 B4
Durnsford Ave SW18,
SW19 . . . . 70 C2
Durnsford Rd SW18,
SW19 . . . . 70 C1
Durnford End Est
SE19 . . . . 71 A1
Durrell Rd SW6 . . . 164 C3
Durrels Ho W14 . . . 141 A4
Durrington Rd E5 . . 18 A4
Durrington Twr 3
SW8 . . . . 171 A2
Durrisdeer Ho
NW2 . . . . 10 B4
Durston NW5 . . . . . 12 C3
Durward St E1 . . . . . 32 A4
Durweston Mews
W1 . . . . 103 A4
Durweston St W1 . . 103 A3
Dutch Yd SW18 . . . . 58 C2
Dutton Ho SW2 . . . . 75 A3
Dutton St SE10 . . . . 52 B2
Dwight Ct 3 SW6 . . 164 B2
Dycer Ho 9 E9 . . . . 17 C2
Dye House La E3 . . . 26 C4
Dyer Ho SE4 . . . . . . 51 A1
Dyer's Bldgs EC1 . . 107 B3
Dyer's La SW15 . . . . 57 A3
Dykes Ct 11 SW2 . . 74 B3
Dylan Rd 2 SE24 . . 63 A3
Dylways SE5 . . . . . . 63 C3
Dymchurch Ho 12
E5 . . . . 17 A3
Dymes Path SW19 . . 69 C2
Dymock St SW6 . . . 59 A4
Dyne Rd NW6 . . . . . 10 B1
Dynevor Rd
Richmond TW10 . . . 54 A2
Shacklewell N16 . . . . 7 B1
Dynham Rd NW6 . . . 10 C1
Dyott St
Soho WC1 . . . . 105 C2
St Giles WC1, WC2 . . 106 A2
Dysart St
EC2 . . . . 24 A1 98 A1
Dyson Ho 3 SE10 . . 43 B1

E

Eade Rd N4 . . . . 6 B4
Eagle Cl SE16 . . . . . 40 B1
Eagle Ct
10 Dulwich SE21 . . . 75 C2
Holborn EC1 . . . . . 108 A4
Eagle Dwellings
N1 . . . . 97 A4
Eagle Ho
22 Bethnal Green
E1 . . . . 25 A1
Finsbury Pk N7 . . . . . 5 B1
Eagle Hts 10 SW11 . 60 A4
Eagle Lo NW11 . . . . 1 B4
Eagle Mans N16 . . . . 16 B3
Eagle Mews N1 . . . . 16 A2
Eagle Pl
South Kensington
SW7 . . . . 143 A2
St James SW1 . . . . . 119 A3
Eagle St WC1 . . . . . 106 C3
Eagle Wharf SE1 . . . 124 C1
Eagle Wharf Rd
N1 . . . . 87 A2
Eagle Works
E1 . . . . 24 B1 99 A1
Eagling Cl E3 . . . . . . 26 C2
Ealing, Hammersmith
and West London
Coll 10 W3 . . . . 28 A1
Ealing, Hammersmith
& West London Coll
W14 . . . . 140 A2
Eamann Casey Ho 24
SW9 . . . . 173 C3
Eamont Ct 14 . . . . . 80 B2
Eamont St NW8 . . . . 80 B2
Eardley Cres SW5 . . 141 C1
Earldom Rd SW15 . . 57 B3
Earle Ho SW1 . . . . . 147 C3
Earlham St WC2 . . . 106 A1
Earl Ho NW1 . . . . . . 90 B1
Earlom Ho WC1 . . . . 95 B3
Earl Rd SW14 . . . . . 55 B3
EARL'S COURT 141 C3
Earl's Court Gdns
SW5 . . . . 142 A3
Earl's Court Rd SW5,
W8 . . . . 141 C4
Earl's Court Sq
SW5 . . . . 142 A2
Earl's Court Sta
SW5 . . . . 141 C3
Earlsferry Way N1 . . 14 A1
EARLSFIELD 71 B3
Earlsfield Prim Sch
SW18 . . . . 71 B2
Earlsfield Rd
SW18 . . . . 71 B4
Earlsfield Sta
SW18 . . . . 71 B3
Earlsmead Rd
NW10 . . . . 22 B2
Earlsthorpe Mews 3
SW12 . . . . 60 C1
Earlstoke St EC1 . . . 96 A4
Earlston Gr E9 . . . . . 25 A4
Earls Wlk W8 . . . . . 127 B1
Earlswood Cl 10
SE10 . . . . 43 A1
Earlswood Ho 2
SW2 . . . . 74 B3

Earlswood St SE10 . 43 A1
Early Mews NW1 . . . 82 B4
Earnshaw Ho EC1 . . 96 B3
Earnshaw St WC1,
WC2 . . . . 105 C2
Earsby St W14 . . . . 140 B4
Earth Galleries
SW7 . . . . 129 C1
Eashing Point 5
SW15 . . . . 69 A3
Easley's Mews W1 . . 103 C2
EAST ACTON 29 A1
East Acton Arc
W3 . . . . 29 B3
East Acton Ct 3 W3 . 29 A2
East Acton La W3 . . 29 A2
East Acton Prim Sch
W3 . . . . 29 A2
East Acton Sta
W12 . . . . 29 B3
East Arbour St E1 . . 32 C3
East Bank N16 . . . . . 7 A4
East Block 5 SE1 . . 121 A1
East Block 3
SE1 . . . . 121 A1
East Block 3 . . . . . . 28 C2
Eastbourne Ave
W3 . . . . 28 C3
Eastbourne Gdns
SW14 . . . . 55 B4
Eastbourne Mews
W2 . . . . 101 A2
Eastbourne Rd
W4 . . . . 45 B4
Eastbourne Terr
W2 . . . . 101 A2
Eastbury Gr W4 . . . 38 A1
Eastbury Terr E1 . . . 25 C1
Eastcastle St W1 . . . 105 A2
East Churchfield Rd
W3 . . . . 28 C1
Eastcote St SW9 . . . 172 C1
East Cross Route
Bow E3 . . . . 26 C4
Hackney Wick E9 . . . 18 B3
Eastdown Ho E8 . . . 16 C4
Eastdown Pk SE13 . . 67 C3
EAST DULWICH . . . 64 C2
East Dulwich Gr
SE22 . . . . 64 A2
East Dulwich Rd SE15,
SE22 . . . . 64 C3
East Dulwich Sta
SE22 . . . . 64 A4
East Ferry Rd E14 . . 42 A2
Eastfields Ave
SW18 . . . . 58 C3
Eastfields Rd W3 . . . 28 B4
Eastfield St E14 . . . . 33 A4
East Harding St
EC4 . . . . 107 C2
East Heath Rd NW3 . 2 C1
East Hill SW18 . . . . . 59 B2
East India Bldgs 9
E14 . . . . 33 C2
East India Ct 17
SE16 . . . . 40 B4
East India Dock Basin
E14 . . . . 35 A2
East India Dock Rd
E14 . . . . 34 B3
East India Dock Road
Tunnel 18 E14 . . . . 34 C3
East La 5 SE16 . . . 139 B3
Eastlake Ho NW8 . . 89 C1
Eastlake Rd SE5 . . . 48 B1

Eastlands Cres
SE21 . . . . 64 B1
Eastleigh Wlk 9
SW15 . . . . 68 C4
Eastman Dental Hospl
WC1 . . . . 94 C2
Eastman Ho 7
SW4 . . . . 61 B1
Eastman Rd W3 . . . 37 C4
Eastmearn Rd SE21,
SE27 . . . . 75 B2
East Mount St E1 . . 32 A4
Eastney St SE10 . . . 42 C1
Easton Ho 8 SE27 . . 75 A1
Easton St WC1 . . . . 95 B2
East Parkside
SE10 . . . . 43 B4
East Pas EC1 . . . . . 108 C4
East Plaza E14 . . . . 34 A1
East Point 4 SE1 . . 153 B2
East Poultry Ave
EC1 . . . . 108 A3
East Putney Sta
SW15 . . . . 58 A2
East Rd
Chelsea SW1 . . . . . 145 B1
Shoreditch N1 . . . . . 97 C4
East Row W10 . . . . . 23 A1
Eastry Ho SW8 . . . . 162 A1
EAST SHEEN 55 C3
East Sheen Ave
SW14 . . . . 55 C3
East Sheen Prim Sch
SW14 . . . . 56 A3
East Smithfield
E1 . . . . 125 A3
East St SE17 . . . . . 151 B2
East Surrey Gr
SE15 . . . . 49 B3
East Tenter St E1 . . 111 A1
Eastvale 1 W3 . . . . 29 B1
East View NW3 . . . . 2 C2
Eastway E9, E9 . . . . 18 B3
Eastwell Ho SE1 . . . 137 C2
Eastwick Ct 2
SW19 . . . . 69 C3
Eastwood Cl 2
N7 . . . . 14 C3
Eaton Cl SW1 . . . . 145 B3
Eaton Dr SW9 . . . . . 63 A3
Eaton Gate SW1 . . 145 B4
Eaton Ho
Battersea SW11 . . . 167 C3
2 Limehouse E14 . . 33 B2
Eaton House The
Manor SW4 . . . . . . 61 A3
Eaton La SW1 . . . . 132 B1
Eaton Mans SW1 . . 145 B3
Eaton Mews N
SW1 . . . . 131 C1
Eaton Mews S
SW1 . . . . 132 A1
Eaton Mews W
SW1 . . . . 145 C4
Eaton Pl SW1 . . . . 131 C1
Eaton Row SW1 . . . 132 A1
Eaton Sq SW1 . . . . 131 C1
Eaton Sq Pre-Prep
Sch SW1 . . . . 146 A4
Eaton Square Sch
SW1 . . . . 146 C2

Eaton Terr
Belgravia SW1 . . . . . **145** C4
Bow E3 . . . . 26 A2
Eaton Terr Mews
SW1 . . . . **145** B4
Eatonville Rd
SW17 . . . . 72 B2
Eatonville Villas
SW17 . . . . 72 B2
Ebbisham Dr SW8 **162** C3
Ebbsfleet Rd NW2 . .10 A4
Ebenezer Ho
SE11 . . . . **150** A3
Ebenezer Mussel Ho
E2 . . . . 25 B3
Ebenezer St N1 . . . . 97 B4
Ebley Cl SE15 . . . . . . 49 B4
Ebner St SW18 . . . . . 59 A2
Ebony Cl NW10 . . . . . 8 B2
Ebony Ho
27 Bethnal Green
E2 . . . . 24 C2 **99** B3
10 West Hampstead
NW6 . . . . 11 A2
Ebor Cotts SW15 . .68 A1
Ebor St E1,
E2 . . . . 24 B1 **98** C2
Ebrahim Academy
E1 . . . . **111** C2
Ebrahim Coll E1 . . **111** C2
Eburne Rd N7 . . . . . . 5 A1
Ebury Bridge Rd
SW1 . . . . **145** C1
Ebury Mews
Belgravia SW1 . . . . . **146** A4
West Norwood
SE27 . . . . 75 A1
Ebury Mews E
SW1 . . . . **132** A1
Ebury Sq SW1 . . . . **145** C3
Ebury St SW1 . . . . **146** A4
Ecclesbourne Rd
N1 . . . . 15 B1
Eccles Ct SE11 . . . **149** A1
Eccles Rd SW11 . . . 60 B3
Eccleston Ho 1
SW2 . . . . 62 C1
Eccleston Mews
SW1 . . . . **131** C1
Eccleston Pl SW1 **146** A4
Eccleston Sq
SW1 . . . . **146** B3
Eccleston Sq Mews
SW1 . . . . **146** A3
Eccleston St SW1 **146** A4
Eckford St N1 . . . . . 85 B2
Eckington La 9
SE14 . . . . 50 C3
Eckstein Rd SW11 .60 A3
Ecole Francaise
Jacques Prevert 3
W6 . . . . 39 C2
Edans Ct W12 . . . . . . 38 B4
Edbrooke Rd W9 . . . 23 C1
Eddisbury Ho 7
SE26 . . . . 76 C1
Eddiscombe Rd
SW6 . . . . **165** A2
Eddison Ct N19 . . . . . 5 A2
Eddystone Rd SE4 . .66 A2
Eddystone Twr
SE8 . . . . 41 A1
Edenbridge Cl 29
SE16 . . . . 40 A1

Edenbridge Rd E9 . .17 C1
Eden Cl
Child's Hill NW3 . . . . . .1 C2
Kensington W8 . . . . **127** C2
Edendale W3 . . . . 28 A2
Eden Gr
Islington N7 . . . . 14 B3
Willesden NW10 . . . . . .9 A2
Edenham Way
W10 . . . . 31 B4
Eden Ho
16 Battersea
SW11 . . . . 60 A4
Lisson Gr NW8 . . . . . 90 A1
Edenhurst Ave
SW6 . . . . 58 B4
Eden Lodge NW6 . . . 9 C1
Eden Mews SW17 . .71 B1
Edensmuir Ct SE3 . .53 C3
Edensor Gdns W4 . .46 A3
Edensor Rd W4 . . . . . 46 A3
Edenvale St SW6 . **166** C1
Eden Way E3 . . . . 26 B4
Edgar Ho
Homerton E9 . . . . 18 A3
South Lambeth
SW8 . . . . **162** A2
Edgar Kail Way
SE22 . . . . 64 A3
Edgarley Terr
SW6 . . . . **164** A3
Edgar Rd E3 . . . . 27 A2
Edgar Wallace Cl 4
SE15 . . . . 49 A3
Edgcott Ho 2
W10 . . . . 30 B4
Edgecombe Ho
4 London SE5 . . . . . 49 A1
Putney SW19 . . . . 70 A4
Edgecote Cl 7
W3 . . . . 28 B1
Edgehill Ho 4
SW9 . . . . 48 A1
Edgeley La SW4 . . . . 61 C4
Edgeley Rd SW4 . . . . 61 C4
Edgel St SW18 . . . . . 59 A3
Edge St
W8 . . . . 31 C1 **113** C2
Edgeworth Ho
NW8 . . . . 78 C4
Edgson Ho SW1 . . **146** A2
Edgware Acad
WC2 . . . . **106** B1
Edgware Rd W1, W2,
NW1, NW8 . . . . . . **102** A3
Edgware Road Sta
(Bakerloo) NW1 . . **102** A3
Edgware Road Sta
(Met, Distr, Circle)
NW1 . . . . **102** B3
Edinburgh Cl 2
E2 . . . . 25 B3
Edinburgh Ct 10
SE16 . . . . 32 C1
Edinburgh Ho
13 Acton W3 . . . . 28 C3
Maida Vale W9 . . . . . 88 B4
Edington 20 NW5 . .12 C2
Edison Bldg 7
E14 . . . . 41 C4
Edison Ct SE10 . . . . 43 B3
Edison Ho SE1 . . . . **151** B4
Edis St NW1 . . . . 81 C4
Editha Mans
SW10 . . . . **156** C3

Edith Cavell Cl 2
N19 . . . . 5 A4
Edith Gr SW10 . . . **157** A2
Edith Ho 6 W6 . . . . 39 B1
Edithna St SW9 . . . . 62 A4
Edith Neville Cotts
NW1 . . . . 93 B4
Edith Neville Prim
Sch NW1 . . . . 83 B1
Edith Ramsay Ho 2
E1 . . . . 33 A4
Edith Rd
Stratford New Town
E15 . . . . 19 C3
West Kensington
W14 . . . . **140** B3
Edith Row SW6 . . . **166** B4
Edith St E2 . . . . 24 C3
Edith Summerskill Ho
6
SW6 . . . . **154** C2
Edith Terr SW10 . . **156** C2
Edith Villas W14 . . **140** C2
Edith Yd SW10 . . . **157** A2
Edmeston Cl E9 . . . . 18 A2
Edmond Ct SE14 . . . 50 B2
Edmonton Ct 5
SE16 . . . . 40 B3
Edmund Halley Way
SE10 . . . . 43 A4
Edmund Ho
Kennington SE17 . . **150** B1
New Cross Gate
SE14 . . . . 51 B2
Edmundsbury Ct Est
15 SW9 . . . . 62 B3
Edmund St SE5 . . . . 48 C3
Edmund Waller Prim
Sch SE14 . . . . 50 C1
Ednam Ho SE15 . . . 49 C4
Edna St SW11 . . . . **168** A3
Edred Ho E9 . . . . 18 A4
Edrich Ho SW4 . . . **172** A3
Edric Ho SW1 . . . . **147** C4
Edric Rd SE14 . . . . . 50 C3
Edridge Ho 9
SE27 . . . . 75 A1
Edward Alleyn Ho
SE21 . . . . 76 A4
Edward Ct 2 E16 . . 35 C4
Edward Dodd Ct
N1 . . . . 97 C4
Edward Edward's Ho
SE1 . . . . **122** A1
Edwardes Pl W8 . . **127** A1
Edwardes Sq W8 . **127** A1
Edward Friend Ho 6
N16 . . . . 7 A1
Edward Ho
Paddington W2 . . . . 89 B1
Vauxhall SE11 . . . . **149** A2
Edward Kennedy Ho
10 W10 . . . . 23 A1
Edward Mann Cl 13
E1 . . . . 32 C3
Edward Mews
NW1 . . . . 82 B1
Edward Mills Way 23
E14 . . . . 33 C3
Edward Pl SE8 . . . . . 51 B4
Edward Robinson Ho
8 SE14 . . . . 50 C3
Edward's Cotts 11
N1 . . . . 15 A1
Edward's La N16 . . . .7 A2
Edwards Mews
Islington N1 . . . . 14 C1

Edwards Mews
continued
Marylebone W1 . . . **103** B1
Edward Sq
Islington N1 . . . . 84 C3
1 Rotherhithe
SE16 . . . . 33 A1
Edward St SE14 . . . . 51 B3
Edward VII Mans
NW10 . . . . 22 C2
Edward Wilson Prim
Sch 2 W2 . . . . . . 100 A4
Edwin Ho SE15 . . . . 49 C3
Edwin's Mead E9 . .18 A4
Edwin St
Bethnal Green E1 . . 25 B1
Newham E16 . . . . 35 C4
Edwy Ho E9 . . . . 18 B4
Edwyn Ho SW18 . . . 59 A1
Eel Brook Cl SW6 **166** A4
Effie Pl SW6 . . . . . **155** C1
Effie Rd SW6 . . . . . **155** C1
Effingham Ho 37
SW8 . . . . **171** B1
Effra Ct SW2 . . . . . . 62 B2
Effra Mans SW2 . . . 62 C2
Effra Par SW2 . . . . . 62 C2
Effra Rd SW2 . . . . . . 62 C2
Effra Road Ret Pk
SW2 . . . . 62 C2
Egbert Ho E9 . . . . . . 18 A3
Egbert St NW1 . . . . . 81 B4
Egbury Ho SW15 . . . 56 B1
Egerton Cres
SW3 . . . . **144** B4
Egerton Ct 5
TW10 . . . . 54 A2
Egerton Dr SE10 . . . 52 A2
Egerton Gdns
Knightsbridge
SW3 . . . . **130** A1
Willesden NW10 . . . . 22 B4
Egerton Gdns Mews
SW3 . . . . **130** B1
Egerton Ho W4 . . . . 45 B4
Egerton Pl SW3 . . **130** B1
Egerton Rd N16 . . . . . 7 B4
Egerton Terr SW3 . **130** B1
Egham Cl SW19 . . . . 70 A2
Eglantine Rd
SW18 . . . . 59 B2
Eglington Ct SE17 . . 48 B4
Eglinton Mews
SW15 . . . . 57 B4
Egliston Rd SW15 . .57 B4
Egmont St SE14 . . . 50 C3
Egremont Ho SE13 . 52 A1
Egremont Rd SE27 . .74 C1
Egret Ho 5 SE16 . . . 40 C2
Eider Ct 38 SE8 . . . . 51 B4
Elaine Ct 15 NW3 . .12 B2
Elaine Gr NW5 . . . . . 12 C3
Elaine Ho N4 . . . . 5 A3
Elam Cl SE5 . . . . 48 A1
Elam St SE5 . . . . 48 A1
Elan Ct E1 . . . . 32 A4
Eland Rd SW11 . . . . 60 B4
Elba Pl SE17 . . . . . **151** A4
Elbe St SW6 . . . . . **166** C2
Elborough St
SW18 . . . . 70 C3
Elbury Dr E16 . . . . . . 35 C3
Elcho St SW11 . . . **158** B1

Elcot Ave SE15 . . . . 50 A3
Elderberry Rd W5 . .36 A4
Elderfield Ho 4
E14 . . . . 33 C2
Elderfield Rd E5 . . . .17 B4
Elder St E1 . . . . 24 B1 **98** C1
Elder Wlk
Islington N1 . . . . 86 B4
2 Lewisham SE13 . . 67 B4
Eldon Ct NW6 . . . . . . 23 C4
Eldon Gr NW3 . . . . . . 11 C3
Eldon Ho SW9 . . . . . 63 A4
Eldon Rd W8 . . . . . **128** B2
Eldon St EC2 . . . . . **109** C3
Eldon Way NW10 . . .20 A3
Eldridge Ct SE16 . **139** B1
Eleanor Cl SE16 . . . . 40 C4
Eleanor Ct 13 E2 . . 24 C4
Eleanor Gr SW13 . . .56 A4
Eleanor Ho
5 Hammersmith
W6 . . . . 39 B1
1 Kentish Town
NW5 . . . . 13 B3
Eleanor Palmer Prim
Sch 12 NW5 . . . . . 13 B3
Eleanor Rathbone Ho
6 N6 . . . . 4 C4
Eleanor Rd
Brixton SW9 . . . . . **173** C3
Hackney E8 . . . . 17 A1
Eleanor St E3 . . . . . . 26 C2
Electra Bsns Pk
E16 . . . . 34 C4
Electra Ct 8 NW2 . . . 9 B2
Electric Ave SW9 . . 62 C3
Electric Ho 19 E3 . . 26 C2
Electric La 2
SW9 . . . . 62 C3
Electric Mans 1
SW9 . . . . 62 C3
Elephant & Castle
Newington SE1 . . . **136** B1
Newington SE1 . . . **150** B4
Elephant & Castle Sh
Ctr SE1 . . . . **150** C4
Elephant & Castle Sta
Lambeth SE1 . . . . . **136** B1
Newington SE17 . . **150** C4
Elephant La SE16 . . 40 B4
Elephant Rd SE17 **150** C4
Elfindale Rd SE24 . .63 B2
Elfort Rd N5 . . . . 14 C4
Elf Row E1 . . . . 32 B2
Elgar Ave W5 . . . . . . 36 A4
Elgar Cl SE8 . . . . 51 C3
Elgar Ct W14 . . . . . **126** A1
Elgar Ho
Pimlico SW1 . . . . . **146** B1
South Hampstead
NW6 . . . . 11 B1
Elgar St SE16 . . . . . . 41 A3
Elgin Ave
Hammersmith
W12 . . . . 39 A3
Westbourne Green
W9 . . . . 88 B4
Elgin Cl W12 . . . . . . 39 A4
Elgin Cres
W11 . . . . 31 A2 **112** B4
Elgin Ct W9 . . . . 88 A2
Elgin Ho E14 . . . . 34 A3
Elgin Mans W9 . . . . 88 A3
Elgin Mews N1 . . . . 15 A2
Elgin Mews N W9 . . 88 B4
Elgin Mews S W9 . . 88 B4

lgood Cl
W11 . . . . 31 A1 112 A1
Igood Ho NW8 . . . 79 C1
liam Ho NW6 . . . . .15 A2
lia Mews N1 . . . . .86 A1
lias PI SW8 . . . 163 B3
lia St N1 . . . . . . .86 A1
lim Est SE1 . . . . 138 A2
lim St SE1 . . . . .138 A2
liot Cotts SE3 . . . .53 A1
liot Ct SW18 . . . . .59 A1
liot Gdns SW15 . . .56 C3
liot Ho I SE11 . . .52 B1
liot Ho III TW10 . . .54 B1
liot Mews NW8 . . .78 C1
liot Pk SE23 . . . . .52 B1
liot PI SE3 . . . . .53 A1
lis Wy E15 . . . . . .19 B3

Elizabeth Ave
Islington N1 . . . . .15 C1
Shoreditch N1 . . . 87 A4
Elizabeth Barnes Ct II
SW6 . . . . 166 B2
Elizabeth Blount Ct III
E14 . . . . .33 A3
Elizabeth Cl
Paddington W9 . . .89 A1
I2 Poplar E14 . . . .34 A3
Elizabeth Cooper Lo
SW12 . . . . .60 C1
Elizabeth Cotts III
TW9 . . . . .44 C2
Elizabeth St
Chelsea SW10 . . 157 C3
East Dulwich SE22 .64 C3
Marylebone NW8 . .90 B2
Westminster SW1 . 133 C1
Elizabeth Finn Ho II
W12 . . . . .38 C3
Elizabeth Garrett
Anderson Language
Coll N1 . . . . . . .85 A1
Elizabeth Gdns
W3 . . . . .29 B1
Elizabeth Ho
II5 Hammersmith
W6 . . . . .39 B1
Lambeth SE11 . . 149 C3
Elizabeth Ind Est
SE14 . . . . .50 C4
Elizabeth Kenny Ho
N1 . . . . .15 B2
Elizabeth Mews
I2 Hackney E2 . . .24 C3
Maitland Pk NW3 . 12 B2
Elizabeth Selby Inf
Sch II E2 . . . .24 C2 99 C4
Elizabeth Sq I3
SE16 . . . . .33 A2
Elkington Point
SE11 . . . . .149 B3
Elkstone Rd W10 . .31 B4
Ellacombe Ho II
SW2 . . . . .74 C4
Elland Ho I3 E14 . .33 B3
Elland Rd SE15 . . .65 B3
Ella Rd N4, N8 . . . .5 A4
Ellenborough Ho II
W12 . . . . .30 A2
Ellenborough PI
SW15 . . . . .56 C3
Ellen St E1 . . . . .111 C1

Ellen Wilkinson Ho
I2 Globe Town
E2 . . . . .25 C2
West Brompton
SW6 . . . . 155 A3
Ellerby St SW6 . . . .47 C2
Ellerdale Cl I5 . . . .11 B4
Ellerdale Rd NW3 . .11 B3
Ellerdale St SE13 . .67 A4
Ellerker Gdns
TW10 . . . . .54 A1
Ellerslie Gdns
NW10 . . . . .21 C4
Ellerslie Ind Est
SW2 . . . . .62 A2
Ellerslie Rd W12 . .30 A1
Ellerton St III E3 . .27 A2
Ellerton Rd
Barnes SW13 . . .46 C2
Wandsworth SW17 .71 C1
Ellery Cl III NW10 .21 B3
Ellery Ho III SE17 151 C3
Ellery St SE15 . . . .50 A1
Ellesmere Ct W4 . .45 C4
Ellesmere Rd
Bow E3 . . . . . . .26 A3
Chiswick W4 . . . .45 C4
Willesden NW10 . . .8 A2
Ellesmere St E14 . .34 A3
Ellingfort Rd E8 . . .17 A1
Ellingham Rd
Leyton E15 . . . . .19 C4
Shepherd's Bush
W12 . . . . .38 C4
Ellington Ho SE1 .137 A1
Ellington St N7 . . .14 C2
Elliott Rd
Acton W4 . . . . . .38 A2
Brixton SW9 . . . . .48 A2
Elliott's PI N1 . . . .86 B3
Elliott Sq NW3 . . .12 A1
Elliott's Row I3 SE11 150 B4
Ellis Cl NW10 . . . . .9 B2
Ellisfield Dr SW15 .68 C4
Ellis Franklin Ct
NW8 . . . . .78 C2
Ellison Ho II SE13 .52 B1
Ellison Rd SW13 . .46 B1
Ellis St SW1 . . . .145 B4
Ellis Terr SE5 . . . 163 C2
Ellsworth St E2 . . .25 A2
Ellwood Ct IIW9 . .88 B1
Elmar Ct NW4 . . . 164 B2
Elm Bank Gdns
SW13 . . . . .46 A1
Elm Bank Mans
SW13 . . . . .46 A1
Elmbourne Rd
SW17 . . . . .73 A1
Elmbridge Wlk E8 .16 C1
Elm Cl III N19 . . . .4 B2
Elmcourt Rd SE21,
SE27 . . . . .75 B2
Elm Cres W5 . . . . .36 A4
Elmcroft Ave NW11 .1 B4
Elmcroft Cres
NW11 . . . . .1 A4
Elmcroft St E5 . . . .17 B4
Elm Ct
Brixton SW9 . . . 173 B4
Lewisham SE13 . . .67 C4
I2 Notting Hill W2 .31 C4

Elm Ct continued
Strand EC4 . . . . 121 B4
Elm Ct Sch SE27 . .74 B4
Elmer Ho NW1 . . .102 A4
Elmfield Ho
I5 Canonbury N5 . .15 B3
Paddington W9 . . .23 C1
Elmfield Mans I5
SW17 . . . . .72 C2
Elmfield Rd SW17 .72 C3
Elmfield Way W9 . .31 C4
Elm Friars Wlk
NW1 . . . . .13 C1
Elm Gn
Cricklewood NW2 . .1 A1
Peckham SE15 . . .49 C1
Elmgreen Sch The
SE27 . . . . .75 A1
Elm Grove Rd
Barnes SW13 . . .46 C1
Ealing W5 . . . . . .36 A4
Elm Ho I E14 . . . .42 B4
Elmhurst Mans
SW4 . . . . .61 C4
Elmhurst St SW4 . .61 C4
Elmhurst Villas
SE15 . . . . .65 B3
Elmington Rd SE5 .48 C3
Elmira St SE13 . . .67 A4
Elm Lo SW6 . . . . .47 C2
Elmore Ho SW9 . .48 A1
Elmore St N1 . . . .15 C1
Elm Park Gdns
SW10 . . . . 143 B1
Elm Park Ho
SW10 . . . . 143 B1
Elm Park La SW3 .143 B1
Elm Park Mans
SW10 . . . . 157 A4
Elm Park Rd SW3 .157 B4
Elm Pk SW2 . . . . .74 B4
Elm PI SW7 . . . . 143 B2
Elm Quay SW8 . . 161 B3
Elm Rd SW14 . . . .55 B3
Elm Row NW3 . . . . .2 B1
Elms Cres SW4 . . .61 C1
Elmshaw Rd SW15 .56 C2
Elmslie Point I2
E3 . . . . .33 B4
Elms Mews I3 W2 115 B4
Elms Rd SW4 . . . .61 B2
Elm St WC1 . . . . .95 A1
Elms The
Barnes SW13 . . .56 B4
I5 Harlesden
NW10 . . . . .21 A3
Elmstone Rd SW6 .165 B4
Elm Terr NW2 . . . . .1 C1
Elmton Ct NW8 . . .89 B2
Elm Tree Cl NW8 . .89 B3
Elm Tree Ct
I5 Camberwell
SE5 . . . . .48 B2
St John's Wood
NW8 . . . . .89 B3
Elm Tree Rd NW8 . .89 B3
Elm Way NW10 . . . .8 A4
Elm Wlk NW3 . . . . .1 C2
Elmwood Ct
SW11 . . . . 170 A4
Elm Wood Prim Sch
SE27 . . . . .75 C2
Elmwood Rd
Chiswick W4 . . . .45 B4
Herne Hill SE24 . .63 C2

Elmworth Gr SE21 .75 C2
Elnathan Mews
W9 . . . . .88 B1
Elrington Rd E8 . . .16 C2
Elsa St E1 . . . . . . .33 A4
Elsdale Ho II E9 . . .17 B2
Elsdale St E9 . . . . .17 B1
Elsden Mews E2 . . .25 B3
Elsenham St SW18,
SW19 . . . . .70 B2
Elsfield NW5 . . . . .13 A3
Elsham Rd W14 . .126 A3
Elsham Terr W14 . 126 A3
Elsie Lane Ct W2 . 100 A3
Elsiemaud Rd SE4 .66 B2
Elsie Rd SE22 . . . .64 B3
Elsinore Gdns NW2 . .1 A1
Elsinore Ho
I2 Camberwell
SE5 . . . . .48 B1
Islington N1 . . . . .85 B3
Elsinore Way TW9 .55 A4
Elsley Rd SW11 . . .60 C4
Elsley Sch I3
SW17 . . . . .72 A2
Elspeth Rd SW11 . .60 B3
Elstead Ho II
SW2 . . . . .74 B4
Elsted St SE17 . . .151 C3
Elstow Grange
NW6 . . . . .9 C1
Elswick Rd SE13 . .52 A1
Elswick St SW6 . . .166 C2
Elsworthy Rd NW3 .80 A4
Elsworthy Rise
NW3 . . . . .12 A1
Elsworthy Terr
NW3 . . . . .12 A1
Elsynge Rd SW18 . .59 C2
Elsynge Road Mans
SW18 . . . . .59 C2
Elthiron Rd SW6 .165 C3
Elthorne Rd N19 . . .4 C2
Elthruda Rd SE13 . .67 C1
Elton Ho I3 E3 . . . .26 B4
Elton PI N16 . . . . .16 A3
Elton St II N16 . . .16 A3
Eltringham St
SW18 . . . . .59 B3
Elvaston Mews
SW7 . . . . .129 A2
Elvaston PI SW7 . 129 A1
Elveden Ho I7
SW9 . . . . .63 A3
Elver Gdns I0
E2 . . . . 24 C2 99 C4
Everson Rd I3 E14 .42 A3
Elverson Rd Sta
SE8 . . . . .51 A1
Elverton St SW1 . 147 B4
Elvin Ho I7 E9 . . . .17 B2
Elvis Rd NW2 . . . . .9 B2
Elwin St E2 . . 24 C2 99 B4
Elwood Ho N5 . . . . .6 A1
Elwood St N4, N5 . . .6 A1
Elworth Ho SW8 . .163 A1
Ely Cotts SW8 . . .162 C1
Ely Court Flats
SW4 . . . . .164 A3
Ely Ct
Holborn EC1 . . . .107 C3
I2 Maida Vale
NW6 . . . . .23 C3
Ely Ho I2 SE15 . . .49 C3

Ely PI
EC1 . . . . .107 C3
Kensington SW1 . 162 C1
Elysium Gate I7
SW6 . . . . 164 C2
Elysium PI SW6 . .164 C1
Elysium St SW6 . .164 C1
Elystan Ct SW15 . .57 A2
Elystan PI SW3 . .144 C2
Elystan St SW3 . .144 B3
Elystan Wlk N1 . . .85 B3
Emanuel Ave W3 . .28 B3
Emanuel Ct W3 . . .28 C3
Emanuel Sch
SW11 . . . . .60 A2
Embankment
SW15 . . . . .47 C1
Embankment Gdns
SW3 . . . . .159 A4
Embankment Pier
WC2 . . . . 120 B2
Embankment PI
WC2 . . . . 120 B2
Embankment Sta
WC2 . . . . 120 B2
Embassy Ct NW8 . .79 C1
Embassy Ho I2
NW6 . . . . .10 C1
Emba St SE16 . . .139 C3
Ember Ct I3 W12 . .38 A3
Emberton SE5 . . . .49 A4
Emberton Ct EC1 . .96 A3
Embleton Rd SE13 .67 A3
Emden St SW6 . . .166 B4
Emerald Rd NW10 . .20 C4
Emerald Sq SW15 .56 C2
Emerald St WC1 . .106 C4
Emerson Ho N16 . .16 A3
Emerson St SE1 . .122 C2
Emery Hill St
SW1 . . . . .133 A1
Emery St SE1 . . . .135 C2
Emily St I3 E16 . . .35 B3
Emirates Airway
SE10 . . . . .35 B1
Emirates Greenwich
Peninsula SE10 . . .43 A4
Emirates Royal Dock
E16 . . . . .35 B1
Emirates Stad
(Arsenal FC) N7 . .14 C4
Emlyn Gdns I3
W12 . . . . .38 A3
Emlyn Rd W12 . . . .38 A3
Emmanuel CE Prim
Sch NW6 . . . . . . .11 A2
Emmanuel Ho
Dulwich SE21 . . . .75 C1
Lambeth SE11 . . 149 B3
Emmanuel Rd
SW12 . . . . .73 C3
Emma St E2 . . . . .25 A3
Emminster NW6 . . .78 A4
Emmott Cl E1 . . . .26 A1
Emperor's Gate
SW7 . . . . .142 C4
Empingham Ho I0
SE8 . . . . .40 C2
Empire Ho SW3 . .130 A1
Empire Sq N19 . . . .5 A1
Empire Wharf E3 . .26 A4
Empire Wharf Rd
E14 . . . . .42 C2

Empress App
SW6 .... **155** B4
Empress Ms 56
.... 48 B1
Empress Pl SW5 ...... 141 B1
Empress St SE17 ..... 48 A4
Empress State
Building SW6 .... **141** B1
Empson St E3 .... 27 A1
Emsworth St SW2 ....74 B2
Emu Rd SW8 .... 170 A1
Enard Ho 28 E3 ......26 B3
Enbrook St W10 .... 23 A2
Enclave Ct E1 .... 96 B2
Endell St WC2 .... 106 A1
Enderby St SE10 ......43 A1
Endlesham Ct 2
SW12 ....72 C4
Endlesham Rd
SW12 ....72 C4
Endsleigh Gdns
WC1 ....93 B2
Endsleigh Mans 4
SW16 ....74 A1
Endsleigh Pl WC1 .... 93 C2
Endsleigh St WC1 .... 93 C2
Endwell Rd SE4 ......51 A1
Endymion Rd
Harringay N4 ....6 A4
Tulse Hill SW2 ....62 B1
Energen Cl NW10 ....8 A2
Enfield Cloisters 7
N1 ....24 A2 98 A4
Enfield Ho 24
SW9 .... 172 B2
Enfield Rd
De Beauvoir Town E8,
N1 ....16 A1
South Acton W3 ....37 A4
England's La NW3 ....12 B2
Englefield Rd N1 .... 92 C3
Englefield Rd N1 ....16 A1
Englewood Rd
SW12 ....61 B1
English Gardening
Sch 12 SW3 .... 158 C4
English Grounds
SE1 .... 124 A1
English Martyrs RC
Prim Sch
Walworth SE17 ..... 151 C3
Whitechapel E1 ...... 111 A1
English St E3 ....26 B1
Enid St SE16 .... 139 A2
Enid Stacy Ho 11
N19 ....5 A4
Enmore Ct SW14 ....55 C2
Enmore Gdns
SW14 ....55 C2
Enmore Rd SW15 ....57 B2
Ennerdale Ho 3
N4 ....6 C4
Ennerdale Rd TW9 ....44 B1
Ennersdale Rd
SE13 ....67 C2
Ennis Ho 10 E14 ....34 A3
Ennismore Ave
W4 ....38 B2
Ennismore Gdns
SW7 .... 130 A2

Ennismore Gdns
Mews 8 SW7 ..... 130 A2
Ennismore Mews
SW7 .... 130 A2
Ennismore St
SW7 .... 130 A2
Ennis Rd N4 ....5 C3
Ensbury Ho SW8 .... 162 C2
Ensign Cl 12 E1 ..... 125 C3
Ensign Ho 15 E14 ....41 C4
Ensign St E1 .... 125 B4
Ensor Mews SW7 ... 143 B2
Enterprise Ho 36
E9 ....17 B1
Enterprise Way
College Pk NW10 .....21 C2
Wandsworth SW18 ....58 C3
Enterprise Way
SE8 ....41 B2
Epirus Mews SW6 .. 155 B2
Epirus Rd SW6 ..... 155 A2
Epping Cl E14 ....41 C2
Epping Ho 5 E5 ....7 C2
Epping Pl N1 ....14 C2
Epple Rd SW6 ...... 165 A4
Epstein Ct N1 ....86 B3
Epworth St EC2 ......97 C1
Equity Sq 29
E2 ....24 B2 99 A3
Erasmus St SW1 ... 147 C3
Erconwald St W12 ...29 B3
Eresby Ho SW7 ..... 130 B3
Eresby Pl NW6 ....10 C1
Erica Ct SW4 .... 172 B3
Erica Ho SE4 ....66 B4
Erica St W12 ....29 C2
Ericcson Cl SW18 ....58 C2
Eric Fletcher Ct 16
N1 ....15 B1
Eric Macdonald Ho
SW6 .... 165 C3
Eric Rd NW10 ....8 B2
Ericson Ho
London SE13 ....67 C3
Stamford Hill N16 .....7 B3
Eric St E3 ....26 B1
Eric Wilkins Ho 14
SE1 .... 153 B1
Eridge Ho SE22 ......64 B4
Eridge House Prep
Sch SW6 .... 164 C2
Eridge Rd W4 ....37 C3
Erin Cl SW6 .... 155 C1
Erin Ct NW2 ....9 B2
Erlanger Rd SE14 ....50 C1
Ermine Rd SE13 ......67 A3
Ernest Bevin Coll
SW17 ....72 A2
Ernest Gdns W4 .....45 A4
Ernest Simmonds Ho
SE14 ....50 B1
Ernest St E1 ....25 C1
Ernshaw Pl SW15 ....58 A2
Eros (Shaftesbury
Meml Fountain)
W1 .... 119 B3
Erpingham Rd
SW15 ....57 B4
Errington Rd W9 .....23 B1
Errol St EC1 ....97 A1
Erskine Ho SW1 .... 146 C1
Erskine Rd NW3 .....12 B1
Escuan Lo N5 ....15 B3
Esher Gdns SW19 ...69 C2
Esher Ho 8 SW8 ... 171 C2
Eskdale NW1 ....82 C1

Esk Ho E3 ....26 B1
Esme Ho SW15 ......56 B3
Esmeralda Rd
SE1 .... 153 C3
Esmond Ct 18
W8 .... 128 B2
Esmond Gdns W4 ...37 C2
Esmond Rd
Acton W4 ....37 C3
Kilburn NW6 ....23 B4
Esmond St SW15 ....58 A3
Esparto St SW18 ....71 A4
Espirit Ct E1 .... 110 C3
Espirit Ho 6
SW15 ....58 A2
Essendine Mans
W9 ....23 C2
Essendine Prim Sch
10 W9 ....23 C2
Essendine Rd W9 ...23 C2
Essex Ct
Barnes SW13 ....46 B1
Hammersmith W6 ....39 B3
Holborn EC4 .... 107 B1
Essex Ho 2 E14 .....34 A3
Essex Park Mews
W3 ....29 A1
Essex Pl W4 ....37 B2
Essex Place Sq 6
W4 ....37 C2
Essex Rd
Acton W3 ....28 B2
Chiswick W4 ....37 C2
Islington N1 ....86 B4
Willesden NW10 ....8 A1
Essex Road Sta N1 .15 B1
Essex St WC2 .... 121 B4
Essex Villas W8 ... 127 B3
Essian St E1 ....33 A4
Essington SW15 ....58 A1
Estcourt Rd SW6 ... 154 C2
Estella Ho 19 W11 ...30 C2
Estelle Rd NW3 ......12 B4
Esterbrooke St
SW1 .... 147 B3
Este Rd SW11 ....60 A4
Estoria Cl 22 SW2 ...74 C4
Etal Ho N1 ....15 A1
Etchingham Rd
E15 ....19 B4
Eternit Wlk SW6 .....47 C2
Ethelbert Ho E9 ......18 A4
Ethelbert St SW12 ...73 A3
Ethelburga St
SW11 .... 168 B4
Ethelburga Twr
SW11 .... 168 B4
Ethelden Rd W12 ....30 A1
Ethel Rankin Ct 8
SW6 .... 164 C2
Ethel St SE17 ...... 151 A3
Ethelworth Ct 4
SW2 ....74 C3
Etherow St SE22 ....76 C4
Ethnard Rd SE15 ....50 A4
Eton Ave NW3 ....12 A1
Eton Cl SW18 ....71 A4
Eton College Rd
NW3 ....12 B2
Eton Ct NW3 ....11 C1
Eton Garages 11
NW3 ....12 A2
Eton Hall NW3 ....12 B2
Eton Ho N5 ....15 A4
Eton Pl NW1 ....12 C1

Eton Rd NW3 ....12 B2
Eton Rise NW3 ....12 B2
Eton St TW10 ....54 A2
Eton Villas NW3 .....12 B2
Ettrick St E14 ....34 B3
Eugene Cotter Ho
SE17 .... 151 C3
Eugenia Rd SE16 ....40 B2
Eurocentres SW1 .. 146 B3
Euro Cl NW10 ....8 C2
Eurolink Bsns Ctr
SW2 ....62 C2
Europa Pl EC1 ......96 C3
European Coll 10
E1 .... 111 B2
Eustace Bldg
SW8 .... 160 A3
Eustace Ho SE11 ... 148 C4
Eustace Rd SW6 ... 155 B2
Euston Rd NW1 .....93 A2
Euston Sq NW1 .....93 A3
Euston Square Sta
NW1 ....93 A2
Euston Sta NW1 .....93 B3
Euston Underpass
NW1 ....93 A2
Evan Cook Cl SE15 ..50 B2
Evandale Rd SW9 .. 173 C2
Evangelist Rd
NW5 ....13 A4
Evans Cl E8 .... 16 B2
Evans Ho
6 Shepherd's Bush
W12 ....30 A2
South Lambeth
SW8 .... 161 C1
Evelina Childrens'
Hospl SE1 .... 134 C2
Evelina Mans 9
SE5 ....48 C3
Evelina Rd SE15 ....50 B1
Evelyn Ct
Marylebone W1 ..... 102 C1
Shacklewell E8 ....16 C4
Shoreditch N1 ....87 B1
Evelyn Denington Ct
2 N1 ....15 A1
Evelyn Fox Ct W10 .30 B4
Evelyn Gdns
Richmond TW9 ....54 A3
South Kensington
SW7 .... 143 B1
Evelyn Grace Acad
SE24 ....63 A3
Evelyn Ho
Bedford Pk W12 .....38 B4
3 Brixton SW2 ......62 B2
16 Spitalfields E1 .. 111 B3
Evelyn Rd
Acton W4 ....37 C3
Richmond TW9 ....54 A4
Evelyn St
Greenland SE10 .....52 B4
SE8 ....41 A1
Evelyn Terr TW9 ....54 A4
Evelyn Wlk N1 ....87 B1
Evelyn Yd W1 ...... 105 B2
Evenwood Cl
SW15 ....58 A2
Everard Ho 2 E1 ... 111 C1
Everatt Cl SW18 .....58 B2
Everdon Rd SW13 ...46 C4
Everest Pl E14 ....34 B4

Everett Ho
Islington N7 ....14 C4
Walworth SE17 ..... 151 B2
Evergreen Sq 3
E8 ....16 B1
Everilda St N1 .... 85 A3
Evering Rd E5, N16 ..7 C1
Everington St W6 ...47 C4
Everington St NW10 ..20 C2
Everleigh St N4 ....5 B3
Eversfield Rd TW9 ..44 B1
Evershed Ho E1 .... 111 A2
Evershed Wlk W4 ...37 C2
Eversholt St NW1 ...93 B4
Evershot Rd N4 ....5 B3
Eversleigh Rd
SW11 .... 169 B1
Eversley Ho 12
E2 ....24 C2 99 B3
Everthorpe Rd
SE15 ....64 B4
Everton Bldgs
NW1 ....92 C3
Evesham Ho
1 Bethnal Green
E2 ....25 B3
Pimlico SW1 .... 146 B2
St John's Wood
NW8 ....78 C2
Evesham Rd SW11 ..30 C2
Evesham Way
SW11 ....60 C4
Evesham Wlk
Brixton SW9 .... 173 B2
Camberwell SE5 .... 48 C1
Ewald Rd SW6 ..... 164 C1
Ewart Pl 13 E3 ......26 B3
Ewe Cl N7 ....14 A2
Ewen Cres SW2 .....74 C4
Ewen Henderson Ct
4 SE14 ....51 A3
Ewen Ho N1 .... 84 C3
Ewer St SE1 .... 122 C1
Ewhurst 18 SW15 ...57 C1
Ewhurst Cl E1 ....32 B4
Ewhurst Rd SE4 .....66 B1
Exbury Ho
Hackney E9 ....17 B2
4 London SW9 .... 172 B3
Excel Ct WC2 ...... 119 C3
Excellence Prim Sch
10 E9 ....25 A4
Excelsior Gdns
SE13 ....52 B1
Excelsior Ind Est
SE16 ....50 B4
Exchange Arc
EC2 .... 110 B4
Exchange Ct WC2 . 120 B3
Exchange Mans 2
NW11 ....1 B4
Exchange Pl EC2 .. 110 A4
Exeter Ct NW6 ......23 C3
Exeter Ho
Paddington W2 ..... 100 C2
1 Peckham SE15 ..49 C4
Putney SW15 ....57 B1
Exeter Mans NW2 ...10 A2
Exeter Mews
Fulham SW6 .... 155 B2
3 Hampstead
NW6 ....11 A2

Exeter Rd
Brondesbury
NW2 . . . . 10 A2
Newham E16 . . . . . . 35 C4
Exeter St WC2 . . . 120 C4

Exeter Way 2
SE14 . . . . 51 B3
Exford Ct SW11 . . 167 C4
Exhibition Cl W12 . 30 B2
Exhibition Rd
SW7 . . . . 129 C2
Exmoor Ho 25 E3 . . 26 A4
Exmoor St W10 . . . 30 C4
Exmouth Ho
Clerkenwell EC1 . . . 95 C2
6 Millwall E14 . . . . 42 A2
Exmouth Market
EC1 . . . . 95 C2
Exmouth Mews
NW1 . . . . 93 A3
Exmouth PI E8 . . . . 17 A1
Exmouth St E1 . . . . 32 B3
Exonbury NW8 . . . . 78 B3
Exon St SE17 . . . . 152 A3
Explorers Ct 6
E14 . . . . 34 C2
Express Wharf 10
E14 . . . . 41 C4
Exton St SE1 . . . . 121 B1
Eymella Rd SE22 . . 76 B4
Eynham Rd W12 . . . 30 B3
Eynsford Coll VI L . 105 B2
Eynsford Ho
Borough The SE1 . . 137 B4
2 Deptford SE15 . . 50 B4
Walworth SE17 . . . 152 A3
Eyot Gdns W6 . . . . 38 B1
Eyot Gn W4 . . . . . . 38 B1
Eyre Ct NW8 . . . . . 79 B2
Eyre St Hill EC1 . . . 95 B1
Eythorne Rd SW9 . 173 C3
Ezra St E2 . . . 24 B2 99 A4

F

Fabian Rd SW6 . . . 155 A2
Fabyc Ho TW9 . . . . 44 C3
Fairacres SW15 . . . 56 C3
Fairbairn Gn 4
SW9 . . . . 48 A2
Fairbourne Rd 10
SW4 . . . . 61 C1
Fairbriar Residence
SW7 . . . . 143 C4
Fairbridge Rd N19 . 4 C2
Fairburn Ct SW15 . . 58 A2
Fairburn Ho
9 Stamford Hill
N16 . . . . 7 A3
West Kensington
SW5 . . . . 141 A1
Fairby Ho SE1 . . . 153 A4
Fairchann Trad Est
SE8 . . . . 52 A3
Fairchild Cl 6
SW11 . . . . 167 C1
Fairchild Ho
16 Hackney E9 . . . 17 B1
Pimlico SW1 . . . . . 147 A3
5 Shoreditch
N1 . . . . 24 A2 98 A4
Fairchild Pl
EC2 . . . . 24 A1 98 B1
Fairchild St
EC2 . . . . 24 A1 98 B1

Fairclough St E1 . 111 C1
Faircourt 14 NW3 . . 12 B2
Faircroft N16 . . . . . . 6 C3
Fairdale Gdns
SW15 . . . . 57 A3
Fairdene Ct N7 . . . . 14 A3
Fairfax Ho
1 Brixton SW9 . . . 173 C1
2 Putney SW15 . . . 56 C2
Fairfax Mews
SW15 . . . . 57 B3
Fairfax Pl
Kensington W14 . . 126 B1
South Hampstead
NW6 . . . . 11 B1
Fairfield
Camden Town
NW1 . . . . 82 C3
4 Stepney E1 . . . . 32 B4
Fairfield Ct
Harlesden NW10 . . 21 C4
1 London SW18 . . . 59 A2
Fairfield Dr SW18 . 59 A2
Fairfield Rd E3 . . . 26 C3
Fairfield St SW18 . 59 A2
Fairfoot Rd E3 . . . . 26 C1
Fairford Ho SE11 . 149 C3
Fairhazel Gdns
NW6 . . . . 11 B1
Fairheathe SW15 . . 57 C1
Fairholme Rd
W14 . . . . 140 B1
Fairholt Cl N16 . . . . 7 A3
Fairholt Rd N16 . . . . 6 C3
Fairholt St SW7 . . 130 B2
Fairhurst 4 NW6 . . 11 B2
Fairlawn 4 NW4 . . 37 B2
Fairlawn Ct 3 W4 . 37 B2
Fairlawn Gr W4 . . . 37 B2
Fairlawn Mans
SE14 . . . . 50 C2
Fairlawns SW15 . . . 57 C2
Fairlead Ho 6
E14 . . . . 41 C3
Fairley House Sch
SW1 . . . . 147 C2
Fairlie Ct
22 Bromley E3 . . . . 27 A2
1 Tufnell Pk N7 . . . 13 C4
Fairlight Ave
NW10 . . . . 21 A3
Fairlight Ct 4
NW10 . . . . 21 A3
Fairlop Pl NW8 . . . . 89 C3
Fairmead Ho E9 . . . 18 A4
Fairmead Rd N7,
N19 . . . . 5 B1
Fairmont Ave E14 . . 34 C1
Fairmont Ho 7
E3 . . . . 26 C1
Fairmount Rd
SW2 . . . . 62 B1
Fair St SE1 . . . . . . 138 C4
Fairstead Wlk N1 . . 86 C4
Fairthorn Rd SE7,
SE10 . . . . 43 C1
Fairview Ho 14
SW2 . . . . 74 B4
Fairview Pl SW2 . . . 74 B4
Fairwall Ho 9
SE5 . . . . 49 A2
Fairway Cl NW11 . . 2 B4

Fairway Ct 13
SE16 . . . . 40 C4
Fairway The W3 . . . 29 A3
Fairweather Ho
N7 . . . . 14 A4
Faith Ct NW2 . . . . . 9 A2
Falconberg Ct W1 . 105 C2
Falconberg Mews
W1 . . . . 105 C2
Falconbrook Prim Sch
28 SW11 . . . . 59 C4
Falcon Cl
Chiswick W4 . . . . . 45 B4
Lambeth SE1 . . . . 122 B2
Falcon Ct
8 Dulwich SE21 . . . 75 C2
Holborn EC4 . . . . . 107 B1
Islington N1 . . . . . . 86 B1
Falcon Wlk 12 N7 . 5 B2
Falcon Gr SW11 . . . 60 A4
Falcon Ho 11 SE15 . 49 B2
Falcon La SW11 . . . 60 A4
Falcon Lo
2 Paddington
W9 . . . . 31 C4
West Hampstead
NW3 . . . . 11 A4
Falcon Pk Ind Est
NW10 . . . . 8 A3
Falcon Point SE1 . 122 B3
Falcon Rd SW11 . . . 60 A4
Falcons Pre-Prep Sch
for Boys The 7
SW4 . . . . 60 A3
Falcons Prep Sch for
Boys The TW9 . . . 54 A3
Falcon St E13 . . . . 68 A4
Falcon Way E14 . . . 42 A2
Falconwood Ct
SE3 . . . . 53 B1
Falkener Ct SW11 . 169 C3
Falkirk Ct 11 SE16 . 32 C1
Falkirk Ho W9 . . . . 88 B4
Falkirk St N1 . . . . . 24 A3
Falkland Ho
Kensington W8 . . . 128 A1
West Kensington
W14 . . . . 140 C2
Falkland Pl 2
NW5 . . . . 13 B3
Falkland Rd NW5 . . 13 B3
Falkner House Sch
SW7 . . . . 143 A2
Falloden Ho
6 London SW8 . . . 171 C2
Paddington W11 . . . 31 B4
Fallow Ct 20 SE16 . 153 C1
Fallowfield N4 . . . . 5 B2
Falmouth Ho
Bayswater W2 . . . 116 A4
Kennington SE11 . . 149 C2
Falmouth Rd SE1 . 137 A1
Falmouth St E15 . . 19 C3
Falstaff Ct SE11 . . 150 A3
Falstaff Ho 18 N1 . 24 A3
Fan Mus The SE10 . 52 B3
Fann St EC1 . . . . . . 97 A1
Fanshaw St
N1 . . . . 24 A2 98 A4
Fanthorpe St
SW15 . . . . 57 B4

Faraday Rd N7 . . . 14 B2
Faraday Ho
2 Balham SW12 . . . 73 A4
3 Gospel Oak
NW5 . . . . 13 A4
Kensal Town W10 . . 31 A4
6 Poplar E14 . . . . 33 B2
Faraday Rd
Acton W3 . . . . 28 B2
Kensal Town W10 . . 31 A4
Faraday Sch 1
E14 . . . . 35 A2
Fareham Ho 13
SW15 . . . . 68 C3
Fareham St W1 . . . 105 B2
Farjeon Ho NW6 . . 11 C1
Farleigh PI N16 . . . 16 B4
Farleigh Rd N16 . . . 16 B4
Farley Ct
Kensington W14 . . 126 C2
Marylebone NW1 . . 91 B1
Farlington Pl
SW15 . . . . 69 A4
Farlow Rd SW15 . . . 57 C4
Farlton Rd SW18 . . 71 A4
Farm Ave NW2 . . . . 1 B1
Farm Cl SW6 . . . . . 155 C2
Farmdale Rd SE10 . 43 C1
Farleigh Rd N16 . . . 16 B4
Farmer Ho 4
SE16 . . . . 40 A3
Farmers Mkt W8 . 112 C2
Farmers Rd SE5 . . . 48 A3
Farmer St
W8 . . . . 31 C1 113 B2
Farm La SW6 . . . . 155 C2
Farm Lane Trad Ctr
SW6 . . . . 155 C3
Farmleigh Ho
SW9 . . . . 63 A2
Farm Pl
W8 . . . . 31 C1 113 B2
Farm Rd NW10 . . . . 20 C4
Farm St W1 . . . . . 118 A3
Farnaby Ho 2
W10 . . . . 23 B2
Farnborough Ho 8
SW15 . . . . 68 C3
Farncombe St
SE16 . . . . 139 C3
Farndale Ho 6
NW6 . . . . 78 A4
Farnell Mews
SW5 . . . . 142 A2
Farnell Pl W3 . . . . . 28 A2
Farnfield Ho 12
SW2 . . . . 62 B2
Farnham Ho
Borough The SE1 . . 122 C1
Marylebone NW1 . . 90 B1
Farnham Pl SE1 . . 122 B1
Farnham Royal
SE11 . . . . 149 A1
Farnhurst Ho 7
SW11 . . . . 169 B2
Farningham Ho 6
N4 . . . . 6 C4
Farnley Ho 8
SW8 . . . . 171 B2
Farnsworth Ct
SE10 . . . . 43 B3
Farnworth Ho 5
E14 . . . . 42 C2
Faroe Rd W14 . . . . 39 C3
Farquhar Rd SW19 . 70 C1

Farrance St E14 . . 33 C3
Farrant Ho 14
SW11 . . . . 59 C4
Farrell Ho E1 . . . . . 32 B3
Farrer Ho SE8 . . . . 51 C3
Farriers Mews
SE15 . . . . 65 B4
Farrier St NW1 . . . . 13 B1
Farrier Wlk SW10 . 156 C4
Farringdon La EC1 . 95 C1
Farringdon Rd EC1 . 95 C1
Farringdon St
EC4 . . . . 108 A2
Farringdon Sta
EC1 . . . . 108 A4
Farrins Rents
SE16 . . . . 33 A1
Farrow La SE14 . . . 50 B3
Farrow PI SE16 . . . 41 A3
Farthingale Wlk
E15 . . . . 19 C1
Farthing Alley 8
SE1 . . . . 139 B3
Farthing Fields 8
E1 . . . . 32 A1
Fashion Retail Acad
The W1 . . . . 105 B2
Fashion St E1 . . . . 111 A3
Fashion & Textile Mus
SE1 . . . . 138 A4
Fassett Rd E8 . . . . 16 C2
Fassett Sq E8 . . . . 16 C2
Fauconberg Ct
W4 . . . . 45 B4
Fauconberg Rd
W4 . . . . 45 B4
Faulkner Ho SW15 . 47 B1
Faulkner's Alley
EC1 . . . . 108 A4
Faulkner St SE14 . . 50 B2
Faunce Ho 1
SE17 . . . . 48 A4
Faunce St SE17 . . 150 A1
Favart Rd SW6 . . . 165 C4
Faversham Ho
Camden Town
NW1 . . . . 83 A3
Walworth SE17 . . . 152 A1
Fawcett Cl SW11 . 167 C1
Fawcett Est E5 . . . . 7 C3
Fawcett Ho 25
SW9 . . . . 172 B2
Fawcett Rd NW10 . . 8 B1
Fawcett St SW10 . 156 C4
Fawe Park Rd
SW15 . . . . 58 B3
Fawe St E14 . . . . . . 34 A4
Fawkham Ho SE1 . 153 A3
Fawley Ct SE27 . . . 75 A2
Fawley Lo 2 E14 . . 42 C2
Fawley Rd NW6 . . . 11 A3
Fawnbrake Ave
SE24 . . . . 63 B2
Fayetville Ho 28
N19 . . . . 4 C4
Faygate Rd SW2 . . 74 B2
Fazerley Ct 50 W2 . 31 C4
Fearnley Ho SE5 . . 49 A1
Fearon St SE10 . . . 43 C1
Feathers Pl SE10 . . 52 C4
Featherstone St
EC1 . . . . 97 B2
Featley Rd SW9 . . . 63 A4

Felbridge Ho **21**
SE22 . . . . .64 A4
Felday Rd SE13 . . . . . .67 A1
Felden St SW6 . . . . . .164 C3
Feldman Cl N16 . . . . . .7 C3
Felgate Mews **4**
W6 . . . . .39 A2
Felix St E2 . . . . .25 A3
Felixstowe Rd
NW10 . . . . .22 A2
Fellbrigg Rd SE22 . . .64 B2
Fellbrigg St **1** E1 . . .25 A1
Fell Ho **11** N19 . . . . . . .4 B1
Fellows Ct E2 . . . . . . .24 B3
Fellows Rd NW3 . . . .12 A1
Fells Haugh **6**
W3 . . . . .28 B3
Felltram Way SE7 . . .43 C2
Felmersham Cl **2**
SW4 . . . . .61 C3
Felsberg Rd SW2 . . . .74 A4
Felsham Ho **5**
SW15 . . . . .57 C4
Felsham Mews **14**
SW15 . . . . .57 C4
Felsham Rd SW15 . . .57 C4
Felstead St E15 . . . . .18 B2
Felstead Wharf
E14 . . . . .42 B1
Felton Ho N1 . . . . . . .87 C3
Felton St N1 . . . . .87 C3
Fenchurch Ave
EC3 . . . . .110 A1
Fenchurch Bldgs
EC3 . . . . .110 B1
Fenchurch Pl EC3 . .124 B4
Fenchurch St EC3 . .124 B4
Fenchurch Street Sta
EC3 . . . . .124 A4
Fendall St SE1 . . . . .138 B1
Fender Ct **5** SW4 . .172 A2
Fendt Cl **8** E16 . . . . .35 B3
Fenelon Pl W14 . . . .141 A3
Fenham Rd SE15 . . . .50 A3
Fenner Cl SE16 . . . . . .40 A2
Fenner Ho **2** E1 . . . . .32 A1
Fenner Sq **8**
SW11 . . . . .59 C4
Fennings Rd **17**
SW4 . . . . .61 C1
Fenning St SE1 . . . . .138 A4
Fen St E16 . . . . .35 B2
Fen St E16 . . . . .3 B3
Fenstanton Prim Sch
20 SW2 . . . . .74 C3
Fentiman Rd SW8 . .162 C2
Fenton Cl
15 Dalston E8 . . . . .16 B2
South Lambeth
SW9 . . . . .172 C1
Fenton Ho SE14 . . . . .51 A3
Fenton House NW3 . . .2 B1
Fentons SE3 . . . . .53 B3
Fenton St E1 . . . . .32 A3
Fenwick Gr SE15 . . . .64 C4
Fenwick Pl SW9 . . . . .62 A4
Fenwick Rd SE15 . . . .64 C4
Ferdinand Ho **1**
NW1 . . . . .13 A1
Ferdinand Pl NW1 . .12 C1
Ferdinand St NW1 . .12 C1
Ferguson Dr W3 . . . .28 C3

Ferguson Ho SE10 . . .52 B2
Ferguson's Cl E14 . . .41 C2
Fergus Rd N5 . . . . . . .15 A3
Fermain Ct E N1 . . . .24 A4
Fermain Ct N N1 . . . .24 A4
Fermain Ct W N1 . . .24 A4
Fermoy Rd W9 . . . . . .23 B1
Fernbank Mews
SW12 . . . . .61 B1
Fern Ct **3** N1 . . . . . . .24 A3
Ferncliff Rd E8 . . . . . .16 C3
Ferncroft Ave
NW3 . . . . .10 C4
Fern Ct SE14 . . . . .50 C1
Ferndale Com Sp Ctr
SW9 . . . . .62 B3
Ferndale Ct **3**
SE3 . . . . .53 B3
Ferndale Ho N16 . . . . .6 C3
Ferndale Rd SW4, SW9
SW9 . . . . .62 B3
Ferndene Rd SE24 . . .63 B3
Ferndown Lo **17**
E14 . . . . .42 B3
Fernhead Rd W9 . . . .23 B2
Fernhill Ho E5 . . . . . . .7 C2
Fernholme Rd
SE15 . . . . .65 C2
Fernhurst Rd
SW6 . . . . .164 B4
Fernie Ho SE22 . . . . . .64 B4
Fernlea Rd SW12 . . . .73 A3
Fernleigh Cl W9 . . . . .23 B2
Fernsbury St **1** WC1 .95 B3
Fernshaw Mans
SW10 . . . . .156 C3
Fernshaw Rd
SW10 . . . . .156 C3
Fernside NW11 . . . . . . .1 C3
Fernside Rd SW12 . . .72 C4
Fern St E3 . . . . .26 C1
Ferntower Rd N5 . . . .15 C3
Fern Wlk **18** SE16 . .153 C1
Fernwood SW19 . . . . .70 B3
Ferrey Mews **19**
SW9 . . . . .173 B1
Ferriby Cl N1 . . . . . . .14 C1
Ferrier Ind Est
SW18 . . . . .59 A3
Ferrier Point **8**
E16 . . . . .35 C4
Ferrier St SW18 . . . . .59 A3
Ferrings SE21 . . . . . . .76 A1
Ferris Rd SE22 . . . . . .64 C3
Ferrybridge Ho
SE11 . . . . .135 A1
Ferry La
Barnes SW13 . . . . . .46 B4
Brentford TW8 . . . . .44 A4
Richmond TW9 . . . . .44 C3
Ferry Rd SW13 . . . . . .46 C2
Ferry Sq **1** TW8 . . . .44 A4
Ferry St E14 . . . . .42 B1
Festing Rd SW15 . . . .57 C4
Festival Ct **5** E8 . . . .16 B1
Festival Pier SE1 . . .120 C2
Fetter La EC4 . . . . . .107 C2
Fettes Ho NW8 . . . . . .79 C1
Ffinch St SE8 . . . . . . .51 C3
Field Ct
Hampstead NW3 . . .11 B3
Holborn WC1 . . . . .107 A3
Lower Holloway N7 . .14 A3
Wimbledon SW19 . . .70 C1
Fieldgate Mans **23**
E1 . . . . .111 C3

Fieldgate St E1 . . . . .111 C3
Field Ho NW10 . . . . . .22 C2
Fieldhouse Rd
SW12 . . . . .73 B3
Fielding Ho
Chiswick W4 . . . . . . .46 A4
1 Kilburn NW6 . . . .23 C2
St John's Wood
NW8 . . . . .78 C4
Fielding Mews
SW13 . . . . .47 A4
Fielding Rd
Acton W4 . . . . .38 A3
Hammersmith W14 . .39 C3
Fielding St SE17 . . . . .48 B4
Field Lo NW10 . . . . . . .8 B2
Field Rd W6 . . . . .154 A4
Fields Est E8 . . . . .16 C1
Field St WC1 . . . . .94 C4
Fieldsway Ho N5 . . . . .14 C3
Fieldview SW17,
SW18 . . . . .71 C3
Fieldview Ct **2**
N5 . . . . .15 A4
Fieldway Cres N5,
N7 . . . . .14 B3
Fieldwick Ho **17**
E9 . . . . .17 C2
Fife Rd
Mortlake SW14 . . . . .55 B2
Newham E16 . . . . . .35 C4
Fife Terr N1 . . . . .85 A2
Fifth Ave W10 . . . . . . .23 A2
Fig Tree Cl NW10 . . . .21 A4
Filey Ave N16 . . . . .7 C3
Filey Ho SW18 . . . . . .59 B3
Filigree Ct SE16 . . . . .33 B1
Filmer Ho SW6 . . . . .164 B4
Filmer Mews
SW6 . . . . .164 B4
Filmer Rd SW6 . . . . .154 C1
Filton Ct **14** SE14 . . .50 B3
Finborough Rd
SW10 . . . . .156 B4
Finchdean Ho
SW15 . . . . .68 B4
Finch Ho **1** SE8 . . . . .52 A3
Finch La EC2, EC3 . .109 C1
Finchley Pl NW8 . . . . .79 B2
Finchley Rd
Hampstead NW3 . . .11 B2
St John's Wood
NW8 . . . . .79 B2
Finchley Road &
Frognal Sta NW3 . .11 B3
Finchley Road Sta
NW3 . . . . .11 B2
Finch Lo **19** W9 . . . . .31 C4
Finch Mews
SE15 . . . . .49 B2
Finch's Ct **10** E14 . .34 A2
Findhorn St **1**
E14 . . . . .34 B3
Findon Cl SW18 . . . . .58 C1
Findon Rd W12 . . . . . .38 C4
Fine Arts Coll
NW3 . . . . .12 B2
Fineran Ct **8**
SW11 . . . . .59 C3
Fingal St SE10 . . . . . .43 B1
Fingest Ho NW8 . . . . .90 A2
Finland Rd SE4 . . . . . .66 A4
Finland St SE16 . . . . .41 A3
Finlay St SW6 . . . . . . .47 C2
Finley Ct **2** SE5 . . . .48 B3
Finmere Ho **1** N4 . . . .6 B4

Finnemore Ho N1 . . .86 C4
Finn Ho N1 . . . . .97 C4
Finnis St E2 . . . . .25 A1
FINSBURY 95 C4
Finsbury Ave EC2 . .109 C3
Finsbury Cir EC2 . . .109 C3
Finsbury Ct EC2 . . . .109 B4
Finsbury L Ctr EC1 . .96 C3
Finsbury Market
EC2 . . . . .110 A4
Finsbury Mkt
EC2 . . . .**2** A1, 98 A1
FINSBURY PARK 5 C2
Finsbury Park Rd N4,
N5 . . . . .6 A2
Finsbury Park Sta
N4 . . . . .5 B2
Finsbury Pavement
EC2 . . . . .109 C4
Finsbury Sq EC2 . . . .109 C4
Finsbury St EC2 . . . .109 B4
Finsen Rd SE5 . . . . . .63 B4
Finstock Rd W10 . . . .30 C3
Finton House Sch
SW17 . . . . .72 B2
Finucane Ct TW9 . . . .54 B4
Finwhale Ho E14 . . . .42 A3
Fiona Ct **3** NW6 . . . .23 B3
Firbank Rd SE15 . . . . .50 A1
Fircroft N1 . . . . .86 B4
Fircroft Prim Sch
SW17 . . . . .72 B1
Fircroft Rd SW17 . . . .72 B1
Fire Brigade Pier
SE1 . . . . .148 B3
Firecrest Dr NW3 . . . . .2 A1
Fire Ho **7** W10 . . . . . .30 A4
Fir Lo SW15 . . . . .57 A3
Firmston Ho **9**
SW14 . . . . .55 C4
Firs Ave SW14 . . . . . .55 B3
Firsby Rd N16 . . . . .7 C3
First Ave
East Acton W3 . . . . .29 B1
Mortlake SW14 . . . . .56 A4
West Kilburn W10 . . .23 B1
First St SW3 . . . . . . .144 B4
Firth Gdns SW6 . . . .164 A3
Fir Tree Ho **1**
SE14 . . . . .50 B3
Fir Trees Cl SE16 . . . .33 A1
Fisher Cl SE16 . . . . . .32 C1
Fishermans Dr
SE16 . . . . .40 C4
Fisherman's Wlk
E14 . . . . .33 C1
Fishers Cl SW16 . . . . .73 C1
Fishers Ct SE14 . . . . .50 C2
Fisher's La W4 . . . . . .37 C2
Fisher St
Holborn WC1 . . . . .106 C3
Newham E16 . . . . . .35 C4
2 Tufnell Pk N19 . . . .4 B1
Fisherton Street Est
NW8 . . . . .89 C1
Fisher Ho
Islington N1 . . . . .85 B3
3 Shadwell E1 . . . . .32 B2
Fishlock Ct **6**
SW4 . . . . .172 A2
Fish St Hill EC3 . . . .123 C3
Fitch Ct SW2 . . . . . . .62 C2
Fitzalan St SE11 . . . .149 B4
Fitzclarence Ho
W11 . . . . .126 A4

Fitz-George Ave
W14 . . . . .140 A3
Fitzgerald Ave
SW14 . . . . .56 A4
Fitzgerald Ho
18 Brixton SW2 . . .173 B4
14 Poplar E14 . . . . .34 A3
Fitzgerald Rd
SW14 . . . . .55 C4
Fitzhardinge Ho
W1 . . . . .103 B2
Fitzhardinge St
W1 . . . . .103 B2
Fitzherbert Ho **11**
TW10 . . . . .54 B1
Fitzhugh Gr SW18 . . .59 C1
Fitzjames Ave
W14 . . . . .140 B3
Fitzjohn's Ave
NW3 . . . . .11 C3
Fitzjohns Mans
NW3 . . . . .11 B2
Fitzjohn's Prim Sch **4**
NW3 . . . . .11 C3
Fitzmaurice Ho **3**
SE16 . . . . .40 A2
Fitzmaurice Pl
W1 . . . . .118 C2
Fitzneal St W12 . . . . .29 B3
FITZROVIA 104 A4
Fitzroy Cl N6 . . . . .3 B3
Fitzroy Cres W4 . . . . .45 C3
Fitzroy Ct W1 . . . . . . .93 A1
Fitzroy Ho
Bermondsey SE1 . . .153 A2
12 Tower Hamlets
E14 . . . . .33 B3
Fitzroy Mews W1 . . . .92 C1
Fitzroy Pk N6 . . . . .3 B3
Fitzroy Rd NW1 . . . . .81 B4
Fitzroy Sq W1 . . . . . . .92 C1
Fitzroy St W1 . . . . . . .92 C1
Fitzroy Yd NW1 . . . . .81 B4
Fitzwarren Gdns
N19 . . . . .4 B3
Fitzwilliam Ave
TW9 . . . . .44 B1
Fitzwilliam Mews
E16 . . . . .35 C1
Fitzwilliam Rd
SW4 . . . . .61 B4
Fives Ct SE11 . . . . . .136 A1
Fiveways Rd SW9 . . .173 C1
Flamborough Ho **12**
SE15 . . . . .49 C2
Flamborough St
E14 . . . . .33 A3
Flamingo Ct **2**
SE8 . . . . .51 C3
Flamsteed Ct **13**
SE13 . . . . .52 A2
Flamsteed Ho
SE10 . . . . .52 C3
Flanchford Rd
W12 . . . . .38 B3
Flanders Ho N16 . . . . .7 A1
Flanders Mans **1**
W4 . . . . .38 B2
Flanders Rd W4 . . . . .38 A2
Flanders Way E9 . . . .17 C2
Flank St **3** E1 . . . . .125 B4
Flansham Ho **2**
E14 . . . . .33 B3
Flask Cotts **4**
NW3 . . . . .11 C4
Flask Wlk NW3 . . . . . .11 C4

Flatiron Sq SE1.... **123** A1
Flatiron Yd SE1.... **123** A1
Flavell Mews SE10.. **43** A1
Flaxman Ct W1 .... **105** B1
Flaxman Ho

10 Chiswick W4 ...... **38** A1
Newington SE1 .... **136** B2
Flaxman Rd SE5 .... **48** A1
Flaxman Sp Ctr

SE5 .... **48** B1
Flaxman Terr WC1 .. **93** C3
Flecker Ho **5** SE5 .. **48** C3
Fleece Wik N1 ...... **24** A4
Fleet Ct **3** W12 .... **38** A3
Fleetfield WC1 ..... **94** B4
Fleet Ho

5 Brixton SW2 .... **62** C2
4 Limehouse E14 .. **33** A2
Fleet Pl EC4 .... **108** A2
Fleet Prim Sch **15**

SW3 .... **12** B3
Fleet Rd NW3 ...... **12** B3
Fleet Sq WC1 ...... **94** C3
Fleet St EC4 .... **107** C1
Fleet Street Hill **10**

E1 .... **24** C1 **99** B1
Fleetway WC1 ...... **94** B4
Fleet Wood **6** N16 .. **7** B2
Fleetwood Rd

NW10 .... **8** C3
Fleetwood St N16 ... **7** A2
Fleming Ct **4** W2 .. **23** C1
Fleming Ct **4** W1 .. **101** B4
Fleming Ho

14 Bermondsey

SE16 .... **139** B3
Finsbury Pk N4 .... **6** B3
Fleming Rd SE17 .... **48** A4
Fletcher Bldgs

WC2 .... **106** B1
Fletcher Ho **8**

NW5 .... **13** A4
Fletcher Ho **10**

N16 .... **16** A4
Fletcher Path **7**

SE8 .... **51** C3
Fletcher Rd W4 .... **37** B3
Fletcher St **18** E1 . **125** C4
Fleur De Lis St

E1 .... **24** B1 **98** C1
Fleur Gates **7**

SW19 .... **69** C4
Flinders Ho **23** E1 .. **32** A1
Flinton St SE17 .... **152** B2
Flint St SE17 ...... **151** C3
Flitcroft St WC2 ... **105** C1
Flitton Ho **7** N1 ... **15** A1
Flock Mill Pl

SW18 .... **71** A3
Flodden Rd SE5 .... **48** B2
Flood St SW3 ...... **158** B4
Flood Wik SW3 ..... **158** B4
Flora Cl E14 .... **34** A3
Flora Gardens Prim

Sch **17** W6 ...... **39** A2
Flora Gdns **2** W6 .. **39** A2
Floral St WC2 ...... **120** A4
Florence Ct W9 .... **89** A3
Florence Gdns W4 .. **45** B4
Florence Ho

20 Bermondsey

SE16 .... **40** A1
2 Brixton SW2 .... **62** B2
10 Shepherd's Bush

W11 .... **30** C2

Florence Ho continued
7 Wandsworth

SW18 .... **59** C3
Florence Mans

SW6 .... **164** C4
Florence Nightingale

Ho **10** N1 .... **15** B2
Florence Nightingale

Mus SE1 .... **135** A3
Florence Rd

Acton W4 .... **37** C3
Finsbury Pk N4 .... **5** C4
New Cross Gate

SE14 .... **51** B2
Florence St N1 ..... **15** A1
Florence Terr

Kingston u T

SW15 .... **68** A1
New Cross Gate

SE14 .... **51** B2
Florence Way

SW12 .... **72** B3
Flores Ho **13** E1 .. **32** C4
Florfield Rd E8 .... **17** A2
Florian SE5 .... **49** A2
Florian Rd SW15 ... **58** A3
Florida St

E2 .... **24** C2 **99** C3
Florida State Univ

WC1 .... **105** C3
Florin Ct SE1 ...... **138** C3
Floris PI **3** SW4 ... **61** B4
Florys Ct **9** SW19 . **70** A3
Floss St SW15 ...... **47** B1
Flower & Dean Wik

E1 .... **111** A3
Flowersmead

SW17 .... **72** C2
Flower Wik The

SW7 .... **129** A4
Floyer Cl TW10 .... **54** B2
Flynn Ct **14** E14 .. **33** C2
Foley Ho **19** E1 ... **32** B3
Foley St W1 .... **104** C3
Folgate St E1 ...... **110** C4
Foliot Ho N1 ...... **84** C2
Foliot St W12 ..... **29** B3
Follett Ho SW10 ... **157** B2
Follett St E14 ..... **34** B3
Folly Wall E14 .... **42** B4
Fonda Ct **14** E14 .. **33** C2
Fontarabia Rd

SW11 .... **60** C3
Fontenelle SE5 .... **49** A2
Fontenoy Ho

SE11 .... **150** A3
Fontenoy Rd SW12,

SW17 .... **73** B2
Fonthill Ho

Kensington W14.... **126** B2
Pimlico SW1 ...... **146** B2
Fonthill Mews N4 .. **5** B2
Fonthill Rd N4 ..... **5** C2
Fontley Way SW15 . **68** C4
Footpath The

SW15 .... **56** C2
Forber Ho **22** E2 .. **25** B2
Forbes Ho **2** W4 .. **36** C1
Forbes St E1 ...... **111** C1
Forburg Rd N16 ... **7** C3
Ford Cl **3** E3 ..... **26** A3
Fordcombe **13**

NW5 .... **12** C2

Fordham Ho **11**

SE14 .... **51** A3
Fordham St **18** E1 **111** C2
Fordingley Rd W9 .. **23** B2
Ford Rd E3 .... **26** A3
Fords Park Rd E16 .. **35** C3
Ford Sq E1 .... **32** A4
Ford St

Bow E3 .... **26** A3
Canning Town E16 .. **35** B3
Fordwych Ct NW2 .. **10** A2
Fordwych Rd NW2 .. **10** A3
Fordyce Rd SE13 ... **67** B2
Forecastle Ct E14 .. **41** C4
Foreign &

Commonwealth

Office SW1 .... **134** A4
Foreland Ho

W11 .... **31** A2 **112** A4
Foreshore SE8..... **41** B2
Fore St EC2 .... **109** B3
Forest Cl NW6..... **10** A1
Forest Dr E12 ...... **41** C3
Forest Gr E8 ...... **16** B2
Forest Hill Rd

SE22 .... **65** A1
Forest Rd

Dalston E8 .... **16** B2
Richmond TW9 .... **44** C3
Fore Street Ave

EC2 .... **109** B3
Forest Way **5** N19 . **4** B2
Forfar Rd SW11 ... **169** C4
Forge PI NW1 ..... **12** C2
Forman Ho SE4..... **65** C3
Forman PI **6** N16 .. **16** B4
Formby Ct **9** N7 .. **14** C3
Formosa Ho **1** E1 . **26** A1
Formosa St W9 .... **88** B1
Formunt Cl E16 .... **35** B4
Forrest Ct N7 ...... **14** C2
Forrest Ho SW15 ... **47** B1
Forset Ct W1 ...... **102** B2
Forset St W1 ...... **102** B2
Forster Rd SW2 ... **74** A4
Forston St N1 ..... **87** A2
Forsyth Gdns SE17 . **48** A4
Forsyth Ho

14 Hackney E9 .... **17** B1
Pimlico SW1....... **147** A3
Forsythia Ho SE4 .. **66** A4
Fortescue Ave **1**

E8 .... **17** A1
Fortess Gr NW5 ... **13** B3
Fortess Rd NW5 ... **13** B3
Fortess Wik NW5 .. **13** A3
Fortess Yd **15**

NW5 .... **13** A4
Forthbridge Rd

SW11 .... **60** C3
Forth Ho **33** E3 ... **26** B3
Forties The **10**

NW5 .... **13** B3
Fortior Ct N6...... **4** B4
Fortnam Rd N19 ... **4** C2
Fort Rd SE1 .... **153** A3
Fortrose Cl E14.... **34** C3
Fortrose Gdns SW12,

SW2 .... **74** A3
Fort St E1 .... **110** B3
Fortuna Cl N7 ..... **14** B2
Fortune Ct **8** E8 .. **16** B1
Fortune Gate Rd

NW10 .... **21** A4
Fortune Green Rd

NW6 .... **10** C4

Fortune Ho

Lambeth SE11 ..... **149** B3
St Luke's EC1 ..... **97** A1
Fortune St EC1 .... **97** A1
Fortune Way

NW10 .... **21** C2
Forty Acre La E16 .. **35** C4
Forum Ct **7** E3 ... **26** C4
Forward Bsns Ctr The

3 E16 .... **27** C1
Fosbrooke Ho

SW8 .... **162** A1
Fosbury Ho **7**

SW9 .... **62** B3
Fosbury Mews

W2 .... **114** B3
Foscote Mews W9 .. **31** C4
Foskett Rd SW6 ... **164** C1
Fossil Rd SE13 .... **66** C4
Foster Ct

6 Camden Town

NW1 .... **13** B1
Canning Town E16 .. **35** B3
Foster Ho SE14 ..... **51** B2
Foster La EC2 ..... **108** C2
Foster Rd

Acton W3 .... **29** A1
Chiswick W4 ...... **37** C1
Foubert's PI W1 ... **104** C1
Foulden Rd N16 ... **16** B4
Foulden Terr N16 .. **16** B4
Foulis Terr SW7 ... **143** C2
Foulser Rd SW17 .. **72** C1
Foundary Ho **6**

E14 .... **34** A4
Founders Ct EC2 ... **109** B2
Founders Ho **1** SW1 **147** B2
Foundling Ct WC1 .. **94** A2
Foundling Mus The

WC1 .... **94** B2
Foundry Bsns Ctr The

SE1 .... **136** A3
Foundry Cl SE16 ... **33** A1
Foundry Mews

NW1 .... **93** A2
Foundry PI

Stepney E1 .... **32** B4
Wandsworth SW18 . **71** A4
Fountain &

Colonnade

Sh Ctr SW1 ...... **146** B4
Fountain Ct

Belgravia SW1 .... **146** A3
14 Shepherd's Bush

W11 .... **39** C4
Strand EC4 .... **121** B4
Fountain Green Sq **3**

SE16 .... **139** C3
Fountain Ho

1 Brondesbury Pk

NW6 .... **10** A1
Mayfair W1 .... **117** B2
Fountain Mews

1 Highbury N5 .... **15** B4
Maitland Pk NW3 .. **12** B2
Fountain PI SW9 ... **173** C3
Fountayne Rd N16 . **7** C2
Fount St SW8 ...... **162** A1
Fournier St E1 ..... **111** A4
Fourscore Mans

E8 .... **16** C1
Four Seasons Cl

E3 .... **26** C3
Fourth Ave W10 ... **23** A2
Fovant Ct **5** SW8 . **170** C1

Fowey Cl E1 .... **32** A1
Fowey Ho SE11 .... **149** C2
Fowler Cl SW11 .... **59** C4
Fowler Ho

5 Camberwell

SE5 .... **49** A1
Islington N1 ...... **86** B4
South Lambeth

SW8 .... **171** C3
Fowler Rd N1 ..... **86** B4
Fownes St SW11 ... **60** A4
Fox and Knot St

EC1 .... **108** B4
Foxberry Ct SE4 ... **66** B3
Foxberry Rd SE4.... **66** A4
Foxborough Gdns

SE4 .... **66** C2
Foxbourne Rd

SW17 .... **72** C2
Fox Cl

Bethnal Green E1... **25** B1
Newham E16 ...... **35** C4
Foxcombe Rd **6**

SW15 .... **68** C3
Foxcote SE5....... **152** B1
Foxcroft N1 .... **85** A1
Fox Ct EC1 .... **107** B3
Foxfield NW1...... **82** B3
Foxglove St W12 ... **29** B2
Foxham Rd N19 ... **4** C1
Fox Ho **2** SW11 ... **59** C3
Foxley Cl E8 ...... **16** C3
Foxley Ho **4** E3 ... **27** A2
Foxley Rd SW9 .... **48** A3
Foxley Sq **3** SW9 . **48** A2
Foxmore St SW11 . **168** C3
Fox Prim Sch

W8 .... **31** C1 **113** B1
Fox Rd E16........ **35** B4
Fox's Yd E2 ... **24** B1 **99** A2
Foxwell Mews SE4.. **66** A4
Foxwell St SE4 .... **66** A4
Foyle Rd SE3 ...... **53** B4
Fradel Lo N16..... **6** C4
Framfield Rd N5.... **15** A3
Frampton NW1 .... **13** C1
Frampton Ct **3**

W3 .... **37** B4
Frampton Ho NW8 . **89** C1
Frampton Park Rd

E9 .... **17** B1
Frampton St NW8 . **89** C1
Francemary Rd

SE4 .... **66** C2
Franche Court Rd

SW17 .... **71** B1
Francis Chichester

Way SW11 .... **169** C3
Francis Cl **6** E14 .. **42** C2
Francis Ct **12** SE14 . **50** C4
Francis Ho

Harlesden NW10 ... **21** B4
11 Shoreditch N1 .. **24** A4
Walham Green

SW10 .... **156** B2
Francis Holland Sch

Belgravia SW1 .... **145** C3
Marylebone NW1 .. **90** C2
Francis Snary Lo **5**

SW18 .... **58** C2
Francis St SW1 .... **147** A4
Francis Terr N19 ... **4** B1
Francis Terrace Mews

6 N19 .... **4** B1

Francis Wlk N1..... 84 C4
Franconia Rd SW4..61 C2
Frank Barnes Sch
N1................. 83 C3
Frank Beswick Ho
SW6 .... 155 A3
Frank Dixon Cl
SE21 ....76 A3
Frank Dixon Way
SE21 ....76 A3
Frankfurt Rd SE24..63 B2
Frankham Ho 8
SE8 ....51 C3
Frankham St SE8...51 C3
Frank Ho SW8 .... 162 A2
Frankland Cl SE16..40 A2
Frankland Ho 4
SE22 ....73 A4
Frankland Rd
SW7 .... 129 B1
Franklin Bldg 5
E14 ....41 C4
Franklin Cl
Greenwich SE13....52 A2
West Norwood
SE27 ....75 A1
Franklin Ho
New Cross SE14....51 A2
28 Wapping E1......32 A1
Franklin Pl SE13....52 A2
Franklin Sq SW5 .. 141 A1
Franklin's Row
SW3 .... 145 A2
Franklin St 43 E3...26 C2
Franklyn Rd NW10..8 B2
Frank Mews 29
SE1 ....40 A2
Frank Soskice Ho
SW6 .... 155 A3
Frank Whymark Ho 4
SE16 ....40 B4
Frans Hals Ct E14 ..42 C3
Fraserburgh Ho 29
E3 ....26 B3
Fraser Ct SW11 ... 168 A4
Fraser Ho
Brentford TW8......36 B1
40 Clapham SW8 .. 171 B1
Fraser Regnart Ct 22
NW5 ....12 B3
Fraser St W4 ....38 A1
Frazier St SE1 .... 135 B3
Frean St SE16 .... 139 B2
Frearson Ho C..... 95 A4
Freda Corbett Cl 10
SE15 ....49 C3
Frederica St 4
N7 ....14 B1
Frederick Blg N1..16 A2
Frederick Charrington
Ho 4 E1...........25 B1
Frederick Cl W2 .. 116 C4
Frederick Cres
SW9 ....48 A3
Frederick Ct SW6..58 A4
Frederick Hugh House
Sch SW5 .... 158 A4
Frederick Rd SW9 ..48 A1
Frederick's Pl
EC2 .... 109 B1
Frederick Sq 11
SE16 ....33 A2
Frederick's Row
EC1 .... 96 A4

Frederick St WC1... 94 C3
Frederick Terr E8..16 B1
Frederic Mews
SW1 .... 131 B3
Freedom St SW11 169 A2
Freegrove Rd N7...14 A3
Freeling Ho NW8...79 B4
Freeling St
Barnsbury N1.......14 A1
7 London N1.......14 B1
Freeman Ho 13
SW2 ....74 A4
Freemantle St
SE17 .... 152 A2
Freemens Hos 1
SW9 ....62 B3
Freight La NW1 ....13 C1
Freightliners City
Farm 1 N7........14 C2
Freke Rd SW11 ....60 C4
Fremantle Ho 14
E1 ....25 A1
Fremont St E8 .....25 B4
French Inst The
SW7 .... 143 B4
French Pl
E1 ....24 A1 98 B2
Frendsbury Rd
SE4 ....66 A3
Frensham Ct N5....15 B3
Frensham Dr
SW15 ....69 A2
Frensham St SE15 ..49 C4
Frere St SW11 .... 168 B2
Freshfield Ave E8..16 B1
Freshfield Cl SE13 ..67 C3
Freshford St SW17,
SW18 ....71 B1
Freston Rd W10,
W11 ....30 C2
Freswick Ho 8
SE8 ....41 A2
Freud Mus The
NW3 ....11 B2
Frewell Bldg EC1 . 107 B4
Frewin Rd SW18 ...71 C3
Friar Mews SE27 ...75 A1
Friars Ave
Putney SW15 ......58 A2
Roehampton SW15..68 B1
Friars Cl SE1 ..... 122 B1
Friars Gdns W3 ...28 C3
Friars Mead E14 ...42 B3
Friars Place La
W3 ....28 C2
Friars Prim
Foundation Sch
SE1 .... 136 B3
Friars Stile Pl 9
TW10 ....54 A1
Friars Stile Rd
TW10 ....54 A1
Friar St EC4 ..... 108 B1
Friars Way W3 ....28 C3
Friary Park Ct 12
W3 ....28 B3
Friary Rd
Acton W3 ....28 C3
Peckham SE15.....49 C3
Friday Grove Mews 1
SW12 ....73 B4
Friday St EC4 .... 122 C4
Frideswide Pl
NW5 ....13 B3
Friendly Pl 16
SE13 ....52 A2

Friendly St SE8.....51 C2
Friendly Street Mews
SE8 ....51 C1
Friendship Way
E15 ....27 B4
Friend St EC1 .....96 A4
Friern Rd SE22 ....64 C1
Frigate Ho 7 E14 ..42 B2
Frigate Mews SE8..51 C4
Frimley Cl SW19 ...70 A2
Frimley Way E1 ....25 C1
Frinstead Ho 6
W10 ....30 C2
Friston St SW6 ... 166 A1
Frith Ho
Bethnal Green
E2 ....24 C2 99 B3
Paddington NW8 ...89 C1
Frith Rd E11........19 C4
Frith St W1 ...... 105 B1
Frithville Ct 2
W12 ....30 B1
Frithville Gdns
W12 ....30 B1
Frobisher Ct 1
Greenwich
SE10 ....52 C4
3 Shepherd's Bush
W12 ....39 B4
Frobisher Ho 27
E1 ....32 A1
Frobisher Pas E14 ..33 C1
Frobisher Pl SE14 ..51 B3
Frobisher St SE10 ..53 A4
Frogley Rd SE22 ...64 B3
Frogmore SW18 ...58 C2
Frogmore Est
NW10 ....20 B2
Frogmore Ind Est
N5 ....15 B4
Frognal NW3 ......11 B3
Frognal Cl NW3 ...11 B3
Frognal Ct NW3 ...11 B2
Frognal Gdns
NW3 ....11 B4
Frognal La NW3 ...11 A3
Frognal Par NW3 ..11 B2
Frognal Rise NW3 ..11 B4
Frognal Way NW3 ..11 B4
Frome St N1 ....86 C2
Fromow's Cnr 14
W4 ....37 B1
Frontenac NW10 ...9 A1
Frostic Wlk 1 E1 . 111 A3
Froude St SW8 ... 170 B1
Frye Ct 5 E3......26 B2
Frying Pan Alley
E1 .... 110 C3
Fry Rd NW10 .....21 B4
Fulbeck Ho N7 ....14 B2
Fulbourne St 1
E1 ....32 A4
Fulbrook Rd N19 ...13 B4
Fulcher Ct 40 SE8 ..51 B4
Fulcher Ho
10 Deptford SE8....41 B1
16 Shoreditch N1...24 A4
Fulford Mans 3
N19 ....5 A1
Fulford St SE16.....40 A4
FULHAM 47 C1
Fulham Broadway
SW6 .... 155 C1
Fulham Broadway Sh
Ctr SW6......... 155 C1

Fulham Broadway Sta
SW6 .... 155 C2
Fulham Bsns
Exchange SW6 .. 167 A3
Fulham College Boys'
Sch SW6 .... 154 A1
Fulham Cross Girls'
Sch SW6 .... 154 A1
Fulham Ct SW6 .. 165 B4
Fulham High St
SW6 .... 164 B1
Fulham Pal SW6.. 164 A1
Fulham Palace Rd SW6,
W6 ....47 C4
Fulham Park Gdns
SW6 .... 164 C2
Fulham Park Rd
SW6 .... 164 C2
Fulham Prep Sch
6 Fulham SW6.... 164 B1
Fulham W14...... 154 B4
Fulham Prim Sch
SW6 .... 155 B3
Fulham Rd
Chelsea SW10 ... 157 A4
Fulham SW6 ..... 165 A4
Fuller Cl 4
E2 ....24 C1 99 B2
Fullers Ho 5
SW18 ....58 C2
Fullerton Rd SW18 59 B2
Fullwood's Mews
N1 .... 97 C4
Fulmar Ct 55 SE21 ..75 C2
Fulmar Ho
12 Bermondsey
SE16 ....40 C2
Marylebone NW8 ...90 B1
Fulmead St SW6 . 166 B3
Fulneck 1 E1 .....32 B4
Fulthorp Rd SE3 ...53 C1
Fulton Mews W2 . 114 C4
Fulwood Pl WC1 . 107 A3
Fulwood Wlk
SW19 ....70 A3
Furber St W6.......39 A3
Furley Ho 7 SE15 ..49 C3
Furley Rd SE15 ....49 C3
Furlong Rd N7 ....14 C2
Furmage St SW18 ..71 A4
Furness Ho SW1 . 146 A2
Furness Lo 4
SW14 ....55 A3
Furness Prim Sch
NW10 ....21 A3
Furness Rd
Harlesden NW10 ...21 C3
Sands End SW6 .. 166 B2
Furnival St EC4 .. 107 B2
Furrow La E9......17 B3
Fursecroft W1 .... 102 C2
Furze St E3 ....33 C4
Fusion Ct SW15 ...68 A1
Futters Ct 1
NW10 ....21 A3
Fyfield N4..........5 C2
Fyfield Rd 5 SW9 ..62 C4
Fynes St SW1 .... 147 B4

G

Gable Ho 12 W4 ...38 A2
Gables Cl SE5 .....49 A2
Gables The
3 Clapham SW4 ...61 B4

Gables The continued
Hampstead NW3 ....2 C2
Gabriel Ho 11 ... 148 C4
Gabrielle Ct NW3 ..11 C2
Gabriel Mews NW2..1 B2
Gabriel's Wharf
SE1 .... 121 B2
Gaddesden Ho EC1 97 C3
Gadsden Ho
6 Homerton E9.....17 C2
8 Kensal Town
W10 ....23 A1
Gagarin Ho SW11 ..59 C4
Gage Rd E16 ......35 A4
Gage St WC1 .... 106 B4
Gainford Ho 10 E2 ..25 A2
Gainford St N1 ....85 B4
Gainsborough Ct
5 Bermondsey
SE16 ....40 A1
Dulwich SE21 .....76 A2
Shepherd's Bush
W12 ....39 B4
Gainsborough Gdns
Golders Green
NW11 ....1 B4
Hampstead NW3 ....2 C1
Gainsborough Ho
Finsbury Pk N4.....5 B3
3 Hampstead
NW3 ....11 B4
5 Limehouse E14 ..33 A2
Westminster SW1 . 147 C3
Gainsborough Prim
Sch E9 ....18 C2
Gainsborough Rd
Bedford Pk W4 ....38 B2
Richmond TW9 ....54 B4
Gainsborough St 5
E9 ....18 B2
Gainsborough Studios
N1 .... 87 B3
Gairloch Rd SE5 . 139 A4
Gairloch Ho 2
NW1 ....13 C1
Gairloch Rd SE5 ...49 A1
Gaisford St NW5 ...13 B2
Gaitskell Ct SW11 168 A2
Gaitskell Ho SE17..48 C4
Gaitskell Way SE1 136 C4
Galata Rd SW13 ...46 C3
Galatea Sq SE15 ...65 A4
Galaxy Bldg 5
E14 ....41 C2
Galaxy Ho EC2.....97 C2
Galbraith St E14 ...42 B3
Gale Ho 10 SW2 ...62 B2
Galena Ho 5 W6...39 A2
Galena Rd W6......39 A2
Galen Pl WC1 .... 106 B3
Galesbury Rd
SW18 ....59 B1
Gales Gdns E2 ....25 A2
Gale St E3 ....33 C4
Galgate Cl 4
SW19 ....70 A3
Galleon Cl SE16 ...40 C4
Galleon Ho 8 E14..42 B2
Gallery Ct SW10 . 156 C3
Gallery Rd SE21 ...75 C3
Galleywall Rd
SE16 ....40 A2
Galleywall Road Trad
Est 12 SE16......40 A2
Galleywood Ho 1
W10 ....30 B4

Gallia Rd N5 .... 15 A3
Galloway Rd W12 .... 29 C1
Galsworthy Ave
E14 .... 33 A4
Galsworthy Ct W3 .... 37 A3
Galsworthy Ho 4
W11 .... 31 A3
Galsworthy Rd
NW2 .... 10 A4
Galton St W10 .... 23 A2
Galveston Ho 2
E1 .... 26 A1
Galveston Rd
SW15 .... 58 B2
Galway Cl 28 SE16 .... 40 A1
Galway Ho
Finsbury EC1 .... 97 A3
Stepney E1 .... 32 C4
Galway St EC1 .... 97 A3
Gambetta St 1
SW8 .... 170 B1
Gambia St SE1 .... 122 B1
Gambier Ho EC1 .... 97 A3
Gamlen Rd SW15 .... 57 C3
Gandolfi St 5
SE15 .... 49 A4
Ganley Ct 18
SW11 .... 59 C4
Gannet Ct 5 SE21 .... 75 C2
Gannet Ho SE15 .... 49 B2
Garand Ct 2 N7 .... 14 B3
Garbett Ho 2
SE17 .... 48 A4
Garbutt Pl W1 .... 103 C3
Garden Cl SW15 .... 69 A4
Garden Ct
4 Richmond
TW9 .... 44 B2
10 South Acton W4 .... 37 B3
St John's Wood
NW8 .... 89 B4
Strand EC4 .... 121 B4
Garden Flats
SW16 .... 74 A1
Garden Ho 12
SW9 .... 172 B2
Garden House Sch
SW3 .... 145 A2
Garden La SW2 .... 74 B3
Garden Mews
W2 .... 31 C2 113 C3
Garden Mus 51 .... 134 C1
Garden Pl 2 E2 .... 24 B4
Garden Rd
Richmond TW9 .... 54 C4
St John's Wood
NW8 .... 89 A4
Garden Row SE1 .... 136 A2
Garden Royal 18
SW15 .... 57 C1
Garden Sch The
N16 .... 16 A4
Garden St E1 .... 32 C4
Gardens The
East Dulwich
SE22 .... 64 C3
Stamford Hill N16 .... 7 B4
Garden Terr
Knightsbridge
SW7 .... 130 B3
Pimlico SW1 .... 147 B2
Garden Wlk
EC2 .... 24 A1 98 A2
Gardiner Ave NW2 .... 9 B3
Gardiner Ct NW10 .... 20 C4

Gardiner Ho
SW11 .... 168 A4
Gardner Ct N5 .... 15 B4
Gardners La EC4 .... 122 C4
Gardnor Mans 11
NW3 .... 11 B4
Gardnor Rd NW3 .... 11 C4
Gard St EC1 .... 96 B4
Gareth Ct SW16 .... 73 C1
Garfield Ho W2 .... 102 C1
Garfield Mews 2
SW11 .... 60 C4
Garfield Rd SW11 .... 60 C4
Garford St E14 .... 33 C2
Garland Cl SW11 .... 137 C1
Garland Ct 12 E14 .... 33 C2
Garland Ho N16 .... 6 C1
Garlands Ho NW8 .... 78 B2
Garlick Hill EC4 .... 123 A4
Garlinge Ho 2
SW9 .... 173 B4
Garlinge Rd NW2 .... 10 B2
Garnault Mews
EC1 .... 95 C3
Garnault Pl EC1 .... 95 C3
Garner St E2 .... 24 C3
Garnet Rd NW10 .... 8 A2
Garnet St E1 .... 32 B2
Garnett Ho 5
NW3 .... 12 B3
Garnett Rd NW3 .... 12 B3
Garnham Cl 2 N16 .... 7 B2
Garnham St 1 N16 .... 7 B2
Garnies Cl SE15 .... 49 B3
Garrad's Rd SW16 .... 73 C1
Garrard Wlk NW10 .... 8 A2
Garratt Ho 8 N16 .... 7 A3
Garratt La SW18 .... 71 A3
Garratt Park Sch 5
SW18 .... 71 B2
Garraway Ct SW13 .... 47 B3
Garraway Ho 21 .... 76 B1
Garrett Cl W3 .... 28 C4
Garrett Ho 8 W12 .... 30 A3
Garrett St EC1 .... 97 A2
Garrett Cl SW18 .... 59 C3
Garrick Ho
Chiswick W4 .... 46 A4
Mayfair W1 .... 118 A1
Garrick Rd TW9 .... 44 C1
Garrick St WC2 .... 120 A4
Garrick Yd WC2 .... 120 A4
Garsdale Terr
SW5 .... 141 A2
Garsington Mews
SE4 .... 66 B4
Garson Ho W2 .... 115 B4
Garston Ho 5 N1 .... 15 A1
Garter Way SE16 .... 40 C4
Garth Ct W4 .... 45 C4
Garth Ho NW2 .... 1 B2
Garth Rd
Child's Hill NW2 .... 1 B2
8 Chiswick W4 .... 37 C1
Gartmoor Gdns
SW19 .... 70 B3
Garton Ho 6 N6 .... 4 C4
Garton Pl SW18 .... 59 B1
Gartons Way
SW11 .... 59 B4
Garway Rd W2 .... 100 A1
Gascoigne Pl 17
E2 .... 24 B2 98 C3
Gascony Ave NW6 .... 10 C1
Gascoyne Ho 2
E9 .... 17 C1

Gascoyne Rd E9 .... 17 C1
Gaselee St E14 .... 34 B2
Gasholder Pl
SE11 .... 149 A1
Gaskarth Rd SW4 .... 61 C4
Gaskell St SW4 .... 172 A2
Gaskin Ho N16 .... 6 C1
Gaskin St N1 .... 86 A4
Gaspar Cl SW7 .... 142 B4
Gaspar Mews
SW5 .... 142 B4
Gasson Ho 24
SE14 .... 50 C4
Gastein Rd W6 .... 47 C4
Gastigny Ho EC1 .... 97 A3
Gaston Bell Cl
TW9 .... 54 B4
Gaston Gate SW8 .... 172 C4
Gataker Ho 5
SE16 .... 40 A3
Gataker St 5
SE16 .... 40 A3
Gatcliff Cl SW1 .... 145 C1
Gatcombe Ho 20
SE22 .... 64 A4
Gatcombe Rd
8 Newham E16 .... 35 C1
Tufnell Pk N19 .... 4 C1
Gatefield Ct SE15 .... 64 C4
Gateforth St NW8 .... 90 A1
Gate Hill Ct
W11 .... 31 B1 113 A2
Gatehouse Sch 2
E2 .... 25 C3
Gatehouse Sq
SE1 .... 123 A2
Gateley Ho 6 SE4 .... 65 C3
Gateley Rd SW9 .... 62 B4
Gates Mews SW7 .... 130 B3
Gatesborough St
EC2 .... 24 A1 98 A2
Gates St SE17 .... 150 C2
Gatesden WC1 .... 94 B3
Gateside Rd SW17 .... 72 B1
Gateway SE17 .... 48 B4
Gateway Arc N1 .... 86 A2
Gateway Ho SW12 .... 61 A1
Gateway Ind Est
NW10 .... 21 C1
Gateway Mews 4
E8 .... 16 B3
Gateway Prim Sch
NW8 .... 89 C2
Gateways The
SW3 .... 144 B3
Gateway Trad Est
NW10 .... 21 B2
Gathorne St 19 E2 .... 25 C3
Gatliff Rd SW1 .... 146 A1
Gatonby St SE15 .... 49 B2
Gatwick Ho 5 E14 .... 33 B3
Gatwick Rd SW18 .... 70 B4
Gauden Cl SW4 .... 61 C4
Gauden Rd SW4 .... 61 C4
Gaugin Ct 19 SE16 .... 40 A1
Gaunt St SE1 .... 136 C2
Gautrey Rd SE15 .... 50 B1
Gavel St SE17 .... 151 C4
Gaverick Mews 3
E14 .... 41 C2
Gaviller Pl 3 E5 .... 17 A4
Gawber St E2 .... 25 B2
Gawthorne Ct E3 .... 26 C3
Gay Cl NW2 .... 9 A3
Gaydon Ho W2 .... 100 A4

Gayfere St SW1 .... 134 A1
Gayford Rd W12 .... 38 B4
Gay Ho N16 .... 16 A3
Gayhurst SE17 .... 48 C4
Gayhurst Ho NW8 .... 90 B2
Gayhurst Prim Sch
E8 .... 16 C1
Gayhurst Rd E8 .... 16 C1
Gaymead NW8 .... 78 B3
Gay Rd E15 .... 27 C3
Gaysley Ho SE11 .... 149 B3
Gay St SW15 .... 57 C4
Gayton Cres NW3 .... 11 C4
Gayton Ho E3 .... 26 C1
Gayton Rd NW3 .... 11 C4
Gayville Rd SW11 .... 60 B1
Gaywood Cl SW2 .... 74 C3
Gaywood St SE1 .... 136 B1
Gaza St SE17 .... 150 A1
Gaze Ho 10 E14 .... 34 C3
Gean Ct 8 E11 .... 19 C4
Geary Ho N7 .... 14 B3
Geary Rd NW10 .... 8 C3
Geary St N7 .... 14 B3
Gedling Ho SE22 .... 64 B4
Gedling Pl SE1 .... 139 A2
Gees Ct W1 .... 103 C1
Gee St EC1 .... 96 C2
Geffrye Ct N1 .... 24 A3
Geffrye Mus E2 .... 24 A3
Geffrye St E2 .... 24 B3
Geldart Rd SE15 .... 50 A3
Geldeston Rd E5 .... 7 C2
Gellatly Rd SE14 .... 50 C1
Gemini Bsns Ctr
E16 .... 27 C1
Gemini Ho 1 E3 .... 26 C4
Gems Hampshire Sch
(Main Sch) SW7 .... 144 A1
Gems Hampshire Sch
(The Early Years)
SW7 .... 143 B3
General Wolfe Rd
SE10 .... 52 C2
Genesis Bsns Pk
NW10 .... 20 A3
Geneva Ct
1 Putney SW15 .... 57 C2
Stoke Newington
N16 .... 6 C3
Geneva Dr SW9 .... 62 C3
Genoa Ave SW15 .... 57 B2
Genoa Ho 1 E1 .... 25 C1
Geoffrey Cl SE5 .... 48 B1
Geoffrey Ct SE4 .... 66 B4
Geoffrey Ho SE1 .... 137 C2
Geoffrey Jones Ct
NW10 .... 21 C4
Geoffrey Rd SE4 .... 66 B4
George Beard Rd 11
SE8 .... 41 B2
George Beare Lo 9
SW4 .... 61 B2
George Belt Ho 8
E2 .... 25 C2
George Ct WC2 .... 120 B3
George Downing Est
N16 .... 7 B2
George Eliot Ho
SW1 .... 147 A3
George Eliot Prim Sch
NW8 .... 79 B4
George Elliot Ho
SE17 .... 150 C2
George Elliston Ho 10
SE1 .... 153 B1

Gal–Ger 217

George Eyre Ho
NW8 .... 79 C1
George Green's Sch
E14 .... 42 B1
George Inn SE1 .... 123 B1
George Inn Yd
SE1 .... 123 B1
George La SE13 .... 67 B1
George Lansbury Ho
2 Bow E3 .... 26 B2
3 Willesden NW10 .... 21 A4
George Lashwood Ct
12 SW9 .... 62 B3
George Leybourne Ho
19 E1 .... 125 C4
George Lindgren Ho
6 SW6 .... 155 A2
George Loveless Ho
6 E2 .... 24 B2 99 A4
George Mathers Rd
SE11 .... 150 A4
George Mews
27 Brixton SW9 .... 173 B1
NW1 .... 92 C3
George Peabody Ct
NW1 .... 102 A4
George Potter Way
SW11 .... 167 C1
George Row SE16 .... 139 B3
George's Rd N7 .... 14 B3
George's Sq SW6 .... 155 A4
George St
6 Canning Town
E16 .... 35 B3
Marylebone W1 .... 103 A2
George Tingle Ho
SE1 .... 139 A2
Georgette Pl SE10 .... 52 B3
George Vale Ho 38
E2 .... 24 C3
George Walter Ho 3
SE16 .... 40 B2
George Wyver Cl
SW18 .... 70 A4
George Yd
City of London
EC3 .... 109 C1
Mayfair W1 .... 117 C4
Georgiana St NW1 .... 83 A4
Georgian Ct 12 E9 .... 25 B4
Georgina Gdns 10
E2 .... 24 B2 99 A4
Geraldine Rd
Brentford W4 .... 44 C4
Wandsworth SW18 .... 59 B2
Geraldine St SE11 .... 136 A1
Gerald Mews
SW1 .... 145 C4
Gerald Rd SW1 .... 145 C4
Gerard Rd SW13 .... 46 B2
Gerards Cl SE16 .... 40 B1
Gernigan Ho
SW18 .... 59 C1
Gernon Rd E3 .... 26 A3
Gerrard Ho 5
SE14 .... 50 C3
Gerrard Pl W1 .... 119 C4
Gerrard Rd N1 .... 86 B2
Gerrard St W1 .... 119 C4
Gerridge Ct SE1 .... 135 C2
Gerridge St SE1 .... 135 C2
Gerry Raffles Sq
E15 .... 19 C2

Gertrude St SW10 ... **157** A3
Gervase St SE15 ... **50** A3
Getters Talmud Torah
 [3] N16 ... 6 C4
Getters Talmud Torah
 Sch [1] N16 ... 6 C4
Ghent Way E8 ... 16 B2
Gherkin The (30 St
 Mary Axe) EC2 ... **110** B2
Giant Arches Rd
 SE24 ... 63 B1
Gibbings Ho C4 ... **136** B3
Gibbins Rd E15 ... 19 B1
Gibbon Ho NW6 ... **89** C1
Gibbon Rd
 Acton W3 ... 29 A2
 Nunhead SE15 ... 50 B1
Gibbons Rd NW10 ... 8 A2
Gibbon's Rents
 SE1 ... **124** A1
Gibbon Wlk SW15 ... 56 C3
Gibbs Gn W14 ... **141** A2
Gibbs Ho SW12 ... 73 A4
Gibbs Green Cl
 W14 ... **141** A2
Gibraltar Ho
 NW10 ... 21 A3
Gibraltar Wlk [28]
 E2 ... 24 B2 **99** A3
Gibson Cl E1 ... 25 B1
Gibson Gdns N16 ... 7 B2
Gibson Rd SE11 ... **149** A3
Gibson Sq N1 ... 85 C4
Gibson St SE10 ... 43 A1
Gideon Rd SW11 ... 60 C4
Giesbach Rd N19 ... 4 C2
Giffen Square Mkt
 SE8 ... 51 C3
Giffin St SE8 ... 51 C3
Gifford Ho
 [5] Clapham SW4 ... 61 C3
 Greenwich SE10 ... 42 C1
 Pimlico SW1 ... **146** C1
Gifford Rd NW10 ... 8 A1
Gifford St N1 ... 14 A1
Gilbert Ho
 Barbican EC2 ... **109** A3
 Deptford SE8 ... 51 C4
 [9] Globe Town E2 ... 25 C2
 Pimlico SW1 ... **146** B1
 South Lambeth
 SW8 ... **162** A2
Gilbert Pl WC1 ... **106** A3
Gilbert Rd SE11 ... **149** C4
Gilbert Sheldon Ho
 W2 ... **101** C4
Gilbertson Ho [11]
 E14 ... 41 C3
Gilbert St W1 ... **103** C1
Gilbeys Yd NW1 ... 12 C1
Gilby Ho [5] E9 ... 17 C2
Gilda Cres N16 ... 7 C3
Gildea St W1 ... **104** B3
Gilden Cres NW5 ... 12 C3
Giles Ho
 [5] Bermondsey
 SE16 ... **139** B2
 Notting Hill W11 ... 31 C3
Gilesmead SE5 ... 48 C2
Gilkes Cres SE21 ... 64 A1
Gilkes Pl SE21 ... 64 A1
Gillam Ho [9] SE16 ... 40 B2
Gill Ave E16 ... 35 C3
Gillender St E3 ... 27 B1

Gillespie Prim Sch
 N5 ... 6 A1
Gillespie Rd N4, N5 ... 6 A1
Gillett Pl [27] E8 ... 16 A3
Gillett St E8, N16 ... 16 A3
Gillfoot NW1 ... 82 C1
Gillian St SE13 ... 67 A2
Gillies St NW5 ... 12 C3
Gilling Ct [3] NW3 ... 12 A2
Gillingham Ho
 SW1 ... **146** C4
Gillingham Mews
 SW1 ... **146** C4
Gillingham Rd NW2 ... 1 A1
Gillingham Row
 SW1 ... **146** C4
Gillingham St
 SW1 ... **146** C4
Gillison Wlk [3]
 SE16 ... **139** C2
Gillis Sq [3] SW15 ... 56 C1
Gillman Ho [3] E2 ... 24 C3
Gillray Ho SW10 ... **157** B3
Gill St E14 ... 33 B2
Gilmore Ho SW4 ... 61 C3
Gilmore Rd SE13 ... 67 C3
Gilpin Ave SW14 ... 55 C3
Gilpin Cl W2 ... **101** A4
Gilpin Rd E5 ... 18 A4
Gilray Ho W2 ... **115** B4
Gilstead Rd SW6 ... **166** B2
Gilston Rd SW10 ... **143** A1
Gilstpur St EC1 ... **108** B2
Giltwell Cl [15] E17 ... 17 A4
Gipsy Cnr W3 ... 28 C4
Gipsy La SW15 ... 57 A4
Giraud St E14 ... 34 A3
Girdlers Rd W14 ... 39 C2
Girdlestone Wlk
 N19 ... 4 C2
Girdwood Rd SW18,
 SW19 ... 70 A4
Girling Ho [9] N1 ... 24 A4
Gironde Rd SW6 ... **155** A1
Girton Ho SW15 ... 57 C1
Girton Villas [6]
 W10 ... 30 C3
Gisburn Ho [23]
 SE15 ... 49 C3
Gissing Wlk N1 ... 14 C1
Glade The W12 ... 39 A4
Glading Terr N16 ... 7 B1
Gladsmuir Rd N19 ... 4 B3
Gladstone Ct
 Westminster
 SW1 ... **147** C3
 Willesden NW2 ... 9 A3
Gladstone Park Sch
 NW10 ... 9 A4
Gladstone Rd W4 ... 37 C3
Gladstone St SE1 ... **136** A2
Gladstone Terr
 SW8 ... **170** B4
Gladwin Ho NW1 ... 83 A1
Gladwyn Rd SW15 ... 57 C4
Gladys Rd NW6 ... 10 C1
Glaisher St SE8 ... 52 A4
Glamis Ct W3 ... 37 A4
Glamis Est [3] E1 ... 32 C2
Glamis Pl E1 ... 32 B2
Glamis Rd E1 ... 32 B2
Glanville Ho [6]
 SW12 ... 73 B4
Glanville Rd SW2 ... 62 A2

Glasbury Ho [5]
 SW9 ... 62 B3
Glaserton Rd N16 ... 7 A4
Glasgow Ho W9 ... 78 B1
Glasgow Terr
 SW1 ... **146** C1
Glasshill St SE1 ... **136** B4
Glasshouse Fields
 E1 ... 32 C2
Glasshouse St
 W1 ... **119** A3
Glasshouse The
 SE13 ... 67 B3
Glasshouse Wlk
 SE11 ... **148** C2
Glasshouse Yd
 EC1 ... 96 C1
Glass St [4] E2 ... 25 A1
Glastonbury Ct [12]
 SE14 ... 50 B3
Glastonbury Ho
 SW1 ... **146** A2
Glastonbury Pl [22]
 E1 ... 32 B3
Glastonbury St
 NW6 ... 10 B3
Glaucus St E3 ... 34 A4
Glazbury Rd W14 ... **140** B2
Glazebrook Cl
 SE21 ... 75 C2
Glebe Cl [1] W4 ... 38 A1
Glebe Ho [5] SE16 ... 40 A3
Glebelands Cl SE5 ... 64 A4
Glebe Pl SW3 ... **158** A4
Glebe Rd
 Barnes SW13 ... 46 C1
 Dalston E8 ... 16 B1
 Willesden NW10 ... 8 C2
Glebe St W4 ... 38 A1
Gledhow Gdns
 SW5 ... **142** C3
Gledstanes Rd
 W14 ... **140** B1
Glegg Pl [3] SW15 ... 57 C3
Glenaffric Ave E14 ... 42 C2
Glen Albyn Rd
 SW19 ... 69 C2
Glenalmond Ho [2]
 SW15 ... 57 C1
Glenarm Rd E5 ... 17 C4
Glenbrook Prim Sch
 SW4 ... 61 C1
Glenbrook Rd
 NW6 ... 10 C3
Glenburnie Rd
 SW17 ... 72 B1
Glencoe Mans [6]
 SW9 ... **163** B1
Glendall St SW9 ... 62 B3
Glendarvon St
 SW15 ... 57 C4
Glendower Gdns [10]
 SW14 ... 55 C4
Glendower Pl
 SW7 ... **143** B4
Glendower Prep Sch
 SW7 ... **143** B4
Glendown Ho [2]
 E8 ... 16 C3
Glendun Ct W3 ... 29 A2
Glendun Rd W3 ... 29 A2
Gleneagles Cl [1]
 SE16 ... 40 A1
Glenelg Rd SW2 ... 62 A2

Glenfield Rd SW12 ... 73 B3
Glenfinlas Way
 SE5 ... 48 A3
Glenforth St SE10 ... 43 B1
Glengall Gr E14 ... 42 B3
Glengall Pass [2]
 NW6 ... 23 C4
Glengall Rd
 Camberwell SE15 ... 49 B4
 Kilburn NW6 ... 23 B4
Glengall Terr SE15 ... 49 B4
Glengarnock Ave
 E14 ... 42 B2
Glengarry Rd SE22 ... 64 B2
Glenhurst Ave
 NW5 ... 12 C4
Glenilla Rd NW3 ... 12 A2
Glenister Rd SE10 ... 43 B1
Glenkerry Ho [1]
 E14 ... 34 B3
Glenloch Rd NW3 ... 12 A3
Glenluce Rd SE3 ... 53 C4
Glenmore SW15 ... 57 C1
Glenmore Ho [6]
 TW10 ... 54 A1
Glenmore Rd NW3 ... 12 A2
Glennie Ct SE21 ... 76 C3
Glennie Ho SE10 ... 52 B2
Glennie Rd SE27,
 SE16 ... 74 C1
Glenridding NW1 ... 83 A1
Glenrosa St SW6 ... **166** C2
Glenroy St W12 ... 30 B3
Glenshaw Mans [7]
 SW9 ... **163** B1
Glentanner Way
 SW17 ... 71 C1
Glentham Gdns
 SW13 ... 47 A4
Glentham Rd
 SW13 ... 47 A4
Glenthorne Mews
 W6 ... 39 A2
Glenthorne Rd
 W6 ... 39 A2
Glenton Mews
 SE15 ... 50 B1
Glentworth St
 NW1 ... 91 A1
Glenville Gr SE8 ... 51 B3
Glenville Mews
 SW18 ... 70 C4
Glenworth Ave
 E14 ... 42 C2
Gliddon Rd W14 ... **140** A2
Globe Pond Rd
 SE16 ... 33 A1
Globe Prim Sch [3]
 E2 ... 25 B2
Globe St SE1 ... **137** B3
Globe Terr [9] E2 ... 25 B2
Globe Theatre The
 SE1 ... **122** C3
Globe View EC4 ... **122** C4
Globe Yd W1 ... **104** A1
Gloucester Ave
 NW1 ... 81 C4
Gloucester Cir
 SE10 ... 52 B3

Gloucester Cres
 NW1 ... 82 A4
Gloucester Ct
 Borough The SE1 ... **137** C4
 City of London EC3 ... **124** B3
 Dulwich SE22 ... 76 C3
 Golders Green NW11 ... 1 A4
 Richmond TW9 ... 44 C3
Gloucester Dr N4 ... 6 A2
Gloucester Gate
 NW1 ... 82 A2
Gloucester Gate
 Mews NW1 ... 82 A2
Gloucester Gdns
 Golders Green
 NW11 ... 1 B4
 Paddington W2 ... **100** C2
Gloucester Ho
 Kilburn NW6 ... 23 C3
 Richmond TW10 ... 54 C2
Gloucester Mews
 W2 ... **101** A1
Gloucester Mews W
 W2 ... **100** C1
Gloucester Pk
 SW7 ... **142** C4
Gloucester Pl NW1 ... **103** A4
Gloucester Pl Mews
 W1 ... **103** A3
Gloucester Rd
 Acton W3 ... 37 B4
 Richmond TW9 ... 44 C3
 South Kensington
 SW7 ... **142** C4
Gloucester Road Sta
 SW7 ... **142** C4
Gloucester Sq
 [6] Hackney E2 ... 24 C4
 Paddington W2 ... **102** A1
Gloucester St
 SW1 ... **146** C2
Gloucester Terr
 W2 ... **101** A1
Gloucester Way
 EC1 ... 95 C3
Gloucester Wlk
 W8 ... **127** C4
Glover Ho
 London SE15 ... 65 A3
 [2] South Hampstead
 NW6 ... 11 B1
Glycena Rd SW11 ... 60 B4
Glyn Ct SE27 ... 74 C1
Glynde Mews
 SW3 ... **130** B1
Glynde Reach WC1 ... 94 B3
Glynde St SE4 ... 66 B1
Glynfield Rd NW10 ... 8 A1
Glyn Mans W14 ... **140** B4
Glyn Rd E5 ... 17 C4
Glyn St SE11 ... **148** C1
Goater's Alley
 SW6 ... **155** A1
Goat Wharf TW8 ... 44 A4
Godalming Rd E14 ... 34 A4
Goddard Ho SW19 ... 69 C2
Goddard Pl N19 ... 4 B1
Godfrey Ho EC1 ... 97 B3
Godfrey St
 Chelsea SW3 ... **144** B2
 Mill Meads E15 ... 27 B3
Goding St SE11 ... **148** B1
Godley Rd SW18 ... 71 C3
Godliman St EC4 ... **122** C4
Godman Rd SE15 ... 50 A1

Godolphin Ho
Primrose Hill
NW3 . . . . 12 A1
🚇 Streatham SW2 . . 74 C3
Godolphin & Latymer
Sch 18 W6 . . . . 39 A2
Godolphin Pl W3 . . 28 C2
Godolphin Rd
W12 . . . . 39 A4
Godson St N1 . . . . . 85 B2
Godstone Ct 1 N16 . 7 A3
Godstone Ho 5 SE1 137 C2
Godwin Cl N1 . . . . . 87 A2
Godwin Ho
2 Haggerston E2 . . 24 B3
Kilburn NW6 . . . . . . 78 A2
Goffers Ho SE3 . . . . 53 A1
Goffers Rd SE3,
SE13 . . . . 53 A1
Goffton Ho 14
SW9 . . . . 173 A1
Golborne Gdns
5 Kensal Town
W10 . . . . 23 A1
West Kilburn W10 . . 23 A1
Golborne Mews 5
W10 . . . . 31 A4
Golborne Rd W10 . . 31 A4
Golden Cross Mews
2 W11 . . . . 31 B3
Golden Hinde II The
SE1 . . . . 123 B2
Golden Hind Pl 5
SE8 . . . . 41 B2
Golden La EC1 . . . . 97 A1
Golden Lane L Ctr
EC1 . . . . 96 C1
Golden Plover Cl
E16 . . . . 35 C3
Golden Sq W1 . . . . 119 A4
Golders Ct NW11 . . . 1 B4
Golders Gdns NW11 . 1 B4
GOLDERS GREEN . . 1 C4
Golders Green Coll
NW11 . . . . 1 C3
Golders Green Cres
NW11 . . . . 1 C3
Golders Green Rd
NW11 . . . . 1 A4
Golders Green Sta
NW11 . . . . 1 C3
Golders Hill Sch
NW11 . . . . 1 C4
Golderslea NW11 . . . 1 C3
Golders Park Cl
NW11 . . . . 1 C3
Golders Way NW11 . . 1 B4
Goldhawk Ind Est
W6 . . . . 39 A3
Goldhawk Mews 2
W12 . . . . 39 A4
Goldhawk Rd W12 . 38 C3
Goldhawk Road Sta
W12 . . . . 39 B4
Goldhurst Terr
NW6 . . . . 11 B1
Goldie Ho N19 . . . . . 4 C4
Golding St E1 . . . . 111 C1
Goldington Cres
NW1 . . . . 83 B2
Goldington Ct
NW1 . . . . 83 B2
Goldington St
NW1 . . . . 83 B2

Goldman Cl
E2 . . . . 24 C1 99 B2
Goldney Rd W9 . . . 23 C1
Goldsboro Rd
SW8 . . . . 161 C1
Goldsborough Ho
SW8 . . . . 171 C3
Goldsmith Ave W3 . 28 C2
Goldsmith Ct
WC1 . . . . 106 B2
Goldsmith Ho 2
W3 . . . . 28 C2
Goldsmith Rd
Acton W3 . . . . 28 C1
Peckham SE15 . . . . 49 C2
Goldsmiths Bldgs
W3 . . . . 28 C1
Goldsmiths Cl 3
W3 . . . . 28 C1
Goldsmith's Pl 6
NW6 . . . . 78 A3
Goldsmith's Row
E2 . . . . 24 C3
Goldsmith's Sq 17
E2 . . . . 24 C3
Goldsmith St EC2 . 109 A2
Goldsmiths Univ of
London SE14 . . . . . 51 A2
Gondar Gdns NW6 . 10 B3
Gondar Mans NW6 . 10 B3
Gonson St SE8 . . . . 52 A4
Gonston Cl SW19 . . 70 A2
Gonville Ho 5
SW15 . . . . 57 C1
Gonville St SW6 . . . 58 A4
Gooch Ho EC1 . . . . 107 B4
Goodall Ho 10 SE4 . 65 C3
Goodenough Coll
WC1 . . . . 94 C2
Goodfaith Ho 18
E14 . . . . 34 A2
Goodge Pl W1 . . . 105 A3
Goodge St W1 . . . 105 A3
Goodge Street Sta
W1 . . . . 105 B4
Goodhall St NW10 . 21 B2
Good Hart Pl E14 . . 33 A2
Goodhope Ho 3
E14 . . . . 34 A2
Gooding Cl N7 . . . . 14 A2
Goodinge Rd N7 . . 14 A2
Goodman Cres
SW2 . . . . 73 C2
Goodman's Ct
E1 . . . . 124 C4
Goodman's Stile 7
E1 . . . . 111 B2
Goodman's Yd E1,
EC3 . . . . 124 C4
Goodrich Com Prim
Sch SE22 . . . . 64 C1
Goodrich Ct 7
W10 . . . . 30 C3
Goodrich Ho
20 Bethnal Green
E2 . . . . 25 B3
Stamford Hill N16 . . . 7 A4
Goodrich Rd SE22 . 64 C1
Good Shepherd RC
Prim Sch The
W12 . . . . 38 B4

Goodson Rd NW10 . . 8 A1
Goodspeed Ho 20
E14 . . . . 34 A2
Goodsway NW1 . . . 84 A2
Goodway Gdns
E14 . . . . 34 C3
Goodwill Ho 22
E14 . . . . 34 A2
Goodwin Cl SE16 . 139 A1
Goodwin Ho 22
SE15 . . . . 65 A4
Goodwin Rd W12 . . 38 C4
Goodwins Ct WC2 . 120 A4
Goodwin St N4 . . . . 5 C2
Goodwood Ct W1 . 104 B4
Goodwood Ho 3
W4 . . . . 37 B1
Goodwood Mans
SW9 . . . . 62 C4
Goodwood Rd
SE14 . . . . 51 A3
Goose Green Prim
Sch SE22 . . . . 64 B3
Goose Green Trad Est
SE22 . . . . 64 C3
Gophir La EC4 . . . . 123 B4
Gopsall St N1 . . . . . 87 C3
Gordon Ave SW14 . 56 A3
Gordonbrock Prim
Sch SE4 . . . . 66 C2
Gordonbrock Rd
SE4 . . . . 66 C2
Gordon Ct 5 W12 . 30 B3
Gordondale Rd SW18,
SW19 . . . . 70 C2
Gordon Gr SE5 . . . . 48 A1
Gordon Hospl
SW1 . . . . 147 B3
Gordon House Rd
NW5 . . . . 12 C4
Gordon Lo N16 . . . . 6 C3
Gordon Mans WC1 . 93 B1
Gordon PI W8 . . . . 127 C4
Gordon Rd
Chiswick W4 . . . . . . 45 A4
Leyton E15 . . . . 19 B4
Peckham SE15 . . . . 50 A1
Richmond TW9 . . . . 44 B1
Gordon Sq WC1 . . . 93 C2
Gordon St WC1 . . . 93 B2
Gore Rd E9 . . . . 25 B4
Gore St SW7 . . . . . 129 A2
Gorham Ho 10
SW4 . . . . 61 B1
Gorham Pl
W11 . . . . . . 31 A2 112 A3
Goring St EC3 . . . . 110 B2
Gorleston St W14 . 140 B4
Gorse Cl E16 . . . . . 35 C3
Gorsefield Ho 6
E14 . . . . 33 C2
Gorst Rd
London NW10 . . . . . 20 B1
North Acton NW10 . . 20 C1
Gorsuch Pl 1
E2 . . . . 24 B2 98 C4
Gorsuch St
E2 . . . . 24 B2 98 C4
Gosberton Rd
SW12 . . . . 72 C3
Gosfield St W1 . . . 104 C3
Gosford Ho 23 E3 . 26 B3
Goslett Yd WC2 . . . 105 C2

Gosling Ho 2 E1 . . 32 B2
Gosling Way SW9 . 173 B4
Gospatric Home Ho
SW14 . . . . 56 A4
GOSPEL OAK 12 C4
Gospel Oak Prim Sch
NW5 . . . . 12 C4
Gospel Oak Sta
NW5 . . . . 12 C4
Gosport Ho 1
SW15 . . . . 68 C3
Gosset St E2 . . 24 C2 99 BA
Gosterwood St
SE8 . . . . 51 A4
Goswell Pl EC1 . . . . 96 B3
Goswell Rd EC1 . . . 96 B4
Gothic Ct 11 SE5 . . 48 B3
Gottfried Mews
NW5 . . . . 13 B4
Gough Ho N1 . . . . . 86 A3
Gough Sq EC4 . . . 107 C2
Gough St WC1 . . . . 95 A1
Gough Wlk 14 E14 . 33 C3
Goulden Ho SW11 . 168 A2
Gouldman Ho 33
E1 . . . . 25 B1
Gould Terr 28 E8 . . . 17 A3
Goulston St E1 . . . 110 C2
Goulton Rd E5 . . . . 17 A4
Govan St E2 . . . . . . 24 C4
Gover Ct 8 SW4 . . 172 B2
Gowan Ave SW6 . . 164 A4
Gowan Ho 22
E2 . . . . 24 B2 99 A3
Gowan Rd NW10 . . . 9 A2
Gower Cl SW4 . . . . 61 B1
Gower Ct WC1 . . . . 93 B3
Gower Ho SE17 . . . 151 A2
Gower Mews
WC1 . . . . 105 C4
Gower PI NW1,
WC1 . . . . 93 B2
Gower Sch The 14
N7 . . . . 14 A2
Gower St WC1 . . . . 93 B1
Gower's Wlk E1 . . 111 B1
Gowlett Rd SE15 . . 64 C4
Gowrie Rd SW11 . . 60 C4
Gracechurch St EC2,
EC4 . . . . 123 C4
Gracefield Gdns
SW16 . . . . 74 A1
Gracehill 2 E1 . . . . 32 B4
Grace Ho SE11 . . . 163 A4
Grace Jones Cl E8 . 16 C2
Grace PI E3 . . . . 27 A2
Graces Mews NW8 . 79 A1
Grace's Mews SE5 . 49 A1
Grace's Rd SE5 . . . 49 A1
Grace St E3 . . . . . . 27 A2
Graemesdyke Ave
SW14 . . . . 55 A3
Grafton Cres NW1 . 13 A2
Grafton Ct 10 E8 . . 16 C3
Grafton Ho
10 Bow E3 . . . . 26 C2
12 Deptford SE8 . . 41 B1
Grafton Mans SW4 . 61 B3
Grafton Mews W1 . 92 C1
Grafton PI NW1 . . . 93 C3
Grafton Prim Sch
N7 . . . . 5 A1
Grafton Rd
Acton W3 . . . . 28 B2
Gospel Oak NW5 . . 12 C3
Grafton Sq SW4 . . . 61 B4

Grafton St W1 . . . 118 B3
Grafton Terr NW5 . . 12 C3
Grafton Way W1 . . 93 A1
Grafton Yd NW5 . . . 13 A2
Graham Ct 6
SE14 . . . . 50 C4
Graham Ho
6 Balham SW12 . . 73 A4
2 Tufnell Pk N19 . . 13 C4
Graham Mans 2
E8 . . . . 17 A2
Graham Rd
Acton W4 . . . . 37 C3
Dalston E8 . . . . 16 C2
Hackney E8 . . . . . . 86 B1
Graham St N1 . . . . 86 B1
Graham Twr W3 . . 145 C3
Grainger Ct 22
SE5 . . . . 48 B3
Grampian Gdns
NW2 . . . . 1 A3
Grampians The 10
W14 . . . . 39 C4
Granard Ave SW15 . 57 A2
Granard Ho 20 E9 . 17 C2
Granard Prim Sch
SW15 . . . . 57 A1
Granard Rd SW11,
SW12 . . . . 72 B4
Granary Rd E1 . . . . 25 A1
Granary Sq
Islington N1 . . . . . . 14 C2
N1 . . . . 84 A3
Granary St NW1 . . . 83 A2
Granary The SE8 . . 51 C3
Granby PI SE1 . . . . 135 B3
Granby St
Bethnal Green
E2 . . . . 24 C1 99 B2
Shoreditch
E2 . . . . 24 B1 99 A2
Granby Terr NW1 . . 82 C1
Grand Ave EC1 . . . 108 B4
Grand Canal Ave
SE13 . . . . 41 A2
Grandfield E14 . . . . 45 C4
Grandison Rd
SW11 . . . . 60 B2
Grand Junction Wharf
N1 . . . . 86 C1
Grand Par SW14 . . 55 B3
Grand Union Cl
W9 . . . . 31 B4
Grand Union Cres
E8 . . . . 24 C4
Grand Union Ind Est
NW10 . . . . 20 A3
Grand Vitesse Ind Est
SE1 . . . . 122 B1
Granfield St
SW11 . . . . 167 C3
Grangecourt Rd
N16 . . . . 7 A3
Grange Ct
Peckham SE15 . . . . 49 B1
Strand WC2 . . . . . . 107 A1
1 Willesden NW10 . . 9 A1
Grangefield NW1 . . 14 A1
Grange Gdns NW3 . . 2 A1
Grange Gr N1 . . . . . 15 B2
Grange Ho
Bermondsey SE1 . . 138 C1
Willesden NW10 . . . 9 A1
Grange La SE21 . . . 76 B2

Grangemill **11**
NW5 . . . . .13 A4
GRANGE MILLS . . .73 B3
Grange Mills
SW12 . . . . .73 B3
Grange Pk NW6 . . . . .10 C1
Grange Prim Sch
SE1 . . . .**138** A1
Grange Rd
Barnes SW13 . . . . . . .46 C2
Bermondsey SE1 . . .**138** C1
Gunnersbury W4 . . . .37 A1
Willesden NW10 . . . . . .9 A2
Grange St N1 . . . . . .87 C3
Grange The
Bermondsey SE1 . . .**138** C1
7 Gunnersbury
W4 . . . . .37 A1
Hammersmith W12 . .39 A3
19 Maitland Pk
NW3 . . . . .12 B2
South Acton W3 . . . . .37 A4
West Kensington
W14 . . . .**140** C3
Grangeway NW6 . . . .10 C1
Grange Wlk SE1 . . .**138** C1
Grange Yd SE1 . . . .**138** C1
Granite Apts E15 . . .19 C2
Grannary The **10**
SE16 . . . . .40 B4
Gransden Ave E8 . . .17 A1
Gransden Ho **1**
SE8 . . . . .41 B1
Gransden Rd W12 . .38 B4
Grantbridge St N1 . .86 B2
Grantham Ct **9**
SE16 . . . . .40 C4
Grantham Ho **12**
SE15 . . . . .49 C4
Grantham Pl W1 . . .**118** A1
Grantham Rd
Chiswick W4 . . . . . . .46 A3
South Lambeth
SW9 . . . .**172** B1
Grant Ho
5B Clapham
SW8 . . . .**171** B1
Clerkenwell EC1 . . . .**108** B2
Grantley Ho
2 Deptford SE14 . .50 C4
5 Putney SW19 . . . .69 C3
Grantley St E1 . . . . .25 C1
Grant Mus of Zoology
WC1 . . . . .93 B1
Grant Rd SW11 . . . . .60 A4
Grant St N1 . . . . .85 B2
Grantully Rd W9 . . . .88 A3
Granville Ct
8 Deptford SE14 . .51 A3
Shoreditch N1 . . . . . .87 C4
Granville Gr SE13 . . .67 B4
Granville Ho **10**
E14 . . . . .33 C3
Granville Ind Est
NW2 . . . . .1 B2
Granville Mans **8**
W12 . . . . .39 B4
Granville Pk SE13 . . .67 C4
Granville Pl
Marylebone W1 . . . .**103** B1
Walham Green
SW6 . . . .**156** A1
Granville Point
NW2 . . . . .1 B2

Granville Rd
Child's Hill NW2 . . . . . .1 B2
Kilburn NW6 . . . . . . .23 C3
Wandsworth SW18 . .70 B4
Granville Sq
3 Camberwell
SE15 . . . . .49 A3
Finsbury WC1 . . . . . .95 A3
Granville St WC1 . . .95 A3
Grape St WC2 . . . . .**106** A2
Grasgarth Cl W3 . . . .28 B2
Grasmere NW1 . . . . .92 B4
Grasmere Ave W3 . . .28 C2
Grasmere Ct
SW13 . . . . .46 C4
Grasmere Ho **20**
N16 . . . . .15 C4
Grasmere Point **3**
SE15 . . . . .50 B3
Grasmere Prim Sch
N16 . . . . .15 C4
Grateley Ho **10**
SW15 . . . . .69 A3
Gratton Rd W14 . . .**126** A1
Graveley Ho **7**
SE8 . . . . .41 A2
Gravesend Rd
W12 . . . . .29 C2
Grayfriars Pas
EC1 . . . .**108** B2
Gray Ho SE17 . . . . .**151** A2
Grayland Ct WC1 . . .94 C3
Grayling Rd N16 . . . . .6 C2
Grayling Sq
E2 . . . .**24** C2 **99** C4
Grayshott Rd
SW11 . . . . .60 C4
Gray's Inn WC1 . . .**107** A4
Gray's Inn Pl WC1 . .**107** A3
Gray's Inn Rd WC1 . .95 A2
Gray's Inn Sq
WC1 . . . .**107** B4
Grayson Ho EC1 . . . .97 A3
Gray St SE1 . . . . . .**135** C3
Grayswood Point **10**
SW15 . . . . .68 C3
Gray's Yd W1 . . . . .**103** C2
Grazebrook Rd N16 . .6 C2
Great Arthur Ho
EC1 . . . . .96 C1
Great Bell Alley
EC2 . . . .**109** B2
Great Castle St
W1 . . . .**104** C2
Great Central St
NW1 . . . .**102** C4
Great Chapel St
W1 . . . .**105** B2
Great Chart St
SW11 . . . . .59 B3
Great Chertsey Rd
SW14,W4 . . . . .45 C2
Great Church La
W6 . . . . .39 C1
Great College St
SW1 . . . .**134** A2
Great Croft WC1 . . . .94 B3
Great Cross Ave
SE3 . . . . .53 A3
Great Cumberland
Mews W1 . . . .**102** C1
Great Cumberland Pl
W1 . . . .**103** A1
Great Dover St
SE1 . . . .**137** B2

Great Eastern Bldgs
10 E8 . . . . .17 A2
Great Eastern Ent Ctr
E14 . . . . .42 A4
Great Eastern Pier
E14 . . . . .41 C1
Great Eastern Rd
E15 . . . . .19 C2
Great Eastern St
EC2 . . . .**24** A1 **98** A2
Great Eastern Wharf
SW11 . . . .**158** B1
Great Field **7**
NW5 . . . . .13 B3
Greatfield Cl
London SE4 . . . . .66 C3
4 Tufnell Pk N19 . . .13 A4
Great George St
SW1 . . . .**134** A3
Great Guildford Bsns
Sq SE1 . . . .**122** C1
Great Guildford St
SE1 . . . .**122** C1
Greatham Wlk **3**
SW15 . . . . .68 C3
Great James St
WC1 . . . .**106** C4
Great Marlborough St
W1 . . . .**104** C1
Great Maze Pond
SE1 . . . .**137** C4
Great Newport St
WC2 . . . .**120** A4
Greatorex Ho **13**
E1 . . . .**111** B4
Greatorex St E1 . . .**111** B4
Great Ormond St
Hospl for Children
WC1 . . . . .94 C1
Great Ormond St
WC1 . . . . .94 C1
Great Percy St
WC1 . . . . .95 B4
Great Peter St
SW1 . . . .**133** C1
Great Portland St
W1 . . . .**104** B4
Great Portland Street
Sta W1 . . . . .92 B1
Great Pulteney St
W1 . . . .**119** A4
Great Queen St
WC2 . . . .**106** B2
Great Russell Mans
WC1 . . . .**106** A3
Great Russell St
WC1 . . . .**106** A3
Great St Helen's
EC3 . . . .**110** A2
Great St Thomas
Apostle EC4 . . . . . .**123** A4
Great Scotland Yd
SW1,WC2 . . . .**120** A2
Great Smith St
SW1 . . . .**133** C2
Great Spilmans
SE22 . . . . .64 A2
Great Suffolk St
SE1 . . . .**122** B1
Great Sutton St
EC1 . . . . .96 B1
Great Swan Alley
EC2 . . . .**109** B2
Great Titchfield St
W1 . . . .**104** C3

Great Tower St
EC3 . . . .**124** A4
Great Trinity La
EC4 . . . .**123** A4
Great Turnstile
WC2 . . . .**107** A3
Great Western Rd W2,
W9 . . . . .31 B4
Great West Rd W6 . .45 C4
Great West Road
Cedars Rd W4 . . . . .45 B4
Great West Road
Hogarth La W4 . . . .46 A4
Great Winchester St
EC2 . . . .**109** C2
Great Windmill St
W1 . . . .**119** B4
Great Yd SE1 . . . . .**138** B4
Greaves Cotts **10**
E14 . . . . .33 A3
Greaves Twr
SW10 . . . .**157** A2
Grebe Ct **11** E14 . . .42 B4
Greek Ct W1 . . . . . .**105** C1
Greek St W1 . . . . . .**105** C1
Greenacre Ct E8 . . .16 C3
Greenacre Sq **26**
SE16 . . . . .40 C4
Green Arbour Ct
EC1 . . . .**108** A2
Greenaway Gdns
NW3 . . . . .11 A4
Greenaway Ho
Finsbury WC1 . . . . . .95 B3
St John's Wood
NW8 . . . . .78 C4
Green Bank E1 . . . . .32 A1
Greenbanks Cl
SE13 . . . . .67 A4
Greenberry St
NW8 . . . . .80 A1
Green Cl NW11 . . . . . .2 B4
Greencoat Pl
SW1 . . . .**147** A4
Greencoat Row
SW1 . . . .**133** A1
Greencourt Ho **2**
E1 . . . . .25 C1
Greencroft Gdns
NW6 . . . . .11 B1
Green Ct **2** Balham SW12 .10 A4
Green Dale SE22 . . . .64 A2
Greendale SE22 . . . .64 A2
Green Dragon Ct
SE1 . . . .**123** B1
Green Dragon Ho
WC1 . . . .**106** B2
Green Dragon La
TW8 . . . . .36 B1
Green Dragon Prim
Sch TW8 . . . . .44 A4
Green Dragon Yd **24**
E1 . . . .**111** B3
Greene Ct **20** SE14 .50 C4
Greene Ho SE1 . . . .**137** B1
Greenend Rd W4 . . .38 A4
Greener Ho **3**
SW4 . . . . .61 C4
Grenfell Mans
SE8 . . . . .52 A4
Greenfield Gdns
NW2 . . . . .1 A1
Greenfield Ho **20**
SW19 . . . . .69 C3
Greenfield Rd E1 . . .**111** C2

Greenham Cl SE1 . . .**135** B3
Greenham Ho **5**
E9 . . . . .25 B4
Greenheath Bsns Ctr
3 E2 . . . . .25 A1
Greenhill NW3 . . . . .11 C4
Greenhill Pk
NW10 . . . . .21 A4
Greenhill Rd
NW10 . . . . .21 A4
Greenhill's Rents
EC1 . . . .**108** A4
Greenhills Terr **15**
N1 . . . . .15 C2
Green Ho The **5**
SW19 . . . . .70 A3
Green Hundred Rd
SE15 . . . . .49 C4
Greening Ho SE13 . .67 C3
Greenland Ho
Bermondsey SE8 . . . . .40 C1
4 Mile End E1 . . . . .26 A1
Greenland Mews
SE8 . . . . .40 C1
Greenland Pier
SE8 . . . . .41 B3
Greenland Pl NW1 . .82 B4
Greenland Quay
SE16 . . . . .40 C2
Greenland Rd
NW1 . . . . .82 C4
Greenland St NW1 . .82 B4
Green Lanes N4, N8,
N15 . . . . .6 A4
Greenleaf Cl **8**
SW2 . . . . .74 C4
Green Link Wlk
TW9 . . . . .45 A2
Greenman St N1 . . .86 C4
Greenmead &
Paddock Schs
SW15 . . . . .57 A2
Green Mews N1 . . . .97 C4
Greenock Rd **11**
W3 . . . . .37 A3
Green Park SW1,
W1 . . . .**132** B2
Green Park Sta
W1 . . . .**118** C2
Greenroof Way
SE10 . . . . .43 B3
Greens Ct W1 . . . . .**119** B4
Green's Ct
W11 . . . . .31 B1 **112** C1
Greenside Prim Sch
W12 . . . . .38 C4
Greenside Rd W12 . .38 C4
Green Spring
Academy Shoreditch
45 E2 . . . .**24** B3 **99** A3
Green St W1 . . . . . .**117** B4
Greenstead Gdns
SW15 . . . . .57 A2
Greenstreet Hill
SE4 . . . . .65 C4
Greensward Ho
SW6 . . . .**166** C2
Green Terr EC1 . . . . .95 C3
Green The W3 . . . . .29 A3
Greenview Cl W3 . . .29 A1
Greenview Ct
East Dulwich
SE22 . . . . .64 C3
Wandsworth SW18 . .72 A4
Greenway Cl N4 . . . . .6 B2
Greenwell St W1 . . .92 B1

GREENWICH......43 C3
Greenwich Acad
SE10......52 A2
Greenwich Bsns Ctr
SE10......52 A4
Greenwich Bsns Pk
SE10......52 B4
Greenwich Church St
SE10......52 B4
Greenwich Com Coll
17 SE10......52 B3
Greenwich Ct **11**
E1......32 A3
Greenwich High Rd
SE10......52 A3
Greenwich Ho
SE13......67 C1
Greenwich Ind Est
SE10......52 A4
Greenwich Mkt **2**
SE10......52 B4
Greenwich Park......53 A3
Greenwich Park St
SE10......53 A4
Greenwich Pier
SE10......42 B1
Greenwich Quay
SE8......52 A4
Greenwich South St
SE10......52 B2
Greenwich Sta
SE10......52 A3
Greenwich Steiner
Sch SE13......53 C4
Greenwich View Pl
E14......42 A3
Green St W1......138 A1
Greenwood **8**
SW19......69 C4
Green Wood NW5......13 B3
Greenwood Ho
Finsbury WC1......95 B3
6 Nunhead SE4......65 C3
Greenwood Pl
NW5......13 A3
Greenwood Rd E8..16 C2
Greenwood Terr
NW10......20 C3
Green W WC1......96 B2
Greet Ho SE1......135 C3
Greet St SE1......121 C1
Gregor Mews SE3..53 C3
Gregory Pl W8......128 A4
Greig Terr SE17......48 A4
Grenada Ho **18**
E14......33 B2
Grenade St E14......33 B2
Grena Gdns TW9..54 B3
Grena Rd TW10,
TW9......54 B3
Grenard Cl SE15..49 C3
Grendon Ho
29 Hackney E9......17 B1
Pentonville N1....84 C1
Grendon St NW8..90 A2
Grenfell Ho SE5....48 B3
Grenfell Rd W11..30 C2
Grenfell Twr **5**
W11......30 C2
Grenfell Wlk **4**
W11......30 C2
Grenier Apartments
11 SE15......50 A3
Grenville Ho
28 Bow E3......26 A3

Grenville Ho continued
4 Deptford SE8....51 C4
Grenville Lo N6....4 B4
Grenville Mans
WC1......94 A3
Grenville Mews
SW7......142 C3
Grenville Pl SW7..142 C4
Grenville Rd N19....5 A3
Grenville St WC1....94 B1
Gresham Almshouses
1 SW9......173 A4
Gresham Coll EC1..107 C3
Gresham Gdns
NW11......1 A3
Gresham Pl **2** N19..4 C2
Gresham Rd SW9..62 C4
Gresham St EC2..109 A2
Gresham Way
SW19......70 C1
Gresham Way Est
SW19......71 A1
Gresley Ho SW8..171 C4
Gresley Rd N19......4 B4
Gressenhall Rd
SW18......70 B4
Gresse St W1......105 B2
Greswell St SW6..47 C2
Greta Ho SE3......53 B4
Gretton Ho **2** E2..25 B2
Greville Hall NW6..78 B2
Greville Ho
Knightsbridge
SW1......131 B2
Putney SW15......57 C4
Greville Lo **5** SW7..100 A2
Greville Mews **5**
NW6......78 A3
Greville Pl W9......78 B2
Greville Rd
Kilburn NW6......78 B2
Richmond TW10....54 B1
Greville St EC1....107 C4
Grey Coat Hospital
The (Sch)
SW1......147 B3
SW1......133 B1
Greycoat Pl SW1..133 B1
Greycoat St SW1..133 B1
Grey Eagle St
E1......24 B1 99 A1
Greyfriars **18** SE26..76 C1
Greyfriars Ho SE3..53 B4
Grey Ho **2** W12..30 A2
Greyhound Ct
WC2......121 B4
Greyhound Rd
College Pk NW10..22 A2
Fulham W6......154 A4
Greyladies Gdns
SE10......52 B2
Greystoke Ho
SE15......49 C4
Greystoke Pl EC4..107 C2
Grey Turner Ho
W12......29 C3
Grice Ct N1......15 B2
Grierson Rd SE23..66 A1
Griffin Cl NW10......9 A3
Griffin Ct
9 Brentford
TW8......44 A4
Chiswick W4......38 B1
Shepherd's Bush
W12......30 A1

Griffin Gate **1**
SW15......57 C4
Griffin Prim Sch
SW8......171 A3
Griffon Ho **3**
SW11......60 A4
Grigg's Pl SE1......138 B1
Grimaldi Ho N1....84 C2
Grimsby St
8 Bethnal Green
E2......24 B1 99 A2
Shoreditch
E2......24 B1 99 A2
Grimsel Path SE5..48 A3
Grimshaw Cl N6....3 C4
Grimston Rd SW6..164 C1
Grinthorpe Ho
EC1......96 A2
Grindall Cl SE15..64 B4
Grindall Ho **21** E1..25 A1
Grindal St SE1......135 B3
Grindley Ho **3** E3..33 B4
Grinling Gibbons Prim
Sch **28** SE8......51 B4
Grinling Pl SE8....51 C4
Grinstead Rd SE8..41 A1
Grisedale NW1......92 C4
Grittleton Rd W9..23 C1
Grocers' Hall Ct
EC2......109 B1
Groombridge Rd
E9......17 C1
Groom Cres SW18..71 C4
Groome Ho SE11..149 A3
Groom Pl SW1....131 C2
Grosse Way SW15..57 A1
Grosvenor Ave
Canonbury N5......15 B3
Mortlake SW14......56 A4
Richmond TW10....54 A2
Grosvenor Bridge
SW1......160 B4
Grosvenor Cotts
SW1......145 B3
Grosvenor Court Mans
W2......102 C1
Grosvenor Cres
SW1......131 C3
Grosvenor Cres Mews
SW1......131 B3
Grosvenor Ct
Brondesbury Pk
NW6......22 C4
Gunnersbury W4..37 A1
22 Poplar E14......33 B3
Putney SW15......58 A2
Grosvenor Gdns
Cricklewood NW2....9 B3
Mortlake SW14......56 A4
Westminster SW1..132 B1
Grosvenor Gdns Mews
E SW1......132 B2
Grosvenor Gdns Mews
N SW1......132 A1
Grosvenor Gdns Mews
S SW1......132 B1
Grosvenor Hill
W1......118 A4
W1......118 A4
Grosvenor Hill Ct
W1......118 A4
Grosvenor Ho E5....7 C3
Grosvenor Park
SE5......48 B3
Grosvenor Pier
SW1......161 B4
Grosvenor Park Mews
SE5......48 B4

Grosvenor Pl
SW1......132 A3
Grosvenor Rd
Acton Green W4..37 B1
Pimlico SW1......161 A4
Richmond TW10....54 A2
Grosvenor Residences
3 W14......39 C3
Grosvenor Sq W1..117 C4
Grosvenor St W1..118 A4
Grosvenor Terr
SE5......48 B3
Grosvenor The
NW11......2 A4
Grosvenor Wy
SW17......71 C1
Grosvenor Wharf Rd
E14......42 C2
Grote's Bldgs SE3..53 A1
Grote's Pl SE3......53 A1
Groton Rd SW18....71 A2
Grotto Ct SE1......136 C4
Grotto Pas W1......103 B4
Grove Crescent Rd
E15......19 C2
Grove Ct
Camberwell SE5......49 A4
Clapham SW4......61 B4
South Kensington
SW10......143 A1
St John's Wood
NW8......89 B3
Grove Cotts SW3..158 A4
Grove Dwellings
E1......32 B4
Grove End Mews NW5..13 A4
Grove End Gdns
NW8......79 B1
Grove End Ho
NW8......89 B3
Grove End Rd NW8..89 B3
Grove Gdns NW8..90 B3
Grove Hall Ct
Bow E3......26 C3
St John's Wood
NW8......89 A4
Grove Hill Rd SE5..64 A4
Grove Ho
Blackheath SE3....53 B1
Chelsea SW3......158 B4
Grove La SE5......64 A4
Groveland Ct EC4..109 A1
Grovelands Cl SE5..49 A1
Grove Lane Terr
SE5......48 C1
Groveley Ho **4** N4..6 B4
Grove Lo SW4......61 B3
Grove Mans
London SW4......60 B3
2 Shepherd's Bush
W6......39 B4
3 Stamford Hill N16..7 C3
GROVE PARK W4..45 B3
Grove Park Bridge
W4......45 B3
Grove Park Gdns
W4......45 A3
Grove Park Mews
W4......45 B3
Grove Park Prim Sch
W4......45 A3
Grove Park Rd W4..45 A3
Grove Park Terr
W4......45 A3
Grove Pk SE5......49 A1

Grove Pl
Acton W3......28 B1
Balham SW12......61 A1
Hampstead NW3......2 C1
Grover Ct SE13......52 A1
Grove Rd
Acton W3......28 B1
Barnes SW13......46 B1
Bow E3......26 A3
Richmond TW10....54 B1
Willesden NW2......9 B2
Grover Ho
4 London SW4......61 B2
Vauxhall SE11......149 A1
Groveside Ct
SW11......167 B2
Grove St SE8......41 B1
Grove Terr NW5......13 A4
Grove Terrace Mews
NW5......4 A1
Grove The
Dulwich SE21......76 C3
Hendon NW11......1 A4
Highgate N6......3 C4
Stroud Green N4......5 B4
Grove Vale SE22....64 B3
Groveway SW9......173 A3
Grovewood **9**
TW9......44 C2
Grovewood Ho
NW2......1 B2
Grummant Rd
SE15......49 B2
Grundy St E14......34 A3
Guardian Angels RC
Prim Sch **8** E3..26 A2
Guards Mus The
SW1......133 A3
Gubyon Ave SE24..63 A2
Gudden Dr E5......17 A4
Guerin Sq E3......26 B2
Guernsey Gr SE24..75 B4
Guernsey Ho **10**
N1......15 B2
Guernsey Rd **11**
N1......15 B2
Guilford Gr SE10..52 B2
Guildford Rd
SW8......172 B4
Guildford Ho **3**
SE5......48 B1
Guildford Wlk **8** SE18..172 A4
Guildhall Art Gall
EC2......109 B2
Guildhall Ho EC2..109 B2
Guildhall Sch Music &
Drama EC2......109 A4
Guildhall Yd EC2..109 B2
Guildhouse St
SW1......146 C3
Guilford Pl WC1....94 C1
Guilford St WC1....94 B1
Guillemot Ct **28**
SE8......51 B4
Guinness Cl E9......18 A1
Guinness Ct
Chelsea SW3......144 C3
Finsbury EC1......97 A3
Primrose Hill NW8..80 B3
Whitechapel E1....111 A1
Guinness Sq SE1..152 A4
Guinness Trust Bldgs
Bermondsey SE1....138 A4
7 Bethnal Green
E2......24 C3
Chelsea SW3......144 C3

Guinness Trust Bldgs
  continued
  Hammersmith W6 . . . .39 B1
  Kennington SE11 . . . 150 A2
Guion Rd SW6 . . . . . .165 A2
Gujarat Ho **1** N16 . . . . .7 A1
Gulland Wlk **2** N1 . .15 B2
Gullane Ho **8** E3 . . . .26 B3
Gulliver St SE16 . . . . .41 B3
Gulston Wlk SW3 . . .145 A3
Gunmakers La E3 . . . .26 A4
GUNNERSBURY 37 A2
Gunnersbury Avenue
  (North Circular Rd)
  W3 . . . . .36 C3
Gunnersbury Cl **8**
  W4 . . . . .37 A1
Gunnersbury Cres
  W3 . . . . .36 B4
Gunnersbury Ct **8**
  W3 . . . . .37 A1
Gunnersbury Dr
  W5 . . . . .36 B4
Gunnersbury Gdns
  W3 . . . . .36 B4
Gunnersbury La
  W3 . . . . .36 C4
Gunnersbury Mews **6**
  W4 . . . . .37 A1
Gunnersbury Park
  W3 . . . . .36 C3
Gunnersbury Park
  Mus W3 . . . . .36 C3
Gunnersbury Sta
  W4 . . . . .37 A1
Gunnersbury Triangle
  Nat Res W12 . . . . . .37 B2
Gunners Rd SW18 . . .71 C2
Gunpowder Sq
  EC4 . . . . .107 C2
Gun St E1 . . . . .110 C3
Gunstor Rd N16 . . . . .16 A4
Gunter Gr SW6 . . . .156 C2
Gunterstone Rd
  W14 . . . . .140 B2
Gunthorpe St E1 . . . 111 A2
Gunton Mews
  SE13 . . . . .67 C2
Gunwhale Cl SE16 . . .32 C1
Gun Wharf
  Old Ford E3 . . . . . . .26 A4
  Wapping E1 . . . . . . .32 B1
Gurdon Ho **7** E14 . . .33 C3
Gurdon Rd SE7 . . . . .43 C1
Gurney Ho
  1 Bayswater
  W2 . . . . .100 A2
  4 Bethnal Green
  E2 . . . . .24 C3
Gurney Rd SW6 . . . . .59 B4
Guthrie Ct SE1 . . . . .135 C3
Guthrie St SW3 . . . .144 A2
Gutter La EC2 . . . . . .108 C2
Guyscliff Rd SE13 . . .67 B2
Guy's Hospl SE1 . . . .137 C4
Guy's St SE1 . . . . . . .137 C4
Gwalior Rd SW15 . . .57 C4
Gwendolen Ave
  SW15 . . . . .57 C2
Gwendolen Cl **1**
  SW15 . . . . .57 C2
Gwendwr Rd W14 . .140 B2
Gwent Ct **13** SE16 . . .32 C1

Gwilym Maries Ho **11**
  E2 . . . . .25 A2
Gwyn Cl SW6 . . . . . .156 C1
Gwynne Cl W4 . . . . . .46 B4
Gwynne Ho
  Finsbury WC1 . . . . . .95 B3
  6 Streatham SW2 .74 B3
  Whitechapel E1 . . . . .32 A4
Gwynne Pl WC1 . . . . .95 A3
Gwynne Rd SW11 . .167 C2
Gye Ho **2** SW4 . . . . .62 A3
Gylcote Cl SE5 . . . . .63 C3

H

Haarlem Rd **12**
  W14 . . . . .39 C3
Haberdasher Pl **4**
  N1 . . . . .24 A2 98 A4
Haberdashers' Aske's
  Hatcham Coll
  6 Deptford SE14 . .51 A1
  6 Deptford SE14 . .51 A2
  SE4 . . . . .51 A1
Haberdasher St
  N1 . . . . .97 C4
Hackford Rd SW9 . .173 A4
Hackford Wlk
  SW9 . . . . .173 B3
HACKNEY 17 A2
Hackney Central Sta
  E8 . . . . .17 A2
Hackney City Farm
  E2 . . . . .24 C3
Hackney Com Coll **33**
  N1 . . . . .24 A2 98 A4
Hackney Downs Sta
  E8 . . . . .17 A3
Hackney Empire
  E8 . . . . .17 A2
Hackney Gr **2** E8 . . .17 A2
Hackney New Sch **8**
  E2 . . . . .24 A4
Hackney Rd E2 . . . . .24 C3
HACKNEY WICK 18 C2
Hackney Wick E9 . . . .18 B2
Hackney Wick Sta
  E8 . . . . .18 C2
Hackworth Point **24**
  E3 . . . . .27 A2
Hacon Sq **12** E8 . . . .17 A1
Haddo Ho
  Gospel Oak NW5 . . .13 A4
  Greenwich SE10 . . . .52 A4
Haddon Ct W3 . . . . . .29 B2
Haddo St SE10 . . . . . .52 B4
Haden Ct N4 . . . . .5 C2
Hadfield Ho **17**
  E1 . . . . 111 C1
Hadleigh Cl **1** E1 . . .25 B1
Hadleigh Ho **10** E1 . .25 B1
Hadleigh St E2 . . . . . .25 B2
Hadley Ct N16 . . . . . . .7 C3
Hadley Gdns W4 . . . .37 C1
Hadley St NW1 . . . . . .13 A2
Hadlow Ho **17** 152 B2
Hadrian Cl **8** E3 . . . .26 C4
Hadrian Ct SE4 . . . . .66 C4
Hadrian Est **12** E2 . .24 C3
Hadrian St SE10 . . . . .43 A1
Hadstock Ho NW1 . . .93 C4
Hadyn Park Ct **13**
  W12 . . . . .38 C4
Hadyn Park Rd
  W12 . . . . .38 C4

Hafer Rd SW11 . . . . . .60 B3
HAGGERSTON 24 B3
Haggerston Rd E8 . . .24 B4
Haggerston Sch **18**
  E2 . . . . .24 C3
Haggerston Studios
  30 E8 . . . . .24 B3
Hague Prim Sch **21**
  E2 . . . . .25 A1
Hague St **20** . .24 C2 99 C3
Haig Ho **8** E2 . . . . . .24 C3
Hailsham Ave SW2 . . .74 B2
Hainford Cl SE4 . . . . .65 C3
Haining Cl **3** W4 . . . .36 C1
Hainton Cl E1 . . . . . . .32 A3
Halcomb St N1 . . . . . .24 A4
Halcrow St E1 . . . . . . .32 A4
Halcyon Cl SW13 . . . .56 C4
Haldane Pl SW18 . . . .71 A3
Haldane Rd SW6 . . . .155 A3
Haldon Rd SW18 . . . .58 B1
Hales Ho **5** SW12 . . .73 A4
Hales Prior N1 . . . . . .84 C1
Hales St SE8 . . . . .51 C3
Hale St E14 . . . . .34 A2
Halesworth Rd
  SE13 . . . . .67 A4
Half Moon Cres
  N1 . . . . .85 A2
Half Moon Ct EC1 . .108 C3
Half Moon La
  SE24 . . . . .63 B1
Halford Ho **1** SW15 .57 C4
Halford Rd
  Richmond TW10 . . . .54 A2
  West Brompton
  SW6 . . . . .155 B3
Haliday Ho N1 . . . . . .15 C2
Haliday Wlk **4** N1 . . .15 C2
Halidon Cl E9 . . . . . . .17 B3
Haliwell Ho **10**
  NW6 . . . . .78 A3
Halkett Ho **5** E2 . . . .25 B4
Halkin Arc SW1 . . . .131 A2
Halkin Mews SW1 . .131 B2
Halkin Pl SW1 . . . . . .131 B2
Halkin St SW1 . . . . . .131 C3
Hallam Ct W1 . . . . . .104 B4
Hallam Ho
  17 London SW9 . .173 B4
  Pimlico SW1 . . . . . .147 A1
Hallam Mews W1 . . .104 B4
Hallam Rd SW13 . . . .57 A4
Hallam St W1 . . . . . .104 B4
Hallane Ho **6**
  SE15 . . . . .65 B3
Hallett Ho **9** 67 C4
Halley Prim Sch
  E3 . . . . .33 A4
Halley St E14 . . . . . . .33 A4
Hallfield Prim Sch **61**
  W2 . . . . .100 B1
Halliday Ho **40** E1 . .111 C1
Halliford St N1 . . . . . .15 C1
Halling Ho **6**
  SE1 . . . . .137 C3

Hallings Wharf
  Studios **2** E15 . . . .27 C4
Halliwell Ct **5**
  SE22 . . . . .64 C2
Halliwell Rd SW2 . . . .62 B1
Hall Oak Wlk NW6 . . .10 B2
Hall Pl W2 . . . . .89 B1
Hall Rd
  Leyton E15 . . . . .19 C4
  St John's Wood
  NW8 . . . . .89 A3
Hall Sch The NW3 . . .11 C1
Hall Sch Wimbledon
  SW15 . . . . .68 C1
Hall St EC1 . . . . .96 B4
Hallsville Prim Sch
  E16 . . . . .35 C3
Hallsville Rd E16 . . . . .35 B3
Hall Twr W2 . . . . .101 C4
Halpin Pl SE17 . . . . . .151 C3
Halsbury Ho N7 . . . . .14 B4
Halsbury Rd W12 . . . .30 A1
Halsey St SW3 . . . . . .144 C4
Halsmere Rd SE5 . . . .48 A2
Halstead Ct N1 . . . . . .87 C1
Halston Cl SW11 . . . . .60 B1
Halstow Prim Sch **5**
  SE10 . . . . .43 C1
Halstow Rd
  Greenwich SE3,
  SE10 . . . . .43 C1
  Kensal Green
  NW10 . . . . .22 C2
Halton Cross St
  N1 . . . . .86 B4
Halton Ho **22** N1 . . .15 A1
Halton Mans N1 . . . . .15 A1
Halton Pl N1 . . . . .86 C4
Halton Rd N1 . . . . . . .86 B4
Halyard Ho E14 . . . . .42 B3
Hambalt Rd SW4 . . . .61 B2
Hambledon SE17 . . . .48 C4
Hambledon Chase
  N4 . . . . .5 A4
Hambledon Ho
  E5 . . . . .17 A4
Hambledon Pl
  SE21 . . . . .76 B3
Hambledon Rd
  SW18 . . . . .70 B4
Hamble St SW6 . . . . .59 A4
Hambley Ho **5**
  SE16 . . . . .40 A2
Hambro Rd SW16 . . . .74 A1
Hambrook Ct **3**
  NW5 . . . . .13 A4
Hamers Ho **3**
  SW2 . . . . .74 C4
Hamilton Cl
  Rotherhithe SE16 . . .41 A4
  St John's Wood
  NW8 . . . . .89 B3
Hamilton Ct W9 . . . . .88 C4
Hamilton Gdns
  NW8 . . . . .89 A3
Hamilton Hall
  NW8 . . . . .78 C1
Hamilton Ho
  1 Bow E3 . . . . . . .26 B2
  Chiswick W4 . . . . . . .46 A4
  Kensington W8 . . . .128 A4
  1 Poplar E14 . . . . .33 B2

Hamilton Ho *continued*
  Putney SW15 . . . . . .56 C2
  10 Richmond TW9 . .44 C2
  St John's Wood
  NW8 . . . . .89 B4
Hamilton La N5 . . . . .15 A4
Hamilton Lo **1** E1 . . .25 B1
Hamilton Mews
  W1 . . . . .132 A4
Hamilton Pk N5 . . . . .15 A4
Hamilton Pk W N5 . . .15 A4
Hamilton Pl **1** 117 C1
Hamilton Rd
  Acton W4 . . . . .38 A4
  Hendon NW11 . . . . . . .1 A4
  Willesden NW10 . . . . .8 C3
Hamilton Sq SE1 . . .137 C4
Hamilton St SE8 . . . . .51 C4
Hamilton Terr
  NW8 . . . . .89 A4
Hamlet Ct
  1 Hammersmith
  W6 . . . . .39 B1
  Kennington SE11 . . .150 A2
Hamlet Gdns W6 . . . .38 C2
Hamlet Ind Ctr E9 . . .18 C1
Hamlet Sq NW2 . . . . . .1 A1
Hamlets Way **3** E3 . .26 B1
Hamlet The SE5 . . . . .63 C3
Hamlet Way SE1 . . . .137 C4
Hammelton Gn **2**
  SW9 . . . . .48 A2
Hammersmith Ho **7**
  SE14 . . . . .50 B3
HAMMERSMITH 39 B2
Hammersmith Acad
  10 W12 . . . . .39 A4
Hammersmith Bridge
  Rd W6, SW13 . . . . . .39 B1
Hammersmith
  Broadway
  11 Hammersmith W6 . .39 B1
  5 Hammersmith
  W6 . . . . .39 B2
Hammersmith Flyover
  W6 . . . . .39 B1
Hammersmith Gr
  W6 . . . . .39 B3
Hammersmith Hospl
  W12 . . . . .30 A3
Hammersmith Rd
  Hammersmith W6 . . .39 B1
  Kensington W14 . . . .140 B4
Hammersmith Sta
  W6 . . . . .39 B2
Hammersmith Terr **6**
  W6 . . . . .38 C1
Hammersmith & West
  London Coll **18**
  W14 . . . . .140 A2
Hammett St EC3 . . . .124 C4
Hammond Ho
  10 Deptford SE14 . .50 B3
  Millwall E14 . . . . . . .42 A3
Hammond Lo **6**
  W9 . . . . .31 C4
Hammond St NW5 . . .13 B2
Hamond Sq N1 . . . . . .24 A3
Hampden Cl NW1 . . . .83 C2
Hampden Gurney CE
  Prim SchW1 . . . . . .102 B2
Hampden Gurney St
  W1 . . . . .102 C1
Hampden Rd N19 . . . .4 C2
Hampshire Ct **4**
  SW13 . . . . .46 B1

Hampshire Hog La
3 Hammersmith
W6 .... 39 A1
11 Hammersmith
W6 .... 39 A2
Hampshire St
NW5 .... 13 C2
Hampson Way
SW8 .... 172 C4
HAMPSTEAD 11 B2
Hampstead Coll of
Fine Arts &
Humanities **12**
NW3 .... 11 C4
Hampstead Com Mkt
NW3 .... 11 C4
Hampstead Gate
NW3 .... 11 B3
Hampstead Gn
NW3 .... 12 A3
Hampstead Gr NW3 . 2 B1
Hampstead Heath 2 C2
Hampstead Heath Sta
NW3 .... 12 A4
Hampstead High St
NW3 .... 11 C3
Hampstead Hill Gdns
NW3 .... 12 A4
Hampstead Hill Sch
1 NW3 .... 12 A3
Hampstead La N6 .... 3 C4
Hampstead Parochial
CE Prim Sch **12**
NW3 .... 11 B3
Hampstead Rd
NW1 .... 92 C4
Hampstead Sch
NW2 .... 10 A4
Hampstead Sq **1**
NW3 .... 2 B1
Hampstead Sta
NW3 .... 11 C3
Hampstead Theatre
NW3 .... 11 C1
Hampstead West **1**
NW6 .... 10 C1
Hampstead Wlk **1**
E3 .... 26 B4
Hampton Cl NW6 .. 23 C2
Hampton Ct
1 Islington N1 ... 15 A2
2 Rotherhithe
SE16 .... 32 C1
Hampton St SE1 .. 150 B3
Hamstead Gates **11**
NW5 .... 13 A2
Ham Yd W1 V 119 B4
Hana Mews E5 .... 17 A4
Hanbury Ho
6 Bethnal Green
E1 .... 111 B4
South Lambeth
SW8 .... 162 B3
Hanbury Mews N1. 87 A3
Hanbury Rd W3 ... 37 A4
Hanbury St E1 ...... 111 A4
Hancock Nunn Ho **1**
NW3 .... 12 B1
Hancock Rd E3 .... 27 B2
Handa Wlk **3** N1... 15 B2
Hand Ct WC1 ...... 107 A3
Handel & Hendrix in
London W1 .... 118 B4
Handel Mans
Barnes SW13 .... 47 B3

Handel Mans continued
Bloomsbury WC1 ... 94 B2
Handel St WC1 ...... 94 B2
Handforth Rd
SW9 .... 163 B2
Handley Rd E9 ...... 25 B4
Hands Wlk E16 .... 35 C3
Handyside St N1 .. 84 A3
Hanford Cl SW18 .. 70 C3
Hankey Pl SE1 .... 137 C3
Hanley Ct N4 .... 5 B3
Hanley Gdns N4 ..... 5 B3
Hanley Rd N4, N19 .. 5 A3
Hanmer Wlk N7 ..... 5 B2
Hannah Mary Way **17**
SE1 .... 153 C3
Hannay La N8 .... 4 C4
Hannay Wlk SW16 . 73 C2
Hannell Rd SW6 .. 154 B2
Hannen Ho SE5 ... 63 A4
Hannen Rd SE27 .. 75 A1
Hannibal Rd E1 ... 32 B4
Hannington Rd
SW4 .... 61 A4
Hanover Ave E16 .. 35 C1
Hanover Cl TW9 ... 44 C3
Hanover Ct
Shepherd's Bush
W12 .... 29 C1
Stamford Hill N16... 7 B4
Hanover Gate Mans
NW1 .... 90 B2
Hanover Gdns
SE11 .... 163 B3
Hanover Ho NW8 . 80 A1
Hanover Mans **5**
SW2 .... 62 C2
Hanover Pk SE15 . 49 C2
Hanover Pl
16 Bow E3 .... 26 B2
St Giles WC2 ...... 106 B1
Hanover Prim Sch
N1 .... 86 C2
Hanover Rd NW10 . 22 B4
Hanover Sq W1 ... 104 B1
Hanover Stps W1. 102 B1
Hanover Terr NW1 . 90 C3
Hanover Terrace
Mews NW1 .... 90 B3
Hanover West Ind Est
NW10 .... 20 C2
Hanover Yd N1 .... 86 C2
Hansard Mews
W14 .... 39 C4
Hanscomb Mews
SW4 .... 61 B3
Hans Cres SW1 .. 130 C2
Hansel Rd NW6 ... 23 C2
Hansler Ct **11**
SW19 .... 70 A3
Hansler Rd SE22 . 64 B2
Hansom Mews
SE11 .... 149 A2
Hanson Cl
Balham SW12 .... 73 A4
Mortlake SW14 ...... 55 B4
Hanson Ho **2** E1 125 C4
Hanson St W1 .... 104 C4
Hans Pl SW1 ...... 130 C2
Hans Rd SW3 .... 130 C2
Hans St SW1 ...... 131 A1
Hanway Ho **25**
SW9 .... 173 C4
Hanway Pl W1 .... 105 B2
Hanway St W1 .... 105 B2

Hanworth Ho SE5 . 48 A3
Harben Rd NW6 .... 11 B1
Harberson Rd
E15 .... 76 C1
SW12 .... 73 A3
Harberton Rd N19 . 4 B3
Harbet Rd W2 .... 101 C3
Harbinger Prim Sch
1 E14 .... 42 A2
Harbinger Rd E14 . 42 A2
Harbin Ho **5** SW2 . 74 C3
Harbledown Ho
SE1 .... 137 B3
Harbledown Rd
SW6 .... 165 B4
Harbord Cl
Camberwell SE5 ... 49 A3
London SE5 .... 48 C1
Harbord Ho **5**
SE16 .... 40 C2
Harbord St SW6 .. 47 C2
Harbour Ave
SW10 .... 167 A3
Harbour Exchange Sq
E14 .... 42 A4
Harbour Rd SE5 .. 63 B4
Harbridge Ave
SW15 .... 68 C4
Harbut Rd SW11 .. 59 C3
Harcombe Rd N16 . 7 A1
Harcourt Ho
2 Clapham
SW8 .... 171 B2
Marylebone W1 ... 104 A2
4 Willesden NW10 . 9 B2
Harcourt Rd SE4 . 66 B4
Harcourt St W1 .. 102 B3
Harcourt Terr
SW10 .... 142 B1
Hardcastle Ho
3 New Cross Gate
SE14 .... 51 A2
8 Peckham SE15 . 49 C2
Hardel Rise SW2 . 75 A3
Hardel Wlk SE24,
SW2 .... 74 C4
Harden Ho SE5 ... 49 A1
Harders Rd SE15 . 50 A1
Hardess St SE24 . 63 B4
Hardham Ho **5**
SE5 .... 62 C1
Harding Cl SE17 . 48 B4
Hardinge Rd
NW10 .... 22 B4
Hardinge St E1 ... 32 B3
Harding Ho SW13. 47 A4
Hardington **2**
NW1 .... 12 C1
Hardwicke Ho **14**
E3 .... 27 A2
Hardwicke Mews
WC1 .... 95 A3
Hardwicke Rd W4 . 37 C2
Hardwick Ho
14 London SW8 .. 171 B2
Marylebone NW8 . 90 B2
Hardwick St EC1 . 95 C3
Hardwick's Way
SW18 .... 58 C2
Hardwidge St
SE1 .... 138 A4
Hardy Ave E16 ... 35 C1
Hardy Cl SE16 .... 40 C4
Hardy Cotts **2**
SE10 .... 52 C4
Hardy Rd SE3 ..... 53 B4

Hare and Billet Rd
SE3 .... 52 C1
Harecourt Rd N1 .. 15 B2
Hare Ct EC4 .... 107 B1
Haredale Ho **24**
SE16 .... 139 B3
Haredale Rd SE24 . 63 B3
Harefield Mews
SE4 .... 66 B4
Harefield Rd SE4 . 66 B4
Hare Marsh
E2 .... 24 C1 99 B2
Hare Pl EC4 .... 107 C1
Hare Row E2 ...... 25 A3
Hare Wlk N1 .... 24 A3
Harewood Ave
NW1 .... 90 B1
Harewood Pl W1 . 104 B1
Harewood Row
NW1 .... 102 B4
Harfield Gdns **1**
SE5 .... 64 A4
Harfleur Ct SE11 . 150 A3
Harford Ho
Camberwell SE5 ... 48 B4
Notting Hill W11 ... 31 B4
Harford Mews **6**
N19 .... 4 C2
Harford St E1 ...... 33 A4
Hargrave Mans **3**
N19 .... 4 C2
Hargrave Park Sch
14 London N19 ... 4 B2
8 Upper Holloway
N19 .... 4 B2
Hargrave Pk N19 .. 4 B2
Hargrave Pl N7 ... 13 C3
Hargraves Ho **14**
W12 .... 30 A2
Hargwyne St SW9 . 62 B4
Harkness Ho **20**
E1 .... 111 C1
Harland Rd SE3 .. 53 C1
Harlech Twr **5**
W3 .... 37 B4
Harlescott Rd
SE15 .... 65 C3
HARLESDEN 21 B4
Harlesden Gdns
NW10 .... 21 B4
Harlesden Plaza **2**
NW10 .... 21 B3
Harlesden Prim Sch
NW10 .... 21 A3
Harlesden Rd
NW10 .... 21 C4
Harlesden Sta
NW10 .... 20 C3
Harleyford Ct
SW8 .... 162 C4
Harleyford Manor **3**
W3 .... 28 B1
Harleyford Rd
SE11 .... 162 C4
Harleyford St
SE11 .... 163 B3
Harley Gdns
SW10 .... 143 A1
Harley Gr E3 .... 26 B2
Harley Ho NW1 ... 91 C1
Harley Pl W1 ...... 104 A3
Harley Rd
Hampstead NW3 ... 11 C1
Harlesden NW10 ... 21 A3
Harley St Clinic The
W1 .... 104 A4

Harley St W1 ...... 104 A3
Harley Villas
NW10 .... 21 A3
Harling Ct **3**
SW11 .... 168 C2
Harlowe Ho **13** E8 . 24 B4
Harlynwood **19**
SE5 .... 48 B3
Harman Cl
11 Bermondsey
SE1 .... 153 B1
Cricklewood NW2 ... 1 A1
Harman Dr NW2 ... 10 A4
Harmon Ho **7** SE8 . 41 B2
Harmood Gr NW1 . 13 A1
Harmood Ho **2**
NW1 .... 13 A1
Harmood St NW1 . 13 A1
Harmsworth St
SE17 .... 150 A1
Harnage Ho NW8 . 36 A1
Harney Ct SE14 ... 51 A2
Harold Ct **14** SE16 . 40 C4
Harold Est SE1 ... 138 B1
Harold Ho **16** E2 ... 25 C3
Harold Laski Ho
EC1 .... 96 B3
Harold Maddison Ho
SE17 .... 150 B2
Harold Rd NW10 . 20 C2
Harold Wilson Ho
SW6 .... 155 A3
Harp Alley EC4 ... 108 A2
Harpenden Rd SE27,
SW16 .... 75 A2
Harpenmead Point
NW2 .... 1 B2
Harper Ho **3** SW9 . 63 A4
Harper Mews
SW17 .... 71 B1
Harper Rd SE1 ... 137 A2
Harp La EC3 ...... 124 A3
Harpley Sq E1 .... 25 C1
Harpsden St
SW11 .... 169 B3
Harpur Mews
WC1 .... 106 C4
Harpur St WC1 ... 106 C4
Harrier Ho **9**
SW11 .... 60 A4
Harriet Cl E8 ...... 24 C4
Harriet Ho SW6 . 156 B1
Harriet St SW1 ... 131 A3
Harriet Tubman Cl **21**
SW2 .... 74 C4
Harriet Wlk SW1 . 131 A3
Harrington Ct
South Kensington
SW7 .... 143 C4
9 West Kilburn
W9 .... 23 C2
Harrington Gdns
SW7 .... 142 C3
Harrington Ho
Regent's Pk NW1 . 92 C4
Westminster SW1 . 147 C2
Harrington Rd
SW7 .... 143 B4
Harrington Sq
NW1 .... 82 C1
Harrington St NW1 . 92 C4
Harriott Cl SE10 .. 43 B2
Harriott Ho **11** E1 . 32 B3

Harris Acad at
 Peckham SE15 .....49 B2
Harris Acad
 Bermondsey
 SE1 ....153 A4
Harris Academy
 Battersea SW11 169 A3
Harris Boys' Academy
 East Dulwich
 SE22 ....65 B2
Harris Girls' Acad East
 Dulwich SE15 ....65 B2
Harris Ho
 🔟 Bow E3 ....26 C2
 🔟 Brixton SW9 ....62 C4
Harrison Ho SE17. 151 B2
Harrison Rd NW10. 20 C4
Harrisons Ct 🔟
 SE14 ....50 C4
Harrison St WC1. 94 B3
Harris St SE5 .....48 C3
Harrodian Sch The
 SW13 ....46 B3
Harrogate Ct 🔟
 SE26 ....76 C1
Harrold Ho 🔟
 NW3 ....11 B1
Harroway Rd
 SW11 ....167 C2
Harrowby St W1. 102 B2
Harrowgate Ho 🟤
 E9 ....17 C2
Harrowgate Rd E9. 18 A2
Harrow La E14 .....34 B2
Harrow Pl E1 ....110 B2
Harrow Rd
 Little Venice W2 . 101 A3
 Westbourne Green W2,
 W9 ....23 C1
Harrow St NW1 ... 102 A4
Harry Gosling Prim
 Sch 🔟 E1 ....111 C1
Harry Hinkins Ho
 SE17 ....151 A1
Harry Lambourn Ho
 🔟 SE15 ....50 A3
Harston Wlk E3 .. 27 A1
Hartfield Terr E3 . 26 C3
Hartham Cl N7 .... 14 A3
Hartham Rd N7 ... 14 A3
Hart Ho SW2 .....74 C3
Hartington Ct
 Chiswick W4 .....45 A3
 South Lambeth
 SW8 ....172 A4
Hartington Rd
 Chiswick W4 .....45 B2
 South Lambeth
 SW8 ....162 A1
Hartismere Rd
 SW6 ....155 A2
Hartlake Rd E9 ... 18 A2
Hartland NW1 ... 83 A3
Hartland Rd
 Camden Town
 NW1 ....13 A1
 Kilburn NW6 .....23 B4
Harley Ho
 Bermondsey SE1 . 153 A4
 Putney SW15 ....56 C2
Hartley St E2 .....25 B2
Hartnoll Ho 🔟 N7. 14 C3
Hartnoll St N7 ....14 B3

Harton Lodge 🟤
 SE8 ....51 C2
Harton St SE8 ....51 C2
Hartopp Ct 🟤 N16 ...7 A1
Hartopp Point
 SW6 ....154 B2
Hartshorn Alley
 EC3 ....110 B1
Hart's La SE14 .... 51 A2
Hart St EC3 ....124 B4
Hartswood Ho 🟤
 SW2 ....74 A3
Hartswood Rd
 W12 ....38 B3
Hartwell Cl 🟤
 SW2 ....74 B3
Hartwell Ct SE22 ....64 C3
Hartwell St E8 ....16 B2
Harvard Ct NW6 .. 11 A3
Harvard Hill W4 ..45 A4
Harvard Ho
 🟤 Camberwell
 SE17 ....48 A4
 Putney SW15 ....57 C1
Harvard Mans
 SW11 ....59 C3
Harvard Rd
 🔟 Acton Green
 W4 ....37 B1
 Gunnersbury W4 . 37 A1
 Lewisham SE13 .. 67 B2
Harvey Ct SW11 . 168 B4
Harvey Ho
 🔟 Bethnal Green
 E1 ....25 A1
 Brentford TW8 ...36 A1
 Pimlico SW1 ....147 C1
 Shoreditch N1 ... 87 C3
Harvey Lo 🟤 W9 ...31 C4
Harvey Point 🟤
 E16 ....35 C4
Harvey Rd 🟤 SE5 .. 48 C2
Harvey St N1 .....87 C3
Harvist Rd NW6 .. 23 A3
Harwood Ct
 Putney SW15 ....57 B3
 Shoreditch N1 ... 87 C3
Harwood Point
 SE16 ....41 B4
Harwood Rd SW6 156 A1
Harwood Terr
 SW6 ....166 A4
Hascombe Ho 🟤
 SW15 ....69 A3
Hascombe Terr 🟤
 SE5 ....48 C1
Haselrigge Rd
 SW4 ....61 C3
Hasker St SW3 .. 144 B4
Haslam Cl N1 ....14 C1
Haslam Ho 🔟 N1. 15 B1
Haslam St SE15 .. 49 B2
Haslemere Ave
 SW18 ....71 A2
Haslemere Ct 🟤
 N16 ....7 A3
Haslemere Ind Est
 SW18 ....71 A2
Haslemere Rd N8 . 5 A4
Hassard St E2 .... 24 B3
Hassett Rd E9 ....18 A2
Hastings Cl 🔟
 SE15 ....49 C3

Hastings Ho 🔟
 W12 ....30 A2
Hastings Hos WC1. 94 A3
Hastings St WC1... 94 A3
Hatcham Mews Bsns
 Ctr SE14 ....50 C1
Hatcham Park Mews
 SE14 ....50 C2
Hatcham Park Rd
 SE14 ....50 C2
Hatcham Rd SE15 50 B4
Hatcham Rd N19 ...5 A2
Hatchers Mews
 SE1 ....138 B3
Hatcliffe Almshouses
 🟤 SE10 ....43 A1
Hatcliffe St SE10 ..43 A1
Hatfield Cl SE14 ..50 C3
Hatfield Ct SE3 ... 53 C3
Hatfield Ho EC1 .. 96 C1
Hatfield Rd W4 ... 37 C4
Hatfields SE1 ... 121 C2
Hathaway Ho 🟤
 N1 ....24 A2 98 A4
Hatherley Ct 🟤
 W2 ....100 A2
Hatherley Gr W2 100 A2
Hatherley Rd TW9 .44 B2
Hatherley St SW1 147 A3
Hathersage Ct N1 .15 C3
Hathersley Ho 🟤
 SW2 ....74 C4
Hathorne Cl 🟤
 SE15 ....50 A1
Hatley Rd N4, N7... 5 B2
Hat & Mitre Ct EC1 96 B1
Hatstone Ct 🟤
 NW3 ....11 B2
Hatteraick St 🟤
 SE16 ....40 B4
Hatton Gdn EC1 . 107 C4
Hatton Ho 🔟 E1. 125 C4
Hatton Pl EC1 ... 107 C4
Hatton Row NW8 .. 89 C1
Hatton St NW8 ... 89 C1
Hatton Wall EC1 . 107 C4
Haunch of Venison Yd
 W1 ....104 A1
Hauteville Court Gdns
 🟤 W6 ....38 B3
Havana Rd SW18,
 SW19 ....70 C2
Havannah St E14 ..41 C4
Havelock Cl 🟤
 W12 ....30 A2
Havelock Ct 🟤
 SE15 ....49 C3
Havelock St N1 ...84 B3
Havelock Terr
 SW8 ....160 B1
Haven Cl SW19 ....69 C1
Havenpool NW8 ...78 B3
Haven The TW9 ...54 C4
Havercourt 🟤
 NW3 ....12 A2
Haverfield Gdns
 TW9 ....44 C3
Haverfield Rd E3 ..26 A2
Haverhill Rd SW12. 73 B3
Havering 🟤 NW1. 13 A1
Havering Ho N4 ...6 B4

Havering St E1 ....32 C3
Haversham Lo NW2 ..9 C3
Haversham Pl N6 ....3 B2
Haverstock Hill
 NW3 ....12 B2
Haverstock Rd
 NW5 ....12 C3
Haverstock Sch 🟤
 NW5 ....12 C2
Haverstock St N1. 86 B1
Haviland Mews
 W12 ....29 B3
Havil St SE5 .....49 A2
Havisham Ho 🟤
 SE16 ....139 B3
Hawarden Gr SE24. 75 B4
Hawberry Lo N7... 14 A2
Hawes St N1 .....15 A1
Hawgood St E3 ... 33 C4
Hawke Ho 🟤 E1 .. 25 C1
Hawke Pl 🟤 SE16 .. 40 C4
Hawkesbury Rd
 SW15 ....57 A2
Hawkesdown House
 Sch W2 ...31 C1 113 C4
Hawkesworth Ho 🟤
 SW4 ....61 C1
Hawke Twr 🟤
 SE14 ....51 A4
Hawk Ho 🟤 SW11. 60 A4
Hawkins Ho 🟤
 SE8 ....51 C4
Hawkley Gdns
 SE27 ....75 A2
Hawkridge 🟤
 NW5 ....12 C2
Hawkshaw Cl 🟤
 SW2 ....74 A4
Hawkshead NW1 .. 92 C4
Hawkshead Rd
 Acton W4 ....38 A3
 Willesden NW10 . 8 B1
Hawkslade Rd
 SE15 ....65 C2
Hawksley Rd N16... 7 A1
Hawks Mews 🔟
 SE10 ....52 B3
Hawksmoor Mews
 E1 ....32 A2
Hawksmoor Pl 🟤
 E2 ....24 C1 99 B2
Hawksmoor St
 W6 ....47 C4
Hawkstone Rd
 SE16 ....40 B2
Hawkwell Wlk N1 . 87 A4
Hawley Cres NW1. 13 A1
Hawley Inf Sch 🟤
 NW1 ....13 A1
Hawley Mews 🟤
 NW1 ....13 A1
Hawley Rd 🟤
 NW1 ....13 A1
Hawley St NW1 ... 13 A1
Haworth Ho 🟤
 SW2 ....62 C1
Hawstead Rd SE6. 67 A1
Hawthorn Ct
 Putney SW15 ....57 C4
 Richmond TW9 ...45 A2
Hawthorne Cl N1 . 16 A2
Hawthorne Cres
 SE10 ....43 B1

Hawthorne Ho
 SW1 ....147 A1
Hawthorn Ho SE14. 51 B2
Hawthorn Rd NW10. 8 C1
Hawthorn Wlk
 W10 ....23 A1
Hawtrey Rd NW3 .. 12 A1
Haycroft Gdns
 NW10 ....22 A4
Haycroft Mans
 NW10 ....21 C4
Haycroft Rd SW2 . 62 A2
Hay Currie St E14. 34 A3
Hayday Rd E16 ... 35 C4
Hayden Piper Ho
 SW3 ....158 C4
Hayden's Pl W11 .. 31 B3
Haydon St EC3 .. 124 C4
Haydon Way SW11. 59 C3
Haydon Wlk E1 .. 111 A1
Hayes Ct
 🟤 Camberwell
 SE5 ....48 B3
 Streatham SW12 .. 74 A3
Hayes Gr SE15,
 SE22 ....64 B3
Hayes Mews SE8 . 51 C2
Hayes Pl NW1 ....90 B1
Hayfield Pas E1 .. 25 B1
Hayfield Yd 🟤 E1. 25 B1
Hay Hill W1 ....118 B3
Hayhurst N1 .....86 B4
Hayles Bldgs
 SE11 ....150 B4
Hayles St SE11 .. 150 A4
Hayling Ct 🟤 N16. 16 C4
Haymans Point
 SE11 ....148 C2
Haymarket SW1 . 119 B3
Haymerle Ho 🟤
 SE15 ....49 C4
Haymerle Rd SE15 .49 C4
Haymerle Sch 🟤
 SE15 ....49 C4
Hayne Ho
 W11 ....31 A1 112 A2
Haynes Ho 🟤 E9 .. 17 C2
Hayne St EC1 ... 108 B4
Hay's Galleria
 SE1 ....124 A2
Hay's La SE1 ... 124 A2
Hay's Mews W1 .. 118 A2
Hay St E2 .....24 C4
Hayter Ho W12 ...29 C2
Hayter Rd SW2 ... 62 B2
Haythorn Ho
 SW11 ....167 C3
Hayton Cl 🔟 E8 .. 16 B2
Hayward Ct 🟤
 SW4 ....172 B2
Hayward Gallery
 SE1 ....121 A2
Hayward Gdns
 SW15 ....57 B1
Hayward Ho N1 .. 85 B2
Hayward Mews 🟤
 SE4 ....66 B2
Haywards Pl EC1 . 96 A2
Haywood Lo 🟤
 N7 ....13 C3
Hazelbourne Rd
 SW12 ....61 A1
Hazel Cl
 Peckham SE15 ....49 C1
 Upper Holloway N19 ..4 B2

Hazel Ct **8** SE16 . . . .33 A1
Hazeldon Rd SE4 . . .66 A2
Hazel Ho
  London SE4 . . . . .66 B4
  12 Maitland Pk
  NW3 . . . . .12 B2
Hazel La SE10 . . . . . .43 B1
Hazellville Rd N19 . . .4 C3
Hazelmere Ct **10**
  SW2 . . . . .74 B3
Hazelmere Rd
  NW6 . . . . .126 A1
Hazel Way SE1 . . . .152 C4
Hazelwood CI W5 . . .36 A4
Hazelwood Ho **11**
  SE8 . . . . .41 A2
Hazelwood Mans
  SW6 . . . . .164 C4
Hazlebury Rd
  SW6 . . . . .166 B2
Hazledene Rd W4 . .45 B4
Hazlewell Rd
  SW15 . . . . .57 B2
Hazlewood Cres
  W10 . . . . .23 A1
Hazlewood Mews
  SW9 . . . . .62 A4
Hazlewood Twr
  W10 . . . . .23 B1
Hazlitt Mews
  W14 . . . . .126 A1
Hazlitt Rd W14 . . .126 A1
Headbourne Ho
  SE1 . . . . .137 C2
Headcorn **10** NW5 . .12 C2
Headfort Pl SW1 . .131 C3
Headington Rd
  SW18 . . . . .71 B2
Headlam Rd SW4 . .73 C4
Headlam St E1 . . . . . .25 A1
Heads Mews W11 . . .31 C3
Head St E1 . . . . .32 C3
Heald St SE8, SE14 . .51 C2
Healey St NW1 . . . . .13 A2
Healy Ho **2** E3 . . . . .26 C1
Heanor Ct **4** E5 . . . .17 C4
Hearne Rd W4 . . . . . .44 C4
Hearn's Bldgs
  SE17 . . . . .151 C3
Hearn St
  EC2 . . . . .24 A1
  E14 . . . . .33 A3
Hearnville Rd
  SW12 . . . . .72 C3
Heart Radio W11 . . .30 C2
Heathbrook Prim Sch
  11 SW4 . . . . .170 C1
Heath Brow NW3 . . .2 B1
Heath CI NW11 . . . . .2 A4
Heathcote Gate
  SW6 . . . . .58 C4
Heathcote Point **25**
  E9 . . . . .17 C2
Heathcote St WC1 . .94 C3
Heathcroft NW11 . . .2 A3
Heath Ct
  8 Hampstead
  NW3 . . . . .11 B2
  Stoke Newington
  N16 . . . . .6 C3
Heath Dr NW3 . . . .11 A4
Heather CI
  Clapham SW4 . . . . .61 A4
  6 Finsbury Pk N7 . . .5 B1

Heather Ct SW4 . . .172 B3
Heather Ho **11** E14 . .34 B3
Heatherley Ho **16** . . .7 C1
Heatherley Sch of
  Fine Art SW10 . . .156 C1
Heather Lo N16 . . . . .7 A3
Heather Wlk W10 . . .23 A1
Heathfield Ave
  SW18 . . . . .71 C4
Heathfield Ct
  8 Bow E3 . . . . . . .26 C3
  3 Chiswick W4 . . . .37 B1
  Wandsworth SW18 . .71 C4
Heathfield Gdns
  Acton Green W4 . . . .37 B1
  Blackheath SE3 . . . . .53 A1
  Wandsworth SW18 . .59 C1
Heathfield Ho SE3 . .53 A1
Heathfield House Sch
  16 W4 . . . . .37 B1
Heathfield Pk NW2 . .9 B2
Heathfield Rd
  South Acton W3 . . . .37 A4
  Wandsworth SW18 . .59 C1
Heathfield Sq
  SW18 . . . . .71 C4
Heathfield Terr
  W4 . . . . .37 C1
Heathgate Pl NW3 . .12 B4
Heath House Prep
  Sch **1** SE8 . . . . . .53 B1
Heath Hurst Rd
  NW3 . . . . .12 A4
Heath La SE3 . . . . . .52 C1
Heathland Rd N16 . . .7 A3
Heath Mans
  5 Hampstead
  NW3 . . . . .11 B4
  Putney SW15 . . . . . .57 C1
Heathman's Rd
  SW6 . . . . .165 A3
Heath Mead SW19 . .69 C1
Heathmere Prim Sch
  SW15 . . . . .68 C3
Heath Park Gdns
  NW3 . . . . .2 A1
Heathpool Ct **8** E1 . .25 A1
Heath Rise SW15 . . .57 C1
Heath Royal SW15 . .57 C1
Heathshott **8**
  TW10 . . . . .54 A1
Heathside NW3 . . . . .11 C4
Heathside Prep Sch
  22 NW3 . . . . .11 B4
Heath St NW3 . . . . . .2 B1
Heathstan Rd W12 . .29 C3
Heath View NW5 . . . .12 C4
Heathview Ct
  SW19 . . . . .69 C2
Heathview Gdns
  SW15 . . . . .69 B4
Heath Villas NW3 . . .11 C4
Heathville Rd N4,
  N19 . . . . .5 A4
Heathwall St
  SW11 . . . . .60 B4
Heathway SE3 . . . . .53 C3
Heathway Ct NW3 . . .1 C2
Heathwood Ct
  SW12 . . . . .73 B3
Heaton Ho
  Chelsea SW10 . . . .157 A4
  6 Peckham SE15 . . .50 A1
Heaton Rd SE15 . . . .50 A1

Heaven Tree CI
  N1 . . . . .15 B3
Heaver Rd **23**
  SW11 . . . . .59 C4
Hebden Ct **24** E2 . . .24 B4
Hebdon Rd SW17 . . .72 A1
Heber Prim Sch
  SE22 . . . . .64 B1
Heber Rd
  Cricklewood NW2 . . . .9 C4
  East Dulwich SE22 . . .64 B1
Hebron Rd W6 . . . . .39 A3
Heckfield Pl SW6 . .155 B1
Heckford Ho E14 . . .34 A3
Heckford St E1 . . . . .32 C2
Hector Ct
  1 London SW9 . . .173 B4
  Putney SW15 . . . . . .57 C2
Hector Ho **14** E2 . . . .25 A3
Heddington Gr N7 . .14 B3
Heddon St W1 . . . .118 C4
Hedger's Gr E9 . . . . .18 A2
Hedger St SE11 . . . .150 A4
Hedingham CI **6**
  N1 . . . . .15 B1
Hedley Ct SW15 . . . .57 C1
Hedley Ho E14 . . . . .42 B3
Hedley Row N5,
  N16 . . . . .15 C3
Hedsor Ho
  E2 . . . . .24 B1
Heidegger Cres
  SW13 . . . . .47 A3
Heights The NW3 . . .11 B4
Heiron St SE17 . . . . .48 A4
Helby Rd SW4 . . . . .61 C1
Heldar Ct SE1 . . . . .137 C3
Helena Pl **8** E9 . . . .25 B4
Helena Rd NW10 . . . .9 A3
Helena Sq **12** SE16 . .33 A2
Helen Gladstone Ho
  SE1 . . . . .136 A4
Helen Ho **9** E2 . . . . .25 A3
Helen Mackay Ho **10**
  E14 . . . . .34 C3
Helen Peele Cotts **7**
  SE16 . . . . .40 B3
Helenslea Ave
  NW11 . . . . .1 C3
Helen's Pl E2 . . . . . . .25 B2
Helen Taylor Ho **5**
  SE16 . . . . .153 B4
Heliport Ind Est
  SW11 . . . . .167 B1
Helix **17** W11 . . . . .30 C1
Helix Gdns SW2 . . . .62 B1
Helix Rd SW2 . . . . . .62 B1
Helix The SW9 . . . . .62 B3
Hellings St E1 . . . . .125 C1
Helmet Row EC1 . . . .97 A2
Helmsdale Ho
  NW6 . . . . .78 A1
Helmsley Pl E8 . . . . .17 A1
Helmsley St **3** E8 . . .17 A1
Helperby Rd NW10 . .8 A1
Helsby Ct NW8 . . . . .89 B2
Helsinki Sq SE16 . . . .41 A3
Helston Ho SE11 . . .149 C2
Helston Rd SE15 . . . .50 B4
Hemans Est SW8 . . .161 C1
Hemans St SW8 . . . .161 C1
Hemberton Rd
  SW9 . . . . .62 A4
Hemingford Rd N1 . .85 A4
Hemlock Rd W12 . . .29 B2

Hemming St
  E1 . . . . .24 C1 99 C1
Hemingway CI
  NW5 . . . . .12 C4
Hemp Wlk SE17 . . . .151 C4
Hemstal Rd NW6 . . .10 C1
Hemsworth Ct N1 . . .24 A3
Hemsworth St N1 . . .24 A3
Hemus Pl SW3 . . . .144 B1
Henchman St W12 . .29 B3
Henderson Ct
  2 Deptford SE14 . . .50 C4
  Hampstead NW3 . . .11 C3
  Wandsworth SW18 . .72 A4
Henderson Dr
  NW8 . . . . .89 B2
Henderson Rd
  SW18 . . . . .72 A4
Hendham Rd
  SW17 . . . . .72 B2
Hendre Ho SE1 . . . .152 B3
Hendre Rd SE1 . . . .152 B3
Hendrick Ave
  SW12 . . . . .72 B4
Heneage La EC3 . . . .110 B1
Heneage Pl EC3 . . . .110 B1
Heneage St E1 . . . .111 A4
Henfield CI N19 . . . . .4 B3
Henley CI
  Brondesbury NW2 . . .9 C2
  Peckham SE15 . . . . .64 C4
Henley Dr SE1 . . . .153 A4
Henley Ho
  E2 . . . . .24 B1 99 A2
Henley Prior N1 . . . .84 C1
Henley Rd NW10 . . .22 B4
Henley St SW11 . . . .169 C2
Henniker Mews
  SW3 . . . . .157 B4
Henniker Rd E15 . . .19 C3
Henning St SW11 . .168 A3
Henrietta CI SE8 . . . .51 C4
Henrietta Ho **11**
  W6 . . . . .39 B1
Henrietta Mews
  WC1 . . . . .94 B2
Henrietta Pl W1 . . .104 A2
Henrietta St
  Strand WC2 . . . . . .120 B4
  Stratford New Town
  E15 . . . . .19 B3
Henriques St E1 . . .111 C1
Henry Dent CI SE5 . .63 C4
Henry Dickens Ct
  W11 . . . . .31 A1 112 A2
Henry Fawcett Prim
  Sch SE11 . . . . . . .163 B4
Henry Ho
  Lambeth SE1 . . . . .121 C1
  South Lambeth
  SW8 . . . . .162 A2
  St John's Wood
  NW8 . . . . .80 A2
Henry Jackson Ho **4**
  SW15 . . . . .57 C4
Henry Jackson Rd
  SW15 . . . . .57 C4
Henry Rd N4 . . . . .6 B3
Henryson Rd SE4 . . .66 C2
Henry Wise Ho
  SW1 . . . . .147 A3
Henshall Point **19**
  E3 . . . . .27 A2
Henshall St N1 . . . . .15 C2
Henshaw St SE17 . .151 B4

Hensley Point **28**
  E9 . . . . .17 C2
Henslowe Rd SE22 . .64 C2
Henslow Ho **12**
  SE15 . . . . .49 C3
Henson Ave NW2 . . .9 B3
Henson Ct **3** N5 . . . . .6 B1
Henstridge Pl
  NW8 . . . . .80 A3
Henty CI SW11 . . . .168 B4
Henty Wlk SW15 . . .57 A2
Hepburn Mews
  SW11 . . . . .60 B2
Hepburn Pl W3 . . . . .28 B1
Hepplestone C
  SW15 . . . . .57 A1
Hepscott Rd E9 . . . . .18 C1
Hepworth Ct
  Chelsea SW1 . . . . .146 A1
  Islington N1 . . . . . . .86 A4
Hera Ct **15** E14 . . . .41 C2
Heralds Pl SE11 . . . .150 A4
Herald St **5** E2 . . . .25 A1
Herald Hill EC1 . . . . .95 C1
Herbert Chapman Ct
  N5 . . . . .15 A4
Herbert Cres
  SW1 . . . . .131 A2
Herbert Gdns
  Chiswick W4 . . . . . .45 A4
  Willesden Green
  NW10 . . . . .22 A3
Herbert Ho E1 . . . .110 C2
Herbert Mews **16**
  SW2 . . . . .62 C1
Herbert Morrison Ho
  SW6 . . . . .154 C3
Herbert Morrison
  Prim Sch SW8 . . .162 A1
Herbert St NW5 . . . .12 C2
Herbrand St WC1 . . .94 A2
Herbrand St WC1 . . .94 A2
Hercules Ct **7**
  SE14 . . . . .51 A4
Hercules Pl N7 . . . . . .5 A1
Hercules Rd SE1 . . .135 A1
Hercules St N7 . . . . . .5 A1
Here Eastford E9 . . . .18 C3
Hereford Bldgs
  SW3 . . . . .157 C4
Hereford Ho
  5 Brixton SW2 . . . .62 C3
  25 Camberwell SE5 . .48 B1
  Knightsbridge
  SW3 . . . . .130 B2
  Walham Green
  SW10 . . . . .156 B2
Hereford Mans
  W2 . . . . .31 C3
Hereford Mews **6**
  W2 . . . . .31 C3
Hereford Pl SE14 . . .51 B3
Hereford Rd
  Acton W3 . . . . .28 B2
  Bayswater
  W2 . . . . .32 C3 113 C4
Hereford Retreat **5**
  SE15 . . . . .49 C3
Hereford Sq SW7 . .143 A3
Hereford St
  E2 . . . . .24 C1 99 B2
Hereward House Sch
  NW3 . . . . .11 C3
Heritage CI SW9 . . . .63 A4

Heritage Ct SE8 . . . . 40 C1
Heritage Ho 22
SW19 . . . . 69 C3
Hermes Cl 5 SW9 . . 23 C1
Hermes Ct 4
SW9 . . . . 173 B4
Hermes St N1 . . . . . 85 B1
Hermitage Ct
2 Child's Hill NW2 . . 1 C1
6 Wapping E1 . . . . 125 C1
Hermitage Gdns
NW2 . . . . 1 C1
Hermitage La NW2 . . 1 C1
Hermitage Prim Sch
10 E1 . . . . 125 C2
Hermitage Row 9
E8 . . . . 16 C3
Hermitage St W2 . 101 B3
Hermitage The
Barnes SW13 . . . . . 46 C3
Richmond TW10 . . . 54 A2
Hermitage Villas
SW6 . . . . 155 B4
Hermitage Wall
E1 . . . . 125 C1
Hermit PI NW6 . . . . 78 A3
Hermit St EC1 . . . . . 96 A4
Herndon Rd SW18 . . 59 B2
HERNE HILL 63 B2
Herne Hill SE24 . . . 63 B3
Herne Hill Ho
SE24 . . . . 63 A1
Herne Hill Mans
SE24 . . . . 63 B3
Herne Hill Rd
SE24 . . . . 63 B2
Herne Hill Sch
SE24 . . . . 63 B2
Herne Hill Sta
SE24 . . . . 63 A1
Herne Hill Velodrome
SE24 . . . . 63 C1
Herne PI SE24 . . . . . 63 A2
Heron Cl NW10 . . . . 8 A2
Heron Ct
6 Cubitt Town
E14 . . . . 42 B3
7 Dulwich SE21 . . . 75 C2
Herondale Ave
SW18 . . . . 72 A3
Heron Dr N4 . . . . . . 6 B2
Herongate N1 . . . . . 87 A4
Heron Ho
Battersea SW11 . . 168 B4
Peckham SE15 . . . . 49 B2
St John's Wood
NW8 . . . . 80 A1
Heron PI
Marylebone W1 . . 103 C2
Rotherhithe SE16 . . 33 A1
Heron Quays Sta
E14 . . . . 33 C1
Heron Rd SE24 . . . . 63 B3
Heron Trad Est
W3 . . . . 28 A4
Herrick Ho
16 Camberwell
SE5 . . . . 48 B3
17 Canonbury N16 . 15 C4
Herrick Rd N5 . . . . . 6 B1
Herrick St SW1 . . . 147 C3
Herries St W10 . . . . 23 A3
Hersant Cl NW10 . . 21 C4

Herschell's Mews
SE5 . . . . 63 B4
Hersham Cl SW15 . . 68 C4
Hershell Ct 1
SW14 . . . . 55 A3
Hertford Ave
SW14 . . . . 56 A3
Hertford Ct 10
SW11 . . . . 60 A4
Hertford Lo 10
SW19 . . . . 70 A3
Hertford PI W1 . . . . 93 A1
Hertford Rd N1 . . . . 24 A4
Hertford St W1 . . . 118 A1
Hertmitage The 3
SE13 . . . . 52 B1
Hertslet Rd N7 . . . . 5 B1
Heswall Cl SW4 . . 171 A1
Hesketh PI
W11 . . . . . . 31 A2 112 A3
Heslop Ct 1
SW12 . . . . 72 C3
Heslop Rd SW12 . . . 72 B3
Hesper Mews
SW5 . . . . 142 A3
Hesperus Cres
E14 . . . . 42 A2
Hessel St E1 . . . . . . 32 A3
Hestercombe Ave
SW6 . . . . 164 B3
Hester Rd SW11 . . 158 A1
Hester Terr TW9 . . . 54 C4
Hestia Ho SE1 . . . 138 A3
Heston Ho
Gunnersbury W4 . . 37 A1
8 St Johns SE8 . . . 51 C2
Heston St SE14 . . . . 51 C2
Hetherington Rd
SW4 . . . . 62 A3
Hethpool Ho W2 . . . 89 B1
Hetley Rd W12 . . . . 39 A4
Hetty Rees Ct 6
N19 . . . . 5 A4
Hevelius Cl SE10 . . . 43 B1
Hever Ho SE15 . . . . 50 C4
Heversham Ho
SE15 . . . . 50 B4
Heward Ct SE13 . . 52 B1
Hewer Ho 8 SW4 . . 61 B2
Hewer St W10 . . . . 30 C4
Hewett Ho SW15 . . 47 B1
Hewett St
EC2 . . . . . . 24 A1 98 B1
Hewison St 3 . . . . 26 B3
Hewlett Rd E3 . . . . 26 A3
Hewling Ho 1
N16 . . . . 16 A3
Hexagon The N6 . . . 3 B3
Hexham Rd SE27 . . 75 B2
Hexton Ct N4 . . . . . 6 B2
Heybridge 2 NW1 . 13 A2
Heydon Ho 3
SE14 . . . . 50 B2
Heyford Ave SW8 . 162 B2
Heyford Terr
SW8 . . . . 162 B2
Heygate St SE17 . 151 A4
Heylyn Sq E3 . . . . . 26 B2
Heysham La NW3 . . 2 A1
Heythorp St SW18 . 70 B2
Heythrop Coll W8 128 A2
Heywood Ho
1 Deptford SE14 . . 50 C4
6 Tulse Hill SW2 . . 62 C1
Heyworth Rd E5 . . . 17 A4

Hibbert Ho 19 E14 . 41 C3
Hibbert St SW11 . . . 59 C4
Hichisson Rd SE15 . 65 B3
Hicken Rd SW2 . . . . 62 B2
Hickes Ho 6 NW6 . . 11 B1
Hickey's Almshouses
3 TW9 . . . . 54 B3
Hickin Cl SE17 . . . . 48 C1
Hickin St 2 E14 . . . . 42 B3
Hickleton N1 . . . . . . 84 C3
Hickling Ho 10
SE16 . . . . 40 A3
Hickmore Wlk
SW4 . . . . 61 B4
Hicks Cl SW11 . . . . 60 A4
Hicks St SE8 . . . . . . 41 A1
Hide PI SW1 . . . . . 147 B3
Hide Twr SW1 . . . . 147 B3
Hieover SE21 . . . . . 75 B2
Higgins Ho 7 N1 . . . 24 A4
Higginson Ho 2
NW3 . . . . 12 B1
Higgs Ind Est 5
SE24 . . . . 63 A4
Highbridge Ct 3
SE14 . . . . 50 B3
High Bridge Wharf
SE10 . . . . 42 C1
Highbury Mans 24
N1 . . . . 15 A1
HIGHBURY 15 A3
Highbury Cnr N5 . . . 15 A2
Highbury Corner
N5 . . . . 15 A2
Highbury Cres N5 . . 14 C2
Highbury Fields Sch
4 N5 . . . . 15 A3
Highbury Gr N5 . . . . 15 A3
Highbury Grange
N5 . . . . 15 B4
Highbury Grove Ct
N5 . . . . 15 A2
Highbury Grove Sch
7 N5 . . . . 15 B3
Highbury Hill N5 . . . 15 A4
Highbury & Islington
Sta N1 . . . . 15 A2
Highbury New Pk
N5 . . . . 15 B4
Highbury Pk N5 . . . . 15 A4
Highbury PI N5 . . . . 15 A3
Highbury Pool N5 . . 15 A2
Highbury Quadrant
N5 . . . . 6 B1
Highbury Quadrant
Prim Sch N5 . . . . . 15 C4
Highbury Station Rd
N1 . . . . 14 C2
Highbury Terrace
Mews N5 . . . . 15 A3
Highcliffe Dr
SW15 . . . . 56 B1
Highcroft Rd N19 . . 5 A4
Highcross Way 4
SW15 . . . . 68 C3
Highdown Rd
SW15 . . . . 57 A1
Highfield Ave NW11 . 1 A4
Highfield Cl SE13 . 67 C1
Highfield Mews
NW6 . . . . 11 A1
Highfield Rd W3 . . . 28 B4
Highfields Gr N6 . . . 3 B3
HIGHGATE 3 C4
Highgate Archway
N6 . . . . 4 B3

Highgate Ave N6 . . . 4 A4
Highgate Cemetery
N19 . . . . 3 C1
Highgate Cl N6 . . . . 3 C4
Highgate High St
N6 . . . . 4 A3
Highgate Hill N19 . . 4 B3
Highgate Ho 11
SE26 . . . . 76 C1
Highgate Pre-Prep &
Jun Sch N6 . . . . . . 3 A4
Highgate Rd NW5 . . 13 A4
Highgate Sch N6 . . . 3 C4
Highgate West Hill
Highgate N6 . . . . . 3 C3
London N6 . . . . . . 3 C3
Highgrove Point 2
NW3 . . . . 11 B4
High Holborn
WC1 . . . . 106 C3
High Holborn Ho
WC1 . . . . 107 A3
Highlands Ave W3 . 28 B2
Highlands Cl N4 . . . 5 A4
Highlands Heath
SW15 . . . . 69 B4
Highlever Rd W10 . 30 B4
High London N6 . . 4 C4
Highmore Rd SE3 . . 53 A3
High Mount 11 N4 . 4 A4
High Park Ave
TW9 . . . . 44 C2
High Park Rd TW9 . 44 C2
High Par The
SW16 . . . . 74 A1
High Point N6 . . . . . 3 C4
High Rd NW10 . . . . . 8 C2
Highshore Rd
SE15 . . . . 49 B1
Highshore Sch
4 Camberwell
SW6 . . . . 48 A3
16 Camberwell SE15 . . 49 B2
High St
Acton W3 . . . . 28 A1
Brentford TW8 . . . . 44 A4
Stratford Marsh
E15 . . . . 27 B4
High Street Harlesden
NW10 . . . . 21 B3
High Street
Kensington Sta
W8 . . . . 128 A3
High The SW16 . . . . 74 C1
High Timber St
EC4 . . . . 122 C4
High Trees SW2 . . . 74 C3
Hightrees Ho
SW12 . . . . 60 C1
Highview N8 . . . . . . 5 A4
Highview 1
SW19 . . . . 70 A3
High View Prim Sch
5 SW11 . . . . 59 C3
Highway Bsns Pk The
7 E1 . . . . 32 C2
Highway The E1 . . . 32 B2
Highway Trad Ctr The
8 E1 . . . . 32 C2
Highwood Cl SE22 . 76 C3
Highwood Rd N19 . . 5 A1
Highworth St
NW1 . . . . 102 B4
Hilary Cl SW6 . . . . 156 A2
Hilary Rd W12 . . . . 29 B2

Hilborough Ct 1
E8 . . . . 24 B4
Hilborough Rd 1
E8 . . . . 16 B1
Hilda Terr 2
SW9 . . . . 173 C2
Hilditch Ho 7
TW10 . . . . 54 B1
Hildred Ho SW1 . . 146 A4
Hildreth St 5
SW12 . . . . 73 A3
Hildreth Street Mews
2 SW12 . . . . 73 A3
Hildyard Rd SW6 . 155 C4
Hiley Rd NW10 . . . . 22 B2
Hilgrove Rd NW6 . . 11 B1
Hillary Ct 12 W12 . . 39 B4
Hillbeck Cl
Deptford SE15 . . . . 50 B3
Deptford SE15 . . . . 50 B4
Hillbrow 7 TW10 . . 54 A1
Hillbury Rd SW17 . . 73 A1
Hillcourt Rd SE22 . 65 A1
Hillcrest
Camberwell SE24 . 63 C3
Highgate N6 . . . . . 3 C4
Notting Hill
W11 . . . . . 31 B2 112 C3
Hillcrest Ct NW2 . . 10 A3
Hillcrest Rd W3 . . . 28 A1
Hill Ct
Hampstead NW3 . . 12 A4
Putney SW15 . . . . 57 C2
Hilldrop Cres N7 . . 13 C3
Hilldrop La N7 . . . . 13 C3
Hilldrop Rd N7 . . . . 13 C3
Hillersdon Ave
SW13 . . . . 46 C1
Hillersdon Ho
SW1 . . . . 146 A2
Hillery Cl SE17 . . . 151 C3
Hill Farm Rd W10 . 30 C4
Hillfield Ct NW3 . . . 12 A3
Hillfield Ho N5 . . . . 15 B3
Hillfield Mans
NW3 . . . . 12 A3
Hillfield Rd NW6 . . . 10 C3
Hillgate PI
Balham SW12 . . . . 73 A4
Kensington
W8 . . . . 31 C1 113 B2
Hillgate St
W8 . . . . 31 C1 113 B2
Hill House Sch
SW1 . . . . 131 A1
Hilliard Ho 15 E1 . . 32 A1
Hilliard's Ct 4 E1 . . 32 B1
Hillier Ho 1 NW1 . . 13 C1
Hillier Rd SW11 . . . 60 B1
Hillingdon St SE17 . 48 A4
Hill Lo SW11 . . . . . 59 C3
Hillman Dr 12
W10 . . . . 22 B1
Hillmarton St 8 . . . 17 A2
Hillmarton Rd N7 . . 14 A3
Hillmead Dr SW9 . . 63 A3
Hill Mead Prim Sch 23
SW9 . . . . 63 A3
Hillrise Mans N19 . . 5 A4
Hill Rd NW8 . . . . . . 79 A1
Hillrise Rd N19 . . . . 5 A4
Hillsboro Rd SE22 . 64 A2
Hillsborough Ct 13
NW6 . . . . 78 A3

Hillside
Greenwich SE10 . . . . . . .52 C3
Stonebridge NW10 . . . .20 C4
Hillside CI NW8 . . . . . . 78 B2
Hillside Ct NW3 . . . . . . 11 A3
Hillside Gdns SW2 . . . .74 C2
Hillside Rd SW2 . . . . . . 74 C2
Hillsleigh Rd
W14 . . . . .31 B1 113 A2
Hills PI W1 . . . . .104 C1
Hill St W1 . . . . .118 A2
Hillstone Ct **3** E3 . .27 A1
Hilltop Ct
12 London SW13 . . . .59 C3
South Hampstead
NW8 . . . . .11 B1
Hilltop Ho **7** N6 . . . . 4 C4
Hilltop Rd NW6 . . . . . .10 C1
Hill View NW1 . . . . . . 81 C2
Hill Wood Ho NW1 . . 83 A2
Hillworth Rd SW2 . . . .74 C4
Hillyard St SW9 . . . . . 173 B3
Hillyfield CI E9 . . . . . . 18 A3
Hilly Fields Cres
SE4 . . . . .66 C4
Hilsea Point **7**
SW15 . . . . .69 A3
Hilsea St E5 . . . . .17 B4
Hilton Docklands Pier
SE16 . . . . .118 B4
Hilton Ho
Lower Holloway
N7 . . . . .14 A4
9 Nunhead SE4 . . . .65 C3
Hilversum Cres **10**
SE22 . . . . .64 A2
Hinckley Rd SE15 . . . .64 C3
Hind Ct EC4 . . . . .107 C1
Hinde Mews W1 . . . .103 C2
Hinde St W1 . . . . .103 C2
Hind Gr E14 . . . . .33 C3
Hindhead Point **6**
SW15 . . . . .69 A3
Hind Ho
13 Deptford SE14 . .50 C4
Islington N7 . . . . .14 C4
Hindle Ho E8 . . . . .16 B3
Hindley Ho N7 . . . . 5 B1
Hindlip Ho SW8 . . . . .171 B3
Hindmans Rd
SE22 . . . . .64 C2
Hindmans Yd **5**
SE22 . . . . .64 C2
Hindmarsh CI E1 . . . .125 C4
Hindrey Rd E5 . . . . . . .17 A3
Hinstock NW6 . . . . . . .78 A4
Hinton Rd SE24 . . . . . .63 A4
Hippodrome Mews
W11 . . . . .31 A2 112 A3
Hippodrome PI
W11 . . . . .31 A2 112 B3
Hirst Ct SW1 . . . . .146 A1
Hitchcock La E15 . . . .19 B2
Hitchin Sq E3 . . . . . . .26 A3
Hithe Gr SE16 . . . . . . .40 B3
Hitherfield Prim Sch
SW16 . . . . .74 C4
Hitherfield Rd SW16,
SW27 . . . . .74 C1
Hither Green La
SE13 . . . . .67 C1
Hitherlands SW12 . . .73 A2
HM Prison
Wormwood Scrubs
W12 . . . . .29 C3

HMS Belfast SE1 . . 124 B2
HMS President
EC4 . . . . .121 C4
Hoadly Rd SW16 . . . .73 C2
Hobart PI SW1 . . . . .132 A2
Hobbes Wlk SW15 . . .57 A2
Hobb's Ct SE1 . . . . . .139 A4
Hobbs' PI N1 . . . . .24 A4
Hobday St E14 . . . . . .34 A3
Hobhouse Ct SW1 119 C3
Hobsons PI E1 . . . . . .111 B4
Hobury St SW10 . . . .157 B3
Hocker St **2**
E2 . . . . .24 B2 98 C3
Hockett CI SE8 . . . . . .41 B2
Hockley Ho **4** E9 . . .17 B2
Hockliffe Ho **5**
W10 . . . . .30 B4
Hockney Ct **1**
SE16 . . . . .40 A1
Hockworth Ho **7**
N16 . . . . 7 A3
Hocroft Ave NW2 . . . . 1 B1
Hocroft Ct NW2 . . . . . 1 B1
Hocroft Rd NW2 . . . . . 1 B1
Hocroft Wlk NW2 . . . . 1 B1
Hodford Lo NW11 . . . 1 C2
Hodford Rd NW11 . . . 1 C3
Hodister CI **5** SE5 . .48 B3
Hodnet Gr SE16 . . . . .40 B2
Hoffman Sq N1 . . . . . .97 C4
Hofland Rd W14 . . . .126 A2
Hogan Mews **2** W2 101 B4
Hogan Way **5** E5 . . . 7 C2
Hogarth Bsns Pk
W4 . . . . .46 A4
Hogarth Ct
3 Camden Town
NW1 . . . . .13 B1
City of London EC3 124 B4
24 Whitechapel E1 111 C1
Hogarth Ho SW1 . . .147 C3
Hogarth Ind Est
NW10 . . . . .21 C1
Hogarth La W4 . . . . . .46 A4
Hogarth Pl SW5 . . . .142 A3
Hogarth Rd SW5 . . . .142 A3
Hogarth Roundabout
W4 . . . . .46 A4
Hogarth's House
W4 . . . . .46 A4
Holbeach Mews **1**
SW12 . . . . .73 A3
Holbeck Row SE15 . .49 C3
Holbein Ho SW1 . . . .145 B2
Holbein Mews
SW1 . . . . .145 B2
Holbein PI SW1 . . . .145 B3
Holberton Gdns
NW10 . . . . .22 A2
HOLBORN 107 C3
Holborn EC1 . . . . . . .107 C3
Holborn Cir EC1 . . . .107 C3
Holborn Ho **1**
W12 . . . . .30 A3
Holborn PI WC1 . . . .106 C3
Holborn Sta WC1 . . .106 C3
Holborn Viaduct
EC1 . . . . .108 A3
Holbrook CI N19 . . . . 4 A3
Holbrooke Ct N7 . . . .14 A4
Holbrook Ho
Acton W3 . . . . .28 C4
3 Streatham SW2 . .74 B3
Holcombe Ho
SW9 . . . . .62 A4

Holcombe PI SE4 . . . .66 A4
Holcombe St W6 . . . . .39 A2
Holcroft Ct W1 . . . .104 C4
Holcroft Ho
Battersea SW11 . . . . . .59 C4
Lewisham SE10 . . . . . .52 B2
Holcroft Rd E9 . . . . . .17 B1
Holdenby Rd SE4 . . . .66 A2
Holden Ho
7 Deptford SE8 . . . .51 C3
Islington N1 . . . . .86 C3
Holden Point E15 . . . 19 C2
Holden St SW11 . . . .169 B1
Holdernesse Rd **6**
SW17 . . . . .72 C2
Holderness Ho
SE5 . . . . .64 A4
Holdsworth Ho **5**
SW2 . . . . .74 C4
Holford Ho
6 Bermondsey
SE16 . . . . .40 A2
Finsbury WC1 . . . . .95 A4
Holford PI WC1 . . . . .95 A4
Holford Rd NW3 . . . . . 2 C1
Holford St WC1 . . . . .95 B4
Holford Yd WC1 . . . . .85 B1
Holgate Ave SW11 . . .59 C4
Holland Gdns
Brentford TW8 . . . . . . .44 A4
3 Kensington W14 . .126 B2
Holland Gr SW9 . . . .163 C1
Holland Park
W11 . . . . .31 B1 112 C1
Holland Park Ave
W11 . . . . .31 A1 112 B1
Holland Park Ct
W14 . . . . .126 B4
Holland Park Gdns
W14 . . . . .126 A4
Holland Park Mews
W11 . . . . .31 B1 112 C1
Holland Park Pre
Prep Sch W14 . . . . .126 C1
Holland Park Rd
W14 . . . . .127 A1
Holland Park Rdbt
W12 . . . . .39 C4
Holland Park Sch
W8 . . . . .127 A4
Holland Park Sta
W11 . . . . .31 B1 112 C1
Holland Pas N1 . . . . .86 C4
Holland Pl **8** W8 . .128 A4
Holland Rd
West Kensington
W14 . . . . .126 B2
Willesden Green
NW10 . . . . .22 A3
Holland Rise Ho
SW9 . . . . .163 A1
Holland St
Kensington W8 . . . . . .127 C4
Lambeth SE1 . . . . . . .122 B2
Holland Villas Rd
Kensington W14 . . . . .126 A4
Holland Wlk
Kensington W14 . . . . .127 C4
Upper Holloway N19 . . 4 C3
Hollar Rd N16 . . . . 7 B1
Hollen St W1 . . . . . . .105 B2
Holles Ho **9** SW9 . . .173 B2
Holles St W1 . . . . . . .104 B2
Holley Rd W3 . . . . . . .38 A4

Holliday Sq **6**
SW11 . . . . .59 C4
Hollies The SW12 . . .73 B2
Hollies Way **1**
SW12 . . . . .72 C4
Hollingbourne Rd
SE24 . . . . .63 B2
Hollins Ho N7 . . . . . . .14 A4
Hollisfield WC1 . . . . .94 B3
Holloway Rd
Lower Holloway
N7 . . . . .14 B4 5 A1
Upper Holloway N19 . . 4 C2
N7 . . . . .14 B3
Holloway Road Sta
N7 . . . . .14 B3
Holly Berry La **8**
NW3 . . . . .11 B4
Hollybush Gdns
E2 . . . . .25 A2
Holly Bush Hill **7**
NW3 . . . . .11 B4
Hollybush Ho **23**
E2 . . . . .25 A2
Hollybush Pl E2 . . . . .25 A2
Holly Bush Steps **6**
NW3 . . . . .11 B4
Holly Bush Vale **10**
NW3 . . . . .11 B4
Holly CI NW10 . . . . 8 A1
Hollycroft Ave NW3 . . 1 C1
Hollydale Prim Sch **7**
SE15 . . . . .50 B1
Hollydale Rd SE15 . . .50 B1
Hollydene
Hither Green
SE13 . . . . .67 C1
8 Peckham SE15 . . .50 A2
Holly Gr SE15 . . . . . . .49 C1
Hollyhedge Ho
SE3 . . . . .52 C1
Holly Hill NW3 . . . . . .11 B4
Holly Lo W8 . . . . . . .127 B4
Holly Lodge SE13 . . . . 67 C4
Holly Lodge Gdns
N6 . . . . 3 C3
Holly Lodge Mans
N6 . . . . 3 C3
Holly Mews SW10 . . .143 A1
Holly Mount NW3 . . . .11 B4
Hollymount CI **9**
SE10 . . . . .52 B2
Holly Park Est N4 . . . . 5 B4
Holly Pk N4 . . . . 5 A4
Holly Park Montessori
Sch **7** N4 . . . . 5 A4
Holly Rd **5** W4 . . . . .37 C2
Holly St E8 . . . . .16 B1
Holly Terr N6 . . . . 3 C3
Holly Tree Ho SE4 . . .66 B4
Holly Village N6 . . . . . 4 A2
Holly Wlk NW3 . . . . . .11 B4
Hollywood Lofts
E1 . . . . .24 B1 98 C1
Hollywood Mews
SW10 . . . . .156 C4
Hollywood Rd
SW10 . . . . .156 C4
Holman Ho **2** E2 . . .25 C2
Holman Hunt Ho
W14 . . . . .140 A1
Holman Rd SW11 . . .167 B1

Holmbrook NW1 . . . .83 A1
Holmbury Ct SW17 . .72 B1
Holmbury Ho SW9 . . .63 A2
Holmbush Rd
SW15 . . . . .58 A1
Holmcote Gdns
N5 . . . . .15 B3
Holmdale Rd NW6 . . .10 C3
Holmdene Ave
SE24 . . . . .63 B2
Holmead Rd SW6 . .156 B1
Holmefield Ct **4**
NW3 . . . . .12 A2
Holmefield Ho
W10 . . . . .23 A1
Holmes CI SE22 . . . . .64 C3
Holmes Ct
5 South Acton
W4 . . . . .37 B3
18 South Lambeth
SW4 . . . . .172 A2
Holmesdale Ave
SW14 . . . . .55 A3
Holmesdale Ho **12**
NW6 . . . . .23 C4
Holmesdale Rd
Highgate N6 . . . . 4 A4
Richmond TW9 . . . . . .44 B2
Holmesley Rd
SE23 . . . . .66 A1
Holmes Pl SW10 . . . .157 A4
Holmes Rd NW5 . . . .13 A3
Holmes Terr SE1 . . . .135 B4
Holmewood Gdns
SW2 . . . . .74 B4
Holmewood Rd
SW2 . . . . .74 B4
Holmhurst SE13 . . . . .67 C1
Holmleigh Prim Sch
N16 . . . . 7 A3
Holmleigh Rd N16 . . . 7 A3
Holm Oak CI SW15 . .58 B1
Holm Oak Mews **11**
SW4 . . . . .62 A2
Holmsdale Ho **24**
N7 . . . . .13 C3
Holmside Ct SW12 . . .60 C1
Holmside Rd
SW12 . . . . .60 C1
Holmsley Ho
SW15 . . . . .68 B4
Holm Wlk SE3 . . . . . . .53 C1
Holmwood Ct **3**
N16 . . . . 7 B4
Holocaust Meml Gdn
W2 . . . . .131 A4
Holroyd Rd SW15 . . .57 B2
Holsgrove Ct W3 . . . .29 A1
Holst Mans SW13 . . . .47 B4
Holsworthy Ho **9**
E3 . . . . .27 A2
Holsworthy Sq
WC1 . . . . .95 A1
Holt Ct SE10 . . . . .52 B4
Holt Ho SW2 . . . . .62 C1
Holton St E1 . . . . .25 C1
Holwood PI **7**
SW4 . . . . .61 C3
Holybourne Ave
SW15 . . . . .68 C4
Holy Cross RC Prim
Sch SW6 . . . . .165 B4

Holy Ghost RC Prim
  Sch **4** SW12 . . . . .72 C4
Holyhead Cl E3 . . . . .26 C2
Holyoake Ct SE16 . . . . .41 B4
Holyoak Rd SE11 . . . .150 B3
Holyport Rd SW6 . . . .47 C3
Holyrood Ho N4 . . . . .6 B3
Holyrood Mews
  6 Greenwich
  SE7 . . . . .43 C1
  10 Newham E16 . . . . .35 C1
Holyrood St SE1 . . . .124 A1
Holy Trinity CE Prim
  Sch
  Belgravia SW1 . . . . .145 B4
  Chelsea SW3 . . . . . .145 A1
  Dalston E8 . . . . .16 B2
  13 Hampstead
  NW3 . . . . .11 B4
  Richmond TW10 . . . .54 C3
  Streatham SW2 . . . . .74 B3
Holy Trinity & Saint
  Silas CE Prim Sch **22**
  NW1 . . . . .13 A1
Holywell Cl
  12 Bermondsey
  SE16 . . . . .40 A1
  2 Greenwich SE3 . . .53 C4
Holywell La
  EC2 . . . . .24 A1 98 B2
Holywell Row
  EC2 . . . . .24 A1 98 B2
Homan Ho **6** SW4 .73 C4
Homecross Ho **7**
  W4 . . . . .37 C2
Homefield Rd W4 . . . .38 B1
Homefield St **14**
  N1 . . . . .24 A3
Homeleigh Ct **8**
  SW16 . . . . .74 A1
Homeleigh Rd
  SE15 . . . . .65 C2
Homemead SW12 . . . . .73 A2
Home Office SW1 .133 C1
Home Park Rd
  SW19 . . . . .70 B1
Home Rd SW11 . . . .168 A2
Homer Dr E14 . . . . . .41 C2
Homer Rd E9 . . . . . . .18 A2
Homer Row W1 . . . .102 B3
Homer St W1 . . . . . .102 B3
HOMERTON 17 C1
Homerton Gr E9 . . . . .17 C3
Homerton High St
  E9 . . . . .17 C3
Homerton Rd E9 . . . . .18 B3
Homerton Sta E9 . . . .17 C2
Homerton Terr E9 . . . .17 B2
Homerton University
  Hospl E9 . . . . .17 C3
Homestall Rd
  SE22 . . . . .65 B2
Homestead Rd
  SW6 . . . . .155 A1
Homewoods **3**
  SW12 . . . . .73 B4
Homildon Ho **10**
  SE26 . . . . .76 C1
Honduras St EC1 . . . . .96 C2
Honeybourne Rd
  NW6 . . . . .11 A3
Honeybrook Rd SW12,
  SW4 . . . . .73 B4

Honeyfield N4 . . . . .5 C2
Honey La EC2 . . . . . .109 A1
Honey Lane Ho
  SW10 . . . . .156 B4
Honeyman Cl NW6 . . . .9 C1
Honeywell Jun & Inf
  Schs **3** SW11 . . . . .60 B1
Honeywell Rd
  SW11 . . . . .60 B2
Honeywood Ho **3**
  SE15 . . . . .49 C2
Honeywood Rd
  NW10 . . . . .21 B3
Honiton Gdns **1**
  SE15 . . . . .50 B1
Honiton Ho **29** SE5 . . .48 B1
Honiton Rd NW6 . . . . .23 B3
HONOR OAK 65 B2
Honor Oak Park Sta
  SE23 . . . . .65 C1
Honor Oak Pk
  SE23 . . . . .65 C1
Honor Oak Rise
  SE23 . . . . .65 B1
Honour Lea Ave
  E15 . . . . .19 A3
Honwell Ho **3**
  W2 . . . . .31 C4
Hood Ave SW14 . . . . .55 B2
Hood Ct N7 . . . . .5 B1
Hood Ho **17** SE5 . . . .48 C3
Hooke Ho **32** E3 . . . . .26 A3
Hookham Ct SW8 . .171 B4
Hooks Cl SE15 . . . . . .50 A2
Hooper Ho **9**
  SW18 . . . . .58 B2
Hooper Rd E16 . . . . . .35 C3
Hooper's Ct SW1 . . .130 C3
Hooper's Mews **4**
  W3 . . . . .28 B1
Hooper St E1 . . . . . .111 B1
Hoop La NW11 . . . . . . .1 C4
Hope Cl
  2 Brentford
  TW8 . . . . .36 A1
  N1 . . . . .15 B2
Hopefield Ave
  NW6 . . . . .23 A3
Hope Gdns **10** W3 . . .37 A4
Hope St
  London SW11 . . . . . . .59 C4
  Poplar E14 . . . . .35 A3
Hopetown St E1 . . . .111 A3
Hopewell St SE5 . . . .48 C3
Hop Gdns WC2 . . . . .120 A3
Hopgood St **3**
  W12 . . . . .30 B1
Hopkins Ho **17**
  E14 . . . . .33 C3
Hopkinson Ho **1**
  SW11 . . . . .169 B2
Hopkinson's Pl
  NW1 . . . . .81 B4
Hopkins St W1 . . . . .105 B1
Hopping La N1 . . . . . .15 A2
Hop St SE10 . . . . .43 B2
Hopton Ho **5**
  SW9 . . . . .48 A1
Hopton's Gdns
  SE1 . . . . .122 B2
Hopton St SE1 . . . . .122 B2
Hopwood Cl SW17 . . .71 B1
Hopwood Rd SE17 . . .48 C4
Hopwood Wlk E8 . . . .16 C1
Horatio Ho **12** E2 . . .24 B3

Horatio Pl **8** E14 . . .34 B1
Horatio St **11** E2 . . .24 B3
Horbury Cres
  W11 . . . . .31 C2 113 B3
Horbury Mews
  W11 . . . . .31 B2 113 A3
Horder Rd SW6 . . . .164 B3
Horde Prom E **18**
  SE15 . . . . .49 B3
Hordle Prom N **4**
  SE15 . . . . .49 B3
Hordle Prom S **7**
  SE15 . . . . .49 B3
Horizon Bldg **22**
  E14 . . . . .33 C2
Horizon Ind Est
  SE15 . . . . .50 A4
Horle Wlk SE5 . . . . . .48 A1
Hormead Rd W9 . . . . .23 B1
Hornbeam Cl
  SE11 . . . . .149 B4
Hornbeam Ho **2**
  NW3 . . . . .12 B2
Hornbeam Sq **8**
  E3 . . . . .26 B4
Hornblower Cl **2**
  SE16 . . . . .41 A2
Hornby Cl NW3 . . . . .11 C1
Hornby Ho **6**
  SE11 . . . . .163 C4
Horndean Cl **3**
  SW15 . . . . .68 C3
Horner Hos **18** N1 . .24 A4
Horne Way SW15 . . . .47 B1
Horn La
  Acton W3 . . . . .28 B3
  Greenwich SE10 . . . .43 C2
Horn Link Way
  SE10 . . . . .43 C2
Hornsby House Sch **7**
  SW12 . . . . .72 C3
Hornsey La N6 . . . . . . .4 B4
Hornsey Lane Gdns
  N6 . . . . .4 B4
Hornsey Rd N7, N19 . . .5 B2
Hornsey Rise Gdns
  N19 . . . . .5 A4
Hornsey St N7 . . . . . . .14 B3
Hornshay St SE15 . . . .50 B4
Hornton Ct W8 . . . . .127 C3
Hornton Pl W8 . . . . .127 C3
Hornton St W8 . . . . .127 C4
Horrocks Ho
  SW15 . . . . .57 A2
Horse & Dolphin Yd
  W1 . . . . .119 C4
Horseferry Pl
  SE10 . . . . .52 B4
Horseferry Rd
  Limehouse E14 . . . . . .33 A2
  Westminster SW1 . . .147 C4
Horseferry Rd Est
  SE1 . . . . .138 C4
Horse Guards Ave
  SW1 . . . . .120 A1
Horse Guards Par
  SW1 . . . . .119 C1
Horse Guards Rd
  SW1 . . . . .133 C4
Horsell Rd N5 . . . . . . .14 C3
Horselydown La
  SE1 . . . . .124 C1
Horselydown Mans
  SE1 . . . . .138 C4
Horsemongers Mews
  SE1 . . . . .137 A3

Horsendon Ho **11**
  N7 . . . . .13 C3
Horseshoe Cl E14 . . . .42 B1
Horse Yd N1 . . . . .86 B4
Horsfield Ho **13**
  N1 . . . . .15 B1
Horsford Rd SW2 . . . .62 B2
Horsley Ct SW1 . . . .147 C3
Horsley Ho **30** SE4 . .65 C3
Horsley St **4** SE17 . .48 C4
Horsman Ho SE5 . . . .48 B4
Horsman St SE5 . . . . .48 B4
Horsmonden Rd
  SE4 . . . . .66 B1
Horston Ho N4 . . . . . . .6 B4
Hortensia Ho
  SW10 . . . . .156 C2
Hortensia Rd
  SW10 . . . . .156 C2
Horticultural Pl **6**
  W4 . . . . .37 C1
Horton Ave NW2 . . . .10 A4
Horton Ho
  13 Deptford SE15 . .50 B4
  South Lambeth
  SW8 . . . . .162 C2
  West Kensington
  W14 . . . . .140 A1
Horton Rd E8 . . . . . . .17 A2
Horton St SE13 . . . . . .67 A4
Horwood Ho
  24 Bethnal Green
  E2 . . . . .25 A2
  Marylebone NW8 . . . .90 B2
Hosack Rd SW12,
  SW17 . . . . .72 C2
Hosier La EC1 . . . . .108 B3
Hoskins St SE10 . . . . .42 C1
Hospl for Tropical
  Diseases NW1 . . . . .93 A1
Hospl of St John & St
  Elizabeth NW8 . . . . .79 B1
Hotham Prim Sch
  SW15 . . . . .57 C3
Hotham Rd SW15 . . . .57 B4
Hothfield Pl SE16 . . . .40 B3
Hotspur St SE11 . . . .149 B2
Houblon Rd TW10 . . . .54 A2
Houghton Cl **10**
  E8 . . . . .16 B2
Houghton Sq SW9 . . .62 A4
Houghton St WC2 . . .107 A1
Houndsditch EC3 . .110 B2
Household Cavalry
  Mus SW1 . . . . .120 A1
Houseman Way **2**
  SE5 . . . . .48 C3
House Mill The **3** . . .27 B2
Houses of Parliament
  SW1 . . . . .134 B2
Hoveden Rd NW2 . . . .10 A3
Howard Bldg
  SW8 . . . . .160 A3
Howard Cl
  Acton W3 . . . . .28 A3
  Cricklewood NW2 . . . .10 A4
Howard Ct
  Lewisham SE10 . . . . .52 B2
  Peckham SE15 . . . . . .64 C4
Howard Ho
  6 Brixton SW9 . . . . .62 C4
  14 Deptford SE8 . . . .51 B4
  Fitzrovia W1 . . . . .92 B1
Howard Mews N5 . . . .15 A4
Howard Rd
  Canonbury N16 . . . . . .15 C4

Howard Rd continued
  Cricklewood NW2 . . . . .9 C2
Howard's La SW15 . . .57 B3
Howbury Rd SE15 . . . .65 B4
Howcroft Ho **3**
  E3 . . . . .26 B2
Howden St SE15 . . . . .64 C4
Howell Ho **5** N7 . . . .13 C3
Howell Wlk SE1 . . . .150 B3
Howgate Rd SW14 . . .55 C4
Howick Pl SW1 . . . . .133 A1
Howie St SW11 . . . . .158 A1
Howitt Cl
  6 Maitland Pk
  NW3 . . . . .12 A2
  Stoke Newington
  N16 . . . . .16 A4
Howitt Rd NW3 . . . . . .12 A2
Howland Ho **3**
  SW16 . . . . .74 A1
Howland Mews E
  W1 . . . . .105 A4
Howland St W1 . . . . .105 A4
Howland Way
  SE16 . . . . .41 A4
Howletts Rd SE24 . . . .63 B1
Howley Pl W2 . . . . . .101 A4
Howsman Rd
  SW13 . . . . .46 C4
Howson Rd SE4 . . . . .66 A3
Howson Terr
  TW10 . . . . .54 A1
How's St E2 . . . . .24 B3
HOXTON 24 A3
Hoxton Garden Prim
  Sch **4** N1 . . .24 A2 98 A3
Hoxton Mkt **10**
  N1 . . . . .24 A2 98 A3
Hoxton Point
  EC1 . . . . .24 A2 98 A3
Hoxton Sq
  N1 . . . . .24 A2 98 A3
Hoxton St N1 . . . . . . .24 A3
Hoxton Sta N1 . . . . . .24 B3
Hoylake Rd W3 . . . . . .29 A3
Hoyland Cl **4**
  SE15 . . . . .50 A3
Hoy St E16 . . . . .35 B3
Hub Buildings The **4**
  SW12 . . . . .73 A3
Hub E15 E15 . . . . .27 A3
Huberd Ho SE1 . . . .137 C2
Hubert Gr SW9 . . . . . .62 A4
Hubert Ho NW8 . . . . .90 A1
Hub The NW1 . . . . . . .81 A1
Hucknall Ct NW8 . . . .89 B2
Huddart St **1** E3 . . . .33 B4
Huddleston Cl E2 . . . .25 B3
Huddleston Rd
  NW2 . . . . .9 A2
Huddleston Rd N7 . . . .13 B4
Hudson Cl **13** W12 . .30 A2
Hudson Ct **1** E14 . . .41 C1
Hudson Ho
  Chelsea SW10 . . . . .156 C2
  3 Notting Hill W11 . .31 A3
Hudsons Ho N1 . . . . . .97 C3
Hudson's Pl SW1 . . .146 C4
Huggin Ct EC4 . . . . .123 A4
Huggin Hill EC4 . . . .123 A4
Huggins Ho **6** E3 . . .26 C2
Huggins Pl SW2 . . . . .74 B3
Hughan Rd E15 . . . . . .19 C3
Hugh Astor Ct
  SE1 . . . . .136 B2

Hugh Dalton Ave
SW6 . . . . 154 C3
Hughenden Ho
NW8 . . . . 90 A2
Hughendon Terr
E15 . . . . 19 B4
Hughes Ho
28 Bethnal Green
E2 . . . . 25 B2
Camberwell SE5 . . . 48 B2
4 Deptford SE8 . . . 51 C4
Newington SE17 . . 150 B3
Hughes Mans
E1 . . . . 24 C1 99 C1
Hughes Terr 6
E16 . . . . 35 B4
Hugh Gaitskell Cl
SW6 . . . . 154 C3
Hugh Gaitskell Ho
Stoke Newington
N16 . . . . 7 B2
Willesden NW10 . . . 8 B1
Hugh Mews SW1 . 146 B3
Hugh Morgan Ho 5
SW4 . . . . 61 C4
Hugh Myddelton Prim
Sch EC1 . . . . 95 C3
Hugh Platt Ho 2
E2 . . . . 25 A3
Hugh St SW1 . . . 146 B3
Hugo Ho 5 SW1 . 131 A2
Hugon Rd SW6 . . . 59 A4
Hugo Rd N19 . . . . . 13 B4
Huguenot Ct 9
E1 . . . . 111 B4
Huguenot Pl
London SW18 . . . . 59 B2
Wandsworth SW17 111 A4
Huguenot Sq SE15 . 65 A4
Hullbridge Mews
N1 . . . . 87 B4
Hull Cl SE16 . . . . . 32 C1
Hull Ct SE5 . . . . . . 48 C1
Hull St EC1 . . . . . . 96 C3
Hulme Pl SE1 . . . 137 A3
Humber Dr W10 . . . 22 C1
Humber Rd SE3 . . . 53 B4
Humberton Cl E9 . . 18 A3
Humbolt Rd W6 . . 154 A3
Hume Ct N1 . . . . . . 15 A1
Hume Ho 14 W11 . . 30 C1
Humphrey Ct
SW11 . . . . 167 C3
Humphrey St SE1 . 152 C2
Humphry Ho 19
SW15 . . . . 57 C2
Hungerford Bridge
WC2 . . . . 120 C2
Hungerford Ho
SW1 . . . . 161 A4
Hungerford La
WC2 . . . . 120 B2
Hungerford Prim Sch
19 N7 . . . . 13 C2
Hungerford Rd
12 Camden Town
N7 . . . . 13 C2
Lower Holloway N7 . 14 A3
Hungerford St 21
E1 . . . . 32 A3
Hunsdon Rd SE14 . 50 C3
Hunslett St 26 E2 . . 25 B3
Hunstanton Ho
NW1 . . . . 102 B4
Hunt Cl W11 . . . . . 30 C1

Hunter Cl
Borough The SE1 . 137 C1
Upper Tooting
SW12 . . . . 72 C3
Huntercombe-
Roehampton Hospl
The SW15 . . . . . . 68 C4
Hunter Ct
5 London SE5 . . . . 63 C3
2 Streatham SW2 . 74 C4
Hunter Ho
Bloomsbury WC1 . . 94 B2
Lambeth SE1 . . . . 136 B3
South Lambeth
SW8 . . . . 161 C1
1 Tufnell Pk N19 . . 4 B1
West Brompton
SW5 . . . . 141 C1
Hunterian Mus
WC2 . . . . 107 A2
Hunter Lo 9 W9 . . 31 C4
Hunter St WC1 . . . 94 B2
Huntingdon Ct
SW14 . . . . 55 B4
Huntingdon Gdns
W4 . . . . 45 B3
Huntingdon Ho
SW5 . . . . 141 C4
Huntingdon St
Canning Town
E16 . . . . 35 B3
Islington N1 . . . . . 14 B1
Huntingfield Rd
SW15 . . . . 56 C2
Huntingford Ho
SW15 . . . . 47 B1
Huntington Ho
NW2 . . . . 9 B2
Huntley St E1 . . . . 93 B1
Hunton St E1 . . . 111 B4
Hunts Cl SE3 . . . . . 53 C1
Hunt's La E15 . . . . 27 B3
Huntshaw Ho 37
E3 . . . . 27 A2
Hunt's La E15 . . . . 27 B3
Huntsman St
SE17 . . . . 152 A3
Huntspill St SW17 . 71 B1
Hunts Slip Rd
SE21 . . . . 76 A2
Huntsworth Mews
NW1 . . . . 90 C1
Hurdwick Ho NW1 . 82 C2
Hurdwick Pl NW1 . 82 C2
Hurleston Ho 11
SE8 . . . . 41 B1
Hurley Cres SE16 . . 40 C4
Hurley Ho
Lambeth SE11 . . . 149 C3
34 Shoreditch
E2 . . . . 24 B2 98 C3
Hurley Lo SE22 . . . 65 B1
Hurlingham Bsns Pk
SW6 . . . . 58 C4
Hurlingham &
Chelsea Sec Sch
SW6 . . . . 58 C4
Hurlingham Court
Mans SW6 . . . . . 165 B1
Hurlingham Ct
SW6 . . . . 58 B4
Hurlingham Gdns
SW6 . . . . 58 B4
Hurlingham Rd
SW6 . . . . 165 A1

Hurlingham Sch
SW15 . . . . 58 B3
Hurlingham Sq
SW6 . . . . 59 A4
Hurlock Ho 1 N5 . . . 6 A1
Hurlock St N5 . . . . . 6 A1
Huron Rd SW17 . . . 72 C1
Hurstbourne Ho 9
SW15 . . . . 56 B1
Hurstbourne Gdns
N15 . . . . 6 C3
Hurst Ho WC1 . . . . 85 A1
Hurst St SE24 . . . . 63 A1
Hurstway Wlk 2
W11 . . . . 30 C2
Husborne Ho 8
SE8 . . . . 41 A2
Huson Cl NW3 . . . . 12 A1
Hutching's St E14 . . 41 C4
Hutching's Wharf 11
E14 . . . . 41 C4
Hutchins Cl E15 . . . 19 B1
Hutchins Ho 8
SW4 . . . . 73 C4
Hutchinson Ho 9
SE14 . . . . 50 B3
Hutton Ct 4 N4 . . . . 5 B3
Hutton Ho 10
E2 . . . . 24 C2 99 B3
Hutton St EC4 . . . 107 C1
Huxbear St SE4 . . . 66 B2
Huxley Ho
4 London SW9 . . 172 C2
Paddington NW8 . . 89 C1
Huxley St W10 . . . . 23 A2
Hyacinth Rd SW15 . 68 C3
Hyde Farm Mews
SW12 . . . . 73 C3
Hyde La SW11 . . . 168 A4
Hyde Park W2 . . . 116 C1
Hyde Park Cnr
SW1 . . . . 131 C4
Hyde Park Corner Sta
SW1 . . . . 131 C4
Hyde Park Cres
W2 . . . . 102 A1
Hyde Park Gate Mews
SW7 . . . . 129 A3
Hyde Park Gdns
W2 . . . . 115 C4
Hyde Park Gdns Mews
W2 . . . . 116 A4
Hyde Park Mans
NW1 . . . . 102 A3
Hyde Park Pl W2 . 116 B4
Hyde Park Sch
SW7 . . . . 129 A1
Hyde Park Sq W2 . 102 A1
Hyde Park Square
Mews W2 . . . . . . 102 A1
Hyde Park St W2 . 102 A1
Hyde Park Twrs
W2 . . . . 114 C3
Hyde Rd
Richmond TW10 . . . 54 B2
Shoreditch N1 . . . . 24 A4
Hyde's Pl 12 N1 . . . 15 A1
Hyde St SE8 . . . . . 51 C4
Hydethorpe Rd
SW12 . . . . 73 B3
Hyde Vale SE10 . . . 52 B3
Hylda Ct NW5 . . . . . 3 C1
Hyndman Ho 4
N19 . . . . 4 C4
Hyndman St SE15 . 50 A4

Hyperion Ho
27 Bow E3 . . . . . . 26 A3
Streatham SW2 . . . 74 B4
Hyson Rd SE16 . . . 40 A1
Hythe Ho 16 SE16 . 40 B4
Hythe Rd NW10 . . . 21 C1
Hythe Road Ind Est
NW10 . . . . 21 C1

I

Ian Hamilton Ho
NW1 . . . . 93 B4
Ian Mikardo High Sch
E3 . . . . 27 A2
Ibberton Ho
Kensington W14 . 126 B1
South Lambeth
SW8 . . . . 162 C2
Ibbotson Ave E16 . 35 B3
Ibbott St 22 E1 . . . 25 B1
Iberia Ho 17 N19 . . . 4 C4
Ibis Ct 18 SE8 . . . . 51 B4
Ibis La W4 . . . . 45 B2
Ibsley Gdns SW15 . 68 C3
Ibstock Place Sch
SW15 . . . . 56 A1
Icarus Ho 21 E3 . . . 26 B2
Iceland Rd E3 . . . . 26 C4
Iceland Wharf
SE16 . . . . 41 A2
Iceni Ct 27 E3 . . . . 26 B4
Ice Wharf NW1 . . . 84 B2
Ickburgh Rd E5 . . . . 7 C1
Ickburgh Sch 7
E9 . . . . 18 A3
Idaho Bldg 7
SE13 . . . . 52 A2
Ida St E14 . . . . 34 B3
Identity & Passport
Office SW1 . . . . . 146 B3
Idmiston Rd SE21,
SE27 . . . . 75 B2
Idol La EC3 . . . . . 124 A3
Idonia St SE8 . . . . 51 C3
Iffley Ho 14
E2 . . . . 24 B2 98 C3
Iffley Rd W6 . . . . . 39 A3
Ifield Ho 50 SE17 . 152 B2
Ifield Rd SW10 . . . 156 B4
Ifor Evans Pl E1 . . 25 C1
Ightham Ho SE17 . 152 A3
Ikon Ho 21 E1 . . . . 32 B2
Ilbert St W10 . . . . . 23 A2
Ilchester Gdns
W2 . . . . 114 A4
Ilchester Mans
W8 . . . . 127 B2
Ilchester Pl W14 . 127 A2
Ilderslly Gr SE21 . . 75 C2
Ilderton Prim Sch
SE16 . . . . 40 B1
Ilderton Rd SE15,
SE16 . . . . 50 B4
Ilex Rd NW10 . . . . . 8 B2
Ilford Ho 14 N1 . . . 15 C2
Ilfracombe Flats
SE1 . . . . 137 A4
Iliffe St SE17 . . . . 150 B2
Iliffe Yd SE17 . . . . 150 B2
Ilkeston Ct 7 E5 . . 17 C4
Ilminster Gdns
SW11 . . . . 60 A3
Ilsley Ct 8 SW8 . . 170 C1
Imber St N1 . . . . . . 87 B3

Imperial Ave 5
N16 . . . . 16 A4
Imperial Cl NW2 . . . 9 A3
Imperial College
London (Charing
Cross) W6 . . . . . . 39 C1
Imperial College
London (Chelsea &
Westminster)
SW10 . . . . 157 A3
Imperial College
London
(Hammersmith)
W12 . . . . 30 A3
Imperial College
London (South
Kensington)
SW7 . . . . 129 B2
Imperial College
London (St Mary's)
W2 . . . . 101 C2
Imperial College Rd
SW7 . . . . 129 B2
Imperial Cres
SW15 . . . . 167 A1
Imperial Ct NW8 . . 80 B2
Imperial Ho
1 Bow E3 . . . . 26 A2
2 Poplar E14 . . . . 33 B2
Strand WC2 . . . . . 106 C1
Imperial Rd SW6 . 166 B3
Imperial Sq SW6 . 166 B4
Imperial St E3 . . . . 27 B2
Imperial Twrs 6
NW3 . . . . 11 B2
Imperial War Mus SE1,
SE11 . . . . 135 C1
Imperial Wharf Sta
SW6 . . . . 167 A3
Imre Cl W12 . . . . . . 30 A1
Inchbald Sch of
Design SW1 . . . . 145 B4
Independent Pl 8 E8 . 16 B3
Indescon Ct E14 . . 42 A4
Indiana Bldg 7
SE8 . . . . 51 C2
Indigo Mews N16 . . 6 C1
India St EC3 . . . . . 110 C1
India Way W12 . . . 30 A2
India Mews W4 . . . . 30 A2
India Way 4 SW15 . 56 C1
Indus Ct 20 SE15 . . 49 B3
Ingelow Ho W8 . . 128 A4
Ingersoll Rd W12 . 30 A1
Ingestre Pl W1 . . . 105 A1
Ingestre Rd
Camden Town
NW5 . . . . 13 A4
Forest Gate E7 . . . 19 C2
Ingham Rd NW6 . . 10 C4
Inglebert St EC1 . . 95 B4
Ingleborough St
SW9 . . . . 173 B2
Ingleby Rd N7 . . . . . 5 A1
Inglefield Sq 15
E1 . . . . 32 A1
Ingle Ho 5 SW12 . . 73 C3
Ingle Mews EC1 . . 95 B4
Inglesham Wlk E9 . 18 B2
Ingleside Gr SE3 . . 53 B4
Inglethorpe Ho 6
E5 . . . . 7 C2
Inglethorpe St
SW6 . . . . 47 C2
Ingleton St SW9 . . 173 B2
Inglewood Cl E14 . . 41 C2

Inglewood Mans **11**
NW6 . . . .**10** C3
Inglewood Rd
NW6 . . . .**10** C3
Inglis Ho SW15 . .**57** B2
Inglis St SE5 . . . . .**48** A2
Ingram Ave NW11 . .**2** B4
Ingram Cl SE11 . .**149** A4
Ingram Ho E3 . . . . .**26** A4
Ingram Lo **8** NW4 . . .**61** C1
Ingrave St SW11 . . .**60** A4
Ingrebourne Ho
NW8 . . . .**101** C4
Ingress St **4** W4 . . .**38** A1
Inigo Pl WC2 . . . .**120** A4
Inkerman Rd NW5 . .**13** A2
Inkerman Terr
W8 . . . .**127** C1
Inkster Ho **8**
SW11 . . . .**60** A4
Inman Rd
Harlesden NW10 . .**21** A4
Wandsworth SW18 . .**71** B4
Inner Circ NW1 . . . .**91** B4
Inner Park Rd
SW19 . . . .**69** C2
Inner Temple EC4 .**121** B4
Inner Temple La
EC4 . . . .**107** B1
Innes Gdns SW15 . .**57** A1
Innisfree Ho NW2 . . .**9** C2
Innis Ho SE17 . . . .**152** A2
Insley Ho **11** E3 . . . .**27** A1
Institute of Cancer
Research The
SW7 . . . .**143** A2
Institute Pl **8** E8 . . .**17** A3
Instituto Espanol
Canada Blanch Sch
W10 . . . .**31** A4
Inst of Child Health
WC1 . . . .**94** C1
Inst of Neurology
Bloomsbury WC1 . .**106** B4
St Pancras WC1 . . . .**94** B1
Int Coll of
Accountancy The
SW17 . . . .**72** B3
Interchange The
NW5 . . . .**13** A2
International Com Sch
W1 . . . .**91** C1
International House
Language Sch
WC2 . . . .**106** B2
International Sch of
London W3 . . . .**36** C2
International Sch of
Screen Acting
E15 . . . .**27** B2
International Wy
E15 . . . .**19** B2
Inver Ct
11 Bayswater
W2 . . . .**100** B1
4 Hammersmith
W6 . . . .**38** C3
Inverforth Cl NW3 . . .**2** B2
Inverforth Ho NW3 . . .**2** B2
Invergarry Ho
NW6 . . . .**78** A1
Invermead Cl W6 . . .**38** C2
Inverness Gdns
W8 . . . .**114** A1

Inverness Mews
W2 . . . .**114** B4
Inverness Pl W2 . .**114** B4
Inverness St NW1 . .**82** B4
Inverness Terr
W2 . . . .**114** B4
Invernia Rd SE15 . . .**65** C3
Invicta Cl **2** E3 . . . .**33** C4
Invicta Plaza SE1 .**122** A2
Invicta Prim Sch
SE3 . . . .**53** C3
Invicta Rd SE3, SE7 .**53** C4
Inville Rd SE17 . . .**151** C1
Inwen Ct SE8 . . . . . .**41** A1
Inwood Ho **11** . . . .
SE22 . . . .**64** A4
Inworth St SW11 . .**168** B2
Inworth Wlk N1 . . . .**86** C4
Ion Ct **2** E2 . . . .**24** C3
Ionian Bldg **19**
E14 . . . .**33** A2
Ionian Ho **22** E1 . . .**25** C1
Ipsden Bldgs SE1 .**135** C4
Ipswich Ho SE4 . . . .**65** C2
Iqra Ind Sch SW9 . .**62** C1
Irby Ho SW2 . . . . . .**62** C1
Ireland Yd EC4 . . .**108** B1
Irene Rd SW6 . . . .**165** C3
Ireton Ho **22** SW9 .**173** C1
Ireton St **12** E3 . . . .**26** C1
Iris Ct **8** SE15 . . . .**64** C4
Iroko Ho **7** NW3 . . .**11** A2
Iron Bridge Cl
NW10 . . . .**8** A3
Irongate Ho EC3 . .**110** B2
Iron Mill Pl SW18 . .**59** A1
Iron Mill Rd SW18 . .**59** A1
Ironmonger La
EC2 . . . .**109** B1
Ironmonger Pas
EC1 . . . .**97** A3
Ironmonger Row
EC1 . . . .**97** A3
Ironmonger Row
Baths EC1 . . . .**97** A3
Ironmongers Pl
E14 . . . .**41** C2
Ironmonger's Pl **2**
E14 . . . .**41** C2
Ironside Cl SE16 . . .**40** C4
Ironside Ho E9 . . . . .**18** A4
Ironworks **11** E3 . . .**26** C4
Irvine Ct N1 . . . .**93** A1
Irvine Ho N7 . . . .**14** B2
Irving Gr SW9 . . . .**172** C1
Irving Ho SE17 . . .**150** A1
Irving Mews N1 . . . .**15** B2
Irving Rd W14 . . . . .**39** C3
Irving St WC2 . . . .**119** C3
Irwell Est **3** SE16 . .**40** B4
Irwin Gdns NW10 . .**22** A4
Isabella Ct **3**
TW10 . . . .**54** B1
Isabella Ho
13 Hammersmith
W6 . . . .**39** B1
8
Kennington SE11 . .**150** A2
Isabella Mews **11**
N1 . . . .**16** A2
Isabella Rd E9 . . . . .**17** B3
Isabella St SE1 . . .**122** A1
Isabel St SW9 . . . .**173** A4

Isambard Mews
E14 . . . .**42** B3
Isambard Pl SE16 . .**32** B1
Iseldon Ct N7 . . . . . .**14** A4
Isel Way **4** SE22 . . .**64** A2
Isis Cl SW15 . . . . . .**57** B3
Isis Ct W4 . . . .**45** A3
Isis Ho NW8 . . . . . .**89** C1
Isis St SW18 . . . . . .**71** B2
Islamia Prim & Girls
Sec Schs NW6 . . . .**23** B4
Islamic Coll for
Advanced Studies **2**
NW10 . . . .**9** A2
Island Gardens Sta
E14 . . . .**42** B1
Island Ho E14 . . . . .**27** B2
Island Rd SE16 . . . .**40** C2
Island Row E14 . . . .**33** B3
Islay Wlk **17** N1 . . . .**15** B2
Isleden Ho N1 . . . . .**86** C4
Isledon Rd N4, N7 . . .**5** C1
ISLE OF DOGS **42** B2
ISLINGTON **14** C2
Islington Arts & Media
Sch **11** N4 . . . .**5** B3
Islington Bsns Ctr
N1 . . . .**87** A4
Islington Est N1 . . . .**86** C4
Islington Gn N1 . . . .**86** A3
Islington High St
N1 . . . .**86** A2
Islington Mus **1**
N1 . . . .**96** A3
Islington Park Mews
1 N1 . . . .**15** A1
Islington Park St
N1 . . . .**15** A1
Islington Tennis Ctr
N7 . . . .**14** A2
Islip St NW5 . . . .**13** B3
Isokon Flats **3**
NW3 . . . .**12** B3
Issac Way SE1 . . . .**137** A4
Italia Conti Acad of
Theatre Arts EC1 . .**96** C1
IUC Languages Sch
W1 . . . .**104** B3
Ivanhoe Ho
11 Balham SW12 . .**73** A4
34 Bow E3 . . . .**26** A3
Ivanhoe Rd SE5 . . .**64** B4
Ivatt Pl W14 . . . . .**141** A1
Iveagh Cl E9 . . . . . .**25** C4
Iveagh Ct EC3 . . . .**110** C1
Iveagh Ho . . . .
2 Brixton SW9 . . . .**48** A1
Chelsea SW10 . . . .**157** A2
Ivebury Ct **8** W10 . .**30** B3
Iveley Rd SW4 . . . .**170** C1
Iver Ct N1 . . . .**15** B2
Iverna Ct W8 . . . . .**127** C2
Iverna Gdns W8 . . .**127** C2
Iverson Rd NW6 . . .**10** C2
Ives Rd E16 . . . .**35** A4
Ives St SW3 . . . . . .**144** B4
Ivimey St E2 . . . . . .**24** C2
Ivinghoe Ho **14** N7 . .**13** C3
Ivor Ct NW1 . . . .**90** C2
Ivor Mayor Lo
SW12 . . . .**60** C1
Ivor Pl NW1 . . . .**90** C1
Ivor St NW1 . . . .**13** B1
Ivory Ho
6 London W11 . . . .**59** B4

Ivory Ho continued
St George in East
E1 . . . .**125** A2
Ivory Sq **13** SW18 . .**59** B4
Ivybridge Ho **18**
SE22 . . . .**64** A4
Ivybridge La WC2 .**120** B3
Ivy Church La SE1, ...
SE17 . . . .**152** C2
Ivy Cres W4 . . . .**37** B2
Ivy Ct **17** SE16 . . . .**153** C1
Ivydale Prim Sch
SE15 . . . .**65** C3
Ivydale Rd SE15 . . .**65** C3
Ivyday Gr SW16 . . . .**74** B1
Ivy Lo W8 . . . .**31** C1 113 B2
Ivymount Rd SE27 . .**74** C1
Ivy Rd
Brockley SE4 . . . . . .**66** C3
Cricklewood NW2 . . . .**9** B4
Newham E16 . . . . . .**35** C3
Ivy St N1 . . . .**24** A3
Ixworth Pl SW3 . . .**144** A3

J

Jacaranda Gr E8 . . .**16** B1
Jackman Ho **24** . . . .
E1 . . . .**32** A1
Jackman St E8 . . . .**25** A4
Jackson Cl E9 . . . . .**17** C1
Jackson Ho **15**
SW11 . . . .**59** C4
Jackson Rd N7 . . . . .**14** B4
Jackson's La N6 . . . . .**4** A4
Jack Taylor Sch
NW8 . . . .**78** C4
Jack Tizard Sch
East Acton W3 . . . . .**29** C2
London W12 . . . .**30** A1
Jack Walker Ct
N5 . . . .**15** A4
Jacobin Lo N7 . . . . .**14** A3
Jacob Mans **15** E1 . .**32** A3
Jacobson Ct . . . .
SW11 . . . .**168** B3
Jacobson Ho E1 . .**110** C2
Jacob St SE1 . . . . .**139** B4
Jacob's Well Mews
W1 . . . .**103** C2
Jacotts Ho W10 . . . .**22** B1
Jacqueline Ho **8** . . . . .
E1 . . . .**32** C4
Jaggard Way
SW12 . . . .**72** C4
Jagger Ho SW11 . .**168** C4
Jago Wlk SE5 . . . . .**48** C3
Jamaica Rd
Bermondsey SE1 . .**139** A3
Bermondsey SE16 . .**40** A3
Jamaica St E1 . . . . .**32** B4
James Allen's Girls'
Sch (prep) **13**
SE22 . . . .**64** A2
James Allen's Girls'
Sch (pre-prep)
SE21 . . . .**63** C1
James Allen's Girls'
Sch (senior) **12**
SE22 . . . .**64** A2
James Anderson Ct **20**
E2 . . . .**24** A3
James Ave NW2 . . . . .**9** B3
James Brine Ho **6**
E2 . . . .**24** B2 99 A4

James Campbell Ho
2 E2 . . . .**25** B3
James Collins Cl
W9 . . . .**23** B1
James Docherty Ho
4 E2 . . . .**25** B3
James Hammett Ho
8 E2 . . . .**24** B3
James Ho
Mile End E1 . . . .**26** A1
33 Rotherhithe
SE16 . . . .**40** C4
James Joyce Wlk **7**
SE24 . . . .**63** A3
James Leicester Hall
of Residence N7 . . .**14** A2
James Lind Ho **6**
SE8 . . . .**41** B2
James Middleton Ho
2 E2 . . . .**25** A2
James Morgan Mews
N1 . . . .**87** A3
Jameson Ct **6** E2 . .**25** B3
Jameson Ho SE11 .**148** C2
Jameson Pl **11** W3 . .**37** B4
Jameson St
W8 . . . .**31** C1 113 C2
James's Cotts
TW9 . . . .**44** C3
James St
Marylebone W1 . . .**103** C1
Strand WC2 . . . . . .**120** B4
James Stewart Ho
NW6 . . . .**10** B1
James Stroud Ho
SE17 . . . .**151** A1
Jamestown Rd
NW1 . . . .**82** A4
Jamestown Way
E14 . . . .**34** C2
James Voller Way **30**
E1 . . . .**32** B3
James Wolfe Prim
Sch **18** SE10 . . . . .**52** B3
Jamuna Cl E14 . . . .**33** A4
Jane St E1 . . . .**32** A3
Janet St E14 . . . . . .**41** C3
Janeway Pl **2**
SE16 . . . .**40** A4
Janeway St SE16 . .**139** C3
Jansen Ho **5**
SW15 . . . .**56** C2
Jansen Wlk SW11 . .**59** C3
Japan Cres N4 . . . . . .**5** B3
Jardine Rd E1 . . . . .**32** C2
Jarmen Ho . . . .
Bermondsey SE16 . .**40** C2
16 Stepney E1 . . . . .**32** B4
Jarrett Cl SW2 . . . . .**75** A3
Jarrow Rd SE16 . . . .**40** B1
Jarrow Way E9 . . . . .**18** A4
Jarvis Ho **3** SE15 . .**49** C2
Jarvis Rd SE22 . . . . .**64** A3
Jasmin SE14 . . . . . .**50** B3
Jasmine Sq **15** E3 . .**26** B4
Jasmin Ho SE14 . . . .**66** B4
Jasmin Lo **10** SE16 .**40** A1
Jason Ct
2 London SW9 . . . .**173** B4
Marylebone W1 . . .**103** C2
Jasper Wlk N1 . . . . .**97** B4
Java Wharf SE1 . . .**139** A4
Jay Ho SW15 . . . . . .**47** B1
Jay Mews SW7 . . . .**129** A3
Jean Darling Ho
SW10 . . . .**157** B3

Jean Pardies Ho 23
E1 ....32 B4
Jebb Ave SW2 ....62 A1
Jebb St E3 ....26 C3
Jedburgh St SW11 ..60 C3
Jeddo Mews W12 ...38 B4
Jeddo Rd W12 ....38 B4
Jefferson Bldg 3
E14 ....41 C4
Jeffrey's Ct 2
SW4 ....172 A2
Jeffrey's Pl NW1 ...13 B2
Jeffrey's Rd SW4 ..172 A2
Jeffrey's St NW1 ....13 B1
Jeger Ave E2 ....24 B4
Jelf Rd SW2 ....62 C2
Jellicoe Ho
3 Bethnal Green
E2 ....24 C3
Fitzrovia NW1 ....92 B1
11 Putney SW15 ....57 C2
Jemotts Ct 9
SE14 ....50 C4
Jenkins Ho SW8 ....171 B4
Jenkinson Ho 12
E2 ....25 B2
Jenner Ave W3 ....28 C4
Jenner Ho SE3 ....53 A4
Jenner Pl SW13 ....47 A4
Jenner Rd N16 ....7 B1
Jennifer Ho SE11 ...149 C3
Jennings Ho SE10 ...42 C1
Jennings Rd SE22 ...64 B1
Jensen Ho 10 E13 ....27 C1
Jephson Ct 17
SW4 ....172 B1
Jephson Ho 6
SE17 ....48 A4
Jephson St SE5 ....48 C2
Jephtha Rd SW18 ...58 C1
Jerdan Pl SW6 ......155 B2
Jeremiah St 11
E14 ....34 A3
Jeremy Bentham Ho
E2 ....24 C2 99 C3
Jermyn St SW1 .....119 A2
Jerningham Ct
SE14 ....51 A2
Jerningham Rd
SE14 ....51 A2
Jerome Cres NW8 ..90 A2
Jerome Ho NW1 ...102 B4
Jerome St
E1 ....24 B1 98 C1
Jerome Twr 5
W3 ....37 A4
Jerrard St SE13 ....67 A4
Jerrold Lo SW15 .....57 B4
Jerrold St 24 N1 .....24 A3
Jersey Ho 15 N1 .....15 B2
Jersey Rd N1 ....15 B2
Jersey St E2 ....25 A2
Jerusalem Pas
EC1 ....96 A1
Jervis Bay Ho 9
E14 ....34 C3
Jervis Ct
2 Greenwich
SE10 ....52 B2
Marylebone W1 ......104 B1
Jervis Rd SW6 ......155 A3
Jessel Ho
St Pancras WC1
Westminster SW1 ...147 C4
Jessica Rd SW18 ....59 B2

Jessie Blythe La 4
N19 ....5 A4
Jessie Duffett Ho 11
SE5 ....48 B3
Jesson Ho SE17 ....151 B3
Jessop Ct N1 ....86 B1
Jessop Ho 10 W4 ....38 A2
Jessop Prim Sch 26
SE24 ....63 A3
Jessop Sq E14 ....33 C1
Jeston Ho 10 SE27 ...75 A1
Jethou Ho 10 N1 ......15 B2
Jevons Ho 5
NW8 ....11 C1
Jewell Ho 8
SW12 ....73 B4
Jewel Tower ★ SW1 134 A2
Jewish Mus ★ NW1 ..82 B3
Jewry St EC3 ....110 C1
Jews Row SW18 .....59 B3
Jeymer Ave NW2 .....9 B3
Jeypore Rd SW18 ...59 B1
Jim Griffiths Ho
SW6 ....155 A3
Jim Veal Dr 3
N7 ....14 A2
Joanna Ho 7 W6 .....39 B1
Joan St SE1 ....122 A1
Jocelin Ho N1 ....85 A3
Jocelyn Rd TW9 ......54 A4
Jocelyn St SE15 ......49 C2
Jockey's Fields
WC1 ....107 A4
Jodane Rd SE8 ....41 B2
Jodrell Rd E3 ....18 B1
Johanna St SE1 .....135 B3
John Adam St
WC2 ....120 B3
John Aird Ct W2 ....101 A4
John Archer Way
SW18 ....59 C1
John Ashby Cl
SW2 ....62 A1
John Ball Prim Sch
SE3 ....53 A1
John Barker Ct
NW6 ....10 A1
John Betts' Ho
W12 ....38 C3
John Betts Prim Sch
W6 ....39 A3
John Bond Ho 2
E3 ....26 B3
John Brent Ho 8
SE8 ....40 C2
John Buck Ho
NW10 ....21 B4
John Burns Prim Sch
17 SW11 ....169 C1
John Campbell Rd 28
N16 ....16 A3
John Carpenter St
EC4 ....122 A4 123 A4
John Cartwright Ho
7 E2 ....25 A2
John Clynes Ct
SW15 ....57 A4
John Conwey Ho 23
SW2 ....62 C1
John Dee Ho 3
SW14 ....55 C4
John Donne Prim Sch
SE15 ....50 A2
John Dwight Ho
W6 ....39 A4

John Fearon Wlk 5
W10 ....23 A2
John Felton Rd 10
SE16 ....139 B3
John Fielden Ho 10
E2 ....25 A2
John Fisher St E1 ..125 B4
6 E15 ....27 C4
John Harris Ho
SE15 ....64 C4
John Harrison Way
SE10 ....43 B3
John Islip St SW1 ..148 A3
John Keall Ho 8
SW15 ....57 C4
John Keble CE Prim
Sch NW10 ....21 B4
John Kennedy Ct 1
N1 ....15 C2
John Kennedy Ho 1
SE16 ....40 C2
John Kennedy Lo 2
N1 ....15 C2
John King Ct
N19 ....5 A2
John Kirk Ho
21 Battersea
SW11 ....59 C4
5 Streatham
SW16 ....74 A1
John Knight Lo
SW6 ....155 C2
John McDonald Ho 3
E14 ....42 B3
John McKenna Wlk 17
SE16 ....139 C2
John Maurice Cl
SE17 ....151 B4
John Nettleford Ho 14
E2 ....25 A2
John Orwell Sports
Ctr E1 ....32 A1
John Parker Sq 7
SW11 ....59 C4
John Parry Ct 28
N1 ....24 A3
John Penn Ho SE8 ..51 B3
John Penn St
SE13 ....52 A2
John Perryn Prim Sch
W3 ....29 A3
John Prince's St
W1 ....104 B2
John Pritchard Ho 24
E1 ....24 C1 99 C1
John Ratcliffe Ho 8
NW6 ....23 C2
John Rennie Wlk 1
E1 ....32 B1
John Roan Sch
SE3 ....53 A3
John Roll Way
SE16 ....139 C2
John Ruskin Prim Sch
SE5 ....48 B4
John Ruskin St
SE5 ....48 B4
John Scurr Ho 18
E14 ....33 A3
John Scurr Prim Sch
E1 ....25 B1
John Silkin La SE8 ..40 C1
John's Mews WC1 ...95 A1

John Smith Ave
SW6 ....154 C2
John Smith Mews
E14 ....34 C2
Johnson Cl E8 ....24 C4
Johnson Ho
1 SW1 ....59 C3
Belgravia SW1 ......145 C3
23 Bethnal Green
E2 ....24 C2 99 C3
Somers Town NW1 ...83 A1
South Lambeth
SW8 ....161 C1
Johnson Lo 19 W9 ..31 C4
Johnson Rd NW10 ...20 C4
Johnsons Ct EC4 ...107 C1
Johnson's Pl SW1 ..146 C1
Johnson St E1 ....32 B3
Johnsons Way
NW10 ....20 A1
John Spencer Sq
N1 ....15 A2
John's Pl E1 ....32 A3
John St WC1 ....95 A1
John Stainer Com
Prim Sch SE4 ....66 A4
Johnston Cl SW9 ..173 A3
Johnstone Ho
SE13 ....67 C4
John Strachey Ho
SW6 ....155 A3
John Trundle Ct
EC2 ....108 C4
John Tucker Ho 8
E14 ....41 C3
John Wesley's House
& Mus of Methodism
EC1 ....97 C2
John Wheatley Ho
14 London N19 ......4 C4
West Brompton
SW6 ....155 A3
John Williams Cl
SE14 ....50 C4
Joiners Arms Yd 12
SE5 ....48 C2
Joiner St SE1 ....123 C1
Joiners Yd N1 ....84 B1
Jolles Ho 9 E3 ....27 A2
Jonathan Ct 9
W4 ....38 A2
Jonathan St SE11 ..148 C2
Jones Ho
4 South Bromley
E14 ....34 C3
Stamford Hill N16 .....7 A3
Jones St W1 ....118 A3
Jones Wlk 6
TW10 ....54 B1
Jonson Ho
Borough The SE1 ..137 C1
18 Canonbury N16 ..15 C4
Jordan Ct SW15 .....57 C3
Jordan Ho
12 London SE4 ......65 C3
Shoreditch N1 ....87 C3
Jordans Ho NW8 ....90 A1
Joscoyne Ho 5
E1 ....32 A3
Joseph Ave W3 ....28 C3
Joseph Conrad Ho
SW1 ....147 A3
Joseph Ct N16 ....7 A4
Joseph Hardcastle Cl
SE14 ....50 C3

Josephine Ave
SW2 ....62 B2
Joseph Irwin Ho 7
E14 ....33 B2
Joseph Mews
Islington N7 ....14 C2
Kennington SE15 ....65 C2
Joseph Powell Cl 1
SW12 ....61 B1
Joseph Priestley Ho
12 E2 ....25 A2
Joseph St E3 ....26 B1
Joseph Trotter Cl
EC1 ....95 C3
Joshua St E14 ....34 B3
Joslings Cl W12 ......29 C2
Josseline Ct 3 E3 ...26 A3
Joubert Mans
SW3 ....144 B2
Joubert St SW11 ...169 A2
Jowett Ho 27
SW9 ....172 B1
Jowitt Ho 27
SE14 ....51 A3
Jubet Ho 8 N16 ......15 C4
Jubilee Bldgs NW8 ..79 B1
Jubilee Cl 4
NW10 ....21 B1
Jubilee Cres E14 ....42 B3
Jubilee Ct N1 ....84 B1
Jubilee Ho SE11 ....149 C3
Jubilee Hts NW2 ....10 B2
Jubilee Mans 10
E1 ....32 B3
Jubilee Market
WC2 ....120 B4
Jubilee Pl SW3 .....144 B2
Jubilee Prim Sch
SE14 ....51 A3
Jubilee Sch N16 ......7 C3
Jubilee St E1 ....32 B4
Jubilee The 2
SE10 ....52 A3
Jubilee Yd SE1 .....138 C4
Judd St WC1 ....94 A3
Jude St E16 ....35 B3
Judges' Wlk NW3 .....2 B1
Julia St NW1 ....158 B1
Julian Ave W3 ....28 A2
Julian Ct SW13 ......46 B2
Julian Pl E14 ....42 A1
Julia St NW5 ....12 C3
Juliet Ho 1 N1 ....24 A3
Julius Ct TW8 ....44 A3
Julius Ho 3 E14 .....34 C3
Julius Nyerere Cl
N1 ....84 C3
Junction App
Battersea SW11 ......60 A4
Lewisham SE13 ......67 B1
Junction Mews
W2 ....102 A2
Junction Pl W2 .....101 C2
Junction Rd N19 ....4 B1
Juniper Cres NW1 ..12 C1
Juniper Ct N16 ....6 C2
Juniper Dr SW18 ....59 B3
Juniper Ho
6 Peckham SE14,
SE15 ....50 B3
9 Richmond TW9 .....45 A2
Juno Ct 11 SW9 ....163 B1
Juno Ho 2 E3 ....26 C4
Juno Way SE14 ......50 C4

Juno Way Ind Est
SE14 . . . . .50 C4
Jupiter Ct 16
SW9 . . . . 163 B1
Jupiter Way N7 . . . . .14 B2
Jupp Rd E15 . . . . . . .19 C1
Jupp Rd W E15 . . . . .27 C4
Jura Ho SE16 . . . . . .41 A2
Jurston Ct SE1 . . . . 135 C3
Justice Wlk SW3 . . 158 A3
Justines Pl E2 . . . . . .25 C2
Jutland Cl N19 . . . . . .5 A3
Jutland Ho 4 SE5 . . .48 B1
Juxon St SE11 . . . . 149 A4

K

Kambala Rd SW11 . .59 C4
Kara Way NW2 . . . . . .9 C4
Karen Ct
 2 Camberwell
 SE5 . . . . .64 A4
 Forest Hill SE23 . . . .66 A1
Karen Ho 7 N16 . . . .15 C4
Kasmin Ct NW10 . . . .8 C1
Kassala Rd SW11 169 A3
Katherine Cl 3
SE16 . . . . .32 C1
Katherine Ho
W10 . . . . .23 A1
Katherine Sq
W11 . . . 31 A1 112 A2
Kathleen Ave W3 . . .28 B4
Kathleen Rd SW11 . .60 B4
Kayani Ave N4 . . . . . .6 B3
Kay Ho SW9 . . . . . . 172 C1
Kay St E2 . . . . .24 C3
Kean Ho 6 SE7 . . . .48 A4
Kean St WC2 . . . . . 106 C1
Keates Est N16 . . . . . .7 B2
Keats Cl
 Bermondsey SE1 . . 152 C3
 Hampstead NW3 . . . .12 A4
Keats Gr NW3 . . . . . .12 A4
Keats Ho
 22 Bethnal Green
 E2 . . . . .25 B2
 30 Camberwell SE5 . .48 C3
 Chelsea SW1 . . . . . 161 A4
Keats House (Mus)
NW3 . . . . .12 A4
Keats Pl EC2 . . . . . 109 B3
Keble Ho 4 SW15 . .57 C1
Keble Pl SW13 . . . . . .47 A4
Kedelston Ct E5 . . . .18 A4
Kedge Ho 16 E14 . . .41 C3
Kedleston Wlk 21
E2 . . . . .25 A2
Keel Cl SE16 . . . . . . .32 C1
Keel Ct 8 E14 . . . . . .34 C2
Keeley St WC2 . . . . 106 C1
Keeling Ho 4 E2 . . . .25 A3
Keelson Ho 9
E14 . . . . .41 C3
Keen's Yd N1 . . . . . .15 A2
Keeper Wharf E1 . . .32 C2
Keepier Wharf 18
E1 . . . . .32 C2
Keep The SE3 . . . . . . .53 C1
Keeton's Rd SE16 . . .40 A3
Keevil Dr SW19 . . . . .70 A4
Keighley Cl N7 . . . . .14 A4
Keildon Rd SW11 . . .60 B3

Keir Hardie Ho
 Fulham W6 . . . . .47 C4
 18 Upper Holloway
 N19 . . . . .4 C4
 Willesden NW10 . . . .22 C2
Keir Hardy Prim Sch
E16 . . . . .35 C4
Keith Connor Cl 5
SW8 . . . . .61 A4
Keith Gr W12 . . . . . .29 C1
Keith Ho NW6 . . . . . .78 A1
Kelby Ho N7 . . . . . . .14 B2
Kelfield Ct 1 W10 . .30 C3
Kelfield Gdns W10 . .30 C3
Kelfield Mews
W10 . . . . .30 C3
Kellett Ho N1 . . . . . .87 C3
Kellett Rd SW2 . . . .62 C3
Kellow Ho SE1 . . . . 137 B4
Kell St SE1 . . . . 136 B2
Kelly Ave SE15 . . . . .49 B2
Kelly Ct 18 E14 . . . . .33 C2
Kelly Mews 4 W9 . .23 B1
Kelly St NW1 . . . . . .13 A2
Kelman Cl SW4 . . . . 171 C1
Kelmore Gr SE22 . . .64 C3
Kelmscott Gdns
W12 . . . . .38 C3
Kelmscott House
W6 . . . . .39 A1
Kelmscott Rd
SW11 . . . . .60 B2
Kelross Rd N5 . . . . . .15 B4
Kelsall Mews TW9 . .45 A2
Kelsey St E2 . . . . . . .24 C1
Kelshall Ct N4 . . . . . . .6 B2
Kelso Ho E14 . . . . . . .42 B3
Kelso Pl W8 . . . . . . 128 B2
Kelvedon Ho SW8 172 B4
Kelvedon Rd SW6 155 A1
Kelvin Ct
 Chiswick W4 . . . . . . .45 B3
Kelvin Rd N5 . . . . . . .15 A4
Kelvington Rd
SE15 . . . . .65 C2
Kelvin Rd N5 . . . . . .15 B4
Kelyway Ho 20
SW2 . . . . .74 C4
Kember St N1 . . . . . .14 B1
Kemble Ho SW9 . . . .63 A4
Kemble St WC2 . . . 106 C1
Kemerton Rd SE5 . . .63 B4
Kemey's St E9 . . . . .18 A3
Kemp Ct SW8 . . . . . 162 A1
Kemp Ho SE1 . . . . . 137 C1
Kemp Ho NW6 . . . . .22 C3
Kemp Ho
 Finsbury EC1 . . . . . . .97 B3
 1 Globe Town E2 . . .25 C3
Kempis Way 5
SE22 . . . . .64 A2
Kemplay Rd NW3 . . .11 C4
Kemp's Ct W1 . . . . . 105 B1
Kemps Dr E14 . . . . . .33 C2
Kempsford Gdns
SW5 . . . . 141 C1
Kempsford Rd
 Lambeth SE11 . . . . 149 C3
 Newington SE11 . . . 150 A3
Kemps Gdns SE13 . .67 B2
Kempson Rd SW6 . 155 C1
Kempthorne Rd
SE8 . . . . .41 B2
Kempton Ct E1 . . . . .32 A4

Kempton Ho 13
N1 . . . . .24 A4
Kemsing Ho SE1 . . 137 C3
Kemsing Rd SE10 . .43 C1
Kemsley SE13 . . . . . .67 A2
Kenbrook Ho
 Kensington W14 . . . 127 A1
 4 Kentish Town
 NW5 . . . . .13 B3
Kenbury Gdns 1
SE5 . . . . .48 B1
Kenbury Mans 18
SE5 . . . . .48 B1
Kenbury St SE5 . . . . .48 B1
Kenchester Cl
SW8 . . . . 162 B1
Kendal NW1 . . . . . . .92 B4
Kendal Ave W3 . . . . .28 A4
Kendal Cl SE5 . . . . . .49 A3
Kendal Ct NW2 . . . . .10 A3
Kendal Ho
 9 Hackney E9 . . . . . .17 B1
 Islington N1 . . . . . . .85 A2
Kendall Ct 3
SE22 . . . . .64 C2
Kendall Pl W1 . . . . . 103 B3
Kendall Pl SW15 . . . .58 B2
Kendal Rd NW10 . . . . .8 C4
Kendal St W2 . . . . . 102 B1
Kendal Stps W2 . . . 102 B1
Kender Prim Sch
 7 Deptford SE14 . . .50 B2
 London SE14 . . . . . . .50 B2
Kender St SE14 . . . . .50 B2
Kendoa Rd 1
SW4 . . . . .61 C3
Kendon Ho E15 . . . . .19 C1
Kendrick Ct 12
SE15 . . . . .50 A2
Kendrick Mews
SW7 . . . . 143 B3
Kendrick Pl SW7 . . 143 B3
Keniford Rd
SW12 . . . . .73 A4
Kenilworth Ct
SW6 . . . . .58 A4
Kenilworth Rd
 Bow E3 . . . . .26 A3
 Kilburn NW6 . . . . . . .23 B4
Kenley Wlk
W11 . . . 31 A2 112 A3
Kenmont Prim Sch
NW10 . . . . .22 A2
Kenmore Ct TW9 . . .44 C3
Kenmure Rd N16 . . . .10 C1
Kenmure Yd E8 . . . . .17 A3
Kennacraig Cl 6
E16 . . . . .35 C1
Kennard Ho 12
SW11 . . . . 169 C3
Kennard Rd E15 . . . .19 C1
Kennard St 9
SW11 . . . . 169 B3
Kennedy Cox Ho 9
E16 . . . . .35 B4
Kennedy Ho SE11 . 148 C2
Kennedy Wlk
SE17 . . . . 151 C3
Kennet Cl SW11 . . . .59 C3
Kennet Ct 27 W2 . . .31 C4
Kenneth Campbell Ho
NW8 . . . . .89 C2
Kenneth Cres NW2 . .9 A3

Kenneth Ct SE11 . . 149 C4
Kennet Ho NW8 . . . .89 C1
Kenneth Younger Ho
SW6 . . . . 155 A3
Kennet Rd W9 . . . . . .23 B1
Kennet St E1 . . . . . 125 C2
Kennett Wharf La
EC4 . . . . 123 A4
Kenning Ho 6 N1 . .24 A4
Kenning St 18
SE16 . . . . .40 B4
Kennings Way
SE11 . . . . 149 C2
KENNINGTON 149 B1
Kennington Ent Ctr
SE17 . . . . 150 A1
Kennington La
SE11 . . . . 149 A1
Kennington Oval
SE11 . . . . 163 A3
Kennington Palace Ct
SE11 . . . . 149 B2
Kennington Park Bsns
Ctr SW9 . . . . 163 C2
Kennington Park
Gdns SE17 . . . . .48 A4
Kennington Park Ho
SE11 . . . . 149 C1
Kennington Park Pl
SE11 . . . . 149 C1
Kennington Park Rd
SE11 . . . . 149 C1
Kennington Rd
SE11 . . . . 149 B3
Kennington Sta
SE17 . . . . 150 A2
Kennlodes SE21 . . . .75 C2
Kenrick Pl W1 . . . . . 103 B3
KENSAL GREEN 22 B2
Kensal Green Cemy
 (All Souls) NW10 . .22 B2
Kensal Green Sta
NW10 . . . . .22 B2
Kensal Ho W10 . . . . .22 C1
Kensal Rd W10 . . . . .23 C1
KENSAL RISE 22 B3
Kensal Rise Prim Sch
NW6 . . . . .22 C3
Kensal Rise Sta
NW10 . . . . .22 C3
KENSAL TOWN 23 A1
KENSINGTON 127 C3
Kensington Aldridge
Acad 22 W11 . . . . .30 C3
Kensington & Chelsea
Coll
 Chelsea SW10 . . . . 156 C2
 14 Kensal Town
 W10 . . . . .31 A4
Kensington Church Ct
W8 . . . . 128 A3
Kensington Church St
W8 . . . . . 31 C1 113 C1
Kensington Church
Wlk W8 . . . . 128 A3
Kensington Court
Mans W8 . . . . 128 B3
Kensington Court
Mews W8 . . . . 128 B3
Kensington Court Pl
W8 . . . . 128 B2
Kensington Ct
W8 . . . . 128 B3
Kensington Ct Gdns
W8 . . . . 128 B2

Kensington Gardens
W2 . . . . 115 A1
Kensington Gate
W8 . . . . 128 C2
Kensington Gdns Sq
W2 . . . . 100 A1
Kensington Gore
SW7 . . . . 129 B3
Kensington Hall Gdns
W14 . . . . 140 C2
Kensington High St
W8 . . . . 127 C2
Kensington Ho 3
NW5 . . . . .13 B3
Kensington Hts
W8 . . . . . 31 C1 113 B1
Kensington L Ctr
W11 . . . 31 A2 112 A4
Kensington Mall
W8 . . . . . 31 C1 113 C2
Kensington Mans
SW5 . . . . 141 C2
Kensington Olympia
Sta W14 . . . . 126 A2
Kensington Pal
W8 . . . . 114 B1
Kensington Palace
Gdns W8 . . . . 114 A2
Kensington Park Gdns
W11 . . . 31 B2 113 A3
Kensington Park
Mews W11 . . . . .31 B3
Kensington Park Rd
W11 . . . 31 B2 113 A4
Kensington Pl
W8 . . . . . 31 C1 113 B2
Kensington Prep Sch
SW6 . . . . 165 A4
Kensington Rd
SW7 . . . . 129 A3
Kensington Sq
W8 . . . . 128 A3
Kensington Village
W14 . . . . 141 A3
Kensington W
W14 . . . . 140 A4
Kensworth Ho EC1 . .97 C3
Kent Ct 3 E2 . . . . . .24 B3
Kent Ho
 Camberwell SE1 . . . 153 A1
 13 Chiswick W4 . . . .38 A1
 Marylebone W1 . . . 104 C2
 Pimlico SW1 . . . . . . 147 B1
 Richmond TW10 . . . .54 C2
Kentish Bldgs
SE1 . . . . 123 B1
KENTISH TOWN 13 B3
Kentish Town CE Prim
Sch 13 NW5 . . . . . .13 B3
Kentish Town City
Farm NW5 . . . . .12 C3
Kentish Town Rd
NW1 . . . . .13 A2
Kentish Town Sp Ctr
NW5 . . . . .13 A2
Kentish Town Sta
NW5 . . . . .13 B3
Kentish Town West
Sta NW5 . . . . .13 A2
Kent Lo 10 SW19 . . .69 C3
Kentmere Ho SE15 . .50 B4
Kenton Ct W14 . . . . 126 C1
Kenton Ho
 20 Globe Town
 E1 . . . . .25 B1
 Highbury N5 . . . . . . .15 A3

Kenton Rd E9 . . . . 17 C2
Kenton St WC1 . . . . . 94 A2
Kent Pas NW1 . . . . . 90 C2
Kent Pk Ind Est
SE15 . . . . 50 A4
Kent Rd
Richmond TW9 . . . . 44 C3
South Acton W4 . . . 37 B3
Kent St E2 . . . . 24 B3
Kent Terr NW1 . . . . . 90 B3
Kentwell CI SE4 . . . . 66 A3
Kentwood Gn
SE13 . . . . 46 C3
Kent Yard SW7 . . . . 130 B3
Kenway Rd SW5 . . . 142 A3
Ken Wilson Ho 19
E2 . . . . 24 C3
Kenwood CI NW3 . . . 2 C3
Kenwood Ho 15
SW9 . . . . 63 A3
Kenwood Ho NW3 . . . 3 A3
Kenworthy Rd E9 . . 18 A2
Kenrick Ho 1 . . . . . . 85 A3
Kenwyn Rd SW4 . . . 61 C3
Kenyon St SE5 . . . 48 B3
Kenyon Ho SE5 . . . 48 B3
Kenyon St SW6 . . . . 47 C2
Kepler Ho 9 SE10 . . 43 B1
Kepler Rd SW2,
SW4 . . . . 62 A3
Keppel Ho
Brompton SW3 . . . . 144 A3
5 Deptford SE8 . . . . 41 B1
Keppel Row SE1 . . 122 C1
Keppel St WC1 . . . 105 C4
Kerbela St 3
E2 . . . . C4 99 B2
Kerbey St E14 . . . . . 34 A3
Kerfield Cres SE5 . . 48 C2
Kerfield Pl SE5 . . . . 48 C2
Kerin Ho E15 . . . . . 19 A3
Kerridge Ct 10 N1 . . 24 A4
Kerrier Ho SW10 . . 157 A1
Kerrington Ct 7
W12 . . . . 39 B4
Kerrison Rd
Battersea SW11 . . . . 60 A4
Mill Meads E15 . . . . 27 C4
Kerry N7 . . . . 14 A2
Kerry Ho 5 N1 . . . . 32 B3
Kerry Path SE8 . . . . 51 B4
Kerry Rd SE8 . . . . . 51 B4
Kerscott Ho 10 E3 . . 27 A2
Kersfield Ho SW15 . . 57 C1
Kersfield Rd SW15 . . 57 C1
Kershaw CI SW18 . . . 59 C1
Kershaw Ho 7
SE27 . . . . 75 A1
Kersley Mews
SW11 . . . . 168 C3
Kersley Rd N16 . . . . 7 A1
Kersley St SW11 . . . 168 C2
Kerwick CI 1 N7 . . . 14 B1
Keslake Mans
NW10 . . . . 22 C3
Keslake Rd NW6 . . . 22 C3
Keston Ho SE17 . . . 152 B2
Keston Rd SE15 . . . . 64 C4
Kestrel Ave SE24 . . . 63 B2
Kestrel Ho
4 Battersea
SW11 . . . . 60 A4
Finsbury EC1 . . . . . 96 C4
Kestrel Pl SE14 . . . . 51 A4
Keswick Broadway 1
SW15 . . . . 58 B2

Keswick Ct 2
SE22 . . . . 64 C2
Keswick Ho 8
SE5 . . . . 48 B2
Keswick Hts 9
SW15 . . . . 58 A2
Keswick Lo E8 . . . . . 16 B2
Keswick Rd SW15 . . 58 A2
Kett Gdns SW2 . . . . 62 B2
Kettleby Ho NW9 . . 63 A4
Ketton Ho 10 W11 . . 22 B1
Kevan Ho SE5 . . . . . 48 B3
KEW 44 C4
Kew Bridge TW8 . . . 36 B1
Kew Bridge Ct 4 W6 36 C1
Kew Bridge
Distribution Ctr
TW8 . . . . 36 B1
Kew Bridge Rd
TW8 . . . . 36 B1
Kew Bridge Sta
TW8 . . . . 36 B1
Kew Coll TW9 . . . . . 44 C3
Kew Foot Rd TW9 . . 54 A4
Kew Gardens Rd
TW9 . . . . 44 C2
Kew Gardens (Royal
Botanic) TW9 . . . . . 44 A2
Kew Gardens Sta
TW9 . . . . 44 C2
Kew Gn TW9 . . . . . . 44 B4
Kew Green TW9 . . . . 44 B4
Kew Green Prep Sch
TW9 . . . . 44 B4
Kew Lo 11 TW9 . . . . 44 B2
Kew Pal TW9 . . . . . . 44 A3
Kew Pier TW9 . . . . . 44 C4
Kew Rd TW9 . . . . . . 44 B2
Kew Ret Pk TW9 . . . 45 A2
Kew Riverside Prim
Sch TW9 . . . . 45 A1
Key CI E1 . . . . 25 A1
Keyes Ct SE22 . . . . . 64 C2
Keyes Rd NW2 . . . . . 9 C3
Keyham Ho 10 W2 . . 31 C4
Key Ho 9 SE11 . . . . 163 B4
Keymer Rd SW2 . . . . 74 B2
Keynsham Ho 2
N4 . . . . 6 B4
Keystone Cres N1 . . 84 C1
Keyworth Cl E5 . . . . 18 A4
Keyworth Pl SE1 . . 136 B2
Keyworth Prim Sch
SE17 . . . . 150 A2
Keyworth St SE1 . . 136 B2
Kezia St SE8 . . . . . . 41 A1
Khyber Rd SW11 . . 168 A1
Kia Oval The (Surrey
Cnty Crkt Club)
SE11 . . . . 163 A4
Kibworth St SW8 . . 162 C1
Kidbrooke Gdns
SE3 . . . . 53 C1
Kidderpore Ave
NW3 . . . . 10 C4
Kidderpore Gdns
NW3 . . . . 10 C4
Kiffen St EC2 . . . . . . 97 C2
Kilbrennan Ho 9
E14 . . . . 34 B3
KILBURN 23 C4
Kilburn Bridge 14
NW6 . . . . 23 C4
Kilburn Gate NW6 . . 78 A2
Kilburn High Rd
NW6 . . . . 23 C4

Kilburn High Road Sta
NW6 . . . . 78 A3
Kilburn Ho 11 W9 . . 23 B2
Kilburn La W10 . . . . 23 A3
Kilburn Park Rd
NW6 . . . . 23 C2
Kilburn Park Sch The
10 NW6 . . . . 23 B3
Kilburn Park Sta
NW6 . . . . 23 C3
Kilburn Pl NW6 . . . . 23 C4
Kilburn Priory
NW6 . . . . 78 A3
Kilburn Sq NW6 . . . . 23 C4
Kilburn Sta NW2 . . . 10 B2
Kilburn Vale NW6 . . 78 A3
Kilburn Vale Est 1
NW6 . . . . 78 A3
Kilby Ct SE10 . . . . . 43 B3
Kildare Gdns W2 . . . 31 C3
Kildare Rd E16 . . . . 35 C4
Kildare Terr W2 . . . . 31 C3
Kildare Wlk E14 . . . 33 C3
Kildoran Rd SW2 . . . 62 A2
Kilgour Rd SE23 . . . 66 A1
Kilkie St SW6 . . . . 166 C1
Killarney Rd SW18 . . 59 B1
Killick St N1 . . . . . . 84 C1
Killieser Ave SW2 . . 74 A2
Killip Cl E16 . . . . . . 35 B3
Killoran Ho 8 E14 . . 42 B3
Killowen Rd E9 . . . . 17 C2
Killyon Rd SW8 . . . 171 B1
Kilmaine Rd SW6 . . 154 B1
Kilmarsh Rd W6 . . . 39 B2
Kilmington Rd
SW13 . . . . 46 C4
Kilmore Ho 17 E14 . . 34 A3
Kilmuir Ho SW1 . . . 145 C3
Kiln Ct E14 . . . . 33 B2
Kilner Ho 3 SE11 . . 163 B4
Kilner St E14 . . . . . 33 C4
Kiln Pl NW5 . . . . . . 12 C3
Kiloh Ct 1 SW11 . . . 60 A4
Kilpatrick Ct N16 . . . 7 B3
Kilpeck Ho 8 N4 . . . . 6 B4
Kilravock St W10 . . . 23 A2
Kilronan 5 W3 . . . . . 28 C3
Kimbell Gdns
SW6 . . . . 164 A3
Kimber Ctr The
SW18 . . . . 70 C4
Kimberley Ave
SE15 . . . . 65 B4
Kimberley Ct NW6 . . 23 A4
Kimberley Ho 6
E14 . . . . 42 B3
Kimberley Rd
Kilburn NW6 . . . . . . 23 A4
Stockwell SW9 . . . . 62 A4
Kimber Rd SW18 . . . 71 A4
Kimble Ho
Lisson Gr NW8 . . . . 90 B2
1 Lower Holloway
N7 . . . . 14 A3
Kimbolton Row
SW3 . . . . 144 A3
Kimpton Ct 12 SE5 . . 48 C2
Kimpton Ho SW15 . . 68 C4
Kimpton Rd SE5 . . . 48 C2
Kinburn St SE16 . . . 40 C4
Kincaid Rd SE15 . . . 50 A3
Kincardine Gdns
W9 . . . . 23 C1

Kindell Ho 4
SW14 . . . . 55 C4
Kinder Ho N1 . . . . . . 87 C2
Kindersley Ho 38
SE1 . . . . 111 C1
Kinefold Ho N7 . . . . 14 A2
Kinfauns Rd SW2 . . 74 C2
King Alfred Sch
NW11 . . . . 1 C3
King Arthur Cl
SE15 . . . . 50 B3
King Charles Ct 16
SE17 . . . . 48 A4
King Charles Ho
SW6 . . . . 156 B2
King Charles St
SW1 . . . . 134 A4
King Charles Terr 11
E1 . . . . 32 A2
King Charles Wlk 6
SW19 . . . . 70 A3
King David La E1 . . . 32 B2
Kingdom St W2 . . . 100 C3
Kingdon Ho 8
E14 . . . . 42 B3
Kingdon Rd NW6 . . . 10 C2
Kingdown Cl W10 . . 30 C3
King Edward Mans 2
E8 . . . . 25 A4
King Edward Mews
SW13 . . . . 46 C2
King Edwards Mans
SW6 . . . . 155 B1
King Edward's Rd
E9 . . . . 25 B4
King Edward St
EC1 . . . . 108 C2
King Edward The
Third Mews 17
SE16 . . . . 40 A4
King Edward VII's
Hospl W1 . . . . 103 C4
King Edward Wlk
SE1 . . . . 135 C2
King Fahed Acad The
W3 . . . . 29 B2
Kingfield St E14 . . . 42 B2
Kingfisher Ct
11 Battersea
SW11 . . . . 60 A4
17 Cubitt Town E14 . . 42 B4
Putney SW19 . . . . . 70 A2
Kingfisher Ho
4 Battersea
SW18 . . . . 59 B4
Peckham SE15 . . . . 49 B2
West Kensington
W14 . . . . 126 C2
Kingfisher Mews
SE13 . . . . 67 A2
Kingfisher Sq 4
SE8 . . . . 51 B4
King Frederik IX Twr
SE16 . . . . 41 B3
King George Sq
TW10 . . . . 54 B1
King George St
SE10 . . . . 52 B3
Kingham Cl
1 Shepherd's Bush
W11 . . . . 39 A3
Wandsworth SW18 . . 71 B4
Kingham Ind Est
NW10 . . . . 20 C2

King Henry's Rd
NW3 . . . . 12 A1
King Henry's Reach
W6 . . . . 47 B4
King Henry St N16 . . 16 A3
King Henry's Wlk
N1 . . . . 16 A2
King Henry's Yd 5
N16 . . . . 16 A3
King Henry Terr 11
E1 . . . . 32 A2
King Ho 5 W12 . . . . 30 A3
Kinghorn St EC1 . . 108 C3
King James Ct
SE1 . . . . 136 B3
King James St
SE1 . . . . 136 B3
King John Ct
EC2 . . . . 24 A1 98 B2
King John St E1 . . . . 32 C4
Kinglake Est SE17 . . 152 B2
Kingly Ct W1 . . . . . 119 A4
Kingly St W1 . . . . . 118 C4
King & Queen St
SE17 . . . . 151 A2
King's Arms Ct 1 . . 111 B3
King's Arms Yd
EC2 . . . . 109 B2
Kings Ave SW4 . . . . 62 A1
Kings Avenue Sch
SW4 . . . . 62 A2
King's Bench St
SE1 . . . . 136 B4
King's Bench Wlk
EC4 . . . . 107 C1
King's Boulevard
NW1 . . . . 84 A1
Kingsbridge N16 . . . . 6 C3
Kingsbridge Ave
W3 . . . . 36 B4
Kingsbridge Ct
E14 . . . . 41 C2
Kingsbridge Rd
W10 . . . . 30 B3
Kingsbury Rd N1 . . . 16 A2
Kingsbury Terr N1 . . 16 A2
Kingsclere Cl
SW15 . . . . 68 C4
Kingscliffe Gdns
SW19 . . . . 70 B3
King's Coll SE24 . . . 63 C1
Kings College Ct
NW3 . . . . 12 A1
King's College Hospl
SE5 . . . . 48 C1
Kings College Rd
NW3 . . . . 11 C1
King's Coll London
(Denmark Hill
Campus) SE5 . . . . . 48 B1
King's Coll London
School of Medicine
SE1 . . . . 123 C1
King's Coll London
(Strand Campus)
WC2 . . . . 121 A4
King's Coll London (St
Thomas' Campus)
SE1 . . . . 134 C1
King's Coll London
(Waterloo Campus)
SE1 . . . . 121 B1
Kingscote NW11 . . . 1 B3
Kingscote Rd W4 . . . 37 C3

Kingscote St EC4 .... **122** A4

King's Court N
SW3 .... **144** A1
Kingscourt Rd
SW16 .... **74** A1
King's Court S
SW3 .... **144** A1
King's Cres N4, N5 .... **6** B1
Kingscroft SW4 ..... **62** A1
Kingscroft Rd
NW2 .... **10** B2
KING'S CROSS **84** C2
King's Cross WC1 .... **94** B4
King's Cross Acad
N1 .... **83** C3
King's Cross Bridge
WC1 .... **94** B4
King's Cross Rd
WC1 .... **95** A3
King's Cross, St
Pancras N1 .... **94** A4
King's Cross Sta
N1 .... **84** B1
Kings Ct
5 Barnsbury N7 .. **14** B1
Chiswick W6 .... **38** C2
East Dulwich SE22 .. **64** C3
Primrose Hill NW8 .. **80** C3
10 Putney SW15 .... **68** C4
King's Ct SE1 .... **136** C4
Kingsdale Gdns
W11 .... **30** C1
Kingsdale Sch
SE21 .... **76** A1
Kingsdown Ave
W3 .... **29** A2
Kingsdown Cl
26 Deptford SE16 .. **40** A1
8 Notting Hill W11 .. **31** A3
Kingsdown Ct
SW11 .... **60** A1
Kingsdown Ho **1**
E8 .... **16** C3
Kingsdown Rd **4**
N19 .... **5** A2
Kings Farm Ave
TW10 .... **54** C3
Kingsfield Ho **18**
N16 .... **19** A4
Kingsford St NW5 .... **12** B3
Kingsgate Est N1 .... **16** A2
Kingsgate Ho **2**
SW9 .... **173** C4
Kingsgate Par
SW1 .... **133** A1
Kingsgate Pl NW6 ... **10** C1
Kingsgate Prim Sch
NW6 .... **10** C1
Kingsgate Rd
NW6 .... **10** C1
King's Gdns **6**
NW6 .... **10** C1
King's Gr
Peckham SE15 ...... **50** A2
Peckham SE15 ...... **50** A3
Kingshall Mews
SE13 .... **67** B4
King's Head Yd
SE1 .... **123** B1
Kingshill SE17 .... **151** A4
Kings Ho
10 Limehouse
E14 .... **33** B2

Kings Ho continued
South Lambeth
SW8 .... **162** B2
Kingshold Rd E9 .... **17** B1
King's House Sch
TW10 .... **54** B2
King's House Sch
(Jun) TW10 .... **54** B2
King's Keep **6**
SW15 .... **57** C2
Kingsland N1 .... **16** A2
Kingsland Gn **1** E8,
N1 .... **16** A2
Kingsland High St
E8 .... **16** C3
Kingsland Pas **2**
E8 .... **16** A2
Kingsland Rd E2 .. **24** A3
Kingsland Sh Ctr **12**
E8 .... **16** B2
Kingslawn Cl
SW15 .... **57** A2
Kingsley Ct NW2 .... **9** A2
Kingsley Flats
SE1 .... **152** B3
Kingsley Ho
Chelsea SW3 ..... **157** C3
3 Clapham SW4 .. **171** C2
Kingsley Mews
Kensington W8 .... **128** B1
St George in t East
E1 .... **32** A2
Kingsley Pl N6 ..... **3** C4
Kingsley Rd SW19 .. **23** B4
Kingsley St SW11 ... **60** B4
Kings Mall Sh Ctr
W6 .... **39** B2
King's Mans SW3 **158** A3
Kingsmead TW10 .... **54** B1
Kingsmead Ct N6 .... **4** C4
Kingsmead Ho E9 .... **18** A4
Kingsmead Prim Sch
E9 .... **18** A4
Kingsmead Rd
SW2 .... **74** C2
King's Mead Way E5,
E9 .... **18** A4
Kingsmere Cl **13**
SW15 .... **57** C4
Kingsmere Pl N16 .... **6** C3
Kingsmere Rd
SW19 .... **69** C2
King's Mews
1 Clapham Pk
SW4 .... **62** A2
Gray's Inn WC1 ..... **95** A1
Kingsmill NW8 ...... **79** C2
Kingsmill Terr
NW8 .... **79** C2
Kingsnorth Ho **12**
W10 .... **30** C3
King Solomon Acad
NW1 .... **102** A4
King's Par
12 Hammersmith
W12 .... **38** C3
Willesden NW10 .... **22** B4
Kings Pl W4 .... **37** B1
King's Pl SE1 .... **136** C3
King's Quay SW10 **167** A4
Kings Rd
Richmond TW10,
TW9 .... **54** B2

Kings Rd continued
Willesden NW10 .... **9** A1
King's Rd
Chelsea SW3 ..... **144** A1
Chelsea SW10 .... **157** B3
Mortlake SW14 .... **55** C4
Kings Ride Gate
TW10 .... **54** C3
Kingsridge SW19 .... **70** A2
King's Scholars' Pas
SW1 .... **146** C4
King St
Acton W3 .... **28** B1
Hammersmith W6 .. **39** C2
St James SW1 .... **119** A2
Strand WC2 ...... **120** A4
Whitechapel EC2 .. **109** A1
King Stairs Cl
SE16 .... **40** A4
King's Terr NW1 .... **82** C3
Kingston Ho **4**
NW6 .... **10** A1
Kingston Ho E
SW7 .... **130** A3
Kingston Ho N
SW7 .... **130** A3
Kingston Ho S
SW7 .... **130** A3
Kingston Rd SW15,
SW19 .... **69** A3
Kingston Univ
(Roehampton Vale)
SW15 .... **68** B1
Kingston Vale
SW15 .... **68** A1
Kingstown St NW1 **81** B4
King Street Cloisters
8 W6 .... **39** A2
Kingswater Pl
SW11 .... **158** A1
Kingsway
Mortlake SW14,
TW9 .... **55** A4
St Giles WC2 ..... **106** C2
Kingsway Mans
WC1 .... **106** C4
Kingsway Pl EC1 ... **96** A2
Kingswear Rd NW5 .. **4** A1
Kings Well **28**
NW3 .... **11** B4
Kings Wlk Sh Mall
SW3 .... **144** C2
Kingswood **21** E2 .. **25** B3
Kingswood Ave
NW6 .... **23** A3
Kingswood Ct
SW8 .... **162** B1
Kingswood Ct
Hither Green
SE13 .... **67** C1
7 Richmond TW10 **54** B2
Kings Wood Ct **4**
NW6 .... **10** C1
Kingswood Rd
South Acton W4 .... **37** B3
Streatham SW2 .... **74** A4
Kingswood Terr
W4 .... **37** B3
Kings Yd E15 ...... **18** C2
Kington Ho **18**
NW6 .... **78** B3
Kingward Ho **1** E1 **111** B4
Kingweston Cl NW2 **1** A1
King William La **3**
SE10 .... **43** A1

King William St
EC4 .... **123** C4
King William Wlk
SE10 .... **52** B4
Kingwood Rd
SW6 .... **154** A1
Kinloch St N7 ...... **5** B1
Kinnaird Ave W4 .... **45** B3
Kinnear Rd W12 .... **38** B4
Kinnerton Pl N
SW1 .... **131** A3
Kinnerton Pl S
SW1 .... **131** A3
Kinnerton St SW1 **131** B3
Kinnerton Yd
SW1 .... **131** B3
Kinnoul Mans **6**
E5 .... **17** A4
Kinnoull Rd W6 ... **154** A4
Kinross Ho N1 ..... **84** C4
Kinsale Rd SE15 ... **64** C4
Kinsham Ho **5**
E2 .... **99** C2
Kintore Way SE1 .. **152** C4
Kintyre Ct **17** SW2 **74** A4
Kintyre Ho **6** E14 .. **34** B1
Kinver Ho N4 ...... **6** C4
Kipling Ho **22** SE5 .. **48** B3
Kipling St SE1 ... **137** C4
Kipling Twr **3** W3 .. **37** B3
Kirby Est SE16 .... **40** A3
Kirby Gr SE1 ..... **138** A4
Kirby St EC1 ..... **107** C4
Kirkeby Bldg EC1 **107** B4
Kirkland Wlk **2**
E8 .... **16** B2
Kirkley Ho N16 ..... **7** A3
Kirkman Ho W1 ... **105** B3
Kirkman Pl W1 ... **105** B3
Kirkmichael Rd
E14 .... **34** B3
Kirkside Rd SE3 ... **53** C4
Kirkstall Gdns
SW2 .... **74** A3
Kirkstall Ho SW1 **146** A2
Kirkstall Rd SW2 .. **74** A3
Kirkstead Ct E5 ... **18** A4
Kirkstone NW1 .... **92** C4
Kirkwall Pl E2 ..... **25** B2
Kirkwood Rd SE15 .. **50** A1
Kirtley Ho SW8 ... **171** A4
Kirtling St SW8 .. **160** C2
Kirton Cl W4 ...... **37** C2
Kirton Gdns **21**
E2 .... **24** B2 99 A3
Kirwin Way SE5 ... **48** A3
Kitcat Terr E3 ..... **26** C2
Kite Ho **5** SW11 ... **60** A4
Kite Pl **7**
E2 .... **24** C2 99 C4
Kitson Rd
Barnes SW13 ...... **46** C2
Camberwell SE5 .... **48** B3
Kittiwake Ct **20**
SE8 .... **51** B4
Kitto Rd SE14 ..... **50** C1
Kiver Rd N19 ...... **5** A2
Klea Ave SW4 ..... **61** B1
Kleffens Ct **2** SE3 .. **53** B3
Kleine Wharf **30**
N1 .... **24** A4
Knapp Cl NW10 .... **8** A2
Knapp Rd E3 ...... **26** C1
Knaresborough Dr
SW18 .... **71** A3

Knaresborough Ho **4**
N4 .... **6** B4
Knaresborough Pl
SW5 .... **142** A4
Knatchbull Rd
Brixton SE5 .... **48** A2
Stonebridge NW10 .. **20** C4
Knebworth Ho
South Lambeth
SW8 .... **171** C3
2 Stoke Newington
N16 .... **16** A4
Knebworth Rd **3**
N16 .... **16** A4
Kneller Ho **9**
SW8 .... **171** C2
Kneller Rd SE4 .... **66** A3
Knighten St E1 .... **32** A1
Knighthead Point **20**
E14 .... **41** C4
Knight Ho SE17 .. **152** A3
Knightleas Ct NW2 .. **9** B2
Knightrider Ct
EC4 .... **122** C4
Knightrider St
EC4 .... **122** B4
Knights Arc SW1 **130** C3
Knight's Ave W5 .... **36** A4
KNIGHTSBRIDGE
.... **130** A2
Knightsbridge
SW7 .... **130** C3
Knightsbridge Ct
SW1 .... **131** A3
Knightsbridge Gn
SW1 .... **130** C3
Knightsbridge Sta
SW1 .... **131** A3
Knightsbridge Under
Sch SW7 .... **143** A3
Knights Ct SE1 .... **137** B4
Knights Ho
Bermondsey SE1 .. **138** C4
South Lambeth
SW8 .... **162** B1
West Kensington
SW5 .... **140** C2
Knight's Ho SW10 **156** C2
Knight's Rd E16 ... **43** C4
Knight's Wlk SE11 **150** A3
Knightswood Ct N4 .. **4** C4
Knivet Rd SW6 ... **155** B3
Knoll Ho NW8 ..... **78** C2
Knoll Rd SW18 ... **59** B2
Knolly's Ct SE27,
SW16 .... **74** C1
Knolly's Rd SE27,
SW16 .... **74** C1
Knot Ho SE1 ..... **124** C1
Knottisford St E2 .. **25** B2
Knowlden Ho **5**
E1 .... **32** B2
Knowle Cl SW9 ... **62** C4
Knowledge Point Sch
6 N7 .... **14** B2
Knowles Hill Cres
SE13 .... **67** C2
Knowles Ho
Wandsworth
SW18 .... **59** A1
Willesden Green
NW10 .... **21** C4
Knowles Wlk SW4 .. **61** B4

Knowlton Ho 🔢
SW9 . . . . 173 C4
Knowsley Rd
SW11 . . . . 168 C1
Knox Ct 🔢 SW4 . . 172 B2
Knox Ho SW15 . . . . . 47 B1
Knox St W1 . . . . 102 C4
Knoyle Ho W14 . . . . 126 B2
Knoyle St SE14 . . . . . 51 A4
Kobi Nazrul Prim Sch
🔢 E1 . . . . 111 C2
Koops Mill Mews
SE1 . . . . 139 A2
Kossuth St SE10 . . . 43 A1
Kotree Way 🔢
SE1 . . . . 153 C4
Kramer Mews
SW5 . . . . 142 A1
Kreedman Wlk 🔢
E8 . . . . 16 C3
Kreisel Wlk TW9 . . . . 44 B4
Kylemore Ct 🔢
W12 . . . . 38 A4
Kylemore Rd NW6 . . 10 C1
Kylestrome Ho
SW1 . . . . 145 C3
Kynance Mews
SW7 . . . . 128 B1
Kynance PI SW7 . . . 128 C1
Kynaston Ho 🔢
SW2 . . . . 74 B3
Kynaston Rd N16 . . . 7 A1
Kyrle Rd SW11 . . . . . 60 C1
Kyverdale Rd N16 . . 7 B3

L

Laburnham Ct NW2 . . 1 B2
Laburnum CI 🔢
SE15 . . . . 50 B3
Laburnum Ct 🔢
E2 . . . . 24 B4
Laburnum Ho
New Cross SE4 . . . . . 51 B1
🔢 Stoke Newington
N16 . . . . 6 C2
Laburnum St E2 . . . . 24 B4
Lacey Ho 🔢 SE13 . . 26 C3
Lacey Mews 🔢 E3 . . 26 C3
Lacine Ct 🔢 SE16 . . 40 C4
Lackington St
EC2 . . . . 109 C4
Lackland Ho 🔢 SE1 . 153 A2
Lacland Ho SW10 . . 157 B2
Lacon Rd SE22 . . . . 64 C3
Lacy Rd SW15 . . . . 57 C3
Ladbroke Cres
W11 . . . . 31 A3
Ladbroke Gdns
W11 . . . . . 31 B2 112 C4
Ladbroke Gr
Kensal Town W10 . . 31 A4
Notting Hill
W11 . . . . . 31 B2 112 C4
Ladbroke Grove Ho
W11 . . . . 31 B2 112 C4
Ladbroke Grove Sta
W10 . . . . 31 A4
Ladbroke Ho 🔢 E1 . 111 A3
Ladbroke Mews
W11 . . . . 31 A1 112 B1
Ladbroke Rd
W11 . . . . . 31 B1 112 C2
Ladbroke Sq
W11 . . . . . 31 B2 113 A3

Ladbroke Terr
W11 . . . . . 31 B1 113 A2
Ladbroke Wlk
W11 . . . . . 31 B1 113 A2
Ladlands SE22 . . . . . 76 C4
Ladybower Ct 🔢
E5 . . . . 17 C4
Ladycroft Rd SE13 . 67 A4
Lady Elizabeth Ho
SW14 . . . . 55 B4
Ladyfern Ho 🔢 E3 . . 33 C4
Lady Florence Ctyd 🔢
SE8 . . . . 51 C3
Lady Margaret Rd
NW5 . . . . 13 B3
Lady Margaret Sch
SW6 . . . . 165 B3
Lady Somerset Rd
NW5 . . . . 13 A4
LADYWELL 66 C1
Ladywell Arena
SE13 . . . . 67 A1
Ladywell CI SE4 . . . . 66 B1
Ladywell Hts SE4 . . . 66 B1
Ladywell Sta SE13 . . 67 A2
Ladywell Water Twr
SE4 . . . . 66 C2
Lafitte Ho 🔢 SW2 . . 62 C2
Lafone Ho 🔢 SW2 . . 74 A4
Lafone St SE1 . . . . . 138 C4
Lagado Mews
SE16 . . . . 32 C1
Lagonda Ho 🔢 E3 . . 26 C1
Lagonier Ho EC1 . . . 97 A3
Laindon Ho 🔢 N16 . 7 B3
Laing Ho SE5 . . . . . . 48 B3
Lainson St SW18 . . . 70 C4
Lairdale CI SE21 . . . . 75 B4
Laird Ho SE5 . . . . . . 48 B3
Lairs Ct N7 . . . . 14 A2
Laitwood Rd SW12 . 73 A3
Lakanal 🔢 SE5 . . . . . 49 A2
Lake Ho SE1 . . . . . . 136 C3
Laker Ct SW4 . . . . . 172 B2
Laker PI SW15 . . . . . 58 A1
Lakeside Ct N4 . . . . . 6 B3
Lakeside Rd W14 . . . 39 C3
Lakeview 🔢 E3 . . . . 25 C3
Lake View Ct
SW1 . . . . 132 B2
Lakis CI NW3 . . . . . . 11 B4
Laleham Ho
E2 . . . . 24 B1 98 C2
Lalor St SW6 . . . . . . 164 B2
Lambard Ho 🔢
SE10 . . . . 52 B3
Lamb CI 🔢 E14 . . . . . 33 A2
Lamberhurst Ho 🔢
SE15 . . . . 50 B4
Lambert Ave TW9 . . 55 A4
Lambert Ho
🔢 Brixton SW9 . . . 173 B1
🔢 Crouch End N19 . . 4 C4
Lambert Rd SW2 . . . 62 B2
Lambert St N1 . . . . . 14 C1
LAMBETH 134 C3
Lambeth Acad
SW4 . . . . 61 B2
Lambeth Coll (Brixton
Ctr) SW2 . . . . 62 B2
Lambeth Coll
(Clapham Ctr)
SW4 . . . . 61 B2

Lambeth Coll
(Vauxhall Ctr)
SW8 . . . . 171 B4
Lambeth Ct 🔢
SW18 . . . . 58 C2
Lambeth High St
SE1 . . . . 148 C4
Lambeth Hill EC4 . . 122 C4
Lambeth Hospl
SW9 . . . . 62 B4
Lambeth North Sta
SE1 . . . . 135 B2
Lambeth Pal SE1 . . 134 C1
Lambeth Palace Rd
SE1 . . . . 134 C2
Lambeth Pier SE1 . 134 B1
Lambeth Rd SE1 . . . 135 C1
Lambeth Twrs
SE11 . . . . 135 B1
Lambeth Wlk
SE11 . . . . 149 A4
Lambfold Ho N7 . . . 14 A2
Lamb Ho
🔢 Camberwell
SE5 . . . . 48 B3
🔢 Camberwell SE5 . . 48 C2
Greenwich SE10 . . . 52 B4
Lamb La E8 . . . . 17 A1
Lamble St NW5 . . . . 12 C4
Lamb Office Ct
WC1 . . . . 106 A4
Lambolle PI NW3 . . . 12 A2
Lambolle Rd NW3 . . 12 A2
Lambourn CI 🔢
NW5 . . . . 13 B4
Lambourne Gr
SE16 . . . . 40 C1
Lambourne Ho
NW8 . . . . 101 C4
Lambourn Rd SW4 . 61 A4
Lambrook Ho 🔢
SE15 . . . . 49 C2
Lambrook Terr
SW6 . . . . 164 A4
Lamb's Bldgs EC1 . . 97 B1
Lamb's Conduit Pas
WC1 . . . . 106 C4
Lamb's Conduit St
WC1 . . . . 94 C1
Lamb's Mews N1 . . 86 A3
Lamb's Pas EC1 . . . . 97 B1
Lamb St E1 . . . . 110 C4
Lambton 🔢 E14 . . . . 33 A4
Lambton Rd N19 . . . 5 A3
Lambton Mews 🔢
N19 . . . . 5 A3
Lamerton Lo 🔢
TW9 . . . . 44 B2
Lamerton St 🔢
SE8 . . . . 51 C4
Lamington St 🔢
W6 . . . . 39 A2
Lamlash St SE11 . . 150 A4
Lamley Ho SE10 . . . 52 A3
Lammas Rd E9 . . . . . 17 C1
Lammermoor Rd
SW12 . . . . 73 A4
Lamont Rd SW10 . . 157 B3
Lamont Rd Pas
SW10 . . . . 157 B3
Lampard Gr N16 . . . . 7 B3
Lampern Sq 🔢
E2 . . . . 24 C2 99 C4

Lampeter Sq W6 . . 154 A3
Lamplighter CI 🔢
E1 . . . . 25 B1
Lampson Ho 🔢
N19 . . . . 13 B4
Lanark Ho 🔢 SE1 . . 153 B1
Lanark Mans
Paddington W9 . . . . 89 A2
🔢 Shepherd's Bush
W12 . . . . 39 B4
Lanark Mews NW8 . . 89 A2
Lanark PI W9 . . . . . . 89 A2
Lanark Rd W9 . . . . . 88 C3
Lanark Sq E14 . . . . . 42 A3
Lanbury Rd SE15 . . . 65 C3
Lancashire Ct W1 . . 118 B4
Lancaster Ave SE21,
SE27 . . . . 75 B2
Lancaster Ct
Bayswater W2 . . . . 115 A4
Parsons Green
SW6 . . . . 155 A1
West Norwood
SE27 . . . . 75 A2
Lancaster Dr
Canary Wharf E14 . . 34 B1
Maitland Pk NW3 . . 12 A2
Lancaster Gate
W2 . . . . 115 A4
Lancaster Gate Sta
W2 . . . . 115 A4
Lancaster Gr NW3 . 12 A2
Lancaster hall 🔢
E16 . . . . 35 C1
Lancaster Ho
SW15 . . . . 47 B1
Lancaster Lo 🔢
W11 . . . . 31 A3
Lancaster Mews
Bayswater W2 . . . . 115 A4
🔢 Richmond TW10 . . 54 A1
🔢 Wandsworth
SW18 . . . . 59 A2
Lancaster Pk
TW10 . . . . 54 A2
Lancaster PI WC2 . 120 C3
Lancaster Rd
Dudden Hill NW10 . . 8 C3
Finsbury Pk N4 . . . . 5 C4
Notting Hill W11 . . . 31 A3
Lancaster St SE1 . . 136 B3
Lancaster Sta 🔢 E1 . 32 A3
Lancaster Stables 🔢
NW3 . . . . 12 A2
Lancaster Terr
W2 . . . . 115 B4
Lancaster Wlk
W2 . . . . 115 A3
Lancefield Ho
SE15 . . . . 65 A4
Lancefield St W10 . . 23 B2
Lancell St N16 . . . . . 7 A2
Lancelot PI SW7 . . . 130 C3
Lancer Sq W8 . . . . . 128 A4
Lanchester Ct W2 . 102 C1
Lanchester Way
SE14 . . . . 50 C2

Lancing St NW1 . . . . 93 B3
Lancresse Ct N1 . . . 24 A4
Landale Ct SE10 . . . 52 B2
Landale Ho 🔢
SE16 . . . . 40 B3
Landcroft Rd SE22 . 64 B1
Landells Rd SE22 . . 64 C1
Landford Rd SW15 . 57 B4
Landin Ho 🔢 E14 . . 33 C3
Landleys Field 🔢
N7 . . . . 13 C3
Landmann Ho 🔢
SE16 . . . . 40 A2
Landmann Way
SE14 . . . . 40 C1
Landmark Hts E5 . . 18 A4
Landon PI SW1 . . . 130 C2
Landons CI E14 . . . . 34 B1
Landon Wlk 🔢
E14 . . . . 34 A2
Landor Ct N16 . . . . . 16 A3
Landor Ho 🔢 SE5 . . 48 C3
Landor Rd SW9 . . . . 62 A4
Landor Wlk 🔢
W12 . . . . 38 C4
Landrake NW1 . . . . 83 A3
Landridge Rd
SW6 . . . . 164 C2
Landseer Ct 🔢 N19 . 5 A2
Landseer Ho
Battersea SW11 . . . 169 C3
Paddington NW8 . . . 89 C2
Westminster SW1 . . 147 C3
Landseer Rd N19 . . . 5 A2
Landulph Ho
SE11 . . . . 149 C2
Landward Ct W1 . . 102 B2
Lane Ct SW11 . . . . . 72 B4
Lanercost CI SW2 . . 74 C2
Lanercost Rd SW2 . 74 C2
Lane The NW8 . . . . . 78 C1
Laneway SW15 . . . . 57 A2
Laney Bldg EC1 . . . 107 B4
Lanfranc Rd E3 . . . . 26 A3
Lanfrey PI W14 . . . 140 C1
Langbourne Ave N6 . 3 C2
Langbourne Ho 🔢
SW2 . . . . 62 C2
Langbourne Mans
N6 . . . . 3 C2
Langbourne PI
E14 . . . . 42 A1
Langdale NW1 . . . . . 92 C4
Langdale CI
Camberwell SE17 . . 48 B4
Mortlake SW14 . . . . 55 A3
Langdale Ho SW1 . 146 C1
Langdale Rd SE10 . . 52 B3
Langdale St 🔢 E1 . . 32 A3
Langdon Ct
Finsbury EC1 . . . . . 86 B1
Harlesden NW10 . . . 21 A4
Langdon Ho 🔢
E14 . . . . 34 B3
Langdon Park Rd
N6 . . . . 4 B4
Langdon Park Sch
E14 . . . . 34 B3
Langdon Park Sta
E14 . . . . 34 A3
Langdon Pk L Ctr
E14 . . . . 34 B3
Langdon Pk Sta
E3 . . . . 34 A3

Langdon Pl SW14 . . . . . . 55 B4
Langdon Way 18
SE1 . . . . 153 C3
Langford Cl
Shacklewell E8 . . . . . . 16 C3
St John's Wood
NW8 . . . . 79 A2
Langford Ct NW8 . . . . . 79 A1
Langford Gn SE5 . . . . . 64 A4
Langford Ho 5
SE8 . . . . 51 C4
Langford Pl NW8 . . . . . 79 A2
Langford Prim Sch
SW6 . . . . 166 B2
Langford Rd 4
SW6 . . . . 166 B2
Langham Ct 4
SW15 . . . . 57 C2
Langham Ho SW4 . . . . 61 B2
Langham Mans
SW5 . . . . 142 A1
Langham Pl
Chiswick W4 . . . . 46 A4
Fitzrovia W1 . . . . 104 B3
Langham St W1 . . . . . 104 B3
Lang Ho
South Lambeth
SW8 . . . . 162 A1
3 Tufnell Pk N19 . . . . . 4 B1
Langholm Cl
SW12 . . . . 73 C4
Langhorne Ct 10
NW8 . . . . 11 C1
Langhurst Ho 10
SW11 . . . . 169 B2
Langland Gdns
NW3 . . . . 11 A3
Langland Ho 10
SE5 . . . . 48 C3
Langland Mans
NW3 . . . . 11 A3
Langler Rd NW10 . . . . 22 B3
Langley Ct
South Lambeth
SW8 . . . . 172 A4
Strand WC2 . . . . 120 A4
Langley Dr W3 . . . . . . 37 A4
Langley Ho
11 Lower Clapton
E5 . . . . 17 A3
36 Paddington W2 . . . . 31 C4
Langley La SW8 . . . . . 162 B4
Langley Mans
SW8 . . . . 162 B4
Langley St WC2 . . . . . 106 A1
Langmead Ho 34
E3 . . . . 27 A2
Langmore Ho 39
E1 . . . . 111 C1
Langport Ho 1
SW9 . . . . 48 A1
Langridge 15 NW5 . . 12 C2
Langroyd Rd SW17 . . 72 B2
Langside Ave
SW15 . . . . 56 C3
Lang St E1 . . . . 25 B1
Langston Hughes Cl
5 SE24 . . . . 63 A2
Langthorn Ct EC2 . . . 109 C2
Langthorne Lo 30
SW2 . . . . 74 C4
Langthorne St
SW6 . . . . 47 C3
Langton Cl WC1 . . . . . . 95 A2

Langton Ct SW15 . . . . . 58 B1
Langton Ho SE11 . . . . 149 A4
Langton Pl SW18 . . . . . 70 C3
Langton Rd SW9 . . . . . 48 A3
Langton St SW10 . . . . 157 A3
Langton Way SE3 . . . . 53 C3
Langtry Pl SW6 . . . . . . 155 C4
Langtry Rd NW8 . . . . . 78 A3
Langtry Wlk NW8 . . . . 78 C4
Lanhill Rd W9 . . . . 23 C1
Lanier Rd SE13 . . . . . . 67 C1
Lanner Ho 2
SW11 . . . . 60 A4
Lannoy Point
SW6 . . . . 154 B2
Lanrick Rd E14 . . . . . . 35 A3
Lansbury Gdns 1
E14 . . . . 34 C3
Lansbury Lawrence
Prim Sch 20 E14 . . . . . 34 A3
Lanscombe Wlk
SW8 . . . . 162 A1
Lansdell Ho 9
SW2 . . . . 62 C1
Lansdowne Coll
W2 . . . . 114 A3
Lansdowne Cres
W11 . . . . 31 A2 112 B3
Lansdowne Dr E8 . . . . 16 C1
Lansdowne Gdns
SW8 . . . . 172 A4
Lansdowne Gr
NW10 . . . . 8 A4
Lansdowne Hill
SE27 . . . . 75 A1
Lansdowne Ho
W11 . . . . 31 B1 112 C2
Lansdowne Mews
W11 . . . . 31 B1 112 C2
Lansdowne Pl
SE1 . . . . 137 C2
Lansdowne Rd
W11 . . . . 31 A2 112 B3
Lansdowne Rise
W11 . . . . 31 A2 112 B3
Lansdowne Row
W1 . . . . 118 B2
Lansdowne Sch 5
SW9 . . . . 62 B4
Lansdowne Terr
WC1 . . . . 94 B1
Lansdowne Way SW4,
SW8 . . . . 172 B3
Lansdowne Wlk
W11 . . . . 31 B1 112 C2
Lansdowne Wood Cl
11 SE27 . . . . 75 A1
Lansdown Ho 28
SE5 . . . . 48 B1
Lantern Cl SW15 . . . . . 56 C3
Lantern Ho E14 . . . . . . 41 C4
Lanterns Ct E14 . . . . . . 41 C3
Lanterns Wy E14 . . . . . 42 A4
Lant Ho SE1 . . . . 136 C3
Lantry Ct 1 W3 . . . . . . 28 A1
Lant St SE1 . . . . 137 A3
Lanvanor Rd SE15 . . . 50 B1
Lanyard Ho 4 SE8 . . . 41 B2
Lapford Cl W9 . . . . 23 B1
Lapsang SE1 . . . . 125 A1
Lapwing Twr 8 1
SE8 . . . . 51 B4
Lapworth Ct W2 . . . . 100 B4
Lara Cl SE13 . . . . 67 B1
Larch Ave W3 . . . . 29 A1

Larch SW12
Balham SW12 . . . . 73 A2
2 Putney SW15 . . . . . 57 C2
19 Upper Holloway
N19 . . . . 4 B2
Larch Cl 4 W2 . . . . 31 C4
Larches Ave SW14 . . . 55 C3
Larchfield Ho 2
N5 . . . . 15 B3
Larch Ho 20 SE16 . . . . 40 B4
Larchmore Ct N19 . . . . 5 A2
Larch Rd NW2 . . . . 9 B4
Larcom St SE17 . . . . . 151 A3
Larden Rd W3 . . . . 38 A4
La Retraite RC Girls
Sch SW12 . . . . 73 B4
Larissa St SE17 . . . . . 151 C3
Larix Ct NW10 . . . . 21 C4
Larkfield Rd TW9 . . . . 54 A3
Larkhall La SW4 . . . . . 172 A3
Larkhall Rise
SW4 . . . . 171 B1
Lark Row E2 . . . . 25 B4
Larmenier & Sacred
Heart RC Prim Sch
4 W6 . . . . 39 C2
Larnaca Ho SE1 . . . . . 138 C2
Larnach Rd W6 . . . . . . 47 C4
Larpent Ave SW15 . . . 57 B2
La Saint Union RC Sec
Sch NW5 . . . . 4 A1
Lascelles Ho NW1 . . . . 90 B1
Lassell St SE10 . . . . . . 42 C1
Lasseter Pl SE3 . . . . . . 53 B4
Latchmere Rd
SW11 . . . . 168 C1
Latchmere St 5
SW11 . . . . 168 C2
Latham Ho E1 . . . . 32 C3
Latimer SE17 . . . . 152 A1
Latimer Ho
1 Homerton E9 . . . . . 17 C2
Notting Hill
W11 . . . . 31 B2 113 A3
Latimer Ind Est 1
NW10 . . . . 30 B3
Latimer Pl W10 . . . . . . 30 B3
Latimer Rd W10 . . . . . 30 B3
Latimer Road Sta
W10 . . . . 30 C2
Latitude Ho NW1 . . . . . 82 A3
Latona Rd SE15 . . . . . . 49 C4
Lattimer Pl W4 . . . . . . 46 A4
Latvia Ct SE17 . . . . . . 151 A1
Latymer Ct W6 . . . . . . 39 C2
Latymer Upper Sch 1
W6 . . . . 38 C2
Lauderdale Mans
W9 . . . . 88 B3
Lauderdale Rd W9 . . . 88 B3
Lauderdale Twr
EC2 . . . . 108 C4
Laud St SE11 . . . . 148 C2
Loughton Ho 1
SW2 . . . . 62 C1
Launcelot St SE1 . . . . 135 B3
Launceston Pl
W8 . . . . 128 C1
Launch St E14 . . . . 42 B3
Laundress La N16 . . . . . 7 C1
Laundry La 7 N1 . . . . . 15 B1
Laundry Rd W6 . . . . . 154 A3
Laura Pl E5 . . . . 17 B4
Laurel Bank Gdns 3
SW6 . . . . 165 A2
Laurel Cl 8 N19 . . . . . . 4 B2

Laurel Ct
Dalston E8 . . . . 16 B1
2 Putney SW15 . . . . . 57 C2
6 Rotherhithe
SE16 . . . . 33 A1
Laurel Ho
2 Deptford SE8 . . . . . 51 B4
6 Hamstead NW3 . . . 11 A2
Laurel Rd SW13 . . . . . 46 C1
Laurel St E8 . . . . 16 B2
Laurence Mews 12
W12 . . . . 38 C4
Laurence Pountney
Hill EC4 . . . . 123 B4
Laurence Pountney La
EC4 . . . . 123 C4
Laurie Ho
Newington SE1 . . . . . 136 B1
Notting Hill
W8 . . . . 31 C1 113 B1
Laurie Rd NW5 . . . . 4 A1
Lauriston Ho 6
E9 . . . . 17 C1
Lauriston Lo NW6 . . . 10 B2
Lauriston Prim Sch 6
E9 . . . . 25 C4
Lauriston Rd E9 . . . . . 17 C1
Lausanne Rd SE15 . . . 50 B2
Lavell St N16 . . . . 15 C4
Lavender Cl SW3 . . . . 157 C3
Lavender Gr E8 . . . . . . 16 C1
Lavender Gdns
SW11 . . . . 60 B3
Lavender Hill
SW11 . . . . 60 C4
Lavender Ho
6 Richmond
TW9 . . . . 45 A2
4 Rotherhithe
SE16 . . . . 32 C1
Lavender Rd
Battersea SW11 . . . . . 59 C4
Rotherhithe SE16 . . . . 33 A1
Lavender Sweep
SW11 . . . . 60 B3
Lavender Terr 12
SW11 . . . . 60 A4
Lavender Wlk
SW11 . . . . 60 B3
Lavendon Ho NW8 . . . 90 B2
Lavengro Rd SE27 . . . 75 B2
Lavenham Rd
SW18 . . . . 70 C3
Lavers Rd N16 . . . . 7 A1
Laverstoke Gdns
SW15 . . . . 68 C4
Laverton Mews
SW5 . . . . 142 B3
Laverton Pl SW5 . . . . 142 B3
Lavina Gr N1 . . . . 84 C2
Lavington Cl E9 . . . . . . 18 B2
Lavington St SE1 . . . . 122 B1
Lavisle Jun Sch
Bethnal Green E2 . . . . 99 C4
26 E2 . . . . 24 C2 99 C4
Lawford Rd
Chiswick W4 . . . . 45 B3
De Beauvoir Town
N1 . . . . 16 A1
Kentish Town NW5 . . 13 B2
Lawfords Wharf 18
NW1 . . . . 13 B1
Lawless Ho 5 E14 . . . 34 B2
Lawless St 12 E14 . . . 34 A2

Lawley St E5 . . . . 17 B4
Lawman Ct 2
TW9 . . . . 44 C3
Lawn Cres TW9 . . . . . . 44 C1
Lawnfield Ct NW6 . . . . 9 C1
Lawn House Cl
E14 . . . . 42 B4
Lawn La SW8 . . . . 162 C4
Lawn Rd NW3 . . . . 12 B3
Lawns The N16 . . . . . . 16 A3
Lawrence Ave
NW10 . . . . 20 C4
Lawrence Bldgs 1
N16 . . . . 7 B2
Lawrence Cl
Bow E3 . . . . 26 C3
6 Shepherd's Bush
W12 . . . . 30 A2
Lawrence Ct
4 South Acton
W3 . . . . 37 B3
Stoke Newington
N16 . . . . 7 B1
Lawrence Ho
20 Camden Town
NW1 . . . . 83 A3
Westminster SW1 . . . 147 C3
Lawrence La EC2 . . . . 109 A2
Lawrence Mans
SW3 . . . . 158 A3
Lawrence Mews
SW15 . . . . 57 B3
Lawrence Pl N1 . . . . . . 84 B4
Lawrence St
Canning Town
E16 . . . . 35 B4
Chelsea SW3 . . . . 158 A3
Lawrence Trad Est
SE10 . . . . 43 A2
Lawrence Univ
SW7 . . . . 143 A4
Lawson Cl SW19 . . . . . 69 C1
Lawson Ct 1 N4 . . . . . . 5 B3
Lawson Ho 17
W12 . . . . 30 A2
Law St SE1 . . . . 137 C2
Lawton Rd E3 . . . . 26 A2
Laxfield Ct E8 . . . . 24 C4
Laxley Cl SE5 . . . . 48 A3
Laxton Path 1
SE4 . . . . 65 C3
Laxton Pl NW1 . . . . 92 B2
Layard Rd SE16 . . . . . . 40 A2
Layard Sq SE16 . . . . . . 40 A2
Laybourne Ho 18
E14 . . . . 41 C4
Laycock Prim Sch 5
N1 . . . . 15 A2
Laycock St N1 . . . . 14 C2
Layfield Ho 1
SE10 . . . . 43 C1
Laystall Ct EC1 . . . . . . 95 B1
Laystall St EC1 . . . . . . 95 B1
Layton Pl TW9 . . . . 44 C2
Lazar Wlk 8 N7 . . . . 5 B2
Leabank Sq E9 . . . . . . 18 C2
Leabourne Rd N16 . . . . 7 C4
Leacroft Ave
SW12 . . . . 72 B4
Lea Ct 3 W12 . . . . 38 A4
Leadenhall Building
The EC3 . . . . 110 A1
Leadenhall Mkt
EC3 . . . . 110 A1
Leadenhall Pl
EC3 . . . . 110 A1

Leadenhall St
EC3 . . . . 110 A1
Leadenhall Ct 15
E3 . . . . 26 C1
Lea Ho NW8 . . . . . . 90 A1
Leahurst Rd SE13 . . 67 C2
Lea Int E9 . . . . 18 C3
Leake St
Lambeth SE1 . . 135 B3
South Bank SE1 . . 135 A4
Leamington Ct
4 Forest Hill
SE26 . . . . 76 C1
North Acton W3 . . 28 C4
Leamington Ho 4
W11 . . . . 31 B4
Leamington Pk
W3 . . . . 28 C4
Leamington Rd Villas
W11 . . . . 31 B4
Leamore St
27 Hackney E9. . . . 17 B1
St Johns SE8 . . . . . 51 C2
Leander Rd SW2 . . 62 C1
Leary Ho SE11. . . . 149 A1
Leaside Bsns Ctr
E10. . . . . 34 B4
Lea Sq 22 E3 . . . . . 26 B4
Leatherdale St
32 Bethnal Green
E1 . . . . 25 B1
11 Globe Town E1 . . 25 C2
Leatherhead Cl N16.7 B3
Leather La EC1 . . . 107 C4
Leather La Mkt
EC1 . . . . 107 C4
Leathermarket Ct
SE1 . . . . 138 A3
Leathermarket St
SE1 . . . . 138 A3
Leather Rd SE16. . . 40 C2
Leathwaite Rd
SW11 . . . . 60 B2
Leathwell Rd SE8 . . 52 A1
Lebanon Gdns
SW18 . . . . 58 C1
Lebanon Rd SW18. . 58 C2
Lebus Ho NW8 . . . . 80 A1
Lechmere Rd NW2. . 9 A2
Leckford Rd SW18 . . 71 B3
Leckhampton Pl 2
SW2 . . . . 74 C4
Lecky Ho NW2. . . . . 9 A4
Lecky St SW7 . . . . 143 B2
L'Ecole de Battersea
SW11 . . . . 168 A3
L'Ecole des Petits Sch
SW6 . . . . 166 A2
L'Ecole du Parc 13
SW11. . . . . 60 C4
Leconfield Ave SW13,
SW15 . . . . 56 B4
Leconfield Ho SE5. . 64 A4
Leconfield Rd N5. . 15 C4
Lector Ct EC1 . . . . 95 C1
Leda Ct 5 SW9 . . . 163 B1
Ledam Bldg E1 . . . 107 B4
Ledbury Ho 12
SE22 . . . . 64 A4
Ledbury Mews N
W11 . . . . 31 C3
Ledbury Mews W
W11 . . . . . 31 C2 113 B4
Ledbury Rd W11. . . 31 C3

Ledbury St SE15. . . 49 C3
Ledo Ho 1 N16 . . . . 15 C4
Lee Conservancy Rd
E9 . . . . 18 B3
Lee Ct SE13 . . . . . . 67 C3
Leeds Ct EC1 . . . . . 96 A2
Lee Ho 3 N19 . . . . 13 C3
Leeke St WC1 . . . . . 94 C4
Leeland Way NW10 . . 8 B4
Leerdam Dr E14. . . 42 B3
Lees Ct W1 . . . . . . 117 B4
Lees Ho SE17. . . . . 151 C1
Leeson Rd 12
SE24 . . . . 62 C3
Lees Pl W1. . . . . . . 117 B4
Lee St E8 . . . . 24 B4
Leet Ct N16 . . . . . . 15 C4
Lefevre Wlk E3 . . . 26 C4
Leffern Rd W12. . . 38 C4
Left Ho 3 NW6 . . . 10 A1
Lefroy Ho SE1 . . . 136 C3
Lefroy Rd W12 . . . 38 B4
Legard Rd N5 . . . . . 6 A1
Leggatt Rd E15. . . . 27 B3
Legge St SE13 . . . . 67 B2
Leghorn Rd NW10 . . 21 C3
Legion Cl N1 . . . . . 14 C1
Legion Terr 3 E3 . . 26 C4
Leicester Ct
1 Paddington
W2 . . . . 31 C4
St James WC2 . . . 119 C4
Leicester Ho
5 Brixton SW9 . . . 63 A4
4 Putney SW15 . . 69 B4
Leicester Pl WC2 . . 119 C4
Leicester Sq WC2 . 119 C3
Leicester Square Sta 119 C4
Leicester St WC2 . . 119 C4
Leigham Ave
SW16 . . . . 74 A1
Leigham Cl 5
SW16 . . . . 74 B1
Leigham Court Rd
SW16 . . . . 74 B1
Leigham Hall 3
SW16 . . . . 74 A1
Leigham Hall Par 2
SW16 . . . . 74 A1
Leigham Vale SW27,
SW16, SW2 . . . . . . 74 C2
Leigh Ct 22 SW2. . . 62 C1
Leighfield Ho 5 N4 . . 6 B4
Leigh Gdns NW10 . . 22 B3
Leigh Ho 10 SW15 . . 56 C2
Leigh Orchard Cl
SW16 . . . . 74 B1
Leigh Pl EC1 . . . . . 107 B4
Leigh Rd N5. . . . . . . 15 A4
Leigh St WC1 . . . . . 94 A3
Leighton Cres
NW5 . . . . 13 B3
Leighton Gdns
NW10 . . . . 22 B3
Leighton Gr NW5 . . 13 B3
Leighton House Mus 127 A2
Leighton Pl NW5 . . 13 B3

Leighton Rd NW5. . . 13 B3
Leinster Ave SW14. . 55 B3
Leinster Gdns W2 . 114 C4
Leinster Mews
W2 . . . . 114 C4
Leinster Pl W2 . . . 100 C1
Leinster Sq W2. . . 100 A1
Leinster Terr W2. . 114 C4
Leitch Ho 8 NW8 . . 11 C1
Leithcote Path
SW16 . . . . 74 B1
Leith Ho
7 Kentish Town
N7. . . . . 13 C3
5 Streatham SW2 . . 74 B4
Leith Mans W9 . . . 88 A3
Leith Yd 3 NW6. . . 23 C4
Lelitia Cl E8 . . . . . . 24 C4
Leman St E1 . . . . . 111 B1
Lemmon Rd SE10. . 53 A4
Le Moal Ho 28 E1 . . 32 B4
Lemsford Ct N4 . . . 6 B2
Lena Gardens Prim
Sch W6 . . . . 39 B3
Lena Gdns W6. . . . 39 B3
Lendal Terr 7
SW4 . . . . 61 C4
Len Freeman Pl
SW6 . . . . 154 C3
Lenham 11 NW5. . . 12 C2
Lenham Ho SE1 . . 137 C3
Lennon Rd NW2 . . . 9 B2
Lennox Gdns
Knightsbridge
SW1 . . . . 130 C1
Willesden NW10. . . 8 B4
Lennox Gdns Mews
SW1 . . . . 144 C4
Lennox Ho 10 E9 . . 17 B2
Lennox Rd
11 Camberwell
SW9 . . . . 48 A2
Finsbury Pk N4, N7. . 5 C2
Lenthall Ho SW1 . . 147 A1
Lenthall Rd E8 . . . . 16 C1
Lenthorp Rd SE10. . 43 B2
Lenton Rise TW9. . . 54 A4
Len Williams Ct
NW6 . . . . 23 C3
Leo Ct 3 Brentford
TW8 . . . . 36 A1
Leonard Ct
Bloomsbury WC1 . . 94 A2
Kensington W8 . . . 127 B2
Leonard Day Ho 5
NW5 . . . . 13 A2
Leonard Pl 16 N16. . 16 A4
Leonard St EC2. . . 97 C2
Leonora Ho W9 . . . 88 C2
Leontine Cl SE15. . 49 C3
Leopards Ct EC1. . 107 B4
Leopold Bldgs 14
E2 . . . . 24 B2 98 C4
Leopold Mews 9
E9 . . . . 25 B4
Leopold Prim Sch
NW10 . . . . 8 B1
Leopold Rd NW10 . . 8 A1
Leopold St 3 E3. . . 33 B4
Leopold Wlk SE11 148 C1
Leo St SE15 . . . . . . 50 A3
Leo Yd EC1 . . . . . . 96 B1
Leppoc Rd SW4 . . . 61 C2
Leroy St SE1 . . . . . 152 A4
Lerry Cl W14 . . . . . 155 A4
Lerwick Ho SW18. . 59 B3
Lesley Ct SW1 . . . 133 B1
Leslie Prince Ct 8
SE5 . . . . 48 C3

Leslie Rd E11. . . . . . 19 C4
Lessar Ave SW4 . . . 61 B1
Lessar Ct SW4 . . . . 61 B1
Lester Ct 2 E3 . . . . 27 A2
Leswin Pl N16. . . . . 7 B1
Leswin Rd N16. . . . . 7 B1
Letchford Gdns
NW10 . . . . 21 C2
Letchford Mews
NW10 . . . . 21 C2
Letchmore Ho 7
W10 . . . . 22 B1
Lethaby Ho 3 SW4 . 62 B3
Lethbridge Cl
SE13 . . . . 52 B1
Letterstone Rd
SW6 . . . . 154 C1
Lettice St SW6 . . . 165 A3
Lett Rd E15 . . . . . . 19 C1
Lettsom St SE5. . . . 49 A1
Levana Cl SW19 . . . 70 A3
Levant Ho 30 E1 . . 25 C1
Levehurst Way SW4,
SW9 . . . . 172 B2
Leven Rd E14. . . . . 34 C3
Lever Ct 15 E9. . . . 17 C2
Leverington Pl N1 . 97 C3
Leverstock Ho
SW3 . . . . 144 B2
Leverton Pl NW5 . . 13 B3
Leverton St NW5 . . 13 B3
Levison Way 2
N19. . . . . 4 C3
Levita Ho NW1 . . . 93 C4
Levyne Ct EC1 . . . . 95 B2
Lewesdon Cl 19
SW19 . . . . 69 C3
Lewes Ho
Bermondsey SE1 . . 138 B4
Peckham SE15 . . . 49 C4
Leweston Pl N16 . . 7 B4
Lewey Ho 2 E3 . . . 26 B1
Lewin Rd SW14. . . 55 C4
Lewis Ct 6 SE16 . . 40 A1
Lewis Gr SE13 . . . . 67 B4
LEWISHAM 67 B3
Lewisham Bsns Ctr
SE14 . . . . 50 C4
Lewisham Coll
(Deptford Campus)
2 SE8 . . . . 51 C2
Lewisham High St
SE13 . . . . 67 B2
Lewisham Hill
SE13 . . . . 52 B1
Lewisham Pk SE13 . 67 B1
Lewisham Rd SE13 . 52 B1
Lewisham Sh Ctr
SE13 . . . . 67 B4
Lewisham Southwark
Coll SE11 . . . . . . 136 A4
Lewisham Southwark
Coll (Tressillian
Building) SE4 . . . . 66 C4
Lewisham St SW1 . 133 C3
Lewisham Sta
SE13 . . . . 67 B4
Lewisham Way SE4,
SE14 . . . . 51 B2
Lewis Pl E8 . . . . 16 C3
Lewis Silkin Ho 9
SE15 . . . . 50 B4

Lewis Silkin Ho 9
SE15 . . . . 50 B4
Lewis St NW1 . . . . . 13 A2
Lexden Rd W3. . . . . 28 A1
Lexham Gardens
Mews W8 . . . . . . 128 B1
Lexham Gdns W8 142 A4
Lexham Mews
W8 . . . . 141 C4
Lexham Wlk W8 . . 128 B1
Leyborne Park TW9. 44 C2
Leybourne Ho 17
NW10 . . . . 13 A1
Leybourne Rd 8
NW1 . . . . 13 A1
Leybourne St 5
NW1 . . . . 13 A1
Leyden Mans 7
N19. . . . . 5 A4
Leyden St E1 . . . . . 110 C3
Leydon Cl
Rotherhithe SE16. . 32 C1
SE16 . . . . 32 C1
Ley Ho SE1 . . . . . . 136 C3
Leyland Ho 6 E14 . 34 A2
Leylands SW18 . . . . 58 B1
Leylang Rd SE14. . . 50 C3
Leys Ct 3 SW9 . . . 173 B1
Leysdown
NW5 . . . . 12 C2
Leysdown Ho
SE17 . . . . 152 B2
Leysfield Rd W12. . 38 C4
Leythe Rd W3 . . . . 37 B4
LEYTON 19 C4
Leyton Mill Ret Pk
E10 . . . . 19 C4
Leyton Mills E10. . . 19 B4
Leyton Rd E15. . . . . 19 C2
Liardet St SE14 . . . 51 A4
Liberia Rd N5 . . . . . 15 A2
Liberty Bridge Rd
E15 . . . . 19 B3
Liberty Mews
SW12 . . . . 61 A1
Liberty St SW9 . . . 173 A4
Libra Rd 7 E3 . . . . 26 B3
Library Mans 4
W12 . . . . 39 B4
Library Par NW10. . 21 A4
Library Pl E1 . . . . . 32 A2
Library St SE1 . . . . 136 B3
Lichfield Ct TW9 . . 54 A4
Lichfield Gdns TW10,
TW9 . . . . 54 A2
Lichfield Ho 27
SE5 . . . . 48 B1
Lichfield Rd
Mile End E3 . . . . . 26 A2
Richmond TW9 . . . 44 B2
West Hampstead
NW2 . . . . 10 A4
Lichfield Terr 1
TW9 . . . . 54 A2
Lickey Ho W14 . . . 155 A4
Lidcote Gdns 22
SW9 . . . . 173 A1
Liddell Gdns
NW10 . . . . 22 B3
Liddell Rd NW6. . . 10 C2
Lidfield Rd N16. . . . 15 C4

Lidgate Rd **22**
SE15 ....49 B3
Lidiard Rd SW18....71 B2
Lidlington Pl NW1..83 A1
Lido The W2 ....100 C4
Lidyard Rd N19 ....4 B3
Liffey Ct NW10 ....8 C1
Liffords Pl SW13....46 B1
Lilford St SW15.....57 C3
Lighter Cl **16** SE16..41 A2
Lighterman Mews **15**
E1 ....32 B3
Lighterman's Rd
E14 ....42 A4
Lightermans Wlk
SW18 ....58 C3
Light Horse Ct
SW1 ....145 B1
Ligonier St
E2 ....24 B1 98 C2
Lilac Ho SE4 ....66 B4
Lilac Pl SE11 ....148 C3
Lilac St W12 ....29 C2
Lilestone Est NW8 ..89 C1
Lilestone Ho NW8 ..89 C2
Lilestone St NW8....90 A2
Lilford Ho SE5 ......48 B1
Lilford Rd SE5 ....48 A1
Lilian Baylis Ho
N1 ....15 B2
Lilian Baylis Tech Sch
SE11 ....149 A1
Lilley Cl E1 ....125 C1
Lillian Ave W3.......36 C4
Lillian Cl **11** N16 ....7 A1
Lillian Rd SW13 .....47 A4
Lillie Ho N5 ....14 C3
Lillie Rd SW6.......154 C3
Lillie Road Mans
SW6 ....154 B3
Lillieshall Rd SW4..61 B4
Lillie Yd SW6 ....155 B4
Lillingston Ho N7..14 C4
Lily Cl W14 ....39 C2
Lily Pl EC1 ....107 C4
Lilyville Rd SW6...164 C4
Limasol St SE1 ....139 A2
Limborough Ho **5**
E14 ....33 C4
Limburg Rd SW11..60 A3
Limeburner La
EC4 ....108 A2
Lime Cl E1 ....125 C2
Lime Ct SW15 ....57 A4
Lime Gr W12 ....39 B4
Limeharbour E14...42 A4
Lime Ho **7** TW9....45 A2
LIMEHOUSE 33 A2
Limehouse Cswy
E14 ....33 B2
Limehouse Ct **3**
E14 ....33 C3
Lime House Ct **8**
E14 ....33 B3
Limehouse Cut **4**
E14 ....34 A4
Limehouse Fields Est
14 E14 ....33 A4
Limehouse Link
(Tunnel) E14 ....33 B2
Limehouse Sta
E14 ....33 A3
Limekiln Wharf **21**
E14 ....33 B2

Limerick Cl SW12...73 B4
Limerick Ct **1**
SW12 ....73 B4
Limerston St
SW10 ....157 A3
Lime St Pas EC3...124 A4
Limes Ave
Barnes SW13 ....46 A1
Golders Green NW11..1 A4
Limes Ct NW6 ....9 C1
Limes Field Rd
SW14 ....56 A4
Limesford Rd
SE15 ....65 C3
Limes Gdns SW18 ..58 C1
Limes Gr SE13 ....67 B3
Lime St EC3 ....110 A1
Limes The
Camberwell SE5 .....64 A4
Kensington
W2 ....2 C1 113 C3
Limes Wlk SE15 ....65 B3
Lime Tree Ct **14**
E3 ....33 C4
Limpsfield Ave
SW19 ....69 C2
Limscott Ho **8** E3..27 A2
Linacre Cl SE15......65 A4
Linacre Ct W6 ....39 C1
Linacre Rd NW2 .....9 A2
Linale Ho N1 ....87 B1
Linberry Wlk **3**
SE8 ....41 B2
Lincoln Ave SW19 ..69 C1
Lincoln Ct N16 ....6 C4
Lincoln Ho
Bloomsbury WC1 ..107 A3
10 Dartmouth Pk
NW5 ....4 B1
2 Islington N1 .....15 B1
Knightsbridge
SW1 ....130 C3
Lincoln Mews
NW6 ....23 B4
Lincoln's Inn WC2 107 A2
Lincoln's Inn Fields
WC2 ....107 A2
Lindale SW19 ....70 A2
Lindal Rd SE4........66 B2
Linden Ave NW10..22 C3
Linden Ct **1**
SW18 ....59 C4
1 Shepherd's Bush
W12 ....30 B1
Linden Gdns
Chiswick W4 ....37 C1
Notting Hill
W2 ....31 C2 113 C3
Linden Gr SE15 .....65 B4
Linden Ho **10** SE8..51 B4
Linden Lodge Sch
SW19 ....70 A3
Linden Mans N6 .....4 A3
Linden Mews
Kensington
W2 ....31 C2 113 C3
Stoke Newington
N1 ....15 C3
Lindens The W4 .....45 B2
Lindfield Gdns
NW3 ....11 B3
Lindfield Hts NW3..11 B3
Lindfield St E14 .....33 C3

Lindisfarne Way
E9 ....18 A4
Lindley Ho
15 Peckham SE15 ....49 C3
9 Stepney E1 ....32 B4
Lindley Pl TW9 ......44 C2
Lindop Ho **3** E1....26 A1
Lindore Rd SW11 ...60 B3
Lindo St SE15 ....50 B1
Lindrop St SW6 ....166 C2
Lindsay Ct SW11..167 C3
Lindsay Sq SW1 ..147 C2
Lindsell St **6**
SE10 ....52 B2
Lindsey Ho SW10 157 C2
Lindsey Mews **18**
N1 ....15 B1
Lindsey St EC1 .....108 B4
Lind St SE8...........52 A1
Linford Christie
Stadium The
W12 ....30 A4
Linford Ho **3** E2 ..24 C4
Linford St SW8 ....170 C3
Linford Street Bsns
Est SW8 ....170 C4
Lingard Ho **11** E14..42 B3
Lingards Rd SE13 ..67 B3
Lingfield Ho
8 Acton Green
W4 ....37 B1
Lambeth SE1 ....136 B3
Lingham St SW9...172 C1
Ling's Coppice
SE21 ....75 C2
Lingwell Rd SW17..72 A1
Lingwood Rd E5 ......7 C4
Linhope St NW1 .....90 C1
Linkenholt Mans **3**
W6 ....38 B3
Link St E9 ....17 B3
Links Yd
10 Spitalfields
E1 ....111 A4
Spitalfields E1 .....111 A4
Link The W3..........28 A3
Linkway N4 ....6 B4
Linkwood Wlk
NW1 ....13 C1
Linnell Ho
Spitalfields E1 .....110 C4
St John's Wood
NW8 ....78 C4
Linnell Rd SE5 ......49 A1
Linnet Mews
SW12 ....72 C4
Linom Rd SW4 ....62 A3
Linscott Rd E5 ....17 B4
Linsey St SE16 .....153 B4
Linslade Ho
10 Hackney E2....24 C4
Marylebone NW8 ....90 B2
Linstead St **1**
NW6 ....10 C1
Linstead Way SW18,
SW19 ....70 A4
Lintaine Cl **16** W6 154 B3
Linthorpe Rd N16 ...7 A4
Linton Ho
Lower Holloway
N7 ....14 B4
2 Tower Hamlets
E3 ....33 C4

Linton St N1 ....87 A3
Linver Rd SW6 .....165 B2
Linwood Cl SE5 .....49 B1
Lion Cl SE4............66 C1
Lionel Ho **10** W10..31 A4
Lionel Mans **14**
W14 ....39 C3
Lionel Mews **13**
W10 ....31 A4
Lionel Prim Sch
TW8 ....36 A2
Lionel Road N
TW8 ....36 A2
Lionel Road S
TW8 ....36 B1
Lion Gate Gdns
TW9 ....54 B4
Lion Gate Mews
SW18 ....70 C4
Lion Mills **50** E2 ..24 C3
Lion Yd SW4 ....61 C3
Lipton Rd **9** E1 ....32 C3
Lisburne Rd NW3...12 B4
Lisford St SE15 .....49 B2
Lisgar Terr W14 ...140 C4
Liskeard Gdns SE3..53 C2
Liskeard Ho SE11 149 C2
Lisle Ct NW2 ....1 A1
Lisle St WC2 ....119 C4
Lismore Cir NW5 ...12 C3
Lismore Wlk **4**
N1 ....15 B2
Lissenden Gdns
NW5 ....12 C4
Lissenden Mans
NW5 ....12 C4
Lisson Cotts NW1 102 B4
Lisson Gr NW1,
NW8 ....90 A2
LISSON GROVE 90 B1
Lisson Ho NW1 ....102 A4
Lisson St NW1 .....102 A4
Lister Cl W3 ....28 C4
Lister Ct N16 ....7 A2
Lister Ho
Greenwich SE3 ......53 A4
Marylebone W1 ....104 A2
Spitalfields E1 .....111 C4
Lister Hospl SW1 146 A1
Lister Mews N7......14 B4
Liston Rd SW4 ....61 B4
Listowel Cl **2**
SW9 ....163 C2
Listria Lo N16 ....7 B2
Listria Pk N16 ....7 B2
Litcham Ho **18** E1..25 C2
Litchfield Gdns
NW10 ....8 C2
Litchfield St WC2 119 C4
Lithos Rd NW3 ......11 B2
Little Albany St
NW1 ....92 B2
Little Argyll St
W1 ....104 C1
Little Boltons The
SW10 ....142 B1
Little Britain EC1 108 B3
Littlebury Rd SW4 ..61 C4
Little Chelsea
Antiques Fair
SW3 ....144 B1
Little Chelsea Ho
SW10 ....157 A3
Little Chester St
SW1 ....132 A2

Little Cloisters
SW1 ....134 A2
Little College St
SW1 ....134 A2
Little Combe Cl **13**
SW15 ....57 C1
Littlecote Cl SW19..70 A4
Little Cottage Pl
SE10 ....52 A3
Little Deans Yd
SW1 ....134 A2
Little Dimocks
SW12 ....73 A2
Little Dorrit Ct
SE1 ....137 A4
Little Edward St
NW1 ....92 B4
Little Essex St
WC2 ....121 B4
Littlefield Cl N19 ...13 B4
Little George St
SW1 ....134 A3
Little Green St
NW5 ....13 A4
Little Marlborough St
W1 ....104 C1
Little Newport St
WC2 ....119 C4
Little New St EC4 107 C2
Little Portland St
W1 ....104 C2
Little Russell St
WC1 ....106 A3
Little St James's
SW1 ....118 C1
Little St Leonards
SW14 ....55 B4
Little Sanctuary
SW1 ....134 A3
Little Smith St
SW1 ....133 C2
Little Somerset St
E1 ....110 C1
Little Titchfield St
W1 ....104 C3
Littleton St SW18...71 B2
Little Trinity La
EC4 ....123 A4
Little Turnstile
WC1 ....106 C3
LITTLE VENICE 101 A4
Little Venice W9 ...100 C4
Littlewood SE13 ....67 B1
Livermere Ct **3**
E8 ....24 B4
Livermere Rd E8 ...24 B4
Liverpool Gr SE17 151 B1
Liverpool Ho N7 ....14 C2
Liverpool Rd
Islington N1 ....85 C3
Islington N1, N7....14 C1
Newham E16 ....35 A4
Liverpool St EC2...110 A3
Liverpool Street Sta
EC2 ....110 A3
Livesey Pl SE15......49 C4
Livingstone Ho **10**
SE5 ....48 B3
Livingstone Lo **13**
W9 ....23 C1
Livingstone Pl E14..42 B1
Livingstone Rd
1 Battersea
SW11 ....59 C4
Mill Meads E15......27 B4

ivity Sch The
London SW2 . . . . .62 A2
Streatham Hill
SW16 . . . . .74 B2
ivonia St W1 . . . . 105 A1
izard St EC1 . . . . 97 A3
landovery Ho 1
E14 . . . . .42 B4
lanelly Rd NW2 . . . . . . 1 B2
lanvanor Rd NW2 . . . . 1 B2
lewellyn Ho 10
N19 . . . . 4 C4
lewellyn St SE16 139 C3
loyd Baker St
WC1 . . . . 95 B3
loyd Ct
Ladywell SE13 . . . . . . 67 A2
6 West Norwood
SE27 . . . . .75 A1
loyd Ho N16 . . . . 6 C1
loyd's Ave EC3 . . 110 B1
loyd's Bldg EC3 . 110 A1
loyd's Pl SE3 . . . . 53 A1
loyd Sq WC1 . . . . 95 B4
loyd St WC1 . . . . 95 B4
loyd's Row EC1 . . . 96 A3
loyd St WC1 . . . . 95 B4
loyd Villas SE4 . . . 51 C1
loyd Williamson Sch
The 7 W10 . . . . 31 A4
loampit Hill SE13 . . 52 A1
loampit Vale SE13 . . 67 B4
loanda Cl 2 E14 . . 34 B4
loats Rd SW2 . . . . . . 62 A1
locarno Rd 6 W3 . . 28 B1
lochaline St W6 . . . 47 B4
lochbie 3 N4 . . . . 5 A4
lochinvar St
SW12 . . . . 73 A4
lochmore Ho
SW1 . . . . 145 C3
lochnagar St E14 . . 34 B4
lockbridge Ct 2
W9 . . . . .31 C4
locke Ho
Nine Elms SW8 . . 170 C4
Stamford Hill N16 . . . 7 B3
lockesfield Pl E14 . .42 A1
lockgate Cl E9 . . . . .18 B3
lockhart Cl N7 . . . . . .14 B2
lockhart St E3 . . . . . .26 B1
lockhurst St E5 . . . . 17 C4
lockington Rd
SW8 . . . . 170 B4
lockmead Rd
SE13 . . . . .67 B4
Lock Mews 9
N1 . . . . 13 C2
Lockside 17 E14 . . . 33 A2
Locksley St E14 . . . .33 B4
Lock View Ct 3
E14 . . . . .33 A2
Lockwood Ho 10
SE11 . . . . 163 B3
Lockwood Sq
SE16 . . . . .40 A3
Lockyer Est SE1 . 137 C3
Lockyer Ho
7 Greenwich
SE10 . . . . .43 B1
10 Putney SW15 . . 57 C4
South Lambeth
SW8 . . . . 162 A2
Lockyer St SE1 . . 137 C3
Locton Gn 4 E3 . . 26 B4
Loddiges Ho 5 E9 . 17 B1
Loddiges Rd E9 . . . 17 B1

Loddon Ho NW8 . . . 89 C1
Loder St SE15 . . . . . . .50 B3
Lodge Ave SW14 . . . .56 A4
Lodge Rd NW8 . . . . . 90 A3
Lodge The 8 W4 . . . 38 A3
Lodore St E14 . . . . . . 34 B3
Lodsworth Ho
SW11 . . . . 169 B3
Loftie St SE16 . . . 139 C3
Lofting Ho 6 N1 . . . 14 C1
Lofting Rd N1 . . . . . . 14 C1
Lofts on the Park 2
E9 . . . . 17 C2
Loftus Rd W12 . . . . . . 30 A1
Loftus Rd (Queens
Park Rangers FC)
W12 . . . . 30 A1
Logan Cl E15 . . . . 19 A3
Logan Mews W8 . 141 B4
Logan Pl W8 . . . . 141 B4
Loggetts SE21 . . . . . . 76 A2
Lohmann Ho 5
SE11 . . . . 163 B4
Lolesworth Cl E1 113 A3
Lollard St SE11 . . . 149 B3
Lollards Twr SE1 . 134 C1
Loman St SE1 . . . 136 B4
Lomas Dr 10 E8 . . . 16 B1
Lomas St E1 . . . . . 111 C4
Lombard Ct
4 Acton W3 . . . . .28 A1
City of London EC3 123 C4
Lombard La EC4 . 107 C1
Lombard Rd
SW11 . . . . 167 B2
Lombard St EC3 . 109 C1
Lombardy Pl W2 . 114 B3
Lomley Ho 3
SW2 . . . . .62 C1
Lomond Gr 3 SE5 . .48 C3
Lomond Ho 10
SE5 . . . . .48 C2
Loncroft Rd SE5 . . 49 A4
Londesborough Ho 1
N16 . . . . .16 A4
Londesborough Rd
N16 . . . . .16 A4
London Acad for
Higher Education
The E15 . . . . .27 C4
London Acad of
Computing &
Electronics
SW17 . . . . 72 B1
London Aquatics Ctr
E15 . . . . .19 B1
London Bridge EC4,
SE1 . . . . 123 C3
London Bridge City
Pier
SE1 . . . . 124 A2
. . . . 124 A2
London Bridge
Experience The
SE1 . . . . 123 C2
London Bridge Hospl
SE1 . . . . 123 C2
London Bridge St
SE1 . . . . 123 C1
London Bridge Sta
SE1 . . . . 123 C1
London Bridge Wlk
SE1 . . . . 123 C2
London Britannia Coll
N1 . . . . 97 B4

London Business Sch
NW1 . . . . 90 C2
London Canal Mus
N1 . . . . 84 C2
London Central
Mosque NW8 . . . . 90 B3
London Chest Hospl
E2 . . . . 25 B3
London City Sh Ctr
EC1 . . . . 97 A1
London Clinic The
(Hospl) NW1 . . . . 91 C1
London Coll of Beauty
Therapy W1 . . . . 105 A1
London Coll of Bsns &
Computer Studies 12
SW4 . . . . 61 C3
London Coll of
Communication (Sch
of Printing &
Publishing)
SE1 . . . . 136 B3
London Coll of
Economics &
Science NW10 . . . . 20 B1
London Coll of
Fashion (Curtain Rd)
EC2 . . . . 24 A1 98 B2
London Coll of
Fashion (Golden La)
EC1 . . . . 96 C1
London Coll of
Fashion (John
Prince's St) W1 . 104 A1
London Coll of
Fashion (Mare St)
E8 . . . . 17 B1
London Coll of
International
Business Studies
WC1 . . . . 106 B3
London Ct 3
SE18 . . . . 58 C2
London Ctr of
Contemporary
Music 123 A1
London City Hall
SE1 . . . . 134 C4
London Dungeon The
SE1 . . . . 134 C4
London East Acad
E1 . . . . 111 C2
London Eye Hospl
W1 . . . . 104 A3
London Eye
(Millennium Wheel)
SE1 . . . . 134 C4
London Fields East
Side E8 . . . . 25 A4
London Fields Prim
Sch 13 E8 . . . . .25 A4
London Fields Sta
E8 . . . . 17 A1
London Fields West
Side E8 . . . . 16 C1
London Film Mus
SE1 . . . . 134 C4
London Film Sch The
WC2 . . . . 106 A1
London Fire Brigade
Pop-up Mus
SE1 . . . . 148 C4
London Glassblowing
Workshop SE1 . . 138 A3
London Ho 5 W6 . . 38 C2
London Ho TW9 . . . 54 B4

London Ho NW8 . . . 80 B2
London Hospital
Dental Inst 5 E1 . 32 A4
London Ho E1 . . . . . . .32 A4
London Independent
Hospl The E1 . . . . . 32 C4
London Irish Rifles
Mus SW9 . . . . 48 B2
London Islamic Sch 7
E1 . . . . 32 B3
London La E8 . . . . 17 A1
London Metropolitan
Univ 51 . . . . 110 C2
London Metropolitan
Univ (Central Ho)
E1 . . . . 111 B2
London Metropolitan
Univ (Commercial
Rd) 43 E1 . . . . . . 111 C2
London Metropolitan
Univ (Ladbrook Ho)
5 N5 . . . . 15 A3
London Metropolitan
Univ (Moorgate)
EC2 . . . . 109 C3
London Metropolitan
Univ North Campus
N7 . . . . 14 C4
London Mews W2 101 C2
London Mus of Water
& Steam TW8 . . . . 36 A1
London Nautical Sch
SE1 . . . . 121 C2
London Oratory Sch
The SW6 . . . . 155 C2
London Oratory The
SW7 . . . . 130 A1
London Rd SE1 . . 136 B2
London Sch of
Economics &
Political Science
WC2 . . . . 107 A1
London South Bank
Univ SE1 . . . . 136 B2
London St
City of London
EC3 . . . . 124 B4
Paddington W2 . . 101 B1
London Stadium
(West Ham FC)
E15 . . . . .19 A1
London Stile 5
W4 . . . . 36 C1
London Stock
Exchange EC2 . . 108 C2
London Terr 1 E2 . 24 C3
London Transport
Mus WC2 . . . . 120 B4
London Wall EC2 . 109 B3
London Wall Bldgs
EC2 . . . . 109 C3
London Wharf 4
E2 . . . . 25 A3
Long Acre WC2 . . 106 A1
Longbeach Rd
SW11 . . . . 60 B4
Longberrys NW2 . . . 1 B1
Longbridge Way
SE13 . . . . 67 B2
Longcliffe Ho
SW18 . . . . 59 A2
Long Dr W3 . . . . 29 A3
Longfellow Way
SE1 . . . . 153 A3

Longfield Dr
SW14 . . . . 55 A2
Longfield Est SE1 153 A3
Longfield St SW18 . 70 C4
Longford Ct
1 Bedford Pk
W12 . . . . 38 A4
2 Clapton Pk E5 . 17 C4
Longford Ho 7
E1 . . . . 32 B3
Longford Ho NW1
SW1 . . . . 92 B2
Longford Wlk 9
SW2 . . . . .74 C4
Longhope Cl SE15 . 49 B4
Longhurst Ho
W9 . . . . 23 B2
Long La
Bermondsey SE1 . 137 C3
Holborn EC1 . . . . 108 B4
Longland Ct
Bermondsey SE1 . 153 B2
Hackney E9 . . . . . . 18 A3
Longlands Ct
W11 . . . . 31 B2 113 A4
Longleat Ho SW1 . 147 B2
Longleigh Ho 3
SE5 . . . . 49 A2
Longlents Ho 3
NW10 . . . . 20 C4
Longley Ho 6
N19 . . . . 13 B4
Longley St SE1 . . 153 B4
Longman Ho
9 Globe Town
E2 . . . . 25 C3
10 Shoreditch E8 . 24 B4
Long Meadow 20
N7 . . . . 14 C3
Longmoor Point 14
SW15 . . . . 69 A3
Longmore St
SW1 . . . . 146 C3
Longnor Rd E1 . . . . . 25 C2
Long Pond Rd SE3 . 53 A2
Long Rd SW4 . . . . . . 61 B3
Longridge Ho
SE1 . . . . 137 A1
Longridge Rd
SW5 . . . . 141 C3
Longs Ct 2 TW9 . . 54 B3
Long's Ct W1 . . . 119 C3
Longshore SE8 . . . . 41 B2
Long St E2 . . . . . 24 B2 98 C4
Longstaff Cres
SW18 . . . . 58 C1
Longstone Ave
NW10 . . . . 21 B4
Longthorne Ho 18
E3 . . . . 26 B2
Longthorpe Ct 9
W6 . . . . 38 B2
Longville Rd SE11 150 B4
Long Wlk SE1 . . . 138 B2
Longwood Dr
SW15 . . . . 56 C1
Long Yd WC1 . . . . . . 94 C1
Lonsdale Ave
Fulham SW6 . . . . . . 58 C4
6 Stoke Newington
N4 . . . . 6 B4
Lonsdale Mews
Notting Hill W11 . . . 31 B3

Lonsdale Mews
continued
4 Richmond TW9 . . .44 C2
Lonsdale Pl N1 . . . .14 C1
Lonsdale Rd
Barnes SW13 . . . . . . .46 B3
Chiswick W4 . . . . .38 B2
Kilburn NW6 . . . . .23 B4
Notting Hill W11 . . . .31 B3
Lonsdale Sq
Islington N1 . . . . .14 C1
Islington N1 . . . . .85 C4
Lopez Ho 4 SW9 . .62 A4
Loraine Rd
Chiswick W4 . . . . .45 A4
Islington N7 . . . . .14 B4
Lord David Pitt Ho 1
SE24 . . . . .62 C3
Lorden Wlk 13
E2 . . . . .24 C2 99 B3
Lord Hills Rd W2 . .100 B4
Lord Holland La 6
SW9 . . . . .173 C2
Lord Napier Pl
W6 . . . . .38 C1
Lord North St
SW1 . . . . .134 A1
Lord Roberts Mews
SW6 . . . . .156 A1
Lords Cl SE21 . . . . .75 B2
Lord's Cricket Mus
NW8 . . . . .89 C3
Lordship Gr N16 . . . . .6 C2
Lordship Ho 5 N16 . . .6 C2
Lordship La SE22 . . .64 B1
Lordship Park Mews
N16 . . . . .6 B2
Lordship Pk N16 . . . . .6 C2
Lordship Pl SW3 . .158 A3
Lordship Rd N16 . . . . .6 C2
Lordship Terr N16 . . .6 C2
Lord's Indoor Cricket
Sch NW8 . . . . .90 A4
Lord's (MCC &
Middlesex Cty
Cricket Ground)
NW8 . . . . .89 C4
Lord's View NW8 . . .89 C3
Loreburn Ho 2
N7 . . . . .14 B4
Lorenzo St N1,
WC1 . . . . .94 C4
Loris Rd W6 . . . . . . .39 B3
Lorn Ct SW9 . . . . . .173 B2
Lorne Cl NW8 . . . . .90 B3
Lorne Ct SW15 . . . .57 C1
Lorne Gdns 5
W11 . . . . .39 C4
Lorne Ho
Hornsey N4 . . . . .5 B4
7 Tower Hamlets
E1 . . . . .33 A4
Lorne Rd
Finsbury Pk N4 . . . . . .5 B4
3 Richmond TW10 . .54 B2
Lorn Rd SW9 . . . . .173 B2
Lorraine Ct 10
NW1 . . . . .13 A1
Lorrimore Rd
SE17 . . . . .48 A4
Lorrimore Sq
SE17 . . . . .48 A4
Lorton Ho 9 NW6 . .23 C4

Lostock Ho 10
SW8 . . . . .171 B2
Lothair Rd S N4 . . . . .6 A4
Lothbury EC2 . . . . .109 B2
Lothian Rd SW9 . . . .48 A2
Lothrop St W10 . . . . .23 A2
Lots Rd SW10 . . . . .157 A1
Loudoun Rd NW8 . . .79 A3
Loughborough Ct 7
SW9 . . . . .63 A4
Loughborough
Junction Sta
SW9 . . . . .63 A4
Loughborough Pk
SW9 . . . . .63 A3
Loughborough Prim
Sch SW9 . . . . .48 A1
Loughborough Rd SE5,
SE24 . . . . .48 A1
Loughborough St
SE11 . . . . .149 A1
Lough Rd N7 . . . . . .14 B2
Louisa Cl E9 . . . . . .25 C4
Louisa Gdns E1 . . . .25 C1
Louisa Ho SW15 . . . .56 B3
Louisa St E1 . . . . . . .25 C1
Louise Bennett Cl 9
SE24 . . . . .63 A3
Louise De Marillac Ho
20 E1 . . . . .32 B4
Louise White Ho 1
N19 . . . . .4 C3
Louisville Rd
SW17 . . . . .72 C1
Louvaine Rd SW11 . .59 C3
Lovat Cl NW2 . . . . . .9 A1
Lovat La EC3 . . . . . .124 A3
Lovatt Ct SW12 . . . . .73 A3
Loveday Ho 2
SW2 . . . . .74 C3
Lovegrove St SE1 . . .49 C4
Lovegrove Wlk
E14 . . . . .34 B1
Love La EC2 . . . . . .109 A2
Lovelace Ho 12 E8 . .24 B4
Lovelace Rd SE21 . . .75 B3
Lovelinch Cl SE15 . . .50 B4
Lovell Ho E8 . . . . . . .24 C4
Lovell Pl SE16 . . . . . .41 A3
Loveridge Mews
NW6 . . . . .10 B2
Loveridge Rd NW6 . .10 B2
Lover's Wlk W1 . . . .117 B1
Lovette Ho 4 E3 . . . .26 C2
Lovetts PI SW18 . . . .59 A3
Love Wlk SE5 . . . . . .48 C1
Low Cross Wood La
SE21 . . . . .76 B1
Lowden Rd SE24 . . . .63 B3
Lowder Ho 6 E1 . . . .32 A1
Lowe Ave E16 . . . . . .35 C4
Lowell Ho 10 SE5 . . . .48 B3
Lowell St E14 . . . . . .33 A3
Lower Addison Gdns
W14 . . . . .126 A3
Lower Belgrave St
SW1 . . . . .132 A1
LOWER CLAPTON .17 B4
Lower Clapton Rd
E5 . . . . .17 B4
Lower Clarendon Wlk
9 W11 . . . . .31 A3
Lower Comm S
SW15 . . . . .57 A4
Lower Grosvenor Pl
SW1 . . . . .132 B2

Lower Grove Rd
TW10 . . . . .54 B2
LOWER
HOLLOWAY 14 A3
Lower James St
W1 . . . . .119 A4
Lower John St
W1 . . . . .119 A4
Lower Lea Crossing
E14, E16 . . . . .35 A2
Lower Mall W6 . . . . .39 A1
Lower Marsh SE1 . .135 B3
Lower Merton Rise
NW3 . . . . .12 A1
Lower Mortlake Rd
TW9 . . . . .54 B4
Lower Pk
Acton W3 . . . . .20 B1
8 Putney SW15 . . . .57 C2
LOWER PLACE 20 B3
Lower Place Bsns Ctr
NW10 . . . . .20 B3
Lower Rd SE16 . . . . . .40 B4
Lower Richmond Rd
Mortlake SW14,
TW9 . . . . .55 A4
Putney SW15 . . . . . . .57 B4
Lower Robert St
WC2 . . . . .120 B3
Lower Sloane St
SW1 . . . . .145 B2
Lower Terr NW3 . . . . .2 B1
Lower Thames St
EC3 . . . . .124 A3
Lowerwood Ct
W11 . . . . .31 A3
Loweswater Ho E3 .26 B1
Lowfield Rd
Dagenham W3 . . . . . .28 B3
Hampstead NW6 . . . .10 C1
Lowlands NW3 . . . . .12 A2
Lowman Rd N7 . . . . .14 B4
Lowndes Cl SW1 . .131 C1
Lowndes Ct
Knightsbridge
SW1 . . . . .131 A2
Marylebone W1 . . . .104 C1
Lowndes Lo SW1 . .131 A2
Lowndes Pl SW1 . .131 B1
Lowndes Sq SW1 . .131 A3
Lowndes St SW1 . .131 B2
Lowood Ho 12 E1 . . .32 B2
Lowood St E1 . . . . . .32 A2
Lowry Ct 3 SE16 . . .40 A1
Lowther Ho
8 Pimlico SW1 . . . . .147 A1
5 Shoreditch E8 . . . .24 B4
Lowther Prim Sch
SW13 . . . . .46 C4
Lowther Rd
Barnes SW13 . . . . . . .46 B2
Islington N7 . . . . .14 C3
Lowth Rd SE5 . . . . . .48 B1
Loxford Gdns 5
N5 . . . . .15 A4
Loxford Ho SW1 . . .145 C3
Loxham St WC1 . . . . .94 B3
Loxley Rd SW18 . . . .71 C3
Lubavitch Boys Prim
Sch 6 E5 . . . . .7 B4
Lubavitch House Sch
(Jun Boys) 9 E5 . . . .7 B4
Lubavitch Senior
Girls' Sch 8 N16 . . . .7 B4
Lubbock Ho 21
E14 . . . . .34 A2

Lubbock St SE14 . . . .50 B3
Lucan Ho N1 . . . . . . .87 C3
Lucan Pl SW3 . . . . .144 B3
Lucas Ct SW11 . . . .169 C3
Lucas Ho
2 Clapham SW8 . . .171 A2
Walham Green
SW10 . . . . .156 B2
Lucas St SE4, SE8 . . .51 C2
Lucas Vale Prim Sch
SE8 . . . . .51 C2
Lucerne Mews
W8 . . . . .31 C1 113 C2
Lucerne Rd N5 . . . . .15 A4
Lucey Rd SE16 . . . . .139 B1
Lucey Way SE16 . . . .153 C4
Lucien Rd SW18 . . . .71 A2
Lucraft Ho 12 SW2 . .74 A4
Lucy Ashe Ho
SE17 . . . . .150 B3
Lucy Brown Ho
SE1 . . . . .123 A1
Lucy Cres W3 . . . . . .20 B1
Ludgate Broadway
EC4 . . . . .108 B1
Ludgate Cir EC4 . . .108 A1
Ludgate Hill EC4 . . .108 A1
Ludgate Sq EC4 . . . .108 B1
Ludham NW5 . . . . . .12 B3
Ludlow Ct W3 . . . . . .37 B4
Ludlow St EC1 . . . . . .96 C2
Ludovick Wlk
SW15 . . . . .56 A3
Ludwell Ho W14 . . .126 B2
Ludwick Mews
SE14 . . . . .51 A3
Lugard Ho 2 W12 . . .30 A1
Lugard Rd SE15 . . . . .50 A2
Luke Ho 82 E1 . . . . . .32 A3
Luke St EC2 . . . .24 A1 98 A2
Lukin St E1 . . . . .32 B3
Lullingstone Ho 20
SE15 . . . . .50 B4
Lullingstone La
SE13 . . . . .67 C1
Lulot Gdns N19 . . . . .4 A2
Lulworth
Camden Town
NW1 . . . . .13 C1
Walworth SE17 . . . . .151 B2
Lulworth Ho SW8 . .162 C1
Lulworth Rd SE15 . . .50 A1
Lumiere Ct 7
SW17 . . . . .72 C2
Lumina Bldg 1
E14 . . . . .34 B1
Lumley Ct WC2 . . . .120 B3
Lumley Flats SW1 . .145 B2
Lumley St W1 . . . . .103 C1
Lumsdon NW8 . . . . . .78 B3
Lunan Ho 14 E3 . . . . .26 B3
Lund Point E15 . . . . . .27 B4
Luntley Pl E1 . . . . . .111 B3
Lupin Cl SW2 . . . . . .75 A2
Lupino Ct SE11 . . . .149 A4
Lupin Point SE1 . . . .139 A3
Lupton St NW5 . . . . .13 B4
Lupus St SW1 . . . . .147 A1
Luralda Gdns E14 . . .42 C1
Lurgan Ave W6 . . . . .47 C4
Lurline Gdns
SW11 . . . . .169 C4
Luscombe Ho
SW18 . . . . .58 B2

Luscombe Way
SW8 . . . . .162 A2
Lusher Ho SW15 . . . .57 C1
Lushington Rd
NW10 . . . . .22 A3
Lushington Terr 8
E8 . . . . .16 C3
Luton Pl SE10 . . . . . .52 B3
Luton St NW8 . . . . . .89 C1
Luttrell Ave SW15 . .57 A2
Lutyens Ho SW1 . . .146 C1
Luxborough Ho
W1 . . . . .103 B4
Luxborough St
W1 . . . . .103 B4
Luxborough Twr
W1 . . . . .103 B4
Luxemburg Gdns
W6 . . . . .39 C2
Luxford St SE16 . . . .40 C2
Luxmore St SE4 . . . .51 B2
Luxor St SE5 . . . . . . .63 B4
Lyall Mews SW1 . . .131 B1
Lyall Mews W
SW1 . . . . .131 B1
Lyall St SW1 . . . . . .131 B1
Lyal Rd E3 . . . . .26 A3
Lycée Français
Charles de Gaulle
SW7 . . . . .143 B4
Lycett Ho 10 SW2 . .74 A4
Lycett Pl 3 W12 . . . . .38 C4
Lycott Gr SE22 . . . . .64 B2
Lydden Gr SW18 . . . .71 A4
Lydden Rd SW18 . . . .71 A4
Lydford NW1 . . . . . . .83 A3
Lydford Rd
Brondesbury NW2 . . . . .9 C2
Paddington W9 . . . . . .23 B1
Lydgate Ho 8
N16 . . . . .16 A3
Lydhurst Ave SW2 . .74 B2
Lydney Cl
Camberwell SE15 . . . .49 A3
Putney SW19 . . . . . . .70 A2
Lydon Rd SW4 . . . . .61 B4
Lydwell Ho 20
SW8 . . . . .171 B1
Lyford Rd SW18 . . . .72 A3
Lygoe Ho 16 N6 . . . . .4 C4
Lygon Ho 2
E2 . . . . .24 C2 99 B4
Lygon Pl SW1 . . . . .132 A1
Lyham Cl SW2 . . . . .62 A1
Lyham Rd SW2 . . . . .62 A1
Lyle Pk SW15 . . . . . .57 C1
Lyly Ho SE1 . . . . . . .137 C1
Lyme Gr E9 . . . . .17 B1
Lyme Grove Ho 2
E9 . . . . .17 B1
Lyme St NW1 . . . . . .82 C4
Lyminge Gdns SW17,
SW18 . . . . .72 A3
Lymington Mans
NW6 . . . . .11 A2
Lymington Rd
NW6 . . . . .11 A2
Lympstone Gdns
SE15 . . . . .49 C3
Lynbrook Gr SE15 . .49 A3
Lynch Wlk 2 SE8 . . .51 B4
Lyncott Cres SW4 . .61 A3
Lyncourt SE3 . . . . . .52 C1
Lyncroft Gdns
NW6 . . . . .10 C3

yncroft Mans **4**
NW6 . . . . .10 C3
yndale NW2 . . . . 1 B1
yndale Ave NW2 . . . . . 1 B1
yndale Cl SE3 . . . . . .53 B4
ynde Ho **2** SW4 . . . .61 C4
ynden Gate SW15 . .69 A4
yndhurst Gdns
NW3 . . . . .11 C3
yndhurst Gr SE5,
SE15 . . . . .49 B1
yndhurst Ho **2**
SW15 . . . . .68 C4
yndhurst House Prep
Sch 11 C3
yndhurst Lo **3**
E14 . . . . .42 C2
yndhurst Rd NW3 .11 C3
yndhurst Sch
SE5 . . . . .48 C1
yndhurst Sq SE15 .49 B2
yndhurst Terr
NW3 . . . . .11 C3
yndhurst Way
SE15 . . . . .49 B1
Lyneham Wlk E5 . . .18 A3
Lynette Ave SW4 . .61 B1
Lynford French Ho
SE17 . . . . .150 C2
Lyngham Ct **10** N4 . . .6 B4
ynhurst Ho NW8 . .79 B3
Lyn Mews **13** E3 . . .26 B2
Lynmouth Rd N16 . .7 B3
Lynne Ct NW6 . . . . .11 A1
Lynnett Ct E9 . . . . . .18 A2
Lynn Ho SE15 . . . . .49 C4
Lynn Rd SW12 . . . . .73 A4
Lynton Cl SE21 . . . . . .3 A1
Lynton Ct **5** W3 . . .28 B3
Lynton Est SE1 . . . .153 B3
Lynton Ho **7** W2 .100 B1
Lynton Lo N5 . . . . . . .15 A3
Lynton Mews SE1 .135 B2
Lynton Rd
Acton W3 . . . . .28 A2
Bermondsey SE1 . . .153 A3
Paddington NW6 . . .23 B3
Lynton Terr **4** W3 .28 B3
Lyn Terr SW19 . . . . .70 C1
Lyon Ho NW8 . . . . . .90 A1
Lyons Pl NW8 . . . . . .89 B1
Lyon St N1 . . . . .14 B1
Lyons Wlk W14 . . .140 A4
Lyric Rd SW13 . . . . .46 B2
Lysander Gr N19 . . . .4 C3
Lysander Ho **10**
E2 . . . . .25 A3
Lysander Mews N19 .4 B3
Lysia Ct SW6 . . . . . .47 C3
Lysias Rd SW12 . . . .61 A1
Lysia St SW6 . . . . . .47 C3
Lysons Wlk SW6 . . .56 C2
Lytham St SE17 . . . .151 B1
Lyttelton Cl NW3 . . .12 A1
Lytten Ct **6** W12 . . .38 C4
Lyttleton Ho **10** E9 .17 B1
Lytton Ct WC1 . . . .106 B3
Lytton Gr SW15 . . . .58 A1

M

Mabel Thornton Ho **12**
N16 . . . . .15 C4
Mabledon Pl NW1,
WC1 . . . . .93 C3

Mablethorpe Rd
SW6 . . . . .154 A1
Mabley St E9 . . . . . .18 A3
MacArthur Ho **4**
SW2 . . . . .74 A4
Macartney Ho
SE10 . . . . .52 C3
Macaulay CE Prim
Sch SW4 . . . . .61 A3
Macaulay Ct SW4 . .61 A4
Macaulay Ho
2 Kensal Town
W10 . . . . .31 A4
10 Stoke Newington
N16 . . . . .7 A1
Macaulay Rd SW4 . .61 A4
Macaulay Sq SW4 . .61 A3
McAuley Cl SE1 . . . .135 B2
Macaulay Mews
SE13 . . . . .52 B1
McAusland Ho **5**
E3 . . . . .26 B3
Macbeth Ho **4** N1 .24 A3
Macbeth St W6 . . . .39 A1
McBride Ho **6** E3 .26 B3
McCall Cl SW4 . . . .172 A2
McCall Ho N7 . . . . . .14 A4
Mccarthy Ct
SW11 . . . . .168 B3
Macclesfield Rd
EC1 . . . . .96 C4
Macclesfield St **2**
W1 . . . . .119 C4
McCoid Way SE1 . .136 C3
Mcconnell Ho
SW8 . . . . .171 B3
McCormick Ho **9**
SW2 . . . . .74 C3
McCrone Mews **8**
NW3 . . . . .11 C2
McCullum Rd E3 . . .26 B4
McDermott Cl
SW11 . . . . .60 A4
McDermott Rd
SE15 . . . . .64 C4
Macdonald Ho **7**
SW11 . . . . .169 B2
Macdonald Rd N19 . .4 B2
McDougall Ct
TW9 . . . . .44 C1
McDougall Ho
E2 . . . . .24 C2 99 B3
McDowall Cl E16 . . .35 B4
McDowall Rd SE5 . .48 B2
Macduff Rd SW11 .169 C4
McGlashon Ho **15**
E2 . . . . .24 C2 99 B1
McGregor Ct **8**
N1 . . . . .24 A2 98 B4
McGregor Rd W11 .31 B4
Machell Rd SE15 . . .65 B4
McIndoe Ct N1 . . . . .87 B4

McIntosh Ho **14**
SE16 . . . . .40 B2
McIntyre Ct **19**
SW4 . . . . .172 B2
Mackay Ho **33**
W12 . . . . .30 A2
Mackay Rd SW4 . . .61 A4
McKenna Ho **3**
E3 . . . . .26 B3
Mackennal St NW8 .80 B2
Mackenzie Cl
W12 . . . . .30 A2
Mackenzie Rd N7 . .14 B2
Mackenzie Wlk
E14 . . . . .33 C1
McKerrell Rd SE15 .49 C2
Mackeson Rd
NW3 . . . . .12 B4
Mackie Ho **16**
SW2 . . . . .74 C4
Mackie Rd SW2 . . . .74 C4
McKiernan Ct **2**
SW11 . . . . .168 A2
Mackinnon Wood Ho
16 E2 . . . . .24 C2 99 B3
Mackintosh La E9 . .17 C3
Macklin St WC2 . . .106 B2
Mackonochie Ho
EC1 . . . . .107 B4
Mackrow Wlk **11**
E14 . . . . .34 B2
Macks Rd SE16 . . . .153 C4
Mackworth Ho
NW1 . . . . .92 C4
Mackworth St
NW1 . . . . .92 C4
Mac Laren Mews
SW15 . . . . .57 B3
Maclean Rd SE23 . .66 A1
Mcleod Ct SE21 . . . .76 C3
McLeod's Mews
SW7 . . . . .142 B4
Mcleod St SE17 . . . .151 A1
Maclise Rd W14 . . .126 A1
McManus Ho **2**
SW11 . . . . .59 C4
Mcmillan Ho SE4 . .66 A4
Macmillan Ho
Cricklewood NW4 . . . .9 A4
Lisson Gr NW8 . . . . .90 B3
McMillan St SE8 . . .51 C4
Mcmorran Ho **4**
N7 . . . . .14 A4
Macnamara Ho
SW10 . . . . .157 B2
McNeil Rd SE5 . . . . .49 A1
McNicol Dr NW10 . .20 B3
Maconochies Rd **8**
E14 . . . . .42 A1
Macquarie Way
E14 . . . . .42 A2
Macready Ho W1 . .102 B3
Macready Pl **2**
N7 . . . . .14 A4
Macroom Ho W9 . . .23 B2
Macroom Rd W9 . . .23 B2
Mac's Pl EC4 . . . . . .107 C2
Madame Tussauds
NW1 . . . . .91 B1
Madani Girls' Sch **11**
E1 . . . . .32 A3
Maddams St E3 . . . .27 A1
Maddocks Ho **3**
E1 . . . . .32 A2
Maddock Way
SE17 . . . . .48 A4

Maddox St W1 . . . .118 B4
Madinah Rd
7 Dalston E8 . . . . . .16 C2
London E8 . . . . .16 C3
Madison Ho E3 . . . .27 B2
Madoc Cl NW2 . . . . .1 C2
Madras Pl N7 . . . . . .14 C2
Madrid Rd SW13 . . .46 C3
Madron St SE17 . . . .152 B2
Mafeking Ave
TW8 . . . . .44 A4
Magdala Ave N19 . . .4 B2
Magdalene Cl **7**
SE15 . . . . .50 A1
Magdalene Ho **7**
SW15 . . . . .57 C1
Magdalen Pas **1**
E1 . . . . .125 A4
Magdalen Rd
SW18 . . . . .71 C3
Magdalen St SE1 . . .124 A1
Magee St SE11 . . . . .163 B4
Magellan Ho **16**
E1 . . . . .25 C1
Magellan Pl **23**
E14 . . . . .41 C2
Magnin Cl **5** E8 . . .24 C4
Magnolia Cl
Richmond TW9 . . . . . .45 A2
Wandsworth SW11 . .60 B1
Magnolia Ho **16**
SE8 . . . . .51 B4
Magnolia Pl SW4 . .62 A2
Magnolia Rd W4 . . .45 A4
Magnolia Wharf
W4 . . . . .45 A4
Magpie Ho **7** E3 . .26 B4
Magpie Pl SE14 . . . .51 A4
Magri Wlk **23** E1 . .32 B4
Maguire St SE1 . . . .139 A4
Mahatma Gandhi Ind
Est **1** SE24 . . . . . .63 A3
Mahogany Cl SE16 .33 A1
Mahoney Ho SE14 . .51 B2
Maida Ave W2 . . . . .89 A1
MAIDA VALE 88 A4
Maida Vale W9 . . . . .88 C3
Maida Vale Sta
W9 . . . . .88 B4
Maiden La
Borough The SE1 . . .123 A2
Camden Town NW1 . .13 C1
Strand WC2 . . . . . . .120 B4
Maidenstone Hill
SE10 . . . . .52 B2
Maidstone Bldgs
SE1 . . . . .123 B1
Maidstone Ho **4**
E14 . . . . .34 A3
Mail Coach Yd **38**
E2 . . . . .24 A2 98 B4
Main Yd E9 . . . . .18 C2
Maismore St SE15 . .49 C4
Maitland Cl **3**
SE10 . . . . .52 A3
Maitland Ct W2 . . . .115 B4
Maitland Ho
Chelsea SW1 . . . . . .160 C4
2 South Hackney
E2 . . . . .25 B3
MAITLAND PARK . .12 B2
Maitland Park Rd
NW3 . . . . .12 B2
Maitland Park Villas
NW3 . . . . .12 B2
Maitland Pl E5 . . . . .17 B4
Majestic Ct N4 . . . . . .6 A3

Major Cl SW9 . . . . . .63 A4
Major Rd
E15 . . . . .19 C3
SE16 . . . . .139 C2
Majorie Mews **6**
E1 . . . . .32 C3
Makepeace Ave N6 . .3 C2
Makepeace Mans
N6 . . . . .3 C2
Makins St SW3 . . . .144 B3
Malabar Ct **20**
W12 . . . . .30 A2
Malabar St E14 . . . . .41 C4
Malam Ct SE11 . . . .149 B3
Malam Gdns **3**
E14 . . . . .34 A2
Malay Ho **2** E1 . . .32 B1
Malbrook Rd
SW15 . . . . .57 A3
Malcolm Ho **13** N1 .24 A3
Malcolm Pl E2 . . . . .25 B1
Malcolm Rd E1 . . . . .25 B1
Malcolmson Ho
SW1 . . . . .147 C1
Malden Cres NW1 . .12 C2
Malden Pl **1**
NW5 . . . . .12 C3
Malden Rd NW5 . . . .12 C2
Maldon Cl
Camberwell SE5 . . . .64 A4
Shoreditch N1 . . . . . .87 A4
Stratford New Town
E15 . . . . .19 C3
Maldon Rd W3 . . . . .28 B2
Malet Pl WC1 . . . . . .93 B1
Malet St WC1 . . . . .105 C4
Maley Ave SE27 . . . .75 A2
Malfort Rd SE5 . . . . .64 A4
Malins Ct SW12 . . . .60 C1
Mallams Mews 1
SW9 . . . . .63 A4
Mallard Cl
1 Hackney E9 . . . . .18 B2
Kilburn NW6 . . . . . . .23 C4
Mallard Ho
8 Camberwell
SE15 . . . . .49 B2
St John's Wood
NW8 . . . . .80 A1
Mallard Point **6**
E3 . . . . .26 C2
Mallet Ho **10**
SW15 . . . . .56 C2
Mallet Rd SE13 . . . . .67 C1
Mall Galleries
SW1 . . . . .119 C2
Malling SE13 . . . . . .67 A2
Mallinson Rd
SW11 . . . . .60 B2
Mallinson Sp Ctr
N6 . . . . .3 B4
Mallon Gdns E1 . . .111 A3
Mallord St SW3 . . . .157 C4
Mallory Bldgs EC1 . .96 A1
Mallory Cl SE4 . . . . .66 A3
Mallory Ho NW8 . . .90 B2
Mallory St NW8 . . . .90 B2
Mallow Ct SE13 . . . .52 B1
Mallow St EC1 . . . . .97 B2
Mall Rd W6 . . . . .39 A1
Mall Studios **1**
NW3 . . . . .12 B3
Mall The
Mortlake SW14 . . . . .55 B2
St James SW1 . . . . .119 B1
Malmesbury **30** E2 .25 B3
Malmesbury Prim Sch
23 E3 . . . . .26 B2

Malmesbury Rd
Bow E3 . . . . **26** B3
Newham E16 . . . . **35** A4
Malmesbury Terr
E16 . . . . **35** B4
Malmsmead Ho
E9 . . . . **18** A3
Malorees Jun & Inf
Schs NW6 . . . . **9** C1
Malpas Rd
Hackney E8 . . . . **17** A2
New Cross SE4 . . . . **51** B1
Malta St EC1 . . . . **96** B2
Maltby St Mkt
SE1 . . . . **138** C3
Maltby St SE1 . . . . . . **138** C2
Malthouse Dr W4 . . **46** B4
Malthouse Pas
SW13 . . . . **46** A1
Malting Ho E14 . . . . . . **33** B2
Maltings W4 . . . . **36** C1
Maltings Cl SW13 . . . **46** A1
Maltings Lo SW4 . . . . **46** A3
Maltings Pl
Bermondsey SE1 . . . . **138** B4
Parsons Green
SW6 . . . . **166** B3
Malt Mill SE1 . . . . . . **124** C1
Malton Mews [1]
W10 . . . . **31** A3
Malton Rd W10 . . . . . **31** A3
Maltravers St
WC2 . . . . **121** B4
Malt St SE1 . . . . **49** C4
Malva Cl SW18 . . . . . . **59** A2
Malvern Cl W10 . . . . . **31** A4
Malvern Ct
[15] Shepherd's Bush
W12 . . . . **38** C4
South Kensington
SW7 . . . . **143** C4
Malvern Gdns NW2 . . **1** A2
Malvern Ho
London N16 . . . . **7** B3
SE17 . . . . **151** A1
Malvern Mews
NW6 . . . . **23** C2
Malvern Pl NW6 . . . . **23** B2
Malvern Rd
Dalston E8 . . . . **16** C1
Maida Vale NW6 . . . . . **23** C2
Upper Holloway N19 . . **4** C2
Malvern Terr N1 . . . . **85** B4
Malwood Rd SW12 **61** A1
Malyons Rd SE13 . . . **67** A2
Malyons Terr SE13 . . **67** A2
Managers St [8]
E14 . . . . **34** B1
Manaton Cl SE15 . . . **65** A4
Manbre Rd W6 . . . . . . **47** B4
Manchester Dr
W10 . . . . **23** A1
Manchester Gr
E14 . . . . **42** B1
Manchester Ho
SE17 . . . . **151** A2
Manchester Mans
N19 . . . . **4** C4
Manchester Mews
W1 . . . . **103** B3
Manchester Rd
E14 . . . . **42** B3

Manchester Sq
W1 . . . . **103** C2
Manchester St
W1 . . . . **103** B3
Manchuria Rd
SW11 . . . . **60** C1
Manciple St SE1 . . . **137** C2
Mandalay Ho [6]
N16 . . . . **15** C4
Mandalay Rd SW4 . . **61** B2
Mandarin Ct [5]
SE8 . . . . **51** C4
Mandela Cl [39]
W12 . . . . **30** A2
Mandela Ho [18]
E2 . . . . **24** B2 **98** C4
Mandela Rd E16 . . . . **35** C3
Mandela St
Camden Town
NW1 . . . . **83** A4
Kennington SW9 . . . **163** B1
Mandela Way SE1 **152** B4
Mander Portman
Woodward Sch
SW7 . . . . **143** B3
Manderville Ho
SE1 . . . . **153** A2
Mandeville Cl [5]
SE3 . . . . **53** B3
Mandeville Ct
N4 . . . . **11** A3
Mandeville Ctyd
SW11 . . . . **169** B3
Mandeville Ho [9]
SW4 . . . . **61** B2
Mandeville Pl W1 . **103** C2
Mandrake Rd
SW17 . . . . **72** B1
Mandrell Rd SW2 . . **62** A2
Manette St W1 . . . . **105** C1
Manfred Ct [7]
SW15 . . . . **58** B2
Manfred Rd SW15 . . **58** B2
Manger Rd N7 . . . . . . **14** A2
Manilla St E14 . . . . . . **41** C4
Manilla Wk SE10 . . . . **43** A2
Manitoba Ct [29]
SE16 . . . . **40** B4
Manley Ct N16 . . . . . . **7** B1
Manley Ho SE11 . . . **149** B2
Manley St NW1 . . . . . **81** B4
Mannebry Prior N1 . **85** A1
Mannering Ho [16]
SW2 . . . . **62** B2
Manningford Cl
EC1 . . . . **96** A4
Manning Ho [9]
W11 . . . . **31** A3
Manning Pl TW10 . . . **54** B1
Manningtree Cl
SW19 . . . . **70** A3
Manningtree St [2]
E1 . . . . **111** B2
Manny Shinwell Ho
SW6 . . . . **155** A3
Manor Ave SE4 . . . . . **51** B1
Manor Circus TW9 . . **54** C4
Manor Ct
[7] Brixton SW2 . . . . . **62** B2
Camberwell SE15 . . . . **49** B3
Gunnersbury W3 . . . . **36** C2
Parsons Green
SW6 . . . . **166** B3
Streatham SW16 . . . . **74** A1
Manorfield Cl [3]
N19 . . . . **13** B4

Manorfield Prim Sch
[8] E14 . . . . **34** A4
Manor Gdns
[8] Chiswick W4 . . . . . . **38** A1
Clapham Pk SW4 . . . **171** A1
Gunnersbury W3 . . . . **36** C2
Richmond TW10,
TW9 . . . . **54** B3
Upper Holloway N7 . . . **5** A1
Manor Gr
Deptford SE15 . . . . **50** B4
Richmond TW9 . . . . . . **54** C4
Manor Gt SW15 . . . . . **58** A2
Manor Ho NW1 . . . . **102** B4
Manor House Ct
W9 . . . . **88** C1
Manor House Dr
NW6 . . . . **9** C1
Manor House Sta
N4 . . . . **6** A3
Manor Lo NW2 . . . . **9** C2
Manor Mans
[7] Hampstead
NW3 . . . . **12** A2
Tufnell Pk N7 . . . . **5** A1
Manor Mews
New Cross SE4 . . . . **51** B1
Paddington NW6 . . . . . **23** C3
Manor Oak Mans
SE22 . . . . **65** A1
Manor Par N16 . . . . . . **7** B2
Manor Park Par
SE13 . . . . **67** C3
Manor Park Rd
NW10 . . . . **21** B4
Manor Pk TW9 . . . . . . **54** B3
Manor Pl SE17 . . . . . **150** C2
Manor Rd
Richmond TW10,
TW9 . . . . **54** B3
Stamford Hill N16 . . . . . **7** A3
Manor Sch
Brondesbury
NW6 . . . . **10** A1
Willesden NW10 . . . . . **22** B4
Manor Street Est
SW3 . . . . **158** B4
Manor The W1 . . . . . **118** A3
Manor Way W3 . . . . . . **36** C2
Manresa Rd SW3 . . . **144** A1
Mansel Ct SW11 . . . **168** B3
Mansell Ho SW8 . . . **171** A4
Mansell Rd W3 . . . . . . **37** C4
Mansell St E1 . . . . . . **111** A1
Manse Rd N16 . . . . **7** B1
Mansfield Ct [27]
E2 . . . . **24** B4
Mansfield Ho
SW15 . . . . **57** C1
Mansfield Mews
W1 . . . . **104** A3
Mansfield Pl [28]
NW3 . . . . **11** B4
Mansfield Rd
Acton W3 . . . . **20** A1
Maitland Pk NW3 . . . . **12** B4
Mansfield St W1 . . . **104** A3
Mansford St E2 . . . . . **24** C3
Mansion Cl SW9 . . . **173** C4
Mansion Gdns NW3 . . **2** A1
Mansion Ho EC4 . . . **109** B1
Mansion House Pl EC3,
EC4 . . . . **109** B1
Mansion House St
EC2 . . . . **109** B1

Mansion House Sta
EC4 . . . . **123** A4
Mansions The
NW6 . . . . **10** B3
Manson Mews
SW7 . . . . **143** B3
Manson Pl SW7 . . . . **143** B3
Manston NW1 . . . . **13** B1
Manstone Rd NW2 . . **10** A3
Manston Ho W14 . . **126** B1
Mantell Ho SW4 . . . . **61** B2
Mantle Rd SE4 . . . . . . **66** A4
Manton Ho N16 . . . . . . **6** C1
Mantua St [22]
SW11 . . . . **59** C4
Mantus Cl E1 . . . . **25** B1
Mantus Rd E1 . . . . **25** B1
Manville Gdns
SW17 . . . . **73** A1
Manville Rd SW17 . . **73** A1
Manwood Rd SE4 . . . **66** B1
Many Gates SW12 . . **73** A2
Mapesbury Ct
NW2 . . . . **10** A3
Mapesbury Rd
NW2 . . . . **10** A2
Mapeshill Pl NW2 . . **9** B2
Mape St E2 . . . . **25** A1
Maple Ave W3 . . . . . . **29** A1
Maple Cl SW4 . . . . . . **61** C1
Maple Ct [3] NW2 . . . . **9** B4
Mapledene Est E8 . **16** C1
Mapledene Rd E8 . . **16** C1
Maple Ho
[11] Maitland Pk
NW3 . . . . **12** B2
[5] New Cross SE8 . . . **51** B3
[4] Richmond TW9 . . . **45** A2
Maple Leaf Sq [27]
SE16 . . . . **40** C4
Maple Lo SW15 . . . . . **58** A1
Maple Mews NW6 . . **78** A2
Maple Pl W1 . . . . **93** A1
Maples Pl E1 . . . . **32** A4
Maple St
[5] Bethnal Green
E2 . . . . **25** A3
Fitzrovia W1 . . . . **93** A1
Maplestead Rd
SW2 . . . . **74** B4
Mapleton Cres
SW18 . . . . **59** A1
Mapleton Rd
SW18 . . . . **59** A1
Maple Walk Sch
NW10 . . . . **21** B4
Maple Wlk W10 . . . . . **22** C1
Maplin St E3 . . . . **26** B2
Marada Ho NW6 . . . . **10** A1
Marais W4 . . . . **45** B3
Marathon Science
Sch of Excellence [22]
SE8 . . . . **41** A2
Marban Rd W9 . . . . . . **23** B2
Marble Arch M1 W1 . **117** A4
Marble Arch Sta
W1 . . . . **103** A1
Marble Cl W3 . . . . **28** A1
Marbleford Ct [4]
N6 . . . . **4** C4
Marble Ho W9 . . . . . . **23** B1
Marcella Rd SW9 . . **173** B1
Marchant Ho [13]
SW2 . . . . **62** B2
Marchant St SE14 . . **51** A4

Marchbank Rd
W14 . . . . **155** A4
March Ct SW15 . . . . . . **57** A3
Marchmont Rd
TW10 . . . . **54** B2
Marchmont St
WC1 . . . . **94** A3
Marchwood Cl [9]
SE5 . . . . **49** A3
Marcia Rd SE1 . . . . . **152** B3
Marcilly Rd SW18 . . **59** C1
Marcol Ho W1 . . . . . **104** B2
Marcon Ct [20] E8 . . **17** A3
Marcon Pl E8 . . . . **17** A3
Marco Rd W6 . . . . **39** B3
Marcus Ct TW8 . . . . . **44** A3
Marcus Garvey Mews
SE22 . . . . **65** A2
Marcus Garvey Way
[3] SE24 . . . . **62** C3
Marcus Ho [4]
SE15 . . . . **49** B2
Marcus St SW18 . . . . **59** A1
Marcus Terr SW18 . . **59** A1
Marden Ho [8] E8 . . . **17** A3
Marden Sq SE16 . . . . **40** A3
Mardyke Ho SE17 . **151** C4
Maresfield Gdns
NW3 . . . . **11** B2
Mare St E8 . . . . **17** A1
Margaret Bondfield
Ho
[8] Bow E3 . . . . **26** A3
[22] Kentish Town
NW5 . . . . **13** C3
Margaret Ct W1 . . . **104** C2
Margaret Herbison Ho
SW6 . . . . **155** A3
Margaret Ho [16]
W6 . . . . **39** B1
Margaret Ingram Cl
SW6 . . . . **154** C3
Margaret Mcmillan
Ho [10] N19 . . . . **4** C4
Margaret Rd N16 . . . . **7** B3
Margaret Rutherford
Pl [8] SW12 . . . . **73** B3
Margaret St W1 . . . **104** C2
Margaretta Terr
SW3 . . . . **158** A4
Margaret White Ho
NW1 . . . . **93** B4
Margate Rd SW2 . . . **62** A2
Margery Fry Ct N7 . . **5** A1
Margery St WC1 . . . . **95** B3
Margravine Gdns
Hammersmith W6 . . . **39** C1
West Kensington
W14 . . . . **140** A2
Margravine Rd
W6 . . . . **154** A4
Marham Gdns SW17,
SW18 . . . . **72** A3
Maria Cl [13] SE1 . . . **153** C4
Maria Fidelis Catholic
Sch (Lower)
NW1 . . . . **93** A3
Maria Fidelis Catholic
Sch (Upper) NW1 . . **93** B4
Maria Montessori Sch
[6] NW3 . . . . **11** C3
Marian Ct E9 . . . . **17** B3
Marian Pl E2 . . . . **25** A3
Marian Sq E2 . . . . **25** A3
Marian St [2] E2 . . . . **25** A3
Marian Way NW10 . . **8** B1

Maria Terr E1 25 C1
Maribor 13 SE10 52 B3
Marie Curie SE5 49 A2
Marie Lloyd Ct 13 SW9 62 B3
Marie Lloyd Gdns 1 N19 5 A4
Marie Lloyd Ho N1 87 B1
Marie Stopes Ct 3 N19 5 A4
Marigold St SE16 40 A4
Marina Ct 12 E3 26 C2
Marina Point 4 E14 42 A3
Marinefield Rd SW6 166 B2
Marinel Ho 25 SE5 48 B3
Mariners Mews E14 42 C2
Marine St SE16 139 B2
Marine Twr 29 SE8 51 B4
Marion Richardson Prim Sch 17 E1 32 C3
Marischal Rd SE13 67 C4
Maritime Ho 5 SW4 61 B4
Maritime Quay 5 E14 41 C1
Maritime St E3 26 B1
Marius Mans 3 SW17 72 C2
Marius Rd SW17 72 C2
Marjorie Gr SW11 60 B3
Market Ct W1 104 C2
Market La W12 39 B4
Market Mews W1 118 A1
Market Pl
- 3 Acton W3 28 B1
- 1 Bermondsey SE16 40 A2
- Marylebone W1 104 C2
Market Rd
- Barnsbury N7 14 A2
- Richmond TW9 54 C4
Market Sq E14 34 A3
Market St E1 110 C4
Market Studios 14 W12 39 B4
Market Way E14 34 A3
Market Yd Mews SE1 138 A2
Markham Pl SW3 144 C2
Markham Sq SW3 144 C2
Markham St SW3 144 B2
Mark Ho 3 E2 25 C3
Mark La EC3 124 B4
Markland Ho W10 30 C2
Mark Mans W12 38 C4
Marksbury Ave TW9 54 C4
Mark Sq EC2 24 A1 98 A2
Mark St EC2 24 A1 98 A2
Markstone Ho SE1 136 A3
Markyate Ho 6 W10 22 B1
Marland Ho SW1 131 A2
Marlborough
- 11 Putney SW19 69 C3
- St John's Wood W9 88 C4
Marlborough Ave 3 E8 24 C4
Marlborough Cl SE17 150 B3
Marlborough Cres W4 38 A3
Marlborough Ct
- Kensington W8 141 B4
- Marylebone W1 104 C1
Marlborough Flats SW3 144 B4
Marlborough Gr SE1 153 B1
Marlborough Hill NW8 79 A3
Marlborough Ho
- Marylebone NW1 92 B2
- Richmond TW10 54 C2
- Stoke Newington N4 6 B3
Marlborough Ho SW1 119 A1
Marlborough Ho SW19 69 C1
Marlborough Lo
- 36 Stepney E1 25 B1
- St John's Wood NW8 78 C1
Marlborough Mans 5 NW6 10 C3
Marlborough Mews 18 SW2 62 B3
Marlborough Pl NW8 79 A2
Marlborough Prim Sch SW3 144 B3
Marlborough Rd
- Acton Green W4 37 B1
- Richmond TW10 54 B1
- St James SW1 119 A1
- Upper Holloway N19 5 A2
Marlborough St SW3 144 B3
Marlborough Trad Est TW9 45 A2
Marlborough Yd N19 4 C2
Marlbury NW8 78 B3
Marley Ho 14 W11 30 C2
Marley Wlk NW2 9 B3
Marlin Ho SW15 58 A2
Marloes Rd W8 128 A1
Marlow Ct NW6 9 C1
Marlowe Bsns Ctr 2 SE14 51 A3
Marlowe Ct SW3 144 B3
Marlowe Ho 15 N16 16 A4
Marlowes The NW8 79 B4
Marlow Ho
- Bermondsey SE1 138 C2
- 15 Kensington W2 100 B1
- 44 Spitalfields E2 24 B2 98 C3
Marlow Studio Workshops 43 E2 24 B2 98 C3
Marlow Way SE16 40 C4
Marl Rd SW18 59 B3
Marlston NW1 92 B3
Marlton St SE10 43 B1
Marmara Apts 4 E16 35 C2
Marmion Ho 13 SW12 73 A4
Marmion Mews 4 SW11 60 C4
Marmion Rd SW11 60 C3
Marmont Rd SE15 49 C3
Marmora Ho E1 33 A4
Marmora Rd SE22 65 B1
Marner Prim Sch 6 E3 27 A1
Marne St W10 23 A2
Marney Rd SW11 60 C3
Marnfield Cres SW2 74 B3
Marnham Ave NW2 10 A4
Marnock Ho SE17 151 B2
Marnock Rd SE4 66 B2
Maroon St E14 33 A4
Marquess Rd N1 15 C2
Marquis Ct N4 5 B3
Marquis Rd
- Finsbury Pk N4 5 C3
- Kentish Town NW1 13 C2
Marrick Cl SW15 56 C3
Marrick Ho 19 NW6 78 B3
Marriott Rd N4 5 B3
Marryat Ct 12 W6 39 A2
Marryat Ho SW1 146 C1
Marryat Sq SW6 164 A4
Marsala Rd SE13 67 A3
Marsalis Ho 3 E3 26 C2
Marsden Rd SE15 64 B4
Marsden St NW5 12 C2
Marshall Cl SW18 59 B1
Marshall Ct SW4 172 B3
Marshall Ho
- Paddington NW6 23 B3
- Shoreditch N1 87 C2
- Walworth SE17 151 B2
Marshall Rd E10 19 A4
Marshall St L Ctr W1 105 A1
Marshall's Pl SE16 139 A1
Marshall St W1 105 A1
Marshalsea Rd SE1 137 A4
Marsham Ct
- 19 Putney SW19 69 C3
- Westminster SW1 147 C4
Marsham St SW1 147 C4
Marsh Ct E8 16 C2
Marshfield St E14 42 B3
Marshgate Bsns Ctr E15 27 B3
Marshgate Primary Sch TW10 54 B2
Marsh Hill E9 18 A3
Marsh Ho
- Nine Elms SW8 171 A4
- Pimlico SW1 147 C1
Marsh St E14 42 A2
Marsh Wall E14 42 A4
Marshwood Ho 10 NW6 23 C4
Marsland Cl SE17 150 B1
Marsom Ho N1 87 B1
Marston SE17 151 A4
Marston Cl NW6 11 B1
Marston Ho 23 SW9 173 C1
Marsworth Ho 8 E2 24 C4
Martaban Rd N16 7 B2
Martello St E8 17 A1
Martello Terr E8 17 A1
Martell Rd SE21 75 C1
Martel Pl E8 16 B2
Martha's Bldgs EC1 97 B2
Martha St E1 32 B3
Martin Ct 15 E14 42 B4
Martindale SW14 55 B2
Martindale Ave 2 E16 35 C2
Martindale Ho 23 E14 34 A2
Martindale Rd SW12 73 A4
Martineau Ho SW1 146 C1
Martineau Mews N5 15 A4
Martineau Rd N5 15 A4
Martin Ho
- Newington SE1 137 A1
- South Lambeth SW8 162 A2
Martin La EC4 123 C4
Martlett Ct WC2 106 B1
Martlett Lo NW3 11 A4
Martley Ho SW8 171 A4
Martock Ct 10 SE15 50 A2
Marton Rd 2 N16 7 A1
Marvel Ho 5 SE5 48 C3
Marville Rd SW6 154 C1
Marvin St 3 E8 17 A2
Marwell Ct SE3 52 C1
Mary Adelaide Cl SW15 68 A1
Mary Adelaide Ho W2 101 C4
Mary Ann Bldgs SE8 51 C4
Mary Datchelor Cl SE5 48 C2
Mary Dine Ct SW8 163 A1
Mary Gn NW8 78 B4
Mary Ho
- 8 Hammersmith W6 39 B1
- 6 Stockwell SW9 172 C1
Mary James Ho 32 E2 24 C3
Mary Jones Ho 20 E14 33 C2
Maryland Rd
- Paddington W9 23 C1
- Stratford New Town E15 19 C3
Marylands Rd W9 88 A1
Maryland Wlk N1 86 C4
Mary Lawrenson Pl 1 SE3 53 C3
MARYLEBONE 104 B2
Marylebone Flyover NW1 102 A3
Marylebone High St W1 103 C4
Marylebone La W1 103 C2
Marylebone Mews W1 104 A3
Marylebone Pas W1 105 A2
Marylebone Rd NW1 103 A4
Marylebone St W1 103 C3
Marylebone Sta NW1 90 C1
Marylee Way SE11 149 A3
Mary McArthur Ho 12 N19 4 C4
Mary Macarthur Ho
- 15 Globe Town E2 25 C2
- W14 154 A4
Maryon Mews NW3 12 A4
Mary Pl W11 31 A2 112 A3
Mary's Ct NW8 90 B2
Mary Secole Cl 21 E8 24 B4
Mary Smith Ct SW5 141 C3
Mary St
- 5 Canning Town E16 35 B4
- Shoreditch N1 87 A3
Mary Terr NW1 82 C3
Mary Wharrie Ho 4 NW3 12 B1
Masbro' Rd W14 39 C3
Mascotte Rd 2 SW15 57 C3
Masefield Ct N5 15 C3
Masefield Ho 4 NW6 23 C2
Mashie Rd W3 29 A3
Maskall Cl SW2 74 C3
Maskell Rd SW17 71 B1
Maskelyne Cl SW11 168 B4
Mason Cl
- Bermondsey SE16 153 C2
- Newham E16 35 C2
Mason Ho
- 15 Bermondsey SE1 153 C3
- 16 Hackney E9 17 B1
Mason's Arms Mews W1 118 B4
Mason's Ave EC2 109 B2
Mason's Pl EC1 96 C4
Mason St SE17 151 C4
Mason's Yd
- Finsbury EC1 96 B4
- St James SW1 119 A2
Massie Rd E8 16 C2
Massinger St SE1, SE17 152 A3
Massingham St E1 25 C1
Mast Ct 17 SE16 41 A2
Masterman Ho 1 SE5 48 C3
Masters Dr SE16 40 A1
Masters Lo 24 E1 32 B3
Master's St 16 E1 32 C4
Mast House Terr E14 41 C2
Masthouse Terrace Pier SE8 41 C1
Mastin Ho SW18 70 C3
Mast L Ctr The SE16 40 C3
Mastmaker Rd E14 41 C4
Matara Mews SE17 150 C1
Matching Ct 14 E3 26 C2
Matham Gr SE22 64 B3
Matheson Lang Ho SE1 135 B3
Matheson Rd W14 140 C3

Mathews Yd WC2 . . . . . . 106 A1
Mathieson Ct SE1 136 B3
Mathison Ho
SW10 . . . . 156 C2
Matilda Gdns 10
E3 . . . . 26 C3
Matilda Ho 1 . . . . . . 125 B2
Matilda St N1 . . . . 85 A4
Matlock Cl SE24 . . . . . . 63 B3
Matlock Ct
1 Herne Hill SE5 . . . . . 63 C3
St John's Wood
NW8 . . . . 78 C2
Matlock St E14 . . . . 33 A3
Maton Ho SW6 . . . . . 154 C2
Matrix Ind Pk
NW10 . . . . 20 A2
Matson Ho
1 Bermondsey
SE16 . . . . 40 A3
10 Homerton E9 . . . . . 17 B2
Matthew Cl W10 . . . . . 22 C1
Matthew Parker St
SW1 . . . . 133 C3
Matthews Ct N5 . . . . . 15 B4
Matthews Ho 3
E14 . . . . 33 C4
Matthews St
SW11 . . . . 168 C2
Matthias Ct 12
TW10 . . . . 54 A1
Matthias Ho 2
N16 . . . . 16 A3
Matthias Rd N16 . . . . . 16 A3
Mattingly Way 8
SE15 . . . . 49 B3
Maude Ho 3 E2 . . . . . 24 C3
Maude Rd SE5 . . . . 49 A2
Maudlins Gn E1 . . . . 125 B2
Maudslay Ho TW8 . . . . 36 A1
Maudsley Hospl
SE5 . . . . 48 C1
Maud St E16 . . . . 35 B4
Maud Wilkes Cl 10
NW5 . . . . 13 B3
Maugham Ct 5
W3 . . . . 37 B3
Maugham Wy 21
W3 . . . . 37 B3
Mauleverer Rd
SW2 . . . . 62 A2
Maundeby Wlk
NW10 . . . . 8 A2
Maunsel St SW1 . . . . 147 B4
Maurer Ct 2 SE2 . . . . 43 B3
Mauretania Bldg 11
E1 . . . . 32 C2
Maurice Ct 4 E1 . . . . 26 A2
Maurice Ho 11
SW9 . . . . 172 C2
Maurice St W12 . . . . . 30 A3
Mauritius Rd SE10 . . . . 43 A2
Maury Rd N16 . . . . 7 C1
Maverton Rd E3 . . . . . 26 C4
Mavor Ho N1 . . . . 85 A3
Mawbey Ho SE1 . . . . 153 A1
Mawbey Pl SE1 . . . . . 153 A1
Mawbey Rd SE1 . . . . 153 A1
Mawbey St SW8 . . . . 162 A1
Mawdley Ho SE1 . . . . 135 C3
Mawson Ct N1 . . . . . . 87 C3
Mawson Ho EC1 . . . . . 95 B1
Mawson La W4 . . . . . . 46 B4
Maxden Ct SE15 . . . . . 64 C4

Maxted Rd SE15 . . . . . 64 B4
Maxwell Ct SE21 . . . . 76 C3
Maxwell Rd SW6 . . . . 156 B1
Maya Ct SE15 . . . . 50 A1
Mayall Rd SE24 . . . . . . 63 A2
Maybury Ct SW1 . . . . 103 C3
Maybury Gdns
NW10 . . . . 9 A2
Maybury Mews N6 . . . 4 B4
Maydew Ho SE16 . . . . 40 B2
Maydwell Ho 5
E14 . . . . 33 C4
MAYFAIR 118 A3
Mayfair Pl W1 . . . . . 118 B2
Mayfield Ave W4 . . . . 38 A2
Mayfield Cl
Clapham Pk SW4 . . . . 61 C2
Dalston E8 . . . . 16 B2
Mayfield Ho
51 Bethnal Green
E2 . . . . 25 A3
Stamford Hill N16 . . . . 7 A4
Mayfield Mans
SW15 . . . . 58 B2
Mayfield Rd
Acton W3 . . . . 28 A2
Bedford Pk W12 . . . . . 38 A4
Dalston E8 . . . . 16 B1
Mayflower Cl SE16 . . . 40 C2
Mayflower Prim Sch
E14 . . . . 34 A3
Mayflower Rd
SW9 . . . . 62 A4
Mayflower St 1
SE16 . . . . 40 B4
Mayford NW1 . . . . . . 83 A2
Mayford Cl SW12 . . . . 72 B4
Mayford Rd SW12 . . . 72 C4
Maygood Ho N1 . . . . . 85 B2
Maygood St N1 . . . . . 85 B2
Maygrove Rd NW6 . . . 10 B2
Mayhew Ct 2 SE5 . . . 63 C3
Maylands Ho
SW3 . . . . 144 B3
Maylie Ho 4 SE16 . . . 40 A4
Maynard Cl SW6 . . . . 156 B1
Maynard Ho E1 . . . . . 26 A2
Maynards Quay E1 . . . 32 B2
Mayo Ho 10 E1 . . . . . 32 B4
Mayola Rd E5 . . . . 17 B4
Mayo Rd NW10 . . . . . . 8 A2
May's Buildings Mews
SE10 . . . . 52 C3
Mays Ct WC2 . . . . . . 120 A3
May's Ct SE10 . . . . . . 52 C3
Maysoule Rd
SW11 . . . . 59 C3
May St
Kensington W14 . . . . 140 C1
W14 . . . . 141 A1
Mayston Mews 8
SE10 . . . . 43 C1
Maythorne Cotts
SE13 . . . . 67 C1
Mayton St N7 . . . . 5 B1
May Tree Ho SE4 . . . . 66 B4
Maytree Wlk SW2 . . . 74 C2
Mayward Ho 7
SE5 . . . . 49 A2
Mazahirul Uloom
London 20 SE15 . . . . 25 C1
Maze Hill SE10,
SE3 . . . . 53 A4
Maze Hill Lodge 7
SE10 . . . . 52 C4

Maze Hill Sta
SE10 . . . . 53 A4
Mazenod Ave
NW6 . . . . 10 C1
Maze Rd TW9 . . . . 44 C3
Mead Cl 3 NW1 . . . . . 12 C1
Meadcroft Rd
SE17 . . . . 48 A4
Meade Cl W4 . . . . 44 C4
Meader Ct SE14 . . . . . 50 C3
Mead Ho
W11 . . . . 31 B1 112 C2
Mead Lo W4 . . . . 37 C4
Meadowbank NW3 . . . 12 B1
Meadow Bank 8
SW15 . . . . 58 B2
Meadowbank Cl
SW6 . . . . 47 B3
Meadow Cl E9 . . . . . . 18 B3
Meadowcroft 18
W4 . . . . 36 C1
Meadow Mews
SW8 . . . . 162 C3
Meadow Pl
Chiswick W4 . . . . 46 A3
South Lambeth
SW8 . . . . 162 B2
Meadow Rd SW8 . . . . 162 C2
Meadow Row SE1 . . . 136 C1
Meadows The E5 . . . . 64 A4
Meadow Rd 1
SW8 . . . . 135 B2
Meadway The SE3 . . . . 52 C1
Meakin Est SE1 . . . . . 138 A2
Meakin Ho N7 . . . . . . 14 B3
Meard St W1 . . . . 105 B1
Meath Cres E1, E2 . . . 25 C2
Meath Ho SE24 . . . . . . 63 A1
Meath St SW11 . . . . . 170 A4
Mecklenburgh Pl
WC1 . . . . 94 C2
Mecklenburgh Sq
WC1 . . . . 94 C2
Mecklenburgh St
WC1 . . . . 94 C2
Medburn St NW1 . . . . 83 B2
Medcroft Gdns
SW14 . . . . 55 B3
Medfield St SW15 . . . . 69 A4
Medhurst Cl 8 E3 . . . . 26 A3
Median Rd E5 . . . . 17 B3
Medina Ct N7 . . . . 5 C1
Medina Gr N7 . . . . 5 C1
Medina Ho SE15 . . . . . 65 B3
Medina Rd N7 . . . . 5 C1
Medlar St SE5 . . . . 48 B2
Medley Rd NW6 . . . . . 10 C2
Medora Rd SW2 . . . . . 74 B4
Medresco Ho
NW6 . . . . 11 C1
Medusa SE6 . . . . 67 A1
Medway Bldgs E3 . . . . 26 A3
Medway Ct WC1 . . . . . 94 A3
Medway Ho
Bermondsey SE1 . . . . 137 C3
Paddington NW8 . . . . 102 A4
Stoke Newington
N16 . . . . 15 C4
Medway Mews 38
E3 . . . . 26 A3
Medway Rd E3 . . . . . . 26 A3
Medway St SW1 . . . . . 133 C1
Medwin St SW4 . . . . . 62 B3
Meecham Ct 1
SW11 . . . . 168 A2

Meeson St E5 . . . . 18 A4
Meeting House Alley
7 E1 . . . . 32 A1
Meeting House La
SE15 . . . . 50 A3
Mehetabel Rd E9 . . . . 17 B3
Melba Way SE13 . . . . . 52 A2
Melbourne Ct
Hackney E5 . . . . 18 A4
Paddington W9 . . . . . 89 A2
Melbourne Gr
SE22 . . . . 64 B3
Melbourne Ho
W8 . . . . 31 C1 113 B1
Melbourne Mews
SW9 . . . . 173 B3
Melbourne Pl
WC2 . . . . 107 A1
Melbourne Sq 11
SW9 . . . . 173 B3
Melbray Mews 1
SW6 . . . . 164 C1
Melbreak Ho 11
SE22 . . . . 64 A4
Melbury Ct W8 . . . . . 127 A2
Melbury Dr SE5 . . . . . . 49 A3
Melbury Ho SW8 . . . . 162 C2
Melbury Rd W14 . . . . 127 A2
Melchester 5
W11 . . . . 31 B3
Melchester Ho 1
N19 . . . . 4 C1
Melcombe Ct
NW1 . . . . 102 C4
Melcombe Ho
SE8 . . . . 162 C1
Melcombe Pl
NW1 . . . . 102 C4
Melcombe Prim Sch
W6 . . . . 47 C4
Melcombe St NW1 . . . 91 A1
Meldon Cl SW6 . . . . . 166 B4
Melford Ct
Bermondsey SE1 . . . . 138 B2
Dulwich SE22 . . . . 76 C4
Melford Rd SE21,
SE22 . . . . 76 C4
Melgund Rd N5 . . . . . 14 C3
Melina Ct
Putney SW15 . . . . 56 C4
St John's Wood
NW8 . . . . 89 B3
Melina Pl NW8 . . . . . . 89 B3
Melina Rd W12 . . . . . . 39 A4
Melior Pl SE1 . . . . 138 A4
Melior St SE1 . . . . 138 A4
Melisa Ct N6 . . . . 4 C4
Mellish Ho 2
N16 . . . . 7 C1
Mellis Ave TW9 . . . . . 45 A2
Mellish Ho 2 E1 . . . . . 32 A3
Mellish St E14 . . . . . . 41 C3
Mellitus St W12 . . . . . 29 B3
Mell St 6 SE10 . . . . . . 43 A1
Melody La N5 . . . . 15 B3
Melody Rd SW18 . . . . 59 B2
Melon Pl W8 . . . . 127 C4
Melon Rd SE15 . . . . . . 49 C2
Melrose Ave
Cricklewood NW2 . . . . 9 B3
Wimbledon SW19 . . . . 70 C1
Melrose Cl SW18 . . . . 58 B1
Melrose Gdns W6 . . . . 39 B3
Melrose Ho
Maida Vale NW6 . . . . . 23 C2
Pimlico SW1 . . . . 146 B2

Melrose Rd
8 Barnes SW13 . . . . . 46 B1
Wandsworth SW18 . . . 58 B1
Melrose Terr W6 . . . . . 39 B3
Melton Ct SW7 . . . . . . 143 C3
Melton Ho E5 . . . . 7 C2
Melton St NW1 . . . . . . 93 B3
Melville Court Flats 1
W12 . . . . 39 A4
Melville Ho
4 Brentford W4 . . . . . 36 C1
Rotherhithe SE8 . . . . . 41 A1
Melville Pl 6 N1 . . . . . 15 B1
Melville Pl N1 . . . . 15 B1
Melville Rd SW13 . . . . 46 C2
Melville Villas Rd
W3 . . . . 28 C1
Melwood Ho 21
E1 . . . . 32 A3
Melyn Cl N7 . . . . 13 B4
Memel Ct EC1 . . . . 96 C1
Memel St EC1 . . . . 96 C1
Menai Pl 2 E3 . . . . . . 26 C3
Mendez Wy 3
SW15 . . . . 56 C2
Mendham Ho SE1 138 A2
Mendip Ct
2 Battersea
SW11 . . . . 59 B4
Deptford SE14 . . . . . . 50 B4
Mendip Dr NW2 . . . . . 1 A2
Mendip Ho 2 N4 . . . . . 6 C4
Mendip Hos 12 E2 . . . 25 B2
Mendip Rd SW11 . . . . 59 B4
Mendora Rd SW6 . . . 154 C2
Menelik Rd NW2 . . . . . 10 B4
Menorah Prim Sch
NW11 . . . . 1 B4
Menotti St 8
E2 . . . . 24 C1 99 C2
Menteath Ho 8
E14 . . . . 33 C3
Mentmore Terr E8 . . . 17 A1
Mentone Ct SW8 . . . . 172 B4
Meon Rd W3 . . . . 37 B4
Mepham St SE1 . . . . . 121 B1
Merbury Ct SE13 . . . . . 52 C1
Mercator Pl 4
E14 . . . . 41 C1
Mercator Rd SE13 . . . . 67 C3
Merceron Ho 3
E2 . . . . 25 B2
Merceron St E1 . . . . . 25 A1
Mercers Cl SE10 . . . . . 43 B2
Mercer's Cotts 8
E3 . . . . 33 A3
Mercers Mews N7 . . . 13 C4
Mercers Pl W6 . . . . . . 39 C2
Mercers Rd N19 . . . . . 4 C1
Mercer St WC2 . . . . . 106 A1
Merchant Ct E1 . . . . . 32 B1
Merchants Ho
SE10 . . . . 42 C1
Merchant Sq 2 . . . . . 101 B3
Merchant Taylors'
Hall EC3 . . . . 109 C1
Merchon Ho N7 . . . . . 13 B4
Mercia Gr SE13 . . . . . . 67 B3
Mercia Ho 9 SE5 . . . . 48 B1
Mercie Ct SE22 . . . . . . 76 C3
Mercier Rd SW15 . . . . 58 A2

Mercury Ct
⑩ Brixton SW9 ... 173 B4
⑩ Millwall E14 ..... 41 C2
Mercury Ho ⓐ 63 C4
Mercury Way SE14.. 50 C4
Mercy Terr SE13 .... 67 A2
Mere CI SW15,
SW19 .... 69 C4
Meredith Ave NW2 .. 9 B3
Meredith Ho ⑰
N16 .... 16 A3
Meredith Mews
SE4 .... 66 B3
Meredith St EC1 .... 96 A3
Meredith Twr ⓐ 37 A3
Meredyth Rd
SW13 .... 46 C1
Meretone Ct SE4 .. 66 A3
Mereton Mans ⓑ
SE8 .... 51 C2
Mereworth Ho ⓑ
SE15 .... 50 B4
Merganser Ct ⑰
SE8 .... 51 B4
Meridan Ct SE13 .. 67 C3
Meriden Ho ⓐ SW3.. 144 A1
Meriden Ho ⓓ N1 .. 24 A4
Meridian Courtyard
SE10 .... 52 C3
Meridian Ho ⓐ SE10 .. 43 A2
Meridian Pl E14 ..... 42 B4
Meridian Prim Sch ⓑ
SE10 .... 52 C4
Meridian Sq E15 .... 19 C1
Merivale Rd SW15 .. 58 A3
Merlin Ho
⑰ Chiswick W4 .... 37 C1
West Hampstead
NW3 .... 11 A4
Merlin Sch The ⑪
SW15 .... 58 A2
Merlins Ct WC1 .... 95 B3
Merlin St EC1 .... 95 B3
Mermaid Ct
Bermondsey SE1 .. 137 B4
Rotherhithe SE16 ... 33 B1
Mermaid Ho ⓑ
E14 .... 34 B2
Mermaid Twr ⓑ
SE8 .... 51 B4
Meroe Ct N16 ...... 7 A2
Merredene St
SW2 .... 62 B1
Merriam Ave ⓑ
E9 .... 18 B2
Merricks Ct ⓑ
SW14 .... 55 A3
Merrick Sq SE1 .. 137 B2
Merrington Rd
SW6 .... 155 C4
Merritt Rd SE4 .... 66 B2
Merrivale NW1 ..... 83 A3
Merrow St SE17 .. 151 C1
Merrow Wlk SE17 151 C2
Merryfield ⓑ SE3 .. 53 B1
Merryweather Ct ⑱
N19 .... 4 B1
Merryweather Pl ⓑ
SE10 .... 52 A3
Mersey Ho N7 .... 14 C3
Merstone Ho
SW18 .... 59 A1
Merthyr Terr
SW13 .... 47 A4
Merton Ave W4..... 38 B2
Merton Ho SW18 .. 70 C3

Merton La N6 ...... 3 B2
Merton Rd SW18 .. 70 C4
Merton Rise NW3.. 12 A1
Merton Road Ind Est
SE18 .... 70 C4
Merts CI SW15 .... 65 C2
Meru CI NW5 ..... 12 C3
Mervan Rd SW2 ... 62 C3
Messaline Ave W3.. 28 B3
Messina Ave NW6 .. 10 C1
Messiter Ho N1 .... 85 A3
Metcalfe Ho ⓘ
SW8 .... 171 B3
Meteor St SW11 .. 60 C3
Methley Ho ⓓ N7 .. 5 B2
Methley St SE11 .. 149 C1
Methodist Central
Hall SW1 .... 133 C3
Methwold Rd W10.. 30 C4
Met Police Heritage
Ctr SW6 .... 141 B1
Metropolis
Apartments ⓑ
SW12 .... 73 A3
Metropolitan Benefit
Societies
Almshouses ⓑ
N1 .... 16 A2
Metropolitan Bsns Ctr
N1 .... 16 A2
Metropolitan CI ⓑ
E14 .... 33 C4
Mews St E1 ...... 125 B2
Mews The
Shoreditch N1 ..... 87 A4
⑥ Upper Holloway
N19 .... 5 A3
Mexborough NW1 .. 82 C3
Mexfield Rd SW15.. 58 B2
Meyer Ho ⑪
SW12 .... 73 A4
Meymott St SE1 .. 122 A1
Meynell Cres E9 .. 17 C1
Meynell Gdns E9 .. 17 C1
Meynell Rd E9 .... 17 C1
Meyrick Ho ⓑ
E14 .... 33 C4
Meyrick Rd
Battersea SW11....60 A4
Willesden NW10.... 8 C2
Miah Terr ⓑ E1 .. 125 C1
Micawber Ct N1 .. 97 A4
Micawber Ho ⓑ
SE16 .... 139 C3
Micawber St N1 .. 97 A4
Michael CI ⓑ E16.. 35 C2
Michael Cliffe Ho
EC1 .... 95 C3
Michael Faraday Ho
SE17 .... 151 C1
Michael Faraday Prim
Est ⑩ SW18 .... 171 A2
Michael Manley Ind
Est ⑫ SW8 .... 170 C4
Michael Rd SW6 .. 166 B4
Michael Tippett Sch
The SE24 .... 63 B3
Michelangelo Ct ⓑ
SE16 .... 40 A1
Michelle Ct W3 .... 28 C2
Michels Almshouses
⑪ N16 .... 54 A2
Michelsdale Dr ⓑ
TW9 .... 54 A3
Michelson Ho
SE11 .... 149 A3

Michel's Row ⓑ
TW9 .... 54 A3
Michigan Ho E14 .. 41 C3
Mickledore NW1 .. 83 A1
Micklethwaite Rd
SW6 .... 155 C3
Middlefield NW8 .. 79 B4
Middle Row W10 .. 23 A1
Middlesex Ct ⓑ
W4 .... 38 B2
Middlesex Ho ⓘ
W1 .... 105 A4
Middlesex Pas
EC1 .... 108 B3
Middlesex PI ⑬
E9 .... 17 B2
Middlesex St E1 .. 110 C2
Middle St EC1 .... 108 C4
Middle Temple La
EC4 .... 121 B4
Middle Temple
EC4 .... 121 B4
Middleton Dr
SE16 .... 40 C4
Middleton Gr N7 .. 14 A3
Middleton Ho
Dalston E8 .... 16 B1
Newington SE1 .. 137 B1
Middleton Mews
N7 .... 14 A3
Middleton PI W1 .. 104 C3
Middleton Rd
Dalston E8 .... 16 B1
Golders Green NW11.. 1 C4
Middleton St E2 .. 25 A2
Middleton Way
SE13 .... 67 C3
Middle Yd SE1 .. 124 A2
Midford PI W1 .... 93 A1
Midhope Ho WC1.. 94 B3
Midhope St WC1 .. 94 B3
Midhurst Ct N8 .... 5 A4
Midhurst Ho ⓑ
E14 .... 33 B3
Midhurst Way E5 ..16 C4
Midland Pl E14 .... 42 B1
Midland Rd NW1.. 94 A4
Midland Terr
NW10 .... 21 A1
Midlothian Ho NW9.. 4 A4
Midlothian Rd E3.. 26 B1
Midmoor Rd SW12.. 73 B3
Midnight Ave ⓑ
SW9 .... 48 A3
Midship CI SE16 .. 32 C1
Midship Point E14.. 41 C4
Midstrath Rd NW10.. 8 A4
Midway Ho EC1 .. 96 A4
Milborne Ho ⑪ ⓑ .. 17 B2
Milborne St E9 .... 17 B2
Milcote St SE1 .. 136 B3
Mildmay Ave N1 .. 15 C2
Mildmay Ct N1 .... 15 C3
Mildmay Gr N N1 .. 15 C3
Mildmay Gr S N1.. 15 C3
Mildmay Ho ⓑ
SW15 .... 57 B2
Mildmay Mission
Hospl E2 ...... 24 B2 98 C3
Mildmay Pk N1 .... 15 C3
Mildmay Rd N1 .... 16 A3
Mildmay St N1 .... 15 C2

MILE END 26 A1
Mile End Hospl E2.. 25 C2
Mile End Park L Ctr &
Stad E3 .... 33 B4
Mile End PI E1 .... 25 C1
Mile End Rd E1, E3.. 25 C1
Mile End Sta E3 .. 26 B2
Miles Bldgs NW1 .. 102 A4
Miles Coverdale Prim
Sch ⓦ W12 ..... 39 B4
Miles Ct E1 .... 32 A3
Miles Ho ⓑ SE10 .. 43 A1
Miles Lo E15 ...... 19 C3
Miles PI NW8 .... 101 C4
Miles St SW8 .... 162 B3
Milestone Green
SW14 .... 55 C3
Milfoil St W12 ..... 29 C2
Milford Ct ⓑ N16 .. 7 A3
Milford La WC2 .. 121 B4
Milford Mews
SW16 .... 74 B1
Milk St EC2 ...... 109 A2
Milkwell Yd ⑰
SE5 .... 48 B2
Milkwood Rd SE24.. 63 A3
Milk Yd E1 .... 32 B2
Millais Rd E11 ..... 19 C4
Milland Ho ⑪
SW15 .... 68 C3
Millard CI ⑳ N16.. 16 A3
Millard Rd SE8 .... 41 B1
Millbank SW1 .... 148 A3
Millbank Acad
SW1 .... 147 C2
Millbank Millennium
Pier SW1 .... 148 B3
Millbrooke Ct ⑰
SW15 .... 58 A2
Millbrook Ho ⓐ
SE15 .... 49 C4
Millbrook PI NW1 .. 82 C2
Millbrook Rd SW9.. 63 A4
Millender Wlk
SE16 .... 40 B2
Millennium Bridge SE1,
EC4 .... 122 C3
Millennium City Acad
W1 .... 104 B2
Millennium Dr
E14 .... 42 C2
Millennium Harbour
E14 .... 41 C4
Millennium PI ⑳
E2 .... 25 A3
Millennium Prim Sch
SE10 .... 43 B3
Millennium Sq
SE1 .... 139 A4
Millennium Way
SE10 .... 43 B3
Miller Ho ⑨ SW2.. 74 A4
Miller's Ave E8,
N16 .... 16 B3
Miller's Ct ⓘ W4.. 38 B1
Miller's Terr ⓘ E8.. 16 B3
Miller's Way W6 .. 39 B4
Millers Wharf Ho
E1 .... 125 B1
Miller Wlk SE1 .. 121 C1
Millfield N4 .... 5 C2
Millfield La N6 .... 3 B3
Millfield Pl N6 ...... 3 C2
Millfields Com Sch
E5 .... 17 B4

Millgrove St ⓑ
SW11 .... 169 B2
Millharbour E14 .. 42 A4
Mill Hill SW13 .... 56 C4
Mill Hill Gr ⑪ W3.. 28 A1
Mill Hill Rd
Barnes SW13 ..... 46 C1
South Acton W3 .. 37 A4
Mill Hill Terr ⓑ
W3 .... 28 A1
Mill Ho ⓑ SE13 .. 67 B4
Milligan St E14 .... 33 B2
Milliners Ho SW18.. 58 C3
Millington Ho N16.. 6 C1
Mill La NW6 .... 10 B3
Millman Ct WC1 .. 94 C1
Millman Mews
WC1 .... 94 C1
Millman PI WC1 .. 95 A1
Millman St WC1 .. 94 C1
Millmark Gr SE14.. 51 A1
MILL MEADS 27 C1
Millner Ct SE4 .... 51 B1
Mill PI E14 .... 33 A3
Mill Pond CI SW8 161 C1
Millpond Est SE16.. 40 A4
Mill Row N1........ 24 A4
Mills Ct EC2 .. 24 A2 98 A3
Mills Gr ⓘ E14 .... 34 B4
Mills Ho SW8 .... 171 A4
Millshott CI SW6 .. 47 B2
Mills Row W4 .... 37 C2
Mill St
Bermondsey SE1 .. 139 A4
Mayfair W1 ...... 118 C4
Millstream Ho ⑭
SE16 .... 40 A4
Millstream Rd
SE1 .... 138 C3
Mill Trad Est The
NW10 .... 20 B2
MILLWALL 41 C3
Millwall Dock Rd
E14 .... 41 C3
Millwood St ⑩
W10 .... 31 A4
Mill Yd E1 .... 125 B4
Milman Rd NW6 .. 23 A3
Milman's Ho
SW10 .... 157 B3
Milman's St SW10 157 B3
Milner Bldg N16 .. 6 C1
Milner Ho ⑪
SW11 .... 59 C4
Milner PI N1 ...... 85 C4
Milner Sq N1 ..... 15 A1
Milner St SW3 ... 144 C4
Milnthorpe Rd W4.. 45 C4
Milo Rd SE22 ..... 64 B1
Milroad Ho ⓑ E11.. 32 C4
Milroy Wlk SE1 .. 122 A2
Milson Rd W14 .. 126 A2
Milsted Ho ⓑ E5.. 17 A3
Milton Ave
Becontree NW10 .. 20 C4
Crouch End N6 .... 4 C4
Stonebridge NW10 .. 20 B4
Milton CI SE1 .... 152 C3
Milton Court Rd
SE14 .... 51 A4
Milton Ct
Fulham SW6 ...... 58 A4
St Luke's EC2 .... 109 B4

Milton Ct continued
 9 Wandsworth
SW18 . . . . .58 C2
Milton Gr N16 . . . . . . .16 A4
Milton Ho
 11 Bethnal Green
E2 . . . . .25 B2
 2 Camberwell SE5 .48 C3
Milton House Mans
E8 . . . . .16 B4
Milton Pk N6 . . . . .4 B4
Milton Pl 13 N7 . . . . .14 C3
Milton Rd
Acton W3 . . . . .28 C1
Crouch End N6 . . . . . . .4 A4
Mortlake SW14 . . . . .55 C4
Tulse Hill SE24 . . . . . .63 A2
Milton St EC1, EC2 109 B4
Milverton NW5 . . . . . .12 C3
Milverton Rd NW6 . . . .9 B1
Milverton St SE11 149 C1
Milward St E1 . . . . . . .32 A4
Mimosa St SW4 . . . . .172 B3
Mimosa St SW4 . . . . .165 A3
Mina Rd SE17 . . . . . .152 B2
Minchin Ho 10
E14 . . . . .33 C3
Mincing La EC3 . . . .124 A4
Minera Mews
SW1 . . . . .145 C4
Minerva Cl SW9 . . . .163 C2
Minerva Rd NW10 . . .20 C2
Minerva St E2 . . . . . . .25 A3
Minerva Wlk EC1 . .108 B2
Minet Ave NW10 . . . . .21 A3
Minet Gdns NW10 . . .21 A3
Minet Ho 20 E1 . . . .111 B1
Minet Rd SE5, SW9 . .48 A1
Minford Gdns
W14 . . . . .39 C4
Mingard Wlk N7 . . . . . .5 B1
Ming St E14 . . . . .33 C2
Minnow Wlk SE17 152 B3
Minories EC3 . . . . . .124 C4
Minshull St SW8 . . . .171 B3
Minson Rd E9 . . . . . . .25 C4
Minstead Gdns
SW15 . . . . .68 B4
Minster Ct EC3 . . . . .124 B4
Minster Rd NW2 . . . . .10 A3
Mint Bsns Pk 12
E16 . . . . .35 C4
Mintern St N1 . . . . . . .87 C2
Minton Ho SE11 . . . .149 B4
Minton Mews 3
NW6 . . . . .11 A2
Mint St SE1 . . . . .137 A4
Mirabelle Gardens
E15 . . . . .19 C3
Mirabel Rd SW6 . . . .155 A2
Miranda Cl 19 E1 . . . .32 B4
Miranda Ho 3 N1 . . . .24 A3
Miranda Rd N19 . . . . . .4 B3
Missenden SE17 . . . .151 C1
Missenden Ho
NW8 . . . . .90 A2
Mission Pl SE15 . . . . .49 C2
Mission Sq 13
TW8 . . . . .44 A4
Mission The
 13 Bermondsey
SE16 . . . . .40 A4
 14 Poplar E14 . . . . .33 B3

Misterton Ct
SW11 . . . . .167 C4
Mistral SE5 . . . . .49 A2
Mitali Pas 51 E1 . . . .111 B1
Mitcham Ho 9
SE5 . . . . .48 B2
Mitchell Brook Prim
Sch NW10 . . . . .8 A2
Mitchell Ho
Gunnersbury W4 . . . . .37 A1
 1 Islington N1 . . . . .14 C1
 2 Shepherd's Bush
W12 . . . . .30 A2
Mitchell's Pl SE21 . .76 A4
Mitchell St EC1 . . . . . .97 A2
Mitchison Rd N1 . . . . .15 C2
Mitford Rd N19 . . . . . . .5 A2
Mitre Bridge Ind Pk
W10 . . . . .22 A1
Mitre Rd SE1 . . . . . .135 C4
Mitre Sq EC3 . . . . . .110 B1
Mitre St EC3 . . . . . . .110 B1
Mitre The 9 E14 . . . . .33 B2
Mitre Way W10 . . . . . .30 A4
Mizzen Ct E14 . . . . . . .41 C4
Moatfield NW6 . . . . . .10 A1
Moat Pl
Acton W3 . . . . .28 A3
Stockwell SW9 . . . . . .62 B4
Moat Sch The 7
SW6 . . . . .164 A2
Moberly Rd SW4 . . . .73 C4
Mobey Ct SW4 . . . . .172 A3
Mocatta Ho 9 E1 . . . .25 A1
Modbury Gdns
NW5 . . . . .12 C2
Modder Pl SW15 . . . .57 C3
Model Cotts SW14 . .55 B4
Modling Ho 8 E2 . . . .25 C3
Moelwyn Hughes Ct
N7 . . . . .13 C3
Moffat Ho 24 SE5 . . .48 B3
Mohawk Ho 33 E3 . . .26 A3
Moiety Rd E14 . . . . . .41 C4
Moira Ct SW17 . . . . . .72 C2
Moira Ho 13 SW9 . . .173 B4
Molasses Ho 1
SW11 . . . . .59 B4
Molasses Row 2
SW11 . . . . .59 B4
Mole Ct 2 W12 . . . . . .38 A4
Mole Ho NW8 . . . . . . .89 C1
Molesey Ho
E2 . . . . .24 B1 98 C2
Molesford Rd
SW6 . . . . .165 B3
Molesworth Ho 6
SE17 . . . . .48 A4
Molesworth St
SE13 . . . . .67 B4
Molly Huggins Cl
SW12 . . . . .73 B4
Molton Ho N1 . . . . . . .85 A3
Molyneux Ho W1 . . .102 B2
Molyneux St W1 . . . .102 B3
Mona Rd SE15 . . . . . .50 B1
Mona St E16 . . . . .35 B4
Monck's Row
SW18 . . . . .58 B1
Monck St SW1 . . . . .133 C1
Monckton Ct W14 126 C2
Monclar Rd SE5 . . . . .63 C3
Moncorvo Cl SW7 130 A3
Moncrieff St SE15 . .49 C1

Mondragon Ho
SW8 . . . . .172 B4
Monet Ct 13 SE16 . . .40 A1
Moneyer Ho N1 . . . . .97 B4
Monica Shaw Ct
NW1 . . . . .83 C1
Monier Rd E3 . . . . . . .18 C1
Monkbretton Ho
E2 . . . . .24 C2 99 B3
Monk Ct W12 . . . . . . .29 C1
Monk Dr E16 . . . . .35 C2
Monkridge 3 N8 . . . . . .4 C4
Monksfield N4 . . . . . . .5 C2
Monkswell Ho
E2 . . . . .24 C2 99 B3
Monkton Ho
 32 Bermondsey
SE16 . . . . .40 C4
 33 Hackney E5 . . . .17 A3
Monkton St SE11 . .149 C4
Monkwell Sq EC2 109 A3
Monmouth Cl W4 . . .37 C3
Monmouth Gr
TW8 . . . . .36 A2
Monmouth Ho
 1 Camden Town
NW5 . . . . .13 A2
Wandsworth SW18 . .58 C1
Monmouth Pl W2 . .100 A1
Monmouth Rd W2 . . .31 C3
Monmouth St
WC2 . . . . .106 A1
Monnery Rd N19 . . . . .4 C1
Monnow Rd SE1 . . . .153 B3
Monro Dr SW14 . . . . .55 A2
Monro Ho
 16 Crouch End N19 . .4 C4
Lisson Gr NW8 . . . . . .90 B3
Monro Ho
Hampstead
NW3 . . . . .11 B4
Putney SW15 . . . . . . .57 A2
Monro Way E5 . . . . . .16 C4
Monsal Ct E5 . . . . . . .18 A4
Monsell Ct 4 N4 . . . . .6 A1
Monsell Rd N4, N5 . . .6 A1
Monson Rd
Deptford SE14 . . . . . .50 C3
Willesden Green
NW10 . . . . .22 A3
Montagu Ct W1 . . . .103 A3
Montague Ave
SE4 . . . . .66 C3
Montague Cl SE1 123 B2
Montague Pl WC1 105 C4
Montague Rd
Richmond TW10 . . . . .54 A1
Shacklewell E8 . . . . . .16 C3
Montague Sq SE15 .50 B3
Montague St
Bloomsbury WC1 . . .106 A4
City of London EC1 108 C3
Montagu Mans
W1 . . . . .103 A3
Montagu Mews N
W1 . . . . .103 A3
Montagu Mews S
W1 . . . . .103 A2
Montagu Mews W
W1 . . . . .103 A2
Montagu Pl W1 . . . .103 A3
Montagu Row W1 . .103 A3
Montagu Sq W1 . . . .103 A3
Montagu St W1 . . . .103 A2
Montaigne Cl
SW1 . . . . .147 C3

Montana Bldg 4
SE13 . . . . .52 A2
Montana Rd SW17 . .72 C1
Montcalm Ho E14 . . .41 C2
Montclare St
E2 . . . . .24 B1 98 C2
Monteagle Ct 27
N1 . . . . .24 A3
Monteagle Way
Nunhead SE15 . . . . . .65 A4
Shacklewell E5 . . . . . . .7 C1
Montefiore Ct 2
N16 . . . . .7 B3
Montefiore St 2
SW8 . . . . .170 B1
Montego Cl 9
SE24 . . . . .62 C3
Montem Prim Sch 5
N7 . . . . .5 B1
Montem St N4 . . . . . . .5 B3
Montenay Studios
W10 . . . . .23 A3
Montesquieu Terr 3
E16 . . . . .35 B3
Montfichet Rd E15 . .19 B2
Montford Pl SE11 . .149 B1
Montfort Ho
 4 Bethnal Green
E2 . . . . .25 B2
Cubitt Town E14 . . . . .42 B3
Montfort Pl SW19 . . .69 C3
Montgomery Ct
W4 . . . . .45 B4
Montgomery Ho 5
E1 . . . . .25 C1
Montgomery Lo 38
E1 . . . . .25 B1
Montgomery Rd
W4 . . . . .37 B2
Montgomery St
E14 . . . . .34 A1
Montholme Rd
SW11 . . . . .60 B1
Monthope Rd 17
E1 . . . . .111 B3
Montolieu Gdns
SW15 . . . . .57 A2
Montpelier Gr
NW5 . . . . .13 B3
Montpelier Mews
SW7 . . . . .130 B2
Montpelier Pl
Knightsbridge
SW7 . . . . .130 B2
 21 Stepney E1 . . . . .32 B3
Montpelier Rd
SE15 . . . . .50 A2
Montpelier Rise
NW11 . . . . .1 A4
Montpelier Row
SE3 . . . . .53 B1
Montpelier Sq
SW7 . . . . .130 B3
Montpelier St
SW7 . . . . .130 B2
Montpelier Terr
SW7 . . . . .130 B3
Montpelier Vale
SE3 . . . . .53 B1
Montpelier Way
NW11 . . . . .1 A4
Montpelier Wlk
SW7 . . . . .130 B2
Montreal Pl WC2 . .120 C4
Montrell Rd SW2 . . . .74 A3

Montrose Ave
NW6 . . . . .23 A4
Montrose Ct SW7 . .129 C3
Montrose Ho
Belgravia SW1 . . . . .131 C3
Millwall E14 . . . . .41 C3
Montrose Pl SW1 . .131 C3
Montrose Villas 3
W6 . . . . .38 C2
Montserrat Rd
SW15 . . . . .58 A3
Monument Gdns
SE13 . . . . .67 B2
Monument St EC3 123 C4
Monument Sta
EC3 . . . . .123 C4
Monument The
EC3 . . . . .123 C4
Monza Bldg The
E1 . . . . .32 B2
Monza St E1 . . . . .32 B2
Moodkee St SE16 . . .40 B3
Moody Rd SE15 . . . . .49 B2
Moody St E1 . . . . .25 C2
Moon St N1 . . . . .86 A4
Moorcroft Rd
SW16 . . . . .74 A1
Moore Cl SW14 . . . . .55 B4
Moore Ct N1 . . . . .86 A3
Moore Ho
 16 Bethnal Green
E2 . . . . .25 B2
 3 Greenwich SE10 .43 B1
 7 Shadwell E1 . . . . .32 B2
Wandsworth SW17 . .71 C1
Moore Park Ct
SW6 . . . . .156 B2
Moore Park Rd
SW6 . . . . .156 A1
Moore St SW3 . . . . .144 C4
Moorfields EC2 . . . . .109 B3
Moorfields Eye Hospl
EC1 . . . . .97 B3
Moorfields Highwalk
EC2 . . . . .109 B3
Moorgate EC2 . . . . .109 B3
Moorgate Pl EC2 . .109 B2
Moorgate Sta
EC2 . . . . .109 B3
Moorgreen Ho
EC1 . . . . .96 A4
Moorhouse Ct 2 . . .109 B3
Moorhouse Rd
W2 . . . . .31 C3
Moorland Rd SW9 . .63 A3
Moor Pl EC2 . . . . . . .109 B3
Moor St W1 . . . . .105 C1
Morant Ho SW9 . . . .172 C2
Morant St E14 . . . . . .33 C2
Mora Prim Sch
NW2 . . . . .9 B4
Mora Rd NW2 . . . . .9 B4
Mora St EC1 . . . . .97 A3
Morat St SW9 . . . . . .173 A4
Moravian Cl SW3 . .157 C3
Moravian Pl
SW10 . . . . .157 C3
Moravian St 12 E2 . .25 B2
Moray Ho 6 E1 . . . . . .26 A1
Moray Mews N4, N7 . .5 B2
Moray Rd N4, N7 . . . . .5 B2
Mordaunt Ho
 3 Becontree
NW10 . . . . .20 C4
 34 Clapham SW8 . .171 B1

Mordaunt Rd
NW10 . . . . .20 C4
Mordaunt St SW9 . .62 B4
Morden Hill 10
SE13 . . . . .52 B1
Morden Ho 11
SW2 . . . . .62 C1
Morden La SE13 . . . .52 B2
Morden Mount Prim
Sch 1 SE13 . . . . . . .52 A1
Morden Rd SE3 . . . . .53 C1
Morden Road Mews
SE3 . . . . .53 C1
Morden St SE13 . . . .52 A2
Morden Wharf Rd
SE10 . . . . .43 A3
Mordern Ho NW1 . . .90 B1
Morecambe Cl 3
E1 . . . . .32 C4
Morecambe St
SE17 . . . . .151 A2
More Cl
Canning Town
E16 . . . . .35 B3
West Kensington
W14 . . . . .140 A3
Moredown Ho 3
E8 . . . . .16 C3
More House Sch
SW1 . . . . .131 A1
Moreland Ct 3
NW2 . . . . .1 C1
Moreland Prim Sch
EC1 . . . . .96 B3
Moreland St EC1 . . . .96 B4
Morella Rd SW11,
SW12 . . . . .72 B4
Morell Ho 5 SW9 172 C1
More London Pl
SE1 . . . . .124 A1
Moresby Rd E5 . . . . . .7 C3
More's Gdn SW3 . . .157 C3
Moreton Ho SE16 . . .40 A3
Moreton Pl SW1 . . . .147 A2
Moreton St SW1 . . . .147 B2
Moreton Terr
SW1 . . . . .147 A2
Moreton Terr Mews N
SW1 . . . . .147 A2
Moreton Terr Mews S
SW1 . . . . .147 A2
Moreton Twr 3
W3 . . . . .28 A1
Morgan Ct 5
SW11 . . . . .167 C2
Morgan Ho
Nine Elms SW8 . . . .171 A4
Pimlico SW1 . . . . . . .147 A3
Morgan Rd
Islington N7 . . . . . . .14 C3
Notting Hill W10 . . . .31 B4
Morgans La SE1 . . .124 A1
Morgan St
Canning Town
E16 . . . . .35 B4
Globe Town E3 . . . . .25 C2
Morgan's Wlk
SW11 . . . . .158 A1
Moriatry Cl N7 . . . . . .14 A4
Morie St SW18 . . . . . .59 A2
Morkyns Wlk SE21 . .76 A1
Morland Cl NW11 . . . .2 A3
Morland Ct W12 . . . . .39 A4
Morland Est E8 . . . . .16 C1
Morland Ho
Kilburn NW6 . . . . . . .23 C4

Morland Ho continued
Notting Hill W11 . . . . .31 A3
Somers Town NW1 . . .83 A1
Westminster SW1 . .148 A4
Morland Mews 1
N1 . . . . .14 C1
Morley Coll SE1 . . . .135 C2
Morley Ct SE13 . . . . .67 B3
Morley Ho
Stoke Newington
N16 . . . . .7 C2
Streatham SW2 . . . .74 A4
W11 . . . . .104 B2
Morley Rd SE13 . . . . .67 B3
Morley St SE1 . . . . . .135 C3
Morna Rd SE5 . . . . . .48 B1
Morning La E9 . . . . . .17 B2
Morningside Prim Sch
17 E9 . . . . .17 B2
Mornington Ave
W14 . . . . .140 C3
Mornington Avenue
Mans W14 . . . . .140 C3
Mornington Cres
Camden Town
NW1 . . . . .82 C2
NW1 . . . . .82 C2
Mornington Crescent
Sta NW1 . . . . .82 C2
Mornington Ct
NW1 . . . . .82 C2
Mornington Gr E3 . . .26 C2
Mornington Mews 2
SE5 . . . . .48 B2
Mornington Pl
1 New Cross
SE8 . . . . .51 B3
Regent's Pk NW1 . . . .82 C2
Mornington Rd SE14,
SE8 . . . . .51 B3
Mornington St
NW1 . . . . .82 B2
Mornington Terr
NW1 . . . . .82 B2
Morocco St SE1 . . . .138 A3
Morpeth Gr E9 . . . . . .25 C4
Morpeth Rd E9 . . . . . .25 C4
Morpeth St E2 . . . . . .25 C2
Morpeth Terr
SW1 . . . . .146 C4
Morrel Ct 11 E2 . . . . .24 C3
Morris Blitz Ct 2
N16 . . . . .16 B4
Morris Ct 3 SE5 . . . . .63 C3
Morris Gdns SW18 . .70 C4
Morris Ho
1 Bethnal Green
E2 . . . . .25 B2
Lisson Gr NW8 . . . . . .90 A1
1 Stockwell SW4 . . .62 A3
10 Tufnell Pk N19 . . .13 B4
Morrish Rd SW2 . . . .74 A4
Morrison Bldgs 5
E1 . . . . .111 B2
Morrison Ho SW2 . . .74 C3
Morrison St SW11 . . .60 C4
Morris Pl N4 . . . . .5 C2
Morris Rd E14 . . . . . .34 A4
Morris Ho
5 Bethnal Green
E2 . . . . .25 B2
SE16 . . . . .40 A4
Morris St E1 . . . . .32 A3
Morshead Mans
W9 . . . . .23 C2
Morshead Rd W9 . . . .23 C2
Mortain Ho 9
SE16 . . . . .40 A2

Morten Cl SW4 . . . . . .61 C1
Mortimer
1 Child's Hill NW2 . . . .1 B1
Streatham SW16 . . . .73 C2
Mortimer Cres
NW6 . . . . .78 B3
Mortimer Ct NW8 . . . .79 A1
Mortimer Est NW6 . . .78 A3
Mortimer Ho
4 Shepherd's Bush
W11 . . . . .30 C1
West Kensington
W14 . . . . .140 B3
Mortimer Lo 11
SW19 . . . . .70 A3
Mortimer Market
WC1 . . . . .93 A1
Mortimer Pl NW6 . . . .78 A3
Mortimer Rd
De Beauvoir Town
N1 . . . . .16 A1
Kensal Green
NW10 . . . . .22 B2
Mortimer Sq W11 . . .30 C2
Mortimer St W1 . . . .105 A3
Mortimer Terr
NW5 . . . . .13 A4
MORTLAKE 55 B4
Mortlake High St
SW14 . . . . .55 C4
Mortlake Ho 7
W4 . . . . .37 B2
Mortlake Rd SW14,
TW9 . . . . .44 C2
Mortlake Sta
SW14 . . . . .55 B4
Mortlake Terr
TW9 . . . . .44 C2
Mortlock Cl SE15 . . . .50 A2
Morton Cl 22 E1 . . . . .32 B3
Morton Ho SE17 . . . . .48 A4
Morton Mews
SW5 . . . . .142 A3
Morton Pl SE1 . . . . . .135 B1
Morton Rd N1 . . . . . . .15 B1
Morval Rd SW2 . . . . .62 C2
Morville Ho SW18 . . .59 C1
Morville St E3 . . . . . . .26 C3
Morwell St WC1 . . . .105 C3
Moscow Pl W2 . . . . .114 A4
Moscow Rd W2 . . . .114 A4
Mosedale NW1 . . . . . .92 B3
Moseley Row SE10 . .43 B2
Mosque Tower 26
E1 . . . . .111 C3
Mossbourne Com
Acad E8 . . . . .16 C3
Mossbourne Victoria
Park Acad E9 . . . . .17 C1
Mossbury Rd
SW11 . . . . .60 A4
Moss Cl E1 . . . . .111 C4
Mossford St E3 . . . . .26 B1
Mossington Gdns
SE16 . . . . .40 B2
Mossop St SW3 . . . .144 B4
Mostyn Gdns
NW10 . . . . .22 C3
Mostyn Gr E3 . . . . . . .26 C3
Mostyn Lo N5 . . . . . . .15 B4
Mostyn Rd SW9 . . . .173 C3
Motcomb St SW1 . . .131 B2
Mothers Sq The 18
E5 . . . . .17 A4

Motley Ave
EC2 . . . . .24 A1 98 A2
Motley St SW8 . . . .170 C2
Moules Ct SE5 . . . . . .48 B3
Moulins Rd E9 . . . . . .17 B1
Moulsford Ho
5 Lower Holloway
N7 . . . . .14 A3
32 Paddington W2 . .31 C4
Mounsey Ho 13
W10 . . . . .23 A2
Mount Adon Pk SE21,
SE22 . . . . .76 C4
Mountague Pl 2
E14 . . . . .34 B2
Mountain Ho
SE11 . . . . .148 C2
Mount Angelus Rd
SW15 . . . . .68 B4
Mount Ararat Rd
TW10 . . . . .54 A2
Mountbatten Ho
N6 . . . . .3 C4
Mountbatten Mews
SW18 . . . . .71 B3
Mount Carmel 3
N7 . . . . .14 B3
Mount Carmel RC
Tech Coll for Girls
8 N19 . . . . .4 C3
Mounteagle Gdns SW16,
SW2 . . . . .74 B1
Mount Ephraim La
SW16 . . . . .73 C1
Mount Ephraim Rd
SW16 . . . . .73 C1
Mountfield Ct
SE13 . . . . .67 C1
Mount Ford St E1 111 B2
Mountford Cres
N1 . . . . .15 B2
Mountfort 1
N1 . . . . .14 C1
Mountgrove Rd N5 . . .6 B1
Mountjoy Ho2 EC2 108 C3
Mount Lodge SW4 . .61 C3
Mount Mills EC1 . . . .96 B3
Mount Nod Rd SW16,
SW2 . . . . .74 B1
Mount Pl 7 W3 . . . . . .28 A1
Mount Pleasant
WC1 . . . . .95 B1
Mount Pleasant Cres
N4 . . . . .5 B4
Mount Pleasant Rd
Lewisham SE13 . . . .67 B1
Willesden NW10 . . . .22 B4
Mount Pleasant Villas
N4 . . . . .5 B4
Mount Rd SW18,
SW19 . . . . .71 A2
Mount Row W1 . . . .118 A3
Mount St Mews
W1 . . . . .117 C3
Mount Sq The 3
NW3 . . . . .2 B1
Mount St W1 . . . . . .117 C3
Mount Terr E1 . . . . . .32 A4
Mount The
Hampstead NW3 . . . .2 B1
Kensington
W8 . . . . . . .31 C1 113 B1
Mount Tyndal NW3 . .2 C3

Mount Vernon
NW3 . . . . .11 B3
Mountview 5
SW16 . . . . .74 B1
Mountview Cl
NW11 . . . . .2 B3
Mount Villas SE27 . .75 A1
Mourne Ho NW3 . . . .11 B2
Mowatt Cl N19 . . . . . .4 C3
Mowbray Rd NW6 . . .10 A1
Mowlem Prim Sch 36
E2 . . . . .25 B3
Mowlem St E2 . . . . . .25 A3
Mowll St SW9 . . . . . .163 B1
Moxon St W1 . . . . . .103 B3
Moye Cl 10 E2 . . . . . .24 C3
Moylan Rd W6 . . . . .154 B3
Moyle Ho SW1 . . . . .161 A4
Moyne Ho SW9 . . . . .63 A3
Mozart St W10 . . . . . .23 B2
Muchute Pk & Farm
E14 . . . . .42 B2
Mudchute Sta E14 . . .42 B2
Mudie Ho 8 SW2 . . . .74 A4
Mudlarks Blvd 3
SE10 . . . . .43 B3
Muirdown Ave
SW14 . . . . .55 C3
Muir Dr SW18 . . . . . . .60 A1
Muirfield W3 . . . . .29 A3
Muirfield Cl 23
SE16 . . . . .40 A1
Muirfield Cres
E14 . . . . .42 A3
Muir Rd E5 . . . . .7 C1
Mulberry Bsns Ctr
SE16 . . . . .40 C4
Mulberry Cl
Chelsea SW3 . . . . .157 C3
East Dulwich SE22 .64 C1
Hampstead NW3 . . .11 C4
Mulberry Ct
Finsbury EC1 . . . . . .96 B3
Islington N5 . . . . . . .15 A3
1 Leyton E11 . . . . . .19 C4
10 Paddington W9 . .23 B2
Mulberry Ho
8 Bethnal Green
E2 . . . . .25 B2
5 Deptford SE8 . . . .51 B4
Mulberry House Sch
The NW2 . . . . .1 A1
Mulberry Mews
SE14 . . . . .51 B2
Mulberry Pl W6 . . . . .38 C1
Mulberry Rd E8 . . . . .16 B1
Mulberry Sch for Girls
50 Stepney E1 . . . . . .32 A3
18 St George in East
E1 . . . . .32 A2
Mulberry St 7
E1 . . . . .111 B2
Mulberry Wlk
SW3 . . . . .157 C4
Mulgrave Rd
West Kensington
W14 . . . . .154 C4
Willesden NW10 . . . . .8 B4
Mulkern Rd N19 . . . . .4 C3
Mullard Ho WC1 . . . .105 A4
Mullens Ho 7
SW15 . . . . .57 B2
Mullen Twr EC1 . . . . .95 B1
Muller Rd SW4 . . . . . .61 C1

Mullet Gdns **7**
E2...............24 C2 99 C4
Mulletsfield WC1....94 B3
Mull Ho **17** E3........26 B3
Mullins Path
SW14....................55 C4
Mulready St NW8...90 A1
Multi Way W3..........38 A4
Multon Ho E9.........17 B1
Multon Rd SW18....71 C4
Mulvaney Way
SE1......................137 C3
Mumford Rd SE24...63 A2
Muncaster Rd
SW11....................60 C2
Mundania Ct SE22..65 A1
Mundania Rd SE22..65 B1
Munday Ho SE1....137 B1
Munday Rd E16......35 C2
Munden Ho **5** E3...27 A2
Munden St W14....140 A4
Mund St W14........141 A1
Mundy Ho **6** W10..23 A2
Mundy St
N1.............24 A2 98 B4
Munro Ho
Bermondsey SE1...137 C3
Lambeth SE1........135 B3
Munro Mews W10...31 A4
Munster Ct SW6...164 C2
Munster Rd SW6...154 B2
Munster Residences
SW6.....................164 B4
Munster Sq NW1...92 B3
Munton Rd SE1,
SE17....................151 A4
Murchison Ho **1**
W10.......................31 A4
Murdoch Ho **8**
SE16......................40 B3
Murdock Cl E16......35 B3
Murdock St SE15...50 A4
Murfett Cl SW19....70 A2
Muriel St N1...........85 A4
Murphy Ho SE1....136 B2
Murphy St SE1.....135 B3
Murray Gr N1..........87 B1
Murray Mews
NW1........................13 C1
Murray St NW1......13 C1
Murray Terr NW3...11 C4
Musard Rd W6.....154 B4
Musbury St E1.......32 B3
Muscal W6...........154 A4
Muscatel Pl SE5.....49 A2
Muschamp Rd
SE15.....................64 B4
Muscott Ho **15** E2..24 C4
Muscovy St EC3...124 B4
Museum & Galleries
of Modern London
EC2......................108 C3
Museum Ho **2** E2..25 B2
Museum La SW7...129 B1
Museum Mans
WC1......................106 A3

Museum of London
EC2......................108 C3
Museum of London
Docklands E14.....33 C2
Museum of the Order
of St John EC1......96 A1
Museum St WC1...106 A2
Museum Way W3...36 C4
Musgrave Cres
SW6.....................165 C4
Musgrave Ct
SW11....................168 A4
Musgrove Ho **6**
E9.........................17 C2
Musgrove Rd SE14..51 A2
Musical Mus The
TW8......................44 B4
Musjid Rd **7**
SW11....................167 C1
Mustow Pl **2**
SW6.....................165 A2
Mutrix Rd NW6.......23 C4
Mutton Pl NW1.......12 C2
Myatt Garden Prim
Sch SE4.................51 B1
Myatt Rd SE5.........48 A1
Myatt Rd SW9........48 A1
Myatts Field Ct
SE5.......................48 A2
Mycenae Rd SE3....53 C4
Myddelton Pas
EC1.......................95 C4
Myddelton Sq EC1..95 C4
Myddelton St EC1...95 C3
Myddleton Ave N4....6 B2
Myers Ho **5** SE5...48 B3
Myers La SE14........50 C4
Mylius Cl SE14.......50 B2
Mylne Cl W6...........38 C1
Mylne St EC1..........85 B1
Myrtene Ct **10**
SW19.....................69 C3
Myrtle Cl **16** E1...111 C2
Myrtle St N1.........111 C2
Myron Pl SE13........67 B4
Myrtle Ho SE14.....50 C2
Myrtle Rd W3..........28 B1
Myrtle Wlk **20** N1...24 A3
Mysore Rd SW11....60 B3
Myton Rd SE21......75 C1
Mytton Ho SW8....162 C1

N

N1 Sh Ctr N1.........85 C2
Nags Head N7........14 B4
Nags Head Ct EC1..97 A1
Nags Head Sh Ctr The
N7.........................14 B4
Nainia Jewish Prep
Sch NW6................78 A2
Nainby Ho **11** SE11..149 B3
Nairne Gr SE5,
SE24.....................63 C3
Nairn St E14..........34 B4
Naldera Gdns SE3..53 C4
Nalton Ho **4** NW6..11 B1
Namco Funscape
SE1......................134 C4
Nankin St E14.........33 C3
Nansen Rd SW11....60 C4
Nant Ct NW2.........1 B2
Nantes Cl SW18.....59 B3
Nant Rd NW2..........1 B2
Nant St E2..............25 A2

Naomi St **20** SE8....41 A2
Naoroji St WC1.......95 B3
Napa Cl E15...........19 B3
Napier Ave
Deptford E14........41 C1
Fulham SW6..........58 B4
Napier Cl
New Cross SE14,
SE8.......................51 B3
West Kensington
W14.....................126 C2
Napier Ct
Fulham SW6..........58 B4
Shoreditch N1........87 B2
Napier Gr N1..........87 A2
Napier Ho SE17.....48 A4
Napier Pl W14......126 C1
Napier Rd
College Pk NW10....22 A2
Kensington W14...126 C1
Napier Terr N1.......15 A1
Narbonne Ave
SW4.....................61 B2
Narborough St
SW6.....................166 A1
Narcissus Rd NW6..10 C3
Narford Rd E5.........7 C2
Narrow St **6**
Acton W3...............28 A1
Limehouse E14......33 A2
Nascot St W12........30 B3
Naseby Cl NW6.......11 B1
Nashe Ho SE1......137 B1
Nash Ho
4 Millwall E14....41 C3
Pimlico SW1........146 B1
Nash Rd SE4...........66 A2
Nash St NW1..........92 B4
Nasmyth St W6......39 A3
Nassau Rd SW13....46 B2
Nassau St W1......104 C3
Nassington Rd
NW3......................12 B4
Nathan Ho SE11...149 C3
Nathaniel Cl E1....111 A3
National Archives The
TW9......................45 A3
National Army Mus
SW3.....................159 A4
National Gallery
W1.......................119 C3
National Hospl for
Neurology &
Neurosurgery
WC1......................94 B1
National Maritime
Mus SE10..............52 C4
National Portrait
Gallery W1.........119 C3
National Tennis Ctr
SW15....................56 A2
National Theatre
SE1......................121 A2
Natural History Mus
SW7.....................129 B1
Nautilus Bldg The
EC1.......................95 C4
Naval Row E14.......34 B2
Navarino Gr E8.......16 C2
Navarino Mans E8..16 C2
Navarino Rd E8.......16 C2
Navarre St
E2.............24 B1 98 C2
Navenby Wlk **13**
E3.........................26 C1
Navy St SW4..........61 C4

Naxos Bldg **9** E14..41 C4
Naylor Bldg W **4**
E1.......................111 B2
Naylor Ho
23 Clapham
SW8.....................171 B1
Walworth SE17.....151 C2
5 West Kilburn
W10.......................23 A2
Naylor Rd SE15......50 A3
Nayor Bldg E **6**
E1.......................111 B2
Nazareth Cl SE15...50 A1
Nazrul St E2....24 B2 98 C4
Nealden St SW9...62 B4
Neal St WC2.........106 A1
Neal's Yd WC2.....106 A1
Neasden Cl NW10....8 A3
Neasden Junc
NW10......................8 A3
Neasden La NW10...8 A3
Neasden Sta NW10...8 A3
Neatham Pl
SW1.....................146 C2
Nebraska Bldg **1**
SE13......................52 A2
Nebraska St SE1...137 B3
Neckinger SE16...139 C2
Neckinger Est
SE16....................139 C2
Nectarine Way
SE13......................52 A1
Nedahall Ct **4**
NW11.....................1 B4
Needham Ho
SE11.....................149 B3
Needham Rd W11...31 C3
Needleman St
SE16......................40 C4
Needwood Ho N4....6 B3
Neilson-Terry Ct **9**
SW9......................62 B3
Nelson Cl NW6......23 C2
Nelson Ct SE16......33 B1
Nelson Docks
SE16......................33 B1
Nelson Gdns
E2.............24 C2 99 C4
Nelson Pas EC1....97 A4
Nelson Pl N1..........86 B1
Nelson Rd SE10....52 B4
Nelson's Column
W1.......................120 A2
Nelson Sq SE1....136 A4
Nelsons Row SW4..61 C3
Nelson St
Canning Town
E16.......................35 B2
Stepney E1............32 A3
Nelsons Yd NW1...82 C2
Nelson Terr N1......86 B1
Nemoure Rd W3.....28 B2
Nepaul Rd **17**
SW11....................60 A4
Nepean St SW15....68 C4
Neptune Ct **13** E14..41 C2
Neptune Ho
2 Rotherhithe
SE16......................40 B3

Neptune Ho continued
11 Stoke Newington
N16.......................16 A3
Neptune St SE16....40 B3
Nesham Ho N1......24 A4
Nesham St E1.......125 B2
Ness St SE16.....139 B2
Nestor Ho **12** E2...25 A3
Netheravon Rd
W4.........................38 B1
Netheravon Rd S
W4.........................38 B1
Netherby Ho **2**
SW8.....................171 B1
Nethercombe Ho **3**
SE3.......................53 C4
Nethercott Ho **27**
E3.........................27 A2
Netherfield Rd
SW17....................72 C1
Netherford Rd
SW4.....................171 A1
Netherhall Gdns
NW3......................11 B3
Netherhall Way
NW3......................11 B3
Netherleigh Cl N6...4 A3
Netherton Gr
SW10...................157 A3
Netherwood Rd
W14.......................39 C4
Netherwood St
NW6......................10 C2
Netley SE5..............49 A2
Netley Prim Sch
NW1......................92 C3
Netley Rd TW8......44 A4
Netley St NW1......92 C3
Nettlecombe Ho **5**
SW19.....................70 A3
Nettleden Ho
SW3.....................144 B3
Nettlefold Pl SE27..75 A1
Nettleton Rd SE14..50 C2
Nevada St SE10......52 B4
Nevena Ct **3** SW2..62 C2
Nevern Mans
SW5.....................141 B2
Nevern Pl SW5....141 C3
Nevern Rd SW5...141 B3
Nevern Sq SW5...141 C3
Neville Cl
Acton W3................28 B1
Paddington NW6...23 B3
Peckham SE15......49 C3
Somers Town NW1...83 C1
Neville Ct **10**
SW12.....................73 B4
Neville Gill Cl
SW18.....................59 A1
Neville Rd NW6......23 C3
Neville St SW7....143 B2
Neville Terr SW7...143 B2
Nevill Ho **3**
N19.........................4 C1
Nevinson Cl SW18..59 C1
Nevis Rd SW17......72 C2
Nevitt Ho N1..........87 C1
Newall Ho SE1....137 A2
Newark Cres
NW10......................20 C2
Newark Ho **3**
SW9......................48 A1
Newark St E1..........32 A4
New Atlas Wharf
E14.......................41 C3

New Bentham Ct **10**
N1 . . . . .15 B1
Newberry Ho N1 . . . . .15 B1
Newbold Cotts **4**
E1 . . . . .32 B3
Newbolt Ho SE17 .**151** B2
New Bond St W1 . .**118** B4
New Bridge St
EC4 . . . .**108** A1
New Broad St
EC2 . . . .**110** A3
New Bsns Ctr The
NW10 . . . . .21 B2
Newburgh Rd W3 . .28 B1
Newburgh St W1 . .**105** A1
New Burlington Mews
W1 . . . .**118** C4
New Burlington Pl
W1 . . . .**118** C4
New Burlington St
W1 . . . .**118** C4
Newburn Ho SE11 **149** A2
Newburn St SE11 . .**149** A2
Newbury Ct E5 . . . . .18 A3
Newbury Ho
Brixton SW9 . . . . . . .48 A1
14 Kensington W2 .**100** B1
Newbury Mews
NW5 . . . . .12 C2
Newbury St EC1 . . .**108** C4
New Butt La SE8 . . .51 C3
Newby Ho E14 . . . . .34 B2
Newby Pl E14 . . . . . .34 B2
Newby St SW8 . . . . .61 A4
New Caledonian Mkt
SE1 . . . .**138** B2
New Caledonian
Wharf SE16 . . . . . . .41 B3
New Campden Ct **9**
NW3 . . . . .11 B4
Newcastle Cl EC4 .**108** A2
Newcastle Ct EC4 .**123** A4
Newcastle Ho W1 .**103** B4
Newcastle Pl W2 . .**101** C4
Newcastle Row
EC1 . . . . .95 C1
New Cavendish St
W1 . . . .**104** A3
New Change EC4 . .**108** C1
New Charles St
EC1 . . . . .96 B4
New Church Rd
32 Camberwell
SE5 . . . . .48 B3
Camberwell SE5 . . .48 C4
New College Ct **6**
NW3 . . . . .11 B2
New College Mews **7**
N1 . . . . .14 C1
New College Par **1**
NW3 . . . . .11 C3
Newcombe Ho N5 . .15 B3
Newcombe St
W8 . . . . .31 C1 **113** C2
Newcomen Ho **5**
NW5 . . . . .13 A4
Newcomen Rd
SW11 . . . . .59 C4
Newcomen St
SE1 . . . .**137** B4
New Compton St
WC2 . . . .**106** A1
New Concordia Wharf
SE1 . . . .**139** A4
Newcourt Ho **2**
E2 . . . . .25 A2

Newcourt St NW8 . .**80** A1
New Covent Garden
Flower Market
SW8 . . . .**162** A3
New Covent Garden
Fruit & Vegetable
Mkt SW8 . . . .**161** B1
New Crane Pl E1 . . .32 B1
New Crescent Yd **1**
NW10 . . . . .21 B3
NEW CROSS 51 B2
New Cross SE14 . . .51 B3
NEW CROSS
GATE 50 C2
New Cross Gate
SE14 . . . . .50 C2
New Cross Gate Sta
SE14 . . . . .51 A3
New Cross Rd
SE14 . . . . .51 A3
New Cross Sta
SE14 . . . . .51 B3
New Ct
City of London
EC4 . . . .**107** B1
28 Hampstead
NW3 . . . . .11 B4
Stoke Newington
N16 . . . . .6 C3
Newdigate Ho **5**
E14 . . . . .33 B3
Newell St E14 . . . . .33 B3
New End NW3 . . . . . .2 B1
New End Prim Sch **33**
NW3 . . . . .11 B4
New End Sq NW3 . . .11 C4
Newent Cl SE15 . . .49 A3
New Fetter La
EC4 . . . .**107** C2
Newfield Prim Sch
NW10 . . . . .8 B1
Newgate St EC1 . .**108** B2
New Globe Wlk
SE1 . . . .**122** C2
New Goulston St
E1 . . . .**110** C2
New Hope Christian
Acad **1** SE22 . . . . .64 B3
Newington Barrow
Way N7 . . . . .5 B1
Newington Butts
SE11 . . . .**150** B3
Newington Cswy
SE1 . . . .**136** C2
Newington Gn
N16 . . . . .15 C3
Newington Green
Mans N16 . . . . .15 C3
Newington Green
Prim Sch N16 . . . . .15 C3
Newington Green Rd
N1 . . . . .15 C2
Newington Ind Est
SE17 . . . .**150** C3
New Inn Broadway
EC2 . . . . .24 A1 **98** B2
New Inn Sq
EC2 . . . . .24 A1 **98** B2

New Inn St
EC2 . . . . .24 A1 **98** B2
New Inn Yd
EC2 . . . . .24 A1 **98** B2
New James Ct
SE15 . . . . .65 A4
New Kent Rd SE1 .**151** A4
New Kings Prim Sch
SW6 . . . .**165** C3
New King's Rd
SW6 . . . .**165** C3
New King St SE8 . . .51 C4
Newland Ct EC1 . . .**97** B2
Newland Ho **17**
SE14 . . . . .50 C4
Newlands NW1 . . . .**92** C4
Newlands Acad
SE15 . . . . .65 C3
Newlands Quay E1 .32 B2
New London St
EC3 . . . .**124** B4
Newlyn NW1 . . . . . .**83** A3
Newman Catholic Coll
NW10 . . . . .21 C4
Newman Pas W1 .**105** A3
Newman St W1 . . .**105** A2
Newman's Row
WC2 . . . .**107** A3
Newnham Ho **11**
SW9 . . . . .63 A3
Newmill Ho **1**
E3 . . . . .27 B1
Newmount NW3 . . .11 C3
New Mount St E15 .19 C1
Newnes Path
SW15 . . . . .57 A3
Newnham Ho **9**
SW15 . . . . .57 A3
Newnham Terr
SE1 . . . .**135** B2
New North Com Sch
N1 . . . .**86** C4
New North Pl
EC2 . . . . .24 A1 **98** A2
New North Rd N1 . .**87** B3
New North Road
N1 . . . .**87** B3
New North St
WC1 . . . .**106** C4
Newnton Cl N4 . . . . .6 C4
New Oxford St
WC1 . . . .**106** A2
New Palace Yd
SW1 . . . .**134** A3
New Park Ct **28**
SW2 . . . . .74 A4
New Park Par **14**
SW2 . . . . .74 A4
New Park Rd SW2 .74 A4
New Place Sq
SE16 . . . . .40 A3
Newport Ave E14 . .34 C2
Newport Ct WC2 . .**119** C4
Newport Pl WC2 . . .**119** C4
Newport Rd SW13 .46 C2
Newport St SE11 .**149** A4
New Priory Ct **8**
NW6 . . . .**10** C1
New Providence
Wharf E14 . . . . .34 C1
Newquay Ho SE11 **149** B2
New Quebec St
W1 . . . .**103** A1
New River Ct N5 . . .15 C4

New River Way N4 . .6 C4
New Row WC2 . . . .**120** A4
New St Sq EC4 . . .**107** C2
New Scotland Yard
SW1 . . . .**133** B2
New Shepherd's Bush
Mkt **9** W12 . . . .**39** B4
New Spring Gdns Wlk
SE1 . . . .**148** B1
New Sq WC2 . . . . .**107** A2
New Square Pas
WC2 . . . .**107** B2
New St EC2 . . . . . .**110** B3
Newstead Ho N1 . .**85** C2
Newton Ave W3 . . . .37 B4
Newton Gr W4 . . . . .38 A2
Newton Ho
5 Clapham
SW8 . . . .**171** B2
Paddington NW8 . .**78** B4
1 Stepney E1 . . . . .32 A2
Newton Pl E14 . . . .41 C2
Newton Point **1**
E16 . . . . .35 B3
Newton Prep Sch
SW8 . . . .**170** B4
Newton Rd
Acton W3 . . . . .37 B4
Kensington W2 . . . .**100** A1
Stratford New Town
E15 . . . . .19 C3
Newton St WC2 . .**106** B2
Newton's Yd **14**
SW18 . . . . .58 C2
New Tower Bldgs **21**
E1 . . . . .32 A1
Newtown Ct
Battersea SW11 . . .**170** A3
Clapham SW4 . . . . .61 A2
New Union Cl E14 .42 B3
New Union St
EC2 . . . .**109** B3
New Wharf Rd N1 . .**84** B2
Niagara Cl N1 . . . . .**87** A2
Niagara Ct **6**
SE16 . . . . .40 B3
Nicholas Ct
Chiswick W4 . . . . . .46 A3
Golders Green NW11 .1 C4
Nicholas Ho **2**
SW15 . . . . .56 C2
Nicholas La EC2,
EC4 . . . .**123** C4
Nicholas Pas EC3 **123** C4
Nicholas Rd
Bethnal Green E1 . .25 B1
20 Shepherd's Bush
W11 . . . . .30 C2
Nicholay Rd N19 . . .4 C3
Nicholl Ho N4 . . . . . .6 B3
Nicholl St E2 . . . . . .24 C4
Nichols Cl N4 . . . . . .5 C3
Nichols Ct E2 . . . . .24 B3
Nicholson Ho
SE17 . . . .**151** B2
Nicholson St SE1 .**122** A1
Nickleby Ho
18 Bermondsey
SE1 . . . .**139** B3
7 Shepherd's Bush
W11 . . . . .30 C2
Nickols Wlk SW18 .59 A3
Nicoll Ct NW10 . . . .21 A4
Nicoll Rd NW10 . . . .21 A4
Nicosia Rd SW18 . .72 A4
Nigel Bldg EC1 . . .**107** B4

Nigel Playfair Ave
W6 . . . . .39 A1
Nigel Rd SE15 . . . . .64 C4
Nightingale Cl W4 .45 B4
Nightingale Ct
1 Cubitt Town
E14 . . . . .42 B3
Finsbury Pk N4 . . . . .5 B2
Nightingale Gr
SE13 . . . . .67 C2
Nightingale Ho
21 Hoxton E1 . . . . .24 A4
4 North Kensington
W12 . . . . .30 B3
1 St George in East
E1 . . . .**125** C2
Nightingale Hospl
NW1 . . . .**102** B4
Nightingale La SW11,
SW12 . . . . .60 C1
Nightingale Lo **5**
W9 . . . . .31 C4
Nightingale Mans **1**
SW12 . . . . .60 C1
Nightingale Mews
1 Bow E3 . . . . .26 A3
Newington SE11 . . .**150** A4
Nightingale Pl
SW10 . . . .**157** A4
Nightingale Prim Sch
E5 . . . . .16 C4
Nightingale Rd
22 Canonbury N1 . .15 B2
Dagenham NW10 . .21 B1
Nightingale Sch
SW17 . . . . .72 A2
Nightingale Sq
SW12 . . . . .72 C4
Nightingale Wlk SW18,
SW4 . . . . .61 A1
Nile Cl N16 . . . . .7 B1
Nile Ho N1 . . . .**97** B4
Nile St N1 . . . .**97** B4
Nile Terr SE1 . . . . .**153** A1
Nimegen Way **9**
SE22 . . . . .64 A2
Nimrod Pas **4** N1 . .16 A2
NINE ELMS **160** C2
Nine Elms La
SW8 . . . .**161** B3
Nine Elms Rte **19** C3
Niton Rd TW9 . . . . .54 C4
Niton St SW6 . . . . . .47 C3
Nobel Ho **8** SE5 . . .48 B1
Noble Ct E1 . . . . . . .32 A2
Noble St EC2 . . . . .**108** C2
Noel Coward Ho
SW1 . . . .**147** A3
Noel Ho **3** NW3 . . .11 C3
Noel Rd
Acton W3 . . . . .28 A3
Islington N1 . . . .**86** B2
Noel St W1 . . . .**105** A1
Noko NW10 . . . . . . .22 C2
Nolan Way E5 . . . . .16 C4
Noll Ho N7 . . . . .5 B2
Norbiton Rd E14 . . .33 B3
Norbroke St W12 . .29 B2
Norburn St W10 . . .31 A4
Norcombe Ho **2**
N19 . . . . .4 C1
Norcott Rd N16 . . . .7 C1

Norcroft Gdns
SE22 . . . .**76** C4
Norden Ho 28 E2 . . . .**25** A2
Nore Ct NW10 . . . .**8** C1
Norfolk Cres W2 . .**102** B2
Norfolk Ho
City of London
EC4 . . . .**122** C4
Greenwich SE3 . . . . .**53** A4
4 Putney SW15 . . . .**69** B4
Richmond TW10 . . . .**54** C2
Shacklewell E8 . . . . .**16** B4
St Johns SE8 . . . .**51** C2
Westminster SW1 . .**147** C3
Norfolk House Rd
SW16 . . . .**74** A1
Norfolk Mans
Battersea SW11 . . .**169** A3
10 Wandsworth
SW18 . . . .**58** C2
Norfolk Mews 12
W10 . . . .**31** A4
Norfolk Pl W2 . . . .**101** C2
Norfolk Rd
St John's Wood
NW8 . . . .**79** C3
Willesden NW10 . . . . .**8** A1
Norfolk Row SE1,
SE11 . . . .**148** C4
Norfolk Sq W2 . . . .**101** C2
Norfolk Sq Mews
W2 . . . .**101** C1
Norgrove St SW12 . .**72** C4
Norland Ho 19
W11 . . . .**30** C1
Norland Pl
W11 . . . . . .**31** A1 **112** B1
Norland Place Sch
W11 . . . . . .**31** A1 **112** A1
Norland Rd 18
W11 . . . .**30** C1
Norland Sq
W11 . . . . . .**31** A1 **112** B1
Norley Vale SW15 . .**68** C3
Norman Butler Ho 10
W10 . . . .**23** A1
Norman Cl
Dulwich SE22 . . . . . .**76** C4
Finsbury Pk N4 . . . . . .**5** C4
Willesden NW10 . . . . .**8** C1
Normand Croft Com
Sch W14 . . . .**155** A4
Normand Mews
W14 . . . .**154** B4
Normand Rd W14 .**154** C4
Normandy Ho 8
E14 . . . .**42** B4
Normandy Rd
SW9 . . . .**173** B3
Norman Gr E3 . . . . .**26** A3
Norman Ho 9 SW8 .**162** A2
Normanhurst Rd
SW2 . . . .**74** B2
Norman Rd SE10 . . .**52** A3
Norman St EC1 . . . .**97** A3
Normanton Ave SW18,
SW19 . . . .**70** C2
Normanton Ho 6
SW4 . . . .**61** B1
Norman Way W3 . . .**28** A3

Norris Ho
12 Hoxton N1 . . . . .**24** A4
15 South Hackney
E9 . . . .**25** B4
Norris St SW1 . . . .**119** B3
Norroy Rd SW15 . . .**57** C3
Norse Ho 13 SE5 . . .**48** B1
Norstead Pl SW15 . .**68** C2
NORTH ACTON **20** C2
North Acton Rd
NW10 . . . .**20** C3
North Acton Sta
W3 . . . .**28** C4
Northampton Gr
N1 . . . .**15** C3
Northampton Pk
N1 . . . .**15** C2
Northampton Rd
EC1 . . . .**95** C2
Northampton Sq
EC1 . . . .**96** A3
Northampton St
N1 . . . .**15** B1
North Audley St
W1 . . . .**117** B4
North Ave 3 TW9 . . .**44** C2
Northaw Ho 4
W10 . . . .**22** B1
North Bank NW8 . . .**90** A3
North Block 13 E1 . .**32** B2
Northbourne Ho 21
E5 . . . .**17** A3
Northbourne Rd
SW4 . . . .**61** C2
North Bridge House
Sch 13 NW3 . . . . . .**11** B2
North Bridge House
School Prep Sch
NW1 . . . .**82** A3
North Bridge House
Senior Sch 6
NW3 . . . .**11** C4
North Carriage Dr
W2 . . . .**116** B4
North Chiswick Bsns
Pk W3 . . . .**37** A3
Northchurch
SE17 . . . .**151** C2
Northchurch Ho 19
E2 . . . .**24** C4
Northchurch Rd
N1 . . . .**15** C1
Northchurch Terr
N1 . . . .**16** A1
North Circular Rd NW2,
NW10 . . . .**8** A3
North Colonnade The
E14 . . . .**34** A1
Northcote Lodge Sch
SW11 . . . .**60** B1
Northcote Rd
Wandsworth
SW11 . . . .**60** A2
Willesden NW10 . . . . .**8** A1
Northcourt W1 . . . .**105** A4
North Cres
Marylebone WC1 . .**105** B4
Newham E16 . . . .**27** C1
Northcroft Ct 8
W12 . . . .**38** C4
North Cross Rd
SE22 . . . .**64** C2
North Ct SW1 . . . .**134** A1
Northdown St N1 . . .**84** C1

North Dulwich Sta
SE21 . . . .**63** C2
NORTH END **2** B2
North End NW3 . . . . .**2** B2
North End Ave NW3 . .**2** B2
North End Cres
W14 . . . .**140** C3
North End Ho
W14 . . . .**140** B3
North End Par
W14 . . . .**140** B3
North End Rd
Golders Green
NW11 . . . .**2** A3
West Kensington
W14 . . . .**141** A1
North End Way
NW3 . . . .**2** B2
Northern Hts N8 . . . .**4** C4
Northesk Ho 6
E1 . . . .**25** A1
North Eyot Gdns 5
W6 . . . .**38** B1
Northey St E14 . . . . .**33** A2
Northfield Hall N6 . . .**3** C4
Northfield Ho 3
SE15 . . . .**49** C4
Northfield Rd N16 . . .**7** A4
Northfields SW18 . . .**58** C3
Northfields Prospect
SW18 . . . .**58** C3
Northfields Rd W3 . .**28** B4
Northfleet Ho
SE1 . . . .**137** B4
North Flower Wlk
W2 . . . .**115** B3
North Gate NW8 . . . .**80** A1
Northgate Ct 14
SW9 . . . .**62** C4
North Gower St
NW1 . . . .**93** A3
North Gr N6 . . . .**3** C4
North Greenwich Pier
SE10 . . . .**35** B1
North Greenwich Sta
SE10 . . . .**43** A4
North Hill Ct N6 . . . . .**3** C4
North Ho 3 SE8 . . . . .**41** B1
Northiam WC1 . . . . .**94** B3
Northiam St E9 . . . . .**25** A4
Northington St
WC1 . . . .**95** A1
NORTH
KENSINGTON **30** C4
Northlands St SE5 . .**48** B1
Northleigh Ho 30
E3 . . . .**27** A2
North Lo SW4 . . . . . .**61** A3
North Lodge Cl
SW15 . . . .**57** C2
North Mews WC1 . . .**95** A1
Northolme Rd N5 . . .**15** B4
Northpoint Sq 8
NW1 . . . .**13** C2
North Pole Rd
W10 . . . .**30** B4
Northport St N1 . . . .**87** C3
North Rd
Barnsbury N7 . . . . . .**14** A2
Brentford TW8 . . . . .**44** A4
Highgate N6 . . . .**3** C4
Richmond TW9 . . . . . .**44** C1
North Ride W2 . . . .**116** A3
North Rise W2 . . . .**102** B1
North Row W1 . . . .**117** B4

NORTH SHEEN **44** C1
North Sheen Sta
TW10 . . . .**54** C3
North Side
Wandsworth Comm
SW18 . . . .**59** C2
North St SW4 . . . . . .**61** B4
Northstead Rd
SW2 . . . .**74** C2
North Tenter St
E1 . . . .**111** A1
North Terr SW3 . . .**130** A1
Northumberland Alley
EC3 . . . .**110** B1
Northumberland Ave
WC2 . . . .**120** A2
Northumberland Ho
NW5 . . . .**13** B2
Northumberland
Mans E5 . . . .**17** B4
Northumberland Pl
W2 . . . .**31** C3
Northumberland St
WC2 . . . .**120** A2
Northumbria Ct 10
TW9 . . . .**54** A3
Northumbria St
E14 . . . .**33** C3
North Verbena Gdns
2 W6 . . . .**38** C1
Northview 1 N7 . . . . .**5** A1
Northview Cres
NW10 . . . .**8** B4
Northview Jun & Inf
Sch NW10 . . . .**8** B4
North Villas NW1 . . .**13** C2
Northway Rd SE5 . . .**63** B4
Northways Par 2
NW3 . . . .**11** C1
North West London
Jewish Day Sch
NW6 . . . .**10** A1
Northwest Pl N1 . . . .**85** C2
North Wharf Rd
W2 . . . .**101** B3
Northwick Cl NW8 . .**89** B2
Northwick Ho
NW8 . . . .**89** A2
Northwick Terr
NW8 . . . .**89** B2
North Wlk W2 . . . . .**114** C3
Northwold Prim Sch
E5 . . . .**7** C2
Northwold Rd E5,
N16 . . . .**7** C2
North Wood Lo
NW3 . . . .**11** A4
Northwood Rd N6 . . . .**4** A4
Northwood Sta SE13 .**51** B1
North Worple Way
SW14 . . . .**55** C4
Norton Folgate
E1 . . . .**110** B4
Norton Ho
14 Globe Town
E2 . . . .**25** C3
30 Stepney E1 . . . . .**32** A3
18 Stockwell SW9 . .**173** A1
Norval Gn 1 SW9 **173** C2
Norvic Ho 5 SE5 . . . .**48** B1
Norway Gate SE16 . .**41** A3
Norway Pl E14 . . . . .**33** B3
Norway St SE10 . . . .**52** A4
Norwich Ho 6
E14 . . . .**34** A3
Norwich St EC4 . . . .**107** B2
Norwood Cl NW2 . . . .**1** A1

Norwood Ho 25
E14 . . . .**34** A2
Norwood NHS Ctr
SE27 . . . .**75** A1
Norwood Rd SE24,
SE27 . . . .**75** A3
Notley Pl 3 SW4 . . . .**62** A1
Notley St SE5 . . . . . .**48** C3
Notre Dame RC Sec
Girls' Sch SE1 . . . .**136** A2
Notting Barn Rd
W10 . . . .**22** C1
Nottingdale Sq
W11 . . . .**31** A1 **112** A2
Nottingham Ct
WC2 . . . .**106** A1
Nottingham Ho
33 Camberwell
SE5 . . . .**48** B1
Stoke Newington N4 . . .**6** B3
Nottingham Pl
W1 . . . .**103** B4
Nottingham Rd
SW17 . . . .**72** B3
Nottingham St
W1 . . . .**103** B4
Nottingham Terr
NW1 . . . .**91** B1
NOTTING HILL **112** C3
Notting Hill Gate
W11 . . . .**31** C1 **113** B2
Notting Hill Gate Sta
W11 . . . .**31** C1 **113** B2
Notting Hill Prep Sch
3 W11 . . . .**31** A3
Nottingwood Ho
W11 . . . . . .**31** A2 **112** A4
Nova Bldg 1 E14 . . . .**41** C2
Nova Ct E 3 E14 . . . .**34** B1
Nova Ct W 2 E14 . . . .**34** B1
Novello St SW6 . . . .**165** B4
Nowell Rd SW13 . . . .**46** C4
Noyna Rd SW17 . . . .**72** B1
Nucleus NW10 . . . . .**20** B2
Nuding Cl SE13 . . . . .**66** C4
Nuffield Lo 14 W9 . . .**31** C4
Nugent Ct 3 N19 . . . .**5** A3
Nugent Rd N19 . . . . . .**5** A3
Nugent Terr NW8 . . .**79** A1
Nun Ct EC2 . . . .**109** B2
NUNHEAD **65** B3
Nunhead Cres
SE15 . . . .**65** A4
Nunhead Gn SE15 . . .**65** A4
Nunhead Gr SE15 . . .**65** B4
Nunhead La SE15 . . .**65** A4
Nunhead Sta SE15 . .**50** B1
Nursery Cl
New Cross SE14 . . . . .**51** B1
Putney SW15 . . . .**57** C3
Nursery La
North Kensington
W10 . . . .**30** B4
Shoreditch E2 . . . . . .**24** B4
Nursery Rd
Hackney E9 . . . .**17** B2
Stockwell SW9 . . . . . .**62** B3
Nursery Row
SE17 . . . .**151** B3
Nutbourne St W10 . .**23** A2
Nutbrook St SE15 . . .**64** C4
Nutcroft Rd SE15 . . .**50** A3
Nutfield Rd
East Dulwich
SE22 . . . .**64** B3
Leyton E15 . . . .**19** B4

Nutford Pl W1..... **102** C2
Nuthurst Ave SW2 .. 74 B2
Nutley Terr NW3 ... 11 C2
Nutmeg La E14....34 C3
Nuttall St N1 .... 24 A3
Nutt St SE15.... 49 B3
Nye Bevan Ho
SW6 ..... **154** C2
Nye's Wharf SE1,
Nylands Ave NW9 ..44 C1
Nynehead St SE14.. 51 A3
Nyton Cl **7** N19 .... 5 A3

Oaklands Ho SE4 ...66 B4
Oaklands Mews **1**
NW2 ....9 C4
Oaklands Pas NW2 ..9 C4
Oaklands Pl **8**
SW4 ..... 61 C3
Oaklands Rd
Cricklewood NW2....9 C4
Mortlake SW14 .. 55 C4
Oaklands Sch **31**
E2 ..... 25 A2
Oakley Cres EC1.. 86 B1
Oakley Dr SE13.... 67 C1
Oakley Gdns SW3. 158 B4
Oakley Ho SW1 ... 145 A4
Oakley Pl SE1 .... 152 C1
Oakley Rd N1 .... 15 C1
Oakley Sq NW1 .... 83 A2
Oakley St SW3 ... 158 A4
Oak Lock Mews **16**
W4 .... 38 A1
Oak Lodge **14**
Oak Lodge Sch
SW19 ..... 72 C4
Oakman Ho **29**
SW19 ..... 69 C3
Oakmead Rd
SW12 ..... 73 A3
Oak Park Gdns
SW19 ..... 69 C3
Oak Park Mews
N16. ..... 7 B1
Oakshaw Rd SW18.. 71 A4
Oakshott Ct **1** .. 83 B1
Oak Sq SW4..... 172 C1
Oaks Sh Ctr The
Oaks The
Brondesbury Pk
NW6 ..... 9 C4
Willesden NW10....9 A1
Oak Tree Ct
Acton W3 ..... 28 A2
3 Clapham Pk

Observatory Gdns
W8 ..... **127** C4
Observatory Mews
E14. ..... 42 C2
Observatory Rd
Kensington SW7.. **129** B1
Mortlake SW14 .. 55 B3
Occupation Rd
SE17 ..... **150** C2
Ocean Est E1 ... 32 C4
Ocean Wharf E14.. 41 C4
Ockbrook **3** E1 .. 32 B4
Ockendon Rd N1 .. 15 C2
Ockley Rd SW16.. 74 A1
Octagon Arc EC2 . 110 A3
Octagon The NW3 . 10 C4
Octavia Ho W10 .. 23 A1
Octavia Mews **1**
W9 ..... 23 B1
Octavia St SW11.. 168 B3
Odell Wlk SE13.... 67 B4
Odeon Ct
Dagenham NW10...21 A4
1 Newham E16...35 C4
Odessa Rd NW10 .. 21 C3
Odessa St SE16.... 41 B3
Odette Duval Ho **6**
E1. ..... 32 B4
Odger St SW11 ... 169 A2
Odhams Wlk WC2 . 106 B1
Odin Ho **6** SE5....48 B1
O'Donnell Ct WC1 . 94 B2
O'Driscoll Ho **4**
W12. ..... 30 A3
Offa's Mead E9....18 A4
Offenbach Ho **6**
E2 ..... 25 C3
Offerton Rd SW4 .. 61 B4
Offham Ho SE17 . 152 A3
Offley Ho **10** E9 .. 17 C2
Offley Rd SW9 ... 163 B2
Offord Rd N1 ..... 14 B1
Offord St N1 ..... 14 B1
Ogilvie Ho **12** E1 .. 32 C3
Oglander Rd SE15.. 64 B4
Ogle St W1 .... 104 C4
O'Gorman Ho
SW10. ..... 157 A2
Ohio Bldg **13** SE13. 52 A2
Oil Mill La W6....38 C1
Okehampton Rd
NW10. ..... 22 C4
Okeover Manor
SW4 ..... 61 A3
Olaf St W11 .... 30 C2
Old Bailey EC4 .. 108 B1
Old Bailey (Central
Criminal Court)
EC4. ..... **108** B1
Old Barrack Yd
SW1 ..... **131** B3
Old Bellgate Wharf
E14. ..... 41 C3
Old Bethnal Green Rd
E2 ..... 25 A2
Old Billingsgate Wlk
EC3. ..... **124** A3
Old Bldgs WC2 ... **107** B2
Old Bond St W1 .. 118 C3
Old Brewery Mews
NW3 ..... 11 C4
Old Broad St EC2 . **109** C2
Old Brompton Rd SW5,
SW7 ..... **143** A3

Old Burlington St
W1. ..... **118** C3
Oldbury Ct E9 .... 18 A3
Oldbury Pl W1 ... 103 C4
Old Canal Mews
SE15. ..... **153** A1
Old Castle St E1 . **111** A2
Old Cavendish St
W1 ..... **104** A1
Old Change Ct
EC4. ..... **108** C1
Old Chiswick Yd
W4 ..... 46 A4
Old Church Rd E1 . 32 C3
Old Church St
SW3 ..... **143** C1
Old Compton St
W1 ..... **105** B1
Old Court Ho W8 . **128** A3
Old Court Pl W8 . 128 A3
Old Curiosity Shop
The WC2 ..... **106** C2
Old Dairy Mews
5 Balham SW12..72 C3
1 Camden Town
NW5 ..... 13 A2
Old Deer Park Gdns
TW9 ..... **54** B4
Old Devonshire Rd
SW12 ..... 73 A4
Old Dock Cl TW9 .. 44 C4
Oldfield Gr SE16....40 C2
Oldfield Ho **14** W4..38 A1
Oldfield Mews **6**
N6. ..... 4 B4
Oldfield Rd
Bedford Pk W3,
Stoke Newington
N16. ..... 7 A1
Willesden NW10....8 B1
Old Fish St Hill
EC4. ..... **123** A4
Old Fleet La EC4. 108 A2
OLD FORD 26 B4
Old Ford Prim Sch **31**
E3 ..... 26 B3
Old Ford Rd E2, E3. **25** C3
Old Ford Trad Est
30 ..... 26 C4
Old Forge Mews
W12 ..... 39 A4
Old Forge Rd N19.. 4 C2
Old Gloucester St
WC1 ..... **106** B4
Oldham Terr W3 .. 28 B1
Old Hospital Cl SW12,
SW17. ..... **72** B3
Olding Ho **5**
SW12 ..... 73 B4
Old Jamaica Bsns Est
23 SE16 ..... **139** B2
Old Jamaica Rd
SE16 ..... **139** B2
Old James St SE15 . 65 A4
Old Jewry EC2 ... **109** B1
Old Kent Rd
Deptford SE1,
SE15..... 50 A4
Walworth SE1.... **152** B2
Old Laundry The **14**
SW18 ..... 59 C3
Old Manor Ct NW8 . **79** A2
Old Manor Yd
SW5 ..... **142** A3

Nut–Olg 251

Old Market Sq **13**
E2. ..... 24 B2 **99** A4
Old Marylebone Rd
NW1 ..... **102** B3
Old Mitre Ct EC4 . **107** C1
Old Montague St
E1. ..... **111** B3
Old Nichol St
E2. ..... 24 B1 **98** C2
Old North St WC1 . **106** C4
OLD OAK
COMMON 21 B1
Old Oak Common La
NW10. ..... 21 A1
Old Oak La NW10...21 B2
Old Oak Prim Sch
W12 ..... 29 B3
Old Oak Rd W3....29 B2
Old Orch The NW3..12 B3
Old Palace Prim Sch
51 E3. ..... 27 A2
Old Paradise St
SE11 ..... **148** C4
Old Park Ave
SW12 ..... 60 C1
Old Park La W1 .. **118** A1
Old Pearson St
SE10 ..... 52 A3
Old Pye St SW1 .. **133** B2
Old Pye Street Est
SW1 ..... **133** B1
Old Quebec St
W1 ..... **103** A1
Old Queen St
SW1 ..... **133** C3
Oldridge Rd SW12..73 A4
Old Royal Free Pl
N1. ..... **85** C3
Old Royal Free Sq
N1. ..... **85** C3
Old School Cl
SE10 ..... 43 A3
Old School Sq **12**
E14. ..... 33 C3
Old School The
NW5 ..... **107** A4
Old Seacoal La
EC4. ..... **108** A1
Old South Lambeth
Rd SW8 ..... **162** B2
Old Spitalfields Mkt
E1. ..... **110** C4
Old Sq WC2 .... **107** B2
Old St EC1 .... **97** C2
Old Stable Mews
N5. ..... 6 B1
Old Station Wy **8**
SW4 ..... 61 C3
Old Street Sta EC1. **97** C2
Old Sun Wharf
E14. ..... 33 A2
Old Swan Wharf
SW11. ..... **167** C4
Old Theatre Ct
SE1. ..... **123** A2
Old Town SW4 .... 61 B4
Old Vicarage Sch
TW10 ..... 54 A1
Old Woolwich Rd
SE10. ..... 42 C1
Old York Rd SW18 . 59 A2
O'Leary Sq E1 ... 32 B4

Olga Prim Sch **37**
E3. ..... 26 A3

O2 Arena The
O2 Ctr NW6 .... 11 A1
O2 Ctr NW6 .... 10 C1
Oakbank Gr SE24. 63 B3
Oakbury Rd SW6. 166 B1
Oakcourt **17** SE15.. 49 B3
Oak Cres E16.... 35 A4
Oakcroft Cl SE3 .. 53 C2
Oakcroft Rd SE13.. 52 C1
Oakdale Ct N19.... 5 A2
Oakdale Rd SE15..50 A1
Oakdene **3** SE15..50 A2
Oakdene Ho **11** N16.7 A3
Oakden St SE11 .. 149 C4
Oakeford Ho W14. 126 B1
Oakend Ho **10** N4 .. 6 C4
Oakeshott Ave N6.. 3 C2
Oakey La SE1..... 135 B2

Oakhill Ct
Clapham Pk SW4 ..62 A1
Finsbury Pk N8.... 5 A4
Oakfield Prep Sch
SE21 ..... 75 C3
Oakfield Rd
Finsbury Pk N4.... 5 C4
Wimbledon SW19.. 69 C1
Oakfield St SW10 156 C4
Oakford Rd NW5 .. 13 B4
Oak Gr NW2..... 10 A4
Oakham Ho **5**
W10 ..... 22 B1
Oakhill Ave NW3 .. 11 A4
Oakhill Ct
Honor Oak SE23....65 B1
Putney SW15 .... 58 B2
Oak Hill Lo NW3.. 11 A4
Oak Hill Park Mews
NW3 ..... 11 B4
Oak Hill Pk NW3 .. 11 A4
Oakhill Pl SW15 .. 58 C2
Oakhill Rd SW15.. 58 B2
Oak Hill Way NW3 . 11 C4
Oak Ho
1 Cubitt Town
E14. ..... 42 B4
2 Maitland Pk
NW3 ..... 12 B2
2 Richmond TW9 . 45 A2
3 Stoke Newington
N16. ..... 6 C2
Oakhurst Gr SE22. 64 C3
Oakington Rd W9 . 23 C1
Oakington Way N8. 5 A4
Oak La E14 .... 33 C2
Oaklands Ct
Dagenham NW10...21 A4
5 Shepherd's Bush
W12 ..... 39 A4
Oaklands Gr W12...29 C1

Olga St 20 E3 . . . . .26 A3
Oliphant St W10 . . . . . . .23 A2
Olive Blythe Ho 14
W10 . . . . .23 A3
Oliver Bsns Pk
NW10 . . . . .20 B3
Oliver Cl W4 . . . . .45 A4
Oliver Rd NW2 . . . . .9 B4
Oliver Goldsmith Prim
Sch 10 SE5 . . . . .49 B2
Oliver Ho
22 Bermondsey
SE16 . . . . .139 B3
Notting Hill
W11 . . . . . .31 A2 112 A3
South Lambeth
SW8 . . . . .162 A2
Oliver House Prep
Sch 18 SW4 . . . . .61 A1
Oliver Mews SE15 . . .49 C1
Oliver's Yd EC1 . . . . . .97 C2
Olive Tree Ho 7
SE15 . . . . .50 A4
Olive Tree Sch The
SE13 . . . . .67 A1
Olivette St 1
SW15 . . . . .57 C3
Olive Waite Ho
NW6 . . . . .11 A1
Ollerton Gn E3 . . . . . . .26 B4
Ollgar Cl W12 . . . . .29 B1
Olliffe St E14 . . . . .42 B3
Olmar St SE1 . . . . .49 C4
Olney Ho NW8 . . . . . . .90 B2
Olney Rd SE17 . . . . . . .48 B4
Olympia Ex Ctr
W14 . . . . .126 B1
Olympian Ct 8
E14 . . . . .41 C2
Olympia Way
W14 . . . . .126 B1
Olympia Yd W2 . . . . .114 B3
Olympic Ho 10
W10 . . . . .30 B3
Olympic Park Ave
E15 . . . . .19 A3
Olympus Sq E5 . . . . . . .7 C1
Oman Ave NW2 . . . . . . .9 B4
Oman Ct NW4 . . . . .9 A4
Ombersley Ho N4 . . . .6 B4
Omeara St SE1 . . . . . .123 A1
Omega Cl E14 . . . . .42 A3
Omega Ho SE10 . . . . .157 A2
Omega Pl N1 . . . . .84 B1
Omega St SE14 . . . . . .51 C2
Omega Works E3 . .18 C1
Ommaney Rd
SE14 . . . . .51 A2
Omnibus Bsns Ctr
N7 . . . . .13 C3
Ondine Rd SE15 . . . . .64 B3
Onedin Point 10
E1 . . . . .125 C3
Onega Gate SE16 . . . .41 A3
O'Neill Ho NW8 . . . . . .79 C1
One New Change Sh
Ctr EC4 . . . . .108 C1
One Tree Cl SE23 . . . . .65 B1
Ongar Ho 15 N1 . . . . . .15 C2
Ongar Rd SW6 . . . . . .155 C4
Onslow Ave TW10 . . . .54 A2
Onslow Avenue Mans
10 TW10 . . . . .54 A2
Onslow Cl W9 . . . . .23 B2

Onslow Ct SW10 . . . .143 A1
Onslow Gdns
SW7 . . . . .143 B2
Onslow Lo 28 SW2 . . .74 C4
Onslow Mews E
SW7 . . . . .143 B3
Onslow Mews W
SW7 . . . . .143 B3
Onslow Sq SW7 . . . . .143 C3
Onslow St EC1 . . . . . . .95 C1
Ontario St SE1 . . . . . .136 B2
Ontario Way E14 . . . . .33 C2
Opal St SE11 . . . . .150 A2
Open Air Theatre,
Regent's Pk NW1 . . .91 B3
Openview SW17,
Opera Ct 7 N19 . . . . . . .4 C1
Operating Theatre
Mus & Herb Garret
The SE1 . . . . .123 C1
Ophelia Gdns NW2 . . . .1 A1
Ophir Terr SE15 . . . . . .49 C2
Oppenheim Rd
SE13 . . . . .52 B1
Oppidan Apartments
NW6 . . . . .10 C2
Oppidans Rd NW3 . . .12 B1
Orange Pl SE16 . . . . . .40 B3
Orangery Gallery The
W8 . . . . .126 C3
Orange St WC2 . . . . .119 C3
Orange Yd WC2 . . . . .105 C1
Oransay Rd 1 N1 . . . . .15 B2
Oratory La SW3 . . . . .143 C2
Oratory RC Prim Sch
SW3 . . . . .144 A2
Orbain Rd SW6 . . . . .154 B1
Orbel St SW11 . . . . . .168 A3
Orb St SE17 . . . . .151 B3
Orchard Cl
Honor Oak SE23 . . . . .65 B1
21 Islington N1 . . . . . .15 B1
Kensal Town W10 . . . .31 A4
Orchard Ct
Barnes SW13 . . . . .56 B4
Marylebone W1 . . . . .103 B2
Orchard Dr SE3 . . . . . .53 A1
Orchard Hill SE13 . . . .52 A2
Orchard Ho
Camberwell SE5 . . . . .48 B2
11 Rotherhithe
SE16 . . . . .40 B3
Shepherd's Bush
W12 . . . . .29 C1
Orchard House Sch 18
W4 . . . . .38 A2
Orchard Mead Ho
NW11 . . . . .1 C2
Orchard Mews
Lewisham SE13 . . . . . .67 B1
London N1 . . . . .15 C1
Orchard Pl E14 . . . . . .35 A2
Orchard Prim Sch 24
E9 . . . . .17 B1
Orchard Rd
Highgate N6 . . . . .4 A4
Richmond TW9 . . . . . .54 C4
Orchard Rise
TW10 . . . . .55 A3
Orchardson Ho
NW8 . . . . .89 C1

Orchardson St
NW8 . . . . .89 C1
Orchard Sq W14 . . . .140 C1
Orchard St W1 . . . . . .103 C2
Orchard The
Acton Green W4 . . . . . .37 C2
Lewisham SE3 . . . . . . .52 C1
Orchid St W12 . . . . . . .29 C2
Orchid Mews 15
NW2 . . . . .20 C4
Orde Hall St WC1 . . .106 C4
Orde Ho 10 N16 . . . . . .15 C4
Ordell Ct 8 E3 . . . . . . .26 B3
Ordell Rd E3 . . . . .26 B3
Ordnance Cres
SE10 . . . . .43 A4
Ordnance Hill
NW8 . . . . .79 C3
Ordnance Mews
NW8 . . . . .79 C2
Ordnance Rd E16 . . . .35 B4
Oregano Dr E14 . . . . . .34 C3
Oregon Bldg 5
SE13 . . . . .52 A2
O'Reilly St SE17 . . . .152 C4
Orestes Mews 11
NW6 . . . . .10 C3
Orford Ct SE27 . . . . . . .75 A2
Oriana Ho 3 E14 . . . . .33 B2
Oriel Ct NW3 . . . . .11 B4
Oriel Dr SW13 . . . . . . .47 B4
Oriel Rd
Hackney E9 . . . . .18 A2
Homerton E9 . . . . .17 C2
Orient St SE11 . . . . . .150 A4
Orion Bsns Ctr
SE14 . . . . .40 C1
Orion Ho 20 E1 . . . . . .25 A1
Orion Point 8
E14 . . . . .41 C2
Orkney Ho N1 . . . . . . .84 C4
Orkney St SW11 . . . .169 B2
Orlando Rd SW4 . . . . .61 C4
Orleston Mews N7 . . .14 C2
Orleston Rd N7 . . . . . .14 C2
Orlop St SE10 . . . . .43 A1
Orme Ct W2 . . . . .114 A3
Orme Ct Mews
W2 . . . . .114 A3
Orme Ho 8 E8 . . . . . . .24 B4
Orme La W2 . . . . .114 A3
Ormeley Rd SW12 . . . .73 A3
Ormerod Ho 3
SW9 . . . . .62 A4
Orme Sq W2 . . . . .114 A3
Ormiston Gr W12 . . . .30 A1
Ormiston Rd SE10 . . . .43 C1
Ormond Cl WC1 . . . .106 B4
Ormond Ho SW15 . . . .57 B3
Ormonde Gate
SW3 . . . . .145 A1
Ormonde Mans
WC1 . . . . .106 B4
Ormonde Pl SW1 . . .145 C3
Ormonde Terr
NW8 . . . . .80 C3
Ormond Ho N16 . . . . . .6 C2
Ormond Mans
WC1 . . . . .94 C1
Ormond Rd N4, N19 . .5 B3
Ormond Yd SW1 . . . .119 A2

Ormrod Ct W11 . . . . . .31 B3
Ormsby Lo 7 W4 . . . . .38 A3
Ormsby Pl N16 . . . . . . .7 B1
Ormsby St E2 . . . . .24 B3
Ormside St SE15 . . . . .50 B4
Ornan Rd NW3 . . . . . .12 A3
Orpen Ho SW5 . . . . .141 C3
Orpen Wlk N16 . . . . . . .7 A1
Orpheus Ho 25 N19 . . .4 C4
Orpheus St SE5 . . . . . .48 C2
Orsett Mews W2 . . . .100 C2
Orsett St SE11 . . . . . .149 A2
Orsett Terr W2 . . . . . .100 C2
Orsman Rd N1 . . . . . . .24 A4
Orton St E1 . . . . .125 B1
Orville Rd SW11 . . . .167 C2
Orwell Ct
Hackney E8 . . . . .24 C4
Highbury N5 . . . . .15 B4
Orwell Ho W12 . . . . . . .29 C2
Osbaldeston Rd
N16 . . . . .7 C3
Osbert St SW1 . . . . . .147 B3
Osborn Cl E8 . . . . .24 C4
Osborne Rd
Finsbury Pk N4 . . . . . . .5 C3
South Acton W3 . . . . . .37 A4
Willesden NW2 . . . . . . .9 A2
Osborn St E1 . . . . . . .111 A4
Osbourne Ho
TW10 . . . . .54 C2
Oscar Faber Pl 8
N1 . . . . .16 A1
Oscar St SE8 . . . . .51 C1
Oseney Cres NW5 . . . .13 C2
Osier Ct E1 . . . . .25 C1
Osier Mews W4 . . . . . .46 B4
Osiers Rd SW18 . . . . . .58 C3
Osier St E1 . . . . .25 B1
Oslo Ct NW8 . . . . .80 A1
Oslo Ho 2 SE5 . . . . . . .48 B1
Oslo Sq SE16 . . . . .41 A3
Osman Rd W6 . . . . . . .39 B3
Osmani Prim Sch
E1 . . . . .111 C4
Osman Rd W6 . . . . . . .39 B3
Osmington Ho
SW8 . . . . .163 A1
Osmund St W12 . . . . . .29 B4
Osnaburgh St NW1 . .92 B2
Osnaburgh Terr
NW1 . . . . .92 B2
Osprey Ct NW3 . . . . . .11 A3
Osprey Ho
Camberwell SE15 . . . .49 B2
2 Limehouse E14 . . . . .33 A2
Ospringe Ho SE1 . . .121 C1
Ospringe Rd NW5 . . . .13 B4
Osric Path 8 N1 . . . . . .24 A3
Ossian Mews N4 . . . . . .5 B4
Ossian Rd N4 . . . . .5 B4
Ossington Bldgs
W1 . . . . .103 B3
Ossington Cl
W2 . . . . .31 C2 113 C3
Ossington St W2 . . . .114 A3
Ossory Rd SE1 . . . . . . .49 C4
Ossulston St NW1 . . . .83 C2
Ostade Rd SW2 . . . . . .74 B4
Osten Mews SW7 . . .128 B1
Osterley Ho 5
E14 . . . . .34 A3
Osterley Rd N16 . . . . .16 A4

Oswald Bldg SW8 . . .160 A3
Oswald's Mead E9 . . .18 A4
Osward Rd SW12,
SW17 . . . . .72 B2
Oswell Ho 9 E1 . . . . . .32 A1
Oswin St SE11 . . . . . .150 B4
Oswyth Rd SE5 . . . . . .49 A1
Otford Cres SE4 . . . . . .66 B1
Otford Ho
Bermondsey SE1 . . . .137 C3
6 Deptford SE15 . . . . .50 B4
Otha Ho 119 SW9 . . . . .172 B1
Othello Cl SE11 . . . . .150 A2
Otis St E3 . . . . .27 B2
Otley Ho N5 . . . . .6 A1
Ottaway St E5 . . . . .7 C1
Ottaway St E5 . . . . .7 C1
Otterburn Ho 12
SE5 . . . . .48 B3
Otter Cl E15 . . . . .27 B4
Otto St SE17 . . . . .48 A4
Our Lady of Dolours
RC Prim Sch
W2 . . . . .100 A4
Our Lady of Lourdes
RC Prim Sch
NW10 . . . . .20 B4
Our Lady of Victories
RC Prim Sch
7 Putney SW15 . . . . . .57 C3
South Kensington
SW7 . . . . .143 A3
Our Lady Queen of
Heaven Primary Sch
10 SW19 . . . . .69 C4
Our Lady RC Prim Sch
Camden Town
NW1 . . . . .83 A4
22 Poplar E14 . . . . .33 B3
Our Lady & St Joseph
Catholic Prim Sch 5
E14 . . . . .33 C2
Our Lady & St Joseph
RC Prim Sch 14
N1 . . . . .16 A2
Our Lady's Convent
High Sch 8 N15 . . . . . . .7 A4
Ouseley Rd SW12 . . . .72 B3
Outer Circ NW1 . . . . . .81 A1
Outgate Rd NW10 . . . .8 B1
Outram Pl N1 . . . . .84 B4
Outwich St EC3 . . . . .110 B2
Outwood Ho 3
SW2 . . . . .74 B4
Oval Mans SE11 . . . .163 A4
Oval Pl SW8 . . . . .163 A2
Oval Rd NW1 . . . . .82 A4
Oval Sta SE11 . . . . . .163 B3
Oval The E2 . . . . .25 A3
Oval Way SE11 . . . . . .149 A1
Overbury Ho 3
E5 . . . . .17 C4
Overbury St E5 . . . . . . .17 C4
Overcliff Rd SE13 . . . .66 C4
Overhill Rd SE21,
SE22 . . . . .76 C4
Overlea Rd E5 . . . . .7 C4
Oversley Ho 17
W2 . . . . .31 C4
Overstone Ho 19
E14 . . . . .33 C3
Overstone Rd W6 . . . .39 B2
Overstrand Mans
SW11 . . . . .169 B3
Overton Ho SW15 . . . .68 B4
Overton Rd SW9 . . . .173 C1

Overy Ho SE1 . . . . . **136** A3
Ovex Cl E14 . . . . 42 B4
Ovington Ct SW3 . . **130** B1
Ovington Gdns
SW3 . . . . **130** B1
Ovington Mews
SW3 . . . . **130** B1
Ovington Sq SW3 . . **130** B1
Ovington St SW3 . . **144** B4
Owen Ho N19 . . . . . 13 A4
Owen's C EC1 . . . . 96 A4
Owen's Row EC1 . . . . 96 A4
Owen St EC1 . . . . 86 A1
Owgan Cl SE5 . . . . . . 48 C3
Oxberry Ave SW6 . **164** B2
Oxbridge Ct 4
W4 . . . . 37 A1
Oxendon St SW1,
W1 . . . . **119** B3
Oxenford St SE15 . . 64 B4
Oxenham Ho 18
SE8 . . . . 51 C4
Oxenholme NW1 3 . 82 B1
Oxestalls Rd SE8 . . . 41 A1
Oxford & Cambridge
Mans NW1 . . . . **102** B3
Oxford Cir W1 . . . . **104** C1
Oxford Circus Ave
W1 . . . . **104** C1
Oxford Circus Sta
W1 . . . . **104** C1
Oxford Ct
City of London
EC4 . . . . **123** B4
Gunnersbury W4 . . . 37 A1
48 Paddington W2 . . 31 C4
Oxford Dr SE1 . . . . . **124** A1
Oxford Gardens Prim
Sch 42 W10 . . . . . . 30 C3
Oxford Gate W6 . . . 39 C2
Oxford Gdns
Brentford W4 . . . . . 44 C4
North Kensington
W10 . . . . 30 C3
Oxford Ho N4 . . . . 5 C3
Oxford Rd
Finsbury Pk N4 . . . . . 5 C3
Paddington NW6 . . . 23 C3
Putney SW15 . . . . . . 58 A3
Stratford E15 . . . . . 19 C2
Oxford Rd N W4 . . . . 37 A1
Oxford Rd S W4 . . . . 37 A1
Oxford Sq W2 . . . . **102** B1
Oxford St W1 . . . . . **104** B1
Oxley Cl SE1 . . . . . . **153** A2
Oxonian St SE22 . . . 64 B3
OXO Tower Wharf
SE1 . . . . **121** C3
Oxted Ct N16 . . . . 7 A3
Oyster Row E1 . . . . . 32 B3
Ozolins Way E16 . . . 35 C3

P

Pablo Neruda Cl 4
SE24 . . . . 63 A3
Pace Pl E1 . . . . 32 A3
Pacific Ho 15 E1 . . . . 25 C1
Pacific Rd E16 . . . . . . 35 C3
Pacific Wharf
SE16 . . . . 32 C1
Packenham Ho
24 Crouch End N19 . . 4 C4

Packenham Ho
continued
21 Spitalfields
E2 . . . . 24 B2 **99** A4
Packington Rd 20
W3 . . . . 37 B3
Packington Sq N1 . 86 C4
Packington St N1 . . 86 B3
Padbury SE17 . . . . . **152** B1
Padbury Ct
E2 . . . . 24 B2 **99** A3
Padbury Ho NW8 . . . 90 B2
Paddenswick Ct 2
W6 . . . . 39 A3
Paddenswick Rd
W6 . . . . 38 C3
PADDINGTON **100** C3
Paddington Acad 7
W9 . . . . 23 C1
Paddington Gn
W2 . . . . **101** B4
Paddington Green
Prim Sch NW8 . . . 89 B1
Paddington St
W1 . . . . **103** B4
Paddington Sta
W2 . . . . **101** B2
Paddock Cl SE3 . . . . 53 C1
Paddock Sch
SW15 . . . . 56 B3
Paddock Way 11
SW15 . . . . 69 B4
Padfield Rd SE5 . . . . 63 B4
Padstow Ho 50
E3 . . . . 27 A2
Padstow Ho 12
E14 . . . . 33 B2
Pageant St SW8 . . **170** B4
Pageant Cres
SE16 . . . . 33 B1
Pageantmaster Ct
EC4 . . . . **108** A1
Page Ho SE10 . . . . . . 52 B4
Page Mews SW11 . **169** C1
Page St SW1 . . . . . . **147** C4
Page's Wlk SE1 . . . **138** B1
Page's Yd W4 . . . . . . 46 A4
Paget Ho 12 E2 . . . . 25 B3
Paget Rd N16 . . . . 6 C3
Paget St EC1 . . . . 96 A4
Pagham Ho 8
W10 . . . . 22 B1
Pagnell St SE14 . . . . 51 B3
Pagoda Ave TW9 . . 54 B4
Pagoda Gdns SE3 . . 52 C1
Pagoda Gr
Brixton SE27 . . . . . . 75 B2
Dulwich SE27 . . . . . 53 B4
Paine Ct SE3 . . . . 53 B4
Painsthorpe Rd 3
N16 . . . . 7 A1
Painswick Ct 1
SE15 . . . . 49 B3
Painters Mews
SE16 . . . . **153** C4
Pakefield Mews
SW3 . . . . 74 B3
Pakeman Ho SE1 . **136** B4
Pakeman Prim Sch 1
N7 . . . . 5 B1
Pakenham Cl
SW12 . . . . 72 C3
Pakenham St WC1 . 95 A2
Palace Ave W8 . . . **128** B4

Palace Ct
Hampstead NW3 . . . 11 A3
Kensington W2 . . . **114** A3
Streatham SW2 . . . . 74 C2
Palace Garden Mews
W8 . . . . 31 C1 **113** C2
Palace Gate W8 . . **128** C3
Palace Gdns Mews
W8 . . . . **114** B1
Palace Gn W8 . . . . **114** A1
Palace Mans W14 **140** B4
Palace Mews
Belgravia SW1 . . . **145** C3
Fulham SW6 . . . . . **155** A2
Palace of
Westminster
SW1 . . . . **134** B3
Palace Pl SW1 . . . . **132** C2
Palace Rd SE27,SW16,
SW2 . . . . 74 C2
Palace St SW1 . . . . **132** C2
Palatine Ave N16 . . 16 A4
Palatine Rd N16 . . . 16 A4
Palazzo Apartments
11 N1 . . . . 16 A1
Palemead Cl SW6 . 47 C2
Palermo Rd NW10 . 21 C3
Palewell Common Dr
SW14 . . . . 55 C2
Palewell Pk SW14 . 55 C3
Palfrey Pl SW8 . . . **163** A2
Palgrave Gdns
NW1 . . . . 90 B2
Palgrave Ho
6 Camberwell
SE5 . . . . 48 B3
4 Maitland Pk
NW3 . . . . 12 B3
Palgrave Rd W12 . . 38 B3
Palissy St 38
E2 . . . . 24 B2 98 C3
Pallant Ho SE1 . . . **137** C1
Pallester Ct NW11 . 1 A3
Palliser Ct W14 . . . **140** A1
Palliser Ho
2 Greenwich
SE10 . . . . 52 C4
4 Stepney E1 . . . . 25 C1
Palliser Rd W14 . . **140** A1
Palliser Terr
SW15 . . . . 68 B2
Pall Mall SW1 . . . . **119** B1
Pall Mall E SW1 . . **119** C2
Pall Mall Pl SW1 . . **119** A1
Palm Ct
18 Camberwell
SE15 . . . . 49 B3
Stoke Newington
N16 . . . . 6 C2
Palm Ho
2 Deptford SE14 . . 50 C3
8 Kentish Town
NW5 . . . . 13 B4
3 Tufnell Pk N19 . . 4 B1
Palmer Pl N7 . . . . . . 14 C3
Palmers Rd
Globe Town E2 . . . . 25 C3
Mortlake SW14 . . . . 55 B4
Palmer St SW1 . . . **133** B2
Palmerston Ct 22
E3 . . . . 25 C3
Palmerston Ho
Battersea SW11 . . **169** C3
Kensington
W8 . . . . 31 C1 **113** B1

Palmerston Rd
Acton Green W3 . . . 37 B3
Brondesbury NW6 . 10 B1
Hampstead NW6 . . 10 C1
Mortlake SW14 . . . . 55 B3
Palmerston Way
SW8 . . . . **160** B1
Palm Gr W5 . . . . 36 A3
Palm Tree Ho 2
SE14 . . . . 50 C3
Pamela Ct NW10 . . . 8 C1
Pamela Ho 18 E8 . . 24 B4
Pamlion Ct N4 . . . . . 5 A4
Panama Ho 5 E1 . . 32 C4
Pancras La EC2 . . **109** B1
Pancras Rd N1 . . . . 83 C2
Pancras Square
N1 . . . . 84 A2
Pancras Way E3 . . . 26 C3
Pandian Way 4
NW1 . . . . 13 C2
Pandora Rd NW6 . . 10 C2
Pangbourne NW1 . 92 C3
Pangbourne Ave
W10 . . . . 30 B4
Pankhurst Cl 7
SE14 . . . . 50 C3
Pankhurst Ho 2
NW10 . . . . 8 C2
Panmure Cl N5 . . . . 15 A4
Pan Peninsula Sq
E14 . . . . 42 A4
Pansy Gdns W12 . . 29 C2
Panter Ho 1 SW11 **119** B3
Panyer Alley EC2 . **108** C2
Paper Mill Wharf
E14 . . . . 33 A2
Papworth Gdns
N7 . . . . 14 B3
Papworth Way
SW2 . . . . 74 C4
Parade Mans 19
SE5 . . . . 48 B1
Parade Mews SE27,
SW2 . . . . 75 A2
Parade The SW11 . **159** A2
Paradise Pas N7 . . 14 C3
Paradise Rd
Richmond TW10 . . . 54 A2
South Lambeth
SW4 . . . . **172** A2
Paradise Row E2 . . 25 A2
Paradise St SE16 . . 40 A4
Paradise Wlk
SW3 . . . . **159** A4
Paragon Christian
Acad E5 . . . . 17 C4
Paragon Cl E16 . . . . 35 C3
Paragon Ho SE3 . . . 53 B1
Paragon Mews
SE1 . . . . **151** C4
Paragon Pl SE3 . . . . 53 B1
Paragon Rd E9 . . . . 17 B2
Paragon The
Kidbrooke SE3 . . . . 53 C1
Walworth SE17 . . . **151** C4
Paramount Bldg
EC1 . . . . 96 A2
Paramount Ct
WC1 . . . . 93 A1
Parbury Rd SE23 . . 66 A1
Pardoner St SE1 . . **137** C2
Pardon St EC1 . . . . . 96 B2
Parfett St E1 . . . . . **111** C2

Parfitt Cl NW11 . . . . . 2 B3
Parfrey St W6 . . . . . . 47 B4
Paris Gdn SE1 . . . . **122** A2
Parison Cl 1 TW9 . . 54 C4
Park Ave
Golders Green
NW11 . . . . 1 C3
Mortlake SW14 . . . . 55 C3
Willesden NW2 . . . . . 9 B2
Park Ave N NW10 . . . 9 A3
Park Cl
Kensington W14 . **127** A2
Knightsbridge
SW1 . . . . **130** C3
15 South Hackney
E9 . . . . 25 B4
Park Cres W1 . . . . . 92 A1
Park Crescent Mews E
W1 . . . . 92 B1
Park Crescent Mews
W W1 . . . . 92 A1
Park Ct
Battersea SW11 . . **170** A4
Clapham Pk SW4 . . 61 C2
Dulwich SE21 . . . . . 75 C1
12 Hammersmith
W6 . . . . 38 C2
Upper Tooting
SW12 . . . . 72 C3
Park Dr
Acton W3 . . . . 36 C3
Golders Green NW11 1 C3
Mortlake SW14 . . . . 55 C3
Park Dwellings 7
NW3 . . . . 12 B3
Park End NW3 . . . . . 12 A4
Parker Ct
Shoreditch N1 . . . . 87 A4
South Lambeth
SW4 . . . . **172** A3
Parke Rd SW13 . . . . 46 C2
Parker Mews
WC2 . . . . **106** B2
Parkers Row 18
SE1 . . . . **139** A3
Parker's Row SE1 **139** A3
Parker St WC2 . . . **106** B2
Parkfield Ave
SW14 . . . . 56 A3
Parkfield Ct SE14 . . 51 B2
Parkfield Ind Est
SW11 . . . . **169** C2
Parkfield Rd
11 Clapham Park
SW4 . . . . 61 C1
New Cross SE14 . . . 51 B2
Willesden NW10 . . . . 9 A1
Parkfields SW15 . . 57 B3
Parkfield St N1 . . . 85 C2
Park Flats N6 . . . . . . 3 A4
Parkgate Gdns
SW14 . . . . 55 C2
Parkgate House Sch
SW11 . . . . 60 C4
Parkgate Mews N6 . 4 B4
Parkgate Rd
SW11 . . . . **158** B1
Park Hall SE10 . . . . 52 C3
Park Hall Rd SE21 . 75 C1
Park Hall Road Trad
Est SE21 . . . . 75 C1
Parkham St SW11 **168** A3

Park Heights Ct 21
E14 . . . . 33 B3
Park Hill
Clapham Pk SW4 . . . . 61 C2
Richmond TW10 . . . . . 54 B1
Park Hill Ct SW17 . . . . 72 B1
Parkhill Rd NW3 . . . . . 12 B3
Park Hill Wlk 10
NW3 . . . . 12 B3
Park Ho
8 Camberwell
SE5 . . . . 48 C2
Finsbury Pk N4 . . . . 6 A2
33 Hackney E9 . . . . . . 17 B1
Richmond TW10 . . . . . 54 A2
Parkholme Rd E8 . . . . 16 C2
Parkhouse St SE5 . . . . 48 C3
Parkhurst Ct N7 . . . . . 14 A4
Parkhurst Rd N7 . . . . . 14 A4
Parkinson Ct
Finsbury N1 . . . . 97 B3
Shoreditch EC1 . . . . . . 97 C4
Parkinson Ho 8
E9 . . . . 17 B1
Park La
Mayfair W1 . . . . 117 B3
Mill Meads E15 . . . . . . 27 C4
Parkland Ct N14 . . . . 126 A4
Parkland Gdns 12
SW19 . . . . 69 C3
Parklands
East Dulwich
SE22 . . . . 65 A2
Highgate N6 . . . . 4 A4
Parklands Cl
SW14 . . . . 55 B2
Park Lea Ct N16 . . . . . . 7 A4
Park Lo
11 South Hampstead
NW8 . . . . 11 C1
10 Wapping E1 . . . . . . 32 A1
Willesden NW2 . . . . 9 B4
Park Lofts 3 SW4 . . . . 62 A2
Park Lorne NW8 . . . . . 90 B3
Park Mans
Battersea SW11 . . . . 168 C3
Bedford Pk W6 . . . . . . 38 B3
Fulham SW6 . . . . 164 B3
Knightsbridge
SW1 . . . . 130 C3
St John's Wood
NW8 . . . . 80 A1
Vauxhall SW8 . . . . . . 162 B4
Parkmead SW15 . . . . . 57 A1
Park Mews
Greenwich SE10 . . . . . 43 B1
Kensal Rise W10 . . . . . 23 A3
Park Par
Acton W3 . . . . 36 C3
Dagenham NW10 . . . . 21 B3
Park Piazza 3
SE13 . . . . 67 C1
Park Pl
Canary Wharf
E14 . . . . 33 C1
Gunnersbury W3 . . . . 36 C2
Shoreditch N1 . . . . 87 C4
St James SW1 . . . . . . 118 C2
Park Place Dr W3 . . . . 36 C3
Park Place Ho 8
SE10 . . . . 52 C4
Park Place Villas
W2 . . . . 101 A4

Park Rd
Chiswick W4 . . . . 45 C4
Dagenham NW10 . . . . 21 A4
Lisson Gr NW1,
NW8 . . . . 90 B2
Richmond TW10 . . . . . 54 B1
Park Rd E W3 . . . . 37 B4
Park Rd N
Chiswick W4 . . . . 37 C1
South Acton W3 . . . . . 37 A4
Park Road E 11
W3 . . . . 37 B4
Park Row SE10 . . . . . . 52 C4
PARK ROYAL 20 A2
Park Royal NW10 . . . . 20 A4
Park Royal Bsns Ctr
Park Royal Metro Ctr
NW10 . . . . 20 A1
Park Royal Rd NW10,
W3 . . . . 20 B1
Park S SW11 . . . . . . 169 B3
Park St James
NW8 . . . . 80 C3
Park Sheen 3
SW14 . . . . 55 A3
Parkshot TW9 . . . . 54 A3
Parkside
East Acton W3 . . . . . . 29 A1
Greenwich SE3 . . . . . . 53 B3
Park Side NW2 . . . . 9 A4
Parkside Ave 19
SE10 . . . . 52 B2
Parkside Bsns Est
SE8 . . . . 51 A4
Parkside Cres N7 . . . . . 5 C1
Parkside Est 19
E9 . . . . 25 C4
Parkside Sq 13
SE10 . . . . 52 B2
Parkside St SW11 . . . 169 B3
Park Sq E NW1 . . . . . . 92 B2
Park Square Mews
NW1 . . . . 92 A1
Park Sq W NW1 . . . . . 92 A1
Park St
Borough The SE1 . . . . 123 A2
Mayfair W1 . . . . 117 B3
Parkstead Rd
SW15 . . . . 57 A1
Parkstone Rd 8
SE15 . . . . 49 C1
Park Stps W2 . . . . . . 116 B4
Park The NW11 . . . . 2 A3
Parkthorne Rd
SW12 . . . . 73 C4
Park Twrs W1 . . . . . . 118 A1
Park View
Dagenham W3 . . . . . . 28 B4
Highbury N5 . . . . 15 B4
Willesden NW2 . . . . 9 B4
Parkview Ct SW6 . . . . 164 B1
Park View Ct
SE24 . . . . 58 C1
Park View Ho
Hornsey N4 . . . . 6 A4
Park View Mews 24
SW9 . . . . 172 C2
Park View Rd NW10 . . . 8 B4
Park Village E
NW1 . . . . 82 B1
Park Village W
NW1 . . . . 82 A2
Parkville Rd SW6 . . . . 154 C1

Park Vista SE10 . . . . . 52 C4
Park Walk Prim Sch
SW10 . . . . 157 B3
Parkwat Cres E15 . . . . 19 B3
Parkway NW1 . . . . 82 B3
Park Way W3 . . . . 36 C2
Parkway Ho SW14 . . . 55 C3
Park West W2 . . . . . . 102 B1
Park West Pl W1,
W2 . . . . 102 B2
Park Wk 1 SW10 . . . . 157 B3
Park Wlk
Chelsea SW10 . . . . . . 157 B4
Highgate N6 . . . . 3 C4
Parkwood NW8 . . . . . . 80 C3
Parkwood Prim Sch
N4 . . . . 6 A2
Parliament Ct
NW3 . . . . 12 A4
Parliament Hill
NW3 . . . . 12 A4
Parliament Hill Mans
NW5 . . . . 12 C4
Parliament Hill Sch
NW5 . . . . 12 C4
Parliament Mews
SW14 . . . . 45 B1
Parliament Sq
SW1 . . . . 134 A3
Parliament St
SW1 . . . . 134 A4
Parliament View
Apartments
SE11 . . . . 148 C4
Parma Cres SW11 . . . . 60 B3
Parminter Ind Est 20
E2 . . . . 25 A3
Parmiter St E2 . . . . 25 A3
Parmoor Ct EC1 . . . . . 96 C2
Parnell Cl W12 . . . . . . 39 A3
Parnell Ho WC1 . . . . 105 C2
Parnell Rd E3 . . . . 26 B4
Parnham St E14 . . . . . 33 A3
Parolles Rd N19 . . . . . . 4 B3
Parr Ct N1 . . . . 87 B2
Parrington Ho 1
SW4 . . . . 61 C1
Parr Pl W4 . . . . 38 B2
Parr St N1 . . . . 87 B2
Parry Ho 55 E1 . . . . . . 32 A1
Parry Rd W10 . . . . 23 A2
Parry St SW8 . . . . 162 B4
Parsifal Ho NW3 . . . . . 10 C4
Parsifal Rd NW6 . . . . . 10 C3
Parsonage St E14 . . . . 42 B2
Parsons Gn SW6 . . . . 165 B3
PARSONS
  GREEN 165 B4
Parsons Green La
SW6 . . . . 165 B4
Parsons Green Sta
SW6 . . . . 165 B3
Parsons Ho
Paddington W2 . . . . . . 89 B1
23 Streatham
SW12 . . . . 74 A4
Parsons Lo NW6 . . . . . 11 A1
Parthenia Rd
SW6 . . . . 165 C3
Partington Cl N19 . . . . 4 C3
Parton Lo 14 E8 . . . . . 16 B2
Partridge Ct EC1 . . . . . 96 A2
Partridge Ho 22
E3 . . . . 26 B3
Pascall Ho SE17 . . . . . 48 B4
Pascal St SW8 . . . . . . 161 C2

Pascoe Rd SE13 . . . . . 67 C2
Pasley Cl SE17 . . . . . . 150 C1
Passfield Dr E14 . . . . . 34 A4
Passfields W14 . . . . . . 140 C1
Passing Alley EC1 . . . . 96 B1
Passmore St SW1 . . . 145 B2
Pastor St SE1,
SE11 . . . . 150 B4
Patcham Terr
SW8 . . . . 170 B4
Patent Ho E14 . . . . 34 A4
Paternoster La
EC4 . . . . 108 B2
Paternoster Sq
EC4 . . . . 108 B2
Pater St W8 . . . . 127 B1
Patience Rd
SW11 . . . . 168 A1
Patience Villas
SE13 . . . . 67 C4
Patio Cl SW4 . . . . 61 C1
Patmore Ho 9
N16 . . . . 16 A3
Patmore St SW8 . . . . 171 A4
Patmos Rd SW9 . . . . . 48 A2
Paton Cl E3 . . . . 26 C2
Paton Ho SW9 . . . . . . 172 C2
Paton St EC1 . . . . 96 C3
Patrick Coman Ho
EC1 . . . . 96 A3
Patrick Connolly Gdns
41 E3 . . . . 27 A2
Patriot Sq E2 . . . . 25 A3
Patrol Pl SE6 . . . . 67 A1
Pat Shaw Ho 7
E1 . . . . 25 C1
Patshull Pl NW5 . . . . . 13 B2
Patshull Rd NW5 . . . . . 13 B2
Patten Ho N4 . . . . 6 B3
Patten Rd SW18 . . . . . 72 A4
Patterdale NW1 . . . . . 92 B3
Patterdale Rd
SE15 . . . . 50 B3
Pattina Wlk SE16 . . . . 33 A1
Pattison Point 10
E16 . . . . 35 C4
Pattison Ho
Borough The SE1 . . . . 137 A4
1 Stepney E1 . . . . 32 C3
Pattison Rd NW2 . . . . . 1 C1
Pat Williams Ho
SE27 . . . . 75 B1
Paul Daisley Ct 2
NW6 . . . . 10 A1
Paulet Rd SE5 . . . . 48 A2
Paul Ho 10 W10 . . . . . 23 A1
Pauline Ho 10 E1 . . . . 111 C4
Paul Julius Cl E14 . . . . 34 C2
Paul St EC2 . . . . 24 A1 98 A2
Paultons Ho SW3 . . . . 157 C4
Paultons Sq SW3 . . . . 157 C4
Paultons St SW3 . . . . 157 C3
Pauntley Ho 6 N19 . . . 4 B3
Pauntley St 4 N19 . . . . 4 B3
Pavan Ct 2 E2 . . . . 25 B2
Pavilion 8 SW11 . . . . 158 A1
Paveley Ho N1 . . . . 84 C1
Paveley St NW8 . . . . . 90 B2
Pavement The
Brentford W5 . . . . 36 A1
Clapham SW4 . . . . 61 B3
Pavilion Ct
7 Hampstead
NW3 . . . . 11 B4
Hampstead NW3 . . . . . 11 C3

Pavilion Ct continued
3 Paddington
NW6 . . . . 23 C2
Pavilion Mans 10
SW9 . . . . 62 B3
Pavilion Rd SW1 . . . . 131 A1
Pavilion Sq SW17 . . . . 72 B1
Pavilion St SW1 . . . . . 131 A1
Pavilion Terr 8
W12 . . . . 30 B3
Pavillion St SW1 . . . . 160 A4
Pavillion La SE10 . . . . 43 A4
Pavitt Ct NW9 . . . . 8 C1
Paxton Cl TW9 . . . . . . 44 B1
Paxton Ho SE17 . . . . . 151 A2
Paxton Rd W4 . . . . 46 A4
Paxton Terr SW1 . . . . 160 B4
Paymal Ho 88 E1 . . . . . 32 B4
Payne Ho N1 . . . . 85 A3
Payne Rd E3 . . . . 27 A3
Paynesfield Ave
SW14 . . . . 55 C4
Payne St SE8 . . . . 51 B4
Paynes Wlk W6 . . . . . 154 A3
Peabody Ave
SW1 . . . . 146 B1
Peabody Bldgs
5 Camberwell
SE5 . . . . 48 C2
Walworth SE17 . . . . . 151 B3
Peabody Cl SW1 . . . . 160 B4
Peabody Ct
9 Camberwell
SE5 . . . . 48 C2
St Luke's EC1 . . . . 97 A1
Peabody Est
18 Bethnal Green
E2 . . . . 25 A3
Borough The SE1 . . . . 122 C1
Fulham SW6 . . . . 155 A4
6 Hammersmith
W6 . . . . 39 B1
Holborn EC1 . . . . 95 C1
Lambeth SE1 . . . . 121 C1
North Kensington
W10 . . . . 30 B4
9 Ratcliff E1 . . . . 32 C2
St George in t East
E1 . . . . 125 B4
St Luke's EC1 . . . . 97 A1
Strand WC2 . . . . 106 C1
Streatham SE24 . . . . . 75 B4
Westminster SW1 . . . 147 A4
Peabody Hill SE21 . . . . 75 B3
Peabody Sq SE1 . . . . 136 A3
Peabody Twr EC1 . . . . 97 A1
Peabody Yd N1 . . . . . . 86 C4
Peace Pagoda
SW3 . . . . 159 A2
Peach Rd W10 . . . . . . 23 A2
Peachum Rd SE3 . . . . . 53 B4
Peach Walk Mews 24
E3 . . . . 25 C3
Peacock St SE17 . . . . 150 B3
Peacock Yd SE17 . . . . 150 B3
Peak Ho N4 . . . . 6 B3
Pearce Ho
Camden Town N19 . . . 4 B1
7 Streatham SW2 . . . . 74 A4
Westminster SW1 . . . 147 C3
Pear Cl SE14 . . . . 51 A3
Pear Ct 21 SE15 . . . . . 49 B3
Peardon St SW8 . . . . 170 B1
Pearfield Ho 1
N5 . . . . 15 B3
Pearl St E1 . . . . 32 A1

Pearmain Ho **9**
  SE13 . . . . .52 B1
Pearman St SE1 . . .135 C3
Pear Pl SE1 . . . . . .135 B4
Pearscroft Ct
  SW6 . . . . .166 B3
Pearscroft Rd
  SW6 . . . . .166 B3
Pearse St SE15 .49 A4
Pearson Cl **4** SE5 .48 B2
Pearson Ho SW15 .47 B1
Pearson's Ave SE8,
  SE14 . . . . .51 C2
Pearson St E2 . . .24 B3
Peartree Ave
  SW17 . . . . . . .71 B1
Pear Tree Cl **23**
  E2 . . . . .24 B4
Pear Tree Ct
  Holborn EC1 . . . . .95 C1
  Putney SW15 . . . .57 A2
Pear Tree Ho SE4 . .66 B3
Peartree La E1 . . . . .32 B2
Peartree St EC1 .96 C2
Peartree Way
  SE10 . . . . .43 C2
Peary Pl E2 . . . . . .25 B2
Peckarmans Wood
  SE21, SE26 . . . . .76 C1
Peckett Sq **5** N5 ..15 A4
Peckford Pl SW9 .173 C1
PECKHAM 49 C2
Peckham Gr SE15 ..49 A3
Peckham High St
  SE15 . . . . .49 C2
Peckham Hill St
  SE15 . . . . .49 C3
Peckham Park Prim
  Sch **2** SE15 . . . .49 C3
Peckham Park Rd
  SE15 . . . . .49 C3
Peckham Rd SE5 .49 A2
Peckham Rye
  East Dulwich
  SE22 . . . . .64 C3
  Peckham SE15,
  SE22 . . . . .65 A3
Peckham Rye Sta
  SE15 . . . . .49 C1
Peckwater Ho **2**
  NW5 . . . . .13 C2
Peckwater St NW5 .13 B3
Pedlars Wlk N7 . . .14 A3
Pedley St E1 .24 B1 **99 A1**
Pedro St E5 . . . . .17 C4
Pedworth Gdns **4**
  SE16 . . . . .40 B2
Peel Gr E2 . . . . . . .25 B3
Peel Pass
  W8 . . . . .31 C1 **113 B1**
Peel Pl SW6 . . . . .155 B4
Peel Prec NW6 . . . .23 C3
Peel St W8 .31 C1 **113 B1**
Peerless St EC1 ..97 B3
Pegasus Cl N16 .15 C4
Pegasus Ct
  11 Acton W3 . . . . .28 B3
  Brentford TW8 . . . . .36 B1
  College Pk NW10 ..22 A2
Pegasus Ho **9** E1 ..25 C1
Pegwell Ho **5** E5 .17 A3
Pekin St E14 . . . . .125 A1
Pekoe SE1 . . . . . .125 A1
Peldon Ct TW10 ..54 B2
Pelham Cl SE5 . . . .64 A4
Pelham Cres SW7 **144 A3**

Pelham Ct SW3 . . .**144 A3**
Pelham Ho W14 ..140 C3
Pelham Pl SW7 . . .**144 A3**
Pelham St SW7 . . .143 C2
Pelican Ho **8** SE8 .41 B2
Pelier St SE17 . . . .48 B4
Pella Ho SE11 . . . .149 A2
Pellant Rd SW6 ..154 B2
Pellatt Rd SE22 ..64 B2
Pellerin Rd N16 ..16 A3
Pellew Ho **15** E1 ..25 A1
Pelling St E14 . . . .33 C3
Pelter St **5** E2 . . . .24 B2 **98 C4**
Pelton Rd SE10 . . .43 A1
Pember Rd NW10 ..22 C2
Pemberton Ct **6**
  E1 . . . . .25 C2
Pemberton Gdns
  N19 . . . . .4 B1
Pemberton Pl **2**
  E8 . . . . .17 A1
Pemberton Row
  EC4 . . . .**107 C2**
Pemberton Terr
  N19 . . . . .4 B1
Pembridge Cres
  W11 . . . . .31 C2 **113 B4**
Pembridge Gdns
  W2 . . . . .31 C2 **113 C3**
Pembridge Hall Sch
  W2 . . . . .31 C2 **113 C3**
Pembridge Mews
  W11 . . . . .31 C2 **113 B4**
Pembridge Pl
  Notting Hill
  W2 . . . . .31 C2 **113 C4**
  17 Wandsworth
  SW15 . . . . .58 C2
Pembridge Rd
  W11 . . . . .31 C2 **113 B3**
Pembridge Sq
  W2 . . . . .31 C2 **113 C3**
Pembridge Villas
  W11 . . . . .31 C2 **113 B4**
Pembroke Ave N1 .84 B4
Pembroke Bldgs
  NW10 . . . . .21 C2
Pembroke Cl
  SW1 . . . .**131 C3**
Pembroke Gardens
  SW14 . . . .**141 A2**
Pembroke Gdns
  W8 . . . .**141 A3**
Pembroke Gdns Cl
  W8 . . . .**127 A2**
Pembroke Ho
  Acton W3 . . . . . . .37 B4
  Chelsea SW1 . . . .**131 B1**
  5 Clapham Pk
  SW2 . . . . .62 A2
  17 Kensington W2 .**100 B1**
  Putney SW15 . . . .56 C2
Pembroke Lo **2**
  SW16 . . . . .74 A1
Pembroke Mews
  8 Bow E3 . . . . . .26 A2
  Kensington W8 . . .**127 A1**
Pembroke Pl W8 .**127 A1**
Pembroke Rd W8 .**141 B4**
Pembroke Sq W8 .**127 B1**
Pembroke St N1 ..84 B4
Pembroke Studios
  W8 . . . .**127 A1**

Pembroke Terr
  NW8 . . . . .79 B3
Pembroke Villas
  W8 . . . .**141 B4**
Pembroke Wlk
  W8 . . . .**141 B4**
Pembury Cl E5 . . .17 A3
Pembury Ho SE5 .49 A1
Pembury Pl **15** E5,
  E8 . . . . .17 A3
Pembury Rd E5 . . .17 A3
Pemell Cl **30** E1 ..25 B1
Pemell Ho **31** E1 ..25 B1
Penally Pl N1 . . . .87 C4
Penang St E1 . . . .32 A1
Penarth Ctr The
  SE15 . . . . .50 B4
Penarth St SE15 .50 B4
Pencombe Mews
  W11 . . . . .31 B2 **113 A4**
Pencraig Way
  SE15 . . . . .50 A4
Penda's Mead E9 .18 A4
Pendennis Ho **15**
  SE8 . . . . .41 A2
Pendergast Ladywell
  Sch SE4 . . . . . . .66 C3
Penderyn Way N7 .13 C4
Pendle Ho **16**
  SE26 . . . . .76 C1
Pendley Ho **18** E2 .24 C4
Pendrell Ho WC2 .**105 C1**
Pendrell Rd SE4 ..51 A1
Penelope Ho **20**
  SW9 . . . .**173 B3**
Penfield Lo **1** W9 .31 C4
Penfields Ho N7 ..14 A2
Penfold Pl NW1 ..**102 A4**
Penfold St NW8 ...89 C1
Penford St SE5 . . .48 A1
Penhurst Mans
  SW6 . . . . .164 C4
Peninsula Ct E14 ..42 A3
Peninsula Ret Pk
  TW9 . . . . .43 C2
Peninsular Park Rd
  SE7 . . . . .43 C2
Penmayne Ho
  SE11 . . . . .149 C2
Pennack Rd SE15 .49 B4
Penn Almshouses **1**
  SE10 . . . . .52 B2
Pennant Mews
  W8 . . . . .142 A4
Pennard Mans **5**
  W12 . . . . .39 C4
Pennard Rd W12 .39 B4
Pennethorne Cl
  E9 . . . . .25 B4
Pennethorne Ho
  SW11 . . . . .59 C4
Pennethorne Rd
  SE15 . . . . .50 A3
Penn Ho NW8 . . . .90 A1
Pennine La NW2 ..1 A2
Pennine Mans NW2 .1 A2
Pennine Par NW2 .1 A2
Pennington Ct
  4 Rotherhithe
  SE16 . . . . .33 A1
  23 St George in East
  E1 . . . .**125 C3**
Pennington St E1 .32 A2

Penn Rd N7 . . . . . .14 A4
Penn St N1 . . . . . .87 C3
Penny Brookes St
  E15 . . . . .19 B2
Penny Ct SW10 ...157 A4
Pennyfields E14 ...33 C2
Pennyford Ct NW8 .89 B2
Penny Mews
  SW12 . . . . .73 A4
Pennymore Wlk
  W9 . . . . .23 B1
Penny Rd NW10 ..20 A2
Penpoll Rd E8 . . . .17 A2
Penrhyn Cres
  SW14 . . . . .55 B3
Penrith Cl SW15 ..58 A2
Penrith Pl SE27 ..75 A2
Penrose Gr SE17 .150 C1
Penrose Ho SE17 .150 C1
Penrose St SE17 ..150 C1
Penryn Ho SE11 ..150 C2
Penryn St NW1 ...83 B2
Penry St SE1 . . . .152 B3
Pensbury Pl SW8 .171 A2
Pensbury St SW8 .171 A2
Pensford Ave TW9 .44 C1
Penshurst **2** NW5 .12 C2
Penshurst Ho **15**
  SE15 . . . . .50 B4
Penshurst Rd E9 ..17 C1
Pentland Cl NW11 .1 A2
Pentland Gdns
  SW18 . . . . .59 B1
Pentland Ho
  17 Camden Town
  NW5 . . . . .12 C2
  7 Stamford Hill N16 .7 B3
Pentland Rd **1**
  NW6 . . . . .23 C2
Pentland St SW18 .59 B1
Pentlow St SW15 .57 B4
Pentney Rd SW12 .73 B3
Penton Gr N1 . . . .85 B1
Penton Ho N1 . . . .85 B1
Penton Pl SE17 ..150 B2
Penton Rise WC1 .95 A4
Penton St N1 . . . .85 B2
PENTONVILLE 85 A1
Pentonville Rd
  WC1 . . . . .84 C1
Pentridge St SE15 .49 B3
Penwith Rd SW18 .71 A2
Penwood Ho
  SW15 . . . . .56 B1
Penywern Rd
  SW5 . . . . .141 C2
Penzance Ho
  SE11 . . . . .149 C2
Penzance Pl
  W11 . . . . .31 A1 **112 B2**
Penzance St
  W11 . . . . .31 A1 **112 B2**
Peony Gdns W12 .29 C2
Peperfield WC1 ...94 C3
Pepler Ho **17** W10 .23 A1
Pepler Mews SE1 .152 C1
Peploe Rd NW6 . . .22 C3
Peppermead Sq
  SE13 . . . . .66 C2
Pepper St
  Borough The SE1 ..136 C4
  Millwall E14 . . . . .42 A3
Peppie Cl N16 . . . .7 A2
Pepys Ct **21** E5,...35 C1
Pepys Ent Ctr **13**
  SE8 . . . . .41 B2

Pepys Ho
  14 Bethnal Green
  E2 . . . . .25 B2
  Clapham Pk SW4 ..61 C2
Pepys Rd SE14 . . .50 C1
Pepys St EC3 . . . .124 B4
Perceval Ave NW3 .12 A3
Percheron Cl **3**
  SW9 . . . . .62 B4
Perch St E8 . . . . . .16 B4
Percival Mews
  SW8 . . . . .162 C4
Percival Rd SW14 .55 B3
Percival St EC1 ...96 B3
Percy Cir WC1 . . . .95 A4
Percy Laurie Ho **6**
  SW15 . . . . .57 C3
Percy Mews W1 ..105 B3
Percy Pas W1 . . . .105 B3
Percy Rd
  Newham E16 . . . . .35 A4
  Shepherd's Bush
  W12 . . . . .38 C2
Percy St W1 . . . . .105 B3
Peregrine Ho
  8 Battersea
  SW11 . . . . .60 A4
  Finsbury EC1 . . . . .96 B4
Perham Rd W14 ..140 B1
Perifield SE21 . . . .75 B3
Perkins Ho **15** E14 .33 B3
Perkins Rents
  SW1 . . . .**133 B1**
Perkins Sq SE1 ..123 A2
Perley Ho **8** E3 ...33 B4
Perotti Ho SW6 ..59 A4
Perran Rd SE24,
  SW2 . . . . .75 A2
Perren St NW5 . . .13 A2
Perrers Rd W6 . . .39 A2
Perring Est **3** E3 .33 C4
Perrin's Ct **20**
  NW3 . . . . .11 B4
Perrin's La NW3 ..11 B4
Perrin's Wlk NW3 .11 B4
Perronet Ho SE1 .136 B1
Perry Ave W3 . . . .28 C3
Perry Ct **6** E14 ...41 C1
Perry Ho **24** SW2 .74 A4
Perrymead St
  SW6 . . . . .166 A3
Perryn Ho W3 . . . .29 A2
Perryn Rd
  Acton W3 . . . . . . .28 C2
  4 Bermondsey
  SE16 . . . . .40 A3
Perry's Pl W1 . . . .105 B2
Perrywood Ho **17**
  E5 . . . . .17 A3
Perseverance Works
  17 E2 . . . .24 A2 **98 B4**
Perth Cl **5** SE5 ...48 B1
Perth Ho N1 . . . . .14 B1
Perth Rd N4 . . . . .5 C3
Petchey Acad The
  E8 . . . . .16 A3
Peter Ave NW10 ..9 A1
Peter Best Ho **1**
  E1 . . . . .32 A3
Peterboat Cl SE10 .43 A2
Peterborough Ct
  EC4 . . . .**107 C1**
Peterborough Mews
  SW6 . . . . .165 B2

Peterborough Rd
SW6 . . . . .58 C4
Peterborough Villas
SW6 . . . . .166 A4
Peter Butler Ho **9**
SE1 . . . . .139 B3
Peterchurch Ho
SE15 . . . . .50 A3
Petergate SW11 . . . . . .59 B3
Peter Harrison
Planetarium
SE10 . . . . .52 C3
Peter Heathfield Ho
4 E15 . . . . .27 C4
Peter Hills Ho **8**
SE16 . . . . .153 B4
Peter Hills with St
Mary's & St Paul's CE
Sch **20** SE16 . . . . . . .32 C1
Peter Ho SW8 . . . . . .162 A2
Peter James Ent Ctr
NW10 . . . . .20 B2
Peterley Bsns Ctr **1**
E2 . . . . .25 A3
Peter Scott Visitor
Centre SW13 . . . . . . .47 A2
Peters Ct **12** W2 . . . .100 B2
Peter's Ct SW4 . . . . . . .62 A1
Petersfield Rd W3 . . . .37 B4
Petersfield Rise
SW15 . . . . .69 A3
Petersham Ho
SW7 . . . . .143 B4
Petersham La
SW7 . . . . .128 C2
Petersham Mews
SW7 . . . . .129 A1
Petersham Pl
SW7 . . . . .129 A2
Peter's La EC1 . . . . . . .108 B4
Peter St W1 . . . . .119 B4
Peterstow Cl
SW19 . . . . .70 A2
Petherton Ct
NW10 . . . . .22 C4
Petherton Ho N4 . . . . . .6 B3
Petherton Rd N5 . . . . . .15 B3
Petiver Cl **28** E9 . . . . .17 B1
Petley Rd W6 . . . . .47 C3
Peto Pl NW1 . . . . .92 B2
Peto St N E16 . . . . . . .35 B3
Petrel Ct **8** SE21 . . . .75 C2
Petrie Cl NW2 . . . . . . .10 A2
Petrie Mus of
Egyptian
Archaeology
WC1 . . . . .93 B1
Petros Gdns **1**
NW3 . . . . .11 B2
Petticoat Lane Mkt
EC2 . . . . .110 C3
Petticoat Sq E1 . . . . . .110 C2
Petticoat Twr E1 . . . . .110 C2
Pettiward Cl SW15 . . . .57 B3
Petty France SW1 . . . .133 B2
Petty Wales EC3 . . . . .124 B3
Petworth Ho **18**
SE22 . . . . .64 A4
Petworth St
SW11 . . . . .168 B4
Petyt Pl SW3 . . . . .158 A3
Petyward SW3 . . . . . .144 B3

Pevensey Ct
4 South Acton
W3 . . . . .37 A4
West Norwood
SW16 . . . . .74 C1
Pevensey Ho **1**
E1 . . . . .33 A4
Peverill Ho SE1 . . . . . .137 C1
Pewsham Ho N4 . . . . . . .6 B3
Peyton Pl SE10 . . . . . . .52 B3
Pharamond NW2 . . . . . .9 C2
Phelps Ho **11**
SW15 . . . . .57 C4
Phelp St SE17 . . . . . . .48 C4
Phene St SW3 . . . . . . .158 B4
Philadelphia Ct
SW10 . . . . .157 A1
Philbeach Gdns
SW5 . . . . .141 B2
Phil Brown Pl **3**
SW8 . . . . .61 A4
Philchurch Pl **33**
E1 . . . . .111 C1
Philia Ho **4** NW1 . . . .13 B1
Philip Blairman Ho
E1 . . . . .24 B1 **98** C1
Philip Ct W2 . . . . .101 B4
Philip Ho **12** NW6 . . . .78 A3
Philip Turner Est **28**
E9 . . . . .17 B1
Philip Wlk SE15 . . . . . .64 C4
Phillimore Ct W8 . . . . .127 C3
Phillimore Gardens Cl
W8 . . . . .127 B2
Phillimore Gdns
Kensington W8 . . . . . .127 B3
Willesden NW10 . . . . . .22 B4
Phillimore Pl W8 . . . . .127 B3
Phillimore Terr
W8 . . . . .127 B2
Phillimore Wlk
W8 . . . . .127 C3
Phillip Ho E1 . . . . .111 A3
Phillipp St N1 . . . . .24 A4
Philpot La EC3 . . . . . .124 A4
Philpot Sq SW6 . . . . . . .59 A4
Philpot St E1 . . . . .32 A3
Philson Mans **13**
E1 . . . . .32 A3
Phipps Ho **15** W12 . . .30 A2
Phipps Mews
SW1 . . . . .132 B1
Phipp St
EC2 . . . . .24 A1 **98** A2
Phoebeth Rd SE4 . . . . . .66 C2
Phoenix Bsns Ctr **22**
E3 . . . . .33 C4
Phoenix Cl **11** E8 . . . .24 B4
Phoenix Ct
4 Brentford
TW8 . . . . .36 A1
2 Deptford SE14 . . . .51 A4
Millwall E14 . . . . .41 C2
Phoenix High Sch
W12 . . . . .29 C2
Phoenix Ho SW1 . . . . .145 B4
Phoenix Lodge Mans
1 W6 . . . . .39 B2
Phoenix Pl WC1 . . . . . .95 A2
Phoenix Prim Sch
26 E3 . . . . .26 B2
22 SE1 . . . . .153 C1
Phoenix Rd NW1 . . . . . .93 B4
Phoenix St WC2 . . . . .105 C1
Phoenix Wharf Rd
SE1 . . . . .139 A3

Phyllis Hodges Ho
NW1 . . . . .83 B1
Physic Pl SW3 . . . . . .158 C4
Piano La **2** N16 . . . . . .6 C1
Piccadilly W1 . . . . . . .118 C2
Piccadilly Arc
SW1 . . . . .118 C2
Piccadilly Cir W1 . . . .119 B3
Piccadilly Circus Sta
SW1 . . . . .119 B3
Piccadilly Ct **5**
N7 . . . . .14 B2
Piccadilly Pl W1 . . . . .119 A3
Pickard St EC1 . . . . . . .96 B4
Pickering Cl **6** E9 . . . .17 C1
Pickering Ho
1 Kensington
W2 . . . . .100 B1
Stoke Newington N4 . . . .6 C4
Pickering Mews **1**
W2 . . . . .100 B2
Pickering Pl SW1 . . . .119 A1
Pickering St N1 . . . . . . .86 B4
Pickets St SW12 . . . . . .73 A4
Pickfords Wharf
N1 . . . . .86 C1
Pickwick Ho
21 Bermondsey
SE16 . . . . .139 B3
6 Shepherd's Bush
W11 . . . . .30 C1
Pickwick Rd SE21 . . . . .76 A4
Pickwick St SE1 . . . . .136 C3
Pickworth Cl
SW8 . . . . .162 B1
Picton Ho **1** SW4 . . . .74 A4
Picton Pl W1 . . . . .103 C1
Picton St SE5 . . . . .48 C3
Picture Ho **6**
SW16 . . . . .74 A2
Pied Bull Ct WC1 . . . .106 B3
Pied Bull Yd WC1 . . . .106 B3
Pier Head E1 . . . . .32 A1
Pierhead Wharf **27**
E1 . . . . .32 A1
Pier Ho SW3 . . . . .158 B3
Piermont Rd SE22 . . . . .65 A2
Pierpoint Bldg **4**
E14 . . . . .41 C4
Pierrepont Rd
W3 . . . . .28 A2
Pierrepont Row
N1 . . . . .86 A2
Pier St E14 . . . . .42 B2
Pier Terr SW18 . . . . . . .59 B3
Piggott Ho **2** E2 . . . . .25 C3
Pigott St E14 . . . . .33 C3
Pilgrimage St
SE1 . . . . .137 B3
Pilgrim Ho SE1 . . . . . .137 C1
Pilgrims Cloisters **10**
SE5 . . . . .49 A3
Pilgrims Ct SE3 . . . . . .53 C2
Pilgrim's La NW3 . . . . .11 C4
Pilgrims Mews **12**
E14 . . . . .34 C2
Pilgrim's Pl **6**
NW3 . . . . .11 C4
Pilgrim St EC4 . . . . . .108 A1
Pilgrims Way N19 . . . . .4 C3
Pilgrims Way Prim
Sch SE15 . . . . .50 B4
Pilkington Rd **4**
SE15 . . . . .50 A1
Pilot Cl **4** SE8 . . . . . .51 B4
Pilot Ind Ctr NW10 . . . .21 A1

Pilot Wk SE10 . . . . . . .43 B3
Pilsden Cl SW19 . . . . . .69 C3
Pilton Pl SE17 . . . . . . .151 A2
Pimlico Sta SW1 . . . . .147 B2
PIMLICO 146 C1
Pimlico Acad
SW1 . . . . .147 A1
Pimlico Rd SW1 . . . . .145 C2
Pimlico Wlk **1**
N1 . . . . .24 A2 **98** A4
Pinchin St E1 . . . . . . .125 C4
Pincombe Ho
SE17 . . . . .151 B2
Pincott Pl SE4 . . . . . . .65 C4
Pindar St EC2 . . . . . . .110 A4
Pindock Mews W9 . . . . .88 B1
Pine Apple Ct
SW1 . . . . .132 C2
Pine Ave E15 . . . . .19 C3
Pine Cl **11** N19 . . . . . . .4 B2
Pinedene **2** SE15 . . . .50 A2
Pinefield Cl E14 . . . . . . .33 C2
Pine Gr N4, N19 . . . . . . .5 B2
Pine Ho
Bow E3 . . . . .26 A4
21 Rotherhithe
SE16 . . . . .40 B4
Pinehurst Ct **6**
W11 . . . . .31 B3
Pinelands Cl **7**
SE3 . . . . .53 B3
Pine Lo SW15 . . . . .58 A1
Pine Rd NW2 . . . . .9 C4
Pines The SE4 . . . . . . .51 B4
Pine St EC1 . . . . .95 B2
Pine Tree Ho SE14 . . . .50 C3
Pine Tree Way **1**
SE13 . . . . .67 A4
Pinewood Ct SW4 . . . .61 C1
Pinkham Mans
W4 . . . . .36 C1
Pinnacle Ho E14 . . . . . .42 B3
Pinnacle Ho EC3 . . . . .124 A3
Pinnacle The **7**
E14 . . . . .15 B2
Pinner Ct NW8 . . . . . . .89 B2
Pinner Ho SE5 . . . . . . .48 B1
Pintail Ct **30** SE8 . . . .51 B4
Pinter Ho **80** SW9 . . .172 B1
Pioneer Cl
14 Bow Comm
E14 . . . . .34 A4
London W12 . . . . .30 A3
Pioneer St SE15 . . . . . .49 C2
Pioneer Way W12 . . . .30 B3
Piper Cl N7 . . . . .14 B3
Pipers Ho SE10 . . . . . .42 C1
Pippin Ho **18** W10 . . .30 C2
Pippin Ho **8** W10 . . . .57 B1
Pirate Castle The **1**
NW1 . . . . .82 A4
Pirbright Rd SW18 . . . .70 C3
Pitcairn Ho **1** E9 . . . . .17 B1
Pitfield Ho N5 . . . . .15 B3
Pitfield St N1 . . . . .24 A3
Pitman Ho **4** SE8 . . . .51 C2
Pitman St SE5 . . . . . . .48 B3
Pitmaston Ho **2**
SE13 . . . . .52 B1
Pitsea Pl E1 . . . . .32 C3
Pitsea St E1 . . . . .32 C3
Pitt's Head Mews
W1 . . . . .117 C1
Pitt St W8 . . . . .127 C4

Pitwell Mews **8**
E8 . . . . .16 C2
Pixley St E14 . . . . .33 B3
Planetree Ct W6 . . . . . .39 C2
Plane Tree Ho
SE8 . . . . .51 A4
Plantain Pl SE1 . . . . . .137 B4
Plantation La EC3 . . . .124 A4
Plantation The
SE3 . . . . .53 C1
Platanos Coll
SW9 . . . . .172 C3
Platehouse The **3**
E14 . . . . .42 A1
Platina St EC2 . . . . .97 C2
Plato Pl **1** SW6 . . . . . .62 A3
Plato Rd SW2 . . . . .62 A3
Platt's La NW3 . . . . .1 C1
Platt St NW1 . . . . .83 B2
Plaxdale Ho SE17 . . . .152 A3
Playfair St W6 . . . . .39 B1
Playfield Cres
SE22 . . . . .64 B2
Playford Rd
Finsbury Pk N4 . . . . .5 B2
Finsbury Pk N4 . . . . .5 C2
Playhouse Yd
EC4 . . . . .108 A1
Playon (Canary Wharf
Indoor Sports)
E14 . . . . .34 B1
Plaza Sh Ctr W1 . . . . .105 A2
Pleasance Rd
SW15 . . . . .57 A2
Pleasance The
SW15 . . . . .57 A3
Pleasant Pl N1 . . . . . . .15 A1
Pleasant Row NW1 . . . .82 B3
Plender Ct NW1 . . . . . .83 A3
Plender St NW1 . . . . . .83 A3
Pleshey Rd N7 . . . . .13 C4
Plevna St E14 . . . . .42 B3
Pleydell Ave W6 . . . . . .38 B2
Pleydell Ct EC4 . . . . . .107 C1
Pleydell St EC4 . . . . . .107 C1
Plimsoll Cl E14 . . . . . . .34 A3
Plimsoll Rd N4 . . . . .6 A1
Plough Cl NW10 . . . . . .22 A2
Plough Ct EC3 . . . . . .123 C4
Plough La SE22 . . . . . . .64 B1
Ploughmans Cl
NW1 . . . . .83 B4
Plough Mews **19**
SW11 . . . . .59 C3
Plough Pl EC4 . . . . . . .107 C2
Plough Rd SW11 . . . . . .59 C3
Plough St **18** E1 . . . .111 B2
Plough Terr SW11 . . . . .59 C3
Plough Way SE16 . . . . .41 A2
Plough Yd
EC2 . . . . .24 A1 **98** B1
Plover Ho **8** SW9 . . . .163 B2
Plover Way SE16 . . . . . .41 A3
Plowman Ho
SW19 . . . . .69 C2
Plumbers Row E1 . . . .111 C2
Plumbridge St **7**
SE10 . . . . .52 B2
Plume Ho SE10 . . . . . . .52 A4
Plummer Ct SE13 . . . . .67 A1
Plummer Rd SW4 . . . . .73 C4
Plumtree Ct EC4 . . . . .108 A2
Plymouth Ho **20**
SE10 . . . . .52 B4
Plymouth Rd E16 . . . . .35 C4

Plymouth Wharf
E14 .... 42 C2
Plympton Ave
NW6 .... 10 B1
Plympton PI NW1 .. 90 A1
Plympton Rd NW6 .. 10 B1
Plympton St NW8 .. 90 A1
Pocklington Ct
SW15 .... 68 C3
Pocklington Lo 🔟
W12 .... 38 C3
Pocock St SE1 ... 136 B4
Podmore Rd SW18 . 59 B3
Poets Cnr SW1 ... 134 A2
Poets Mews 🔞
SE24 .... 63 A2
Poet's Rd N5 .... 15 C3
Point Cl SE10 .... 52 B2
Point Hill SE10 .. 52 B2
Pointer Sch The
SE3 .... 53 C1
Pointers Cl E14 ... 42 A1
Point PI NW8 ..... 89 B1
Point Rd SE10 .... 52 B2
Point Pleasant
SW18 .... 58 C3
Point Wharf La
TW8 .... 44 A3
Poland Ho 🔞 E15 . 27 C4
Poland St W1 .... 105 A1
Polesworth Ho 🔞
W2 .... 31 C4
Polish Inst & Sikorski
Mus SW7 .... 129 C3
Polish Univ Abroad 🔟
W6 .... 38 C2
Pollard Cl
Islington N7 ...... 14 B4
Newham E16 ...... 35 C2
Pollard Ho N1 ... 84 C1
Pollard Row
E2 .... 24 C2 99 C4
Pollard St
E2 .... 24 C2 99 C4
Pollen St W1 .... 104 B1
Pollitt Dr NW8 .... 89 C2
Pollock Ho W10 .. 23 A1
Pollock's Toy Mus
W1 .... 105 A4
Polperro Mans 🔞
NW6 .... 10 C3
Polperro Mews
SE11 .... 150 A4
Polygon Rd NW1 .. 83 B1
Polygon The 🔞
🔞 Clapham SW4 .. 61 B3
St John's Wood
NW8 .... 79 C4
Pomell Way E1 .. 111 A2
Pomeroy Ct W11 .. 31 A3
Pomeroy Ho 🔞 E2 25 C3
Pomeroy St SE14 . 50 B2
Pomfret Rd SE5 .. 63 A4
Pomoja La N19 .. 5 A2
Pomona Ho 🔞
SE8 .... 41 A2
Pond Cl SE3 ...... 53 C1
Pond Cotts SE21 .. 76 A3
Ponder St 🔞 N7 .. 14 B1
Pondfield Ho 🔞
N5 .... 15 B3
Pond Ho SW3 ... 144 A3
Pond Mead SE21 .. 63 C1
Pond Rd SE3 ..... 53 B1
Pond Sq N6 .... 3 C3
Pond St NW3 ..... 12 A3

Ponler St E1 ...... 32 A3
Ponsard Rd NW10 22 A2
Ponsford St E9 ... 17 B2
Ponsonby Ho 🔞
E2 .... 25 B3
Ponsonby PI SW1 147 C2
Ponsonby Rd
SW15 .... 69 A4
Ponsonby Terr
SW1 .... 147 C2
Ponton Ho SW2 .. 74 C3
Ponton Rd SW8 .. 161 C3
Pont St Mews
SW1 .... 130 C1
Pont St SW1 .... 131 A1
Pontypool PI SE1 136 A4
Poole Ct N1 ...... 16 A1
Poole Ho SE11 .. 135 A1
Poole Rd E9 ...... 17 C2
Pooles Bldgs EC1 . 95 B1
Pooles La SW10 . 156 C1
Pooles Park Prim Sch
🔞 N4 .... 5 B2
Pooles Pk N4 ..... 5 C2
Poole St N1 ...... 87 B3
Pooley Ho E1 ..... 25 C2
Pool Ho NW8 .... 101 C4
Poolmans St SE16 40 C4
Poonah St E1 .... 32 B3
Pope Ho
🔞 Bermondsey
SE16 .... 40 A2
🔞 Camberwell SE5 48 C3
Pope John RC Prim
Sch W12 .... 30 A2
Pope's Head Alley
EC3 .... 109 C1
Pope's La W5 .... 36 A3
Pope's Rd SW9 .. 62 C4
Pope St SE1 .... 138 B3
Popham Ct N16 .. 7 A1
Popham Gdns
TW9 .... 55 A4
Popham Rd N1 .. 86 C4
Popham St
Islington N1 ...... 86 B4
Shoreditch N1 .... 86 C4
POPLAR 33 C3
Poplar Bath St 🔞
E14 .... 34 A2
Poplar Bsns Pk
E14 .... 34 A2
Poplar Cl E9 ..... 18 B3
Poplar Ct 🔞 SW16 76 A1
Poplar Gr W6 .... 39 B4
Poplar High St
E14 .... 34 A2
Poplar Ho
Brockley SE4 ..... 66 B3
🔞 Rotherhithe
SE16 .... 40 C4
Poplar Mews 🔞
W12 .... 30 B1
Poplar PI W2 .... 114 B4
Poplar Sta E14 ... 34 A2
Poplars The NW5 . 13 B3
Poplar Wlk SE24 . 63 B3
Poppins Ct EC4 . 108 A1
Porchester Ct 🔞
W2 .... 100 B1
Porchester Gate
W2 .... 114 C3
Porchester Gdn Mews
W2 .... 100 B1
Porchester Gdns
W2 .... 114 B4

Porchester Ho 🔞
E1 .... 32 A3
Porchester Mews
W2 .... 100 B2
Porchester PI W2 102 B1
Porchester Rd
W2 .... 100 B2
Porchester Sq
W2 .... 100 B2
Porchester Terr
W2 .... 114 C4
Porchester Terr N
W2 .... 100 B2
Porden Rd SW2 .. 62 B3
Porland St SE17 137 B2
Porlock Ho 🔞
SE26 .... 76 C1
Porlock St SE1 .. 137 C4
Porson Ct SE13 .. 67 A4
Portal Cl SE27 ... 74 C1
Portal Way W3 ... 28 C4
Portbury Cl 🔞
SE15 .... 49 C2
Portchester Cl
SE24 .... 63 C3
Porten Hos W14 .126 A1
Porten Rd W14 .. 126 A1
Porter Sq N19 .... 5 A3
Porter St
Borough The SE1 123 A2
Marylebone W1 .. 103 A4
Porteus Rd W2 .. 101 A4
Portfleet Pl 🔞 N1 24 A4
Portgate Cl W9 ... 23 B1
Portia Way E3 ... 26 B1
Porticos The SW3 157 B3
Portinscale Rd
SW15 .... 58 B2
Portishead Ho 🔞
W2 .... 31 C4
Portland Ave N16 . 7 B4
Portland Ct
🔞 De Beauvoir Town
N1 .... 16 A1
🔞 Deptford SE14 . 51 A4
Portland Gr SW8 172 C4
Portland Ho 🔞
SW2 .... 74 C3
**Portland Hospl for
Women & Children**
The W1 .... 92 B1
Portland Mews
W1 .... 105 A1
Portland PI W1 .. 104 B3
Portland Place Sch
W1 .... 104 B4
Portland Rd
Notting Hill
W11 .... 31 A1 112 B2
Notting Hill
W11 ... 31 A1 112 A2 🔞
Portland Rise N4 .. 6 B3
Portland Sq 🔞 E1 32 A1
Portland St SE17 151 B1
Portland Village
W6 .... 39 B3
Portman Ave
SW14 .... 55 C4
Portman Cl W1 .. 103 B2

Portman Gate
NW1 .... 90 B1
Portman Hts 🔞
NW3 .... 1 C1
Portman Mews S
W1 .... 103 B1
Portman PI E2 ... 25 B2
Portman Sq W1 .. 103 B2
Portman St W1 .. 103 B1
Portman The NW11 1 C4
Portman Twrs
W1 .... 103 A2
Portnall Rd W9 .. 23 B2
Portobello Ct Est
W11 .... 31 B3
Portobello Mews
W11 .... 31 C2 113 B3
Portobello Rd
W11 .... 31 B2 113 A4
Portobello Road Mkt
W11 .... 31 A2 🔞
Portpool La EC1 .. 107 B4
Portree St E14 ... 34 C3
Port Royal Pl 🔞
N1 .... 16 A3
Portsea Hall W2 . 102 B1
Portsea Ho 🔞
SW15 .... 69 A3
Portsea Mews
W2 .... 102 B1
Portsea PI W2 .. 102 B1
Portslade Ho
SW8 .... 170 C2
Portsmouth Rd
SW15 .... 69 A4
Portsmouth St
WC2 .... 107 A1
Portsoken St E1,
EC3 .... 124 C4
Portswood Pl 🔞
SW15 .... 56 B1
Portugal St WC2 107 A1
Poseidon Ct 🔞
E14 .... 41 C2
Postal Museum The 🔞
WC1 .... 95 B2
Postern The EC2 . 109 A3
Post Office Way
SW8 .... 161 B2
Potier St SE1 .... 137 C1
Potterne Cl 🔞
SW19 .... 69 C4
Potters Cl 🔞 SE15 49 A3
Potters Fields
SE1 .... 124 B1
Potters Lo E14 ... 42 B2
Potters Rd SW6 . 166 C1
Pottery La
W11 .... 31 A1 112 B2
Pottery Rd TW8 ... 44 A4
Pottery St SE16 .. 40 A4
Pott St E2 .... 25 A2
Poullett Ho SW2 .. 75 A3
Poulton Cl E8 ... 17 A2
Poultry EC2 .... 109 B1
Pound La NW10 .. 8 C2
Pountney Rd
SW11 .... 60 C4
Povey Ho
🔞 Tulse Hill SW2 . 62 C1
Walworth SE17 .. 152 A3
Powell's Wlk W4 .. 46 B4
Powergate Bsns Pk
NW10 .... 20 C2
Power Ho 🔞 W4 . 38 A2
Power Ho The W4 . 38 B2

Power Rd W4 .... 36 C2
Powerscroft Rd
E5 .... 17 B4
Powis Gdns
Golders Green
NW11 .... 1 B4
Notting Hill W11 .. 31 B3
Powis Ho WC2 .. 106 B2
Powis Mews W11 . 31 B3
Powis Pl WC1 .... 94 B1
Powis Rd E3 .... 27 A2
Powis Sq W11 .... 31 B3
Powis Terr W11 .. 31 B3
Powlesland Ct 🔞
E14 .... 33 A3
Powlett Ho NW1 .. 13 A2
Powlett PI NW1 .. 13 A1
Pownall Rd E8 ... 24 C4
Pownall Terr
SE11 .... 163 C3
Powrie Ho 🔞
SW11 .... 167 C2
Poynder Ct 🔞 N7 14 A3
Poynders Ct 🔞
SW4 .... 61 B1
Poynders Gdns
SW12 .... 73 B4
Poynders Rd SW12,
SW4 .... 73 C4
Poynings Rd N19 .. 4 B1
Poynter Ho
Paddington NW8 . 89 B2
🔞 Shepherd's Bush
W11 .... 30 C1
Poyntz Rd SW11 168 C1
Poyser St E2 .... 25 A3
Praed Mews W2 . 101 C2
Praed St W2 .... 101 C2
Prague PI SW2 ... 62 A2
Prah Rd N4 .... 5 C2
Prairie St SW8 .. 170 A1
Pratt Mews NW1 . 82 C3
Pratt St NW1 .... 82 C4
Pratt Wlk SE1,
SE11 .... 149 A4
Preachers Ct EC1 . 96 B1
Prebend Gdns W4,
W6 .... 38 B2
Prebend Mans 🔞
W4 .... 38 B2
Prebend St N1 ... 86 C4
Precinct The
Islington N1 ..... 86 B3
Islington N5 ..... 15 A3
Premier Corner
NW6 .... 23 B3
Premier Ho 🔞 N1 15 A1
Premier Park Rd
NW10 .... 20 A3
Premier PI NW10 . 20 A3
Premier PI 🔞 E14 33 C2
Prendergast Ho 🔞
SW4 .... 61 C3
Prendergast Prim Sch
SE4 .... 66 C3
Prendergast Sch
SE4 .... 66 C3
Prendergast Vale Sch
🔞 SE13 .... 67 A4
Prescot St E1 ... 125 A4
Prescott Ho 🔞
SE17 .... 48 A4
Prescott PI SW4 . 61 C3

Presentation Mews
SW2 ... 74 B3
President Dr E1 ... 33 A2
President Ho EC1 ... 96 B3
President St EC1 ... 96 C4
Prestage Way 13
E14 ... 34 B2
Prested Rd SW11 ... 60 A3
Preston Cl SE1 ... 152 A4
Preston Gdns NW10 .8 A2
Preston Ho
Bermondsey SE1 ... 138 C2
Walworth SE1 ... 152 A4
Preston Pl
Richmond TW10 ... 54 A2
Willesden NW2 ... 8 C2
Preston's Rd E14 ... 34 B1
Prestwich Terr
SW4 ... 61 C2
Prestwood Ho 3
SE16 ... 40 A3
Prestwood St N1 ... 87 A1
Priam Ho E2 ... 25 A3
Price Ho N1 ... 86 C3
Prices Ct SW11 ... 59 C4
Price's St SE1 ... 122 B2
Price's Yd N1 ... 85 A3
Prichard Ct
Battersea SW11 ... 167 C3
Islington N7 ... 14 B3
Prideaux Ho WC1 .. 95 A4
Prideaux Pl
Acton W3 ... 28 C2
St Pancras WC1 ... 95 A4
Prideaux Rd SW9 .. 62 A4
Pride Ct N1 ... 85 C2
Priestley Cl N16 .. 7 B4
Priestley Ho
2 Camden Town
NW5 ... 13 A2
St Luke's EC1 ... 97 A2
Priestman Point 23
E3 ... 27 A2
Priests Bridge
SW14 ... 56 A4
Priest's Ct EC2 ... 108 C2
Prima Rd SW9 ... 163 B2
Primrose Cl E3 ..26 C3
Primrose Ct
2 Child's Hill NW2 .. 1 B1
11 Primrose Hill NW8 .. 80 C3
1 Streatham
SW12 ... 73 C4
Primrose Gdns
NW3 ... 12 A2
PRIMROSE HILL .. 12 B1
Primrose Hill EC4 107 C1
Primrose Hill Ct
NW3 ... 12 B2
Primrose Hill Prim
Sch NW1 ... 81 C4
Primrose Hill Rd NW1,
NW3 ... 12 B1
Primrose Hill Studios
NW1 ... 81 B4
Primrose Ho
7 Peckham SE15 ..49 C2
1 Richmond TW9 .. 44 B2
Primrose Mans
SW11 ... 169 B4
Primrose Mews 9
NW1 ... 12 B1
Primrose Sq E9 ..25 B4

Primrose St EC2.. 110 B4
Primrose Wlk 6
SE14 ... 51 A3
Primrose Wy 10
SE13 ... 52 B1
Primula St W12 ..29 C3
Prince Albert Ct
NW8 ... 80 C3
Prince Albert Rd
NW8 ... 80 C3
Prince Arthur Ct 18
NW3 ... 11 B4
Prince Arthur Mews
17 NW3 ... 11 B4
Prince Arthur Rd
NW3 ... 11 B4
Prince Charles Rd
SE3 ... 53 B2
Prince Consort Ho
SE1 ... 148 B2
Prince Consort Rd
SW7 ... 129 B2
Princedale Rd
W11 ... 31 A1 112 B2
Prince Edward Mans
2 W2 ... 31 C2 113 C4
Prince Edward Rd
E9 ... 18 B2
Prince George Rd
N16 ... 16 A4
Princelet St E1 ... 111 A4
Prince of Orange La
8 SE10 ... 52 B3
Prince of Wales Dr
SW11 ... 169 B4
Prince of Wales Mans
Battersea SW11 .. 169 C4
Clapham SW4 ... 61 A2
Prince of Wales Pas
NW1 ... 92 C3
Prince of Wales Rd
Blackheath Vale
SE3 ... 53 B2
Camden Town NW5 ..12 C2
Prince of Wales Terr
Chiswick W4 ... 38 A1
Kensington W8 .. 128 B3
Prince Regent Ct 2
SE16 ... 33 A1
Prince Regent Mews
NW1 ... 92 C3
Princes Arc SW1 .. 119 A2
Princes Ave W3 ... 36 C3
Princes Cir WC2.. 106 A2
Princes Cl N4 ... 6 A3
Princes Coll WC1 106 A2
Princes Court Bsns
Ctr E1 ... 32 A2
Princes Ct
Brondesbury
NW2 ... 10 A3
Hampstead NW3 .. 11 C4
Stepney E1 ... 32 A2
7 Prince's Ct SE16 ..41 B3
Princes Gate SW7 129 C3
Prince's Gate
SW7 ... 130 A3
Princes Gate Ct
SW7 ... 129 C3
Princes Gate Mews
SW7 ... 129 C2
Princes Gdns
SW7 ... 129 C2
Princes Ho
W11 ... 31 C2 113 B3

Prince's Mews
W6 Hammersmith
W6 ... 39 A1
Islington N1 ... 86 A3
Kensington W2... 114 A4
Princes Pl
Notting Hill
W11 ... 31 A1 112 A2
St James SW1 ... 119 A2
Princes Rd
Kew TW9 ... 44 B2
Richmond TW10 ... 54 B2
Prince's Rd SW14 .. 55 C4
Princes Rise SE13 .. 52 B1
Princes Riverside Rd
7 SE16 ... 32 C1
Princess Alexandra
School of Nursing
The 6 E1 ... 32 A4
Princess Alice Ho 1
W10 ... 22 B1
Princess Beatrice Ho
SW10 ... 142 A1
Princes Cres N4 ... 6 A2
Princess Ct
Hampstead NW6 ... 11 A1
Kensington W2 ... 114 B4
Marylebone W1 ... 102 C3
Princess Frederica CE
VA Prim Sch
NW10 ... 22 B3
Princess Grace Hospl
The W1 ... 91 B1
Princess Louise Cl
W2 ... 101 C4
Princess Louise Wk 2
W10 ... 30 B4
Princess Mary Ho
SW1 ... 147 C3
Princess May Prim
Sch 8 N16 ... 16 B4
Princess May Rd
N16 ... 16 A4
Princess Mews 3
NW3 ... 11 C2
Prince's Sq W2 ... 114 A4
Princess Rd
Camden Town
NW1 ... 81 C4
Paddington NW6 ... 23 C3
Princess St SE1 .. 136 B1
Prince St SE8 ... 51 B4
Prince's St
City of London
EC2 ... 109 B1
Richmond TW10,
TW9 ... 54 A2
Prince St SE8 ... 51 B4
Princes Way
Acton W3 ... 36 C3
Putney SW15,
SW19 ... 70 A4
Princes Yd
W11 ... 31 A1 112 B1
Princethorpe Ho
W2 ... 100 A4
Princeton Ct 12
SW15 ... 57 C4
Princeton Mans
WC1 ... 106 C3
Princeton St WC1 106 C4
Principal Sq E9 ..17 C3
Printers Mews E3 ..26 A4
Printers Rd SW4 .. 173 A4
Printer St EC4 ... 107 C2

Printing House Yd 16
E2 ... 24 A2 98 B3
Printon Ho 13 E3 ..33 B4
Print Village Ind Est
SE15 ... 49 B1
Prior Bolton St N1 .. 15 A2
Prioress Ho 2 E3 ..27 A2
Prioress Rd SE27 .. 75 A1
Prioress St SE1 .. 137 C1
Priors Lo 4 TW10 .. 54 A1
Prior St SE10 ... 52 B3
Prior Weston Prim
Sch
Broadgate EC1 ... 97 B2
St Luke's EC1 ... 97 A2
Priory Ave W4 ... 38 A3
Priory Ct
City of London
EC4 ... 108 B1
Homerton E9 ... 17 C3
Nunhead SE15 ... 65 B3
Roehampton SW15.. 56 B3
South Lambeth
SW8 ... 171 C4
Priory Gdns
Barnes SW13 ... 56 B4
2 Chiswick W4 ... 38 A2
Priory Gn N1 ... 84 C2
Priory Gr SW8 ... 172 A3
Priory Ho
Clerkenwell EC1 ... 96 A2
Pimlico SW1 ... 147 B2
Spitalfields E1 .. 110 C4
Priory Hospl
Roehampton The
SW15 ... 56 B3
Priory Hts N1 ... 85 A2
Priory La SW15 ... 56 B2
Priory Lo 7 W4 ... 36 C1
Priory Lodge Sch
SW15 ... 56 B3
Priory Mans
17 Maitland Pk
NW3 ... 12 B2
South Kensington
SW10 ... 143 A1
Priory Park Rd
NW6 ... 23 B4
Priory Rd
Bedford Pk W4 ... 37 C3
Hampstead NW6 ... 11 A1
Richmond TW9 ... 44 C3
Priory St 13 E3 ... 27 A2
Priory Terr NW6 ... 78 A4
Priory The 13 SE3 ..53 B3
Priory Wlk SW10 .. 143 A1
Pritchard Ho 30
E2 ... 24 C3
Pritchard's Rd E2 .. 24 C4
Priter Rd SE16 ... 139 C1
Priter Road Hostel 5
SE16 ... 139 C1
Probert Rd SW2 ..62 C2
Probyn Ho SW1 .. 147 C4
Probyn Rd SW2 ... 75 A2
Procter Ho 12 SE5..48 C3
Procter St WC1 .. 106 C3
Proctor Ho 5
SE1 ... 153 B1
Prodgis Bsns Pk
E16 ... 27 B1
Prome Ho 13 N16 .. 15 C4
Promenade Approach
Rd W4 ... 46 A3
Promenade The
W4 ... 46 A2

Prospect Cotts
SW18 ... 58 C3
Prospect Ho
1 Dalston E8 ... 16 B2
Islington N1 ... 85 B3
Newington SE1 .. 136 B1
14 North Kensington
W10 ... 30 C3
Prospect House Sch
11 SW15 ... 69 C4
Prospect Pl
5 Child's Hill NW2 ... 1 B1
2 Chiswick W4 ... 37 C1
6 Deptford SE8 ... 51 B4
6 Lower Holloway
NW3 ... 11 B4
7 Lower Holloway
N7 ... 14 A4
Wapping E1 ... 32 B1
Prospect Quay
SW18 ... 58 C3
Prospect Rd NW2 ... 1 C1
Prospect St SE16 .. 40 A4
Prospect Wharf
E1 ... 32 B2
Prospero Rd N19 ... 4 C3
Prothero Rd SW6 154 C2
Proud Ho 16 E1 ... 32 A3
Prout Gr NW10 ... 8 B4
Provence St N1 ... 86 C2
Providence Ct W1 ..117 C4
Providence Pl
Islington N1 ... 86 A3
Mayfair W1... 117 C4
Providence Pl N1.. 86 A3
Providence Row
N1 ... 84 C1
Providence Row Cl 10
E2 ... 25 A2
Providence Sq 30
SE1 ... 139 B4
Providence Yd 1
E2 ... 24 C2 99 B4
Province Dr 9
SE16 ... 40 C4
Provost Ct NW3 ... 12 B2
Provost Rd NW3 ... 12 B1
Provost St N1 ... 97 B4
Prowse Pl NW1 ... 13 B1
Prudent Pas 2 ... 109 A1
Prusom's Island 8
E1 ... 32 B1
Prusom St E1 ... 32 B1
Pryors The NW3 ... 2 C1
Pudding La EC3 .. 123 C4
Pudding Mill La
E15 ... 27 A4
Pudding Mill Lane Sta
E15 ... 27 A4
Puddle Dock EC4. 122 B4
Pugin Ct N1 ... 14 C1
Pulborough Rd
SW18 ... 70 B4
Pulham Ho SW8 .. 162 C1
Pullman Ct SW2 ..74 B3
Pullman Gdns
SW15 ... 57 B1
Pulross Rd SW9 ..62 B4
Pulteney Cl 20 E3 ..26 B4
Pulteney Terr N1 .. 85 A4
Pulton Ho SE4 ..66 A3
Pulton Pl SW6 ... 155 B1
Puma Ct E1 ... 110 C4
Pump Ct EC4 ... 107 B1
Pump House Cl
SE16 ... 40 B4

Pump House Cres
TW8 . . . . .44 B4

Pumphouse
Educational Mus The
SE16 . . . . .33 C1

Pump House Gall
SW11 . . . .**159** B1

Pumping Ho **3**
E14 . . . . .34 C2

Pumping Station Rd
W4 . . . . .46 A4

Pump La SE14 . . . . . .50 B3

Punderson's Gdns
E2 . . . . .25 A2

Purbeck Ho SW8 . .**162** C1

Purbrook Est SE1 . .**138** B3

Purbrook Ho **2**
SW15 . . . . .69 A3

Purbrook St SE1 . .**138** B2

Purcell Cres SW6 . .**154** A2

Purcell Ho SW10 . .**157** B3

Purcell Mews **2**
NW10 . . . . .8 A1

Purcell St N1 . . . . . . .24 A3

Purchese St NW1 . .**83** C1

Purday Ho **4** W10 . .23 B2

Purdon Ho **1**
SE15 . . . . .49 C2

Purdy St E3 . . . . .27 A1

Purley Ave NW2 . . . . .1 A2

Purley Pl N1 . . . . .15 A1

Purser Ho **3** SW2 . .62 C1

Pursers Cross Rd
SW6 . . . .**165** A4

Purves Rd NW10 . . . .22 B3

Pusey Ho **2** E14 . . . .33 C3

Puteaux Ho **6** E2 . . .25 C3

PUTNEY 57 B2

Putney Bridge App
SW6 . . . . .58 A4

Putney Bridge Rd
SW15 . . . . .58 B3

Putney Bridge Sta
SW6 . . . . .58 B4

Putney Comm
SW15 . . . . .57 B4

Putney Exchange
Shopping Ctr
SW15 . . . . .57 C3

PUTNEY HEATH 57 B1

Putney Heath
SW15 . . . . .57 C1

Putney Heath La
SW15 . . . . .57 C1

Putney High Sch
SW15 . . . . .57 C2

Putney High St
SW15 . . . . .58 A3

Putney Hill **12**
1 Putney SW15 . . .69 B4
Putney SW15 . . . . . .57 C2

Putney L Ctr SW15 . .57 B3

Putney Park Ave
SW15 . . . . .56 C3

Putney Park La
SW15 . . . . .57 A3

Putney Pier SW15 . . .58 A4

Putney School of Art
& Design SW15 . . . .58 A3

Putney Sta SW15 . . . .58 A3

PUTNEY VALE 68 C1

Putney Wharf Twr
SW15 . . . . .58 A4

Pykewell Lo **18** E8 . .16 C3

Pylon Trad Est
E16 . . . . .34 C4

Pymers Mead
SE21 . . . . .75 B3

Pynfolds SE16 . . . . . .40 A4

Pynnersmead
SE24 . . . . .63 B2

Pyrford Ho **12**
SW9 . . . . .63 A3

Pyrland Rd
Richmond TW10 . . . .54 B1
Stoke Newington
N5 . . . . .15 C3

Pyrmont Gr SE27 . . .75 A1

Pyrmont Rd W4 . . . . .44 C4

Pytchley Rd SE22 . . .64 A4

Q

Quadrangle Cl
SE1 . . . .**152** A4

Quadrangle The
Chelsea SW10 . . . .**167** A4
Fulham SW6 . . . . . .**154** A1
Herne Hill SE24 . . . .63 B2
3 North Kensington
W12 . . . . .30 B3
Paddington W2 . . . .**102** A2

Quadrant Arc W1 .**119** A3

Quadrant Bsns Ctr
NW6 . . . . .23 A4

Quadrant Gr NW5 . .12 B3

Quadrant The
4 Kensal Green
W10 . . . . .22 C2
Richmond TW9 . . . .54 A3

Quaker Ct EC1 . . . . .**97** A2

Quaker St
E1 . . . . .24 B1 **98** C1

Quality Ct WC2 . . . .**107** B2

Quantock Ho N16 . . .7 B3

Quantock Mews **3**
SE15 . . . . .49 C1

Quarrendon St
SW6 . . . .**165** C2

Quarry Rd SW18 . . . .59 B1

Quarterdeck The
E14 . . . . .41 C4

Quayside Ct **8**
SE16 . . . . .32 C1

Quebec & Crown
Wharves E1 . . . . .33 B3

Quebec Ind Est
SE16 . . . . .41 A3

Quebec Mews
W1 . . . .**103** A1

Quebec Wharf **17**
E8 . . . . .24 A4

Quedgeley Ct **3**
SE15 . . . . .49 B4

Queen Alexandra
Mans WC1 . . . . . .**94** A3

Queen Anne Mews
W1 . . . .**104** B3

Queen Anne Rd
E9 . . . . .17 C2

Queen Anne's Gate
SW1 . . . .**133** B3

Queen Anne's Gdns
Bedford Pk W4 . . . .38 A3
Ealing W5 . . . . .36 A4

Queen Anne's Gr
Bedford Pk W4 . . . .38 A3
Ealing W5 . . . . .36 A4

Queen Anne's Sq
SE1 . . . .**153** B4

Queen Anne St
W1 . . . .**104** A3

Queen Anne Terr **9**
E1 . . . . .32 A2

Queen Caroline St
W6 . . . . .39 B1

Queen Charlotte's &
Chelsea Hospl
W12 . . . . .29 C3

Queen Ct WC1 . . . .**94** B1

Queen Elizabeth Ct **5**
N1 . . . . .15 C2

Queen Elizabeth Hall
& Purcell Room
SE1 . . . .**121** A2

Queen Elizabeth II
Con Ctr SW1 . . . .**133** C3

Queen Elizabeth II
Jubilee Sch **5**
W9 . . . . .23 B1

Queen Elizabeth
Olympic Pk E15 . . .19 A3

Queen Elizabeth's Cl
N16 . . . . .6 C2

Queen Elizabeth's Coll
3 SE10 . . . . .52 B3

Queen Elizabeth St
SE1 . . . .**138** C4

Queen Elizabeth's Wlk
N16 . . . . .6 C2

Queen Elizabeth Wlk
SW13 . . . . .47 A2

Queen Isabella Wy
EC1 . . . .**108** C2

Queen Margaret Flats
22 E2 . . . . .25 A2

Queen Margarets Ct
N1 . . . . .16 A3

Queen Margaret's Gr
N1 . . . . .16 A3

Queen Mary's Gdns
NW1 . . . .**91** B3

Queen Mary's Univ
Hospl SW15 . . . . .56 C1

Queen Mary Univ of
London E1 . . . . . . .26 A1

Queen Mary, Univ of
London E1 . . . . . . .26 A1

Queen Mother Sp Ctr
SW1 . . . .**146** C4

Queen of Denmark Ct
SE16 . . . . .41 B3

Queen St PI EC4 . .**123** A4

Queensberry Mews W
SW7 . . . .**143** B4

Queensberry Pl
SW7 . . . .**143** B4

Queensberry Way
SW7 . . . .**143** B4

Queensborough Mews
W2 . . . .**114** C4

Queensborough Pas
W2 . . . .**114** C4

Queensborough Terr
W2 . . . .**114** B4

Queensbridge Ct **1**
E2 . . . . .24 B3

Queensbridge Inf Sch
11 E8 . . . . .16 B1

Queensbridge Rd
Dalston E8 . . . . . . .16 B1
Shoreditch E2, E8 . .24 B4

Queensbury St **22**
N1 . . . . .15 B1

Queen's CE Prim Sch
The TW9 . . . . .44 C3

Queen's Cir SW11 **160** A1

Queen's Club Gdns
W14 . . . .**154** B4

Queen's Club The
W14 . . . .**140** B1

Queen's Coll W1 . .**104** A3

Queen's Coll Prep Sch
W1 . . . .**104** A4

Queens Cres TW10 . .54 B3

Queen's Cres NW5 . .12 C2

Queens Ct
Battersea SW11 . .**170** A4
Camberwell SE5 . . .49 A1
4 Limehouse E14 . .33 B2
Richmond TW10 . . .54 B1

Queen's Ct
Barnes SW13 . . . . .56 C4
Kensington W2 . . .**114** B3
3 Richmond TW10 .54 B1
St John's Wood
NW8 . . . .**79** B2

Queensdale Cl W11 .30 C1

Queensdale Cres
W11 . . . . .30 C1

Queensdale Pl
W11 . . . . . .31 A1 **112** A1

Queensdale Rd
Notting Hill W11 . . .30 C1
Notting Hill
W11 . . . . . .31 A1 **112** A1

Queensdale Wlk
W11 . . . . . .31 A1 **112** A1

Queen's Dr N4 . . . . . .6 A2

Queen's Elm Par
SW3 . . . .**143** C2

Queen's Elm Sq
SW3 . . . .**143** C1

Queen's Gallery
SW1 . . . .**132** B3

Queen's Gate
SW7 . . . .**129** A1

Queensgate Gdns
SW15 . . . . .57 A3

Queen's Gate Gdns
SW7 . . . .**129** A1

Queensgate Ho **34**
E3 . . . . .26 B3

Queen's Gate Mews
SW7 . . . .**129** A2

Queen's Gate Pl **1**
NW6 . . . .**10** C1

Queen's Gate Pl
SW7 . . . .**129** A1

Queen's Gate Pl Mews
SW7 . . . .**129** A1

Queen's Gate Sch
SW7 . . . .**143** B4

Queen's Gate Terr
SW7 . . . .**129** A2

Queen's Gate Villas
E9 . . . . .18 A1

Queen's Gdns W2 .**114** C4

Queen's Gr NW8 . . . .**79** C3

Queen's Head Pas
EC2 . . . .**108** C2

Queen's Head St
N1 . . . .**86** B3

Queen's Head Yd
SE1 . . . .**123** B1

Queens Ho **1**
SE17 . . . . .48 C4

Queen's House The
SE10 . . . . .52 C4

Queensland Rd
N7 . . . . .14 C4

Queen's Manor Prim
Sch SW6 . . . . .47 C3

Queens Mans
NW6 . . . . .11 A3

Queen's Mans W6 . .39 C2

Queensmead NW8 . .**79** C4

Queensmere Ct
SW19 . . . . .69 C2

Queensmere Rd
SW19 . . . . .69 C2

Queens Mews
W2 . . . .**114** A4

Queensmill Rd
SW6 . . . . .47 C3

Queensmill Sch
1 East Acton
W12 . . . . .29 C1
London SW6 . . . . .**165** C1

Queensmill Sec Sch
W14 . . . .**141** A2

Queens Par **1** NW2 .9 B2

Queens Park Com Sch
NW6 . . . . .22 C4

Queen's Park **5**
W10 . . . . .22 C2

Queen's Park Prim
Sch **2** W10 . . . . .23 A1

Queen's Park Sta
NW6 . . . . .23 B3

Queen Sq **1** WC1 .**106** B4

Queen's Quay EC4 **123** A4

Queen's Ride
Mortlake SW14 . . . .55 B4
New Cross Gate SE14,
SE15 . . . . .51 B2
Richmond TW10 . . .54 B1

Queen's Ride
SW13 . . . . .57 A4

Queen's Rise
TW10 . . . . .54 B1

Queen's Road
Peckham Sta
SE15 . . . . .50 B2

Queen's Row SE17 . .48 C4

Queen St
City of London
EC4 . . . .**123** A4
Mayfair W1 . . . . . .**118** A2

Queens Terr NW8 . . .**79** B2

Queenstown Mews
SW8 . . . .**170** A3

Queenstown Rd
SW8 . . . .**160** A2

Queenstown Road
(Battersea) Sta
SW8 . . . .**170** B4

Queensville Rd SW12,
SW4 . . . . .73 C4

Queensway **2** W2 .**114** B4

Queensway Sta
W2 . . . .**114** B3

Queen's Wlk SW1 **118** C1

Queenswood Ct **1**
SW4 . . . . .62 A2

Queen Yd E9 . . . . . . .18 C2

Queen's Yd W1 . . . . .93 A1

Queen Victoria Meml
SW1 . . . .**132** C4

Queen Victoria St
EC4 . . . . **122** C4
Queen Victoria Terr
12 E1 . . . .**32** A2
Quelch Ho **2** N19 . .13 C3
Quemerford Rd
N7. . . . . .14 B3
Quendon Ho **9**
W10 . . . . .22 B1
Quenington Ct **5**
SE15 . . . . .49 B4
Quenington Mans
SW6 . . . . **164** C4
Quennel Ho **7**
SW12 . . . . .73 B4
Querrin St SW6. . **166** C1
Quested Ct **7** E8 . .17 A3
Quex Mews NW6 . .23 C4
Quex Rd NW6 . . . . .23 C4
Quick Rd W4 . . . . . .38 A1
Quick St N1 . . . . . . .86 B1
Quick Street Mews
N1. . . . . .86 A1
Quickswood NW3 . .12 A1
Quill La SW15 . . . . .57 C3
Quill St N4 . . . . .5 C1
Quill St SE1 . . . . . **136** C4
Quilter St
E2 . . . . .24 C2 **99** B4
Quilting Ct **23**
SE16 . . . . .40 C4
Quince Rd SE13 . . .52 A1
Quinn Cl **2** 25 B3
Quintin Ct W4 . . . . .45 B3
Quintin Kynaston Sch
NW8 . . . . .79 B3
Quintock Ho **2**
TW9 . . . . .44 C2
Quinton Ho SW8 . **162** A2
Quinton St SW18 . .71 B2
Quixley St **1** E14 . .34 C2
Quorn Rd SE22 . . . .64 A4

R

Rabbit Row
W8 . . . . .31 C1 **113** C2
Raby St E14 . . . . . . .33 A3
Racine **15** SE5 . . . . .49 A2
Racton Rd SW6 . . **155** B3
Radbourne Ct **15** . .17 C4
Radbourne Rd
SW12. . . . . .73 C3
Radcliff Bldg EC1. **107** B4
Radcliffe Ave
NW10. . . . . .21 C3
Radcliffe Coll
Marylebone W1 . . **104** C1
Soho W1 . . . . **105** B2
Radcliffe Ho **10**
SE16 . . . . .40 A2
Radcliffe Path **5**
SW8 . . . . **170** B1
Radcliffe Rd SE1 . **138** B2
Radcliffe Sq SW15 . .57 C1
Radcot St SE11 . . **149** C1
Raddington Rd
W10 . . . . .31 A4
Radford Ho
7 Bow Comm
E14. . . . . .34 A4
Islington N7 . . . . . . .14 B3
Radford Rd SE13 . .67 B1

Radipole Rd SW6 . **164** C4
Radland Rd E16 . . .35 C3
Radlett Pl NW8. . . . .80 A4
Radley Ct **23** SE16 . .40 C4
Radley Ho NW1 . . . .90 C2
Radley Lo **30** . . . .
Radley Mews W8 . **127** C1
Radley Terr **1**
E16. . . . . .35 B4
Radnor Ho W2. . . **101** C1
Radnor Mews W2 . **101** C1
Radnor Pl W2 . . . **102** A1
Radnor Rd
Kensal Rise NW6. . .23 A4
Peckham SE15 . . . . .49 C3
Radnor St EC1. . . . .97 A3
Radnor Wlk W14 . **140** C4
Radnor Way NW10 . .20 A1
Radnor Wlk
Chelsea SW3 . . . . **144** C1
21 Millwall E14 . . . .41 C2
Radstock St
SW11 . . . . **158** A1
Radway Ho **33** W2 . .31 C4
Radwell Ho SW2. . .62 C2
Raebarn Ct **8** . . . . .
SW16 . . . . .74 A1
Raeburn St SW2. . .62 A3
RAF Bomber
Command Memorial
SW1 . . . . **132** A4
Ragged School Mus
E3 . . . . .33 A4
Raglan Ct SW9. . . . .62 C4
Raglan St NW5 . . . .13 A2
Ragley Cl W3. . . . . . .37 B4
Rahere Ho EC1. . . . .96 C4
Railey Mews NW5 . .13 B3
Rail Sidings Rd
SE16 . . . . **139** C1
Railton Rd SE24 . . .63 A2
Railway App SE1 **123** C2
Railway Ave SE16 . .40 B4
Railway Cotts SW19 . .70 C1
Railway Gr SE14. . . .51 B3
Railway Rise SE22 . .64 A3
Railway Side
SW13 . . . . .56 A4
Railway St N1 . . . . .84 B1
Railway Terr SE13 . .67 A2
Rainbow Ave E14 . .42 A1
Rainbow Ct **3** . . . . . .
SE14 . . . . .51 A4
Rainbow Montessori
Sch NW6 . . . . .11 A1
Rainbow Quay
SE16 . . . . .41 A3
Rainbow Sch **5** . . . .
SW17 . . . . .71 B2
Rainbow St SE5 . . . .49 A3
Raines St N16 . . . . . .7 B2
Raine's Foundation
Lower Sch **2** E2 . . .25 A2
Raine's Foundation
Sch **24** E2 . . . . .25 B3
Raine St E1. . . . . . . .32 A1
Rainford Ho **9** N7 . . .5 B2
Rainham Cl SW11 . .60 A1
Rainham Ho NW1 . .83 A3
Rainham Rd NW10 . .22 C2
Rainsborough Ave
SE8 . . . . .41 A2
Rainsford Ct . . . .
NW10 . . . . .20 A3

Rainsford Ho **3** . . . .
SW2 . . . . .62 B2
Rainsford Rd
NW10 . . . . .20 A3
Rainsford St W2. . **102** A2
Rainton Rd SE7. . . . .43 C1
Rainville Rd W6 . . . .47 B4
Raleigh Ct
7 Hammersmith
W12 . . . . .39 A4
2 Rotherhithe
SE16 . . . . .32 C1
Raleigh Gdns SW2. .62 B1
Raleigh Ho . . . .
30 Clapham
SW8 . . . . **171** B2
Isle of Dogs E14. . . .42 A4
Raleigh Mews N1 . . .86 B3
Raleigh Rd TW9 . . . .54 B4
Raleigh St N1 . . . . . .86 B3
Ralph Ct **8** W2 . . . **100** B2
Ralston St SW3 . . **144** C1
Ramar Ho **12** E1. . **111** B4
Ramilles Cl SW2. . . .62 A1
Ramilles Ho W1 . . **105** A1
Ramilles Pl W1 . . **104** C1
Ramillies Rd W4 . . .37 C3
Ramillies St W1 . . **104** C1
Rampart St E1. . . . . .32 A3
Rampayne St
SW1 . . . . **147** B2
Ramsay Ho **10**
NW8 . . . . .80 A2
Ramsay Mews
SW3 . . . . **158** A4
Ramsay Rd W3 . . . . .37 B4
Ramsdean Ho **1** . . . .
SW15 . . . . .69 A3
Ramsden Rd
SW12 . . . . .72 C4
Ramsey Ct
Putney SW15 . . . . . .57 B1
6 Upper Holloway
N19. . . . . .4 C2
Ramsey Ho . . . .
5 Battersea
SW11 . . . . .59 C3
14 Kensington
SW9 . . . . **163** C1
Ramsey St
E2 . . . . .24 C1 **99** C2
Ramsey Wlk N1 . . . .15 C2
Ramsfort Ho **4** . . . . .
SE16 . . . . .40 A2
Ramsgate St E8 . . . .16 B2
Ram St SW18. . . . . .59 A2
Randal Cremer Prim
Sch **15** E2 . . . . .24 B3
Randall Cl SW11 . **168** A4
Randall Pl SE10 . . .52 B3
Randall Rd SE11 . **148** C3
Randall Row SE11 **148** C3
Randell's Rd N1. . . .84 B4
Randolf St
Paddington NW6 . . .78 A1
St John's Wood
NW8 . . . . .78 C3
Randolph Ave W9. .88 C3
Randolph Cres W9 **88** C2
Randolph Gdns
NW6 . . . . .78 A1
Randolph Mews
W9 . . . . .89 A1
Randolph Rd W9 . .89 A1
Randolph St NW1 . .13 B1
Ranelagh Ave . . . . . .
Barnes SW13 . . . . . .46 C1

Ranelagh Ave continued
Fulham SW6. . . . . . .58 B4
Ranelagh Gardens
Mans SW6 . . . . .58 A4
Ranelagh Gardens
(site of Chelsea
Flower Show)
SW1 . . . . **145** C2
Ranelagh Gdns
3 Bedford Pk
W6 . . . . .38 B3
Chiswick W4 . . . . . .45 B3
Fulham SW6. . . . . . .58 B4
Ranelagh Gr SW1 **145** C2
Ranelagh Ho SW3 **144** C2
Ranelagh Mans
SW6 . . . . **165** A2
Ranelagh Rd
Dagenham NW10 . . .21 B3
Pimlico SW1 . . . . . **147** A1
Rangdon St E3 . . . . .27 A2
Ranger's House (The
Wernher Collection)
SE10 . . . . .52 C2
Rangoon Ho **5** . . . . .
N16. . . . . .15 C4
Rankine Ho SE1 . . **136** C1
Ranmere St SW12 . .73 A3
Rann Ho **1** SW14 . . .55 C4
Rannoch Rd W6 . . . .47 C4
Ransomes Dock Bsns
Ctr SW11 . . . . **158** B1
Ransomes Mews
SW11 . . . . **158** B2
Ranston St NW1. . **102** A4
Ranulf Rd NW2 . . . . .10 B4
Ranwell Cl **18** E3 . .26 B4
Ranwell Ho **8** E3 . .26 B4
Raphael Ct **2** . . . . . .
SE16 . . . . .40 A1
Raphael St SW7 . . **130** C3
Rapley Ho **8** . . . .
E2. . . . . .24 C2 **99** B3
Rashleigh Ct **8** . . . . .
SW8 . . . . .61 A4
Rashleigh Ho WC1. **94** A3
Rastell Ave SW12. . .73 C3
RATCLIFF . . . .
E1 . . . . .32 C3
Ratcliffe Cross St
E1 . . . . .33 A3
Ratcliffe Ho **10** . . . . .
E14 . . . . .33 A3
Ratcliffe La **16** . . . . . .
E14 . . . . .33 A3
Ratcliffe Orch **9** . . . .
E1 . . . . .32 C2
Rathbone Ho . . . .
5 Canning Town
E16 . . . . .35 B3
Kilburn NW6 . . . . . . .23 C4
Rathbone Mkt **2** . . . .
E16 . . . . .35 B4
Rathbone Pl W1. . **105** B2
Rathbone St . . . .
Canning Town
E16 . . . . .35 B3
Fitzrovia W1. . . . . **105** A3
Rathgar Rd SW9. . . .63 A4
Rathmell Dr SW4 . .61 C1
Rattray Rd SW2. . . .62 C2
Raul Rd SE15 . . . . . .49 C2
Raveley St NW5 . . . .13 B4
Ravenet St
Battersea SW11. . . **170** A3
Clapham SW4. . . . . .61 A2

Ravenet St SW11 . **170** A3
Ravenfield Rd
SW17 . . . . .72 B1
Raven Ho **10** SE16 . .40 C2
Ravenna Rd SW15 . .57 C2
Raven Row E1. . . . . .32 A4
Ravensbourne . . . . . .
SE10 . . . . .43 A4
Ravensbourne Ho . . .
9 SE8 . . . . .51 C4
Ravensbourne Mans
9 SE8 . . . . .51 C4
Ravensbourne Pl **2**
SE13 . . . . .52 A1
Ravensbury Rd
SW18 . . . . .71 A2
Ravensbury Terr
SW18 . . . . .71 A2
Ravenscar NW1 . . **82** C3
Ravenscourt **1** . . . . .
N16. . . . . .7 C1
Ravenscourt Ave
W6 . . . . .38 C2
Ravenscourt Gdns
W6 . . . . .38 C2
Ravenscourt Ho **13** . .
W6 . . . . .38 C2
Ravenscourt Park
W6 . . . . .39 A3
Ravenscourt Park
Prep Sch W6. . . . . .38 C2
Ravenscourt Park Sta
W6 . . . . .38 C2
Ravenscourt Pk
W6 . . . . .38 C2
Ravenscourt Pl
W6 . . . . .39 A2
Ravenscourt Rd
W6 . . . . .39 A2
Ravenscourt Sq
W6 . . . . .38 C3
Ravenscourt Theatre
Sch **13** W6 . . . . .39 A2
Ravenscroft Ave
NW11 . . . . .1 B4
Ravenscroft Cl **4** . . . .
E16 . . . . .35 C4
Ravenscroft Ct
NW11 . . . . .1 B4
Ravenscroft Point **20**
E9 . . . . .17 C2
Ravenscroft Rd . . . . .
Acton W4 . . . . .37 B2
Newham E16 . . . . . . .35 C4
Ravenscroft St
E2. . . . . .24 B2 **99** A4
Ravensdon St
SE11 . . . . **149** C1
Ravenshaw St
NW6 . . . . .10 B3
Ravenslea Rd SW11,
SW12 . . . . .72 B4
Ravensmede Way
W4 . . . . .38 B2
Ravenstone SE17 . **152** B1
Ravenstone Prim Sch
SW12 . . . . .72 C2
Ravenstone St
SW12 . . . . .72 C3
Ravenswood Rd
SW12 . . . . .73 A4
Ravensworth Ct
SW6 . . . . **155** B1
Ravensworth Rd
NW10 . . . . .22 A2
Raven Wharf SE1 **138** C4

Ravey St
EC2 . . . . .24 A1 98 A4
Rav Pinter Cl N16 . . . .7 A4
Rawlings St SW3 . . . . 144 C4
Rawlinson Ho
SE13 . . . . .67 C3
Rawlinson Point 8
E16 . . . . .35 B4
Rawreth Wlk N1 . . . . . .87 A4
Rawson Ct SW11 . . . . 169 C3
Rawson St SW11 . . . . 170 A3
Rawstone Pl EC1 . . . . . .96 A4
Rawstorne St EC1 . . . . .96 A4
Rayburne Ct W14 . . . . 126 A2
Raydon St N19 . . . . .4 A2

Ray Ho
7 North Kensington
W10 . . . . .30 C3
Shoreditch N1 . . . . 87 C3
Raymede Twr 2
W10 . . . . .30 C4
Raymond Bldgs
WC1 . . . . 107 A4
Raymouth Rd
SE16 . . . . .40 A2
Raynald Ho 3
SW16 . . . . .74 A1
Rayne Ct SE1 . . . . 138 C4
Rayne Ho
1 Balham SW12 . . . .60 C1
Paddington W9 . . . . .88 A2
Rayner Ct 10 W12 . . . .39 B4
Rayner's Rd SW15 . . . .58 A2
Raynes Ct NW2 . . . . . . .10 A4
Raynham W2 . . . . 102 A2
Raynham Ho 1
E1 . . . . .25 C1
Raynham Rd W6 . . . . . .39 A2
Raynor Pl
2 Canonbury N1 . . .15 B1
N1 . . . . .87 A4
Ray St EC1 . . . . .95 C1
Ray Wlk N7 . . . . .5 B2
Reachview Cl 17
NW1 . . . . .13 B1
Reade Ct 6 W3 . . . . . .37 B3
Reade Wlk 5
NW10 . . . . .8 A1
Read Ho 4 SE11 . . . . 163 B4
Reading Ho
Paddington W2 . . . . 100 C1
Peckham SE15 . . . . . .49 C4
Reading La E8 . . . . .17 A2
Reapers Cl NW1 . . . . . .83 A4
Reardon Ho 5 . . . .32 A1
Reardon Path 31
E1 . . . . .32 A1
Reardon St E1 . . . . . . .32 A1
Reaston St SE14 . . . . . .50 C3
Reay Prim Sch
SW9 . . . . 163 A1
Reckitt Rd W4 . . . . .38 A1
Record St SE16 . . . . . . .50 B4
Rector St N1 . . . . 86 C3
Rectory Gdns 6
SW4 . . . . .61 B4
Rectory Gr SW4 . . . . . .61 B4
Rectory Rd
Barnes SW13 . . . . . . .46 C1
1 London SW3 . . . .28 B1
Shacklewell N16 . . . . .7 B1
N16 . . . . .7 B1
Rectory Sq E1 . . . . . . .32 C4
Reculver Ho 2
SE15 . . . . .50 B4

Reculver Rd SE16 . . . .40 C1
Red Anchor Cl
SW3 . . . . 158 A3
Redan Pl W2 . . . . 100 A1
Redan St W14 . . . . .39 C3
Redan Terr SE5 . . . . . . .48 A1
Redbourne Ho 7
E14 . . . . .33 B3
Redbourn Ho 10
W10 . . . . .22 B1
Redbridge Gdns
SE5 . . . . .49 A3
Redburn St SW3 . . . . 158 C4
Redcar St SE5 . . . . .48 B3
Redcastle Cl E1 . . . . . .32 B2
Redchurch St
E2 . . . . .24 B1 98 C2
Redcliffe Cl 5 SW5 . . 142 A1
Redcliffe Gdns
Fulham SW10 . . . . . 141 B1
Fulham SW10 . . . . . 156 B4
Redcliffe Mews
SW10 . . . . 142 B1
Redcliffe Pl SW10 . . . 156 C3
Redcliffe Rd
SW10 . . . . 157 A4
Redcliffe Sch
SW10 . . . . 156 C4
Redcliffe Sq
SW10 . . . . 142 B1
Redcliffe St SW10 . . . 156 B4
Redclyf Ho 13 E1 . . . .25 B1
Redcroft 5 NW6 . . . . .10 C2
Red Cross Cotts
SE1 . . . . 137 A4
Redcross Way
SE1 . . . . 123 A1
Reddins Rd SE15 . . . . . .49 C4
Rede Pl
W2 . . . . .31 C2 113 C4
Redesdale St
SW3 . . . . 158 C4
Redfern Rd NW10 . . . . .8 A1
Redfield La SW5 . . . . . 142 A4
Redfield Mews
SW5 . . . . 141 C4
Redfiff Est SE16 . . . . . .41 B3
Redford Wlk N1 . . . . . .86 C4
Redgate Terr
SW15 . . . . .57 C1
Redgrave Rd
SW15 . . . . .57 C4
Redhill Ct SW2 . . . . . . .74 C2
Redhill St NW1 . . . . . . .92 B4
Red House Sq 20
N1 . . . . .15 B1
Redington Gdns
NW3 . . . . .11 A4
Redington Ho N1 . . . . .85 A2
Redington Rd
NW3 . . . . .11 A4
Redlands Prim Sch 38
E1 . . . . .32 B4
Redlands Way
SW2 . . . . .74 B4
Red Lion Cl 9
SE17 . . . . .48 C4
Red Lion Ct EC4 . . . . 107 C1
Red Lion Row
SE17 . . . . .48 B4
Red Lion Sq WC1 . . . 106 C3
Red Lion St WC1 . . . . 106 C3
Red Lion Yd W1 . . . . . 117 C2
Redlynch Ct W14 . . . . 126 B3
Redlynch Ho 27
SW9 . . . . 173 C4

Redman Bldg EC1 107 B4
Redman Ho SE1 . . . . 137 A3
Redman's Rd E1 . . . . . .32 B4
Redmayne Ho 18
SW9 . . . . 173 A2
Redmead La E1 . . . . . 125 B1
Redmill Ho 22 E1 . . . . .25 A1
Redmond Ho N1 . . . . . 85 A3
Redmore Rd W6 . . . . . .39 A2
Red Pl W1 . . . . 117 B4
Red Post Hill SE21,
SE24 . . . . .63 C2
Redriff Prim Sch
SE16 . . . . .41 A4
Redriff Rd SE16 . . . . . .41 A3
Red Rover SW13 . . . . . .56 C4
Redrup Ho 21
SE14 . . . . .50 C4
Redruth Rd E9 . . . . .25 B4
Red Sq The N16 . . . . . . .6 C1
Redstart Cl SE14 . . . . . .51 A3
Redvers St
E2 . . . . .24 A2 98 B4
Redwald Rd E5 . . . . . . .17 C4
Redwing Ct SE1 . . . . . .48 B4
Redwood Cl
4 Bow E3 . . . . .26 C3
Rotherhithe SE16 . . . .33 A1
Redwood Ct
Brondesbury
NW6 . . . . .10 A1
Crouch End N19 . . . . .4 C4
Redwood Mews 2
SW4 . . . . .61 A4
Redwoods SW15 . . . . . .68 C3
Reece Mews SW7 . . . 143 B4
Reed Cl E16 . . . . .35 C4
Reedham St SE15 . . . . .64 C4
Reed Ho SW15 . . . . . . .56 C1
Reedholm Villas
N16 . . . . .15 C4
Reed Pl
Battersea SW11 . . . . .60 A3
Clapham SW4 . . . . . .61 C3
Reed's Pl NW1 . . . . . . .13 B1
Reedworth St
SE11 . . . . 149 C3
Reef Ho E14 . . . . .42 B3
Rees St N1 . . . . 87 A3
Reeves Ho
Lambeth SE1 . . . . . . 135 B3
Mayfair W1 . . . . 117 B3
Reeves Mews W1 117 C3
Reeves Rd E3 . . . . .27 A1
Reflection Ho 9
E2 . . . . .24 C1 99 B2
Reform St SW11 . . . . 169 A2
Regal Cl E1 . . . . . .111 C4
Regal La NW1 . . . . 81 C3
Regal Pl
6 Tower Hamlets
E3 . . . . .26 B2
Walham Green
SW6 . . . . 156 B1
Regan Way N1 . . . . . . .24 A3
Regatta Point
TW8 . . . . .44 B4
Regency Ct
9 Bow E3 . . . . .26 B3
4 South Hackney
E9 . . . . .25 B4
Regency Ho NW1 . . . . 92 B2
Regency Lo NW3 . . . . .11 C1
Regency Mews
Camberwell SW9 . . . . .48 A3
1 Willesden NW10 . . .8 C2
Regency Pl SW1 . . . . 147 C4

Regency St SW1 . . . . 147 C2
Regency Terr
SW7 . . . . 143 B2
Regency Wlk 8
TW10 . . . . .54 A2
Regeneration Rd
SE16 . . . . .40 C2
Regent Ct
Lisson Gr NW8 . . . . . 90 A3
1 Stamford Hill N16 . .7 B4
Regent High Sch
NW1 . . . . .83 B2
Regent Ho W14 . . . . . 140 A4
Regent Pl W1 . . . . 119 A4
Regent Rd SE24 . . . . . .63 A2
Regents Bridge Gdns
SW8 . . . . 162 B2
Regents Canal Ho 6
E14 . . . . .33 A3
Regents Ct E8 . . . . . . .24 C4
Regents Gate Ho 20
E14 . . . . .33 A2
Regents Lo 9
SW2 . . . . .74 B3
Regents Mews
NW8 . . . . 79 A2
REGENT'S PARK 92 A4
Regent's Park
NW1 . . . . 81 B1
Regent's Park
Barracks NW1 . . . . . .82 C2
Camden Town
NW1 . . . . .82 C4
Primrose Hill NW3 . . 12 C1
Regent's Park Sta
NW1 . . . . 92 A1
Regent's Park Terr
NW1 . . . . 82 A4
Regent's Pl SE3 . . . . . .53 C1
Regents Plaza 2
NW6 . . . . 78 A2
Regent Sq
2 Bromley E3 . . . . .27 A2
St Pancras WC1 . . . . 94 B3
Regent's Row E8 . . . . .24 C4
Regent St
Brentford W4 . . . . . . .36 C1
7 Kensal Green
NW10 . . . . .22 C2
Mayfair W1 . . . . 118 C4
Regent's University
London NW1 . . . . . . 91 B3
Regents Wharf
3 Hackney E2 . . . . .25 A4
Islington N1 . . . . 84 C2
Reginald Pl 6
SE8 . . . . .51 C3
Reginald Rd SE8 . . . . . .51 C3
Reginald Sq SE8 . . . . . .51 C3
Regina Point SE16 . . . .40 B3
Regina Rd N4 . . . . .5 B3
Regis Ct NW1 . . . . 102 C4
Regis Rd NW5 . . . . .13 A3
Regnart Bldgs
NW1 . . . . 93 A3
Reid Ct SW14 . . . . .45 B1
Reighton Rd E5 . . . . . . .7 C2
Reizel Cl N16 . . . . .7 B3
Relay Rd W12 . . . . .30 B1
Relf Rd SE15 . . . . .64 C4
Reliance Sq
E2 . . . . .24 A1 98 B2
Relton Ct W3 . . . . .36 C4

Relton Mews
SW7 . . . . 130 B2
Rembrandt Cl E14 . . . . .42 C1
Rembrandt Ct 10
SE16 . . . . .40 A1
Rembrant Cl SW1 . . . 145 B3
Remington St N1 . . . . . 86 B1
Remnant St WC2 . . . . 106 C2
Remsted Ho 9
NW6 . . . . 78 A3
Remus Rd E3 . . . . .18 C1
Renaissance Wlk 4
SE10 . . . . .43 B3
Renbold Ho 5
SE10 . . . . .52 B2
Rendlesham Ho 3 E5,
N16 . . . . .7 C2
Rendlesham Rd E5 . . . .7 C1
Renforth St SE16 . . . . .40 B4
Renfrew Ho NW6 . . . . 78 A1
Renfrew Rd SE11 . . . . 150 A3
Rennell Ho 18 E9 . . . . .17 C2
Rennell St SE13 . . . . . .67 B4
Rennie Cotts 29
E1 . . . . .25 B1
Rennie Ct SE1 . . . . . . 122 A2
Rennie Ho SE1 . . . . . 136 C1
Rennie St SE1 . . . . . . 122 A2
Renoir Ct 7 SE16 . . . .40 A1
Renton Cl SW2 . . . . . . .62 B1
Rephidim St SE1 . . . . 138 A1
Replingham Rd
SW18 . . . . .70 C3
Reporton Rd SW6 154 B1
Repton Ho SW1 . . . . 147 A3
Repton St E14 . . . . .33 A3
Reservoir Rd SE4 . . . . .51 A1
Reservoir Studios 10
E1 . . . . .32 C3
Resolution Way 4
SE8 . . . . .51 C3
Restell Cl SE3 . . . . .53 A4
Reston Pl SW7 . . . . . . 128 C3
Restoration Sq
SW11 . . . . 167 C3
Retcar Pl N19 . . . . .4 A2
Retford St E2 . . . . .24 A3
Retreat Ho 5 E9 . . . . .17 B2
Retreat Pl E9 . . . . .17 B2
Retreat The SW14 . . . . .56 A4
Reunion Row E1 . . . . . .32 A2
Reveley Sq SE16 . . . . . .41 A4
Revelon Rd SE4 . . . . . .66 A4
Revelstoke Rd SW18,
SW19 . . . . .70 C2
Reverdy Rd SE1 . . . . . 153 B3
Rewell St SW6 . . . . . . 156 C1
Rex Pl W1 . . . . 117 C2
Reynard Cl SE4 . . . . . .66 A4
Reynard Pl SE14 . . . . . .51 A4
Reynolds Cl NW11 . . . . .2 A4
Reynolds Ho
Finsbury Pk N4 . . . . . .5 A3
18 South Hackney
E2 . . . . .25 B3
St John's Wood
NW8 . . . . 79 C1
Westminster SW1 . . . 147 C3
Reynolds Pl 12
TW10 . . . . .54 B1
Reynolds Rd
Acton Green W4 . . . .37 B3
Nunhead SE15 . . . . . .65 B3

Reynolds Sp Ctr
W3 ....36 C4
Rffra Rd Ret Pk
SW2 ....62 C2
Rheidol Mews N1 ......86 C3
Rheidol Terr N1 ....86 C3
Rhizotron & Xstrata
Treetop Walkway
TW9 ....44 A2
Rhoda Ct E2 ..24 B1 99 A2
Rhodes Ho
Shepherd's Bush
W12 ....30 A1
Shoreditch N1 ....97 B4
Rhodesia Rd SW9 .....172 B1
Rhodes St N7 ....14 B3
Rhodeswell Rd
E14 ....33 B3
Rhondda Gr E3 ....26 B2
Rhyl Prim Sch 21
NW5 ....12 C2
Rhyl St NW5 ....12 C2
Ribblesdale Ho 11
NW6 ....23 C4
Ribbon Dance Mews
SE5 ....48 C2
Ribstone Ho 10 SE22 .64 C2
Ricardo St E14 ....34 A3
Riceyman Ho WC1 .....95 B3
Richard Anderson Ct
1 SE14 ....50 C3
Richard Atkins Prim
Sch 20 SW2 ....74 A4
Richard Burbidge
Mans SW13 ....47 B4
Richard Cloudesley
Sch
Shoreditch N1 ....86 C3
St Luke's EC1 ....97 A1
Richard Cloudesley
Sch (Prim Dept)
EC1 ....97 A1
Richard Cobden Prim
Sch NW1 ....83 A3
Richard Fox Ho N4 .....6 B1
Richard Ho 10
SE16 ....40 B2
Richard Knight Ho
SW6 ....165 C4
Richard Neale Ho 2
E1 ....32 A2
Richardson Cl 19
E8 ....24 B4
Richardson Ct 20
SW4 ....172 B2
Richardson Ho 10
E14 ....33 C4
Richardson's Mews
W1 ....92 C1
Richard's Pl SW3 ......144 B4
Richard St 20 E1 ....32 A3
Richbell WC1 ....106 B4
Richbell Pl WC1 ....106 C4
Richborne Terr
SW8 ....163 A2
Richborough Ho
10 Deptford SE15 .....50 B4
14 Hackney E5 ....17 A4
Richborough Rd
NW2 ....10 A4
Richbourne Ct
W1 ....102 B2
Richford Gate W6 ......39 B3
Richford St W6 ....39 B3

Rich Ind Est SE15 ......50 A4
Rich La SW5 ....142 A2
Richland Ho 4
SE15 ....49 C2
Richman Ho 10
SE8 ....41 B1
Rich Mix E1 ....99 A2
RICHMOND 54 B3
Richmond Ave
Islington N1 ....85 A4
Willesden NW10 ....9 B2
Richmond Bldgs
W1 ....105 B1
Richmond Circus
TW9 ....54 A3
Richmond Cres N1 ....85 B4
Richmond Ct
SW1 ....131 A3
Richmond Gr N1 ....15 A1
Richmond Healthcare
Hamlet Hospl
TW9 ....54 A4
RICHMOND HILL 54 A1
Richmond Hill
TW10 ....54 A1
Richmond Hill Ct 5
TW10 ....54 A1
Richmond Ho
7 Forest Hill
SE26 ....76 C1
Regent's Pk NW1 ....82 B1
Walworth SE17 ....151 B2
Richmond
International Bsns
Ctr 9 TW9 ....54 B3
Richmond Mans
Earl's Ct SW5 ....142 A2
Putney SW15 ....58 A4
Richmond Mews
W1 ....105 B1
Richmond Park Acad
SW14 ....56 A3
Richmond Park Rd
SW14 ....55 C3
Richmond Rd
Dalston E8 ....16 C1
Ealing W5 ....36 A4
Richmond Sta
TW9 ....54 A3
Richmond Terr
SW1 ....134 A4
Richmond Univ
Kensington W8 ....128 B2
Kensington W8 ....128 B3
Richmond Way W12,
W14 ....39 C4
Rich St E14 ....33 B2
Rickard Cl SW2 ....74 C3
Rickett St SW6 ....155 C4
Rickman Ho 22 E1 .....25 B1
Rickman St 8 E1 ....25 B1
Rick Roberts Way
E15 ....27 C3
Rickthorne Rd 7
N19 ....5 A2
Riddell Ct SE1 ....152 C2
Ridgdale St E3 ....27 A3
Ridge Hill NW11 ....1 A3
Ridge Rd NW2 ....1 B1
Ridgeway 11
TW10 ....54 A1
Ridgeway Dr W3 ....36 C3
Ridgeway Gdns N6 .....4 B4
Ridgeway The
Acton W3 ....36 C3
Golders Green NW11 ...1 B3

Ridgewell Cl N1 ......87 A4
Ridgmount Gdns
WC1 ....105 B4
Ridgmount Pl
WC1 ....105 B4
Ridgmount Rd
SW18 ....59 A2
Ridgmount St
WC1 ....105 B4
Ridgway Rd SW9 ......63 A4
Riding House St
W1 ....104 C3
Ridings Cl N6 ....4 B4
Riding The NW11 ....1 B4
Ridley Ho 14
SW11 ....60 A4
Ridley Rd
Dalston E8 ....16 B3
Willesden Green
NW10 ....21 C3
Riffel Rd NW2 ....9 B3
Riffle Rd SE11 ....163 C4
Riffle Way W11 ....30 C1
Riffle St E14 ....34 A4
Rigault Rd SW6 ....164 B1
Rigden St E14 ....34 A3
Rigeley Rd NW10 ......21 C2
Rigge Pl SW4 ....61 C3
Rigg Ho 2 SW4 ....74 A4
Rignold Ho 6 SE5 .....49 A1
Riley Ho
3 Bow E3 ....26 C1
Chelsea SW10 ....157 B3
1 Streatham SW4 ......73 C4
Riley Rd SE1 ....138 C2
Riley St SW10 ....157 B2
Rill Ho 18 SE5 ....49 A3
Rimini Ct SW12 ....72 B3
Rinaldo Rd SW12 ......73 A4
Ringcroft St N7 ....14 C3
Ringford Ho SW18 .....58 B2
Ringford Rd SW18 .....58 C1
Ring Ho 11 E1 ....32 B2
Ringmer Ave SW6 ....164 B3
Ringmer Gdns 3
N19 ....5 A2
Ringmer Ho 18
SE22 ....64 A4
Ring Rd W12 ....30 B1
Ringsfield Ho
SE17 ....151 A1
Ringwood Gdns
17 Millwall E14 ....41 C2
14 Roehampton SW15 .68 C3
Ripley Gdns SW14 ....55 C4
Ripley Ho
Mortlake SW14 ....56 A4
Nine Elms SW11 ....160 C4
Ripley's Believe It or
Not! SW1 ....119 B3
Riplington Ct
SW15 ....69 A4
Ripplevale Gr N1 ......14 B1
Risborough SE17 ......150 C4
Risborough Ho
NW8 ....90 B2
Risborough St
SE1 ....136 B4
Risdon Ho 38 SE16 ...40 B4
Risdon St 27 SE16 .....40 B4
Riseholme Ct E9 ....18 B2
Riseholme Ho 14
SE22 ....64 A4

Riseldine Rd SE23 ...66 A1
Risinghill St N1 ....85 B2
Rising Sun Ct EC1 ...108 B3
Risley Ho 7 E9 ....17 C2
Risley Rd SW8 ....162 C2
Ritchie Ho
Crouch End N19 ....4 C4
6 Rotherhithe
SE16 ....40 B3
12 South Bromley
E14 ....34 C3
Ritchie St N1 ....85 C2
Ritherdon Rd
SW17 ....73 A2
Ritson Ho N1 ....84 C3
Ritson Rd E8 ....16 C2
Rivaz Pl E9 ....17 B2
Riven Ct 10 W2 ....100 B1
Riverains The
SW11 ....167 B3
River Barge Cl
E14 ....42 B4
Rivercourt Rd W6 .....39 A1
River Ct SE1 ....122 A3
Riverdale Dr
SW18 ....71 A3
Riverfleet WC1 ....94 B4
Riverford Ho 28
W2 ....31 C4
River Ho SW13 ....46 A1
River House
Montessori Sch
E14 ....42 A4
Rivermead Ct SW6 ...58 B4
Rivermead Ho E9 ......18 A3
River Plate Ho
EC2 ....109 C3
River Reach Bsns Pk
SW6 ....59 A4
River St Mews EC1 ...95 B4
Riversdale Prim Sch
SW18 ....70 C3
Riversdene Rd N5 ......6 B1
Rivers Ho 10 TW8 .....36 C1
Riverside
Battersea SW11 ....158 B2
6 Rotherhithe
SE16 ....40 B4
St Pancras WC1 ....94 B4
Riverside Bsns Ctr
SW18 ....71 A3
Riverside Ct SW8 ....161 C4
Riverside Dr W4 ....46 A2
Riverside Gdns
W6 ....39 A1
Riverside Health &
Racquets Club
Chiswick TW
W4 ....46 A2
Riverside Ho 14
N1 ....15 B1
Riverside Mans 4
E1 ....32 B1
Riverside Prim Sch 17
SE16 ....139 C3
Riverside Rd
Mill Meads E15 ....27 C2
Wandsworth SW17,
SW19 ....71 B1
Riverside Wlk Mkt
WC2 ....121 A2
Riverside Workshops
SE1 ....123 A2
River St EC1 ....95 B4

River Terr
London W6 ....39 B1
St James SW1 ....120 C3
Riverton Cl W9 ....23 B2
Riverview Gdns
SW13 ....47 A4
Riverview Gr W4 ....45 A4
Riverview Rd W4 ....45 A4
River Way SE10 ....43 B3
Rivington Ct
NW10 ....21 C4
Rivington Pl
EC2 ....24 A2 98 B3
Rivington St
EC2 ....24 A2 98 B3
Rivington Wlk 4
E8 ....24 C4
Rixon St N7 ....5 C1
Roach Rd E3 ....18 C1
Roads Pl N19 ....5 A2
Roan St SE10 ....52 B4
Robert Adam St
W1 ....103 B2
Roberta St
E2 ....24 A2 99 C3
Robert Bell Ho 2
SE16 ....153 B4
Robert Blair Prim Sch
N7 ....14 A2
Robert Browning Prim
Sch SE17 ....151 B3
Robert Cl W9 ....89 A1
Robert Dashwood
Way SE17 ....150 C3
Robert Gentry Ho
W14 ....140 B1
Robert Jones Ho 3
SE16 ....153 B4
Robert Keen Cl 18
SE15 ....49 C2
Robert Lowe Cl
SE14 ....50 C3
Robert Owen Ho
Fulham SW6 ....47 C2
8 Spitalfields
E2 ....24 B2 99 A4
Robert Owen Lo 4
E5 ....17 A4
Roberts Ct
Islington N1 ....86 B3
Willesden NW10 ....8 A2
Roberts Ho 5
SE27 ....75 A1
Roberts Mews
SW1 ....131 B1
Robertson Ho 11
SE10 ....52 B2
Robertson St
SW8 ....170 B1
Robert's Pl EC1 ....95 C2
Robert St
Regent's Pk NW1 ....92 B3
Strand WC2 ....120 B3
Robert Sutton Ho 20
E1 ....32 B3
Robeson St 3 E3 ....33 B4
Robin Ct 15 E14 ....42 B3
Robin Gr
Dartmouth Pk N6 ....3 C2
Highgate N6 ....3 C2
Robin Ho NW8 ....80 A1
Robin Hood SW15 .....68 A1
Robin Hood Gdns 12
E14 ....34 B2

Robin Hood La
E14 . . . . .34 B2
Robinscroft Mews 10
SE10 . . . . .52 A2
Robins Ct TW10 . . . . .54 A1
Robin's Ct SW4 . . . . . .62 A1
Robinsfield Inf Sch
NW8 . . . . .80 A2
Robinson Ct
Islington N1 . . . . .86 B4
4 Richmond TW9 . . . .54 B3
Robinson Ho
2 North Kensington
W10 . . . . .30 C3
12 Tower Hamlets
E14 . . . . .33 B3
Robinson Rd E2 . . . . .25 B3
Robinson St SW3 . . . .158 C4
Robinson Wy 8
SE14 . . . . .50 C4
Robinswood Mews 6
N5 . . . . .15 A3
Robsart St SW9 . . . . .173 B2
Robson Ave NW10 . . . .8 C1
Robson Rd SE21,
SE27 . . . . .75 B1
Roby Ho EC1 . . . . .96 C2
Rochdale Way 4
SE8 . . . . .51 C3
Roche Ho 12 E14 . . . . .33 B2
Rochelle Cl SW11 . . . .59 C3
Rochelle Ct 11 E1 . . . .32 B3
Rochelle St 11
E2 . . . . .24 B2 98 C3
Rochemont Wlk 2
E8 . . . . .24 C4
Roche Sch The 15
SW18 . . . . .58 C2
Rochester Ct
1 Bethnal Green
E2 . . . . .25 A1
3 Camden Town
NW1 . . . . .13 B1
Rochester Ho
Bermondsey SE1 . . .137 C3
18 Deptford SE15 . . . .50 B4
Rochester Mews
NW1 . . . . .13 B1
Rochester Pl NW1 . . .13 B1
Rochester Rd
NW1 . . . . .13 B2
Rochester Row
SW1 . . . . .147 A4
Rochester Sq NW1 . .13 B1
Rochester St
SW1 . . . . .133 B1
Rochester Terr
NW1 . . . . .13 B2
Rochester Wlk
SE1 . . . . .123 B2
Rochford Wlk 8
E8 . . . . .16 C1
Rochfort Ho 4
SE8 . . . . .41 B1
Rock Ave SW14 . . . . . .55 C4
Rockell's Pl SE22 . . . .65 A1
Rockfield Ho SE10 . . .52 B4
Rock Grove Way
SE16 . . . . .153 C4
Rockhall Rd NW2 . . . . .9 C4
Rockingham Cl
SW15 . . . . .56 B3
Rockingham St
SE1 . . . . .136 C1
Rockland Rd
SW15 . . . . .58 A3

Rockley Ct 9
W14 . . . . .39 C4
Rockley Rd W14 . . . . .39 C4
Rocks La SW13 . . . . . .56 C4
Rock St N4 . . . . .5 C2
Rockstraw Ho 5
NW3 . . . . .12 B1
Rockwood Ct N16 . . . .7 C4
Rocliffe St N1 . . . . . . .86 B1
Rocque Ho SW6 . . . .154 C2
Rodborough Rd
NW11 . . . . .1 C3
Rodenhurst Ct
SW4 . . . . .61 C2
Rodenhurst Rd
SW4 . . . . .61 C1
Roden St N7 . . . . .5 B1
Roderick Ho 3
SE16 . . . . .40 B2
Roderick Rd NW3 . . . .12 B4
Rodgers Ho 4
SW4 . . . . .73 C4
Rodin Ct N1 . . . . .86 A3
Roding Ct 6 W12 . . . .38 A4
Roding Ho N1 . . . . . . .85 B3
Roding Mews E1 . . . .125 C2
Roding Rd E5 . . . . . . .18 A3
Rodmarton St W1 . . .103 A3
Rodmell WC1 . . . . . . .94 B3
Rodmere St SE10 . . . .43 A1
Rodmill La 10
SW2 . . . . .74 A4
Rodney Ct NW8 . . . . .89 A2
Rodney Ho
1 Cubitt Town
E14 . . . . .42 A2
Islington N1 . . . . .85 A1
Notting Hill
W11 . . . . .31 C2 113 B4
2 Deptford SE17 . . . .151 A4
Rodney Rd SE17 . . . .151 B3
Rodney St N1 . . . . . . .85 A1
Rodway Rd SW15 . . . .56 C1
Rodwell Rd SE22 . . . .64 B1
Roedean Cres
SW15 . . . . .56 A2
ROEHAMPTON 68 A4
Roehampton Church
Sch SW15 . . . . .69 A4
Roehampton Cl
SW15 . . . . .56 C3
Roehampton Ct
SW13 . . . . .56 C4
Roehampton Gate
SW15 . . . . .56 A1
Roehampton High St
SW15 . . . . .68 C4
Roehampton La
Putney SW15,SW15 . .69 A3
Roehampton SW15 . .69 A3
Roehampton Vale
SW15 . . . . .68 B2
Roffey St E14 . . . . .42 B4
Rogate Ho E5 . . . . .7 C1
Roger Dowley Ct 8
E2 . . . . .25 B3
Roger's Almshouses
7 SW9 . . . . .62 B3
Rogers Ct 16 E14 . . . .33 C2
Rogers Est 28 E2 . . . .25 B2
Rogers Ho SW1 . . . . .147 C4
Rogers Rd E16 . . . . . . .35 B3
Roger St WC1 . . . . . . .95 A1
Rokeby Ho
8 Balham SW12 . . . .73 A4
Bloomsbury WC1 . . . .94 C1

Rokeby Ct 9
SE4 . . . . .51 B1
Rokeby Sch
11 Canning Town
E16 . . . . .35 B4
Stratford E15 . . . . . . .19 C1
Rokeland Ho SE4 . . . .66 A3
Roland Gdns SW7 . . .143 A2
Roland Ho SW7 . . . . .143 A2
Roland Mews 1
E1 . . . . .32 C4
Roland Way
South Kensington
SW7 . . . . .143 A2
Walworth SE17 . . . . .151 C1
Rollins St SE15 . . . . . .50 B4
Rollit Ho N7 . . . . .14 C3
Rollit St N7 . . . . .14 C3
Rollo Ct SW11 . . . . . .170 A3
Rolls Bldgs EC4 . . . . .107 C2
Rollscourt Ave
SE24 . . . . .63 B2
Rolls Pas EC4 . . . . . . .107 B2
Rolls Rd SE1 . . . . .153 A2
Rolt St SE8 . . . . .51 A4
Roman Cl W3 . . . . .37 A4
Roman Ct 4 N7 . . . . . .14 B2
Romanfield Rd
SW2 . . . . .74 B4
Roman Rd
Chiswick W4 . . . . .38 B2
Globe Town E2,E3 . . .25 C3
25 Old Ford E3 . . . . . .26 B3
Roman Road Mkt 11
E3 . . . . .26 B3
Roman Way
Barnsbury N7 . . . . . . .14 B2
4 Deptford SE15 . . . .50 B3
Roma Read Cl
SW15 . . . . .69 A4
Romayne Ho SW4 . . . .61 C4
Romberg Rd SW17 . . .72 C1
Romborough Gdns
SE13 . . . . .67 B2
Romborough Way
SE13 . . . . .67 B2
Romer Ho 9 SW2 . . . .62 B2
Romero Cl SW9 . . . . .62 B4
Romeyn Rd SW16 . . . .74 B1
Romford Ho 17
N1 . . . . .15 C2
Romford St E1 . . . . . . .32 A4
Romilly Rd N4 . . . . .6 A2
Romilly St W1 . . . . . . .119 C4
Romily Ct SW6 . . . . . .164 B2
Romney Cl
7 Deptford SE14 . . . .50 B3
North End NW11 . . . . .2 B3
Romney Ct
9 Hammersmith
W12 . . . . .39 B4
9 Hampstead
NW3 . . . . .12 A2
Romney Ho 2
E14 . . . . .34 C2
Romney Mews
W1 . . . . .103 B4
Romney Rd SE10 . . . .52 C4
Romney St SW1 . . . . .134 A1
Romola Rd SE24,
SW2 . . . . .75 A3
Ronald Ross Prim Sch
6 SW19 . . . . .70 A4
Ronaldshay N4 . . . . . . .5 C3
Ronalds Rd N5 . . . . . .14 C3
Ronald St E1 . . . . .32 B3
Rona Rd NW3 . . . . . . .12 C4

Rona Wlk 20 N1 . . . . .15 C2
Rondu Rd NW2 . . . . . .10 A3
Rood La EC3 . . . . .124 A4
Rookery Rd SW4 . . . . .61 B3
Rookery Sch
SW4 . . . . .73 C4
Rooke Way SE10 . . . . .43 B1
Rookwood Rd N16 . . . .7 C4
Roosevelt Ct 18
SW19 . . . . .70 A3
Rootes Dr W10 . . . . . .30 C4
Ropemaker Rd
SE16 . . . . .41 A3
Ropemaker's Fields 7
E14 . . . . .33 B2
Ropemaker St
EC2 . . . . .109 B4
Roper La SE1 . . . . . . .138 B3
Roper's Orch
SW3 . . . . .158 A3
Ropers Wlk 13
SW2 . . . . .74 C4
Ropery St E3 . . . . .26 B1
Rope St SE16 . . . . .41 A3
Ropewalk Gdns 18
E1 . . . . .111 C2
Ropley St 2 E2 . . . . . .24 C3
Rosa Alba Mews
N5 . . . . .15 B4
Rosalind Ho 21 N1 . . .24 A3
Rosaline Rd SW6 . . . .154 B1
Rosaline Terr
SW6 . . . . .154 B1
Rosa Parks Ho 9
SW9 . . . . .172 C1
Rosary Ct 17 E1 . . . . .32 C4
Rosary Gdns SW7 . . .143 A3
Rosary RC Prim Sch
NW3 . . . . .12 A3
Rosaville Rd SW6 . . .154 C1
Rosbury SW15 . . . . . . .58 A1
Roscastle Rd SE4 . . . .66 A2
Roscoe St EC1 . . . . . . .97 A1
Roscommon Ho 2
NW3 . . . . .11 C3
Rose Alley
Borough The SE1 . . .123 A2
Broadgate EC2 . . . . .110 B3
Rosebank
2 Dagenham W3 . . . .28 C3
Fulham SW6 . . . . . . .47 B3
Rosebank Gdns
Bow E3 . . . . .26 B3
1 Dagenham W3 . . . .28 C3
Rosebank Way
W3 . . . . .28 C3
Rosebank Wlk
NW1 . . . . .13 C1
Rosebay Ho 10 E3 . . .33 C4
Roseberry Pl E8 . . . . .16 B2
Roseberry St SE16 . . .40 A2
Rosebery Ave EC1 . . .95 C3
Rosebery Ct
Holborn EC1 . . . . .95 B2
Mayfair W1 . . . . .118 A2
Rosebery Ho 21
E2 . . . . .25 B3
Rosebery Ho Bsns Ctr
EC1 . . . . .95 C2
Rosebery Rd SW2 . . . .62 A1
Rosebery Sq EC1 . . . .95 B1
Rosebery Sch SW6 . .166 B3
Rose Bush Ct NW3 . . .12 B3
Rosecroft Ave NW3 . . .1 C1
Rose & Crown Ct
EC2 . . . . .108 C2
Rose & Crown Yd
SW1 . . . . .119 A1

Rose Ct
7 Dalston E8 . . . . .16 B1
Islington N1 . . . . .86 A3
Spitalfields E1 . . . . . .111 A3
Rosedale Ct N5 . . . . . .15 A4
Rosedale Ho N16 . . . . .6 C3
Rosedale Rd TW9 . . . .54 A3
Rosedale Terr W6 . . . .39 A3
Rosedene NW6 . . . . . .22 C4
Rosedene Ave
SW16 . . . . .74 B1
Rosedew Rd W6 . . . . .47 C4
Rosefield Gdns
E14 . . . . .33 C2
Roseford Ct 18
W12 . . . . .39 C4
Rosegate Ho 32
E3 . . . . .26 B3
Rosehart Mews 8
W11 . . . . .31 C3
Rosehill Rd SW18 . . . .59 B2
Rose Joan Mews
NW6 . . . . .10 C4
Roseland Ho SW6 . . . .58 A4
Roseleigh Ave N5 . . . .15 A4
Rosemary Branch
Bridge N1 . . . . .87 C4
Rosemary Ct 33
SE8 . . . . .51 A4
Rosemary Dr 18
E14 . . . . .34 C3
Rosemary Gdns
SW14 . . . . .55 B4
Rosemary Ho
Shoreditch N1 . . . . . .87 C3
Willesden NW10 . . . . .22 A4
Rosemary La
SW14 . . . . .55 B4
Rosemary Rd
Camberwell SE15 . . . .49 B3
Wandsworth SW17 . . .71 B1
Rosemary St N1 . . . . .87 C4
Rosemead Prep Sch
SE27 . . . . .75 B2
Rosemont Mans 11
NW3 . . . . .11 A2
Rosemont Rd
Acton W3 . . . . .28 A2
Richmond TW10 . . . . .54 A1
South Hampstead
NW3 . . . . .11 B2
Rosemoor St
SW3 . . . . .144 C3
Rosemount Ct 3
W3 . . . . .28 A1
Rosemount Lo W3 . . .28 A2
Rosenau Cres
SW11 . . . . .168 C3
Rosenau Rd
SW11 . . . . .168 C4
Rosendale Prim Sch
SE21 . . . . .75 B4
Rosendale Rd SE21,
SE24 . . . . .75 B3
Roseneath Rd
SW11 . . . . .60 C1
Rosenthal Ho SE6 . . .67 A1
Rosenthal Rd SE6 . . .67 B1
Rosenthorpe Rd
SE15 . . . . .65 C2
Roserton St E14 . . . . .42 B4
Rose Sq SW7 . . . . . . .143 C2

Rose St
Holborn EC4 . . . . **108** B2
Strand WC2 . . . . **120** A4
Rose Theatre SE1 . . . . . **122** C2

Rosethorn Cl
SW12 . . . . .73 C4
Rosetta Cl SW8 . . . . **162** B1
Roseway SE21 . . . . .63 C1
Rosewood Ct 2
E11 .19 C4
Rosewood Gdns
SE13 . . . . .52 B1
Rosewood Ho 9
NW3 . . . . .11 A2
Rosewood Sq
W12 . . . . .29 C3
Rosher Cl E15 . . . . .19 C1
Rosina St E9 . . . . .17 C2
Roskell Rd SW15 . . . . .57 C4
Roslin Ho 2 E1 . . . . . . .32 C2
Roslin Rd W3 . . . . .37 A3
Rosmead Rd
W11 . . . . . . .31 A2 **112** B4
Rosoman Pl EC1 . . . . . .95 C2
Rosoman St EC1 . . . . . .95 C3
Ross Ct
8 Hackney E5 . . . . .17 A4
4 Putney SW15 . . . . . .69 C4
Rossdale Rd SW15 . . .57 B3
Rosse Gdns SE13 . . . . .67 C1
Rossendale Way
NW1 . . . . .83 A4
Rossetti Ct WC1 . . . . **105** B4
Rossetti Gdns Mans
SW3 . . . . **158** C4
Rossetti Ho SW1 . . . . **147** C3
Rossetti Mews
NW8 . . . . .79 C3
Rossetti Rd SE16 . . . . .40 A1
Rossetti Studios
SW3 . . . . **158** B4
Ross Ho 8 E1 . . . . .32 A1
Rossington St E5 . . . . . .7 C2
Rossiter Gr 2 . . . .
SW9 . . . . .62 C4
Rossiter Rd SW12 . . . .73 A3
Rosslyn Ave SW13 . . .56 B4
Rosslyn Ct NW3 . . . . . .12 A3
Rosslyn Hill NW3 . . . .11 C3
Rosslyn Ho 8
TW9 . . . . .44 B2
Rosslyn Mans
6 Hampstead
NW3 . . . . .11 B2
South Hampstead
NW6 . . . . .11 B2
Rosslyn Mews 7
NW3 . . . . .11 C4
Rosslyn Park Mews
NW3 . . . . .11 C3
Rossmore Ct NW1 . . .90 C2
Rossmore Rd NW1 . . .90 B2
Ross Wy 2 SE14 . . . . .33 A3
Rostrevor Mans
SW6 . . . . **164** C4
Rostrevor Mews
SW6 . . . . **164** C3
Rostrevor Rd
SW6 . . . . **164** C4
Rotary Lo 12 SE27 . . .75 A1
Rotary St SE1 . . . . . . **136** B2
Rothay NW1 . . . . .92 B4
Rothbury Rd E9 . . . . . .18 C1
Rotheley Ho 38 E9 . .17 B1

Rotherfield Ct
De Beauvoir Town
N1 . . . . .15 C1
Shoreditch N1 . . . . . . .87 B4
Rotherfield Prim Sch
N1 . . . . .87 A4
Rotherfield St
Islington N1 . . . . .15 B1
Shoreditch N1 . . . . . . .87 B4
Rotherham Wlk
SE1 . . . . **122** A1
ROTHERHITHE
SE16 . . . . .40 C4
Rotherhithe Bsns Est
6 SE16 . . . . .40 B2
Rotherhithe New Rd
SE16 . . . . .40 C2
Rotherhithe Old Rd
SE16 . . . . .40 C2
Rotherhithe Prim Sch
2 SE16 . . . . .40 C4
Rotherhithe St
SE16 . . . . .40 B4
Rotherhithe Sta
SE16 . . . . .40 B4
Rotherhithe Tunnel
SE16 . . . . .32 C1
Rother Ho SE15 . . . . . .65 A3
Rotherwick Rd
NW11 . . . . .1 C4
Rotherwood Rd
SW15 . . . . .57 C4
Rothery St N1 . . . . . . **86** B4
Rothesay Ave SW14,
SW15 . . . . .56 A3
Rothesay Ct 13
SE11 . . . . **163** B3
Rothley Ct NW8 . . . . . .89 B2
Rothsay St SE1 . . . . . **138** A1
Rothsay Wlk 10
E14 . . . . .41 C2
Rothschild Rd W4 . . . .37 B3
Rothwell St
1 Hampstead
NW1 . . . . .12 B1
Primrose Hill NW1 . . **81** A4
Roth Wlk N7 . . . . .5 B2
Rotten Row SW1 . . . **130** C4
Rotterdam Dr E14 . .42 B3
Rouel Rd
Bermondsey
SE16 . . . . **153** B4
Bermondsey SE16 . . . .40 A2
Roundacre SW19 . . .69 C2
Roundel Cl SE4 . . . . . . .66 B3
Roundhouse La
NW1 . . . . **82** C1
Roundhouse Theatre
NW1 . . . . .12 C1
Roundwood Rd
NW10 . . . . .8 B1
Rounton Rd E3 . . . . . . .26 C1
Roupell Rd SW2 . . . . . .74 B3
Roupell St SE1 . . . . . **121** C1
Rousden St NW1 . . . . .13 B1
Routh Rd SW18 . . . . . .72 A4
Rover Ho 6 N1 . . . . . . .24 A4
Rowallan Rd SW6 . .154 A1
Rowan Cl W5 . . . . .36 A4
Rowan Ct
19 Camberwell
SE15 . . . . .49 B3
Wandsworth SW11 . . .60 B1
Rowan Ho
2 Bow E3 . . . . .26 B3
Dagenham NW10 . . . .21 A1

Rowan Ho continued
5 Maitland Pk
NW3 . . . . .12 B2
Rowan Rd W6 . . . . . . .39 C2
Rowan Terr W6 . . . . . .39 C2
Rowan Wlk
7 Dartmouth Pk
N19 . . . . .4 B2
Rowberry Cl SW6 . . . .47 B3
Rowcross St SE1 . . **153** A2
Rowditch La
SW11 . . . . **169** B2
Rowdon Ave NW10 . . .9 A1
Rowe Ho E9 . . . . .17 B2
Rowe La E9 . . . . .17 B3
Rowena Cres
SW11 . . . . **168** B1
Rowfant Rd SW12,
SW17 . . . . .72 C2
Rowhill Mans 11
E5 . . . . .17 A4
Rowhill Rd E5 . . . . .17 A4
Rowington Cl W2 . . **100** A4
Rowland Hill Ho
SE1 . . . . **136** A4
Rowland Hill St
NW3 . . . . .12 A3
Rowley Gdns N4 . . . . . .6 B4
Rowley Ho SE8 . . . . . . .51 C4
Rowley Ind Pk W3 . . . .37 A3
Rowley Way NW8 . . . .78 C4
Rowntree Cl NW6 . . . .10 C2
Rowse Cl E15 . . . . .27 B4
Rowstock SW11 . . . . . .13 C2
Rowstock Gdns
N7 . . . . .13 C3
Roxby Pl SW6 . . . . . . **155** C4
Roxford Ho 2 E3 . . . .27 A1
Roxley Rd SE13 . . . . . .67 A1
Roxwell 10 NW1 . . . . .13 A2
Roxwell Rd W12 . . . . .38 C4
Royal Academy of
Dramatic Art
WC1 . . . . **105** B4
Royal Acad of Arts
W1 . . . . **118** C3
Royal Acad of Dance
SW11 . . . . **169** C3
Royal Acad of Music
NW1 . . . . .91 C1
Royal Albert Hall
SW7 . . . . **129** B3
Royal Arc W1 . . . . . . **118** C3
Royal Armouries The
E1 . . . . **124** C2
Royal Avenue Ho
SW3 . . . . **144** C2
Royal Ballet Upper
Sch The WC2 . . . . . . **106** B1
Royal Brompton Hospl
Chelsea SW3 . . . . . . **143** B2
Chelsea SW3 . . . . . . **144** A2
Royal Cir SE27 . . . . . .75 A1
Royal Cl
Deptford SE8 . . . . .51 B4
Putney SW19 . . . . .69 C2
Stamford Hill N16 . . . .7 A3
Royal College of Art,
Battersea SW11 . . . **158** A1
Royal College of
Physicians Liby
NW1 . . . . .92 B2
Royal College St
NW1 . . . . .83 A4

Royal Coll of
Anaesthetists
WC1 . . . . **106** C3
Royal Coll of
Midwives E1 . . . . . **106** C3
Royal Coll of Music
SW7 . . . . **129** B2
Royal Coll of
Obstetricians &
Gynaecologists
NW1 . . . . .90 C3
Royal Coll of
Paediatrics & Child
Health W1 . . . . **107** A4
Royal Coll of
Physicians W1 . . . .92 B1
Royal Coll of
Radiologists W1 . . **104** B4
Royal Coll of Science
SW7 . . . . **129** B2
Royal Coll of Speech
Language Therapists
SE1 . . . . **123** B1
Royal Coll of
Surgeons WC2 . . . **107** A2
Royal Coll of
Veterinary Surgeons
SW1 . . . . **134** A1
Royal Courts of
Justice WC2 . . . . . **107** B1
Royal Cres
W11 . . . . .31 A1 **112** A1
Royal Crescent Mews
W11 . . . . .30 C1
Royal Ct
City of London
EC3 . . . . **109** C1
Royal Duchess Mews
16 SW12 . . . . .73 A4
Royal Exchange
EC3 . . . . **109** C1
Royal Exchange Bldgs
EC3 . . . . **109** C1
Royal Festival Hall
SE1 . . . . **121** A1
Royal Free Hospl
NW3 . . . . .12 A3
Royal Fusiliers Mus
E1 . . . . **124** C2
Royal Geographical
Society SW7 . . . . . **129** C3
Royal George Mews
10 SE5 . . . . .63 C3
Royal Hill SE10 . . . . . .52 B3
Royal Hill Ct 2
SE10 . . . . .52 B3
Royal Horticultural
Society (Lawrence
Hall & Conf Ctr)
SW1 . . . . **133** B1
Royal Horticultural
Society (Lindley
Hall) SW1 . . . . **147** B4
Royal Hospital
Chelsea The
SW1 . . . . **145** B1
Royal Hospital Rd
SW3 . . . . **145** A1
Royal Hospl for Neuro-
Disability The
SW15 . . . . .58 A1
Royal Hospl Mus
SW3 . . . . **145** A1

Royal Institute of
British Architects
W1 . . . . **104** B4
Royal Institution
Faraday Mus The
SW1 . . . . **118** C3
Royal Langford
Apartments 3
NW6 . . . . .78 A2
Royal London Est The
NW10 . . . . .20 C3
Royal London Hospl
for Integrated
Medicine WC1 . . . . **106** C3
Royal London Hospl
Mus E1 . . . . .32 A4
Royal London Hospl
(Whitechapel) The
E1 . . . . .32 A4
Royal Marsden Hospl
SW3 . . . . **143** C2
Royal Mews The
SW1 . . . . **132** B2
Royal Mint Pl 6
E1 . . . . **125** B4
Royal Mint St E1 . . **125** A4
Royal National
Orthopaedic Hospl
W1 . . . . .92 B1
Royal National TNE
Hospl The WC1 . . . **94** C4
Royal Naval Pl
SE14 . . . . .51 B3
Royal Oak Ct 8
N1 . . . . .24 A2 **98** A4
Royal Oak Pl SE22 . .65 A1
Royal Oak Rd 5
E8 . . . . .17 A2
Royal Oak Sta
W2 . . . . **100** B3
Royal Oak Yd SE1 **138** A3
Royal Observatory
The SE10 . . . . .52 C3
Royal Opera Arc
SW1 . . . . **119** B2
Royal Orchard Cl
SW18 . . . . .70 A4
Royal Par
Blackheath Vale
SE3 . . . . .53 B1
Fulham SW6 . . . . **154** A2
13 Richmond TW9 . .44 C2
Royal Pharmaceutical
Society Mus E1 . . **125** B3
Royal Pl 11 SE10 . . . .52 B3
Royal Rd SE17 . . . . . . .48 A4
Royal St SE1 . . . . . . **135** A2
Royalty Ho W1 . . . . **105** B1
Royalty Mews W1 . **105** B1
Royalty Studios
W11 . . . . .31 A3
Royal United Services
Institute SW1 . . . . **120** A1
Royal Veterinary Coll
The NW1 . . . . .83 B3
Royal Victoria Sta
E16 . . . . .35 C2
Royal Victor Pl E3 . .25 C3
Roycroft Cl SW2 . . . .74 C3
Roydon Ct 7
SW11 . . . . **168** C2
Roy Ridley Ho 6
SW4 . . . . .61 C4
Roy Sq E14 . . . . .33 A2
Royston Ct
New Cross SE4 . . . . . . .51 B1

Royston Ct *continued*
　Richmond TW9 . . . . 44 B2
Royston Ho 14
　SE15 . . . . 49 C4
Royston Rd 3
Royston Rd TW10 . . . 54 A2
Royston St 24 . . . . 25 B3
Rozel Ct 3 N1 . . . . 24 A4
Rozel Rd SW4 . . . . 61 B4
Ruby St SE15 . . . . . 50 A4
Ruby Triangle
　SE15 . . . . 50 A4
Ruckholt Rd E9,
　E10 . . . . 18 C4
Rucklidge Ave
　NW10 . . . . 21 C3
Rudall Cres NW3 . . 11 C4
Rudbeck Ho 11
　SE15 . . . . 49 C3
Ruddington Cl E5 . . 18 A4
Rudge Ho 1
　SE16 . . . . 139 C2
Rudgwick Terr
　NW8 . . . . 80 B3
Rudhall Ho 4
　SW2 . . . . 62 C1
Rudloe Rd SW12 . . 73 B4
Rudolf Pl SW8 . . . 162 B3
Rudolph Rd NW6 . . 23 C3
Rudstone Ho 10
　E3 . . . . 27 A2
Rudyard Ct SE1 . . 137 C3
Rufford St N1 . . . . 84 B4
Rufford Street Mews
　N1 . . . . 14 A1
Rufford Twr 5
　W3 . . . . 28 A1
Rufus Bsns Ctr
　SW18 . . . . 71 A2
Rufus Ho SE1 . . . 139 A2
Rufus St N1 . . 24 A2 98 A3
Rugby Mans W14 . 140 B4
Rugby Rd W4 . . . . 38 A4
Rugby St WC1 . . . . 94 C1
Rugg St E14 . . . . . 33 C2
Rugless Ho 2 E14 . 42 B4
Rugmere 4 NW1 . . 12 C1
Rumball Ho 14
　SE5 . . . . 49 A3
Rumbold Rd SW6 . 156 B1
Rum Cl E1 . . . . . . 32 B2
Rumford Ho SE1 . 136 C1
Rumsey Rd SW9 . . 62 B4
Runacres Ct SE17 . 150 C1
Runcorn Pl
　W11 . . . . . 31 A2 112 A4
Rundell Twr SW8 . 172 C4
Running Horse Yd 1
　TW8 . . . . 44 A4
Runnymede Ct
　SW15 . . . . 68 C3
Runnymede Ho
　Hackney E9 . . . . . . 18 A4
　Richmond TW10 . . . 54 C2
Rupack St 3 SE16 . 40 B4
Rupert Ct W1 . . . 119 B4
Rupert Gdns SW9 . 48 A1
Rupert Ho
　SE11 . . . . 149 C3
　5 Upper Holloway
　N19 . . . . 4 C4
Rupert Rd
　Bedford Pk W4 . . . . 38 A3
　Paddington NW6 . . . 23 B3
　3 Upper Holloway N19 . . 4 C2
Rupert St W1 . . . . 119 B4
Rusbridge Cl E8 . . 16 C3

Ruscoe Rd E16 . . . . 35 B3
Rusham Rd SW12 . . 72 B4
Rushbrook Ho 20
　SW8 . . . . 171 B2
Rushby Ct SW4 . . . 172 B4
Rush Common Mews
　18 SW2 . . . . 74 B4
Rushcroft Rd SW2,
　SW9 . . . . 62 C3
Rushcutters Ct 18
　SE16 . . . . 41 A2
Rushey Mead SE4 . 66 C2
Rushford Rd SE4 . . 66 B1
Rush Hill Mews 3
　SW11 . . . . 60 C4
Rush Hill Rd SW11 . 60 C4
Rushlake Ho 3
　SW11 . . . . 169 B2
Rushmead 5 E2 . . . 25 A2
Rushmere Ho 2
　SW15 . . . . 68 C3
Rushmore Cres 9
　E5 . . . . 17 C4
Rushmore Ho
　9 Kentish Town
　N7 . . . . 13 C3
　W14 . . . . 126 B1
Rushmore Prim Sch
　7 E5 . . . . 17 C4
Rushmore Rd
　Clapton Pk E5 . . . . 17 C4
　Hackney E5 . . . . . . 17 C4
Rusholme Rd
　SW15 . . . . 58 A1
Rushton Ho 28
　SW8 . . . . 171 B1
Rushton St N1 . . . . 87 C2
Rushworth St SE1 . 136 B3
Ruskin Ave TW9 . . 44 C3
Ruskin Ct SE5 . . . . 63 C4
Ruskin Ho SW1 . . 147 C3
Ruskin Park Ho
　SE5 . . . . 63 C4
Ruskin Wlk SE24 . . 63 B2
Rusper Ct SW9 . . 172 B1
Russell Cl W4 . . . . 46 B4
Russell Ct
　Battersea SW11 . . 170 A4
　Bloomsbury WC1 . . . 94 A1
　8 Peckham SE15 . . 50 A1
　St James SW1 . . . 119 A1
Russell Gdns Mews
　W14 . . . . 126 A2
Russell Gr 5
　SW9 . . . . 173 C4
Russell Ho
　20 Poplar E14 . . . . 33 C3
　SW1 . . . . 146 C2
Russell Kerr Cl
　W4 . . . . 45 B3
Russell Lo SE1 . . 137 B2
Russell Mans
　WC1 . . . . 106 B4
Russell Pickering Ho
　2 SW4 . . . . 62 A4
Russell Pl
　Hampstead NW3 . . 12 A3
　Rotherhithe SE16 . . 41 A3
Russell Rd W14 . . 126 C1
Russell Sq WC1 . . . 94 A1
Russell Square Ho
　WC1 . . . . 94 A1
Russell Square Mans
　WC1 . . . . 106 B4

Russell Square Sta
　WC1 . . . . 94 A1
Russell St WC2 . . 120 B4
Russell's Wharf 7
　W9 . . . . 23 B1
Russell Wlk 4
　TW10 . . . . 54 B1
Russell Yd SW15 . . 58 A3
Russet Cres N7 . . . 14 B3
Russett Way SE13 . 52 A1
Russia Dock Rd
　SE16 . . . . 33 A1
Russia La E2 . . . . . 25 B3
Russia Row EC2 . . 109 A1
Rusthall Ave W4 . . 37 C3
Rusthall Mans 3
　W4 . . . . 37 C2
Ruston Mews W11 . 31 A3
Ruston St E3 . . . . . 26 B4
Rust Sq SE5 . . . . . 48 C3
Ruth Ct 15 E3 . . . . 26 A3
Rutherford Ho 12
　E1 . . . . 25 A1
Rutherford House Sch
　8 SW17 . . . . 72 C2
Rutherford St
　SW1 . . . . 147 B4
Ruth Ho W10 . . . . . 23 A1
Ruthin Rd SE3 . . . . 53 C4
Ruthven St E9 . . . . 25 C4
Rutland Cl SW14 . . 55 B4
Rutland Ct
　Herne Hill SE5 . . . . 63 C3
　SW7 . . . . 130 B3
Rutland Gate
　SW7 . . . . 130 B3
Rutland Gate Mews
　SW7 . . . . 130 A3
Rutland Gdns
　SW7 . . . . 130 B3
Rutland Gdns Mews
　SW7 . . . . 130 B3
Rutland Gr W6 . . . 39 A1
Rutland Ho
　10 Putney SW15 . . 69 B4
　W8 . . . . 128 A1
Rutland Mews E
　NW8 . . . . 78 C3
Rutland Mews S
　SW7 . . . . 130 A2
Rutland Mews W
　SW7 . . . . 130 A2
Rutland Park Gdns 1
　NW2 . . . . 9 B2
Rutland Park Mans 2
　NW2 . . . . 9 B2
Rutland Pl EC1 . . . 108 B4
Rutland Rd E9 . . . . 25 C4
Rutland St SW7 . . 130 B2
Rutland Studios
　NW10 . . . . 21 C2
Rutley Cl SE11 . . . 48 A4
Rutt's Terr SE14 . . 50 C2
Ruvigny Gdns
　SW15 . . . . 57 C4
Ruvigny Mans 7
　SW15 . . . . 57 C4
Rycott Path SE22 . . 76 C4
Rycuff Sq SE3 . . . . 53 C1
Rydal Ho 22 SW8 . 171 B1
Rydal Water NW1 . 92 C3
Rye Ho 11 SE16 . . 40 B4
Ryder Ct SW1 . . . 119 A2

Ryder Dr SE16 . . . . 40 A1
Ryder Ho 18 E1 . . . 25 B1
Ryder St SW1 . . . 119 A2
Ryder's Terr NW8 . . 78 C2
Ryder St SW1 . . . 119 A2
Ryde Vale Rd
　SW12 . . . . 73 B2
Rydon St N1 . . . . . 87 A4
Rydston Cl 7 N7 . . 14 B1
Ryecotes Mead
　SE21 . . . . 76 A3
Ryecroft Rd SE13 . 67 B2
Ryecroft St SW6 . . 166 A3
Ryedale SE22 . . . . 65 A1
Ryefield Path 9
　SW15 . . . . 68 C3
Ryegates 2 SE5 . . 50 A1
Rye Hill Pk SE15 . . 65 B3
Rye La SE15 . . . . . 49 C1
Rye Lane Mkt
　SE15 . . . . 49 C1
Rye Oak Prim Sch 7
　SE15 . . . . 65 A4
Rye Passage 6
　SE15 . . . . 64 C4
Rye Rd SE15 . . . . . 65 C3
Rye Wlk SW15 . . . 57 C2
Ryfold Rd SW19 . . 70 C1
Ryland Rd NW5 . . . 13 A2
Rylett Cres W12 . . 38 B3
Rylett Rd W12 . . . 38 B3
Rylston Rd SW6 . . 154 C3
Rymer St SE24 . . . 63 A1
Rysbrack St SW1 . 130 C2

S

Saatchi Gallery
　SW3 . . . . 145 A2
Sabbarton St 9
　E16 . . . . 35 B3
Sabella Ct E3 . . . . 26 B3
Sabine Rd SW11 . . 60 C4
Sable St N1 . . . . . 15 A1
Sackets Ho 24
　SW9 . . . . 173 C4
Sackville Ho 16
　SW16 . . . . 74 A1
Sackville St W1 . . 119 A3
Sacred Heart Catholic
　Prim Sch SW15 . . . 57 C2
Sacred Heart Catholic
　Sch 18 SW6 . . . . 154 A1
Sacred Heart High
　Sch 19 W6 . . . . . 39 B2
Sacred Heart RC Prim
　Sch SW15 . . . . . . 56 C2
Sacred Heart Sch
　N7 . . . . 14 B3
Saddlers Mews
　SW8 . . . . 172 B4
Sadler Ho
　17 Bromley E3 . . . . 27 A2
　EC1 . . . . 96 A4
Sadler Pl E9 . . . . . 18 A3
Saffron Ave E14 . . 34 C2
Saffron Ct 10 N1 . . 15 C2
Saffron Hill EC1 . . 107 C4
Saffron Ho
　TW9 . . . . 45 A2
Saffron St EC1 . . . 107 C4
Saffron Wharf
　SE1 . . . . 139 A4
Sage Mews SE22 . . 64 B2

Sage St E1 . . . . . . 32 B2
Sage Way WC1 . . . 94 C3
Sailacre Ho 10
　SE10 . . . . 43 B1
Sail Ct 10 E14 . . . 34 C2
Sailmakers Ct
　SW6 . . . . 59 B4
Sail St SE11 . . . . 149 A4
Sainfoin Rd SW17 . 72 C2
St Agnes Cl E9 . . . 25 B4
St Agnes Pl SE11 . . 48 A4
St Agnes RC Sch
　15 E3 . . . . 27 A2
St Agnes RC Sch
　NW2 . . . . 1 B1
St Aidan's Rd SE22 . 65 A2
St Albans Ave W4 . 37 C3
St Alban's CE Prim
　Sch EC1 . . . . 107 B4
St Alban's Cl NW11 . 1 C3
St Alban's Gr W8 . 128 B2
St Alban's La NW11 . 1 C3
St Alban's Pl N1 . . 86 A3
St Alban's Rd
　Dagenham NW10 . . 21 A4
　Dartmouth Pk NW5 . . 4 A1
St Alban's St SW1 . 119 B3
St Albans Studios
　W8 . . . . 128 B2
St Albans Terr
　W6 . . . . 154 A4
St Alban's Villas
　NW5 . . . . 3 C1
St Alfege Pas
　SE10 . . . . 52 B4
St Alfege with St
　Peter's CE Prim Sch
　SE10 . . . . 52 B4
St Aloysius Convent
　NW1 . . . . 93 B4
St Aloysius RC Coll 18
　N19 . . . . 5 A3
St Aloysius RC Inf Sch
　NW1 . . . . 93 B4
St Aloysius RC Jun
　Sch NW1 . . . . 83 B1
St Alphage Gdn
　EC2 . . . . 109 A3
St Alphage Highwalk
　EC2 . . . . 109 A3
St Alphonsus Rd
　SW4 . . . . 61 C3
St Andrew's
　(Barnsbury) CE Prim
　Sch N1 . . . . 85 A4
St Andrews Chambers
　W1 . . . . 105 A2
St Andrews Ct 5
　SW18 . . . . 71 B2
St Andrew's Ct 2
　SW18 . . . . 71 B2
St Andrew's Gr N16 . 6 C3
St Andrew's Hill
　EC4 . . . . 108 B1
St Andrews Ho 6
　SE16 . . . . 40 A3
St Andrews Mans 1
　E5 . . . . 17 A4

St Andrew's Mans
W1 . . . . **103** B3
St Andrews Mews
Greenwich SE3 . . . . **53** C3
4 Streatham
SW12 . . . . **73** C3
St Andrew's Mews
N16 . . . . **7** A3
St Andrew's Pl
NW1 . . . . **92** B2
St Andrew's Sq
SW9 . . . . **172** B1
St Andrews Rd
W3 . . . . **29** A3
St Andrew's Rd
W14 . . . . **154** B4
Willesden NW2 . . . . **9** A2
**St Andrews & St
Francis CE Prim Sch**
6 NW2 . . . . **8** C2
St Andrew's Sq
W11 . . . . **31** A3
St Andrew St EC4 . . **107** C3
St Andrews Way
E3 . . . . **27** A1
St Andrew's Wharf
SE1 . . . . **139** A4
St Anne's CE Prim Sch
6 SW18 . . . . **59** A2
St Anne's Cl N6 . . . . . **3** C1
St Anne's Ct
Kensal Rise NW6 . . . . **23** A4
W1 . . . . **105** B1
St Anne's Flats
NW1 . . . . **93** B4
St Anne's Pas E14 . . **33** B3
St Anne's RC Prim Sch
10 E1 . . . . **24** C1 **99** B1
SE11 . . . . **162** C4
St Anne's Row E14 . . **33** B3
St Anne St E14 . . . . . **33** B3
St Anne's Trad Est **22**
E14 . . . . **33** B3
St Ann's Cres
SW18 . . . . **59** B1
St Ann's Gdns
NW5 . . . . **12** C2
St Ann's Hill SW18 . . **59** B1
St Ann's La SW1 . . . **133** C1
St Ann's Park Rd
SW18 . . . . **59** B1
St Anns Rd
Barnes SW13 . . . . **46** B2
Shepherd's Bush
W11 . . . . **30** C2
St Ann's St SW1 . . . **133** C2
St Ann's Terr NW8 . . **79** C2
St Ann's Villas
W11 . . . . **31** A1 **112** A1
St Anselm's Pl
W1 . . . . **118** A4
**St Anselm's RC Prim
Sch** SW17 . . . . **72** C1
St Anthonys Cl **6**
SW17 . . . . **72** A2
St Anthony's Cl
8 E1 . . . . **125** B2
5 Hackney Wick
E9 . . . . **18** B3
St Anthony's Ct **5**
6 Balham SW12 . . . . **60** C1
Upper Tooting
SW17 . . . . **72** C2

St Anthony's Flats
NW1 . . . . **83** B1
**St Anthony's RC Prim
Sch** SE22 . . . . **64** C1
St Anthony's Sch **8**
NW3 . . . . **11** C3
St Asaph St SE4 . . . . **65** C4
St Asaph Rd SE4 . . . . **65** C4
St Aubins Ct N1 . . . . **87** C4
**St Augustine's
High Sch** **5**
N6 . . . . **23** C3
St Augustine's Ho
NW1 . . . . **93** B4
**St Augustine's Prim
Sch** NW6 . . . . **78** A2
**St Augustine's RC
Prim Sch** W6 . . . . . . **154** B3
St Augustine's Rd
NW1 . . . . **13** C1
St Austell Rd SE13 . . **52** C1
**St Barnabas' CE Prim
Sch** SW1 . . . . **145** C2
St Barnabas **11**
SE22 . . . . **64** A2
St Barnabas Mews
SW11 . . . . **145** C2
**St Barnabas & St
Philip's CE Prim Sch**
W8 . . . . **127** B1
St Barnabas St
SW1 . . . . **145** C2
St Barnabas Terr
E9 . . . . **17** C3
St Barnabas Villas
SW8 . . . . **172** B4
**St Bartholomew's
Hospl** EC1 . . . . **108** B3
St Bartholomew's Mus
EC1 . . . . **108** B3
St Bede's RC Inf Sch
SW12 . . . . **73** C3
St Benets Cl **6**
SW17 . . . . **72** A2
St Benet's Pl EC3 . . **123** C4
**St Bernadette RC Jun
Sch** SW12 . . . . **73** B4
St Bernard Ho **6**
E14 . . . . **42** B3
St Botolph St E1,
EC3 . . . . **110** C2
St Brelades Ct N1 . . **87** C4
St Bride's EC4 . . . . **108** A1
St Bride's Ave
EC4 . . . . **108** A1
St Bride's Pas
EC4 . . . . **108** A1
St Bride St EC4 . . . . **108** A2
St Catherines Cl **7**
SW17 . . . . **72** A2
St Catherine's Ct **8**
W4 . . . . **38** A3
St Catherine's Dr
SE14 . . . . **50** C1
St Catherines Mews
SW3 . . . . **144** C4
St Cecilia's CE Sch
SW18 . . . . **70** B3
St Chad's Pl WC1 . . . **94** C4
St Chad's St WC1 . . . **94** B4
St Charles' Hospl
W10 . . . . **30** C4
St Charles Pl W10 . . **31** A4
**St Charles RC Prim
Sch** **7** W10 . . . . . . **30** C4

**St Charles RC Sixth
Form Coll** **8**
W10 . . . . **30** C4
St Charles Sq W10 . . **30** C4
St Christina's Sch
NW8 . . . . **80** B2
St Christopher's Ho
N19 . . . . **4** B1
St Christopher's Ho
NW1 . . . . **83** B1
St Christopher's Pl
W1 . . . . **103** C2
St Christopher's Sch
5 NW3 . . . . **11** C3
St Clair Ho **17** E3 . . **26** B2
St Clare St EC3 . . . . **110** C1
**St Clement Danes CE
Prim Sch** WC2 . . . . . **106** C1
**St Clement & St
James CE Prim Sch**
W11 . . . . **31** A1 **112** A2
St Clements Ct
Barnsbury N7 . . . . **14** A2
7 SE14 . . . . **50** C4
6 Shepherd's Bush
W11 . . . . **30** C2
St Clements Ct
EC4 . . . . **123** C4
St Clements Ho
E1 . . . . **110** C3
St Clement's La
WC2 . . . . **107** A1
St Clements Mans **7**
SW6 . . . . **47** C4
St Clements Ho N7 . . **14** C1
St Columb's Ho **11**
W10 . . . . **31** A4
St Crispins Ct
SW3 . . . . **12** A4
St Cross St EC1 . . . . **107** C4
St Cuthbert's Rd
NW2 . . . . **10** B2
**St Cuthbert with St
Matthias CE Prim Sch**
SW5 . . . . **142** A2
St Davids Ct **27**
E16 . . . . **40** A1
St Dionis Rd SW6 . . **165** A2
**St Dominic's Catholic
Prim Sch** **9** E9 . . . . **18** A2
**St Dominic's RC Prim
Sch** **11** NW5 . . . . . . **12** B3
St Donatt's Rd
London SE14 . . . . **51** B2
New Cross Gate
SE4 . . . . **51** B1
St Dunstan Ave
W3 . . . . **28** C2
St Dunstan Gdns
W3 . . . . **28** C2
St Dunstan's Alley
EC3 . . . . **124** A3
St Dunstan's Ct
EC4 . . . . **107** C1
St Dunstan's Hill
EC3 . . . . **124** A3
St Dunstan's La
EC3 . . . . **124** A3
St Dunstan's Rd
W6 . . . . **39** C1
**St Edmund's Catholic
Prim Sch** E14 . . . . . . **41** C2
St Edmunds Cl **3**
SW17 . . . . **72** A2

St Edmund's Cl
NW8 . . . . **80** C3
St Edmund's Ct
NW8 . . . . **80** C3
St Edmund's Sq
SW13 . . . . **47** B4
St Edmund's Terr
NW8 . . . . **80** C3
**St Edward's RC Prim
Sch** NW1 . . . . **90** B1
**St Elizabeth RC Prim
Sch** SE22 . . . . **64** C2
**St Elizabeth's RC Prim
Sch** TW10 . . . . **54** B1
St Elmo Rd W12 . . . . **38** B4
St Elmos Rd SE16 . . **41** A4
St Ermin's Hill
SW1 . . . . **133** B2
St Ervan's Rd W10 . . **31** B4
**St Eugene de
Mazenod RC Prim
Sch** **12** NW6 . . . . . . **10** C1
St Faith's CE Prim Sch
SW18 . . . . **59** C2
St Faith's Rd SE24 . . **75** A3
**St Francesca Cabrini
RC Prim Sch**
SE23 . . . . **65** B1
St Francis Ho
NW1 . . . . **83** B1
**St Francis of Assisi RC
Prim Sch** **9** W11 . . **30** C2
St Francis Pl
SW12 . . . . **61** A1
**St Francis RC Prim
Sch** **20** SE15 . . . . . **49** C3
St Francis Rd
SE22 . . . . **64** A3
St Francis Xavier Coll
SW12 . . . . **61** A1
St Frideswides Mews
5 E14 . . . . **34** B3
**St Gabriel's CE Prim
Sch** SW1 . . . . **146** C1
St Gabriel's Cl **3**
E14 . . . . **34** A4
**St Gabriel's Coll
(Dennen Site)** **19**
SE5 . . . . **48** A2
St Gabriel's Rd
NW2 . . . . **9** C3
St George Ho
SW11 . . . . **169** C3
**ST GEORGE IN THE
EAST** **32** A2
St George's Ave
N7 . . . . **13** C4
St George's Bldgs
SE11 . . . . **136** B1
St George's Cath
NW1 . . . . **92** B4
**St George's Cath RC
Prim Sch** SE1 . . . . . **136** A2
**St George's CE Prim
Sch**
15 SE5 . . . . **49** A3
SW8 . . . . **161** A1
St George's Circ
SE1 . . . . **136** A2
St Georges Cl
SW8 . . . . **171** A4
St Georges Coll N7 . . **5** C1
St Georges Ct
SW3 . . . . **58** B3
St George's Ct
Brompton SW3 . . . . . **144** A4

St George's Ct
continued
Kensington SW7 . . . . **128** C2
Newington SE17 . . . . **136** A1
St George's Dr
SW1 . . . . **146** C2
St George's Field
W2 . . . . **102** B3
St George's Gr
SW17 . . . . **71** C1
**St George's Hanover
Square CE Sch**
W1 . . . . **117** C3
St George's Ho
NW1 . . . . **83** A1
St George's La
EC3 . . . . **124** A4
St George's Mews
1 NW1 . . . . **12** C1
2 Rotherhithe SE8 . . **41** B2
SE1 . . . . **135** C2
St Georges Pl N7 . . . **13** C4
St George's Pools
E1 . . . . **32** A2
St George's RC Cath
SE1 . . . . **135** C2
**St George's RC Sec
Sch** W9 . . . . **78** C1
St Georges Rd W4 . . **37** C4
St George's Rd
Newington SE1 . . . . . **136** A1
Richmond TW9 . . . . . . **54** B4
**St George's
Residences** **4**
SW2 . . . . **62** C2
St Georges Sq **1**
EC4 . . . . **108** A2
St Georges Sq **2**
E14 . . . . **33** A2
St George's Sq
Rotherhithe SE8 . . . . . **41** B2
SW1 . . . . **147** B1
**St George's Square
Mews** SW1 . . . . **147** B1
St George St W1 . . . **118** B4
St Georges Terr
NW1 . . . . **81** A4
St George's Terr
NW1 . . . . **12** B1
St George's Way
SE15 . . . . **49** A4
**St George the Martyr
CE Prim Sch**
WC1 . . . . **95** A1
St George Wharf
SW8 . . . . **162** A4
St George Wharf Pier
SW8 . . . . **162** A4
St Gerards Cl SW4 . . **61** B2
St German's Pl
SE3 . . . . **53** C2
St Gildas' RC Jun Sch
13 N8 . . . . **5** A4
St GILES **106** A2
St Giles Cir WC1 . . . **105** C2
St Giles Ct WC2 . . . **106** A2
St Giles High St
WC2 . . . . **105** C2
St Giles Ho SW16 . . . **74** A1
St Giles International
WC2 . . . . **106** A2
St Giles Pas WC2 . . **105** C1
St Giles Rd SE5 . . . . **49** A2
St Giles Terr EC1 . . . **109** A3
St Giles Twr **3**
SE5 . . . . **49** A2

St Gilles Ho 15 E2 . . .25 C3
St Helena Ho WC1. . .95 B3
St Helena Rd SE16. .40 C2
St Helena St WC1. . .95 B3
St Helens Gdns
W10 . . . . .30 C3
St Helen's PI EC3 110 A2
St Helen's RC Primary
Sch 21 SW9 . . . . .62 C4
St Helier Ct 2 N1. . .24 A4
St Hildas Ct 7
SW17 . . . . .72 A2
St Hilda's CI NW6 . . .9 C1
St Hilda's Rd
SW13 . . . . .47 A4
St Hildas Wharf
E1 . . . . .32 B1
St Hubert's Ho 2
E14 . . . . .41 C3
St Hughes CI 4
SW17 . . . . .72 A2
St Ives Ct NW2 . . . .10 A2
St Ives PI E14 . . . . .34 B4
St JAMES 119 B2
St James's CE Prim
Sch
Bermondsey
SE16. . . . . .139 B2 125 C4
St James Ct
26 Bethnal Green
E2 . . . . .24 C2 99 C3
2 Brentford W4 . . .36 C1
St James' Ct
Bedford Pk W4 . . . .37 C3
SW1 . . . . .133 A2
St James Ho 5 N5 . .14 C3
St James Ind Mews 4
SE1 . . . . .153 C1
St James Jun &
Senior Girls Schs
W14 . . . . .140 B4
St James' Mans
NW6 . . . . .10 C1
St James Mews
E14 . . . . .42 B3
St James's CE 51 A2
St James's & St
Michael's CE Prim
Sch 57 . . . . .115 A4
St James's App
EC2. . . . . . . .24 A1 98 A1
St James's Ave 2 . .25 B3
St James's CE Prim
Sch SE14. . . . . . . .51 A2
St James School Flats
5 N7 . . . . .14 C3
St James's CI
NW8 . . . . .80 C3
Upper Tooting
SW17 . . . . .72 B2
St James's Cloisters
2 SE22 . . . . .64 B3
St James's Cres
SW9 . . . . .62 C4
St James's Dr
Balham SW12,
SW17 . . . . .72 A4
Upper Tooting
SW17 . . . . .72 B2
St James's Gdns
W11 . . . . . . .31 A1 112 A2
St James's Gr
SW11 . . . . .169 A2
St James's Market
SW1 . . . . .119 B3

St James's Pal
SW1 . . . . .119 A1
St James's Park Sta
SW1 . . . . .133 B2
St James's Pas
EC3 . . . . .110 B1
St James's Pk
SW1 . . . . .133 B4
St James's Rd
Bermondsey SE1,
SE16 . . . . .153 C4
Peckham SE1 . . . . .49 C4
St James's Sq
SW1 . . . . .119 A2
St James's St
SW1 . . . . .118 C2
St James St 6
W6 . . . . .39 B1
St James's Terr
NW8 . . . . .80 C4
3 Upper Tooting
SW12 . . . . .72 B4
St James's Terrace
Mews NW8 . . . . .80 C3
St James The Great
RC Prim Sch 17
SE15 . . . . .49 B2
St James the Less
Prim Sch SW1. . .147 B2
St Joan of Arc RC
Prim Sch N5 . . . . .15 B4
St John Bosco Coll
SW11 . . . . .168 A3
St John of Jerusalem
CE Prim Sch 8
E9 . . . . .17 B1
ST JOHN'S 51 C1
St John's & St James
CE Prim Sch 6
E9 . . . . .17 B3
St John's Angell Town
CE Prim Sch
16 Brixton SW9 . . .62 C3
22 London SW9 . . .173 B1
St John's Ave
Dagenham NW10 . . .21 B4
Putney SW15 . . . . .57 C2
St John's CE Prim Sch
58 E2 . . . . .25 B3
St John's Church Rd
E9 . . . . .17 B3
St John's CI SW6. .155 B2
St John's Cres
SW9 . . . . .62 C4
St John's Ct 6 E1 . .32 A1
St John's Dr
Finsbury Pk N4. . . . .6 A2
Hammersmith W6 . .39 A2
Lewisham SE13 . . . . .7 A1
6 South Hampstead
NW6 . . . . .11 B2
Saint John's Ct N5 . .15 A4
St John's Dr SW18. .71 A3
St John's Est SE1 .138 C3
St John's Gdns
W11 . . . . . .31 B2 112 C3
St John's Gr
3 Barnes SW13 . . .46 B1
11 Richmond TW9 . .54 A3
Upper Holloway N19 . .4 B2
St John's Highbury
Vale CE Prim Sch
N5 . . . . .6 A1

St John's Hill
SW11 . . . . .59 C3
St John's Hill Gr
SW11 . . . . .59 C3
St Johns Ho 5
SE17 . . . . .48 C4
St John's Ho 1
E14 . . . . .42 B1
St John's Lo 2 E1 . .108 B4
St John's Lodge 8
SE8 . . . . .51 C2
St John's Mans E5 . .17 A3
St John's Park Mans
N19 . . . . .4 B3
St John's Path 4
EC1 . . . . .96 A1
St John's Pk SE3 . . .53 C3
St John's PI EC1 . . .96 A1
St John's RC Prim Sch
16 . . . . .41 A4
St John's Rd
Battersea SW11. . . .60 A3
Canning Town E16 . .35 C3
Richmond TW9 . . . .54 A3
St John's & St
Clement's CE Prim
Sch 4 SE15. . . . . .64 C4
St John's Smith Sq
Concert Hall
SW1 . . . . .134 A1
St John's Sq EC1. . .96 A1
St Johns Sta SE8 . . .51 C1
St John St EC1 . . . .96 A1
St John's Terr
W10 . . . . .22 C1
SW15 . . . . .69 B4
St John's Therapy Ctr
SW11 . . . . .59 C3
St John's Upper
Holloway CE Prim
Sch 7 N19. . . . . . . .4 C2
St John's Vale SE8. .51 C1
St John's Villas
Upper Holloway
N19 . . . . .4 C2
W8 . . . . .128 B1
St John's Walham
Green CE Prim Sch
SW6 . . . . .164 B4
St John's Walworth
CE Prim Sch
SE17 . . . . .151 A3
St John's Way N19 . . .4 C3
ST JOHN'S WOOD . .79 B1
St John's Wood Ct
NW8 . . . . .89 C3
St John's Wood High
St NW8 . . . . .80 A1
St John's Wood Park
NW8 . . . . .79 B4
St John's Wood Pre-
Prep Sch NW8. . . .90 A4
St John's Wood Rd
NW8 . . . . .89 C3
St John's Wood Sta
NW8 . . . . .79 B2
St John the Baptist
VA CE Prim Sch
N1 . . . . .24 A3
St John the Divine CE
Jun & Inf Sch
SE5 . . . . .48 A3
St John the Evangelist
RC Prim Sch N1. . .86 A2

St Joseph's
Camberwell RC
Schools' Federation
38 SE5 . . . . .49 A3
St Joseph's CI
W10 . . . . .31 A4
St Josephs Ct 3
NW10 . . . . .21 B3
St Joseph's Flats
NW1 . . . . .93 B4
St Joseph's Ho
W6 . . . . .39 C2
St Joseph's Hospice Dr,
E8 . . . . .25 A4
St Joseph's RC Prim
Sch
Chelsea SW3 . . . .144 C3
16 Deptford SE8. . .51 C3
11 Greenwich SE10 .43 B1
Paddington W9. . . . .88 C3
Rotherhithe SE16. . .40 B3
St Giles WC2. . . . .106 B2
Upper Holloway N19 . .4 A3
16 Wandsworth
SW18 . . . . .58 C2
8 Willesden NW10 . .8 A4
St Joseph's St
SW8 . . . . .170 B4
St Joseph's Vale
SE3 . . . . .67 C4
St Jude & St Paul's CE
Prim Sch 27 N1 . .16 A2
St Jude's CE Prim Sch
4 London SE24. . . .63 A2
St Jude's CE Prim Sch
SE1 . . . . .136 A1
St Judes Ho 6
W10 . . . . .23 B2
St Jude's Rd E2 . . . .25 A3
St Jude St N16 . . . .16 A3
St Julian's Rd
NW6 . . . . .23 C4
St Katharine's Ho
N1 . . . . .85 B2
St Katharine's Prec
NW1 . . . . .82 A2
St Katharine's Way
E1 . . . . .125 A2
St Katherine's Pier
E1 . . . . .125 A2
St Katherine's Row
EC3 . . . . .110 B1
St Katherine's Wlk 1
W11 . . . . .30 C1
St Kilda's Rd N16. . . .7 A3
St Laurence's CI
NW6 . . . . .22 C4
St Lawrence Ct 5
N1 . . . . .87 C4
St Lawrence Ho
SE1 . . . . .138 B2
St Lawrence St
E14 . . . . .34 B1
St Lawrence Terr
W10 . . . . .31 A4
St Lawrence Way
SW9 . . . . .173 C2
St Leonards Ct
SW14 . . . . .55 B4
St Leonard's Ct 1
N1 . . . . .97 C4
St Leonard's Hospl
N1 . . . . .24 A3
St Leonards Rd
SW14 . . . . .55 B4
St Leonard's Rd
Becontree NW10 . . .20 C1
South Bromley E14. . .34 B4

St Leonard's Sq
NW5 . . . . .12 C2
St Leonard's St 3
SW3 . . . . .E3 . .27 A2
St Loo Ave SW3 . . .158 B4
St Loo Ct SW3 . . . .158 C4
St LUKE'S 97 A2
St Luke's Ave SW4. .61 C3
St Luke's CE Prim Sch
7 Cubitt Town
E14 . . . . .42 C2
North Sheen TW9. . .44 C1
Paddington W9. . . . .23 C1
Shoreditch EC1. . . . .97 A3
1 West Hampstead
NW6 . . . . .10 C2
St Luke's CI EC1 . . .97 A2
St Luke's Ct 1 . . . . .31 B3
St Luke's Mews
W11 . . . . .31 B3
St Luke's Prim Sch 5
E16 . . . . .35 B4
St Luke's Sq E16 . . .35 B3
St Luke's St SW3 . .144 B2
St Margaret's Cres
SW15 . . . . .57 A2
St Margaret's Ct
Putney SW15 . . . . .57 A3
SE1 . . . . .123 B1
St Margaret's La
W8 . . . . .128 A1
St Margarets Lo
W3 . . . . .37 A4
St Margaret's Rd
Brockley SE4. . . . . .66 B3
Kensal Green
NW10 . . . . .22 B2
St Margaret's Sch
NW3 . . . . .11 A4
St Margaret St
SW1 . . . . .134 A3
St Mark's CE Prim Sch
Kennington SE11 . .163 A4
11 Upper Holloway
N19 . . . . .5 A3
St Mark's CI 5
SE10 . . . . .52 B3
St Mark's Cres
NW1 . . . . .81 C4
St Marks Gate E9 . .18 B1
St Mark's Gr
SW10 . . . . .156 B2
St Mark's Ho 6
SE17 . . . . .48 C4
St Mark's Mans 14
N4 . . . . .5 B2
St Mark's PI W11. . .31 A3
St Marks Rd
15 North Kensington
NW10 . . . . .30 C3
North Kensington
W10 . . . . .30 C4
St Mark's Rd W11 . .31 A3
St Mark's Rise E8 . .16 C3
St Mark's Sq NW1. .81 B3
St Mark St E1 . . . .111 A1
St Martin-in-the-
Fields High Sch 27
SW2 . . . . .74 C3
St Martin's
Almshouses NW1 .82 C4
St Martin's CI NW1 .82 C4

St Martins Ct N1 . . .24 A4

St Martin's Ct
WC2 . . . . **120** A4
West Norwood
SE27 . . . . .75 A2

St Martin's La
WC2 . . . . **120** A3

St Martin's Le Grand
EC1 . . . . **108** C2

St Martin's Pl
WC2 . . . . **120** A3

St Martin's Rd
SW9 . . . . **172** C2

St Martin's St
WC2 . . . . **119** C3

St Martin's Way
SW17 . . . . .71 B1

St Mary Abbots CE
Prim Sch W8 . . . . **128** A3

St Mary Abbot's Ct
W14 . . . . **126** C1

St Mary Abbot's Pl
W8 . . . . **127** A1

St Mary Abbots Terr
W14 . . . . **127** A1

St Mary at Hill
EC3 . . . . **124** A3

St Mary Axe EC3. . **110** B2

St Marychurch St
SE16 . . . . .40 B4

St Mary Graces Ct
E1 . . . . **125** A3

St Marylebone CE Sch
The W1 . . . . **103** C4

St Mary le Bow
Church EC2 . . . . . **109** A1

St Mary- le-Park Ct
SW11 . . . . **158** B1

St Mary Magdalene
Acad N7 . . . . .14 C2

St Mary Magdalene
CE Prim Sch
6 Greenwich
SE10 . . . . .43 B3
3 Paddington W2 **100** A4
10 Peckham SE15 . . .50 A1

St Mary Magdalen's
RC Prim Sch
Brockley SE4 . . . . .66 A3
14 Mortlake SW14 . . .55 C4

St Mary Magdelen's
RC Jun Sch **11**
. . . . .9 A2

St Mary Newington Cl
SE17 . . . . **152** B2

St Mary of the Angels
RC Prim Sch **2**
W2 . . . . .31 C3

St Mary & St Michael
Prim Sch **27** E1. . .32 B3

St Mary & St Pancras
CE Prim Sch
NW1 . . . . .83 B1

St Mary's Bryanston
Square CE Sch
W1 . . . . **102** C4

St Mary's CE Prim Sch
Islington N1 . . . . . **86** B4
2 London N16. . . . .7 A2
London SE13. . . . . .67 A2
19 Putney SW15 . . .57 C4
Willesden NW10. . . . .8 A2
St Mary's Ct W6 . . .38 B3

St Mary's Est **2**
SE16 . . . . .40 B4

St Mary's Flats
NW1 . . . . **93** B4

St Mary's Gate
W8 . . . . **128** A1

St Mary's Gdns
SE11 . . . . **149** C4

St Mary's Gr
Barnes SW13 . . . . .57 A4
Chiswick W4 . . . . .45 A4
Islington N1 . . . . . .15 A2
Richmond TW10,
TW9 . . . . .54 B3

St Mary's Ho **11**
W2 . . . . **101** C2

St Mary's Hospl
Medical Sch **81**
W2 . . . . **101** C2

St Mary's Kilburn CE
Prim Sch **16**
NW6 . . . . .23 C4

St Mary's Mans
Dagenham NW10. . .21 A4
Paddington W2 . . . **101** B4

St Mary's Mews
NW6 . . . . .11 A1

St Mary's Path N1 . **86** B4

St Mary's RC Prim Sch
Chiswick W4 . . . . .46 A4
10 Clapham Pk
SW4 . . . . .61 B2
Clapham SW8 . . . **170** B4
Hammersmith W14 . .39 C3
Paddington NW6 . . .23 C3
9 W10 . . . . .23 A1

St Mary's Rd
Golders Green
NW11 . . . . .1 A4
Harlesdon NW10 . . .21 A4
Nunhead SE15 . . . . .50 B1

St Mary's Sch
Hampstead NW3 . . .11 C3

St Mary's Sq W2. . **101** B4

St Mary's Terr
W2 . . . . **101** B4

St Mary's Twr EC1 . **97** A1

St Mary's Wlk
SE11 . . . . **149** C4

St Matthews Ct
SE1 . . . . **136** C1

St Matthew's Ho **2**
SE17 . . . . .48 C4

St Matthew's Lo
NW1 . . . . **83** A2

St Matthew's Prim
Sch SW1 . . . . **133** C2

St Matthew's Rd
SW2 . . . . .62 B2

St Matthew's Row
E2 . . . . .24 C1 **99** B2

St Matthew St
SW1 . . . . **133** B1

St Matthias CE Prim
Sch E2 . . . .24 B1 **99** A2

St Matthias's CE Prim
Sch **20** N16 . . . . . .16 A4

St Mauritius Ho
SE13 . . . . .67 B2

St Maur Rd SW6 . . **165** A3

St Michael & All
Angels CE Acad **27**
SE5 . . . . **48** A3

St Michael's Alley
EC3 . . . . **109** C1

St Michael's Cath Coll
85 SE16 . . . . **139** B3

St Michael's CE Prim
Sch
Camden Town
NW1 . . . . **82** C4
Highgate N6 . . . . . . **3** C4
Wandsworth SW18 . .70 B4

St Michael's Ct **2**
E14 . . . . .34 B4

St Michael's Ct
NW11 . . . . .1 B4

St Michael's Flats
NW1 . . . . **83** B1

St Michael's Gdns
W10 . . . . .31 A4

St Michael's Rd
Cricklewood NW2 . . .9 B4
Stockwell SW9 . . . **172** C2

St Michael's St
W2 . . . . **102** A2

St Mildred's Ct
EC2 . . . . **109** B1

St Monica's RC Prim
Sch **24** N1 . . . .24 A2 **98** A4

St Nicholas' Flats
NW1 . . . . **83** B1

St Nicholas Ho
SE8 . . . . .51 C4

St Nicholas Mans
SW17 . . . . .72 B2

St Nicholas St SE8. .51 C2

St Norbert Gn SE4. .66 A3

St Norbert Rd SE4. .66 A3

St Olaf's Rd SW6 . **154** B2

St Olaves Ct **2** . .45 C4

St Olave's Ct EC2 . **109** B1

St Olave's Est SE1 **138** B4

St Olave's Gdns
SE11 . . . . **149** B4

St Olave's Mans
SE11 . . . . **149** B4

St Olav's Sq **2**
SE16 . . . . .40 B4

St Osmund's CE Prim
Sch SW13 . . . . .46 B2

St Oswald's Pl
SE11 . . . . **148** C1

St Oswulf St SW1 **147** C3

St Owen Ho SE1 . . **138** B2

ST PANCRAS 94 B4

St Pancras
Almshouses **2**
NW5 . . . . .12 B3

St Pancras
Commercial Ctr
NW1 . . . . **83** A4

St Pancras Hospl
NW1 . . . . **83** B3

St Pancras
International Sta
WC1 . . . . **94** A4

St Pancras Way
NW1 . . . . **83** B4

St Patrick's RC Prim
Sch NW5 . . . . .13 A3

St Paul's Cath . . . **108** C1

St Paul's Cath Sch
EC4 . . . . **108** C1

St Paul's CE Prim Sch
W6 . . . . .39 B1

St Paul's CE Prim Sch
continued
Hampstead NW3 . . .12 B1
SE17 . . . . **150** C2

St Paul's Church Yd
EC4 . . . . **108** C1

St Pauls Cl W5 . . . .36 B4

St Pauls Cres
NW1 . . . . .13 C1

St Paul's Ct
Clapham SW4. . . . .61 C3
6 Upper Holloway
N19 . . . . .4 B2

St Paul's Dr E15. . .19 C3

St Paul's Girls' Sch **1**
W6 . . . . .39 C2

St Pauls Mews
NW1 . . . . .13 C1

St Paul's Pl N1 . . . .15 C2

St Pauls Rd TW9. . .54 B4

St Paul's Rd N1 . . . .15 B2

St Paul's Sch
SW13 . . . . .39 A1

St Paul's Sta EC2 **108** C2

St Pauls Steiner Sch
2 N1 . . . . .15 C2

St Paul St N1. . . . . **87** A3

St Paul's Terr
SE17 . . . . **48** A4

St Pauls View WC1 . **95** B3

St Paul's Way **3**
E3 . . . . .33 C4

St Paul's Way Com
Sch **28** E3. . . . . . .33 C4

St Paul's Whitechapel
CE Prim Sch E1 . . **125** C4

St Paul's with St
Michael's CE Prim
Sch **24** E8 . . . . .24 C4

St Paul with St Luke
CE Prim Sch **18**
E3 . . . . .33 B4

St Peter & St Paul RC
Prim Sch EC1 . . . . **96** B2

St Peter's Alley
EC3 . . . . **109** C1

St Peter's Ave **37**
E2 . . . . .25 A3

St Petersburgh Mews
W2 . . . . **114** A3

St Petersburgh Pl
W2 . . . . **114** A3

St Peter's CE Prim
Sch
15 Chiswick W6 . .38 C1
6 Paddington W9 . .23 C1
SE17 . . . . **151** B1

St Peter's Church Ct
N1 . . . . **86** B3

St Peter's Ct **1**
SW17 . . . . .72 A2

St Peter's Cl E2 . . . .24 C3

St Peters Ct
New Cross SE4 . . . .51 B1
22 Stepney E1 . . . . .25 B1

St Peter's Eaton Sq CE
Prim Sch SW1 . . . **132** B1

St Peter's Gdns
SE22 . . . . .74 C1

St Peters Ho WC1 . **94** B3

St Peter's Ho
4 SE17 . . . . .48 C4
Stamford Hill N16. . . . .7 A4

St Peter's London
Docks CE Prim Sch
11 E1 . . . . .32 B1

St Peter's Pl W9. . . **88** A1

St Peter's Rd W6 . .38 C1

St Peter's Sq
Chiswick W6 . . . . .38 B1
Hackney E2 . . . . . . .24 C3

St Peter's St N1 . . . **86** B2

St Peter's Street
Mews N1. . . . . **86** B2

St Peter's Terr
SW6 . . . . **154** B1

St Peter's Villas **3**
W6 . . . . .38 C2

St Peter's Way N1 . .16 A1

St Peter's Wharf **8**
W6 . . . . .38 C1

St Philip Ho WC1 . . **95** B3

St Philip Sq **1**
SW8 . . . . **170** A1

St Philip's Rd E8 . .16 C2

St Philip's Sch
SW7 . . . . **143** A3

St Philip St SW8. . **170** A1

St Philip's Way N1 . **87** A3

St Quentin Ho
SW18 . . . . .59 C1

St Quintin Ave
W10 . . . . .30 C4

St Quintin Gdns **1**
W10 . . . . .30 B4

St Regis Hts NW3. . .2 A1

St Richard's Ho
NW1 . . . . **93** B4

St Rule St SW8 . . . **170** C1

St Saviours & St Olaves
CE Sch SE1. . . . . **137** C1

St Saviour's CE Prim
Sch
8 Bow Comm
E14 . . . . .34 A4
Camberwell SE24 . .63 B3
28 Paddington W9 . .88 B1

St Saviours Ho **36**
SE1 . . . . **139** B3

St Saviour's RC Prim
Sch
SW2 . . . . .62 B2

St Saviour's Rd
SW2 . . . . .62 B2

St Saviour's Wharf
SE1 . . . . **139** A4

St Scholastica's RC
Prim Sch **6** E5. . . .7 C1

St Silas Pl NW5. . . .12 C2

St Simon's Ave
SW15 . . . . .57 B2

St Stephen's Ave
W12 . . . . .39 A4

St Stephen's CE Prim
Sch
18 London W12 . .39 B4
Paddington W2 . . . .31 C4
2 St Johns SE8 . . . .51 C1
SW8 . . . . **162** C2

St Stephen's Cl
Maitland Pk NW5 . . .12 B3
NW8 . . . . **80** B3

St Stephen's Cres
W2 . . . . .31 C3

St Stephen's Gdns
Notting Hill W2 . . . .31 C3
4 Putney SW15 . . .58 B2

St Stephen's Gr
SE13 . . . . .67 B4

St Stephens Ho **7**
SE17 . . . . .48 C4

St Stephen's Mews 34
W2 . . . . .31 C4
St Stephen's Rd
E3 . . . . .26 B3
St Stephen's Row
EC4 . . . . .109 B1
St Stephen's Terr
SW8 . . . . .162 C1
St Stephen's Wlk
SW7 . . . . .142 C4
St Swithin's La
EC4 . . . . .109 B1
St Swithin's Rd
SE13 . . . . .67 C2
St Theresas Cl E9 . .18 C4
St Thomas' CE Prim
Sch 2 W10 . . . . . . .23 A1
St Thomas Ct 14 . . .13 B1
St Thomas Ho 2
E1 . . . . .32 C3
St Thomas More
Language Coll
SW3 . . . . .144 C3
St Thomas of
Canterbury RC Prim
Sch SW6 . . . . .154 C2
St Thomas Rd E16 . .35 C3
St Thomas' Rd W4 . .45 B4
St Thomas's Gdns
NW5 . . . . .12 C2
St Thomas's Hospl
SE1 . . . . .134 C2
St Thomas's Pl 20
E9 . . . . .17 B1
St Thomas's Rd
Dagenham NW10 . . .21 A4
Highbury N4, N5 . . . . .5 C1
St Thomas's Sq E9 . .17 B1
St Thomas St SE1 . .123 C1
St Thomas's Way
SW6 . . . . .155 A1
St Thomas the
Apostle Coll
SE15 . . . . .50 B2
St Ursula's Convent
Sch SE10 . . . . .52 C3
St Vincent De Paul Ho
24 E1 . . . . .32 B4
St Vincent De Paul RC
Prim Sch SW1 . .133 A2
St Vincent Ho
SE1 . . . . .138 C2
St Vincent's Catholic
Prim Sch W3 . . . . . .28 A2
St Vincent's RC Prim
Sch W1 . . . . .103 C3
St Vincent SW1 . . . .103 C3
Salamanca Pl SE1 . .148 C3
Salamanca St
SE11 . . . . .148 C3
Salcombe Gdns
SW4 . . . . .61 A3
Salcombe Lo NW5 . .12 C4
Salcombe Rd 23
N16 . . . . .16 A3
Salcombe Villas
TW10 . . . . .54 A2
Salcot N4 . . . . .5 B2
Salcott Rd SW11 . . .60 B2
Salehurst Rd SE4 . . .66 B1
Salem Ho 13 E1 . . . .17 C2
Salem Rd W2 . . . . . .114 B4
Sale Pl W2 . . . . .102 A2
Sale St E2 . . . .24 C1 99 C2
Salford Ho 5 E14 . .42 B2

Salford Rd SW12,
SW2 . . . . .73 C3
Salisbury Ct SE17 . .151 B4
Salisbury Ct
Bermondsey
SE16 . . . . .139 C1
Chiswick W4 . . . . . . .38 A2
EC4 . . . . .108 A1
Hackney E9 . . . . . . .18 A3
Salisbury Ho
2 Islington N1 . . . . .15 A2
Islington N1 . . . . . . .86 A4
8 Poplar E14 . . . . . .34 A3
Westminster SW1 . .147 C2
Wimbledon SW19 . .69 C1
Salisbury Mews
SW6 . . . . .154 C1
Salisbury Pl
Camberwell SW9 . . .48 A3
Marylebone W1 . . . .102 C4
Salisbury Rd W4 . . .45 B4
Salisbury Sq EC4 . .107 C1
Salisbury St
10 Acton W3 . . . . . . .37 B4
NW8 . . . . .90 A1
Salisbury Terr
SE15 . . . . .65 B4
Salisbury Wlk N19 . . .4 B2
Salisbury Yd 5
SE13 . . . . .67 B4
Salmon La E14 . . . . .33 A3
Salmon St 13 E14 . . .33 B3
Saltcoats Rd W4 . . .38 A4
Saltdene N4 . . . . .5 B3
Salter Rd
Rotherhithe SE16 . . .32 C1
SE16 . . . . .33 A1
Salters' Hall Ct
EC4 . . . . .123 B4
Salters Rd W10 . . . . .22 C1
Salter St
College Pk NW10 . . .21 C2
11 Poplar E14 . . . . . .33 C2
Saltoun Rd SW2,
SW9 . . . . .62 C3
Saltram Cres W9 . . .23 C2
Saltwell St E14 . . . . .33 C2
Saltwood Gr SE17 . .151 B1
Saltwood Ho 16
SE15 . . . . .50 B4
Salusbury Prim Sch
NW6 . . . . .23 B4
Salusbury Rd NW6 . .23 A4
Salutation Rd
SE10 . . . . .43 A2
Salvin Rd SW15 . . . . .57 C4
Salway Rd E15 . . . . .19 C2
Salween Ho 2
N16 . . . . .15 C4
Sambrook Ho 29
E1 . . . . .32 B4
Samels Ct W6 . . . . . .38 C1
Samford Ho N1 . . . . .85 B3
Samford St NW8 . . . .90 A1
Sam Manners Ho 7
SE10 . . . . .43 A1
Sam March Ho 5
E14 . . . . .34 C3
Sampson St E1 . . . .125 C1
Samuel Cl
SE14 . . . . .50 C4
Shoreditch E8 . . . . . .24 B4
Samuel Ct
N1 . . . . .24 A2 98 A3

Samuel Jones Ind Est
7 SE15 . . . . .49 A3
Samuel Lewis Bldgs
N1 . . . . .14 C2
Samuel Lewis Trust
Dwellings
6 Camberwell
SE5 . . . . .48 B2
Chelsea SW3 . . . . .144 A3
Walham Green
SW6 . . . . .155 C2
West Kensington
W14 . . . . .140 B4
Samuel Rhodes Sch
8 Finsbury Pk N7 . . .5 C2
8 Islington N5 . . . . .15 A3
N1 . . . . .85 B4
Samuel Richardson
Ho W14 . . . . .140 C3
Samuel's Cl 6 W6 . .39 B2
Samuel St SE15 . . . .49 B3
Sancroft Ct SW11 . .168 B4
Sancroft Ho SE11 . .149 A2
Sancroft St SE11 . . .149 A2
Sanctuary Mews 18
E8 . . . . .16 B2
Sanctuary The
2 Wapping E1 . . . . .32 A1
Westminster SW1 . .133 C2
Sandale Cl N16 . . . . .6 C1
Sandall Ho 7
E3 . . . . .26 A3
Sandall Rd NW5 . . . .13 B2
Sandalwood Cl
E1 . . . . .26 A1
Sandalwood Ho 5
NW3 . . . . .11 A2
Sandbourne
4 Kensington
W11 . . . . .31 C3
Sandbourne 17
Paddington NW8 . . .78 B4
Sandbourne Rd
SE4 . . . . .65 C3
Sandbrook Rd N16 . .7 A1
Sandby Ho
6 Camberwell
SE5 . . . . .49 A2
7 Kilburn NW6 . . . . .23 C4
Sandell St SE1 . . . . .135 B4
Sanderling Ct 20
SE8 . . . . .51 B4
Sanders Ho WC1 . . .95 B4
Sanderson Ho
7 SE8 . . . . .41 B1
NW5 . . . . .13 A4
Sanderson Ho 7
SE10 . . . . .43 B2
Sanderstead Ave
NW2 . . . . .1 A2
Sanderstead Cl
SW12 . . . . .73 B4
Sanders Way 3
N19 . . . . .4 C3
Sandfield WC1 . . . . .94 B3
Sandford Ct N16 . . . .7 A3
Sandford Row
SE17 . . . . .151 C2
Sandford St SW6 . .156 B1
Sandgate Ho 15
E5 . . . . .17 A4
Sandgate La SW17,
SW18 . . . . .72 A3
Sandgate St SE15 . . .50 A4
Sandgate Trad Est
SE15 . . . . .50 A4
Sandham Ct SW4 . .172 B3

Sandhills The
SW10 . . . . .157 A4
Sandhurst Ct SW2 . .62 A3
Sandhurst Ho 12
E1 . . . . .32 B4
Sandilands Rd
SW6 . . . . .166 A3
Sandison St SE15 . . .64 C4
Sandland St WC1 . .107 A3
Sandlings Cl SE15 . .50 A1
Sandmere Rd SW4 . .62 A3
Sandon Ho 5
SW2 . . . . .74 A4
Sandown Ho 2
W4 . . . . .37 B1
Sandpiper Cl SE16 . .41 B4
Sandpiper Ct
Cubitt Town
E14 . . . . .42 B3
10 SE8 . . . . .51 C3
Sandridge St 3
N19 . . . . .4 B2
Sandringham Cl 1
SW19 . . . . .69 C3
Sandringham Ct
Marylebone W1 . . . .105 A1
Putney SW15 . . . . . .57 C1
10 Rotherhithe
SE16 . . . . .32 C1
8 St John's Wood W9 .89 A3
Sandringham Flats
WC2 . . . . .119 C4
Sandringham Ho
Richmond TW10 . . . .54 C2
W14 . . . . .140 A4
Sandringham Rd
Dalston E8 . . . . .16 B3
Golders Green NW11 . .1 A4
Willesden NW2 . . . . . .9 C2
Sandrock Rd SE13 . .66 C4
Sands End La
SW6 . . . . .166 B4
Sandstone TW9 . . . .44 C3
Sandstone Pl N19 . . .4 A2
Sandways 8 TW9 . . .44 C2
Sandwell Cres 2
NW6 . . . . .10 C2
Sandwell Mans 3
NW6 . . . . .10 C2
Sandwich Ho
12 Rotherhithe
SE16 . . . . .40 B4
WC1 . . . . .94 A3
Sandwich St WC1 . .94 A3
Sandy Lo N6 . . . . .4 B4
Sandy Rd NW3 . . . . . .2 A2
Sandy's Row E1 . . . .110 B3
Sanford La N16 . . . . .7 B2
Sanford St SE14,
SE8 . . . . .51 A4
Sanford Terr N16 . . . .7 B1
Sanford Wlk
SE14 . . . . .51 A4
8 Stoke Newington
N16 . . . . .7 B2
Sangora Rd 17
SW11 . . . . .59 C3
San Ho 26 E2 . . . . . .25 B3
Sankey Ho 22 E2 . . .25 B3
Sansom Rd E11 . . . . .19 C4
Sansom St
Camberwell SE5 . . . .48 C2

Sansom St continued
SE5 . . . . .48 C3
Sans Wlk EC1 . . . . . .96 A2
Santley Ho SE1 . . . .135 C3
Santley St SW4 . . . . .62 A3
Santos Rd SW18 . . . .58 C2
Sapcote Trad Ctr
NW10 . . . . .8 B2
Saperton Wlk
SE11 . . . . .149 A4
Sapperton Ct EC1 . .96 C2
Sapphire Ct 13
E1 . . . . .125 B4
Sapphire Rd SE8 . . . .41 A1
Saracen's Head Yd
EC3 . . . . .110 B1
Saracen St 14 . . . . .33 C3
Sarah Ho
Roehampton
SW15 . . . . .56 B3
3 Stepney E1 . . . . . .32 A3
Sarah Swift Ho
SE1 . . . . .137 C4
Sara Lane Ct 81
N1 . . . . .24 A3
Saratoga Rd E5 . . . .17 B4
Sardinia Ho WC2 . . .106 C1
Sardinia St WC2 . . .106 C1
Sarjant Path SW19 . .69 C2
Sark Ho 3 N1 . . . . . .15 B2
Sarnesfield Ho
SE15 . . . . .50 A4
Sarratt Ho 8 W10 . .30 B4
Sarre Rd NW2 . . . . . .10 B3
Sarsden Bldgs
W1 . . . . .103 C1
Sarsfeld Rd SW12,
SW17 . . . . .72 B3
Sartor Rd SE15 . . . . .65 C3
Sarum Hall Sch
NW3 . . . . .12 A1
Sarum Ho
W11 . . . . .31 B2 113 A3
Sassoon Ho SE15 . . .50 B1
Satchwell Rd 17
E2 . . . . .24 C2 99 B3
Saturn Ho 4 E3 . . . .26 C4
Saul Ct 4 SE15 . . . . .49 B4
Saunders Cl 14
E14 . . . . .33 B2
Saunders Ho 11
W2 . . . . .74 C3
Saunders Ness Rd
E14 . . . . .42 C2
Saunders St SE11 . .149 B4
Savage Gdns EC3 . .124 B4
Savana N16 . . . . .7 A2
Savannah Cl 9
SE15 . . . . .49 B3
Savernake Ho N4 . . . .6 C4
Savernake Rd
NW3 . . . . .12 B4
Saville Rd W4 . . . . . .37 C3
Saville Row W1 . . . . .118 C4
Savill Ho 2 SW4 . . . .61 C1
Savona St SW8 . . . .160 C1
Savoy Circus W3 . . .29 B2
Savoy Ct
Earl's Ct SW5 . . . . .141 C4
Strand WC2 . . . . . . .120 B3
Savoy Hill WC2 . . . .120 B3
Savoy Mews SW9 . . .62 A4
Savoy Pier WC2 . . . .120 C3
Savoy Pl WC2 . . . . .120 B3

Savoy Row WC2 . . 120 C4
Savoy St WC2 . . . . 120 C3
Savoy Steps WC2 . . 120 C3
Savoy Way WC2 . . . 120 C3
Sawkins Cl SW19 . . . 70 A2
Sawley Rd W12 . . . . 29 C1
Sawmill Yd E3 . . . . . 26 A4
Sawyer St SE1 . . . . 136 C4
Saxby Rd SW2 . . . . . 74 A4
Saxonbury Ct

Kentish Town

N7 . . . . 13 C3

Lower Holloway

N7 . . . . 14 A3
Saxoncroft Ho
SW16 . . . . 73 C1
Saxon Dr W3 . . . . . . 28 A4
Saxonfield Cl SW2 . . 74 B4
Saxon Hall W2 . . . . 114 A3
Saxon Ho 4 SW4 . . . 61 C3
Saxon Rd E3 . . . . . . 26 B3
Saxton Cl SE13 . . . . 67 C4
Sayer Ho SE4 . . . . . . 66 A3
Sayes Court St
SE8 . . . . 51 B4
Sayes Ct St SE8 . . . . 51 B4
Scafell NW1 . . . . . . 92 C4
Scala St W1 . . . . . . 105 A4
Scampston Mews 5
W10 . . . . 30 C3
Scandrett St 3
E1 . . . . 32 A1
Scarba Wlk N1 . . . . . 15 C2
Scarborough Rd N4 . . 5 C3
Scarborough St
E1 . . . . 111 A1
Scarlet Cl E15 . . . . . 19 A3
Scarlette Manor Wlk
10 SE24 . . . . 74 C4
Scarsbrook Ho 2
SW2 . . . . 62 C1
Scarsdale Pl W8 . . . 128 A2
Scarsdale Villas
W8 . . . . 127 C1
Scarth Rd SW13 . . . . 56 B4
Scawen Rd SE8 . . . . 41 A1
Scawfell St E2 . . . . . 24 B3
Sceptre Ho 10 E1 . . . 25 B1
Sceptre Rd E2 . . . . . 25 B2
Schiller Univ SE1 . . . 121 B1
Schofield Wlk SE3 . . 53 C3
Sch of Pharmacy
WC1 . . . . 94 B2
Sch of the Islamic
Republic of Iran The
6 NW6 . . . . 23 C3
Scholars Cl 5 N16 . . . 7 A1
Scholars Pl 9 N16 . . . 7 A1
Scholars Rd SW12 . . 73 B3
Scholefield Rd N19 . . 4 C2
Scholey Ho SW11 . . . 60 A4
Schomberg Ho
SW1 . . . . 147 C4
Schonfeld Sq N16 . . . 6 C3
School App 3
E2 . . . . 24 A2 98 B4
Schoolbank Rd
SE10 . . . . 43 B2
School Bell Cloisters
17 E3 . . . . 26 B3
Schoolbell Mews 18
E3 . . . . 26 A3
School Flats SW8 . . 172 A3
School Ho SE1 . . . . 152 A4

Schoolhouse La
E1 . . . . 32 C2
School of Economic
Science W1 . . . . . . 103 C2
School Rd NW10 . . . 20 C1
School Sq SE10 . . . . 43 B3
Schooner Cl

Cubitt Town E14 . . . 42 C3

Rotherhithe

SE16 . . . . 40 C4
Schubert Rd SW15 . . 58 B2
Science Mus SW7 . . 129 B1
Sclater St
E1 . . . . 24 B1 99 A2
Scoles Cres SW2 . . . 74 C3
Scoresby St SE1 . . . 122 A1
Scorton Ho 2 N1 . . . 24 A3
Scotch Ho SW1 . . . . 130 C3
Scoter Cl 2 SE8 . . . . 51 B4
Scotia Bldg 10 E1 . . . 32 C2
Scotia Ct 3 SE16 . . . 40 B3
Scotia Rd 2 SW2 . . . 74 C4
Scotland Pl SW1 . . . 120 A1
Scotney Ho E9 . . . . . 17 B2
Scotson Ho SE11 . . . 149 B3
Scotswood St EC1 . . 95 C2
Scott Ave SW15,
SW18 . . . . 58 A1
Scott Ct

Acton W4 . . . . 37 C4

Clapham SW11 . . . 170 B1

Stoke Newington

N16 . . . . 7 A1
Scott Ellis Gdns
NW8 . . . . 89 B3
Scott Ho

Barnsbury N7 . . . . . 14 B2

Islington N1 . . . . . . 87 B4

Lisson Gr NW8 . . . . 90 A1

Millwall E14 . . . . . . 41 C4
Scott Lidgett Cres
SE16 . . . . 139 C3
Scotts Ct 6 W12 . . . 39 A4
Scott's Rd W12 . . . . 39 A4
Scott's Sufferance
Wharf SE1 . . . . 139 A3
Scott St E1 . . . . 25 A1
Scott's Yd EC4 . . . . 123 B4
Scoulding Ho 6
E14 . . . . 41 C3
Scoulding Rd E16 . . . 35 C3
Scouler St E14 . . . . . 34 C2
Scout App NW10 . . . . 8 A4
Scout La SW4 . . . . . 61 B4
Scovell Cres SE1 . . . 136 C3
Scovell Rd SE1 . . . . 136 C3
Scrimgeour Pl N4 . . . 6 B3
Scriven Ct 8 E8 . . . . 24 B4
Scriven St E8 . . . . . . 24 B4
Scrooby St SE6 . . . . 67 A1
Scrope Bldg EC1 . . . 107 B4
Scrubs La NW10, W10,
W12 . . . . 22 A1
Scrutton Cl SW12 . . . 73 C4
Scrutton St
EC2 . . . . 24 A1 98 A1
Scutari Rd SE22 . . . . 65 B2
Scylla Rd SE15 . . . . 65 A4
Seabright St 27
E2 . . . . 25 A2
Seacole Cl W3 . . . . . 28 C4
Seacon Twr 8
E14 . . . . 41 C4
Seaford Ho 13
SE16 . . . . 40 B4
Seaford St WC1 . . . . 94 B3

Seaforth Cres N5 . . . 15 B3
Seaforth Lo 2
SW13 . . . . 46 B1
Seaforth Pl SW1 . . . 133 A2
Seager Pl 8 E3 . . . . . 51 C4
Seagrave Cl 6 E1 . . . 32 C4
Seagrave Lo SW6 . . 155 C4
Seagrave Rd SW6 . . 155 C4
Seagrave Rd SW6 . . 155 C4
Seagull La E16 . . . . . 35 C2
Seal Ho SE1 . . . . . . 137 C2
SEA LIFE London
Aquarium 5
SE1 . . . . 134 C3
Seal St E8 . . . . 16 B4
Searle Pl N4 . . . . 5 B3
Searles Cl SW11 . . . 158 B1
Searles Rd SE1 . . . . 151 C4
Searson Ho SE17 . . . 150 B3
Sears St SE5 . . . . . . 48 C3
Seasalter Ho 10
SW9 . . . . 173 B4
Seaton Cl SW15 . . . . 69 A4
Seaton Point E5 . . . . 16 C4
Seavington Ho 3
SE5 . . . . 64 A4
Sebastian Ho 2
N1 . . . . 24 A3
Sebastian St EC1 . . . 96 B3
Sebbon St N1 . . . . . . 15 A1
Sebright Ho 20 E2 . . 24 C3
Sebright Pas 30
E2 . . . . 24 C3
Secker Ho SW9 . . . . 48 A1
Secker St SE1 . . . . . 121 B1
Second Ave

East Acton W3 . . . . 29 B1

Kensal Town W10 . . 23 A1

Mortlake SW14 . . . . 56 A4
Sedan Way SE17 . . . 152 A2
Sedding St SW1 . . . 145 B4
Seddon Ho EC2 . . . . 108 C4
Seddon St WC1 . . . . 95 A3
Sedgeford Rd
W12 . . . . 29 B1
Sedgewick Ho
SW19 . . . . 69 C2
Sedgley Ho N4 . . . . . 5 B2
Sedgmoor Pl SE5 . . . 49 A3
Sedgwick St E9 . . . . 17 C3
Sedleigh Rd SW18 . . 58 B1
Sedlescombe Rd
SW6 . . . . 155 B4
Sedley Ho SE11 . . . 149 A2
Sedley Pl W1 . . . . . 104 A1
Seething La EC3 . . . 124 B4
Sefton St SW15 . . . . 57 B4
Sekforde St EC1 . . . . 96 A2
Selbie Ave NW10 . . . 8 B3
Selborne 2 SW11 . . 60 C4
Selborne Ho SE1 . . . 137 B3
Selborne Rd 1
SE5 . . . . 48 C1
Selby Ho 10 SW4 . . . 61 B1
Selby Pl SW11 . . . . 104 A1
Selby Sq 1 W10 . . . . 23 A2
Selby St E1 . . . . 24 C1 99 C1
Selden Ho 8 SE15 . . 50 B1
Selden Rd SE15 . . . . 50 B1
Seldon Ho

Nine Elms SW8 . . . 160 C1

Pimlico SW1 . . . . . 146 C1
Selhurst Cl SW19 . . . 69 C3
Selina Ho NW8 . . . . . 89 C2

Selkirk Ho
N1 . . . . 84 C4

Stoke Newington

N16 . . . . 7 A1
Sellons Ave NW10 . . 21 A4
Selma Ho 7 W12 . . . 30 A3
Selman Ho 3 E9 . . . . 18 A2
Selsdon Way 1 E14 . . 42 A3
Selsea Pl N16 . . . . . 16 A3
Selsey St E14 . . . . . 33 C4
Selway Ho SW8 . . . 172 B4
Selwood Ho 6 N4 . . . 6 C4
Selwood Pl SW7 . . . 143 B2
Selwood Terr
SW7 . . . . 143 B2
Selworthy Ho
SW11 . . . . 167 C4
Selwyn Ave TW9 . . . 54 B4
Selwyn Ct 3
TW10 . . . . 54 B2
Selwyn Ho 3
SW15 . . . . 57 C1
Selwyn Rd

Bow E3 . . . . 26 B3

Willesden NW10 . . . 8 A1
Semley Gate E9 . . . . 18 B2
Semley Ho SW1 . . . 146 A3
Semley Pl SW1 . . . . 146 A3
Senate St SE15 . . . . 50 B1
Senators Lo 23 E3 . . 26 A3
Sendall Ct 7
SW11 . . . . 59 C4
Senior St W2 . . . . . 100 A4
Senrab St 1 . . . . 32 C3
Sentamu Cl SE24 . . . 75 A3
Seraph Ct EC1 . . . . . 96 C4
Serenaders Rd 20
SW9 . . . . 173 B1
Sergeant Ind Est The
SW18 . . . . 59 A1
Serica Ct 14 SE10 . . 52 B3
Serjeant's Inn
EC4 . . . . 107 C1
Serlby Ct W14 . . . . 126 C2
Serle St WC2 . . . . . 107 A2
Sermon La EC4 . . . . 108 C1
Serpentine Ct 10
SE16 . . . . 40 C4
Serpentine Gallery
W2 . . . . 129 C3
Serpentine Rd
W2 . . . . 116 C1
Serpentine Sackler
Gallery M
W2 . . . . 116 A2
Serpentine The
W2 . . . . 116 B1
Service Route No 1
E15 . . . . 19 C1
Service Route No 2 1
E15 . . . . 19 C1
Service Route No 3 2
E15 . . . . 19 C1
Servite Ho SE13 . . . . 52 A2
Servite RC Prim Sch
SW10 . . . . 156 B4
Setchell Rd SE1 . . . 152 C4
Setchell Way SE1 . . 152 C4
Seth St 5 SE16 . . . . . 40 B4
Settlers Ct 8 E14 . . . 34 C2
Settles St E1 . . . . . . 111 C2
Settrington Rd
SW6 . . . . 166 A1
Seven Dials WC2 . . . 106 A1
Seven Islands L Ctr
SE16 . . . . 40 B3

Seven Mills Prim Sch
2 E14 . . . . 41 C4
Sevenoaks Rd SE4 . . 66 B1
Seven Sisters Rd
Finsbury Pk N4 . . . . 6 A2
Stoke Newington N4, N7,
N15 . . . . 6 B4
Seven Stars Cnr
W12 . . . . 38 C3
Seven Stars Yd
E1 . . . . 111 A4
Severnake Cl E14 . . . 41 C2
Severn Ave 2
W10 . . . . 23 A2
Severn Way NW10 . . . 8 B3
Severus Rd SW11 . . . 60 A3
Seville Ho 10 E1 . . . 125 C2
Seville Mews N1 . . . 16 A1
Seville St SW1 . . . . 131 A3
Sevington St W9 . . . 88 A1
Seward St EC1 . . . . . 96 C3
Sewardstone Rd
E2 . . . . 25 B3
Sewell Ho 2 N16 . . . 16 A3
Sextant Ave E14 . . . 42 C2
Sexton Ct 7 E14 . . . . 34 C2
Sexton's Ho 5
SE13 . . . . 52 B4
Seymour Ct

Putney SW15 . . . . . 57 A3

Upper Clapton N16 . . 7 C3
Seymour Gdns
SE4 . . . . 66 A4
Seymour Ho

Bloomsbury WC1 . . . 94 A2

Clapham SW8 . . . . 171 A2

Somers Town NW1 . . 93 C3
Seymour Mews
W1 . . . . 103 B2
Seymour Pl W1 . . . . 102 C2
Seymour Rd

Acton W4 . . . . 37 B2

Wandsworth SW18 . . 58 B1

Wimbledon SW19 . . 69 C1
Seymour St W1 . . . . 103 A1
Seymour Wlk
SW10 . . . . 156 C4
Seyssel St E14 . . . . . 42 B2
Shaa Rd W3 . . . . 28 C2
Shabana Ct 3
W12 . . . . 30 A1
Shackleton Ct

Dulwich SE21 . . . . 75 C2

Isle of Dogs E14 . . . 41 C1

Shepherd's Bush

W12 . . . . 39 A4
Shackleton Ho 5
E1 . . . . 32 B1
SHACKLEWELL 16 B4
Shacklewell Ho 2
E8 . . . . 16 B4
Shacklewell La E8 . . 16 B3
Shacklewell Prim Sch
5 E8 . . . . 16 B4
Shacklewell Rd
N16 . . . . 16 B4
Shacklewell Row
E8 . . . . 16 B4
Shacklewell St 10
E2 . . . . 24 B2 99 A3
Shad Thames SE1 . . 139 A4
SHADWELL 32 B2
Shadwell Gdns E1 . . 32 B2
Shadwell Pierhead
E1 . . . . 32 B2
Shadwell Pl 1 E1 . . . 32 B2

Shadwell Sta E1....32 A2
Shaftesbury Ave
  W1............119 C4
Shaftesbury Ct ■
  Borough The SE1...137 B2
  ■ Herne Hill SE5...63 C3
  Shoreditch N1.....87 B1
  Streatham SW16...73 C1
Shaftesbury Ctr.....22 C1
Shaftesbury Gdns
  NW10...........21 A1
Shaftesbury Ho
  ■ Canning Town
    E16..........35 B3
  ■ Stoke Newington
    N16...........7 A1
  W2............114 B4
Shaftesbury Lo ❾
  E14............34 A3
Shaftesbury Mews
  ❷ Clapham Pk
    SW4..........61 B2
  W8............127 C1
Shaftesbury Park
Chambers
  SW11..........60 C4
Shaftesbury Rd
  Finsbury Pk N4,
    N19...........5 A3
  Richmond TW9....54 A4
Shaftesbury St N1..87 B1
Shafteswood Ct
  SW17..........72 B1
Shafto Mews
  SW1...........131 A1
Shafton Rd E9.....25 C4
Shaftsbury Park Prim
  Sch ⑭ SW11...169 B1
Shafts Ct EC3.....110 A1
Shahjalal Ho ⑱
  E2............24 C3
Shakespeare Ave ❼
  NW10..........20 C4
Shakespeare Ho ❸
  E9............17 B1
Shakespeare Rd
  Acton W3.......28 B1
  Brixton SE24....63 A3
  Stonebridge NW10..20 C4
Shakespeare's Globe
  Theatre (site of)
    SE1..........123 A2
Shakespeare Twr
  EC2...........109 A4
Shakspeare Mews ❼
  N16............16 A4
Shakspeare Wlk
  N16............16 A4
Shalbourne Sq E9..18 B2
Shalcomb St
  SW10..........157 A3
Shalden Ho SW15...56 B1
Shalfleet Dr W10...30 C2
Shalford NW10.....21 C4
Shalford Ct N1.....86 A2
Shalford Ho SE1...137 C2
Shalimar Gdns W3..28 B2
Shalimar Lo W3....28 B2
Shalimar Rd W3....28 B2
Shalstone Rd SW14,
  TW9...........55 A4
Shamrock St SW4..61 C4
Shandon Ct SE4....51 A1
Shandon Rd SW4...61 B1
Shand St SE1.....138 B4

Shandy St E1......25 C1
Shan Ho WCL.....94 C1
Shannon Ct
  ⑪ Peckham SE15..49 B3
  Stoke Newington
    N16...........7 A1
  Willesden NW10...8 C1
Shannon Gr SW9...62 B3
Shannon Pl NW8...80 B2
Shanti Ct
  E1............125 C3
Shapla Prim Sch ⑳
  E1............125 C3
Shardcroft Ave
  SE24..........63 A2
Shardeloes Rd
  SE14..........51 B1
Shard's Sq SE15...49 C4
Shard The SE1....123 C1
Sharebourne Ho
  SW2............62 B2
Sharman Ho ⑬
  E14............34 B3
Sharnbrook Ho
  W6............155 B4
Sharon Gdns E9...25 B4
Sharon Rd W4.....37 C1
Sharp Ho SW8.....61 A4
Sharples Hall St ❽
  NW1............12 B1
Sharpness Ct ❷
  SE15..........49 B3
Sharratt St SE15...50 B4
Sharsted St SE17..150 A1
Sharwood WC1....85 A1
Shaver's Pl SW1...119 B3
Shawbury Ct SE22..64 B2
Shawbury Rd SE22..64 B2
Shaw Cres
  ❻ E14.........33 A3
Shaw Ct
  ❽ Acton Green
    W3...........37 B3
  ⑪ Battersea SW11..59 C4
  Upper Holloway N19..5 A2
Shawfield St SW3..144 B1
Shawford Ct
  SW15..........68 C4
Shaw Rd SE22.....64 A3
Shearing Way N7...14 A2
Shearsmith Ho ⑮
  E1............125 C4
Shearwater Ct ⑳
  SE8............51 B4
Sheba Pl E1......111 A4
Sheen Common Dr
  SW14, TW10.....54 C2
Sheen Court Rd
  TW10..........54 C3
Sheen Ct TW10....54 C3
Sheendale Rd
  TW9...........54 B3
Sheen Gate Gdns
  SW14..........55 B3
Sheengate Mans
  SW14..........55 C3
Sheen Gr N1......85 B4
Sheen La SW14....55 B3
Sheen Mount Prim
  Sch SW14.......55 A2
Sheen Pk TW10,
  TW9...........54 B3
Sheen Rd TW10,
  TW9...........54 B3
Sheen Wood
  SW14..........55 B2
Sheepcote La
  SW11..........169 A1

Sheep La E8......25 A4
Sheffield Ho ⑮
  SE15..........49 B2
Sheffield Sq ❷ E3..26 B2
Sheffield St WC2...106 C1
Sheffield Terr
  W8.....31 C1 113 C1
Shelburne Ho ⑳
  N19............4 C4
Shelburne Ct
  SW15..........57 C2
Shelburne Rd N7...14 B4
Shelbury Rd SE22..65 A2
Sheldon Ct SW8...162 A1
Sheldon Ho ⑲ E9..17 C2
Sheldon Pl E2.....25 A3
Sheldon Rd NW2...9 C4
Sheldon Sq W2....101 A3
Sheldrake Ho ⑯
  SE16..........40 C2
Sheldrake Pl W8...127 B4
Shelduck Ct ❸
  SE8............51 B4
Shelford Pl N16....6 C1
Shelgate Rd SW11..60 B2
Shell Ct SE1.....121 A1
Shelley Cl SE15....50 A1
Shelley Ct
  Finsbury Pk N4,
    SW3..........159 A4
Shelley Ho
  ❶ Bethnal Green
    E2...........25 B2
  Chelsea SW1....160 C4
  ⑨ Stoke Newington
    N16...........16 A4
  Walworth SE17...151 A2
Shelley Rd NW10...20 C4
Shellgrove Rd ❽
  N16............16 A3
Shellness Rd E5....17 A3
Shell Rd SE13.....67 A4
Shellwood Rd
  SW11..........168 C1
Shelmerdine Cl
  E3............33 C4
Shelton St WC2....106 A1
Shene Bldg EC1...107 B4
Shenfield St N1....24 A3
Shenley Rd SE5....49 A2
Shepard Ho ❼
  SW11..........59 C4
Sheperdes Pl N1...97 A4
Shepherd Cl W1...117 B4
Shepherdess Wlk
  N1............87 A1
Shepherd Ho
  ■ Barnsbury N7...14 A2
  ⑩ Poplar E14....34 A3
Shepherd Mkt
  W1............118 A1
SHEPHERD'S
BUSH.........39 B4
Shepherd's Bush Gn
  W12...........39 B4
Shepherd's Bush
Market W12.....39 B4
Shepherd's Bush Mkt
  Sta W12.......30 B1
Shepherd's Bush
  Overground Sta
    W12.........39 B4
Shepherd's Bush Pl
  W12...........39 C4
Shepherd's Bush Rd
  W6............39 B3

Shepherd's Bush Sta
  W12...........39 C4
Shepherds Ct ❽
  W12...........39 C4
Shepherd's La E9..17 C2
Shepherd's Pl W1..117 B4
Shepherd St W1...118 A1
Shepherd's Wlk
  NW3............11 C4
Sheppard Dr SE16..40 A1
Sheppard Ho
  ❽ Hackney E2...24 C3
  ❷ Streatham SW2..74 C3
Shepperton Rd N1..87 B4
Sheppey Ho SE5...49 A2
Shepton Ct SW11..167 C4
Shepton Hos ⑪ E2
  ....22 B2
Sherard Ct N19....5 A1
Sherard Ho ❷ E9..17 B1
Sheraton Ho SW1..160 B4
Sheraton St W1...105 B1
Sherborne Ho
  Pimlico SW1....146 B2
  South Lambeth
    SW8.........162 C1
Sherborne La EC4..123 C4
Sherborne St N1...87 B4
Sherbourne Ct
  SW5...........142 A4
Sherbrooke Ho ❾
  E2............25 B3
Sherbrooke Rd
  SW6...........154 B1
Sherbrooke Terr
  SW6...........154 B1
Shere Ho SE1.....137 B2
Sherfield Gdns
  SW15..........56 B1
Sheridan Bldgs
  WC2...........106 B1
Sheridan Ct
  Earl's Ct SW5...142 A3
  South Hampstead
    NW6..........11 B1
  South Lambeth
    SW9..........173 A3
Sheridan Ho
  SE11..........149 C3
  ❼ Stoke Newington
    N16...........7 A1
Sheridan Pl SW13..56 A4
Sheridan St ❻ E1..32 A3
Sheringham Prim Sch
  SW18..........70 B3
Sheringham Ho
  NW1...........102 B4
Sheringham Mews ❹
  SW18..........71 B2
Sheringham Rd
  N7............14 C2
Sherlock Ct NW8...79 B4
Sherlock Holmes Mus
  NW1...........91 A1
Sherlock Mews
  W1............103 B4
Sherrick Green Rd
  NW10...........9 A3
Sherriff Ct NW6...10 C2
Sherriff Rd NW6...10 C2
Sherrin Rd E10....19 A4
Sherston Ct
  Finsbury WC1....95 B3
  Newington SE1...150 B4

Sherwin Ho ❶
  SE11..........163 B4
Sherwin Rd SE14..50 C2
Sherwood NW6....10 A1
Sherwood Cl
  SW13..........57 A4
Sherwood Ct
  ❶ Battersea
    SW11.........59 B4
  St Johns SE13...52 A1
  W1............102 C3
Sherwood Gdns
  Bermondsey SE16..40 A1
  Millwall E14.....41 C2
Sherwood Ho N4...6 B4
Sherwood St W1...119 A4
Shetland Rd E3....26 B3
Shillaker Ct W3....29 B1
Shillibeer Pl W1...102 B3
Shillingford Ho ⑳
  E3............27 A2
Shillingford St ⑱
  N1............15 A1
Shillingstone Ho
  W14...........126 B1
Shinfield St W12...30 B3
Shipka Rd SW12...73 A3
Ship La SW14.....45 B1
Shiplake Ho ❻
  E2.....24 B2 98 C3
Shipley St ❼
  SW8...........171 B1
Ship & Mermaid Row
  SE1...........138 A4
Ship St SE8......51 C1
Ship Tavern Pas
  EC3...........124 A4
Shipton Ho
  ❼ Camden Town
    NW5..........12 C2
  Haggerston E2...24 B3
Shipton St
  E2.....24 B2 99 A4
Shipwright Rd
  SE16..........41 A4
Shipwright Yd
  SE1...........124 A1
Shirbutt St E14...34 A2
Shire Pl SW18....71 B4
Shirland Mews
  W9............23 B2
Shirland Rd W9....23 C1
Shirley Gr SW11...60 C4
Shirley Ho ⑤ SE5..48 C3
Shirley Rd W4.....37 C4
Shirley St E16....35 B3
Shirlock Rd NW3..12 B4
Shoe La EC4......107 C2
Shooters Hill Rd SE3,
  SE10..........53 A3
Shoot-Up Hill
  NW2...........10 A2
Shopstop SW11...60 A3
Shore Bsns Ctr ❸
  E9............17 B1
SHOREDITCH.....87 C1
Shoreditch Ct ❷
  E8............16 B1
Shoreditch High St
  Sta E2........24 B1
Shoreditch High St
  E2.....24 A1 98 B2
Shoreditch Ho N1..97 C3

Shoreham Cl
SW18 . . . . **59** A2
Shore Ho SW4 . . . . **61** A4
Shore Mews 30 E9 . .**17** B1
Shore Pl E9 . . . . **17** B1
Shore Rd E9 . . . . **17** B1
Shorncliffe Rd
SE1 . . . . **152** C2
Shorrolds Rd
SW6 . . . . **155** A2
Shortcroft Mead Ct
NW10 . . . . **8** C3
Shorter St EC3 . . . . **125** A4
Shortlands W6 . . . . . **39** C2
Short Rd W4 . . . . **46** A4
Shorts Gdns WC2 **106** A1
Short St SE1 . . . . **135** C4
Shottendane Rd
SW6 . . . . **165** B4
Shottfield Ave
SW14 . . . . **56** A3
Shottsford 1 W11. . **31** C3
**Shoulder of Mutton
Alley** 10 E14 . . . . . . **33** A2
Shouldham St
W1 . . . . **102** B3
Shrek's Adventure!
London SE1 . . . . . . **134** C3
Shreveport Ho 22
N19 . . . . **4** C4
Shrewsbury Ave
SW14 . . . . **55** C3
Shrewsbury Cres
NW10 . . . . **20** C4
Shrewsbury Ho
Chelsea SW3 . . . . . **158** A3
Kennington SE11 . . **163** A3
Shrewsbury Mews 33
W2 . . . . **31** C4
Shrewsbury Rd
Notting Hill W2 . .**31** C3
2 Stonebridge
NW10 . . . . **20** C4
Shrewsbury St
W10 . . . . **22** B1
Shropshire Ho
WC1 . . . . **93** A1
Shroton St NW1 . . . **102** B4
Shrubbery Cl N1. . . . **87** A3
Shrubland Rd E8 . . . **24** C4
Shrubs Ho SW1 . . . . **147** C3
Shurland Gdns
SE15 . . . . **49** B3
Shushan Cl 4 N16 . . **7** A4
Shuters Sq W14 . . . **140** C1
Shuttle St
E1 . . . . **24** C1 **99** B1
Shuttleworth Rd
SW11 . . . . **168** A2
Sibella Rd SW4. . . . **171** C1
Sicilian Ave WC1 . . **106** B3
Sidbury St SW6. . . . **164** A4
Siddons Ct WC2 . . . **106** C1
Siddons Ho 8
NW3 . . . . **12** B3
Siddons La NW1 . . . . **91** A1
Sidford Ho SE1 . . . . **135** A1
Sidford Pl SE1 . . . . . **135** A1
Sidgwick Ho 24
SW9
Sidings Mews N7 . . **14** C4
Sidlaw Ho N16 . . . . . . **7** B3

Sidmouth Ho
18 Camberwell
SE15 . . . . **49** C3
Marylebone W1 . . . **102** B2
20 Streatham SW2 . .**74** C4
Sidmouth Mews
WC1 . . . . **94** C3
Sidmouth Par NW2 . .**9** B1
Sidmouth Rd NW2. . . .**9** B1
Sidmouth St WC1. . . **94** C3
Sidney Boyd Ct
NW6 . . . . **10** C1
Sidney Godley (VC)
Ho 33 E2 . . . . **25** B2
Sidney Gr EC1. . . . . . **86** A1
Sidney Ho 4 E2 . . . . **25** C3
Sidney Miller Ct 8
W3 . . . . **28** A1
Sidney Rd SW9 . . . **173** A1
Sidney Sq E1 . . . . . . **32** B4
Sidney St E1 . . . . **32** B4
Siege Ho 14 E1 . . . . . **32** A3
Sienna Pl 1 SE23 . . **66** A1
Sigdon Rd E8 . . . . . . **16** C3
Signal Ho
9 London SE1 . . . . . **17** A1
E1 . . . . **136** C3
Signmakers Yd
NW1 . . . . **82** B3
Silbury Ho 9
SE26 . . . . **76** C1
Silbury St N1. . . . . . . **97** B4
Silchester Rd W10 . .**30** C3
Silesia Bldgs E8 . . . . **17** A1
Silex St SE1 . . . . **136** B3
Silkin Mews 24
SE15 . . . . **49** C3
Silk Mews SE11 . . . **149** C1
Silk Mills Path
SE13 . . . . **67** B4
Silk Mills Sq E9 . . . . **18** B2
Silk St EC2 . . . . **109** A4
Sillitoe Ho N1 . . . . . . **87** C3
Silsoe Ho NW1 . . . . . **82** B1
Silverbirch Wlk 1
NW3 . . . . **12** C2
Silverburn Ho 4
SW9 . . . . **48** A2
Silver Cl SE14 . . . . . . **51** A3
Silver Cres W4 . . . . . **37** A2
Silver Ct N19 . . . .**4** B1
Silverdale NW1 . . . . . **92** C4
Silverdale Ct EC1. . . **96** B2
Silvermere Rd SE6. . **67** A1
Silver Pl W1. . . . . **119** A4
Silver Rd
Shepherd's Bush
W12 . . . . **30** C2
St Johns SE13 . . . . . **67** A4
Silverthorn 17
NW6
Silverthorne Rd
SW8 . . . . **170** B1
Silverton Rd W6 . . . . **47** C4
Silvertown Way
E16 . . . . **35** C1
Silver Wlk SE16 . . . . **33** B1
Silverwood Pl 10
SE10 . . . . **52** B2
Silvester Ho
21 Bethnal Green
E2 . . . . **25** B2
3 Notting Hill W11. .**31** B3
6 Stepney E1 . . . . . . **32** A3

Silvester Rd SE22. . . **64** B2
Silvester St SE1 . . . **137** B3
Silvex Ho
E1 . . . . **24** B1 **98** C1
Silwood St SE16 . . . **40** B1
Simla Ho SE1 . . . . . . **137** C3
Simmonds Ct
SW5 . . . . **142** A3
Simmons Ho
20 Bethnal Green
E2 . . . . **24** C2 **99** B3
Finsbury Pk N7 . . . . . .**5** B2
Simms Ct SW6 . . . . . **58** A4
Simms Rd SE1 . . . . . **153** C3
Simon Cl
W11 . . . . . . **31** B2 **113** A4
Simon Ct W9 . . . . . . **23** C2
Simon Lo 31 SW19. . **69** C3
Simon Marks Jewish
Prim Sch 8 N16 . . . .**7** B2
Simons Wlk E15 . . . **19** C3
Simpson Dr W3 . . . . . **28** C3
Simpson Ho
Lisson Gr NW8 . . . . **90** A3
Vauxhall SE11 . . . . **148** C1
Simpson's Rd E14 . .**34** A2
Simpson St SW11 . . **168** A1
Sinclair Ct N5 . . . . . . **15** B2
Sinclair Gdns W14. .**39** C4
Sinclair Ho 1
SW12 . . . . **73** A3
Sir John Soane's Mus
WC2 . . . . **106** C2

Sinclair Mans 13
W12 . . . . **39** C4
Sinclair Pl SE4 . . . . . **66** C1
Sinclair Rd W14 . . . **126** A2
Sinclairs Ho 13 E3. . **26** B3
Singer Mews
SW4 . . . . **172** A1
Singer St EC2 . . . . . . **97** C3
Sion Ho SE13 . . . . . . **67** B3
Sion-Manning RC Sch
for Girls
10 Kensal Town
W10 . . . . **31** A4
2 North Kensington
W10 . . . . **30** C4
**Sir Abraham Dawes
Cotts** SW15. . . . . **58** A3
Sir Alexander Cl
W3 . . . . **29** B1
Sir Alexander Rd
W3 . . . . **29** B1
Sirdar Rd
W11 . . . . . . **31** A2 **112** A3
**Sir Francis Drake
Prim Sch** 1 SE8 . . . **41** A1
Sirinham Point
SW8 . . . . **163** A3
Sirius Bldg 11 E1 . . **32** C2
**Sir John Cass
Foundation &
Redcoat CE Sec Sch**
10 E1 . . . . **32** C4
**Sir John Cass's
Foundation Prim**
Sch EC3 . . . . **110** B1
Sir John Kirk Cl 28
SE5 . . . . **48** B3
Sir John Lillie Ho
Sch SW6 . . . . **154** B3

**Sir Oswald Stoll
Foundation The**
SW6 . . . . **156** A2
**Sir Thomas Abney
Prim Sch** N16 . . . .**6** C3
Sir Thomas More Est
SW3 . . . . **157** C3
**Sir William Burrough
Prim Sch** 27 E14. . **33** B3
**Sir William Powell's
Almshos** SW6 . . . . **58** A4
Sise La EC4 . . . . **109** B1
Siskin Ho 14 SE16 . . **40** C2
Sispara Gdns
SW18 . . . . **58** B1
Sissinghurst Ho 17
SE15 . . . . **50** B4
Sister Mabel's Way 16
SE15 . . . . **49** C3
Sisters Ave SW11 . . **60** B3
Sistova Rd SW12 . . . **73** A3
Sisulu Pl SW9 . . . . . **62** C4
Sitarey Ct 4 W12 . . **30** A1
**Site of Changing of
the Guard** SW1 . . . **132** C3
Sivill Ho 6
E2 . . . . **24** B2 **99** A4
Siward Rd SW17 . . . . **71** B1
Six Bridges Ind Est 16
SE1 . . . . **153** C1
Sixth Ave W10 . . . . . . **23** A2
Skardu Rd NW2 . . . . **10** A3
Skeena Hill SW18,
SW19 . . . . **70** A3
Skeggs Ho 5 E14 . . **42** B3
Skegness Ho 3
N7 . . . . **14** B1
Skelbrook St
SW18 . . . . **71** B2
Skelgill Rd SW15 . . **58** B3
Skelton Cl 7 E8 . . . . **16** B2
Skelton Ho N16 . . . . **16** A3
Skelwith Rd W6 . . . . **47** B4
Skenfrith Ho SE15 . .**50** A4
Sketchley Gdns
SE16 . . . . **40** C1
Skiffington Cl
SW2 . . . . **74** C3
Skinner Pl SW1 . . . . **145** B3
Skinners' Acad 10
N4 . . . .**6** B4
**Skinners Company
Sch (Upper)** 10
N16 . . . .**7** B4
Skinners La EC4. . . . **123** A4
Skinner St EC1 . . . . . **95** C2
Skipsea Ho SW18. . . **59** C1
Skipton Ho SE4 . . . . **66** A3
Skipwith Bldg
EC1 . . . . **107** B4
Skipworth Rd E9 . . . **25** B4
Skua Ct 13 SE8 . . . . **51** B4
Skyline Ct SE1 . . . . . **138** C1
Skyline Plaza Bldg 10
E1 . . . . **111** C2
Skylines E14 . . . . **42** B4
Slade Ct NW2 . . . . . . **10** A3
Sladen Pl 13 E5 . . . . **17** A4
Slagrove Pl SE13 . . **67** A2
Slaidburn St
SW10 . . . . **157** A3
Slaithwaite Rd
SE13 . . . . **67** B3
Slaney Ct NW10 . . . . . .**9** B1
Slaney Pl 1 N7 . . . . . **14** C3
Sleaford Ho 11 E3. . **26** C1

Sleaford Ind Est
SW8 . . . . **161** A1
Sleaford St SW8. . . . **161** A1
Sleat Ho 11 E3 . . . . . **26** B3
Sleevemore Ct 8
SW4
Sligo Ho 8 E1 . . . . . . **25** C1
Slingsby Pl WC2 . . . **120** A4
Slippers Pl SE16 . . . **40** A3
Slipway Ho 1 E14 . . **42** A1
Sloane Ave SW3 . . . **144** B3
Sloane Avenue Mans
SW3 . . . . **144** C3
Sloane Ct E SW3 . . . **145** B2
Sloane Ct W SW3 . . . **145** B2
Sloane Gate Mans
SW1 . . . . **145** B4
Sloane Gdns SW1 . .**145** B3
Sloane Ho 7 E9 . . . . **17** B1
Sloane Sq SW1 . . . . **145** B3
Sloane Square Sta
SW1 . . . . **145** C3
Sloane St SW1 . . . . . **131** A1
Sloane Terr SW1 . . . **145** B4
Sloane Terr Mans
SW1 . . . . **145** B4
Sly St 17 E1. . . . . **32** A3
Smallbrook Mews
W2 . . . . **101** B1
Smalley Cl N16 . . . . . .**7** B1
Smart's Pl WC1,
WC2 . . . . **106** B2
Smart St E2 . . . . **25** C2
Smeaton Ct SE1 . . . **136** C1
Smeaton Rd SW18 . .**70** C4
Smeaton St E1 . . . . . **32** A1
Smedley St SW4 . . . **171** C2
Smeed Rd E3 . . . . . . **18** C1
Smiles Pl SE13 . . . . . **67** B4
Smith Cl SE16 . . . . . . **32** C1
Smithfield Mkt
EC1 . . . . **108** B3
Smithfield St EC1 . **108** A3
Smith's Ct W1 . . . . . **119** B4
Smith Sq SW1 . . . . . **134** A1
Smith St SW3. . . . . . **144** C1
Smith's Yd SW18 . . . **71** B2
Smith Terr SW3 . . . . **144** C1
Smithwood Cl
SW19 . . . . **70** A2
Smithy St E1 . . . . **32** B4
Smithy Street Sch 9
E1 . . . . **32** B4
Smugglers Way
SW18 . . . . **59** A3
Smyrk's Rd SE17 . . . **152** B1
Smyrna Mans 6
NW6 . . . . **10** C1
Smyrna Rd NW6. . . . **10** C1
Smythe St E14 . . . . . **34** A2
Snarsgate St W10 . . **30** B4
Sneath Ave NW11. . . . **1** B4
Sneyd Rd NW2 . . . .**9** B4
Snowberry Cl E11 . . **19** C4
Snowbury Rd 8
SW6 . . . . **166** B3
Snowden St
EC2 . . . . **24** A1 **98** A1
Snowe Ho SE27 . . . . **75** A1
Snow Hill EC1 . . . . . **108** A3
Snowman Ho NW6 . **78** B4
Snowsfields SE1 . . . **137** C4
Snowsfields Prim Sch
SE1 . . . . **138** A4
Soames St SE15. . . . **64** B4
Soane Ct 10 NW1. . . **13** B1

Soane Ho SE17 ....151 C1
Soaphouse La
  TW8 ....44 A3
Sobell L Ctr N7.....5 B1
SOHO 105 B1
Soho W1 ....105 B2
Soho Parish CE Prim
  Sch W1 ....119 B4
Soho Sq W1 ....105 B2
Soho St W1 ....105 B2
Sojourner-Truth Cl 10
  E8 ....17 A2
Solander Gdns
  13 Shadwell E1 ...32 B2
  Stepney E1 ......32 A2
Soldene Ct N7.....14 B2
Solebay St E1 .....26 A1
Solent Ho E1 ......33 A4
Solent Rd NW6 ....10 C3
Soley Mews WC1 ...95 B4
Solidarity Ho
  NW10 ....8 C2
Solna Ave SW15 ....57 B2
Solomon's Pas
  SE15 ....65 A3
Solon New Rd
  SW4 ....62 A3
Solon Rd SW2 .....62 A3
Solway Ho 10 E1 ...25 C1
Solway Rd SE22 ....64 C3
Somali Rd NW2 ....10 B3
Somborne Ho 11
  SW15 ....68 C4
Sombrook Ho
  SE11 ....149 B3
Somer Ct SW6.....155 B3
Somerfield Rd N4 ..6 A2
Somerfield St
  SE16 ....41 A1
Somerford Gr N16..16 B4
Somerford Grove Est
  N16 ....16 B4
Somerford St E1 ...25 A1
Somerford Way
  SE16 ....41 A4
Somerleyton Rd
  SW9 ....62 C3
Somers Cl NW1 ....83 B2
Somers Cres W2 ...102 A1
Somerset Gdns
  Highgate N6 .....3 C4
  St Johns SE13 ...52 A1
Somerset Ho
  WC2 ....121 A4
Somerset Ho
  SW19 ....70 A1
Somerset Lo
  SW15 ....57 A3
Somerset Rd
  Bedford Pk W4 ...37 C3
  Wimbledon SW19..70 A1
Somerset Sq W14 .126 C3
Somers Pl SW2 ....74 B4
Somers Rd SW2 ....62 B1
SOMERS TOWN 93 C4
Somers Town Est
  NW1 ....83 A1
Somerton Ave
  TW9 ....55 A4
Somerton Rd
  Cricklewood NW2...1 A1
  Nunhead SE15 ....65 A3
Somerville Ave
  SW13 ....47 B4
Somerville Cl
  SW9 ....173 A2

Somerville Ho 10
  SW15 ....57 C1
Somerville Point
  SE16 ....41 B4
Sonderburg Rd 13
  N7 ....5 B2
Sondes St SE17.....48 C4
Sonia Gdns NW10 ..8 B4
Sonning Ho 5
  E2 ....24 B2 98 C3
Sophia Cl N7......14 B2
Sophia Ho 10 W6 ..39 B1
Sophia Sq 10 SE16.33 A2
Sopwith Way
  SW8 ....160 A2
Sorrel La E14 ......34 C3
Sorrell Cl
  6 Brixton SW9 ...173 C2
  SE14 ....51 A3
Sotherby Rd N5 ....15 B4
Sotheran Cl E8 .....24 C4
Sotheron Pl SW6 ..156 B1
Soudan Rd SW11 ..168 C3
Souldern Rd 10
SOUTH ACTON 37 A3
South Acton Sta W3,
  ....37 B3
South Africa Rd
  W12 ....30 A2
Southall Pl SE1 ...137 B3
Southam Ho 10
  W10 ....23 A1
Southampton Bldgs
  WC2 ....107 B3
Southampton Pl
  WC1 ....106 B3
Southampton Rd
  NW5 ....12 B3
Southampton Row
  WC1 ....106 B4
Southampton St
  WC2 ....120 B4
Southampton Way
  SE5 ....49 A3
South Audley St
  W1 ....117 C2
South Ave TW9 ....44 C1
SOUTH BANK 120 C1
South Bank Bsns Ctr
  SW8 ....161 C3
Southbank Ctr
  SE1 ....121 A1
Southbank
  International Sch 14
  NW3 ....11 B2
Southbank
  International Sch
  (Westminster
  Campus) W1 ....104 A4
Southbank Int Sch
  W11 ....12 C3 113 B3
South Bermondsey
  Sta SE16 ....40 B1
South Black Lion La
  7 W6 ....38 C1
South Bldg SW1 ..133 A2
South Block E1 ....32 B2
South Bolton Gdns
  SW10 ....142 B2
Southborough Ho
  SE17 ....152 B2
Southborough Rd
  E9 ....25 C4
SOUTH BROMLEY..34 C4

South Building
  SE10 ....52 C3
Southbury NW8 ....79 A4
South Carriage Dr SW1,
  SW7 ....130 C4
South Chelsea Coll 22
  ....44 A3
South Colonnade The
  E14 ....34 A1
Southcombe St
  W14 ....140 A4
Southcote Rd N19..13 B4
Southcott Ho
  51 Bromley E3 ....27 A2
  W9 ....89 A1
South Cres
  Newham E16 .....27 C1
  WC1 ....105 B3
Southcroft 8
  SW11 ....60 B1
South Ct 10 SW15..57 C1
Southdean Gdns
  SW19 ....70 B2
Southdown N7 .....14 A2
South Eastern Univ 3
  N7 ....5 B1
South Eaton Pl
  SW1 ....145 C4
South Edwardes Sq
  W8 ....127 B1
South End W8......128 B2
South End Cl NW3..12 A4
South End Gn
  NW3 ....12 A4
South End Rd
  NW3 ....12 A4
South End Row
  W8 ....128 B2
Southerngate Way
  SE14 ....51 A3
Southern Gr E3 ....26 B1
Southern Row
  W10 ....23 A1
Southern Way
  SE10 ....43 B1
Southernwood Ret Pk
  SE1 ....152 C1
Southerton Rd W6..39 B2
Southey Ho SE17 .151 A2
Southey Mews
  E16 ....35 C1
Southey Rd SW9...173 B4
Southfield Prim Sch
  W4 ....38 A4
Southfield Rd W4 ..37 C4
SOUTHFIELDS 71 A3
Southfields Acad
  SW18 ....70 C3
Southfields Rd
  SW18 ....58 C1
Southfields Sta
  SW18 ....70 B3
Southgate Ct 10 N1.15 C1
Southgate Gr N1 ...15 C1
Southgate Rd N1...87 C4
South Gr N6 ....3 C3
SOUTH HACKNEY..25 B4
SOUTH
  HAMPSTEAD....11 B1
South Hampstead
  High Sch
  7 Hampstead
  NW6 ....11 B2

South Hampstead
  High Sch continued
  11 London NW3...11 C1
South Hampstead Sta
  NW3 ....11 B1
South Hill Pk NW3..12 A4
South Hill Pk Gdns
  NW3 ....12 A4
South Island Pl
  SW9 ....163 B1
SOUTH
  KENSINGTON ...143 A3
South Kensington Sta
  SW7 ....143 C4
South Kensington
  Station Arc SW7 .143 C4
SOUTH
  LAMBETH 172 B3
South Lambeth Pl
  SW8 ....162 B4
South Lambeth Rd
  SW8 ....162 B4
Southlands Dr
  SW19 ....69 C2
South Lo NW8 .....89 B4
South London Gall
  SE5 ....49 A2
South London
  Montessori Sch
  SW11 ....168 A3
Southmead Prim Sch
  SW19 ....70 A3
Southmead Rd
  SW19 ....70 A3
South Molton La
  W1 ....104 A1
South Molton Rd
  E16 ....35 C3
South Molton St
  W1 ....104 A1
Southmoor Way
  E9 ....18 B2
Southolm St
  SW11 ....170 B3
South Par W4......37 C2
South Parade
  SW3 ....143 C2
South Park Mews
  SW6 ....59 A4
South Pl EC2 .....109 C3
South Pl Mews
  EC2 ....109 C3
South Quay Plaza
  E14 ....42 A4
South Quay Sta
  E14 ....42 A4
South Rise W2 ....116 B4
South Row SE3 ....53 B1
South Sea St SE16.41 B3
Southside N7 ......13 C4
South Side W6 ....38 B3
Southside Ind Est
  SW8 ....170 C4
Southside Quarter 4
  SW11 ....168 C2
Southside Sh Ctr
  SW18 ....59 A1
South Sq WC1 ....107 B3
South St W1 ......117 C2
South Tenter St
  E1 ....111 A1
South Terr SW7 ...144 A4
South Thames Coll
  (Roehampton Ctr)
  SW15 ....56 C1

South Thames Coll
  (Wandsworth Ctr)
  SW18 ....59 B2
Southvale Rd SE3 ..53 A1
Southview Ave
  NW10 ....8 B3
South Villas NW1 ..13 C2
Southville
  London SW8 ....171 C3
  South Lambeth
  SW8 ....172 A1
SOUTHWARK 123 A3
Southwark Bridge SE1,
  EC4 ....123 A3
Southwark Bridge Rd
  SE1 ....123 A2
Southwark Cath
  SE1 ....123 B2
Southwark Coll
  (Blackfriars Ctr)
  SE1 ....122 A1
Southwark Coll
  (Camberwell Ctr) 17
  SE5 ....49 A3
Southwark Park Est
  11 SE16 ....40 A2
Southwark Park Prim
  Sch 10 SE16.....40 A3
Southwark Park Rd
  SE16 ....40 A3
Southwark Park Sch
  13 SE16 ....40 C3
Southwark Pk Sports
  Complex SE16 ...40 B2
Southwark St SE1 .122 C1
Southwater Cl
  E14 ....33 B3
Southway Cl 9
  W12 ....39 A4
Southwell Gdns
  SW7 ....142 C3
Southwell Ho
  5 Bermondsey
  SE16 ....40 A2
  13 Stoke Newington
  N16 ....16 A3
Southwell Rd SE5 .63 B4
South Wharf Rd
  W2 ....101 C2
Southwick Mews
  W2 ....101 C2
Southwick Pl W2 ..102 A1
Southwick St W2 ..102 A1
Southwick Yd W2 .102 A1
Southwold Mans
  W9 ....23 C2
Southwood Ave
  N6 ....4 B4
Southwood Ct EC1 .96 A3
Southwood Ho
  W11 ....31 A2 112 A4
Southwood Hts N6..4 A4
Southwood La N6 ..3 C4
Southwood Lawn Rd
  N6 ....4 A4
Southwood Park
  N6 ....3 C4
Southwood Smith Ho
  11 E2 ....25 A2
Southwood Smith St
  N1 ....86 A3
South Worple Ave
  SW14 ....56 A4

Southwyck Ho
SW9 . . . . .62 C3
South Yd E1 . . . .**109** B4
Sovereign Cl E1 . . . .32 A2
Sovereign Cres
SE16 . . . . .33 A2
Sovereign Ct
3 Richmond
TW9 . . . . .54 B3
1 Stepney E1 . . . . . . .32 C2
Sovereign Ho 23
E1 . . . . .25 A1
Sovereign Mews 6
E2 . . . . .24 B3
Sovereign Pk
NW10 . . . . .20 A1
Space Bsns Pk
NW10 . . . . .20 A1
Spa Ct 12 SE16 . . . .**139** B1
Spafield St EC1 . . . .95 B2
Spalding Ho SE4 . . .66 A2
Spanby Rd E3 . . . . . .26 C1
Spaniards Cl NW11 . .2 C3
Spaniards End NW3 . .2 C3
Spaniards Rd NW3 . .2 B2
Spanish Pl W1 . . . .**103** C2
Spanish Rd SW18 . . .59 B2
Spa Rd SE16 . . . . . .**139** A1
Spare St SE17 . . . .**150** C3
Sparke Terr 2
E16 . . . . .35 B3
Sparkford Ho
SW11 . . . .**167** C4
Sparks Cl W3 . . . . . .28 C3
Sparsholt Rd N19 . . .5 A3
Sparta St 12 SE10 . .52 B2
Spa Sch SE1 . . . . . .**153** B4
Spa View 6 SW16 . .74 C1
Speakers' Corner
W1 . . . .**117** A4
Speakman Ho SE4 . .66 A4
Spear Mews SW5 . .**141** C3
Spears Rd N19 . . . . . .5 A3
Spectrum Ho NW5 . .12 C4
Spectrum Wy 19
SW18 . . . . .58 C2
Spedan Cl NW3 . . . . .2 B1
Speechly Mews
E8 . . . . .16 B3
Speed Ho EC2 . . . .**109** B4
Speedwell St 8
SE8 . . . . .51 C3
Speedy Pl WC1 . . . .**94** A3
Speldhurst Rd
Bedford Pk W4 . . . . . .37 C3
Homerton E9 . . . . .17 C1
Spellbrook Wlk N1 . **87** A4
Spelman Ho 6
E1 . . . .**111** B3
Spelman St E1 . . . .**111** B4
Spence Cl SE16 . . . .41 B4
Spencer Gdns
SW14 . . . . .55 B2
Spencer Ho
51 Clapham
SW8 . . . .**171** B1
24 Putney SW19 . . . .69 C3
Vale of Health NW3 . . .2 C1
Wimbledon SW19 . . . .69 C1
Spencer House Mus
SW1 . . . .**118** C1
Spencer Mews
Fulham W6 . . . .**154** A4

Spencer Mews
continued
South Lambeth
SW9 . . . .**172** C3
Spencer Park Ct
SW18 . . . . .59 C2
Spencer Pk SW18 . . .59 C2
Spencer Pl
16 Islington N1 . . . . .15 A1
SW1 . . . .**133** A1
Spencer Rd
Acton W3 . . . . .28 B1
Chiswick W4 . . . . .45 B3
Wandsworth SW18 . . .59 C3
Spencer Rise NW5 . . .4 A1
Spencer St EC1 . . . .**96** A3
Spencer Way 3
E1 . . . . .32 A3
Spencer Wlk
23 Hampstead
NW3 . . . . .11 B4
Putney SW15 . . . . . . .57 C3
Spencer Yd SE3 . . . .53 B1
Spenlow Ho 2
SE16 . . . .**139** C2
Spenser Gr N16 . . . .16 A4
Spenser Mews
SE21 . . . . .75 C3
Spenser Rd SE24 . . .63 A2
Spenser St SW1 . . .**133** A2
Spens Ho WC1 . . . . .**94** C1
Spensley Wlk N16 . . .6 C1
Spert St E14 . . . . . . .33 A2
Spey St E14 . . . . . . .34 B4
Spezia Rd NW10 . . . .21 C3
Spice Ct
19 Battersea
SW11 . . . . .59 B4
2 St George in East
E1 . . . .**125** C2
Spice Quay Htss
SE1 . . . .**125** A1
Spicer Cl SE5, SW9 . .48 A1
Spicer Ho
E2 . . . .**24** C2 B3
Spindrift Ave E14 . . .42 A2
Spinnaker Ho 1
E14 . . . . .41 C4
Spinney The
Barnes SW13 . . . . . . .47 A4
Streatham SW16 . . . . .73 C1
Spire Ho 12 W2 . . .**115** A4
Spire Ho W2 . . . . . .**115** A4
Spirit Quay E1 . . . . .32 A1
Spital Sq E1 . . . . . .**110** B4
Spital St E1 . . . . . .**111** B4
Spital Yd E1 . . . . . .**110** B4
Splendour Wlk
SE16 . . . . .40 B1
Spode Ho SE11 . . . .**135** B1
Spode Wlk NW3 . . . .11 A3
Sporle Ct 5 SW11 . .59 C4
Sprewell SW18 . . . .58 A1
Spriggs Ho 11 N1 . . .15 B1
Sprimont Pl SW3 . . .**144** C2
Springall St 9
SE15 . . . . .50 A3
Springalls Wharf 2
SE16 . . . .**139** B4
Springbank Wlk
NW1 . . . . .13 C1
Spring Cott 10
W12 . . . . .38 C4

Spring Ct NW2 . . . .10 B2
Springdale Rd
N16 . . . . .15 C4
Spring Ct
SW2 . . . . .62 B2
Springett Ho 15
SW2 . . . . .62 B2
Springfield Ct
3 Dagenham W3 . . .28 B3
Hampstead NW3 . . . . .12 A1
Springfield Ho
Acton W3 . . . . .28 B1
1 Camberwell SE5 . .49 A1
13 Dalston E8 . . . . . .16 B2
Springfield La
NW6 . . . . .78 A3
Springfield Rd
NW8 . . . . .79 A3
Springfield University
Hosp SW17 . . . . .72 A1
Springfield Wlk
NW6 . . . . .78 A3
Spring Gdns
Islington N5 . . . . .15 B3
SW1 . . . .**120** A2
Spring Gr W4 . . . . . .44 C4
Spring Grove Rd
TW10 . . . . .54 B2
Spring Hill E5 . . . . . . .7 C4
Springhill Cl SE5 . . .63 C4
Spring Ho WC1 . . . . .**95** B3
Spring Mews W1 . .**103** A4
Springpark Dr N4 . . . .6 B3
Spring Pl NW5 . . . . .13 A3
Springrice Rd
SE13 . . . . .67 C1
Spring St W2 . . . . .**101** B1
Spring Terr TW10 . . .54 A2
Springtide Cl 10
SE15 . . . . .49 C2
Springvale Ave
TW8 . . . . .36 A1
Springvale Terr 5
W14 . . . . .39 C3
Springwater WC1 . .**106** C4
Springwell Ave
NW10 . . . . .21 B4
Spring Wlk E1 . . . . .**111** C4
Springwood Cl 8
E3 . . . . .26 C3
Spruce Ct W5 . . . . . .36 A3
Spruce Ho 15
SE16 . . . . .40 C4
Sprules Rd SE4 . . . .51 A1
Spurgeon St SE1 . .**137** B2
Spurling Rd SE22 . . .64 B3
Spur Rd SE1 . . . . . .**135** B4
Spurstowe Rd E8 . . .17 A2
Spurstowe Terr
E8 . . . . .17 A3
Square Rigger Row 7
SW11 . . . . .59 B4
Square The
Hammersmith W6 . . . .39 B1
36 Bethnal Green . . .16 A1
Squarey St SW17 . . .71 B1
Squire Gdns NW8 . . .89 B3
Squires Ct SW4 . . .**172** B3
Squire's Mount
NW3 . . . . .2 C1
Squirrels The
SE13 . . . . .67 C4
Squirries St
E2 . . . .**24** C2 **99** C3
Stable Ho 9 SE16 . . .40 B4
Stable St N1 . . . . . . .84 A3
Stables Way SE11 . .**149** B2
Stable Way SW17 . . .30 B1

Stable Yd Rd
SW1 . . . .**133** A4
Stacey St
Highbury N7 . . . . .5 C1
Soho WC2 . . . .**105** C1
Stack Ho SW1 . . . . .**145** C3
Stackhouse St
SW3 . . . .**130** C2
Stadium St SW10 . .**157** A1
Stafford Cripps Ho
30 Bethnal Green
E2 . . . . .25 B2
SW6 . . . .**155** A3
Stafford Ct
Kensington W8 . . . . .**127** C2
South Lambeth
SW8 . . . .**172** A2
Stafford Ho SE1 . . .**153** A2
Stafford Mans
3 Hammersmith
W14 . . . . .39 C3
14 Stockwell SW4 . .62 A3
SW1 . . . .**158** C1
Stafford Pl SW1 . . .**132** C2
Stafford Rd
Bow E3 . . . . .26 B3
Maida Vale NW6 . . . . .23 C2
Staffordshire St
Peckham SE15 . . . . . .49 C2
Peckham SE15 . . . . . .50 A2
Stafford St W1 . . . .**118** C2
Stafford Terr W8 . . .**127** B2
Stag La SW15 . . . . . .68 B2
Stagshaw Ho 17
SE22 . . . . .64 A4
Stainer St SE1 . . . .**123** C1
Staining La EC2 . . .**109** A2
Stainsby Ct E14
Stainsby Rd E14 . . . .33 C3
Stalbridge Flats
W1 . . . .**103** C1
Stalbridge Ho
NW1 . . . . .82 C1
Stalbridge St
NW1 . . . .**102** B4
Stalham St SE16 . . . .40 A3
Stambourne Ho
SW8 . . . .**172** B4
Stamford Bridge
Stadium (Chelsea
FC) SW6 . . . .**156** A2
Stamford Brook Ave
W6 . . . . .38 B3
Stamford Brook Gdns
1 W6 . . . . .38 B3
Stamford Brook Mans
2 W6 . . . . .38 B3
Stamford Brook Rd
W6 . . . . .38 B3
Stamford Brook Sta
W6 . . . . .38 C3
Stamford Cl 2
NW3 . . . . .2 B1
Stamford Cotts
SW10 . . . .**156** B2
Stamford Gr E 1
N16 . . . . .7 C3
Stamford Gr W 4
N16 . . . . .7 C3
STAMFORD HILL 7 A3
Stamford Hill
N16 . . . . .7 B3

Stamford Hill Mans 1
N16 . . . . .7 A4
Stamford Hill Sta
N16 . . . . .7 A4
Stamford Lo 2 N16 . .7 B4
Stamford Mans 2
N16 . . . . .7 C3
Stamford Rd N1 . . . .16 A2
Stamford St SE1 . . .**121** C2
Stamp PE2 . . . . .24 B4
Stanard Cl N16 . . . . . .7 A4
Stanborough Ho 4
E3 . . . . .27 A1
Stanborough Pas
E8 . . . . .16 B2
Stanbridge Mans
SW15 . . . . .57 B4
Stanbridge Rd
SW15 . . . . .57 B4
Stanbrook Ct W1 . .**118** C2
Stanbury Ct 10
NW3 . . . . .12 B2
Stanbury Rd
Nunhead SE15 . . . . . .50 B1
Peckham SE15 . . . . . .50 A1
Standard Pl 1
EC2 . . . . **24** A2 **98** B3
Standard Rd
NW10 . . . . .20 C1
Standen Rd SW18 . . .70 C4
Standish Ho 6
W6 . . . . .38 C2
Standish Rd W6 . . . .38 C2
Stanesgate Ho 20
SE15 . . . . .49 C3
Stanfield Ho NW8 . .**89** C2
Stanfield Rd E3 . . . .26 A3
Stanford Ct
Kensington W8 . . . . .**128** B1
Walham Green
SW6 . . . .**166** B3
Stanford Pl SE1 . . .**152** A3
Stanford Rd W8 . . .**128** B2
Stanford St SW1 . . .**147** B3
Stangate SE1 . . . . .**135** A2
Stanhope Cl 23
SE16 . . . . .40 C4
Stanhope Gate
W1 . . . .**117** C2
Stanhope Gdns
SW7 . . . .**143** A4
Stanhope Ho
4 Putney SW15 . . . . .57 B2
SE8 . . . . .51 B3
Stanhope Mews E
SW7 . . . .**143** A4
Stanhope Mews S
SW7 . . . .**143** A3
Stanhope Mews W
SW7 . . . .**143** A4
Stanhope Par NW1 .**92** C4
Stanhope Pl W2 . . .**102** C1
Stanhope Rd N6 . . . . .4 B4
Stanhope Row
W1 . . . .**118** A1
Stanhope St NW1 . .**92** C3
Stanhope Terr
W2 . . . .**115** C4
Stanier Cl SW5 . . . .**141** A1
Stanlake Mews 7
W12 . . . . .30 B1
Stanlake Rd W12 . . .30 B1
Stanlake Villas 8
W12 . . . . .30 B1
Stanley Cl SW8 . . . .**162** C3

Stanley Cohen Ho
EC1 . . . . **96** C1
Stanley Cres
W11 . . . . . .31 B2 **112** C4
Stanley Gdns
Bedford Pk W3 . . . . . .38 A4
Cricklewood NW2 . . . . .9 B3
W11 . . . . . .31 B2 **112** C4
Stanley Gr SW11. . **169** C1
Stanley Ho
35 Clapham
SW8 . . . . **171** B1
22 Poplar E14 . . . . .33 C3
Stanley Holloway Ct
E16 . . . . .35 C3
Stanley Mans
SW10 . . . . **157** A4
Upper Tooting
SW17 . . . . .72 B2
Stanley Rd
Acton Green W3 . . . . .37 B3
Mill Meads E15 . . . . .27 C4
Mortlake SW14 . . . . .55 A3
Stanley St SE14,
SE8 . . . . .51 B3
Stanley Studios
SW10 . . . . **157** A4
Stanley Terr 8 N19. .5 A2
Stanliff Ho 8 E14. .41 C3
Stanmer St SW11 . **168** B2
Stanmore Gdns
TW9 . . . . .54 B4
Stanmore Ho 21
SW8 . . . . **171** C2
Stanmore Pl NW1 . . **82** B4
Stanmore Rd TW9 . .54 B4
Stanmore St N1 . . . .84 C4
Stannard Cotts 27
E1 . . . . .25 B1
Stannard Mews
E8 . . . . .16 C2
Stannard Rd E8 . . . .16 C2
Stannary Pl SE11 . **149** C1
Stannary St SE11 . **149** C1
Stanswick Sq 3
W10 . . . . .23 A2
Stansfeld Ho SE1 . . **153** A3
Stansfield Rd SW9 . .62 B4
Stanstead Ho E3 . . .27 B1
Stansted Express
Terminal EC2 . . . . **110** A4
Stanswood Gdns
SE5 . . . . .49 A3
Stanton Ct N16 . . . . .6 C4
Stanton Ho 5
SE10 . . . . .52 B4
Stanton Rd SW13 . .46 B1
Stanway Ct 23 N1 . .24 A3
Stanway St N1 . . . . .24 A3
Stanwick Rd W14 . **140** C3
Stanworth St SE1 . **139** A3
Staplefield Cl 3
SW2 . . . . .74 A3
Stapleford Cl
SW19 . . . . .70 A4
Staplehurst Ct 1
SW11 . . . . .60 B1
Staplehurst Ho 18
E5 . . . . .17 A3
Staple Inn WC2 . . . **107** B3
Staple Inn Bldgs
WC2 . . . . **107** B3
Staple St SE1 . . . . **137** C3
Stapleton Hall N4 . . .5 B4

Stapleton Hall Rd
N4 . . . . .5 B4
Stapleton Ho 19
E2 . . . . .25 A2
Stapleton Rd
SW17 . . . . .72 C1
Star Alley EC3 . . . **124** B4
Starboard Way
E14 . . . . .41 C3
Starcross St NW1 . . .93 A3
Starfield Rd W12 . . .38 C4
Star & Garter Mans 8
SW15 . . . . .57 C4
Star Lane Sta E16 . .27 C1
Starliner Ct N7 . . . .14 C2
Starling Ho NW8 . . .80 A2
Star Pl E1 . . . . . . **125** A3
Star Rd W14 . . . . **140** C1
Star St W2 . . . . . **102** A2
Star Works NW10 . .21 C2
Star Yd WC2 . . . . **107** B2
Statham Ct N7 . . . . . .5 A1
Statham Gr N16 . . . .6 C1
Statham Ho SW8 . **170** C4
Station App
Dagenham NW10 . . . .21 B2
Fulham SW6 . . . . . . .58 A4
Richmond TW9 . . . . .44 C2
Station Approach Rd
W4 . . . . .45 B3
Station Approach
Road SE1 . . . . . . **135** B4
Station Ave
3 Brixton SW9 . . . . .63 A4
35 Richmond TW9 . .44 C2
Station Cres SE3 . . .43 C1
Station Ct 5 SE15 . .50 B1
Stationers Hall Ct
EC4 . . . . **108** B1
Station Gdns W4 . . .45 B3
Station Mews Terr 4
SE3 . . . . .43 C1
Station Par
Cricklewood NW2 . . . .9 B2
4 Upper Tooting
SW12 . . . . .72 C3
Station Pas SE15 . . .50 B2
Station Pl N4 . . . . . . .5 C2
Station Rd
Barnes SW13 . . . . . .46 B1
Camden Town N19 . . .4 B1
Harlesden NW10 . . . .21 B3
Lewisham SE13 . . . . .67 B4
Station Rise SE27 . .75 A2
Station St E15 . . . . .19 C1
Station Terr
Camberwell SE5 . . . .48 B2
Kensal Rise NW10 . . .22 C3
Staunton Ho SE17 . **152** A3
Staunton St SE8 . . .51 B4
Staveley NW1 . . . . . **92** C4
Staveley Cl
Hackney E9 . . . . .17 B3
Lower Holloway N7 . .14 A4
New Cross Gate
SE15 . . . . .50 B3
6 Peckham SE15 . . .50 A2
Staveley Gdns W4 . .45 C2
Staveley Ho SE4 . . .66 A2
Staveley Rd W4 . . . .45 C3
Stavers Ho 11 E3 . . .26 B3
Staverton Rd NW2 . . .9 B1
Staveyard Rd
SE16 . . . . .33 A1

Stavordale Lo
W14 . . . . **127** A2
Stavordale Rd N5 . . .15 A4
Stayner's Rd E1 . . . .25 C1
Steadman Ct EC1 . . **97** A2
Stead St SE17 . . . . **151** B3
Stean St E8 . . . . . . .24 B4
Stebbing Ho 8
W11 . . . . .30 C1
Stebondale St E14 . .42 B2
Stebon Prim Sch 26
E14 . . . . .33 C4
Stedham Pl WC1 . . **106** A2
Steedman St
SE17 . . . . **150** C3
Steele Rd
Acton Green W4 . . . . .37 B3
Becontree NW10 . . . .20 B3
Steele's Mews N
NW3 . . . . .12 B2
Steele's Mews S
NW3 . . . . .12 B2
Steele's Rd NW3 . . .12 B2
Steel's La 21 E1 . . .32 B3
Steen Way 7
SE22 . . . . .64 A2
Steep Hill SW16 . . .73 C1
Steeple Cl SW6 . . . **164** B1
Steeple Ct 11 E1 . . .25 A1
Steeple Wlk N1 . . . . **87** A4
Steerforth St
SW18 . . . . .71 B2
Steers Way SE16 . . .41 A4
Stelfax Ho WC1 . . . . .95 A4
Stellman Cl E5 . . . . .16 C4
Stephan Cl E8 . . . . .24 C4
Stephen Ct 18
SW19 . . . . .69 C3
Stephendale Rd
SW6 . . . . **166** C2
Stephen Fox Ho 7
W4 . . . . .38 A1
Stephen Hawking Sch
23 E14 . . . . .33 A3
Stephen Mews
W1 . . . . **105** B3
Stephen Pl SW4 . . . .61 B4
Stephen Saunders Ct
SW11 . . . . .60 A2
Stephens Ct SE4 . . .66 A4
Stephenson Ho
2 Gospel Oak
NW5 . . . . .13 A4
8 Maitland Pk
NW3 . . . . .12 B2
Newington SE1 . . . **136** C2
Stephenson St
Dagenham NW10 . . . .21 B2
Newham E16 . . . . . . .35 A4
Stephenson Way
NW1 . . . . .93 A3
Stephen St W1 . . . **105** B3
STEPNEY 32 B4
Stepney City E1 . . . .32 B4
Stepney City Farm
E1 . . . . .32 C4
Stepney Cswy E1 . . .32 C3
Stepney Gn E1 . . . . .32 C4
Stepney Greencoat CE
Prim Sch The 26
E14 . . . . .33 C4
Stepney Green Ct **4**
E1 . . . . .32 C4

Stepney Green Maths
& Computing Coll 18
E1 . . . . .32 C4
Stepney Green Sta
E1 . . . . .32 C4
Stepney High St
E1 . . . . .32 C4
Stepney Way E1 . . . .32 B4
Sterling Cl NW10 . . .8 C1
Sterling Gdns
SE14 . . . . .51 A4
Sterling Pl W5 . . . . .36 A2
Sterling St SW7 . . **130** B2
Sterndale Rd W14 . .39 C3
Sterne St W12 . . . . .39 C4
Sternhall La SE15 . .64 C4
Sternhold Ave SW12,
SW2 . . . . .73 C2
Sterry St SE1 . . . . **137** B3
Steve Biko Ct W10 . .22 C1
Steve Biko Rd N7 . . .5 C1
Stevedore St 3
E1 . . . . .32 A1
Stevenage Rd
SW6 . . . . .47 C2
Stevens Ave E9 . . . .17 B2
Stevenson Cres
SE16 . . . . .40 A1
Stevenson Ho
1 Battersea
SW11 . . . . **168** C1
6 Clapham Pk
SW2 . . . . .62 A2
NW8 . . . . .78 C4
Stevens St SE1 . . . **138** B2
Steventon Rd W12 . .29 B2
Steward St E1 . . . . **110** B3
Stewart Headlam
Prim Sch 28 E1 . . .25 A1
Stewart Ho SE1 . . . **138** A1
Stewart Rd E15 . . . .19 C4
Stewart's Gr SW3 . **144** A2
Stewart's Pl 1
SW2 . . . . .74 A4
Stewart's Rd SW8 . **170** C4
Stewart St E14 . . . . .42 B4
Stew La EC4 . . . . . **122** C4
Steyne Ho
15 Acton W3 . . . . . .28 A1
16 Acton W3 . . . . . .28 A1
Steyne Rd W3 . . . . .28 A1
Stifford Ho E1 . . . . .32 B4
Stile Hall Gdns
W4 . . . . .36 C1
Stile Hall Par 6
W4 . . . . .36 C1
Stileman Ho 4 E3 . .33 B4
Stillingfleet Rd
SW13 . . . . .46 C4
Stillington St
SW1 . . . . **147** A4
Stillness Jun & Inf
Sch SE23 . . . . . . .66 B1
Stillness Rd SE23 . .66 B1
Stirling Ct
Clerkenwell EC1 . . . . **96** A2
2 Strand WC2 . . . **120** C3
Stirling Mans NW6 .11 B2
Stirling Rd
South Acton W3 . . . . .37 A3
Stockwell SW9 . . . . .72 B4
Stoatley Ho 10
SW15 . . . . .68 C3
Stockbeck NW1 . . . . **83** A1
Stockfield Rd
SW16 . . . . .74 B1

Stockholm Ho E1 . . **125** C4
Stockholm Rd
SE16 . . . . .40 B1
Stockholm Way
E1 . . . . **125** B2
Stockhurst Cl
SW15 . . . . .47 C1
Stockleigh Hall
NW8 . . . . **80** B2
Stock Orchard Cres
N7 . . . . .14 B3
Stock Orchard St
N7 . . . . .14 B3
Stocks Ct 5 E1 . . . . .25 C1
Stocks Pl 11 E14 . . .33 B2
Stockton Ho 12 E2 . .25 A2
STOCKWELL 62 A4
Stockwell Ave
SW9 . . . . .62 B4
Stockwell Gdns
SW9 . . . . **172** C2
Stockwell Gn
SW9 . . . . **172** C1
Stockwell La SW9 . **172** C1
Stockwell Park Cres
SW9 . . . . **173** A2
Stockwell Park Rd
SW9 . . . . **173** A3
Stockwell Park Wlk
SW9 . . . . .62 C4
Stockwell Prim Sch 6
SW9 . . . . **172** C2
Stockwell Rd SE10 . .52 B4
SW9 . . . . **172** C2
Stockwell Terr
SW9 . . . . **172** C2
Stoddart Ho SW8 . **163** A3
Stodmarsh Ho 28
SW9 . . . . **173** C4
Stoford Cl 4
SW19 . . . . .70 A4
Stokenchurch St
SW6 . . . . **166** A3
STOKE
NEWINGTON 7 A2
Stoke Newington
Church St N16 . . . . .7 A2
Stoke Newington
Comm N16 . . . . .7 C3
Stoke Newington
High St N16 . . . . . . .7 B2
Stoke Newington Rd
N16 . . . . .16 B4
Stoke Newington Sch
N16 . . . . .7 A2
Stoke Newington Sta
N16 . . . . .7 B2
Stoke Pl NW10 . . . . .21 B2
Stokesley St W12 . . .29 B3
Stone Bldgs WC2 . **107** A3
STONEBRIDGE 20 B4
Stonebridge Ctr 9
NW10 . . . . .20 C4
Stonebridge Prim Sch
NW10 . . . . .20 C4
Stone Cl SW4 . . . . **171** A1
Stonecutter St
EC4 . . . . **108** A2
Stonefield N4 . . . . . . .5 B2
Stonefield Mans
N1 . . . . **85** B3
Stonefield St N1 . . . **85** C4

Stonegate 8 NW5...12 C2
Stonehill Cl SW14...55 C2
Stonehill Rd
  Brentford W4........36 C1
  Mortlake SW14.....55 C2
Stonehills Ct SE21...76 A1
Stonehill's Mans 3
....................74 A2
Stonehouse NW1...83 A3
Stonehouse Ct
  EC2...................110 B2
Stonehouse Ho 27
....................31 C4
Stoneleigh Lo 13
....................44 B2
Stoneleigh Mews 15
....................26 A3
Stoneleigh Pl W11..30 C2
Stoneleigh St W11..30 C2
Stoneleigh Terr
  N19....................4 A2
Stonell's Rd SW11...60 B2
Stonemasons Yd
  SW18...............71 C4
Stonenest St N7......5 A3
Stones End St
  SE1..................136 C3
Stoneyard La E14....34 A2
Stoney La EC3.......110 B2
Stoney St SE1.......123 B2
Stonhouse St SW4...61 C3
Stonor Rd W14.......140 C3
Stopes St SE15......49 B3
Stopford Rd SE17...150 B1
Stopher Ho SE1.....136 B3
Storace Ho 6
  SW4..................62 A3
Storers Quay E14...42 C2
Store St
  Bloomsbury WC1....105 B4
  Stratford New Town
  ....19 C3
Storey Ct NW8......89 B3
Storey Ho 8 E14....34 A2
Storey's Gate
  SW1.................133 C3
Stories Mews SE5...49 A1
Stories Rd SE5......64 A4
Storks Rd SE16.....139 C1
Stormont House Sch
  E5.....................17 A4
Stormont Rd
  Clapham SW11.....60 C3
  Highgate N6..........3 B4
Storrington WC1....94 B3
Story St N1..........14 B1
Stothard Rd 2 E1...25 B1
Stothard Pl E2......110 B4
Stothard St 1 E1...25 B1
Stott Cl SW18.......59 C1
Stoughton Cl
  Roehampton
  SW15................68 C3
  SE11...............149 A3
Stourcliffe Cl W1...102 C2
Stourcliffe St W1...102 C2
Stourhead Cl 6
  SW19................69 C4
Stour Rd E3..........18 C1
Stowage SE8.........52 A4
Stowe Ho 11 N16....7 A1
Stowe Rd W12.......39 A4
Stracey Rd NW10...20 C4
Stradbroke Rd N5...15 B4

Stradella Rd SE24...63 B1
Straffan Lo 8
....................74 A2
Stafford Ho 9
....................31 A2
Strafford Rd 3 W3..37 B4
Strafford St E14.....41 C4
Strahan Rd E3.......26 A2
Straightsmouth
  SE10.................52 B3
Straker's Rd SE15...65 A3
Strale Ho 17 N1.....24 A4
STRAND............120 C4
Strand
  Strand WC2........120 C4
  Strand WC2........107 A1
Strand Dr TW9.......45 A3
Strand La WC2......121 A4
STRAND ON THE
  GREEN..............44 C4
Strand-on-the-Green
....................44 C4
Strand on the Green
  Jun & Inf Sch 5
  W4....................44 C4
Strang Ho N1........86 C3
Strangways Terr
  W14.................126 C1
Stranraer Way N1...14 A1
Strasburg Rd
  SW11...............170 A3
STRATFORD.........19 B2
Stratford Bus Sta
  E15...................19 B2
Stratford Coll
  (Newham 6th Form
  Coll) E15...........19 B2
Stratford Gr SW15...57 C3
Stratford High St Sta
  E15...................27 C4
Stratford
  International Sta
  E15...................19 B2
STRATFORD
  MARSH..............27 A4
STRATFORD NEW
  TOWN................19 C3
Stratford Pl W1....104 A1
Stratford Rd W8....127 C1
Stratford Sh Ctr
  E15...................19 C1
Stratford Studios
  W8...................128 A1
Stratford Villas
  NW1...................13 C1
Stratford Workshops
  E15...................27 C4
Strathan Cl SW18..58 A1
Strathblaine Rd
  SW11................59 C3
Strathdon Dr
  SW17.................71 C1
Strathearn Ho
  W2...................116 A4
Strathearn Pl W2...116 A4
Stratheden Par
  SE3...................53 C3
Stratheden Rd
  SE3...................53 C3
Strathleven Rd
  SW2..................62 A2
Strathmore Ct
  NW8..................90 A4
Strathmore Gdns
  W8...31 C1 113 C2

Strathmore Rd
  SW19.................70 C1
Strathnairn St
  SE1..................153 C3
Strathray Gdns
  NW3..................12 A2
Strath Terr SW11...60 A3
Strathville Rd
  SW18.................71 A2
Stratton Ct 4 N1...16 A1
Stratton St W1.....118 B2
Strattondale St
  E14...................42 B3
Strauss Rd W4......37 C4
Streamline Mews
  SE22.................76 C4
Streatham Cl
  SW16.................74 A2
Streatham & Clapham
  High Sch SW16...73 C1
Streatham Ct
  SW16.................74 A1
STREATHAM HILL...74 A3
Streatham Hill
  SW2..................74 A3
Streatham Hill &
  Clapham High Sch
  14 SW2.............74 A4
Streatham Hill Sta
  SW2..................74 A2
Streatham Pl SW2..74 A4
Streatham St
  WC1.................106 A2
Streathbourne Rd
  SW17.................72 C1
Streatham Wells Prim
  Sch SW2............74 A2
Streatleigh Par 4
  SW16.................74 A1
Streatley Pl
  7 Hampstead
  NW3..................11 B4
  Hampstead NW3...11 C4
Streatley Rd NW6...10 B1
Streimer Rd E15.....27 B3
Strelley Way W3....29 A2
Stretton Mans 16
  SE8...................51 C4
Strickland Ct SE15...65 A4
Strickland Ho 26
  E2...................99 A3
Strickland Row
  SW18.................71 C4
Strickland St SE8...51 C2
Stringer Hos 19
  N1.....................24 A4
Strode Ho 3 SW2..74 C3
Strode Rd
  SW6.................154 A2
  Willesden NW10...8 C2
Strome Ho NW6.....78 A1
Stronsa Rd W12....38 B4
Strood Ho SE1.....137 C3
Stroud Cres SW15...68 C1
Stroud Green Prim
  Sch N4................5 C4
Stroud Green Rd
  N4......................5 C3
Stroudley Ho
  SW8.................171 A4
Stroudley Wlk E3...27 A2
Strout's Pl 2
  E2....................98 C4
Strudwick Ct
  SW4..................172 B3

Strutton Ground
  SW1.................133 B1
Strype St E1........110 C3
Stuart Ave W5.......36 B4
Stuart Ho
  Hammersmith W6...39 B3
  1 Homerton E9.....17 C1
  5 Stockwell SW4...62 A3
  W14.................140 A4
Stuart Mill Ho 1
  N1.....................84 C1
Stuart Rd
  Acton W3............28 B1
  Maida Vale NW6...23 C2
  Nunhead SE15.....65 B3
  Wimbledon SW19...70 C1
Stubbs Dr SE16.....40 A1
Stubbs Ho
  Finsbury Pk N4......5 B3
  1 Globe Town E2...25 C2
Stucley Pl 19 NW1...13 A1
Studd St N1..........86 A4
Studdridge St
  SW6..................165 C2
Studholme Ct
  NW3..................10 C4
Studholme St
  SE15...................50 A3
Studio Pl SW1.....131 A3
Studios The
  4 Clapham SW4...61 B3
  SW8..................171 C3
Studland SE17.....151 B2
Studland Ho E14....33 A3
Studland St W6.....39 A2
Studley Cl E5........18 A3
Studley Ct 13 E14...34 C2
Studley Rd SW4....172 A2
Stukeley St WC2...106 B2
Stunell Ho 20
  SE14...................50 C4
Sturdee Ho 2 E2....24 C3
Sturdy Ho 28 E3....26 A3
Sturdy Rd SE15.....65 A4
Sturgeon Rd SE17 150 C1
Sturge St SE1......136 C4
Sturmer Way N7....14 B3
Sturminster Ho
  SW8.................163 A1
Sturry St E14........34 A3
Sturt St N1...........87 A1
Stutfield St E1......111 C1
Stuttle Ho 9
  E1................24 C1 99 B1
Styles Gdns SW9...63 A4
Styles Ho SE1......122 A1
Stylus Apartments 28
  E8....................24 C4
Sudbourne Prim Sch
  13 SW2..............62 B2
Sudbourne Rd
  SW2..................62 B2
Sudbrooke Rd
  SW12.................60 C1
Sudbury Ct SW8...171 C4
Sudbury Ho SW18...59 A2
Sudeley St N1.......86 B1
Sudlow Rd SW18...58 C2
Sudrey St SE1......136 C3
Suffield Ho SE17...150 B2
Suffolk Ho 4 E1...123 B4
Suffolk Pl SW1.....119 C2
Suffolk Rd
  Barnes SW13.......46 C3
  Willesden NW10....8 A1

Suffolk St SW1.....119 C2
Sugar House La
  E15...................27 B3
Sugar Loaf Wlk 6
  E2....................25 B2
Sugden Rd SW11...60 C3
Sulby Ho SE4........66 A3
Sulgrave Gdns 11
....................39 B4
Sulgrave Rd W6.....39 B3
Sulina Rd SW2......74 A4
Sulivan Ct SW6....165 B1
Sulivan Ent Ctr
  SW6..................58 C1
Sulivan Prim Sch
  SW6..................58 C1
Sulkin Ho 11 E2....25 C2
Sullivan Cl SW11...60 A4
Sullivan Ct
  Stamford Hill N16....7 B3
  SW5.................141 C4
Sullivan Ho
  Chelsea SW1.......160 B4
  Vauxhall SE11.....149 A3
Sullivan Rd SE11...149 C4
Sultan St SE5........48 B3
Sumatra Rd NW6...10 C2
Sumburgh Rd
  SW12.................60 C1
Summercourt Rd
  E1....................32 B3
Summerfield Ave
  NW6..................23 A3
Summer Ho SE13...67 C3
Summerhouse Rd
  N16.....................7 A2
Summerlands Ave
  W3....................28 B2
Summerley St
  SW18.................71 B2
Summersby Rd N6...4 B4
SUMMERSTOWN...71 B1
Summit Ct NW2......10 A3
Summit Est N16.....7 C4
Sumner Ave SE15...49 B2
Sumner Bldgs
  SE1..................122 C2
Sumner Ct SW8....172 A4
Sumner Ho 1 E3....34 A4
Sumner Pl SW7....143 C3
Sumner Place Mews
  SW7.................143 C3
Sumner Rd SE15...49 B3
Sumner St SE1......122 C2
Sun Alley 6 TW9...54 A3
Sun Alliance Ho
  WC2.................107 B2
Sunbeam Cres
  W10..................22 B1
Sunbeam Rd
  NW10.................20 C1
Sunbury Ave
  SW14.................55 C3
Sunbury Ct 3
  SE14...................50 C4
Sunbury Ho 38
  E2....................98 C3
Sunbury La SW11 167 C4
Sunbury Workshops
  E2................24 B2 98 C3
Sun Ct EC3...........109 C1
Sunderland Ct
  SE22...................76 C4

Sunderland Ho 28
W2 . . . . 31 C4
Sunderland Terr
W2 . . . . 100 A2
Sundew View 29 E1 . .29 C2
Sundra Wlk 29 E1 . .25 C1
Sundridge Ho 4
E9 . . . . 17 C1
Sunley Ho 6 . . . . . 111 A3
Sunlight Sq 2 E2 . .25 A2
Sunningdale Ave
W3 . . . . 29 A2
Sunningdale Cl 22
SE16 . . . . 40 A1
Sunningdale Gdns
W8 . . . . 127 C1
Sunninghill Ct 9
W3 . . . . 37 B4
Sunninghill Rd
SE13 . . . . 52 A1
Sunnyhill Cl E5 . .18 A4
Sunnymead Rd
SW15 . . . . 57 A2
Sunnyside 4 NW2 . . 1 B1
Sunnyside Ho 3
NW2 . . . . 1 B1
Sunnyside Rd N19 . . 4 C4
Sun Pas 8 SE16 . .139 B2
Sunray Ave SE5,
Sun Rd W14 . . . . . 140 C1
Sunrise Cl E15 . . .19 B3
Sun St Pas EC2 . .110 A3
Sunset Rd SE5 . . .63 C3
Sun St EC2 . . . . . 109 C4
Sunwell Cl SE15 . . .50 A2
Surcot Ho 2
SW4 . . . . 171 C1
Surma Cl E1 . . .24 C1 99 C1
Surma Rd E1 . . . . . 99 C1
Surrey Canal Rd SE14,
SE8 . . . . 50 C4
Surrey Cres
3 Brentford W4 . . .36 C1
1 London W4 . . . .36 C1
Surrey Docks Farm
SE16 . . . . 41 B4
Surrey Docks
Watersports Ctr
SE8 . . . . 41 B2
Surrey Gr 8 SE17 .152 A1
Surrey Ho 6 SE16 . .32 C1
Surrey La SW11 . .168 B3
Surrey Quays Rd
SE16 . . . . 40 C4
Surrey Quays Sh Ctr
SE16 . . . . 40 C3
Surrey Quays Sta
SE16 . . . . 40 C2
Surrey Rd SE15 . . .65 C2
Surrey Row SE1 . .136 B4
Surrey Sq SE17 . . 152 B2
Surrey Square Prim
Sch SE17 . . . . . . 152 A2
Surrey St WC2 . . .121 A4
Surrey Terr SE17 . .152 B2
Surrey Water Rd
SE16 . . . . 32 C1
Surridge Ct 15
SW9 . . . . 172 B2
Surr St N7 . . . . . . .14 A2
Susan Constant Ct 18
E14 . . . . .34 C2
Susannah St E14 . .34 B3
Sussex Cl N19 . . . .5 A2

Sussex Ct
4 Barnes SW13 . .46 B1
Greenwich SE10 . . .52 B4
Paddington W2 . . .101 B1
Sussex Gdns SW2 . .101 C1
Sussex Ho
Hampstead NW3 . . .12 A2
Richmond TW9 . . . .44 B1
Sussex House Sch
SW3 . . . . 144 C4
Sussex Lo W2 . . .101 C1
Sussex Mans
South Kensington
SW7 . . . . 143 B3
Strand WC2 . . . . .120 B4
Sussex Mews E
W2 . . . . 101 C1
Sussex Mews W
W2 . . . . 115 C4
Sussex Pl
22 Hammersmith
W6 . . . . .39 B1
Lisson Gr NW1 . . . .90 C2
Paddington W2 . . .101 C1
Sussex Sq W2 . . .115 C4
Sussex St SW1 . . .146 B2
Sussex Way
Upper Holloway N7 . .5 B1
Upper Holloway N7,
N19 . . . . .5 A2
Upper Holloway N19 . .4 C3
Sutherland Ave
W9 . . . . .88 C2
Sutherland Ct
2 Paddington
W9 . . . . .23 C1
Stoke Newington
N16 . . . . .6 C1
Sutherland Gdns
SW14 . . . . .56 A4
Sutherland Gr SW18,
SW19 . . . . .70 B4
Sutherland Ho
Kensington W8 . . .128 A1
1 Putney SW15 . . .69 B4
8 South Hampstead
NW6 . . . . .11 B2
Sutherland Pl W2 . .31 C3
Sutherland Rd
Bow E3 . . . . .26 B3
Chiswick W4 . . . . .46 A4
Sutherland Row
SW1 . . . . 146 B2
Sutherland Sq
SE17 . . . . 150 C1
Sutherland St
SW1 . . . . 146 B2
Sutherland Wlk
SE17 . . . . 151 A1
Sutterton St N7 . . .14 B2
Sutton Court Mans
W4 . . . . .45 B4
Sutton Court Rd
W4 . . . . .45 B4
Sutton Ct
Chiswick W4 . . . . .45 B4
6 Hackney E5 . . . .17 A4
Sutton Est The 13
W10 . . . . .30 C4
Sutton Ho & Breaker's
Yd E9 . . . . .17 B3
Sutton La EC1 . . . .96 B1
Sutton La N 4 W4 . .37 B1
Sutton La S W4 . . .45 B4
Sutton Pl E9 . . . . . .17 B3

Sutton Row W1 . . .105 C2
Sutton Sq E9 . . . . .17 B3
Sutton St E1 . . . . . .32 B3
Suttons Way EC1 . . .97 A1
Sutton Wlk SE1 . . .121 A1
Swaby Rd SW17,
SW18 . . . . .71 B2
Swaffield Prim Sch
SW18 . . . . .71 B4
Swaffield Rd
SW18 . . . . .71 B4
Swain's La N6 . . . . .4 A2
Swainson Ho N7 . . .14 C4
Swainson Rd W3 . . .38 B4
Swain St NW8 . . . . .90 A2
Swallow Cl SE14 . . .50 C2
Swallow Ct 4 W9 . .31 C4
Swallowfield NW1 . .92 B3
Swallow Ho NW8 . . .80 A2
Swallow Pl
24 Poplar E14 . . . .33 B3
W1 . . . . 104 B1
Swallow St W1 . . .119 A3
Swanage Ct 6 N1 . .16 A1
Swanage Ho SW8 .162 C1
Swanage Rd SW18 . .59 B1
Swanbourne SE17 .150 C3
Swanbourne Ho
NW8 . . . . .90 A2
Swan Bsns Ctr 8
W4 . . . . .37 C2
Swan Ct
Chelsea SW3 . . . .144 B1
Parsons Green
SW6 . . . . 155 B1
Poplar E14 . . . . . . .33 C3
1 South Hampstead
NW6 . . . . .11 B2
Swandon Way
SW18 . . . . .59 A3
Swanfield St 3
E2 . . . . . . .24 B2 99 A3
Swan Ho N1 . . . . . .15 C1
Swan La EC4 . . . . .123 C3
Swan Lane Pier
EC4 . . . . 123 B3
Swanlea Sch E1 . . .25 A1
Swanley Ho SE17 . .152 B2
Swan Mead SE1 . . .138 A1
Swan Mews
Stockwell SW9 . . . .172 C2
SW6 . . . . 165 B4
Swanmore Ct
SW18 . . . . .59 B1
Swanne Ho 12
SE13 . . . . .67 B4
Swannell Way NW2 . .9 C4
Swanscombe Ho 11
W11 . . . . .30 C1
Swanscombe Point 7
E16 . . . . .35 B2
Swanscombe Rd
6 Chiswick W4 . . .38 A1
Shepherd's Bush
W11 . . . . .30 C1
Swan St SE1 . . . . .137 A3
Swanton Gdns
SW19 . . . . .69 C3
Swanwick Cl
SW15 . . . . .68 B4
Swan Wlk SW3 . . .158 C4
Swan Yd N1 . . . . . .15 A2
Swaton Rd E3 . . . . .26 C1

Swathling Ho
SW15 . . . . .56 B1
Swedenborg Gdns
E1 . . . . .32 A2
Sweden Gate SE16 . .41 A2
Swedish Quays
SE16 . . . . .41 A3
Swedish Sch The
SW13 . . . . .47 A4
Sweeney Cres
SE1 . . . . 139 A3
Sweyn Pl SE3 . . . . .53 C1
Swift Ho
12 Stepney E1 . . . .25 B1
3 Stoke Newington
N16 . . . . .7 A1
1 SW9 . . . . .163 C2
Swift St SW6 . . . .164 C4
Swinbrook Rd
W10 . . . . .31 A4
Swinburne Ct 4
SE5 . . . . .63 C3
Swinburne Ho 15
E2 . . . . .25 B2
Swinburne Rd
SW15 . . . . .56 C3
Swindon St W12 . . .30 B1
Swinford Gdns
SW9 . . . . .63 A4
Swingfield Ho 4
E9 . . . . .25 B4
Swinley Ho NW1 . . .92 B4
Swinnerton St E9 . .18 A3
Swinton Ho 2
E2 . . . . . . .24 C2 99 B3
Swinton Pl WC1 . . .94 C4
Swinton St WC1 . . .94 C4
Swiss Cottage
NW3 . . . . .11 C1
Swiss Cottage L Ctr
NW3 . . . . .11 C1
Swiss Cottage Sch
3 South Hampstead
NW3 . . . . .11 C1
St John's Wood
NW8 . . . . .79 C4
Swiss Cottage Sta
NW3 . . . . .11 C1
Swiss Ct SW1 . . . .119 C3
Swiss Terr 7
NW3 . . . . .11 C1
Switch Ho 2 E14 . .34 C2
Sybil Phoenix Cl
SE8 . . . . .40 C1
Sybil Thorndike
Casson Ho SW5 . .141 C1
Sybil Thorndike Ho 6
N1 . . . . .15 B2
Sycamore Ave E3 . .26 B4
Sycamore Cl W3 . . .29 A1
Sycamore Ct
Kilburn NW6 . . . . . .23 C4
Tufnell Pk N19 . . . . .4 C1
Sycamore Gdns W6,
W12 . . . . .39 A3
Sycamore Gr SE6 . .67 B1
Sycamore Ho
10 Maitland Pk
NW3 . . . . .12 B2
6 Rotherhithe
SE16 . . . . .40 C4
4 Shepherd's Bush
W6 . . . . .39 A4
2 Stoke Newington
N16 . . . . .7 C2

Sycamore Lo
SW15 . . . . .57 A4
Sycamore Mews 4
SW4 . . . . .61 B4
Sycamore St EC1 . .96 C1
Sycamore Wlk 1
W10 . . . . .23 A2
Sydcote SE21 . . . .75 B3
Sydenham Hill SE21,
SE22, SE23, SE26,
SE19 . . . . .76 C3
Sydenham Hill Sta
SE21 . . . . .76 B1
Sydenham Hill Wood
Nature Reserve
SE26 . . . . .76 C1
Sydner Mews N16 . .16 B4
Sydner Rd N16 . . . .16 B4
Sydney Cl SW3 . . .143 C3
Sydney Ho 4 W4 . .38 A3
Sydney Mews
SW3 . . . . 143 C3
Sydney Pl SW7 . . .144 A3
Sydney Rd TW10,
TW9 . . . . .54 B3
Sydney St SW3 . . .144 A2
Sylva Gdns SW3 . .143 C2
Sylvan Ct 5 SW15 . .69 C4
Sylvan Gr
Hampstead NW2 . . .9 C4
SE15 . . . . .50 A4
Sylvester Ho 7
E8 . . . . .17 A2
Sylvester Path 8
E8 . . . . .17 A2
Sylvester Rd E8 . . .17 A2
Sylvia Ct N1 . . . . . .87 B1
Sylvia Pankhurst Ho
14 E2 . . . . .25 C2
Symes Mews NW1 . .82 C2
Symington Ho
SE1 . . . . 137 B1
Symington Mews
E9 . . . . .17 C3
Symister Mews
N1 . . . . . . .24 A2 98 A3
42 Shoreditch
N1 . . . . .24 A2
Symons Cl 6 SE15 .50 B1
Symons St SW3 . . .145 A3
Symphony Mews 15
W10 . . . . .23 A2
Syringa Ho SE4 . . .66 B4

T

Tabard Ct 6 E14 . .34 B3
Tabard Ho SE1 . . . .137 C2
Tabard Sq SE1 . . .137 C2
Tabard St SE1 . . . .137 B2
Tabernacle St EC2 . .97 C2
Tableer Ave SW4 . .61 C2
Tabley Rd N7 . . . . .14 A4
Tabor Rd W6 . . . . .39 A3
Tachbrook Est
SW1 . . . . 147 C1
Tachbrook Mews
SW1 . . . . 146 C4
Tachbrook St
SW1 . . . . 147 A3
Tack Mews SE4 . . .66 C4
Tadema Ho NW8 . . .89 C1

Tadema Rd SW10 ....157 A1
Tadmor St W12 ......30 C1
Tadworth Ho SE1 ...136 A3
Taeping St E14 ......42 A2
Taffrail Ho **2** E14 ...42 A1
Taft Way **44** E3 .....27 A2
Tailworth St **16**
 E1 ....111 B3
Tait Ct
 16 Old Ford E3 ....26 B4
 SW8 ....171 C4
Tait Ho
 SE1 ....121 C1
 2 Tufnell Pk N19 ..13 B4
Takhar Mews
 SW11 ....168 B1
Talacre Com Sp Ctr
 NW5 ....13 A2
Talacre Rd NW5 .....12 C2
Talbot Ct EC3.......123 C4
Talbot Grove Ho **10**
 W11 ....31 A3
Talbot Ho
 Highbury N7 ....5 C1
 Poplar E14 ....34 A3
Talbot Pl SE3 ....53 A1
Talbot Rd
 Camberwell SE22...64 A3
 Notting Hill W2 ....31 C3
 Notting Hill W11....31 B3
Talbot Sq W2.......101 B1
Talbot Wlk
 NW10 ....8 A2
 Notting Hill W11....31 A3
Talbot Yd SE1 ......123 B1
Talcott Path **2**
 SW2 ....74 B3
Talfourd Pl SE15 ....49 B2
Talfourd Rd SE15 ...49 B2
Talgarth Rd
 Hammersmith W6 ..39 B1
 W14 ....140 B2
Talia Ho E14........42 B3
Talleyrand Ho SE5 ..48 B1
Tallis Ct EC4.......121 C4
Talma Rd SW2......62 C3
Talmud Torah Bobov
 Prim Sch **4** N16 ...7 B4
Talmud Torah
 Machzikei Hadass
 Sch E5 ....7 C4
Talmud Torah Toldas
 Yakov Yosef Sch
 N16 ....7 A3
Talmud Torah Yetev
 Lev **6** N16 ....7 C3
Talwin St E3 ....27 A2
Tamar Cl **24** E3 ....26 B4
Tamar Ho
 10 Cubitt Town
 E14 ....42 B4
 SE11 ....149 C2
Tamarind Ct **8**
 W3 ....28 B3
Tamarind Ho **4**
 SE15 ....49 B3
Tamarind Yd **5**
 E1 ....125 C2
Tamarisk Sq W12 ...29 B2
Tamworth **5** N7.....14 A2
Tamworth St
 SW6 ....155 B3
Tangier Rd TW10 ...55 A4
Tangley Gr SW15 ...68 B4

Tangmere WC1 .....94 C3
Tanhurst Ho **27**
 SW2 ....74 A4
Tankerton St WC1 ..94 B3
Tanner Ho SE1 ....138 B3
Tanner's Hill SE8 ...51 C2
Tanners Mews
 SE8 ....51 B2
Tanner St SE1 .....138 B3
Tanners Yd **22** E2 ...25 A3
Tannery Ho **22** E1 ..111 B4
Tannington Terr
 N5 ....5 C1
Tansley Cl N7 ......13 C3
Tanswell St SE1 ....135 B3
Tantallon Rd
 SW12 ....72 C3
Tant Ave E16 ....35 B3
Tanza Rd NW3 .....12 B4
Tapley Ho **1** SE1 ..139 B3
Taplow NW3 ....11 C1
Taplow Ho **38**
 E2 ....24 B2 98 C3
Taplow St N1 ....87 A1
Tappesfield Rd
 SE15 ....65 B4
Tapp St E1 ....25 A1
Taranto Ho **14** E1 ...32 C4
Tarbert Rd SE22 ....64 A2
Tarbert Wlk E1 .....32 B2
Tarling Rd E16 .....35 B3
Tarling St E1 ....32 B3
Tarnbrook Ct
 SW1 ....145 B3
Tarn St SE1 ....136 C1
Tarns The NW1 .....92 C4
Tarplett Ho **2**
 SE14 ....50 C4
Tarragon Cl SE14 ...51 A3
Tarranbrae Ho **6** ...10 A1
Tarrant Ho E2 ......25 B2
Tarrant Pl W1 .....102 C3
Tarrantt Ho W14 ..126 A2
Tarriff Cres SE8 ....41 B2
Tarrington Cl
 SW16 ....73 D1
Tartan Ho **10** E14 ...34 B3
Tarver Rd SE17 ....150 B2
Tarves Way SE10 ...52 A3
Tasker Ho **11** E14 ...33 B4
Tasker Lo W8 ......127 B4
Tasker Rd NW3 ....12 B3
Tasman Ct **8** E14 ...42 A2
Tasman Ho **17** E1 ..32 A1
Tasman Rd SW9 ....62 A4
Tasso Rd W6 ......154 A4
Tasso Yd W6 ......154 A3
Tatchbury Ho **8**
 SW15 ....56 B1
Tate Britain SW1 ..148 A3
Tate Ho **13** E2 ......25 C3
Tate Modern SE1 ..122 B2
Tatham Pl NW8 ....79 C2
Tatnell Rd SE23 ....66 A1
Tatton Cres E5, N16 ..7 B4
Tatum St SE17 ....151 C3
Tauheed Cl N4 ......6 B2
Taunton Ho W2 ...100 C1
Taunton Mews
 NW1 ....90 C1
Taunton Pl NW1 ....90 C2
Tavern Cl SE4 .....137 A1
Taverner Ho N16 ....6 C1
Taverners Cl
 W11 ....31 A1 112 A1
Taverner Sq **4** N5...15 B4

Tavern La SW9 ....173 C2
Tavistock Cl N16...16 A3
Tavistock Cres
 W11 ....31 B4
Tavistock Ct WC1 ..93 C2
Tavistock Ho **3**
 W11 ....31 B4
Tavistock Mews **3**
 W11 ....31 B3
Tavistock Pl WC1 ..94 A2
Tavistock Rd
 Dagenham NW10 ...21 B3
 Notting Hill W11 ...31 B4
Tavistock Sq WC1 ..93 C2
Tavistock St WC2 ..120 B4
Tavistock Terr N19 ..4 C1
Tavistock Twr
 SE1 ....141 A1
Taviton St WC1 ....93 B2
Tavy Cl SE11 ......149 C2
Tawhid Boys Sch
 N16 ....7 B2
Tawny Way SE16 ...40 C2
Taybridge Rd
 SW11 ....60 C3
Tayburn Cl E14 .....34 B3
Tayler Ct NW8 .....79 B4
Tayler Ho
 Stepney E1 ....25 A1
Tayler St NW8 .....79 A4
Taylor Ave TW9 ....45 A1
Taylor Cl SE8 ......51 B4
Taylor Ho **10** SW2 ..74 C3
Taylor's Gn W3 ....29 A3
Taylor's La NW10 ...8 A1
Tayport Cl N1 .....14 A1
Tayside Ct **6** SE5 ..63 C3
Tayyibah Girls Sch **8**
 E5 ....7 C3
Teak Cl SE16 ......33 A1
Tealby Ct N7 ......14 B2
Teal Ct SE8 ....51 B4
Teale St E2 ....24 C3
Teal St **1** SE10 .....43 B3
Teather St **12** SE5 ..49 A3
Tebbs Ho **2** SW2 ...74 C4
Tedman Ct SE13 ...67 B3
Ted Roberts Ho **25**
 E2 ....25 A3
Tedworth Gdns
 SW3 ....144 C1
Tedworth Sq SW3 .144 C1
Teesdale Cl E2 .....25 A3
Teesdale St E2 .....25 A3
Teesdale Yd **18** E2 ..25 A3
Tee The W3 ....29 A3
Teignmouth Cl **6**
 SW4 ....61 C3
Teignmouth Rd
 NW2 ....9 C2
Telcon Way SE10 ...43 A2
Telegraph Hill NW3 ..2 A1
Telegraph Pl E14 ...42 A2
Telegraph Rd
 SW15 ....69 B4
Telegraph St EC2 ..109 B2
Telephone Pl
 SW6 ....155 A4
Television Ctr
 W12 ....30 B1
Telfer Cl **4** W3 .....37 B4
Telfer Ho EC1 ......96 B3
Telferscroft Prim Sch
 5 SW2 ....73 C3
Telferscroft Rd
 SW2 ....73 C3
Telford Ave SW12,
 SW2 ....74 A3

Telford Avenue Mans
 7 SW2 ....74 A3
Telford Ho
 8 Kensal Town
 W10 ....31 A4
 SE1 ....136 C2
Telford Parade Mans
 7 SW2 ....74 A3
Telford Rd W10.....31 A4
Telford Terr SW1 ..160 C4
Telford Way W3 ....29 A4
Tell Gr SE22 ....64 B3
Telscombe Ho
 SW11 ....169 B3
Temair Ho **1**
 SE10 ....52 B3
Temeraire Pl TW8 ..36 B1
Temeraire St SE16 ..40 B4
Temperley Rd
 SW12 ....72 C4
Templar Ho NW2 ..10 B2
Templar St SE5 ....48 A1
Temple Bar EC4 ...108 B1
Temple Bar EC4 ...108 B1
Templecombe Rd
 E9 ....25 B4
Temple Ct
 Stepney E1 ....32 C4
 SW8 ....162 A1
Temple Dwellings **7**
 E2 ....25 A3
Temple Gr Hatcham
 Sch SE14 ....50 C1
Temple Ho
 13 Battersea
 SW11 ....60 A4
 4 Tufnell Pk N7 ....4 B1
Temple La EC4 ....107 C1
Templemead Cl
 W3 ....29 A3
Templemead Ho
 E9 ....18 A4
TEMPLE MILLS 19 A3
Temple Mills La
 London E10, E15....19 B4
 Stratford E15 ......19 A4
Temple Mills Rd
 E9 ....18 C4
Temple Pl WC2 ...121 A4
Temple Rd
 Acton Green W4 ...37 B3
 Richmond TW9 ....54 B3
Temple Sheen
 SW14 ....55 B2
Temple Sheen Rd
 SW14 ....55 B3
Temple Sta WC2...121 B4
Templeton Cl **25**
 N16 ....16 A3
Templeton Pl
 SW5 ....141 C3
Temple West Mews
 SE11 ....136 A1
Templewood Ave
 NW3 ....2 A1
Templewood Gdns
 NW3 ....2 A1
Templewood Point
 NW2 ....1 B3
Tenbury Ct SW12 ...73 C3
Tenby Ho
 Islington N7 ....14 C3
 W2 ....100 C1
Tench St E1 ....32 A1

Tenda Rd SE16 .....40 A2
Tendring Ho SW2 ..62 C1
Tenham Ave SW2 ..73 C2
Tenison Ct W1 ....118 C4
Tenison Way SE1 ..121 B1
Tenniel Cl W2 .....114 B4
Tennis St SE1 .....137 B4
Tennyson Ho
 SE17 ....151 A2
Tennyson Rd NW6 .23 B4
Tennyson St SW8 ..170 A1
Tensing Ho N1 .....15 A2
Tenterden Ho
 SE17 ....152 B2
Tenterden St W1 ..104 B1
Tenter Ground
 E1 ....110 C3
Tequila Wharf E14..33 A3
Terborch Way **6**
 SE22 ....64 A3
Tercelet Terr NW3 ..11 B4
Teredo St SE16 ....40 C3
Terling Ho **9** W10 ..30 B4
Terling Wlk N1 .....86 C4
Terminus Pl SW1 ..132 B1
Tern Ho **9** SE15 ....49 B2
Terrace Gdns
 SW13 ....46 B1
Terrace La TW10 ...54 A2
Terrace Rd E9 ......17 B1
Terrace The
 Barnes SW13,
 SW14 ....46 A1
 EC4 ....107 C1
 Kilburn NW6 ......23 C4
 10 Rotherhithe SE8 .41 B2
Terrano Ho **1**
 TW9 ....45 A2
Terrapin Ct SW17 ..73 A1
Terrapin Rd SW17 ..73 A1
Terrick St W12 .....30 A3
Territorial Ho
 SE11 ....149 C3
Terry Ho SW2 .....74 C3
Tersha St TW9 .....54 B3
Tessa Sanderson Pl **6**
 SW8 ....61 A4
Testerton Wlk **3**
 W11 ....30 C2
Tetcott Rd SW10 ..156 C1
Teversham La
 SW8 ....172 B4
Teviot St E14 ......34 B4
Teyham Ct **2**
 SW11 ....60 B1
Thackeray Ct
 Chelsea SW3 .....144 C2
 West Kensington
 W14 ....126 A1
Thackeray Ho
 College Pk NW10 ..21 C2
 WC1 ....94 A2
Thackeray Mews **6**
 E8 ....16 C2
Thackeray Rd
 SW8 ....170 B1
Thackeray's
 Almshouses SE6....67 A1
Thackeray St W8 ..128 B2
Thalia Cl SE10 .....52 C4
Tham Cl **10** SE24 ...63 A1
Thame Rd SE16 ....40 C4
Thames Ave
 SW10 ....167 A4

Thames Bank SW14 .....45 B1
Thames Christian Coll SW11 .....59 C4
Thames Circ E14 .....41 C2
Thames Cres W4 .....46 A3
Thames Ct 10 E15 .....49 B3
Thames Hts SE1 .. 138 C4
Thameside Ctr W8 .....4 B4
Thames Link Ho 7 W9 .....23 A3
Thames Pl SW15 ..57 C4
Thames Quay Millwall E14 .....42 A4
W10 .....167 A3
Thames Rd W4 .....45 A4
Thames Reach W6 ..41 B3
Thames Row TW9 ..44 B4
Thames Village W4 .....45 B2
Thames Wlk SW11 .....158 A2
Thane Mans N7 .. 5 B1
WC1 .....94 A3
7 West Norwood SE27 .....75 A1
Thanet Ho WC1 .. 10 A2
Thanet St WC1 .....94 A3
Thane Villas N1 .. 5 B1
Thane Works N1 .. 5 B2
Thavies Inn EC4 .. 107 C2
Thaxted Ct N1 .. 87 C1
Thaxted Ho SE16 .. 40 A2
Thaxton Rd W14 .. 155 A4
Thayer St W1 .. 103 C2
Theatre Royal E10 .. 19 C2
Theatre Sq E15 .. 19 C2
Theatre St SW11 .. 60 B4
Theberton St N1 .. 86 B4
Theed St SE1 .. 121 C1
Thelbridge Ho 20 E3 .....27 A2
Theobalds Ct WC1 .....106 C4
Theobald's Rd WC1 .....106 C4
Theobald St SE1. 137 B1
Theodore Ct SE13 .. 67 C1
Theodore Ho 1 SW15 .....56 C2
Theodore Rd SE13 .. 67 C1
Therapia Rd SE22 ..65 B1
Theresa Rd W6 .. 38 C2
Therfield Ct N5 .. 6 B2
Thermopylae Gate E14 .....42 A2
Theseus Ho 7 E14 .....34 C3
Theseus Wlk N1 .. 86 B1
Thessaly Ho SW8 160 C1
Thessaly Rd SW8 171 A4
Thetford St NW1 .. 83 C1
Thetis Terr TW9 .. 44 C4
Third Ave East Acton W3 .. 29 B1
West Kilburn W10 .. 23 A2
Thirleby Rd SW1 133 A1
Thirlmere NW1 .. 92 B4
N16 .....15 C4
Thirsk Rd SW11 .. 60 C3
Thistle Gr SW7 .. 143 A1
Thistle Ho 10 E14 .. 34 B3

Thistlewood Cl 3 N7 .....5 B2
Thistly Ct SE8 .....52 A4
Thomas Baines Rd SW11 .....59 C4
Thomas Burt Ho 8 E2 .....25 A2
Thomas Buxton Prim Sch 17 E1.. 24 C1 99 C1
Thomas Crowell Ct 16 N16 .....16 A3
Thomas Doyle St SE1 .....136 B2
Thomas Fairchild Com Sch 1 N1.. 87 A2
Thomas Ho 8 Hackney E9 .....17 B2
4 Stockwell SW4 ..62 A3
Thomas Hollywood Ho 2 E2 .....25 B3
Thomas Jones Sch 1 W11 .....31 A3
Thomas Milner Ho 8 SE15 .....49 C3
Thomas More Ho EC2 .....108 C3
Thomas More Sq E1 .....125 B3
Thomas More St E1 .....125 B3
Thomas Neal's Ctr WC2 .....106 A1
Thomas North Terr 4 E16 .....35 B4
Thomas Pl W8.. 128 A1
Thomas Rd E14.. 33 C4
Thomas Road Ind Est 2 E14 .....33 C3
Thomas's, Battersea SW11 .....167 C3
Thomas's London Day Sch SW6.. 59 A4
Thomas's London Ind Day Sch 1 W8.. 128 C3
Thomas's Prep Sch Clapham SW11..60 B2
Thompson Ave Richmond TW9 ..54 C4
6 SE5 .....48 B3
Thompson Ho 3 Kensal Town W10 .....23 A1
SE14 .....50 C4
Thompson Rd SE22 .....64 B1
Thomson Ct 4 E8.. 16 C2
Thomson Ho SW1 .....147 C1
Walworth SE17 .....152 A3
Thomson House Sch SW1 .....147 C1
Thorburn Ho SW1 131 B3
Thorburn Sq SE1.. 153 B3
Thoresby Ho N16.. 6 C1
Thoresby St N1 .... 97 A4
Thornaby Ho 15 E2 .....25 A2
Thornbill Ho 4 SE15 .....49 C3
Thornbury Ct W11 .....31 C2 113 B4
Thornbury Ho N6.. 4 B3
Thornbury Rd SW2 .....62 A1

Thornbury Sq London N6 .....4 B3
7 Upper Holloway N6 .....4 B3
Thorncliffe Ct SW2 .....62 A1
Thorncliffe Rd SW2 .....62 A1
Thorncombe Rd SE22 .....64 A2
Thorncroft St SW8 .....162 A1
Thorndale Ho 10 N16 .....15 C2
Thorndean St SW18 .....71 B2
Thorndike Cl SW10 .....156 C2
Thorndike Ho SW1 .....147 B2
Thorndike Rd 21 N1 .....15 C2
Thorndike St SW1 .....147 B3
Thorne Cl E16 .....35 C3
Thorne Ho 34 Bethnal Green E2 .....25 B2
4 Cubitt Town E14 ..42 B3
Thorne Pas 7 SW13 .....46 B1
Thorne Rd SW8 .....162 B1
Thorness Ct SW18.. 59 B1
Thorne St SW13, SW14 .....56 A4
Thornewill Ho 6 E1 .....32 B2
Thorney Cres SW11 .....157 C1
Thorneycroft Ho 1 W4 .....38 A1
Thorney Ct W8 .. 128 C3
Thorney Hedge Rd W4 .....37 A2
Thorney St SW1 .. 148 A4
Thornfield Ho 5 E14 .....33 C2
Thornfield Rd W12 .....39 A4
Thorngate Rd W9 ..23 C1
Thornham Gr E15 ..19 C3
Thornham St SE10.. 52 A4
Thorn Ham Ho SE1 .....137 C2
Thornhaugh St WC1 .....93 C1
Thornhill Bridge Wharf N1 .....84 C3
Thornhill Cres N1 .. 14 C1
Thornhill Gr N1 .... 14 C1
Thornhill Ho 12 Chiswick W4 ..38 A1
Islington N1 .....14 C1
Thornhill Mews SW15 .....58 B3
Thornhill Prim Sch 11 N1 .....14 C1
Thornhill Rd N1 .... 85 B4
Thornhill Sq N1 .... 14 B1
Thornicroft Ho 12 SW9 .....173 A1
Thornley Pl 2 SE10 .....43 A1

Thornsett Rd SW18 .....71 B2
Thornton Ave Chiswick W4 .....38 A2
Streatham SW2 ..73 C3
Thornton Ct N7 .... 13 C3
Thornton Gdns SW12 .....73 C3
Thornton Ho SE17 .....152 A3
Thornton Pl W1 .. 103 A4
Thornton Rd Mortlake SW14 ....55 C4
Streatham SW12, SW2 .....73 C3
Thornton St SW9 173 B2
Thornville St SE8.. 51 C2
Thornwood Gdns W8 .....127 B4
Thornwood Ho N6 .....4 B4
Thornycroft Ct TW9 .....44 B1
Thorold Ho SE1 .....136 C4
6 Streatham SW2 ..74 A4
Thorparch Rd SW8 .....161 C1
Thorpebank Rd W12 .....29 C1
Thorpe Cl W10 ....31 A3
Thorpedale Rd N4.. 5 B3
Thorpe Ho N1 .....85 A3
Thorverton Rd NW2.. 1 A1
Thoydon Rd E3 ....26 A3
Thrale St SE1 .....123 A1
Thrasher Cl 20 E8 ..24 B4
Thrawl St E1 .....111 A3
Thrayle Ho 2 SW9 .....62 B4
Threadgold Ho 8 N1 .....15 C2
Threadneedle St EC2, EC3 .....109 C1
Three Colts La E2 ..25 A1
Three Colt St E14.. 33 B2
Three Cups Yd WC1 .....107 A3
Three Kings Yd W1 .....118 A4
Three Mill La E3 ..27 B2
Three Nun Ct EC2 ..109 B2
Three Oak La SE1 138 C4
Threshers Pl W11 .....31 A2 112 A4
Thring Ho 8 SW9 .....172 C2
Throgmorton Ave EC2 .....109 C2
Throgmorton St EC2 .....109 C2
Thrush St SE17 .. 150 C2
Thurland Ho 3 SE16 .....40 A2
Thurland Rd SE16 139 B2
Thurleigh Ave SW12 .....60 C1
Thurleigh Ct SW12 .....60 C1
Thurleigh Rd SW12 .....60 C1
Thurloe Cl SW7 .. 144 A3
Thurloe Ct SW3 .. 144 A3
Thurloe Pl SW7 .. 143 C4
Thurloe Place Mews SW7 .....143 C4

Thurloe Sq SW7 .. 144 A4
Thurloe St SW7 .. 143 C4
Thurlow Hill SE21.. 75 B2
Thurlow Ho 17 SW16 .....74 A1
Thurlow Park Rd SE21, SE24 .....75 A2
Thurlow Rd NW3 .. 11 C3
Thurlow St SE17 .. 152 A1
Thurlow Terr NW5 12 C3
Thurlow Twrs SE27 .....74 B1
Thurlow Wlk SE17 .....152 A1
Thurnscoe NW1 .. 82 C3
Thursley Gdns SW19 .....69 C2
Thursley Ho 10 SW2 .....74 B4
Thurso Ho NW6 .. 78 A1
Thurston Ind Est SE13 .....67 A4
Thurston Rd SE8, SE13 .....52 A1
Thurtle Rd E2 .....24 B3
Tibbatts Rd E3 .... 27 A1
Tibberton Sq N1 .. 86 C4
Tibbets Cl SW19 .. 69 C3
Tibbet's Corner SW19 .....69 C4
Tibbet's Ride SW19 .....69 C4
Tiber Cl 10 E3 ....26 C4
Tiber Gdns N1 .... 84 B3
Tickford Ho NW8.. 90 A3
Tidal Basin Rd E16 .....35 B2
Tidbury Ct SW8 .. 160 C1
Tidemill Acad 20 SE8 .....51 C3
Tideswell 11 NW5 .. 13 A4
Tideswell Rd SW15 .....57 A3
Tideway Ct 9 SE16 .....32 C1
Tideway Ind Est SW8 .....161 A3
Tideway Wharf SW13 .....46 A1
Tideway Yd SW13.. 46 A1
Tidey St E3 .....33 C4
Tidworth Ho 13 SE15 .....50 B4
Tidworth Rd E3 .. 26 C1
Tierney Rd SW2 .. 74 A3
Tierney Terr SW2.. 74 A3
Tiger Ho WC1 .... 93 C3
Tiger Way E5 .....17 A4
Tignel Ct W3 .....36 C4
Tilbury Cl 14 SE15.. 49 B3
Tilbury Ho 4 SE14 .....50 C4
Tildesley Rd SW15.. 57 B1
Tilehurst NW1 .....92 B3
Tilehurst Rd SW17, SW18 .....71 C3
Tile Kiln La N6 .... 4 B3
Tileyard Rd N7 ....14 A1
Tilford Gdns SW19.. 69 C3
Tilford Ho 3 SW2.. 74 B4
Tilia Rd E5 .....17 A4
Tilia Wlk 3 SW9 ..63 A3
Tiller Ho 24 N1 ....24 A4

Tiller L Ctr E14......41 C3
Tiller Rd E14.........41 C3
Tillet Sq SE16........41 A4
Tillet Way 6
E2.........24 C2 99 B4
Tilling Ho 8 SE15...65 A4
Tilman Ho 8
SW2.................74 B3
Tillman St E1.........32 A3
Tilloch St 9 N1......14 B1
Tillotson Ct SW8....161 C1
Tilney Ct EC1........97 A2
Tilney Gdns 12 N1...15 C2
Tilney St W1........117 C2
Tilson Cl 5 SE5....49 A3
Tilson Gdns SW2,
SW4.................74 A4
Tilton St SW6.......154 B3
Tiltwood The W3....28 B2
Timberland Cl 16
SE15.................49 C3
Timberland Rd E1...32 A3
Timber Mill Way
SW4.................61 C4
Timber Pond Rd
SE16.................40 C4
Timber St EC1.......96 C2
Time Sq E8..........16 B3
Timothy Cl 1
SW4.................61 B2
Timsbury Wlk 5
SW15................68 C3
Tina Ct SW16........74 C1
Tindal St SW9.......48 A2
Tinniswood Cl N5...14 C3
Tintage Cl 1
SE22................76 C4
Tintagel Cres
SE22................76 C4
Tintagel Ct EC1....96 A2
Tintern Cl SW15....58 A2
Tinworth St SE11..148 B2
Tipthorpe Rd
SW11................60 C4
Tiptree 3 NW1.....13 A1
Tisbury Ct W1......119 B4
Tisdall Pl SE17....151 C3
Tissington Ct 4
SE16................40 C2
Titan Bsns Est 3
SE8.................51 A4
Titan Ct TW8........36 B1
Titchborne Row
W2.................102 B1
Titchfield Rd NW8..80 C4
Titchwell Rd
SW18................71 C3
Tite St SW3.......158 C4
Titmuss St W12....39 B4
Tiverton Rd NW6,
NW10................22 C4
Tiverton St SE1.....136 C2
Tivoli Ct SE16.......33 B1
Tivoli Wy E14.......33 B3
Tobago St 15 E14...41 C4
Tobin Cl NW3........12 A1
Toby La E1...........26 A1
Todber Ho W14....126 A2
Todds Wlk N7.......5 B2

Tokenhouse Yd
EC2.................109 B2
Token Yd SW15.....58 A3
Toland Sq SW15....56 C2
Tolchurch 2 W11...31 C3
Tolhurst Dr 4
W10.................23 A2
Tollbridge Cl W10..23 A1
Tollet St E1..........25 C1
Tollgate Dr SE21....76 A2
Tollgate Ho 4
NW6.................78 A2
Tollhouse Way N19..4 B2
Tollington St N4......5 B2
Tollington Ho 4
N19..................5 A1
Tollington Pk N4......5 B2
Tollington Pl N4......5 B2
Tollington Rd N7....14 B4
Tollington Way N7...5 A1
Tolmers Sq NW1.....93 A2
Tolpaide Ho SE11...149 B3
Tolpuddle St N1.....85 B2
Tolsford Rd E5......17 A3
Tom Groves Cl
E15..................19 C3
Tom Hood Cl E15...19 C3
Tom Jenkinson Rd 6
E16..................35 C1
Tonkyns Ho SE11...149 B3
Tomline Ho 4........122 C1
Tomlin's Gr E3......26 C2
Tomlinson Cl
5 Gunnersbury
W4..................37 A1
Spitalfields
E2.............24 B2 99 A3
Tomlin's Terr E14....33 A3
Tomlins Wlk 4 N7...5 B2
Tompion Ho EC1.....96 B2
Tompion St
EC1..................96 B3
Finsbury EC1.........96 B3
Tom Smith Cl
SE10.................53 A4
Tomson Ho SE1....138 C2
Tom Williams Ho
SW6.................154 C3
Tonbridge Hos
WC1..................94 A3
Tonbridge St WC1...94 A3
Toneborough 16
NW8.................78 B3
Tonsley Hill SW18..59 A2
Tonsley Pl SW18....59 A2
Tonsley Rd SW18...59 A2
Tonsley St SW18....59 A2
Took's Ct EC4......107 B2
Topley St SE9......124 A1
Tooting Bec Sta
SW17.................72 C1
Topham Ho 8
SE10.................52 B3
Topham St EC1......95 B2
Topiary Sq TW9......54 B4
Topmast Point 22
E14..................41 C4
Tora Temimah Prim
Sch NW2..............9 A3
Torbay Ct 13 NW1..13 A1
Torbay Mans NW6..23 B4
Torbay Rd NW6.....10 B1
Torbay St 13 NW1..13 A1
Tor Ct W8..........127 C4
Tor Gdns W8.......127 B4

Tornay Ho
Hackney E9.........17 B1
N1...................84 C2
Torquay St W2.....100 A3
Torrence Ho 6
N19..................4 B2
Torrens Ct SE5.....63 C4
Torrens Rd SW2....62 B2
Torrens St EC1......86 A1
Torres Sq E14.......41 C1
Torriano Ave NW5..13 C3
Torriano Cotts
NW5.................13 B3
Torriano Mews
NW5.................13 B3
Torriano Sch 24
NW5.................13 C3
Torridge Gdns
SE15.................65 B3
Torridon Ho NW6...78 A1
Torrington Pl
Bloomsbury WC1...105 B4
St George in t East
E1..................125 C2
Torrington Sq
WC1..................93 C1
Tortington Ho 6
SE15.................50 A3
Torwood Rd SW15..56 C2
Tothill Ho SW1....147 C4
Tothill St SW1.....133 C3
Totland Ho SW18...59 A1
Tottan Terr E1......32 C3
Tottenhall 6 NW1..12 C1
Tottenham Court Rd
W1..................105 A4
Tottenham Court
Road Sta W1......105 C2
Tottenham Mews
W1..................105 A4
Tottenham Rd N1...16 A2
Tottenham St W1...105 A4
Totteridge Ho
SW11................167 C2
Touchard Ho N1.....97 C3
Toulmin St SE1....136 C3
Toulon St SE5.......48 B3
Toulouse Ct 2
SE16.................40 A1
Tounson Ct SW1...147 C3
Tournay Rd SW6...155 A2
Toussaint Wlk 18
SE16................139 C2
Tovy Ho 6 SE1....153 B1
Towcester Rd E3...27 B1
Tower 42 EC2.....110 A2
Tower Bldgs 21
E1..................32 A1
Tower Br App E1,
EC3.................124 C3
Tower Bridge E1, EC3,
SE1.................124 C3
Tower Bridge Bsns
Complex SE16......40 A3
Tower Bridge Bsns Sq
SE16.................40 A2
Tower Bridge Piazza
SE1.................124 C2
Tower Bridge Prim
Sch SE1............138 C4
Tower Bridge Rd
SE1.................138 A3
Tower Bridge Sq
SE1.................138 C4

Tower Cl NW3......11 C3
Tower Ct
Brockley SE4.......66 A3
Stamford Hill E5....7 B4
St Giles WC2......106 A1
St John's Wood
NW8.................80 B2
Towergate SE1....152 A4
Towergate Ho 8
E3..................26 B3
Tower Gateway Sta
EC3.................124 C3
TOWER HAMLETS..33 B4
Tower Hamlets Coll
20 Poplar E14......34 A3
22 Poplar E14......34 A2
6 Stepney E1.......32 C3
Tower Hill EC3....125 A3
Tower Hill Sta
EC3.................124 C3
Tower House Sch
SW14................55 B3
Tower Mans SE1...138 C1
Tower Mews E18...18 A3
Tower Millennium
Pier EC3...........124 B2
Tower Mill Rd 7
6 Camberwell
SE15.................49 A4
1 SE15..............49 A3
Tower of London The
EC3.................124 C3
Tower Pl E EC3....124 B3
Tower Pl W EC3....124 B3
Tower Rd NW10....8 C1
Tower Rise 19......54 A3
Tower Royal EC4..123 B4
Tower Pl 7W10.....54 A2
Tower St WC2.....106 A1
Towers The
Dartmouth Pk NW5..4 A1
1 Richmond TW9...54 B3
Tower Terr SE4.....66 A3
Towerview SE13....66 C2
Tower Wharf SE1..138 C4
Tower Wlk SE1....152 A4
Tower Workshops
SE1.................138 B4
Towncourt Path N4..6 B3
Townhall Ave 8
W4..................37 C1
Town Hall Rd
SW11................60 B4
Town Hos EC1......96 B1
Townley Rd SE22...64 A2
Townley St SE17...151 B2
Townmead Bsns Ctr
SW6.................59 B4
Townmead Rd
Richmond TW9.....45 A1
Sands End SW6....166 C1
Townsend Ho 14
SE1.................153 C3
Townsend Ind Est
NW10................20 B3
Townsend Mews 3
SW18................71 B2
Townsend Prim Sch
SE17................152 A3
Townsend Rd NW8..80 B2
Townsend St SE1,
SE17................152 A4
Townsend Yd N6....4 A3
Townshend Ct
NW8.................80 B2

Townshend Est
NW8.................80 A1
Townshend Rd
Primrose Hill
NW8.................80 A1
Richmond TW9.....54 B3
Townshend Terr
TW9.................54 B3
Towns Ho 4 SW4..61 C4
Towpath Wlk E9....18 B3
Towton Rd SE27...75 B2
Toxteth Ho N4......6 B4
Toynbee St E1....110 C3
Toynbee Studios
E1..................111 A3
Tracey Ave NW2....9 B3
Tracy Ho 8 E3......26 B2
Tradescant Ho 15
E9...................17 B1
Tradescant Rd
SW8.................162 B1
Trade Twr 8
SW11................59 B4
Trade Winds Ct 1
E1..................125 C2
Trading Estate Rd
NW10................20 B1
Traemore Ct
SW16................74 C1
Traemore Ave
SE15.................49 B3
Trafalgar Cl 1
SE16.................41 A2
Trafalgar Gdns
Stepney E1..........32 C4
W8..................128 B2
Trafalgar Ho SE10..52 C2
Trafalgar Mews
E9...................18 B2
Trafalgar Point 2
N1...................15 C1
Trafalgar Rd SE10..43 A1
Trafalgar Sq SW1..119 C2
Trafalgar St SE17..151 C2
Trafalgar Way E14..34 B1
Trafford Ho N1.....87 C2
Tragail SW15.......58 A2
Trahorn Cl E1.......25 A1
Tralee Ct 31 SE16..40 A1
Tramway Ave E15..19 C1
Trance Way W3....36 C3
Tranmere Ho 7
N7...................14 C3
Tranmere Rd SW7,
SW18................71 B2
Tranquil Pas SE3...53 B1
Tranquil Vale SE3...53 A1
Transept St NW1..102 B3
Transom Cl SE16...41 A2
Transom Sq E14...41 A1
Tranton Rd SE16...40 A3
Trappes Ho 2
SE16.................40 A2
Travers Ho 6
SE10.................52 C4
Travers Rd N7......5 C1
Travis Ho SE10.....52 B2
Treadgold Ho 7
W11..................30 C2
Treadgold St W11..30 C2
Treadway St E2.....25 A3
Treasury Bldgs
SW1.................134 A4

...eaty St N1........... **84** C3
...ebeck St W1 .... **118** A1
...eborough Ho
   N1 .... **103** B4
...ebovir Rd SW5 . **141** C3
...eby St E3........... **26** B1
...ecastle Way **2**
   .... .13 C4
...edegar Mews Ho
   E3 ....26 B2
...edegar Rd E3 ...26 B3
...edegar Rd E3 ...26 B3
...edegar Terr E3 ...26 B2
...ederwen Rd E8 ...24 C4
...een Ave SW13 ...56 B4
...ees The N16....... .6 C4
...efil N1, N7 ...... .14 A4
...efoil Rd SW18 ...59 B2
...egarvon Rd
   SW11 ....60 C3
...ego Rd E9 ......18 C1
...egothnan Rd
   SW9 ....62 A4
...eguenter Rd
   SW10 .... **142** C1
...eherne Ct SW9 ...48 A2
...ehern Rd **12**
   SW14 ....55 C4
...ehurst St E5....... .18 A3
...elawney Est E3 ...26 C2
...elawney Ho
   SE1 .... **136** C4
...elawney Sq **2**
   SW2 ....62 C2
...ellis Sq **1** E8 ...26 C4
...emadoc Rd SW4 ...61 C3
...emaine Cl SE4 ...51 C1
...ematon Ho
   SE11 .... **149** C2
...emlett Ct N19 ... .4 B1
...emlett Mews **2**
   N19 ....4 B1
...enchard St SE10 . .42 C1
...enchford St
   SW8 .... **162** A3
...endell Ho **8**
   E14 ....33 C3
...enmar Gdns
   NW10 ....22 A2
...entham Ct W3 ...28 C4
...entham St SW18 ...70 C3
...ent Ho SE15 ...65 B3
...ent Rd SW2 ......62 B2
...eport St SW18 ...71 A4
...resco Ho SE11 .. **149** B2
...resco Rd SE15 ...65 A3
...resham Cres
   NW8 ....90 A2
...resham Wlk E9 ...17 B3
...residder Ho **10**
   SW4 ....73 C4
...ressel Cl SW11 ...61 A1
...ressillian Cres
   SE4 ....66 C4
...ressillian Rd SE4 ...66 C4
...revanion Rd
   W14 .... **140** B2
...revelyan Gdns
   NW10 ....22 B4
...revelyan Ho
   16 Globe Town
   E2 ....25 C2
.... .SE5 ....48 A3
...reveris St SE1 .. **122** B1
...reverton St W10 ...22 C1
...reverton Twr **4**
   W10 ....30 C4

Treves Ho
   E1 ....24 C1
Treville St SW15 ...69 A4
Trevithick Ho
   13 Bermondsey
   SE16 ....40 A2
   3 Gospel Oak
   NW5 ....13 A4
.... SW8 .... **171** B4
Trevithick St **8** ...51 C4
Trevithick Wy **2**
   E3 ....26 C2
Trevor Pl SW7 .. **130** B3
Trevor-Roberts Sch
   NW8 ....11 C1
Trevor Sq SW7 .. **130** B3
Trevor Sq SW7 .. **130** B3
Trevor St SW7 .. **130** B3
Trewint St SW18 ...71 B2
Triangle Ct SE1 .. **123** A1
Triangle Est The
   SE11 .... **149** B1
Triangle Pl SW4 ...61 C3
Triangle Rd **7** E8 ...25 A4
Triangle The
   Crouch End N19 ... .4 C4
   EC1 .... **96** B2
   10 Hackney E8 ...25 A4
Trident Ho SE14 ... **51** A3
Trident St SE16 ...40 C2
Trieste Ct SW12 ...72 B3
Trig La EC4 ...... **122** C4
Trigon Rd SW8 .. **163** A2
Trillington Ho
   W12 ....29 C1
Trimdon NW1 ... **83** A3
Trinder Gdns N19 ... .5 A3
Trinder Rd N4, N19 .. .5 A3
Trinidad Ho **17**
   E14 ....33 B2
Trinidad St E14 ...33 B2
Trinity Church Rd
   SW13 ....47 A4
Trinity Church Sq
   SE1 .... **137** A2
Trinity Cl
   3 Clapham SW4 ...61 B3
   Lewisham SE13 ...67 C3
Trinity Coll of Music
   SE10 ....52 B4
Trinity Cotts TW9 ...54 B4
Trinity Cres TW12 ...72 C2
Trinity Ct
   Finsbury WC1 .... **94** C2
   2 Hoxton N1 ......24 A4
   Rotherhithe SE16 ...41 A4
   Willesden NW2 ... .9 B3
Trinity Gdns
   E16 ....35 B4
   Stockwell SW2,
   SW9 ....62 B3
Trinity Gn **2** E1 ...32 B4
Trinity Gr **8** SE10 ...52 B2
Trinity Ho SE1 .. **137** A2
Trinity Homes **14**
   SW2 ....62 B3
Trinity Laban
   Conservatoire of
   Music & Dance **7**
.... .SE18 ....52 A4
Trinity Mews
   SW18 ....70 C3

Trinity Pl EC3 ... **124** C3
Trinity Rd
   Richmond TW9 ......54 B4
   Wandsworth SW17,
   SW18 ....72 A4
Trinity Rise SE24,
   SW2 ....75 B2
Trinity St Mary's CE
   Prim Sch **8**
   SW12 ....73 A3
Trinity Sq EC3 .. **124** B4
Trinity St
   9 Newham E16.......35 C4
   SE1 .... **137** B2
Trinity Way W3 ...29 B2
Trio Pl SE1 .... **137** B2
Tristan Ct **2** SE8 ...51 B4
Triton Ct EC2 ...97 C1
Triton Ho **2** E14 ...42 A2
Tritton Rd SE21,
   SE27 ....75 C1
Trocette Mans
   SE1 .... **138** B2
Trojan Ct NW6 ... **10** A1
Trojan Ind Est
.... .NW10 ....8 B2
Troon Cl **2** SE6 ...40 A1
Troon Ho **9** E14 ...33 A3
Troon St E1 ......33 A3
Tropical Ct **2**
   W10 ....22 C1
Trossachs Rd
   SE22 ....64 A2
Trothy Rd SE1 .. **153** C3
Trotman Ho **1**
.... .SE14 ....50 B2
Trott St SW11 .. **168** A3
Trotwood Ho **3**
   SE16 ....40 A4
Troubridge Ct **12**
.... .W4 ....37 B1
Troutbeck NW1 .. **92** B3
Troutbeck Rd
   SE14 ....51 A2
Trouville Rd SW4 ...61 B1
Trowbridge Est **8**
   E15 ....18 B2
Trowbridge Rd E9 ...18 B2
Trower Ho **5** E9 ...18 A2
Troy Ct W8 .... **127** B2
Troyes Ho NW3 ...12 B3
Troy Town SE15 ...64 C4
Troy Town Flats
   SE15 ....64 C4
Truman's Rd **2**
   N16 ....16 A3
Trump St EC2 .. **109** A1
Trundle St SE1 .. **137** A4
Trundleys Rd SE8 ...51 A4
Trundley's Rd SE8 ...41 A1
Trundley's Terr
   SE8 ....40 C2
Truro Ho **2** W2 ...31 C4
Truro St NW5 ......12 C2
Trussley Rd W6 ...39 B3
Trust Wlk SE21 ...75 A3
Tryon Cres E9 ...25 B4
Tryon St SW3 .. **144** C2
Tubbs Rd NW10 ...21 B3
Tudor Cl
   Crouch End N6 ... .4 B4
   Hampstead NW3 ...12 A2
   Tulse Hill SW2 ......62 B1
Tudor Coll WC1 .. **94** A3

Tudor Ct
   Kingsland N1 ...... .16 A2
   5 Rotherhithe
   SE16 ....32 C1
   South Acton W5 ...36 C4
   Tudor St Ent W10 ...20 A3
Tudor Gdns SW14 ...56 A4
Tudor Gr **9** E9 ...17 B1
Tudor Ho
   Brook Green W14 ...39 C2
   34 Hackney E9 ...17 B1
Tudor Mews **2**
   NW10 ....8 C2
Tudor Rd E9 ......25 A4
Tudor St EC4 .. **121** C4
Tudor Way W3 ......36 C4
Tufnell Ct **14** E3 ...26 B3
Tufnell Park Mans
   N7 ....5 A1
TUFNELL PARK ...13 C4
Tufnell Park Mans **2**
   N7 ....5 A1
Tufnell Park Prim Sch
   N7 ....13 C4
Tufnell Park Rd N19,
   N7 ....13 C4
Tufnell Park Sta
.... .N19 ....13 B4
Tufton Ct SW1 .. **134** A1
Tufton St SW1 .. **134** A1
Tuke Sch SE15 ......49 B4
Tullis Ho **12** E9 ...17 B1
TULSE HILL 75 A4
Tulse Hill
   Tulse Hill SW2 ......74 C4
   Tulse Hill SW27 ...75 A2
Tulse Hill Sta
   SE27 ....75 A2
Tulse Ho SW2 ......62 C1
Tulsemere Rd SE21,
   SE27 ....75 C2
Tunbridge Ct **1**
   SE26 ....76 C1
Tunbridge Ho EC1 . **96** A4
Tunis Rd W12 ......30 A1
Tunley Gn **2** E14 ...33 B4
Tunley Rd
   Dagenham NW10 ...21 A4
   Upper Tooting SW12,
   SW17 ....72 C2
Tunnel Avenue Trad
   Est SE10 ....42 C4
Tunnel Rd SE16 ......40 B4
Tunstall Ct **14** ...... .54 B4
Tunstall Rd SW9 ...62 B3
Tunstall Wlk **10**
   TW8 ....44 A4
Tunworth Cres
   SW15 ....56 B1
Tun Yd SW8 ......61 A4
Tupman Ho **28**
   SE16 .... **139** B3
Turberville Ho **1**
   SW9 ....62 B4
Turenne Cl SW18 ...59 B3
Turin St E2 ......24 C2
Turk's Head Yd
   EC1 .... **108** A4
Turks Row SW3 .. **145** A2
Turle Rd N4 ...... .5 B2
Turlewray Cl N4 .. .5 B3
Turnagain La EC4 . **108** A2
Turnberry Cl **24**
   SE16 ....40 A1

Turnberry Quay **1**
   E14 ....42 A3
Turnbull Ho N1 ......86 B4
Turnchapel Mews **7**
   SW4 ....61 A4
Turner Cl **7** SW9.. .48 A2
Turner Ct
   9 Herne Hill SE5... .63 C3
   24 Rotherhithe
   SE16 ....40 B4
Turner Ho
   Finsbury Pk N4... .5 B3
   24 Millwall E14 ...41 C4
   St John's Wood
   NW8 ....90 A2
   Strand WC2 .... **120** B3
   Westminster SW1 .. **147** C3
Turner Lo **10**
   SW19 ....69 C3
Turner Pl SW11 ...60 A2
Turners Ct E15 ...19 B4
Turner's Rd E3 ...33 B4
Turner St
   Canning Town
   E16 ....35 B3
   Stepney E1 ......32 A4
Turneville Rd
   W14 .... **154** C4
Turney Rd SE21 ...75 C3
Turney Sch SE21...75 B4
Turnham Green Sta
   W4 ....38 A2
Turnham Green Terr
   W4 ....38 A2
Turnham Ho SE4 ...66 A3
Turnham Prim Sch **6**
   SE4 ....66 A3
Turnmill Ho **8**
   SW2 ....62 C2
Turnmill St EC1 .. **108** A4
Turnour Ho **1** E1 ...32 A3
Turnpike Cl SE8 ...51 B3
Turnpike Ho EC1 .. **96** B3
Turpin Ho
   SE10 ....52 B4
Turpentine La
   SW1 .... **146** B1
Turpin Ho SW11 .. **170** A4
Turpin Way N19 ...4 C3
Turquand St SE17 .. **151** A3
Turret Gr SW4 ......61 B4
Turville Ho NW8 .. **90** A2
Turville St
   E2 .... **24** B1
Tuscan Ho **38** E2 ...25 B2
Tuskar St SE10 ...43 A1
Tuttle Ho SW1 .. **147** C1
Tweed Ho E14 ......34 B1
Tweezer's Alley
   WC2 .... **121** B4
Twelvetrees Bsns Pk
   E3 ....27 C1
Twelvetrees Cres
   E3 ....27 C1
Twig Folly Cl **2**
   E2 ....25 C3
Twilley St SW18 ...71 A4
Twine Ct E1 ......32 B2
Twinings Mus
   WC2 .... **107** B1
Twisden Rd NW5 ...13 A4
Twycross Mews
   SE10 ....43 A2

Twyford CE High Sch W3 ...28 A1
Twyford Ho N5 ...6 A1
Twyford Sp Ctr W3 ...28 A1
Twyford St N1 ...84 C4
Twynholm Mans SW6 ...154 A2
Tyburn Tree (site of) W2 ...116 C4
Tyburn Way W1 ...117 A4
Tyer's Est SE1 ...138 A4
Tyers Gate SE1 ...138 A3
Tyers St SE11 ...148 C2
Tyers Terr SE11 ...149 A1
Tyler Cl E2 ...24 B3
Tyler Ho SE3 ...52 C1
Tyler St
  Greenwich SE10 ...43 A1
  SE10 ...53 A4
Tylney Ho 10 E1 ...32 A3
Tymperley Ct SW19 ...70 A3
Tyndale La N1 ...15 A1
Tyndale Mans N1 ...15 A1
Tyndale Terr 13 N1 ...15 A1
Tyneham Cl 10 SW11 ...60 C4
Tyneham Rd SW11 ...60 C4
Tynemouth St SW6 ...166 C2
Tyne St E1 ...111 A2
Tynsdale Rd NW10 ...8 A2
Tynte Ct E9 ...18 A3
Tynwald Ho 10 SE26 ...76 C1
Type St E2 ...25 C3
Tyrawley Rd SW6 ...166 A3
Tyrells Ct 3 SE15 ...65 A4
Tyrrell Ho SW1 ...161 A4
Tyrrell Rd SE22 ...64 C3
Tyrwhitt Rd SE4 ...66 C4
Tysoe St EC1 ...95 C3
Tyssen Com Prim Sch N16 ...7 C2
Tyssen Rd N16 ...7 B1
Tyssen St
  Dalston E8 ...16 B2
  Hoxton N1 ...24 A3
Tysson Ho E9 ...18 A1
Tytherton 29 E2 ...25 B3
Tytherton Rd N19 ...4 C1

U
Uamvar St E14 ...34 A4
UCL Acad 13 NW3 ...11 C1
UCL Elizabeth Garrett Anderson Wing NW1 ...93 A1
Udall St SW1 ...147 A3
Udimore Ho 11 W10 ...30 B4
Uffington Rd NW10 ...22 A4
Ufford St SE1 ...135 C4
Ufton Gr N1 ...15 C1
Ufton Rd N1 ...16 A1
Uhura Sq 19 N16 ...7 A1
Ujima Ct N19 ...5 A3
Ullin St E14 ...34 B4
Ullswater SW15 ...57 C1
Ullswater Ho SE15 ...50 B4
Ullswater Rd
  Barnes SW13 ...46 C3
  West Norwood SE27, SW16 ...75 A2
Ulster Pl NW1 ...92 A1
Ulster Terr NW1 ...92 A2
Ulundi Rd SE3 ...53 A4
Ulva Rd SW15 ...57 C3
Ulverscroft Rd SE22 ...64 C2
Ulverstone Rd SE27 ...75 A2
Ulysses Rd NW6 ...10 B3
Umberston St E1 ...32 A3
Umbria St SW15 ...56 C1
Una Ho 7 NW5 ...13 A2
Undercliff SE10 ...52 B2
Undercliff Rd SE13 ...67 A4
Underhill Ho 7 E14 ...33 C4
Underhill Pas NW1 ...82 B4
Underhill St NW1 ...82 B3
Undershaft EC3 ...110 A1
Underwood Ho W6 ...39 A3
Underwood Rd E1 ...24 C1 99 C1
Underwood Row N1 ...97 A4
Underwood St N1 ...97 A4
Undine Rd E14 ...42 A2
Unicorn Bldg 14 E1 ...32 C2
Unicorn Sch TW9 ...44 B2
Union Cl E11 ...19 C4
Union Ct
  46 Paddington W2 ...31 C4
  2 Richmond TW10 ...54 A2
  South Lambeth SW4 ...172 A1
  Whitechapel EC2 ...110 A2
Union Dr E1 ...26 A1
Union Gr SW8 ...171 C2
Union Mews SW9 ...172 A1
Union Pk 11 SE10 ...43 B1
Union Rd SW8 ...171 C1
Union Sq N1 ...87 A3
Union St
  Mill Meads E15 ...27 C4
  SE1 ...122 C1
Union Wharf N1 ...87 A2
Union Wlk E2 ...24 A2 98 B4
Union Yd W1 ...104 B1
Unity Cl NW10 ...8 C2
Unity Mews NW1 ...83 B2
Univ Coll Hospl at Westmoreland St W1 ...103 C3
Univ Coll London (Bloomsbury WC1) ...93 B2
Univ Coll London (Bloomsbury WC1) ...94 B2
Univ Coll London (Windeyer Inst) W1 ...105 A4
Univ Coll London (Wolfson Ho) NW1 ...93 A3
Univ Coll Sch Junior Branch 31 NW3 ...11 B4
University College London WC1 ...93 C1
University Coll Hospl WC1 ...93 A2
University Coll Sch NW3 ...11 B3
University Mans 9 SW15 ...57 C4
University of Cumbria London 24 E14 ...33 C2
University St W1 ...93 A1
Univ Hospl Lewisham SE13 ...67 A2
Univ of California WC1 ...105 C3
Univ of Greenwich SE10 ...52 C4
Univ of London Birkbeck College WC1 ...105 C4
Univ of London (King's Coll Hall) SE5 ...63 C4
Univ of Notre Dame SW1 ...119 C3
Univ of Notre Dame SW1 ...119 C3
Univ of Roehampton (Digby Stuart Coll) SW15 ...56 C2
Univ of Roehampton (Froebel Coll) SW15 ...56 B1
Univ of Roehampton (Southlands Coll) SW15 ...56 B1
Univ of Roehampton (Whitelands Coll) SW15 ...68 C4
Univ of Wales Trinity St David's SW1 ...163 C2
Univ of Westminster (Cavendish Campus) W1 ...104 C4
Univ of Westminster (Marylebone Campus) W1 ...103 B4
Univ of Westminster (Regent Campus) W1 ...104 C3
Univ of Westminster (Regent Campus, Univ HQ) W1 ...104 B2
Univ of Westminster (Wigram House Halls of Residence) SW1 ...133 A1
Unwin Cl SE15 ...49 C4
Unwin Rd SW7 ...129 C2
Upbrook Mews W2 ...101 A1
Upcerne Rd SW10 ...157 A1
Upcott Ho
  3 Bromley E3 ...27 A2
  4 Hackney E9 ...17 B1
Upgrove Manor Way 12 SE24 ...74 C4
Upham Park Rd W4 ...38 A2
Upland Rd SE22 ...64 C1
Uplands Cl SW14 ...55 A2
Upnall Ho 10 SE15 ...50 B2
Upnor Way SE17 ...152 B2
Upper Addison Gdns W14 ...126 A4
Upper Bank St E14 ...34 A1
Upper Bardsey Wlk 7 N1 ...15 B2
Upper Belgrave St SW1 ...131 C2
Upper Berkeley St W1 ...103 A1
Upper Brockley Rd SE4 ...51 B1
Upper Brook St W1 ...117 B4
Upper Caldy Wlk 18 N1 ...15 B2
Upper Camelford Wlk 14 W10 ...31 A3
Upper Cheyne Row SW3 ...158 A4
Upper Clarendon Wlk 22 W11 ...31 A3
Upper Dengie Wlk N1 ...86 C4
Upper Grosvenor St W1 ...117 B3
Upper Ground SE1 ...121 B2
Upper Gulland Wlk 23 N1 ...15 B2
Upper Hampstead Wlk 30 NW3 ...2 B1
Upper Handa Wlk 2 N1 ...15 B2
Upper Harley St NW1 ...91 C1
Upper Hawkwell Wlk N1 ...87 A4
UPPER HOLLOWAY ...4 C2
Upper Holloway Sta N19 ...4 C2
Upper James St W1 ...119 A4
Upper John St W1 ...119 A4
Upper Lismore Wlk 6 N1 ...15 B2
Upper Mall W6 ...39 A1
Upper Marsh SE1 ...135 A2
Upper Montagu St W1 ...102 C3
Upper North St E14 ...33 C4
Upper Park Rd NW3 ...12 B3
Upper Phillimore Gdns W8 ...127 B3
Upper Ramsey Wlk 10 N1 ...15 C2
Upper Rawreth Wlk N1 ...87 A4
Upper Richmond Rd SW15 ...57 B3
Upper Richmond Rd W TW10, SW14, SW15 ...55 B3
Upper St Martin's La WC2 ...120 A4
Upper St N1 ...86 A3
Upper Tachbrook St SW1 ...147 A4
Upper Talbot Wlk 7 W10 ...31 A3
Upper Terr NW3 ...2 B1
Upper Thames St EC4 ...123 A4
Upper Tollington Pk N4 ...5 C3
UPPER TOOTING ...72 B1
Upper Tooting Park Mans 1 SW17 ...72 C2
Upper Tooting Pk SW17 ...72 B2
Upper Tooting Rd SW17 ...72 B1
Upper Tulse Hill SW2 ...74 C3
Upper Wimpole St W1 ...103 C4
Upper Woburn Pl NW1, WC1 ...93 C3
Upstall St SE5 ...48 A2
Upton Cl NW2 ...1 A1
Urban Mews N4 ...6 A4
Urlwin St SE5 ...48 B4
Urlwin Wlk SW9 ...48 A1
Urmston Dr SW19 ...70 A3
Urmston Ho 4 E14 ...42 B2
Ursula Gould Wy 27 E14 ...33 C4
Ursula Mews N4 ...6 B3
Ursula St SW11 ...168 A3
Urswick Rd E9 ...17 B3
Urswick Sch The 18 E9 ...17 B3
Usborne Mews SW8 ...163 A2
Usher Rd E3 ...26 B3
Usk Rd SW11 ...59 B3
Usk St E2 ...25 C2
Utah Bldg 3 SE13 ...52 A1
Utopia Ho 3 NW2 ...8 C2
Utopia Village NW1 ...81 B4
Uverdale Rd SW10 ...157 A1
Uxbridge Rd W12 ...30 A1
Uxbridge St W8 ...31 C1 113 B2

V
Vadnie Bish Ho NW5 ...13 B3
Vaine Ho 4 E9 ...18 A2
Vale Cl W9 ...88 C3
Vale Ct
  3 Hammersmith W3 ...29 B3
  St John's Wood W9 ...88 C3
Vale End SE22 ...64 B3
Vale Est The W3 ...29 A1
Vale Gr
  Acton W3 ...29 A1
  Stoke Newington N4 ...6 A4
Valens Ho 1 SW2 ...74 C3
Valentia Pl SW9 ...62 C3
Valentine Ho
  11 Clapham Pk SW4 ...61 B1
  20 Old Ford E3 ...26 B4
Valentine Pl SE1 ...136 A4
Valentine Rd E9 ...17 C2
Valentine Row SE1 ...136 A3
VALE OF HEALTH ...2 C1
Vale of Health NW3 ...2 C1
Vale Rd N4 ...6 B4
Vale Rise NW11 ...1 B3
Vale Row N5 ...6 A1
Vale Royal N7 ...14 A1
Vale Sch The SW7 ...128 C1

ale The
Cricklewood NW11....1 A2
East Acton W3....29 A1
SW3....157 C4
aletta Rd W3....38 B4
alette Ho E9....17 B2
alette St E8....17 A2
aliant Ho
10 Cubitt Town
E14....42 B4
SW11....167 C3
alliance Rd
E1....24 C1 99 C1
alliere Rd NW10....21 C2
al McKenzie Ave
N7....5 C1
almar Rd SE5....48 B2
almar Trad Est
SE5....48 B2
alois Ho 11....138 C2
alonia Gdns
SW18....58 B1
anbern Ho NW5....12 C2
anbrugh Ct SE11....149 C3
anbrugh Fields
SE3....53 B3
anbrugh Hill SE10,
SE3....53 B4
anbrugh Ho 8
E9....17 B1
anbrugh Park Rd
SE3....53 B3
anbrugh Park Rd W
SE3....53 B3
anbrugh Pk SE3....53 B3
anbrugh Rd W4....37 C3
anbrugh Terr
SE3....53 B2
anburgh Ho 14....110 C4
ancover Ho 33
E1....32 A1
anderbilt Rd
SW18....71 B3
anderbilt Villas 1
W12....39 C4
andon Ct SE1....138 A2
andon Pas SW1....133 A2
andon St SW1....133 A2
andyke Cl SW15....57 C1
andy St
EC2....24 A1 98 A1
ane Cl W3....11 C4
ane St SW1....147 A4
ange Ho 12 W10....30 B4
an Gogh Ct E14....42 C3
anguard Bldg 8
E14....41 C4
anguard Ho 1
E8....17 A1
anguard St SE8....51 C2
anneck Sq SW15....56 C2
anner Point 27
E9....25 B4
ansittart St 7
SE14....51 A3
anston Ho SW6....155 C2
antage Mews 3
E14....34 B1
antage Pl W8....127 C1
antrey Ho SE11....149 B3
arcoe Rd SE16....40 B1
ardens Rd SW11....59 C3
arden St E1....32 A3
ardon Cl W3....28 C3
ardon Ho E10....52 B2
arey Ho E1....26 A2

Varley Ho 5 NW6....23 C4
Varma Ct SE3....53 C2
Varna Rd SW6....154 C1
Varndell St NW1....92 C4
Varnishers Yard
N1....84 B1
Varsity Row SW14....45 B1
Vascroft Est NW10....20 A1
Vassall Ho 8 E3....26 A2
Vassall Rd SW9....163 C1
Vat Ho SW8....162 B2
Vauban Est SE16....139 A1
Vauban St SE16....139 A1
Vaudeville Ct N4....5 C2
Vaughan Ave W6....38 B2
Vaughan Est 8
E2....24 B2 98 C4
Vaughan Ho SE1....136 A4
Vaughan Rd SE5....63 B4
Vaughan St SE16....41 B4
Vaughan Way E1....125 C2
Vaughan Williams Cl
SE8....51 C3
VAUXHALL....148 B1
Vauxhall Bridge Rd
SW1....147 A3
Vauxhall City Farm
SE11....148 C1
Vauxhall Cross SE1,
SE11....148 B1
Vauxhall Gr SW8....162 C4
Vauxhall Prim Sch
SE11....149 A1
Vauxhall St SE11....149 A2
Vauxhall Sta SE11....148 B1
Vauxhall Wlk
SE11....148 C2
Vawdrey Cl E1....25 B1
Vaynor Ho N7....14 A4
Vectis Ct SW18....59 A1
Veda Rd SE13....66 C3
Velde Way 1
SE22....64 A2
Vellacott Ho 3
W12....30 A3
Velletri Ho 1 E2....25 C3
Venables St NW8....101 C4
Vencourt Pl W6....38 C2
Venetian Rd SE5....48 B1
Venice Ct 14 SE5....48 B3
Venn Ho N1....85 A3
Venn St SW4....61 B3
Ventnor Rd SE14....50 C3
Ventura Ho 12
SE22....62 A3
Venue St E14....34 B4
Venus Ho
2 Millwall E14....41 C2
8 Old Ford E3....26 C4
Vera Ct 1 W2....100 A2
Vera Rd SW6....164 B4
Verbena Gdns 4
W6....38 C1
Verdun Rd SW13....46 C3
Vere Bank SW19....70 B3
Vereker Rd W14....140 B1
Vere Ho 2
Lisson Gr NW8....90 A2

Verney Ho continued
South Kensington
SW10....156 C4
Verney Rd SE16....40 A1
Verney Way SE16....40 A1
Vernon Ct NW2....1 B1
Vernon Ho SE11....149 A1
Vernon Mews
W14....140 B3
Vernon Pl WC1....106 B3
Vernon Rd
Bow E3....26 B3
Mortlake SW14....55 C4
Vernon Rise WC1....95 A4
Vernon St W14....140 B3
Vernon Yd
W11....31 B2 112 C4
Verona Ct
Chiswick W4....38 A1
14 SE14....50 C4
Veronica Ho
Brockley SE4....66 B4
46 Bromley E3....27 A2
Veronica Rd SW17....73 A2
Verran Rd SW12....73 A4
Verulam Bldgs
WC1....107 A4
Verulam Ho 1
W6....39 B4
Verulam St EC1....107 B4
Vervain Ho 2
SE15....49 C3
Verwood Ho SW8....163 A1
Verwood Lo 6
E14....42 C2
Vesage Ct EC1....107 C3
Vesey Path 15 E14....34 A3
Vespan Rd W12....38 C4
Vesta Ct SE1....138 A3
Vesta Rd SE4, SE14....51 A1
Vestry Mews 12
SE5....49 A2
Vestry Rd SE5....49 A2
Vestry St N1....97 B4
Viaduct Pl 2 E2....25 A2
Viaduct St E2....25 A2
Vian St SE13....67 A4
Vibart Gdns SW2....74 B4
Vibart Wlk N1....84 B4
Vicarage Ave SE3....53 C3
Vicarage Cres
SW11....167 B3
Vicarage Ct
8 Putney SW15....68 C4
W8....128 A4
Vicarage Dr SW14....55 C2
Vicarage Gate
W8....114 A1
Vicarage Gdns
Mortlake SW14....55 C2
W8....31 C1 113 C1
Vicarage Gr SE5....48 C2
Vicarage Wlk
SW11....167 C4
Vicar's Cl E9....25 B4
Vicars Hill SE13....67 A3
Vicar's Rd NW5....12 C3
Viceroy Ct NW8....80 B2
Viceroy Rd SW8....172 A4
Vic Johnson Ho 3
E3....26 B4
Vickery Ct EC1....97 A2
Vickery Ho

Vickery Ho 13
SW4....62 A3
Vickery's Wharf 7
E14....33 C3
Victor Cazalet Ho
N1....86 A4
Victoria & Albert Mus
SW7....129 C1
Victoria Arc SW1....132 B1
Victoria Ave EC2....110 B3
Victoria Bldgs 18
E8....25 A4
Victoria Chambers
EC2....24 A1 98 A2
Victoria Coach Sta
SW1....146 A3
Victoria Cotts
7 Richmond
TW9....44 C2
5 Spitalfields E1....111 B4
Victoria Ct
5 Clapham Pk
SW4....61 C1
South Acton W3....36 C4
4 St George in E
E1....125 B3
Victoria Dr SW19....69 C3
Victoria Emb
WC2....121 B3
Victoria Gate Gardens
SW2....52 A3
Victoria Gdns
W11....31 C1 113 B2
Victoria Gr W8....128 C2
Victoria Gr Mews
W2....114 A3
Victoria Hall 16
E16....35 C1
Victoria Ho
6 Clapham Pk
SW4....61 C1
2 Shepherd's Bush
W12....30 A1
SW1....146 A2
Victoria Ind Est
W3....29 A4
Victoria Mans
1 Islington N7....14 C3
Willesden NW10....9 A1
Victoria Mews
Kilburn NW6....23 C4
Wandsworth SW18....71 B3
Victoria Mills 1
E15....27 C4
Victoria Miro Gall
N1....87 A1
Victorian Gr N16....7 A1
Victorian Rd N16....7 B1
Victoria Park Ct 11
E9....17 B1
Victoria Park Ind Ctr
E9....18 B2
Victoria Park Lofts
E9....18 C2
Victoria Park Rd
E9....17 C1
Victoria Park Sq
E2....25 B2
Victoria Pas NW8....89 B2
Victoria Place Sh Ctr
SW1....146 B4
Victoria Rd
Finsbury Pk N4....5 B3
Kensington W8....128 C2
Kilburn NW6....23 B4
Mortlake SW14....55 C4

Victoria Rd continued
North Acton NW10....21 A1
Victoria Rise SW4....61 A4
Victoria Sq SW1....132 B2
Victoria St SW1....133 A1
SW1....146 B4
Victoria Terr
Dagenham NW10....21 A1
Finsbury Pk N4....5 C4
Victoria
(Underground)
SW1....132 B1
Victoria Villas
TW9....54 B3
Victoria Wharf
E14....33 A2
Victoria Yd 1 E1....111 C1
Victor Rd NW10....22 A2
Victory Pl
6 Limehouse
E14....33 A2
SE17....151 B4
Victory Prim Sch
SE17....151 A4
Victory Way SE16....41 A4
Victory Wlk SE8....51 C2
Video Ct N4....5 A4
View Cl N6....3 B4
Viewfield Rd
SW18....58 B1
Viewpoint 3 N5....15 A3
Vigo St W1....118 C3
Viking Cl 13 E3....26 A3
Viking Ho 3 SE5....48 B1
Village Cl NW3....11 C3
Village Mount 1
NW3....11 B4
Village Sch The
NW3....12 B2
Village The SW11....60 B4
Village Way SE21....63 C1
Villa Rd SW9....62 C4
Villa Sch The
Villas On The Heath
NW3....2 B1
Villa St SE17....151 C1
Villiers Ct SW11....168 B4
Villiers Gardens
E15....19 A3
Villiers Rd NW2....8 C2
Villiers St WC2....120 B2
Vince Ct N1....97 C3
Vincent Ct
Finsbury Pk N4....5 A3
Marylebone W1....102 C2
South Lambeth
SW9....173 A3
Vincent Mews 1
E3....26 C3
Vincent Rd W3....37 B3
Vincents Cl SE16....41 A4
Vincent St
Canning Town
E16....35 B4
Westminster SW1....147 C4
Vincent Terr N1....86 B2
Vince St EC1....97 C3
Vine Cl E5....16 C4
Vine Ct E1....111 C3
Vinegar St E1....32 A1
Vinegar Yd SE1....138 A4
Vine Hill EC1....95 B1

Vine La SE1 . . . . **124** B1
Vine Rd SW13 . . . . . . **56** B4
Vinery Wy W6 . . . . . . **39** A3
Vine St Bridge EC1 **95** C1
Vine Sq W14 . . . . . . **141** A1
Vine St
W1 . . . . **119** A3
Whitechapel EC3 . **110** C1
Vineyard Path
SW14 . . . . **55** C4
Vineyard Sch The
TW10 . . . . **54** A1
Vineyard The
TW10 . . . . **54** A2
Vineyard Wlk EC1 **95** B2
Viney Ct **B** SW4 . . . . **61** C1
Vine Yd SE1 . . . . **137** A4
Viney Rd SE13 . . . . . . **67** A4
Vining St SW2,
SW9 . . . . **62** C3
Vinson Ho N1 . . . . . . **87** C1
Vintners Ct EC4 . . . . **123** A4
Viola Sq W12 . . . . **29** B2
Violet CI **B** SE8 . . . . **51** B4
Violet Hill NW8 . . . . . **78** C1
Violet Hill Ho NW8 **78** C1
Violet Rd E3 . . . . **27** A1
Violet St E2 . . . . **25** A1
Virgil Pl W1 . . . . **102** C3
Virgil St SE1 . . . . **135** A2
Virginia Ct **B**
SE16 . . . . **40** C4
Virginia Ho **B** E14 . . **34** B2
Virginia Prim Sch **B**
E2 . . . . **24** B2 **98** C3
Virginia Rd **ID**
E2 . . . . **24** B2 **98** C3
Virginia St E1 . . . . . . **125** C3
Virginia Wlk SW2 . . **62** B1
Viscount Ct **B**
W11 . . . . **31** C3
Viscount St EC1 . . . . **108** C4
Vista Bldgs **ID** E3 . . **26** B2
Vitae Apartments **Z**
W6 . . . . **38** C3
Vitali CI SW15 . . . . . . **56** C1
Vittoria Ho N1 . . . . . . **85** A3
Vittoria Prim Sch
N1 . . . . **85** B2
Vivian Comma CI **B**
N4 . . . . **6** A1
Vivian Ct NW6 . . . . . . **78** A2
Vivian Ho N4 . . . . **6** C4
Vivian Rd E3 . . . . **26** A3
Vivian Sq SE15 . . . . . . **65** A4
Vogans Mill SE1 . . . . **139** A4
Vogler Ho **B** E1 . . . . **32** B2
Vollasky Ho **B**
E1 . . . . **111** B4
Voltaire
B Camberwell
SE5 . . . . **49** B2
ID Richmond TW9 . . **44** B2
Voltaire Ct **ID**
SW11 . . . . **169** C2
Voltaire Rd SW4 . . . . **61** C4
Volt Ave NW10 . . . . . . **21** A2
Vorley Rd N19 . . . . **4** B2
Voss St E2 . . . . **24** C2 **99** B3
Voyager Bsns Est **ID**
SE16 . . . . **139** B2

Vulcan Rd SE4 . . . . . . **51** B1
Vulcan Sq E14 . . . . . . **41** C2
Vulcan Terr SE4 . . . . **51** B1
Vulcan Way N7 . . . . . . **14** B2
Vyner Ct E5 . . . . **7** C2
Vyner Rd W3 . . . . **28** C2
Vyner St E2 . . . . **25** A4

W

Wadcroft Ct SE4 . . . . **66** B4
Wadding St SE17 . . . . **151** B3
Waddington Rd
E15 . . . . **19** C2
Waddington St
E15 . . . . **19** C2
Made Ho **ID** SE1 . . . **139** B3
Wadeson St E2 . . . . . . **25** A3
Wade's Pl E14 . . . . . . **34** A2
Wadham Gdns
NW3 . . . . **80** A4
Wadham Mews
SW14 . . . . **45** B1
Wadham Rd SW15 . . **58** A3
Wadhurst Rd
Battersea SW8 . . . . **170** C4
London W4 . . . . **37** C3
Wager St E3 . . . . **26** B1
Waghorn St SE15 . . . . **64** C4
Wagner St SE15 . . . . . **50** B3
Wainford CI SW19 . . **69** C3
Wainwright Ho **B**
E1 . . . . **32** B1
Waite St SE15 . . . . . . **49** B4
Waithman St EC4 . . **108** A1
Wakefield Ho **G**
SE15 . . . . **49** C2
Wakefield Mews
WC1 . . . . **94** B3
Wakefield St WC1 . . . **94** B3
Wakeford CI SW4 . . . **61** B2
Wakeham St **B**
N1 . . . . **15** C2
Wakehurst Rd
SW11 . . . . **60** B2
Wakeling Ho **B**
SE27 . . . . **75** A1
Wakeling St **ID**
E14 . . . . **33** A3
Wakelin Ho **ID** N1 . . **15** A1
Wakeman Rd
NW10 . . . . **22** C2
Wakley St EC1 . . . . . . **96** A4
Walberswick St
SW8 . . . . **162** B1
Walbrook EC4 . . . . . . **123** B4
Walbrook Ct **B**
N1 . . . . **24** A3
Walbrook Wharf
EC4 . . . . **123** B4
Walburgh St E1 . . . . **32** A3
Walcorde Ave
SE17 . . . . **151** A3
Walcot Gdns
SE11 . . . . **149** B4
Walcot Ho **G**
SE22 . . . . **64** A4
Walcot Sq SE11 . . . . **149** C4
Walcott St SW1 . . . . **147** A4
Waldeck Gr SE27 . . . . **75** A1
Waldeck Rd
Brentford W4 . . . . . . **44** C4
Mortlake SW14 . . . . . **55** B4
Waldeck Terr
SW14 . . . . **55** B4

Waldegrave Ho **B**
SW15 . . . . **57** B2
Waldemar Ave
SW6 . . . . **164** B2
Waldemar Avenue
Mans SW6 . . . . **164** A3
Walden CI SW8 . . . . **171** C4
Walden Ho
B Clapham
SW11 . . . . **169** B2
SW1 . . . . **145** C3
Walden St E1 . . . . **32** A3
Waldo CI SW4 . . . . . . **61** B2
Waldo Rd NW10 . . . . . **22** A2
Waldron Ho **B**
SW2 . . . . **62** B2
Waldron Mews
SW3 . . . . **157** C4
Waldron Rd SW18 . . **71** B1
Walerand Rd SE13 . . **52** B1
Waleran Flats
SE1 . . . . **152** A4
Wales CI SE15 . . . . . . **50** A4
Wales Farm Rd
W3 . . . . **28** C4
Waley St **ID** E1 . . . . . **33** A4
Walford Ho **2G** E1 . . **32** A3
Walford Rd N16 . . . . **16** A4
Walham Ct **ID**
NW3 . . . . **12** B2
Walham Gr **B** SW6 . . **155** B2
**WALHAM
GREEN** **156** A1
Walham Green Arc
SW6 . . . . **155** B2
Walham Yd SW6 . . . **155** B2
Walker Ho NW1 . . . . **83** B1
Walker Mews **Z**
SW2 . . . . **62** C2
Walkerscroft Mead
SE21 . . . . **75** B3
Walker's CI SW11 . . **119** B4
Walker's Ct **ID** E14 . . **42** B4
Walker's PI SW15 . . **58** A3
Walkinshaw Ct **B**
N1 . . . . **15** B1
Walkynscroft **B**
SE15 . . . . **50** A1
Wallace Collection
The W1 . . . . **103** B2
Wallace Ct NW1 . . . **102** B3
Wallace Ho N7 . . . . . . **14** B2
Wallace Lo N4 . . . . . . **5** C3
Wallace Rd N1, N5 . . **15** B2
Wallbutton Rd
SE4 . . . . **51** A1
Wall Ct N4 . . . . **5** B3
Waller Rd SE14 . . . . . **50** C1
Waller Wy **B** SE10 . . **52** A3
Wallett Ct **ID** NW1 . . **13** B1
Wallflower St W12 . . **29** B2
Wallgrave Rd
SW5 . . . . **142** A3
Wallingford Ave
W10 . . . . **30** C3
Wallis Alley SE1 . . . **137** A4
Wallis CI SW11 . . . . . **59** C4
Wallis Ho **B** SE14 . . **51** A2
Wallis Rd E9 . . . . **18** C2
Wallis's Cottages **B**
SW2 . . . . **74** A4
Wallorton Gdns
SW14 . . . . **55** C3
Wallside EC2 . . . . . . **109** A3
Wall St N1 . . . . **15** C2
Wallwood St E14 . . . . **33** B4

Walmer Ho **B**
W10 . . . . **30** C3
Walmer PI W1 . . . . . **102** C4
Walmer Rd
North Kensington
W10 . . . . **30** B3
W11 . . . . . . **31** A2 **112** A4
Walmer Road Sch The
W11 . . . . **112** A4
Walm La NW2 . . . . **9** B2
Walney Wlk **G** N1 . . **15** B2
Walnut CI SE8 . . . . . . **51** B4
Walnut Ho **ID** E3 . . . **26** B4
Walnut Tree CI
SW13 . . . . **46** B2
Walnut Tree Ho
SW10 . . . . **156** B4
Walnut Tree Rd
Brentford TW8 . . . . . **44** A4
Greenwich SE10 . . . . **43** A1
Walnut Tree Walk
Prim Sch SE11 . . . **149** B4
Walnut Tree Wlk
SE11 . . . . **149** B4
Walpole Ave TW9 . . **44** B1
Walpole Ct
B Hammersmith
W14 . . . . **39** C3
B South Hampstead
NW6 . . . . **11** B1
Walpole Gdns W4 . . **37** B1
Walpole Mews
NW8 . . . . **79** B3
Walpole St SW3 . . . **145** A2
Walsham CI N16 . . . . . **7** C3
Walsham Ho
New Cross Gate
SE14 . . . . **50** C1
SE17 . . . . **151** B2
Walsham Rd SE14 . . **50** C1
Walsingham NW8 . . **79** C4
Walsingham Lo
SW13 . . . . **46** C2
Walsingham Mans
SW6 . . . . **156** B2
Walsingham PI SW4,
SW11 . . . . **60** C1
Walsingham Rd E5 . . **7** C1
Walter Besant Ho **2D**
E1 . . . . **25** C2
Walter Ct **B** W3 . . . . **28** B3
Walter Green Ho
SE15 . . . . **50** B2
Walter Ho SW10 . . . **157** B2
Walter Northcott Ho
Z NW6 . . . . **10** C3
Walters CI SE17 . . . **151** A3
Walters Ho
B Camberwell
SE5 . . . . **49** A1
Islington N1 . . . . . . **86** B4
ID Kennington
SE17 . . . . **48** A4
Walter Sickert Hall
B N1 . . . . **86** C1
Walter St E2 . . . . **25** C2
Walters Way SE23 . . **65** C1
Walter Taylor Ct
SE4 . . . . **66** B3
Walter Terr E1 . . . . . . **32** C3
Walterton Rd W9 . . . **23** C1
Waltham Green Ct
SW6 . . . . **156** A1
Waltham Ho
NW8 . . . . **78** C4
ID Stockwell SW9 . **173** A1

Walton CI SW8 . . . . . **162** B1
Walton Gdns W3 . . . . **28** A4
Walton Ho
E2 . . . . **24** B1 **99** A4
Upper Holloway N7 . . **5** B1
Wandsworth SW18 . . **58** B1
Walton St SW3 . . . . **130** C1
Walton St SW3 . . . . . **144** A4
Walton Way W3 . . . . . **28** A4
Walt Whitman CI **B**
SE24 . . . . **63** A3
WALWORTH **152** A4
Walworth Acad
SE17 . . . . **152** B1
Walworth PI SE17 . . **151** A1
Walworth Rd
SE17 . . . . **151** A2
Wanborough Dr
SW15 . . . . **69** A3
Wandle Ct **B** W12 . . **38** A4
Wandle Ho
NW8 . . . . **102** A4
Wandsworth SW18 . . **71** A4
Wandle Rd SW17 . . . **72** A2
Wandle Way SW18 . . **71** A3
Wandle Ho SW18 . . . **156** B3
WANDSWORTH . . **58** C1
Wandsworth Bridge
Rd SW6 . . . . **166** A3
Wandsworth Common
Sta SW12 . . . . **72** B4
Wandsworth Common
West Side SW18 . . . **59** B2
Wandsworth Gyratory
SW18 . . . . **59** A2
Wandsworth High St
SW18 . . . . **59** A2
Wandsworth Plain
SW18 . . . . **59** A2
Wandsworth Prep Sch
ID SW12 . . . . **61** A1
Wandsworth Rd
SW8 . . . . **162** A1
Wandsworth Road Sta
SW4 . . . . **171** A1
Wandsworth Town
Sta SW18 . . . . **59** A3
Wangford Ho **B**
SW9 . . . . **63** A3
Wanless Rd SE24 . . . **63** B4
Wanley Rd SE5 . . . . . **63** C3
Wansbeck Rd E3,
E9 . . . . **18** B1
Wansdown PI
SW6 . . . . **156** A2
Wandsworth Riverside
Quarter Pier
SW6 . . . . **58** C4
Wansey St SE17 . . . . **151** A3
WAPPING **32** A1
Wapping Dock St **ID**
E1 . . . . **32** A1
Wapping High St
E1 . . . . **32** A1
Wapping La E1 . . . . . **32** A1
Wapping Sta E1 . . . . **32** B1
Wapping Wall E1 . . . **32** B1
Warbeck Rd W12 . . . . **39** A4
Warburg Ho
E2 . . . . **24** C2 **99** B3
Warburton CI
N1 . . . . **16** A2
Warburton Ct
SE15 . . . . **64** C4
Warburton Ho **B**
E8 . . . . **25** A4

Warburton Rd **8**
■8 ....25 A4
Warburton St **6**
■8 ....25 A4
Vardalls Gr SE14 ...48 B3
Vardalls Ho **12**
SE8 ....51 B4
Vardell Ho **7**
SE10 ....52 B4
Vardell Mews **14**
.................61 A4
Varden Rd NW5 ......12 C2
Vardens Gr SE1 ...122 C1
Ward La E9 ....18 A3
Wardle St E9 ....17 C3
Wardley St SW18 ....71 A4
Wardlow St NW5 .....13 A4
Wardo Ave SW6 ....164 A4
Wardour Mews
W1 ....105 A1
Wardour St W1 ......105 B1
Ward Point SE11 ....149 B3
Ward Rd
 Camden Town N19 ....4 B1
 Mill Meads E15 ......27 C4
Wardrobe Pl EC4 ...108 B1
Wardrobe Terr
EC4 ....122 B4
Wareham Ct **2**
N1 ....16 A1
Wareham Ho
SW8 ....162 C2
Warfield Rd NW10 ...22 C2
Warfield Yd **6**
NW10 ....22 C2
Wargrave Ho **48**
E2 ....24 B2 98 C3
Warham Rd N4 ....5 C4
Warham St SE5 ....48 A3
Waring Ho **52**
E2 ....24 C2 99 C3
Warley Ho N1 ....15 C2
Warley St E2 ....25 C2
Warlock Rd W9 ......23 C1
Warlters Cl N7 .....14 A4
Warlters Rd N7 .....14 A4
Warltersville Mans
N19 ....5 A4
Warltersville Rd N4, N8,
N19 ....5 A4
War Meml Homes
W4 ....45 C3
Warmington Rd
SE24 ....63 B1
Warmsworth NW1 ...82 C4
Warndon St SE16 ...40 B2
Warneford St E9 ....25 A4
Warner Ho
■4 Homerton E9 ....17 C2
 Lewisham SE13 .....52 A1
 NW8 ....88 C4
Warner Pl
E2 ....24 C2 99 C4
Warner Rd SE5 .....48 B2
Warner St EC1 .....95 B1
Warner Yd EC1 .....95 B1
Warnford Ho
SW15 ....56 A1
Warnham WC1 ....94 C3
Warnham Ho **6**
SW2 ....74 B4
Warple Mews W3, ...38 A4
Warple Way W3,
W12 ....38 A4
Warren Ave SW14, ..55 A3
TW10
Warren Cl SE21 ....75 B4

Warren Ct N1 ....85 B2
Warrender Rd N19 ..13 B4
Warren Gdns E15 ...19 C3
Warren Ho **21** E3 ...27 A2
Warren Mews W1 ....92 C1
Warren St W1 ......92 C1
Warren Street Sta
NW1 ....93 A2
Warriner Gdns
SW11 ....169 B3
Warrington Cres
W9 ....88 C2
Warrington Gdns
W9 ....88 C2
Warspite Ho **3**
E14 ....42 A2
Warton Rd E15 .....27 B4
Warwick W14 ......141 A3
Warwick Ave W9 ....88 C1
Warwick Avenue Sta
W9 ....88 C1
Warwick Bldg
SW8 ....160 A3
Warwick Chambers
W8 ....127 B2
Warwick Cres W2 ..100 C4
Warwick Ct WC1 ...107 A3
Warwick Dr SW15 ...57 A4
Warwick Gdns
W14 ....141 A4
Warwick Ho
 10 Brixton SW9 ...173 B1
 6 Putney SW15 ...69 B4
 Stoke Newington N4 ..6 B3
Warwick House St
SW1 ....119 C2
Warwick La EC4 ...108 B1
Warwick Lo NW2 ...10 A3
Warwick Mans
SW5 ....141 B4
Warwick Pas EC4 ...108 B2
Warwick Pl N1 ....100 C4
Warwick Pl N
SW1 ....146 C3
Warwick Rd W14,
SW5 ....141 A4
Warwick Row
SW1 ....132 B2
Warwickshire Path
SE8 ....51 B3
Warwick Sq
 Holborn EC4 ......108 B2
 Pimlico SW1 ......146 C2
Warwick Sq Mews
SW1 ....146 C3
Warwick St W1 ....119 A4
Warwick Way
SW1 ....146 B4
Warwick Yd EC1 ....97 A1
Wasdale NW1 ....92 B3
Washbrook Ho
SW2 ....62 C1
Washington Bldg **1**
SE13 ....52 A2
Washington Cl **3**
E3 ....27 A2
Washington Ho
SW1 ....130 C3
Washington Rd
SW13 ....46 C3
Watchfield Ct **7**
W4 ....37 B1
Watcombe Cotts
TW9 ....44 C4
Watercress Pl **12**
N1 ....16 A1

Waterford Rd
SW6 ....156 A1
Waterford Way
NW10 ....8 C3
Water Gardens The
W2 ....102 B2
Watergate EC4 ....122 A4
Watergate St SE8 ..51 C4
Watergate Wlk
WC2 ....120 B2
Waterhead Ho **20**
E9 ....18 A3
Waterhouse Cl
 Hammersmith W6 ...39 C1
 Hampstead NW3 ....11 C3
Waterhouse Sq
EC1 ....107 B3
Wateridge Cl E14 ..41 C3
Water La
 Bermondsey E2 ....124 B3
 10 Camden Town
 NW1 ....13 A1
 SE14 ....50 B3
Waterloo Bridge SE1,
WC2 ....121 A3
Waterloo Cl E9 ....17 B3
Waterloo East Sta
SE1 ....121 C1
Waterloo Gdns
 22 Islington N1 ....15 A1
 South Hackney E2 ...25 B3
Waterloo Millennium
Pier SE1 ....134 C4
Waterloo Pl
 Kew TW9 ....44 C4
 9 Richmond TW9 ...54 A3
 SW1 ....119 B2
Waterloo Rd SE1 ..135 C4
Waterloo St SW1 ..135 C4
Waterloo Terr N1 ..15 A1
Waterlow Rd N19 ....4 B3
Waterman Bldg **2**
E14 ....41 C4
Watermans Arts Ctr
TW8 ....44 A4
Watermead Ho E9 ..18 B3
Watermeadow La
SW6 ....166 C1
Water Mews SE15 ..65 B3
Watermill Ct SE13 ..67 A4
Watermint Quay
N16 ....7 C4
Water's Edge SW6 ..47 B2
Waterside N1 ......86 C1
Waterside Cl
 30 Bermondsey
 SE16 ....139 C3
 Old Ford E3 ....26 B4
Waterside Ct SE13 ..67 C3
Waterside Pl NW1 ..81 C4
Waterside Point
SW11 ....158 B2
Waterson St
E2 ....24 B2 98 C4
Waters Pl SW15 ....47 B1
Water St WC2 .....121 B4
Water Tower Pl
N1 ....86 A3

Waterview Ho **13**
E14 ....33 A4
Waterway Ave **2**
SE13 ....67 A4
Waterworks Rd
SW2 ....62 B1
Watford Cl SW11 ..168 B4
Watford Rd E16 ....35 C4
Watkins Ho **1** E14 ..42 B4
Watkinson Rd N7 ...14 B2
Watling Ct EC4 ...109 A1
Watling Gdns
NW2 ....10 A2
Watling St
 4 Camberwell
 SE15 ....49 A4
 City of London EC4 ..109 A1
Watney Cotts
SW14 ....55 B3
Watney Mkt E1 ....32 A3
Watney Rd SW14 ...55 B3
Watney St E1 .....32 A3
Watson Cl N16 ....15 C3
Watson Ho **5**
SW2 ....74 A4
Watsons Mews
W1 ....102 B3
Watson's St SE8 ...51 C3
Watts Gr E3 ....34 A4
Watts Ho **6** W10 ...31 A4
Watts St
 SE15 ....49 B2
 Wapping E1 ....32 A1
Wat Tyler Rd SE10 ..52 C2
Wavel Ct
 7 Streatham
 SW16 ....74 A1
 7 Wapping E1 ....32 B1
Wavel Mews NW6 ..11 A1
Wavendon Ave
W4 ....37 C1
Waveney Ave SE15 ..65 A3
Waveney Cl **20** E1 ..125 C2
Waveney Ho SE15 ..65 A3
Waverley Ct
 5 Brondesbury
 NW6 ....10 A1
 W1 ....103 C4
Waverley Pl
 Finsbury Pk N4 ....6 A3
 St John's Wood
 NW8 ....79 B2
Waverley Rd N8 ....5 A4
Waverly Ct NW3 ...12 B2
Waverton Ho **2**
E3 ....26 B4
Waverton Rd
SW18 ....71 B4
Waverton St W1 ..118 A2
Wavertree Ct **9**
SW2 ....74 A3
Wavertree Rd
SW2 ....74 A3
Waxham NW5 ....12 B3
Waxlow Rd NW10 ...20 C3
Wayford St SW11 ..168 B1
Wayland Ave E8 ...16 C3
Wayland Ho **12**
SW9 ....173 B2
Waylett Ho SE11 ..149 B1
Waylett Pl SE27 ...75 A1
Wayman Ct E8 .....17 A2
Waynflete Sq
 10 North Kensington
 W10 ....30 C2

Waynflete Sq continued
 16 Shepherd's Bush
 W10 ....30 C2
Waynflete St
SW18 ....71 B2
Wayside
 Golders Green
 NW11 ....1 A3
 Mortlake SW14 ....55 B2
Weald Cl **18** SE16 ..40 A1
Weardale Ho N4 ....6 B4
Weardale Rd SE13 ..67 C3
Wearmouth Ho **1**
E3 ....33 B4
Wear Pl **16** E2 ....25 A2
Wearside Rd SE13 ..67 A3
Weatherbury **6**
W2 ....31 C3
Weatherbury Ho **9**
N19 ....4 C1
Weatherley Cl E3 ..33 B4
Weaver Ct **2**
E2 ....25 A1
Weaver Ho **12**
E1 ....24 C1 99 B1
Weaver's La SE1 ..124 B1
Weaver St
E1 ....24 C1 99 B1
Weavers Way
 6 Camden Town
 NW1 ....13 C1
 NW1 ....83 B1
Webb Cl NW10 .....22 B1
Webb Ct W3 ....37 A4
Webber Row SE1 ..136 A3
Webber St SE1 ....136 A3
Webb Est E5 ....7 C4
Webb Ho SW8 .....161 C1
Webb Pl NW10 .....21 B2
Webb Rd SE3 ......53 B4
Webb's Rd SW11 ...60 B2
Webheath **7** NW6 ..10 B1
Webster Ho **18**
N16 ....16 A3
Webster Rd SE16 ..139 C1
Weddell Ho **22** E1 ..25 C1
Wedderburn Rd
NW3 ....11 C3
Wedgewood Ho
SW1 ....146 C1
Wedgewood Mews
W1 ....105 C1
Wedgewood Wlk
NW3 ....11 A3
Wedgwood Ho
 17 Globe Town
 E2 ....25 C2
 SE11 ....135 B1
Wedlake St W10 ...23 A1
Wedmore Gdns
N19 ....4 C2
Wedmore Mews
N19 ....4 C1
Wedmore St N19 ...4 C1
Weech Rd NW6 ....10 C4
Weedington Rd
NW5 ....12 C3
Weedon Ho W12 ...29 C3
Weekley Sq SW11 ..59 C4
Weighhouse St
W1 ....103 C1
Weimar St SW15 ...58 A4
Weir Ho **4** SW12 ..73 B4

Weir Rd
 Streatham SW12 . . . . . . **73** B4
 Wimbledon SW18,
 SW19 . . . . **71** A1
Weiss Rd SW15 . . . . **57** C4
Welbeck Ct W14 . . . . **140** C4
Welbeck Mans **10**
 NW6 . . . . **10** C3
Welbeck St W1 . . . . . . **104** A2
Welbeck Way W1 . . . **104** A2
Welbury Ct E8 . . . . **16** A1
Welby Ho N19 . . . . **4** C4
Welby St SE5 . . . . **48** A2
Weldon Ct SE8 . . . . **51** C1
Weld Works Mews **4**
 SW2 . . . . **62** B1
Welford Ct
 12 Camden Town
 NW1 . . . . **13** A1
 7 Clapham SW8 . . **170** C1
Welland Ho SE15 . . . . **65** B3
Welland Mews **21**
 E1 . . . . **125** C2
Welland St SE10 . . . . . **52** B4
Wellclose Sq E1 . . . . **125** C3
Wellclose St **20**
 E1 . . . . **125** C3
Well Ct EC4 . . . . **109** A1
Wellday Ho **2** E9 . . **18** A2
Welldon Ct **1**
 SE21 . . . . **75** C2
Weller Ho **2**
 SE16 . . . . **139** B3
Weller St SE1 . . . . . . **136** C4
Welles Ct **11** E14 . . . **33** C2
Wellesley Ave W6 . . . **39** A3
Wellesley Ct W9 . . . . . **88** C4
Wellesley Ho NW1 . . . **93** B3
Wellesley Pl
 Camden Town
 NW5 . . . . **12** C3
 NW1 . . . . **93** B3
Wellesley Rd
 Gospel Oak NW5 . . . . **12** C3
 Gunnersbury W4 . . . . **37** A1
Wellesley St E1 . . . . **32** C4
Wellesley Terr N1 . . . **97** A4
Wellfit St **6** SE24 . . . **63** A4
Wellgarth Rd NW11 . . **2** A3
Wellington Arch
 SW1 . . . . **131** C4
Wellington Bldgs
 18 Bow E3 . . . . **26** C2
 SW1 . . . . **145** C1
Wellington Cl
 Kensington W11 . . . . **31** C3
 New Cross Gate
 SE14 . . . . **50** C2
Wellington Ct
 Knightsbridge
 SW1 . . . . **130** C3
 St John's Wood
 NW8 . . . . **79** C1
 Strand WC2 . . . . **120** A4
Wellington Gr
 SE10 . . . . **52** C3
Wellington Ho **18**
 NW3 . . . . **12** B2
Wellington Hospl The
 NW8 . . . . **79** C1
Wellington Mans
 N16 . . . . **16** B4

Wellington Mews
 East Dulwich
 SE22 . . . . **64** C3
 3 Islington N7 . . . . . **14** B2
 Streatham SW16 . . . . **73** C1
Wellington Pl NW8 . . **89** C4
Wellington Prim Sch
 20 E3 . . . . **26** C2
Wellington Rd
 Kensal Green
 NW10 . . . . **22** C2
 St John's Wood
 NW8 . . . . **79** C1
 Wimbledon SW19 . . . **70** C2
Wellington Row
 E2 . . . . **24** C2 **99** B4
Wellington Sq
 Islington N1 . . . . **84** B4
 SW3 . . . . **144** C2
Wellington St
 WC2 . . . . **120** C4
Wellington Terr **1**
 E1 . . . . **32** A1
Wellington Way
 E3 . . . . **26** C2
Well La SW14 . . . . **55** B2
Well Rd NW3 . . . . **2** C1
Wells Ct
 1 Hampstead
 NW3 . . . . **11** B4
 3 Paddington
 NW6 . . . . **23** C3
 Stoke Newington
 N1 . . . . **16** A3
Wells Ho
 Finsbury EC1 . . . . . . **96** A4
 12 Kensal Town
 W10 . . . . **23** A1
 New Cross Gate
 SE4 . . . . **51** A1
 9 Rotherhithe
 SE16 . . . . **40** B3
Wells Ho The **2**
 NW3 . . . . **11** C4
Wells House Rd
 NW10 . . . . **29** A4
Wellside Gdns
 SW14 . . . . **55** B2
Wells Mews W1 . . . . **105** A2
Wells Pl SW18 . . . . . . **71** B4
Wells Rd W12 . . . . **39** B4
Wells Rise NW8 . . . . . **80** C3
Wells Sq WC1 . . . . . . **95** A3
Wells St W1 . . . . **105** A2
Well St E9 . . . . **17** B1
Wells Terr N4 . . . . **5** C2
Wells Way
 Brompton SW7 . . . . **129** B2
 Camberwell SE5 . . . . **49** A4
Well Wlk NW3 . . . . **2** C1
Wellwood Ct
 SW15 . . . . **57** B3
Welmar Mews **13**
 SW4 . . . . **61** C3
Welmar Works
 SW4 . . . . **61** C3
Welsh Ho **11** E1 . . . . **32** A1
Welshpool Ho **22**
 E8 . . . . **24** C4
Welshpool St **1**
 2 E8 . . . . **25** A4
 3 Hackney E8 . . . . . **24** C4
Welstead Ho
 E1 . . . . **32** A3
Welstead Way W4 . . . **38** B2

Weltje Rd W6 . . . . **38** C1
Welton Ct SE5 . . . . . . **49** A2
Welton Ho E1 . . . . . . **32** C4
Welwyn St E2 . . . . **25** B2
Wembury Mews N6 . . **4** B4
Wembury Rd N6 . . . . . **4** A4
Wemyss Rd SE3 . . . . . **53** B1
Wendell Park Prim
 Sch W12 . . . . **38** B4
Wendell Rd W12 . . . . **38** B4
Wendling NW5 . . . . . . **12** B3
Wendon St E3 . . . . **26** B4
Wendover SE17 . . . . **152** A1
Wendover Ct
 Acton W3 . . . . **20** A1
 Becontree W3 . . . . . . **20** B1
 4 Child's Hill NW2 . **1** C1
 W1 . . . . **103** B3
Wendover Ho
 W1 . . . . **103** B3
Wendover Rd
 NW10 . . . . **21** B3
Wengham Ho W12 . . . **29** C2
Wenham Ho SW8 . . **160** C1
Wenlake Ho EC1 . . . . **96** C2
Wenlock Ct N1 . . . . . . **87** C1
Wenlock Rd N1 . . . . . **87** A1
Wenlock St N1 . . . . . . **87** B1
Wennington Rd
 E3 . . . . **25** C3
Wensdale Ho E5 . . . . . **7** C2
Wensleydale Ho **8**
 . . . . **6** B4
Wentworth Cres
 SE15 . . . . **49** C3
Wentworth Ct
 W6 . . . . **154** A3
 Wandsworth SW18 . . **59** A1
Wentworth Dwellings
 E1 . . . . **110** C2
Wentworth Ho **4**
 SE3 . . . . **53** B3
Wentworth Mews
 E3 . . . . **26** B2
Wentworth St E1 . . **111** A3
Werrington St
 NW1 . . . . **83** A1
Werter Rd SW15 . . . . **58** A3
Wesleyan Pl NW5 . . . **13** A4
Wesley Ave NW10 . . . **20** C2
Wesley Cl
 Finsbury Pk N7 . . . . . **5** B2
 SE17 . . . . **150** B3
Wesley Ct W1 . . . . . . **103** C3
Wesley Ho SE24 . . . . . **63** C1
Wesley Rd NW10 . . . . **20** B4
Wesley Sq W11 . . . . . . **31** A3
Wesley St W1 . . . . . . **103** C3
Wessex Ct SW15 . . . . **57** C2
Wessex Gardens Prim
 Sch NW11 . . . . **1** A3
Wessex Gdns NW11 . . **1** A3
Wessex Ho
 SE1 . . . . **153** A1
 4 Tufnell Pk N19 . . . **4** C1
Wessex St E2 . . . . **25** B2
Wessex Way NW11 . . . **1** A3
West 12 Sh Ctr
 W12 . . . . **39** C4
Westacott Ct N19 . . . . **4** C3
West Acton Prim Sch
 W3 . . . . **28** A3
West Arbour St
 E1 . . . . **32** C3
West Bank N16 . . . . . . **7** A4
Westbere Rd NW2 . . . **10** A3

West Block **18** E1 . . **32** B2
Westbourne Ave
 W3 . . . . **28** C3
Westbourne Cres
 W2 . . . . **115** B4
Westbourne Ct
 W2 . . . . **100** C2
Westbourne Gdns
 W2 . . . . **100** A2
Westbourne Gr
 Notting Hill W2,
 W11 . . . . **31** C3
 W11 . . . . **31** B2 **113** A4
Westbourne Gr Mews
 7 W11 . . . . **31** C3
Westbourne Gr Terr
 W2 . . . . **100** A1
Westbourne Ho
 SW1 . . . . **146** A2
Westbourne Park Rd
 Notting Hill W2 . . . . . **31** C3
 Notting Hill W11 . . . . **31** B3
Westbourne Park Sta
 W11 . . . . **31** B4
Westbourne Park
 Villas W2 . . . . **100** A2
Westbourne St
 W2 . . . . **115** C4
Westbourne Terr
 W2 . . . . **101** A2
Westbourne Terrace
 Mews W2 . . . . **100** C2
Westbourne Terrace
 Rd W2 . . . . **100** C3
Westbridge Cl
 W12 . . . . **29** C1
Westbridge Rd
 SW11 . . . . **168** A4
WEST
BROMPTON . . . **156** A4
 West Brompton Sta
 SW5 . . . . **141** C1
Westbrook Ho
 6 Bethnal Green
 E2 . . . . **25** B2
 3 Clapham Pk
 SW4 . . . . **61** B2
Westbury Ct SW4 . . . **61** A1
Westbury Ho **4**
 NW10 . . . . **8** A1
Westbush Ct **3**
 W12 . . . . **39** A4
West Carriage Dr
 W2 . . . . **116** A2
West Central St
 WC1 . . . . **106** A2
Westchester Ho
 W2 . . . . **102** C1
Westcliff Ho **13**
 N1 . . . . **15** C2
Westcombe Ct **1**
 SE3 . . . . **53** B3
Westcombe Hill SE3,
 SE10 . . . . **53** C4
Westcombe Park Rd
 SE3 . . . . **53** A3
Westcombe Park Sta
 SE3 . . . . **43** C1
Westcott Ho **1**
 E14 . . . . **33** C2
Westcott Rd SE17 . . . . **48** A4
West Cotts NW6 . . . . . **10** C3

Westcroft Cl NW2 . . . **10** A4
Westcroft Ct **3**
 W6 . . . . **38** C2
Westcroft Sq W6 . . . . **38** C2
Westcroft Way
 NW2 . . . . **10** A4
West Cromwell Rd
 W14 . . . . **141** A2
West Cross Route W10,
 W11 . . . . **30** C2
Westdean Cl
 SW18 . . . . **59** A1
Westdean Cl **59** A1
Westdown Rd E15 . . . **19** B4
WEST DULWICH
 Sta **75** B2
West Dulwich Sta
 SE21 . . . . **75** C3
West Eaton Pl
 SW1 . . . . **145** B4
West Eaton Pl Mews
 SW1 . . . . **145** B4
West Ella Rd NW10 . . **8** A1
West End Ct NW6 . . . **11** A1
West End La NW6 . . . **11** A2
Westerdale Ct N5 . . . **15** A4
Westerdale Rd **2**
 SE10 . . . . **43** C1
Westerham NW1 . . . . **82** C3
Westerham Ho
 SE1 . . . . **137** C2
Western Ave W3 . . . . . **28** C3
Western Avenue Bsns
 Pk W3 . . . . **20** A4
Western Beach Apts
 E16 . . . . **35** C1
Western Ct
 3 Dagenham W3 . . **28** C3
 1 Kilburn W9 . . . . . **23** B3
Western Eye Hospl
 The NW1 . . . . **102** C4
Western Gateway
 E16 . . . . **35** C2
Western Ho **5**
 W9 . . . . **23** B3
Western La SW12 . . . **72** C4
Western Mews
 W9 . . . . **23** B1
Western Pl
 36 Bermondsey
 SE16 . . . . **40** B4
 SE16 . . . . **40** B4
Western Rd
 Becontree NW10 . . . . **20** A3
 Brixton SW9 . . . . **62** C4
Western Terr **3**
 W6 . . . . **38** C1
Western Wharf **2**
 SE15 . . . . **49** C4
Westferry Cir E14 . . . **33** C1
Westferry Rd E14 . . . **41** C2
Westferry Sta E14 . . . **33** C2
Westfield NW3 . . . . . . **10** C4
Westfield Ave E15 . . . **19** C4
Westfield Cl
 SW10 . . . . **156** C1
Westfield Ct **1**
 W10 . . . . **22** C2
Westfield Ho **6**
 SE16 . . . . **40** C2
Westfield London Sh
 Ctr W12 . . . . **30** C1
Westfields SW13 . . . . **56** B4
Westfields Ave
 SW13 . . . . **56** A4
Westfields Rd W3 . . . . **28** A4
Westfield Stratford Sh
 Ctr EH15 . . . . **19** B2

Westfield Way E1....26 A1
West Garden Pl
W2 .... 102 B1
Westgate Bsns Ctr
2 Kensal Town
W10 ....23 A1
North Kensington
W10 ....22 C1
Westgate Ct 18
SW9 ....62 C4
Westgate St E8....25 A4
Westgate Terr
SW10 ....156 B4
West Gdns E1......32 A2
West Gr SE10......52 C2
Westgrove La
SE10 ....52 B2
West Halkin St
SW1 ....131 B2
West Hall Rd TW9 ..45 A2
WEST
HAMPSTEAD 10 C4
West Hampstead
Mews NW6........11 A2
West Hampstead Sta
NW6 ....10 C2
West Hampstead
Thameslink Sta
NW6 ....10 C2
West Harding St
EC4 ....107 C2
Westhay Gdns
SW14 ....55 A2
West Heath Ave
NW11 ....1 C3
West Heath Cl NW3 ..1 C1
West Heath Ct
NW11 ....1 C3
West Heath Dr
NW11 ....1 C3
West Heath Gdns
NW3 ....1 C1
West Heath Rd
NW3 ....2 A1
WEST HILL 58 B1
West Hill SW15 ....58 A1
Westhill Ct
W11 .....31 B2 113 A4
West Hill Ct N6 ....3 C2
Westhill Pk
Dartmouth Pk N6 ..3 C2
Highgate N6 ....3 B2
West Hill Prim Sch 17
SW18 ....58 B2
West Hill Rd SW18 ..58 B1
West Ho 9 SW12 ..73 B4
Westhope Ho 20
E2 ......24 C2 99 C3
Westhorpe Rd
SW15 ....57 B4
West House Cl
SW19 ....70 A3
West India Ave
E14 ....33 C1
West India Dock Rd
E14 ....33 C2
West India Ho 1
E14 ....33 C2
West India Quay Sta
E14 ....33 C2
WEST
KENSINGTON 140 B3
West Kensington Ct
W14 ....140 C2
West Kensington
Mans W14........140 C1

West Kensington Sta
W14 ....140 C2
WEST KILBURN 23 A2
West La SE16.......40 A4
Westlake 12 SE16..40 B2
Westland Pl N1......97 B4
Westlands Terr 3
SW12 ....61 B1
Westleigh Ave
SW15 ....57 B2
West London Free
Sch 6 W6 ....38 C2
Westly Ct NW2 .....9 C2
Westmacott Ho
NW8 ....89 C1
West Mall
W11 .....31 C1 113 C2
Westmark Point 13
SW15 ....69 A3
West Mews SW1 ..146 C3
Westmill Ct N4 .....6 B2
WESTMINSTER 133 A1
Westminster Abbey
SW1 ....134 A1
Westminster Abbey
Choir Sch SW1 ..133 C2
Westminster Acad
W2 ....31 C4
Westminster Acad
(Sch of English)
W1 ....105 A2
Westminster Boating
Base SW1 ....161 B4
Westminster Bridge
SE1, SW1 ....134 B3
Westminster Bridge
Rd SE1 ....134 C3
Westminster Cath
SW1 ....132 C1
Westminster Cath
Choir Sch SW1 ..147 A4
Westminster Cath RC
Prim Sch SW1 ...147 C2
Westminster City Hall
SW1 ....133 A2
Westminster City Sch
SW1 ....133 A2
Westminster Coll
W1 ....119 B4
Westminster
Dragoons Mus
SE6 ....58 A4
Westminster Gdns
SW1 ....148 A3
Westminster
Kingsway Coll
(King's Cross
Centre) WC1 .....94 C3
Westminster
Kingsway Coll
(Regent's Park Ctr)
NW1 ....92 C2
Westminster
Kingsway Coll
(Victoria Centre)
SW1 ....147 B4
Westminster
Millennium Pier
SW1 ....134 B3

Westminster Pier
SW1 ....134 B3
Westminster Sch
SW1 ....134 A2
Westminster Sta
SW1 ....134 B3
Westminster Under
Sch SW1 ....147 B3
Westmore Ct
SW15 ....58 A2
Westmoreland Ho
NW10 ....21 C2
Westmoreland Pl
SW1 ....146 B1
Westmoreland Rd
Barnes SW13 .....46 C4
Camberwell SE17..48 C4
Westmoreland St
W1 ....103 C3
Westmoreland Terr
SW1 ....146 B1
WEST NORWOOD ..75 B2
West Norwood Sta
SE27 ....75 A1
Westonbirt Ct 6
SE15 ....49 B4
Weston Ct N4 .....6 B1
West One Ho W1 ..104 C3
West One Sh Ctr
W1 ....104 A1
Weston Ho
6 Brondesbury
NW6 ....10 A1
8 South Hackney
E9 ....25 B4
Weston Rise N1,
WC1 ....95 A4
Weston St SE1 ....137 C4
Weston Wlk 3 E8,
E9 ....17 A1
Westover Hill NW3 ..1 C2
Westover Rd
SW18 ....59 B1
West Park Ave
TW9 ....45 A2
West Park Rd
TW9 ....44 C2
West Parkside
Greenwich SE10 ..43 B3
Greenwich SE10 ..43 C2
West Plaza E14 ....34 A1
Westpoint SW15...57 C1
West Point 2
SE1 ....153 B2
Westpoint Trad Est
W3 ....28 A4
Westport St E1 ....32 C3
West Poultry Ave
EC1 ....108 A3
West Quarters
W12 ....29 C3
West Rd
Chelsea SW3 ....159 A4
Clapham Pk SW4 ..61 C2
West Row W10 ....23 A1
West Sheen Vale
TW9 ....54 B3
Westside 11 W6 ..38 C2
Westside E1 1
W9 ....23 B3
West Silvertown Sta
E16 ....35 C1
West Smithfield
EC1 ....108 B3

West Sq SE11.....136 A1
West St
30 Bethnal Green
E2 ....25 A3
Soho WC2 ....105 C1
West Temple Sheen
SW14 ....55 A4
West Tenter St
E1 ....111 A1
Westvale Mews
W3 ....38 A4
Westview Cl
North Kensington
W10 ....30 B3
Willesden NW10 ..22 B1
Westville Rd W12 ..38 C4
West Warwick Pl
SW1 ....146 C3
Westway W10,
W12 ....29 C2
Westway (Elevated
Rd) W10 ....31 B4
Westway Lo 35
W2 ....31 C4
Westwell 4 NW5 ..12 C2
Westwick Gdns
W14 ....39 C4
Westwood Bsns Ctr
NW10 ....21 A1
Westwood Gdns
SW13 ....56 B4
Westwood Ho
6 Shepherd's Bush
W12 ....30 B1
5 Stoke Newington
N4 ....6 C4
Westwood Park Trad
Est W3 ....20 A1
Westwood Rd
SW13 ....56 B4
Wetherby Gdns
SW5 ....142 C3
Wetherby Mans
SW5 ....142 A2
Wetherby Mews
SW5 ....142 B2
Wetherby Pl SW7 ..143 A3
Wetherby
(Reception & Little
Wetherby)
W11 .....31 C2 113 B4
Wetherby Sch (Years
1, 2 & 3) W2 ....113 C3
Wetherell Rd E9 ....25 C4
Wevco Wharf
SE15 ....50 A4
Wexford Ho 11 E1 ..32 B4
Wexford Rd SW12 ..72 B4
Weybourne St
SW18 ....71 B2
Weybridge Ct 19
SE16 ....40 A1
Weybridge Ho N4 ..6 B4
Weybridge Point 1
SW11 ....169 A2
Weydown Cl SW19 ..70 A3
Weyhill Ho 26 SE5 ..48 B1
Weyhill Rd 11 E1 ..111 C2
Wey Ho NW8 ......89 C1
Weymouth Ct
5 Haggerston E2 ..24 B3
13 Streatham SW2 ..74 B4
Weymouth Ho
Fitzrovia W1 .....104 B4
South Lambeth
SW8 ....162 C1

Weymouth Mews
W1 ....104 A4
Weymouth St W1 ..104 A4
Weymouth Terr
E2 ....24 B3
Whadcoat St N4 ....5 C2
Whaddon Ho
10 Camberwell
SE5 ....64 A4
SW1 ....131 A3
Wharfdale Rd N1...84 B2
Wharfedale Ct 5
E5 ....17 C4
Wharfedale St
SW10 ....142 A1
Wharf La E19 E14...33 B3
Wharf PI E2 ....25 A4
Wharf Rd N1 ......86 C1
Wharfside Rd E16 ..35 C4
Wharf St
E16 ....35 A4
Isle of Dogs SE8 ..41 C1
Wharf View Ct 15
E14 ....34 B3
Wharncliffe Ho 3
SW15 ....57 B2
Wharton Cl NW10 ..8 A2
Wharton St WC1 ..95 A4
Wharton St WC1...95 A3
Whateley Rd SE22 ..64 B2
Whatman Ho 10
E14 ....33 B3
Wheatland Ho 7
SE22 ....64 A4
Wheatlands Rd
SW17 ....72 C1
Wheatley Ho
Gospel Oak NW5 ..13 A4
3 Putney SW15 ..68 C4
Wheatley St W1 ..103 C3
Wheat Sheaf Cl
E14 ....42 A2
Wheatsheaf La
Fulham SW6 ......47 B3
SW8 ....162 B2
Wheatsheaf Terr
SW6 ....155 A1
Wheatstone Ho 7
W10 ....31 A4
Wheatstone Rd
W10 ....31 A4
Wheeler Ct 4
SW11 ....59 C4
Wheeler Gdns N1 ..84 B4
Wheeler La E1 ....110 C4
Wheelhouse The 4
E14 ....42 A1
Wheelwright St
N7 ....14 B1
Wheldon Ct SE1 ..138 C4
Wheler Ho
E1 ....24 B1 98 C1
Wheler St E1 ......98 C1
Whellock Rd W4 ..38 A3
Whetstone Park
WC2 ....106 C2
Whewell Rd N19...5 A2
Whichcote St SE1 ..121 B1
Whidborne Bldgs
WC1 ....94 A3
Whidborne Cl SE8..51 C1
Whidborne St WC1 ..94 A3

Whippingham Ho 22
  E3 . . . . 26 B2
Whiskin St EC1 . . . . . 96 A3
Whistler Mews 23
  SE15 . . . . 49 B3
Whistlers Ave
  SW11 . . . . 157 C1
Whistler St N5 . . . . . 15 A3
Whistler Twr
  SW10 . . . . 156 C1
Whistler Wlk
  SW10 . . . . 157 A2
Whiston Ho 16 N1 . . 15 A1
Whiston Rd E2 . . . . . 24 C4
Whitbread Ctr EC1 . . 97 B1
Whitbread Rd SE4 . . 66 B3
Whitburn Rd SE13 . . 67 B3
Whitby Ave NW10 . . 20 A2
Whitby Ct 16 N7 . . . . 14 A4
Whitby Ho NW8 . . . . 78 C3
Whitby St
  E1 . . . . 24 B1 98 C2
Whitcher Cl SE14 . . . 51 A4
Whitcher Pl NW1 . . . 13 B2
Whitchurch Ho 18
  W10 . . . . 30 C3
Whitchurch Rd
  W11 . . . . 30 C2
Whitcomb Ct 17
  W1 . . . . 119 C3
Whitcomb St
  WC2 . . . . 119 C3
Whitcome Mews
  TW9 . . . . 45 A2
Whiteacre Mews
  SE11 . . . . 149 C1
Whiteadder Way
  E14 . . . . 42 A2
Whitear Wlk E15 . . . 19 C2
Whitebeam Cl
  SW9 . . . . 163 A1
Whitebeam Ho 3
  NW3 . . . . 12 B2
White Bear Pl 1
  NW3 . . . . 11 C4
White Bear Yd EC1 . . 95 B1
WHITECHAPEL . . . 110 C1
Whitechapel Gall
  E1 . . . . 111 A2
Whitechapel High St
  E1 . . . . 111 A2
Whitechapel Mkt
  E1 . . . . 111 C3
Whitechapel Rd
  E1 . . . . 32 A4
Whitechapel Sta
  E1 . . . . 32 A4
Whitechurch La 3
  E1 . . . . 111 B2
Whitchurch Pas 1
  E1 . . . . 111 B2
White City W12 . . . . 30 B3
White City Cl W12 . . 30 B3
White City Est
  W12 . . . . 30 A2
White City Rd
  W12 . . . . 30 B2
White City Sta
  W12 . . . . 30 B2
Whitecliff Ho
  SW18 . . . . 59 A1
White Conduit St
  N1 . . . . 85 C2
Whitecross Pl
  EC2 . . . . 109 C4

White Cube (Gall)
  SE1 . . . . 138 A3
  SW1 . . . . 119 A2
Whitefield Cl
  SW15 . . . . 58 A1
Whitefriars St
  EC4 . . . . 107 C1
Whitehall SW1 . . . . 134 A4
Whitehall Ct SW1 . . 120 B1
Whitehall Gdns
  Chiswick W4 . . . . 45 A4
  SW1 . . . . 120 A1
Whitehall Mans 3
  N19 . . . . 4 B3
Whitehall Park Rd
  W4 . . . . 45 A4
Whitehall Pk N19 . . . 4 B3
Whitehall Pl WC2,
  SW1 . . . . 120 A1
White Hart Ct
  EC2 . . . . 110 A3
White Hart La
  Mortlake SW13 . . 56 A4
  Willesden NW10 . . 8 B2
White Hart St
  Holborn EC4 . . . . 108 B2
  Kennington SE11 149 C2
White Hart Yd
  SE1 . . . . 123 B1
Whitehaven St
  NW8 . . . . 90 A1
Whitehead Cl
  SW18 . . . . 71 B4
Whitehead Ho 8
  SW15 . . . . 57 C2
Whitehead's Gr
  SW3 . . . . 144 B3
White Ho
  1 Battersea
    SW11 . . . . 167 C2
  3 Streatham SW4 . 73 C4
Whitehorn Ho 6
  E1 . . . . 32 B1
White Horse La
  E1 . . . . 32 C4
Whitehorse Mews
  SE1 . . . . 136 A2
Whitehorse Rd E1 . . 33 A4
White Horse Rd
  E1 . . . . 33 A3
White Horse St
  W1 . . . . 118 B1
White Horse Yd
  EC2 . . . . 109 B2
White Ho The
  NW1 . . . . 92 B2
White House Prep Sch
  SW12 . . . . 73 A3
White Kennett St
  E1 . . . . 110 B2
Whitelands Cres
  SW18 . . . . 70 A4
Whitelands Ho
  SW3 . . . . 145 A2
Whiteley Ho 5
  SW4 . . . . 73 C4
Whiteleys Ctr 10
  W2 . . . . 100 B1
White Lion Ct
  EC3 . . . . 110 A1
White Lion Hill
  EC4 . . . . 122 B4
White Lion St N1 . . . 85 C1
White Lo NW11 . . . . 1 B3

Whitelock Ho 21
  E9 . . . . 17 C2
White Lyon Ct
  EC2 . . . . 108 C4
Whiteness Ho 18
  SW9 . . . . 173 B4
White Post La E9 . . . 18 C2
White Post St SE14,
  SE15 . . . . 50 B3
White Rd EC2 . . . . . 110 A3
White's Grounds
  SE1 . . . . 138 B4
White's Grounds Est
  SE1 . . . . 138 B4
White's Row E1 . . . 110 C3
White's Sq SW4 . . . . 61 C3
Whitestone La NW3 . 2 B1
Whitestone Wlk
  NW3 . . . . 2 B1
Whitethorn St E3 . . . 33 C4
White Twr Way E1 . . 33 A4
Whitfield Ct SW4 . . 172 A3
Whitfield Gdns
  W1 . . . . 105 A4
Whitfield Ho NW8 . . 90 A1
Whitfield Pl W1 . . . . 93 A1
Whitfield St W1 . . . 105 A4
Whitgift Ho
  Battersea SW11 . . 168 A4
  Lambeth SE11 . . 148 C4
Whitgift St SE11 . . 148 C4
Whitington Ave
  EC3 . . . . 110 A1
Whiting Way SE8 . . . 41 A2
Whitley Ho SW1 . . . 161 A4
Whitlock Dr SW19 . . 70 A3
Whitman Ho 20 E2 . . 25 B2
Whitman Rd E3 . . . . 26 A1
Whitmore Gdns
  NW10 . . . . 22 B3
Whitmore Ho 20
  E1 . . . . 24 A4
Whitmore Prim Sch
  N1 . . . . 87 C3
Whitmore Rd N1 . . . 24 A4
Whitnell Ct 7
  SW15 . . . . 57 C2
Whitnell Way
  SW15 . . . . 57 C2
Whitney Ho 6
  SE22 . . . . 64 A4
Whitstable Ho 11
  W10 . . . . 30 C3
Whitsters Ho SE1 . . 138 C4
Whittaker Ct SW4 . . 172 B3
Whittaker St SW1 . . 145 B3
Whittaker Way 1
  SE1 . . . . 153 C4
Whittingham Ct
  W4 . . . . 46 A3
Whittingstall Mans
  SW6 . . . . 165 A3
Whittingstall Rd
  SW6 . . . . 165 A3
Whittington Hospl
  The N19 . . . . 4 B2
Whittlebury Ho N4 . . 6 B4
Whittlesey St SE1 . . 121 C1
Whitton NW3 . . . . . . 12 B1
Whitton W5 . . . . 13 A4
Whitworth Ho
  SE1 . . . . 137 A1
Whitworth St
  SE10 . . . . 43 A1
Whorlton Rd SE15 . . 65 A4
Whytlaw Ho 10 E3 . . 33 B4

Wicker St 24 E1 . . . . 32 A3
Wickfield Ho 32
  SE16 . . . . 139 C3
Wickford Ho 5
  E1 . . . . 25 B1
Wickford St E1 . . . . 25 B1
Wickham Ct E1 . . . . 25 A1
Wickham Gdns
  SE4 . . . . 66 B4
Wickham Ho
  SW15 . . . . 57 C1
Wickham Mews
  SE4 . . . . 51 B1
Wickham Rd SE4 . . . 66 B3
Wickham St SE11 . . 148 C2
Wick La
  Hackney E3 . . . . . 18 B1
  Stratford Marsh E3 . 26 C4
Wicklow Ho N16 . . . 7 B3
Wicklow St WC1 . . . 94 C4
Wick Rd
  Hackney E9 . . . . . 17 C2
  Hackney E9 . . . . . 18 A2
Wickstead Ho
  TW8 . . . . 36 B1
Wicksteed Ho
  SE1 . . . . 137 A1
Wick Village 7
  E9 . . . . 18 B3
Wickway Ct 7
  SE15 . . . . 49 B4
Wickwood St SE5 . . 48 A1
Widdenham Rd
  N7 . . . . 14 B4
Widecombe Ho 33
  SE5 . . . . 48 B1
Widegate St E1 . . . 110 B3
Widford 8 NW1 . . . . 13 A2
Widford Ho N1 . . . . 86 A1
Widley Rd W9 . . . . . 23 C1
Widnes Ho 6 N7 . . . 14 C3
Wigmore Hall W1 . . 104 A2
Wigmore Pl W1 . . . 104 A2
Wigmore St W1 . . . 103 C2
Wigram Ct SW11 . . 168 A4
Wigram Ho 7 E14 . . 34 A2
Wigton Pl SE11 . . . 149 C1
Wilberforce Ho 8
  SW11 . . . . 59 C4
Wilberforce Mews 9
  SW4 . . . . 61 C3
Wilberforce Prim Sch
  W10 . . . . 23 A2
Wilberforce Rd
  Finsbury Pk N4 . . . 6 A2
  Highbury N4, N5 . . 6 B3
Wilbraham Ho
  SW8 . . . . 162 A1
Wilbraham Pl
  SW1 . . . . 145 B4
Wilby Mews
  W11 . . . . . 31 B1 113 A2
Wilcox Cl SW8 . . . . 162 B2
Wilcox Ho 5 E3 . . . . 33 B4
Wilcox Pl SW1 . . . . 133 A1
Wilcox Rd SW8 . . . 162 A2
Wildcroft Manor
  SW15 . . . . 69 B4
Wildcroft Rd
  SW15 . . . . 69 B4
Wild Ct WC2 . . . . . 106 C2
Wilde Cl E8 . . . . 24 C4
Wilde Pl SW18 . . . . 71 C4
Wilderness Mews
  SW4 . . . . 61 A3
Wilderton Rd N16 . . 7 A4

Wild Goose Dr
  SE14 . . . . 50 B2
Wilding Ho 17 E9 . . . 17 C2
Wild's Rents SE1 . . 138 A2
Wild St WC2 . . . . . 106 C1
Wildwood Gr NW3 . . 2 C2
Wildwood Rd NW11 . 2 B4
Wildwood Rise
  NW11 . . . . 2 B4
Wildwood Terr NW3,
  NW11 . . . . 2 C2
Wilfred Fienburgh Ho
  N7 . . . . 13 C4
Wilfred St SW1 . . . 132 C2
Wilfrid Gdns W3 . . . 28 B4
Wilkes Rd 3 TW8 . . 44 A4
Wilkes St E1 . . . . . 111 A4
Wilkie Ho SW1 . . . 147 C2
Wilkin St Mews
  NW5 . . . . 13 A2
Wilkins Ho SW1 . . . 160 C4
Wilkinson Ho N1 . . . 87 C1
Wilkinson St SW8 . 162 C1
Wilkinson Way
  W4 . . . . 37 C4
Wilkin St NW5 . . . . 13 A2
Wilks Pl N1 . . . . 24 A3
Willan Wall E16 . . . 35 B2
Willard St SW8 . . . . 61 A4
Willbury Ho 4 N7 . . 13 C3
Willcott Rd W3 . . . . 28 A1
Willenfield Rd
  NW10 . . . . 20 B3
WILLESDEN 8 C1
Willesden Community
  Hospl The NW10 . . 8 C1
WILLESDEN
  GREEN 22 A4
Willesden Green Sta
  NW2 . . . . 9 C3
Willesden Junction
  Sta NW10 . . . . . . 21 B2
Willesden La NW2,
  NW6 . . . . 9 C2
Willesden Sports Ctr
  W10 . . . . 22 B2
Willes Rd NW5 . . . . 13 A2
Willett Ho SW9 . . . 62 C4
William Banfield Ho
  10 SW6 . . . . 164 C2
William Blake Ho 2
  SE15 . . . . 49 C1
William Bonney Est 10
  SW4 . . . . 61 C3
William Booth Meml
  Training Coll
  SE5 . . . . 48 C1
William Brown Ct
  SE27 . . . . 75 A2
William Caslon Ho 3
  E2 . . . . 25 A3
William Channing Ho
  6 E2 . . . . 25 A2
William Cl SE13 . . . 67 B4
William Congreve
  Mews N1 . . . . 86 C3
William Davis Prim
  Sch 18 E2 . . . . . . 99 B2
William Davis Prim
  Sch 19 E2 . . . . . . 24 C2 99 B2
William Dromey Ct
  NW6 . . . . 10 B1
William Dunbar Ho
  NW6 . . . . 23 B3
William Ellis Sch
  NW5 . . . . 3 C1

William Ellis Way 18
SE16 . . . . 139 C1
William Evans Ho 9
SE8 . . . . 40 C2
William Gdns
SW15 . . . . 57 A2
William Guy Gdns 1
E3 . . . . 27 A2
William Harvey Ho 1
SW19 . . . . 70 A3
William Hogarth Sch
The 15 W4 . . . . 38 A1
William Hunt Mans
SW13 . . . . 47 B4
William IV St
WC2 . . . . 120 A3
William Margrie Cl 1
SE15 . . . . 49 C1
William Mews
SW1 . . . . 131 A3
William Morris Ho
W6 . . . . 47 C4
William Morris Sixth
Form W6 . . . . 39 C1
William Morris Way
SW6 . . . . 166 C1
William Patten Prim
Sch 19 N16 . . . . 7 B2
William PI 17 E3 . . . . 26 B3
William Rathbone Ho
3 E2 . . . . 25 A2
William Rd NW1 . . . . 92 C3
William Rushbrooke
Ho 4 SE16 . . . . 153 B4
William Saville Ho 2
NW6 . . . . 23 B3
William's Bldgs 1
E2 . . . . 25 B1
Williams Cl SW6 . . . 154 B2
Williams Coll EC1 107 C3
Williams Ho
10 Bow E3 . . . . 26 C2
9 Hackney E9 . . . . 25 A4
14 Streatham SW2 . . . 74 C3
Williams La SW14 . . 45 B1
Williamson Cl
SE10 . . . . 43 B1
Williamson Ct
SE17 . . . . 150 C1
Williamson St N7 . . . 14 A4
William St 15
SE16 . . . . 33 A2
William St SW1 . . . . 131 A3
William Tyndale Prim
Sch 27 N1 . . . . 15 A1
William Winter Ct 20
SW2 . . . . 74 C4
Willingham Cl 4
NW5 . . . . 13 B3
Willingham Terr
NW5 . . . . 13 B3
Willington Rd
SW9 . . . . 62 A4
Willis Ho 8 E14 . . . . . 34 A2
Willis St E14 . . . . 34 A3
Willoughby Ho
EC2 . . . . 109 B3
10 Wapping E1 . . . . . . 32 A1
Willoughby Rd
NW3 . . . . 11 C4
Willoughby St
WC1 . . . . 106 A3
Willoughbys The
SW14 . . . . 56 A3
Willow Ave SW13 . . . 46 B1
Willowbank SW6 . . . 58 A4

Willowbank Rd
SE15 . . . . 49 B4
Willow Bridge Rd
N1 . . . . 15 B2
Willow Cotts TW9 . . 44 C4
Willow Ct
Brixton SW9 . . . . 173 B3
Chiswick W4 . . . . 46 A3
EC2 . . . . 24 A1 98 A2
Islington N7 . . . . 14 B3
40 Paddington W2 . . . 31 C4
5 Streatham
SW16 . . . . 74 B1
Willowdene
Highgate N6 . . . . 3 B4
5 Peckham SE15 . . . . 50 A2
6 SE15 . . . . 50 A3
Willow Farm La
SW15 . . . . 57 A4
Willow Hall
NW3 . . . . 11 C4
Willow Lo
Fulham SW6 . . . . 47 C2
Putney SW15 . . . . 57 A4
Willow Lodge 10
SW8 . . . . 61 A4
Willow Lodge 13
SE13 . . . . 67 A2
Willow PI SW1 . . . . . 147 A4
Willow Rd
Ealing W5 . . . . 36 A4
Hampstead NW3 . . . . . 11 C4
Willow St
EC2 . . . . 24 A1 98 A2
Willows Terr
NW10 . . . . 21 B3
Willow Tree Cl
18 Old Ford E3 . . . . . . 26 B4
Wandsworth SW18 . . . 71 A3
Willow Vale W12 . . . 29 C1
Willow Way 9
W11 . . . . 30 C2
Willow Wlk SE1 . . . 152 C4
Willsbridge Ct 1
SE15 . . . . 49 B4
Wilman Gr E8 . . . . . . 16 C1
Wilmcote Ho W2 . . 100 A4
Wilmer Gdns 22
N1 . . . . 24 A4
Wilmer Ho 8 E3 . . . . 26 A3
Wilmer Lea Cl E15 . . 19 C1
Wilmer PI N16 . . . . 7 B2
Wilmers Ct 5
NW10 . . . . 20 C4
Wilmington Ave
W4 . . . . 45 C3
Wilmington Sq
WC1 . . . . 95 B3
Wilmington St
WC1 . . . . 95 B3
Wilmot Cl SE15 . . . . 49 C3
Wilmot Pl NW1 . . . . . 13 B1
Wilmot St E2 . . . . 25 A1
Wilna Rd SW18 . . . . 71 B4
Wilsham St
N11 . . . . 31 A1 112 A2
Wilshaw Ho 10
SE8 . . . . 51 C3
Wilshaw St SE14 . . . 51 C2
Wilson Gr SE16 . . . . 40 A4
Wilson Ho
39 Clapham
SW8 . . . . 171 B1

Wilson Ho continued
NW6 . . . . 23 A4
Wilson Rd SE5 . . . . . 49 A2
Wilson's Pl E14 . . . . 33 B3
Wilson's Rd W6 . . . . 39 C1
Wilson St EC2 . . . . . 109 C4
Wiltern Ct NW2 . . . . 10 A2
Wilton Ave W4 . . . . . 38 A1
Wilton Cres SW1 . . 131 B3
Wilton Ct
4 Richmond
TW10 . . . . 54 A2
7 Stepney E1 . . . . 32 A3
Wilton Est E8 . . . . . . 16 C2
Wilton Ho 8 SE22 . . 64 A4
Wilton Mews
SW1 . . . . 131 C2
Wilton Pl SW1 . . . . . 131 B3
Wilton Row SW1 . . 131 B3
Wilton Sq N1 . . . . . . 87 B4
Wilton St SW1 . . . . 132 A2
Wilton Terr SW1 . . . 131 B3
Wilton Villas N1 . . . . 87 B3
Wilton Way E8 . . . . . 16 C2
Wiltshire Cl SW3 . . 144 C3
Wiltshire Ct 2 N4 . . . . 5 B3
Wiltshire Rd SW9 . . . 62 C4
Wiltshire Row N1 . . . 87 C3
Wimbart Rd SW2 . . . 74 B4
Wimbledon Park
Tennis Mus & Tours
SW19 . . . . 70 A1
Wimbledon Park Ct
SW19 . . . . 70 B3
Wimbledon Park
Montessori Sch
SW19 . . . . 69 C3
Wimbledon Park Prim
Sch SW19 . . . . 71 A2
Wimbledon Park Rd
SW18, SW19 . . . . 70 B3
Wimbledon Park Side
SW19 . . . . 69 C3
Wimbledon Lawn
Tennis Sta
SW19 . . . . 70 C1
Wimbledon Stadium
Bsns Ctr SW17 . . . . 71 A1
Wimbledon Windmill
Mus SW19 . . . . 69 B1
Wimbolt St
E2 . . . . 24 C2 99 B4
Wimborne Ho
Canning Town
E16 . . . . 35 B3
Marylebone NW1 . . . . 90 B1
South Lambeth
SW8 . . . . 163 A1
Upper Tooting
SW12 . . . . 73 B2
Wimbourne Ct N1 . . 87 B2
Wimbourne St N1 . . 87 B2
Wimpole Mews
W1 . . . . 104 A3
Wimpole St W1 . . . . 104 A3
Winans Wlk SW9 . . 173 B1
Wincanton Rd
SW18 . . . . 70 B4
Winchelsea Cl
SW15 . . . . 57 C2
Winchelsea Ho 16
SE16 . . . . 40 B4
Winchelsea Rd
NW10 . . . . 20 C4

Winchendon Rd
SW6 . . . . 165 A4
Winchester Ave
NW6 . . . . 10 A1
Winchester Cl
SE17 . . . . 150 B3
Winchester Ct
Richmond TW9 . . . . . . 54 B4
W8 . . . . 128 A4
Winchester Ho
Bayswater W2 . . . . . 100 C1
Chelsea SW3 . . . . . . 157 C3
10 Tower Hamlets
E3 . . . . 26 B2
Winchester Pal
SE1 . . . . 123 B2
Winchester Pl
8 Dalston E8 . . . . 16 B3
Highgate N6 . . . . 4 A3
Winchester Rd
Highgate N6 . . . . 4 A3
South Hampstead
NW3 . . . . 11 C1
Winchester Sq
SE1 . . . . 123 B2
Winchester St
Acton W3 . . . . 37 B4
SW1 . . . . 146 B2
Winchester Wlk
SE1 . . . . 123 B2
Winchfield Ho
SW15 . . . . 56 B1
Winch Ho
Isle of Dogs E14 . . . . 42 A3
SW10 . . . . 157 A2
Winchilsea Ho
NW8 . . . . 89 C3
Wincott St SE11 . . . 149 C3
Windermere
NW1 . . . . 92 B4
12 Putney SW15 . . . . 57 C1
Windermere Ave
NW6 . . . . 23 A4
Windermere Ct
SW13 . . . . 46 B4
Windermere Ho
E3 . . . . 26 B1
Windermere Point 3
SE15 . . . . 50 B3
Windermere Rd
N19 . . . . 4 B2
Winders Rd SW11 168 A2
Windham Rd TW9 . . 54 B4
Windlass Pl SE8 . . . 41 A2
Windlesham Gr
SW19 . . . . 69 C3
Windmill WC1 . . . . . 106 C4
Windmill Alley 7
W4 . . . . 38 A2
Windmill Cl
12 Bermondsey
SE1 . . . . 153 C4
4 Lewisham SE13 . . . 52 B1
Windmill Ct NW2 . . . 10 A2
Windmill Dr
Clapham SW4 . . . . . . 61 A2
Cricklewood NW2 . . . . . 1 A2
Windmill Gdns
SW2 . . . . 62 B1
Windmill Hill
8 Hampstead
NW3 . . . . 11 B4
Hampstead NW3 . . . . . 2 B1
Windmill Ho
4 Millwall E14 . . . . . 41 C2
SE1 . . . . 121 C1

Windmill La E15 . . . . 19 C2
Windmill Pas 10
W4 . . . . 38 A2
Windmill Rd
Chiswick W4 . . . . 38 A2
Roehampton SW19 . . . 69 A1
Wandsworth SW18 . . . 59 C1
Windmill Row
SE11 . . . . 149 B1
Windmill St W1 . . . . 105 B3
Windmill Wlk SE1 . 135 C4
Windrose Cl SE16 . . . 40 C4
Windrush Cl
Battersea SW11 . . . . . 59 C3
Chiswick W4 . . . . 45 B3
4 Hackney E8 . . . . 16 C1
Windrush Ho
NW8 . . . . 101 C4
Windrush Rd
NW10 . . . . 20 C4
Windrush Sq
Brixton SW9 . . . . 62 C3
SW2 . . . . 62 C3
Windsock Cl 1
SE16 . . . . 41 B2
Windsor Ct
Battersea SW11 . . . . 167 C2
Bayswater W2 . . . . . . 114 A4
Chelsea SW3 . . . . . . 144 B2
2 Clapham SW4 . . . . . 61 B3
Fulham SW6 . . . . 58 A4
20 Rotherhithe
SE16 . . . . 32 C1
4 Wandsworth
SW18 . . . . 58 C2
West Hampstead
NW3 . . . . 10 C4
Windsor Gdns W9 . . 23 C1
Windsor Ho
4 Acton Green
W4 . . . . 37 B1
Brondesbury NW2 . . . . 10 A2
4 Globe Town E2 . . . . 25 C2
Regent's Pk NW1 . . . . 92 B4
Shoreditch N1 . . . . 87 A2
Stoke Newington N4 . . . 6 B3
Windsor Pl SW1 . . . 147 A4
Windsor Rd
Richmond TW9 . . . . . . 44 B1
Upper Holloway N7 . . . 5 A1
Willesden NW2 . . . . 9 A2
Windsor St N1 . . . . . 86 B4
Windsor Terr N1 . . . . 97 A4
Windsor Way
W14 . . . . 140 A4
Windsor Wharf E9 . . 18 B3
Windsor Wlk SE5 . . 48 C1
Windspoint Dr
SE15 . . . . 50 A4
Windus Rd N16 . . . . . 7 B3
Windus Wlk N16 . . . . 7 B3
Wine Cl E1 . . . . 32 B2
Wine Office Ct
EC4 . . . . 107 C2
Winfield Ho 3
SW11 . . . . 167 C2
Winford Ct 18
SE15 . . . . 49 C2
Winforton St SE10 . . 52 B2
Winfrith Rd SW18 . . 71 B3
Wingate Ho
20 Bromley E3 . . . . . . 27 A2

Wingate Ho *continued*
8 Stoke Newington
N16.............................C4
Wingate Rd W6 ....39 A3
Wingfield Ct **5**
E14............................34 C2
Wingfield Ho
Paddington NW6 ... **78** A2
5 Spitalfields
E2..............24 B2 **98** C3
Wingfield Mews
SE15.........................64 C4
Wingfield St SE15 ...64 C4
Wingford Rd SW2 ...62 A1
Wingham **5** NW5 ...12 C2
Wingmore Rd
SE24.........................63 B4
Wingrad Ho **18** E1...32 B4
Wingrave SE17 .... **151** B3
Wingrave Rd W6 .....47 B4
Wingreen **15** NW8 ..78 B4
Winicotte Ho W2 **101** C4
Winifrede Paul Ho **7**
NW5.........................13 A4
Winkley St **E** E2 ...25 A3
Winkworth Cotts **14**
E1.............................25 B1
Winnett St W1 .... **119** B4
Winnington Ho
19 Kensal Town
W10..........................23 A1
8 SE5 ....48 B3
Winscombe St N19 ..4 A2
Winsham Gr SW11..60 C2
Winsham Ho NW1 ...93 C4
Winslade Rd SW2 ...62 A2
Winsland Mews
W2 .... **101** B3
Winsland St **2** W2 . **101** B3
Winsley St W1....... **105** A2
Winslow SE17 ...... **152** A1
Winslow Rd W6 .....47 B4
Winstanley Rd
SW11 ....59 C4
Winston Ho WC1 ...**93** C3
Winston Rd N16....15 C4
Winston Wlk **2**
W4 ....37 C2
Winterbourne Ho
W11 ....31 A2 **112** A3
Winter Box Wlk
TW10........................54 B2
Winterbrook Rd
SE24.........................63 B1
Winterfold Ct **7**
SW19 ....70 A2
Winterleys **7**
Winter Lo **17**
SE18...................... **153** C1
Winterslow Ho **20**
SE5 ....48 B1
Winterton Ho **5**
E1.............................32 B3
Winterton Pl
SW10 .... **157** A4
Winterwell Rd
SW2..........................62 A2
Winthorpe Rd
SW15 ....58 A3
Winthrop Ho **10**
W12..........................30 A2
Winthrop St E1........32 A4

Winton Prim Sch
N1.............................84 C1
Wirrall Ho **15**
SE26..........................76 C1
Wisbech **5** N4........5 B3
Wisden Ho SW8 .. **163** A3
Wise Rd E15............27 C4
Wisteria Rd SE4 .....66 A4
Wistow Ho **14** E2...24 C4
Witanhurst La N6.....3 C3
Witan St E2 ....25 A2
Witchwood Ho **14**
SW9 ....62 C4
Witcombe Point **14**
SE15..................... **49** C2
Witechapel Sp Ctr
E1.............................32 B4
Witham Ct SW17 ....72 B1
Witham Ho **31** SE5..48 B1
Witherington Rd
N5.............................14 C3
Withers Pl EC1 .... **97** A2
Withycombe Rd
SW19 .... **69** C4
Witley Ho **6** E1.....25 C1
Witley St WC1...... **94** A1
Witley Ho **2** SW2 ..74 B4
Witley Point **8**
SW15 ....69 A3
Witley Rd N19..........4 B2
Wittering Ho **11**
SW11 .... **169** A2
Wivenhoe Cl SE15 ..65 A4
Wix Prim Sch SW4 ..61 A3
Wix's La SW4...........61 A3
Woburn Ct
32 Bermondsey
SE16.........................40 A1
Richmond TW9 ....54 B4
Woburn Pl WC1 .....94 A1
Woburn Sq WC1.....93 C1
Woburn Wlk WC1....93 C3
Wodeham Gdns **1**
E1.............................32 A4
Wodehouse Ave
SE15.........................49 B2
Wodehouse Ct **11**
W3 ....37 B3
Woking Cl SW15......56 B3
Wolcot Ho NW1 ... **83** A1
Wolfe Cres
7 Bermondsey
SE16.........................40 C4
14 Rotherhithe
SE16.........................40 C4
Wolfe Ho **19** W12 ...30 A2
Wolfe Ho **19**
Golders Green
NW11 ....1 B4
SE1 .... **139** A4
Wolfe Cres
Wolftencroft Cl
SW11 ....59 C4
Wollaston Cl SE1 . **150** C4
Wollstonecraft St
N1.......................... **85** C2
Wolseley Ave SW18,
SW19 ....70 C2
Wolseley Gdns
W4 ....45 A4

Wolseley Rd W4....37 B2
Wolseley St SE1 .. **139** A3
Wolsey Cl NW4.......11 B1
Wolsey Ho **3**
NW5...........................13 C2
Wolsey Mews
NW5...........................13 B2
Wolsey Rd N1..........15 C3
Wolsey St E1........ **32** B4
Wolverley St E2 .....25 A2
Wolverton SE17 ... **152** A2
Wolverton Gdns
W6 ....39 C2
Wontner Cl **5** N1...15 B1
Wontner Rd SW12,
SW17.........................72 C2
Woodall Cl **18** E14..34 A2
Woodberry Down
Com Prim Sch N4 ...6 B4
Woodberry Down N4 .6 B4
Woodberry Gr N4 ....6 B4
Woodberry Terr E9 ..17 B2
Woodborough Rd
SW15 ....57 A3
Woodbourne Ave
SW16.........................73 C1
Woodbourne Cl
SW16.........................73 C1
Woodbridge Cl **10**
N7...............................5 B2
Woodbridge Ct SW15 ...58 B2
Woodbridge St
EC1 .... **96** A2
Woodchester Sq
W2 .... **100** A4
Woodchurch Ho **9**
SW9 .... **173** B4
Woodchurch Rd
NW6...........................11 A1
Wood Cl E2 ...24 C1 **99** B2
Woodcock Ho **4**
E14............................33 C4
Woodcote Ho **4**
SE8............................51 B4
Woodcott Ho **1**
SW15 ....68 C4
Woodcroft Mews
SE8............................41 A2
Wood Dene **8**
SE15.........................50 A2
Woodfall Rd N4 ......5 C2
Woodfall St SW3 . **144** C1
Woodfarrs SE5 ....63 C3
Wood Field NW3 ....12 B3
Woodfield Ave
SW16.........................73 C1
Woodfield Ct
SW16.........................73 C1
Woodfield Gr
SW16.........................73 C1
Woodfield La
SW16.........................73 C1
Woodfield Pl W9 ...23 B1
Woodfield Rd W9 ...23 B1
Woodford Ct **18**
W12..........................39 C4
Woodger Rd W12...39 B4
Woodhall Ho **1**
SW18 .... **92** C3
Woodhall Ave
SE21.........................76 B1
Woodhall Dr SE21 ..76 B1
Woodhall Ho **1**
SW18 ....59 C1
Woodheyes Rd
NW10..........................8 A3

Wood Ho
4 Clapham SW4... **171** C2
5 Paddington
NW6...........................23 B3
Woodison St E3 ......26 A1
Wood La N6 ....4 A4
Wood La W12 ....30 B2
Woodland Cres
18 Rotherhithe
SE16.........................40 C4
Woodland Gr SE10..43 A1
Woodland Hts SE3...53 A4
Woodland Mews
SW16.........................74 A1
Woodlands Ave
W3 ....28 A1
Woodlands Ct
SE22.........................64 A3
Woodlands Gt
SW15 ....58 B2
Woodlands Park Rd
SE10..........................53 A4
Woodlands Rd
SW13 ....56 B4
Woodland St **2**
E8..............................16 B2
Woodlands The
Highbury N5............15 B4
12 Hornsey N8..........5 A4
Woodlands Way
SW15 ....58 B2
Woodland Wlk
9 Greenwich
SE10.........................43 A1
Hampstead NW3 ....12 A3
Wood Lane High Sch
W12...........................30 A3
Wood Lane Sta
W12...........................30 A3
Woodlawn Cl
SW15 ....58 B2
Woodlawn Rd
SW6 ....47 C2
Woodlea Rd N16 .....7 A1
Woodleigh Gdns
SW16.........................74 A1
Woodmans Gr
NW10..........................8 B3
Woodmans Mews
W12...........................30 A4
Woodmere Cl **11**
SW11 ....60 C4
Woodmill **1**
SW15 ....56 C1
Woodmill St SE1 . **139** A2
Woodpecker Mews
SE13..........................67 C3
Woodpecker Rd **6**
SE14.........................51 A4
Wood Point **8**
E16............................35 C4
Woodquest Ave
SE24.........................63 B2
Woodruff Ho **12**
SW2..........................62 C1
Woodrush Cl **4**
SE14.........................51 A3
Woodseer St E1 ... **111** A4
Woodsford SE17 . **151** B1
Woodsford Sq
W14 .... **126** B4
Woods Ho SW8... **170** C4

Wood's Mews W1 **117** B4
Woodsome Rd NW5 ..4 A1
Wood's Pl SE1 .... **138** B1
Woodspring Rd
SW19 ....70 A2
Wood's Rd SE15 .....50 A2
Wood St
Chiswick W4...........38 A1
City of London EC2 **109** A2
Woodstar Ho **3**
SE15...................... **49** C3
Woodstock Ave
NW11 ....1 A4
Woodstock Ct
SE11 .... **149** A2
Woodstock Gr
W12...........................39 C4
Woodstock Ho **2**
N5.............................15 B4
Woodstock Mews
W1 .... **103** C3
Woodstock Rd
Bedford Pk W4.......38 A3
Finsbury Pk N4........5 C3
Golders Green NW11 ..1 B4
Woodstock St W1 **104** A1
Woodstock Studios **17**
W12...........................39 C4
Woodstock Terr
E14............................34 A2
Woodthorpe Rd
SW15 ....57 A3
Woodview Cl N4 ......6 A4
Woodville Ct **3**
SE10.........................52 B2
Woodville Ho SE1 **138** C2
Woodville Rd
Golders Green
NW11 ....1 A4
Paddington NW6 ....23 B3
Stoke Newington
N16............................16 A3
Woodwarde Rd
SE22.........................64 A1
Woodwell St
SW18 ....59 B2
Wood Wharf SE10 ...52 B4
Woodyard Cl NW5 ...12 C3
Woodyard La SE21...76 A4
Woolcombes Ct **4**
SE16.........................32 C1
Wooler St SE17... **151** C2
Woolf Ct **7** W3 .....37 B3
Woolf Mews WC1 ...94 A2
Woolley Ho SW9.....63 A4
Woollon Ho **1** E1...32 B3
Woolmore Prim Sch
11 E14 ....34 B2
Woolmore St E14...34 B2
Woolneigh St
SW6 .... **166** A1
Woolpack Ho **1**
E9.............................17 B2
Woolridge Way E9...17 B1
Woolstaplers Way
SE16...................... **153** B4
Woolstone Ho **7**
E2..............................24 C4
Woolven Ho SE3.....53 B4
WoolYd SE17 ....40 A2
Wooster Gdns E14.34 C3
Wooster Pl SE1... **151** C4
Wootton St SE1 .. **121** C1
Worcester Ct **44**
W2 ....31 C4
Worcester Dr W4....38 A4

Worcester Gdns
  SW11 . . . . 60 B2
Worcester Ho
  Bayswater W2 . . . . 100 C1
  3 Islington N1 . . . . 15 B1
  Lambeth SE11 . . . . 135 B1
  5 Putney SW15 . . . . 69 B4
Worcester Mews 2
  NW6 . . . . 11 A2
Wordsworth Ho
  NW6 . . . . 23 C2
Wordsworth Pl 11
  NW5 . . . . 12 B3
Wordsworth Rd
  Bermondsey SE1 . . 153 A3
  Stoke Newington
  N16 . . . . 16 A4
Worfield St SW11 . . 158 B1
Worgan St
  Rotherhithe SE16 . . 40 C2
  SE11 . . . . 148 C2
Working Men's Coll
  The NW1 . . . . 83 A2
World's End Pas
  SW10 . . . . 157 B2
World's End Pl
  SW10 . . . . 157 A2
World Trade Ctr
  London E14 . . . . . . 42 A4
Worlidge St W6 . . . 39 B1
Worlingham Rd
  SE22 . . . . 64 B3
Wormholt Park Prim
  Sch W12 . . . . 29 C2
Wormholt Rd W12 . 29 C1
Wormwood St
  EC2 . . . . 110 A2
Wornington Rd
  W10 . . . . 31 A4
Woronzow Rd
  NW8 . . . . 80 A3
Worple St SW14 . . . 55 C4
Worple Way TW10 . . 54 A3
Worship St
  EC2 . . . . 24 A1 98 A1
Worsley Gr E5 . . . . . 16 C4
Worsopp Dr SW4 . . 61 B2
Worth Gr SE17 . . . . 151 B1
Worthington Ho
  EC1 . . . . 95 C4
  10 Streatham SW2 . . 74 C4
Wotton Ct 14 E14 . . 34 C2
Wotton Rd 18 SE8 . . 51 B4
Wouldham Rd E16 . 35 B3
Wraxall Rd 2 E3 . . . 26 B1
Wrayburn Ho 20
  SE16 . . . . 139 C3
Wray Cres N4 . . . . . . 5 B2
Wray Ct N4 . . . . 5 B2
Wray Ho 11 SW2 . . . 74 A3
Wren Ave NW2 . . . . . 9 B4
Wren Cl E16 . . . . 35 B3
Wren Ho
  20 Bow E3 . . . . 26 A3
  SW1 . . . . 147 B1

Wren Landing E14 . . 33 C1
Wrenn Ho SW13 . . . 47 B4
Wren Rd SE5 . . . . . . 48 C2
Wren St WC1 . . . . . . 95 A2
Wrentham Ave
  NW10 . . . . 22 C3
Wren View N6 . . . . . . 4 B3
Wrestlers Ct EC3 . . 110 A2
Wrexham Rd E3 . . . . 26 C3
Wriglesworth St
  SE14 . . . . 50 C3
Wright Cl SE13 . . . . 67 C3
Wright Ho SW11 . . . 57 A2
Wright's Gr SW4 . . . 61 C3
Wright's La W8 . . . 128 A2
Wright's Rd E3 . . . . 26 B3
Wrights Wlk SW14 . 55 C4
Wrotham Ho SE1 . . 137 C2
Wrotham Rd 18
  NW1 . . . . 13 B1
Wrottesley Rd
  NW10 . . . . 21 C3
Wroughton Rd
  SW11 . . . . 60 B1
Wroxton Rd SE15 . . 50 B1
Wulfstan St W12 . . . 29 B3
Wyatt Ho
  Blackheath Vale SE3 . 53 B1
  NW8 . . . . 89 C1
Wyatt Park Mans 1
  SW2 . . . . 74 A2
Wyatt Park Rd
  SW2 . . . . 74 B2
Wyatt Rd N5 . . . . 6 B1
Wybert St NW1 . . . . 92 C2
Wycherley Cl SE3 . . 53 B3
Wychwood End N6 . . 4 B4
Wychwood Ho N4 . . 6 B4
Wyclif Ct EC1 . . . . . 96 A3
Wycliffe Ho 15
  N16 . . . . 16 A4
Wyclif St EC1 . . . . . 96 A3
Wycombe Ct SE3 . . 53 C3
Wycombe Gdns
  NW11 . . . . 1 C2
Wycombe Ho NW8 . 90 A2
Wycombe Pl SW18 . 59 B1
Wycombe Sq
  W8 . . . . 31 C1 113 B1
Wyersdale Ho N4 . . . 6 B4
Wye St SW11 . . . . . 167 C1
Wyfold Rd SW6 . . . 154 A1
Wyke Rd E3 . . . . 18 C1
Wyldes Cl NW11 . . . . 2 B3
Wyllen Cl E1 . . . . . . 25 B1
Wymering Mans 9
  W9 . . . . 23 C2
Wymering Rd W9 . . 23 C2
Wymondham Ct
  NW8 . . . . 79 C4
Wymond St SW15 . . 57 B4

Wynan Rd E14 . . . . . 42 A1
Wyndham Cres N19 . 4 B1
Wyndham Deedes Ho
  50 E2 . . . . 24 C3
Wyndham Ho
  SW1 . . . . 145 B3
Wyndham Mews
  W1 . . . . 102 C3
Wyndham Pl W1 . . 102 C3
Wyndham Rd SE5 . . 48 B3
Wyndhams Ct 8
  E8 . . . . 16 B1
Wyndham St W1 . . 102 C4
Wyndham Yd W1 . . 102 C3
Wyneham Rd SE24. . 63 C2
Wynford Rd N1 . . . . 85 A2
Wynne Ho SE14 . . . 50 C2
Wynne Rd SW9 . . . 173 B1
Wynnstay Gdns
  W8 . . . . 127 C2
Wynter Ho 20
  SW9 . . . . 173 A1
Wynter St SW11 . . . 59 B3
Wynton Pl W3 . . . . . 28 A3
Wynyard Ho SE11 . 149 A2
Wynyard Terr
  SE11 . . . . 149 A2
Wynyatt Ho EC1 . . . 96 A4
Wynyatt St EC1 . . . . 96 A4
Wytham Ho NW8 . . 89 C1
Wythburn Ct W1 . . 102 C2
Wythburn Pl W1 . . 102 C2
Wyvil Prim Sch
  SW8 . . . . 162 B2
Wyvil Rd SW8 . . . . 162 A2
Wyvis St E14 . . . . . . 34 A4

Y

Yabsley St E14 . . . . . 34 B1
Yaldam Ho SE1 . . . 152 A3
Yalding Ho 20 E5 . . 17 A3
Yalding Rd SE16 . . 153 B4
Yale Ct NW6 . . . . . . 11 A3
Yardley St WC1 . . . . 95 B3
Yard The N1 . . . . . . 84 B1
Yarmouth Pl W1 . . 118 A1
Yarnfield Sq 16
  SE15 . . . . 49 C2
Yarrow Ho
  12 Cubitt Town
  E14 . . . . 42 B3
  16 North Kensington
  W10 . . . . 30 B4
Yatesbury Ct E5 . . . 18 A3
Yates Ct NW2 . . . . . . 9 C2
Yates Ho 22
  E2 . . . . . 24 C2 99 C4
Yatton Ho 18 W10 . 30 B4
Yeadon Ho 14
  W10 . . . . 30 B4
Yearby Ho W10 . . . . 22 B1
Yeate St N1 . . . . 15 C1
Yeldham Ho W6 . . . . 39 C1

Yeldham Rd W6 . . . . 39 C1
Yelverton Rd
  SW11 . . . . 167 C1
Yeoman Cl SE27 . . . 75 A1
Yeoman's Row
  SW3 . . . . 130 B1
Yeoman St SE8 . . . . 41 A2
Yeoman's Yd E1 . . . 125 A4
Yeo St E3 . . . . 34 A4
Yeovil Ho
  Finsbury Pk N7 . . . . 5 B2
  North Kensington
  W10 . . . . 22 B1
Yerbury Prim Sch
  N19 . . . . 4 C1
Yerbury Rd N19 . . . . 4 C1
Yesoday Hatorah
  Senior Girls Sch 5
  N16 . . . . 7 B4
Yet Lev Ct E5 . . . . . . 7 C3
Yewfield Rd NW10 . . 8 B2
Yew Gr NW2 . . . . 9 C4
Yew Tree Cl 3
  SE13 . . . . 67 B4
Yew Tree Ct 8 N16 . 6 C2
Yew Tree Rd W12 . . 29 B2
Yoakley Rd N16 . . . . 7 A2
Yoke Cl N7 . . . . 14 A2
Yonge Pk N4, N7 . . . 5 C1
York Ave
  Mortlake SW14 . . . 55 B2
  Walworth SE17. . . 151 A2
York Bldgs WC2 . . 120 B3
York Bridge NW1 . . 91 B2
York Cl 17 SE5 . . . . 48 B1
York Gate NW1 . . . . 91 C1
York Gr SE15 . . . . . 50 B2
York Hall L Ctr E2 . 25 B3
York Ho
  Acton W3 . . . . 28 B2
  Chelsea SW3 . . . . 145 A2
  Islington N1 . . . . . . 14 C3
  Kensington W8 . . 128 A4
  11 Kentish Town
  N7 . . . . 13 C2
  Kew TW9 . . . . 44 C3
  Lambeth SE1 . . . . 135 A1
  Marylebone W1 . . 102 C4
  Pentonville N1 . . . 84 C1
  Richmond TW10 . . 54 C2
York House Pl
  W8 . . . . 128 A4
York Ho 3
  W10 . . . . 22 B1
Yorkley Ho 3
  W10 . . . . 22 B1
York Mans
  Battersea SW11 . . 169 C4
  Marylebone W1 . . 103 B4
  Walworth SE17. . . 151 A2
York Mews NW5 . . . 13 A3
York Pl
  Battersea SW11 . . 59 C4
  WC2 . . . . 120 B3

York Place Mans
  NW1 . . . . 103 A4
York Rd
  Battersea SW11,
  SW18 . . . . 59 C4
  Dagenham W3 . . . . 28 C3
  Richmond TW10 . . 54 B2
  SE1 . . . . 135 A4
York Rise NW5 . . . . . 4 A1
York Road Bsns Ctr
  SW11 . . . . 167 B1
York St Chambers
  W1 . . . . 102 C4
Yorkshire Cl N16 . . . 7 A1
Yorkshire Grey Pl 13
  NW3 . . . . 11 B4
Yorkshire Grey Yd
  WC1 . . . . 106 C3
Yorkshire Rd E14 . . 33 A3
York Sq 12 E14 . . . . 33 A3
York St W1 . . . . 103 A4
York Terr E NW1 . . . 91 C1
York Terr W NW1 . . . 91 B1
Yorkton St E2 . . . . . 24 C3
York Water Gate The
  SW1 . . . . 120 B2
York Way
  Barnsbury N1, N7,
  N1 . . . . 14 A1
  N1 . . . . 84 B3
York Way Ct
  Islington N1 . . . . . . 84 B3
  Islington N1 . . . . . . 84 C3
Young's Bldgs EC1 . 97 A2
Youngs Ct SW11 . . 169 C3
Young St W8 . . . . . 128 A3
Yoxall Ho 2 W10 . . 22 B1
Yukon Rd SW12 . . . 73 A4

Z

Zabludowicz
  Collection NW5 . . 12 C2
Zampa Rd SE16 . . . . 40 B1
Zander Ct
  E2 . . . . . 24 C2 99 C4
Zangwill Ho NW6 . . 23 B3
Zealand Ho 11 SE5 . 48 B1
Zealand Rd E3 . . . . 26 A3
Zennor Rd SW12 . . 73 B3
Zennor Trade Pk 2
  SW12 . . . . 73 B3
Zenoria St SE22 . . . 64 B3
Zetland Ho W8 . . . 128 A2
Zetland St E14 . . . . 34 B4
Zeus Ho N1 . . . . 97 B3
Zion Ho 6 E1 . . . . . 32 B3
Zoar St SE1 . . . . . . 122 C2
Zodiac Ho 3 E3 . . . 26 C1
Zoffany St N19 . . . . 4 C2
ZSL London Zoo
  NW1 . . . . 81 B2

List of numbered locations

This atlas shows thousands more place names than any other London street atlas. In some busy areas it is impossible to fit the name of every place.

Where not all names will fit, some smaller places are shown by a number. If you wish to find out the name associated with a number, use this listing.

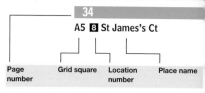

34

A5 **8** St James's Ct

| Page number | Grid square | Location number | Place name |

1

B1 **1** Mortimer Cl
2 Primrose Ct
3 Sunnyside Ho
4 Sunnyside
5 Prospect Pl
B4 **1** Berkeley Ct
2 Exchange Mans
3 Beechcroft Ct
4 Nedahall Ct
C1 **1** Portman Hts
2 Hermitage Ct
3 Moreland Ct
4 Wendover Ct

2

B1 **1** Hampstead Sq
2 Stamford Cl
3 Mount Sq The

4

B1 **1** Hunter Ho
2 Fisher Ho
3 Lang Ho
4 Temple Ho
5 Palmer Ho
6 Carlisle Ho
7 Durham Ho
8 Suffolk Ho
9 Lincoln Ho
10 Llewellyn Ho
11 Fell Ho
12 Aveling Ho
13 Merryweather Ct
14 Brennands Ct
15 St Christophers Ct
16 Francis Terrace Mews
17 Tremlett Mews
B2 **1** Flowers Mews
2 Archway Cl
3 Sandridge St
4 Bovingdon Cl
5 Cavell Ct
6 Torrence Ho
7 Rowan Wlk
8 Laurel Cl
9 Forest Way
10 Larch Cl
11 Pine Cl
12 Alder Mews
13 Aspen Cl
14 Hargrave Park Sch

B3 **1** Calvert Ct
2 Academy The
3 Whitehall Mans
4 Pauntley St
5 Archway Hts
6 Pauntley Ho
7 Thornbury Sq
8 St Aloysius RC Coll
C1 **1** Melchester Ho
2 Norcombe Ho
3 Weatherbury Ho
4 Wessex Ho
5 Archway Bsns Ctr
6 Harford Mews
7 Opera Ct
8 Rupert Ho
9 All Saints Church
C2 **1** Bowerman Ct
2 Gresham St
3 Hargrave Mans
4 Church Garth
5 John King Ct
6 Ramsey Ct
7 St John's Upper Holloway CE Prim Sch
8 Hargrave Park Sch
C3 **1** Louise White Ho
2 Levison Way
3 Sanders Way
4 Birbeck Ho
5 Scholars Ct
6 Mount Carmel RC Tech Coll for Girls
C4 **1** Eleanor Rathbone House
2 Christopher Lo
3 Monkridge
4 Marbleford Ct
5 High London
6 Garton Ho
7 Hilltop Ho
8 Caroline Martyn Ho
9 Arthur Henderson House
10 Margaret Mcmillan House
11 Enid Stacy Ho
12 Mary McArthur Ho
13 Bruce Glasier Ho
14 John Wheatley Ho
15 Keir Hardie Ho
16 Monroe Ho

17 Iberia Ho
18 Lygoe Ho
19 Lambert Ho
20 Shelbourne Ho
21 Arkansas Ho
22 Lafitte Ho
23 Shreveport Ho
24 Packenham Ho
25 Orpheus Ho
26 Fayetville Ho
27 Bayon Ho

5

A1 **1** Northview
2 Tufnell Park Mans
3 Fulford Mans
4 Tollington Ho
5 Grafton Prim Sch
A2 **1** Bracey Mews
2 Christie Ct
3 Ringmer Gdns
4 Kingsdown Rd
5 Cottenham Ho
6 St Paul's Ct
7 Rickthorne Rd
8 Stanley Terr
9 Arundel Lo
10 Landseer Ct
11 St Mark's CE Prim Sch
A3 **1** Beeches The
2 Lambton Ct
3 Nugent Ct
4 Lambton Mews
5 Mews The
6 Duncombe Prim Sch
7 Nyton Cl
8 Charles St
A4 **1** Marie Lloyd Gdns
2 Edith Cavell Cl
3 Marie Stopes Ct
4 Jessie Blythe La
5 Barbara Rudolph Ct
6 Hetty Rees Ct
7 Leyden Mans
8 Brambledown
9 Lochbie
10 Lyngham Ct
11 High Mount
12 Woodlands The
13 St Gildas' RC Jun Sch

14 Holly Park Montessori Sch
B1 **1** Pakeman Prim Sch
2 South Eastern Univ
3 Samuel Rhodes Sch
4 Montem Prim Sch
5 Heather Cl
B2 **1** Berkeley Wlk
2 Lazar Wlk
3 Thistlewood Cl
4 Tomlins Wlk
5 Andover Ho
6 Barmouth Ho
7 Chard Ho
8 Christ the King RC Prim Sch
9 Methley Ho
10 Rainford Ho
11 Woodbridge Cl
12 Allerton Wlk
13 Falconer Wlk
14 Sonderburg Rd
15 St Mark's Mans
16 Athol Ct
17 Pooles Park Prim Sch
B3 **1** Lawson Ct
2 Wiltshire Ct
3 Fenstanton
4 Hutton Ct
5 Wisbech
6 Islington Arts & Media Sch
7 Old Dairy Ct
C2 **1** Brookfield
2 Churnfield
3 Cornwallis Sq

6

A1 **1** Hurlock Ho
2 Blackstock Ho
3 Vivian Comma Cl
4 Monsell Ct
5 Century Mews
A2 **1** Parkwood Prim Sch
2 Ambler Prim Sch
3 City & Islington Coll (Ctr for Life-long Learning)
B4 **1** Finmere Ho
2 Keynsham Ho
3 Kilpeck Ho
4 Knaresborough Ho

5 Leighfield Ho
6 Lonsdale Ho
7 Groveley Ho
8 Wensleydale Ho
9 Badminton Ct
10 Skinners' Acad
C1 **1** Betty Layward Prim Sch
2 Piano La
C2 **1** Chestnut Cl
2 Sycamore Ho
3 Lordship Ho
4 Clissold Ho
5 Beech Ho
6 Laburnam Ho
7 Ormond Ho
8 Yew Tree Ct
9 Oak Ho
10 Beis Yaakov Girls Sch
C4 **1** Selwood Ho
2 Bnois Jerusalem Girls Sch
3 Mendip Ho
4 Ennerdale Ho
5 Getters Talmud Torah
6 Delamere Ho
7 Westwood Ho
8 Bernwood Ho
9 Allerdale Ho
10 Chattenden Ho
11 Farningham Ho
12 Oakend Ho
13 Getters Talmud Torah Sch

7

A1 **1** Gujarat Ho
2 Marton Rd
3 Painsthorpe Rd
4 Selkirk Ho
5 Defoe Ho
6 Edward Friend Ho
7 Sheridan Ho
8 Barrie Ho
9 Arnold Ho
10 Macaulay Ho
11 Stowe Ho
12 Carlyle Ho
13 Shaftesbury Ho
14 Lillian Cl
15 Swift Ho

14 Cannington
15 Langridge
16 Athlone Ho
17 Pentland Ho
18 Beckington
19 Hawkridge
20 Edington
21 Rhyl Prim Sch
22 Haverstock Ho

13

A1 1 Ferdinand Ho
2 Harmood Ho
3 Hawley Rd
4 Hawley Mews
5 Leybourne St
6 Barling
7 Tiptree
8 Havering
9 Candida Ct
10 Lorraine Ct
11 Donnington Ct
12 Welford Ct
13 Torbay Ct
14 Bradfield Ct
15 Torbay St
16 Water La
17 Leybourne Rd
18 Haven St
19 Stucley Pl
20 Lawrence Ho
21 Holy Trinity & Saint
Silas CE Prim Sch
22 Hawley Inf Sch

A2 1 Ashington
2 Priestley Ho
3 Leonard Day Ho
4 Old Dairy Mews
5 Alpha Ct
6 Una Ho
7 Widford
8 Heybridge
9 Roxwell
10 Hamstead Gates
11 College Francais
Bilingue de
Londres

A4 1 Denyer Ho
2 Stephenson Ho
3 Trevithick Ho
4 Brunel Ho
5 Newcomen Ho
6 Faraday Ho
7 Winifrede Paul Ho
8 Wardlow
9 Fletcher Ct
10 Tideswell
11 Grangemill
12 Hambrook Ct
13 Calver

B1 1 Cherry Tree Ct
2 Chichester Ct
3 Durdans Ho
4 Philia Ho
5 Bernard Shaw Ct
6 Foster Ct
7 Bessemer Ct
8 Hogarth Ct
9 Rochester Ct
10 Soane Ct
11 Wallett Ct
12 Inwood Ct

13 Wrotham Rd
14 St Thomas Ct
15 Caulfield Ct
16 Bruges Pl
17 Reachview Ct
18 Lawfords Wharf

B3 1 Eleanor Ho
2 Falkland Pl
3 Kensington Ho
4 Willingham Ct
5 Kenbrook Ho
6 Aborfield
7 Great Field
8 Appleford
9 Forties The
10 Maud Wilkes Cl
11 Dunne Mews
12 Dowdeny Cl
13 Kentish Town CE
Prim Sch

B4 1 Benson Ct
2 Tait Ho
3 Manorfield Cl
4 Greatfield Cl
5 Longley Ho
6 Lampson Ho
7 Davidson Ho
8 Palmer Ho
9 Lambourn Cl
10 Morris Ho
11 Owen Ho
12 Eleanor Palmer
Prim Sch

C1 1 Hillier Ho
2 Gairloch Ho
3 Cobham Mews
4 Bergholt Mews
5 Blakeney Cl
6 Weavers Way
7 Allensbury Pl

C2 1 Rowstock
2 Peckwater Ho
3 Wolsey Ho
4 Pandian Way
5 Busby Mews
6 Caledonian Sq
7 Canal Byd
8 Northpoint Sq
9 Lock Mews
10 Carters Cl
11 York Ho
12 Hungerford Ed
13 Cliff Road Studios
14 Cliff Ct
15 Camelot Ho
16 Church Studios
17 Camden Terr
18 Brecknock
Prim Sch
19 Hungerford
Prim Sch

C3 1 Blake Ho
2 Quelch Ho
3 Lee Ho
4 Wilbury Ho
5 Howell Ho
6 Holmsbury Ho
7 Leith Ho
8 Betchworth Ho
9 Rushmore Ho
10 Dugdale Ho
11 Horsendon Ho
12 Colley Ho
13 Coombe Ho
14 Ivinghoe Ho
15 Buckhurst Ho
16 Saxonbury Ct

17 Charlton Ct
18 Apollo Studios
19 Barn Cl
20 Long Meadow
21 Landleys Field
22 Margaret Bondfield
House
23 Haywood Lo
24 Torriano Sch
25 Brecon Mews

C4 1 Fairlie Ct
2 Trecastle Way
3 Dalmeny Avenue
Estate
4 Hyndman Ho
5 Carpenter Ho
6 Graham Ho
7 Tufnell Mans

14

A2 1 Clock Tower Pl
2 Clock View Cres
3 Jim Veal Dr
4 Gower Sch The
5 Tamworth
6 Chris Pullen Wy

A3 1 Kimble Ho
2 Saxonbury Ct
3 Poynder Ct
4 Pangbourne Ho
5 Moulsford Ho

A4 1 Arcade The
2 Macready Pl
3 Cardwell Rd
4 Mcmorran Ho
5 Crayford Ho
6 Whitby Ct
7 Prospect Pl
8 City & Islington
Coll (Ctr for Bsns,
Arts & Technology)

B1 1 Kerwick Cl
2 Rydston Cl
3 Skegness Ho
4 Frederica St
5 Ponder St
6 Kings Ct
7 Freeling St
8 Coatbridge Ho
9 Tilloch St

B2 1 Burns Ho
2 Scott Ho
3 Wellington Mews
4 Roman Ct
5 Piccadilly Ct
6 Knowledge Point
Sch

B3 1 Culverin Ct
2 Garand Ct
3 Mount Carmel
B4 1 Buckmaster Ho
2 Loreburn Ho
3 Cairns Ho
4 Halsbury Ho
5 Chelmsford Ho
6 Cranworth Ho
7 City & Islington
Coll (Ctr for Health,
Social & Child
Care)

C1 1 Mountfort Terr
2 Avon Ho
3 Buckland St
4 Dovey Lo
5 Carfree Ct
6 Mitchell Ho
7 New College Mews

8 Lofting Ho
9 Brooksby Ho
10 Cara Ho
11 Thornhill Prim Sch

C2 1 Freightliners
City Farm

C3 1 Slaney Pl
2 Eastwood Cl
3 Milton Pl
4 Hartnoll Ho
5 St James
School Flats
6 Widnes Ho
7 Tranmere Ho
8 Victoria Mans
9 Formby Ct
10 Mersey Ho
11 Birkenhead Ho
12 Drayton Park Mews
13 Drayton Park
Prim Sch

15

A1 1 Islington Park
Mews
2 Evelyn Denington
Court
3 Bassingbourn Ho
4 Cadmore Ho
5 Adstock Ho
6 Garston Ho
7 Flitton Ho
8 Datchworth Ho
9 Battishill St
10 Almeida St
11 Edward's Cotts
12 Hyde's Pl
13 Tyndale Terr
14 Spriggs Ho
15 Barratt Ho
16 Chadston Ho
17 Spencer Pl
18 Whiston Ho
19 Wakelin Ho
20 Tressel Cl
21 Canonbury Ct
22 Halton Ho
23 Shillingford St
24 Highbury Mans
25 Premier Ho
26 Waterloo Gdns
27 William Tyndale
Prim Sch

A2 1 Hampton Ct
2 Salisbury Ho
3 Canonbury
Prim Sch
A3 1 Laycock Prim Sch
2 De Barowe Mews
3 Fieldview Ct
4 Viewpoint
5 Ashurst Lo
6 Highbury
Fields Sch
7 London
Metropolitan Univ
(Ladbrook Ho)
8 Robinswood Mews

A4 1 Chestnuts The
2 Bowen Ct
3 Peckett Sq
4 De Barowe Mews
5 Loxford Gardens

B1 1 Astey's Row
2 Lincoln Ho
3 Worcester Ho
4 Melville Pl

5 Wontner Cl
6 Hedingham Cl
7 Laundry La
8 Base Apartments
9 Walkinshaw Ct
10 New Bentham Ct
11 Bentham Ct
12 Haslam Ho
13 Horsfield Ho
14 Riverside Ho
15 Eric Fletcher Ct
16 Annette Cres
17 Ashby Ho
18 Lindsey Mews
19 Cardigan Wlk
20 Red House Sq
21 Orchard Cl
22 Queensbury St
23 Raynor Pl

B2 1 Crowline Wlk
2 Upper Handa Wlk
3 Handa Wlk
4 Lismore Wlk
5 Bardsey Wlk
6 Walney Wlk
7 Upper Bardsey Wlk
8 Upper Lismore Wlk
9 Sark Ho
10 Guernsey Ho
11 Guernsey Rd
12 Sybil Thorndike Ho
13 Clephane Rd
14 Florence
Nightingale Ho
15 Jersey Ho
16 Jethou Ho
17 Islay Wlk
18 Upper Caldy Wlk
19 Caldy Wlk
20 Alderney Ho
21 Gulland Wlk
22 Nightingale Rd
23 Upper Gulland Wlk
24 Church Rd
25 Oransay Rd
26 Canonbury Yd E

B3 1 Pearfield Ho
2 Larchfield Ho
3 Beresford Terr
4 Pondfield Ho
5 Ashfield Ho
6 Elmfield Ho
7 Highbury
Grove Sch
8 Samuel Rhodes Sch

B4 1 Fountain Mews
2 Woodstock Ho
3 Henson Ct
4 Taverner Sq

C1 1 Downham Ct
2 Trafalgar Point

C2 1 John Kennedy Ct
2 John Kennedy Lo
3 Ball's Pond Pl
4 Haliday Wlk
5 Queen Elizabeth Ct
6 Canonbury Hts
7 Pinnacle The
8 Threadgold Ho
9 Wakeham St
10 Saffron Ct
11 Callaby Terr
12 Tilney Gdns
13 Westcliff Ho
14 Ilford Ho
15 Ongar Ho
16 Greenhills Terr

17
Romford Ho
18 Bute Wlk
19 Upper Ramsey Wlk
20 Rona Wlk
21 Thorndike Rd
22 St Pauls Steiner Sch
C3 **1** Newington Green Prim Sch
C4 **1** Ledo Ho
2 Salween Ho
3 Prome Ho
4 Arakan Ho
5 Rangoon Ho
6 Mandalay Ho
7 Karen Ho
8 Wingate Ho
9 Jubet Ho
10 Orde Ho
11 Chindit Ho
12 Mabel Thornton Ho
13 Crawshay Ho
14 Avon Ho
15 Connaught Mans
16 Jonson Ho
17 Herrick Ho
18 Donne Ho
19 Thirlmere Ho
20 Grasmere Ho
21 Copper La

16
A1 **1** Dorchester Ct
2 Wareham Ho
3 Dorset Ct
4 Stratton Ct
5 Swanage Ct
6 Blandford Ct
7 Portland Ct
8 Oscar Faber Pl
9 Metropolitan Bsns Ctr
10 Lancaster Ct
11 Palazzo Apartments
12 Watercress Pl
A2 **1** Kingsland Gn
2 Kingsland Pas
3 Metropolitan Benefit Societies Almshouses
4 Nimrod Pas
5 De Beauvoir Wrf
6 Warburton Ct
7 Buckingham Mews
8 Aztec Ct
9 Kerridge Ct
10 Isabella Mews
11 St Jude & St Paul's CE Prim Sch
12 De Beauvoir Prim Sch
13 Our Lady & St Joseph RC Prim Sch
14 Childrens House Upper Sch
A3 **1** Hewling Ho
2 Matthias Ho
3 Port Royal Pl
4 Cressington Cl
5 King Henry's Yd
6 Bronte Ho
7 Sewell Ho
8 Lydgate Ho
9 Patmore Ho
10 Congreve Ho

11 Elton St
12 Conrad Ho
13 Southwell Ho
14 Neptune Ho
15 Campion Ho
16 Webster Ho
17 Meredith Ho
18 Beckford Ho
19 Ashley Ct
20 Hayling Ct
21 Millard Cl
22 Lydford Cl
23 Salcombe Rd
24 Truman's Rd
25 Templeton Cl
26 John Campbell Rd
27 Gillett Pl
28 Bradbury St
29 Thomas Crowell Ct
30 Shellgrove Rd
A4 **1** Londesborough Ho
2 Knebworth Ho
3 Knebworth Rd
4 Bransby Ct
5 Imperial Ave
6 Leonard Pl
7 Shakspeare Mews
8 Binyon Ho
9 Shelley Ho
10 Browning Ho
11 Burns Ho
12 Andrew Marvell Ho
13 Wycliffe Ho
14 Blake Ho
15 Marlowe Ho
16 Fletcher Ho
17 Chaucer Ct
18 St Matthias's CE Prim Sch
B1 **1** Hilborough Rd
2 Shoreditch Ct
3 Evergreen Sq
4 Wyndhams Ct
5 Festival Ct
6 Rose Ct
7 Ability Plaza
8 Briar Ct
9 Lomas Dr
10 Queensbridge Inf Sch
B2 **1** Prospect Ho
2 Woodland St
3 Crosby Wlk
4 Kirkland Wlk
5 Bowness Cl
6 Carlisle Wlk
7 Skelton Cl
8 Camerton Cl
9 Buttermere Wlk
10 Houghton Cl
11 Hayton Cl
12 Kingsland Sh Ctr
13 Springfield Ho
14 Parton Lo
15 Sanctuary Mews
16 Fenton Cl
B3 **1** Miller's Terr
2 Chow Sq
3 Drysdale Flats
4 Gateway Mews
5 Birkbeck Mews
6 Winchester Pl
B4 **1** Coronation Ave
2 Morris Blitz Ct
3 Shacklewell Ho
4 Alexandra Ct

5 Shacklewell Prim Sch
6 Forman Pl
7 Princess May Prim Sch
C1 **1** Aldington Ct
2 Bayton Ct
3 Rochford Wlk
4 Windrush Cl
5 Gayhurst Prim Sch
C2 **1** Burdon Ct
2 Thomson Ct
3 Bruno Ct
4 Thackeray Mews
5 Madinah Rd
6 Pitwell Mews
C3 **1** Kingsdown Ho
2 Glendown Ho
3 Moredown Ho
4 Blakeney Cl
5 Beeston Cl
6 Benabo Ct
7 David Devine Ho
8 Kreedman Wlk
9 Hermitage Row
10 Grafton Ct
11 Lushington Terr
12 Aspen Ct
13 Pykewell Lo
14 Albion Works Studios

17
A1 **1** Fortescue Ave
2 Pemberton Pl
3 Weston Wlk
4 Bayford St Ind Ctr
5 Bayford St
6 Sidworth St
7 Helmsley St
8 Cyntra Pl
9 Signal Ho
10 All Nations Ho
11 Vanguard Ho
A2 **1** Bohemia Pl
2 Graham Mans
3 Marvin St
4 Boscobel Ho
5 Royal Oak Ct
6 Colonnades The
7 Sylvester Ho
8 Sylvester Path
9 Doctor Spurstowe Almshouses
10 Great Eastern Bldgs
11 Sojourner-Truth Cl
A3 **1** Birchington Ho
2 Bicknor Ho
3 Boxley Ho
4 Adisham Ho
5 Cranbrook Ho
6 Marden Ho
7 Brome Ho
8 Crandale Ho
9 Cheriton Ho
10 Ditton Ho
11 Langley Ho
12 Dymchurch Ho
13 Elham Ho
14 Davina Ho
15 Pembury Pl
16 Downs Ct
17 Perrywood Ho
18 Stapplehurst Ho
19 Pegwell Ho
20 Yalding Ho

21 Northbourne Ho
22 Monkton Ho
23 Milsted Ho
24 Athlone Cl
25 Clarence Pl
26 Gould Terr
27 Quested Ct
28 Brett Pas
29 Marcon Ct
30 Appleton Ct
31 Institute Pl
A4 **1** Ross Ct
2 Downs La
3 Gaviller Pl
4 Robert Owen Lo
5 Apprentice Way
6 Arrowe Ct
7 Gilwell Ct
8 Sutton Ct
9 St Andrews Mans
10 Kinnoull Mans
11 Rowhill Mans
12 Sladen Pl
13 Mothers Sq The
14 Richborough Ho
15 Sandgate Ho
16 Sheppey Ho
B1 **1** Pitcairn Ho
2 Lyme Grove Ho
3 Shakespeare Ho
4 Upcott Ho
5 Loddiges Ho
6 Parkinson Ho
7 Sloane Ho
8 Vanbrugh Ho
9 Cambridge Pas
10 Lyttleton Ho
11 Victoria Park Ct
12 Tullis Ho
13 Fairchild Ho
14 Forsyth Ho
15 Tradescant Ho
16 Mason Ho
17 Capel Ho
18 Cordwainers Ct
19 Bridgeman Ho
20 St Thomas's Pl
21 Barclay Ho
22 Clayton Ho
23 Danby Ho
24 Sherard Ho
25 Catesby Ho
26 Petiver Ct
27 Leander Ct
28 Philip Turner Est
29 Grendon Ho
30 Shore Mews
31 Shore Bsns Ctr
32 Kendal Ho
33 Classic Mans
34 Tudor Ho
35 Park Ho
36 Enterprise Ho
37 Alpine Gr
38 Clarendon Cl
39 Rotheley Ho
40 Bernie Grant Ho
41 Orchard Prim Sch
42 St John of Jerusalem CE Prim Sch
B2 **1** Wayland Ho
2 Elvin Ho
3 Thomas Ho
4 Hockley Ho
5 Retreat Ho
6 Butfield Ho

18 A2 **295**
7 Brooksbank Ho
8 Cresset Ho
9 Brooksbank St
10 Lennox Ho
11 Milborne Ho
12 Collett Ho
13 Middlesex Pl
14 Elsdale Ho
15 Devonshire Hall
16 Brent Ho
17 Morningside Prim Sch
B3 **1** St John & St James CE Prim Sch
2 City Academy, Hackney The
C1 **1** Stuart Ho
2 Gascoyne Ho
3 Chelsfield Point
4 Sundridge Ho
5 Banbury Ho
6 Lauriston Ho
7 Mossbourne Victoria Park Acad
C2 **1** Musgrave Ho
2 Cheyney Ho
3 Haynes Ho
4 Warner Ho
5 Gilby Ho
6 Gadsden Ho
7 Risley Ho
8 Baycliffe Ho
9 Sheldon Ho
10 Offley Ho
11 Latimer Ho
12 Ribstone Ho
13 Salem Ho
14 Fieldwick Ho
15 Lever Ct
16 Matson Ho
17 Wilding Ho
18 Rennell Ho
19 Dycer Ho
20 Granard Ho
21 Whitelock Ho
22 Harrowgate Ho
23 Cass Ho
24 Lofts on the Park
25 Heathcote Point
26 Ravenscroft Point
27 Vanner Point
28 Hensley Point
29 San Ho
30 Berger Prim Sch
31 Cardinal Pole RC Sch
C4 **1** Cromford Path
2 Longford Ct
3 Overbury Ho
4 Heanor Ct
5 Wharfedale Ct
6 Ladybower Ct
7 Ilkeston Ct
8 Derby Ct
9 Rushmore Cres
10 Blackwell Cl
11 Belper Ct
12 Rushmore Prim Sch

18
A2 **1** Chigwell Ct
2 Wellday Ho

3 Selman Ho
4 Vaine Ho
5 Trower Ho
6 St Dominic's Catholic Prim Sch

A3 **7** Ickburgh Sch

B2 **1** Mallard Cl
2 Merriam Ave
3 Gainsborough St
4 Palace Cl
5 St Anthony's Cl
6 Trowbridge Est

B3 **7** Wick Village

19

C1 **1** Service Route No 2
2 Service Route No 3
3 Newham Sixth Form Coll (Stratford Ctr)

C4 **1** Mulberry Ct
2 Rosewood Ct
3 Gean Ct
4 Blackthorn Ct
5 Cypress Ct

20

C4 **1** Carlyle Rd
2 Bernard Shaw Ho
3 Longlents Ho
4 Mordaunt Ho
5 Wilmers Ct
6 Stonebridge Ctr
7 Shakespeare Ave
8 Southcroft
9 Shrewsbury Rd
10 Orchid Mews

21

A3 **1** Futters Ct
2 Barrett Ct
3 Elms The
4 Fairlight Ct
B3 **1** New Crescent Yd
2 Harlesden Plaza
3 St Josephs Ct
4 Jubilee Cl
5 Ellery Cl

22

B1 **1** Princess Alice Ho
2 Yoxall Ho
3 Yorkley Ho
4 Northaw Ho
5 Oakham Ho
6 Markyate Ho
7 Letchmore Ho
8 Pagham Ho
9 Quendon Ho
10 Redbourn Ho
11 Ketton Ho
12 Hillman Dr
C2 **1** Westfield Ct
2 Tropical Ct
3 Chamberlayne Mans
4 Quadrant The
5 Queens Park Ct
6 Warfield Yd
7 Regent St
8 Cherrytree Ho

9 Artisan Mews
10 Artisan Quarter

23

A1 **1** Sycamore Wlk
2 Westgate Bsns Ctr
3 Buspace Studios
4 Bosworth Ho
5 Golborne Gdns
6 Appleford Ho
7 Adair Twr
8 Gadsden Ho
9 Southam Ho
10 Norman Butler Ho
11 Thompson Ho
12 Wells Ho
13 Paul Ho
14 Olive Blythe Ho
15 Katherine Ho
16 Breakwell Ct
17 Pepler Ho
18 Edward Kennedy Ho
19 Winnington Ho
20 Queen's Park Prim Sch
21 Ark Brunel Prim Acad
22 St Mary's RC Prim Sch
23 St Thomas' CE Prim Sch
A2 **1** Selby Sq
2 Severn Ave
3 Stansbury Sq
4 Tolhurst Dr
5 John Fearon Wlk
6 Mundy Ho
7 Macfarren Ho
8 Bantock Ho
9 Banister Ho
10 Batten Ho
11 Croft Ho
12 Courtville Ho
13 Mounsey Ho
14 Bliss Mews
15 Symphony Mews
B1 **1** Octavia Mews
2 Russell's Wharf
3 Western Ho
4 Kelly Mews
5 Queen Elizabeth II Jubilee Sch
B2 **1** Boyce Ho
2 Farnaby Ho
3 Danby Ho
4 Purday Ho
5 Naylor Ho
6 Leeve Ho
7 Longhurst Ho
8 Harrington Ct
9 Mulberry Ct
10 Kilburn Ho
11 Carlton Vale Inf Sch
B3 **1** Claremont Ct
2 William Saville Ho
3 Western Ct
4 Bond Ho
5 Crone Ct
6 Wood Ho
7 Winterleys
8 Carlton Ho
9 Fiona Ct
10 Kilburn Park Sch The
C1 **1** Westside Ct

3 Byron Mews
4 Sutherland Ct
5 Fleming Cl
6 Hermes Cl
7 St Peter's CE Prim Sch
C2 **1** Pentland Rd
2 Nelson Cl
3 Pavilion Ct
4 Masefield Ho
5 Austen Ho
6 Fielding Ho
7 Argo Bsns Ctr
8 John Ratcliffe Ho
9 Wymering Mews
10 City of Westminster Coll, Queens Park Ctr
11 Essendine Prim Sch
C3 **1** Wells Ct
2 Cambridge Ct
3 Ely Ct
4 Durham Ct
5 St Augustine's CE High Sch
6 Sch of the Islamic Republic of Iran The
C4 **1** Ryde Ho
2 Glengall Pass
3 Leith Yd
4 Daynor Ho
5 Varley Ho
6 Sandby Ho
7 Colas Mews
8 Bishopsdale Ho
9 Lorton Ho
10 Marshwood Ho
11 Ribblesdale Ho
12 Holmesdale Ho
13 Kilburn Vale Est
14 Kilburn Bridge
15 Coll of NW London
16 St Mary's Kilburn CE Prim Sch

24

A2 **1** Pimlico Wlk
2 Aske Ho
3 Hathaway Ho
4 Haberdasher Pl
5 Fairchild Ho
6 Burtt Ho
7 Enfield Cloisters
8 McGregor Ct
9 Royal Oak Ct
10 Hoxton Mkt
11 Bath Pl
12 Chapel Pl
13 Standard Pl
14 Cleeve Workshops
15 Cleeve Ho
16 Printing House Yd
17 Perseverance Works
18 Crooked Billet Yd
19 Drysdale Ho
20 Castlefrank Ho
21 School App
22 Basing House Yd
23 Mail Coach Yd
24 St Monica's RC Prim Sch
25 Symister Mews
26 Hackney Com Coll
B2 **1** Gorsuch Pl
2 Strout's Pl
3 Vaughan Est
4 George Loveless Ho
5 Baroness Rd
6 James Brine Ho
7 Arthur Wade Ho
8 Robert Owen Ho

A3 **1** Bracer Ho
2 Scorton Ho
3 Fern Cl
4 Macbeth Ho
5 Oberon Ho
6 Buckland Ct
7 Crondall Ct
8 Osric Path
9 Caliban Twr
10 Celia Ho
11 Juliet Ho
12 Bacchus Wlk
13 Malcolm Ho
14 Homefield St
15 Crondall Pl
16 Blanca Ho
17 Miranda Ho
18 Falstaff Ho
19 Charmian Ho
20 Myrtle Wlk
21 Arden Ho
22 Sebastian Ho
23 Stanway Ct
24 Jerrold St
25 Rosalind Ho
26 Cordelia Ho
27 Monteagle Ct
28 John Parry Ct
29 James Anderson Ct
30 Ben Jonson Ct
31 Sara Lane Ct
32 Walbrook Ct
33 Hoxton Garden Prim Sch
A4 **1** Portelet Ct
2 Trinity Ct
3 Rozel Ct
4 St Helier Ct
5 Corbiere Ho
6 Kenning Ho
7 Higgins Ho
8 Cavell Ho
9 Girling Ho
10 Fulcher Ho
11 Francis Ho
12 Norris Ho
13 Kempton Ho
14 Nesham Ho
15 Crossbow Ho
16 Catherine Ho
17 Strale Ho
18 Horner Hos
19 Stringer Hos
20 Whitmore Ho
21 Nightingale Ho
22 Wilmer Gdns
23 Arrow Ho
24 Archer Ho
25 Meriden Ho
26 Rover Ho
27 Bowyer Ho
28 Tiller Ho
29 Canalside Studios
30 Kleine Wharf
31 Benyon Wharf
32 Quebec Wharf
33 Belvedere Ct
34 Portfleet Pl
35 Hackney New Sch

9 Sivill Ho
10 Georgina Gdns
11 Old Market Sq
12 Cuff Point
13 Bakers Rents
14 Leopold Bldgs
15 Dunmore Point
16 Wingfield Ho
17 Gascoigne Pl
18 Mandela Ho
19 Virginia Rd
20 Briggs Ho
21 Packenham Ho
22 Gowan Ho
23 Kirton Gdns
24 Chambord Ho
25 Ducal St
26 Strickland Ho
27 Alliston Ho
28 Gibralter Wlk
29 Equity Sq
30 Shacklewell St
31 Rochelle St
32 Sonning Ho
33 Culham Ho
34 Hurley Ho
35 Palissy St
36 Taplow Ho
37 Chertsey Ho
38 Sunbury Ho
39 Sunbury Workshops
40 Datchett Ho
41 Hocker St
42 Coll Sharp Ct
43 Marlow Studio Workshops
44 Marlow Ho
45 Shiplake Ho
46 Wargrave Ho
47 Iffley Ho
48 Virginia Prim Sch
49 Green Spring Academy Shoreditch
50 Columbia Prim Sch
B3 **1** Queensbridge Ct
2 Godwin Ho
3 Kent Ct
4 Brunswick Ho
5 Weymouth Ct
6 Sovereign Mews
7 Dunloe Ct
8 Cremer Bsns Ctr
9 James Hammett Ho
10 Allgood St
11 Horatio St
12 Cadell Ho
13 Horatio Ho
14 Shipton Ho
15 Haggerston Sch
16 Randal Cremer Prim Sch
B4 **1** Hilborough Ct
2 Scriven Ct
3 Livermere Ct
4 Angravc Ct
5 Angrave Pas
6 Benfleet Ct
7 Belford Ho
8 Orme Ho
9 Clemson Ho
10 Longman Ho
11 Lowther Ho
12 Lovelace Ho
13 Harlowe Ho
14 Pamela Ho

- 13 Samuel Ho
- 14 Acton Ho
- 15 Loanda Cl
- 16 Phoenix Cl
- 17 Richardson Cl
- 18 Thrasher Cl
- 19 Mary Secole Cl
- 20 Canal Path
- 21 Pear Tree Cl
- 22 Hebden Ct
- 23 Charlton Ct
- 24 Laburnum Ct
- 25 Mansfield Ct
- 26 Garden Pl
- 27 Amber Wharf
- 28 Haggerston Studios
- 29 Bridge Acad The

C1
- 1 Bentworth Ct
- 2 Hawksmoor Pl
- 3 Kerbela St
- 4 Fuller Cl
- 5 Kinsham Ho
- 6 Menotti St
- 7 Barwell Ho
- 8 Grimsby St
- 9 Reflection Ho
- 10 Fleet Street Hill
- 11 Bratley St
- 12 Weaver Ho
- 13 Cornerstone Ct
- 14 Stuttle Ho
- 15 McGlashon Ho
- 16 John Pritchard Ho
- 17 Thomas Buxton Prim Sch
- 18 St Anne's RC Prim Sch
- 19 William Davis Prim Sch

C2
- 1 Providence Yd
- 2 Lygon Ho
- 3 Brabner Ho
- 4 Delta St
- 5 Delta Point
- 6 Tillet Way
- 7 Mullet Gdns
- 8 Lampern Sq
- 9 Kite Pl
- 10 Elver Gdns
- 11 Cobden Ho
- 12 Eversley Ho
- 13 Lorden Wlk
- 14 Rapley Ho
- 15 Dence Ho
- 16 McKinnon Wood Ho
- 17 Satchwell Rd
- 18 Dickinson Ho
- 19 Hutton Ho
- 20 Simmons Ho
- 21 Swinton Ho
- 22 Yates Ho
- 23 Johnson Ho
- 24 Jeremy Bentham House
- 25 Waring Ho
- 26 St James Ct
- 27 Ebony Ho
- 28 Azure Ho
- 29 Westhope Ho
- 30 Hague St
- 31 Elizabeth Selby Inf Sch
- 32 Lawdale Jun Sch

C3
- 1 London Terr
- 2 Sturdee Ho
- 3 Maude Ho
- 4 Haig Ho
- 5 Jellicoe Ho
- 6 Ropley St
- 7 Guinness Trust Bldgs
- 8 Ion Ct
- 9 Columbia Rd
- 10 Moye Cl
- 11 Morrel Ct
- 12 Courtauld Ho
- 13 Drummond Ho
- 14 Gurney Ho
- 15 Atkinson Ho
- 16 Halley Ho
- 17 Goldsmith's Sq
- 18 Shahjalal Ho
- 19 Ken Wilson Ho
- 20 April Ct
- 21 Crofts Ho
- 22 Sebright Ho
- 23 Beechwood Ho
- 24 Gillman Ho
- 25 Cheverell Ho
- 26 Besford Ho
- 27 Dinmont Ho
- 28 Elizabeth Mews
- 29 Sebright Pas
- 30 Wyndham Deedes Ho
- 31 Sheppard Ho
- 32 Mary James Ho
- 33 Hadrian St
- 34 Blythendale Ho
- 35 George Vale Ho
- 36 Lion Mills
- 37 St Peter's Ave
- 38 Pritchard Ho
- 39 Sebright Sch

C4
- 1 Broke Wlk
- 2 Rochemont Wlk
- 3 Marlborough Ave
- 4 Rivington Wlk
- 5 Magnin Cl
- 6 Gloucester Sq
- 7 Woolstone Ho
- 8 Marsworth Ho
- 9 Cheddington Ho
- 10 Linslade Ho
- 11 Cosgrove Ho
- 12 Blisworth Ho
- 13 Eleanor Ct
- 14 Wistow Ho
- 15 Muscott Ho
- 16 Boxmoor Ho
- 17 Linford Ho
- 18 Pendley Ho
- 19 Northchurch Ho
- 20 Debdale Ho
- 21 Broadway Market Mews
- 22 Welshpool Ho
- 23 Ada Ho
- 24 St Paul's with St Michael's CE Prim Sch
- 25 Welshpool St

25

A1
- 1 Rochester Ct
- 2 Weaver Ct
- 3 Greenheath Bsns Ctr
- 4 Glass St
- 5 Herald St
- 6 Northesk Ho
- 7 Codrington Ho
- 8 Heathpool Ct
- 9 Mocatta Ho
- 10 Harvey Ho
- 11 Blackwood Ho
- 12 Rutherford Ho
- 13 Bullen Ho
- 14 Fremantle Ho
- 15 Pellew Ho
- 16 Ashington Ho
- 17 Dinnington Ho
- 18 Bartholomew Sq
- 19 Steeple Ct
- 20 Orion Ho
- 21 Fellbrigg St
- 22 Hague Prim Sch
- 23 Eagle Ho
- 24 Sovereign Ho
- 25 Redmill Ho
- 26 Berry Ho
- 27 Grindall Ho
- 28 Collingwood Ho
- 29 Stewart Headlam Prim Sch

A2
- 1 Charles Dickens Ho
- 2 Adrian Bolt Ho
- 3 William Rathbone Ho
- 4 Southwood Smith House
- 5 Rushmead
- 6 William Channing House
- 7 John Cartwright Ho
- 8 Charles Darwin Ho
- 9 Thomas Burt Ho
- 10 John Fielden Ho
- 11 Gwilym Maries Ho
- 12 Joseph Priestley House
- 13 Wear Pl
- 14 John Nettleford Ho
- 15 Thornaby Ho
- 16 Stockton Ho
- 17 Barnard Ho
- 18 Gainford Ho
- 19 Stapleton Ho
- 20 James Middleton House
- 21 Kedleston Wlk
- 22 Queen Margaret Flats
- 23 Hollybush Ho
- 24 Horwood Ho
- 25 Norden Ho
- 26 Newcourt Ho
- 27 Seabright St
- 28 Viaduct Pl
- 29 Sunlight Sq
- 30 Providence Row Cl
- 31 Oaklands Sch
- 32 Raine's Foundation Lower Sch
- 33 Beatrice Tate Sch

A3
- 1 Dinmont St
- 2 Marian St
- 3 Claredale Ho
- 4 Keeling Ho
- 5 Maple St
- 6 Winkley St
- 7 Temple Dwellings
- 8 Argos Ho
- 9 Helen Ho
- 10 Lysander Ho
- 11 Antenor Ho
- 12 Paris Ho
- 13 Nestor Ho
- 14 Hector Ho
- 15 Ajax Ho
- 16 Achilles Ho
- 17 Priam Ho
- 18 Peabody Est
- 19 Felix St
- 20 Cambridge Cres
- 21 Peterley Bsns Ctr
- 22 Beckwith Ho
- 23 Brookfield Ho
- 24 Parminter Ind Est
- 25 Ted Roberts Ho
- 26 Cambridge Ct
- 27 Millennium Pl
- 28 William Caslon Ho
- 29 Hugh Platt Ho
- 30 West St
- 31 Mayfield Ho
- 32 Apollo Ho
- 33 Tanners Yd
- 34 Teesdale St

A4
- 1 Welshpool St
- 2 Broadway Ho
- 3 Regents Wharf
- 4 London Wharf
- 5 Warburton Ho
- 6 Warburton St
- 7 Triangle Rd
- 8 Warburton Rd
- 9 Williams Ho
- 10 Booth Cl
- 11 Albert Cl
- 12 King Edward Mans
- 13 Victoria Bldgs
- 14 Andrews Wharf
- 15 London Fields Prim Sch
- 16 Triangle The
- 17 Com Coll Hackney The
- 18 Excellence Prim Sch

B1
- 1 William's Bldgs
- 2 Donegal Ho
- 3 Pelican Pas
- 4 Frederick Charrington Ho
- 5 Wickford Ho
- 6 Braintree Ho
- 7 Doveton Ho
- 8 Doveton St
- 9 Cephas Ho
- 10 Sceptre Ho
- 11 Bancroft Ho
- 12 Stothard St
- 13 Redclyf Ho
- 14 Winkworth Cotts
- 15 Amiel St
- 16 Hadleigh Ho
- 17 Hadleigh Cl
- 18 Ryder Ho
- 19 Kenton St
- 20 Colebert Ho
- 21 Ibbott St
- 22 Rickman Ho
- 23 Rickman St
- 24 Stothard Ho
- 25 Barbanel Ho
- 26 Stannard Cotts
- 27 St Peters Ct
- 28 Rennie Cotts
- 29 Pemell Cl
- 30 Pemell Ho
- 31 Leatherdale St
- 32 Gouldman Ho
- 33 Lamplighter Cl
- 34 Sherren Ho
- 35 Marlborough Lo
- 36 Hamilton Lo
- 38 Montgomery Lo
- 39 Cleveland Gr
- 40 Cromwell Lo
- 41 Bardsey Pl
- 42 Charrington Ho
- 43 Hayfield Yd
- 44 Allport Mews
- 45 Colin Winter Ho
- 46 John Scurr Prim Sch

B2
- 1 Mulberry Ho
- 2 Gretton Ho
- 3 Merceron Ho
- 4 Montfort Ho
- 5 Westbrook Ho
- 6 Sugar Loaf Wlk
- 7 Museum Ho
- 8 Burnham Est
- 9 Globe Terr
- 10 Moravian St
- 11 Shepton Hos
- 12 Mendip Hos
- 13 Academy Ct
- 14 Pepys Ho
- 15 Swinburne Ho
- 16 Moore Ho
- 17 Morris Ho
- 18 Burns Ho
- 19 Milton Ho
- 20 Whitman Ho
- 21 Shelley Ho
- 22 Keats Ho
- 23 Dawson Ho
- 24 Bradbeer Ho
- 25 Forber Ho
- 26 Hughes Ho
- 27 Silvester Ho
- 28 Rogers Est
- 29 Pavan Ct
- 30 Stafford Cripps Ho
- 31 Sidney Godley (VC) House
- 32 Butler Ho
- 33 Butler St
- 34 Thorne Ho
- 35 Bevin Ho
- 36 Tuscan Ho
- 37 Globe Prim Sch
- 38 Bangabandhu Prim Sch
- 39 Bonner Prim Sch

B3
- 1 Evesham Ho
- 2 James Campbell House
- 3 Thomas Hollywood House
- 4 James Docherty Ho
- 5 Ebenezer Mussel House
- 6 Jameson Ct
- 7 Edinburgh Cl
- 8 Roger Dowley Ct
- 9 Sherbrooke Ho
- 10 Calcraft Ho
- 11 Burrard Ho
- 12 Dundas Ho
- 13 Ponsonby Ho
- 14 Barnes Ho
- 15 Paget Ho
- 16 Maitland Ho
- 17 Chesil Ct
- 18 Reynolds Ho
- 19 Cleland Ho
- 20 Goodrich Ho

30 Kerscott Ho
31 Southcott Ho
32 Birchdown Ho
33 Upcott Ho
34 Langmead Ho
35 Limscott Ho
36 Northleigh Ho
37 Huntshaw Ho
38 Chagford Ho
39 Ashcombe Ho
40 Shillingford Ho
41 Patrick Connolly Gdns
42 Lester Ct
43 Franklin St
44 Taft Way
45 Washington Cl
46 Veronica Ho
47 William Guy Gdns
48 Denbury Ho
49 Holsworthy Ho
50 Padstone Ho
51 Old Palace Prim Sch
52 Ian Mikardo High Sch
C1 1 Crescent Court Bsns Ctr
2 Ashmead Bsns Ctr
3 Forward Bsns Ctr The
C4 1 Victoria Mills
2 Hallings Wharf Studios
3 Poland Ho
4 Peter Heathfield Ho
5 Burford Rd
6 John F Kennedy Sch

28
A1 1 Lantry Ct
2 Rosemount Ct
3 Moreton Twr
4 Acton Central Ind Est
5 Rufford Twr
6 Narrow St
7 Mount Pl
8 Sidney Miller Ct
9 Mill Hill Terr
10 Cheltenham Pl
11 Mill Hill Gr
12 Benjamin Ho
13 Arlington Ct
14 Lombard Ct
15 Steyne Ho
16 Ealing, Hammersmith and West London Coll
B1 1 Rectory Rd
2 Derwentwater Mans
3 Market Pl
4 Hooper's Mews
5 Cromwell Pl
6 Locarno Rd
7 Edgecote Cl
8 Harleyford Manor
9 Coopers Ct
10 Avingdor Ct
11 Steyne Ho
B3 1 Avon Ct
2 Bromley Lo
3 Walter Ct
4 Lynton Terr
5 Acton Ho

6 Fells Haugh
7 Springfield Ct
8 Tamarind Ct
9 Lynton Ct
10 Aspen Ct
11 Pegasus Ct
12 Friary Park Ct
C3 1 Rosebank Gdns
2 Rosebank
3 Edinburgh Ho
4 Western Ct
5 Kilronan

29
B1 1 Eastvale
2 Vale Ct
3 Broad Passage
C1 1 Queensmill Sch

30
A1 1 Arlington Ho
2 Lugard Ho
3 Shabana Ct
4 Sitarey Ct
5 Oaklands Ct
6 Davenport Mews
A2 1 Abercrombie Ho
2 Bathurst Ho
3 Brisbane Ho
4 Bentinck Ho
5 Ellenborough Ho
6 Lawrence Ct
7 Mackenzie Ct
8 Carteret Ho
9 Calvert Ho
10 Winthrop Ho
11 Auckland Ho
12 Blaxland Ho
13 Havelock Ct
14 Hargraves Ho
15 Hudson Ct
16 Phipps Ho
17 Lawson Ho
18 Hastings Ho
19 Wolfe Ho
20 Malabar Ct
21 Charnock Ho
22 Canning Ho
23 Cornwallis Ho
24 Commonwealth Ave
25 Champlain Ho
26 Grey Ho
27 Durban Ho
28 Baird Ho
29 Campbell Ho
30 Mitchell Ho
31 Denham Ho
32 Mackay Ho
33 Evans Ho
34 Davis Ho
35 Mandela Ho
A3 1 Holborn Ho
2 Clement Danes Ho
3 Vellacott Ho
4 O'Driscoll Ho
5 King Ho
6 Daley Ho
7 Selma Ho
8 Garrett Ho
B1 1 Linden Ct
2 Frithville Ct
3 Blomfield Mans
4 Poplar Mews
5 Hopgood St
6 Westwood Ho
7 Stanlake Mews

8 Stanlake Villas
9 Alexandra Mans
B3 1 Latimer Ind Est
2 Pankhurst Ho
3 Quadrangle The
4 Nightingale Ho
5 Gordon Ct
6 Ducane Cl
7 Browning Ho
8 Pavilion Terr
9 Ivebury Ct
10 Olympic Ho
B4 1 Galleywood Ho
2 Edgcott Ho
3 Cuffley Ho
4 Addlestone Ho
5 Hockliffe Ho
6 Sarratt Ho
7 Firle Ho
8 Sutton Est The
9 Terling Ho
10 Danes Ho
11 Udimore Ho
12 Vange Ho
13 Binbrook Ho
14 Yeadon Ho
15 Yatton Ho
16 Yarrow Ho
17 Clement Ho
18 Danebury
19 Coronation Ct
20 Calderon Pl
21 St Quintin Gdns
22 Princess Louise Wk
C1 1 St Katherine's Wlk
2 Dorrit Ho
3 Pickwick Ho
4 Dombey Ho
5 Caranday Villas
6 Mortimer Ho
7 Nickleby Ho
8 Stebbing Ho
9 Boxmoor Ho
10 Poynter Ho
11 Swanscombe Ho
12 Darnley Terr
13 Norland Ho
14 Hume Ho
15 Boundary Ho
16 Norland Rd
17 Helix Ct
C2 1 Frinstead Ho
2 Hurstway Wlk
3 Testerton Wlk
4 Grenfell Wlk
5 Grenfell Twr
6 Barandon Wlk
7 Treadgold Ho
8 St Clements Ct
9 Willow Way
10 Florence Ho
11 Dora Ho
12 Carton Ho
13 Agnes Ho
14 Marley Ho
15 Estella Ho
16 Waynflete Sq
17 Pippin Ho
18 Baseline Business Studios
19 St Francis of Assisi RC Prim Sch
20 Nicholas Rd
C3 1 Kelfield Ct
2 Downing Ho
3 Crosfield Ct
4 Robinson Ho

5 Scampston Mews
6 Girton Villas
7 Ray Ho
8 Walmer Ho
9 Goodrich Ct
10 Arthur Ct
11 Whitstable Ho
12 Kingsnorth Ho
13 Bridge Cl
14 Prospect Ho
15 St Marks Rd
16 Whitchurch Ho
17 Blechynden Ho
18 Waynflete Sq
19 Bramley Ho
20 Dixon Ho
21 Oxford Gardens Prim Sch
22 Bassett House Sch
23 Kensington Aldridge Acad
C4 1 Treverton Twr
2 Raymede Twr
3 Bruce Ho
4 Balfour Ho
5 Burleigh Ho
6 Sion-Manning RC Sch for Girls
7 St Charles RC Prim Sch
8 St Charles RC Sixth Form Coll

31
A3 1 Malton Mews
2 Lancaster Lo
3 Manning Ho
4 Galsworthy Ho
5 Hudson Ho
6 Cambourne Mews
7 Upper Talbot Wlk
8 Kingsdown Cl
9 Lower Clarendon Wlk
10 Talbot Grove Ho
11 Clarendon Wlk
12 Upper Clarendon Wlk
13 Camelford Wlk
14 Upper Camelford Wlk
15 Camelford Ct
16 Thomas Jone Sch
17 Notting Hill Prep Sch
A4 1 Murchison Ho
2 Macaulay Ho
3 Chesterton Ho
4 Chiltern Ho
5 Lionel Ho
6 Watts Ho
7 Wheatstone Ho
8 Telford Ho
9 Golborne Mews
10 Millwood St
11 St Columb's Ho
12 Norfolk Mews
13 Lionel Mews
14 Kensington & Chelsea Coll
15 Bevington Prim Sch
16 Sion-Manning RC Sch for Girls
17 Lloyd Williamson Sch The
18 Athlone Gate
B3 1 Silvester Ho

2 Golden Cross Mews
3 Tavistock Mews
4 Clydesdale Ho
5 Colville Prim Sch
6 Melchester
7 Pinehurst Ct
8 Denbigh Ho
B4 1 Blagrove Rd
2 All Saints Ho
3 Tavistock Ho
4 Leamington Ho
C3 1 Shottsford
2 Tolchurch
3 Casterbridge
4 Sandbourne
5 Anglebury
6 Weatherbury
7 Westbourne Gr Mews
8 Rosehart Mews
9 Viscount Ct
10 Hereford Mans
11 Hereford Mews
12 St Mary of the Angels RC Prim Sch
C4 1 Ascot Ho
2 Ashgrove Ct
3 Lockbridge Ct
4 Swallow Ct
5 Nightingale Lo
6 Hammond Lo
7 Penfield Lo
8 Harvey Lo
9 Hunter Lo
10 Barnard Lo
11 Falcon Lo
12 Johnson Lo
13 Livingstone Lo
14 Nuffield Lo
15 Finch Lo
16 Polesworth Ho
17 Oversley Ho
18 Derrycombe Ho
19 Buckshead Ho
20 Combe Ho
21 Culham Ho
22 Dainton Ho
23 Devonport Ho
24 Honwell Ho
25 Truro Ho
26 Sunderland Ho
27 Stonehouse Ho
28 Riverford Ho
29 Portishead Ho
30 Mickleton Ho
31 Keyham Ho
32 Moulsford Ho
33 Shrewsbury Mews
34 St Stephen's Mews
35 Westway Lo
36 Langley Ho
37 Brindley Ho
38 Radway Ho
39 Astley Ho
40 Willow Ct
41 Larch Ct
42 Elm Ct
43 Beech Ct
44 Worcester Ct
45 Union Ct
46 Leicester Ct

37 Kennet Ct
40 Oxford Ct
40 Fazerley Ct

32

A1 1 China Ct
2 Wellington Terr
3 Stevedore St
4 Portland Sq
5 Reardon Ho
6 Lowder Ho
7 Meeting House Alley
8 Farthing Fields
9 Oswell Ho
10 Park Lo
11 Doughty Ct
12 Inglefield Sq
13 Chopin's Ct
14 Welsh Ho
15 Hilliard Ho
16 Clegg St
17 Tasman Ho
18 Ross Ho
19 Wapping Dock St
20 Bridewell Pl
21 New Tower Bldgs
22 Tower Bldgs
23 Chimney Ct
24 Jackman Ho
25 Fenner Ho
26 Franklin Ho
27 Frobisher Ho
28 Flinders Ho
29 Chancellor Ho
30 Beechey Ho
31 Reardon Path
32 Parry Ho
33 Vancover Ho
34 Willoughby Ho
35 Sanctuary The
36 Dundee Ct
37 Pierhead Wharf
38 Scandrett St
39 St Johns Ct

A2 1 Newton Ho
2 Richard Neale Ho
3 Maddocks Ho
4 Cornwall St
5 Brockmer Ho
6 Dellow Ho
7 Bewley Ho
8 Artichoke Hill
9 Queen Anne Terr
10 King Henry Terr
11 King Charles Terr
12 Queen Victoria Terr
13 Sovereign Ct
14 Princes Court Bsns Ctr
15 Kingsley Mews
16 Mulberry Sch for Girls

A3 1 Peter Best Ho
2 Mellish Ho
3 Porchester Ho
4 Dickson Ho
5 Joscoyne Ho
6 Silvester Ho
7 Wilton Ct
8 Sarah Ho
9 Bridgen Ho
10 Tylney Ho
11 Greenwich Ct

12 Damien Ct
13 Philson Mans
14 Siege Ho
15 Jacob Mans
16 Proud Ho
17 Sly St
18 Barnett St
19 Kinder St
20 Richard St
21 Hungerford St
22 Colstead Ho
23 Melwood Ho
24 Wicker St
25 Langdale St
26 Chapman Ho
27 Burwell Cl
28 Walford Ho
29 Welstead Ho
30 Norton Ho
31 Turnour Ho
32 Luke Ho
33 Dunch St
34 Sheridan St
35 Brinsley St
36 Spencer Way
37 Madani Girls' Sch
38 Mulberry Sch for Girls
39 Bigland Green Prim Sch
40 London Islamic Sch

A4 1 Wodeham Gdns
2 Castlemaine St
3 Court St
4 Ashfield St
5 London Hospital Dental Inst
6 Princess Alexandra School of Nursing The
7 Wodeham Gardens

B1 1 John Rennie Wlk
2 Malay Ho
3 Wainwright Ho
4 Riverside Mans
5 Shackleton Ho
6 Whitehorn Ho
7 Wavel Ct
8 Prusom's Island
9 St Peter's London Docks CE Prim Sch

B2 1 Shadwell Pl
2 Gosling Ho
3 Vogler Ho
4 Donovan Ho
5 Knowlden Ho
6 Chamberlain Ho
7 Moore Ho
8 Thornewill Ho
9 Fisher Ho
10 All Saints Ct
11 Coburg Dwellings
12 Lowood Ho
13 Solander Gdns
14 Chancery Bldgs
15 Ring Ho
16 Juniper St
17 Gordon Ho
18 West Block
19 North Block
20 South Block
21 Ikon Ho
22 Blue Gate Fields Jun & Inf Schs

B3 1 Woollon Ho
2 Dundalk Ho
3 Anne Goodman Ho

4 Newbold Cotts
5 Kerry Ho
6 Zion Ho
7 Longford Ho
8 Bromehead St
9 Athlone Ho
10 Jubilee Mans
11 Harriott Ho
12 Brayford Sq
13 Clearbrook Way
14 Rochelle Ct
15 Winterton Ho
16 Swift Ho
17 Brinsley Ho
18 Dean Ho
19 Foley Ho
20 Robert Sutton Ho
21 Montpelier Pl
22 Glastonbury Pl
23 Steel's La
24 Masters Lo
25 Stylus Apartments
26 Arta Ho
27 St Mary & St Michael Prim Sch
28 Bishop Challoner Catholic Federation of Schools
29 Morton Cl
30 James Voller Way

B4 1 Fulneck
2 Gracehill
3 Ockbrook
4 Fairfield
5 Dunstan Hos
6 Cressy Ct
7 Cressy Ho
8 Callahan Cotts
9 Lindley Ho
10 Mayo Ho
11 Wexford Ho
12 Sandhurst Ho
13 Addis Ho
14 Colverson Ho
15 Beckett Ho
16 Jarman Ho
17 Armsby Ho
18 Wingrad Ho
19 Miranda Cl
20 Drake Ho
21 Ashfield Yd
22 Magri Wlk
23 Jean Pardies Ho
24 St Vincent De Paul Ho
25 Sambrook Ho
26 Louise De Marillac House
27 Dagobert Ho
28 Le Moal Ho
29 Odette Duval Ho
30 Charles Auffray Ho
31 Boissanu Ho
32 Clichy Ho
33 Paymal Ho
34 Smithy Street Sch
35 Redlands Prim Sch
36 Cressy Ct

C1 1 Clarence Mews
2 Raleigh Ct
3 Katherine Ct
4 Woolcombes Ct
5 Tudor Ct
6 Quayside Ct
7 Princes Riverside Rd

8 Surrey Ho
9 Tideway Ho
10 Edinburgh Ct
11 Falkirk Ct
12 Byelands Cl
13 Gwent Ct
14 Lavender Ho
15 Abbotsede Rd
16 Bellamy's Ct
17 Blenheim Ct
18 Sandringham Ct
19 Hampton Ct
20 Windsor Ct
21 Balmoral Ct
22 Westminster Ct
23 Beatson Wlk
24 Peter Hills with St Mary's & St Paul's CE Sch

C2 1 Barnado Gdns
2 Roslin Ho
3 Glamis Est
4 Peabody Est
5 East Block
6 Highway Trad Ctr The
7 Highway Bsns Pk
8 Cranford Cotts
9 Ratcliffe Orch
10 Scotia Bldg
11 Mauretania Bldg
12 Compania Bldg
13 Sirius Bldg
14 Unicorn Bldg
15 Keeper Wharf

C3 1 Pattison Ho
2 St Thomas Ho
3 Arbour Ho
4 Bladen Ho
5 Antill Terr
6 Majorie Mews
7 Billing Ho
8 Dowson Ho
9 Lipton Rd
10 Chalkwell Ho
11 Corringham Ho
12 Ogilvie Ho
13 Edward Mann Cl
14 Reservoir Studios
15 Lighterman Mews
16 Tower Hamlets Coll
17 Marion Richardson Prim Sch
18 Barnado Gardens

C4 1 Roland Mews
2 Beatrice Ho
3 Morecambe Cl
4 Stepney Green Ct
5 Milrood Ho
6 Panama Ho
7 Galway Ho
8 Jacqueline Ho
9 Crown Mews
10 Caspian Ho
11 Darien Ho
12 Riga Ho
13 Flores Ho
14 Taranto Ho
15 Aden Ho
16 Master's St
17 Rosary Ct
18 Stepney Green Maths & Computing Coll

19 Sir John Cass Foundation & Redcoat CE Sec Sch
21 Seagrave Cl

33

A1 1 Edward Sq
2 Prince Regent Ct
3 Codrington Ct
4 Pennington Ct
5 Cherry Ct
6 Ash Ct
7 Beech Ct
8 Hazel Ct
9 Laurel Ct

A2 1 St Georges Sq
2 Drake Ho
3 Osprey Ho
4 Fleet Ho
5 Gainsborough Ho
6 Victory Pl
7 Challenger Ho
8 Conrad Ho
9 Lock View CE
10 Shoulder of Mutton Alley
11 Frederick Sq
12 Helena Sq
13 Elizabeth Sq
14 Sophia Sq
15 William Sq
16 Lamb Ct
17 Lockside
18 Adriatic Bldg
19 Ionian Bldg
20 Regents Gate Ho

A3 1 Hearnshaw St
2 Berry Cotts
3 Causton Cotts
4 Elizabeth Blount Ct
5 Carr St
6 Shaw Cres
7 Darnley Ho
8 Mercer's Cotts
9 Troon Ho
10 Ratcliffe Ho
11 Wakeling St
12 York Sq
13 Anglia Ho
14 Cambria Ho
15 Caledonia Ho
16 Ratcliffe La
17 Bekesbourne St
18 John Scurr Ho
19 Regents Canal Ho
20 Basin App
21 Powlesland Ct
22 Cayley Prim Sch
23 Stephen Hawking Sch
24 Dalgleish St
25 Ross Wy

A4 1 Waley St
2 Edith Ramsay Ho
3 Andaman Ho
4 Atlantic Ho
5 Pevensey Ho
6 Solent Ho
7 Lorne Ho
8 Cromarty Ho
9 Dakin Pl
10 Greaves Cotts
11 Donaghue Cotts
12 Ames Cotts
13 Waterview Ho

14 Limehouse Fields Est

32 **1** Hamilton Ho
2 Imperial Ho
3 Oriana Ho
4 Queens Ct
5 Brightlingsea Pl
6 Faraday Ho
7 Ropemaker's Fields
8 Oast Ct
9 Mitre The
10 Bate St
11 Joseph Irwin Ho
12 Padstow Ho
13 Bethlehem Ho
14 Saunders Ct
15 Roche Ho
16 Stocks Pl
17 Trinidad Ho
18 Grenada Ho
19 Kings Ho
20 Dunbar Wharf
21 Limekiln Wharf
22 Belgrave Ct
23 Eaton Ho
24 Cyril Jackson Prim Sch (North Bldg)
25 Cyril Jackson Prim Sch (South Bldg)
B3 **1** Dora Ho
2 Flansham Ho
3 Gatwick Ho
4 Ashpark Ho
5 Newdigate Ho
6 Midhurst Ho
7 Redbourne Ho
8 Southwater Cl
9 Andersens Wharf
10 Whatman Ho
11 Butler Ho
12 Fitzroy Ho
13 Salmon St
14 Mission The
15 Aithan Ho
16 Britley Ho
17 Cheadle Ho
18 Elland Ho
19 Wharf La
20 Docklands Ct
21 Park Heights Ct
22 Grosvenor Ct
23 Lime House Ct
24 Swallow Pl
25 St Anne's Trad Est
26 Stepney Greencoat CE Prim Sch The
27 Sir William Burrough Prim Sch
28 Our Lady RC Prim Sch
B4 **1** Wearmouth Ho
2 Elmslie Point
3 Grindley Ho
4 Stileman Ho
5 Wilcox Ho
6 Huddart St
7 Robeson St
8 Couzens Ho
9 Perley Ho
10 Whytlaw Ho
11 Booker Cl
12 Tunley Gn
13 Callingham Cl
14 Bowry Ho
15 Perkins Ho
16 Printon Ho
17 Tasker Ho

18 St Paul with St Luke CE Prim Sch
C2 **1** West India Ho
2 Berber Pl
3 Birchfield Ho
4 Elderfield Ho
5 Thornfield Ho
6 Gorsefield Ho
7 Arborfield Ho
8 Colborne Ho
9 East India Bldgs
10 Compass Point
11 Salter St
12 Garland Ct
13 Bogart Ct
14 Fonda Ct
15 Welles Ct
16 Rogers Ct
17 Premier Pl
18 Kelly Ct
19 Flynn Ct
20 Mary Jones Ho
21 Cannon Dr
22 Horizon Bldg
23 Our Lady & St Joseph Catholic Prim Sch
24 University of Cumbria London
C3 **1** Landin Ho
2 Thomas Road Ind Est
3 Vickery's Wharf
4 Abbotts Wharf
5 Limehouse Ct
6 Charlesworth Ho
7 Gurdon Ho
8 Trendell Ho
9 Menteath Ho
10 Minchin Ho
11 Donne Ho
12 Old School Sq
13 Anglesey Ho
14 Gough Wlk
15 Baring Ho
16 Gladstone Ho
17 Hopkins Ho
18 Granville Ho
19 Overstone Ho
20 Pusey Ho
21 Russell Ho
22 Stanley Ho
23 Edward Mills Wy
C4 **1** Bredel Ho
2 Linton Ho
3 Matthews Ho
4 Woodcock Ho
5 Limborough Ho
6 Maydwell Ho
7 Underhill Ho
8 Meyrick Ho
9 Ambrose Ho
10 Richardson Ho
11 Carpenter Ho
12 Robinson Ho
13 Bellmaker Ct
14 Lime Tree Ct
15 Bracken Ho
16 Bramble Ho
17 Berberis Ho
18 Bilberry Ho
19 Ladyfern Ho
20 Rosebay Ho
21 Invicta Cl
22 Phoenix Bsns Ctr
23 Metropolitan Cl
24 Busbridge Ho

25 St Paul's Way Com Sch
26 Stebon Prim Sch
27 Ursula Gould Wy

34
A2 **1** Westcott Ho
2 Corry Ho
3 Malam Gdns
4 Blomfield Ho
5 Devitt Ho
6 Leyland Ho
7 Wigram Ho
8 Willis Ho
9 Balsam Ho
10 Finch's Ct
11 Poplar Bath St
12 Lawless St
13 Storey Ho
14 Abbot Ho
15 Woodall Cl
16 Landon Wlk
17 Goodhope Ho
18 Goodfaith Ho
19 Winant Ho
20 Goodspeed Ho
21 Lubbock Ho
22 Goodwill Ho
23 Martindale Ho
24 Holmsdale Ho
25 Norwood Ho
26 Constant Ho
27 Tower Hamlets Coll
A3 **1** Colebrook Ho
2 Essex Ho
3 Salisbury Ho
4 Maidstone Ho
5 Osterley Ho
6 Norwich Ho
7 Clarissa Ho
8 Elgin Ho
9 Shaftesbury Lo
10 Shepherd Ho
11 Jeremiah St
12 Elizabeth Ct
13 Chilcot Cl
14 Fitzgerald Ho
15 Vesey Path
16 Ennis Ho
17 Kilmore Ho
18 Cygnet House N
19 Cygnet House S
20 Lansbury Lawrence Prim Sch
21 Bygrove Prim Sch
22 Mayflower Prim Sch
23 Tower Hamlets Coll
A4 **1** Sumner Ho
2 David Hewitt Ho
3 St Gabriels Ct
4 Limehouse Cut
5 Colmans Wharf
6 Foundary Ho
7 Radford Ho
8 Manorfield Prim Sch
9 St Saviour's CE Prim Sch
10 Pioneer Cl
B1 **1** Lumina Bldg
2 Nova Ct W
3 Nova Ct E
4 Aurora Bldg
5 Arran Ho
6 Kintyre Ho
7 Vantage Mews

8 Managers St
9 Horatio Pl
10 Concordia Wharf
B2 **1** Discovery Ho
2 Mountague Pl
3 Virginia Ho
4 Collins Ho
5 Lawless Ho
6 Carmichael Ho
7 Commodore Ho
8 Mermaid Ho
9 Bullivant St
10 Anderson Ho
11 Mackrow Wlk
12 Robin Hood Gdns
13 Prestage Wy
14 Woolmore Prim Sch
B3 **1** Glenkerry Ho
2 Carradale Ho
3 Langdon Ho
4 Balfron Twr
5 St Frideswides Mews
6 Tabard Ct
7 Delta Bldg
8 Findhorn St
9 Kilbrennan Ho
10 Thistle Ho
11 Heather Ho
12 Tartan Ho
13 Sharman Ho
14 Trident Ho
15 Wharf View Ct
16 Culloden Prim Sch
B4 **1** Mills Gr
2 St Michaels Ct
3 Duncan Ct
C2 **1** Quixley St
2 Romney Ho
3 Pumping Ho
4 Switch Ho
5 Wingfield Ct
6 Explorers Ct
7 Sexton Ct
8 Keel Ct
9 Bridge Ct
10 Sail Ct
11 Settlers Ct
12 Pilgrims Mews
13 Studley Ct
14 Wotton Ct
15 Cape Henry Ct
16 Bartholomew Ct
17 Adventurers Ct
18 Susan Constant Ct
19 Atlantic Ct
C3 **1** Lansbury Gdns
2 Theseus Ho
3 Adams Ho
4 Jones Ho
5 Sam March Ho
6 Araplies Ho
7 Athenia Ho
8 Julius Ho
9 Jervis Bay Ho
10 Helen Mackay Ho
11 Gaze Ho
12 Ritchie Ho
13 Blairgowrie Ct
14 Circle Ho
15 Dunkeld Ho
16 Rosemary Dr
17 Sorrel La
18 East India Dock Road Tunnel

35
A2 **1** Faraday Sch
B3 **1** Newton Point
2 Sparke Terr
3 Montesquieu Terr
4 Crawford Point
5 Rathbone Ho
6 George St
7 Emily St
8 Fendt Cl
9 Sabbarton St
10 St Luke's Prim Sch
11 Briary Ct
12 Shaftesbury Ho
B4 **1** Radley Terr
2 Bernard Cassidy St
3 Rathbone Mkt
4 Thomas North Terr
5 Mary St
6 Hughes Terr
7 Swanscombe Point
8 Rawlinson Point
9 Kennedy Cox Ho
10 Cooper St
11 Rokeby St
C1 **1** Capulet Mews
2 Pepys Cres
3 De Quincey Mews
4 Hardy Ave
5 Tom Jenkinson Rd
6 Kennacraig Cl
7 Charles Flemwell Mews
8 Gatcombe Rd
9 Badminton Mews
10 Holyrood Mews
11 Britannia Gate
12 Dalemain Mews
13 Bowes-Lyon Hall
14 Lancaster Hall
15 Victoria Hall
C2 **1** Clements Ave
2 Martindale Ave
3 Balearic Apts
4 Marmara Apts
5 Baltic Apts
6 Coral Apts
7 Aegean Apts
8 Capital East Apts
C4 **1** Odeon Ct
2 Edward Ct
3 Newhaven La
4 Ravenscroft Cl
5 Douglas Rd
6 Ferrier Point
7 Harvey Point
8 Wood Point
9 Trinity St
10 Pattinson Point
11 Clinch Ct
12 Mint Bsns Pk
13 Keir Hardy Prim Sch

36
A1 **1** Burford Ho
2 Hope Cl
3 Centaur Ct
4 Phoenix Ct
C1 **1** Surrey Cres
2 Forbes Ho
3 Haining Cl
4 Melville Ct
5 London Stile

302 36 C1

6 Stile Hall Par
7 Priory Lo
8 Meadowcroft
9 St James Ct
10 Rivers Ho
11 Surrey Cres

37

A1 1 Churchdale Ct
2 Cromwell Cl
3 Cambridge Rd S
4 Oxbridge Ct
5 Tomlinson Cl
6 Gunnersbury Mews
7 Grange The
8 Gunnersbury Cl
9 Bellgrave Lo
A2 10 Orchard House Sch
A4 1 Cheltenham Pl
2 Beaumaris Twr
3 Arundel Ho
4 Pevensey Ct
5 Jerome Twr
6 Anstey Ct
7 Bennett Ct
8 Gunnersbury Ct
9 Barrington Ct
10 Hope Gdns
11 Park Road E
B1 1 Arlington
Park Mans
2 Sandown Ho
3 Goodwood Ho
4 Windsor Ho
5 Lingfield Ho
6 Ascot Ho
7 Watchfield Ct
8 Belgrave Ct
9 Beverley Ct
10 Beaumont Ct
11 Harvard Rd
12 Troubridge Sq
13 Branden Lo
14 Fromow's Cnr
15 Heathfield House
Sch
B2 1 Chiswick Green
Studios
2 Bell Ind Est
3 Fairlawn Ct
4 Dukes Gate
5 Dewsbury Ct
6 Chiswick Terr
7 Mortlake Ho
B3 1 Blackmore Twr
2 Bollo Ct
3 Kipling Twr
4 Lawrence Ct
5 Maugham Ct
6 Reade Ct
7 Woolf Ct
8 Shaw Ct
9 Verne Ct
10 Wodehouse Ho
11 Greenock Rd
12 Garden Ct
13 Barons Gate
14 Cleveland Rd
15 Carver Cl
16 Chapter Cl
17 Beauchamp Cl
18 Holmes Ct
19 Copper Mews
20 Packington Rd

21 Maugham Wy
B4 1 Belgrave Cl
2 Buckland Wlk
3 Frampton Ct
4 Telfer Cl
5 Harlech Twr
6 Corfe Twr
7 Barwick Ho
8 Charles Hocking
House
9 Sunninghill Ct
10 Salisbury St
11 Jameson Pl
12 Castle Cl
13 Ark Priory
Prim Acad
C1 1 Chatsworth Ct
2 Prospect Pl
3 Townhall Ave
4 Devonhurst Pl
5 Heathfield Ct
6 Horticultural Pl
7 Merlin Ho
8 Garth Rd
9 Autumn Rise
C2 1 Disraeli Ct
2 Winston Wlk
3 Rusthall Mans
4 Bedford Park Mans
5 Essex Place Sq
6 Holly Rd
7 Homecross Ho
8 Swan Bsns Ctr
9 Jessop Ho
10 Belmont Prim Sch

38

A1 1 Glebe Cl
2 Devonshire Mews
3 Binns Terr
4 Ingress St
5 Swanscombe Rd
6 Brackley Terr
7 Stephen Fox Ho
8 Manor Gdns
9 Coram Ho
10 Flaxman Ho
11 Thorneycroft Ho
12 Thornhill Ho
13 Kent Ho
14 Oldfield Ho
15 William Hogarth
Sch The
16 Oak Lock Mews
A2 1 Chestnut Ho
2 Bedford Ho
3 Bedford Cnr
4 Sydney Ho
5 Bedford Park Cnr
6 Priory Gdns
7 Windmill Alley
8 Castle Pl
9 Jonathan Ct
10 Windmill Pas
11 Chardin Rd
12 Gable Ho
13 Chiswick & Bedford
Park Prep Sch
14 Arts Educational
Schools London
15 Orchard Ho Sch
A3 1 Fleet Ct
2 Ember Ct
3 Emlyn Gdns
4 Clone Ct
5 Brent Ct
6 Abbey Ct

7 Ormsby Lo
8 St Catherine's Ct
9 Lodge The
A4 1 Longford Ct
2 Mole Ct
3 Lea Ct
4 Wantle Ct
5 Beverley Ct
6 Roding Ct
7 Crane Ct
B1 1 Miller's Ct
2 British Grove Pas
3 British Grove S
4 Beresteide Rd
5 North Eyot Gdns
B2 1 Flanders Mans
2 Stamford Brook
Mans
3 Linkenholt Mans
4 Prebend Mans
5 Middlesex Ct
B3 1 Stamford Brook
Gdns
2 Hauteville Court
Gdns
3 Ranelagh Gdns
C1 1 Chisholm Ct
2 North Verbena
Gdns
3 Western Terr
4 Verbena Gdns
5 Montrose Villas
6 Hammersmith Terr
7 South Black
Lion La
8 St Peter's Wharf
9 St Peter's CE Prim
Sch
C2 1 Hamlet Ct
2 Derwent Ct
3 Westcroft Ct
4 Black Lion Mews
5 St Peter's Villas
6 Standish Ho
7 Chambon Pl
8 Court Mans
9 Longthorpe Ct
10 Charlotte Ct
11 Westside
12 Park Ct
13 London Ho
14 Latymer Upper Sch
15 Polish Univ Abroad
16 West London
Free Sch
C3 1 Elizabeth Finn Ho
2 Ashchurch Ct
3 King's Par
4 Inver Ct
5 Ariel Ct
6 Pocklington Lo
7 Vitae Apartments
C4 1 Becklow Gdns
2 Victoria Ho
3 Lycett Pl
4 Kylemore Ct
5 Alexandra Ct
6 Lytten Ct
7 Becklow Mews
8 Northcroft Ct
9 Bailey Ct
10 Spring Cott
11 Landor Wlk
12 Laurence Mews
13 Hadyn Park Ct
14 Askew Mans
15 Malvern Ct

39

A1 1 Prince's Mews
2 Aspen Gdns
3 Hampshire Hog La
4 Blades Ct
A2 1 Albion Gdns
2 Flora Gdns
3 Lamington St
4 Felgate Mews
5 Galena Ho
6 Albion Mews
7 Albion Ct
8 King Street
Cloisters
9 Dimes Pl
10 Clarence Ct
11 Hampshire Hog La
12 Marryat Ct
13 Ravenscourt Ho
14 Ravenscourt
Theatre Sch
15 Cambridge Sch
16 Godolphin &
Latymer Sch
17 Flora Gardens
Prim Sch
A3 1 Ravenscourt Park
Mans
2 Paddenswick Ct
3 Ashbridge Ct
4 Brackenbury
Prim Sch
A4 1 Westbush Ct
2 Goldhawk Mews
3 Sycamore Ho
4 Shackleton Ct
5 Drake Ct
6 Scotts Ct
7 Raleigh Ct
8 Melville Court Flats
9 Southway Cl
10 Hammersmith Acad
B1 1 Bridge Avenue
Mans
2 Bridgeview
3 College Ct
4 Beatrice Ho
5 Amelia Ho
6 Edith Ho
7 Joanna Ho
8 Mary Ho
9 Adela Ho
10 Sophia Ho
11 Henrietta Ho
12 Charlotte Ho
13 Alexandra Ho
14 Bath Pl
15 Elizabeth Ho
16 Margaret Ho
17 Peabody Est
18 Eleanor Ho
19 Isabella Ho
20 Caroline Ho
21 Chancellors Wharf
22 Sussex Pl
23 St Paul's CE
Prim Sch
B2 1 Phoenix Lodge
Mans
2 Samuel's Cl
3 Broadway Arc
4 Brook Ho
5 Hammersmith
Broadway
6 Broadway Sh Ctr
7 Cambridge Ct

8 Ashcroft Sq
9 Sacred Heart
High Sch
B4 1 Verulam Ho
2 Grove Mans
3 Frobisher Ct
4 Library Mans
5 Pennard Mans
6 New Shepherd's
Bush Mkt
7 Kerrington Ct
8 Granville Mans
9 Romney Ct
10 Rayner Ct
11 Sulgrave Gdns
12 Bamborough Gdns
13 Hillary Ct
14 Market Studios
15 Lanark Mans
16 St Stephen's CE
Prim Sch
17 Miles Coverdale
Prim Sch
18 Hammersmith &
West London Coll
C2 1 St Paul's Girls' Sch
2 Bute House
Prep Sch
3 Ecole Francaise
Jacques Prevert
4 Larmenier &
Sacred Heart RC
Prim Sch
C3 1 Grosvenor
Residences
2 Blythe Mews
3 Burnand Ho
4 Bradford Ho
5 Springvale Terr
6 Ceylon Rd
7 Walpole Ct
8 Bronte Ct
9 Boswell Ct
10 Souldern Rd
11 Brook Green Flats
12 Haarlem Rd
13 Stafford Mans
14 Lionel Mans
15 Barradell Ho
C4 1 Vanderbilt Villas
2 Bodington Ct
3 Kingham Ct
4 Clearwater Terr
5 Lorne Gdns
6 Cameret Ct
7 Bush Ct
8 Shepherds Ct
9 Rockley Ct
10 Grampians The
11 Charcroft Ct
12 Addison Park Mans
13 Sinclair Mans
14 Fountain Ct
15 Woodford Ct
16 Roseford Ct
17 Woodstock Studios

40

A1 1 Hockney Ct
2 Toulouse Ct
3 Lowry Ct
4 Barry Ho
5 Lewis Ct
6 Gainsborough Ct
7 Renoir Ct
8 Blake Ct
9 Raphael Ct

4 Thorne Ho
5 Skeggs Ho
6 St Bernard Ho
7 Kimberley Ho
8 Kingdon Ho
9 Killoran Ho
10 Aliastor Ho
11 Lingard Ho
12 Yarrow Ho
13 Sandpiper Ct
14 Nightingale Ct
15 Robin Ct
16 Heron Ct
17 Ferndown Lo
18 Crosby Ho
B4 1 Llandovery Ho
2 Rugless Ho
3 Ash Ho
4 Elm Ho
5 Cedar Ho
6 Castalia Sq
7 Aspect Ho
8 Normandy Ho
9 Valiant Ho
10 Tamar Ho
11 Watkins Ho
12 Alice Shepherd Ho
13 Oak Ho
14 Ballin Ct
15 Martin Ct
16 Grebe Ct
17 Kingfisher Ct
18 Walkers Lo
19 Antilles Bay
C2 1 Verwood Lo
2 Fawley Lo
3 Lyndhurst Lo
4 Blyth Ct
5 Farnworth Ho
6 Francis Cl
7 St Luke's CE Prim Sch

43

A1 1 Bellot Gdns
2 Thornley Pl
3 King William La
4 Bolton Ho
5 Miles Ho
6 Mell St
7 Sam Manners Ho
8 Hatcliffe Almshouses
9 Woodland Wlk
10 Earlswood Cl
11 St Joseph's RC Prim Sch
12 Christ Church CE Prim Sch
B1 1 Baldrey Ho
2 Christie Ho
3 Dyson Ho
4 Cliffe Ho
5 Moore Ho
6 Collins Ho
7 Lockyer Ho
8 Halley Ho
9 Kepler Ho
10 Sailacre Ho
11 Union Pk
B3 1 Teal St
2 Maurer Ct
3 Mudlarks Blvd
4 Renaissance Wlk

5 Alamaro Lo
6 St Mary Magdalene CE Prim Sch
C1 1 Layfield Ho
2 Westerdale Rd
3 Mayston Mews
4 Station Mews Terr
5 Halstow Prim Sch
6 Holyrood Mews

44

A4 1 Ferry Sq
2 Watermans Ct
3 Wilkes Rd
4 Albany Par
5 Charlton Ho
6 Albany Ho
7 Alma Ho
8 Griffin Ct
9 Cressage Ho
10 Tunstall Wlk
11 Trimmer Wlk
12 Running Horse Yd
13 Mission Sq
14 Distillery Wlk
B2 1 Primrose Ho
2 Lawman Ct
3 Royston Ct
4 Capel Lo
5 Devonshire Ct
6 Celia Ct
7 Rosslyn Ho
8 Branstone Ct
9 Lamerton Lo
10 Kew Lo
11 Dunraven Ho
12 Stoneleigh Lo
13 Tunstall Ct
14 Voltaire
C2 1 Clarendon Ct
2 Quintock Ho
3 Broome Ct
4 Lonsdale Mews
5 Elizabeth Cotts
6 Sandways
7 Victoria Cotts
8 North Ave
9 Grovewood
10 Hamilton Ho
11 Melvin Ct
12 Royal Par
13 Power Ho
14 Station Ave
15 Blake Mews
C4 1 Strand on the Green Jun & Inf Sch

A2 1 Terrano Ho
2 Oak Ho
3 Aura Ho
4 Maple Ho
5 Cedar Ho
6 Saffron Ho
7 Lime Ho
8 Lavender Ho
9 Juniper Ho
A4 1 Falcons Pre-Prep Sch for Boys The

B1 1 Melrose Rd
2 Seaforth Lo
3 St John's Gr
4 Sussex Ct

5 Carmichael Ct
6 Hampshire Ct
7 Thorne Pas
8 Brunel Ct
9 Beverley Path
10 Birch Yd

C4 1 Cobb's Hall
2 Dorset Mans
3 St Clements Mans
4 Bothwell St
5 Hawksmoor St
6 Melcombe Prim Sch

A1 1 Langport Ho
2 Iveagh Ho
3 Newark Ho
4 Edgehill Ho
5 Hopton Ho
6 Ashby Ho
7 Nevil Ho
A2 1 Fairbairn Gn
2 Hammelton Gn
3 Foxley Sq
4 Silverburn Ho
5 Butler Ho
6 Dalkeith Ho
7 Turner Cl
8 Bathgate Ho
9 Black Roof Ho
10 St Gabriel's Coll (Dennen Site)
11 Charles Edward Brooke Sch
12 Lennox Rd
A3 1 Highshore Sch
2 Midnight Ave
32 St Michael & All Angels CE Acad
A4 1 Faunce Ho
2 Garbett Ho
3 Harvard Ho
4 Doddington Pl
5 Kean Ho
6 Jephson Ho
7 Cornish Ho
8 Bateman Ho
9 Molesworth Ho
10 Walters Ho
11 Cruden Ho
12 Brawne Ho
13 Prescott Ho
14 Chalmer's Wlk
15 Copley Cl
16 King Charles Ct
B1 1 Bergen Ho
2 Oslo Ho
3 Viking Ho
4 Jutland Ho
5 Norvic Ho
6 Odin Ho
7 Baltic Ho
8 Nobel Ho
9 Mercia Ho
10 Kenbury Gdns
11 Zealand Ho
12 Elsinore Ho
13 Norse Ho
14 Denmark Mans
15 Dane Ho
16 Canterbury Cl
17 York Cl
18 Kenbury Mans
19 Parade Mans

20 Winterslow Ho
21 Lilford Ho
22 Bartholomew Ho
23 Guildford Ho
24 Boston Ho
25 Hereford Ho
26 Weyhill Ho
27 Lichfield Ho
28 Lansdown Ho
29 Honiton Ho
30 Pinner Ho
31 Baldock Ho
32 Widecombe Ho
33 Nottingham Ho
34 Witham Ho
35 Barnet Ho
36 Empress Mews
B2 1 Bertha Neubergh House
2 Mornington Mews
3 Badsworth Rd
4 Pearson Cl
5 Elm Tree Ct
6 Samuel Lewis Trust Dwellings
7 Milkwell Yd
8 Keswick Ho
9 Mitcham Ho
10 Sacred Heart Catholic Sch
11 Crawford Prim Sch
B3 1 Boundary Ho
2 Day Ho
3 Burgess Ho
4 Carlyle Ho
5 Myers Ho
6 Thompson Ave
7 Palgrave Ho
8 Winnington Ho
9 Brantwood Ho
10 Lowell Ho
11 Jessie Duffett Ho
12 Otterburn Ho
13 Crossmount Ho
14 Venice Ct
15 Bowyer St
16 Livingstone Ho
17 Gothic Ct
18 Coniston Ho
19 Harlynwood
20 Carey Ct
21 Finley Ct
22 Grainger Ct
23 Hayes Ct
24 Moffat Ho
25 Marinel Ho
26 Hodister Cl
27 Arnot Ho
28 Lamb Ho
29 Kipling Ho
30 Keats Ho
31 Kenyon Ho
32 New Church Rd
33 Sir John Kirk Cl
34 Comber Grove Prim Sch
35 Ark All Saints Acad
36 St Joseph's Camberwell RC Schools' Federation
C1 1 Selborne Ho
2 Hascombe Terr
C2 1 Butterfly Wlk
2 Cuthill Wlk
3 Colonades The

5 Artichoke Mews
6 Peabody Bldgs
7 Brighton Ho
8 Park Ho
9 Peabody Ct
10 Lomond Ho
11 Lamb Ho
12 Kimpton Ct
13 Belham Wlk
14 Datchelor Pl
15 Harvey Rd
C3 1 Masterman Ho
2 Milton Ho
3 Pope Ho
4 Chester Ct
5 Marvel Ho
6 Flecker Ho
7 Landor Ho
8 Leslie Prince Ct
9 Evelina Mans
10 Langland Ho
11 Drinkwater Ho
12 Procter Ho
13 Shirley Ho
14 Drayton Ho
15 Bridges Ho
16 Cunningham Ho
17 Hood Ho
18 Herrick Ho
19 Dekker Ho
20 Houseman Way
21 Coleby Path
22 Brunswick Park Prim Sch
C4 1 Queens Ho
2 Arnside Ho
3 Horsley St
4 St Peter's Ho
5 St Johns Ho
6 St Marks Ho
7 St Matthew's Ho
8 St Stephens Ho
9 Red Lion Cl
10 Boyson Rd
11 Bradenham

49

A1 1 Springfield Ho
2 Craston Ho
3 Walters Ho
4 Edgecombe Ho
5 Fowler Ho
6 Rignold Ho
7 Chatham Ho
A2 1 Barnwell Ho
2 Brunswick Villas
3 St Giles Twr
4 Bentley Ho
5 Dawson Ho
6 Dryden Ho
7 Mayward Ho
8 Longleigh Ho
9 Fairwall Ho
10 Bodeney Ho
11 Sandby Ho
12 Vestry Mews
13 Netley
14 Lakanal
15 Racine
16 Camberwell Coll of Arts
A3 1 Tower Mill Rd
2 Tilson Cl
3 Granville Sq
4 Edgar Wallace Ct
5 Potters Cl
6 Dorton Cl

7 Samuel Jones
Ind Est
8 Dibden Ho
9 Marchwood Cl
10 Pilgrims Cloisters
11 Beacon Ho
12 Teather St
13 Stacy Path
14 Rumball Ho
15 Ballow Cl
16 Rill Ho
17 Southwark Coll
(Camberwell Ctr)
18 St George's
CE Prim Sch
A4 1 Downend Ct
2 Andoversford Ct
3 Pearse St
4 Watling St
5 Gandolfi St
6 Comfort St
7 Tower Mill Rd
B1 1 Villa Sch The
32 1 Colbert
2 Voltaire
3 Finch Mews
4 Charles Coveney Rd
5 Bamber Rd
6 Crane St
7 Curlew Ho
8 Mallard Ho
9 Tern Ho
10 Crane Ho
11 Falcon Ho
12 Bryanston Ho
13 Basing Ct
14 Marcus Ho
15 Sheffield Ho
16 Highshore Sch
17 St James The Great
RC Prim Sch
18 Oliver Goldsmith
Prim Sch
B3 1 Painswick Ct
2 Sharpness Ct
3 Mattingly Way
4 Hordle Prom N
5 Burcher Gale Gr
6 Calypso Cres
7 Hordle Prom S
8 Cinnamon Cl
9 Savannah Ct
10 Thames Ct
11 Shannon Ct
12 Amstel Ct
13 Danube Ct
14 Tilbury Cl
15 Hordle Prom E
16 Indus Ct
17 Oakcourt
18 Palm Ct
19 Rowan Ct
20 Blackthorn Ct
21 Pear Ct
22 Lidgate Rd
23 Whistler Mews
24 Boathouse Wlk
25 Camberwell
Coll of Arts
B4 1 Willsbridge Ct
2 Cam Ct
3 Quedgeley Ct
4 Saul Ct
5 Quenington Ct
6 Westonbirt Ct
7 Wickway Ct
C1 1 William Margrie Cl

2 William Blake Ho
3 Quantock Mews
4 Choumert Sq
5 Parkstone Rd
6 Atwell Rd
C2 1 Canal Head
Public Sq
2 Angelina Ho
3 Jarvis Ho
4 Richland Ho
5 Honeywood Ho
6 Wakefield Ho
7 Primrose Ho
8 Hardcastle Ho
9 Dunstall Ho
10 Springtide Cl
11 Purdon Ho
12 Flamborough Ho
13 Lansdoll St
14 Witcombe Point
15 Yarnfield Sq
16 Winford Ct
17 Portbury Cl
C3 1 Thornbill Ho
2 Vervain Ho
3 Woodstar Ho
4 Tamarind Ho
5 Hereford Retreat
6 Haymerle Ho
7 Furley Ho
8 Thomas Milner Ho
9 Applegarth Ho
10 Freda Corbett Cl
11 Rudbeck Ho
12 Henslow Ho
13 Lindley Ho
14 Collinson Ho
15 Sister Mabel's Way
16 Timberland Cl
17 Hastings Cl
18 Sidmouth Ho
19 Budleigh Ho
20 Stanesgate Ho
21 Breamore Ho
22 Ely Ho
23 Gisburn Ho
24 Silkin Mews
25 Peckham Park
Prim Sch
26 St Francis RC
Prim Sch
C4 1 Bowles Rd
2 Western Wharf
3 Northfield Ho
4 Millbrook Ho
5 Denstone Ho
6 Deerhurst Ho
7 Caversham Ho
8 Battle Ho
9 Cardiff Ho
10 Bridgnorth Ho
11 Exeter Ho
12 Grantham Ho
13 Aylesbury Ho
14 Royston Ho
15 Haymerle Sch

50

A1 1 Walkynscroft
2 Ryegates
3 Hathorne Cl
4 Pilkington Rd
5 Russell Ct
6 Heaton Ho
7 Magdalene Cl

8 Iris Ct
9 Flaxman Ct
10 St Mary Magdalene
CE Prim Sch
A2 1 Willowdene
2 Pinedene
3 Oakdene
4 Beechdene
5 Hollydene
6 Wood Dene
7 Staveley Cl
8 Carnicot Ho
9 Martock Ct
10 Cherry Tree Ct
11 Kendrick Ct
12 John Donne
Prim Sch
A3 1 Tortington Ho
2 Credenhill Ho
3 Bromyard Ho
4 Hoyland Ct
5 Willowdene
6 Ashdene
7 Acorn Par
8 Havelock St
9 Springall St
10 Harry Lambourn Ho
11 Grenier Apartments
12 Burnhill Cl
B1 1 Honiton Gdns
2 Selden Ho
3 Hathway Ho
4 Hathway St
5 Station Ct
6 Symons Cl
7 Hollydale Prim Sch
B2 1 Trotman Ho
2 Boddington Ho
3 Heydon Ho
4 Boulter Ho
5 Astbury Bsns Pk
6 Kender Prim Sch
B3 1 Ambleside Point
2 Grasmere Point
3 Windermere Point
4 Roman Way
5 Laburnum Ct
6 Juniper Ho
7 Romney Cl
8 Hammersley Ho
9 Hutchinson Ho
10 Hammond Ho
11 Fir Tree Ho
12 Glastonbury Ct
13 Highbridge Ct
14 Filton Ct
15 Chiltern Ct
B4 1 Penhurst Ho
2 Reculver Ho
3 Mereworth Ho
4 Camber Ho
5 Chiham Ho
6 Otford Ho
7 Olive Tree Ho
8 Aspen Ho
9 Lewis Silkin Ho
10 Henderson Ct
11 Dover Ho
12 Eynsford Ho
13 Horton Ho
14 Lamberhurst Ho
15 Canterbury Ind Pk
16 Upnall Ho
17 Sissinghurst Ho
18 Rochester Ho
19 Saltwood Ho
20 Leybourne Ho

21 Lullingstone Ho
22 Pilgrims Way Prim
Sch
C3 1 Richard Anderson
Ct
2 Palm Tree Ho
3 Edward Robinson
House
4 Antony Ho
5 Gerrard Ho
6 Palmer Ho
7 Pankhurst Cl
8 Robinson Wy
9 Eckington La
C4 1 Harrisons Ct
2 Grantley Ho
3 Sunbury Ct
4 Tilbury Ho
5 Graham Ct
6 Connell Ct
7 St Clements Ct
8 Henderson Ct
9 Jemotts Ct
10 Verona Ct
11 Heywood Ho
12 Francis Ct
13 Hind Ho
14 Donne Ho
15 Carew Ct
16 Burbage Ho
17 Newland Ho
18 Dobson Ho
19 Dalton Ho
20 Greene Ct
21 Redrup Ho
22 Tarplett Ho
23 Stunell Ho
24 Gasson Ho
25 Bryce Ho
26 Barnes Ho
27 Barkwith Ho
28 Bannister Ho
29 Apollo Ind Bsns Ctr

51

A1 4 Haberdashers'
Aske's Hatcham
College
A2 1 Archer Ho
2 Browning Ho
3 Hardcastle Ho
4 Brooke Ho
5 Wallis Ho
6 Haberdashers'
Aske's Hatcham
College
A3 1 Batavia Ho
2 Marlowe Bsns Ctr
3 Batavia Mews
4 Woodrush Cl
5 Alexandra St
6 Primrose Wlk
7 Vansittart St
8 Granville Ct
9 Cottesbrook St
10 Ewen Henderson Ct
11 Fordham Ho
12 Deptford Green
Sch (Annex)
A4 1 Portland Ct
2 Phoenix Ct
3 Rainbow Ct
4 Hawke Twr
5 Chubworthy St
6 Woodpecker Rd
7 Hercules Ct
B3 1 Austin Ho

2 Exeter Way
3 Crossleigh Ct
4 Mornington Pl
5 Maple Ho
B4 1 Chester Ho
2 Lynch Wlk
3 Arlington Ho
4 Woodcote Ho
5 Cornbury Ho
6 Prospect Pl
7 Akintaro Ho
8 Mulberry Ho
9 Laurel Ho
10 Linden Ho
11 Ashford Ho
12 Wardalls Ho
13 Magnolia Ho
14 Howard Ho
15 Larch Cl
16 Ibis Ct
17 Merganser Ct
18 Wotton Rd
19 Kingfisher Sq
20 Sanderling Ct
21 Dolphin Twr
22 Mermaid Twr
23 Scoter Ct
24 Shearwater Ct
25 Brambling Ct
26 Kittiwake Ct
27 Diana Cl
28 Guillemot Ct
29 Marine Twr
30 Teal Ct
31 Lapwing Twr
32 Violet Cl
33 Skua Ct
34 Tristan Ct
35 Rosemary Ct
36 Cormorant Ct
37 Shelduck Ct
38 Eider Ct
39 Pintail Ct
40 Fulcher Ct
41 Grinling Gibbons
Prim Sch
42 Pilot Cl
C1 1 Ashmead Mews
2 St Stephen's CE
Prim Sch
C2 1 Admiralty Cl
2 Harton Lodge
3 Sylva Cotts
4 Pitman Ho
5 Heston Ho
6 Mereton Mans
7 Indiana Bldg
8 St John's Lodge
9 Dean's Gateway
10 Lucas Vale
Prim Sch
11 Addey &
Stanhope Sch
12 Lewisham Coll
(Deptford Campus)
C3 1 Sandpiper Ct
2 Flamingo Ct
3 Titan Bsns Est
4 Rochdale Way
5 Speedwell St
6 Reginald Pl
7 Fletcher Path
8 Frankham Ho
9 Cremer Ho

51

C3
10 Wilshaw Ho
11 Castell Ho
12 Holden Ho
13 Browne Ho
14 Resolution Way
15 Lady Florence Ctyd
16 Covell Ct
17 Albion Ho
18 St Joseph's RC Prim Sch
20 Tidemill Acad

C4
1 Dryfield Wlk
2 Blake Ho
3 Hawkins Ho
4 Grenville Ho
5 Langford Ho
6 Mandarin Ct
7 Bittern Ct
8 Lamerton St
9 Ravensbourne Mans
10 Armada St
11 Armada Ct
12 Benbow Ho
13 Oxenham Ho
14 Caravel Mews
15 Hughes Ho
16 Stretton Mans

52

A1
1 Morden Mount Prim Sch
2 Ravensbourne Pl
3 Bliss Cres

A2
1 Washington Bldg
2 California Bldg
3 Utah Bldg
4 Montana Bldg
5 Oregon Bldg
6 Dakota bldg
7 Idaho Bldg
8 Atlanta Bldg
9 Colorado Bldg
10 Arizona Bldg
11 Nebraska Bldg
12 Alaska Bldg
13 Ohio Bldg
14 Charter Bldgs
15 Flamsteed Ct
16 Friendly Pl
17 Dover Ct
18 Robinscroft Mews
19 Doleman Ho
20 Plymouth Ho

A3
1 Finch Ho
2 Jubilee The
3 Maitland Ho
4 Ashburnham Retreat
5 Waller Wy
6 Merryweather Pl
7 Victoria Gate Gardens

A4
1 Trinity Laban Conservatoire of Music & Dance

B1
1 Ellison Ho
2 Pitmaston Ho
3 Aster Ho
4 Windmill Cl
5 Hermitage The
6 Burnett Ho
7 Lacey Ho
8 Darwin Ho
9 Pearmain Ho
10 Primrose Wy

B2
1 Penn Almshouses
2 Jervis Ct
3 Woodville Ct
4 Darnall Ho
5 Renbold Ho
6 Lindsell St
7 Plumbridge St
8 Trinity Gr
9 Hollymount Cl
10 Cade Tyler Ho
11 Robertson Ho
12 Sparta St
13 Parkside Sq
14 Copperwood Pl
15 Parkside Ave
16 Silverwood Pl

B3
1 Temair Ho
2 Royal Hill Ct
3 Prince of Orange La
4 Lambard Ho
5 St Marks Cl
6 Ada Kennedy Ct
7 Arlington Pl
8 Topham Ho
9 Darnell Ho
10 Hawks Mews
11 Royal Pl
12 Swanne Ho
13 Maribor
14 Serica Ct
15 Queen Elizabeth's College
16 James Wolfe Prim Sch
17 Greenwich Com Coll
18 David Mews
19 Arlington Pl

B4
1 Crescent Arc
2 Greenwich Mkt
3 Turnpin La
4 Durnford St
5 Sexton's Ho
6 Bardsley Ho
7 Wardell Ho
8 Clavell St
9 Stanton Ho
10 Macey Ho
11 Boreman Ho
12 Clipper Appts

C3
1 Park Wk

C4
1 Frobisher Ct
2 Hardy Cotts
3 Palliser Ho
4 Bernard Angell Ho
5 Corvette Sq
6 Travers Ho
7 Maze Hill Lodge
8 Park Place Ho
9 Meridian Prim Sch

53

B1
1 Heath House Prep Sch

B3
1 Westcombe Ct
2 Kleffens Ct
3 Ferndale Ct
4 Combe Mews
5 Mandeville Ct
6 Pinelands Cl

C3
1 Mary Lawrenson Pl
2 Bradbury Ct
3 Dunstable Ct
4 Wentworth Ho

C4
1 Nethercombe Ho
2 Holywell Cl

54

A1
1 Lancaster Cotts
2 Lancaster Mews
3 Bromwich Ho
4 Priors Lo
5 Richmond Hill Ct
6 Glenmore Ho
7 Hillbrow
8 Heathshott
9 Friars Stile Pl
10 Spire Ct
11 Ridgeway
12 Matthias Ct
13 Old Vicarage Sch

A2
1 Lichfield Terr
2 Union Ct
3 Carrington Lo
4 Wilton Ct
5 Egerton Ct
6 Beverley Lo
7 Bishop Duppa's Almshouses
8 Regency Wlk
9 Clear Water Ho
10 Onslow Avenue Mans
11 Michels Almshouses
12 Albany Pas
13 Salcombe Villas

A3
1 St John's Gr
2 Michel's Row
3 Michelsdale Dr
4 Blue Anchor Alley
5 Clarence St
6 Sun Alley
7 Thames Link Ho
8 Benns Wlk
9 Waterloo Pl
10 Northumbria Ct

B1
1 Chester Cl
2 Evesham Ct
3 Queen's Ct
4 Russell Wlk
5 Charlotte Sq
6 Jones Wlk
7 Hilditch Ho
8 Isabella Ct
9 Damer Ho
10 Eliot Ho
11 Fitzherbert Ho
12 Reynolds Pl
13 Chisholm Rd

B2
1 Alberta Ct
2 Beatrice Rd
3 Lorne Rd
4 York Rd
5 Connaught Rd
6 Albany Terr
7 Kingswood Ct
8 Selwyn Ct
9 Broadhurst Cl

B3
1 Towers The
2 Longs Ct
3 Sovereign Ct
4 Robinson Ct
5 Calvert Ct
6 Bedford Ct
7 Hickey's Almshouses
8 Church Estate Almshouses
9 Richmond International Bsns Ctr
10 Abercorn Mews

C4
1 Parison Cl

55

A3
1 Hershell Ct
2 Deanhill Ct
3 Park Sheen
4 Furness Lo
5 Merricks Ct

C4
1 Rann Ho
2 Craven Ho
3 John Dee Ho
4 Kindell Ho
5 Montgomery Ho
6 Avondale Ho
7 Addington Ct
8 Dovecote Gdns
9 Firmston Ho
10 Glendower Gdns
11 Chestnut Ave
12 Treharn Rd
13 Rock Ave
14 St Mary Magdalen's RC Prim Sch

56

C1
1 Woodmill Cl
2 Bader Wy
3 Mendez Wy
4 India Wy
5 Gillis Sq
6 Benkart Mews
7 Drury Cl

C2
1 Theodore Ho
2 Nicholas Ho
3 Bonner Ho
4 Downing Ho
5 Jansen Ho
6 Fairfax Ho
7 Devereux Ho
8 David Ho
9 Leigh Ho
10 Clipstone Ho
11 Mallet Ho
12 Arton Wilson Ho

57

B2
1 Inglis Ho
2 Ducie Ho
3 Wharncliffe Ho
4 Stanhope Ho
5 Waldegrave Ho
6 Mildmay Ho
7 Mullens Ho

C1
1 Balmoral Ct
2 Glenalmond Ho
3 Selwyn Ho
4 Keble Ho
5 Bede Ho
6 Gonville Ho
7 Magdalene Ho
8 Armstrong Ho
9 Newnham Ho
10 Somerville Ho
11 Balliol Ho
12 Windermere
13 Little Combe Cl
14 Classinghall Ho
15 Chalford Ct
16 Garden Royal
17 South Ct
18 Anne Kerr Ct
19 Ewhurst

C2
1 Geneva Ct
2 Laurel Ct
3 Cambalt Ho
4 Langham Ct
5 Lower Pk
6 King's Keep
7 Whitnell Ct
8 Whitehead Ho
9 Halford Ho
10 Humphry Ho
11 Jellicoe Ho

C3
1 Olivette St
2 Mascotte Rd
3 Glegg Pl
4 Crown Ct
5 Charlwood Terr
6 Percy Laurie Ho
7 Our Lady of Victories RC Prim Sch
8 Griffin Gate
9 Darfur St
10 John Keall Ho
11 Henry Jackson Ho
12 Felsham Ho
13 Ardshiel Cl
14 Ruvigny Mans
15 Star & Garter Mans
16 University Mans
17 Lockyer Ho
18 Phelps Ho
19 Princeton Ct
20 Kingsmere Cl
21 Felsham Mews
22 St Mary's CE Prim Sch

58

A2
1 Claremont
2 Downside
3 Cavendish Cl
4 Ashcombe Cl
5 Carltons The
6 Espirit Ho
7 Millbrooke Ct
8 Coysh Ct
9 Keswick Hts
10 Avon Ct
11 Merlin Sch The

B2
1 Keswick Broadway
2 Burlington Mews
3 Cambria Lo
4 St Stephen's Gdns
5 Atlantic Ho
6 Burton Lo
7 Manfred Ct
8 Meadow Bank
9 Hooper Ho
10 Aspire Bld

C2
1 Pembridge Pl
2 Adelaide Rd
3 London Ct
4 Windsor Ct
5 Westminster Ct
6 Fullers Ho
7 Bridge Pk
8 Lambeth Ct
9 Milton Ct
10 Norfolk Mans
11 Francis Snary Lo
12 Bush Cotts
13 Downbury Mews
14 Newton's Yd
15 Roche Sch The
16 St Joseph's RC Prim Sch

17 West Hill
Prim Sch
18 Spectrum Wy

59
A2 **1** Fairfield Ct
2 Blackmore Ho
3 Lancaster Mews
4 Cricketers Mews
5 College Mews
6 Arndale Wlk
7 St Anne's CE
Prim Sch
8 South Thames Coll
(Wandsworth Ctr)
B1 **1** Wandsworth
Prep Sch
B2 **1** St Faith's CE
Prim Sch
B4 **1** Molasses Ho
2 Molasses Row
3 Cinnamon Row
4 Calico Ho
5 Calico Row
6 Port Ho
7 Square Rigger Row
8 Trade Twr
9 Ivory Ho
10 Spice Ct
11 Sherwood Ct
12 Mendip Ct
13 Chalmers Ho
14 Coral Row
15 Ivory Sq
16 Kingfisher Ho
C3 **1** Burke Ho
2 High View Prim Sch
3 Centre Acad
4 Fox Ho
5 Buxton Ho
6 Pitt Ho
7 Ramsey Ho
8 Beverley Cl
9 Florence Ho
10 Linden Ct
11 Dorcas Ct
12 Johnson Ct
13 Agnes Ct
14 Hilltop Ct
15 Courtyard The
16 Old Laundry The
17 Oberstein Rd
18 Fineran Ct
19 Sangora Rd
20 Harvard Mans
21 Plough Mews
C4 **1** Milner Ho
2 McManus Ho
3 Wilberforce Ho
4 Wheeler Ct
5 Sporle Ct
6 Holliday Sq
7 John Parker Sq
8 Carmichael Cl
9 Fenner Sq
10 Clark Lawrence Ct
11 Shaw Ct
12 Sendall Ct
13 Livingstone Rd
14 Farrant Ho
15 Jackson Ho
16 Darien Ho
17 Shepard Ho
18 Ganley Ct
19 Arthur Newton Ho
20 Chesterton Ho
21 John Kirk Ho

22 Mantua St
23 Heaver Rd
24 Candlemakers
25 Thames Christian
Coll
26 Falconbrook Prim
Sch
27 Benham Cl

60
A4 **1** Kiloh Ct
2 Lanner Ho
3 Griffon Ho
4 Kestrel Ho
5 Kite Ho
6 Peregrine Ho
7 Hawk Ho
8 Inkster Ho
9 Harrier Ho
10 Eagle Hts
11 Kingfisher Ct
12 Lavender Terr
13 Temple Ho
14 Ridley Ho
15 Eden Ho
16 Hertford Ct
17 Nepaul Rd
B1 **1** Staplehurst Ct
2 Teyham Ct
3 Honeywell Jun
& Inf Schs
B2 **1** Clapham Computer
& Secretarial Coll
C1 **1** Rayne Ho
2 St Anthony's Ct
3 Earlsthorpe Mews
4 Nightingale Mans
5 Clavering Pl
C4 **1** Shaftesbury Park
Chambers
2 Selborne
3 Rush Hill Mews
4 Marmion Mews
5 Crosland Rd
6 Craven Mews
7 Garfield Mews
8 Audley Cl
9 Basnett Rd
10 Tyneham Cl
11 Woodmere Cl
12 L'Ecole du Parc
D1 **5** Broomwood Hall
(Lower Sch)

61
A1 **1** Oliver Thomas
Prep Sch
A4 **1** Turnchapel Mews
2 Redwood Mews
3 Phil Brown Pl
4 Bev Callender Cl
5 Keith Connor Cl
6 Tessa Sanderson Pl
7 Daley Thompson
Way
8 Rashleigh Ct
9 Abberley Mews
10 Willow Lodge
11 Beaufoy Rd
12 Wardell Mews
B1 **1** Joseph Powell Cl
2 Cavendish Mans
3 Westlands Terr
4 Cubitt Ho
5 Hawkesworth Ho
6 Normanton Ho
7 Eastman Ho

8 Couchman Ho
9 Poynders Ct
10 Selby Ho
11 Valentine Ho
12 Gorham Ho
13 Deauville Mans
14 Deauville St
B2 **1** Timothy Cl
2 Shaftesbury Mews
3 Brook Ho
4 Grover Ho
5 Westbrook Ho
6 Hewer Ho
7 Batten Ho
8 Mandeville Ho
9 George Beare Lo
10 St Mary's RC
Prim Sch
B3 **1** Polygon The
2 Windsor Ct
3 Trinity Cl
4 Studios The
5 Bourne Ho
6 Porteus Pl
B4 **1** Clapham Manor Ct
2 Clarke Ho
3 Gables The
4 Sycamore Mews
5 Maritime Ho
6 Rectory Gdns
7 Floris Pl
8 Clapham Manor
Prim Sch
C1 **1** Parrington Ho
2 Savill Ho
3 Blackwell Ho
4 Bruce Ho
5 Victoria Ct
6 Victoria Ho
7 Belvedere Ct
8 Ingram Lo
9 Viney Ct
10 Bloomsbury Ho
11 Belgravia Ho
12 Barnsbury Ho
13 Parkfield Rd
14 Brickfield Rd
15 Dragmore St
16 Fairbourne Rd
17 Fennings Rd
C3 **1** Kenloa Rd
2 Felmersham Cl
3 Abbeville Mews
4 Saxon Ho
5 Gifford Ho
6 Teignmouth Cl
7 Holwood Pl
8 Oaklands Pl
9 Wilberforce
Mews
10 William Bonney
Estate
11 London Coll of
Bsns & Computer
Studies
12 Welmar Mews
C4 **1** Chelsham Ho
2 Lynde Ho
3 Greener Ho
4 Towns Ho
5 Hugh Morgan Ho
6 Roy Ridley Ho
7 Lendal Terr
8 Slievemore Cl
9 Cadmus Cl
10 Clapham North
Bsns Ctr

6 Bicycle Mews
7 Old Station Wy

62
A1 **1** Notley Pl
A2 **1** King's Mews
2 Clapham Court Terr
3 Clapham Ct
4 Clapham Park Terr
5 Pembroke Ho
6 Stevenson Ho
7 Queenswood Ct
8 Oak Tree Ct
9 Park Lofts
10 Ashby Mews
11 Holm Oak Mews
A3 **1** Morris Ho
2 Gye Ho
3 Clowes Ho
4 Thomas Ho
5 Stuart Ho
6 Storace Ho
7 Bedford Ho
8 Ascot Ct
9 Ascot Par
10 Ashmere Ho
11 Ashmere Gr
12 Ventura Ho
13 Vickery Ho
14 Stafford Mans
15 Beresford Ho
A4 **1** Callingham Ho
2 Russell
Pickering Ho
3 Ormerod Ho
4 Lopez Ho
5 Coachmaker Mews
B1 **1** Stewart's Ct
2 Weld Works Mews
B2 **1** Beatrice Ho
2 Florence Ho
3 Evelyn Ho
4 Diana Ho
5 Brixton Hill Ct
6 Austin Ho
7 Manor Ct
8 Camsey Ho
9 Romer Ho
10 Gale Ho
11 Byrne Ho
12 Farnfield Ho
13 Marchant Ho
14 Rainsford Ho
15 Springett Ho
16 Mannering Ho
17 Waldron Ho
18 Sudbourne
Prim Sch
19 Corpus Christi RC
Prim Sch
B3 **1** Freemens Hos
2 Roger's
Almshouses
3 Gresham
Almshouses
4 Exbury Ho
5 Glasbury Ho
6 Dalbury Ho
7 Fosbury Ho
8 Chalbury Ho
9 Neilson-Terry Ct
10 Pavilion Mans
11 Daisy Dormer Ct
12 George
Lashwood Ct
13 Marie Lloyd Ct
14 Trinity Homes

15 Lethaby Ho
16 Edmundsbury
Ct Est
17 Regis Pl
18 Marlborough Mews
19 Alpha Ho
20 Beta Pl
21 Cedars Ho
22 South Chelsea Coll
B4 **1** Turberville Ho
2 Thrayle Ho
3 Percheron Ct
4 Draymans Ct
5 Lansdowne Sch
6 Stockwell Prim Sch
C1 **1** Eccleston Ho
2 Scarsbrook Ho
3 Purser Ho
4 Rudhall Ho
5 Hardham Ho
6 Heywood Ho
7 Haworth Ho
8 Birch Ho
9 Lansdell Ho
10 Lomley Ho
11 Laughton Ho
12 Woodruff Ho
13 Bascome St
14 Dudley Mews
15 Herbert Mews
16 Blades Lo
17 Dick Shepherd Ct
18 Charman Ho
19 Morden Ho
20 Bishop Ct
21 Blackburn Ct
22 Leigh Ct
23 John Conwey Ho
24 Bristowe Ct
C2 **1** Crownstone Ct
2 Brockwell Ct
3 Nevena Ct
4 St George's
Residences
5 Hanover Mans
6 Fleet Ho
7 Langbourne Ho
8 Turnmill Ho
9 Walker Mews
10 Cossar Mews
11 Carter Ho
12 Arungford Mews
C3 **1** Electric Mans
2 Electric La
3 Connaught Mans
4 Clifton Mans
5 Hereford Ho
6 Chaplin Ho
7 Lord David Pitt Ho
8 Marcus Garvey Way
9 Montego Cl
10 Bob Marley Way
11 Leeson Rd
12 St John's Angell
Town CE Prim Sch
C4 **1** Buckmaster Cl
2 Albemarle Ho
3 Goodwood Mans
4 Angell Park Gdns
5 Fyfield Rd
6 Howard Ho
7 Harris Ho
8 Broadoak Ct
9 Burgate Ct

5 Telferscot Prim Sch

4 1 Riley Ho
2 Bennett Ho
3 White Ho
4 Rodgers Ho
5 Dumphreys Ho
6 Homan Ho
7 Prendergast Ho
8 Hutchins Ho
9 Whiteley Ho
10 Tresidder Ho
11 Primrose Ct
12 Angus Ho
13 Currie Ho

74

A1 1 De Montfort Ct
2 Leigham Hall Par
3 Leigham Hall
4 Endsleigh Mans
5 John Kirk Ho
6 Raebarn Ct
7 Wavel Ct
8 Homeleigh Ct
9 Howland Ho
10 Beauclerk Ho
11 Bertrand Ho
12 Drew Ho
13 Dowes Ho
14 Dunton Ho
15 Raynald Ho
16 Sackville Ho
17 Thurlow Ho
18 Astoria Mans
A2 1 Wyatt Park Mans
2 Broadlands Mans
3 Stonehill's Mans
4 Streatleigh Par
5 Dorchester Ct
6 Picture Ho
A3 1 Beaumont Ho
2 Christchurch Ho
3 Staplefield Cl
4 Chipstead Ho
5 Coulsdon Ho
6 Conway Ho
7 Telford Avenue Mans

8 Telford Parade Mans
9 Wawertree Ct
10 Hartswood Ho
11 Wray Ho
A4 1 Picton Ho
2 Rigg Ho
3 Watson Ho
4 MacArthur Ho
5 Sandon Ho
6 Thorold Ho
7 Pearce Ho
8 Mudie Ho
9 Miller Ho
10 Lycett Ho
11 Lafone Ho
12 Lucraft Ho
13 Freeman Ho
14 New Park Par
15 Argyll Ct
16 Dumbarton Ct
17 Kintyre Ct
18 Cotton Ho
19 Crossman Hos
20 Cameford Ct
21 Parsons Ho
22 Brindley Ho
23 Arkwright Ho
24 Perry Ho
25 Brunel Ho
26 New Park Ct
27 Tanhurst Ho
28 Hawkshaw Cl
29 Richard Atkins Prim Sch
30 Rodmill La
31 Wallis's Cottages
B1 1 Carisbrooke Ct
2 Pembroke Lo
3 Willow Ct
4 Poplar Ct
5 Leigham Cl
6 Mountview
7 Spa View
B3 1 Charlwood Ho
2 Earlswood Ho
3 Balcombe Ho
4 Claremont Ct

5 Holbrook Ho
6 Gwynne Ho
7 Kynaston Ho
8 Tillman Ho
9 Regents Lo
10 Hazelmere Ct
11 Dykes Ct
12 Hartwell Cl
13 Christ Church Streatham CE Prim Sch
14 Streatham Hill & Clapham High Sch
B4 1 Archbishop's Pl
2 Witley Ho
3 Outwood Ho
4 Dunsfold Ho
5 Deepdene Lo
6 Warnham Ho
7 Albury Lo
8 Tilford Ho
9 Elstead Ho
10 Thursley Ho
11 Brockham Ho
12 Capel Lo
13 Leith Ho
14 Fairview Ho
15 Weymouth Ct
16 Ascalon Ct
17 China Mews
18 Rush Common Mews
C3 1 Valens Ho
2 Loveday Ho
3 Strode Ho
4 Ethelworth Ct
5 Harbin Ho
6 Brooks Ho
7 Godolphin Ho
8 Sheppard Ho
9 McCormick Ho
10 Taylor Ho
11 Saunders Ho
12 Talcott Path
13 Derrick Ho
14 Williams Ho
15 Baldwin Ho
16 Churston Cl

17 Neil Wates Cres
18 Burnell Ho
19 Portland Ho
20 Fenstanton Prim Sch
21 St Martin-in-the-Fields High Sch
22 City Heights Acad
C4 1 Ellacombe Ho
2 Booth Ho
3 Hathersley Ho
4 Brererton Ho
5 Holdsworth Ho
6 Dearmer Ho
7 Cherry Cl
8 Greenleaf Cl
9 Longford Wlk
10 Scarlette Manor Wlk
11 Chandlers Way
12 Upgrove Manor Way
13 Ropers Wlk
14 Tebbs Ho
15 Bell Ho
16 Worthington Ho
17 Courier Ho
18 Mackie Ho
19 Hamers Ho
20 Kelyway Ho
21 Harriet Tubman Cl
22 Estoria Cl
23 Leckhampton Pl
24 Scotia Rd
25 Charles Haller St
26 Sidmouth Ho
27 Hunter Ct
28 Onslow Lo
29 William Winter Ct
30 Langthorne Lo

75

A1 1 Thanet Ho
2 Chapman Ho
3 Beaufoy Ho
4 Easton Ho
5 Roberts Ho
6 Lloyd Ho

76 C1 309

7 Kershaw Ho
8 Wakeling Ho
9 Edridge Ho
10 Jeston Ho
11 Lansdowne Wood Cl
12 Rotary Lo
13 Culzean Cl
A3 1 Sentamu Cl
B1 1 Cranfield Cl
C2 1 Welldon Ct
2 Coppedhall
3 Shackleton Ct
4 Bullfinch Ct
5 Gannet Ct
6 Fulmar Ct
7 Heron Ct
8 Petrel Ct
9 Falcon Ct
10 Eagle Ct
11 Dunnock Ct
12 Dunlin Ct
13 Cormorant Ct
14 Oak Lodge
15 Corfe Lodge

76

C1 1 Tunbridge Ct
2 Harrogate Ct
3 Bath Ct
4 Leamington Ct
5 Porlock Ho
6 Cissbury Ho
7 Eddisbury Ho
8 Dundry Ho
9 Silbury Ho
10 Homildon Ho
11 Highgate Ho
12 Richmond Ho
13 Pendle Ho
14 Tynwald Ho
15 Wirrall Ho
16 Greyfriars

NOTES

MAYOR OF LONDON

tfl.gov.uk

24 hour travel information
0343 222 1234*

Sign up for email updates
tfl.gov.uk/emailupdates

*Service and network charges may apply. See tfl.gov.uk/terms for details.

Improvement works may affect your journey, please check before you travel

Legend:
- Bakerloo
- Central
- Circle
- District
- Hammersmith & City
- Jubilee
- Metropolitan
- Northern
- Piccadilly
- Victoria
- Waterloo & City
- DLR
- Emirates Air Line cable car (Special fares apply)
- London Overground
- TfL Rail
- London Trams
- District open at weekends and on some public holidays
- Interchange stations
- Step-free access from street to train
- Step-free access from street to platform
- National Rail
- Airport
- Riverboat services
- Victoria Coach Station
- Emirates Air Line cable car

LTravelAlerts

UNDERGROUND

TRANSPORT FOR LONDON

EVERY JOURNEY MATTERS

7/3163/P

Version A TfL 3.2017   Correct at time of going to print

www.philips-maps.co.uk

First published in 2001 by Philip's, a division of
Octopus Publishing Group Ltd
www.octopusbooks.co.uk
Carmelite House, 50 Victoria Embankment, London, EC4Y 0DZ
An Hachette UK Company
www.hachette.co.uk

Sixth edition with interim revision 2017
Second impression 2019
LONFA

© Philip's 2017

Spiral-bound
ISBN 978-1-84907-453-7

Perfect-bound
ISBN 978-1-84907-454-4

Hardback (Union Jack)
ISBN 978-1-84907-455-1

This product includes mapping data licensed
from Ordnance Survey® with the permission of
the Controller of Her Majesty's Stationery Office.
© Crown copyright 2017.
All rights reserved. Licence number 100011710.

Map data